GARDNER'S
ART through the AGES

GARDNER'S

FRED S. KLEINER

Volume I

ART through the AGES

A GLOBAL HISTORY

FOURTEENTH EDITION

WADSWORTH
CENGAGE Learning

Australia • Brazil • Japan • Korea • Mexico • Singapore • Spain • United Kingdom • United States

**Gardner's Art through the Ages:
A Global History, Fourteenth Edition, Volume I**
Fred S. Kleiner

Publisher: Clark Baxter

Senior Development Editor: Sharon Adams Poore

Assistant Editor: Ashley Bargende

Editorial Assistant: Elizabeth Newell

Associate Media Editor: Kimberly Apfelbaum

Senior Marketing Manager: Jeanne Heston

Marketing Coordinator: Klaira Markenzon

Senior Marketing Communications Manager: Heather Baxley

Senior Content Project Manager: Lianne Ames

Senior Art Director: Cate Rickard Barr

Senior Print Buyer: Mary Beth Hennebury

Rights Acquisition Specialist, Images: Mandy Groszko

Production Service & Layout: Joan Keyes, Dovetail Publishing Services

Text Designer: tani hasegawa

Cover Designer: tani hasegawa

Cover Image: © Scala/Art Resource, NY

Compositor: Thompson Type, Inc.

For product information and technology assistance, contact us at
Cengage Learning Customer & Sales Support, 1-800-354-9706

For permission to use material from this text or product, submit all requests online at **www.cengage.com/permissions**. Further permissions questions can be emailed to
permissionrequest@cengage.com.

Library of Congress Control Number: 2011931487

Student Edition
ISBN-13: 978-1-111-77157-7
ISBN-10: 1-111-77157-X

Wadsworth
20 Channel Center Street
Boston, MA 02210
USA

Cengage Learning is a leading provider of customized learning solutions with office locations around the globe, including Singapore, the United Kingdom, Australia, Mexico, Brazil and Japan. Locate your local office at **international.cengage.com/region**

Cengage Learning products are represented in Canada by Nelson Education, Ltd.

For your course and learning solutions, visit **www.cengage.com**. Purchase any of our products at your local college store or at our preferred online store **www.cengagebrain.com**.

Instructors: Please visit **login.cengage.com** and log in to access instructor-specific resources.

Printed in the United States of America
1 2 3 4 5 6 7 15 14 13 12 11

Although the best-known paintings from ancient Pompeii are the frescoes depicting Greek mythological subjects, portraits adorned the walls of many Roman houses, especially in the atrium, the grand reception hall in which families often also displayed wax masks of their ancestors. Perhaps the finest of the preserved painted portraits from Pompeii is this tondo (painting in a circular frame) depicting a young woman wearing her hair in curls over her forehead and ears, a coiffure popular during the mid-first century CE. Nicknamed "Sappho" (after the famous ancient Greek poetess) because of the stylus and wax writing tablet she holds, she gazes at the viewer but seems lost in thought. The objects she holds are standard attributes in private portraits of Romans who wished to present themselves as cultured individuals.

Woman with stylus and writing tablet ("Sappho"), from a house in Insula Occidentale VI, Pompeii, Italy, ca. 55–70 CE. Fresco, 1′ ¼″ diameter. Museo Nazionale Archeologico, Naples.

Her gold hairnet and earrings attest to her wealth, real or imagined. In similar portraits from other Pompeian houses, the woman often appears beside her husband. The male portraits also conform to a set pattern. They hold a scroll beneath the chin and therefore share the literary pretensions of their spouse. In fact, a tondo portrait of a man with a scroll was a pendant image on the same wall as the "Sappho" tondo before excavators cut both portraits out of the wall and transferred them to the Archaeological Museum in Naples. The man and "Sappho" were undoubtedly husband and wife.

The identity of the painter is also unknown, but that is the norm in the history of art before the Renaissance, when the modern notion of individual artistic genius took root. *Art through the Ages* surveys the art of all periods from prehistory to the present, and worldwide, and examines how artworks of all kinds have always reflected the historical contexts in which they were created.

FRED S. KLEINER (Ph.D., Columbia University) is the author or co-author of the 10th, 11th, 12th, and 13th editions of *Art through the Ages: A Global History,* as well as the 1st, 2nd, and 3rd editions of *Art through the Ages: A Concise History,* and more than a hundred publications on Greek and Roman art and architecture, including *A History of Roman Art,* also published by Wadsworth, a part of Cengage Learning. He has taught the art history survey course for more than three decades, first at the University of Virginia and, since 1978, at Boston University, where he is currently Professor of Art History and Archaeology and Chair of the Department of History of Art and Architecture. From 1985 to 1998, he was Editor-in-Chief of the *American Journal of Archaeology.* Long acclaimed for his inspiring lectures and dedication to students, Professor Kleiner won Boston University's Metcalf Award for Excellence in Teaching as well as the College Prize for Undergraduate Advising in the Humanities in 2002, and he is a two-time winner of the Distinguished Teaching Prize in the College of Arts and Sciences Honors Program. In 2007, he was elected a Fellow of the Society of Antiquaries of London, and, in 2009, in recognition of lifetime achievement in publication and teaching, a Fellow of the Text and Academic Authors Association.

CONTENTS

PREFACE

THE GARDNER LEGACY IN THE 21ST CENTURY

I take great pleasure in introducing the extensively revised and expanded 14th edition of *Gardner's Art through the Ages: A Global History,* which, like the enhanced 13th edition, is a hybrid art history textbook—the first, and still the only, introductory survey of the history of art of its kind. This innovative new kind of "Gardner" retains all of the best features of traditional books on paper while harnessing 21st-century technology to increase by 25% the number of works examined—without increasing the size or weight of the book itself and at very low additional cost to students compared to a larger book.

When Helen Gardner published the first edition of *Art through the Ages* in 1926, she could not have imagined that more than 85 years later instructors all over the world would still be using her textbook in their classrooms. Indeed, if she were alive today, she would not recognize the book that, even in its traditional form, long ago became—and remains—the most widely read introduction to the history of art and architecture in the English language. During the past half-century, successive authors have constantly reinvented Helen Gardner's groundbreaking global survey, always keeping it fresh and current, and setting an ever-higher standard with each new edition. I am deeply gratified that both professors and students seem to agree that the 13th edition, released in 2008, lived up to that venerable tradition, for they made it the number-one choice for art history survey courses. I hope they will find the 14th edition of this best-selling book exceeds their high expectations.

In addition to the host of new features (enumerated below) in the book proper, the 14th edition follows the enhanced 13th edition in incorporating an innovative new online component. All new copies of the 14th edition are packaged with an access code to a web site with *bonus essays* and *bonus images* (with zoom capability) of more than 300 additional important paintings, sculptures, buildings, and other art forms of all eras, from prehistory to the present and worldwide. The selection includes virtually all of the works professors have told me they wished had been in the 13th edition, but were not included for lack of space. I am extremely grateful to Cengage Learning/Wadsworth for the considerable investment of time and resources that has made this remarkable hybrid textbook possible.

In contrast to the enhanced 13th edition, the online component is now fully integrated into the 14th edition. Every one of the more than 300 bonus images is cited in the text of the traditional book and a thumbnail image of each work, with abbreviated caption, is inset into the text column where the work is mentioned. The integration extends also to the maps, index, glossary, and chapter summaries, which seamlessly merge the printed and online information. The 14th edition is in every way a unified, comprehensive history of art and architecture, even though the text is divided into paper and digital components.

KEY FEATURES OF THE 14TH EDITION

In this new edition, I have added several important features while retaining the basic format and scope of the previous edition. Once again, the hybrid Gardner boasts roughly 1,700 photographs, plans, and drawings, nearly all in color and reproduced according to the highest standards of clarity and color fidelity, including hundreds of new images, among them a new series of superb photos taken by Jonathan Poore exclusively for *Art through the Ages* during three photographic campaigns in France and Italy in 2009, 2010, and 2011. The online component also includes custom videos made at each site by Sharon Adams Poore. This extraordinary new archive of visual material ranges from ancient Roman ruins in southern France to Romanesque and Gothic churches in France and Tuscany to Le Corbusier's modernist chapel at Ronchamp and the postmodern Pompidou Center and the Louvre Pyramide in Paris. The 14th edition also features the highly acclaimed architectural drawings of John Burge. Together, these exclusive photographs, videos, and drawings provide readers with a visual feast unavailable anywhere else.

The captions accompanying those illustrations contain, as before, a wealth of information, but, as in the 13th edition, scales accompany not only all architectural plans, as is the norm, but also appear next to each photograph of a painting, statue, or other artwork—another unique feature of the Gardner text. The works discussed in the 14th edition of *Art through the Ages* vary enormously in size, from colossal sculptures carved into mountain cliffs and paintings that cover entire walls or ceilings to tiny figurines, coins, and jewelry that one can hold in the hand. Although the captions contain the pertinent dimensions, it is difficult for students who have never seen the paintings or statues in person to translate those dimensions into an appreciation of the real size of the objects. The scales provide an effective and direct way to visualize how big or how small a given artwork is and its relative size compared with other objects in the same chapter and throughout the book.

Also retained in this edition are the Quick-Review Captions introduced in the 13th edition. Students have overwhelmingly reported that they found these brief synopses of the most significant aspects of each artwork or building illustrated invaluable when preparing for examinations. These extended captions accompany not only every image in the printed book but also all the digital images in the online supplement. Another popular tool introduced in the 13th edition to aid students in reviewing and mastering the material reappears in the 14th edition. Each chapter ends with a full-page feature called *The Big Picture,* which sets forth in bullet-point format the most important characteristics of each period or artistic movement discussed in the chapter. Small illustrations of characteristic works accompany the summary of major points. The 14th edition, however, introduces two new features in every chapter: a timeline summarizing the major developments during the era treated (again in bullet-point format for easy review) and a chapter-opening essay on a characteristic painting, sculpture, or building. Called *Framing the Era,* these in-depth essays are accompanied by a general view and four enlarged details of the work discussed.

The 14th edition of *Art through the Ages* is available in several different traditional paper formats—a single hardcover volume; two paperback volumes designed for use in the fall and spring semesters of a yearlong survey course; a six-volume "backpack" set; and an interactive e-book version. Another pedagogical tool not found in any other introductory art history textbook is the *Before 1300* section that appears at the beginning of the second volume of the paperbound version of the book and at the beginning of Book D of the backpack edition. Because many students taking the second half of a survey course will not have access to Volume I or to Books A, B, and C, I have provided a special set of concise primers on architectural terminology and construction methods in the ancient and medieval worlds, and on mythology and religion—information that is essential for understanding the history of art after 1300, both in the West and the East. The subjects of these special boxes are Greco-Roman Temple Design and the Classical Orders; Arches and Vaults; Basilican Churches; Central-Plan Churches; The Gods and Goddesses of Mount Olympus; The Life of Jesus in Art; Buddhism and Buddhist Iconography; and Hinduism and Hindu Iconography.

Boxed essays once again appear throughout the book as well. In this edition the essays are more closely tied to the main text than ever before. Consistent with that greater integration, almost all boxes now incorporate photographs of important artworks discussed in the text proper that also illustrate the theme treated in the boxed essays. These essays fall under six broad categories:

Architectural Basics boxes provide students with a sound foundation for the understanding of architecture. These discussions are concise explanations, with drawings and diagrams, of the major aspects of design and construction. The information included is essential to an understanding of architectural technology and terminology. The boxes address questions of how and why various forms developed, the problems architects confronted, and the solutions they used to resolve them.

Materials and Techniques essays explain the various media artists employed from prehistoric to modern times. Since materials and techniques often influence the character of artworks, these discussions contain essential information on why many monuments appear as they do.

Religion and Mythology boxes introduce students to the principal elements of the world's great religions, past and present, and to the representation of religious and mythological themes in painting and sculpture of all periods and places. These discussions of belief systems and iconography give readers a richer understanding of some of the greatest artworks ever created.

Art and Society essays treat the historical, social, political, cultural, and religious context of art and architecture. In some instances, specific monuments are the basis for a discussion of broader themes.

Written Sources present and discuss key historical documents illuminating important monuments of art and architecture throughout the world. The passages quoted permit voices from the past to speak directly to the reader, providing vivid and unique insights into the creation of artworks in all media.

Finally, in the *Artists on Art* boxes, artists and architects throughout history discuss both their theories and individual works.

For every new edition of *Art through the Ages,* I also reevaluate the basic organization of the book. In the 14th edition, the unfolding narrative of the history of art in Europe and America is no longer interrupted with "excursions" to Asia, Africa, and Oceania. Those chapters are now grouped together at the end of Volumes I and II and in backpack Books D and F. And the treatment of the art of the later 20th century and the opening decade of the 21st century has been significantly reconfigured. There are now separate chapters on the art and architecture of the period from 1945 to 1980 and from 1980 to the present. Moreover, the second chapter (Chapter 31, "Contemporary Art Worldwide") is no longer confined to Western art but presents the art and architecture of the past three decades as a multifaceted global phenomenon. Furthermore, some chapters now appear in more than one of the paperbound versions of the book in order to provide enhanced flexibility to instructors who divide the global history of art into two or three semester-long courses. Chapter 14—on Italian art from 1200 to 1400—appears in both Volumes I and II and in backpack Books B and D. The Islamic and contemporary art chapters appear in both the Western and non-Western backpack subdivisions of the full global text.

Rounding out the features in the book itself is a greatly expanded Bibliography of books in English with several hundred new entries, including both general works and a chapter-by-chapter list of more focused studies; a Glossary containing definitions of all italicized terms introduced in both the printed and online texts; and, for the first time, a complete museum index listing all illustrated artworks by their present location .

The 14th edition of *Art through the Ages* also features a host of state-of-the-art online resources (enumerated on page xv).

WRITING AND TEACHING THE HISTORY OF ART

Nonetheless, some things have not changed in this new edition, including the fundamental belief that guided Helen Gardner so many years ago—that the primary goal of an introductory art history textbook should be to foster an appreciation and understanding of historically significant works of art of all kinds from all periods and from all parts of the globe. Because of the longevity and diversity of the history of art, it is tempting to assign responsibility for telling its story to a large team of specialists. The original publisher of *Art through the Ages* took this approach for the first edition prepared after Helen Gardner's death, and it has now become the norm for introductory art history surveys. But students overwhelmingly say the very complexity of the global history of art makes it all the more important for the story to be told with a consistent voice if they are to master so much diverse material. I think Helen Gardner would be pleased to know that *Art through the Ages* once again has a single storyteller—aided in no small part by invaluable advice from well over a hundred reviewers and other consultants whose assistance I gladly acknowledge at the end of this Preface.

I continue to believe that the most effective way to tell the story of art through the ages, especially to anyone studying art history for the first time, is to organize the vast array of artistic monuments according to the civilizations that produced them and to consider each work in roughly chronological order. This approach has not merely stood the test of time. It is the most appropriate way to narrate the *history* of art. The principle underlying my approach to every period of art history is that the enormous variation in the form and meaning of the paintings, sculptures, buildings, and other artworks men and women have produced over the past 30,000 years is largely the result of the constantly changing contexts in which artists and architects worked. A historically based narrative is therefore best suited for a global history of art because it enables the author to situate each work discussed in its historical, social, economic, religious, and cultural context. That is, after all, what distinguishes art history from art appreciation.

In the 1926 edition of *Art through the Ages,* Helen Gardner discussed Henri Matisse and Pablo Picasso in a chapter entitled "Contemporary Art in Europe and America." Since then many other artists have emerged on the international scene, and the story of art through the ages has grown longer and even more complex. As already noted, that is reflected in the addition of a new chapter at the end of the book on contemporary art in which developments on all continents are treated together for the first time. Perhaps even more important than the new directions artists and architects have taken during the past several decades is that the discipline of art history has also changed markedly—and so too has Helen Gardner's book. The 14th edition fully reflects the latest art historical research emphases while maintaining the traditional strengths that have made previous editions of *Art through the Ages* so popular. While sustaining attention to style, chronology, iconography, and technique, I also ensure that issues of patronage, function, and context loom large in every chapter. I treat artworks not as isolated objects in sterile 21st-century museum settings but with a view toward their purpose and meaning in the society that produced them at the time they were produced. I examine not only the role of the artist or architect in the creation of a work of art or a building, but also the role of the individuals or groups who paid the artists and influenced the shape the monuments took. Further, in this expanded hybrid edition, I devote more space than ever before to the role of women and women artists in societies worldwide over time. In every chapter, I have tried to choose artworks and buildings that reflect the increasingly wide range of interests of scholars today, while not rejecting the traditional list of "great" works or the very notion of a "canon." Indeed, the expanded hybrid nature of the 14th edition has made it possible to illustrate and discuss scores of works not traditionally treated in art history survey texts without reducing the space devoted to canonical works.

CHAPTER-BY-CHAPTER CHANGES IN THE 14TH EDITION

All chapters feature many new photographs, revised maps, revised Big Picture chapter-ending summaries, and changes to the text reflecting new research and discoveries.

Introduction: What is Art History? New painting by Ogata Korin added.

1: Art before History. New Framing the Era essay "The Dawn of Art" and new timeline. Göbekli Tepe added.

2: Mesopotamia and Persia. New Framing the Era essay "The Cradle of Civilization" and new timeline.

3: Egypt under the Pharaohs. New Framing the Era essay "Divine Kingship on the Nile" and new timeline. Hatshepsut's expedition to Punt added.

4: The Prehistoric Aegean. New Framing the Era essay "Greece in the Age of Heroes" and new timeline. Mycenean ivory goddesses added.

5: Ancient Greece. New Framing the Era essay "The Perfect Temple" and new timeline. Euphronios *Death of Sarpedon* and Olympia Apollo added.

6: The Etruscans. New Framing the Era essay "The Rediscovery of Etruscan Art" and new timeline. Tomb of the Augurs added.

7: The Roman Empire. New Framing the Era essay "The Ancient World's Greatest Empire" and new timeline. New box on "Roman Ancestor Portraits" added. Column of Trajan frieze and new portrait of Caracalla added.

8: Late Antiquity. New Framing the Era essay "Romans, Jews, and Christians" and new timeline. Villa Torlonia Jewish catacomb and Mildenhall treasure added.

9: Byzantium. New Framing the Era essay "Church and State United" and new timeline. Revised discussion of iconoclasm and of Byzantine women. New box on "Born to the Purple: Empress Zoe."

10: The Islamic World. New Framing the Era essay "The Rise and Spread of Islam" and new timeline. Muqarnas tilework of Imam Mosque, Isfahan, added.

11: Early Medieval Europe. New Framing the Era essay "Missionaries and the Spread of Christian Art" and new timeline. Detail photos of Book of Kells added.

12: Romanesque Europe. New Framing the Era essay "The Rebirth of Monumental Sculpture" and new timeline. New photos of newly cleaned Autun tympanum and many other French churches. Revised boxes on "Pilgrimage Roads in France and Spain" and "The Veneration of Relics." Reliquary of St. Foy added.

13: Gothic Europe. New Framing the Era essay "The Age of the Great Cathedrals" and new timeline. Extensive new photographic documentation of French churches and portal sculpture. Expanded treatment of German Gothic art and architecture.

14: Late Medieval Italy. New Framing the Era essay "Late Medieval or Proto-Renaissance?" and new timeline. New series of photos of architecture and sculpture in Florence, Orvieto, Pisa, and Siena. Andrea Pisano Baptistery doors added.

15: South and Southeast Asia before 1200. New Framing the Era essay "The Life of the Buddha" and new timeline. New series of photos of Buddhist and Hindu monuments.

16: China and Korea to 1279. New Framing the Era essay "Chinese Silk for the Afterlife" and new timeline. Flying horse of Governor-General Zhang and Korean statuette of bodhisattva Maitreya added.

17: Japan before 1333. New Framing the Era essay "Buddhism Spreads to Japan" and new timeline. Kosho's portrait of the priest Kuya added.

18: Native Arts of the Americas before 1300. New Framing the Era essay "Ancient Cities in a New World" and new timeline. Expanded discussions of Teotihuacán and Chichén Itzá.

19: Africa before 1800. New Framing the Era essay "Sacred Kingship in Benin" and new timeline. Seated statue of a man from Tada added.

Go to the online instructor companion site or PowerLecture for a more detailed list of chapter-by-chapter changes and the figure number transition guide.

ACKNOWLEDGMENTS

A work as extensive as a global history of art could not be undertaken or completed without the counsel of experts in all areas of world art. As with previous editions, Cengage Learning/Wadsworth has enlisted more than a hundred art historians to review every chapter of *Art through the Ages* in order to ensure that the text lives up to the Gardner reputation for accuracy as well as readability. I take great pleasure in acknowledging here the important contributions to the 14th edition made by the following : Michael Jay Adamek, Ozarks Technical Community College; Charles M. Adelman, University of Northern Iowa; Christine Zitrides Atiyeh, Kutztown University; Gisele Atterberry, Joliet Junior College; Roann Barris, Radford University; Philip Betancourt, Temple University; Karen Blough, SUNY Plattsburgh; Elena N. Boeck, DePaul University; Betty Ann Brown, California State University Northridge; Alexandra A. Carpino, Northern Arizona University; Anne Walke Cassidy, Carthage College; Harold D. Cole, Baldwin Wallace College; Sarah Cormack, Webster University, Vienna; Jodi Cranston, Boston University; Nancy de Grummond, Florida State University; Kelley Helmstutler Di Dio, University of Vermont; Owen Doonan, California State University Northridge; Marilyn Dunn, Loyola University Chicago; Tom Estlack, Pittsburgh Cultural Trust; Lois Fichner-Rathus, The College of New Jersey; Arne R. Flaten, Coastal Carolina University; Ken Friedman, Swinburne University of Technology; Rosemary Gallick, Northern Virginia Community College; William V. Ganis, Wells College; Marc Gerstein, University of Toledo; Clive F. Getty, Miami University; Michael Grillo, University of Maine; Amanda Hamilton, Northwest Nazarene University; Martina Hesser, Heather Jensen, Brigham Young University; Grossmont College; Mark Johnson, Brigham Young University; Jacqueline E. Jung, Yale University; John F. Kenfield, Rutgers University; Asen Kirin, University of Georgia; Joanne Klein, Boise State University; Yu Bong Ko, Tappan Zee High School; Rob Leith, Buckingham Browne & Nichols School; Adele H. Lewis, Arizona State University; Kate Alexandra Lingley, University of Hawaii–Manoa; Ellen Longsworth, Merrimack College; Matthew Looper, California State University–Chico; Nuria Lledó Tarradell, Universidad Complutense, Madrid; Anne McClanan, Portland State University; Mark Magleby, Brigham Young University; Gina Miceli-Hoffman, Moraine Valley Community College; William Mierse, University of Vermont; Amy Morris, Southeastern Louisiana University; Charles R. Morscheck, Drexel University; Johanna D. Movassat, San Jose State University; Carola Naumer, Truckee Meadows Community College; Irene Nero, Southeastern Louisiana University; Robin O'Bryan, Harrisburg Area Community College; Laurent Odde, Kutztown University of Pennsylvania; E. Suzanne Owens, Lorain County Community College; Catherine Pagani, The University of Alabama; Martha Peacock, Brigham Young University; Mabi Ponce de Leon, Bexley High School; Curtis Runnels, Boston University; Malia E. F. Serrano, Grossmont College; Molly Skjei, Normandale Community College; James Swensen, Brigham Young University; John Szostak, University of Hawaii–Manoa; Fred T. Smith, Kent State University; Thomas F. Strasser, Providence College; Katherine H. Tachau, University of Iowa; Debra Thompson, Glendale Community College; Alice Y. Tseng, Boston University; Carol Ventura, Tennessee Technological University; Marc Vincent, Baldwin Wallace College; Deborah Waite, University of Hawaii–Manoa; Lawrence Waldron, Saint John's University; Victoria Weaver, Millersville University; and Margaret Ann Zaho, University of Central Florida.

I am especially indebted to the following for creating the instructor and student materials for the 14th edition: William J. Allen, Arkansas State University; Ivy Cooper, Southern Illinois University Edwardsville; Patricia D. Cosper, The University of Alabama at Birmingham; Anne McClanan, Portland State University; and Amy M. Morris, Southeastern Louisiana University. I also thank the members of the Wadsworth Media Advisory Board for their input: Frances Altvater, University of Hartford; Roann Barris, Radford University; Bill Christy, Ohio University-Zanesville; Annette Cohen, Great Bay Community College; Jeff Davis, The Art Institute of Pittsburgh–Online Division; Owen Doonan, California State University-Northridge; Arne R. Flaten, Coastal Carolina University; Carol Heft, Muhlenberg College; William Mierse, University of Vermont; Eleanor F. Moseman, Colorado State University; and Malia E. F. Serrano, Grossmont College.

I am also happy to have this opportunity to express my gratitude to the extraordinary group of people at Cengage Learning/Wadsworth involved with the editing, production, and distribution of *Art through the Ages*. Some of them I have now worked with on various projects for nearly two decades and feel privileged to count among my friends. The success of the Gardner series in all of its various permutations depends in no small part on the expertise and unflagging commitment of these dedicated professionals, especially Clark Baxter, publisher; Sharon Adams Poore, senior development editor (as well as videographer extraordinaire); Lianne Ames, senior content project manager; Mandy Groszko, rights acquisitions specialist; Kimberly Apfelbaum, associate media editor; Robert White, product manager; Ashley Bargende, assistant editor; Elizabeth Newell, editorial assistant; Amy Bither and Jessica Jackson, editorial interns; Cate Rickard Barr, senior art director; Jeanne M. Heston, senior marketing manager, Heather Baxley, senior marketing communications manager, and the incomparable group of local sales representatives who have passed on to me the welcome advice offered by the hundreds of instructors they speak to daily during their visits to college campuses throughout North America.

I am also deeply grateful to the following out-of-house contributors to the 14th edition: the peerless and tireless Joan Keyes, Dovetail Publishing Services; Helen Triller-Yambert, development editor; Ida May Norton, copy editor; Do Mi Stauber and Michael Brackney, indexers; Susan Gall, proofreader; tani hasegawa, designer; Catherine Schnurr, Mary-Lise Nazaire, Lauren McFalls, and Corey Geissler, PreMediaGlobal, photo researchers; Alma Bell, Scott Paul, John Pierce, and Lori Shranko, Thompson Type; Jay and John Crowley, Jay's Publishing Services; Mary Ann Lidrbauch, art manuscript preparer; and, of course, Jonathan Poore and John Burge, for their superb photos and architectural drawings.

Finally, I owe thanks to my former co-author, Christin J. Mamiya of the University of Nebraska–Lincoln, for her friendship and advice, especially with regard to the expanded contemporary art section of the 14th edition, as well as to my colleagues at Boston University and to the thousands of students and the scores of teaching fellows in my art history courses since I began teaching in 1975. From them I have learned much that has helped determine the form and content of *Art through the Ages* and made it a much better book than it otherwise might have been.

Fred S. Kleiner

RESOURCES

FOR FACULTY

PowerLecture with Digital Image Library

This flashdrive is an all-in-one lecture and class presentation tool that makes it easy to assemble, edit, and present customized lectures for your course using Microsoft® PowerPoint®. The Digital Image Library provides high-resolution images (maps, diagrams, and most of the fine art images from the text, including the over 300 new images) for lecture presentations, either in PowerPoint format, or in individual file formats compatible with other image-viewing software. A zoom feature allows you to magnify selected portions of an image for more detailed display in class, or you can display images side by side for comparison. You can easily add your own images to those from the text. The Google Earth™ application allows you to zoom in on an entire city, as well as key monuments and buildings. There are links to specific figures for every chapter in the book. PowerLecture also includes an Image Transition Guide, an electronic Instructor's Manual and a Test Bank with multiple-choice, matching, short-answer, and essay questions in ExamView® computerized format. The text-specific Microsoft® PowerPoint® slides are created for use with JoinIn™, software for classroom personal response systems (clickers).

WebTutor™ with eBook on WebCT® and Blackboard®

WebTutor™ enables you to assign preformatted, text-specific content that is available as soon as you log on. You can also customize the WebTutor™ environment in any way you choose. Content includes the Interactive ebook, Test Bank, Practice Quizzes, Video Study Tools, and CourseMate™.

To order, contact your Cengage Learning representative.

FOR STUDENTS

CourseMate™ with eBook

Make the most of your study time by accessing everything you need to succeed in one place. Open the interactive eBook, take notes, review image and audio flashcards, watch videos, and take practice quizzes online with CourseMate™. You will find hundreds of zoomable, high-resolution bonus images (represented by thumbnail images in the text) along with discussion of the images, videos created specifically to enhanced your reading comprehension, audio chapter summaries, compare-and-contrast activities, Guide to Studying, and more.

Slide Guides

The Slide Guide is a lecture companion that allows you to take notes alongside thumbnails of the same art images that are shown in class. This handy booklet includes reproductions of the images from the book with full captions, page numbers, and space for note taking. It also includes Google Earth™ exercises for key cities, monuments, and buildings that will take you to these locations to better understand the works you are studying.

To order, go to www.cengagebrain.com

Why did this Benin kingdom sculptor vary the sizes of the figures? Why is the central equestrian figure much larger than his horse? How did the artist inform the viewer the rider is a king?

Art historians seek to understand not only why individual artworks appear as they do but also why those works exist at all. Who paid this African artist to make this bronze plaque? Why?

Dating and signing artworks are relatively recent practices. How can art historians determine when an unlabeled work such as this one was made, and by whom? Style, technique, and subject are clues.

1 in.

I-1 King on horseback with attendants, from Benin, Nigeria, ca. 1550–1680. Bronze, 1′ 7½″ high. Metropolitan Museum of Art, New York (Michael C. Rockefeller Memorial Collection, gift of Nelson A. Rockefeller).

Introduction

What tools and techniques did the African sculptor employ to transform molten bronze into this plaque representing a king and his attendants projecting in high relief from the background plane?

WHAT IS ART HISTORY?

What is art history? Except when referring to the modern academic discipline, people do not often juxtapose the words *art* and *history*. They tend to think of history as the record and interpretation of past human actions, particularly social and political actions. In contrast, most think of art, quite correctly, as part of the present—as something people can see and touch. Of course, people cannot see or touch history's vanished human events, but a visible, tangible artwork is a kind of persisting event. One or more artists made it at a certain time and in a specific place, even if no one now knows who, when, where, or why. Although created in the past, an artwork continues to exist in the present, long surviving its times. The first painters and sculptors died 30,000 years ago, but their works remain, some of them exhibited in glass cases in museums built only a few years ago.

Modern museum visitors can admire these objects from the remote past—and countless others humankind has produced over the millennia, whether small bronze sculptures from Africa (FIG. I-1) or large paintings on canvas by American artists (FIG. I-2)—without any knowledge of the circumstances leading to the creation of those works. The beauty or sheer size of an object can impress people, the artist's virtuosity in the handling of ordinary or costly materials can dazzle them, or the subject depicted can move them emotionally. Viewers can react to what they see, interpret the work in the light of their own experience, and judge it a success or a failure. These are all valid responses to a work of art. But the enjoyment and appreciation of artworks in museum settings are relatively recent phenomena, as is the creation of artworks solely for museum-going audiences to view.

Today, it is common for artists to work in private studios and to create paintings, sculptures, and other objects commercial art galleries will offer for sale. This is what American painter CLYFFORD STILL (1904–1980) did when he created large canvases (FIG. I-2) of pure color titled simply with the year of their creation. Usually, someone the artist has never met will purchase the artwork and display it in a setting the artist has never seen. This practice is not a new phenomenon in the history of art—an ancient potter decorating a vase for sale at a village market stall probably did not know who would buy the pot or where it would be housed—but it is not at all typical. In fact, it is exceptional. Throughout history, most artists created paintings, sculptures, and other objects for specific patrons and settings and to fulfill a specific purpose, even if today no one knows the original contexts of those artworks. Museum visitors can appreciate the visual and tactile qualities of these objects, but they cannot understand why they were made or why they appear as they do without knowing the circumstances of their creation. Art *appreciation* does not require knowledge of the historical context of an artwork (or a building). Art *history* does.

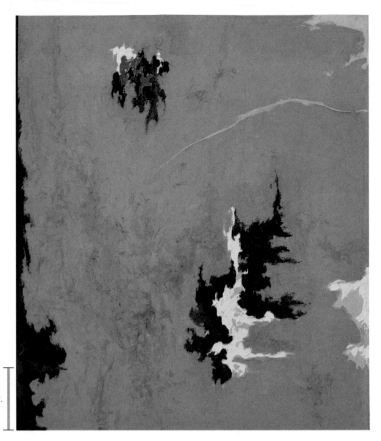

1 ft.

I-2 CLYFFORD STILL, *1948-C*, 1948. Oil on canvas, 6′ 8⅞″ × 5′ 8¾″. Hirshhorn Museum and Sculpture Garden, Smithsonian Institution, Washington, D.C. (purchased with funds of Joseph H. Hirshhorn, 1992).

Clyfford Still painted this abstract composition without knowing who would purchase it or where it would be displayed, but throughout history, most artists created works for specific patrons and settings.

ART HISTORY IN THE 21ST CENTURY

Art historians study the visual and tangible objects humans make and the structures humans build. Scholars traditionally have classified these works as architecture, sculpture, the pictorial arts (painting, drawing, printmaking, and photography), and the craft arts, or arts of design. The craft arts comprise utilitarian objects, such as ceramics, metalwork, textiles, jewelry, and similar accessories of ordinary living. Artists of every age have blurred the boundaries among these categories, but this is especially true today, when multimedia works abound.

Beginning with the earliest Greco-Roman art critics, scholars have studied objects their makers consciously manufactured as "art" and to which the artists assigned formal titles. But today's art historians also study a multitude of objects their creators and owners almost certainly did not consider to be "works of art." Few ancient Romans, for example, would have regarded a coin bearing their emperor's portrait as anything but money. Today, an art museum may exhibit that coin in a locked case in a climate-controlled room, and scholars may subject it to the same kind of art historical analysis as a portrait by an acclaimed Renaissance or modern sculptor or painter.

The range of objects art historians study is constantly expanding and now includes, for example, computer-generated images, whereas in the past almost anything produced using a machine would not have been regarded as art. Most people still consider the performing arts—music, drama, and dance—as outside art history's realm because these arts are fleeting, impermanent media. But during the past few decades, even this distinction between "fine art" and "performance art" has become blurred. Art historians, however, generally ask the same kinds of questions about what they study, whether they employ a restrictive or expansive definition of art.

The Questions Art Historians Ask

HOW OLD IS IT? Before art historians can write a history of art, they must be sure they know the date of each work they study. Thus, an indispensable subject of art historical inquiry is *chronology*, the dating of art objects and buildings. If researchers cannot determine a monument's age, they cannot place the work in its historical context. Art historians have developed many ways to establish, or at least approximate, the date of an artwork.

Physical evidence often reliably indicates an object's age. The material used for a statue or painting—bronze, plastic, or oil-based pigment, to name only a few—may not have been invented before a certain time, indicating the earliest possible date (the *terminus post quem*: Latin "point after which") someone could have fashioned the work. Or artists may have ceased using certain materials—such as specific kinds of inks and papers for drawings—at a known time, providing the latest possible date (the *terminus ante quem*: Latin "point before which") for objects made of those materials. Sometimes the material (or the manufacturing technique) of an object or a building can establish a very precise date of production or construction. The study of tree rings, for instance, usually can determine within a narrow range the date of a wood statue or a timber roof beam.

Documentary evidence can help pinpoint the date of an object or building when a dated written document mentions the work. For example, official records may note when church officials commissioned a new altarpiece—and how much they paid to which artist.

Thus, a central aim of art history is to determine the original context of artworks. Art historians seek to achieve a full understanding not only of why these "persisting events" of human history look the way they do but also of why the artistic events happened at all. What unique set of circumstances gave rise to the construction of a particular building or led an individual patron to commission a certain artist to fashion a singular artwork for a specific place? The study of history is therefore vital to art history. And art history is often indispensable for a thorough understanding of history. Art objects and buildings are historical documents that can shed light on the peoples who made them and on the times of their creation in ways other historical documents may not. Furthermore, artists and architects can affect history by reinforcing or challenging cultural values and practices through the objects they create and the structures they build. Thus, the history of art and architecture is inseparable from the study of history, although the two disciplines are not the same.

The following pages introduce some of the distinctive subjects art historians address and the kinds of questions they ask, and explain some of the basic terminology they use when answering these questions. Readers armed with this arsenal of questions and terms will be ready to explore the multifaceted world of art through the ages.

Internal evidence can play a significant role in dating an artwork. A painter might have depicted an identifiable person or a kind of hairstyle, clothing, or furniture fashionable only at a certain time. If so, the art historian can assign a more accurate date to that painting.

Stylistic evidence is also very important. The analysis of *style*—an artist's distinctive manner of producing an object—is the art historian's special sphere. Unfortunately, because it is a subjective assessment, stylistic evidence is by far the most unreliable chronological criterion. Still, art historians find style a very useful tool for establishing chronology.

WHAT IS ITS STYLE? Defining artistic style is one of the key elements of art historical inquiry, although the analysis of artworks solely in terms of style no longer dominates the field the way it once did. Art historians speak of several different kinds of artistic styles.

Period style refers to the characteristic artistic manner of a specific era or span of years, usually within a distinct culture, such as "Archaic Greek" or "High Renaissance." But many periods do not display any stylistic unity at all. How would someone define the artistic style of the second decade of the new millennium in North America? Far too many crosscurrents exist in contemporary art for anyone to describe a period style of the early 21st century—even in a single city such as New York.

Regional style is the term art historians use to describe variations in style tied to geography. Like an object's date, its *provenance*, or place of origin, can significantly determine its character. Very often two artworks from the same place made centuries apart are more similar than contemporaneous works from two different regions. To cite one example, usually only an expert can distinguish between an Egyptian statue carved in 2500 BCE and one made in 500 BCE. But no one would mistake an Egyptian statue of 500 BCE for one of the same date made in Greece or Mexico.

Considerable variations in a given area's style are possible, however, even during a single historical period. In late medieval Europe, French architecture differed significantly from Italian architecture. The interiors of Beauvais Cathedral (FIG. I-3) and the church of Santa Croce (FIG. I-4) in Florence typify the architectural styles of France and Italy, respectively, at the end of the 13th century. The rebuilding of the east end of Beauvais Cathedral began in 1284. Construction commenced on Santa Croce only 10 years later. Both structures employ the *pointed arch* characteristic of this era, yet the two churches differ strikingly. The French church has towering stone ceilings and large expanses of colored windows, whereas the Italian building has a low timber roof and small, widely separated windows. Because the

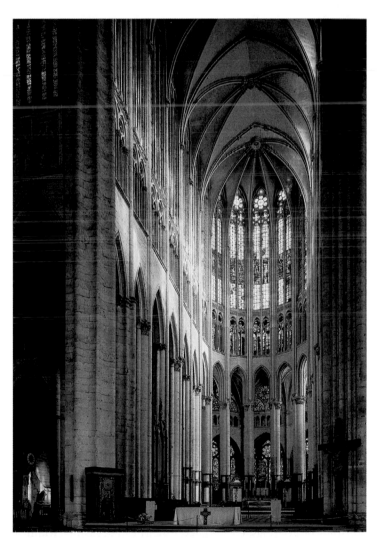

I-3 Choir of Beauvais Cathedral (looking east), Beauvais, France, rebuilt after 1284.

The style of an object or building often varies from region to region. This cathedral has towering stone vaults and large stained-glass windows typical of 13th-century French architecture.

I-4 Interior of Santa Croce (looking east), Florence, Italy, begun 1294.

In contrast to Beauvais Cathedral (FIG. I-3), this contemporaneous Florentine church conforms to the quite different regional style of Italy. The building has a low timber roof and small windows.

I-5 GEORGIA O'KEEFFE, *Jack-in-the-Pulpit No. 4,* 1930. Oil on canvas, 3′ 4″ × 2′ 6″. National Gallery of Art, Washington (Alfred Stieglitz Collection, bequest of Georgia O'Keeffe).

O'Keeffe's paintings feature close-up views of petals and leaves in which the organic forms become powerful abstract compositions. This approach to painting typifies the artist's distinctive personal style.

two contemporaneous churches served similar purposes, regional style mainly explains their differing appearance.

Personal style, the distinctive manner of individual artists or architects, often decisively explains stylistic discrepancies among monuments of the same time and place. In 1930 the American painter GEORGIA O'KEEFFE (1887–1986) produced a series of paintings of flowering plants. One of them—*Jack-in-the-Pulpit No. 4* (FIG. I-5)—is a sharply focused close-up view of petals and leaves. O'Keeffe captured the growing plant's slow, controlled motion while converting the plant into a powerful abstract composition of lines, forms, and colors (see the discussion of art historical vocabulary in the next section). Only a year later, another American artist, BEN SHAHN (1898–1969), painted *The Passion of Sacco and Vanzetti* (FIG. I-6), a stinging commentary on social injustice inspired by the trial and execution of two Italian anarchists, Nicola Sacco and Bartolomeo Vanzetti. Many people believed Sacco and Vanzetti had been unjustly convicted of killing two men in a robbery in 1920. Shahn's painting compresses time in a symbolic representation of the trial and its aftermath. The two executed men lie in their coffins. Presiding over them are the three members of the commission (headed by a college president wearing academic cap and gown) who declared the original trial fair and cleared the way for the

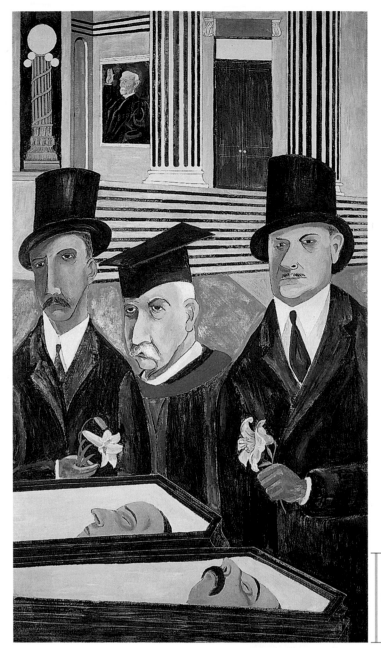

I-6 BEN SHAHN, *The Passion of Sacco and Vanzetti,* 1931–1932. Tempera on canvas, 7′ ½″ × 4′. Whitney Museum of American Art, New York (gift of Edith and Milton Lowenthal in memory of Juliana Force).

O'Keeffe's contemporary, Shahn developed a style markedly different from hers. His paintings are often social commentaries on recent events and incorporate readily identifiable people.

executions. Behind, on the wall of a stately government building, hangs the framed portrait of the judge who pronounced the initial sentence. Personal style, not period or regional style, sets Shahn's canvas apart from O'Keeffe's. The contrast is extreme here because of the very different subjects the artists chose. But even when two artists depict the same subject, the results can vary widely. The *way* O'Keeffe painted flowers and the *way* Shahn painted faces are distinctive and unlike the styles of their contemporaries. (See the "Who Made It?" discussion on page 6.)

The different kinds of artistic styles are not mutually exclusive. For example, an artist's personal style may change dramatically during a long career. Art historians then must distinguish among

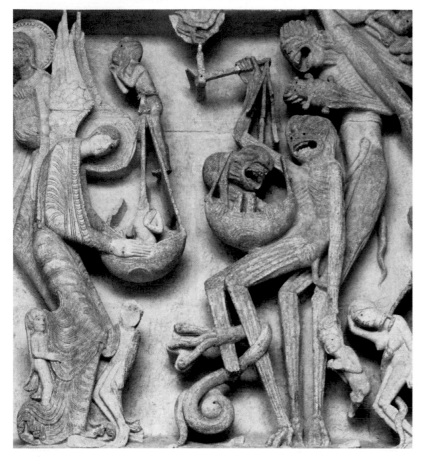

I-7 Gislebertus, *The weighing of souls*, detail of *Last Judgment* (fig. 12-1), west tympanum of Saint-Lazare, Autun, France, ca. 1120–1135.

In this high relief portraying the weighing of souls on judgment day, Gislebertus used disproportion and distortion to dehumanize the devilish figure yanking on the scales of justice.

the different period styles of a particular artist, such as the "Rose Period" and the "Cubist Period" of the prolific 20th-century artist Pablo Picasso.

WHAT IS ITS SUBJECT? Another major concern of art historians is, of course, subject matter, encompassing the story, or narrative; the scene presented; the action's time and place; the persons involved; and the environment and its details. Some artworks, such as modern *abstract* paintings (fig. I-2), have no subject, not even a setting. The "subject" is the artwork itself—its colors, textures, composition, and size. But when artists represent people, places, or actions, viewers must identify these features to achieve complete understanding of the work. Art historians traditionally separate pictorial subjects into various categories, such as religious, historical, mythological, *genre* (daily life), portraiture, *landscape* (a depiction of a place), *still life* (an arrangement of inanimate objects), and their numerous subdivisions and combinations.

Iconography—literally, the "writing of images"—refers both to the content, or subject, of an artwork, and to the study of content in art. By extension, it also includes the study of *symbols,* images that stand for other images or encapsulate ideas. In Christian art, two intersecting lines of unequal length or a simple geometric cross can serve as an emblem of the religion as a whole, symbolizing the cross of Jesus Christ's crucifixion. A symbol also can be a familiar object the artist imbued with greater meaning. A balance or scale, for example, may symbolize justice or the weighing of souls on judgment day (fig. I-7).

Artists may depict figures with unique *attributes* identifying them. In Christian art, for example, each of the authors of the biblical gospel books, the four evangelists (fig. I-8), has a distinctive attribute. People can recognize Saint John by the eagle associated with him, Luke by the ox, Mark by the lion, and Matthew by the winged man.

Throughout the history of art, artists have used *personifications*—abstract ideas codified in human form. Worldwide, people visualize Liberty as a robed woman wearing a rayed crown and holding a torch because of the fame of the colossal statue set up in New York City's harbor in 1886.

I-8 The four evangelists, folio 14 verso of the *Aachen Gospels*, ca. 810. Ink and tempera on vellum, 1' × 9½". Domschatzkammer, Aachen.

Artists depict figures with attributes in order to identify them for viewers. The authors of the four gospels have distinctive attributes—eagle (John), ox (Luke), lion (Mark), and winged man (Matthew).

1 in.

Art History in the 21st Century **5**

I-9 ALBRECHT DÜRER, *The Four Horsemen of the Apocalypse*, ca. 1498. Woodcut, 1′ 3¼″ × 11″. Metropolitan Museum of Art, New York (gift of Junius S. Morgan, 1919).

Personifications are abstract ideas codified in human form. Here, Albrecht Dürer represented Death, Famine, War, and Pestilence as four men on charging horses, each one carrying an identifying attribute.

The Four Horsemen of the Apocalypse (FIG. I-9) is a terrifying late-15th-century depiction of the fateful day at the end of time when, according to the Bible's last book, Death, Famine, War, and Pestilence will annihilate the human race. German artist ALBRECHT DÜRER (1471–1528) personified Death as an emaciated old man with a pitchfork. Dürer's Famine swings the scales for weighing human souls (compare FIG. I-7), War wields a sword, and Pestilence draws a bow.

Even without considering style and without knowing a work's maker, informed viewers can determine much about the work's period and provenance by iconographical and subject analysis alone. In *The Passion of Sacco and Vanzetti* (FIG. I-6), for example, the two coffins, the trio headed by an academic, and the robed judge in the background are all pictorial clues revealing the painting's subject. The work's date must be after the trial and execution, probably while the event was still newsworthy. And because the two men's deaths caused the greatest outrage in the United States, the painter–social critic was probably American.

WHO MADE IT? If Ben Shahn had not signed his painting of Sacco and Vanzetti, an art historian could still assign, or *attribute* (make an *attribution* of), the work to him based on knowledge of the artist's personal style. Although signing (and dating) works is quite common (but by no means universal) today, in the history of art countless works exist whose artists remain unknown. Because personal style can play a major role in determining the character of an artwork, art historians often try to attribute anonymous works to known artists. Sometimes they assemble a group of works all thought to be by the same person, even though none of the objects in the group is the known work of an artist with a recorded name. Art historians thus reconstruct the careers of artists such as "the Achilles Painter," the anonymous ancient Greek artist whose masterwork is a depiction of the hero Achilles. Scholars base their attributions on internal evidence, such as the distinctive way an artist draws or carves drapery folds, earlobes, or flowers. It requires a keen, highly trained eye and long experience to become a *connoisseur,* an expert in assigning artworks to "the hand" of one artist rather than another. Attribution is subjective, of course, and ever open to doubt. At present, for example, international debate rages over attributions to the famous 17th-century Dutch painter Rembrandt van Rijn.

Sometimes a group of artists works in the same style at the same time and place. Art historians designate such a group as a *school. School* does not mean an educational institution or art academy. The term connotes only shared chronology, style, and geography. Art historians speak, for example, of the Dutch school of the 17th century and, within it, of subschools such as those of the cities of Haarlem, Utrecht, and Leyden.

WHO PAID FOR IT? The interest many art historians show in attribution reflects their conviction that the identity of an artwork's maker is the major reason the object looks the way it does. For them, personal style is of paramount importance. But in many times and places, artists had little to say about what form their work would take. They toiled in obscurity, doing the bidding of their *patrons,* those who paid them to make individual works or employed them on a continuing basis. The role of patrons in dictating the content and shaping the form of artworks is also an important subject of art historical inquiry.

In the art of portraiture, to name only one category of painting and sculpture, the patron has often played a dominant role in deciding how the artist represented the subject, whether that person was the patron or another individual, such as a spouse, son, or mother. Many Egyptian pharaohs and some Roman emperors, for example, insisted artists depict them with unlined faces and perfect youthful bodies no matter how old they were when portrayed. In these cases, the state employed the sculptors and painters, and the artists had no choice but to portray their patrons in the officially approved manner. This is why Augustus, who lived to age 76, looks so young in his portraits (FIG. I-10). Although Roman emperor for more than 40 years, Augustus demanded artists always represent him as a young, godlike head of state.

All modes of artistic production reveal the impact of patronage. Learned monks provided the themes for the sculptural decoration of medieval church portals (FIG. I-7). Renaissance princes and popes dictated the subject, size, and materials of artworks destined for display in buildings also constructed according to their specifications. An art historian could make a very long list of commissioned works, and it would indicate patrons have had diverse tastes and needs throughout the history of art and consequently have demanded different kinds of art. Whenever a patron contracts an artist or architect to paint, sculpt, or build in a prescribed manner, personal style often becomes a very minor factor in the ultimate

1 in.

I-10 Bust of Augustus wearing the corona civica, early first century CE. Marble, 1′ 5″ high. Glyptothek, Munich.

Patrons frequently dictate the form their portraits will take. The Roman emperor Augustus demanded he always be portrayed as a young, godlike head of state even though he lived to age 76.

painted on a canvas) or in three dimensions (such as a statue carved from a marble block). Two forms may take the same shape but may differ in their color, texture, and other qualities. *Composition* refers to how an artist *composes* (organizes) forms in an artwork, either by placing shapes on a flat surface or by arranging forms in space.

MATERIAL AND TECHNIQUE To create art forms, artists shape materials (pigment, clay, marble, gold, and many more) with tools (pens, brushes, chisels, and so forth). Each of the materials and tools available has its own potentialities and limitations. Part of all artists' creative activity is to select the *medium* and instrument most suitable to the purpose—or to develop new media and tools, such as bronze and concrete in antiquity and cameras and computers in modern times. The processes artists employ, such as applying paint to canvas with a brush, and the distinctive, personal ways they handle materials constitute their *technique*. Form, material, and technique interrelate and are central to analyzing any work of art.

LINE Among the most important elements defining an artwork's shape or form is *line*. A line can be understood as the path of a point moving in space, an invisible line of sight. More commonly, however, artists and architects make a line visible by drawing (or chiseling) it on a *plane,* a flat surface. A line may be very thin, wirelike, and delicate. It may be thick and heavy. Or it may alternate quickly from broad to narrow, the strokes jagged or the outline broken. When a continuous line defines an object's outer shape, art historians call it a *contour line.* All of these line qualities are present in Dürer's *The Four Horsemen of the Apocalypse* (FIG. I-9). Contour lines define the basic shapes of clouds, human and animal limbs, and weapons. Within the forms, series of short broken lines create shadows and textures. An overall pattern of long parallel strokes suggests the dark sky on the frightening day when the world is about to end.

COLOR Light reveals all *colors.* Light in the world of the painter and other artists differs from natural light. Natural light, or sunlight, is whole or *additive light.* As the sum of all the wavelengths composing the visible *spectrum,* it may be disassembled or fragmented into the individual colors of the spectral band. The painter's light in art—the light reflected from pigments and objects—is *subtractive light.* Paint pigments produce their individual colors by reflecting a segment of the spectrum while absorbing all the rest. Green pigment, for example, subtracts or absorbs all the light in the spectrum except that seen as green.

Hue is the property giving a color its name. Although the spectrum colors merge into each other, artists usually conceive of their hues as distinct from one another. Color has two basic variables—the apparent amount of light reflected and the apparent purity. A change in one must produce a change in the other. Some terms for these variables are *value,* or *tonality* (the degree of lightness or darkness), and *intensity,* or *saturation* (the purity of a color, its brightness or dullness).

Artists call the three basic colors—red, yellow, and blue—the *primary colors.* The *secondary colors* result from mixing pairs of primaries: orange (red and yellow), purple (red and blue), and green (yellow and blue). *Complementary colors* represent the pairing of a primary color and the secondary color created from mixing the two other primary colors—red and green, yellow and purple, and blue and orange. They "complement," or complete, each other, one absorbing colors the other reflects.

appearance of the painting, statue, or building. In these cases, the identity of the patron reveals more to art historians than does the identity of the artist or school. The portrait of Augustus illustrated here (FIG. I-10)—showing the emperor wearing a *corona civica,* or civic crown—was the work of a virtuoso sculptor, a master wielder of hammer and chisel. But scores of similar portraits of this Roman emperor also exist today. They differ in quality but not in kind from this one. The patron, not the artist, determined the character of these artworks. Augustus's public image never varied.

The Words Art Historians Use

As in all fields of study, art history has its own specialized vocabulary consisting of hundreds of words, but certain basic terms are indispensable for describing artworks and buildings of any time and place. They make up the essential vocabulary of *formal analysis,* the visual analysis of artistic form. Definitions and discussions of the most important art historical terms follow.

FORM AND COMPOSITION *Form* refers to an object's shape and structure, either in two dimensions (for example, a figure

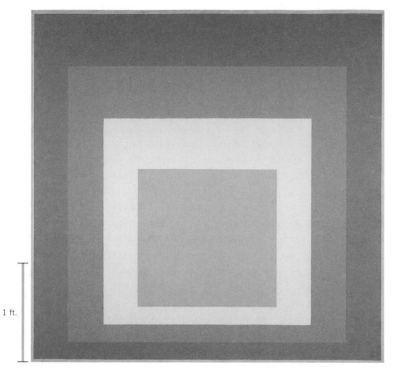

1 ft.

I-11 JOSEF ALBERS, *Homage to the Square: "Ascending,"* 1953. Oil on composition board, 3′ 7½″ × 3′ 7½″. Whitney Museum of American Art, New York.

Albers painted hundreds of canvases using the same composition but employing variations in hue, saturation, and value in order to reveal the relativity and instability of color perception.

Artists can manipulate the appearance of colors, however. One artist who made a systematic investigation of the formal aspects of art, especially color, was JOSEF ALBERS (1888–1976), a German-born artist who emigrated to the United States in 1933. In connection with his studies, Albers created the series *Homage to the Square*—hundreds of paintings, most of which are color variations on the same composition of concentric squares, as in the illustrated example (FIG. I-11). The series reflected Albers's belief that art originates in "the discrepancy between physical fact and psychic effect."[1] Because the composition in most of these paintings remains constant, the works succeed in revealing the relativity and instability of color perception. Albers varied the hue, saturation, and value of each square in the paintings in this series. As a result, the sizes of the squares from painting to painting appear to vary (although they remain the same), and the sensations emanating from the paintings range from clashing dissonance to delicate serenity. Albers explained his motivation for focusing on color juxtapositions:

> They [the colors] are juxtaposed for various and changing visual effects.... Such action, reaction, interaction ... is sought in order to make obvious how colors influence and change each other; that the same color, for instance—with different grounds or neighbors—looks different.... Such color deceptions prove that we see colors almost never unrelated to each other.[2]

TEXTURE The term *texture* refers to the quality of a surface, such as rough or shiny. Art historians distinguish between true texture, that is, the tactile quality of the surface, and represented texture, as when painters depict an object as having a certain tex-

ture even though the pigment is the true texture. Sometimes artists combine different materials of different textures on a single surface, juxtaposing paint with pieces of wood, newspaper, fabric, and so forth. Art historians refer to this mixed-media technique as *collage*. Texture is, of course, a key determinant of any sculpture's character. People's first impulse is usually to handle a work of sculpture—even though museum signs often warn "Do not touch!" Sculptors plan for this natural human response, using surfaces varying in texture from rugged coarseness to polished smoothness. Textures are often intrinsic to a material, influencing the type of stone, wood, plastic, clay, or metal sculptors select.

SPACE, MASS, AND VOLUME *Space* is the bounded or boundless "container" of objects. For art historians, space can be the real three-dimensional space occupied by a statue or a vase or contained within a room or courtyard. Or space can be *illusionistic*, as when painters depict an image (or illusion) of the three-dimensional spatial world on a two-dimensional surface.

Mass and *volume* describe three-dimensional objects and space. In both architecture and sculpture, mass is the bulk, density, and weight of matter in space. Yet the mass need not be solid. It can be the exterior form of enclosed space. Mass can apply to a solid Egyptian pyramid or stone statue, to a church, synagogue, or mosque—architectural shells enclosing sometimes vast spaces—and to a hollow metal statue or baked clay pot. Volume is the space that mass organizes, divides, or encloses. It may be a building's interior spaces, the intervals between a structure's masses, or the amount of space occupied by three-dimensional objects such as a statue, pot, or chair. Volume and mass describe both the exterior and interior forms of a work of art—the forms of the matter of which it is composed and the spaces immediately around the work and interacting with it.

PERSPECTIVE AND FORESHORTENING *Perspective* is one of the most important pictorial devices for organizing forms in space. Throughout history, artists have used various types of perspective to create an illusion of depth or space on a two-dimensional surface. The French painter CLAUDE LORRAIN (1600–1682) employed several perspective devices in *Embarkation of the Queen of Sheba* (FIG. I-12), a painting of a biblical episode set in a 17th-century European harbor with a Roman ruin in the left foreground. For example, the figures and boats on the shoreline are much larger than those in the distance. Decreasing the size of an object makes it appear farther away. Also, the top and bottom of the port building at the painting's right side are not parallel horizontal lines, as they are in a real building. Instead, the lines converge beyond the structure, leading the viewer's eye toward the hazy, indistinct sun on the horizon. These perspective devices—the reduction of figure size, the convergence of diagonal lines, and the blurring of distant forms—have been familiar features of Western art since the ancient Greeks. But it is important to note at the outset that all kinds of perspective are only pictorial conventions, even when one or more types of perspective may be so common in a given culture that people accept them as "natural" or as "true" means of representing the natural world.

In *Waves at Matsushima* (FIG. I-13), a Japanese seascape painting on a six-part folding screen, OGATA KORIN (1658–1716) ignored these Western perspective conventions. A Western viewer might interpret the left half of Korin's composition as depicting the distant horizon, as in Claude's painting, but the sky is a flat, unnatural gold, and in five of the six sections of the composition, waves fill the

I-12 CLAUDE LORRAIN, *Embarkation of the Queen of Sheba,* 1648. Oil on canvas, 4' 10" × 6' 4". National Gallery, London.

To create the illusion of a deep landscape, Claude Lorrain employed perspective, reducing the size of and blurring the most distant forms. Also, all diagonal lines converge on a single point.

1 ft.

full height of the screen. The rocky outcroppings decrease in size with distance, but all are in sharp focus, and there are no shadows. The Japanese artist was less concerned with locating the boulders and waves in space than with composing shapes on a surface, playing the water's swelling curves against the jagged contours of the rocks. Neither the French nor the Japanese painting can be said to project "correctly" what viewers "in fact" see. One painting is not a "better" picture of the world than the other. The European and Asian artists simply approached the problem of picture-making differently.

1 ft.

I-13 OGATA KORIN, *Waves at Matsushima,* Edo period, ca. 1700–1716. Six-panel folding screen, ink, color, and gold leaf on paper, 4' 11$\frac{1}{8}$" × 12' $\frac{7}{8}$". Museum of Fine Arts, Boston (Fenollosa-Weld Collection).

Korin was more concerned with creating an intriguing composition of shapes on a surface than with locating boulders and waves in space. Asian artists rarely employed Western perspective.

I-14 PETER PAUL RUBENS, *Lion Hunt*, 1617–1618. Oil on canvas, 8′ 2″ × 12′ 5″. Alte Pinakothek, Munich.

Foreshortening—the representation of a figure or object at an angle to the picture plane—is a common device in Western art for creating the illusion of depth. Foreshortening is a type of perspective.

1 ft.

Artists also represent single figures in space in varying ways. When Flemish artist PETER PAUL RUBENS (1577–1640) painted *Lion Hunt* (FIG. I-14), he used *foreshortening* for all the hunters and animals—that is, he represented their bodies at angles to the picture plane. When in life one views a figure at an angle, the body appears to contract as it extends back in space. Foreshortening is a kind of perspective. It produces the illusion that one part of the body is farther away than another, even though all the forms are on the same surface. Especially noteworthy in *Lion Hunt* are the gray horse at the left, seen from behind with the bottom of its left rear hoof facing viewers and most of its head hidden

I-15 Hesire, relief from his tomb at Saqqara, Egypt, Dynasty III, ca. 2650 BCE. Wood, 3′ 9″ high. Egyptian Museum, Cairo.

Egyptian artists combined frontal and profile views to give a precise picture of the parts of the human body, as opposed to depicting how an individual body appears from a specific viewpoint.

1 ft.

by its rider's shield, and the fallen hunter at the painting's lower right corner, whose barely visible legs and feet recede into the distance.

The artist who carved the portrait of the ancient Egyptian official Hesire (FIG. I-15) did not employ foreshortening. That artist's purpose was to present the various human body parts as clearly as possible, without overlapping. The lower part of Hesire's body is in profile to give the most complete view of the legs, with both the heels and toes of the foot visible. The frontal torso, however, allows viewers to see its full shape, including both shoulders, equal in size, as in nature. (Compare the shoulders of the hunter on the gray horse or those of the fallen hunter in *Lion Hunt*'s left foreground.) The result—an "unnatural" 90-degree twist at the waist—provides a precise picture of human body parts. Rubens and the Egyptian sculptor used very different means of depicting forms in space. Once again, neither is the "correct" manner.

PROPORTION AND SCALE *Proportion* concerns the relationships (in terms of size) of the parts of persons, buildings, or objects. People can judge "correct proportions" intuitively ("that statue's head seems the right size for the body"). Or proportion can be a mathematical relationship between the size of one part of an artwork or building and the other parts within the work. Proportion in art implies using a *module,* or basic unit of measure. When an artist or architect uses a formal system of proportions, all parts of a building, body, or other entity will be fractions or multiples of the module. A module might be a *column*'s diameter, the height of a human head, or any other component whose dimensions can be multiplied or divided to determine the size of the work's other parts.

In certain times and places, artists have devised *canons,* or systems, of "correct" or "ideal" proportions for representing human figures, constituent parts of buildings, and so forth. In ancient Greece, many sculptors formulated canons of proportions so strict and all-encompassing that they calculated the size of every body part in advance, even the fingers and toes, according to mathematical ratios.

Proportional systems can differ sharply from period to period, culture to culture, and artist to artist. Part of the task art history students face is to perceive and adjust to these differences. In fact, many artists have used disproportion and distortion deliberately for expressive effect. In the medieval French depiction of the weighing of souls on judgment day (FIG. I-7), the devilish figure yanking down on the scale has distorted facial features and stretched, lined limbs with animal-like paws for feet. Disproportion and distortion make him appear "inhuman," precisely as the sculptor intended.

In other cases, artists have used disproportion to focus attention on one body part (often the head) or to single out a group member (usually the leader). These intentional "unnatural" discrepancies in proportion constitute what art historians call *hierarchy of scale,* the enlarging of elements considered the most important. On the bronze plaque from Benin, Nigeria, illustrated here (FIG. I-1), the sculptor enlarged all the heads for emphasis and also varied the size of each figure according to the person's social status. Central, largest, and therefore most important is the Benin king, mounted on horseback. The horse has been a symbol of power and wealth in many societies from prehistory to the present. That the Benin king is disproportionately larger than his horse, contrary to nature, further aggrandizes him. Two large attendants fan the king. Other figures of smaller size and status at the Benin court stand on the king's left and right and in the plaque's upper corners. One tiny figure next to the horse is almost hidden from view beneath the king's feet.

One problem students of art history—and professional art historians too—confront when studying illustrations in art history books is that although the relative sizes of figures and objects in a painting or sculpture are easy to discern, it is impossible to determine the absolute size of the work reproduced because they all appear at approximately the same size on the page. Readers of *Art through the Ages* can learn the exact size of all artworks from the dimensions given in the captions and, more intuitively, from the scales positioned at the lower left or right corner of each illustration.

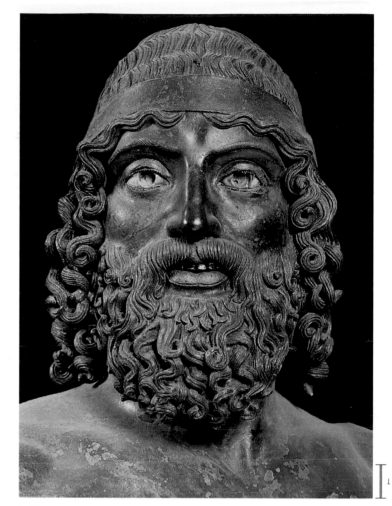

I-17 Head of a warrior, detail of a statue (FIG. 5-35) from the sea off Riace, Italy, ca. 460–450 BCE. Bronze, full statue 6′ 6″ high. Museo Nazionale della Magna Grecia, Reggio Calabria.

The sculptor of this life-size statue of a bearded Greek warrior cast the head, limbs, torso, hands, and feet in separate molds, then welded the pieces together and added the eyes in a different material.

I-16 MICHELANGELO BUONARROTI, unfinished statue, 1527–1528. Marble, 8′ 7½″ high. Galleria dell'Accademia, Florence.

Carving a freestanding figure from stone or wood is a subtractive process. Michelangelo thought of sculpture as a process of "liberating" the statue within the block of marble.

CARVING AND CASTING Sculptural technique falls into two basic categories, *subtractive* and *additive. Carving* is a subtractive technique. The final form is a reduction of the original mass of a block of stone, a piece of wood, or another material. Wood statues were once tree trunks, and stone statues began as blocks pried from mountains. The unfinished marble statue illustrated here (FIG. I-16) by renowned Italian artist MICHELANGELO BUONARROTI (1475–1564) clearly reveals the original shape of the stone block. Michelangelo thought of sculpture as a process of "liberating" the statue within the block. All sculptors of stone or wood cut away (subtract) "excess material." When they finish, they "leave behind" the statue—in this example, a twisting nude male form whose head Michelangelo never freed from the stone block.

In additive sculpture, the artist builds up (*models*) the forms, usually in clay around a framework, or *armature.* Or a sculptor may fashion a *mold,* a hollow form for shaping, or *casting,* a fluid substance such as bronze or plaster. The ancient Greek sculptor who made the bronze statue of a warrior found in the sea near Riace, Italy, cast the head (FIG. I-17) as well as the limbs, torso, hands, and feet (FIG. 5-35) in separate molds and then *welded* them together (joined them by heating). Finally, the artist added features, such as the pupils of the eyes (now missing), in other materials. The warrior's teeth are silver, and his lower lip is copper.

RELIEF SCULPTURE *Statues* and *busts* (head, shoulders, and chest) that exist independent of any architectural frame or setting and that viewers can walk around are *freestanding* sculptures, or *sculptures in the round,* whether the artist produced the piece by carving (FIG. I-10) or casting (FIG. I-17). In *relief* sculpture, the subjects project from the background but remain part of it. In *high-relief* sculpture, the images project boldly. In some cases, such as the medieval weighing-of-souls scene (FIG. I-7), the relief is so high the forms not only cast shadows on the background, but some parts are even in the round, which explains why some pieces, for example, the arms of the scales, broke off centuries ago. In *low-relief,* or *bas-relief, sculpture,* such as the portrait of Hesire (FIG. I-15), the projection is slight. Artists can produce relief sculptures, as they do sculptures in the round, either by carving or casting. The plaque from Benin (FIG. I-1) is an example of bronze-casting in high relief.

ARCHITECTURAL DRAWINGS Buildings are groupings of enclosed spaces and enclosing masses. People experience architecture both visually and by moving through and around it, so they perceive architectural space and mass together. These spaces and masses can be represented graphically in several ways, including as plans, sections, elevations, and cutaway drawings.

A *plan,* essentially a map of a floor, shows the placement of a structure's masses and, therefore, the spaces they circumscribe and enclose. A *section,* a kind of vertical plan, depicts the placement of the masses as if someone cut through the building along a plane. Drawings showing a theoretical slice across a structure's width are *lateral sections.* Those cutting through a building's length are *longitudinal sections.* Illustrated here are the plan and lateral section of Beauvais Cathedral (FIG. I-18), which readers can compare with the photograph of the church's *choir* (FIG. I-3). The plan shows the choir's shape and the location of the *piers* dividing the *aisles* and supporting the *vaults* above, as well as the pattern of the crisscrossing vault *ribs.* The lateral section shows not only the interior of the choir with its vaults and tall *stained-glass* windows but also the structure of the roof and the form of the exterior *flying buttresses* holding the vaults in place.

Other types of architectural drawings appear throughout this book. An *elevation* drawing is a head-on view of an external or internal wall. A *cutaway* combines in a single drawing an exterior view with an interior view of part of a building.

This overview of the art historian's vocabulary is not exhaustive, nor have artists used only painting, drawing, sculpture, and architecture as media over the millennia. Ceramics, jewelry, textiles, photography, and computer graphics are just some of the numerous other arts. All of them involve highly specialized techniques described in distinct vocabularies. As in this introductory chapter, new terms are in *italics* when they first appear. The comprehensive Glossary at the end of the book contains definitions of all italicized terms.

Art History and Other Disciplines

By its very nature, the work of art historians intersects with the work of others in many fields of knowledge, not only in the humanities but also in the social and natural sciences. Today, art historians must go beyond the boundaries of what the public and even professional art historians of previous generations traditionally considered the specialized discipline of art history. In short, art historical research in the 21st century is typically interdisciplinary in nature. To cite one example, in an effort to unlock the secrets of a particular statue, an art historian might conduct archival research hoping to uncover new documents shedding light on who paid for the work and why, who made it and when, where it originally stood, how its contemporaries viewed it, and a host of other questions. Realizing, however, that the authors of the written documents often were not objective recorders of fact but observers with their own biases and agendas, the art historian may also use methodologies developed in fields such as literary criticism, philosophy, sociology, and gender studies to weigh the evidence the documents provide.

At other times, rather than attempting to master many disciplines at once, art historians band together with other specialists in multidisciplinary inquiries. Art historians might call in chemists

I-18 Plan (*left*) and lateral section (*right*) of Beauvais Cathedral, Beauvais, France, rebuilt after 1284.

Architectural drawings are indispensable aids for the analysis of buildings. Plans are maps of floors, recording the structure's masses. Sections are vertical "slices" across either a building's width or length.

to date an artwork based on the composition of the materials used, or might ask geologists to determine which quarry furnished the stone for a particular statue. X-ray technicians might be enlisted in an attempt to establish whether a painting is a forgery. Of course, art historians often reciprocate by contributing their expertise to the solution of problems in other disciplines. A historian, for example, might ask an art historian to determine—based on style, material, iconography, and other criteria—if any of the portraits of a certain king date after his death. Such information would help establish the ruler's continuing prestige during the reigns of his successors. (Some portraits of Augustus [FIG. I-10], the founder of the Roman Empire, postdate his death by decades, even centuries.)

DIFFERENT WAYS OF SEEING

The history of art can be a history of artists and their works, of styles and stylistic change, of materials and techniques, of images and themes and their meanings, and of contexts and cultures and patrons. The best art historians analyze artworks from many viewpoints. But no art historian (or scholar in any other field), no matter how broad-minded in approach and no matter how experienced, can be truly objective. As were the artists who made the works illustrated and discussed in this book, art historians are members of a society, participants in its culture. How can scholars (and museum visitors and travelers to foreign locales) comprehend cultures unlike their own? They can try to reconstruct the original cultural contexts of artworks, but they are limited by their distance from the thought patterns of the cultures they study and by the obstructions to understanding—the assumptions, presuppositions, and prejudices peculiar to their own culture—their own thought patterns raise. Art historians may reconstruct a distorted picture of the past because of culture-bound blindness.

A single instance underscores how differently people of diverse cultures view the world and how various ways of seeing can result in sharp differences in how artists depict the world. Illustrated here are two contemporaneous portraits of a 19th-century Maori chieftain (FIG. I-19)—one by an Englishman, JOHN HENRY SYLVESTER (active early 19th century), and the other by the New Zealand chieftain himself, TE PEHI KUPE (d. 1829). Both reproduce the chieftain's facial tattooing. The European artist (FIG. I-19, *left*) included the head and shoulders and downplayed the tattooing. The tattoo pattern is one aspect of the likeness among many, no more or less important than the chieftain's European attire. Sylvester also recorded his subject's momentary glance toward the right and the play of light on his hair, fleeting aspects having nothing to do with the figure's identity.

In contrast, Te Pehi Kupe's self-portrait (FIG. I-19, *right*)—made during a trip to Liverpool, England, to obtain European arms to take back to New Zealand—is not a picture of a man situated in space and bathed in light. Rather, it is the chieftain's statement of the supreme importance of the tattoo design announcing his rank among his people. Remarkably, Te Pehi Kupe created the tattoo patterns from memory, without the aid of a mirror. The splendidly composed insignia, presented as a flat design separated from the body and even from the head, is Te Pehi Kupe's image of himself. Only by understanding the cultural context of each portrait can art historians hope to understand why either representation appears as it does.

As noted at the outset, the study of the context of artworks and buildings is one of the central concerns of art historians. *Art through the Ages* seeks to present a history of art and architecture that will help readers to understand not only the subjects, styles, and techniques of paintings, sculptures, buildings, and other art forms created in all parts of the world during 30 millennia but also their cultural and historical contexts. That story now begins.

1 in.

I-19 *Left:* JOHN HENRY SYLVESTER, *Portrait of Te Pehi Kupe,* 1826. Watercolor, $8\frac{1}{4}'' \times 6\frac{1}{4}''$. National Library of Australia, Canberra (Rex Nan Kivell Collection). *Right:* TE PEHI KUPE, *Self-Portrait,* 1826. From Leo Frobenius, *The Childhood of Man* (New York: J. B. Lippincott, 1909).

These strikingly different portraits of the same Maori chief reveal the different ways of seeing by a European artist and an Oceanic one. Understanding the cultural context of artworks is vital to art history.

The species of animals depicted in the cave paintings of France and Spain are not among those Paleolithic humans typically consumed as food. The meaning of these paintings remains an enigma.

Prehistoric painters consistently represented animals in strict profile, the only view showing the head, body, tail, and all four legs. But at Lascaux, both horns are included to give a complete picture of the bull.

The Lascaux animals are inconsistent in size and move in different directions. Some are colored silhouettes; others are outline drawings. They were probably made at different times by different painters.

1 ft.

1-1 Left wall of the Hall of the Bulls in the cave at Lascaux, France, ca. 16,000–14,000 BCE. Largest bull 11′ 6″ long. ◼◀

Most of the animals painted on prehistoric cave walls do not stand on a common ground line, nor do they share a common orientation. Paleolithic paintings have no background and no indication of place.

1

ART BEFORE HISTORY

THE DAWN OF ART

The Old Stone Age, which began around 30,000 BCE, was arguably the most important era in the entire history of art. It was then that humans invented the concept of recording the world around them in pictures, often painted on or carved into the walls of caves.

The oldest and best known painted caves are in southern France, and the cave at Lascaux is the most famous of them all. More than 17,000 years ago, prehistoric painters covered many of the walls of the cave with images of animals. The main chamber (FIG. 1-1), nicknamed the Hall of the Bulls, is an unusually large space and easily accessible, but many of the paintings at Lascaux and in other caves are almost impossible to reach. Even the Hall of the Bulls is far from the cave entrance, and its paintings could only have been seen with the flickering light of a primitive lamp. The representations of animals cannot have been merely decorative, but what meaning they carried for those who made and viewed them remains an enigma. Bulls and horses, the most commonly depicted species, were not diet staples in the Old Stone Age. Why, then, did the painters choose to represent these particular animals? In the absence of written records, no one will ever know.

Art historians can, however, learn a great deal about the working methods and conceptual principles of the world's first artists by closely studying the Lascaux paintings and others like them. The immediate impression a modern viewer gets of a rapidly moving herd is almost certainly false. The "herd" consists of several different kinds of animals of various sizes moving in different directions. Also, two fundamentally different approaches to picture making are on display. Many of the animals are colored silhouettes, whereas others are outline drawings. These differences in style and technique suggest different painters created the images in the Hall of the Bulls at different times, perhaps over the course of generations.

Nonetheless, all prehistoric representations of animals for thousands of years depict the beasts in the same way—in strict profile, the only view of an animal wherein the head, body, tail, and all four legs are visible. The Lascaux painters, however, showed the bulls' horns from the front, not in profile, because two horns are part of the concept "bull." Only much later in the history of art did painters become concerned with how to depict animals and people from a fixed viewpoint or develop an interest in recording the environment around the figures. The paintings created at the dawn of art are in many ways markedly different in kind from all that followed.

PALEOLITHIC ART

Humankind originated in Africa in the very remote past. From that great continent also has come the earliest evidence of human recognition of abstract images in the natural environment, if not the first examples of what people generally call "art." In 1925, explorers of a cave at Makapansgat in South Africa (MAP 19-1) discovered bones of *Australopithecus,* a predecessor of modern humans who lived some three million years ago. Associated with the bones was a waterworn, reddish-brown jasperite pebble (FIG. **1-2**) that bears an uncanny resemblance to a human face. The nearest known source of this variety of ironstone is 20 miles from the cave. Perhaps an early human who took refuge in the rock shelter at Makapansgat noticed the pebble in a streambed and, awestruck by the "face" on the stone, carried it back for safekeeping.

Is the Makapansgat pebble "art"? In modern times, many artists have created works critics universally consider art by removing objects from their normal contexts, altering them, and then labeling them. In 1917, for example, Marcel Duchamp chose a ceramic urinal, set it on its side, called it *Fountain* (FIG. 29-27), and declared his "readymade" worthy of exhibition among more conventional artworks. But the artistic environment of the past century cannot be projected into the remote past. For art historians to classify as an "artwork" a found object such as the Makapansgat pebble, it must have been modified by human intervention beyond mere selection—and it was not. In fact, evidence indicates that, with few exceptions, it was not until three million years later, around 30,000 BCE, when large parts of northern Europe were still covered with glaciers during the Ice Age, that humans intentionally manufactured sculptures and paintings. Only then does the story of art through the ages really begin.

The several millennia following 30,000 BCE brought a powerful outburst of creativity. The works produced by the peoples of the Old Stone Age, or *Paleolithic* period (from the Greek *paleo,* "old," and *lithos,* "stone"), are of an astonishing variety. They range from simple shell necklaces to human and animal forms in ivory, clay, and stone to monumental paintings, engravings, and relief sculptures covering the huge wall surfaces of caves. During the Paleolithic period, humankind went beyond the *recognition* of human and animal forms in the natural environment to the *representation* (literally, the presenting again—in different and substitute form—of something observed) of humans and animals. The immensity of this achievement cannot be overstated.

Africa

Some of the earliest paintings yet discovered come from Africa, and, like the treasured pebble resembling a face found at Makapansgat, the oldest African paintings were portable objects.

1-2 Waterworn pebble resembling a human face, from Makapansgat, South Africa, ca. 3,000,000 BCE. Reddish-brown jasperite, $2\frac{3}{8}''$ wide. Natural History Museum, London.

Three million years ago, someone recognized a face in this pebble and brought it to a rock shelter for safekeeping, but the stone is not an artwork because it was neither manufactured nor modified.

APOLLO 11 CAVE Between 1969 and 1972, scientists working in the Apollo 11 Cave in Namibia (MAP 19-1) found seven fragments of stone plaques with paint on them, including four or five recognizable images of animals. In most cases, including the example illustrated here (FIG. **1-3**), the species is uncertain, but the painters always rendered the forms with care. One plaque depicts a striped beast, possibly a zebra. The approximate date of the charcoal from the archaeological layer containing the Namibian plaques is 23,000 BCE.

As has every artist in every age in every medium, the painter of the Apollo 11 plaque had to answer two questions before beginning work: *What* shall be my subject? *How* shall I represent it? In Paleolithic art, the almost universal answer to the first question was an animal—bison, horse, mammoth, and ibex are the most common. In fact, Paleolithic painters and sculptors depicted humans infrequently, and men almost never. In equally stark contrast to today's world, there was also agreement on the best answer to the second question. Artists represented virtually every animal in every Paleolithic, *Mesolithic* (Middle Stone Age), and *Neolithic* (New Stone Age) painting in the same manner—in strict profile. The profile is the only view of an animal wherein the head, body, tail, and all four legs are visible. The frontal view conceals most of the body, and a three-quarter view

ART BEFORE HISTORY

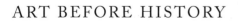

		BCE
30,000 **Paleolithic** 8000	**Neolithic** 2300	

▌ Humans create the first sculptures and paintings, long before the invention of writing ▌ The works range in scale from tiny figurines to life-size paintings and relief sculptures on cave walls	▌ Beginning of agriculture and the formation of the earliest settled communities, first in Anatolia and Mesopotamia and later in Europe ▌ The birth of monumental sculpture and architecture and the introduction of coherent narratives in painting

1-3 Animal facing left, from the Apollo 11 Cave, Namibia, ca. 23,000 BCE. Charcoal on stone, $4\frac{1}{4}'' \times 5''$. State Museum of Namibia, Windhoek.

Like most other paintings for thousands of years, this very early example from Africa represents an animal in strict profile so that the head, body, tail, and all four legs are clearly visible.

1 in.

1-4 Human with feline head, from Hohlenstein-Stadel, Germany, ca. 30,000–28,000 BCE. Mammoth ivory, $11\frac{5}{8}''$ high. Ulmer Museum, Ulm.

One of the oldest known sculptures is this large ivory figure of a human with a feline head. It is uncertain whether the work depicts a composite creature or a human wearing an animal mask.

1 in.

shows neither the front nor side fully. Only the profile view is completely informative about the animal's shape, and that is why Stone Age painters universally chose it. A very long time passed before artists placed any premium on "variety" or "originality," either in subject choice or in representational manner. These are quite modern notions in the history of art. The aim of the earliest painters was to create a convincing image of their subject, a kind of pictorial definition of the animal capturing its very essence, and only the profile view met their needs.

Western Europe

Even older than the Namibian painted plaques are some of the first sculptures and paintings of western Europe (MAP **1-1**), although examples of still greater antiquity may yet be found in Africa, bridging the gap between the Makapansgat pebble and the Apollo 11 Cave painted plaques.

HOHLENSTEIN-STADEL

One of the earliest sculptures discovered yet is an extraordinary ivory statuette (FIG. **1-4**), which may date back as far as 30,000 BCE. Found in fragments inside a cave at Hohlenstein-Stadel in Germany and meticulously restored, the statuette is mammoth ivory and nearly a foot tall—a truly huge image for its era. It represents something that existed only in the vivid imagination of the Paleolithic sculptor who conceived it. It is a human (whether male or female cannot be determined) with a feline head. Composite creatures with animal heads and human bodies (and vice versa) are familiar in the art of ancient Mesopotamia and Egypt (compare, for example, FIGS. 2-10 and 3-36). In those civilizations, surviving texts usually enable historians to name the figures and describe their role in religion and mythology. But for Stone Age representations, no one knows what their makers had in mind. Some scholars identify the animal-headed humans as sorcerers, whereas others describe them as magicians wearing masks. Similarly, Paleolithic human-headed animals have been interpreted as humans dressed up as animals. In the absence of any contemporaneous written explanations—this was a time before writing, before (or pre-) history—researchers can only speculate on the purpose and function of statuettes like the one from Hohlenstein-Stadel.

Art historians are certain, however, that these sculptures were important to those who created them, because manufacturing an ivory figure, especially one a foot tall, was a complicated process. First, the hunter or the sculptor had to remove the tusk from the dead animal by cutting into the ivory where it joined the head. Then the sculptor cut the tusk to the desired size and rubbed it into its approximate final shape with sandstone. Finally, the carver used a sharp stone blade to shape the body, limbs, and head, and a stone burin (a pointed engraving tool) to incise (scratch) lines into the surfaces, as on the Hohlenstein-Stadel creature's arms. All this probably required at least several days of skilled work.

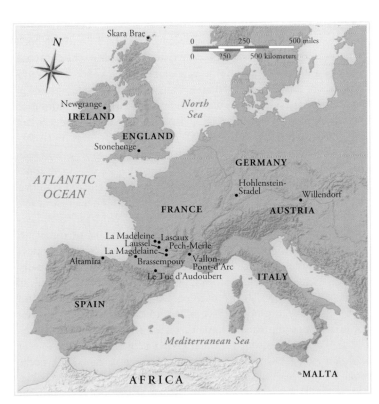

MAP 1-1 Prehistoric sites in Europe.

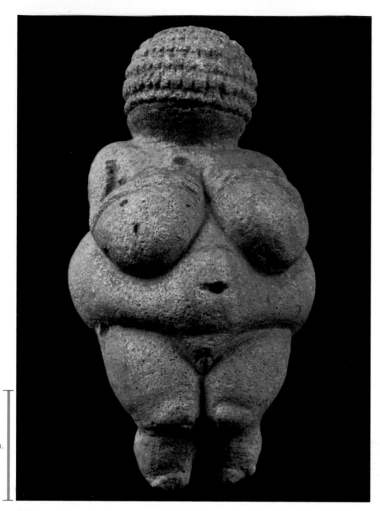

1 in.

1-5 Nude woman (*Venus of Willendorf*), from Willendorf, Austria, ca. 28,000–25,000 BCE. Limestone, 4¼″ high. Naturhistorisches Museum, Vienna. ◼◀

The anatomical exaggerations in this tiny figurine from Willendorf are typical of Paleolithic representations of women, whose child-bearing capabilities ensured the survival of the species.

WILLENDORF The composite feline-human from Germany is exceptional for the Stone Age. The vast majority of prehistoric sculptures depict either animals or humans. In the earliest art, humankind consists almost exclusively of women as opposed to men, and Paleolithic painters and sculptors almost invariably showed them nude, although historians generally assume that during the Ice Age both women and men wore garments covering parts of their bodies. When archaeologists first encountered Stone Age statuettes of women, they dubbed them "Venuses," after the Greco-Roman goddess of beauty and love, whom later artists usually depicted nude. The nickname is inappropriate and misleading. Indeed, it is doubtful the Paleolithic figurines represent deities of any kind.

One of the oldest and most famous prehistoric female images is the tiny limestone figurine of a woman that long ago became known as the *Venus of Willendorf* (FIG. **1-5**) after its *findspot* (place of discovery) in Austria. Its cluster of almost ball-like shapes is unusual, the result in part of the sculptor's response to the natural shape of the stone selected for carving. The anatomical exaggeration has suggested to many observers that this and similar statuettes served as fertility images. But other Paleolithic stone women of far more slender proportions exist, and the meaning of these images is as elusive as everything else about Paleolithic art. Yet

the preponderance of female over male figures in the Old Stone Age seems to indicate a preoccupation with women, whose child-bearing capabilities ensured the survival of the species.

One thing at least is clear: The *Venus of Willendorf* sculptor did not aim for naturalism in shape and proportion. As with most Paleolithic figures, the sculptor did not carve any facial features. A similar but even smaller ivory figurine found in 2008 in a cave at Hohle Fels, near Ulm, Germany, contemporaneous with or perhaps even several thousand years older than the Hohlenstein-Stadel statuette, lacks any head at all. The ivory head (FIG. **1-5A**) of a woman from Brassempouy, France, is a notable exception. The carver of the

1-5A Head of a woman, Brassempouy, ca. 25,000–20,000 BCE.

Willendorf figurine suggested only a mass of curly hair or, as some researchers have argued, a hat woven from plant fibers—evidence for the art of textile manufacture at a very early date. In either case, the emphasis is on female anatomy. The breasts of the Willendorf woman are enormous, far larger in proportion than the tiny forearms and hands that rest upon them. The carver also took pains to scratch into the stone the outline of the pubic triangle. Sculptors often omitted this detail in other early figurines, leading some scholars to question the nature of these figures as fertility images. Whatever the purpose of these statuettes, the makers' intent seems to have been to represent not a specific woman but the female form.

LAUSSEL Probably later in date than the *Venus of Willendorf* is a female figure (FIG. **1-6**) from Laussel in France. The Willendorf and Hohlenstein-Stadel figures are *sculptures in the round* (*freestanding sculptures*). The Laussel woman is one of the earliest *relief sculptures* known. The sculptor employed a stone *chisel* to cut into the relatively flat surface of a large rock in order to create an image that projects from the background. Today, the Laussel relief is on display in a museum, divorced from its original context, a detached piece of what once was a much more imposing monument. When discovered, the Laussel woman (who is about 1½ feet tall, more than four times larger than the Willendorf statuette) was part of a great stone block that measured about 140 cubic feet. The carved block stood in the open air in front of a Paleolithic rock shelter. Rock shelters were a common type of dwelling for early humans, along with huts and the mouths of caves. The Laussel relief is one of many examples of open-air art in the Old Stone Age. The popular notions that early humans dwelled exclusively in caves and that all Paleolithic art comes from mysterious dark caverns are false. Reliefs depicting nude women do, however, occur inside Old Stone Age caves. Perhaps the most interesting is the reclining nude woman (FIG. **1-6A**) on the wall of a corridor in a cave at La Magdeleine, France. She has a counterpart in the relief on the opposite wall (not shown).

1-6A Reclining woman, La Magdeleine, ca. 12,000 BCE.

After chiseling out the female form and incising the details with a sharp burin, the Laussel sculptor applied red ocher, a naturally colored mineral, to the body. (Traces of red ocher coloration also remain on parts of the *Venus of Willendorf*.) Contrary to modern misconceptions, ancient artists usually painted stone sculptures (compare FIG. 5-63A). The Laussel woman has the same bulbous forms as the earlier Willendorf figurine, with a similar exaggeration of the breasts, abdomen, and hips. The head is once again featureless, but the arms have taken on greater importance. The left arm draws attention to the midsection and pubic

1-7 Two bison, reliefs in the cave at Le Tuc d'Audoubert, France, ca. 15,000–10,000 BCE. Clay, right bison 2' $\frac{7}{8}$" long.

Representations of animals are far more common than those of humans in Paleolithic art. The sculptor built up these clay bison using a stone spatula-like smoothing tool and fingers to shape the details.

1-6 Woman holding a bison horn, from Laussel, France, ca. 25,000 20,000 BCE. Painted limestone, 1' 6" high. Musée d'Aquitaine, Bordeaux.

One of the oldest known relief sculptures depicts a woman who holds a bison horn and whose left arm draws attention to her belly. Scholars continue to debate the meaning of the gesture and the horn.

carvers also used antlers as a sculptural medium. The broken spear-thrower carved from a reindeer antler in the form of a bison (FIG. **1-8**) found at La Madeleine in France is only 4 inches long. The sculptor incised lines into the bison's mane using a sharp burin. Compared with the bison at Le Tuc d'Audoubert, the engraving is much more detailed and extends to the horns, eye, ear, nostrils, mouth, tongue, and the hair on the face. Especially interesting is the engraver's decision to represent the bison with its head turned and licking its flank. The small size and irregular shape of the reindeer horn may have been the primary motivation for this space-saving device rather than a desire to record a characteristic anecdotal activity. Whatever the reason, it is noteworthy that the sculptor turned the neck a full 180 degrees to maintain the strict profile Paleolithic sculptors and painters insisted on for the sake of clarity and completeness.

area, and the raised right hand holds what most scholars identify as a bison horn with 13 parallel incised lines. Scholars continue to debate the meaning of the horn as well as the gesture of the left hand.

LE TUC D'AUDOUBERT Paleolithic sculptors sometimes created reliefs by building up forms out of clay rather than by cutting into stone blocks or cave walls. Sometime 12,000 to 17,000 years ago in the low-ceilinged circular space at the end of a succession of cave chambers at Le Tuc d'Audoubert, a master sculptor modeled a pair of bison (FIG. **1-7**) in clay against a large, irregular freestanding rock. The two bison, like the much older painted animal (FIG. 1-3) from the Apollo 11 Cave, are in strict profile. Each is about 2 feet long. They are among the largest Paleolithic sculptures known. The sculptor brought the clay from elsewhere in the cave complex and used both hands to form the overall shape of the animals. The artist then smoothed the surfaces with a spatula-like tool and finally used fingers to shape the eyes, nostrils, mouths, and manes. The cracks in the two reliefs resulted from the drying process and probably appeared within days of the sculptures' completion.

LA MADELEINE As already noted, sculptors fashioned ivory mammoth tusks into human (FIG. 1-5A), animal, and composite human-animal (FIG. 1-4) forms from very early times. Prehistoric

1-8 Bison licking its flank, fragmentary spear-thrower, from La Madeleine, France, ca. 12,000 BCE. Reindeer horn, 4 $\frac{1}{8}$" long. Musée d'Archéologie Nationale, Saint-Germain-en-Laye.

This fragment of a spear-thrower was carved from a reindeer antler. The sculptor turned the bison's head a full 180 degrees to maintain the profile view and incised the details with a stone burin.

Paleolithic Cave Painting

The caves of Altamira (FIG. 1-9), Lascaux (FIGS. 1-1, 1-12, and 1-12A), and other sites in prehistoric Europe are a few hundred to several thousand feet long. They are often choked, sometimes almost impassably, by mineral deposits, such as stalactites and stalagmites. Far inside these caverns, well removed from the cave mouths early humans often chose for habitation, painters sometimes made pictures on the walls and ceilings. Examples of Paleolithic painting now have been found at more than 200 sites, but art historians still regard painted caves as rare occurrences because the images in them, even if they number in the hundreds, were created over a period of some 10,000 to 20,000 years.

To illuminate the surfaces while working, Paleolithic painters used stone lamps filled with marrow or fat, with a wick, perhaps of moss. For drawing, they used chunks of red and yellow ocher. For painting, they ground these same ochers into powders they mixed with water before applying. Analyses of the pigments used show that Paleolithic painters employed many different minerals, attesting to a technical sophistication surprising at so early a date.

Large flat stones served as *palettes*. The painters made brushes from reeds, bristles, or twigs and may have used a blowpipe of reeds or hollow bones to spray pigments on out-of-reach surfaces. Some caves have natural ledges on the rock walls upon which the painters could have stood in order to reach the upper surfaces of the naturally formed chambers and corridors. One Lascaux gallery wall has holes that once probably anchored a scaffold made of saplings lashed together. Despite the difficulty of making the tools and pigments, modern attempts at replicating the techniques of Paleolithic painting have demonstrated that skilled workers could cover large surfaces with images in less than a day.

1-9 Bison, detail of a painted ceiling in the cave at Altamira, Spain, ca. 13,000–11,000 BCE. Standing bison 5′ 2½″ long.

As in other Paleolithic caves, the painted ceiling at Altamira has no ground line or indication of setting. The artist's sole concern was to represent the animals, not to locate them in a specific place.

1 ft.

ALTAMIRA The works examined here thus far, whether portable or fixed to rocky outcroppings or cave walls, are all small, with the exception of the Lascaux Hall of the Bulls (FIG. 1-1). The Lascaux animals dwarf all the other illustrated examples, as do the other "herds" of painted animals that roam the walls and ceilings of other caves in southern France and northern Spain, where some of the most spectacular examples of prehistoric art have been discovered (see "Paleolithic Cave Painting," above). An amateur archaeologist accidentally found the first examples of Stone Age mural painting at Altamira, Spain, in 1879. Don Marcelino Sanz de Sautuola was exploring a cave on his estate where he had previously collected specimens of flint and carved bone. His little daughter Maria was with him when they reached a chamber some 85 feet from the cave's entrance. Because it was dark and the ceiling of the debris-filled cavern was only a few inches above the father's head, the child was the first to discern, from her lower vantage point, the shadowy forms of painted beasts on the cave roof (FIG. 1-9, a detail of a much larger painting approximately 60 feet long). Sanz de Sautuola was certain the bison painted on the ceiling of the cave dated to prehistoric times. Professional archaeologists, however, doubted

the authenticity of these works, and at the Lisbon Congress on Prehistoric Archaeology in 1880, they officially dismissed the paintings as forgeries. But by the close of the century, other caves had been discovered with painted walls partially covered by mineral deposits that would have taken thousands of years to accumulate. This finding finally persuaded skeptics that the world's oldest paintings were of an age far more remote than anyone had ever dreamed.

The bison at Altamira are 13,000 to 14,000 years old, but the painters of Paleolithic Spain approached the problem of representing an animal in essentially the same way as the painter of the Namibian stone plaque (FIG. 1-3), who worked in Africa more than 10,000 years earlier. Every one of the Altamira bison is in profile, whether alive and standing or curled up on the ground—probably dead, although this is disputed. (One suggestion is that these bison are giving birth.) To maintain the profile in the latter case, the painter had to adopt a viewpoint above the animal, looking down, rather than the view of a person standing on the ground.

Modern critics often refer to the Altamira animals as a "group" of bison, but that is very likely a misnomer. The several bison in FIG. 1-9 do not stand on a common *ground line* (a painted or carved

Art in the Old Stone Age

Ever since the discovery in 1879 of the first cave paintings, scholars have wondered why the hunters of the Old Stone Age decided to cover the surfaces of dark caverns with animal images such as those found at Lascaux (FIG. 1-1), Altamira (FIG. 1-9), and Pech-Merle (FIG. 1-10). Researchers have proposed various theories, including that the painted and engraved animals were mere decoration, but this explanation cannot account for the inaccessibility of many of the representations. In fact, the remote locations of many images, and indications the caves were used for centuries, are precisely why many experts have suggested the prehistoric hunters attributed magical properties to the images they painted and sculpted. According to this argument, by confining animals to the surfaces of their cave walls, the Paleolithic hunters believed they were bringing the beasts under their control. Some prehistorians have even hypothesized that rituals or dances were performed in front of the images and that these rites served to improve the hunters' luck. Still other scholars have suggested the animal representations may have served as teaching tools to instruct new hunters about the character of the various species they would encounter or even to serve as targets for spears.

In contrast, some prehistorians have argued that the magical purpose of the paintings and reliefs was not to facilitate the *destruc-tion* of bison and other species. Instead, they believe prehistoric painters and sculptors created animal images to assure the *survival* of the herds on which Paleolithic peoples depended for their food supply and for their clothing. A central problem for both the hunting-magic and food-creation theories is that Old Stone Age diet staples do not include the animals most frequently portrayed. For example, faunal remains show that the Altamirans ate red deer, not bison.

Other scholars have sought to reconstruct an elaborate mythology based on the cave paintings and sculptures, suggesting that Paleolithic humans believed they had animal ancestors. Some researchers have equated certain species with men and others with women and postulated various meanings for the abstract signs that sometimes accompany the images. Almost all of these theories have been discredited over time, and most prehistorians admit that no one knows the intent of these representations. In fact, a single explanation for all Paleolithic animal images, even ones similar in subject, style, and *composition* (how the motifs are arranged on the surface), is unlikely to apply universally. The works remain an enigma—and always will, because before the invention of writing, no contemporaneous explanations could be recorded.

1-10 Spotted horses and negative hand imprints, wall painting in the cave at Pech-Merle, France, ca. 23,000–22,000 BCE. 11′ 2″ long.

The purpose and meaning of Paleolithic art are unknown. Some researchers think the painted hands near the Pech-Merle horses are "signatures" of community members or of individual painters.

1 ft.

baseline on which figures appear to stand in paintings and reliefs), nor do they share a common orientation. They seem almost to float above viewers' heads, like clouds in the sky. And the dead(?) bison are seen in an "aerial view," whereas the others are seen from a position on the ground. The painting has no setting, no background, no indication of place. *Where* the animals are or how they relate to one another, if at all, was of no concern to the Paleolithic painter. Instead, several *separate* images of a bison adorn the ceiling, perhaps painted at different times spanning generations, and each is as complete and informative as possible—even if their meaning remains a mystery (see "Art in the Old Stone Age," above).

PECH-MERLE That the paintings did have meaning to the Paleolithic peoples who made and observed them cannot, however, be doubted. In fact, signs consisting of checks, dots, squares, or other arrangements of lines often accompany the pictures of animals. Representations of human hands also are common. At Pech-Merle (FIG. 1-10) in France, painted hands accompany representations of spotted horses. (The "spots" also surround the horses and may not be spots at all but stones or abstract signs.) Most of the painted hands in Paleolithic caves are "negative," that is, the painter placed one hand against the wall and then brushed or blew or spat pigment around it. Occasionally, the painter dipped a hand in the

The World's Oldest Paintings?

One of the most spectacular archaeological finds of the past century came to light in December 1994 at Vallon-Pont-d'Arc, France. Unlike some other recent "finds" of prehistoric art that proved to be forgeries, the paintings in the Chauvet Cave (named after the leader of the exploration team, Jean-Marie Chauvet) seemed to be authentic. But no one, including Chauvet and his colleagues, guessed at the time of their discovery that *radiocarbon dating* (a measure of the rate of degeneration of carbon 14 in organic materials) of the paintings would establish the murals in the cave as thousands of years older than any previously discovered. Tests conducted by French scientists revealed that the Chauvet Cave paintings date between 30,000 and 28,000 BCE.

This unexpectedly early date immediately caused scholars to reevaluate the scheme of "stylistic development" from simple to more complex forms that art historians had almost universally accepted for decades. In the Chauvet Cave, in contrast to the Lascaux Cave (FIG. 1-1), the Paleolithic painters depicted the horns of the aurochs (extinct long-horned wild oxen) naturalistically, one be-

hind the other, not in the twisted perspective normally used in Old Stone Age art. Moreover, the two rhinoceroses at the lower right of FIG. 1-11 appear to attack each other, suggesting that the painter intended a narrative, another "first" in either painting or sculpture. If the paintings are twice as old as those of Lascaux and Altamira (FIG. 1-9) and almost 10,000 years earlier than the Pech-Merle murals (FIG. 1-10), the assumption that Paleolithic art "evolved" from simple to more sophisticated representations is wrong.

Much research remains to be conducted in the Chauvet Cave, but already the paintings have become the subject of intense controversy. Recently, some archaeologists have contested the early dating of the Chauvet paintings on the grounds the tested samples were contaminated. If the Chauvet animals are later than those at Lascaux, their advanced stylistic features can be more easily explained. The dispute exemplifies the frustration—and the excitement—of studying the art of an age so remote that almost nothing remains and almost every new find causes art historians to reevaluate what they had previously taken for granted.

1-11 Aurochs, horses, and rhinoceroses, wall painting in the Chauvet Cave, Vallon-Pont-d'Arc, France, ca. 30,000–28,000 or ca. 15,000–13,000 BCE. Right rhinoceros 3′ 4″ long. ■◀

The date of the Chauvet Cave paintings is the subject of much controversy. If the murals are the oldest paintings known, they exhibit surprisingly advanced features, such as overlapping animal horns.

1 ft.

pigment and then pressed it against the wall, leaving a "positive" imprint. These handprints, too, must have served a purpose. Some researchers have considered them "signatures" of cult or community members or, less likely, of individual painters. But like so much in Paleolithic art, their meaning is unknown.

The *mural* (wall) paintings at Pech-Merle also furnish some insight into the reasons Paleolithic peoples chose subjects for specific places in a cave. One of the horses (at the right in FIG. 1-10) may have been inspired by the rock formation in the wall surface resembling a horse's head and neck. Old Stone Age painters and sculptors frequently and skillfully used the naturally irregular surfaces of caves to help give the illusion of real presence to their forms, as they did at La Magdeleine (FIG. 1-6A) and at Altamira (FIG. 1-9), where many of the bison paintings cover bulging rock surfaces. In fact, prehistori-

ans have observed that bison and cattle appear almost exclusively on convex surfaces, whereas nearly all horses and hands are painted on concave surfaces. What this signifies has yet to be determined.

LASCAUX Perhaps the most impressive collection of Paleolithic animal paintings is in the Hall of the Bulls (FIG. 1-1) at Lascaux. The large chamber, far from the cave entrance and mysteriously dark, has good acoustics, and would have provided an excellent setting for the kinds of rituals that many archaeologists assume took place in front of the paintings. One noteworthy aspect of the Lascaux murals is that they exhibit, side by side, the two basic approaches to drawing and painting found repeatedly in the history of art—silhouettes and outlines—indicating that different painters created these pictures, probably at different times. The Lascaux

1-12 Rhinoceros, wounded man, and disemboweled bison, painting in the well of the cave at Lascaux, France, ca. 16,000–14,000 BCE. Bison 3′ 4½″ long. ◼

If these paintings of two animals and a bird-faced (masked?) man deep in a Lascaux well shaft depict a hunting scene, they constitute the earliest example of narrative art ever discovered.

1 ft.

bulls also show a convention of representing horns that art historians call *twisted perspective,* or *composite view,* because viewers see the heads in profile but the horns from the front. Thus, the painter's approach is not strictly or consistently optical (seen from a fixed viewpoint). Rather, the approach is descriptive of the fact that cattle have two horns. Two horns are part of the concept "bull." In strict optical-perspective profile, only one horn would be visible, but to paint the animal in that way would amount to an incomplete definition of it. This kind of twisted perspective was the norm in prehistoric painting, but it was not universal. In fact, the 1994 discovery of Paleolithic paintings in the Chauvet Cave (FIG. 1-11) at Vallon-Pont-d'Arc in France, where the painters represented horns in a more natural way, has caused art historians to rethink many of the assumptions they had made about Paleolithic art (see "The World's Oldest Paintings?" page 22).

1-12A "Chinese horse," Lascaux, ca. 16,000–14,000 BCE.

Paintings of animals appear throughout the cave complex at Lascaux, including in the so-called Axial Gallery, which features a representation of a running, possibly pregnant horse (FIG. 1-12A) surrounded by what may be arrows or traps. But the most perplexing painting at Lascaux and perhaps in all Paleolithic art is the one (FIG. 1-12) deep in a well shaft, where man (as opposed to woman) makes one of his earliest appearances in prehistoric art. At the left, and moving to the left, is a rhinoceros. Beneath its tail are two rows of three dots of uncertain significance. At the right is a bison, also facing left but with less realistic proportions, probably the work of someone else. The second painter nonetheless successfully suggested the bristling rage of the animal, whose bowels are hanging from it in a heavy coil. Between the two beasts is a bird-faced (masked?) man (compare the feline-headed human, FIG. 1-4, from Hohlenstein-Stadel) with outstretched arms and hands having only four fingers. The man is depicted with far less care and detail than either animal, but the painter made the hunter's gender explicit by the prominent penis. The position of the man is ambiguous. Is he wounded or dead or merely tilted back and

unharmed? Do the staff(?) with the bird on top and the spear belong to him? Is it he or the rhinoceros who has gravely wounded the bison—or neither? Which animal, if either, has knocked the man down, if indeed he is on the ground? Are these three images related at all? Modern viewers can be sure of nothing, but if the painters placed the figures beside each other to tell a story, this is evidence for the creation of complex narrative compositions involving humans and animals at a much earlier date than anyone had imagined only a few generations ago. Yet it is important to remember that even if the artists intended to tell a story, very few people would have been able to "read" it. The painting, in a deep shaft, is very difficult to reach and could have been viewed only in flickering lamplight. Like all Paleolithic art, the scene in the Lascaux well shaft remains enigmatic.

NEOLITHIC ART

Around 9000 BCE, the ice that covered much of northern Europe during the Paleolithic period melted as the climate warmed. The sea level rose more than 300 feet, separating England from continental Europe, and Spain from Africa. The reindeer migrated north, and the woolly mammoth disappeared. The Paleolithic gave way to a transitional period, the Mesolithic, and then, for several thousand years at different times in different parts of the globe, a great new age, the Neolithic, dawned.* Human beings began to domesticate plants and animals and to settle in fixed abodes. Their food supply assured, many groups changed from hunters to herders to farmers and finally to townspeople. Wandering hunters settled down to organized community living in villages surrounded by cultivated fields.

The basis for the conventional division of prehistory into the Paleolithic, Mesolithic, and Neolithic periods is the development of

---

*This chapter treats the Neolithic art of Europe, Anatolia, and Mesopotamia only. For the Neolithic art of Africa, see Chapter 19; for Asia, see Chapters 15 to 17.

stone implements. However, a different kind of distinction may be made between an age of food gathering and an age of food production. In this scheme, the Paleolithic period corresponds roughly to the age of food gathering. Intensified food gathering and the taming of the dog are the hallmarks of the Mesolithic period. In the Neolithic period, agriculture and stock raising became humankind's major food sources. The transition to the Neolithic occurred first in Anatolia and Mesopotamia.

Anatolia and Mesopotamia

The remains of the oldest known settled communities lie in the grassy foothills of the Antilebanon, Taurus, and Zagros mountains in present-day Turkey, Syria, Iraq, and Iran (MAP 1-2). These regions provided the necessary preconditions for the development of agriculture. Species of native plants, such as wild wheat and barley, were plentiful, as were herds of animals (goats, sheep, and pigs) that could be domesticated. Sufficient rain occurred for the raising of crops. When village farming life was well developed, some settlers, attracted by the greater fertility of the soil and perhaps also by the need to find more land for their rapidly growing populations, moved into the valleys and deltas of the Tigris and Euphrates rivers.

In addition to systematic agriculture, the new sedentary societies of the Neolithic age originated weaving, metalworking, pottery, and counting and recording with clay tokens. These innovations spread with remarkable speed throughout Anatolia (roughly equivalent to present-day Turkey) and Mesopotamia (primarily present-day Syria and Iraq). Village farming communities such as Jarmo in Iraq and Çatal Höyük in southern Anatolia date to the mid-seventh millennium BCE. The remarkable fortified town of Jericho, before whose walls the biblical Joshua appeared thousands of years later, is even older. Archaeologists are constantly uncovering surprises, and the discovery and exploration of new sites each year are

MAP 1-2 Neolithic sites in Anatolia and Mesopotamia.

compelling them to revise their views about the emergence of Neolithic society. Especially noteworthy are the ongoing excavations at Göbekli Tepe in southeastern Turkey, where German archaeologists have uncovered the remains of what appears to be the world's oldest stone temple, dating around 9000 BCE, with animal reliefs on T-shaped pillars. If the dating and the interpretation are correct, Göbekli Tepe overturns one of the most basic assumptions about prehistoric societies. It now appears possible that hunter-gatherers erected stone temples long before sedentary farmers established permanent village communities. Of those sites known for some time, Jericho, Ain Ghazal, and Çatal Höyük together probably offer the most complete picture of the rapid and exciting transformation of human society and of art during the Neolithic period.

JERICHO By 7000 BCE, agriculture was well established from Anatolia to ancient Palestine and Iran. Its advanced state by this date presupposes a long development. Indeed, the very existence of a major settlement such as Jericho gives strong support to this assumption. Jericho, situated on a plateau in the Jordan River valley with an unfailing spring, was the site of a small village as early as the ninth millennium BCE. This village underwent spectacular development around 8000 BCE, when the inhabitants established a new Neolithic settlement covering about 10 acres. Its mud-brick houses sat on round or oval stone foundations and had roofs of branches covered with earth.

As Jericho's wealth grew, the need for protection against marauding nomads resulted in the first known permanent stone fortifications. By 7500 BCE, a wide rock-cut ditch and a 5-foot-thick wall surrounded the town, which probably had a population exceeding 2,000. Set into the circuit wall, which has been preserved to a height of almost 13 feet, was a 30-foot-tall circular tower (FIG. 1-13) constructed of roughly shaped stones laid without mortar. Almost 33 feet in diameter at the base, the tower has an inner stairway leading to its summit. (Today, a grate covers the entrance to the stairway.) Not enough of the site has been excavated to determine whether this tower was solitary or one of several similar towers that formed a complete defense system. In either case, a stone structure as large as the Jericho tower was a tremendous technological achievement and a testimony to the builders' ability to organize a significant workforce.

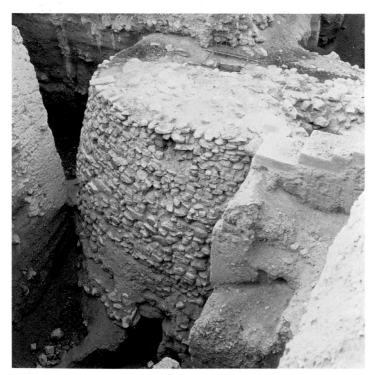

1-13 Stone tower built into the settlement wall, Jericho, ca. 8000–7000 BCE.

Protecting Neolithic Jericho were 5-foot-thick walls and at least one tower 30 feet high and 33 feet in diameter constructed of stone laid without mortar—an outstanding technological achievement.

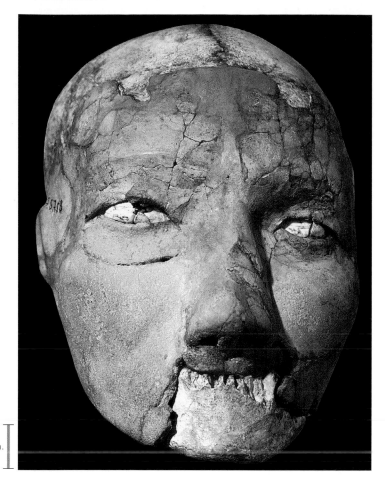

1 in.

1-14 Human skull with restored features, from Jericho, ca. 7200–6700 BCE. Features modeled in plaster, painted, and inlaid with seashells. Life-size. Archaeological Museum, Amman.

The Neolithic farmers of Jericho removed the skulls of their dead before burial, modeled them in plaster, and inlaid the eyes to create lifelike "portraits" of their ancestors, whom they may have worshiped.

Sometime around 7000 BCE, Jericho's inhabitants abandoned their fortified site, but new settlers arrived in the early seventh millennium and established a new farming community of rectangular mud-brick houses on stone foundations with plastered and painted floors and walls. Several of the excavated buildings contained statuettes of animals and women and seem to have served as shrines. The new villagers buried their dead beneath the floors of their houses with the craniums detached from their skeletons and their features reconstructed in plaster. Subtly modeled with inlaid seashells for eyes and painted hair, the appearance of these reconstructed heads is strikingly lifelike. One head (FIG. **1-14**) features a painted mustache, distinguishing it from the others. The Jericho skulls constitute the world's earliest known "portrait gallery," but the artists' intention was certainly not portraiture in the modern sense. The plastered skulls must have served a ritualistic purpose. The community of several hundred Neolithic farmers who occupied Jericho at this time honored and perhaps worshiped their ancestors as intercessors between the living and the world beyond. They may have believed that the dead could exert power over the living and that they had to offer sacrifices to their ancestors to receive favorable treatment. These skulls were probably the focus of rites in honor of those ancestors.

AIN GHAZAL A second important Neolithic settlement in ancient Palestine was Ain Ghazal, near the modern Jordanian capi-

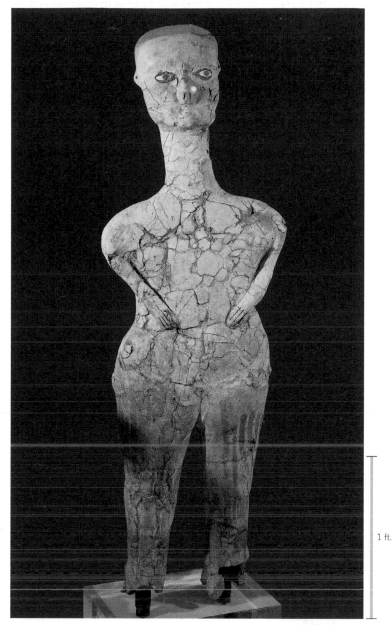

1 ft.

1-15 Human figure, from Ain Ghazal, Jordan, ca. 6750–6250 BCE. Plaster, painted and inlaid with bitumen, 3' 5⅜" high. Musée du Louvre, Paris.

The dozens of large white plaster statuettes (some with two heads and with details added in paint or inlaid with bitumen) found at Ain Ghazal are the earliest large-scale sculptures known.

tal of Amman. Occupied from around 7200 to 5000 BCE, the site featured houses of irregularly shaped stones with plastered floors and walls painted red. The most striking finds, however, are two caches containing three dozen plaster statuettes (FIG. **1-15**) and busts, some with two heads, datable to ca. 6500 BCE. The sculptures, which appear to have been ritually buried, are white plaster built up over a core of reeds and twine, with black bitumen, a tarlike substance, for the pupils of the eyes. Some of the figures have painted clothing. Only rarely did the sculptors indicate the gender of the figures. Whatever their purpose, by their size (as much as three feet tall) and sophisticated technique, the Ain Ghazal statuettes and busts tower over Paleolithic figurines such as the tiny *Venus of Willendorf* (FIG. 1-5) and even the foot-tall Hohlenstein-Stadel ivory statuette (FIG. 1-4). They mark the beginning of monumental sculpture in Mesopotamia.

ÇATAL HÖYÜK During the past half century, archaeologists also have made remarkable discoveries in Turkey, not only at Göbekli Tepe but also at Hacilar and especially Çatal Höyük (FIG. **1-16A**), the site of a flourishing Neolithic culture on the central Anatolian plain between 6500 and 5700 BCE. Although animal husbandry was well established, hunting continued to play an important part in the early Neolithic economy of Çatal Höyük. The importance of hunting as a food source is reflected in the wall paintings of the site's older decorated rooms, where hunting scenes predominate. In style and concept, however, the deer hunt mural (FIG. **1-16**) at Çatal Höyük is worlds apart from the wall paintings the hunters of the Paleolithic period produced. Perhaps what is most strikingly new about the Çatal Höyük painting and other Neolithic examples like it is the regular appearance of the human figure—not only singly but also in large, coherent groups with a wide variety of poses, subjects, and settings. As noted earlier, humans were unusual in Paleolithic cave paintings, and pictorial narratives are almost unknown. Even the "hunting scene" (FIG. 1-12) in the well at Lascaux is doubtful as a narrative. In contrast, human themes and concerns and action scenes with humans dominating animals are central subjects of Neolithic paintings.

In the Çatal Höyük hunt, the group of hunters—and no one doubts it is, indeed, an organized hunting party, not a series of individual figures—is a rhythmic repetition of basic shapes, but the painter took care to distinguish important descriptive details—for example, bows, arrows, and garments—and the heads have clearly defined noses, mouths, chins, and hair. The Neolithic painter placed all the heads in profile for the same reason Paleolithic painters universally chose the profile view for representations of animals. Only the side view of the human head shows all its shapes clearly. However, at Çatal Höyük the painter presented the torsos from the front—again, the most informative viewpoint—whereas the profile view was the choice for the legs and arms. This composite view of the human body is highly artificial—the human body cannot make an abrupt 90-degree shift at the hips—but it well describes what a human body is, as opposed to how it appears from a particular viewpoint. The technique of painting also changed dramatically from the Paleolithic to the Neolithic. The Çatal Höyük painters used brushes to apply their pigments to a background of dry white plaster. The careful preparation of the wall surface is in striking contrast to the direct application of pigment to the irregularly shaped walls and ceilings of Old Stone Age caves.

1-16 Deer hunt, detail of a wall painting from level III, Çatal Höyük, Turkey, ca. 5750 BCE. Museum of Anatolian Civilization, Ankara.

This Neolithic painter depicted human figures as a composite of frontal and profile views, the most descriptive picture of the shape of the human body. This format would become the rule for millennia.

1-17 Landscape with volcanic eruption(?), detail of a watercolor copy of a wall painting from level VII, Çatal Höyük, Turkey, ca. 6150 BCE.

One of the oldest mural paintings from Çatal Höyük may represent the settlement during a volcanic eruption. It is the first known landscape painting in which neither humans nor animals appear.

More remarkable still is a painting (FIG. **1-17** is a watercolor copy) in one of the older rooms at Çatal Höyük. Art historians generally have acclaimed this mural as the world's first *landscape* (a picture of a natural setting in its own right, without any narrative content). As such, it remained unique for thousands of years. According to radiocarbon analysis, the painting dates to around 6150 BCE. Scholars interpret the foreground as a town with rectangular houses neatly laid out side by side, probably representing Çatal Höyük itself. Behind the town appears a mountain with two peaks. Many archaeologists think the dots and lines issuing from the higher of the two cones represent a volcanic eruption, and have suggested that the mountain is the 10,600-foot-high Hasan Dağ, which is within view of Çatal Höyük and is the only twin-peaked volcano in central Anatolia. The conjectured volcanic eruption shown in the mural does not necessarily depict a specific historical event. If, however, the Çatal Höyük painting relates a story, even a recurring one, then it cannot be considered a pure landscape. Nonetheless, this mural is the first depiction of a setting devoid of both humans and animals.

Western Europe

In western Europe, where Paleolithic paintings and sculptures abound, no comparably developed towns of the time of Çatal Höyük have been found. However, in succeeding millennia, perhaps as early as 4000 BCE, the local Neolithic populations in several areas developed a monumental architecture employing massive rough-cut stones. The very dimensions of the stones, some as high as 17 feet and weighing as much as 50 tons, have prompted historians to call them *megaliths* (great stones) and to designate Neolithic architecture employing them as *megalithic*.

NEWGRANGE One of the most impressive megalithic monuments in Europe is also one of the oldest. The megalithic tomb at Newgrange in Ireland, north of Dublin, may date to as early as 3200 BCE and is one of the oldest burial monuments in Europe. It takes the form of a *passage grave,* that is, a tomb with a long stone corridor leading to a dome-covered burial chamber (FIG. **1-18**) beneath a great *tumulus* (earthen burial mound). Some mounds contain more than one passage grave. Similar graves have been found also in England, France, Spain, and Scandinavia. All attest to the importance of honoring the dead in Neolithic society. The Newgrange tumulus is 280 feet in diameter and 44 feet tall. Its passageway is 62 feet long, and it and the primitive dome over

the main chamber are early examples of *corbel vaulting* (FIGS. 4-16 and 4-17*b*). At Newgrange, the huge megaliths forming the vaulted passage and the dome are held in place by their own weight, each stone countering the thrust of neighboring stones. Decorating some of the megaliths are incised spirals and other abstract motifs (not visible in FIG. 1-18). A special feature of the Newgrange tomb is that at the winter solstice the sun illuminates the passageway and the burial chamber.

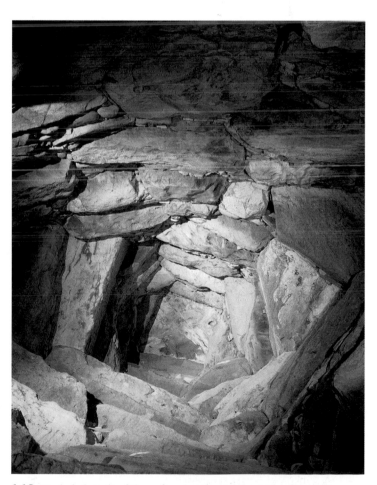

1-18 Corbeled vault of the main chamber in the passage grave, Newgrange, Ireland, ca. 3200–2500 BCE.

The Newgrange passage grave is an early example of corbeled vaulting. The huge stones (megaliths) of the dome of the main burial chamber beneath the tumulus are held in place by their own weight.

HAGAR QIM By the end of the fourth millennium BCE, Neolithic civilization had spread to the most remote parts of Europe, including, in the far north, Skara Brae (FIG. **1-19A**) in the Orkney Islands, and, in the far south, Malta. The megalithic temple (FIG. **1-19**)

of Hagar Qim is one of many constructed on Malta between 3200 and 2500 BCE. The Maltese builders erected their temples by piling carefully cut stone blocks in *courses* (stacked horizontal rows). To construct the doorways at Hagar Qim, the builders employed the *post-and-lintel* system (FIG. 4-17*a*) in which two upright stones (posts) support a horizontal beam (lintel). The layout of this and other Neolithic Maltese temples is especially noteworthy for the combination of rectilinear and curved forms, including multiple *apses* (semicircular recesses). Inside the Hagar Qim temple, archaeologists found altars (hence the identification of the structure as a religious shrine) and several stone statues of headless nude women, one standing, the others seated. The level of architectural and sculptural sophistication seen on this isolated island at so early a date is extraordinary.

STONEHENGE The most famous megalithic monument in Europe is Stonehenge (FIG. **1-20**) on the Salisbury Plain in southern England. A *henge* is an arrangement of megalithic stones in a circle, often surrounded by a ditch. The type is almost entirely limited to Britain. Stonehenge is a complex of rough-cut sarsen (a form of sandstone) stones and smaller "bluestones" (various volcanic rocks) built in several stages over hundreds of years. The final henge took the form of concentric post-and-lintel circles. The outer ring, almost 100 feet in diameter, consists of huge sarsen megaliths. Inside is a ring of bluestones, and this ring, in turn, encircles a horseshoe (open end facing east) of *trilithons* (three-stone constructions)—five lintel-topped pairs of the largest sarsens, each weighing 45 to 50 tons. Standing apart and to the east (outside the aerial view in FIG. 1-20) is the "heel stone," which, for a person looking outward from the center of the complex, would have marked the point where the sun rose at the summer solstice. Stonehenge, perhaps originally a funerary site where Neolithic peoples cremated their dead, seems in its latest phase to have been a kind of astronomical observatory and a remarkably accurate solar calendar. According to a recent theory, it also served as a center of healing that attracted the sick and dying from throughout the region.

Whatever role they played in society, the megalithic tombs, temples, houses, and henges of Europe are enduring testaments to the rapidly developing intellectual powers of Neolithic humans as well as to their capacity for heroic physical effort.

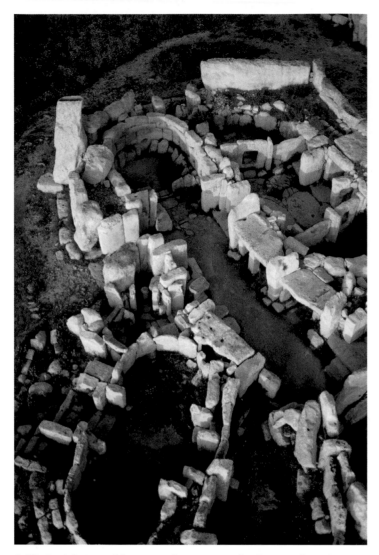

1-19 Aerial view of the ruins of Hagar Qim (looking east), Malta, ca. 3200–2500 BCE.

The 5,000-year-old stone temple at Hagar Qim on the remote island of Malta is remarkably sophisticated for its date, especially in the way the Neolithic builders incorporated both rectilinear and curved forms.

1-20 Aerial view of Stonehenge (looking northwest), Salisbury Plain, Wiltshire, England, ca. 2550–1600 BCE. Circle 97′ in diameter; trilithons 24′ high.

The circles of trilithons at Stonehenge probably functioned as an astronomical observatory and solar calendar. The sun rises over its "heel stone" at the summer solstice. Some of the megaliths weigh 50 tons.

ART BEFORE HISTORY

PALEOLITHIC (OLD STONE AGE) ART ca. 30,000–9000 BCE

I The first sculptures and paintings antedate the invention of writing by tens of thousands of years. Paleolithic humans' decision to represent the world around them initiated an intellectual revolution of enormous consequences.

I No one knows why humans began to paint and carve images or what role those images played in the lives of Paleolithic hunters. Women were far more common subjects than men, but animals, not humans, dominate Paleolithic art.

I The works created range in size from tiny portable figurines, such as the so-called *Venus of Willendorf,* to large, sometimes over-life-size, carved and painted representations of animals, as in the caves of Lascaux, Pech-Merle, Altamira, and elsewhere in southern France and northern Spain.

I Paleolithic artists regularly depicted animals in profile in order to present a complete picture of each beast, including its head, body, tail, and all four legs. This format persisted for millennia.

Nude woman (*Venus of Willendorf*), ca. 28,000–25,000 BCE

Hall of the Bulls, Lascaux, ca. 16,000–14,000 BCE

NEOLITHIC (NEW STONE AGE) ART ca. 8000–2300 BCE

I Around 9000 BCE, the ice that had covered much of northern Europe for millennia receded. After a transitional period, the Neolithic Age began in Anatolia and Mesopotamia and spread gradually to Europe, where it continued longer in remote places like Stonehenge in England.

I The Neolithic Age revolutionized human life with the beginning of agriculture and the formation of the first settled communities, such as that at Çatal Höyük in Anatolia, where archaeologists have uncovered an extensive town with numerous shrines. Some Neolithic towns also had fortified stone circuit walls, like those at Jericho.

I In art, the Neolithic period brought the birth of monumental sculpture, notably the painted plaster figurines from Ain Ghazal and the restored life-size skulls from Jericho.

I In painting, coherent narratives became common, and artists began to represent human figures as composites of frontal and profile views—another formula that would remain universal for a very long time.

Skull with restored features, Jericho, ca. 7200–6700 BCE

Stonehenge, Salisbury Plain, ca. 2550–1600 BCE

The human figures
in Sumerian art are a
composite of frontal and
profile views. Artists
used hierarchy of scale
to distinguish the most
important (largest) figures
from those of lesser rank
in society.

The entertainers at this
banquet of Sumerian nobility
include a musician playing
a bull-headed harp of a type
found in royal graves at Ur.
The long-haired, bare-chested
singer is a court eunuch.

The Sumerians may have been the first
culture to use pictures to tell coherent
stories. Sumerian artists divided the
pictorial field into a series of registers
with figures on a common ground line.

1 in.

2-1 Peace side of the *Standard of Ur,* from tomb 779, Royal Cemetery, Ur (modern Tell Muqayyar), Iraq, ca. 2600–2400 BCE. Wood, lapis lazuli, shell, and red limestone, 8″ × 1′ 7″. British Museum, London. ◼◀

MESOPOTAMIA AND PERSIA

As in prehistoric art, representations of animals in Mesopotamian art are always strict profile views, save for the animals' eyes, which are seen from the front, as are also sometimes an animal's two horns.

THE CRADLE OF CIVILIZATION

Mesopotamia, the core of the region often called the Fertile Crescent and the presumed locale of the biblical Garden of Eden (Gen. 2:10–15), was where humans first learned how to use the wheel and plow and how to control floods and construct irrigation canals. In the fourth millennium BCE, the inhabitants of ancient Sumer, the first great Mesopotamian civilization, also established the earliest complex urban societies, called *city-states,* and invented writing. They may also have been the first culture to use pictures to tell coherent stories, far surpassing Stone Age artists' tentative efforts at pictorial narration.

The so-called *Standard of Ur* (FIG. 2-1), from the Sumerian city that was home to the biblical Abraham, is one of the earliest extant works incorporating all of the pictorial conventions that would dominate ancient narrative art for more than 2,000 years. The artist divided the pictorial field into three successive bands (called *registers,* or *friezes*) and placed all the figures on a common *ground line,* a compositional format that marks a significant break with the haphazard figure placement of Stone Age art. The Sumerians also pioneered the use of *hierarchy of scale,* a highly effective way of distinguishing the most important (largest) figure from those of lesser rank. This pictorial convention would also have a long future in the history of art.

In FIG. 2-1, the narrative reads from left to right and bottom to top. In the lowest band, men carry provisions on their backs. Above, attendants transport a variety of animals and fish for the great banquet depicted in the uppermost register. There, seated dignitaries and a larger-than-life personage—probably a king (third from the left)—feast, while a harp player and singer entertain the group. Some art historians have interpreted the scene as a celebration after the victory in warfare represented on the other side of the wooden box (FIG. 2-8). But the two sides may be independent narratives illustrating the two principal roles of a Sumerian ruler—the mighty warrior who defeats enemies of his city-state, and the chief administrator who, with the blessing of the gods, assures the bountifulness of the land in peacetime. The absence of an inscription prevents connecting the scenes with a specific occasion or person, but the *Standard of Ur* is undoubtedly among the world's oldest depictions of contemporaneous events—another of the many seminal innovations of the Sumerians.

MESOPOTAMIA

When humans first gave up the dangerous and uncertain life of the hunter and gatherer for the more predictable and stable life of the farmer and herder, the change in human society was so significant that historians justly have dubbed it the Neolithic Revolution (see Chapter 1). This fundamental change in the nature of daily life first occurred in Mesopotamia—a Greek word that means "the land between the [Tigris and Euphrates] rivers."

Mesopotamia, the land mass that forms a huge arc from the mountainous border between Turkey and Syria through Iraq to Iran's Zagros Mountains (MAP 2-1), is the region that gave birth to three of the world's great modern faiths—Judaism, Christianity, and Islam—and consequently has long been of interest to historians. Not until the 19th century, however, did systematic excavation open the public's eyes to the extraordinary art and architecture of this ancient land between the rivers. After the first discoveries in Syria and Iraq, the great museums of Europe and North America began avidly to collect Mesopotamian art. The most popular 19th-century acquisitions were the stone reliefs depicting warfare and hunting (FIGS. 2-22 and 2-23) and the colossal statues of monstrous man-headed bulls (FIG. 2-20) from the palaces of the Assyrians, rulers of a northern Mesopotamian empire during the ninth to the seventh centuries BCE. But nothing archaeologists extracted from the earth garnered as much attention as the treasure of gold objects, jewelry, artworks, and musical instruments (FIGS. 2-1 and 2-8 to 2-11) that British archaeologist Leonard Woolley (1880–1960) discovered in the 1920s at the Royal Cemetery at Ur in southern Iraq. The interest in the lavish third-millennium Sumerian cemetery he excavated rivaled the fascination with the 1922 discovery of the second-millennium tomb of the Egyptian boy-king Tutankhamen (see Chapter 3).

Sumer

The discovery of the treasures of ancient Ur put the Sumerians once again in a prominent position on the world stage, from which they had been absent for more than 4,000 years. The Sumerians were the people who in the fourth millennium BCE transformed the vast and previously sparsely inhabited valley between the Tigris and Euphrates into the Fertile Crescent of the ancient world. Ancient Sumer, which roughly corresponds to southern Iraq today, was not a unified nation, however. Rather, it comprised a dozen or so independent city-states under the protection of different Mesopotamian deities (see "The Gods and Goddesses of Mesopotamia," page 34).

MAP 2-1 Mesopotamia and Persia.

The Sumerian rulers were the gods' representatives on earth and the stewards of their earthly treasure.

The rulers and priests directed all communal activities, including canal construction, crop collection, and food distribution. Because the Sumerians developed agriculture to such an extent that only a portion of the population had to produce food, some members of the community were free to specialize in other activities, including manufacturing, trade, and administration. Specialization of labor is the hallmark of the first complex urban societies. In the city-states of ancient Sumer, activities that once had been individually initiated became institutionalized for the first time. The community, rather than the family, assumed functions such as defense against enemies and the caprices of nature. Whether ruled by a single person or a council chosen from among the leading families, these communities gained permanent identities as discrete cities. The city-state was one of the great Sumerian inventions.

Another was writing. The oldest written documents known are Sumerian records of administrative acts and commercial transactions. At first, around 3400 to 3200 BCE, the Sumerians made inventories of cattle, food, and other items by scratching *pictographs*

MESOPOTAMIA AND PERSIA

			Neo-Sumerian and		Hittite and		Neo-Babylonian and		BCE	CE
3500 Sumerian	2332 Akkadian	2150 Babylonian		1600 Assyrian		612 Achaemenid	559	330 Greco-Roman and Sasanian 636			

▮ World's first city-states founded and writing invented ▮ Construction of oldest temples on ziggurats ▮ Artists present narratives in register format	▮ First Mesopotamian rulers to call themselves kings ▮ Earliest preserved hollow-cast bronze statuary	▮ Largest extant ziggurat erected at Ur ▮ Gudea rebuilds temples and commissions portraits ▮ Hammurabi sets up a stele recording his laws	▮ Hittites sack Babylon and fortify their capital at Hattusa ▮ Assyrians rule a vast empire from citadels guarded by lamassu ▮ Extensive relief cycles celebrate Assyrian military campaigns	▮ Nebuchadnezzar II rebuilds Babylon, which boasts two of the Seven Wonders of the ancient world ▮ Persians build an immense palace complex at Persepolis	▮ After conquest by Alexander the Great, Mesopotamia and Persia are absorbed into the Greco-Roman world ▮ New Persian Empire challenges Rome from Ctesiphon

Using only mud bricks, the Sumerians erected temple platforms called ziggurats several centuries before the Egyptians built stone pyramids. The most famous ziggurat was the biblical Tower of Babel.

2-3 Restored view of the White Temple and ziggurat, Uruk (modern Warka), Iraq, ca. 3200–3000 BCE.

The White Temple at Uruk was probably dedicated to Anu, the sky god. It had a central hall (cella) with a stepped altar. There, the Sumerian priests would await the apparition of the deity.

(simplified pictures standing for words) into soft clay with a sharp tool, or *stylus*. The clay plaques hardened into breakable, yet nearly indestructible, tablets. Thousands of these plaques dating back nearly five millennia exist today. The Sumerians wrote their pictorial signs from the top down and arranged them in boxes they read from right to left. By 3000 to 2900 BCE, they had further simplified the pictographic signs by reducing them to a group of wedge-shaped (*cuneiform*) signs (FIGS. 2-7 and 2-11 are early examples; see also FIGS. 2-13, 2-16, and 2-18). The development of cuneiform marked the beginning of writing, as historians strictly define it. The surviving cuneiform tablets testify to the far-flung network of Sumerian contacts reaching from southern Mesopotamia eastward to the Iranian plateau, northward to Assyria, and westward to Syria. Trade was essential for the Sumerians, because despite its fertile soil, Sumeria was poor in such vital natural resources as metal, stone, and wood.

The Sumerians also produced great literature. Their most famous work, known from fragmentary cuneiform texts, is the late-third-millennium *Epic of Gilgamesh,* which antedates the Greek poet Homer's *Iliad* and *Odyssey* by some 1,500 years. It recounts the heroic story of Gilgamesh, legendary king of Uruk and slayer of the monster Huwawa. Translations of the Sumerian epic into several other ancient languages attest to the fame of the original version.

WHITE TEMPLE, URUK The layout of Sumerian cities reflected the central role of the gods in daily life. The main temple to each state's chief god formed the city's monumental nucleus. In fact, the temple complex was a kind of city within a city, where a staff of priests and scribes carried on official administrative and commercial business as well as oversaw all religious functions.

The outstanding preserved example of early Sumerian temple architecture is the 5,000-year-old White Temple (FIG. 2-2) at Uruk, a city that in the late fourth millennium BCE had a population of about 40,000. Usually, only the foundations of early Mesopotamian temples remain. The White Temple is a rare exception. Sumerian builders did not have access to stone quarries and instead formed mud bricks for the superstructures of their temples and other buildings. Almost all these structures have eroded over the course of time. The fragile nature of the building materials did not, however, prevent the Sumerians from erecting towering works, such as the Uruk temple, several centuries before the Egyptians built their famous stone pyramids. The construction of monumental shrines without stone says a great deal about the Sumerians' desire to provide grandiose settings for the worship of their deities.

Enough of the White Temple at Uruk remains to permit a fairly reliable reconstruction (FIG. 2-3). The temple (whose white-washed walls suggested its modern nickname) stands atop a high platform, or *ziggurat,* 40 feet above street level in the city center. A stairway on one side leads to the top but does not end in front of any of the temple doorways, necessitating two or three angular changes in direction. This *bent-axis plan* is the standard arrangement for Sumerian temples, a striking contrast to the linear approach the Egyptians preferred for their temples and tombs (see Chapter 3).

As in other Sumerian temples, the corners of the White Temple are oriented to the cardinal points of the compass. The building, probably dedicated to Anu, the sky god, is of modest proportions (61 by 16 feet). By design, it did not accommodate large throngs of worshipers but only a select few, the priests and perhaps the leading community members. The temple had several chambers. The central hall, or *cella,* was the divinity's room and housed a stepped altar. The Sumerians referred to their temples as "waiting rooms," a reflection of their belief the deity would descend from the heavens to appear before the priests in the cella. Whether the Uruk temple had a roof, and if it did, what kind, are uncertain.

The Sumerian notion of the gods residing above the world of humans is central to most of the world's religions. Moses ascended Mount Sinai to receive the Ten Commandments from the Hebrew God, and the Greeks placed the home of their gods and goddesses on Mount Olympus. The elevated placement of Mesopotamian temples on giant platforms reaching toward the sky is consistent with this widespread religious concept. Eroded ziggurats still dominate most of the ruined cities of Sumer. The loftiness of the great temple platforms made a profound impression on the peoples of

The Gods and Goddesses of Mesopotamia

The Sumerians and their successors in Mesopotamia worshiped numerous deities, mostly nature gods. Listed here are the Mesopotamian gods and goddesses discussed in this chapter.

■ *Anu.* The chief deity of the Sumerians. Anu was the god of the sky and of the city of Uruk. One of the earliest Sumerian temples (FIGS. 2-2 and 2-3) may have been dedicated to his worship.

■ *Enlil.* Anu's son. Enlil was the lord of the winds and the earth. He eventually replaced his father as king of the gods.

■ *Inanna.* The Sumerian goddess of love and war, later known as *Ishtar.* Inanna was the most important female deity in all periods of Mesopotamian history. As early as the fourth millennium BCE, the Sumerians constructed a sanctuary to Inanna at Uruk. Amid the ruins, excavators uncovered statues and reliefs (FIGS. 2-4 and 2-5) connected with her worship.

■ *Nanna.* The moon god, also known as *Sin.* Nanna was the chief deity of Ur, where the Sumerians erected his most important shrine.

■ *Utu.* The sun god, later known as *Shamash.* Utu was especially revered at Sippar. On a Babylonian stele (FIG. 2-18) of ca. 1780 BCE, King Hammurabi presents his laws to Shamash, whom the sculptor depicted as a bearded god wearing a horned headdress. Flames radiate from the sun god's shoulders.

■ *Marduk, Nabu,* and *Adad.* Marduk was the chief god of the Babylonians. His son Nabu was the god of writing and wisdom. Adad was the Babylonian god of storms. Marduk and Nabu's dragon and Adad's sacred bull adorn the sixth-century BCE Ishtar Gate (FIG. 2-24) at Babylon.

■ *Ningirsu.* The local god of Lagash and Girsu. Ningirsu helped Eannatum, one of the early rulers of Lagash, defeat an enemy army. The *Stele of the Vultures* (FIG. 2-7) of ca. 2600–2500 BCE records Ningirsu's role in the victory. Gudea (FIGS. 2-16 and 2-17), one of Eannatum's Neo-Sumerian successors, built a great temple around 2100 BCE in honor of Ningirsu after the god instructed him to do so in a dream.

■ *Ashur.* The local deity of Assur, the city that took his name. Ashur became the king of the Assyrian gods. He sometimes is identified with Enlil.

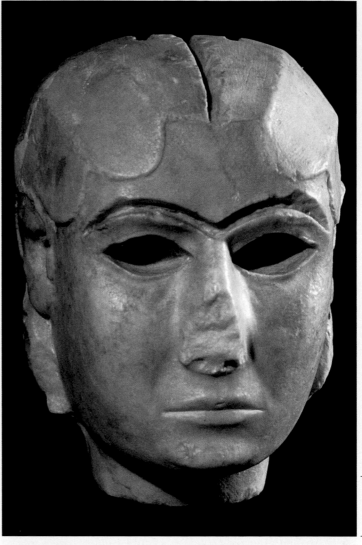

1 in.

2-4 Female head (Inanna?), from Uruk (modern Warka), Iraq, ca. 3200–3000 BCE. Marble, 8″ high. National Museum of Iraq, Baghdad.

The Sumerians imported the marble for this head at great cost. It may represent the goddess Inanna and originally had inlaid colored shell or stone eyes and brows, and a wig, probably of gold leaf.

ancient Mesopotamia. The tallest ziggurat of all, at Babylon, was about 270 feet high. Known to the Hebrews as the Tower of Babel, it became the centerpiece of a biblical story about the insolent pride of humans (see "Babylon, City of Wonders," page 49).

INANNA A fragmentary white marble female head (FIG. **2-4**) from Uruk is also an extraordinary achievement at so early a date. The head, one of the treasures of the recently reopened National Museum of Iraq in Baghdad, disappeared during the Iraq war of 2003, but was later recovered, along with other priceless items (FIGS. 2-5 and 2-12). The Sumerians lacked a ready source of fine stones suitable for carving sculptures, and consequently used stone sparingly. The lustrous hard stone selected for this head had to be brought to Uruk at great cost. In fact, the "head" is really only a face with a flat back. It has drilled holes for attachment to the rest of the head and the body, which may have been of much less costly wood. Although found in the sacred precinct of the goddess Inanna, the subject is unknown. Many have suggested that the face is an image of Inanna, but it may instead portray a mortal woman, perhaps a priestess.

Often the present condition of an artwork can be very misleading, and this female head from Uruk is a dramatic example. Its original appearance would have been much more vibrant than the pure white fragment preserved today. Colored shell or stone filled the deep recesses for the eyebrows and the large eyes. The deep groove at the top of the head anchored a wig, probably made of gold leaf.

The hair strands engraved in the metal fell in waves over the forehead and sides of the face. The bright coloration of the eyes, brows, and hair likely overshadowed the soft modeling of the cheeks and mouth. The missing body was probably clothed in expensive fabrics and bedecked with jewels.

WARKA VASE As noted in the discussion of the *Standard of Ur* (FIG. 2-1), the Sumerians, pioneers in so many areas, were the first masters of pictorial narration. The so-called *Warka Vase* (FIG. **2-5**)

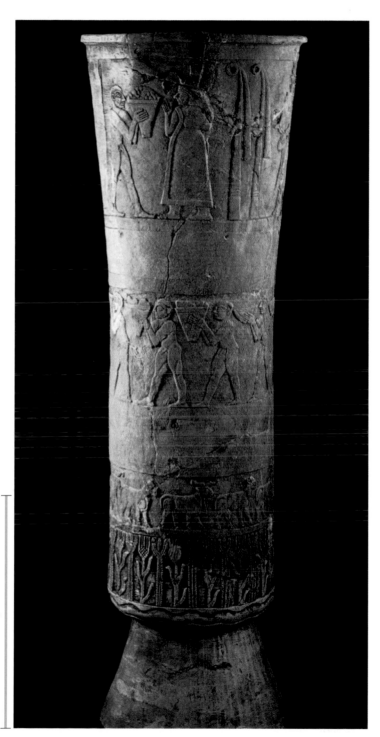

2-5 Presentation of offerings to Inanna (*Warka Vase*), from Uruk (modern Warka), Iraq, ca. 3200–3000 BCE. Alabaster, 3' $\frac{1}{4}$" high. National Museum of Iraq, Baghdad.

In this oldest known example of Sumerian narrative art, the sculptor divided the tall stone vase's reliefs into registers, a significant break with the haphazard figure placement found in earlier art.

1 ft.

from Uruk (modern Warka), several hundred years older than the *Standard of Ur,* is the first great work of narrative relief sculpture known. Found within the Inanna temple complex, it depicts a religious festival in honor of the goddess.

The division of the vase's surface into registers with figures standing on a common ground line—a compositional device still used today in comic strips—contrasts starkly with the haphazard arrangement of figures found in earlier paintings and reliefs. This Sumerian formula remained the norm for narrative art in Mesopotamia, Persia, Egypt, and Greece for millennia. The lowest band on the *Warka Vase* shows wheat and other crops above a wavy line representing water. Then comes a register with ewes and rams moving from left to right in strict profile, consistent with an approach to representing animals that was then some 20,000 years old. Agriculture and animal husbandry were the staples of the Sumerian economy, but the produce and the alternating female and male animals are also symbols of fertility. They underscore that Inanna had blessed Uruk's inhabitants with good crops and increased herds.

A procession of naked men moving in the opposite direction of the animals fills the band at the center of the vase. The men carry baskets and jars overflowing with the earth's abundance. They will present their bounty to the goddess as a *votive offering* (gift of gratitude to a deity usually made in fulfillment of a vow) and will deposit it in her temple. The spacing of each figure involves no overlapping. The Uruk men, like the Neolithic deer hunters (FIG. 1-16) at Çatal Höyük, are a composite of frontal and profile views, with large staring frontal eyes in profile heads. The artist depicted those human body parts necessary to communicate the human form and avoided positions, attitudes, or views that would conceal the characterizing parts. For example, if the figures were in strict profile, an arm and perhaps a leg would be hidden. The body would appear to have only half its breadth. And the eye would not "read" as an eye at all, because it would not have its distinctive oval shape. Art historians call this characteristic early approach to representation *conceptual representation* (as opposed to *optical representation*— the portrayal of people and objects seen from a fixed point) because artists who used it did not seek to record the immediate, fleeting aspect of figures. Instead, they rendered the human body's distinguishing and fixed properties. The fundamental forms of figures, not their accidental appearance, dictated the artist's selection of the composite view as the best way to represent the human body.

In the uppermost (and tallest) band of the *Warka Vase* is a female figure with a tall horned headdress next to two large poles that are the sign of the goddess Inanna. (Some scholars think the woman is a priestess and not the goddess herself.) A nude male figure brings a large vessel brimming with offerings to be deposited in the goddess's shrine. At the far right and barely visible in FIG. 2-5 is an only partially preserved clothed man. Near him is the early pictograph for the Sumerian official that scholars usually, if ambiguously, refer to as a "priest-king," that is, both a religious and secular leader. The greater height of the priest-king and Inanna compared with the offering bearers indicates their greater importance. Some art historians interpret the scene as a symbolic marriage between the priest-king and the goddess, ensuring her continued goodwill—and reaffirming the leader's exalted position in society.

ESHNUNNA STATUETTES Further insight into Sumerian religious beliefs and rituals comes from a cache of sculptures reverently buried beneath the floor of a temple at Eshnunna

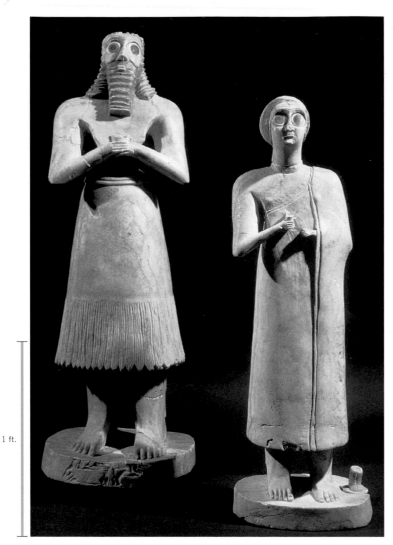

2-6 Statuettes of two worshipers, from the Square Temple at Eshnunna (modern Tell Asmar), Iraq, ca. 2700 BCE. Gypsum, shell, and black limestone, man 2′ 4¼″ high, woman 1′ 11¼″ high. National Museum of Iraq, Baghdad.

The oversized eyes probably symbolize the perpetual wakefulness of these substitute worshipers offering prayers to the deity. The beakers the figures hold were used to pour libations for the gods.

2-6A Urnanshe, from Mari, ca. 2600–2500 BCE.

1 ft.

the name of the donor or the god. The texts inscribed on some statuettes are specific prayers to the deity on the owner's behalf. With their heads tilted upward, the figures represented in these statuettes wait in the Sumerian "waiting room" for the divinity to appear.

The Sumerian sculptors employed simple forms, primarily cones and cylinders, for the figures. The statuettes, even those bearing the names of individuals (for example, Urnanshe), are not portraits in the strict sense of the word, but the sculptors did distinguish physical types. At Eshnunna, the sculptors portrayed at least one child, because next to the woman in FIG. 2-6 are the remains of two small legs. Most striking is the disproportionate relationship between the inlaid oversized eyes and the tiny hands. Scholars have explained the exaggeration of the eye size in various ways. But because the purpose of these votive figures was to offer constant prayers to the gods on their donors' behalf, the open-eyed stares most likely symbolize the eternal wakefulness necessary to fulfill their duty.

STELE OF THE VULTURES The city-states of ancient Sumer were often at war with one another, and warfare is the theme of the so-called *Stele of the Vultures* (FIG. 2-7) from Girsu. A *stele* is a carved stone slab set up to commemorate a historical event or, in some cultures, to mark a grave. The Girsu stele presents a labeled historical narrative with cuneiform inscriptions filling almost every blank space. (It is not, however, the first historical representation in the history of art. That honor belongs—at the moment—to an Egyptian relief [FIG. 3-1] carved more than three centuries earlier.) The inscriptions reveal that the *Stele of the Vultures* celebrates the victory of Eannatum, the *ensi* (ruler; king?) of Lagash, over the neighboring city-state of Umma. The stele has reliefs on both sides and takes its modern name from a fragment depicting a gruesome scene of vultures carrying off the severed heads and arms of the defeated enemy soldiers. Another fragment shows the giant figure of the local god Ningirsu holding tiny enemies in a net and beating one of them on the head with a mace.

The fragment in FIG. 2-7 depicts Eannatum leading an infantry battalion into battle (*above*) and attacking from a war chariot (*below*). The foot soldiers protect themselves by forming a wall of shields—there are far more hands and spears than heads and feet—and trample naked enemies as they advance. (The fragment representing vultures devouring corpses belongs just to the right in the same register.) Both on foot and in a chariot, Eannatum is larger than anyone else, except Ningirsu on the other side of the stele. The artist presented the ensi as the fearless general who paves the way for his army. Many Girsu attackers nonetheless lost their lives, and Eannatum himself sustained wounds in the campaign. Still, the outcome was never in doubt, because Ningirsu fought with the men of Lagash.

Despite its fragmentary state, the *Stele of the Vultures* is an extraordinary find, not only as a very early effort to record historical events in relief but also for the insight it yields about Sumerian society. Through both words and pictures, it provides information about warfare and the special nature of the Sumerian ruler. Eannatum was greater in stature than other men, and Ningirsu watched over him. According to the text, the ensi was born from the god Enlil's semen, which Ningirsu implanted in the womb. When Eannatum incurred injuries in battle, the god shed tears for him. The inscription also says it was Ningirsu who chose Eannatum to rule Lagash and preside over all aspects of the city-state, both in war and in peace. This also seems to have been the role of the ensi in the other Sumerian city-states.

(modern Tell Asmar) during remodeling of the structure. Carved of soft gypsum and inlaid with shell and black limestone, the statuettes range in size from well under a foot to about 30 inches tall. FIG. 2-6 shows the two largest figures. All of the statuettes represent mortals, rather than deities, with their hands folded in front of their chests in a gesture of prayer, usually holding the small beakers the Sumerians used for *libations* (ritual pouring of liquid) in honor of the gods. (Archaeologists found hundreds of these goblets in the temple complex at Eshnunna.) The men wear belts and fringed skirts. Most have beards and shoulder-length hair. The women wear long robes, with the right shoulder bare. Similar figurines have been unearthed at other sites. Some stand, as do the Eshnunna statuettes. Others are seated, for example, the figurine portraying Urnanshe (FIG. 2-6A) from the Ishtar temple at Mari in Syria. Many bear inscriptions giving valuable information, such as

Cuneiform inscriptions on this stele describe Eannatum's victory over the city of Umma with the aid of the god Ningirsu. This fragment shows Eannatum, at gigantic size, leading his troops into battle.

1 ft.

still debate whether these deceased individuals were true kings and queens or simply aristocrats, priests, and priest-esses, but the Sumerians laid them to rest in regal fashion. Archaeologists exploring the Ur cemetery uncovered gold helmets and daggers with handles of lapis lazuli (a rich azure-blue stone imported from Afghanistan), golden bea-kers and bowls, jewelry of gold and lapis, musical instru-ments, chariots, and other luxurious items. The excavators also found dozens of bodies in the richest tombs—a reti-nue of musicians, servants, and soldiers ritually sacrificed in order to accompany the "kings and queens" into the af-terlife. (Comparable rituals occurred in other societies, for example, in ancient America; see Chapter 18.)

Not the costliest object found in the "royal" graves, but probably the most significant from the viewpoint of the history of art, is the *Standard of Ur* (FIGS. 2-1 and **2-8**), discussed briefly at the beginning of this chapter. This wooden box inlaid with lapis lazuli, shell, and red limestone has broad rectangular faces and narrow trapezoidal ends. It is of uncertain function. The excavator, Leonard Woolley, thought the object was originally mounted on a pole, and he considered it a kind of military standard—hence its nickname.

STANDARD OF UR Agriculture and trade brought consid-erable wealth to some of the city-states of ancient Sumer. Nowhere is this more evident than in what the excavators dubbed the Royal Cemetery at Ur. In the third millennium BCE, the leading families of Ur buried their dead in vaulted chambers beneath the earth. Scholars

2-8 War side of the *Standard of Ur,* from tomb 779, Royal Cemetery, Ur (modern Tell Muqayyar), Iraq, ca. 2600–2400 BCE. Wood, lapis lazuli, shell, and red limestone, 8″ × 1′ 7″. British Museum, London. ◼◀

1 in.

Using a mosaic-like technique, this Sumerian artist depicted a battlefield victory in three registers. The narrative reads from bottom to top, and the size of the figures varies with their importance in society.

Art historians usually refer to the two long sides of the box as the "war side" and "peace side," which celebrate the two principal roles of a Sumerian ruler, but the two sides may represent the first and second parts of a single narrative. The artist divided each side into three horizontal bands. The narrative reads from left to right and bottom to top. On the war side (FIG. 2-8), four ass-drawn, four-wheeled war chariots crush enemies, whose bodies appear on the ground in front of and beneath the animals. The gait of the asses accelerates along the band from left to right. Above, foot soldiers gather up and lead away captured foes. In the uppermost register, soldiers bring bound captives (whom the victors have stripped naked to degrade them) to a kinglike figure, who has stepped out of his chariot. His central place in the composition and his greater stature (his head breaks through the border at the top) set him apart from all the other figures.

BULL-HEADED HARPS On the peace side of the *Standard of Ur*, the head of the largest figure also interrupts the upper border. The "king" presides over a banquet at which a musician plays a harp

and a long-haired eunuch (compare FIG. 2-6A) sings (FIG. 2-1, *top right*). From the tomb of "Queen" Pu-abi (many historians prefer to designate her more conservatively and ambiguously as "Lady" Pu-abi) comes a fragmentary harp that, as reconstructed (FIG. 2-9), resembles the instrument depicted on the *Standard of Ur*. A magnificent bull's head fashioned of gold leaf over a wooden core caps the harp's sound box. The hair and beard of the bull are of lapis lazuli, as is the inlaid background of the sound box, which features figures of shell and red limestone.

The excavators unearthed a similar harp in the adjacent "King's Grave." It too has a costly inlaid sound box (FIG. 2-10). In the uppermost of the four panels is a heroic figure embracing two man-bulls in a *heraldic composition* (symmetrical on either side of a central figure). The hero's body and that of the scorpion-man in the lowest panel are in composite view. The animals are, equally characteristically, solely in profile: the dog wearing a dagger and carrying a laden table, the lion bringing in the beverage service, the ass playing the harp, the jackal playing the zither, the bear steadying the harp

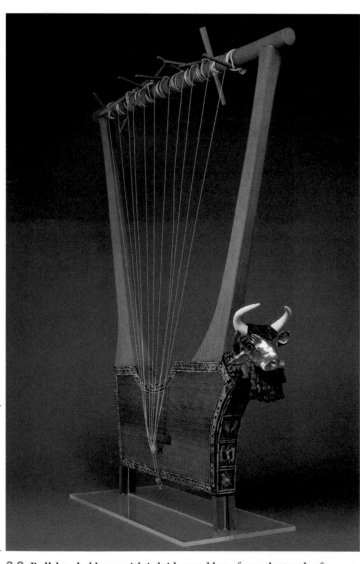

2-9 Bull-headed harp with inlaid sound box, from the tomb of Pu-abi (tomb 800), Royal Cemetery, Ur (modern Tell Muqayyar), Iraq, ca. 2600–2400 BCE. Wood, gold, lapis lazuli, red limestone, and shell, 3′ 8⅛″ high. British Museum, London.

A bearded bull's head fashioned of gold leaf and lapis lazuli over a wooden core adorns this harp from the tomb of "Queen" Pu-abi of Ur. The inlaid sound box features four narrative scenes.

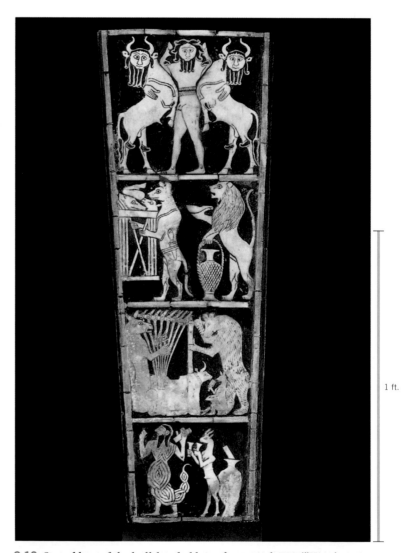

2-10 Sound box of the bull-headed harp from tomb 789 ("King's Grave"), Royal Cemetery, Ur (modern Tell Muqayyar), Iraq, ca. 2600–2400 BCE. Wood, lapis lazuli, and shell, 1′ 7″ high. University of Pennsylvania Museum of Archaeology and Anthropology, Philadelphia.

The four inlaid panels on the sound box of the harp found in the "King's Grave" at Ur represent a Gilgamesh-like hero between man-bulls and animals acting out scenes of uncertain significance.

Mesopotamian Seals

Archaeologists (and farmers and treasure hunters) have unearthed seals in great numbers at sites throughout Mesopotamia. Generally made of stone, seals of ivory, glass, and other materials also survive. The seals take two forms: flat *stamp seals* and *cylinder seals*. The latter have a hole drilled lengthwise through the center of the cylinder so that they could be strung and worn around the neck or suspended from the wrist. Cylinder seals (FIG. 2-11) were prized possessions, signifying high positions in society, and when their owners died, they frequently carried the seals with them into the afterlife.

The primary function of cylinder seals, however, like the earlier stamp seals, was not to serve as items of adornment. The Sumerians (and other ancient Mesopotamian peoples) used both stamp and cylinder seals to identify their documents and protect storage jars and doors against unauthorized opening. The oldest seals predated the invention of writing and conveyed their messages with pictographs that ratified ownership. Later seals often bore long cuneiform inscriptions and recorded the names and titles of rulers, bureaucrats, and deities. Although sealing is increasingly rare, the tradition lives on today whenever someone seals an envelope with a lump of wax and then stamps it with a monogram or other identifying mark. Customs officials often still seal packages and sacks with official stamps when goods cross national borders.

In Mesopotamia, artists decorated both stamp and cylinder seals with incised designs, producing a raised pattern when the owner pressed the seal into soft clay. (Cylinder seals largely displaced stamp seals because they could be rolled over the clay and could thus cover a greater area more quickly.) Illustrated here are a cylinder seal with the name of Queen Pu-abi from the Royal Cemetery at Ur and a modern impression made from it. Note how cracks in the stone cylinder become raised lines in the impression and how the engraved figures, chairs, and cuneiform characters appear in relief. Continuous rolling of the seal over a clay strip results in a repeating design, as the impression also demonstrates at the edges.

The miniature reliefs the seals produce are a priceless source of information about Mesopotamian religion and society. Without them, archaeologists would know much less about how Mesopotamians dressed and dined; what their shrines looked like; how they depicted their gods, rulers, and mythological figures; how they fought wars; and what role women played in society. Clay seal impressions excavated in architectural contexts shed a welcome light on the administration and organization of Mesopotamian city-states. Finally, Mesopotamian seals are an invaluable resource for art historians, providing them with thousands of miniature examples of relief sculpture spanning three millennia.

1 in.

2-11 Banquet scene, cylinder seal (*left*) and its modern impression (*right*), from the tomb of Pu-abi (tomb 800), Royal Cemetery, Ur (modern Tell Muqayyar), Iraq, ca. 2600–2400 BCE. Lapis lazuli, 1⅞" high, 1" diameter. British Museum, London.

The Mesopotamians used seals to identify and secure goods. Artists incised designs into stone cylinders and then rolled them over clay to produce miniature artworks such as this banquet scene.

(or perhaps dancing), and the gazelle bearing goblets. The banquet animals almost seem to be burlesquing the kind of regal feast reproduced on the *Standard of Ur*. The meaning of the sound box scenes is unclear. Some scholars have suggested, for example, that the creatures inhabit the land of the dead and that the narrative has a funerary significance. In any event, the sound box is a very early specimen of the recurring theme in both literature and art of animals acting as people. Later examples include Aesop's fables in ancient Greece, medieval bestiaries, and Walt Disney's cartoon animal actors.

CYLINDER SEALS The excavators of the Ur cemetery found Pu-abi's remains on a bier in her tomb, wearing an elaborate headdress and jewelry of gold, silver, lapis lazuli, carnelian, and agate.

Near her body were pins to fasten her garment and three *cylinder seals,* one of which (FIG. **2-11**) gives her name in cuneiform script. The seal is typical of the period, consisting of a cylindrical piece of stone engraved to produce a raised impression when rolled over clay (see "Mesopotamian Seals," above). In the upper zone, a woman, probably Pu-abi, and a man sit and drink from beakers, attended by servants. Below, male attendants serve two more seated men. Even in miniature and in a medium very different from that of the *Standard of Ur* (FIG. 2-1), the Sumerian artist employed the same figure types and followed the same compositional rules to depict a banquet. All the figures are in composite views with large frontal eyes in profile heads, and the seated dignitaries are larger in scale to underscore their elevated position in the social hierarchy.

Akkad

In 2332 BCE, the loosely linked group of cities known as Sumer came under the domination of a great ruler, Sargon of Akkad (r. 2332–2279 BCE). Archaeologists have yet to locate the specific site of the city of Akkad, but it was in the vicinity of Babylon. The Akkadians were Semitic in origin—that is, they were a Mesopotamian people who spoke a language related to Hebrew and Arabic. Their language, Akkadian, was entirely different from the language of Sumer, but they used the Sumerians' cuneiform characters for their written documents. Under Sargon (whose name means "true king") and his followers, the Akkadians introduced a new concept of royal power based on unswerving loyalty to the king rather than to the city-state. Naram-Sin (r. 2254–2218 BCE), Sargon's grandson, regarded the governors of his cities as mere royal servants, and called himself "King of the Four Quarters"—in effect, ruler of the earth, akin to a god.

AKKADIAN PORTRAITURE A magnificent copper head (FIG. 2-12) found at Nineveh that portrays an Akkadian king em-bodies this new concept of absolute monarchy. The head is all that survives of a statue knocked over in antiquity, perhaps when the Medes, a people that occupied the land south of the Caspian Sea (MAP 2-1), sacked Nineveh in 612 BCE. But the damage to the portrait was not the result solely of the statue's toppling. There are also signs of deliberate mutilation. To make a political statement, the attackers gouged out the eyes (once inlaid with precious or semiprecious stones), broke off the lower part of the beard, and slashed the ears of the royal portrait. Later parallels for this kind of political vandalism abound, for example—in the same region—the destruction of images of Saddam Hussein after the Iraqi ruler's downfall in 2003. Even in its mutilated state, however, the Akkadian portrait conveys the king's majestic serenity, dignity, and authority. The portrait is also remarkable for the masterful way the sculptor balanced naturalism and abstract patterning. The artist carefully observed and recorded the Akkadian's distinctive features—the profile of the nose and the long, curly beard—and brilliantly communicated the differing textures of flesh and hair, even the contrasting textures of the mustache, beard, and braided hair on the top of the head. The

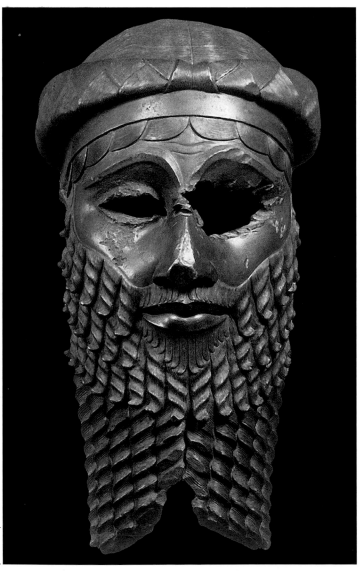

1 in.

2-12 Head of an Akkadian ruler, from Nineveh (modern Kuyunjik), Iraq, ca. 2250–2200 BCE. Copper, 1′ 2⅜″ high. National Museum of Iraq, Baghdad.

The sculptor of this oldest known life-size hollow-cast head captured the distinctive features of the ruler while also displaying a keen sense of abstract pattern. Vandals damaged the head in antiquity.

1 ft.

2-13 Victory stele of Naram-Sin, from Susa, Iran, 2254–2218 BCE. Pink sandstone, 6′ 7″ high. Musée du Louvre, Paris.

To commemorate his conquest of the Lullubi, Naram-Sin set up this stele showing him leading his army up a mountain. The sculptor staggered the figures, abandoning the traditional register format.

Enheduanna, Priestess and Poet

In the man's world of ancient Akkad, one woman stands out prominently—Enheduanna, daughter of King Sargon and priestess of the moon god Nanna at Ur. Her name appears in several inscriptions, and she was the author of a series of hymns in honor of the goddess Inanna. Enheduanna's is the oldest recorded name of a poet, male or female—indeed, the earliest known name of the author of any literary work in world history.

The most important surviving object associated with Enheduanna is the alabaster disk (FIG. 2-14) found in several fragments in the residence of the priestess of Nanna at Ur. The reverse bears a cuneiform inscription identifying Enheduanna as the "wife of Nanna" and "daughter of Sargon, king of the world." It also credits Enheduanna with erecting an altar to Nanna in his temple. The dedication of the relief to the moon god explains its unusual round format, which corresponds to the shape of the full moon. The front of the disk shows four figures approaching a four-story ziggurat. The first figure is a nude man who is either a priest or Enheduanna's assistant. He pours a libation into a plant stand. The second figure, taller than the rest and wearing the headgear of a priestess, is Enheduanna herself. She raises her right hand in a gesture of greeting and respect for the god. Two figures, probably female attendants, follow her.

Artworks created to honor women are rare in Mesopotamia and in the ancient world in general, but they are by no means unknown. The Sumerians, for example, buried Pu-abi of Ur in her own tomb filled with a treasure of jewelry, metal vessels, and musical instruments (FIG. 2-9), accompanied by 10 female retainers to attend her in the afterlife. The works created in honor of Pu-abi and Enheduanna are among the oldest known, but they pale in comparison with the monuments erected in the mid-second millennium BCE in honor of Queen Hatshepsut of Egypt (see "Hatshepsut," Chapter 3, page 69).

1 in.

2-14 Votive disk of Enheduanna, from Ur (modern Tell Muqayyar), Iraq, ca. 2300–2275 BCE. Alabaster, diameter 10″. University of Pennsylvania Museum of Archaeology and Anthropology, Philadelphia.

Enheduanna, daughter of Sargon of Akkad and priestess of Nanna at Ur, is the first author whose name is known. She is the tallest figure on this votive disk, which she dedicated to the moon god.

coiffure's triangles, lozenges, and overlapping disks of hair and the great arching eyebrows that give such character to the portrait reveal the sculptor was also sensitive to formal pattern.

No less remarkable is the fact this is a life-size, hollow-cast metal sculpture (see "Hollow-Casting Life-Size Bronze Statues," Chapter 5, page 130), one of the earliest known. The head demonstrates the bronze-worker's sophisticated skill in casting and polishing copper and in engraving the details. The portrait is the oldest known monumental work of hollow-cast sculpture.

NARAM-SIN STELE The godlike sovereignty the kings of Akkad claimed is also evident in the victory stele (FIG. 2-13) Naram-Sin set up at Sippar. The stele commemorates the Akkadian ruler's defeat of the Lullubi, a people of the Iranian mountains to the east. It carries two inscriptions, one in honor of Naram-Sin and one naming the Elamite king who captured Sippar in 1157 BCE and took the stele as booty back to Susa in southwestern Iran (MAP 2-1), the stele's findspot. The sculptor depicted Naram-Sin leading his army up the slopes of a wooded mountain. His routed enemies fall, flee, die, or beg for mercy. The king stands alone, far taller than his men, treading on the bodies of two of the fallen Lullubi. He wears the horned helmet signifying divinity—the first time a king appears as a god in Mesopotamian art. At least three favorable stars (the stele is damaged at the top) shine on his triumph.

By storming the mountain, Naram-Sin seems also to be scaling the ladder to the heavens, the same conceit that lies behind the great Mesopotamian ziggurats. His troops march up the mountain behind him in orderly files, suggesting the discipline and organization of the king's forces. In contrast, his enemies are in disarray, depicted in a great variety of postures. One falls headlong down the mountainside. The Akkadian artist adhered to older conventions in many details, especially by portraying the king and his soldiers in composite views and by placing a frontal two-horned helmet on Naram-Sin's profile head. But the sculptor showed daring innovation in creating a landscape setting for the story and placing the figures on successive tiers within that landscape. For the first time, an artist rejected the standard Mesopotamian format of telling a story in a series of horizontal registers, the compositional formula that had been the rule for a millennium. The traditional frieze format was the choice, however, for an alabaster disk (FIG. 2-14) that is in other respects an equally unique find (see "Enheduanna, Priestess and Poet," above).

2-15 Ziggurat (looking southwest), Ur (modern Tell Muqayyar), Iraq, ca. 2100 BCE.

The Ur ziggurat is one of the largest in Mesopotamia. It has three (restored) ramplike stairways of a hundred steps each that originally ended at a gateway to a brick temple, which does not survive.

Third Dynasty of Ur

Around 2150 BCE, a mountain people, the Gutians, brought an end to Akkadian power. The cities of Sumer, however, soon united in response to the alien presence, drove the Gutians out of Mesopotamia, and established a Neo-Sumerian state ruled by the kings of Ur. Historians call this period the Neo-Sumerian age or the Third Dynasty of Ur.

ZIGGURAT, UR The most imposing extant Neo-Sumerian monument is the ziggurat (FIG. **2-15**) at Ur. One of the largest ever erected, with a massive mud-brick base 50 feet high, it is about a millennium later than Uruk's more modest White Temple (FIGS. 2-2 and 2-3). The Neo-Sumerian builders used baked bricks laid in bitumen, an asphaltlike substance, for the facing of the entire monument. (Today, most of the bricks are part of a modern reconstruction.) Three ramplike stairways of a hundred steps each converge on a tower-flanked gateway. From there another flight of steps (not restored) probably led to the temple proper, which does not survive.

GUDEA OF LAGASH Of all the preserved sculptures of the Third Dynasty of Ur, the most conspicuous are those portraying Gudea, the ensi of Lagash around 2100 BCE (see "The Piety of Gudea," page 43). His statues show him seated (FIG. **2-16**) or standing (FIG. **2-17**), hands usually tightly clasped, head shaven, sometimes wearing a brimmed sheepskin hat, and always dressed in a long garment that leaves one shoulder and arm exposed. He has a youthful face with large, arching, herringbone-patterned eyebrows framing wide-open eyes. Gudea was zealous in granting the gods their due, and the numerous statues he commissioned are an enduring testimony to his piety—and to his wealth and pride. All his portraits are of polished diorite, a rare and costly dark stone that had to be imported from present-day Oman. Diorite is also extremely hard and difficult to carve. Underscoring the prestige of the material—which in turn lent prestige to Gudea's portraits—is an inscription on one of his statues: "This statue has not been made from silver nor from lapis lazuli, nor from copper nor from lead, nor yet from bronze; it is made of diorite."

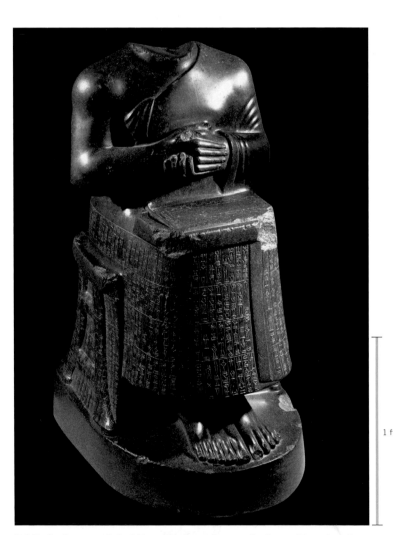

1 ft.

2-16 Gudea seated, holding the plan of a temple, from Girsu (modern Telloh), Iraq, ca. 2100 BCE. Diorite, 2′ 5″ high. Musée du Louvre, Paris.

Gudea built or rebuilt many temples and placed statues of himself in all of them. The inscription on this seated portrait states that Gudea has on his lap a plan of the new temple he erected to Ningirsu.

The Piety of Gudea

Acentral figure of the Neo-Sumerian age was Gudea of Lagash. Nearly two dozen portraits of him survive. All stood in temples where they could render perpetual service to the gods and intercede with the divine powers on his behalf. Although a powerful ruler, Gudea rejected the regal trappings of Sargon of Akkad and his successors, as well as their pretensions of divinity, in favor of a return to the Sumerian model of the ruler as the agent of the gods in the service of his people. Gudea's portraits follow the votive tradition of the Eshnunna (FIG. 2-6) and Mari (FIG. 2-6A) statuettes. Like the earlier examples, many of his statues bear inscriptions with messages to the gods of Sumer. One from Girsu says, "I am the shepherd loved by my king [Ningirsu, the god of Girsu]; may my life be prolonged." Another, also from Girsu, as if in answer to the first, says, "Gudea, the builder of the temple, has been given life." Some of the inscriptions clarify why Gudea was portrayed as he was. For example, his large chest is a sign the gods have given him fullness of life, and his muscular arms reveal his god-given strength. Other inscriptions explain that his large eyes signify that his gaze is perpetually fixed on the gods (compare FIG. 2-6).

Gudea built or rebuilt, at great cost, all the temples in which he placed his statues. One characteristic portrait (FIG. 2-16) depicts the pious ruler of Lagash seated with his hands clasped in front of him in a gesture of prayer. But the statue is unique because Gudea has a temple plan drawn on a tablet on his lap. It is the plan for a new temple dedicated to Ningirsu. Gudea buried accounts of his building enterprises in the temple foundations. The surviving texts describe how the Neo-Sumerians prepared and purified the sites, obtained the materials, and dedicated the completed temples. They also record Gudea's dreams of the gods asking him to erect temples in their honor, promising him prosperity if he fulfilled his duty. In one of these dreams, Ningirsu addresses Gudea:

> When, O faithful shepherd Gudea, thou shalt have started work for me on Erinnu, my royal abode [Ningirsu's new temple], I will call up in heaven a humid wind. It shall bring the abundance from on high. . . . All the great fields will bear for thee; dykes and canals will swell for thee; . . . good weight of wool will be given in thy time.*

2-17A Investiture of Zimri-Lim, Mari, ca. 1775–1760 BCE.

One of Gudea's portraits (FIG. 2-17) differs from the rest in depicting the ensi holding a jar from which water flows freely in two streams, one running down each side of his cloak. Fish swim in the coursing water. In Mesopotamian art, gods and goddesses often hold similar overflowing vessels (FIG. 2-17A), which symbolize the prosperity they bring to their people. This small statue (less than half life-size) is the only known instance in which a Mesopo-

2-17 Gudea standing, holding an overflowing water jar, from the Temple of Geshtinanna, Girsu (modern Telloh), Iraq, ca. 2100 BCE. Calcite, 2' 3/8" high. Musée du Louvre, Paris.

The overflowing water jar that Gudea holds symbolizes the prosperity he brings to the people of Lagash. In Mesopotamian art, normally only gods and goddesses are the sources of life-giving water.

1 ft.

mian ruler appears as the source of the prosperity. For that reason and because the statue is made of calcite instead of the costly imported diorite used for Gudea's other portraits (FIG. 2-16), some scholars have questioned the authenticity of this piece. But the cuneiform inscription, which states that Gudea dedicated the statue in the temple he built in honor of the goddess Geshtinanna, the divine interpreter of dreams, is genuine, and so too must be the statue.

*Translated by Thorkild Jacobsen, in Henri Frankfort, *The Art and Architecture of the Ancient Orient*, 5th ed. (New Haven, Conn.: Yale University Press, 1996), 98.

Babylon

The resurgence of Sumer was short-lived. The last of the kings of the Third Dynasty of Ur fell at the hands of the Elamites, who ruled the territory east of the Tigris River. In the following two centuries, the traditional Mesopotamian political pattern of several independent city-states existing side by side reemerged.

HAMMURABI Babylon was one of those city-states until its most powerful king, Hammurabi (r. 1792–1750 BCE), reestablished a centralized government in southern Mesopotamia in the area known as Babylonia, after its chief city. Perhaps the most renowned king in Mesopotamian history, Hammurabi was famous for his conquests. But he is best known today for his laws (FIG. 2-18),

Hammurabi's Laws

In the early 18th century BCE, the Babylonian king Hammurabi formulated a set of nearly 300 laws for his people. At the time, parts of Europe were still in the Stone Age. Even in Greece, it was more than a thousand years later that Draco provided Athens with its first comprehensive law code. Two earlier sets of Sumerian laws survive in part, but Hammurabi's laws are the only ones known in great detail, thanks to the chance survival of a tall black-basalt stele (FIG. 2-18) that the Elamites carried off as booty to Susa in 1157 BCE, together with the Naram-Sin stele (FIG. 2-13). At the top is a representation in high relief of Hammurabi in the presence of Shamash, the flame-shouldered sun god. The king raises his hand in respect. The god extends to Hammurabi the rod and ring that symbolize authority. (Ishtar presents Hammurabi's contemporary, Zimri-Lim, with the same emblems of power in a mural painting [FIG. 2-18A] in that king's palace at Mari.) The symbols are builders' tools—measuring rods and coiled rope—and connote the ruler's capacity to build the social order and to measure people's lives, that is, to render judgments and enforce the laws spelled out on the stele. The collection of Hammurabi's judicial pronouncements is inscribed on the Susa stele in Akkadian in 3,500 lines of cuneiform characters. Hammurabi's laws governed all aspects of Babylonian life, from commerce and property to murder and theft to marital infidelity, inheritances, and the treatment of slaves.

Here is a small sample of the infractions described and the penalties imposed, which vary with the person's standing in society and notably deal with the rights and crimes of women as well as men:

- If a man puts out the eye of another man, his eye shall be put out.

- If he kills a man's slave, he shall pay one-third of a *mina*.

- If someone steals property from a temple, he will be put to death, as will the person who receives the stolen goods.

- If a married woman dies before bearing any sons, her dowry shall be repaid to her father, but if she gave birth to sons, the dowry shall belong to them.

- If a man strikes a freeborn woman so that she loses her unborn child, he shall pay ten *shekels* for her loss. If the woman dies, his daughter shall be put to death.

- If a man is guilty of incest with his daughter, he shall be exiled.

Hammurabi's stele is noteworthy artistically as well. The sculptor depicted Shamash in the familiar convention of combined front and side views but with two important exceptions. His great headdress with its four pairs of horns is in true profile so that only four, not all eight, of the horns are visible. Also, the artist seems to have tentatively explored the notion of *foreshortening*—a device for suggesting depth by representing a figure or object at an angle, instead of frontally or in profile. Shamash's beard is a series of diagonal rather than horizontal lines, suggesting its recession from the picture plane. The sculptor also depicted the god's throne at an angle.

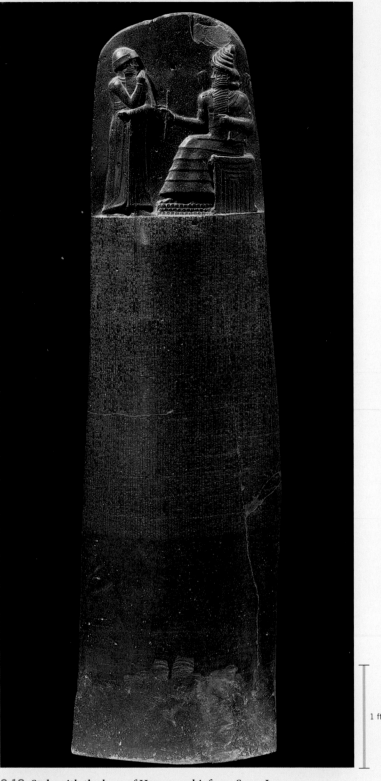

1 ft.

2-18 Stele with the laws of Hammurabi, from Susa, Iran, ca. 1780 BCE. Basalt, 7′ 4″ high. Musée du Louvre, Paris. ◼◀

Crowning the stele recording Hammurabi's laws is a representation of the flame-shouldered sun god Shamash extending to the Babylonian king the symbols of his authority to govern and judge.

which prescribed penalties for everything from adultery and murder to the cutting down of a neighbor's trees (see "Hammurabi's Laws," page 44).

Elam

2-18A Lion Gate, Hattusa, ca. 1400 BCE.

2-19A Beaker with animal decoration, Susa, ca. 4000 BCE.

The Babylonian Empire toppled in the face of an onslaught by the Hittites, an Anatolian people whose heavily fortified capital was at Hattusa (FIG. 2-18A) near modern Boghazköy, Turkey. After sacking Babylon around 1595 BCE, the Hittites abandoned Mesopotamia and returned to their homeland, leaving Babylon in the hands of the Kassites. To the east of Babylon was Elam, which appears in the Bible as early as Genesis 10:22. Archaeologists have discovered painted pottery (FIG. 2-19A) at the Elamite capital of Susa in present-day Iran dating as far back as the Neolithic period. Elam reached the height of its political and military power during the second half of the second millennium BCE. At that time the Elamites were strong enough to plunder Babylonia and to carry off the stelae of Naram-Sin (FIG. 2-13) and Hammurabi (FIG. 2-18) and display them as war booty in Susa.

NAPIR ASU In the ruins of Susa, archaeologists discovered a life-size bronze-and-copper statue (FIG. 2-19) of Queen Napir-Asu, wife of one of the most powerful Elamite kings, Untash-Napirisha (r. ca. 1345–ca. 1305 BCE). The statue weighs 3,760 pounds even in its fragmentary and mutilated state, because the sculptor, incredibly, cast the statue with a solid bronze core inside a hollow-cast copper shell. The bronze core increased the cost of the statue enormously, but the queen wished her portrait to be a permanent, immovable votive offering in the temple where archaeologists found it. In fact, the Elamite inscription on the queen's skirt explicitly asks the gods to protect the statue:

> He who would seize my statue, who would smash it, who would destroy its inscription, who would erase my name, may he be smitten by the curse of [the gods], that his name shall become extinct, that his offspring be barren. . . . This is Napir-Asu's offering.[1]

Napir-Asu's portrait thus falls within the votive tradition dating back to the third-millennium BCE Eshnunna (FIG. 2-6) and Mari (FIG. 2-6A) figurines. In the Elamite statue, the Mesopotamian instinct for cylindrical volume is again evident. The tight silhouette, strict frontality, and firmly crossed hands held close to the body are all enduring characteristics common to the Sumerian statuettes. Yet within these rigid conventions of form and pose, the Elamite artist incorporated features based on close observation. The sculptor conveyed the feminine softness of arm and bust, the grace and elegance of the long-fingered hands, the supple bend of the wrist, the ring and bracelets, and the gown's patterned fabric. The loss of the head is especially unfortunate. The figure presents a portrait of the ideal queen. The hands crossed over the belly may allude to fertility and the queen's role in assuring peaceful dynastic succession.

1 ft.

2-19 Statue of Queen Napir-Asu, from Susa, Iran, ca. 1350–1300 BCE. Bronze and copper, 4′ 2¾″ high. Musée du Louvre, Paris.

This life-size bronze-and-copper statue of the wife of a powerful Elamite king weighs 3,760 pounds. The queen wanted her portrait to stand in a temple at Susa as an immovable votive offering to the deity.

Assyria

During the first half of the first millennium BCE, the fearsome Assyrians vanquished the various warfaring peoples that succeeded the Babylonians and Hittites, including the Elamites, whose capital of Susa they sacked in 641 BCE. The Assyrians took their name from Assur, the city on the Tigris River in northern Iraq dedicated to the god Ashur. At the height of their power, the Assyrians ruled an empire that extended from the Tigris River to the Nile and from the Persian Gulf to Asia Minor.

PALACE OF SARGON II The Assyrian kings cultivated an image of themselves as merciless to anyone who dared oppose them but forgiving to those who submitted to their will. Ever mindful of possible attack, the Assyrians constructed their palaces as fortified citadels. A reconstruction on paper of the palace that Sargon II (r. 721–705 BCE) built at Dur Sharrukin (FIG. 2-20A) gives a good idea of the original appearance of Assyrian royal citadels.

Guarding the gate to Sargon's palace were colossal limestone monsters (FIG. 2-20), which the Assyrians probably called *lamassu*. These winged, man-headed bulls served to ward off the king's enemies. The task of moving and installing these immense stone sculptures was so daunting that several reliefs in the palace of Sargon's successor celebrate the feat, showing scores of men dragging lamassu figures with the aid of ropes and sledges. The Assyrian lamassu sculptures are partly in the round, but the sculptor nonetheless conceived them as high reliefs on adjacent sides of a corner. They combine the front view of the animal at rest with the side view of it in motion. Seeking to present a complete picture of the lamassu from both the front and the side, the sculptor gave the monster five legs—two seen from the front, four seen from the side. This sculpture, then, is yet another case of early artists' providing a conceptual picture of an animal or person and of all its important parts, as opposed to an optical view of the lamassu as it would really stand in space.

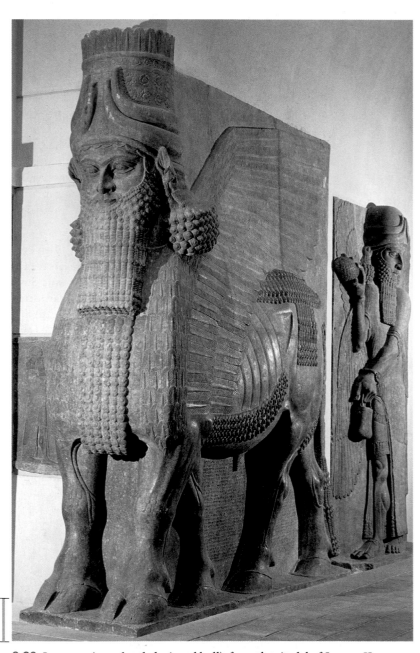

1 ft.

2-20 Lamassu (man-headed winged bull), from the citadel of Sargon II, Dur Sharrukin (modern Khorsabad), Iraq, ca. 720–705 BCE. Limestone, 13′ 10″ high. Musée du Louvre, Paris.

Ancient sculptors insisted on complete views of animals. This four-legged composite monster that guarded an Assyrian palace has five legs—two when seen from the front and four in profile view.

PALACE OF ASHURNASIRPAL II For their palace walls, the Assyrian kings commissioned extensive series of mural paintings and narrative reliefs exalting royal power. Unfortunately, few Assyrian paintings exist today. A notable exception is the depiction (FIG. 2-21) of King Ashurnasirpal II (r. 883–859 BCE) and his retinue paying homage to the gods. It comes from the northwest palace at Kalhu. The painting medium is glazed brick, a much more durable format than direct painting on plastered mud-brick walls, the technique used a millennium earlier in Zimri-Lim's palace at Mari (FIG. 2-17A). The Assyrian painter first applied lines and colors to a clay panel and then baked the clay in a kiln, fusing the colors to the clay.

The Kalhu panel shows Ashurnasirpal—his name means "Ashur guards the heir"—delicately holding a cup. With it, he will make a libation in honor of the protective Assyrian gods. The artist represented the king as taller than everyone else, befitting his rank, and rendered the figures in outline, lavishing much attention on the patterns of the rich fabrics they wear. The color palette is limited to yellow and brown. The king and the attendant behind him are in consistent profile view, but the painter adhered to the convention of showing the eye from the front in a profile head. Painted scenes such as this hint at the original appearance (before the color disappeared) of the stone reliefs (FIGS. 2-21 to 2-23) in Assyrian palaces, although the reliefs would have featured a wider range of hues than those available to the ceramic painter.

The degree of documentary detail in the Assyrian reliefs is without parallel in the ancient world before the Roman Empire (see Chapter 7). Ashurnasirpal's Kalhu palace also boasts one of the earliest and most extensive cycles of Assyrian relief sculptures. The painted gypsum reliefs sheathed the lower parts of the mud-brick palace walls below brightly colored plaster. Rich textiles on the floors contributed to the luxurious ambience. Every relief bore an inscription naming Ashurnasirpal and describing his accomplishments.

The relief illustrated here (FIG. 2-22) probably depicts an episode that occurred in 878 BCE when Ashurnasirpal drove his enemy's forces into the Euphrates River. Two Assyrian archers shoot arrows at the fleeing foe. Three enemy soldiers are in the water. One swims with an arrow in his back. The other two attempt to float to safety by inflating animal skins. Their destination is a fort where their compatriots await them. The artist showed the fort as if it were in the middle of the river, but it was, of course, on land, perhaps at some distance from where the escapees entered the water. The artist's purpose was to tell the story clearly and

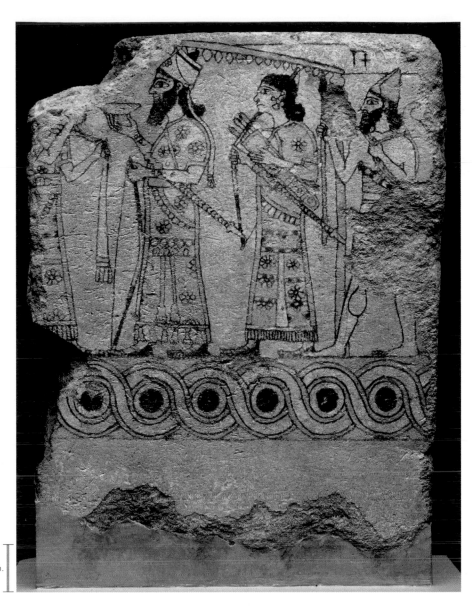

2-21 Ashurnasirpal II with attendants and soldier, from the northwest palace of Ashurnasirpal II, Kalhu (modern Nimrud), Iraq, ca. 875–860 BCE. Glazed brick, 11¾″ high. British Museum, London.

Paintings on glazed bricks adorned the walls of Assyrian palaces. This rare example shows Ashurnasirpal II paying homage to the gods. The artist represented the king as taller than his attendants.

economically. Ancient sculptors and painters often compressed distances and enlarged the human actors so they would stand out from their environment. Literally interpreted, the defenders of the fort are too tall to walk through its archway. (Compare Naram-Sin and his men scaling a mountain, FIG. 2-13.) The sculptor also combined different viewpoints in the same frame, just as the figures are composites of frontal and profile views. The spectator views the river from above, and the men, trees, and fort from the side. The artist also made other adjustments for clarity. The archers' bowstrings are in front of their bodies but behind their heads in order not to hide their faces. (The men will snare their heads in their bows when they launch their arrows.) All these liberties with optical reality, however, result in a vivid and easily legible retelling of a decisive moment in the king's victorious campaign. That was the artist's primary goal.

PALACE OF ASHURBANIPAL Two centuries later, sculptors carved hunting reliefs for the Nineveh palace of the conqueror of Elamite Susa, Ashurbanipal (r. 668–627 BCE), whose name means "Ashur is creator of the son." The Greeks called him Sardanapalus, and the French painter Eugène Delacroix immortalized the Assyrian king in the 19th

2-22 Assyrian archers pursuing enemies, relief from the northwest palace of Ashurnasirpal II, Kalhu (modern Nimrud), Iraq, ca. 875–860 BCE. Gypsum, 2′ 10⅝″ high. British Museum, London.

Extensive reliefs exalting the king and recounting his great deeds have been found in several Assyrian palaces. This one depicts Ashurnasirpal II's archers driving the enemy into the Euphrates River.

2-23 Ashurbanipal hunting lions, relief from the north palace of Ashurbanipal, Nineveh (modern Kuyunjik), Iraq, ca. 645–640 BCE. Gypsum, 5′ 4″ high. British Museum, London.

In addition to ceremonial and battle scenes, the hunt was a common subject of Assyrian palace reliefs. The Assyrians viewed hunting and killing lions as manly royal virtues on a par with victory in warfare.

century in one of the most dramatic canvases (FIG. 27-15) of the Romantic era in Europe. The Assyrians, like many other societies before and after, regarded prowess in hunting as a manly virtue on a par with success in warfare. The royal hunt did not take place in the wild, however, but in a controlled environment, ensuring the king's safety and success. In FIG. **2-23**, lions released from cages in a large enclosed arena charge the king, who, in his chariot and protected by his attendants, thrusts a spear into a savage lion. The animal leaps at the king even though it already has two arrows in its body. All around the royal chariot is a pathetic trail of dead and dying animals, pierced by what appear to be far more arrows than needed to kill them. Blood streams from some of the lions, but they refuse to die. The artist brilliantly depicted the straining muscles, the swelling veins, the muzzles' wrinkled skin, and the flattened ears of the powerful and defiant beasts. Modern sympathies make this scene of carnage a kind of heroic tragedy, with the lions as protagonists. It is unlikely, however, that the king's artists had any intention other than to glorify their ruler by showing the king of men pitted against and repeatedly besting the king of beasts. Portraying Ashurbanipal's beastly foes as possessing courage and nobility as well as the power to kill made the king's accomplishments that much grander.

The Assyrian Empire was never very secure, and most of its kings had to fight revolts throughout Mesopotamia. Assyria's conquest of Elam in the seventh century BCE and frequent rebellions in Babylonia apparently overextended its resources. During the last years of Ashurbanipal's reign, the empire began to disintegrate. Under his successors, it collapsed from the simultaneous onslaught of the Medes from the east and the resurgent Babylonians from the south. Neo-Babylonian kings held sway over the former Assyrian Empire until the Persian conquest.

Neo-Babylonia

The most renowned of the Neo-Babylonian kings was Nebuchadnezzar II (r. 605–562 BCE), whose exploits the biblical book of Daniel recounts. Nebuchadnezzar restored Babylon to its rank as one of the great cities of antiquity. The city's famous hanging gardens were counted among the Seven Wonders of the ancient world, and the Bible (Gen. 11:1–9) immortalized its enormous ziggurat as the Tower of Babel (see "Babylon, City of Wonders," page 49).

ISHTAR GATE Nebuchadnezzar's Babylon was a mud-brick city, but dazzling blue-glazed bricks faced the most important monuments, such as the Ishtar Gate (FIG. **2-24**), really a pair of gates, one of which has been restored and installed in a German museum. The Ishtar Gate consists of a large *arcuated* (*arch*-shaped) opening flanked by towers, and features glazed bricks with reliefs of animals, real and imaginary. The Babylonian builders molded and glazed each brick separately, then set them in proper sequence on the wall. On the Ishtar Gate, profile figures of Marduk and Nabu's dragon and Adad's bull alternate. Lining the processional way leading up to the gate were reliefs of Ishtar's sacred lion, glazed in yellow, brown, and red against a blue ground.

PERSIA

Although Nebuchadnezzar—the "king of kings" in the book of Daniel (2:37)—had boasted in an inscription that he "caused a mighty wall to circumscribe Babylon . . . so that the enemy who would do evil would not threaten," Cyrus of Persia (r. 559–529 BCE) captured the city in the sixth century. Cyrus, who may have been descended from an Elamite line, was the founder of the Achaemenid dynasty and traced his ancestry back to a mythical King Achaemenes.

Babylon, City of Wonders

The uncontested list of the Seven Wonders of the ancient world was not codified until the 16th century. But already in the second century BCE, Antipater of Sidon, a Greek poet, compiled a roster of seven must-see monuments, including six of the seven later Wonders. All of the Wonders were of colossal size and constructed at great expense. The oldest were of great antiquity, nearly 2,500 years old in Antipater's day: the pyramids of Gizeh (FIG. 3-7), which he described as "man-made mountains." Only one site on Antipater's list could boast two Wonders: Babylon, with its "hanging gardens" and "impregnable walls." Later list makers preferred to distribute the Seven Wonders among seven different cities. Most of these Wonders date to Greek times—the Temple of Artemis at Ephesos, with its 60-foot-tall columns; Phidias's colossal gold-and-ivory statue of Zeus at Olympia; the "Mausoleum" at Halikarnassos, the gigantic tomb (FIG. 5-64B) of the fourth-century BCE ruler Mausolus; the Colossus of Rhodes, a bronze statue of the Greek sun god 110 feet tall; and the lighthouse at Alexandria, perhaps the tallest building in the ancient world. The Babylonian gardens were the only Wonder in the category of "landscape architecture."

Several ancient texts describe Babylon's wondrous gardens. Quintus Curtius Rufus reported in the mid-first century CE:

> On the top of the citadel are the hanging gardens, a wonder celebrated in the tales of the Greeks. . . . Columns of stone were set up to sustain the whole work, and on these was laid a floor of squared blocks, strong enough to hold the earth which is thrown upon it to a great depth, as well as the water with which they irrigate the soil; and the structure supports trees of such great size that the thickness of their trunks equals a measure of eight cubits [about twelve feet]. They tower to a height of fifty feet, and they yield as much

fruit as if they were growing in their native soil. . . . To those who look upon [the trees] from a distance, real woods seem to be overhanging their native mountains.*

Not qualifying as a Wonder, but in some ways no less impressive, was Babylon's Marduk ziggurat, the biblical Tower of Babel, erected by King Nebuchadnezzar, who also constructed Babylon's Ishtar Gate (FIG. 2-24). According to the Bible, humankind's arrogant desire to build a tower to Heaven angered God. The Lord put an end to it by causing the workers to speak different languages, preventing them from communicating with one another. The fifth-century BCE Greek historian Herodotus described the Babylonian temple complex:

> In the middle of the sanctuary [of Marduk] has been built a solid tower . . . which supports another tower, which in turn supports another, and so on: there are eight towers in all. A stairway has been constructed to wind its way up the outside of all the towers; halfway up the stairway there is a shelter with benches to rest on, where people making the ascent can sit and catch their breath. In the last tower there is a huge temple. The temple contains a large couch, which is adorned with fine coverings and has a golden table standing beside it, but there are no statues at all standing there. . . . [The Babylonians] say that the god comes in person to the temple [compare the Sumerian notion of the temple as a "waiting room"] and rests on the couch; I do not believe this story myself.†

*Quintus Curtius 5.1.31–35. Translated by John C. Rolfe, *Quintus Curtius I* (Cambridge: Harvard University Press, 1971), 337–339.
† Herodotus 1.181–182. Translated by Robin Waterfield, *Herodotus: The Histories* (New York: Oxford University Press, 1998), 79–80.

2-24 Ishtar Gate (restored), Babylon, Iraq, ca. 575 BCE. Vorderasiatisches Museum, Staatliche Museen zu Berlin, Berlin.

Nebuchadnezzar II's Babylon was one of the ancient world's greatest cities and boasted two of the Seven Wonders. Its Ishtar Gate featured glazed-brick reliefs of Marduk and Nabu's dragon and Adad's bull.

2-25 Aerial view of Persepolis (looking west with the apadana in the background), Iran, ca. 521–465 BCE.

The heavily fortified complex of Persian royal buildings on a high plateau at Persepolis included a royal audience hall, or apadana, with 36 colossal columns topped by animal protomes (FIG. 2-26).

Achaemenid Empire

Babylon was but one of the Achaemenids' conquests. Egypt fell to them in 525 BCE, and by 480 BCE they boasted the largest empire the world had yet known, extending from the Indus River in South Asia to the Danube River in northeastern Europe. If the Greeks had not succeeded in turning back the Persians in 479 BCE, they would have taken control of southeastern Europe as well. The Achaemenid line ended with the death of Darius III in 330 BCE, after his defeat at the hands of Alexander the Great (FIG. 5-70).

PERSEPOLIS The most important source of knowledge about Persian art and architecture is the ceremonial and administrative complex on the citadel at Persepolis (FIG. **2-25**), which the successors of Cyrus, Darius I (r. 522–486 BCE) and Xerxes (r. 486–465 BCE), built between 521 and 465 BCE. Situated on a high plateau, the heavily fortified complex of royal buildings stood on a wide platform overlooking the plain. Alexander the Great razed the site in a gesture symbolizing the destruction of Persian imperial power. Some said it was an act of revenge for the Persian sack of the Athenian Acropolis in 480 BCE (see Chapter 5). Nevertheless, even in ruins, the Persepolis citadel is impressive.

The approach to the citadel led through a monumental gateway called the Gate of All Lands, a reference to the harmony among the

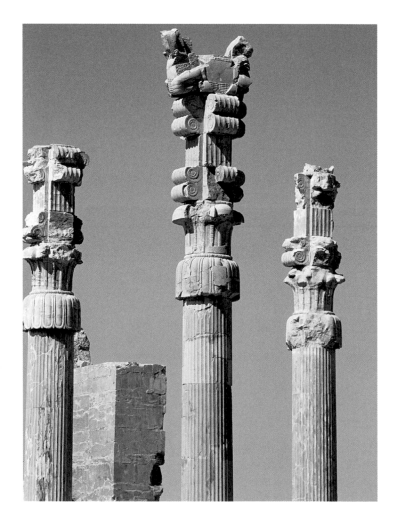

2-26 Columns with animal protomes, from the apadana of the palace (FIG. 2-25), Persepolis, Iran, ca. 521–465 BCE.

The 64-foot columns of the Persepolis apadana drew on Greek, Egyptian, and Mesopotamian models but are unique in form. The back-to-back protomes of the capitals supported gigantic wood beams.

peoples of the vast Persian Empire. Assyrian-inspired colossal man-headed winged bulls flanked the great entrance. Broad ceremonial stairways provided access to the platform and the immense royal audience hall, or *apadana,* in which at least 10,000 guests could stand at one time. Although the hall had mud-brick walls, the floors were paved in stone or brick, and the apadana's chief feature—its forest of 36 colossal *columns* (FIG. **2-26**)—was entirely of stone. The columns consisted of tall *bases* with a ring of palm leaves, *fluted* 57-foot *shafts,* and enormous *capitals* composed of double vertical *volutes* (see "Doric and Ionic Orders," Chapter 5, page 116, for the architectural terminology) topped by polished and painted back-to-back animal *protomes* (the head, forelegs, and part of the body). The columns are unique in form, but the designers drew on Greek, Egyptian, and Mesopotamian traditions.

The capitals with animal protomes in the Persepolis apadana are nearly 7 feet tall, bringing the total height of the columns to almost 64 feet. The animals—*griffins* (eagle-headed winged lions), bulls, lions, and composite man-headed bulls—vary from capital to capital. The Persepolis architect must have wanted to suggest that the Persian king had captured the fiercest animals and monsters to hold up the roof of his palace. The paired protomes form a U-shaped socket that held massive cedar beams (imported from Lebanon), which in turn supported a timber roof sealed with mud plaster. Animal protomes were also popular motifs for the luxurious tableware used to serve the Achaemenid king and his of-ficial guests. A preserved gold *rhyton* (conical pouring vessel) in the form of a winged lion (FIG. **2-26A**) suggests the ostentatious wealth on display in Persian palaces.

2-26A Gold rhyton, Hamadan, fifth to third century BCE.

The reliefs (FIG. **2-27**) decorating the walls of the terrace and staircases leading to the apadana represent processions of royal guards, Persian nobles and dignitaries, and representatives from 23 subject nations, including Medes, Elamites, Babylonians, Egyptians, and Nubians, bringing tribute to the king. Every emissary wears a characteristic costume and carries a typical regional gift for the conqueror. The section of the procession reproduced here represents Persian nobles (in pleated skirts) and Medes wearing their distinctive round caps, knee-length tunics, and trousers. The carving of the Persepolis reliefs is technically superb, with subtly modeled surfaces and crisply chiseled details. Traces of color prove the reliefs were painted, and the original effect surely was more striking than it is today.

Although the Assyrian palace reliefs may have inspired those at Persepolis, the Persian sculptures differ in style. The forms are more rounded, and they project more from the background. Some of the details, notably the treatment of drapery folds, echo forms characteristic of Archaic Greek sculpture (compare FIG. 5-11), and Greek influence seems to be one of the many ingredients of Achaemenid style.

2-27 Persians and Medes, detail of the processional frieze on the east side of the terrace of the apadana of the palace (FIG. 2-25), **Persepolis, Iran, ca. 521–465 BCE. Limestone, 8′ 4″ high.**

The reliefs decorating the walls of the terrace and staircases leading up to the Persepolis apadana (FIG. 2-25) included depictions of representatives of 23 nations bringing tribute to the Persian king.

1 ft.

2-28 Palace of Shapur I, Ctesiphon, Iraq, ca. 250 CE.

The last great pre-Islamic civilization of Mesopotamia was that of the Sasanians. Their palace at Ctesiphon, near Baghdad, features a brick audience hall (iwan) covered by an enormous pointed vault.

Persian art testifies to the active exchange of ideas and artists among all the civilizations of the Mediterranean, Mesopotamia, and Persia at this date. In an inscription at Susa, for example, Darius I boasted of the diverse origin of the stonemasons, carpenters, and sculptors who constructed and decorated his palace. He names Ionian Greeks, Medes, Egyptians, and Babylonians. This heterogeneous workforce created a new and coherent style that perfectly suited the expression of Persian imperial ambitions.

Sasanian Empire

Alexander the Great's conquest of the Achaemenid Empire in 330 BCE marked the beginning of a long period of first Greek and then Roman rule of large parts of Mesopotamia and Persia, beginning with one of Alexander's former generals, Seleucus I (r. 312–281 BCE), founder of the Seleucid dynasty. In the third century CE, however, a new power rose up in Persia that challenged the Romans and sought to force them out of Asia. The new rulers called themselves Sasanians. They traced their lineage to a legendary figure named Sasan, said to be a direct descendant of the Achaemenid kings. The first Sasanian king, Artaxerxes I (r. 211–241 CE), founded the New Persian Empire in 224 CE after he defeated the Parthians (another of Rome's eastern enemies).

SHAPUR I The son and successor of Artaxerxes, Shapur I (r. 241–272 CE), built a great palace (FIG. **2-28**) at Ctesiphon, the capital his father had established near modern Baghdad in Iraq. The central feature of Shapur's palace was the monumental *iwan*, or brick audience hall, covered by a *vault* (here, a deep arch over an oblong space)

2-28A Triumph of Shapur I, Bishapur, ca. 260 CE.

that came almost to a point more than 100 feet above the ground. A series of horizontal bands made up of *blind arcades* (a series of arches without openings, applied as wall decoration) divide the *facade* to the left and right of the iwan. Shapur was also an accomplished general who further extended Sasanian territory. In 260 CE, he even captured the Roman emperor Valerian—a singular feat, which he immortalized in a series of reliefs (FIG. **2-28A**) at Bishapur, Iran.

The New Persian Empire endured more than 400 years, until the Arabs drove the Sasanians out of Mesopotamia in 636 CE, just four years after the death of Muhammad. But the prestige of Sasanian art and architecture long outlasted the empire. A thousand years after Shapur I built his palace at Ctesiphon, Islamic architects still considered its soaring iwan as the standard for judging their own engineering feats (see Chapter 10).

MESOPOTAMIA AND PERSIA

SUMERIAN ART ca. 3500–2332 BCE

▮ The Sumerians founded the world's first city-states in the valley between the Tigris and Euphrates rivers and invented writing in the fourth millennium BCE.

▮ They were also the first to build towering temple platforms, called ziggurats, and to place figures in registers to tell coherent stories.

Standard of Ur, ca. 2600–2400 BCE

AKKADIAN ART ca. 2332–2150 BCE

▮ The Akkadians were the first Mesopotamian rulers to call themselves kings of the world and to assume divine attributes. The earliest recorded name of an author is the Akkadian priestess Enheduanna.

▮ Akkadian artists may have been the first to cast hollow life-size bronze sculptures and to place figures at different levels in a landscape setting.

Portrait of an Akkadian king, ca. 2250–2200 BCE

NEO-SUMERIAN AND BABYLONIAN ART ca. 2150–1600 BCE

▮ During the Third Dynasty of Ur, the Sumerians rose again to power and constructed one of the largest ziggurats in Mesopotamia at Ur.

▮ Gudea of Lagash (r. ca. 2100 BCE) built numerous temples and placed diorite portraits of himself in all of them as votive offerings to the gods.

▮ Babylon's greatest king, Hammurabi (r. 1792–1750 BCE), formulated wide-ranging laws for the empire he ruled. Babylonian artists were among the first to experiment with foreshortening.

Ziggurat, Ur, ca. 2100 BCE

ASSYRIAN AND NEO-BABYLONIAN ART ca. 900–539 BCE

▮ At the height of their power, the Assyrians ruled an empire that extended from the Persian Gulf to the Nile and Asia Minor.

▮ Assyrian palaces were fortified citadels with gates guarded by monstrous lamassu sculptures. Paintings and reliefs depicting official ceremonies and the king in battle and hunting lions decorated the walls of the ceremonial halls.

▮ In the sixth century BCE, the Babylonians constructed two of the Seven Wonders of the ancient world. The Ishtar Gate, with its colorful glazed brick reliefs, gives an idea of Babylon's magnificence under Nebuchadnezzar II (r. 605–562 BCE).

Ashurnasirpal II with attendants, ca. 875–860 BCE

ACHAEMENID AND SASANIAN ART ca. 559–330 BCE and 224–636 CE

▮ The capital of the Achaemenid Persians was at Persepolis, where Darius I (r. 522–486 BCE) and Xerxes (r. 486–465 BCE) built a huge palace complex with an audience hall that could accommodate 10,000 guests. Painted reliefs of subject nations bringing tribute adorned the terraces.

▮ The Sasanians, enemies of Rome, ruled the New Persian Empire from their palace at Ctesiphon until the Arabs defeated them four years after the death of Muhammad.

Apadana, Persepolis, ca. 521–465 BCE

King Narmer's palette is the earliest surviving labeled work of historical art. This hieroglyph gives his name (catfish = *nar*; chisel = *mer*) within a frame representing the royal palace.

The head of a cow with a woman's face appears twice on each side of Narmer's palette. She is probably the goddess Hathor, whom the Egyptians believed was the divine mother of the pharaoh.

Narmer, the largest figure in the composition, shown in a composite of frontal and profile views, effortlessly slays an enemy as the attendant carrying the pharaoh's sandals looks on.

1 in.

3-1 Back of the palette of King Narmer (compare FIG. 3-2), from Hierakonpolis, Egypt, Predynastic, ca. 3000–2920 BCE. Slate, 2′ 1″ high. Egyptian Museum, Cairo.

3

EGYPT UNDER THE PHARAOHS

The falcon with human arms is the god Horus, the pharaoh's protector, who takes captive a man-headed hieroglyph with a papyrus plant growing from it that stands for defeated Lower Egypt.

DIVINE KINGSHIP ON THE NILE

Blessed with ample sources of stone of different hues suitable for carving statues and fashioning building blocks, the Egyptians left to posterity a profusion of spectacular monuments spanning three millennia. Many of them glorify the kings whom they called *pharaohs* and believed to be divine. Indeed, the Egyptians devoted enormous resources to erecting countless monuments and statues to honor the pharaohs during their lifetimes and to constructing and furnishing magnificent tombs to serve as their god-kings' eternal homes in the afterlife.

It is not surprising, then, that the earliest preserved artwork labeled with the name of a ruler is Egyptian—the two-foot-tall slate *palette* (stone slab with a circular depression—FIG. **3-1**; compare FIG. 3-2) portraying Narmer, a pharaoh of the first of Egypt's 31 dynasties, and commemorating the unification of the two previously independent kingdoms of Upper and Lower Egypt. At the top of the 5,000-year-old palette are two heads of a cow with a woman's face, whom scholars usually identify as the goddess Hathor, the divine mother of all pharaohs, but who may be the sky goddess Bat. Between the heads is a *hieroglyph* giving Narmer's name (catfish = *nar*; chisel = *mer*) within a frame representing the pharaoh's royal palace.

At the center and dominating the palette is Narmer, whom the sculptor depicted as larger than everyone else, appropriate for his divine status. The pharaoh wears the high, white, bowling-pin-shaped crown of Upper Egypt. Accompanying the king is an official who carries his sandals. The representation of the pharaoh (and of the attendant) combines profile views of the head, legs, and arms with front views of the eye and torso, the same composite view of the human figure found in Mesopotamian and Persian art. Narmer effortlessly slays an unarmed foe, a motif that became a standard pictorial formula in Egyptian art signifying the inevitable triumph of the Egyptian god-kings over their enemies. Above and to the right, the falcon with human arms is the god Horus, the king's protector. The deity takes captive a hieroglyph of the land of Lower Egypt consisting of a man's head and a papyrus plant. Below the king are two fallen enemies.

Furnishing anecdotal details of a specific event was not the goal of this Egyptian artist. Rather, the objective was to characterize the pharaoh as supreme and protected by the gods, isolated from and larger than all ordinary men, and solely responsible for the triumph over the enemy. The Narmer palette set the standard for narrative art in Egypt for 3,000 years.

EGYPT AND EGYPTOLOGY

The backbone of Egypt was, and still is, the Nile River, which, through its annual floods, supported all life in that ancient land (MAP 3-1). Even more so than the Tigris and the Euphrates rivers of Mesopotamia (MAP 2-1), the Nile defined the cultures that developed along its banks. Originating deep in Africa, the world's longest river flows through regions that may not receive a single drop of rainfall in a decade. Yet crops thrive from the rich soil the Nile brings thousands of miles from the African hills. In antiquity, the land bordering the Nile consisted of marshes dotted with island ridges. Amphibious animals swarmed in the marshes, where the Egyptians hunted them through tall forests of *papyrus* and rushes (FIGS. 3-14 and 3-28). The fertility of Egypt was famous. When the Kingdom of the Nile became a province of the Roman Empire after the death of Queen Cleopatra (r. 51–30 BCE), it served as the granary of the Mediterranean world.

During the Middle Ages, the detailed knowledge the Romans possessed about the Egyptians and their gods (see "The Gods and Goddesses of Egypt," page 57) was largely forgotten. With the Enlightenment of the 18th century (see Chapter 26), scholars began to piece together Egypt's history from references in the Old Testament, from the fifth-century BCE Greek historian Herodotus and other Greco-Roman authors, and from preserved portions of a third-century BCE history of Egypt written in Greek by Manetho, an Egyptian high priest. Manetho described the succession of pharaohs, dividing them into the still-useful groups called dynasties, but his chronology was inaccurate, and today historians still do not agree on the absolute dates of the pharaohs. The chronologies scholars have proposed for the earliest Egyptian dynasties can vary by as much as two centuries. Exact years cannot be assigned to the reigns of individual pharaohs until 664 BCE (26th Dynasty).[1]

The European rediscovery of ancient Egypt and the modern discipline of Egyptology date to the late 18th century, when archaeological exploration of the land of the Nile began. In 1799, on a military expedition to Egypt, Napoleon Bonaparte (1769–1821) took with him a small troop of scholars, linguists, antiquarians, and artists. Their chance discovery of the famed *Rosetta Stone,* now in the British Museum, provided the key to deciphering Egyptian hieroglyphic writing. The stone bears an inscription in three sections: one in Greek, which Napoleon's team easily read; one in *demotic* (Late Egyptian); and one in formal hieroglyphic. On the assumption the text was the same in all three sections, scholars attempted to decipher the two non-Greek sections. Eventually, Jean-François Champollion (1790–1832) deduced the hieroglyphs were not simply pictographs, but the signs of a once-spoken language whose traces survived in Coptic, the language of Christian Egypt. The ability to read hieroglyphic inscriptions revolutionized the study of Egyptian civilization and art.

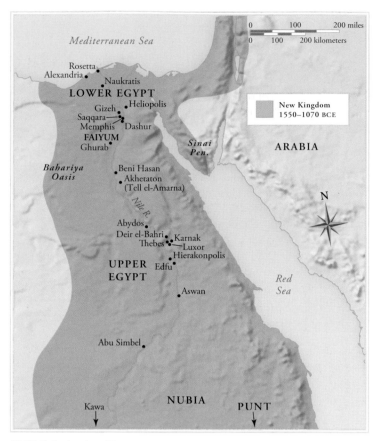

MAP 3-1 Ancient Egypt.

PREDYNASTIC AND EARLY DYNASTIC PERIODS

The Predynastic, or prehistoric, beginnings of Egyptian civilization are obscure. Nevertheless, tantalizing remains of tombs, paintings, pottery, and other artifacts attest to the existence of a sophisticated culture on the banks of the Nile around 3500 BCE.

Painting and Sculpture

In Predynastic times, Egypt was divided geographically and politically into Upper Egypt (the southern, upstream part of the Nile Valley), a narrow tract of grassland that encouraged hunting, and Lower (northern) Egypt, where the rich soil of the Nile Delta islands promoted agriculture and animal husbandry. The major finds of Predynastic art come from Upper Egypt, especially Hierakonpolis, where archaeologists discovered not only the Narmer palette (FIG. 3-1) but also the most extensive series of early

EGYPT UNDER THE PHARAOHS

	Predynastic and Early Dynastic		Old Kingdom		Middle Kingdom		New Kingdom		First Millennium	BCE	CE
3500		2575		2040		1550		1070		30	

Predynastic and Early Dynastic	Old Kingdom	Middle Kingdom	New Kingdom	First Millennium
❙ Earliest Egyptian narrative reliefs and paintings ❙ Imhotep, first recorded artist's name	❙ Statuary types expressing the eternal nature of pharaonic kingship ❙ Construction of the Great Pyramids at Gizeh	❙ Rock-cut tombs become the preferred Egyptian burial sites	❙ Construction of grandiose pylon temples ❙ Akhenaton introduces a new religion and new art forms	❙ Egyptian artistic traditions continue under foreign rule

The Gods and Goddesses of Egypt

The worldview of the Egyptians was distinct from the outlook of their neighbors in the ancient Mediterranean, Mesopotamian, and Persian worlds. Egyptians believed that before the beginning of time the primeval waters, called *Nun,* existed alone in the darkness. At the moment of creation, a mound rose out of the limitless waters—just as muddy mounds emerge from the Nile after the annual flood recedes. On this mound the creator god appeared and brought light to the world. In later times, the Egyptians symbolized the original mound as a pyramidal stone called the *ben-ben,* which supported the supreme god, *Amen,* the god of the sun (*Re*).

The supreme god also created the first of the other gods and goddesses of Egypt. According to one version of the myth, the creator masturbated and produced *Shu* and *Tefnut,* the primary male and female forces in the universe. They coupled to give birth to *Geb* (Earth) and *Nut* (Sky), who bore Osiris, Seth, Isis, and Nephthys. The eldest, *Osiris,* was the god of order, whom the Egyptians revered as the king who brought civilization to the Nile valley. His brother, *Seth,* was his evil opposite, the god of chaos. Seth murdered Osiris and cut him into pieces, which he scattered across Egypt. *Isis,* the sister and consort of Osiris, with the help of Seth's wife, *Nephthys,* succeeded in collecting Osiris's body parts, and

with her powerful magic brought him back to life. The resurrected Osiris fathered a son with Isis—*Horus,* who avenged his father's death and displaced Seth as king of Egypt. Osiris then became the lord of the Underworld. Horus appears in art either as a falcon, considered the noblest bird of the sky, or as a falcon-headed man. The Egyptians identified all their living pharaohs with Horus, then with Osiris after they died.

Other Egyptian deities include *Mut,* the consort of the sun god Amen, and *Khonsu,* the moon god, who was their son. *Thoth,* another lunar deity and the god of knowledge and writing, appears in art as an ibis, a baboon, or an ibis-headed man crowned with the crescent moon and the moon disk. When Seth tore out Horus's falcon-eye (*wedjat*), Thoth restored it. The Egyptians associated Thoth too with rebirth and the afterlife. *Hathor,* daughter of Re, was a divine mother of the pharaoh, nourishing him with her milk. Egyptian artists represented her as a cow-headed woman or as a woman with a cow's horns. *Anubis,* a jackal or jackal-headed deity, was the god of the dead and of mummification. *Maat,* another daughter of Re, was the goddess of truth and justice. Her feather was used to measure the weight of the deceased's heart on Anubis's scales to determine if the *ka* (life force) would be blessed in the afterlife.

Egyptian mural paintings (FIG. 3-1A) on the walls of a tomb dating between 3500 and 3200 BCE.

3-1A Tomb 100, Hierakonpolis, ca. 3500–3200 BCE.

PALETTE OF KING NARMER

The Predynastic period ended with the unification of Upper and Lower Egypt, which until recently historians thought occurred during the rule of the First Dynasty pharaoh Menes. Many Egyptologists have identified Menes with King Narmer, the larger-than-life victor named on the ceremonial palette (FIG. 3-1) already discussed (see "Divine Kingship on the Nile," page 55). Scholars still debate exactly what event or events the reliefs on the two sides of Narmer's palette depict. No longer regarded as commemorating the founding of the first of Egypt's 31 dynasties around 2920 BCE (the last ended in 332 BCE), the scenes probably record the unification of the two kingdoms. Egyptologists now believe this unification occurred over several centuries, but the palette presents the creation of the "Kingdom of the Two Lands" as a single great event.

Narmer's palette is an elaborate, formalized version of a utilitarian object commonly used in the Predynastic period to prepare eye makeup, which Egyptians used to protect their eyes against irritation and the glare of the sun. On the front (FIG. 3-2), the elongated necks of two felines form the circular depression that would

3-2 Front of the palette of King Narmer (compare FIG. 3-1), from Hierakonpolis, Egypt, Predynastic, ca. 3000–2920 BCE. Slate, 2′ 1″ high. Egyptian Museum, Cairo.

Narmer, king of Upper Egypt, wears the crown of Lower Egypt as he reviews the beheaded enemy bodies. Below, the intertwined animal necks may symbolize the unification of the two kingdoms.

1 in.

have held eye makeup in an ordinary palette not made for display. The intertwined necks of the animals (a motif common in Mesopotamian art) may be a pictorial reference to Egypt's unification. In the uppermost register, Narmer, wearing the red crown of Lower Egypt, reviews the beheaded bodies of the enemy. The dead are seen from above, a perspective reminiscent of the Paleolithic paintings (FIG. 1-9) on the ceiling of the Altamira cave in Spain representing bison lying on the ground. The Egyptian artist depicted each body with its severed head neatly placed between its legs. By virtue of his superior rank, the king, on both sides of the palette, performs his ritual task alone and towers over his men and the enemy. The king's superhuman strength is symbolized in the lowest band by a great bull knocking down a rebellious city whose fortress walls also are seen in an "aerial view."

As in Mesopotamian art (see Chapter 2), the Egyptian artist's portrayal of Narmer combines profile views of his head, legs, and arms with front views of his eye and torso. Although the proportions of the human figure changed, this composite representation of the body's parts became standard in Egyptian art as well. In the Hierakonpolis painting (FIG. 3-1A), the artist scattered the figures across the wall more or less haphazardly. On Narmer's palette, the sculptor subdivided the surface into registers and inserted the pictorial elements into their organized setting in a neat and orderly way. The horizontal lines separating the narratives also define the ground supporting the figures. This too was the preferred mode for narrative art in Mesopotamia. Narmer's palette established this compositional scheme as the norm in Egypt for millennia. Egyptian artists who departed from this convention did so deliberately, usually to express the absence of order, as in a chaotic battle scene (FIG. 3-36).

Architecture

Narmer's palette is exceptional among surviving Egyptian artworks because it is commemorative rather than funerary in nature. Far more typical is the Predynastic mural (FIG. 3-1A) from tomb 100 at Hierakonpolis. In fact, Egyptian tombs provide the principal, if not the exclusive, evidence for the historical reconstruction of Egyptian civilization. The majority of monuments the Egyptians left behind were dedicated to ensuring safety and happiness in the next life (see "Mummification and Immortality," page 61).

MASTABAS The standard tomb type in early Egypt was the *mastaba* (Arabic for "bench"), a rectangular brick or stone structure with sloping sides erected over an underground burial chamber (FIG. **3-3**). The form probably developed from earthen mounds that had covered even earlier tombs. Although mastabas originally housed single burials, as in FIG. 3-3, they later became increasingly complex in order to accommodate multiple family burials. The main feature of these tombs, other than the burial chamber itself, was the chapel, which had a false door through which the ka could join the world of the living and partake in the meals placed on an offering table. Some mastabas also had a *serdab*, a small room housing a statue of the deceased.

IMHOTEP AND DJOSER One of the most renowned figures in Egyptian history was IMHOTEP, master builder for King Djoser (r. 2630–2611 BCE) of the Third Dynasty. Imhotep's is the first recorded name of an artist anywhere in the world. A man of legendary talent, Imhotep also served as the pharaoh's official seal bearer and as high priest of the sun god Re. After his death, the Egyptians deified Imhotep as the son of the god Ptah and in time probably inflated the list of his achievements, but architectural historians accept Manetho's attribution to Imhotep of the stepped pyramid (FIG. **3-4**)

1. Chapel
2. False door
3. Shaft into burial chamber
4. Serdab (chamber for statue of deceased)
5. Burial chamber

3-3 Section (*top*), plan (*center*), and restored view (*bottom*) of typical Egyptian mastaba tombs.

Egyptian mastabas had underground chambers containing the mummified body, portrait statues, and offerings to the deceased. Scenes of daily life often decorated the interior walls.

of Djoser at Saqqara. Saqqara was the ancient *necropolis* (Greek for "city of the dead") of Memphis, Egypt's capital at the time. Built before 2600 BCE, Djoser's pyramid is one of the oldest stone structures in Egypt and, in its final form, the first truly grandiose royal tomb. Begun as a large mastaba with each of its faces oriented toward one of the cardinal points of the compass, the tomb was enlarged at least twice before assuming its ultimate shape. About 200 feet high, the stepped pyramid seems to be composed of a series of mastabas of diminishing size, stacked one atop another to form a structure that resembles the great Mesopotamian ziggurats (FIGS. 2-15 and 2-20A). Unlike a ziggurat, however, Djoser's pyramid is a tomb, not a temple platform, and its dual function was to protect the mummified king and his possessions and to symbolize, by its gigantic presence, his absolute and godlike power. Beneath the pyramid was a network of several hundred underground rooms and galleries cut out of the Saqqara bedrock. The vast subterranean complex resembles a palace. It was to be Djoser's home in the afterlife.

Djoser's pyramid stands near the center of an immense (37-acre) rectangular enclosure (FIG. **3-5**) surrounded by a wall of white limestone 34 feet high and 5,400 feet long. The huge precinct, with its protective walls and tightly regulated access (FIGS. 3-5, no. 5, and **3-5A**), stands in sharp contrast to the roughly contemporaneous Sumerian Royal Cemetery at Ur, where no

3-5A Entrance hall, Djoser precinct, Saqqara, ca. 2630–2611 BCE.

3-4 IMHOTEP, stepped pyramid (looking northeast) of Djoser, Saqqara, Egypt, Third Dynasty, ca. 2630–2611 BCE. ■◀

Imhotep, the first artist whose name is recorded, built the first pyramid during the Third Dynasty for King Djoser. The pharaoh's pyramid resembles a series of stacked mastabas of diminishing size.

1. Stepped pyramid
2. Funerary temple of Djoser
3. Court with serdab
4. Large court with altar
5. Entrance portico
6. Heb-Sed court and sham chapels
7. Small temple
8. Court before North Palace
9. North Palace
10. Court before South Palace
11. South Palace
12. South tomb
13. Royal Pavilion
14. Magazines

0   100   200   300 feet

0   50   100 meters

N

3-5 Restored view (*top*) and plan (*bottom*) of the mortuary precinct of Djoser, Saqqara, Egypt, Third Dynasty, ca. 2630–2611 BCE.

Djoser's pyramid was the centerpiece of an immense funerary complex that included a mortuary temple, other buildings, and courtyards. A network of underground galleries resembled a palace.

3-6 Detail of the facade of the north palace of the mortuary precinct of Djoser (FIG. 3-5), Saqqara, Egypt, Third Dynasty, ca. 2630–2611 BCE.

The earliest known stone columns are in Djoser's funerary precinct. Those on the north palace facade are engaged (attached) to the walls and have shafts and capitals resembling papyrus plants.

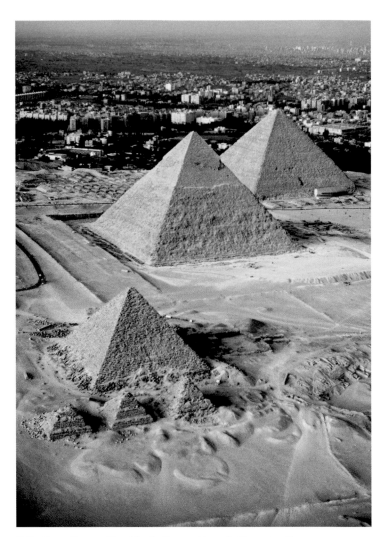

3-7 Great Pyramids, Gizeh, Egypt, Fourth Dynasty. *From bottom:* pyramids of Menkaure, ca. 2490–2472 BCE; Khafre, ca. 2520–2494 BCE; and Khufu, ca. 2551–2528 BCE. ◼◀

The Great Pyramids of Gizeh took the shape of the ben-ben, the emblem of the sun, Re. The sun's rays were the ramp the Egyptian pharaohs used to ascend to the heavens after their death and rebirth.

barriers kept people away from the burial area. Nor did the Mesopotamian cemetery have a temple for the worship of the deified dead. At Saqqara, a funerary temple stands against the northern face of Djoser's pyramid (FIG. 3-5, no. 2). Priests performed daily rituals at the temple in celebration of the divine pharaoh.

Djoser's funerary temple was but one of many buildings arranged around several courts. Most of the others were dummy structures (FIG. 3-5, no. 6) with stone walls enclosing fills of rubble, sand, or gravel. The buildings imitated in stone various types of temporary structures made of plant stems and mats erected in Upper and Lower Egypt to celebrate the Jubilee Festival, which perpetually reaffirmed the royal existence in the hereafter. The translation into stone of structural forms previously made out of plants may be seen in the columns (FIG. **3-6**) of the north palace (FIG. 3-5, no. 9) of Djoser's funerary precinct. The columns end in *capitals* ("heads") that take the form of the papyrus blossoms of Lower Egypt. The column shafts resemble papyrus stalks. Djoser's columns are not freestanding, as are most later columns. They are *engaged* (attached) to walls, but are nonetheless the earliest known stone columns in the history of architecture.

OLD KINGDOM

The Old Kingdom is the first of the three great periods of Egyptian history, called the Old, Middle, and New Kingdoms, respectively. Many Egyptologists now begin the Old Kingdom with the first pharaoh of the Fourth Dynasty, Sneferu (r. 2575–2551 BCE), although the traditional division of kingdoms places Djoser and the Third Dynasty in the Old Kingdom. It ended with the demise of the Eighth Dynasty around 2134 BCE.

Architecture

The pharaohs of the Old Kingdom amassed great wealth and expended it on grandiose architectural projects, of which the most spectacular were the Great Pyramids of Gizeh, the oldest of the Seven Wonders of the ancient world (see "Babylon, City of Wonders," Chapter 2, page 49). The prerequisites for membership in this elite club were colossal size and enormous cost.

GIZEH The Egyptians constructed the three pyramids (FIG. 3-7) at Gizeh in the course of about 75 years (see "Building the Great

Mummification and Immortality

The Egyptians did not make the sharp distinction between body and soul that is basic to many religions. Rather, they believed that from birth a person possessed a kind of other self, the *ka* or life force, which, on the death of the body, could inhabit the corpse and live on. For the ka to live securely, however, the body had to remain as nearly intact as possible. To ensure that it did, the Egyptians developed the technique of embalming (*mummification*) to a high art. Although they believed the god Anubis invented embalming to preserve the body of the murdered Osiris (see "The Gods and Goddesses of Egypt," page 57), Egyptians did not practice mummification systematically until the Fourth Dynasty, when they also buried their dead in underground chambers beneath monumental brick or stone tombs (FIG. 3-3).

The first step in the 70-day process was the surgical removal of the lungs, liver, stomach, and intestines through an incision in the left flank. The Egyptians thought these organs were most subject to decay, and wrapped them individually and placed them in four containers known as *canopic jars* for eventual deposit in the burial chamber with the corpse. (The jars take their name from the port of Canopus, where the Egyptians worshiped human-headed jars as personifications of Osiris. These jars were not, however, used in embalming.) Egyptian surgeons extracted the brain through the nostrils and then discarded it because they did not attach any special significance to that organ. But they left in place the heart, necessary for life and also regarded as the seat of intelligence.

Next, the body was treated for 40 days with natron, a naturally occurring salt compound that dehydrated the body. Then the embalmers filled the corpse with resin-soaked linens, and closed and covered the incision with a representation of the *wedjat* eye of Horus, a powerful *amulet* (a device to ward off evil and promote rebirth). Finally, they treated the body with lotions and resins and wrapped it tightly with hundreds of yards of linen bandages to maintain its shape. The Egyptians often placed other amulets within the bandages or on the corpse. The most important were heart *scarabs* (gems in the shape of beetles). Spells written on them ensured that the heart would be returned to its owner if lost. Between the legs of the deceased the embalmers often put a scroll copy of the *Book of the Dead* (FIG. 3-37), which contained some 200 spells intended to protect the mummy and the ka in the afterlife. Masks (FIG. 3-35) covered the faces of the wealthy.

The Egyptian practice of mummification endured for thousands of years, even under Greek and Roman rule. Roman mummies with painted portraits (FIGS. 7-62 to 7-62B) have been popular attractions in museums worldwide for a long time, but the discovery in 1996 of a cemetery at Bahariya Oasis in the desert southwest of Cairo greatly expanded their number. The site, which archaeologists call the Valley of the Golden Mummies, extends for at least four square miles. The largest tomb found to date contained 32 mummies, but another held 43, some stacked on top of others because the tomb was used for generations and space ran out.

The care with which families laid their dead to rest in the Bahariya cemetery varied markedly with social position and wealth. The bodies of the poorer members of the community were carelessly wrapped in linen and have almost completely decayed. The 60 most elaborate mummies, probably those of successful merchants and their families, have gilded stucco masks. Some also have gilded chest plates with reliefs depicting Egyptian deities, including Thoth holding Maat's feather (compare the weighing scene in FIG. 3-37). Others have painted decoration (compare FIG. 7-62A), and some have eyes of white marble with black obsidian irises and copper eyelashes. The excavators believe the cemetery was still in use as late as the fourth or fifth century CE.

Preserving the deceased's body by mummification was only the first requirement for immortality in ancient Egypt. Food and drink also had to be provided, as did clothing, utensils, and furniture. Nothing that had been enjoyed on earth was to be lacking. The Egyptians also placed statuettes called *ushabtis* (answerers) in the tomb. These figurines performed any labor required of the deceased in the afterlife, answering whenever his or her name was called.

Beginning in the third millennium BCE, the Egyptians also set up statues of the dead (for example, FIGS. 3-11 to 3-13) in their tombs. The statues were meant to guarantee the permanence of the person's identity by providing substitute dwelling places for the ka in case the mummy disintegrated. Wall paintings and reliefs (for example, FIGS. 3-14 and 3-15) recorded the recurring round of human activities. The Egyptians hoped and expected that the images and inventory of life, collected and set up within the protective stone walls of the tomb, would ensure immortality.

Pyramids," page 62) to serve as the tombs of the Fourth Dynasty pharaohs Khufu (r. 2551–2528 BCE; FIG. 3-8), Khafre (r. 2520–2494 BCE), and Menkaure (r. 2490–2472 BCE). They represent the culmination of an architectural evolution that began with the mastaba (FIG. 3-3), but the classic pyramid form is not simply a refinement of the stepped pyramid (FIG. 3-4). The new tomb shape probably reflects the influence of Heliopolis, the seat of the powerful cult of Re, whose emblem was a pyramidal stone, the *ben-ben* (see "The Gods and Goddesses of Egypt," page 57). The Great Pyramids are symbols of the sun. The Pyramid Texts, inscribed on the burial chamber walls of many royal tombs beginning with the Fifth Dynasty pyramid of Unas (r. 2356–2323 BCE), refer to the sun's rays as the ladder the pharaoh uses to ascend to the heavens.

Ho, Unas! You have not gone away dead: You have gone away alive.[2]

So, you shall go forth, Unas, to the sky and step up on it in this its identity of the ladder.[3]

[Unas] has flown . . . to the sky amidst his brothers the gods. . . . Unas's seat is with you, Sun.[4]

The pyramids were where Egyptian kings were reborn in the afterlife, just as the sun is reborn each day at dawn.

Imhotep may have conceived Djoser's stepped pyramid as a giant stairway. As with the Saqqara pyramid, the four sides of each of the Great Pyramids are oriented to the cardinal points of the compass. But the funerary temples associated with the three Gizeh

Building the Great Pyramids

The Great Pyramids (FIG. 3-7) across the Nile from modern Cairo attest to the extraordinary engineering and mathematical expertise of the Egyptians of the mid-third millennium BCE. The structures also are testaments to the Old Kingdom builders' mastery of masonry construction and ability to mobilize, direct, house, and feed a huge workforce engaged in one of the most labor-intensive enterprises ever undertaken. Like all building projects of this type, the process of erecting the pyramids began with the quarrying of stone, in this case primarily the limestone of the Gizeh plateau itself. Teams of skilled workers had to cut into the rock and remove large blocks of roughly equal size using stone or copper chisels and wooden mallets and wedges. Often, the artisans had to cut deep tunnels to find high-quality stone free of cracks and other flaws. To remove a block, the workers cut channels on all sides and partly underneath. Then they pried the stones free from the bedrock with wooden levers. New tools for this difficult work had to be manufactured constantly because the chisels and mallets broke or became dull very quickly.

After workers liberated the stones, the rough blocks had to be transported to the building site and *dressed* (shaped to the exact dimensions required, with smooth faces for a perfect fit). Small blocks could be carried on a man's shoulders or on the back of a donkey, but the Egyptians moved the massive blocks for the Great Pyramids using wooden rollers and sleds. The artisans dressed the blocks by chiseling and pounding the surfaces and, in the last stage, by rubbing and grinding the surfaces with fine polishing stones. Architectural historians call this kind of construction *ashlar masonry*—carefully cut and regularly shaped blocks of stone piled in successive rows, or *courses*.

To set the ashlar blocks in place, workers under the direction of master builders such as Hemiunu (FIG. 3-13B), who supervised the construction of Khufu's pyramid, erected great rubble ramps against the core of the pyramid. They adjusted the ramps' size and slope as work progressed and the tomb grew in height. Scholars debate whether the Egyptians used simple linear ramps inclined at a right angle to one face of the pyramid or zigzag or spiral ramps akin to staircases. Linear ramps would have had the advantage of simplicity and would have left three sides of the pyramid unobstructed. But zigzag ramps placed against one side of the structure or spiral ramps winding around the pyramid would have greatly reduced the slope of the incline and would have made the dragging of the blocks easier. Some scholars also have suggested a combination of straight and spiral ramps, and one recent theory posits a system of spiral ramps within, instead of outside, the pyramid.

The Egyptians used ropes, pulleys, and levers both to lift and to lower the stones, guiding each block into its designated place.

Finally, the pyramid received a casing of white limestone blocks (FIG. 3-8, no. 1), cut so precisely that the eye could scarcely detect the joints. The reflection of sunlight on the facing would have been dazzling, underscoring the pyramid's solar symbolism. A few casing stones still can be seen in the cap that covers the pyramid of Khafre (FIGS. 3-7, *center*, and 3-10, *left*).

Of the three Fourth Dynasty pyramids at Gizeh, the tomb of Khufu (FIGS. 3-8 and 3-9, no. 7) is the oldest and largest. Except for the galleries and burial chamber, it is an almost solid mass of limestone masonry. Some dimensions will suggest the immensity of the Gizeh pyramids: At the base, the length of one side of Khufu's tomb is approximately 775 feet, and its area is some 13 acres. Its present height is about 450 feet (originally 480 feet). The structure contains roughly 2.3 million blocks of stone, each weighing an average of 2.5 tons. Some of the stones at the base weigh about 15 tons. Napoleon's scholars calculated that the blocks in the three Great Pyramids were sufficient to build a wall 1 foot wide and 10 feet high around France.

1. Silhouette with original facing stone
2. Thieves' tunnels
3. Entrance
4. Grand gallery
5. King's chamber
6. So-called Queen's chamber
7. False tomb chamber
8. Relieving blocks
9. Air shafts(?)

3-8 Section of the pyramid of Khufu, Gizeh, Egypt, Fourth Dynasty, ca. 2551–2528 BCE.

Khufu's pyramid is the largest at Gizeh. Constructed of roughly 2.3 million blocks of stone weighing an average of 2.5 tons, the structure is an almost solid mass of stone quarried from the Gizeh plateau itself.

pyramids are not on the north side, facing the stars of the northern sky, as was Djoser's temple. The temples are on the east side, facing the rising sun and underscoring their connection with Re.

From the remains surrounding the pyramid of Khafre at Gizeh, archaeologists have been able to reconstruct an entire funerary complex (FIG. 3-9). The complex included the pyramid itself with the pha-

raoh's burial chamber; the *mortuary temple* adjoining the pyramid on the east side, where priests made offerings to the god-king and stored cloth, food, and ceremonial vessels; the roofed causeway leading to the mortuary temple; and the *valley temple* at the edge of the floodplain. Many Egyptologists believe the complex served not only as the king's tomb and temple but also as his palace in the afterlife.

3-9 Model of the pyramid complex, Gizeh, Egypt. Harvard University Semitic Museum, Cambridge. (1) pyramid of Menkaure, (2) pyramid of Khafre, (3) mortuary temple of Khafre, (4) causeway, (5) Great Sphinx, (6) valley temple of Khafre, (7) pyramid of Khufu, (8) pyramids of the royal family and mastabas of nobles. ◼◀

Like Djoser's pyramid (FIG. 3-4), the Great Pyramids were not isolated tombs but parts of funerary complexes with a valley temple, a covered causeway, and a mortuary temple adjoining the pyramid.

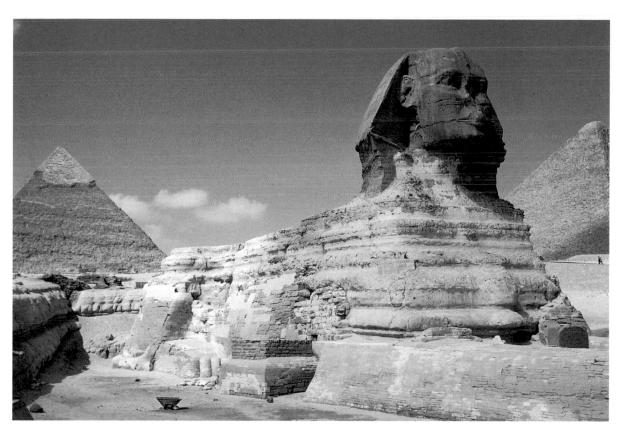

3-10 Great Sphinx (with pyramid of Khafre in the background at left), Gizeh, Egypt, Fourth Dynasty, ca. 2520–2494 BCE. Sandstone, 65′ × 240′.

Carved out of the Gizeh stone quarry, the Great Sphinx is of colossal size. The sphinx has the body of a lion and the head of a pharaoh (probably Khafre) and is associated with the sun god.

GREAT SPHINX Beside the causeway and dominating the valley temple of Khafre rises the Great Sphinx (FIG. 3-10). Carved from a spur of rock in an ancient quarry, the colossal statue—the largest in Egypt, Mesopotamia, or Persia—is probably an image of Khafre (originally complete with the pharaoh's ceremonial beard and *uraeus* cobra headdress), although some scholars think it portrays Khufu and predates the construction of Khafre's complex. Whichever king it portrays, the *sphinx*—a lion with a human head—was associated with the sun god and therefore was an appropriate image for a pharaoh. The composite form suggests that the pharaoh combines human intelligence with the fearsome strength and authority of the king of beasts.

Sculpture

Old Kingdom statues survive in significant numbers because they fulfilled an important function in Egyptian tombs as substitute abodes for the ka (see "Mummification and Immortality," page 61). Although Egyptian sculptors worked with wood, clay, and other materials, mostly for images of individuals not of the royal or noble classes, the primary material for funerary statuary was stone.

KHAFRE ENTHRONED The seated statue of Khafre (FIG. **3-11**) is one of a series of similar statues carved for the pharaoh's valley temple (FIG. 3-9, no. 6) near the Great Sphinx. The stone is diorite, an exceptionally hard dark stone brought some 400 miles down the Nile from royal quarries in the south. (The Neo-Sumerian ruler Gudea [FIG. 2-16] so admired diorite that he imported it to faraway Girsu.) Khafre wears a simple kilt and sits rigidly upright on a throne formed of two stylized lions' bodies. Intertwined lotus and papyrus plants—symbolic of the united Egypt—appear between the throne's legs. The falcon-god Horus (compare FIG. 3-1) extends his protective wings to shelter the pharaoh's head. Khafre has the royal false beard fastened to his chin and wears the royal linen *nemes* headdress with the uraeus cobra of kingship on the front. The headdress covers his forehead and falls in pleated folds over his shoulders. (The head of the Great Sphinx is similarly attired.) As befitting a divine ruler, the sculptor portrayed Khafre with a well-developed, flawless body and a perfect face, regardless of his real age and appearance. Because Egyptians considered ideal proportions appropriate for representing their god-kings, the statue of Khafre is not a true likeness and was not intended to be. The purpose of pharaonic portraiture was not to record individual features or the distinctive shapes of bodies, but rather to proclaim the divine nature of Egyptian kingship.

3-11A Rahotep and Nofret, Maidum, ca. 2575–2550 BCE.

The enthroned Khafre radiates serenity. The sculptor created this effect, common to Egyptian royal statues (compare FIG. **3-11A**), in part by giving the figure great compactness and solidity, with few projecting, breakable parts. The form manifests the purpose: to last for eternity. Khafre's body is one with the unarticulated slab that forms the back of the king's throne. His arms follow the bend of his body and rest on his thighs, and his legs are close together. Part of the original stone block still connects the king's legs to his chair. Khafre's pose is frontal, rigid, and *bilaterally symmetrical* (the same on either side of an axis, in this case the vertical axis). The sculptor suppressed all movement and with it the notion of time, creating an aura of eternal stillness.

3-11B Sculptors at work, Thebes, ca. 1425 BCE.

Some extant reliefs and paintings (FIG. **3-11B**) show Egyptian sculptors at work and provide detailed information about the successive stages of carving a statue. To produce the statue, the artist first drew the front, back, and two profile views of the pharaoh on the four vertical faces of the stone block. Next, apprentices chiseled away the excess stone on each side, working inward until the planes met at right angles. Finally, the master sculpted the parts of Khafre's body, the falcon, and so forth. The polished surface was achieved by *abrasion* (rubbing or grinding). This *subtractive* method of

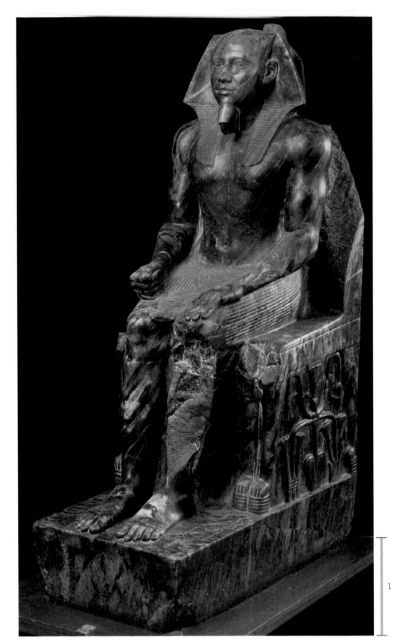

3-11 Khafre enthroned, from Gizeh, Egypt, Fourth Dynasty, ca. 2520–2494 BCE. Diorite, 5′ 6″ high. Egyptian Museum, Cairo. ◼◄

This portrait from his pyramid complex depicts Khafre as an enthroned divine ruler with a perfect body. The rigidity of the pose creates an aura of eternal stillness, appropriate for the timeless afterlife.

1 ft.

creating statuary accounts in large part for the blocklike look of the standard Egyptian statue. Nevertheless, other sculptors, both ancient and modern, with different aims, have transformed stone blocks into dynamic, twisting human forms (for example, FIGS. I-15 and 5-84).

MENKAURE AND KHAMERERNEBTY The seated statue is one of only a small number of basic formulaic types Old Kingdom sculptors employed to represent the human figure. Another is the image of a person or deity standing, either alone or in a group, for example the double portrait (FIG. **3-12**) of Menkaure and one of his wives, probably the queen Khamerernebty. The statue once stood in the valley temple of Menkaure's pyramid complex at Gizeh. Here, too, the figures remain wedded to the stone

3-12 Menkaure and Khamerernebty(?), from Gizeh, Egypt, Fourth Dynasty, ca. 2490–2472 BCE. Graywacke, 4′ 6½″ high. Museum of Fine Arts, Boston. ■◀

The double portrait of Menkaure and his wife displays the conventional postures used for statues designed as substitute homes for the ka. The frozen gestures signify the couple are married.

block. In fact, the statue could be classified as a *high-relief* sculpture. Menkaure's pose—duplicated in countless other Egyptian statues—is rigidly frontal with the arms hanging straight down and close to his well-built body. He clenches his hands into fists with the thumbs forward and advances his left leg slightly. But no shift occurs in the angle of the hips to correspond to the uneven distribution of weight. Khamerernebty stands in a similar position. Her right arm, however, circles around the king's waist, and her left hand gently rests on his left arm. This frozen stereotypical gesture indicates their marital status. The husband and wife show no other sign of affection or emotion and look not at each other but out into space. The artist's aim was not to portray living figures, but to suggest the timeless nature of the stone statue that might have to serve as an eternal substitute home for the ka.

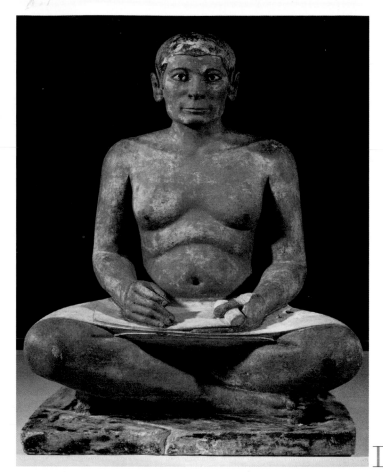

3-13 Seated scribe, from Saqqara, Egypt, Fourth Dynasty, ca. 2500 BCE. Painted limestone, 1′ 9″ high. Musée du Louvre, Paris.

The idealism that characterizes the portraiture of the Egyptian god-kings did not extend to the portrayal of nonelite individuals. This more realistic painted depiction of a scribe shows clear signs of aging.

SEATED SCRIBE Traces of paint remain on the portraits of Menkaure and Khamerernebty. Egyptian artists painted most of their statues, although sometimes sculptors left the natural color of the stone exposed, enhancing the sense of abstraction and timelessness. Striking examples of painted sculpture are the seated statues of Rahotep and Nofret (FIG. 3-11A) and the statue found at Saqqara portraying a Fourth Dynasty scribe (FIG. 3-13). Despite the stiff upright postures of all these statues and the frontality of head and body, the coloration lends a lifelike quality to the stone images.

The head of the Saqqara scribe displays an extraordinary sensitivity. The sculptor conveyed the personality of a sharply intelligent and alert individual with a penetration and sympathy seldom achieved at this early date. The scribe sits directly on the ground, not on a throne or even on a chair. Although he occupied a position of honor in a largely illiterate society, the scribe was a much lower figure in the Egyptian hierarchy than the pharaoh, whose divinity made him superhuman. In the history of art, especially portraiture, it is almost a rule that as a person's importance decreases, formality is relaxed and realism increases. It is telling that the sculptor reproduced the scribe's sagging chest muscles and protruding belly. These signs of age would have been disrespectful and wholly inappropriate in a depiction of an Egyptian god-king or members of his family. But the statue of the scribe is not a true portrait either. Rather, it is a composite of conventional types. Obesity, for example, characterizes many nonroyal Old Kingdom male portraits (for example, FIGS. **3-13A** and especially **3-13B**), perhaps because it attested to the comfortable life of the person represented and his relatively high position in society.

TOMB OF TI In Old Kingdom tombs, images of the deceased also frequently appear in relief sculpture and in mural painting, sometimes singly (FIG. I-15) and sometimes in a narrative context. The painted limestone relief scenes that decorate the walls of the mastaba of a Fifth Dynasty official named Ti typify the subjects Old Kingdom patrons favored for the adornment of their final resting places. Depictions of agriculture and hunting fill Ti's tomb. The Egyptians associated these activities with the provisioning of the ka in the hereafter, but the subjects also had powerful symbolic overtones. In ancient Egypt, success in the hunt, for example, was a metaphor for triumph over the forces of evil.

On one wall (FIG. **3-14**) of his tomb, Ti, his men, and his boats move slowly through the marshes, hunting hippopotami and birds in a dense growth of towering papyrus. The sculptor delineated the reedy stems of the plants with repeated fine grooves that fan out gracefully at the top into a commotion of frightened birds and stalking foxes. The water beneath the boats, signified by a pattern of wavy lines, is crowded with hippopotami and fish. Ti's men seem frantically busy with their spears, whereas Ti, depicted twice their size, stands aloof. The basic conventions of Egyptian figure representation—used a half millennium earlier for the palette of King Narmer (FIG. 3-1)—appear again here. As in the Predynastic work, the artist exaggerated the size of Ti to announce his rank, and combined frontal and profile views of Ti's body to show its most characteristic parts clearly. This approach to representation was well suited for Egyptian funerary art because it emphasizes the essential nature of the deceased, not his accidental appearance. Ti's conventional pose contrasts with the realistically rendered activities of his tiny servants and with the naturalistically carved and painted birds and animals among the papyrus buds. Ti's immobility suggests that he is not an actor in the hunt. He does not *do* anything. He simply *is*, a figure apart from time and an impassive observer of life, like his ka.

The idealized and stiff image of Ti is typical of Egyptian relief sculpture. Egyptian artists regularly ignored the endless variations in body types of real human beings. Painters and sculptors did not sketch their subjects from life but applied a strict *canon*, or system of proportions, to the human figure. They first drew a grid on the wall. Then they placed various human body parts at specific points on the network of squares. The height of a figure, for example, was a fixed number of squares, and the head, shoulders, waist, knees, and other parts of the body also had a predetermined size and place within the scheme. This approach to design lasted for more than 2,500 years. Specific proportions

might vary from workshop to workshop and change over time, but the principle of the canon persisted.

On another wall (FIG. **3-15**) of Ti's mastaba, goats tread in seeds in the upper register and, below, cattle ford a canal in the Nile. Once again, the scenes may be interpreted on a symbolic as well as a literal level. The fording of the Nile, for example, was a metaphor for the deceased's passage from life to the hereafter. Ti is absent from the scenes, and all the men and animals participate in the narrative. Despite the sculptor's repeated use of similar poses for most of the human and animal figures, the reliefs are full of anecdotal details. Especially charming is the group at the lower right. A youth, depicted in a complex unconventional posture, carries a calf on his back. The animal, not a little afraid, turns its head back a full 180 degrees (compare FIG. 1-8) to seek reassurance from its mother, who returns the calf's gaze. Scenes such as this demonstrate that Egyptian artists could be close observers of daily life. The suppression of the anecdotal (that is, of the time-bound) from their representations of the deceased both in relief and in the round was a deliberate choice. Their primary purpose was to suggest the deceased's eternal existence in the afterlife, not to portray his activities while alive.

1 ft.

3-14 Ti watching a hippopotamus hunt, relief in the mastaba of Ti, Saqqara, Egypt, Fifth Dynasty, ca. 2450–2350 BCE. Painted limestone, 4′ high.

In Egypt, a successful hunt was a metaphor for triumph over evil. In this painted tomb relief, the deceased stands aloof from the hunters busily spearing hippopotami. Ti's size reflects his high rank.

The fording of the Nile was a metaphor for the passage to the afterlife. These reliefs combine stereotypical poses for humans and animals with unconventional postures and anecdotal details.

MIDDLE KINGDOM

About 2150 BCE, the Egyptians challenged the pharaohs' power, and for more than a century the land was in a state of civil unrest and near anarchy. But in 2040 BCE, the pharaoh of Upper Egypt, Mentuhotep II (r. 2050–1998 BCE), managed to unite Egypt again under the rule of a single king and established the Middle Kingdom (11th to 14th Dynasties), which lasted 400 years.

Sculpture

3-15A Lady Sennuwy, Kerma, 1960–1916 BCE.

Although in most respects Middle Kingdom sculptors adhered to the conventions established during the Old Kingdom, portraying both men and women in the familiar seated (FIG. 3-15A) and standing poses, there were some notable innovations.

SENUSRET III One of Mentuhotep II's successors was Senusret III (r. 1878–1859 BCE), who fought four brutal military campaigns in Nubia (MAP 3-1). Although Egyptian armies devastated the land and poisoned the wells, Senusret never fully achieved secure control over the Nubians. In Egypt itself, he attempted, with greater success, to establish a more powerful central government. His portraits (FIG. 3-16) are of special interest because they represent a sharp break from Old Kingdom practice. Although the king's preserved statues have idealized bodies, the sculptors brought a stunning and unprecedented realism to the rendition of Senusret's features. His pessimistic expression reflects the dominant mood of the time, echoed in Middle Kingdom literature. The strong mouth, the drooping lines about the nose and eyes, and the shadowy brows show a determined

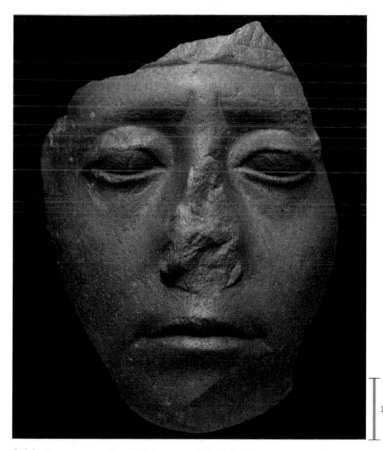

1 in.

3-16 Fragmentary head of Senusret III, 12th Dynasty, ca. 1860 BCE. Red quartzite, $6\frac{1}{2}''$ high. Metropolitan Museum of Art, New York.

Senusret III's portraits exhibit an unprecedented realism. The king's brooding expression reflects the mood of the time and contrasts sharply with the impassive faces of Old Kingdom pharaohs.

ruler who had also shared in the cares of the world, sunk in brooding meditation. The portrait is different in kind from the typically impassive faces of the Old Kingdom. It is personal, almost intimate, in its revelation of the mark of anxiety that a troubled age might leave on the soul of a king.

Architecture

Senusret III's tomb, at Dashur, is a mud-brick pyramid, but the most characteristic burials of the Middle Kingdom are rock-cut tombs. This kind of tomb, documented also in the Old Kingdom, became especially popular during the Middle Kingdom and largely replaced the mastaba as the standard Egyptian tomb type.

BENI HASAN Some of the best preserved Middle Kingdom tombs are at Beni Hasan (FIG. **3-17**). Hollowed out of the cliffs, the typical tomb there has a shallow columnar porch, which leads into a columned hall and then into a burial chamber featuring statues of the deceased in niches and paintings and painted reliefs on the walls. In the 12th Dynasty tomb of Amenemhet, the columns in the hall (FIG. **3-18**) serve no supporting function because, like the porch columns, they are continuous parts of the rock fabric. (Note the broken column in the rear suspended from the ceiling like a stalactite.) The column shafts are *fluted,* like those in the entrance corridor (FIG. **3-5A**) of Djoser's mortuary precinct at Saqqara. The Beni Hasan columns are more formalized versions of Imhotep's earlier columns, which still look like bundles of reeds. The Middle Kingdom columns closely resemble later Greek columns of the Doric order (FIG. 5-13, *left*), and there is no doubt the Greeks knew about and emulated many aspects of Egyptian architecture (see Chapter 5). Archaeologists believe the kind of *fluting* used for the Beni Hasan column shafts derived from the dressing of softwood trunks with the rounded cutting edge of the adze.

3-17 Rock-cut tombs BH 3 to 5, Beni Hasan, Egypt, 12th Dynasty, ca. 1950–1900 BCE.

The tombs of Beni Hasan are characteristic of the Middle Kingdom. Hollowed out of the cliffs, these tombs often have a shallow columnar porch, which leads into a columned hall and burial chamber.

3-18 Interior hall of the rock-cut tomb of Amenemhet (tomb BH 2), Beni Hasan, Egypt, 12th Dynasty, ca. 1950–1900 BCE.

Stonemasons carved the columnar hall of Amenemhet's tomb out of the living rock, which explains the suspended broken column at the rear. The shafts have flutes, a form Greek architects later emulated.

Hatshepsut, the Woman Who Would Be King

In 1479 BCE, Thutmose II, the fourth pharaoh of the 18th Dynasty (r. 1492–1479 BCE), died. His principal wife (and half sister), Queen Hatshepsut (r. 1473–1458 BCE), had not given birth to any sons who survived, so the title of king went to Thutmose III, son of Thutmose II by a minor wife. Hatshepsut became regent for the boy-king. Within a few years, however, the queen proclaimed herself pharaoh and insisted her father, Thutmose I, had chosen her as his successor during his lifetime. Underscoring her claim, one of the reliefs decorating Hatshepsut's enormous funerary complex (FIG. 3-19) depicts Thutmose I crowning his daughter as king in the presence of the Egyptian gods.

Hatshepsut is the first great female monarch whose name has been recorded. (In the 12th Dynasty, Sobekneferu was crowned king of Egypt, but she reigned as pharaoh for only a few years.)

Hatshepsut boasted of having made the "two Lands to labor with bowed back" for her, and for two decades she ruled what was then the most powerful and prosperous empire in the world.

Hatshepsut commissioned numerous building projects, and sculptors produced portraits of the female pharaoh in great numbers for display in those complexes. Unfortunately, Thutmose III (r. 1458–1425 BCE), for reasons still not fully understood, late in his reign ordered Hatshepsut's portraits destroyed. In her surviving portraits, Hatshepsut uniformly wears the costume of the male pharaohs, with royal headdress and kilt, and in some cases (FIG. 3-21) even a false ceremonial beard. (Many inscriptions refer to Hatshepsut as "*His* Majesty.") In other statues, however, Hatshepsut has delicate features, a slender frame, and breasts, leaving no doubt artists also represented her as a woman.

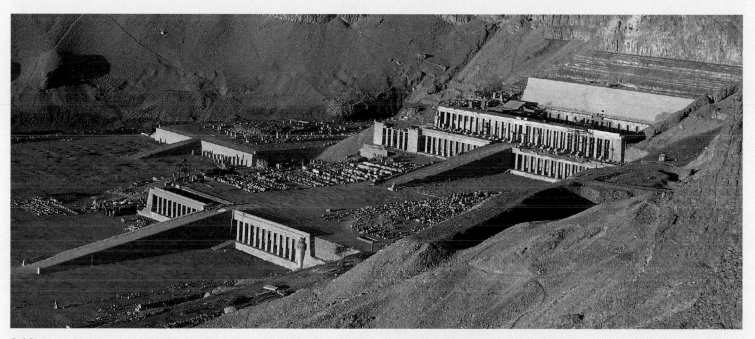

3-19 Mortuary temple of Hatshepsut (looking southwest), Deir el-Bahri, Egypt, 18th Dynasty, ca. 1473–1458 BCE.

Hatshepsut was the first great female monarch whose name is recorded. Her immense funerary temple incorporated shrines to Amen, whom she claimed was her father, and to Hathor and Anubis.

NEW KINGDOM

The Middle Kingdom disintegrated when the Hyksos descended on Egypt from the Syrian and Mesopotamian uplands. They ruled the Nile Delta and Lower Egypt during what historians call the Second Intermediate Period until, in the mid-16th century, native Egyptian kings of the 17th Dynasty rose up in revolt. Ahmose I (r. 1550–1525 BCE), final conqueror of the Hyksos and first king of the 18th Dynasty, ushered in the New Kingdom, the most glorious period in Egypt's long history. At this time, Egypt extended its borders by conquest from the Euphrates River in the east deep into Nubia to the south (MAP 3-1). A new capital—Thebes, in Upper Egypt—became a great metropolis with magnificent palaces, tombs, and temples along both banks of the Nile.

Architecture

If the most impressive monuments of the Old Kingdom are its pyramids, those of the New Kingdom are its grandiose temples, built to honor pharaohs and queens as well as gods. Great pharaonic mortuary temples arose along the Nile in the Thebes district. These shrines provided the rulers with a place for worshiping their patron gods during their lifetimes and then served as temples in their own honor after their death.

DEIR EL-BAHRI The most majestic of these royal mortuary temples (FIG. 3-19) is at Deir el-Bahri, erected by and for the female pharaoh Hatshepsut, one of the most remarkable women of the ancient world (see "Hatshepsut, the Woman Who Would Be King," above). Some Egyptologists attribute the temple to SENMUT

3-20 King and queen of Punt and attendants, relief from the mortuary temple of Hatshepsut, Deir el-Bahri, Egypt, 18th Dynasty, ca. 1473–1458 BCE. Painted limestone, 1′ 3″ high. Egyptian Museum, Cairo.

Painted limestone reliefs throughout Hatshepsut's mortuary temple complex celebrated her reign, her divine birth, and her successful expedition to the kingdom of Punt on the Red Sea.

1 in.

(FIG. 3-27), Hatshepsut's chancellor and possible lover, described in two inscriptions as the queen's architect. His association with this project is uncertain, however. Hatshepsut's temple rises from the valley floor in three colonnaded terraces connected by ramps on the central axis. It is striking how visually well suited the structure is to its natural setting. The long horizontals and verticals of the *colonnades* and their rhythm of light and dark repeat the pattern of the limestone cliffs above.

As imposing as it is today, Hatshepsut's mortuary temple was once part of an even larger complex with a causeway connecting it to a now-lost valley temple. The multi-level funerary temple proper incorporated shrines to Amen, Hathor, and Anubis as well as to Hatshepsut and her father, Thutmose I. Statues portraying the queen and reliefs glorifying her and her reign were on display throughout the vast complex. Together the statues and reliefs constitute the first great tribute to a woman's achievements in the history of art. In the middle colonnade of the second level, for example, painted limestone reliefs commemorated Hatshepsut's divine birth. Hatshepsut claimed to be the daughter of Amen, who had assumed the form of the pharaoh Thutmose I in order to impregnate her mother, the king's principal wife. Other reliefs depicted the impressive engineering feat of transporting huge granite obelisks from the Aswan quarries to the temple of Amen-Re (FIG. 3-24) at Karnak.

The relief illustrated here (FIG. **3-20**) is one of those documenting Hatshepsut's successful expedition to Punt, famed for its gold, myrrh, and other exotic natural resources. The reliefs record the sea journey, the precious cargo of gold ingots and frankincense trees the Egyptians brought back with them, and the people, animals, and houses the Egyptians found in Punt. In this detail, bare-chested men carry the local goods that the Egyptians will load onto

their ships. Leading the procession are two figures that art historians traditionally identify as the king and queen of Punt. The Egyptian sculptor depicted the queen as an obese and misshapen woman. Scholars debate whether this is an accurate portrayal or an exaggeration designed to underscore the foreignness of the Punt queen.

As many as 200 statues in the round depicting Hatshepsut in various guises complemented the extensive relief program. On the lowest terrace, to either side of the processional way, statues repeatedly portrayed Hatshepsut as a sphinx. On the uppermost level, the royal sculptors represented the female pharaoh standing, seated, and in the form of a mummy. At least eight colossal kneeling statues in red granite lined the way to the entrance of the Amen-Re sanctuary. The statue reproduced here (FIG. **3-21**) suffered the same fate as most of Hatshepsut's portraits during the reign of Thutmose III. Vandals smashed it and threw the pieces in a dump, but conservators have skillfully reassembled the portrait. Hatshepsut holds a globular offering jar in each hand as she takes part in a ritual in honor of the sun god. (A king kneeled only before a god, never a mortal.) She wears the royal male nemes headdress and the pharaoh's ceremonial beard (compare FIGS. 3-10 to 3-12 and 3-35). The agents of Thutmose III hacked off the uraeus cobra that once adorned the

3-21 Hatshepsut with offering jars, from the upper court of her mortuary temple, Deir el-Bahri, Egypt, 18th Dynasty, ca. 1473–1458 BCE. Red granite, 8′ 6″ high. Metropolitan Museum of Art, New York.

1 ft.

Her successor destroyed many of Hatshepsut's portraits. Conservators reassembled this one, which depicts the queen as a male pharaoh, consistent with inscriptions calling her "His Majesty."

front of the headdress. The figure is also anatomically male, although other surviving portraits of Hatshepsut represent her with a woman's breasts. The male imagery, however, is consistent with the queen's formal assumption of the title of king and with the many inscriptions that address her as a man.

ABU SIMBEL The sheer size of Hatshepsut's mortuary temple never fails to impress visitors, and this is no less true of the rock-cut temple (FIG. **3-22**) of Ramses II (r. 1290–1224 BCE) at Abu Simbel. In 1968, engineers moved the immense Nubian temple nearly 700 feet—an amazing achievement in its own right—to save it from submersion in the Aswan High Dam reservoir. Ramses, Egypt's last great warrior pharaoh, ruled for two-thirds of a century, an extraordinary accomplishment even in peacetime in an era when life expectancy was far shorter than it is today. The pharaoh, proud of his many campaigns to restore the empire, proclaimed his greatness by placing four colossal images of himself on the temple facade. The portraits are 65 feet tall—almost a dozen times the height of an ancient Egyptian, even though the pharaoh is seated. Spectacular as they are, the rock-cut statues nonetheless lack the refinement of earlier periods, because the sculptors sacrificed detailed carving to overwhelming size. This trade-off is characteristic of colossal statuary of every period and every place (compare FIG. 16-14).

The rock-cut interior (FIG. **3-23**) of the Abu Simbel temple is also of colossal size. The distance from the facade to the back wall is an astounding 206 feet. In the main gallery stand 32-foot-tall figures of the king in the guise of Osiris, carved as one with the *pillars,* facing each other across the narrow corridor. The pillars,

3-22 Facade of the temple of Ramses II, Abu Simbel, Egypt, 19th Dynasty, ca. 1290–1224 BCE. Sandstone, colossi 65′ high.

Four rock-cut images of Ramses II dominate the facade of his mortuary temple at Abu Simbel in Nubia. The colossal portraits are a dozen times the height of a man, even though the pharaoh is seated.

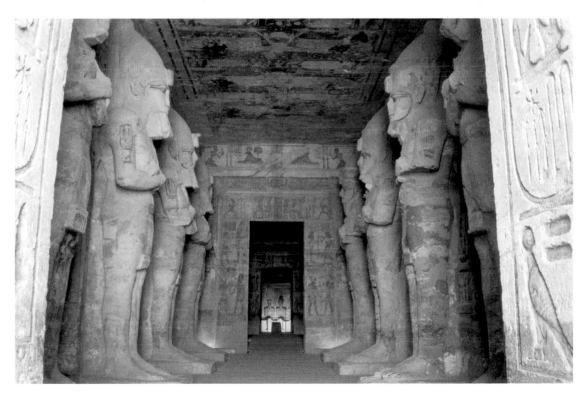

3-23 Interior of the temple of Ramses II, Abu Simbel, Egypt, 19th Dynasty, ca. 1290–1224 BCE. Sandstone, pillar statues 32′ high.

Inside Ramses II's mortuary temple are colossal statues of the long-reigning pharaoh in the guise of Osiris, carved as one with the pillars, facing each other across the narrow corridor.

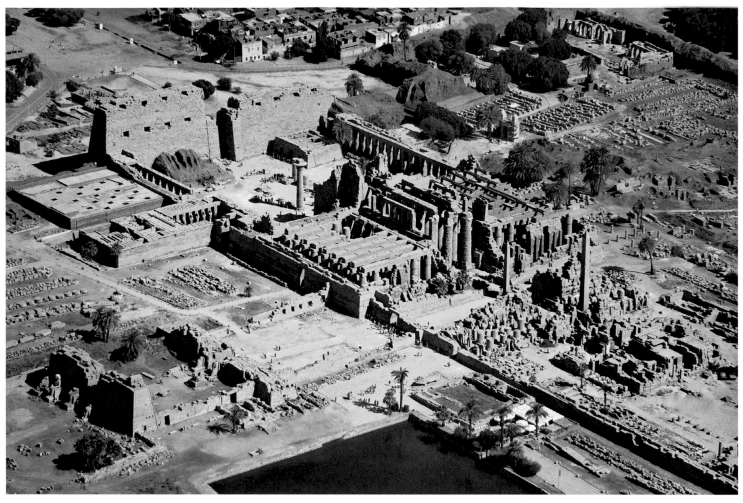

3-24 Aerial view of the temple of Amen-Re (looking north), Karnak, Egypt, begun 15th century BCE.

The vast Karnak temple complex contains an artificial lake associated with the primeval waters of the Egyptian creation myth and a pylon temple with a bilaterally symmetrical axial plan.

carved from the cliff like the pharaoh's facade portraits, have no load-bearing function. In this respect, they resemble the columns in the tombs at Beni Hasan (FIG. 3-18). The statue-column, in its male (*atlantid*) or female (*caryatid*) variants, reappears throughout the history of art. Often, as here, the human figure is attached to a column or *pier*. At other times the figure replaces the architectural member and forms the sole source of support (FIG. 5-54).

Ramses, like other pharaohs, had many wives, and he fathered scores of sons. The pharaoh honored the most important members of his family with immense monuments of their own. At Abu Simbel, for example, north of his temple, Ramses ordered the construction of a grand temple for his principal wife, Nefertari. Huge rock-cut statues—four standing images of the king and two of the queen—dominate the temple's facade. For his sons, Ramses constructed a huge underground tomb complex in the Valley of the Kings at Thebes, which an American team rediscovered in 1987. Robbers looted the tomb within a half century of its construction, but archaeologists have yet to find the royal burial chambers in the complex, so the tomb may one day yield important artworks.

KARNAK Distinct from the New Kingdom temples honoring pharaohs and queens are the edifices built to honor one or more of the gods. Successive kings often added to them until they reached gigantic size. The temple of Amen-Re (FIG. **3-24**) at Karnak, for ex-

ample, was largely the work of the 18th Dynasty pharaohs, including Thutmose I and III and Hatshepsut, but Ramses II (19th Dynasty) also contributed sections, and other pharaohs added chapels to the complex as late as the 26th Dynasty. Enclosing the 247-acre complex and shutting it off from the outside world was a perimeter wall 39 feet high and 26 feet thick. Inside, next to the temple proper, was an artificial sacred lake (FIG. 3-24, *bottom*)—a reference to the primeval waters before creation (see "The Gods and Goddesses of Egypt," page 57). The temple of Amen-Re rises from the earth as the original sacred mound rose from the waters at the beginning of time.

The Karnak temple and similar New Kingdom temples such as the equally huge one at nearby Luxor (FIG. **3-24A**) all had similar *axial plans.* A typical *pylon temple* (the name derives from the sanctuaries' simple and massive gateways, or *pylons,* with sloping walls) is bilaterally symmetrical along a single axis

3-24A Temple of Amen-Re, Luxor, begun early 14th century BCE.

that runs from an approaching avenue through a colonnaded court and hall into a dimly lit sanctuary. Axial plans are characteristic of much of Egyptian architecture. Narrow corridors on the longitudinal axis are also the approaches to the Great Pyramids (FIG. 3-9)

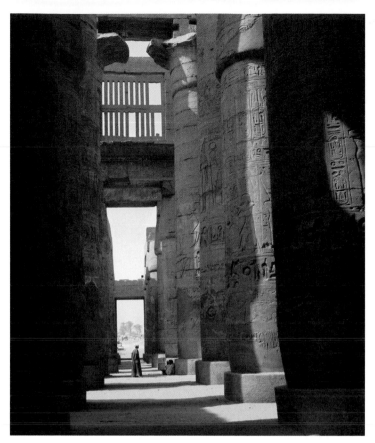

3-25 Hypostyle hall of the temple of Amen-Re, Karnak, Egypt, 19th Dynasty, ca. 1290–1224 BCE.

Columns crowd the hypostyle hall of the Amen-Re temple. The tallest are 66 feet high and have capitals that are 22 feet in diameter. The columns support a roof of stone slabs carried on lintels.

and to Hatshepsut's multilevel mortuary temple (FIG. 3-19). Marking the end of the statuary-lined approach to a New Kingdom temple was the monumental facade of the pylon (FIG. 3-24, *top left*), which Egyptian sculptors routinely covered with reliefs glorifying their rulers (FIG. 3-40). Inside was an open court with columns on two or more sides, followed by a hall (FIG. 3-24, *center*) between the court and sanctuary, its long axis placed at right angles to the corridor of the entire building complex. Only the pharaohs and the priests could enter the sanctuary. A chosen few were admitted to the great columnar *hypostyle hall* (a hall with a roof resting on columns). The majority of the people could proceed only as far as the open court.

Filling Karnak's gigantic (58,000 square feet) hypostyle hall were massive columns, which supported a roof of stone slabs carried on *lintels* (FIGS. **3-25** and **3-26**). The 134 sandstone columns have bud-cluster or bell-shaped capitals resembling lotus or papyrus, the plants of Upper and Lower Egypt. The 12 central columns are 75 feet high, and the capitals are 22 feet in diameter at the top, large enough to hold a hundred people. The Egyptians, who used no cement, depended on precise cutting of the joints and the weight of the huge stone blocks to hold the columns in place. The two central rows of columns are taller than those at the sides. Raising the roof's central section created a *clerestory*. Openings in the clerestory permitted sunlight to filter into the interior, although the stone grilles (FIG. 3-25) would have blocked much of the light. This method of construction appeared in primitive form in the Old Kingdom valley temple of Khafre at Gizeh. The clerestory is evidently an Egyptian innovation, and its significance cannot be overstated. Before the invention of the electric light bulb, illuminating a building's interior was always a challenge for architects. The clerestory played a key role in the history of architecture until very recently.

In the hypostyle hall at Karnak, the columns are indispensable structurally, unlike the rock-cut columns of the tombs at Beni Hasan (FIGS. 3-17 and 3-18) and Abu Simbel (FIG. 3-23). But horizontal bands of painted *sunken relief* sculpture almost hide their function as vertical supports. To create these reliefs, the New Kingdom sculptors chiseled deep outlines below the stone's surface, rather than cut back the stone around the figures to make the figures project from the surface. Sunken reliefs have the advantage of preserving the contours of the columns they adorn. Otherwise, the columns would have an irregular, wavy profile. Despite this effort to maintain sharp architectural lines, the overwhelming of the surfaces with reliefs indicates the Egyptian architects' intention was not to emphasize the functional role of the columns. Instead, they used columns as image- and message-bearing surfaces.

3-26 Model of the hypostyle hall, temple of Amen-Re, Karnak, Egypt, 19th Dynasty, ca. 1290–1224 BCE. Metropolitan Museum of Art, New York.

The two central rows of columns of Karnak's hypostyle hall are taller than the rest. Raising the roof's central section created a clerestory that admitted light through windows with stone grilles.

Sculpture and Painting

Although the Egyptians lavishly decorated the great temple complexes of the New Kingdom with statues and painted reliefs, many of the finest examples of statuary and mural painting adorned tombs, as in the Old and Middle Kingdoms.

SENMUT AND NEFRURA *Block statues* were popular during the New Kingdom. In these works Egyptian sculptors expressed the idea that the ka could find an eternal home in the cubic stone image of the deceased in an even more radical simplification of form than was common in Old Kingdom statuary. In the statue illustrated here (FIG. **3-27**) depicting Hatshepsut's chancellor Senmut and her daughter Nefrura, the streamlined design

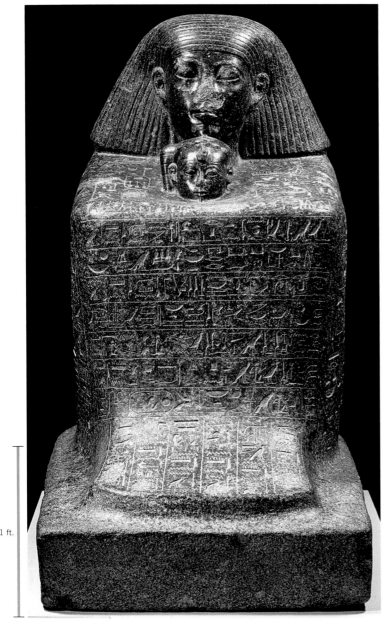

1 ft.

3-27 Senmut with Princess Nefrura, from Thebes, Egypt, 18th Dynasty, ca. 1470–1460 BCE. Granite, 3′ $\frac{1}{2}$″ high. Ägyptisches Museum, Berlin.

Hatshepsut's chancellor holds the queen's daughter in his "lap" and envelops her in his cloak. New Kingdom block statues exhibit a more radical simplification of form than do Old Kingdom statues.

concentrates attention on the heads. The sculptor treated the two bodies as a single cubic block, given over to inscriptions. Senmut holds the pharaoh's daughter by Thutmose II in his "lap" and envelops the girl in his cloak. The polished stone shape has its own simple beauty, with the surfaces turning subtly about smoothly rounded corners. The work—one of many surviving statues depicting Senmut with the princess—is also a reflection of the power of Egypt's queen. The frequent depiction of Senmut with Nefrura enhanced the chancellor's stature through his association with the pharaoh's daughter (he was her tutor) and, by implication, with Hatshepsut herself.

TOMB OF NEBAMUN Some of the best preserved mural paintings of the New Kingdom come from the Theban tomb of Nebamun, whose official titles were "scribe and counter of grain." On one wall (FIG. **3-28**), the painter depicted Nebamun standing in his boat, flushing birds from a papyrus swamp. The hieroglyphic text beneath his left arm says that Nebamun is enjoying recreation in his eternal afterlife. (Here, as elsewhere in Egyptian art, the accompanying text amplifies the message of the picture—and vice versa.) In contrast to the static pose of Ti watching others hunt hippopotami (FIG. 3-14), Nebamun strides forward and vigorously swings his throwing stick. In his right hand, he holds three birds he has caught. A wild cat, impossibly perched on a papyrus stem just in front of and below him, has caught two more in its claws and is holding the wings of a third in its teeth. Nebamun's wife and daughter accompany him on this hunt and hold the lotuses they have gathered. The artist scaled down the figures in proportion to their rank, as did Old Kingdom artists. As in Ti's tomb, the painter depicted the animals naturalistically, based on careful observation.

The painting technique, also employed in earlier Egyptian tombs, is *fresco secco* (dry fresco), in which artists let the plaster dry before painting on it. This procedure, in contrast to true fresco painting on wet plaster (see "Fresco Painting," Chapter 14, page 408), permitted slower and more meticulous work than painting on fresh plaster, which had to be completed before the plaster dried. Fresco secco, however, is not as durable as true fresco painting, because the colors do not fuse with the wall surface.

Another fresco fragment (FIG. **3-29**) from Nebamun's tomb shows a funerary banquet in which four noblewomen (*lower left*) watch and apparently participate in a musical performance in which two nimble and almost nude girls dance in front of the guests at a banquet. When his family buried Nebamun, they must have eaten the customary ceremonial meal at his tomb. His relatives would have returned one day each year to partake in a commemorative banquet during which the living communed with the dead. This fresco represents one of these feasts, with an ample supply of wine jars at the right. It also shows that New Kingdom artists did not always adhere to the old norms for figural representation. This painter carefully recorded the dancers' overlapping figures, their facing in opposite directions, and their rather complicated gyrations, producing a pleasing intertwined motif at the same time. The profile view of the dancers is consistent with their lower stature in the Egyptian hierarchy. The New Kingdom artist reserved the composite view for Nebamun and his family. Of the four seated women, the painter represented the two at the left conventionally, but the other two face the observer in what is a rarely attempted frontal pose. They clap and beat time to the dance, while one of them plays the reeds. The painter took careful note of the soles of their feet as they sit cross-legged and suggested the movement of the women's heads by the loose arrangement

3-28 Nebamun hunting fowl, from the tomb of Nebamun, Thebes, Egypt, 18th Dynasty, ca. 1400–1350 BCE. Fresco secco, 2′ 8″ high. British Museum, London.

Nebamun's wife and daughter—depicted smaller than the deceased—accompany him on his hunt for fowl. An inscription states that Nebamun is enjoying recreation in his eternal afterlife.

1 ft.

lithe dancers, and leisure time to hunt and fish in the marshes. Still, as in the earlier tomb of Ti, the scenes should be read both literally and allegorically. Although Nebamun enjoys himself in the afterlife, the artist symbolically asked viewers to recall how he got there. Hunting scenes reminded Egyptians of Horus, the son of Osiris, hunting down his father's murderer, Seth, the god of disorder (see "The Gods and Goddesses of Egypt," page 57). Successful hunts were metaphors for triumphing over death and disorder, ensuring a happy existence in the afterlife. Music and dance were sacred to Hathor, who aided the dead in their passage to the other world. The sensual women at the banquet are a reference to fertility, rebirth, and regeneration.

of their hair strands. This informality constitutes a relaxation of the Old Kingdom's stiff rules of representation.

The frescoes in Nebamun's tomb testify to the luxurious life of the Egyptian nobility, filled with good food and drink, fine musicians,

1 ft.

3-29 Funerary banquet, from the tomb of Nebamun, Thebes, Egypt, 18th Dynasty, ca. 1400–1350 BCE. Fresco secco, 2′ 10⅝″ × 3′ 10⅞″. British Museum, London.

A second fresco in Nebamun's tomb represents a funerary banquet in which the artist experimented with frontal views of faces and bodies—a relaxation of the Old Kingdom's stiff rules of representation.

Akhenaton and the Amarna Period

Not long after his family laid Nebamun to rest in his tomb at Thebes, a revolution occurred in Egyptian society and religion. In the mid-14th century BCE, Amenhotep IV, later known as Akhenaton (r. 1353–1335 BCE), abandoned the worship of most of the Egyptian gods in favor of Aton, identified with the sun disk, whom the pharaoh declared to be the universal and only god. Akhenaton deleted the name of Amen from all inscriptions and even from his own name and that of his father, Amenhotep III. He emptied the great temples, enraged the priests, and moved his capital downriver from Thebes to present-day Amarna, a site he named Akhetaton (after his new god). The pharaoh claimed to be both the son and sole prophet of Aton. To him alone could the god make revelation. Moreover, in stark contrast to earlier practice, painters and sculptors represented Akhenaton's god neither in animal nor in human form but simply as the sun disk emitting life-giving rays. The pharaohs who followed Akhenaton reestablished the Theban cult and priesthood of Amen at Karnak (FIG. 3-24) and elsewhere and restored Amen's temples and inscriptions. Akhenaton's brief religious revolution was soon undone, and his new city largely abandoned.

During the brief heretical episode of Akhenaton, profound changes also occurred in Egyptian art. A colossal statue (FIG. **3-30**) of Akhenaton from Karnak, toppled and buried after his death, retains the standard frontal pose of canonical pharaonic portraits. But the effeminate body, with its curving contours, and the long face with full lips and heavy-lidded eyes are a far cry indeed from the heroically proportioned figures of the pharaoh's predecessors (compare FIG. 3-12). Akhenaton's body is curiously misshapen, with weak arms, a narrow waist, protruding belly, wide hips, and fatty thighs. Modern physicians have tried to explain his physique by attributing a variety of illnesses to the pharaoh. They cannot agree on a diagnosis, and their premise—that the statue is an accurate depiction of a physical deformity—is probably faulty. Some art historians think Akhenaton's portrait is a deliberate artistic reaction against the established style, paralleling the suppression of traditional religion. They argue that Akhenaton's artists tried to formulate a new androgynous image of the pharaoh as the manifestation of Aton, the sexless sun disk. But no consensus exists other than that the style was revolutionary and short-lived.

NEFERTITI AND TIYE A painted limestone bust (FIG. **3-31**) of Akhenaton's queen, Nefertiti (her name means "the beautiful one has come"), also breaks with the past. The portrait exhibits an expression of entranced musing and an almost mannered sensitivity and delicacy of curving contour. Excavators discovered the bust in the Amarna workshop of the sculptor THUTMOSE. Although one scholar has recently questioned its authenticity, art historians still consider the portrait to be a genuine work, a deliberately unfinished model very likely by the master's own hand. The left eye socket still lacks the inlaid eyeball, making the face a kind of before-and-after demonstration piece. With this elegant bust, Thutmose may have been alluding to a heavy flower on its slender stalk by exaggerating

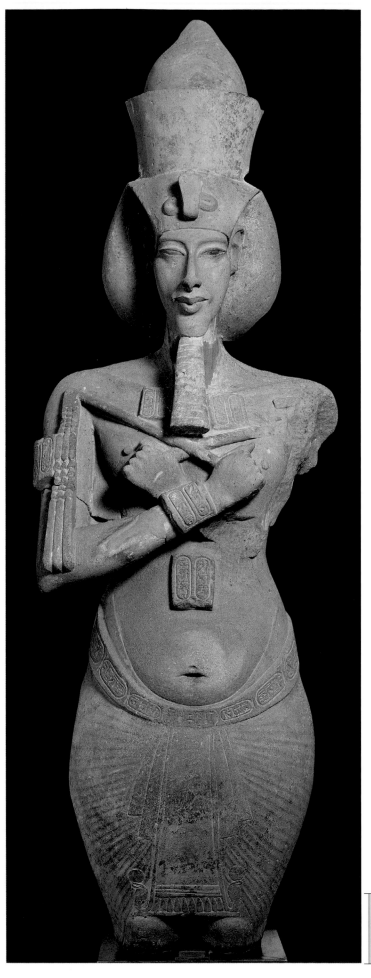

3-30 Akhenaton, from the temple of Aton, Karnak, Egypt, 18th Dynasty, ca. 1353–1335 BCE. Sandstone, 13′ high. Egyptian Museum, Cairo.

Akhenaton initiated both religious and artistic revolutions. This androgynous figure is a deliberate reaction against tradition. It may be an attempt to portray the pharaoh as Aton, the sexless sun disk.

1 ft.

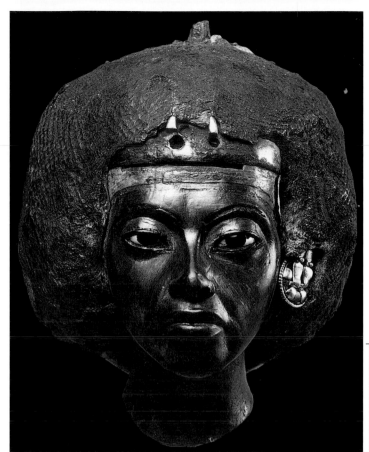

3-32 Tiye, from Ghurab, Egypt, 18th Dynasty, ca. 1353–1335 BCE. Wood, with gold, silver, alabaster, and lapis lazuli, 3¾″ high. Ägyptisches Museum, Berlin.

This portrait of Akhenaton's mother is carved of dark yew wood, possibly to match the queen's complexion. The head was remodeled during her son's reign to remove all references to traditional deities.

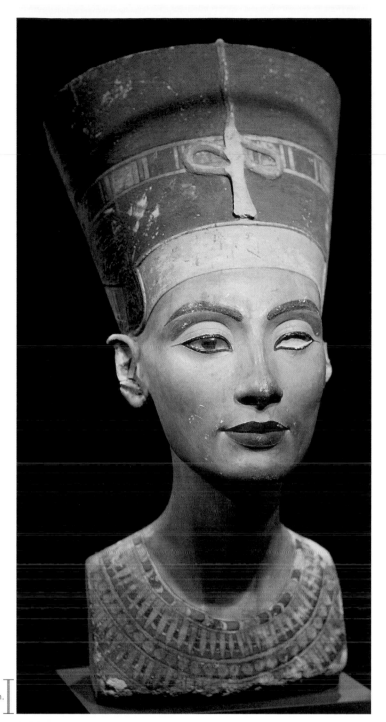

3-31 THUTMOSE, Nefertiti, from Amarna, Egypt, 18th Dynasty, ca. 1353–1335 BCE. Painted limestone, 1′ 8″ high. Ägyptisches Museum, Berlin.

Found in the sculptor's workshop, Thutmose's bust of Nefertiti portrays Akhenaton's influential wife as an elegant beauty with a pensive expression and a long, delicately curved neck.

the weight of the crowned head and the length of the almost serpentine neck. The sculptor seems to have adjusted the likeness of his subject to meet the era's standard of spiritual beauty.

In contrast, the miniature head (FIG. **3-32**) of Queen Tiye, mother of Akhenaton, is a moving portrait of old age. Although not of royal birth, Tiye was the daughter of a high-ranking official and became the chief wife of Amenhotep III. Archaeologists unearthed

her portrait, carved of dark yew wood (possibly to match her complexion), at Ghurab with other objects connected with the funerary cult of Amenhotep III. A sculptor probably remodeled the portrait during her son's reign to eliminate all reference to deities of the old religion. That is when the head acquired the present wig of plaster and linen with small blue beads. Tiye appears as an older woman with lines and furrows, consistent with the new relaxation of artistic rules in the Amarna age. The sculptor inlaid her heavy-lidded slanting eyes with alabaster and ebony, and painted the lips red. The earrings (one is hidden by the later wig) are of gold and lapis lazuli. The wig covers what was originally a silver-foil headdress. A gold band still adorns the forehead. Luxurious materials such as these were common for royal portraits.

Both Nefertiti and Tiye figured prominently in the art and life of the Amarna age. Tiye, for example, regularly appeared in art beside her husband during his reign, and she apparently played an important role in his administration as well as her son's. Letters survive from foreign rulers advising the young Akhenaton to seek his mother's counsel in the conduct of international affairs. Nefertiti, too, was an influential woman. She frequently appears in the decoration of the Aton temple at Karnak, and she not only equals her husband in size but also sometimes wears pharaonic headgear.

3-33 Akhenaton, Nefertiti, and three daughters, from Amarna, Egypt, 18th Dynasty, ca. 1353–1335 BCE. Limestone, 1′ ¼″ high. Ägyptisches Museum, Berlin.

In this sunken relief, the Amarna artist provided a rare intimate look at the royal family in a domestic setting. Akhenaton, Nefertiti, and three of their daughters bask in the life-giving rays of Aton, the sun disk.

1 in.

FAMILY OF AKHENATON A sunken relief stele (FIG. **3-33**), perhaps from a private shrine, provides a rare look at this royal family. The style is familiar from the colossus of Akhenaton (FIG. 3-30) and the portrait head of Nefertiti (FIG. 3-31). Undulating curves have re-placed rigid lines, and the figures possess the prominent bellies that characterize figures of the Amarna period. The pharaoh, his wife, and three of their daughters bask in the life-giving rays of Aton, the sun disk. The mood is informal and anecdotal. Akhenaton lifts one of his daughters in order to kiss her. Another daughter sits on Nefertiti's lap and gestures toward her father, while the youngest daughter reaches out to touch a pendant on her mother's crown. This kind of intimate portrayal of the pharaoh and his family is unprecedented in Egyptian art. Matching the political and religious revolution under Akhenaton was an equally radical upheaval in art.

The Tomb of Tutankhamen and the Post-Amarna Period

The most famous figure of the Post-Amarna period is Tutankhamen (r. 1333–1323 BCE), who was probably Akhenaton's son by a minor wife. Tutankhamen ruled for a decade and died at age 18. (Although some have speculated foul play, examination of the king's mummy in 2005 ruled out murder.) Tutankhamen was a very minor figure in Egyptian history, however. The public remembers him today solely because in 1922 Howard Carter (1874–1939), a British ar-chaeologist, discovered the boy-king's tomb with its fabulously rich treasure of sculpture, furniture, and jewelry largely intact.

TUTANKHAMEN'S MUMMY The principal item Carter found in Tutankhamen's tomb was the enshrined body of the pharaoh himself. The royal mummy reposed in the innermost of three coffins, nested one within the other. The innermost coffin (FIG. **3-34**) was the most luxurious of the three. Made of beaten gold (about a quarter ton of it) and inlaid with semiprecious stones such as lapis lazuli, turquoise, and carnelian, it is a supreme monu-ment to the sculptor's and goldsmith's crafts. The portrait mask (FIG. 3-35), which covered the king's face, is also made of gold with inlaid semiprecious stones. It is a sensitive portrayal of the serene adolescent king dressed in his official regalia, including the nemes headdress and false beard. The general effect of the mask and the tomb treasures as a whole is one of grandeur and richness expres-sive of Egyptian power, pride, and affluence.

TUTANKHAMEN AT WAR Although Tutankhamen prob-ably was too young to fight, his position as king required that art-ists represent him as a conqueror, and he appears as a victorious general in the panels of a painted chest (FIG. **3-36**) deposited in

his tomb. The lid panel shows the king as a successful hunter pursu-ing droves of fleeing animals in the desert. On the side panel, the pharaoh, larger than all other fig-ures on the chest, rides in a war chariot pulled by spirited, plumed horses. He draws his bow against a cluster of bearded Asian enemies, who fall in confusion before him. (The absence of a ground line in an Egyptian painting or relief implies chaos and death.) Tutankhamen slays the enemy, like game, in great numbers. Behind him are three tiers of undersized war chariots, which serve to magnify the king's figure and to increase the count of his warriors. The themes are tra-ditional, but the fluid, curvilinear forms are features reminiscent of the Amarna style.

3-34 Innermost coffin of Tutankhamen, from his tomb at Thebes, Egypt, 18th Dynasty, ca. 1323 BCE. Gold with inlay of enamel and semiprecious stones, 6′ 1″ long. Egyptian Museum, Cairo.

The boy-king Tutankhamen owes his fame today to his treasure-laden tomb. His mummy was encased in three nested coffins. The innermost one, made of gold, portrays the pharaoh as Osiris.

1 ft.

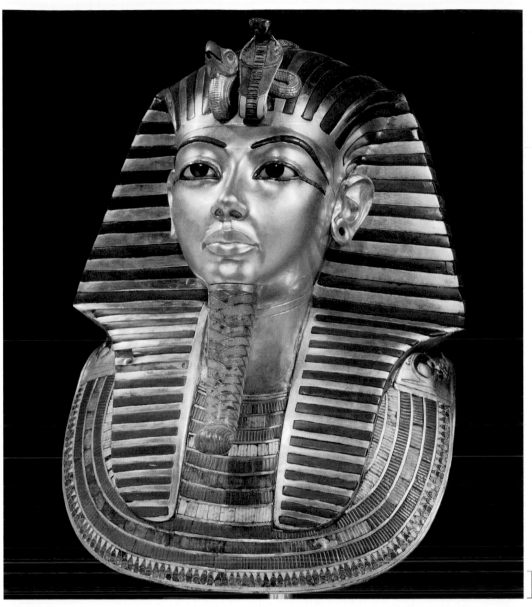

3-35 Death mask of Tutankhamen, from the innermost coffin in his tomb at Thebes, Egypt, 18th Dynasty, ca. 1323 BCE. Gold with inlay of semiprecious stones, 1′ 9¼″ high. Egyptian Museum, Cairo.

The treasures in Tutankhamen's tomb include this mummy mask portraying the teenaged pharaoh with idealized features and wearing the traditional false beard and uraeus cobra headdress.

1 in.

3-36 Painted chest, from the tomb of Tutankhamen, Thebes, Egypt, 18th Dynasty, ca. 1333–1323 BCE. Wood, 1′ 8″ long. Egyptian Museum, Cairo.

In this representation of Tutankhamen triumphing over Asian enemies, the artist contrasted the orderly registers of Egyptian chariots with the chaotic pile of foreign soldiers who fall before the king.

1 in.

1 in.

3-37 Last judgment of Hunefer, from his tomb at Thebes, Egypt, 19th Dynasty, ca. 1300–1290 BCE. Painted papyrus scroll, 1′ 6″ high. British Museum, London.

The Book of the Dead contained spells and prayers. This scroll depicts the weighing of Hunefer's heart against Maat's feather before the deceased can be presented to Osiris, god of the Underworld.

SCROLL OF HUNEFER Tutankhamen's mummy case (FIG. 3-34) shows the boy-king in the guise of Osiris, god of the dead and king of the Underworld, as well as giver of eternal life. The so-called *Book of the Dead,* a collection of spells and prayers, records the ritual of the cult of Osiris. Illustrated papyrus scrolls (some are 70 feet long) containing these texts were essential items accompanying well-to-do persons into the afterlife (see "Mummification and Immortality," page 61). One surviving scroll (FIG. **3-37**) represents the final judgment of the deceased. It comes from the Theban tomb of Hunefer, the royal scribe and steward of Seti I (r. 1306–1290 BCE), the father of Ramses II. At the left of the section reproduced here, Anubis, the jackal-headed god of embalming, leads Hunefer into the hall of judgment. The god then adjusts the scales to weigh the dead man's heart against the feather of the goddess Maat, protectress of truth and right. A hybrid crocodile-hippopotamus-lion monster, Ammit, devourer of the sinful, awaits the decision of the scales. If the weighing had been unfavorable to the deceased, the monster would have eaten his heart. The ibis-headed god Thoth records the proceedings. Above, the gods of the Egyptian pantheon sit in a row as witnesses, while Hunefer kneels in adoration before them. Having been justified by the scales, Hunefer is brought by Osiris's son, the falcon-headed Horus, into the presence of the green-faced Osiris and his sisters Isis and Nephthys to receive the award of eternal life.

In Hunefer's scroll, the figures have all the formality of stance, shape, and attitude of traditional Egyptian art. Abstract figures and hieroglyphs alike are aligned rigidly, and the flexible, curvilinear style suggestive of movement that characterized the art of Amarna and Tutankhamen has disappeared. The return to conservatism is unmistakable.

FIRST MILLENNIUM BCE

During the first millennium BCE, Egypt lost the commanding role it once had played in the ancient world. The empire dwindled away, and foreign powers invaded and occupied the land until, beginning in the fourth century BCE, Alexander the Great of Macedon and his Greek successors and, eventually, the emperors of Rome replaced the pharaohs as rulers of the Kingdom of the Nile.

Thebes

One of those foreign powers was Assyria (see Chapter 2), which sacked Thebes in 660 BCE. A rich and powerful man named Mentuemhet had the misfortune to be mayor of Thebes during the Assyrian invasion of his city.

MENTUEMHET In addition to serving as mayor, Mentuemhet was the Fourth Prophet (priest) of Amen, and according to the inscriptions on works he commissioned, he was responsible for restoring the temples the Assyrians had razed. He placed portrait statues of himself in those temples and also in the tomb he constructed in a prominent place in the Theban necropolis. More than a dozen of his portraits survive, including the somewhat under life-size granite statue illustrated here (FIG. **3-38**).

Mentuemhet's portrait statues exemplify Egyptian sculpture at about the time the Greeks first encountered the art of the Nile region (see Chapter 5). The pose is traditional, as is his costume of kilt and wig, but the face, with its frank portrayal of the mayor's advanced age, is much more realistic than most earlier representations of elite men. In fact, almost all of Mentuemhet's portraits have idealized features. This one is an exception, but even here the

3-38 Portrait statue of Mentuemhet, from Karnak, Egypt, 26th Dynasty, ca. 660–650 BCE. Granite, 4′ 5″ high. Egyptian Museum, Cairo.

Mentuemhet's portrait combines a realistic face with an idealized body. The costume and pose, however, recall Old Kingdom statuary, a testimony to the longevity of stylistic modes in Egypt.

1 ft.

trim, muscular body is that of a young man in the tradition of Old Kingdom royal portraits (FIG. 3-12). The sculptor removed the slab of stone that forms a backdrop to most earlier pharaonic portraits, but left the stone block intact between the arms and the torso and between the legs, an artistic decision that contributes significantly to the rigid look of the statue, so appropriate for a timeless image of the deceased in his eternal afterlife. The stylistic similarity between Egyptian statues created 2,000 years apart is without parallel in the history of art.

Kingdom of Kush

Another foreign power that occupied the Nile valley during the first millennium BCE was Egypt's gold-rich neighbor to the south, the kingdom of Kush, part of which is in present-day Sudan. Called Nubia by the Romans, perhaps from the Egyptian word for gold, Kush appears in Egyptian texts as early as the Old Kingdom. During the New Kingdom, the pharaohs colonized Nubia and appointed a viceroy of Kush to administer the Kushite kingdom, which included Abu Simbel (FIG. 3-22) and controlled the major trade route between Egypt and sub-Saharan Africa. But in the eighth century BCE, the Nubians conquered Egypt and established themselves as the 25th Dynasty.

TAHARQO Around 680 BCE, the Kushite pharaoh Taharqo (r. 690–664 BCE) constructed a temple at Kawa and placed a portrait of himself in it. Emulating traditional Egyptian types, the sculptor portrayed Taharqo as a sphinx (FIG. **3-39**; compare FIG. 3-10) with the ears, mane, and body of a lion but with a human face and a headdress featuring two uraeus cobras. The king's name is inscribed on his chest, and his features are distinctly African, although, as in all pharaonic portraiture, they are generic and idealized rather than a specific likeness.

3-39 Taharqo as a sphinx, from temple T, Kawa, Sudan, 25th Dynasty, ca. 680 BCE. Granite, 1′ 4″ × 2′ 4¾″. British Museum, London.

The Nubian kings who ruled Egypt during the 25th Dynasty adopted traditional Egyptian statuary types, such as the sphinx, but sculptors incorporated the Kushite pharaohs' distinctly African features.

1 in.

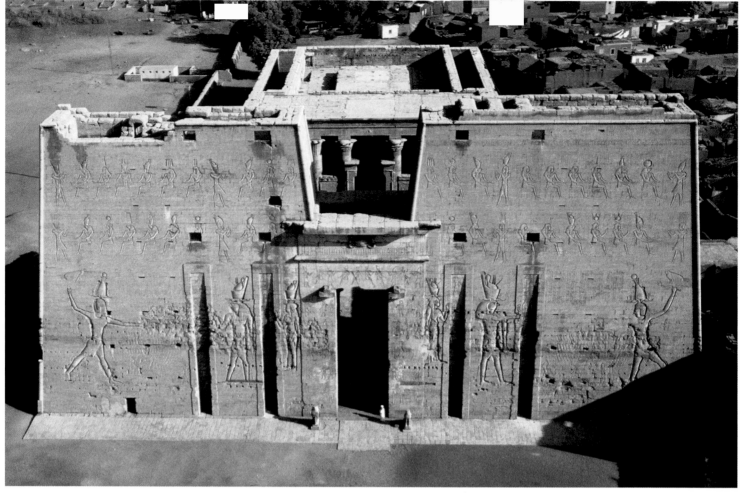

3-40 Temple of Horus (looking east), Edfu, Egypt, ca. 237–47 BCE.

The pylon temple at Edfu is more than a thousand years later than that at Karnak (FIG. 3-24), but it adheres to the same basic architectural scheme. Egyptian artistic forms tended to have very long lives.

After Alexander

Once formulated, Egyptian traditions tended to have very long lives, in architecture as in the other arts—even after Alexander the Great brought Greek rule and Greek culture to the Kingdom of the Nile.

TEMPLE OF HORUS, EDFU The temple of Horus (FIG. 3-40) at Edfu, built during the third, second, and first centuries BCE, still follows the basic pylon temple scheme architects worked out more than a thousand years before (compare the New Kingdom temples at Karnak, FIG. 3-24, and Luxor, FIG. 3-24A). The great entrance pylon at Edfu is especially impressive. The broad surface of its massive facade, with its sloping walls, is broken only

by the doorway with its overshadowing *moldings* at the top and sides, deep channels to hold great flagstaffs, and sunken reliefs. The reliefs depict Horus and Hathor witnessing an oversized King Ptolemy XIII (r. 51–47 BCE) smiting undersized enemies—a motif first used in Egyptian reliefs and paintings in Predynastic times (FIGS. 3-1 and 3-1A). The Edfu temple is eloquent testimony to the persistence of Egyptian architectural and pictorial types even under Greek rule.

Indeed, the exceptional longevity of formal traditions in Egypt is one of the marvels of the history of art. It attests to the invention of an artistic style so satisfactory that it endured in Egypt for millennia. Everywhere else in the ancient Mediterranean, stylistic change was the only common denominator.

EGYPT UNDER THE PHARAOHS

PREDYNASTIC AND EARLY DYNASTIC PERIODS ca. 3500–2575 BCE

▌ The unification of Upper and Lower Egypt into a single kingdom under the rule of a divine pharaoh occurred around 3000–2920 BCE. The earliest labeled work of narrative art, the palette of King Narmer, commemorates the event. The Narmer palette also established the basic principles of Egyptian representational art for 3,000 years.

▌ Imhotep, the first artist in history whose name is known, was the earliest master of monumental stone architecture. He designed the funerary complex and stepped pyramid of King Djoser (r. 2630–2611 BCE) at Saqqara.

Palette of King Narmer,
ca. 3000–2920 BCE

OLD KINGDOM ca. 2575–2134 BCE

▌ The Old Kingdom was the first golden age of Egyptian art and architecture, the time when three pharaohs of the Fourth Dynasty erected the Great Pyramids at Gizeh, the oldest of the Seven Wonders of the ancient world. The pyramids were emblems of the sun on whose rays the pharaohs ascended to the heavens when they died.

▌ Old Kingdom sculptors created seated and standing statuary types in which all movement was suppressed in order to express the eternal nature of pharaonic kingship. These types would dominate Egyptian art for 2,000 years.

Great Pyramids, Gizeh,
ca. 2551–2472 BCE

MIDDLE KINGDOM ca. 2040–1640 BCE

▌ After an intermediate period of civil war, Mentuhotep II (r. 2050–1998 BCE) reestablished central rule and founded the Middle Kingdom.

▌ The major artistic innovation of this period was the rock-cut tomb in which sculptors hewed both the facade and interior chambers out of the living rock. The fluted columns in Middle Kingdom tombs closely resemble the columns later used in Greek temples.

Tomb of Amenemhet, Beni Hasan,
ca. 1950–1900 BCE

NEW KINGDOM ca. 1550–1070 BCE

▌ During the New Kingdom, Egypt extended its borders to the Euphrates River in the east and deep into Nubia in the south.

▌ The most significant architectural innovation of this period was the axially planned pylon temple incorporating an immense gateway, columnar courtyards, and a hypostyle hall with clerestory lighting.

▌ Powerful pharaohs such as Hatshepsut (r. 1473–1458 BCE) and Ramses II (r. 1290–1224 BCE) built gigantic temples in honor of their patron gods and, after their deaths, for their own worship.

▌ Akhenaton (r. 1353–1335 BCE) abandoned the traditional Egyptian religion in favor of Aton, the sun disk, and initiated a short-lived artistic revolution in which undulating curves and anecdotal content replaced the cubic forms and impassive stillness of earlier Egyptian art.

Temple of Ramses II, Abu Simbel,
ca. 1290–1224 BCE

FIRST MILLENNIUM BCE 1000–30 BCE

▌ After the demise of the New Kingdom, Egypt's power in the ancient world declined, and the Nile came under the control of foreigners. These included the Kushite kings of Nubia and, after 332 BCE, Alexander the Great and his Greek successors. In 30 BCE, Egypt became a province of the Roman Empire.

▌ The traditional forms of Egyptian art and architecture lived on even under foreign rule, for example, in the pylon temple erected at Edfu in honor of Horus.

Temple of Horus, Edfu,
ca. 237–47 BCE

Next to a woman who may be pouring ox blood from a jar into a vessel between two double axes is a second woman, also with fair skin, and a male (dark-skinned) harp player.

Archaeologists have not yet deciphered Minoan inscriptions, but the scenes on this sarcophagus from Hagia Triada in southern Crete provide information about Minoan funerary rituals.

Three men moving in the opposite direction carry sculptures of two sacrificial animals and a model of a boat, offerings to the deceased man whose remains this sarcophagus housed.

1 ft.

4-1 Sarcophagus, from Hagia Triada (Crete), Greece, ca. 1450–1400 BCE. Painted limestone, 4′ 6″ long. Archaeological Museum, Herakleion.

THE PREHISTORIC AEGEAN

The Minoan painter included the deceased himself in this depiction of the funerary rites in his honor. He stands in front of his tomb facing the three men presenting him with gifts.

GREECE IN THE AGE OF HEROES

When, in the eighth century BCE, Homer immortalized in the *Iliad* and the *Odyssey* the great war between the Greeks and the Trojans and the subsequent adventures of Odysseus on his tortuous journey home, the epic poet was describing a time long before his own—a golden age of larger-than-life heroes. Since the late 19th century, archaeologists have gradually uncovered impressive remains of that heroic age, including the palaces of the legendary King Minos at Knossos (FIGS. 4-4 to 4-6) on Crete and of King Agamemnon at Mycenae (FIGS. 4-19 and 4-22A) on the Greek mainland. But they have also recovered thousands of less glamorous objects and inscriptions that provide a contemporaneous view of life in the prehistoric Aegean unfiltered by the romantic lens of Homer and later writers.

One of the most intriguing finds to date is the painted Minoan (named after King Minos) sarcophagus (FIG. 4-1) from Hagia Triada on the southern coast of Crete. The paintings adorning the sides of the small coffin are closely related in technique, color scheme, and figure style to the more monumental frescoes on the walls of Minoan palaces, but the subject is foreign to the royal repertoire. The paintings illustrate the funerary rites in honor of the dead. They furnish welcome information about Minoan religion, which still remains obscure despite more than a century of excavation on Crete.

On one long side (not shown) of the sarcophagus, four women and a male double-flute player take part in a ritual centered on an ox tied up on a table. One of the women makes an offering at an altar. In contrast to this unified narrative, the painter divided the side illustrated in FIG. 4-1 into two scenes. At the left, a woman pours liquid (perhaps the blood of the ox on the other side) from a jar into a large vessel on a stand between two double axes. Behind her, a second woman carries two more jars, and a male figure plays the harp. In conformance with the common convention in many ancient cultures, the women have light skin and the men dark skin (compare FIG. 3-11A). To their right, three men carry two sculpted sacrificial animals and a model of a boat to offer to a dead man, whom the painter represented as standing in front of his tomb, just as the biblical Lazarus later appears in medieval art.

The precise meaning of the sarcophagus paintings is uncertain, but there is no doubt that they document well-established Minoan rites in honor of the dead, which included the sacrifice of animals accompanied by music and the deposit of gifts in the tomb. Until scholars can decipher the written language of the Minoans, artworks such as the Hagia Triada sarcophagus will be the primary tools for reconstructing life on Crete, and in Greece as a whole, during the two millennia before the birth of Homer.

GREECE BEFORE HOMER

In the *Iliad,* Homer describes the might and splendor of the Greek armies poised before the walls of Troy.

> Clan after clan poured out from the ships and huts onto the plain . . . innumerable as the leaves and blossoms in their season . . . the Athenians . . . the men of Argos and Tiryns of the Great Walls . . . troops from the great stronghold of Mycenae, from wealthy Corinth . . . from Knossos . . . Phaistos . . . and the other troops that had their homes in Crete of the Hundred Towns.[1]

The Greeks had come from far and wide, from the mainland and the islands (MAP **4-1**), to seek revenge against Paris, the Trojan prince who had abducted Helen, wife of King Menelaus of Sparta. The *Iliad,* composed around 750 BCE, is the first great work of Greek literature. Until about 1870, the world regarded Homer's epic poem as pure fiction. Scholars paid little heed to the bard as a historian, instead attributing the profusion of names and places in his writings to the rich abundance of his imagination. The prehistory of Greece remained shadowy and lost in an impenetrable world of myth.

TROY AND MYCENAE In the late 1800s, however, Heinrich Schliemann (1822–1890), a wealthy German businessman turned archaeologist, proved that scholars had not given Homer his due. Between 1870 and his death 20 years later, Schliemann (whose methods later archaeologists have harshly criticized) uncovered some of the very cities Homer named. In 1870, he began work at Hissarlik on the northwestern coast of Turkey, which a British archaeologist, Frank Calvert (1828–1908), had postulated was the site of Homer's Troy. Schliemann dug into a vast mound and found a number of fortified cities built on the remains of one another. Fire had destroyed one of them in the 13th century BCE. This, scholars now generally agree, was the Troy of King Priam and his son Paris.

Schliemann continued his excavations at Mycenae on the Greek mainland, where, he believed, King Agamemnon, Menelaus's brother, had once ruled. Here his finds were even more startling, among them a massive fortress-palace with a monumental gateway (FIGS. 4-19 and 4-22A); tombs with lofty stone domes beneath earthen mounds (FIGS. 4-20 and 4-21); quantities of gold jewelry, masks (FIG. 4-22), and cups; and inlaid bronze weapons (FIG. 4-23). Schliemann's discoveries revealed a magnificent civilization far older than the famous vestiges of Classical Greece that had remained visible in Athens and elsewhere. Subsequent excavations

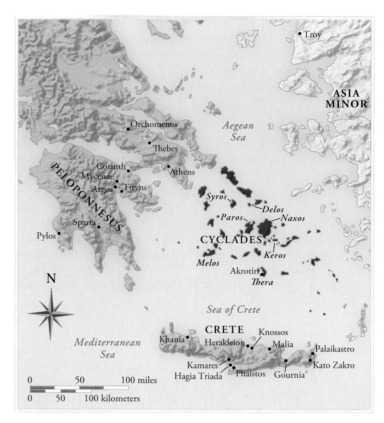

MAP 4-1 The prehistoric Aegean.

proved that Mycenae had not been the only center of this fabulous civilization.

MINOAN CRETE Another legendary figure was Minos, the king of Knossos on the island of Crete, who exacted from Athens a tribute of youths and maidens to be fed to the *Minotaur,* a creature half bull and half man that inhabited a vast labyrinth. In 1900, an Englishman, Arthur Evans (1851–1941), began work at Knossos, where he uncovered a palace (FIGS. 4-4 to 4-6) that resembled a maze. Evans named the people who had constructed it the Minoans after their mythological king. Other archaeologists soon discovered further evidence of the Minoans at Phaistos, Hagia Triada (FIG. 4-1), and other sites, including Gournia, which Harriet Boyd Hawes (1871–1945), an American archaeologist (and one of the first women of any nationality to direct a major excavation), explored between 1901 and 1904.

THE PREHISTORIC AEGEAN

3000	2000	1600	1400	B C E 1200
Early Cycladic sculptors create marble figurines for placement in graves to accompany the dead into the afterlife	Minoans construct major palaces on Crete and adorn the walls with frescoes focusing on palace rituals and nature	Minoan potters manufacture Marine Style vases, and sculptors carve small-scale images of gods and goddesses	Mycenaeans erect fortification walls around their citadels at Mycenae, Tiryns, and elsewhere, and build tombs featuring corbeled domes	
	Cretan ceramists produce Kamares painted pottery	Mycenaeans bury their dead in deep shaft graves with gold funerary masks, ornately inlaid daggers, and gold cups	Mycenaeans fashion the oldest known monumental sculptures in Greece	
	Volcanic eruption destroys Thera, ca. 1628 BCE	Mycenaeans occupy Crete	Destruction of the Mycenaean palaces, ca. 1200 BCE	

More recently, archaeologists have excavated important Minoan remains at many other locations on Crete, and have explored contemporaneous sites on other islands in the Aegean, most notably miThera. Together, the Minoan and Mycenaean buildings, paintings, sculptures, and other finds attest to the wealth and sophistication of the people who occupied Greece and the Aegean Islands in that once-obscure heroic age celebrated in later Greek mythology.

AEGEAN ARCHAEOLOGY TODAY Arguably more important for the understanding of Aegean society than the art objects tourists flock to see in the museums of Athens and Herakleion (near Knossos) are the many documents archaeologists have found written in scripts conventionally called Linear A and Linear B. The progress made during the past several decades in deciphering these texts has provided a welcome corrective to the romantic treasure-hunting approach of Schliemann and Evans. Scholars now regard Linear B as an early form of Greek, and they have begun to reconstruct Aegean civilization by referring to records made at the time and not just to Homer's heroic account. Archaeologists now also know that humans inhabited Greece as far back as the early Paleolithic period and that village life was firmly established in Greece and on Crete in Neolithic times. The heyday of the ancient Aegean, however, did not arrive until the second millennium BCE, well after the emergence of the river valley civilizations of Mesopotamia, Egypt, and South Asia (see Chapters 2, 3, and 15).

The prehistoric Aegean has three geographic areas, and each has its own distinctive artistic identity. *Cycladic* art is the art of the Cyclades Islands (so named because they "circle" around Delos), as well as of the adjacent islands in the Aegean, excluding Crete. *Minoan* art encompasses the art of Crete. *Helladic* art is the art of the Greek mainland (*Hellas* in Greek). Scholars subdivide each area chronologically into early, middle, and late periods, designating the art of the Late Helladic period Mycenaean after Agamemnon's great citadel of Mycenae.

CYCLADIC ART

Marble was abundantly available in the superb quarries of the Aegean Islands, especially on Naxos, which the sculptors of the Early Cycladic period used to produce statuettes (FIGS. 4-2 and 4-3) that collectors revere today (see "Archaeology, Art History, and the Art Market," page 88) because of their striking abstract forms, which call to mind some modern sculptures (FIGS. 29-20 and 29-61A).

SYROS WOMAN Most of the Cycladic sculptures, like many of their Stone Age predecessors in the Aegean, Anatolia, Mesopotamia, and western Europe (FIG. 1-5), represent nude women. The Cycladic examples often are women with their arms folded across their abdomens. The sculptures, which excavators have found both in graves and in settlements, vary in height from a few inches to almost life-size. The statuette illustrated here (FIG. 4-2) is about a foot and a half tall—but only about a half inch thick—and comes from a grave on the island of Syros. The sculptor rendered the human body in a highly schematic manner. Large simple triangles dominate the form—the head, the body itself (which tapers from exceptionally broad shoulders to tiny feet), and the incised triangular pubis. The feet have the toes pointed downward, so the figurine cannot stand upright and must have been placed on its back in the grave—lying down, like the deceased. Archaeologists speculate whether the Syros statuette and the many other similar Cycladic figurines known today represent dead women or fertility figures or goddesses. In any

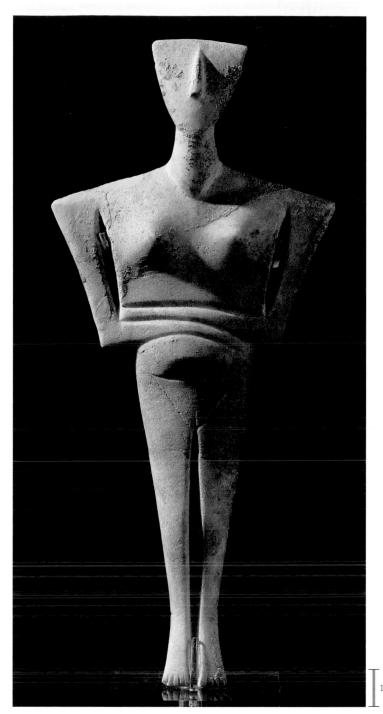

4-2 Figurine of a woman, from Syros (Cyclades), Greece, ca. 2600–2300 BCE. Marble, 1′ 6″ high. National Archaeological Museum, Athens.

Most Cycladic statuettes depict nude women. This one comes from a grave, but whether it represents the deceased is uncertain. The sculptor rendered the female body schematically as a series of triangles.

case, the sculptors took pains to emphasize the breasts as well as the pubic area. In the Syros statuette, a slight swelling of the belly may suggest pregnancy. Traces of paint found on some of the Cycladic figurines indicate that at least parts of these sculptures were colored. The now almost featureless faces would have had painted eyes and mouths in addition to the sculpted noses. Red and blue necklaces and bracelets, as well as painted dots on the cheeks and necks, characterize a number of the surviving figurines.

Archaeology, Art History, and the Art Market

One way the ancient world is fundamentally different from the world today is that ancient art is largely anonymous and undated. The systematic signing and dating of artworks—a commonplace feature in the contemporary art world—has no equivalent in antiquity. That is why the role of archaeology in the study of ancient art is so important. Only the scientific excavation of ancient monuments can establish their context. Exquisite and strikingly "modern" sculptures, such as the marble Cycladic figurines illustrated in FIGS. 4-2 and 4-3, may be appreciated as masterpieces when displayed in splendid isolation in glass cases in museums or private homes. But to understand the role these or any other artworks played in ancient society—in many cases, even to determine the date of an object—the art historian must learn the provenance of the piece. Only when the context of an artwork is known can anyone go beyond an appreciation of its formal qualities and begin to analyze its place in art history—and in the society that produced it.

The extraordinary popularity of Cycladic figurines in recent decades has had unfortunate consequences. Clandestine treasure hunters, anxious to meet the insatiable demands of collectors, have plundered many sites and smuggled their finds out of Greece to sell to the highest bidder on the international art market. Such looting has destroyed entire prehistoric cemeteries and towns because of the high esteem the marketplace has established for these sculptures. Two British scholars have calculated that only about 10 percent of the known Cycladic marble statuettes come from secure archaeological contexts. Many of the rest could be forgeries produced after World War II when developments in modern art fostered a new appreciation of these abstract renditions of human anatomy and created a boom in demand for "Cycladica" among collectors. For some categories of Cycladic sculptures—those of unusual type or size—not a single piece with a documented provenance exists. Those groups may be 20th-century inventions designed to fetch even higher prices due to their rarity. Consequently, most of the conclusions art historians have drawn about chronology, attribution to different workshops, range of types, and how the figurines were used are purely speculative. The importance of the information the original contexts would have provided cannot be overestimated. That information, however, can probably never be recovered.

4-3 Male harp player, from Keros (Cyclades), Greece, ca. 2600–2300 BCE. Marble, 9″ high. National Archaeological Museum, Athens.

The meaning of all Cycladic figurines is elusive, but this musician may be playing for the deceased in the afterlife. The statuette displays simple geometric shapes and flat planes, as in FIG. 4-2.

KEROS MUSICIAN Cycladic sculptors also represented men. The most elaborate figurines portray seated musicians, such as the harp player (FIG. 4-3) from Keros. Wedged between the echoing shapes of chair and instrument, he may be playing for the deceased in the afterlife, although, again, the meaning of these statuettes remains elusive. The harpist reflects the same preference for simple geometric shapes and large flat planes as do the female figures. Still, the artist showed a keen interest in recording the elegant shape of what must have been a prized possession: the harp with a duck-bill or swan-head ornament. (Compare the form of Sumerian harps, FIGS. 2-1, *top*, 2-9, and 2-10.)

One woman's grave contained figurines of both a musician and a reclining woman. The burial of a male figure together with

the body of a woman suggests that the harp players are not images of dead men, but it does not prove that the female figurines represent dead women. The musician might be entertaining the deceased herself, not her image, or be engaged in commemorative rites honoring the dead. (The harp player on the Hagia Triada sarcophagus, FIG. 4-1, may indicate some continuity in funerary customs and beliefs from the Cycladic to the Minoan period in the Aegean.) Given the absence of written documents in Greece at this date, as everywhere else in prehistoric times, and the lack of information about the provenance of most Cycladic sculptures, art historians cannot be sure of the meaning of these statuettes. It is likely, in fact, that the same form took on different meanings in different contexts.

MINOAN ART

During the third millennium BCE, both on the Aegean Islands and on the Greek mainland, most settlements were small and consisted only of simple buildings. Rarely were the dead buried with costly offerings such as the Cycladic statuettes just examined. In contrast, the hallmark of the opening centuries of the second millennium BCE (the Middle Minoan period on Crete) is the construction of large palaces.

Architecture

The first, or Old Palace, period ended abruptly around 1600 BCE, when fire destroyed these grand structures, probably following an earthquake. Rebuilding began almost immediately, and archaeologists consider the ensuing Late Minoan (New Palace) period the golden age of Crete, an era when the first great Western civilization emerged. The rebuilt palaces were large, comfortable, and handsome, with residential suites for the king and his family and courtyards for pageants, ceremonies, and games. They also had storerooms, offices, and shrines, which enabled these huge complexes to serve as the key administrative, commercial, and religious centers of Minoan life. The principal palace sites on Crete are at Knossos, Phaistos, Malia, Kato Zakro, and Khania. The Minoans laid out all of these complexes along similar lines. The size and number of the palaces, as well as the rich finds they have yielded, attest to the power and prosperity of the Minoans.

KNOSSOS The largest Cretan palace—at Knossos (FIGS. 4-4 and 4-5)—was the legendary home of King Minos. Here, the hero Theseus hunted the bull-man Minotaur in his labyrinth. According to the myth, after defeating the monster, Theseus found his way out of the mazelike complex only with the aid of the king's daughter,

4-4 Aerial view of the palace (looking northeast), Knossos (Crete), Greece, ca. 1700–1370 BCE. ◼◀

The Knossos palace, the largest on Crete, was the legendary home of King Minos. Its layout features a large central court surrounded by scores of residential and administrative units.

{ Reconstruction
Earlier { Existing
structures { Reconstruction

1. West porch
2. Corridor of the procession
3. South propylon
4. Central court
5. "Theater area"
6. North-south corridor
7. Pillar hall
8. Magazines
9. Throne room
10. Palace shrine and lower verandas
11. Stepped porch
12. Grand staircase
13. Light well
14. East-west corridor
15. Hall of the Double Axes (principal reception room)
16. "Queen's Megaron"

0 25 50 75 100 feet
0 10 20 30 meters

4-5 Plan of the palace, Knossos (Crete), Greece, ca. 1700–1370 BCE.

The mazelike plan of the Knossos palace gave rise to the Greek myth of the Cretan labyrinth inhabited by the Minotaur, a half-man half-bull monster that King Theseus of Athens slew.

Ariadne. She had given Theseus a spindle of thread to mark his path through the labyrinth and safely find his way out again. In fact, the English word labyrinth derives from the intricate plan and scores of rooms of the Knossos palace. *Labrys* ("double ax") serves as a recurring motif in the Minoan palace and in Minoan art generally (FIG. 4-1, *left*), referring to sacrificial slaughter. The *labyrinth* was the "House of the Double Ax."

The Knossos palace was a rambling structure built against the upper slopes and across the top of a low hill that rises from a fertile plain (FIG. 4-4). All around the palace proper were mansions and villas of the Minoan elite. The central feature of the palace was its great rectangular court (FIG. 4-5, no. 4). The builders carefully planned the structure with clusters of rooms of similar function grouped around this primary space. A secondary organization of the palace plan involves two long corridors. On the west side of the court, a north-south corridor (FIG. 4-5, no. 6) separates official and ceremonial rooms from the magazines (no. 8), where the Minoans stored wine, grain, oil, and honey in large jars. On the east side of the court, a smaller east-west corridor (no. 14) separates the administrative areas (to the south) from the workrooms (to the north). At the northwest corner of the palace is a theater-like area (no. 5) with steps on two sides that may have served as seats. This arrangement is a possible forerunner of the later Greek theater (FIG. 5-71). Its purpose is unknown, but the feature also appears in the Phaistos palace.

The Knossos palace was complex in elevation as well as plan. It had as many as three stories around the central court and even more on the south and east sides where the terrain sloped off sharply. Interior light and air wells with staircases (FIG. 4-6) provided necessary illumination and ventilation. The Minoans also addressed practical issues such as drainage of rainwater. At Knossos, a remarkably efficient system of *terracotta* (baked clay) pipes underlies the enormous building.

The Cretan palaces were sturdy structures, with thick walls composed of rough, unshaped fieldstones embedded in clay. For corners and around door and window openings, the builders used large ashlar blocks. The painted wooden columns (which Evans restored in cement at Knossos) have distinctive capitals and shafts (FIG. 4-6). The bulbous, cushionlike Minoan capitals resemble those of the later Greek Doric order (FIG. 5-13, *left*), but the column shafts—essentially stylized inverted tree trunks—taper from a wide top to a narrower base, the opposite of both Egyptian and later Greek columns.

Painting

Mural paintings liberally adorned the palace at Knossos, constituting one of its most striking features. The brightly painted walls and the red shafts and black capitals of the wooden columns produced an extraordinarily rich effect. The paintings depict many aspects of Minoan life (bull-leaping, processions, and ceremonies) and of nature (birds, animals, flowers, and marine life).

LA PARISIENNE From a ceremonial scene of uncertain significance comes the fragment (FIG. 4-7) dubbed *La Parisienne* (The Parisian Woman) on its discovery because of the elegant dress, elaborate coiffure, and full rouged lips of the young woman depicted. Some have identified her as a priestess taking part in a religious ritual, but because the figure has no arms, it is most likely a statue of a goddess. Although the representation is still convention-bound (note especially the oversized frontal eye in the profile head), the charm and freshness of the mural are undeniable. Unlike the Egyptians, who painted in fresco secco (dry fresco), the Minoans

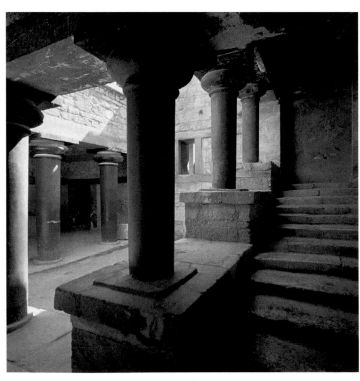

4-6 Stairwell in the residential quarter of the palace, Knossos (Crete), Greece, ca. 1700–1370 BCE. ◼◀

The Knossos palace was complex in elevation as well as plan. It had at least three stories on all sides of the court. Minoan columns taper from top to bottom, the opposite of Egyptian and Greek columns.

4-7 Minoan woman or goddess (*La Parisienne*), from the palace, Knossos (Crete), Greece, ca. 1400–1370 BCE. Fragment of a fresco, 10″ high. Archaeological Museum, Herakleion. ◼◀

Frescoes decorated the Knossos palace walls. This fragment depicts a woman or a goddess—perhaps a statue—with a large frontal eye in her profile head, as in Mesopotamian and Egyptian art.

1 in.

coated the rough fabric of their rubble walls with a fine white lime plaster and used a true (wet) fresco method in which the painter applies the pigments while the walls are still wet. The color consequently becomes chemically bonded to the plaster after it dries (see "Fresco Painting," Chapter 14, page 408). The Minoan painters therefore had to execute their work rapidly, in contrast to Egyptian practice, which permitted slower, more deliberate work.

BULL-LEAPING Another fresco (FIG. 4-8) from the palace at Knossos depicts the Minoan ceremony of bull-leaping, in which young men grasped the horns of a bull and vaulted onto its back— a perilous and extremely difficult acrobatic maneuver. Excavators recovered only fragments of the full composition (the dark patches are original; the rest is a modern restoration). The Minoan artist provided no setting, instead focusing all attention on the three protagonists and the fearsome bull. The young women have fair skin and the leaping youth has dark skin in accord with the widely accepted ancient convention for distinguishing male and female, as on the Hagia Triada sarcophagus (FIG. 4-1; compare FIG. 3-11A). The painter brilliantly suggested the powerful charge of the bull by elongating the animal's shape and using sweeping lines to form a funnel of energy, beginning at the very narrow hindquarters of the bull and culminating in its large, sharp horns and galloping fore-

legs. The highly animated human figures also have stylized shapes, with typically Minoan pinched waists. Although the profile pose with the full-view eye was a familiar convention in Egypt and Mesopotamia, the elegance of the Cretan figures, with their long, curly hair and proud and self-confident bearing, distinguishes them from all other early figure styles. In contrast to the angularity of the figures in Egyptian wall paintings, the curving lines the Minoan artist employed suggest the elasticity of living and moving beings.

THERA Much better preserved than the Knossos frescoes are the mural paintings Greek archaeologists discovered in their ongoing excavations at Akrotiri on the volcanic island of Thera in the Cyclades, some 60 miles north of Crete. In the Late Cycladic period, Thera was artistically (and possibly also politically) within the Minoan orbit. The Akrotiri murals are invaluable additions to the fragmentary and frequently misrestored frescoes from Crete. The excellent condition of the Theran paintings is due to an enormous seismic explosion on the island that buried Akrotiri in volcanic pumice and ash, making it a kind of Pompeii of the prehistoric Aegean (see "The Theran Eruption and the Chronology of Aegean Art," page 92). The Akrotiri frescoes decorated the walls of houses, not the walls of a great palace like Minos's at Knossos, and therefore the number of painted walls from the site is especially impressive.

4-8 Bull-leaping, from the palace, Knossos (Crete), Greece, ca. 1400–1370 BCE. Fresco, 2′ 8″ high, including border. Archaeological Museum, Herakleion. ◼◀

The subjects of the Knossos frescoes are often ceremonial scenes, such as this one of bull-leaping. The women have fair skin and the man has dark skin, a common convention in ancient painting.

1 ft.

The Theran Eruption and the Chronology of Aegean Art

Today, ships bound for the beautiful Greek island of Thera, with its picture-postcard white houses, churches, shops, and restaurants, weigh anchor in a bay beneath steep cliffs. Until about 20,000 BCE, however, Thera had gentler slopes. Then, suddenly, a volcanic eruption blew out the center of the island, leaving behind the crescent-shaped main island and several lesser islands grouped around a bay that roughly corresponds to the shape of the gigantic ancient volcano. The volcano erupted again, thousands of years later, during the zenith of Aegean civilization.

The site of Akrotiri, which Greek excavators have been gradually uncovering for a half century, was buried in that later explosion by a layer of pumice more than a yard deep in some areas and by an even larger volume of volcanic ash (*tephra*) that often exceeds five yards in depth, even after nearly 37 centuries of erosion. Tephra filled whole rooms, and boulders the volcano spewed forth pelted the walls of some houses. Closer to the volcano's cone, the tephra is almost 60 yards deep in places. In fact, the force of the eruption was so powerful that sea currents carried the pumice and wind blew the ash throughout much of the eastern Mediterranean, not only to Crete, Rhodes, and Cyprus but also as far away as Anatolia, Egypt, Syria, and Israel.

A generation ago, most scholars embraced the theory formulated by Spyridon Marinatos (1901–1974), an eminent Greek archae-

ologist, that the otherwise unexplained demise of Minoan civilization on Crete around 1500 BCE was the by-product of the volcanic eruption on Thera. According to Marinatos, devastating famine followed the rain of ash that fell on Crete. But archaeologists now know that after the eruption, life went on in Crete, if not on Thera.

Teams of researchers, working closely in an impressive and most welcome interdisciplinary effort, have determined that a major climatic event occurred during the last third of the 17th century BCE. In addition to collecting evidence from Thera, they have studied tree rings at sites in Europe and in North America for evidence of retarded growth and have examined ice cores in Greenland for peak acidity layers. The scientific data pinpoint a significant disruption in weather patterns in 1628 BCE. Most scholars now believe the cause of this disruption was the cataclysmic volcanic eruption on Thera. The date of the Aegean catastrophe remains the subject of much debate, however, and many archaeologists favor placing the eruption in the 16th century BCE. In either case, the date of Thera's destruction has profound consequences for determining the chronology of Aegean art. If the Akrotiri frescoes (FIGS. 4-9 to 4-9B) date between 1650 and 1625 BCE, they are at least 150 years older than scholars thought not long ago, and are much older than the Knossos palace murals (FIGS. 4-7 and 4-8).

4-9 Landscape with swallows (*Spring Fresco*) from room Delta 2, Akrotiri, Thera (Cyclades), Greece, ca. 1650–1625 BCE. Fresco, 7′ 6″ high. National Archaeological Museum, Athens.

Aegean muralists painted in wet fresco, which required rapid execution. In this wraparound landscape, the painter used vivid colors and undulating lines to capture the essence of nature.

The almost perfectly preserved mural painting from Akrotiri known as the *Spring Fresco* (FIG. 4-9) is the largest and most complete prehistoric example of a pure landscape painting (compare FIG. 1-17). Landscapes—and seascapes—are key elements of many

of the mural paintings found at Akrotiri (FIGS. 4-9A and 4-9B). In each case, however, the artist's aim was not to render the rocky island terrain realistically but rather to capture its essence. In FIG. 4-9, the irrationally undulating and vividly colored rocks, the graceful lilies swaying in the cool island breezes, and the darting swallows express the vigor of growth, the delicacy of flowering, and the lightness of birdsong and flight. In the lyrical language of curving line, the artist celebrated the rhythms of nature. The *Spring Fresco* represents the polar opposite of the first efforts at mural painting in the caves of Paleolithic Europe (see Chapter 1), where animals (and occasionally humans) appeared as isolated figures with no indication of setting.

MINOAN POTTERY The love of nature manifested itself in Crete on the surfaces of painted vases even before the period of the new palaces. During the Middle Minoan period, Cretan potters fashioned sophisticated shapes using newly introduced potters' wheels, and decorated their vases in a distinctive and fully polychromatic style. These Kamares Ware vessels, named for the cave on the slope of Mount Ida where they were first discovered, have been found in

quantity at Phaistos and Knossos. Some examples come from as far away as Egypt. On the jar in FIG. 4-10, as on other Kamares vases, the painter applied creamy white and reddish-brown decoration to a rich black ground. The central motif is a great leaping fish and perhaps a fishnet surrounded by a host of curvilinear abstract patterns including waves and spirals. The swirling lines evoke life in the sea, and both the abstract and the natural forms beautifully complement the shape of the vessel.

The sea and the creatures that inhabit it also inspired the Late Minoan Marine Style octopus flask (FIG. 4-11) from Palaikastro. The tentacles of the octopus reach out over the curving surfaces of the vessel, embracing the piece and emphasizing its volume. The flask is a masterful realization of the relationship between the vessel's decoration and its shape, always a problem for the vase painter. This later jar, which is contemporaneous with the new palaces at Knossos and elsewhere, differs markedly from its Kamares Ware predecessor in color. Not only is the octopus vase more muted in tone, but the Late Minoan artist also reversed the earlier scheme and placed dark silhouettes on a light ground. Dark-on-light coloration remained the norm for about a millennium in Greece, until about 530 BCE when, albeit in a very different form, light figures on a dark ground emerged once again as the preferred manner (FIG. 5-21).

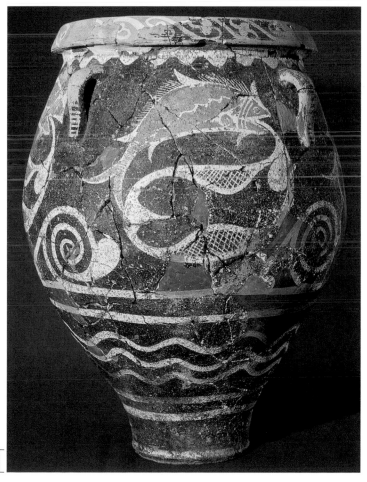

1 in.

4-10 Kamares Ware jar, from Phaistos (Crete), Greece, ca. 1800–1700 BCE. 1′ 8″ high. Archaeological Museum, Herakleion.

Kamares vases have creamy white and reddish-brown decoration on a black background. This jar combines a fish (and a net?) with curvilinear abstract patterns including spirals and waves.

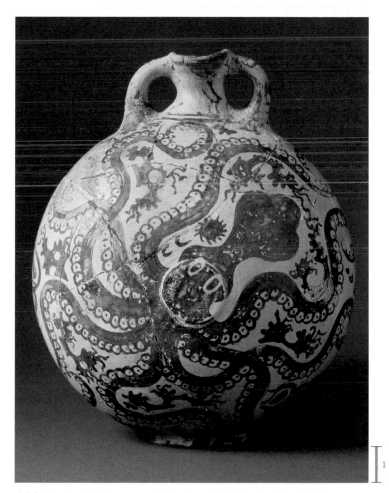

1 in.

4-11 Marine Style octopus flask, from Palaikastro (Crete), Greece, ca. 1450 BCE. 11″ high. Archaeological Museum, Herakleion.

Marine Style vases have dark figures on a light ground. On this octopus flask, the tentacles of the sea creature reach out over the curving surface of the vessel to fill the shape perfectly.

Sculpture

In contrast to Mesopotamia and Egypt, Minoan Crete has yielded no trace of temples or monumental statues of gods, kings, or monsters. Large wooden images may once have existed—*La Parisienne* (FIG. 4-7) perhaps is a depiction of one of them—but what remains of Minoan sculpture is uniformly small in scale.

SNAKE GODDESS One of the most striking finds from the palace at Knossos is the *faience* (low-fired opaque glasslike silicate) statuette popularly known as the *Snake Goddess* (FIG. **4-12**). Reconstructed from many pieces, it is one of several similar figurines that some scholars believe may represent mortal priestesses rather than a deity, although the prominently exposed breasts suggest that these figurines stand in the long line of prehistoric fertility images usually considered divinities. The Knossos woman holds snakes in her hands and supports a tamed leopardlike feline on her head. This implied power over the animal world also seems appropriate for a deity. The frontality of the figure is reminiscent of Egyptian and Mesopotamian statuary, but the costume, with its open bodice and flounced skirt, is distinctly Minoan. If the statuette represents a goddess, as seems likely, it is yet another example of how human beings fashion their gods in their own image.

PALAIKASTRO YOUTH British excavations at Palaikastro between 1987 and 1990 yielded fragments of one of the most remarkable objects ever found on Crete. It is a statuette (FIG. **4-13**) nearly 20 inches tall, fashioned from hippopotamus-tusk ivory, gold, serpentine, and rock crystal. The figurine is a very early example of *chryselephantine* (gold-and-ivory) sculpture, a technique the Greeks would later use for their largest and costliest cult images (FIG. 5-46). The Minoans probably imported the ivory and gold from Egypt, the source also of the pose with left foot advanced

1 in.

4-12 *Snake Goddess,* from the palace, Knossos (Crete), Greece, ca. 1600 BCE. Faience, 1' 1½" high. Archaeological Museum, Herakleion.

This figurine may represent a priestess, but it is more likely a bare-breasted goddess. The snakes in her hands and the feline on her head imply that she has power over the animal world.

1 in.

4-13 Young god(?), from Palaikastro (Crete), Greece, ca. 1500–1450 BCE. Ivory, gold, serpentine, and rock crystal, restored height 1' 7½". Archaeological Museum, Siteia.

This statuette, probably representing a young god, is a very early example of chryselephantine (gold-and-ivory) sculpture, a technique later used for the largest and costliest Greek cult statues.

4-14 *Harvesters Vase,* from Hagia Triada (Crete), Greece, ca. 1500–1450 BCE. Steatite, originally with gold leaf, greatest diameter 5". Archaeological Museum, Herakleion.

The relief sculptor of the singing harvesters on this small stone vase was one of the first artists in history to represent the underlying muscular and skeletal structure of the human body.

1 in.

(FIG. 3-12), but the style and iconography are unmistakably Cretan. The work is the creation of a sculptor of extraordinary ability who delighted in rendering minute details of muscles and veins. The Palaikastro youth (his coiffure, with shaved head save for a central braid, indicates his age) stood alone in a shrine and therefore seems to have been a god rather than a mortal. The excavators found the statuette in scattered and blackened fragments, suggesting fire following a willful destruction of the sacred image in the 15th century BCE.

HARVESTERS VASE The finest surviving example of Minoan relief sculpture is the so-called *Harvesters Vase* (FIG. **4-14**) from Hagia Triada. Only the upper half of the egg-shaped body and neck of the vessel remain. Missing are the lower parts of the harvesters (or, as some think, sowers) and the ground on which they stand as well as the gold leaf that originally covered the relief figures. Formulaic scenes of sowing and harvesting were staples of Egyptian funerary art (FIG. 3-15), but the Minoan artist shunned static repetition in favor of a composition bursting with the energy of its individually characterized figures. The relief shows a riotous crowd singing and shouting as they go to or return from the fields. The artist vividly captured the forward movement and lusty exuberance of the youths.

Although most of the figures conform to the age-old convention of combined profile and frontal views, the relief sculptor singled out one figure (FIG. 4-14, *right of center*) from his companions. He shakes a *sistrum* (an Egyptian percussion instrument or rattle) to beat time, and the artist depicted him in full profile with his lungs so inflated with air that his ribs show. This is one of the first instances in the history of art of a sculptor showing a keen interest in the underlying muscular and skeletal structure of the human body. The Minoan artist's painstaking study of human anatomy is a singular achievement, especially given the size of the *Harvesters*

Vase, barely five inches at its greatest diameter. Equally noteworthy is how the sculptor recorded the tension and relaxation of facial muscles with astonishing exactitude, not only for this figure but for his nearest companions as well. This degree of animation of the human face is without precedent in ancient art.

MINOAN DECLINE Scholars dispute the circumstances ending the Minoan civilization, although most now believe Mycenaeans had already moved onto Crete and established themselves at Knossos at the end of the New Palace period. From the palace at Knossos, these intruders appear to have ruled the island for at least a half century, perhaps much longer. Parts of the palace continued to be occupied until its final destruction around 1200 BCE, but its importance as a cultural center faded soon after 1400 BCE, as the focus of Aegean civilization shifted to the Greek mainland.

MYCENAEAN ART

The origin of the Mycenaeans is also the subject of continuing debate among archaeologists and historians. The only certainty is the presence of these forerunners of the Greeks on the mainland about the time of the construction of the old palaces on Crete—that is, about the beginning of the second millennium BCE. Doubtless, Cretan civilization influenced these people even then, and some scholars believe the mainland was a Minoan economic dependency for a long time. In any case, Mycenaean power developed in the north in the days of the new palaces on Crete, and by 1500 BCE a distinctive Mycenaean culture was flourishing in Greece. Several centuries later, Homer described Mycenae as "rich in gold." The dramatic discoveries of Schliemann and his successors have fully justified this characterization, even if today's archaeologists no longer view the Mycenaeans solely through the eyes of Homer.

4-15 Aerial view of the citadel (looking east), Tiryns, Greece, ca. 1400–1200 BCE.

In the *Iliad*, Homer called the fortified citadel of Tiryns the city "of the great walls." Its huge, roughly cut stone blocks are examples of Cyclopean masonry, named after the mythical one-eyed giants.

Architecture

The destruction of the Cretan palaces left the mainland culture supreme. Although historians usually refer to this Late Helladic civilization as Mycenaean, Mycenae was but one of several large palace complexes. Archaeologists have also unearthed Mycenaean remains at Tiryns, Orchomenos, Pylos, and elsewhere, and a section of a Mycenaean fortification wall is still in place on the Acropolis of Athens. The best-preserved and most impressive Mycenaean remains are those of the fortified palaces at Tiryns and Mycenae. Construction of both citadels began about 1400 BCE. Both palaces burned (along with all the others) between 1250 and 1200 BCE when northern invaders overran the Mycenaeans or they fell victim to internal warfare.

TIRYNS Homer knew the citadel of Tiryns (FIG. 4-15), located about 10 miles from Mycenae, as "Tiryns of the Great Walls." In the second century CE, when Pausanias, author of an invaluable guidebook to Greece, visited the long-abandoned site, he marveled at the towering fortifications and considered the walls of Tiryns as spectacular as the pyramids of Egypt. Indeed, the Greeks of the historical age believed mere humans could not have built these enormous edifices. They attributed the construction of the great Mycenaean

4-16 Corbel-vaulted gallery in the circuit wall of the citadel, Tiryns, Greece, ca. 1400–1200 BCE.

In this long gallery within the circuit wall of Tiryns, the Mycenaeans piled irregular Cyclopean blocks in horizontal courses and then cantilevered them until the two walls met in a pointed arch.

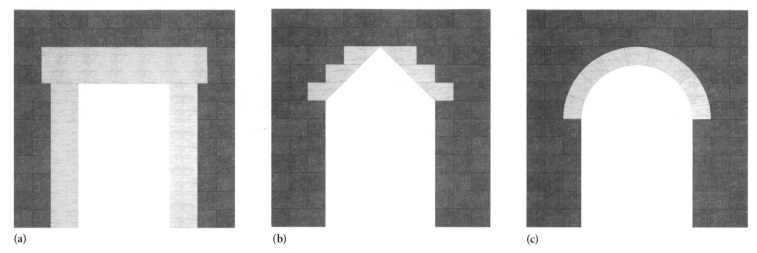

(a)   (b)   (c)

4-17 Three methods of spanning a passageway: (a) post and lintel, (b) corbeled arch, (c) arch (John Burge).

Post-and-lintel construction **(a)** was the norm in ancient Greece, but the Mycenaeans also used corbeled arches **(b)**. The round arch **(c)**, used already in Mesopotamia, was popular later in Rome.

citadels to the mythical *Cyclopes,* a race of one-eyed giants. Architectural historians still employ the term *Cyclopean masonry* to refer to the huge, roughly cut stone blocks forming the massive fortification walls of Tiryns and other Mycenaean sites.

The heavy walls of Tiryns and Mycenae contrast sharply with the open Cretan palaces (FIG. 4-4) and clearly reveal their defensive character. Those of Tiryns average about 20 feet in thickness, and in one section they incorporate a long gallery (FIG. 4-16) covered by corbeled vaults (FIG. 4-17*b*) similar to those constructed long before at Neolithic sites such as Newgrange (FIG. 1-18). At Tiryns, the builders piled the large, irregular Cyclopean blocks in horizontal courses and then cantilevered them inward until the two walls met in a pointed arch. The builders used no mortar. The vault is held in place only by the weight of the blocks (often several tons each), by the smaller stones used as wedges, and by the clay that fills some of the empty spaces. This primitive but effective vaulting scheme possesses an earthy monumentality. It is easy to see how a later age came to believe that the uncouth Cyclopes were responsible for these massive but unsophisticated fortifications.

The Mycenaean engineers who designed the circuit wall of Tiryns compelled would-be attackers to approach the palace (FIG. 4-18) within the walls via a long ramp that forced the soldiers (usually right-handed; compare FIG. 4-26) to expose their unshielded sides to the Mycenaean defenders above. Then—if they got that far—the enemy forces had to pass through a series of narrow gates that also could be defended easily. Inside, at Tiryns as elsewhere, the most important element in the palace plan was the *megaron,* or reception hall and throne room, of the king. The main room of the megaron had a throne against the right wall and a central hearth bordered by four Minoan-style wooden columns serving as supports for the roof. A vestibule with a columnar facade preceded the throne room. The remains of the megaron at Tiryns are scant, but at Pylos, home of Homer's King Nestor, archaeologists found sufficient evidence to permit a reconstruction (FIG. 4-18A) of the original appearance of that palace's megaron, complete with mural and ceiling paintings.

4-18A Megaron, Palace of Nestor, Pylos, ca. 1300 BCE.

4-18 Plan of the palace and southern part of the citadel, Tiryns, Greece, ca. 1400–1200 BCE.

The king's reception room, or megaron, was the main feature of a Mycenaean palace. It had a columnar porch leading to a hall containing the throne and a central hearth bordered by four columns.

Megaron

Citadel walls

Approach ramp

Main gate

Citadel walls

Outer propylon

N

0   25   50   75   100 feet
0   10   20   30 meters

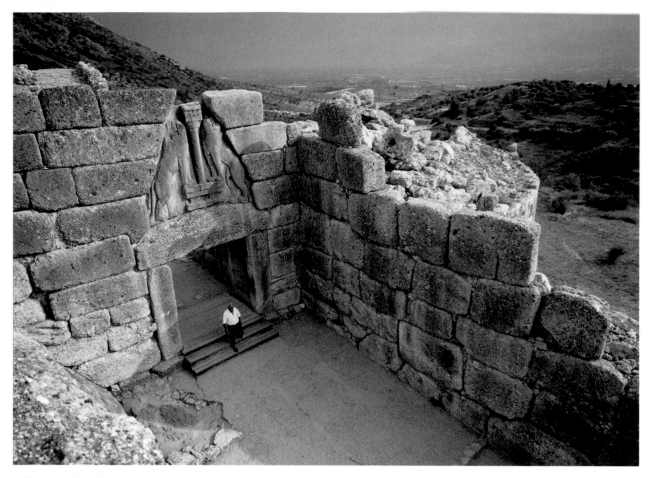

4-19 Lion Gate (looking southeast), Mycenae, Greece, ca. 1300–1250 BCE. Limestone, relief panel 9′ 6″ high. ■◀

The largest sculpture in the prehistoric Aegean is the relief of confronting lions that fills the relieving triangle of Mycenae's main gate. The gate itself consists of two great monoliths and a huge lintel.

4-20 Treasury of Atreus, Mycenae, Greece, ca. 1300–1250 BCE. ■◀

The best-preserved Mycenaean tholos tomb is named after Homer's King Atreus. An earthen mound covers the burial chamber, reached through a doorway at the end of a long passageway.

LION GATE, MYCENAE Although frescoed walls were commonplace in the Mycenaean fortress-palaces, as in the Cretan palaces, monumental sculpture was rare. Agamemnon's Mycenae was the exception. The so-called Lion Gate (FIG. 4-19) is the outer gateway of the stronghold at Mycenae. It is protected on the left by a wall built on a natural rock outcropping and on the right by a projecting bastion of large blocks. Any approaching enemies would have had to enter this 20-foot-wide channel and face Mycenaean defenders above them on both sides. The gate itself consists of two great upright monoliths (*posts*) capped with a huge horizontal *lintel* (FIG. 4-17*a*). Above the lintel, the masonry courses form a *corbeled arch* (FIG. 4-17*b*), leaving an opening that lightens the weight the lintel carries. Filling this *relieving triangle* is a great limestone slab with two lions in high relief facing a central Minoan-type column. The whole design admirably matches its triangular shape, harmonizing in dignity, strength, and scale with the massive stones that form the walls and gate. Similar groups appear in miniature on Cretan seals, but the concept of placing monstrous guardian figures at the entrances to palaces, tombs, and sacred places has its origin in Mesopotamia and Egypt (FIGS. 2-18A, 2-20, and 3-10). At Mycenae, the sculptors fashioned the animals' heads separately. Because those heads are lost, some scholars have speculated that the "lions" perhaps were composite beasts, possibly sphinxes or *griffins* (winged lions with eagles' heads).

TREASURY OF ATREUS The Mycenaeans erected the Lion Gate and the towering fortification wall of which it formed a part a few generations before the presumed date of the Trojan War. At that time, elite families buried their dead outside the citadel walls in beehive-shaped tombs covered by enormous earthen mounds. Nine such tombs remain at Mycenae and scores more at other sites. The best preserved of these *tholos tombs* is Mycenae's so-called Treasury of Atreus (FIG. 4-20), which already in antiquity people mistakenly believed was the repository of the treasure of Atreus, father of Agamemnon and Menelaus. A long passageway (*dromos*) leads to a doorway surmounted by a relieving triangle similar to that in the roughly contemporaneous Lion Gate, but without figural ornamentation. Both the doorway and the relieving triangle, however, once had engaged columns on each side, preserved in fragments today. The burial chamber, or *tholos* (FIG. 4-21), consists of a series of stone corbeled courses laid on a circular base to form a lofty *dome*. The builders probably constructed the vault using rough-hewn blocks. After they set the stones in place, the masons had to finish the surfaces with great precision to make them conform to both the horizontal and vertical curvature of the wall. The principle involved is no different from that of the corbeled gallery (FIG. 4-16) of Tiryns. But the problem of constructing a complete dome is far more complicated, and the execution of the vault in the Treasury of Atreus is much more sophisticated than that of the vaulted gallery at Tiryns. About 43 feet high, this Mycenaean dome was at the time the largest vaulted space without interior supports that had ever been built. The achievement was not surpassed until the Romans constructed the Pantheon (FIG. 7-51) almost 1,500 years later using a new technology—concrete construction—unknown to the Mycenaeans.

Metalwork, Sculpture, and Painting

The Treasury of Atreus was thoroughly looted long before its modern rediscovery, but archaeologists have unearthed spectacular grave goods elsewhere at Mycenae. Just inside the Lion Gate, Schliemann uncovered what archaeologists call Grave Circle A (FIG. 4-22A). It predates the Lion Gate and the walls of Mycenae by some three centuries, and encloses six deep shafts that served as tombs for the kings and their families. The Mycenaeans lowered the royal corpses into their deep graves with masks covering the men's faces, recalling the Egyptian funerary practice (see "Mummification and Immortality," Chapter 3, page 61). Jewelry adorned the bodies of the women, and weapons and golden cups accompanied the men into the afterlife.

4-22A Grave Circle A, Mycenae, ca. 1600 BCE.

4-21 **Interior of the Treasury of Atreus, Mycenae, Greece, ca. 1300–1250 BCE.** ◼◀

The beehive-shaped tholos of the Treasury of Atreus consists of corbeled courses of stone blocks laid on a circular base. The 43-foot-high dome was the largest in the world for almost 1,500 years.

4-22 Funerary mask, from Grave Circle A, Mycenae, Greece, ca. 1600–1500 BCE. Beaten gold, 1′ high. National Archaeological Museum, Athens. ◼◂

Homer described the Mycenaeans as "rich in gold." This beaten (repoussé) gold mask of a bearded man comes from a royal shaft grave. It is one of the first attempts at life-size sculpture in Greece.

MASKS AND DAGGERS The Mycenaeans used the *repoussé* technique to fashion the masks Schliemann found—that is, goldsmiths hammered the shape of each mask from a single sheet of metal and pushed the features out from behind. Art historians have often compared the mask illustrated here (FIG. 4-22) to Tutankhamen's gold mummy mask (FIG. 3-35), but it is important to remember that the Mycenaean metalworker was one of the first

in Greece to produce a sculpted image of the human face at life-size. Tutankhamen's mask stands in a long line of monumental Egyptian sculptures going back more than a millennium. No one knows whether the Mycenaean masks were intended as portraits, but the artists recorded different physical types with care. The masks found in Grave Circle A portray youthful faces as well as mature ones. The mask in FIG. 4-22, with its full beard, must depict a mature man, perhaps a king—although not Agamemnon, as Schliemann wished. If Agamemnon was a real king, he lived some 300 years after the death of the man who wore this mask. Clearly, the Mycenaeans were "rich in gold" long before Homer's heroes fought at Troy.

Also found in Grave Circle A were several magnificent bronze dagger blades inlaid with gold, silver, and *niello* (a black metallic alloy), again attesting to the wealth of the Mycenaean kings as well as to their warlike nature. The largest and most elaborate of the group features on one side (FIG. 4-23) a scene of four hunters attacking a lion that has struck down a fifth hunter, while two other lions flee. The other side (not illustrated) depicts lions attacking deer. The slim-waisted, long-haired figures are Minoan in style, but the artist borrowed the subject from the repertoire of Egypt and Mesopotamia. It is likely that a Minoan metalworker made the dagger for a Mycenaean patron who admired Minoan art but whose tastes in subject matter differed from those of his Cretan counterparts. Excavations at other Mycenaean sites have produced other luxurious objects decorated with Minoan-style figures. Chief among them is the pair of gold drinking cups (FIG. 4-23A) from a tholos tomb at Vapheio.

4-23A Gold drinking cup, Vapheio, ca. 1600–1500 BCE.

IVORY GODDESSES Gold was not the only opulent material elite Mycenaean patrons demanded for the objects they commissioned. For a shrine within the palace at Mycenae, a master sculptor carved an intricately detailed group of two women and a

4-23 Inlaid dagger blade with lion hunt, from Grave Circle A, Mycenae, Greece, ca. 1600–1500 BCE. Bronze, inlaid with gold, silver, and niello, 9″ long. National Archaeological Museum, Athens.

The burial goods in Grave Circle A included costly weapons. The lion hunters on this bronze dagger are Minoan in style, but the metalworker borrowed the subject from Egypt and Mesopotamia.

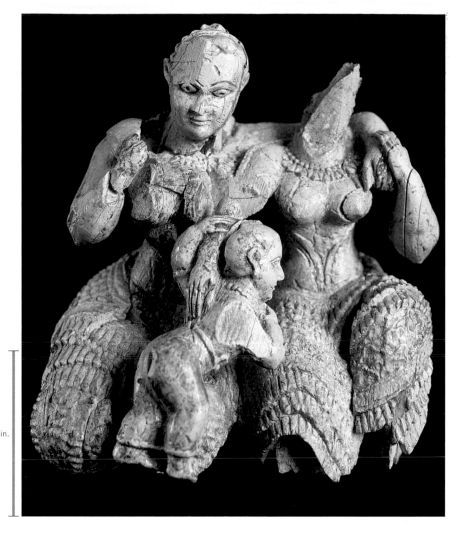

1 in.

4-24 Two goddesses(?) and a child, from Mycenae, Greece, ca. 1400–1250 BCE. Ivory, $2\frac{3}{4}''$ high. National Archaeological Museum, Athens.

Made of rare imported ivory, perhaps by a Cretan artist, this statuette may represent deities later paralleled in Greek mythology, but their identity and even the gender of the child are uncertain.

child (FIG. **4-24**) from a single piece of costly imported ivory. The women's costumes with breasts exposed have the closest parallels in Minoan art, and this statuette is probably of Cretan manufacture. The intimate and tender theme also is foreign to the known Mycenaean repertoire, in which scenes of hunting and warfare dominate.

The identity of the three figures remains a mystery. Some scholars have suggested that the two women are the "two queens" mentioned in inscriptions found in the excavation of the Mycenaean palace at Pylos (FIG. 4-18A). Others have speculated that the two women are deities, Mycenaean forerunners of the Greek agricultural goddesses Demeter and Persephone (see "The Gods and Goddesses of Mount Olympus," Chapter 5, page 107) and that the child is Triptolemos, the hero who spread the gift of agriculture to the Greeks. That myth, however, probably postdates the Mycenaean era.

MONUMENTAL STATUARY Large-scale figural art is very rare on the Greek mainland, as on Crete, other than the paintings that once adorned the walls of Mycenaean palaces (FIG. 4-18A). The triangular relief of the Lion Gate at Mycenae is exceptional, as is the painted plaster head (FIG. **4-25**) of a woman, goddess, or, perhaps, sphinx found at Mycenae. The white flesh tone indicates the head is female. The hair and eyes are dark blue, almost black, and the lips, ears, and headband are red. The artist decorated the cheeks and chin with red circles surrounded by a ring of red dots, recalling the facial paint or tattoos recorded on Early Cycladic figurines of women. Although the large staring eyes give the face a menacing, if not terrifying, expression appropriate for a guardian figure such as a sphinx, the closest parallels to this work in the prehistoric Aegean are terracotta images of goddesses. This head may therefore be a fragment of a very early monumental cult statue in Greece, many times the size of the Palaikastro youth (FIG. 4-13).

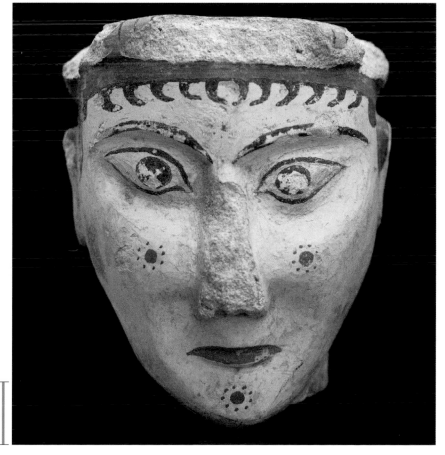

1 in.

4-25 Female head, from Mycenae, Greece, ca. 1300–1250 BCE. Painted plaster, $6\frac{1}{2}''$ high. National Archaeological Museum, Athens.

This painted white plaster head of a woman with staring eyes may be a fragment of a very early monumental statue of a goddess in Greece, but some scholars think it is the head of a sphinx.

Mycenaean Art **101**

4-26 *Warrior Vase* (krater), from Mycenae, Greece, ca. 1200 BCE. 1′ 4″ high. National Archaeological Museum, Athens.

This mixing bowl shows a woman bidding farewell to a column of heavily armed Mycenaean warriors depicted using both silhouette and outline and a combination of frontal and profile views.

Were it not for this plaster head and a few other exceptional pieces, art historians might have concluded, wrongly, that the Mycenaeans had no monumental freestanding statuary—a reminder that it is always dangerous to generalize from the chance remains of an ancient civilization. Nonetheless, life-size Aegean statuary must have been rare. After the collapse of Mycenaean civilization and for the next several hundred years, no attempts at monumental statuary are evident until, after the waning of the Dark Ages, Greek sculptors became exposed to the great sculptural tradition of Egypt (see Chapter 5).

WARRIOR VASE An art form that did continue throughout the period after the downfall of the Mycenaean palaces was vase painting. One of the latest examples of Mycenaean painting is the *krater* (bowl for mixing wine and water) commonly called the *Warrior Vase* (FIG. **4-26**) after its prominent frieze of soldiers

marching off to war. At the left a woman bids farewell to the column of heavily armed warriors moving away from her. The painting on this vase has no indication of setting and lacks the landscape elements that commonly appear in earlier Minoan and Mycenaean art. All the soldiers repeat the same pattern, a far cry from the variety and anecdotal detail of the lively procession shown on the Minoan *Harvesters Vase* (FIG. 4-14).

This simplification of narrative has parallels in the increasingly schematic and abstract treatment of marine life on other painted vases. The octopus, for example, eventually became a stylized motif composed of concentric circles and spirals that are almost unrecognizable as a sea creature. By Homer's time, the apogee of Aegean civilization was but a distant memory, and the men and women of Crete and Mycenae—Minos and Ariadne, Agamemnon and Helen—had assumed the stature of heroes from a lost golden age.

THE PREHISTORIC AEGEAN

EARLY CYCLADIC ART ca. 3000–2000 BCE

▌ Marble statuettes are the major surviving artworks of the Cyclades Islands during the third millennium BCE, but little is known about their function.

▌ Many of the Cycladic figurines come from graves and may represent the deceased, but others, for example, musicians, almost certainly do not. Whatever their meaning, these statuettes mark the beginning of the long history of marble sculpture in Greece.

Harp player, Keros,
ca. 2600–2300 BCE

LATE MINOAN ART ca. 1600–1200 BCE

▌ The Old Palace period (ca. 2000–1600 BCE) on Crete brought the construction of the first palaces on the island, but the golden age of Crete was the Late Minoan period.

▌ The greatest Late Minoan palace was at Knossos. A vast multistory structure arranged around a central court, the Knossos palace was so complex in plan that it gave rise to the myth of the Minotaur in the labyrinth of King Minos.

▌ The largest art form in the Minoan world was fresco painting. The murals depicted rituals (such as bull-leaping), landscapes, seascapes, and other subjects.

▌ Vase painting also flourished. Sea motifs—the octopus, for example—were popular subjects.

▌ Surviving examples of Minoan sculpture are of small scale. They include statuettes of "snake goddesses" and reliefs on stone vases.

Bull-leaping fresco, Knossos,
ca. 1400–1370 BCE

Snake Goddess, Knossos,
ca. 1600 BCE

MYCENAEAN (LATE HELLADIC) ART ca. 1600–1200 BCE

▌ The Mycenaeans, who with their Greek allies later waged war on Troy, were already by 1600–1500 BCE burying their kings in deep shaft graves with gold funerary masks and bronze daggers inlaid with gold and silver.

▌ By 1450 BCE, the Mycenaeans had occupied Crete, and between 1400 and 1200 BCE, they constructed great citadels on the mainland at Mycenae, Tiryns, and elsewhere with "Cyclopean" walls of huge, irregularly shaped stone blocks.

▌ Masters of corbel vaulting, the Mycenaeans also built beehive-shaped tholos tombs covered by earthen mounds. One example is the Treasury of Atreus at Mycenae, which boasted the largest dome in the pre-Roman world.

▌ The oldest preserved monumental sculptures in Greece, most notably Mycenae's Lion Gate, date to the end of the Mycenaean period.

Gold funerary mask, Mycenae,
ca. 1600–1500 BCE

Treasury of Atreus, Mycenae,
ca. 1300–1250 BCE

The reliefs depicting Greeks battling semihuman centaurs are allegories of the triumph of civilization and rational order over barbarism and chaos—and of the Greek defeat of the Persians in 479 BCE.

The architects of the Parthenon calculated the dimensions of every part of the temple using harmonic numerical ratios, which determined, for example, the height and diameter of each column.

The statues in the two pediments of the Parthenon depicted important events in the life of Athena, the patron goddess of Athens. The east pediment represented Athena's birth from the head of Zeus.

5-1 IKTINOS and KALLIKRATES, Parthenon (Temple of Athena Parthenos; looking southeast), Acropolis, Athens, Greece, 447–438 BCE. ◼◄

5

ANCIENT GREECE

The costliest part of the Parthenon's lavish sculptural program was inside the temple—Phidias's colossal gold-and-ivory statue depicting Athena presenting the personification of Victory to Athens.

THE PERFECT TEMPLE

Although the Greeks borrowed many ideas from Egypt and Mesopotamia, they quickly developed an independent artistic identity. Their many innovations in painting, sculpture, and architecture became the foundation of the Western tradition. Indeed, no building type has ever had a longer and more profound impact on the later history of architecture than the Greek temple, which was itself a multimedia monument, richly adorned with painted statues and reliefs.

The greatest Greek temple was the Parthenon (FIG. 5-1), erected on the Acropolis of Athens in the mid-fifth century BCE. It represents the culmination of a century-long effort by Greek architects to build a temple having perfect proportions. Consistent with the thinking of the influential philosopher Pythagoras of Samos, who believed that beauty resided in harmonic numerical ratios, the architect IKTINOS calculated the dimensions of every part of the Parthenon in terms of a fixed proportional scheme. Thus, the ratio of the length to the width of the building, the number of columns on the long versus the short sides, even the relationship between the diameter of a column and the space between neighboring columns, conformed to an all-encompassing mathematical formula. The result was a "perfect temple."

The Athenians did not, however, construct the Parthenon to solve a purely formal problem of architectural design. Nor was this perfect temple, dedicated to Athena Parthenos (the Virgin), a shrine honoring the goddess alone. The temple also celebrated the Athenian people, who a generation earlier had led the Greeks in their successful effort to defeat the Persians after they had sacked the Acropolis in 480 BCE. Under the direction of PHIDIAS, a team of gifted sculptors lavishly decorated the building with statues and reliefs that in many cases alluded to the victory over the Persians. For example, the sculptural program included a series of reliefs depicting nude Greek warriors battling with the part-horse part-human *centaurs*—an allegory of the triumph of civilization (that is, Greek civilization) over barbarism (in this case, the Persians). The statues in one of the *pediments* (the triangular area above the columns beneath the roof) told the story of the birth of Athena, who emerged from the head of her father Zeus, king of the gods, fully armed and ready to protect her people. The costliest sculpture, and most prestigious of all, however, Phidias reserved for himself: the colossal gold-and-ivory statue of Athena inside the temple in which the warrior goddess presented the Athenians with the winged personification of Victory—an unmistakable reference to the Greek victory over the Persians.

MAP 5-1 The Greek world.

THE GREEKS AND THEIR GODS

Ancient Greek art occupies a special place in the history of art through the ages. Many of the cultural values of the Greeks, especially the exaltation of humanity as the "measure of all things," remain today fundamental tenets of Western civilization. This humanistic worldview led the Greeks to create the concept of democracy (rule by the *demos,* the people) and to make groundbreaking contributions in the fields of art, literature, and science. Ancient Greek ideas are so completely part of modern Western habits of mind that most people are scarcely aware the concepts originated in Greece 2,500 years ago.

The Greeks, or *Hellenes,* as they called themselves, were the product of an intermingling of Aegean and Indo-European peoples who established independent city-states, or *poleis* (singular, *polis*). The Dorians of the north, who many believe brought an end to Mycenaean civilization, settled in the Peloponnesos (MAP 5-1). The Ionians settled the western coast of Asia Minor (modern Turkey) and the islands of the Aegean Sea, possibly because the northern invaders

forced them out of Greece. But the Ionians may have been native to Asia Minor, developing out of a mixed stock of settlers between the 11th and 8th centuries BCE. Whatever the origins of the various regional populations, in 776 BCE the separate Greek-speaking states held their first athletic games in common at Olympia. From then on, despite their differences and rivalries, the Greeks regarded themselves as citizens of *Hellas,* distinct from the surrounding "barbarians" who did not speak Greek.

Even the gods of the Greeks (see "The Gods and Goddesses of Mount Olympus," page 107) differed in kind from those of neighboring civilizations. Unlike Egyptian and Mesopotamian deities, the Greek gods and goddesses differed from human beings only in being immortal. The Greeks made their gods into humans and their humans into gods. The perfect individual became the Greek ideal—and the portrayal of beautiful humans became the focus of many of the greatest Greek artists.

The sculptures, paintings, and buildings discussed in this chapter come from cities all over Greece and their many colonies abroad (MAP 5-1), but Athens, where the plays of Aeschylus, Sophocles,

ANCIENT GREECE

	900	Geometric and Orientalizing	600	Archaic	480	Early and High Classical	400	Late Classical	323	Hellenistic	30	BCE

Geometric and Orientalizing	Archaic	Early and High Classical	Late Classical	Hellenistic
▎ Revival of figure painting in Greece during the Geometric period	▎ Construction of the oldest peripteral Doric and Ionic temples	▎ Contrapposto introduced in Greek statuary	▎ Sculptors humanize the Greek gods and goddesses	▎ Hellenistic kingdoms replace Athens as leading cultural centers
▎ Eastern motifs enter Greek art during the Orientalizing period	▎ First Greek life-size stone statues with "Archaic smiles"	▎ Polykleitos formulates his canon of proportions	▎ Corinthian capitals introduced in Greek architecture	▎ Artists explore new subjects in sculpture and painting
	▎ Innovations in black- and red-figure vase painting	▎ Pericles rebuilds the Athenian Acropolis after the Persian sack	▎ Lysippos appointed the official court artist of Alexander the Great	▎ Architects break the rules of the Classical orders

The Gods and Goddesses of Mount Olympus

The names of scores of Greek gods and goddesses appear as early as the eighth century BCE in Homer's epic tales of the war against Troy (*Iliad*) and of the adventures of the Greek hero Odysseus on his long and tortuous journey home (*Odyssey*). The poet Hesiod enumerated even more names, especially in his *Theogony* (*Genealogy of the Gods*), composed around 700 BCE.

The Greek deities most often represented in art are all ultimately the offspring of the two key elements of the Greek universe: Earth (*Gaia/Ge*; all names are given in their Greek and Latin forms respectively) and Heaven (*Ouranos/Uranus*). Earth and Heaven mated to produce 12 Titans, including Ocean (*Okeanos/Oceanus*) and his youngest brother *Kronos* (*Saturn*). Kronos castrated his father in order to rule in his place, married his sister *Rhea,* and then swallowed all his children as they were born, lest one of them seek in turn to usurp him. When *Zeus* (*Jupiter*) was born, Rhea deceived Kronos by feeding him a stone wrapped in clothes in place of the infant. After growing to manhood, Zeus forced Kronos to vomit up Zeus's siblings. Together they overthrew their father and the other Titans and ruled the world from their home on Mount Olympus, Greece's highest peak.

This cruel and bloody tale of the origin of the Greek gods has parallels in Mesopotamian mythology and is clearly pre-Greek in origin, one of many Greek borrowings from the East. The Greek version of the creation myth, however, appears infrequently in painting and sculpture. Instead, the later 12 Olympian gods and goddesses figure most prominently in art—not only in antiquity but also in the Middle Ages, the Renaissance, and up to the present.

▌ *Zeus (Jupiter)* King of the gods, Zeus ruled the sky and allotted the sea to his brother Poseidon and the Underworld to his other brother Hades. His weapon was the thunderbolt, and with it he led the other gods to victory over the giants, who had challenged the Olympians for control of the world.

▌ *Hera (Juno)* Wife and sister of Zeus, Hera was the goddess of marriage.

▌ *Poseidon (Neptune)* Poseidon, one of the three sons of Kronos and Rhea, was lord of the sea. He controlled waves, storms, and earthquakes with his three-pronged pitchfork (*trident*).

▌ *Hestia (Vesta)* Sister of Zeus, Poseidon, and Hera, Hestia was goddess of the hearth.

▌ *Demeter (Ceres)* Third sister of Zeus, Demeter was the goddess of grain and agriculture.

▌ *Ares (Mars)* God of war, Ares was the son of Zeus and Hera and the lover of Aphrodite. His Roman counterpart, Mars, was the father of the twin founders of Rome, Romulus and Remus.

▌ *Athena (Minerva)* Goddess of wisdom and warfare, Athena was a virgin (*parthenos* in Greek), born not from a woman's womb but from the head of her father, Zeus.

▌ *Hephaistos (Vulcan)* God of fire and of metalworking, Hephaistos, son of Zeus and Hera, fashioned the armor Achilles wore in battle against Troy. He also provided Zeus his scepter and Poseidon his trident, and was the "surgeon" who split open Zeus's head to facilitate the birth of Athena. Hephaistos was born lame and, uncharacteristically for a god, ugly. His wife Aphrodite was unfaithful to him.

▌ *Apollo (Apollo)* God of light and music, Apollo was the son of Zeus with *Leto/Latona,* daughter of one of the Titans. His epithet, *Phoibos,* means "radiant," and the young, beautiful Apollo was sometimes identified with the sun (*Helios/Sol*).

▌ *Artemis (Diana)* Sister of Apollo, Artemis was goddess of the hunt and of wild animals. As Apollo's twin, she was occasionally regarded as the moon (*Selene/Luna*).

▌ *Aphrodite (Venus)* Daughter of Zeus and *Dione* (daughter of Okeanos and one of the *nymphs*—the goddesses of springs, caves, and woods), Aphrodite was the goddess of love and beauty. In one version of her myth, she was born from the foam (*aphros* in Greek) of the sea. She was the mother of Eros by Ares and of the Trojan hero Aeneas by a mortal named Anchises.

▌ *Hermes (Mercury)* Son of Zeus and another nymph, Hermes was the fleet-footed messenger of the gods and possessed winged sandals. He was also the guide of travelers, including the dead journeying to the Underworld. He carried the *caduceus,* a magical herald's rod, and wore a winged traveler's hat.

Several non-Olympian deities also appear frequently in Greek art.

▌ *Hades (Pluto)* One of the children of Kronos who fought with his brothers against the Titans, Hades was equal in stature to the Olympians but never resided on Mount Olympus. He was the god of the dead and lord of the Underworld (also called Hades).

▌ *Dionysos (Bacchus)* The son of Zeus and a mortal woman, Dionysos was the god of wine.

▌ *Eros (Amor* or *Cupid)* The son of Aphrodite and Ares, Eros was the winged child-god of love.

▌ *Asklepios (Aesculapius)* The son of Apollo and a mortal woman, Asklepios was the Greek god of healing, whose serpent-entwined staff is the emblem of modern medicine.

and Euripides were first performed, and where many of the most famous artists and architects worked, has justifiably become the symbol of ancient Greek culture. There, Socrates engaged his fellow citizens in philosophical argument, and Plato formulated his prescription for the ideal form of government in his *Republic.* Complementing the rich intellectual life of Athens was a strong interest in athletic exercise. The Athenian aim of achieving a balance of intellectual and physical discipline, an ideal of humanistic education, is well expressed in the familiar phrase "a sound mind in a sound body."

The distinctiveness and originality of Greek contributions to art, science, and politics should not, however, obscure the enormous debt the Greeks owed to the cultures of Egypt and Mesopotamia. The ancient Greeks themselves readily acknowledged borrowing ideas, motifs, conventions, and skills from those older civilizations. Nor should a high estimation of Greek art and culture blind anyone to the realities of Hellenic life and society. Even Athenian "democracy" was a political reality for only one segment of the demos. Slavery was a universal institution among the Greeks, and Greek women were in no way the equals of Greek men. Women normally remained secluded in their homes, emerging usually only for weddings, funerals, and religious festivals. They played little part in public or political life. Despite the fame of the poet Sappho, only a handful of female artists' names are known, and none of their works survive. The existence of slavery and the exclusion of women from public life are both reflected in Greek art. Freeborn men and women often appear with their slaves in monumental sculpture. The *symposium* (a dinner party only men and prostitutes attended) is a popular subject on painted vases.

GEOMETRIC AND ORIENTALIZING PERIODS

The destruction of the Mycenaean palaces brought with it the disintegration of the Bronze Age social order. The disappearance of powerful kings and their retinues led to the loss of the knowledge of how to cut masonry, to construct citadels and tombs, to paint frescoes, and to sculpt in stone. Depopulation, poverty, and an almost total loss of contact with the outside world characterized the succeeding centuries, sometimes called the Dark Age of Greece. Only in the eighth century BCE did economic conditions improve and the population begin to grow again. This era was in its own way a heroic age, when the Greeks established the Olympic Games and wrote down Homer's epic poems, formerly passed orally from bard to bard. During the eighth century BCE, the Greeks broke free of their isolation and once again began to trade with cities in both the east and the west.

Geometric Art

The eighth century also brought the return of the human figure to Greek art—not in monumental statuary, which was exceedingly rare even in Bronze Age Greece, but in small bronze figurines and in paintings on ceramic pots.

DIPYLON KRATER One of the earliest examples of Greek figure painting is a huge krater (FIG. 5-2) that marked the grave of a man buried around 740 BCE in the Dipylon cemetery of Athens. At well over three feet tall, this vase is a considerable technical achievement and a testament both to the potter's skill and to the wealth and position of the deceased's family in the community. The bottom of the great vessel is open, perhaps to permit visitors to the grave to pour libations in honor of the dead, perhaps simply to provide a drain for rainwater, or both.

The artist covered much of the krater's surface with precisely painted abstract angular motifs in horizontal bands. Especially prominent is the *meander,* or key, pattern around the rim of the krater. The decoration of most early Greek vases consists exclusively of abstract motifs—hence the designation of this formative phase of Greek art as the *Geometric* period. On this krater, however, Geometric ornament does not dominate. Instead, the painter reserved the widest part of the vase for two bands of human figures and horse-drawn chariots rather than for geometric ornament. Befitting the vase's function, the scenes depict the mourning for a man laid out on his bier and the grand chariot procession in his honor, scenes that appear frequently on other large Geometric vessels that served as grave markers, for example, the namepiece of the DIPYLON PAINTER, a five-foot-tall vase (FIG. 5-2A) that also stood in the Dipylon cemetery. The painter of the krater filled every empty space around the

5-2 Geometric krater, from the Dipylon cemetery, Athens, Greece, ca. 740 BCE. 3′ 4½″ high. Metropolitan Museum of Art, New York.

Figure painting returned to Greek art in the Geometric period, named for the abstract motifs on vessels such as this funerary krater featuring a mourning scene and procession in honor of the deceased.

figures with circles and M-shaped ornaments, negating any sense that the mourners or soldiers inhabit open space. The human figures, animals, and furniture are as two-dimensional as the geometric shapes elsewhere on the vessel. In the upper band, the shroud, raised to reveal the corpse, is an abstract checkerboard-like backdrop. The figures are silhouettes constructed of triangular (frontal) torsos with attached profile arms, legs, and heads (with a single large frontal eye in the center), following the age-old convention. To distinguish male from female, the painter added a penis growing out of one of the deceased's thighs. The mourning women, who tear their hair out in grief, have breasts emerging beneath their armpits. In both cases the artist's concern was specifying gender, not anatomical accuracy. Below, the warriors look like walking shields and, in the old conceptual manner, the two wheels of the chariots appear side by side. The horses have the correct number of heads and legs but seem to share a common body, so that there is no sense of overlapping or depth. Despite the highly stylized and conventional manner of representation, vessels like this one and the Dipylon Painter's funerary vase (FIG. 5-2A) mark a significant turning point

5-2A DIPYLON PAINTER, Geometric funerary amphora, ca. 750 BCE.

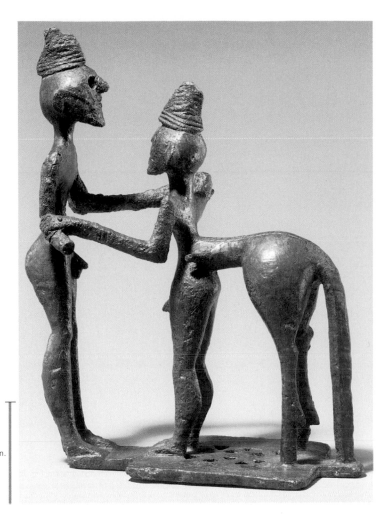

5-3 Hero and centaur (Herakles and Nessos?), from Olympia, Greece, ca. 750–730 BCE. Bronze, $4\frac{1}{2}''$ high. Metropolitan Museum of Art, New York (gift of J. Pierpont).

Sculpture of the Geometric period is small in scale, and the figures have simple stylized shapes. This statuette depicts a hero battling a centaur— an early example of mythological narrative.

in the history of Greek art. Not only did the human figure reenter the painter's repertoire, but the Geometric artists also revived the art of storytelling in pictures.

HERAKLES AND NESSOS One of the most impressive surviving Geometric sculptures is a characteristically small solid-cast bronze group (FIG. **5-3**) made up of two schematic figures locked in a hand-to-hand struggle. The man is a hero, probably Herakles (see "Herakles," page 128). His opponent is a centaur, possibly Nessos, who had volunteered to carry the hero's bride across a river and then assaulted her. Whether or not the hero is Herakles and the centaur is Nessos, the mythological nature of the group is certain. The repertoire of the Geometric artist was not limited to scenes inspired by daily life (and death). Composite monsters were enormously popular in Mesopotamia and Egypt, and renewed contact with foreign cultures may have inspired the human-animal monsters of Geometric Greece. The centaur, however, is a purely Greek invention—and one that posed a problem for the artist, who had, of course, never seen such a creature. The Geometric artist conceived the centaur as a man in front and a horse in back, a rather unhappy and unconvincing configuration in which the forelegs and hind legs belong to different species. In this example, the

sculptor rendered the figure of the hero and the human part of the centaur in a similar fashion. Both have beards and wear helmets, but (contradictory to nature) the man is larger than the horse to indicate that he will be the victor. Like other Geometric male figures, both painted and sculpted, this hero is nude, in contrast to the Mesopotamian statuettes that might have inspired the Greek works. Here, at the very beginning of Greek figural art, the Hellenic instinct for the natural beauty of the human figure is evident. Greek athletes exercised without their clothes and even competed nude in the Olympic Games from very early times.

Orientalizing Art

During the seventh century BCE, the pace and scope of Greek trade and colonization accelerated and Greek artists became exposed more than ever before to Eastern artworks, especially small portable objects such as Syrian ivory carvings. The closer contact had a profound effect on the development of Greek art. Indeed, so many motifs borrowed from or inspired by Egyptian and Mesopotamian art entered the Greek pictorial vocabulary at this time that art historians have dubbed the seventh century BCE the *Orientalizing* period.

MANTIKLOS APOLLO One of the masterworks of the early seventh century BCE is the *Mantiklos Apollo* (FIG. **5-4**), a small bronze statuette dedicated to Apollo by an otherwise unknown man named Mantiklos. Scratched into the thighs of the figure is a message to the deity: "Mantiklos dedicated me as a tithe to the far-shooting Lord of the Silver Bow; you, Phoibos [Apollo], might give some pleasing favor in return." Because the Greeks conceived their gods in human form, it is uncertain whether the figure represents the youthful Apollo or Mantiklos (or neither). But if the left hand at one time held a bow, the statuette is certainly an image of the deity. In any case, the purpose of the votive offering is clear. Equally apparent is the increased interest Greek artists at this time had in reproducing details of human anatomy, such as the long hair framing the unnaturally elongated neck, and the pectoral and abdominal muscles, which define the stylized triangular

5-4 *Mantiklos Apollo,* statuette of a youth dedicated by Mantiklos to Apollo, from Thebes, Greece, ca. 700–680 BCE. Bronze, 8″ high. Museum of Fine Arts, Boston.

Mantiklos dedicated this statuette to Apollo, and it probably represents the god. The treatment of the body reveals the interest seventh-century BCE Greek artists had in representing human anatomy.

Greek Vase Painting

The techniques Greek ceramists used to shape and decorate fine vases required great skill, acquired over many years as apprentices in the workshops of master potters. During the Archaic and Classical periods, when the art of vase painting was at its zenith in Greece, both potters and painters frequently signed their work. These signatures reveal the pride of the artists. In the ancient world, the Greeks were unique in celebrating individual artists as creative geniuses and in systematically recording artists' names for posterity. Many artists achieved great renown even during their lifetimes. No earlier civilization held artists in such high esteem (Egypt's deification of Imhotep was exceptional)—nor would any later culture bestow such high regard on painters, sculptors, and other artisans until the Renaissance in Italy 2,000 years later.

The signatures on Greek vases also might have functioned as "brand names" for a large export market. The products of the workshops in Corinth and Athens in particular were highly prized and have been found all over the Mediterranean world. The Corinthian Orientalizing amphora shown here (FIG. 5-5) was found on Rhodes, an island at the opposite side of the Aegean from mainland Corinth (MAP 5-1). The Etruscans of central Italy (MAP 6-1) were especially good customers. Athenian vases were staples in Etruscan tombs, and all of the illustrated sixth-century BCE examples (FIGS. 5-19 to 5-23A) came from Etruscan sites. Other painted Athenian pots have been found as far away as France, Russia, and the Sudan.

The first step in manufacturing a Greek vase was to remove any impurities found in the natural clay and then to knead it, like dough, to remove air bubbles and make it flexible. The Greeks used dozens of different kinds and shapes of pots, and produced most of them in several parts. Potters formed the vessel's body by placing the clay on a rotating horizontal wheel. While an apprentice turned the wheel by hand, the potter pulled up the clay with the fingers until achieving the desired shape. The master or the apprentice shaped the handles separately and attached them to the vase body by applying *slip* (liquefied clay) to the joints.

Painting was usually the job of a specialist, although many potters decorated their own work. (Today most people tend to regard painters as more elevated artists than potters, but in Greece the potters owned the shops and employed the painters.) Art historians customarily refer to the "pigment" the painter applied to the clay surface as *glaze,* but the black areas on Greek pots are neither pigment nor glaze but a slip of finely sifted clay that originally was of the same rich red-orange color as the clay of the pot. In the three-phase firing process Greek ceramists used, the first (*oxidizing*) phase turned both pot and slip red. During the second (*reducing*) phase, the potter shut off the oxygen supply into the kiln, and both pot and slip turned black. In the final (*reoxidizing*) phase, the pot's coarser material reabsorbed oxygen and became red again, while

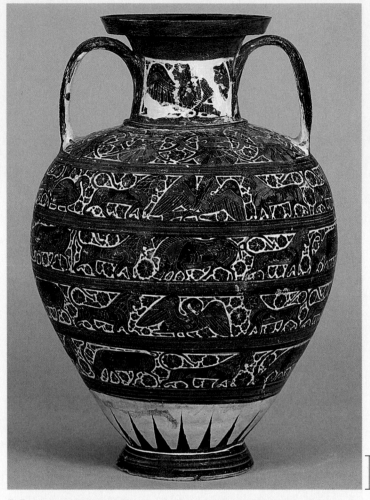

5-5 Corinthian black-figure amphora with animal friezes, from Rhodes, Greece, ca. 625–600 BCE. 1′ 2″ high. British Museum, London.

The Corinthians invented the black-figure technique of vase painting in which artists incised linear details into black-glaze silhouettes. This early example features Orientalizing animals.

the smoother, silica-laden slip did not and remained black. After long experimentation, Greek ceramists developed a velvety jet-black "glaze" of this kind, produced in kilns heated to temperatures as high as 950° Celsius (about 1,742° Fahrenheit). The firing process was the same whether the painter worked in black-figure or in red-figure. In fact, sometimes Greek vase painters employed both manners on the same vessel (FIG. 5-21).

torso. The triangular face once had inlaid eyes, and the figure may have worn a separately fashioned helmet.

ORIENTALIZING AMPHORA An elaborate Corinthian *amphora* (FIG. 5-5), or two-handled storage jar, typifies the new

Greek fascination with the Orient. In a series of bands recalling the organization of Geometric painted vases, animals such as the native boar appear beside exotic lions and panthers and composite creatures inspired by Eastern monsters such as the sphinx and lamassu—in this instance the *siren* (part bird, part woman) prominently

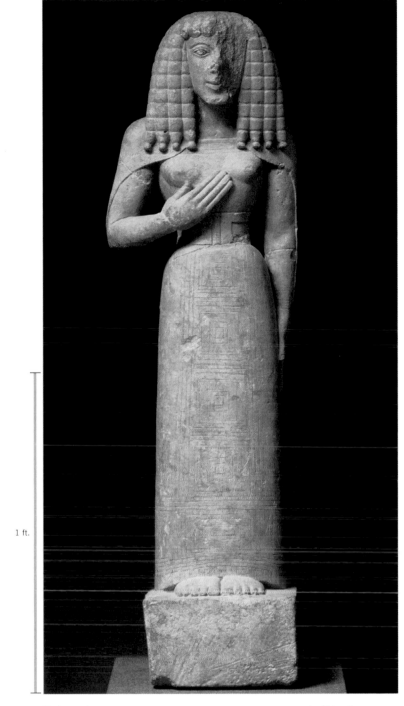

5-6 *Lady of Auxerre*, ca. 650–625 BCE. Limestone, 2′ 1½″ high. Musée du Louvre, Paris.

Probably from Crete, this kore (maiden) typifies the Daedalic sculptural style of the seventh century BCE with its triangular face and hair and lingering Geometric fondness for abstract pattern.

displayed on the amphora's neck. The wide appeal of these vases was due not solely to their Orientalizing animal friezes but also to a new ceramic technique the Corinthians invented. Art historians call this type of vase decoration *black-figure painting* (see "Greek Vase Painting," page 110). The black-figure painter first put down black silhouettes on the clay surface, as in Geometric times, but then used a sharp pointed instrument to incise linear details within the forms, usually adding highlights in white or purplish red over the black figures before firing the vase. The combination of the weighty black silhouettes with the delicate detailing and the bright

polychrome overlay proved to be irresistible, and Athenian painters soon copied the technique the Corinthians pioneered.

DAEDALIC ART The founding of the Greek trading colony of Naukratis in Egypt (MAP 3-1) before 630 BCE brought the Greeks into direct contact with the monumental stone architecture of the Egyptians. Soon after, Greek builders be-

5-6A Temple A, Prinias, ca. 625 BCE.

gan to erect the first stone edifices since the fall of the Mycenaean kingdoms. One of the oldest is Temple A (FIG. 5-6A) at Prinias on Crete. That island, once the center of Minoan civilization (see Chapter 4), is probably also where an early Greek sculptor carved the limestone statuette of a goddess or maiden (*kore;* plural, *korai*) popularly known as the *Lady of Auxerre* (FIG. 5-6) after the French town that is her oldest recorded location. The *Lady of Auxerre* is the masterpiece of the style usually referred to as *Daedalic*, after the legendary artist Daedalus, whose name means "the skillful one." In addition to his status as a great sculptor, Daedalus reputedly built the labyrinth in Crete to house the Minotaur and also designed a temple at Memphis in Egypt. The historical Greeks attributed to him almost all the great achievements in early sculpture and architecture.

As with the figure Mantiklos dedicated (FIG. 5-4), it is uncertain whether the Auxerre "lady" is a mortal or a deity. She is clothed, as are all Greek goddesses and women of this period, but she does not wear a headdress, as do the contemporaneous

5-6B Lintel of Temple A, Prinias, ca. 625 BCE.

goddesses (FIG. 5-6B) of Temple A at Prinias. Moreover, the placement of the right hand across the chest is probably a gesture of prayer, also indicating that this is a kore. The style is much more naturalistic than in Geometric times, but the love of abstract shapes is still evident. Note, for example, the triangular flat-topped head framed by long strands of hair that form triangles complementary to the shape of the face, and the decoration of the long skirt with its incised concentric squares, once brightly painted, as were all Greek stone statues. The modern notion that Greco-Roman statuary was pure white is mistaken. The Greeks did not, however, color their statues garishly. They left the flesh in the natural color of the stone, which they waxed and polished, and painted the eyes, lips, hair, and drapery in *encaustic* (see "Iaia of Cyzicus and the Art of Encaustic Painting," Chapter 7, page 218, and FIG. 5-63A). In this technique, the painter mixed the pigment with hot wax and applied it to the statue to produce a durable coloration.

ARCHAIC PERIOD

The legend that Daedalus worked in Egypt reflects the enormous influence of Egyptian art and architecture on the Greeks not only during the Orientalizing age of the seventh century BCE but also in the succeeding *Archaic* period, which lasted from 600 to 480 BCE.

Statuary

According to the first-century BCE Greek historian Diodorus Siculus, Daedalus used the same compositional patterns for his statues as the Egyptians used for their own.[1] The earliest surviving truly monumental stone statues of the Greeks do, in fact, follow very closely the standard Egyptian format.

5-7 Kouros, from Attica, Greece, ca. 600 BCE. Marble, 6′ ½″ high. Metropolitan Museum of Art, New York. ◼◀

The sculptors of the earliest life-size statues of kouroi (young men) adopted the Egyptian pose for standing figures (FIG. 3-12), but the kouroi are nude and liberated from the stone block.

NEW YORK KOUROS One of the earliest Greek examples of life-size statuary (FIG. 5-7) is the marble *kouros* ("youth"; plural, *kouroi*) now in New York, which emulates the stance of Egyptian statues (FIG. 3-12). In both Egypt and Greece, the figure is rigidly frontal with the left foot advanced slightly. The arms are held

beside the body, and the fists are clenched with the thumbs forward. Like most Egyptian statues, the New York kouros was a funerary statue. It stood over a grave in the countryside of Attica, the region around Athens. Statues such as this one replaced the huge vases (FIGS. 5-2 and 5-2A) of Geometric times as the preferred form of grave marker in the sixth century BCE. The Greeks also used kouroi as votive offerings in sanctuaries. The kouros type, because of its generic quality, could be employed in several different contexts.

Despite the adherence to Egyptian prototypes, Greek kouros statues differ from their models in two important ways. First, the Greek sculptors liberated the figures from the stone block. The Egyptian obsession with permanence was alien to the Greeks, who were preoccupied with finding ways to represent motion rather than stability in their sculpted figures. Second, the kouroi are nude, and in the absence of identifying attributes, they, like Mantiklos's bronze statuette (FIG. 5-4), are formally indistinguishable from Greek images of deities with their perfect bodies exposed for all to see.

The New York kouros shares many traits with the *Mantiklos Apollo* and other Orientalizing works such as the *Lady of Auxerre*, especially the triangular shape of head and hair and the flatness of the face—the hallmarks of the Daedalic style. Eyes, nose, and mouth all sit on the front of the head, and the ears on the sides. The long hair forms a flat backdrop behind the head. The placement of the various anatomical parts is the result of the sculptor's having drawn these features on four independent sides of the marble block, following the same workshop procedure used in Egypt for millennia. The New York kouros also has the slim waist of earlier Greek statues and exhibits the same love of pattern. The pointed arch of the rib cage, for example, echoes the V-shaped ridge of the hips, which suggests but does not accurately reproduce the rounded flesh and muscle of the human body.

CALF BEARER A generation later than the New York kouros is the statue of a *moschophoros* (FIG. **5-8**), or calf bearer, found in fragments on the Athenian Acropolis. Its inscribed base (not visible in the photograph) states that a man named Rhonbos dedicated the statue to Athena in thanksgiving for his prosperity. Rhonbos is almost certainly the calf bearer himself, bringing an offering to the goddess. He stands in the left-foot-forward manner of the kouroi, but he is bearded and therefore no longer a youth. He wears a thin cloak (once painted to set it off from the otherwise nude body). No one dressed in this way in ancient Athens. The sculptor adhered to the artistic convention of male nudity and attributed to the calf bearer the noble perfection nudity imparts but nevertheless indicated that this mature gentleman is clothed, as any respectable citizen would be in this context. The Archaic sculptor's love of pattern is evident once again in the handling of the difficult problem of representing man and animal together. The calf's legs and the moschophoros's arms form a bold X that unites the two bodies both physically and formally.

The calf bearer's face differs markedly from those of earlier Greek statues (and those of Egypt and Mesopotamia) in one notable way. The man smiles—or at least seems to. From this time on, Archaic Greek statues always smile, even in the most inappropriate contexts (see, for example, FIG. 5-27, where a dying warrior with an arrow in his chest grins broadly). Art historians have interpreted this so-called *Archaic smile* in various ways, but the smile should not be taken literally. Rather, the Archaic smile seems to be the sculptor's way of indicating that the person portrayed is alive. By adopting this convention, Greek artists signaled a very different intention from their Egyptian counterparts.

1 ft.

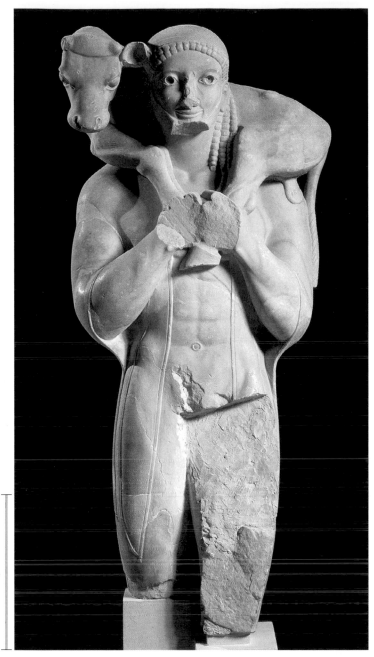

5-8 Calf bearer, dedicated by Rhonbos on the Acropolis, Athens, Greece, ca. 560 BCE. Marble, restored height 5′ 5″; fragment 3′ 11½″ high. Acropolis Museum, Athens.

This statue of a bearded man bringing a calf to sacrifice to Athena is one of the first to employ the so-called Archaic smile—the Greek sculptor's way of indicating a person is alive.

ANAVYSOS KOUROS Sometime around 530 BCE, a young man named Kroisos died a hero's death in battle, and his family erected a kouros statue (FIG. **5-9**) over his grave at Anavysos, not far from Athens. Fortunately, some of the paint remains, giving a better sense of the statue's original appearance. The inscribed base invites visitors to "stay and mourn at the tomb of dead Kroisos, whom raging Ares destroyed one day as he fought in the foremost ranks." The smiling statue is no more a portrait of a specific youth than is the New York kouros. But two generations later, without rejecting the Egyptian stance, the Greek sculptor rendered the human body in a far more naturalistic manner. The head is no longer too large

5-9 Kroisos, from Anavysos, Greece, ca. 530 BCE. Marble, 6′ 4″ high. National Archaeological Museum, Athens. ◼◀

This later kouros stood over the grave of Kroisos, a young man who died in battle. The statue displays more naturalistic proportions and more rounded modeling of face, torso, and limbs.

for the body, and the face is more rounded, with swelling cheeks replacing the flat planes of the earlier work. The long hair does not form a stiff backdrop to the head but falls naturally over the back. The V-shaped ridges of the New York kouros have become rounded, fleshy hips.

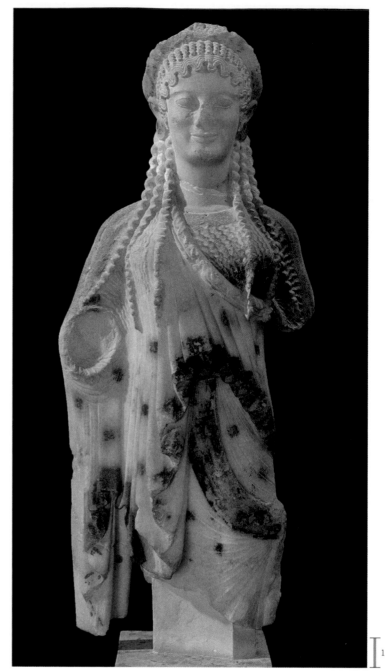

1 ft.

1 in.

5-10 *Peplos Kore,* from the Acropolis, Athens, Greece, ca. 530 BCE. Marble, 4′ high. Acropolis Museum, Athens.

Unlike men, women are always clothed in Archaic statuary. This kore is a votive statue of a goddess wearing four garments. She held her identifying attribute in her missing left hand.

5-11 Kore in Ionian dress, from the Acropolis, Athens, Greece, ca. 520–510 BCE. Marble, 1′ 9″ high. Acropolis Museum, Athens.

Archaic sculptors delighted in rendering the intricate asymmetrical patterns created by the cascading folds of garments such as the Ionian chiton and himation worn by this smiling Acropolis kore.

PEPLOS KORE A stylistic "sister" to the Anavysos kouros is the statue of a woman traditionally known as the *Peplos Kore* (FIG. **5-10**) because until recently scholars thought this kore wore a peplos. A *peplos* is a simple, long, woolen belted garment. Careful examination of the statue has revealed, however, that she wears four different garments, one of which only goddesses wore. The attribute the goddess held in her missing left hand would immediately have identified her. Whichever goddess she is, the contrast with the *Lady of Auxerre* (FIG. 5-6) is striking. Although in both cases the drapery conceals the entire body save for head, arms, and feet, the sixth-century BCE sculptor rendered the soft female form much more naturally. This

softer treatment of the flesh also sharply differentiates later korai from kouroi, which have hard, muscular bodies.

Traces of paint remain on the *Peplos Kore* because the statue lay buried for more than two millennia, which protected the painted surface from the destructive effects of exposure to the atmosphere and bad weather. The Persians had knocked over this statue, Rhonbos's (FIG. 5-8), and many other votive offerings in Athena's sanctuary during their sack of the Acropolis in 480 BCE. Shortly thereafter, the Athenians buried all the damaged Archaic sculptures, which accounts for the preservation of the coloration today.

Greek Temple Plans

The core of an ancient Greek temple plan (FIG. 5-12) was the *naos*, or *cella*, a windowless room that usually housed the cult statue of the deity. In front of the naos was a *pronaos,* or porch, often with two columns between the *antae,* or extended walls (columns *in antis*). A smaller second room might be placed behind the cella (FIG. 5-15), but in its canonical form, the Greek temple had a porch at the rear (*opisthodomos*) set against the blank back wall of the cella. The second porch served only a decorative purpose: It satisfied the Greek passion for balance and symmetry.

Around this core, Greek builders might erect a colonnade across the front of the temple (*prostyle;* FIG. 5-52), across both front and back (*amphiprostyle;* FIG. 5-55), or, more commonly, all around the cella and its porch(es) to form a *peristyle,* as in FIG. 5-12 (compare FIGS. 5-1 and 5-14). Single (*peripteral*) colonnades were the norm, but double (*dipteral*) colonnades were features of especially elaborate temples (FIG. 5-75).

The Greeks' insistence on proportional order guided their experiments with the proportions of temple plans. The earliest temples tended to be long and narrow, with the proportion of the ends to the sides roughly expressible as 1:3. From the sixth century BCE on, plans approached but rarely had a proportion of exactly 1:2.

5-12 Plan of a typical Greek peripteral temple.

The basic form of the canonical Greek temple derives from that of the Mycenaean megaron (FIG. 4-18), but Greek temples housed statues of deities, and most were surrounded by columns.

Classical temples tended to be a little longer than twice their width. To the Greek mind, proportion in architecture and sculpture was comparable to harmony in music—reflections and embodiments of the cosmic order.

KORE IN IONIAN DRESS By the late sixth century BCE, the light linen Ionian *chiton,* worn in conjunction with a heavier *himation* (mantle), was the garment of choice for fashionable women. Archaic sculptors of korai in Ionian dress (FIG. 5-11) delighted in rendering the intricate patterns created by the cascading folds of thin, soft material. The asymmetry of the folds greatly relieves the stiff frontality of the body and makes the figure appear much more lifelike than the typical kouros. The sculptor achieved added variety by showing the kore grasping part of her chiton in her left hand (unfortunately broken off) to lift it off the ground in order to take a step forward. This is the equivalent of the advanced left foot of the kouroi and became standard for statues of korai. Despite the varied surface treatment of brightly colored garments on the korai, the kore postures are as fixed as those of their male counterparts.

Architecture and Architectural Sculpture

The earliest Greek temples do not survive because their builders constructed them of wood and mud brick. Pausanias noted in his second-century CE guidebook to Greece that in the even-then-ancient Temple of Hera at Olympia, one oak column was still in place.[2] (Stone columns had replaced the others.) For Archaic and later Greek temples, however, Greek builders used more permanent materials—limestone or, where it was available, marble, which was more impressive and durable (and more expensive). In Greece proper, if not in its western colonies, marble was readily at hand. Bluish-white marble came from Mount Hymettus, just east of Athens, and glittering white marble from Mount Pentelicus, northeast of the city, and from the Aegean Islands, especially Paros.

Already in the Orientalizing seventh century BCE, at Prinias, the Greeks had built a stone temple (FIG. 5-6A) embellished with stone sculptures, but the Cretan temple resembled the megaron of a Mycenaean palace more than anything Greek traders had seen in their travels overseas. In the Archaic age of the sixth century BCE, with the model of Egyptian columnar halls such as those at Luxor (FIG. 3-24A) and Karnak (FIGS. 3-25 and 3-26) before them, Greek architects began to build the columnar stone temples that have become synonymous with Greek architecture and influenced countless later structures in the Western world.

THE CANONICAL GREEK TEMPLE Greek temples differed in function from most later religious shrines. The altar lay outside the temple—at the east end, facing the rising sun—and the Greeks gathered outside, not inside, the building to worship. The temple proper housed the so-called *cult statue* of the deity, the grandest of all votive offerings. Both in its early and mature manifestations, the Greek temple was the house of the god or goddess, not of his or her followers.

In basic plan (see "Greek Temple Plans," above, and FIG. 5-12), the Greek temple still discloses a close affinity with the Mycenaean megaron (FIG. 4-18), and even in its most elaborate form, it retains the megaron's basic simplicity. In all cases, the remarkable order, compactness, and symmetry of the Greek scheme strike the eye first, reflecting the Greeks' sense of proportion and their effort to achieve ideal forms in terms of regular numerical relationships and geometric rules (see "The Perfect Temple," page 105).

Figural sculpture played a major role in the exterior program of the Greek temple from early times, partly to embellish the god's shrine, partly to tell something about the deity represented within, and partly to serve as a votive offering. But Greek architects also conceived the building itself, with its finely carved capitals and moldings, as sculpture, abstract in form and possessing the power

Doric and Ionic Orders

Architectural historians describe the elevation (FIG. 5-13) of a Greek temple in terms of the platform, the colonnade, and the superstructure (*entablature*). In the Archaic period, two basic systems, or *orders*, evolved for articulating the three units. The Greek architectural orders differ both in the nature of the details and in the relative proportions of the parts. The names of the orders derive from the Greek regions where they were most commonly employed. The *Doric*, formulated on the mainland, remained the preferred manner there and in Greece's western colonies. The *Ionic* was the order of choice in the Aegean Islands and on the western coast of Asia Minor. The geographical distinctions are by no means absolute. The Ionic order, for example, was often used in Athens (where, according to some ancient authors, the Athenians considered themselves Ionians who never migrated).

In both orders, the columns rest on the *stylobate*, the uppermost course of the platform. Metal clamps held together the stone blocks in each horizontal course, and metal dowels joined vertically the blocks of different courses. The columns have two or three parts, depending on the order: the *shaft*, usually marked with vertical channels (*flutes*); the *capital*; and, in the Ionic order, the *base*. Greek column shafts, in contrast to their Minoan and Mycenaean forebears, taper gradually from bottom to top. They usually are composed of separate *drums* joined by metal dowels to prevent turning as well as shifting, although occasionally the Greeks erected *monolithic* (single-piece) columns.

Greek column capitals have two elements. The lower part (the *echinus*) varies with the order. In the Doric, it is convex and cushionlike, similar to the echinus of Minoan (FIG. 4-6) and Mycenaean (FIG. 4-18A) capitals. In the Ionic, it is small and supports a bolster ending in scroll-like spirals (the *volutes*). The upper element, present in both orders, is a flat, square block (the *abacus*) that provides the immediate support for the entablature.

The entablature has three parts: the *architrave*, the main weight-bearing and weight-distributing element; the *frieze*; and the *cornice*, a molded horizontal projection that together with two sloping (*raking*) cornices forms a triangle that frames the *pediment*. In the Ionic order, the architrave is usually subdivided into three horizontal bands. Doric architects subdivided the frieze into *triglyphs* and *metopes*, whereas Ionic builders left the frieze open to provide a continuous field for relief sculpture.

The Doric order is massive in appearance, its sturdy columns firmly planted on the stylobate. Compared with the weighty and severe Doric, the Ionic order seems light, airy, and much more decorative. Its columns are more slender and rise from molded bases. The most obvious differences between the two orders are, of course, the capitals—the Doric, severely plain, and the Ionic, highly ornamental.

DORIC ORDER

IONIC ORDER

5-13 Elevations of the Doric and Ionic orders (John Burge).

The major differences between the Doric and Ionic orders are the form of the capitals and the treatment of the frieze. The Doric frieze is subdivided into triglyphs and metopes.

5-14 Temple of Hera I ("Basilica," looking northeast), Paestum, Italy, ca. 550 BCE.

The peristyle of this huge early Doric temple consists of heavy, closely spaced, cigar-shaped columns with bulky, pancakelike capitals, characteristic features of Archaic Greek architecture.

of sculpture to evoke human responses. To underscore the commanding importance of the sculptured temple and its inspiring function in public life, the Greeks usually erected their temples on elevated sites, often on a hill above the city (*acropolis* means "high city").

Most of the sculptural ornament was on the upper part of the building, in the frieze and pediments (see "Doric and Ionic Orders," page 116). The Greeks painted their architectural sculptures (FIG. 5 26), as they did their freestanding statues, and usually placed sculpture only in the building parts that had no structural function. This is true particularly of the Doric order (FIG. **5-13**, *left*), in which decorative sculpture appears only in the "voids" of the metopes and pediments. Ionic (FIG. 5-13, *right*) builders were willing to decorate the entire frieze and sometimes even the lower column drums. Occasionally, Ionic architects replaced columns with female figures (*caryatids;* FIGS. 5-17 and 5-54). Designers also painted capitals, decorative moldings, and other architectural elements, which enabled architects to bring out more clearly the relationships of the structural parts and soften the stone's glitter at specific points, as well as provide a background to set off the figures.

Although the Greeks used color for emphasis and to relieve what might have seemed too bare, Greek architecture primarily depended on clarity and balance. To the Greeks, it was unthinkable to use surfaces in the way the Egyptians used their gigantic columns—as fields for complicated ornamentation (FIG. 3-25). The history of Greek temple architecture is the history of Greek architects' unflagging efforts to find the most satisfactory (that is, what they believed were perfect) proportions for each part of the building and for the structure as a whole.

BASILICA, PAESTUM The premier example of early Greek efforts at Doric temple design is not in Greece but in Italy, south of Naples, at Paestum (Greek Poseidonia). The huge (80 by 170 feet) Archaic temple (FIG. **5-14**) erected there around 550 BCE retains its entire peripteral colonnade, but most of the entablature, including the frieze, pediment, and all of the roof, has vanished. Called the "Basilica" after the Roman columnar hall building type (see Chapter 7) that early investigators felt it resembled, the structure was a shrine to the goddess Hera—known as the Temple of Hera I to dis-

1. Cella with central row of columns
2. Pronaos with three columns in antis

5-15 Plan of the Temple of Hera I, Paestum, Italy, ca. 550 BCE.

The Hera temple's plan also reveals its early date. The building has an odd number of columns on the facade and a single row of columns in the cella, leaving no place for a central cult statue.

tinguish it from its neighbor, the later Temple of Hera II (FIG. 5-29). The misnomer is partly due to the building's plan (FIG. **5-15**), which differs from that of most other Greek temples. The unusual feature, found only in early Archaic temples, is the central row of columns dividing the cella into two aisles. Placing columns underneath the *ridgepole* (the timber beam running the length of the building below the peak of the gabled roof) might seem the logical way to provide interior support for the roof structure, but it had several disadvantages. The cella columns allowed no place for a central cult statue. Further, in order to correspond with the interior, the temple's facade required an odd number of columns (nine in this case). At Paestum, there are also three columns in antis instead of the standard two, which in turn ruled out a central doorway for viewing the statue. (This design, however, was well suited for two statues, perhaps of Zeus and Hera.) In any case, the architect still achieved a simple 1:2 ratio of facade and flank columns by placing 18 columns on each side of the temple.

Another early aspect of the Paestum temple is the shape of its heavy, closely spaced columns (FIG. 5-14) with their large, bulky, pancakelike Doric capitals, which seem compressed by the overbearing weight of what probably was a high, massive entablature. The columns have a pronounced swelling (*entasis*) at the middle of the shafts, giving them a profile akin to that of a cigar. The columns and capitals thus express in a vivid manner their weight-bearing function. One structural reason, perhaps, for the heaviness of the design and the narrowness of the spans between the columns might be that the Archaic builders were afraid thinner and more widely spaced columns would result in the superstructure's collapse. In later Doric temples (FIGS. 5-1, 5-24, 5-29, and 5-44), the builders placed the columns farther apart and refined the forms. The shafts became more slender, the entasis subtler, the capitals smaller, and the entablature lighter. Greek architects sought the ideal proportional relationship among the parts of their buildings. The sculptors of Archaic kouroi and korai grappled with similar problems. Architecture and sculpture developed in a parallel manner in the sixth century BCE.

TEMPLE OF ARTEMIS, CORFU In fact, architects and sculptors frequently worked together, as at Corfu (ancient Corcyra), where, soon after 600 BCE, the Greeks constructed a large Doric temple in honor of Artemis. Corfu is an island off the western coast of Greece and was an important stop on the trade route between the mainland and the Greek settlements in Italy (MAP 5-1). Prosperity made possible one of the earliest stone peripteral temples in Greece, one also lavishly embellished with sculpture. Sculptors decorated the metopes with reliefs (unfortunately very fragmentary today) and filled both pediments with huge high-relief sculptures (more than 9 feet high at the center). It appears the pediments on both ends of the temple were decorated in an identical manner. The west pediment (FIG. **5-16**) is better preserved.

Designing figural decoration for a pediment was never an easy task for the Greek sculptor because of the pediment's awkward triangular shape. The central figures had to be of great size. In contrast, as the pediment tapered toward the corners, the available area became increasingly cramped. At the center of the Corfu pediment is the *gorgon* Medusa, a demon with a woman's body and a bird's wings. Medusa also had a hideous face and snake hair, and anyone who gazed at her turned into stone. The Corfu sculptor depicted her in the conventional Archaic bent-leg, bent-arm, pinwheel-like posture that signifies running or, for a winged creature, flying.

To her left and right are two great felines. Together they serve as temple guardians, repulsing all enemies from the sanctuary of the goddess. Similar panthers stood sentinel on the lintel (FIG. 5-6B) of the seventh-century BCE temple at Prinias. The Corfu felines are in the tradition of the guardian lions of Mycenae (FIG. 4-19) and the beasts that stood guard at the entrances to Hittite and Assyrian palaces (FIGS. 2-18B and 2-20). Medusa herself is also an *apotropaic* figure that protects the temple and wards off evil spirits. The triad of Medusa and the felines recalls as well Mesopotamian heraldic human-and-animal compositions (FIG. 2-10). The Corfu figures are, in short, still further examples of the Orientalizing manner in early Greek sculpture.

Between Medusa and the two felines are two smaller figures—the human Chrysaor at her left and the winged horse Pegasus at her right (only the rear legs remain, next to Medusa's right foot). Chrysaor and Pegasus were Medusa's children. According to legend, they sprang from her head when the Greek hero Perseus severed it with his sword. Their presence here on either side of the living Medusa is therefore a chronological impossibility. The Archaic artist was not interested in telling a coherent story but in identifying the central figure by depicting her offspring. Narration was, however, the purpose of the much smaller groups situated in the pediment corners. To the viewer's right is Zeus, brandishing his thunderbolt and slaying a kneeling giant. In the extreme corner (not preserved) was a dead giant. The *gigantomachy* (battle of gods and giants) was a popular theme in Greek art from Archaic through Hellenistic times and was a metaphor for the triumph of reason and order over chaos. In the pediment's left corner is one of the Trojan War's climactic events: Achilles' son Neoptolemos kills the enthroned King Priam. The fallen figure to the left of this group may be a dead Trojan.

The master responsible for the Corfu pediments was a pioneer, and the composition shows all the signs of experimentation. The lack of narrative unity in the Corfu pediment and the figures' extraordinary diversity of scale eventually gave way to pedimental designs with freestanding figures in place of reliefs all acting out a single event and appearing the same size. But the Corfu designer already had shown the way. That sculptor realized, for example, the area beneath the raking cornice could be filled with gods and heroes of similar size by employing a combination of standing, leaning, kneeling, seated, and prostrate figures. The Corfu master also discovered that animals could be very useful space fillers because, unlike humans, they have one end taller than the other.

1 ft.

5-16 West pediment, Temple of Artemis, Corfu, Greece, ca. 600–580 BCE. Limestone, greatest height 9′ 4″. Archaeological Museum, Corfu.

The hideous Medusa and two panthers at the center of this early pediment served as temple guardians. To either side, and much smaller, are scenes from the Trojan War and the battle of gods and giants.

SIPHNIAN TREASURY, DELPHI With the sixth century BCE also came the construction of grandiose Ionic temples on the Aegean Islands and the west coast of Asia Minor. The gem of Archaic Ionic architecture and architectural sculpture is, however, not a temple but a treasury (FIG. 5-17) erected by the city of Siphnos in the Sanctuary of Apollo (FIG. 5-17A) at Delphi. Greek *treasuries* were small buildings set up for the safe storage of votive offerings. At Delphi many poleis expressed their civic pride by erecting these templelike but nonperipteral structures. Athens built one with Doric columns in the porch and sculptured metopes in the frieze. The Siphnians equally characteristically employed the Ionic order for their Delphic treasury. Based on the surviving fragments now on display in the Delphi museum, archaeologists have been able to reconstruct the treasury's original appearance (FIG. 5-17). Wealth from the island's gold and silver mines made such a luxurious building possible. In the porch, where one would expect to find fluted Ionic columns, far more elaborate caryatids were employed instead. Caryatids are rare, even in Ionic architecture, but they are unknown in Doric architecture, where they would have been discordant elements in that much more severe order. The Siphnian statue-columns resemble contemporary korai dressed in Ionian chitons and himations (FIG. 5-11).

5-17A Sanctuary of Apollo, Delphi (looking north).

Another Ionic feature of the Siphnian Treasury is the continuous sculptured frieze on all four sides of the building. The north frieze represents the popular theme of the gigantomachy, but it is a much more detailed rendition than that in the corner of the Corfu pediment (FIG. 5-16). In the section reproduced here (FIG. 5-18), Apollo and Artemis pursue a fleeing giant at the right, while behind them one of the lions pulling a goddess's chariot attacks a giant and bites into his midsection. Paint originally enlivened the crowded composition, and painted labels identified the various protagonists, as they do on Archaic black-figure vases (FIGS. 5-19 and 5-20). Some figures had metal weapons. The effect must have been dazzling. On one of the shields the sculptor inscribed his name (unfortunately lost), a clear indication of pride in accomplishment.

5-17 Restored view of the Siphnian Treasury, Sanctuary of Apollo, Delphi, Greece, ca. 530 BCE (John Burge).

Treasuries were storehouses for a city's votive offerings. The Ionic treasury the Siphnians erected in Apollo's sanctuary had caryatids in the porch and sculptures in the pediment and frieze.

1 ft.

5-18 Gigantomachy, detail of the north frieze of the Siphnian Treasury, Delphi, Greece, ca. 530 BCE. Marble, 2′ 1″ high. Archaeological Museum, Delphi.

Greek friezes were brightly painted (FIG. 5-17). As in Archaic vase painting, the Siphnian frieze also had painted labels identifying the various gods and giants. Some of the figures held metal weapons.

Vase Painting

By the mid-sixth century BCE, the Athenians, having learned the black-figure technique from the Corinthians (FIG. 5-5), had taken over the export market for fine painted ceramics (see "Greek Vase Painting," page 110).

FRANÇOIS VASE The masterpiece of early Athenian black-figure painting is the *François Vase* (FIG. 5-19), named for the excavator who discovered it (in hundreds of fragments) in an Etruscan tomb at Chiusi. The vase is a new kind of krater with volute-shaped handles, probably inspired by costly metal prototypes. The signatures of both its painter ("KLEITIAS painted me") and potter ("ERGOTIMOS made me") appear twice among the more than 200 figures in five registers. Labels abound, naming humans and animals alike, even some inanimate objects. The painter devoted only the lowest band to the Orientalizing repertoire of animals and sphinxes. The rest constitute a selective encyclopedia of Greek mythology, focusing on the exploits of Peleus and his son Achilles, the great hero of Homer's *Iliad,* and of Theseus, the legendary king of Athens.

In the detail of the *centauromachy* shown here (FIG. 5-19, *bottom*), Lapiths (a northern Greek tribe) and centaurs battle after a wedding celebration at which the man-beasts, who were invited guests, got drunk and attempted to abduct the Lapith maidens and young boys. Theseus, also on the guest list, was prominent among the centaurs' Greek adversaries. Kleitias did not fill the spaces between his figures with decorative ornament, as did his Geometric predecessors (FIGS. 5-2 and 5-2A). But his heroes still conform to the age-old composite type (profile heads with frontal eyes, frontal torsos, and profile legs and arms). His centaurs, however, are much more believable than their Geometric counterparts (FIG. 5-3). The man-horse combination is top/bottom rather than front/back. The lower (horse) portion has four legs of uniform type, and the upper part of the monster is fully human. In characteristic fashion, Kleitias painted the animal section of the centaur in strict profile, whereas the human head and torso are a composite of frontal and profile views. (He used a consistent profile for the more adventurous detail of the collapsed centaur at the right.)

EXEKIAS The acknowledged master of the black-figure technique was an Athenian named EXEKIAS, whose vases were not only widely exported but copied as well. Perhaps his greatest work is an amphora (FIG. 5-20), found in an Etruscan tomb at Vulci, which Exekias signed as both painter and potter. Unlike Kleitias, Exekias did not divide the surface of the vase into a series of horizontal bands. Instead, he placed figures of monumental stature in a single large

framed panel. At the left is Achilles, fully armed, the mightiest Greek soldier in the war against Troy. He appears again on another of Exekias's amphoras (FIG. 5-20A) battling Penthesilea, queen of the Amazons. On the Vulti amphora Achilles plays a dice game with his comrade Ajax during a lull in the Trojan conflict. Out of the lips of Achilles comes the word *tesara* (four). Ajax calls out *tria* (three). Although Ajax has taken off his helmet, both men hold

5-20A EXEKIAS, Achilles killing Penthesilea, ca. 540–530 BCE.

their spears. Their shields are nearby. Each man is ready for action at a moment's notice. This depiction of "the calm before the storm" is the antithesis of the Archaic preference for dramatic action. The gravity and tension that will characterize much Classical Greek art of the next century, but that are generally absent in Archaic art, already may be seen in this vase.

Exekias had no equal as a black-figure painter. This is evident in details such as the extraordinarily intricate engraving of the patterns on the heroes' cloaks (highlighted with delicate touches of white) and in the brilliant composition. The arch formed by the

1 ft.

5-19 KLEITIAS and ERGOTIMOS, *François Vase* (Athenian black-figure volute krater), from Chiusi, Italy, ca. 570 BCE. General view (*top*) and detail of the centauromachy on the other side of vase (*bottom*). Krater 2′ 2″ high; detail 3″ high. Museo Archeologico Nazionale, Florence. ◼◀

The painter and potter both signed this huge krater found in an Etruscan tomb. The vase has more than 200 mythological figures in five registers, the same format as on Geometric and Orientalizing vases.

1 in.

5-20 EXEKIAS, Achilles and Ajax playing a dice game (detail of an Athenian black-figure amphora), from Vulci, Italy, ca. 540–530 BCE. Amphora 2′ high; detail 8½″ high. Musei Vaticani, Rome. ■◀

The dramatic tension, coordination of figural poses and vase shape, and intricacy of the engraved patterns of the cloaks are hallmarks of Exekias, the greatest master of black-figure painting.

1 in.

backs of the two warriors echoes the shape of the rounded shoulders of the amphora. The shape of the vessel (compare FIGS. 5-20A and 5-21) is echoed again in the void between the heads and spears of Achilles and Ajax. Exekias also used the spears to lead the viewer's eyes toward the thrown dice, where the heroes' eyes are fixed. Of course, those eyes do not really look down at the table but stare out from the profile heads in the old manner. For all his brilliance, Exekias was still wedded to many of the old conventions. Real innovation in figure drawing would have to await the invention of a new ceramic painting technique of greater versatility than black-figure, with its dark silhouettes and incised details.

BILINGUAL PAINTING The birth of this new technique occurred around 530 BCE, and art historians refer to the person responsible as the ANDOKIDES PAINTER, that is, the anonymous painter who decorated the vases signed by the potter ANDOKIDES. The differences between the two techniques can best be studied on a series of experimental vases with the same composition painted on both sides, once in black-figure and once in the new technique, *red-figure*. The Athenians produced these so-called *bilingual vases* for only a short time. An especially interesting example is an amphora (FIG. 5-21) by the Andokides Painter that features copies of the Achilles and Ajax panel by Exekias, his teacher.

5-21 ANDOKIDES PAINTER, Achilles and Ajax playing a dice game (Athenian bilingual amphora), from Orvieto, Italy, ca. 525–520 BCE. Black-figure side (*left*) and red-figure side (*right*). 1′ 9″ high. Museum of Fine Arts, Boston. ■◀

Around 530 BCE, the Andokides Painter invented the red-figure technique. Some of his early vases are "bilingual," that is, they have the same scene on both sides, one in black-figure and one in red-figure.

1 in.

5-22 EUPHRONIOS, Herakles wrestling Antaios (detail of an Athenian red-figure calyx krater), from Cerveteri, Italy, ca. 510 BCE. Krater 1′ 7″ high; detail 7¾″ high. Musée du Louvre, Paris.

Euphronios rejected the age-old composite view for his depiction of Herakles and the giant Antaios and instead attempted to reproduce the way the human body appears from a specific viewpoint.

In neither black-figure nor red-figure did the Andokides Painter capture the intensity of the model, and the treatment of details is decidedly inferior. Yet the new red-figure technique had obvious advantages over the old black-figure manner. Red-figure is the opposite of black-figure. What was previously black became red, and vice versa. The artist used the same black glaze for the figures, but instead of using the glaze to create silhouettes, the painter outlined the figures and then colored the background black. The ceramist reserved the red clay for the figures themselves and used a soft brush instead of a stiff metal graver to draw the interior details. This gave the red-figure painter much greater flexibility. The artist could vary the thickness of the lines and even build up the glaze to give relief to curly hair or dilute it to create brown shades, thereby expanding the chromatic range of the Greek vase painter's craft. The Andokides Painter—very likely the potter Andokides himself—did not yet appreciate the full potential of his own invention. Still, he created a technique that, in the hands of other, more skilled artists, helped revolutionize the art of drawing.

EUPHRONIOS One of those younger and more adventurous painters was EUPHRONIOS, whose krater depicting the struggle between Herakles and Antaios (FIG. 5-22) reveals the exciting possibilities of the new red-figure technique. Antaios was a Libyan giant, a son of Earth, and he derived his power from contact with the ground. To defeat him, Herakles had to lift him into the air and strangle him while no part of the giant's body touched the earth. In Euphronios's representation of the myth, the two wrestle on the ground, and Antaios still possesses enormous strength. Nonetheless, Herakles has the upper hand. The giant's face is a mask of pain. His eyes roll and his teeth are bared. His right arm is paralyzed, with the fingers limp.

On this krater, as on his other signed masterworks, including the most expensive vase ever purchased (FIG. 5-22A), Euphronios used the new red-figure technique brilliantly. For example, he took advantage of the ability to dilute the glaze and produced a golden brown hue for Antaios's hair—intentionally contrasting the giant's unkempt hair with the neat coiffure and

5-22A EUPHRONIOS, Death of Sarpedon, ca. 515 BCE.

carefully trimmed beard of the emotionless Greek hero. The artist also used thinned glaze to delineate the muscles of both figures. But rendering human anatomy convincingly was not his only interest. Euphronios also wished to show that his figures occupy space. He deliberately rejected the conventional composite posture for the human figure, which communicates so well the individual parts of the human body, and attempted instead to reproduce how a particular human body is *seen*. He presented, for example, not only Antaios's torso but also his right thigh from the front. The lower leg disappears behind the giant, and only part of the right foot is visible. The viewer must mentally make the connection between the upper leg and the foot. Euphronios did not create a two-dimensional panel filled with figures in stereotypical postures, as his Archaic and pre-Greek predecessors always did. His panel is a window onto a mythological

5-23 EUTHYMIDES, Three revelers (Athenian red-figure amphora), from Vulci, Italy, ca. 510 BCE. 2′ high. Staatliche Antikensammlungen, Munich. ◼◀

Euthymides chose this theme as an excuse to represent bodies in unusual positions, including a foreshortened three-quarter rear view. He claimed to have surpassed Euphronios as a draftsman.

world with protagonists moving in three-dimensional space—a revolutionary new conception of what a picture is supposed to be.

EUTHYMIDES A preoccupation with the art of drawing per se is evident in a remarkable amphora (FIG. **5-23**) painted by EUTHYMIDES, a rival of Euphronios's. The subject is appropriate for a wine storage jar—three tipsy revelers. But the theme was little more than an excuse for the artist to experiment with the representation of unusual positions of the human form. It is no coincidence that the bodies do not overlap, for each is an independent figure study. Euthymides cast aside the conventional frontal and profile composite views. Instead, he painted torsos that are not two-dimensional surface patterns but are *foreshortened,* that is, drawn in a three-quarter view with some parts of the figures closer to the viewer and others farther away. Most noteworthy is the central figure, shown from the rear with a twisting spinal column and buttocks in three-quarter view. Earlier artists had no interest in attempting to depict figures seen from behind and at an angle because those postures not only

are incomplete views but also do not show the "main" side of the human body. For Euthymides, however, the challenge of drawing a figure from this unusual viewpoint was a reward in itself. With understandable pride he proclaimed his achievement by adding to the formulaic signature "Euthymides painted me" the phrase "as never Euphronios [could do!]" Other vase painters also challenged themselves to outdo their contemporaries in representing the human form. ONESIMOS, for example, successfully drew a young woman's nude torso from a three-quarter view (FIG. **5-23A**).

5-23A ONESIMOS, Girl preparing to bathe, ca. 490 BCE.

Aegina and the Transition to the Classical Period

The years just before and after 500 BCE were also a time of dynamic transition in architecture and architectural sculpture. Some of the changes were evolutionary in nature, others revolutionary. Both kinds are evident in the Doric temple at Aegina dedicated to Aphaia, a local nymph.

TEMPLE OF APHAIA, AEGINA The temple (FIG. **5-24**) sits on a prominent ridge with dramatic views out to the sea. The peripteral colonnade consists of 6 Doric columns on the facade and 12 on the flanks. This is a much more compact structure than the impressive but ungainly Archaic temple (FIG. 5-14) at Paestum, even though the ratio of width to length is similar. Doric architects had learned a great deal in the half century that elapsed between construction of the two temples. The columns of the Aegina temple are more widely spaced and more slender. The capitals create a smooth transition from the vertical shafts below to the horizontal architrave above. Gone are the Archaic flattened echinuses and bulging shafts of the Paestum columns. The Aegina architect also refined the internal elevation and plan (FIG. 5-25). In place of a

5-24 Temple of Aphaia (looking southwest), Aegina, Greece, ca. 500–490 BCE.

In this refined early-fifth-century BCE Doric design (compare FIG. 5-14), the columns are more slender and widely spaced, and there are only 6 columns on the facade and 12 on the flanks.

5-25 Model showing internal elevation (*top*) and plan (*bottom*) of the Temple of Aphaia, Aegina, Greece, ca. 500–490 BCE. Model: Glyptothek, Munich.

Later Doric architects also modified the plan of their temples (compare FIG. 5-15). The Aegina temple's cella has two colonnades, each of two stories (originally with a statue of the deity between them).

5-26 GUILLAUME-ABEL BLOUET, restored view (1828) of the facade of the Temple of Aphaia, Aegina, Greece, ca. 500–490 BCE.

The restored view suggests how colorful Greek temples were. The designer solved the problem of composing figures in a pediment by using the whole range of body postures from upright to prostrate.

single row of columns down the center of the cella is a double colonnade—and each row has two stories. This arrangement allowed a statue to be placed on the central axis and also gave worshipers gathered in front of the building an unobstructed view through the pair of columns in the pronaos.

Painted life-size statuary (FIG. **5-26**) filled both pediments, in contrast to the high reliefs characteristic of most Archaic temple pediments. The theme of both statuary groups was the battle of Greeks and Trojans, but the sculptors depicted different episodes. The compositions were nonetheless almost identical, with Athena at the center of the bloody combat. She is larger than all the other figures because she is superhuman, but all the mortal heroes are the same size, regardless of the statue's position in the pediment. Unlike the experimental design at Corfu (FIG. **5-16**), the Aegina pediments feature a unified theme and consistent scale. The designer was able to keep the size of the figures constant by using the whole range of body postures from upright (Athena) to leaning, falling, kneeling, and lying (Greeks and Trojans).

The Aegina sculptors set the pedimental statues in place around 490 BCE, as soon as construction of the temple concluded. Many scholars believe the statues at the eastern end were damaged and replaced with a new group a decade or two later, although some think both groups date after 480 BCE. In either case, it is instructive to compare the eastern and western figures. The sculptor of the west pediment's dying warrior (FIG. **5-27**) still conceived the statue in the Archaic mode. The warrior's torso is rigidly frontal, and he looks out directly at the spectator—with his face set in an Archaic smile despite the bronze arrow that punctures his chest. He is like a mannequin in a store window whose arms and legs have been arranged by someone else for effective display. There is no sense whatsoever of a thinking and feeling human being.

The comparable figure (FIG. **5-28**) in the east pediment is radically different. This warrior's posture is more natural and more complex, with the torso placed at an angle to the viewer (compare FIG. **5-22**). Moreover, he reacts to his wound as a flesh-and-blood human would. He knows that death is inevitable, but he still struggles to rise once again, using his shield for support. He does not look out at the spectator. This dying warrior is concerned with his plight, not with the viewer. No more than a decade separates the two statues, but they belong to different eras. The eastern warrior is not a creation of the Archaic world, when sculptors imposed anatomical patterns (and smiles) on statues. This statue belongs to the Classical world, where statues move as humans move and possess the self-consciousness of real men and women. This constitutes a radical change in the conception of the nature of statuary. In sculpture, as in painting, the Classical revolution had occurred.

EARLY AND HIGH CLASSICAL PERIODS

Art historians date the beginning of the Classical* age from a historical event: the defeat of the Persian invaders of Greece by the allied Hellenic city-states. Shortly after the Persians occupied and

---

*Note: In *Art through the Ages,* the adjective "Classical," with uppercase *C,* refers specifically to the Classical period of ancient Greece, 480–323 BCE. Lowercase "classical" refers to Greco-Roman antiquity in general, that is, the period treated in Chapters 5, 6, and 7.

5-27 Dying warrior, from the west pediment of the Temple of Aphaia, Aegina, Greece, ca. 490 BCE. Marble, 5′ 2½″ long. Glyptothek, Munich.

The statues of the west pediment of the early-fifth-century BCE temple at Aegina exhibit Archaic features. This fallen warrior still has a rigidly frontal torso and an Archaic smile.

5-28 Dying warrior, from the east pediment of the Temple of Aphaia, Aegina, Greece, ca. 480 BCE. Marble, 6′ 1″ long. Glyptothek, Munich.

The eastern dying warrior already belongs to the Classical era. His posture is more natural, and he exhibits a new self-consciousness. Concerned with his own pain, he does not face the viewer.

sacked Athens in 480 BCE, the Greeks won a decisive naval victory over the Persians at Salamis. It had been a difficult war, and at times it appeared Asia would swallow up Greece and the Persian king Xerxes (see Chapter 2) would rule over all. When the Persians destroyed the Greek city Miletos in 494 BCE, they killed the male inhabitants and sold the women and children into slavery. The narrow escape of the Greeks from domination by Asian "barbarians" nurtured a sense of Hellenic identity so strong that from then on the history of European civilization would be distinct from the civilization of Asia, even though they continued to interact. Typical of the time were the views of the great dramatist Aeschylus, who celebrated, in his *Oresteia* trilogy, the triumph of reason and law over barbarous crimes, blood feuds, and mad vengeance. As a veteran himself of the epic battle of Marathon, Aeschylus repudiated in majestic verse all the slavish and inhuman traits of nature the Greeks at that time of crisis associated with the Persians.

Architecture and Architectural Sculpture

The decades following the removal of the Persian threat are universally considered the high point of Greek civilization. This is the era of the dramatists Sophocles and Euripides, as well as Aeschylus; the historian Herodotus; the statesman Pericles; the philosopher Socrates; and many of the most famous Greek architects, sculptors, and painters.

TEMPLE OF ZEUS, OLYMPIA The first great monument of Classical art and architecture is the Temple of Zeus at Olympia, site of the Olympic Games. The architect was LIBON OF ELIS, who began work on the temple about 470 BCE and completed it by 457 BCE. Today, the structure is in ruins, its picturesque tumbled column drums an eloquent reminder of the effect of the passage of time on even the grandest monuments humans have built. A good idea of its original appearance can be gleaned, however,

The model for the second Hera(?) temple at Paestum was Libon's Zeus temple at Olympia. The Paestum temple reflects the Olympia design but lacks the pedimental sculpture of its model.

from a slightly later Doric temple (FIG. 5-29) modeled closely on the Olympian shrine of Zeus—the temple usually identified as the second Temple of Hera at Paestum but possibly a temple dedicated to Apollo. The plans and elevations of both temples follow the pattern of the Temple of Aphaia (FIG. 5-25) at Aegina: an even number of columns (six) on the short ends, two columns in antis, and two rows of columns in two stories inside the cella. But the Temple of Zeus was more lavishly decorated than even the Aphaia temple. Statues filled both pediments, and narrative reliefs adorned the six metopes over the doorway in the pronaos and the matching six of the opisthodomos.

The subject of the Temple of Zeus's east pediment (FIG. 5-30) is the chariot race between Pelops (from whom the Peloponnesos region takes its name) and King Oinomaos. The story, which had deep local significance, is a sinister one. Oinomaos had one daughter, Hippodameia, and a prophecy foretold that he would die if she married. Consequently, Oinomaos challenged any suitor who wished to make Hippodameia his bride to a chariot race from Olympia to Corinth. If the suitor won, he also won the hand of the king's daughter. But if he lost, Oinomaos killed him. The outcome of each race was predetermined, because Oinomaos possessed the divine horses of his father Ares. To ensure his victory when all others had failed, Pelops resorted to bribing the king's groom, Myrtilos, to rig the royal chariot so that it would collapse during the race. Oinomaos was killed and Pelops won his bride, but he drowned

Myrtilos rather than pay his debt to him. Before he died, Myrtilos brought a curse on Pelops and his descendants. This curse led to the murder of Pelops's son Atreus and to events that figure prominently in some of the greatest Greek tragedies of the Classical era, Aeschylus's three plays known collectively as the *Oresteia*: the sacrifice by Atreus's son Agamemnon of his daughter Iphigeneia; the slaying of Agamemnon by Aegisthus, lover of Agamemnon's wife Clytaemnestra; and the murder of Aegisthus and Clytaemnestra by Orestes, the son of Agamemnon and Clytaemnestra.

Indeed, the pedimental statues (FIG. 5-30), which faced toward the starting point of all Olympic chariot races, are posed as if actors on a stage—Zeus in the center, Oinomaos and his wife on one side, Pelops and Hippodameia on the other, and their respective chariots to each side. All are quiet. The horrible events known to every spectator have yet to occur. Only one man reacts—a seer (FIG. 5-31) who knows the future. He is a remarkable figure. Unlike the gods, heroes, and noble youths and maidens who are the almost exclusive subjects of Archaic and Classical Greek statuary, this seer is a rare depiction of old age. He has a balding, wrinkled head and sagging musculature—and a shocked expression on his face. This is a true show of emotion, unlike the stereotypical Archaic smile, without precedent in earlier Greek sculpture and not a regular feature of Greek art until the Hellenistic age.

In the west pediment, Apollo (FIG. 5-32), the central figure, is also at rest, but all around him is a chaotic scene of Greeks battling

10 ft.

5-30 **Chariot race of Pelops and Oinomaos, east pediment, Temple of Zeus, Olympia, Greece, ca. 470–456 BCE. Marble, 87′ wide. Archaeological Museum, Olympia.**

The east pediment of the Zeus temple depicts the legendary chariot race across the Peloponnesos from Olympia to Corinth. The actors in the pediment faced the starting point of Olympic chariot races.

5-31 Seer, from the east pediment (FIG. 5-30) of the Temple of Zeus, Olympia, Greece, ca. 470–456 BCE. Marble, 4′ 6″ high. Archaeological Museum, Olympia.

The balding seer in the Olympia east pediment is a rare depiction of old age in Classical sculpture. He has a shocked expression because he foresees the tragic outcome of the chariot race.

1 ft.

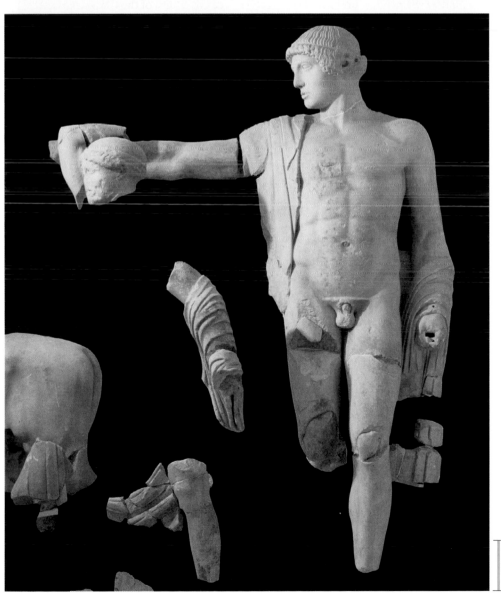

5-32 Apollo, from the west pediment (FIG. 5-32A) of the Temple of Zeus, Olympia, Greece, ca. 470–456 BCE. Marble, restored height 10′ 8″. Archaeological Museum, Olympia.

The epitome of calm rationality, Apollo, with a commanding gesture of his right hand, attempts to bring order out of the chaotic struggle all around him between the Lapiths and the beastly centaurs.

1 ft.

Early and High Classical Periods **127**

Herakles, Greatest of Greek Heroes

Greek heroes were a class of mortals intermediate between ordinary humans and the immortal gods. Most often the children of gods, some were great warriors, such as Achilles and Ajax (FIG. 5-20) and others who fought at Troy and were celebrated in Homer's epic poems. Some heroes went from one fabulous adventure to another, ridding the world of monsters and generally benefiting humankind. Perseus, for example, was the slayer of the hideous Medusa (FIG. 5-16). Bellerophon killed the chimera (FIG. 6-12), a composite lion-goat-serpent beast. Many heroes were worshiped after their deaths, especially in the cities with which they were most closely associated.

The greatest Greek hero was Herakles (the Roman Hercules), who may be the subject of one of the earliest preserved works of Greek narrative art—the bronze figure (FIG. 5-3) depicting a hero battling a centaur. Born in Thebes, Herakles was the son of Zeus and Alkmene, a mortal woman. Zeus's jealous wife Hera hated Herakles and sent two serpents to attack him in his cradle, but the infant strangled them. Later, Hera caused the hero to go mad and to kill his wife and children. As punishment, he was condemned to perform 12 great labors. In the first, he defeated the legendary lion of Nemea and ever after wore its pelt. The lion's skin and his weapon, a club, are Herakles' distinctive attributes (FIGS. 5-63A and 5-66). His last task was to obtain the golden apples the goddess Gaia gave to Hera at her marriage (FIG. 5-33). They grew from a tree in the garden of the Hesperides at the western edge of the ocean, where a dragon guarded them. After completion of the 12 seemingly impossible tasks, Herakles was awarded immortality. Athena, who had watched over him carefully throughout his life and assisted him in performing the labors, introduced him into the realm of the gods on Mount Olympus.

The legendary strongman was the model for many Greek athletes. In fact, the Greeks believed Herakles was the founder of the Olympic Games.

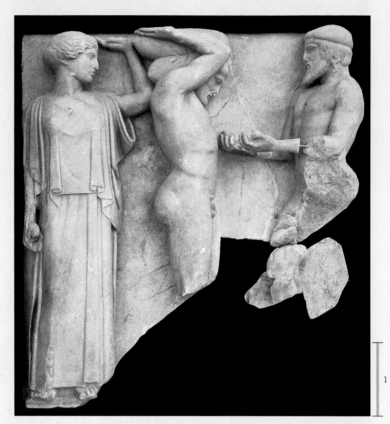

5-33 Athena, Herakles, and Atlas with the apples of the Hesperides, metope from the Temple of Zeus, Olympia, Greece, ca. 470–456 BCE. Marble, 5′ 3″ high. Archaeological Museum, Olympia.

Herakles founded the Olympic Games, and his 12 labors were the subjects of the 12 metopes of the Zeus temple. This one shows the hero holding up the world (with Athena's aid) for Atlas.

5-32A West pediment, Temple of Zeus, Olympia, ca. 470–456 BCE.

centaurs (FIG. **5-32A**). A mixture of calm, even pensive, figures and others involved in violent action also characterizes the narrative reliefs of the 12 metopes of the Zeus temple. They are thematically connected with Olympia, for they depict the 12 labors of Herakles (see "Herakles, Greatest of Greek Heroes," above), the legendary founder of the Olympic Games. In the metope illustrated here (FIG. **5-33**), Herakles holds up the sky (with the aid of the goddess Athena—and a cushion) in place of Atlas, who had undertaken the dangerous journey to fetch the golden apples of the Hesperides for the hero. Herakles will soon transfer the load back to Atlas (at the right, still holding the apples), but now each of the very high relief figures in the metope stands quietly with the same serene dignity as the statues in the east pediment (FIG. 5-30) and Apollo (FIG. 5-32) in the west pediment. In both attitude and dress (simple Doric peploi for the women), these Olympia figures display a severity that contrasts sharply with the smiling and elaborately clad fig-

ures of the Late Archaic period. Consequently, many art historians call this Early Classical phase of Greek art the *Severe Style*.

Statuary

The hallmark of Early Classical statuary is the abandonment of the rigid and unnatural Egyptian-inspired pose of Archaic statues. The figures in the Olympia pediments exemplify this radical break with earlier practice, but the change occurred even earlier—at the very moment Greece was under attack by the Persians.

KRITIOS BOY Although it is well under life-size, the marble statue known as the *Kritios Boy* (FIG. **5-34**)—because art historians once thought it was the work of the sculptor Kritios—is one of the most important statues in the history of art. Never before had a sculptor been concerned with portraying how a human being (as opposed to a stone image) truly stands. Real people do not stand in the stiff-legged pose of the kouroi and korai or their Egyptian predecessors. Humans shift their weight and the position of the torso around the vertical (but flexible) axis of the spine. When

1 ft.

1 ft.

5-34 *Kritios Boy*, from the Acropolis, Athens, Greece, ca. 480 BCE. Marble, 2′ 10″ high. Acropolis Museum, Athens.

This is the first statue to show how a person naturally stands. The sculptor depicted the weight shift from one leg to the other (contrapposto). The head turns slightly, and the Archaic smile is gone.

5-35 Warrior, from the sea off Riace, Italy, ca. 460–450 BCE. Bronze, 6′ 6″ high. Museo Archeologico Nazionale, Reggio Calabria.

The bronze Riace warrior statue has inlaid eyes, silver teeth and eyelashes, and copper lips and nipples (FIG. I-17). The contrapposto is more pronounced than in the *Kritios Boy* (FIG. 5-34).

humans move, the body's elastic musculoskeletal structure dictates a harmonious, smooth motion of all its parts. The sculptor of the *Kritios Boy* was the first, or one of the first, to grasp this anatomical fact and to represent it in statuary. The youth has a slight dip to the right hip, indicating the shifting of weight onto his left leg. His right leg is bent, at ease. The head also turns slightly to the right and tilts, breaking the unwritten rule of frontality dictating the form of virtually all earlier statues. This weight shift, which art historians describe as *contrapposto* (counterbalance), separates Classical from Archaic Greek statuary.

RIACE WARRIOR An unknown sculptor carried the innovations of the *Kritios Boy* even further in the bronze statue (FIG. 5-35) of a warrior found in the sea near Riace at the "toe" of the Italian "boot." It is one of a pair of statues divers accidentally discovered in the cargo of a ship that sank in antiquity on its way from Greece probably to Rome, where Greek sculpture was much admired. Known as the Riace Bronzes, the two statues had to undergo several years of cleaning and restoration after nearly two millennia of submersion in salt water, but they are nearly intact. The statue shown here lacks only its shield, spear, and helmet. It is a masterpiece of

Hollow-Casting Life-Size Bronze Statues

Monumental bronze statues such as the Riace warrior (FIG. 5-35), the Delphi charioteer (FIG. 5-37), and the Artemision god (FIG. 5-38) required great technical skill to produce. They could not be manufactured using a single simple mold of the sort Geometric and Archaic sculptors used for their small-scale figures (FIGS. 5-3 and 5-4). Weight, cost, and the tendency of large masses of bronze to distort when cooling made life-size castings in solid bronze impractical, if not impossible. Instead, the Greeks hollow-cast large statues by the *cire perdue* (*lost-wax*) method. The lost-wax process entailed several steps and had to be repeated many times, because sculptors typically cast monumental statues in parts—head, arms, hands, torso, and so forth.

First the sculptor fashioned a full-size clay model of the intended statue. Then an assistant formed a clay master mold around the model and removed the mold in sections. When dry, the various pieces of the master mold were reassembled for each separate body part. Next, assistants applied a layer of beeswax to the inside of each mold. When the wax cooled, the sculptor removed the mold, revealing a hollow wax model in the shape of the original clay model. The artist could then correct or refine details—for example, engrave fingernails on the wax hands or individual locks of hair on the head.

In the next stage, an assistant applied a final clay mold (*investment*) to the exterior of the wax model and poured liquid clay inside the model. Apprentices then hammered metal pins (*chaplets*)

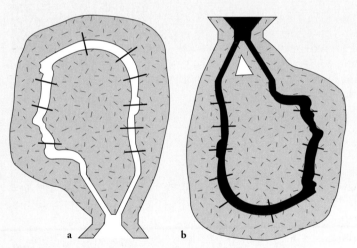

5-36 Two stages of the lost-wax method of bronze casting (after Sean A. Hemingway).

Drawing *a* shows a clay mold (investment), wax model, and clay core connected by chaplets. Drawing *b* shows the wax melted out and the molten bronze poured into the mold to form the cast bronze head.

5-37 Charioteer, from a group dedicated by Polyzalos of Gela in the Sanctuary of Apollo (FIG. 5-17A), Delphi, Greece, ca. 470 BCE. Bronze, 5′ 11″ high. Archaeological Museum, Delphi.

The charioteer was part of a large bronze group that also included a chariot, a team of horses, and a groom. The assemblage required hundreds of individually cast pieces soldered together.

1 ft.

through the new mold to connect the investment with the clay core (FIG. 5-36*a*). Next, the wax was melted out ("lost") and molten bronze poured into the mold in its place (FIG. 5-36*b*). When the bronze hardened and assumed the shape of the wax model, the bronze-caster removed the investment and as much of the core as possible, completing the hollow-casting process. The last step was to fit together and solder the individually cast pieces, smooth the joins and any surface imperfections, inlay the eyes, and add teeth, eyelashes, and accessories such as spears and wreaths. Life-size bronze statues produced in this way were very costly but highly prized.

hollow-casting (see "Hollow-Casting Life-Size Bronze Statues," above, and FIG. 5-36), with inlaid eyes, silver teeth and eyelashes, and copper lips and nipples (FIG. I-17). The weight shift is more pronounced than in the *Kritios Boy*. The warrior's head turns more forcefully to the right, his shoulders tilt, his hips swing more markedly, and his arms have been freed from the body. Natural motion in space has replaced Archaic frontality and rigidity.

CHARIOTEER OF DELPHI A bronze statuary group that equals or exceeds the Riace warrior in technical quality is the chariot group set up a decade or two earlier by the tyrant Polyzalos of Gela (Sicily) to commemorate his victory in the Pythian Games at Delphi (FIG. 5-17A). Almost all that remains of the large group composed of Polyzalos's driver, the chariot, the team of horses, and a young groom is the bronze charioteer (FIG. 5-37). He stands in an almost Archaic

5-38 Zeus (or Poseidon?), from the sea off Cape Artemision, Greece, ca. 460–450 BCE. Bronze, 6' 10" high. National Archaeological Museum, Athens.

In this statue, the god—probably Zeus hurling a thunderbolt—boldly extends both arms and raises his right heel off the ground, underscoring the lightness and stability of hollow-cast bronze statues.

5-39 MYRON, *Diskobolos* (*Discus Thrower*). Roman copy of a bronze statue of ca. 450 BCE. Marble, 5' 1" high. Museo Nazionale Romano—Palazzo Massimo alle Terme.

This marble copy of Myron's lost bronze statue captures how the sculptor froze the action of discus throwing and arranged the nude athlete's body and limbs so they form two intersecting arcs.

pose, but the turn of the head and feet in opposite directions as well as a slight twist at the waist are in keeping with the Severe Style. The moment the sculptor chose for depiction was not during the frenetic race but after, when the driver modestly held his horses quietly in the winner's circle. The charioteer grasps the reins in his outstretched right hand (the lower left arm, cast separately, is missing), and he wears the standard charioteer's garment, girdled high and held in at the shoulders and the back to keep it from flapping. The folds emphasize both the verticality and calm of the figure and recall the flutes of a Greek column. The fillet that holds the charioteer's hair in place is inlaid with silver. The eyes are glass paste, shaded by delicate bronze lashes individually cut from a sheet of bronze and soldered to the head.

ARTEMISION ZEUS The male human form in motion is, in contrast, the subject of another Early Classical bronze statue (FIG. 5-38), which, like the Riace warrior, divers found in an ancient shipwreck, this time off the coast of Greece itself at Cape Artemision. The bearded god once hurled a weapon held in his right hand, probably a thunderbolt, in which case he is Zeus. A less likely suggestion is that this is Poseidon with his trident (see "Gods and Goddesses," page 107). The pose could be employed equally well for

a javelin thrower. Both arms are boldly extended, and the right heel is raised off the ground, underscoring the lightness and stability of hollow-cast monumental statues.

MYRON, *DISKOBOLOS* A bronze statue similar to the Artemision Zeus was the renowned *Diskobolos* (*Discus Thrower*) by the Early Classical master MYRON. The original is lost. Only marble copies (FIG. 5-39) survive, made in Roman times, when demand so far exceeded the supply of Greek statues that a veritable industry was born to meet the call for Greek statuary to display in public places and private villas alike. Usually, the copies were of less costly painted marble, which presented a very different appearance from shiny bronze. In most cases, the copyist also had to add an intrusive tree trunk to support the great weight of the stone statue and to place struts between arms and body to strengthen weak points. The copies rarely approach the quality of the originals, and the Roman sculptors sometimes took liberties with their models according to their own tastes and needs. Occasionally, for example, sculptors created a mirror image of the original for a specific setting. Nevertheless, the copies are indispensable today. Without them it would be impossible to reconstruct the history of Greek sculpture after the Archaic period.

Polykleitos's Prescription for the Perfect Statue

One of the most influential philosophers of the ancient world was Pythagoras of Samos, who lived during the latter part of the sixth century BCE. A famous geometric theorem still bears his name. Pythagoras also is said to have discovered that harmonic chords in music are produced on the strings of a lyre at regular intervals that may be expressed as ratios of whole numbers—for example, 2:1, 3:2, 4:3. He and his followers, the Pythagoreans, believed more generally that underlying harmonic proportions could be found in all of nature, determining the form of the cosmos as well as of things on earth, and that beauty resided in harmonious numerical ratios.

By this reasoning, a perfect statue would be one constructed according to an all-encompassing mathematical formula. In the mid-fifth century BCE, the sculptor Polykleitos of Argos set out to make just such a statue (FIG. 5-40). He recorded the principles he followed and the proportions he used in a treatise titled the *Canon,* that is, the standard of perfection. His treatise is unfortunately lost, but Galen, a physician who lived during the second century CE, summarized the sculptor's philosophy as follows:

> [Beauty arises from] the commensurability [*symmetria*] of the parts, such as that of finger to finger, and of all the fingers to the palm and the wrist, and of these to the forearm, and of the forearm to the upper arm, and, in fact, of everything to everything else, just as it is written in the *Canon* of Polykleitos. . . . Polykleitos supported his treatise [by making] a statue according to the tenets of his treatise, and called the statue, like the work, the *Canon*.*

This is why Pliny the Elder, whose first-century CE multivolume *Natural History* is one of the most important sources for the history of Greek art, maintained that Polykleitos "alone of men is deemed to have rendered art itself [that is, the theoretical basis of art] in a work of art."[†]

Polykleitos's belief that a successful statue resulted from the precise application of abstract principles is reflected in an anecdote (probably a later invention) told by the Roman historian Aelian:

> Polykleitos made two statues at the same time, one which would be pleasing to the crowd and the other according to the principles of his art. In accordance with the opinion of each person who came into his workshop, he altered something and changed its form, submitting to the advice of each. Then he put both statues on display. The one was marvelled at by everyone, and the other was laughed at. Thereupon Polykleitos said, "But the one that you find fault with, you made yourselves; while the one that you marvel at, I made."[‡]

5-40 POLYKLEITOS, *Doryphoros* (*Spear Bearer*). Roman copy from the palaestra, Pompeii, Italy, of a bronze statue of ca. 450–440 BCE. Marble, 6′ 11″ high. Museo Archeologico Nazionale, Naples.

Polykleitos sought to portray the perfect man and to impose order on human movement. He achieved his goals through harmonic proportions and a system of cross balance for all parts of the body. ◼◀

1 ft.

Galen, Pliny, and Aelian are only three of the many Greek and Roman authors who wrote about Greek art and artists. Although none of those writers was an art historian in the modern sense, the existence in the Greco-Roman world of theoretical treatises by artists and of a tradition of art criticism is noteworthy and without parallel in antiquity or during the Middle Ages.

*Galen, *De placitis Hippocratis et Platonis*, 5. Translated by J. J. Pollitt, *The Art of Ancient Greece: Sources and Documents* (New York: Cambridge University Press, 1990), 76.
†Pliny the Elder, *Natural History*, 34.55. Translated by Pollitt, 75.
‡Aelian, *Varia historia*, 14.8. Translated by Pollitt, 79.

Myron's *Discus Thrower* is a vigorous action statue, like the Artemision Zeus, but the sculptor posed the body in an almost Archaic manner, with profile limbs and a nearly frontal chest, suggesting the tension of a coiled spring. Like the arm of a pendulum clock, the right arm of the *Diskobolos* has reached the apex of its arc but has not yet begun to swing down again. Myron froze the action and arranged the body and limbs to form two intersecting arcs (one from the discus to the left hand, one from the head to the right knee), creating the impression of a tightly stretched bow a moment

before the archer releases the string. This tension, however, is not mirrored in the athlete's face, which remains expressionless. Once again, as in the warrior statue (FIG. 5-28) from the Aegina east pediment, the head is turned away from the spectator. In contrast to Archaic athlete statues, the Classical *Diskobolos* does not perform for the spectator but concentrates on the task at hand.

POLYKLEITOS, *DORYPHOROS* One of the most frequently copied Greek statues was the *Doryphoros* (*Spear Bearer*) by

POLYKLEITOS, the sculptor whose work epitomizes the intellectual rigor of Classical art. The best marble replica (FIG. 5-40) stood in a *palaestra* (gymnasium) at Pompeii, where it served as a model for Roman athletes. The *Doryphoros* was the embodiment of Polykleitos's vision of the ideal statue of a nude male athlete or warrior. (The *Spear Bearer* may also have held a shield.) In fact, the sculptor made it as a demonstration piece to accompany a treatise on the subject. *Spear Bearer* is a modern descriptive title for the statue. The name Polykleitos assigned to it was *Canon* (see "Polykleitos's Prescription for the Perfect Statue," page 132).

The *Doryphoros* is the culmination of the evolution in Greek statuary from the Archaic kouros to the *Kritios Boy* to the Riace warrior. The contrapposto is more pronounced than ever before in a standing statue, but Polykleitos was not content with simply rendering a figure that stands naturally. His aim was to impose order on human movement, to make it "beautiful," to "perfect" it. He achieved this through a system of cross balance. What appears at first to be a casually natural pose is, in fact, the result of an extremely complex and subtle organization of the figure's various parts. Note, for instance, how the straight-hanging arm echoes the rigid supporting leg, providing the figure's right side with the columnar stability needed to anchor the left side's dynamically flexed limbs. If read anatomically, however, the tensed and relaxed limbs may be seen to oppose each other diagonally—the right arm and the left leg are relaxed, and the tensed supporting leg opposes the flexed arm, which held a spear. In like manner, the head turns to the right while the hips twist slightly to the left. And although the *Doryphoros* seems to take a step forward, he does not move. This dynamic asymmetrical balance, this motion while at rest, and the resulting harmony of opposites are the essence of the Polykleitan style.

The Athenian Acropolis

While Polykleitos was formulating his *Canon* in Argos, the Athenians, under the leadership of Pericles, were at work on one of the most ambitious building projects ever undertaken, the reconstruction of the Acropolis after the Persian sack. In September 480 BCE, the Athenian commander Themistocles decisively defeated the Persian navy off the island of Salamis, southwest of Athens, and forced it to retreat to Asia. Athens, despite the damage it suffered at the hands of the army of Xerxes, emerged from the war with enormous power and prestige. Less than two years later, in 478 BCE, the Greeks formed an alliance for mutual protection against any renewed threat from the East. The new confederacy came to be known as the Delian League, because its headquarters were on the sacred island of Delos, midway between the Greek mainland and the coast of Asia Minor. Although at the outset each league member had an equal vote, Athens was "first among equals," providing the allied fleet commander and determining which cities were to furnish ships and which were instead to pay an annual tribute to the treasury at Delos.

Continued fighting against the Persians kept the Delian alliance intact, but Athens gradually assumed a dominant role. In 454 BCE, the league's treasury was transferred to Athens, ostensibly for security reasons. Pericles, who was only in his teens when the Persians laid waste to the Acropolis, was by mid-century the recognized leader of the Athenians, and he succeeded in converting the alliance into an Athenian empire. Tribute continued to be paid, but the Athenians did not spend the surplus reserves for the common good of the allied Greek states. Instead, Pericles expropriated the money to pay the enormous cost of executing his grand plan to embellish the Acropolis of Athens.

The reaction of the allies—in reality the subjects of Athens—was predictable. Plutarch, who wrote a biography of Pericles in the early second century CE, reported not only the wrath the Greek victims of Athenian tyranny felt but also the protest voiced against Pericles' decision even in the Athenian assembly. Greece, Pericles' enemies said, had been dealt "a terrible, wanton insult" when Athens used the funds contributed out of necessity for a common war effort to "gild and embellish itself with images and extravagant temples, like some pretentious woman decked out with precious stones."[3] That the Delian League was the source of the funds used for the Acropolis building program is important to keep in mind when examining those great and universally admired buildings erected to realize Pericles' vision of his polis reborn from the ashes of the Persian sack. They are not the glorious fruits of Athenian democracy but are instead the by-products of tyranny and the abuse of power. Too often art and architectural historians do not ask how patrons, whether public or private, paid for the monuments they commissioned. The answer can be very revealing—and very embarrassing.

PORTRAIT OF PERICLES A number of extant Roman marble sculptures are copies of a famous bronze portrait statue of Pericles by KRESILAS, who was born on Crete but worked in Athens. The Athenians set up the portrait on the Acropolis, probably immediately after their leader's death in 429 BCE. Kresilas depicted Pericles in heroic nudity, and his portrait must have resembled the Riace warrior (FIG. 5-35). The copies reproduce the head only, sometimes, as in FIG. 5-41, in the form of a *herm* (a bust on a square pillar). The inscription on the herm reads "Pericles, son of Xanthippos, the Athenian." Pericles wears the helmet of a *strategos* (general), the elective position he held 15 times. The Athenian leader was said to have had an abnormally elongated skull, and Kresilas recorded this feature (while also concealing it) by providing a glimpse through the helmet's eye slots of the hair at the top of the head. This, together with the unblemished features of Pericles' aloof face and, no doubt, his body's perfect physique, led Pliny to assert that

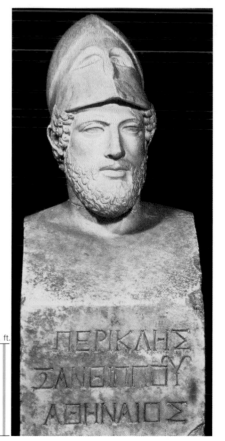

5-41 KRESILAS, *Pericles.* Roman herm copy of the head of a bronze statue of ca. 429 BCE. Marble, full herm 6' high; detail 4' 6½" high. Musei Vaticani, Rome.

In his portrait of Pericles, Kresilas was said to have made a noble man appear even nobler. Classical Greek portraits were not likenesses but idealized images in which humans appeared godlike.

5-42 Aerial view of the Acropolis (looking southeast), Athens, Greece. ◼◀

Under the leadership of Pericles, the Athenians undertook the costly project of reconstructing the Acropolis after the Persian sack of 480 BCE. The funds came from the Delian League treasury.

5-43 Restored view of the Acropolis, Athens, Greece (John Burge). (1) Parthenon, (2) Propylaia, (3) pinakotheke, (4) Erechtheion, (5) Temple of Athena Nike.

Of the four main fifth-century BCE buildings on the Acropolis, the first to be erected was the Parthenon, followed by the Propylaia, the Erechtheion, and the Temple of Athena Nike.

Kresilas had the ability to make noble men appear even more noble in their portraits. This praise was apt because the Acropolis statue was not a portrait in the modern sense of a record of specific features, but an image of an individual that conformed to the Classical ideal of beauty. Pliny refers to Kresilas's "portrait" as "the Olympian Pericles," because the statue made Pericles appear almost godlike.[4]

PERICLEAN ACROPOLIS The centerpiece of the Periclean building program on the Acropolis (FIG. **5-42**) was the Parthenon (FIGS. 5-1 and **5-43**, no. 1), dedicated to Athena Parthenos, and erected in the remarkably short period between 447 and 438 BCE. (Work on the temple's ambitious sculptural ornamentation continued until 432 BCE.) As soon as the Athenian builders completed work on the Parthenon, construction commenced on the Propylaia (FIG. 5-43, no. 2), the grand new western gateway to the Acropolis (the only accessible side of the natural plateau). Begun in 437 BCE, work stopped in 431 at the outbreak of the Peloponnesian War between Athens and Sparta and never resumed. Two later temples, the Erechtheion (FIG. 5-43, no. 4) and the Temple of Athena Nike (FIG. 5-43, no. 5), built after Pericles died, were probably also part of the original project. The greatest Athenian architects and sculptors of the Classical period focused their attention on the construction and decoration of these four buildings.

That these ancient buildings exist at all today is something of a miracle. In the Middle Ages, the Parthenon, for example, became a Byzantine and later a Roman Catholic church and then, after the Ottoman conquest of Greece, a mosque. With each rededication, religious officials remodeled the building. The Christians early on removed the colossal statue of Athena inside. The churches had a great curved *apse* at the east end housing the altar. The Ottomans added a *minaret* (tower used to call Muslims to prayer). In 1687,

the Venetians besieged the Acropolis. One of their rockets scored a direct hit on the ammunition depot the Ottomans had installed in part of the Parthenon. The resultant explosion blew out the building's center. To make matters worse, the Venetians subsequently tried to remove some of the statues from the Parthenon's pediments. In more than one case, the workmen dropped the statues, which smashed on the ground. From 1801 to 1803, Thomas Bruce (1766–1841), Lord Elgin, brought most of the surviving sculptures to England. For the past two centuries, they have been on exhibit in the British Museum (FIGS. 5-47 to 5-50), although Greece has appealed many times for the return of the "Elgin Marbles" and built a new museum near the Acropolis to house them. Today, a uniquely modern blight threatens the Parthenon and the other buildings of the Periclean age. The corrosive emissions of factories and automobiles are decomposing the ancient marbles. A comprehensive campaign has been under way for some time to protect the columns and walls from further deterioration. What little original sculpture remained in place when modern restoration began is now in the new museum's climate-controlled rooms.

PARTHENON: ARCHITECTURE Despite the ravages of time and humanity, most of the Parthenon's peripteral colonnade (FIG. 5-1) is still standing (or has been reerected), and art historians know a great deal about the building and its sculptural program. The architect was Iktinos, assisted, according to some sources, by KALLIKRATES. The statue of Athena (FIG. 5-46) in the cella was the work of Phidias, who was also the overseer of the temple's sculptural decoration. In fact, Plutarch stated that Phidias was in charge of the entire Acropolis project.

Just as the contemporaneous *Doryphoros* (FIG. 5-40) may be seen as the culmination of nearly two centuries of searching for the ideal proportions of the various human body parts, so, too, the Parthenon may be viewed as the ideal solution to the Greek architect's quest for perfect proportions in Doric temple design (see "The Perfect Temple," page 105). Its well-spaced columns (FIG. **5-44**), with their slender shafts, and the capitals, with their straight-sided conical echinuses,

5-44 Iktinos and Kallikrates, east facade of the Parthenon, Acropolis, Athens, Greece, 447–438 BCE. 📹

Iktinos believed harmonic proportions produced beautiful buildings. In the Parthenon, the ratio of larger and smaller parts is $x = 2y + 1$ (8 columns on the facade, 17 on the side).

are the ultimate refinement of the bulging and squat Doric columns and compressed capitals of the Archaic Hera temple (FIG. 5-14) at Paestum. The Parthenon architects and Polykleitos were kindred spirits in their belief that beautiful proportions resulted from strict adherence to harmonic numerical ratios, whether in a temple more than 200 feet long or a life-size statue of a nude man. For the Parthenon, the controlling ratio for the *symmetria* of the parts may be expressed algebraically as $x = 2y + 1$. Thus, for example, the temple's plan (FIG. **5-45**) called for 8 columns on the short ends and 17 on the long sides, because $17 = (2 \times 8) + 1$. The stylobate's ratio of length to width is 9:4, because $9 = (2 \times 4) + 1$. This ratio also characterizes the cella's proportion of length to width, the distance between the centers of two adjacent column drums (the *interaxial*) in proportion to the columns' diameter, and so forth.

The Parthenon's harmonious design and the mathematical precision of the sizes of its constituent elements tend to obscure the fact that this temple, as actually constructed, is quite irregular in shape. Throughout the building are pronounced deviations from the strictly horizontal and vertical lines assumed to be the basis of all Greek post-and-lintel structures. The stylobate, for example, curves upward at the center on the sides and both facades, forming a kind of shallow dome, and this curvature carries up into the entablature. Moreover, the peristyle columns (FIGS. 5-1 and 5-44) lean inward slightly. Those at the corners have a diagonal inclination and are also about 2 inches thicker than the rest. If their lines continued, they would meet about 1.5 miles above the temple. These deviations from the norm meant that virtually every Parthenon block and drum had to be carved according to the special set of specifications dictated by its unique place in the structure. This was obviously a daunting task, and the builders must have had a reason for introducing these so-called refinements in the Parthenon. Some modern observers note, for example, how the curving of horizontal lines and the tilting of vertical ones create a dynamic balance in the building—a kind of architectural contrapposto—and give it a greater sense of life. The oldest recorded explanation, however, may be the most likely. Vitruvius, a Roman architect of the late first century BCE who claims to have had access to Iktinos's treatise on the Parthenon (again, note the kinship with the *Canon* of Polykleitos), maintained that these adjustments were made to compensate for optical illusions. Vitruvius noted, for example, that if a stylobate is laid out on a level surface, it will appear to sag at the center. He also recommended that the corner columns of a building should be thicker because they are surrounded by light and would otherwise appear thinner than their neighbors.

5-45 Plan of the Parthenon, Acropolis, Athens, Greece, with diagram of the sculptural program (after Andrew Stewart), 447–432 BCE.

A team of sculptors directed by Phidias lavishly decorated the Parthenon with statues in both pediments, figural reliefs in all 92 Doric metopes, and an inner 524-foot sculptured Ionic frieze.

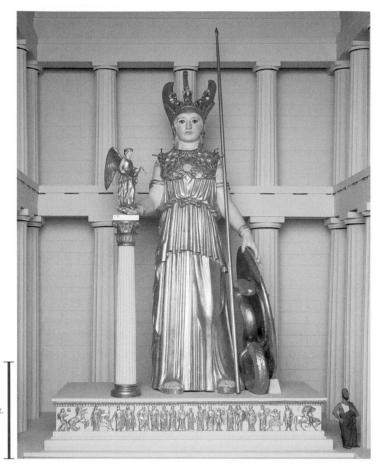

10 ft.

5-46 PHIDIAS, *Athena Parthenos,* in the cella of the Parthenon, Acropolis, Athens, Greece, ca. 438 BCE. Model of the lost chryselephantine statue. Royal Ontario Museum, Toronto.

Inside the cella of the Parthenon stood Phidias's 38-foot-tall gold-and-ivory *Athena Parthenos* (the Virgin). The goddess is fully armed and holds Nike (Victory) in her extended right hand.

The Parthenon is "irregular" in other ways as well. One of the ironies of this most famous of all Doric temples is that it is "contaminated" by Ionic elements. Although the cella (FIG. **5-46**) had a two-story Doric colonnade, the back room (which housed the goddess's treasury and the tribute collected from the Delian League) had four tall and slender Ionic columns as sole supports for the superstructure (FIG. 5-45). And whereas the temple's exterior had a standard Doric frieze (FIG. 5-44), the inner frieze (FIG. 5-50) that ran around the top of the cella wall was Ionic. Perhaps this fusion of Doric and Ionic elements reflects the Athenians' belief that the Ionians of the Aegean Islands and Asia Minor were descendants of Athenian settlers and were therefore their kin. Or it may be Pericles and Iktinos's way of suggesting that Athens was the leader of *all* the Greeks. In any case, a mix of Doric and Ionic features characterizes the fifth-century BCE buildings of the Acropolis as a whole.

ATHENA PARTHENOS The costly decision to incorporate two sculptured friezes in the Parthenon's design is symptomatic. This Pentelic-marble temple was more lavishly adorned than any Greek temple before it, Doric or Ionic. A mythological scene appears in every one of the 92 Doric metopes, and every inch of the 524-foot-long Ionic frieze depicts a procession and cavalcade. Dozens of larger-than-life-size statues filled both pediments. And inside was the most expensive item of all—Phidias's *Athena Parthenos,* a colossal gold-and-ivory (chryselephantine) statue of the

virgin goddess. Art historians know a great deal about Phidias's lost statue from descriptions by Greek and Latin authors and from Roman copies. A model (FIG. 5-46) gives a good idea of its appearance and setting. Athena stood 38 feet tall, and to a large extent Iktinos designed the Parthenon around her. To accommodate the statue's huge size, the cella had to be wider than usual. This, in turn, dictated the width of the facade—eight columns at a time when six columns were the norm (FIGS. 5-25 and 5-29).

Athena was fully armed with shield, spear, and helmet, and she held Nike (the winged female personification of Victory) in her extended right hand. No one doubts that this Nike referred to the victory of 479 BCE. The memory of the Persian sack of the Acropolis was still vivid, and the Athenians were intensely conscious that by driving back the Persians, they had saved their civilization from the Eastern "barbarians" who had committed atrocities at Miletos. In fact, Phidias's *Athena Parthenos* incorporated multiple allusions to the Persian defeat. On the thick soles of Athena's sandals was a representation of a centauromachy. High reliefs depicting the battle of Greeks and Amazons (*Amazonomachy*), in which Theseus drove the Amazons out of Athens, emblazoned the exterior of her shield. On the shield's interior, Phidias painted a gigantomachy. Each of these mythological contests was a metaphor for the triumph of order over chaos, of civilization over barbarism, and of Athens over Persia.

PARTHENON: METOPES Phidias took up these same themes again in the Parthenon's metopes (FIG. 5-45). The best-preserved metopes—although the paint on these and all the other Parthenon marbles long ago disappeared—are those of the south side,

1 ft.

5-47 Centauromachy, metope from the south side of the Parthenon, Acropolis, Athens, Greece, ca. 447–438 BCE. Marble, 4′ 8″ high. British Museum, London. ◼◀

The Parthenon's centauromachy metopes allude to the Greek defeat of the Persians. Here, the sculptor brilliantly distinguished the vibrant living centaur from the lifeless Greek corpse.

which depicted the battle of Lapiths and centaurs, a combat in which Theseus played a major role. On one extraordinary slab (FIG. 5-47), a triumphant centaur rises up on its hind legs, exulting over the crumpled body of the Greek it has defeated. The relief is so high that parts are fully in the round. Some have broken off. The sculptor brilliantly distinguished the vibrant, powerful form of the living beast from the lifeless corpse on the ground. In other metopes, the Greeks have the upper hand, but the full set suggests that the battle was a difficult one against a dangerous enemy and that losses as well as victories occurred. The same was true of the war against the Persians, and the centauromachy metopes—and also the gigantomachy, Amazonomachy, and Trojan War metopes—are allegories for the Greek-Persian conflict of the early fifth century BCE.

PARTHENON: PEDIMENTS The subjects of the two pediments were especially appropriate for a temple that celebrated Athena—and the Athenians. The east pediment depicted the birth of the goddess. At the west was the contest between Athena and Poseidon to determine which one would become the city's patron deity. Athena won, giving her name to the polis and its citizens. It is significant that in the story and in the pediment the Athenians are the judges of the relative merits of the two gods. The selection of this theme for the temple reflects the same arrogance that led to the use of Delian League funds to adorn the Acropolis.

The Christians removed the center of the east pediment when they added an apse to the Parthenon at the time of its conversion into a church. What remains are the spectators to the left and the right who witnessed Athena's birth on Mount Olympus. At the far left (FIG. 5-48) are part of the head and arms of Helios (the Sun) and his chariot horses rising from the pediment floor (FIG. 5-44). Next to them is a powerful male figure usually identified as Dionysos or possibly Herakles, who entered the realm of the gods on completion of his 12 labors (see "Herakles," page 128). At the right (FIG. 5-49) are three goddesses, probably Hestia, Dione, and Aphrodite (see "Gods and Goddesses," page 107), and either Selene (the Moon) or Nyx (Night) and more horses, this time sinking below the pediment's floor. Here, Phidias, who must have designed the composition even if his assistants executed it, discovered an entirely new way to deal with the awkward triangular frame of the pediment. Its floor is now the horizon line, and charioteers and their horses move through it effortlessly. The individual figures, even the animals, are brilliantly characterized. The horses of the Sun, at the beginning of the day, are energetic. Those of the Moon or Night, having labored until dawn, are weary. The reclining figures fill the space beneath the raking cornice beautifully. Dionysos/Herakles and Aphrodite in the lap of her mother Dione are monumental Olympian presences yet totally relaxed organic forms. The Athenian sculptors fully understood not only the surface appearance of human anatomy, both male and female, but also the mechanics of how muscles and bones make the body move. The Phidian workshop mastered the rendition of clothed forms as well. In the Dione-Aphrodite group, the thin and heavy folds of the garments alternately reveal and conceal the main and lesser body masses while swirling in a compositional tide that subtly unifies the two figures. The articulation and integration of the bodies produce a wonderful variation of surface and play of light and shade.

5-48 Helios and his horses, and Dionysos (Herakles?), from the east pediment of the Parthenon, Acropolis, Athens, Greece, ca. 438–432 BCE. Marble, greatest height 4′ 3″. British Museum, London.

The east pediment of the Parthenon depicts the birth of Athena. At the left, Helios and his horses emerge from the pediment's floor, suggesting the sun rising above the horizon at dawn.

5-49 Three goddesses (Hestia, Dione, and Aphrodite?), from the east pediment of the Parthenon, Acropolis, Athens, Greece, ca. 438–432 BCE. Marble, greatest height 4′ 5″. British Museum, London.

The statues of Hestia, Dione, and Aphrodite conform perfectly to the sloping right side of the Parthenon's east pediment. The thin and heavy folds of the garments alternately reveal and conceal the body forms.

5-50 Three details of the Panathenaic Festival procession frieze, from the Parthenon, Acropolis, Athens, Greece, ca. 447–438 BCE. Marble, 3′ 6″ high. *Top:* horsemen (north frieze), British Museum, London. *Center:* Poseidon, Apollo, Artemis, Aphrodite, and Eros (east frieze), Acropolis Museum, Athens. *Bottom:* elders and maidens (east frieze), Musée du Louvre, Paris. ◼◀

The Parthenon's Ionic frieze represents the Panathenaic procession of citizens on horseback and on foot under the gods' watchful eyes. The temple celebrated the Athenians as much as Athena.

PARTHENON: IONIC FRIEZE In many ways the most remarkable part of the Parthenon's sculptural program is the inner Ionic frieze (FIG. **5-50**). Scholars still debate its subject, but most agree it represents the Panathenaic Festival procession that took place every four years in Athens. If this identification is correct, the Athenians judged themselves fit for inclusion in the temple's sculptural decoration—the first instance in Greek art of the depiction of a human event on a temple. It is another example of the Athenians' extraordinarily high sense of self-worth.

The procession began at the Dipylon Gate, passed through the *agora* (central square), and ended on the Acropolis, where the Athenians placed a new peplos on an ancient wooden statue of Athena. That statue (probably similar in general appearance to the *Lady of Auxerre*, FIG. 5-6) had been housed in the Archaic temple the Persians razed in 480 BCE, but the Athenians removed it before the attack for security reasons and eventually installed it in the Erechtheion (FIG. 5-53, no. 1). On the Parthenon frieze the procession begins on the west, that is, at the temple's rear, the side facing the gateway to the Acropolis. It then moves in parallel lines down the long north and south sides of the building and ends at the center of the east frieze, over the doorway to the cella housing Phidias's statue (FIG. 5-45). It is noteworthy that the upper part of the frieze is in higher relief than the lower part so that the more

distant and more shaded upper zone is as legible from the ground as the lower part of the frieze. This is another instance of how the Parthenon's designers took optical effects into consideration.

The frieze vividly communicates the procession's acceleration and deceleration. At the outset, on the west side, marshals gather and youths mount their horses. On the north (FIG. 5-50, *top*) and south, the momentum picks up as the cavalcade moves from the lower town to the Acropolis, accompanied by chariots, musicians, jar carriers, and animals destined for sacrifice. On the east, seated gods and goddesses (FIG. 5-50, *center*), the invited guests, watch the procession slow almost to a halt (FIG. 5-50, *bottom*) as it nears its goal at the shrine of Athena's ancient wooden idol. Most remarkable of all is the role assigned to the Olympian deities. They do not

take part in the festival or determine its outcome but are merely spectators. Aphrodite, in fact, extends her left arm to draw her son Eros's attention to the Athenians, just as today a parent at a parade would point out important people to a child. Indeed, the Athenian people *were* important—self-important, one might say. They were the masters of an empire, and in Pericles' famous funeral oration, he painted a picture of Athens that elevated its citizens almost to the stature of gods. The Parthenon celebrated the greatness of Athens and the Athenians as much as it honored Athena.

PROPYLAIA Even before all the sculptures were in place on the Parthenon, work began on a new monumental entrance to the Acropolis, the Propylaia (FIG. **5-51**). The architect entrusted with

5-51 MNESIKLES, Propylaia (looking southwest), Acropolis, Athens, Greece, 437–432 BCE.

Mnesikles disguised the change of ground level by splitting the Propylaia into eastern and western sections. Each facade resembles a Doric temple but with a wider space between the central columns.

this important commission was MNESIKLES. The site was a difficult one, on a steep slope, but Mnesikles succeeded in disguising the change in ground level by splitting the building into eastern and western sections (FIG. 5-43, no. 2), each one resembling a Doric temple facade. Practical considerations dictated that the space between the central pair of columns on each side be enlarged. This was the path the chariots and animals of the Panathenaic Festival procession took, and they required a wide ramped causeway. To ei-

ther side of the central ramp were stairs for pedestrian traffic. Inside, tall, slender Ionic columns supported the split-level roof. Once again an Athenian architect mixed the two orders on the Acropolis. But as with the Parthenon, the Doric order was the choice for the stately exterior.

Mnesikles' full plan for the Propylaia was never executed because of the change in the fortunes of Athens after the outbreak of the Peloponnesian War in 431 BCE. Of the side wings that were part of the original project, only the northwest one (FIG. 5-43, no. 3) was completed. That wing is of special importance in the history of art. In Roman times it housed a *pinakotheke* (picture gallery). In it were displayed paintings on wood panels by some of the major artists of the fifth century BCE. It is uncertain whether this was the wing's original function. If it was, the Propylaia's pinakotheke is the first recorded structure built for the specific purpose of displaying paintings, and it is the forerunner of modern museums.

ERECHTHEION In 421 BCE, work finally began on the temple that was to replace the Archaic Athena temple the Persians had destroyed. The new structure, the Erechtheion (FIGS. 5-52 and

5-52 Erechtheion (looking northwest), Acropolis, Athens, Greece, ca. 421–405 BCE.

The Erechtheion is in many ways the antithesis of the Doric Parthenon directly across from it. An Ionic temple, it has some of the finest decorative details of any ancient Greek building.

1. Shrine housing wooden image of Athena
2. Athena's olive tree
3. Poseidon's trident mark
4. Ruins of Archaic temple

N

5-53 Plan of the Erechtheion, Acropolis, Athens, Greece, ca. 421–405 BCE.

The asymmetrical form of the Erechtheion is unique for a Greek temple. It reflects the need to incorporate preexisting shrines into the plan, including those of the kings Erechtheus and Kekrops.

5-53), built to the north of the old temple's remains, was to be a multiple shrine, however. It honored Athena and housed the ancient wood image of the goddess that was the goal of the Panathenaic Festival procession. But it also incorporated shrines to a host of other gods and demigods who loomed large in the city's legendary past. Among these were Erechtheus, an early king of Athens, during whose reign the ancient idol of Athena was said to have fallen from the heavens, and Kekrops, another king of Athens, who served as judge of the contest between Athena and Poseidon. In fact, the site chosen for the new temple was the very spot where that contest occurred. Poseidon had staked his claim to Athens by striking the Acropolis rock with his trident and producing a salt-water spring. The imprint of his trident remained for Athenians of the historical period to see. Nearby, Athena had miraculously caused an olive tree to grow. This tree still stood as a constant reminder of her victory over Poseidon.

The asymmetrical plan (FIG. 5-53) of the Ionic Erechtheion is unique for a Greek temple and the antithesis of the simple and harmoniously balanced plan of the Doric Parthenon across the way. Its irregular form reflected the need to incorporate the tomb of King Kekrops and other preexisting shrines, the trident mark, and the olive tree into a single complex. The unknown architect responsible for the building also had to struggle with the problem of uneven terrain. The area could not be leveled by terracing because that would disturb the ancient sacred sites. As a result, the Erechtheion has four sides of very different character, and each side rests on a different ground level.

1 ft.

5-54 Caryatids of the south porch of the Erechtheion, Acropolis, Athens, Greece, ca. 421–405 BCE. Marble, 7′ 7″ high.

The south porch of the Erechtheion features caryatids with contrapposto stances. They are updated versions of the Archaic caryatids of the porch of the Siphnian Treasury (FIG. 5-17) at Delphi.

5-55 KALLIKRATES, Temple of Athena Nike (looking southwest), Acropolis, Athens, Greece, ca. 427–424 BCE.

The Ionic temple at the entrance to the Acropolis is an unusual amphiprostyle building. It celebrates Athena as bringer of victory, and one of the friezes depicts the defeat of the Persians at Marathon.

Perhaps to compensate for the awkward character of the building as a whole, the architect took great care with the Erechtheion's decorative details. The Ionic capitals were inlaid with gold, rock crystal, and colored glass, and the frieze received special treatment. The stone chosen was the dark-blue limestone of Eleusis to contrast with the white Pentelic marble of the walls and columns and the marble relief figures attached to the dark frieze.

The Erechtheion's most striking and famous feature is its south porch (FIG. 5-54), where the architect replaced Ionic columns with caryatids, as on the Ionic Siphnian Treasury (FIG. 5-17) at Delphi. The Archaic caryatids resemble sixth-century BCE korai, and their Classical counterparts equally characteristically look like Phidian-era statues. Although the caryatids exhibit the weight shift that was standard for the fifth century BCE, the flutelike drapery folds concealing their stiff, weight-bearing legs underscores their role as architectural supports. The figures have enough rigidity to suggest the structural column and just the degree of flexibility needed to suggest the living body.

TEMPLE OF ATHENA NIKE Another Ionic building on the Athenian Acropolis is the small Temple of Athena Nike (FIG. **5-55**), designed by Kallikrates, who designed the Parthenon with Iktinos and may have been responsible for that temple's Ionic elements. The Athena Nike temple is amphiprostyle (see "Greek Temple Plans," page 115) with four columns on both the east and west facades. It stands on what used to be a Mycenaean bastion near the Propylaia and greets all visitors entering Athena's great sanctuary. Like the Parthenon, this temple commemorated the victory over the Persians—and not just in its name. The sculptors devoted part of the frieze to a representation of the decisive battle at Marathon, which turned the tide against the Persians—a human event, as in the Parthenon's Panathenaic Festival procession frieze. But on the Athena Nike temple, the Athenians chronicled a specific occasion, not a recurring event involving anonymous citizens.

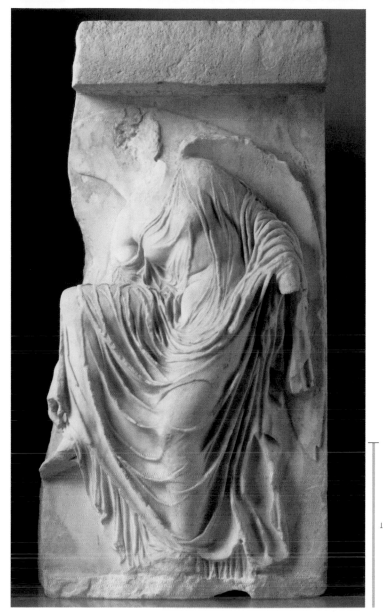

1 ft.

5-56 Nike adjusting her sandal, from the south side of the parapet of the Temple of Athena Nike, Acropolis, Athens, Greece, ca. 410 BCE. Marble, 3′ 6″ high. Acropolis Museum, Athens.

Dozens of images of winged Victory adorned the parapet on three sides of the Athena Nike temple. The sculptor carved this Nike with garments that appear almost transparent.

Around the building, at the bastion's edge, was a *parapet* decorated with exquisite reliefs. The theme of the balustrade matched that of the temple proper—victory. Dozens of images of Nike adorn the parapet, always in different attitudes. Sometimes she erects trophies bedecked with Persian spoils. Other times she brings forward sacrificial bulls for Athena. One relief (FIG. **5-56**) shows Nike adjusting her sandal—an awkward posture that the sculptor rendered elegant and graceful. The artist carried the style of the Parthenon pediments (FIG. 5-49) even further and created a figure whose garments cling so tightly to the body that they seem almost transparent, as if drenched with water. The sculptor was, however, interested in much more than revealing the supple beauty of the young female body. The drapery folds form intricate linear patterns unrelated to the body's anatomical structure and have a life of their own as abstract designs.

The Hegeso Stele

In Geometric times, huge painted vases (FIGS. 5-2 and 5-2A) marked the graves of wealthy Athenians. In the Archaic period, the Greeks placed kouroi (FIGS. 5-7 and 5-9) and, to a lesser extent, korai, or stelae ornamented with relief depictions of the deceased over their graves. The stele (FIG. 5-57) erected in the Dipylon cemetery at the end of the fifth or beginning of the fourth century BCE to commemorate the death of Hegeso, daughter of Proxenos, is in this tradition. An inscription giving the names of the daughter and father is on the cornice of the pediment that crowns the stele. Antae at left and right complete the architectural framework.

Hegeso is the well-dressed woman seated on an elegant chair (with footstool). She examines a piece of jewelry (once rendered in paint, not now visible) selected from a box a servant girl brings to her. The maid's simple unbelted chiton contrasts sharply with the more elaborate attire of her mistress. The garments of both women reveal the body forms beneath them. The faces are serene, without a trace of sadness. Indeed, the sculptor depicted both mistress and maid during a characteristic shared moment out of daily life. Only the epitaph reveals that Hegeso is the one who has departed.

The simplicity of the scene on the Hegeso stele is deceptive, however. This is not merely a bittersweet scene of tranquil domestic life before an untimely death. The setting itself is significant—the secluded women's quarters of a Greek house, from which Hegeso rarely would have emerged. Contemporaneous grave stelae of men regularly show them in the public domain, often as warriors. The servant girl is not so much the faithful companion of the deceased in life as she is Hegeso's possession, like the jewelry box. The slave girl may look solicitously at her mistress, but Hegeso has eyes only for her ornaments. Both slave and jewelry attest to the wealth of Hegeso's father, unseen but prominently cited in the epitaph. (It is noteworthy that there is no mention of the mother's name.) Indeed, even the jewelry box carries a deeper significance, for it probably represents the dowry Proxenos would have provided to his daughter's husband when she left her father's home to enter her husband's home. In the patriarchal society of ancient Greece, the dominant position of men is manifest even when only women are depicted.

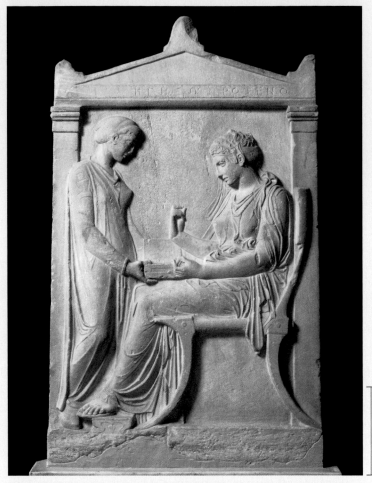

5-57 Grave stele of Hegeso, from the Dipylon cemetery, Athens, Greece, ca. 400 BCE. Marble, 5′ 2″ high. National Archaeological Museum, Athens.

On her tombstone, Hegeso examines jewelry from a box her servant girl holds. Mistress and maid share a serene moment out of daily life. Only the epitaph reveals that Hegeso is the one who died.

HEGESO STELE Although the decoration of the great building projects on the Acropolis must have occupied most of the finest sculptors of Athens in the second half of the fifth century BCE, other commissions were available in the city, notably in the Dipylon cemetery. There, around 400 BCE, a beautiful and touching grave stele (FIG. 5-57) in the style of the Temple of Athena Nike parapet reliefs was set up in memory of a woman named Hegeso. Its subject—a young woman in her home, attended by her maid (see "The Hegeso Stele," above)—and its composition have close parallels in Classical vase painting.

Painting

In the Classical period, some of the most renowned artists were the painters of monumental wood panels displayed in public buildings, both secular and religious. Those works were by nature perishable, and all of the great panels of the masters are unfortunately lost.

Nonetheless, one can get some idea of the polychrome nature of Classical panel paintings by studying Greek vases, especially those painted using the *white-ground* technique, which takes its name from the chalky-white slip used to provide a background for the painted figures. Experiments with white-ground painting date back to the Andokides Painter, but the method became popular only toward the middle of the fifth century BCE.

ACHILLES PAINTER One of the masters of white-ground painting was the so-called ACHILLES PAINTER, who decorated the *lekythos* (flask to hold perfumed oil) in FIG. 5-58. White-ground is essentially a variation of the red-figure technique. First the painter covered the pot with a slip of very fine white clay, then applied black glaze to outline the figures, and diluted brown, purple, red, and white to color them. The artist could use other colors—for example, the yellow the Achilles Painter chose for the garments of

5-58 ACHILLES PAINTER, Warrior taking leave of his wife (Athenian white-ground lekythos), from Eretria, Greece, ca. 440 BCE. 1′ 5″ high. National Archaeological Museum, Athens. ◼◀

White-ground painters applied the colors after firing because most colored glazes could not withstand the kiln's heat. The Achilles Painter here displayed his mastery at drawing an eye in profile.

both figures on this lekythos—but these had to be applied after firing because the Greeks did not know how to make them withstand the heat of the kiln. Despite the obvious attractions of the technique, the impermanence of the expanded range of colors discouraged white-ground painting on everyday vessels, such as drinking cups and kraters. In fact, Greek artists explored the full polychrome possibilities of the white-ground technique almost exclusively on lekythoi, which families commonly placed in graves as offerings to the deceased. For vessels designed for short-term use, the fragile nature of white-ground painting was of little concern.

5-59 NIOBID PAINTER, Artemis and Apollo slaying the children of Niobe (Athenian red-figure calyx krater), from Orvieto, Italy, ca. 450 BCE. 1′ 9″ high. Musée du Louvre, Paris. ◼◀

The placement of figures on different levels in a landscape on this red-figure krater depicting the massacre of the Niobids reflects the compositions of the panel paintings of Polygnotos of Thasos.

The Achilles Painter, like the REED PAINTER (FIG. 5-58A) later in the century, selected a scene appropriate for the funerary purpose of a lekythos. A youthful warrior takes leave of his wife. The red scarf, mirror, and jug hanging on the wall behind the woman indicate that the setting is the interior of their home. The motif of the seated woman is strikingly similar to that of Hegeso on her grave stele (FIG. 5-57), but here the woman is the survivor. It is her husband, preparing to go to war with helmet, shield, and spear, who will depart, never to return. On his shield is a large painted eye, roughly life-size. Greek shields often bore decorative devices such as the horrific face of Medusa, intended to ward off evil spirits and frighten the enemy (compare FIG. 5-16). This eye undoubtedly recalls this tradition, but for the Achilles Painter it was little more than an excuse to display superior drawing skills. Since the late sixth century BCE, Greek painters had abandoned the Archaic habit of placing frontal eyes on profile faces and attempted to render the eyes in profile. The Achilles Painter's mastery of this difficult problem in foreshortening is on exhibit here.

5-58A REED PAINTER, Warrior seated at his tomb, ca. 410–400 BCE.

POLYGNOTOS The leading panel painter of the first half of the fifth century BCE was POLYGNOTOS OF THASOS, whose works adorned important buildings both in Athens and Delphi. One of these was the pinakotheke of Mnesikles' Propylaia, but the most famous was a portico in the Athenian marketplace that came to

be called the Stoa Poikile (Painted Stoa). Descriptions of Polygnotos's paintings make clear that he introduced a revolutionary compositional format. Before Polygnotos, figures stood on a common ground line at the bottom of the picture plane, whether they appeared in horizontal bands or single panels. Polygnotos placed his figures on different levels, staggered in tiers in the manner of Ashurbanipal's lion hunt relief (FIG. 2-23) of two centuries before. He also incorporated landscape elements into his paintings, making his pictures true windows onto the world and not simply surface designs peopled with foreshortened figures. Polygnotos's abandonment of a single ground line was as momentous a break from the past as Early Classical Greek sculptors' rejection of frontality in statuary.

NIOBID PAINTER Polygnotos's influence is evident on a red-figure krater (FIG. 5-59) painted around the middle of the fifth century BCE by the NIOBID PAINTER—so named because one side of this krater depicts the massacre of the Niobids, the children of Niobe. Niobe, who had at least a dozen children, had boasted that she was superior to the goddess Leto, who had only two offspring, Apollo and Artemis. To punish her *hubris* (arrogance) and teach the lesson that no mortal could be superior to a god or goddess, Leto sent her two children to slay all of Niobe's many sons and daughters. On the Niobid Painter's krater, the horrible slaughter occurs in a schematic landscape setting of rocks and trees. The painter disposed the figures on several levels, and they actively interact with their setting. One slain son, for example, not only has fallen upon a rocky outcropping but is partially hidden by it. The Niobid Painter also drew the son's face in a three-quarter view, something that even Euphronios and Euthymides had not attempted.

5-60 PHIALE PAINTER, Hermes bringing the infant Dionysos to Papposilenos (Athenian white-ground calyx krater), from Vulci, Italy, ca. 440–435 BCE. 1′ 2″ high. Musei Vaticani, Rome.

In the Phiale Painter's white-ground representation of Hermes and the infant Dionysos at Nysa, the use of diluted brown to color and shade the rocks may also reflect the work of Polygnotos.

1 in.

that could survive the heat of a Greek kiln—red, brown, purple, and a special snowy white reserved for the flesh of the nymphs and for the hair, beard, and shaggy body of Papposilenos. The use of diluted brown wash to color and shade the rocks may reflect the coloration of Polygnotos's landscapes. This vase and the Niobid krater together provide a shadowy idea of the character of Polygnotos's lost paintings.

TOMB OF THE DIVER, PAESTUM Although all of the panel paintings of the masters disappeared long ago, some Greek mural paintings survive. An early example is in the Tomb of the Diver at Paestum. Covering the four walls of this small, coffinlike tomb are banquet scenes of the kind that appear regularly on Greek vases. On the tomb's cover slab (FIG. **5-61**), a youth dives from a stone platform into a body of water. The scene most likely symbolizes the plunge from this life into the next. Trees resembling those of the Niobid krater are included within the decorative frame.

PHIALE PAINTER Further insight into the appearance of monumental panel paintings of the fifth century BCE comes from a white-ground krater (FIG. **5-60**) by the PHIALE PAINTER. The subject is Hermes handing over his half brother, the infant Dionysos, to Papposilenos ("grandpa-satyr"). The other figures represent the nymphs in the shady glens of Nysa, where Zeus had sent Dionysos, one of his numerous natural sons, to be raised, safe from the possible wrath of his wife, Hera. Unlike the decorators of funerary lekythoi, the Phiale Painter used for this krater only colors

LATE CLASSICAL PERIOD

The Peloponnesian War, which began in 431 BCE, ended in 404 BCE with the complete defeat of a plague-weakened Athens. The victor, Sparta, and then Thebes undertook the leadership of Greece, both unsuccessfully. In the middle of the fourth century BCE, a threat from without caused the rival Greek states to put aside their animosities and unite for their common defense, as they had earlier against the Persians. But at the battle of Chaeronea in 338 BCE, the Greek cities suffered a devastating loss and had to relinquish their indepen-

5-61 Youth diving, cover slab of the Tomb of the Diver, Tempe del Prete necropolis, Paestum, Italy, ca. 480–470 BCE. Fresco, 3′ 4″ high. Museo Archeologico Nazionale, Paestum. ◼◀

This tomb in Italy is a rare example of Classical mural painting. The diving scene most likely symbolizes the deceased's plunge into the Underworld. The trees resemble those on the Niobid krater (FIG. 5-59).

1 ft.

dence to the Macedonian king, Philip II (r. 359–336 BCE). Philip was assassinated in 336, and his son, Alexander III (r. 336–323 BCE), better known simply as Alexander the Great, succeeded him. Alexander led a powerful army on an extraordinary campaign that overthrew the Persian Empire (the ultimate revenge for the Persian invasion of Greece in the early fifth century), wrested control of Egypt, and even reached India (see Chapter 15).

Sculpture

The fourth century BCE in Greece was thus a time of political upheaval, which had a profound impact on the psyche of the Greeks and on the art they produced. In the fifth century BCE, Greeks had generally believed that rational human beings could impose order on their environment, create "perfect" statues such as the *Canon* of Polykleitos, and discover the "correct" mathematical formulas for constructing temples such as the Parthenon. The Parthenon frieze celebrated the Athenians as a community of citizens with shared values. The Peloponnesian War and the unceasing strife of the fourth century BCE brought an end to the serene idealism of the previous century. Disillusionment and alienation followed. Greek thought and Greek art began to focus more on the individual and on the real world of appearances instead of on the community and the ideal world of perfect beings and perfect buildings.

PRAXITELES The new approach to art is immediately apparent in the work of PRAXITELES, one of the great masters of the fourth century BCE. Praxiteles did not reject the favored sculptural themes of the High Classical period, and his Olympian gods and goddesses retained their superhuman beauty. But in his hands, those deities lost some of their solemn grandeur and took on a worldly sensuousness. Nowhere is this new humanizing spirit plainer than in the statue of Aphrodite (FIG. 5-62) that Praxiteles sold to the Knidians after another city had rejected it. The lost original, carved from Parian marble, is known only through copies of Roman date, but Pliny considered it "superior to all the works, not only of Praxiteles, but indeed in the whole world." It made Knidos famous, and many people sailed there just to see the statue in its round temple (compare FIG. 5-72), where "it was possible to view the image of the goddess from every side." According to Pliny, some visitors were "overcome with love for the statue."[5]

The *Aphrodite of Knidos* caused such a sensation in its time because Praxiteles took the unprecedented step of representing the goddess of love completely nude. Female nudity was rare in earlier Greek art and had been confined almost exclusively to paintings on vases designed for household use. The women so depicted also were usually not noblewomen or goddesses but courtesans or slave girls, like the one Onesimos depicted on a red-figure drinking cup (FIG. 5-23A). No one had ever dared place inside a temple a statue of a goddess wearing no clothes. Moreover, Praxiteles' Aphrodite is not a cold and remote image. In fact, the goddess engages in a trivial act out of everyday life. She has removed her garment, draped it over a large *hydria* (water pitcher), and is about to step into the bath.

Although shocking in its day, the *Aphrodite of Knidos* is not openly erotic (the goddess modestly shields her pelvis with her right hand), but she is quite sensuous. Lucian, writing in the second century CE, noted that she had a "welcoming look" and a "slight smile" and that Praxiteles was renowned for his ability to transform marble into soft and radiant flesh. Lucian mentioned, for example, the "dewy quality of Aphrodite's eyes."[6] Unfortunately, the rather

5-62 PRAXITELES, *Aphrodite of Knidos*. Roman copy of a marble statue of ca. 350–340 BCE. Marble, 6′ 8″ high. Musei Vaticani, Rome. ◼◀

This first nude statue of a Greek goddess caused a sensation. But Praxiteles was also famous for his ability to transform marble into soft and radiant flesh. His Aphrodite had "dewy eyes."

mechanical Roman copies do not capture the quality of Praxiteles' modeling of the stone, but some originals of the period do—for example, a female head (FIG. 5-62A) from Chios.

The Praxitelean "touch" is also evident in a statue once thought to be by the hand of the master himself but now generally considered either a copy of the highest quality or an original work by a son or grandson of

5-62A Head of a woman, Chios, ca. 320–300 BCE.

1 ft.

5-63 PRAXITELES(?), Hermes and the infant Dionysos, from the Temple of Hera, Olympia, Greece. Copy of a marble statue by Praxiteles of ca. 340 BCE or an original work of ca. 330–270 BCE by a son or grandson. Marble, 7′ 1″ high. Archaeological Museum, Olympia.

Praxiteles humanized the Olympian deities. This Hermes is as sensuous as the sculptor's Aphrodite. The god gazes dreamily into space while he dangles grapes as temptation for the infant wine god.

the master with the same name. The statue of Hermes and the infant Dionysos (FIG. 5-63) found in the Temple of Hera at Olympia brings to the realm of monumental statuary the theme the Phiale Painter had chosen for a white-ground krater (FIG. 5-60) a century earlier. Hermes has stopped to rest in a forest on his journey to Nysa to entrust the upbringing of Dionysos to Papposilenos and the nymphs. Hermes leans on a tree trunk (here it is an integral part of the composition and not a copyist's addition), and his slender body forms a sinuous, shallow S-curve that is the hallmark of many of Praxiteles' statues. He gazes dreamily into space while he dangles a bunch of grapes (now missing) as a temptation for the

infant, who is to become the Greek god of the vine. This is the kind of tender and very human interaction between an adult and a child that one encounters frequently in real life but that had been absent from Greek statuary before the fourth century BCE.

The quality of the carving is superb. The modeling is deliberately smooth and subtle, producing soft shadows that follow the planes as they flow almost imperceptibly one into another. All that is missing to give a complete sense of the "look" of a Praxitelean statue is the original paint, which a specialist, not the sculptor, applied to the statue (compare FIG. 5-63A). The delicacy of the marble facial features stands in sharp contrast to the metallic precision of Polykleitos's bronze *Doryphoros*

5-63A Artist painting a statue of Herakles, ca. 350–320 BCE.

(FIG. 5-40). The High Classical sculptor even subjected the *Spear Bearer*'s locks of hair to the laws of symmetry, and the hair does not violate the skull's perfect curve. The comparison of these two statues reveals the sweeping change in artistic attitude and intent that took place from the fifth to the fourth century BCE. In the statues of Praxiteles, the deities of Mount Olympus still possess a beauty mortals can aspire to, although not achieve, but they are no longer aloof. Praxiteles' gods have stepped off their pedestals and entered the world of human experience.

SKOPAS In the Archaic period and throughout most of the Early and High Classical periods, Greek sculptors generally shared common goals, but in the Late Classical period of the fourth century BCE, distinctive individual styles emerged. The dreamy, beautiful divinities of Praxiteles had enormous appeal, and the master had many followers (FIG. 5-62A). Other sculptors, however, pursued very different interests. One of these was SKOPAS OF PAROS, an architect as well as a sculptor, who designed a temple at Tegea (fragments of the pedimental sculptures remain; FIG. 5-64A) and contributed to the decoration of one of the Seven Wonders of the ancient world, the Mausoleum (FIG. 5-64B) at Halikarnassos (see "Wonders," Chapter 2, page 49). Although his sculptures reflect the general Late Classical trend toward the humanization of the Greek gods and heroes, Skopas's hallmark was intense emotionalism. None of his statues survives, but a grave

5-64A Herakles, Temple of Athena Alea, Tegea, ca. 340 BCE.

5-64B Mausoleum, Halikarnassos, ca. 353–340 BCE.

stele (FIG. 5-64) found near the Ilissos River in Athens exhibits the psychological tension for which the master's works were famous.

The Ilissos stele was originally set into an architectural frame similar to that of the earlier Hegeso stele (FIG. 5-57). A comparison of the two works is revealing. In the later stele the relief is much higher, with parts of the figures carved fully in the round. The major difference, however, is the pronounced change in mood, which reflects Skopas's innovations. The Late Classical work makes a clear distinction between the living and the dead and depicts overt mourning. The deceased is a young hunter who has the large, deeply set eyes and fleshy overhanging brows that characterized Skopas's sculpted figures (compare FIG. 5-64A). At his feet a small boy, either his servant or perhaps a younger brother, sobs openly. The hunter's dog also droops its head in sorrow. Beside the youth, an old man, undoubtedly his father, leans on a walking stick and, in a gesture

5-64 Grave stele of a young hunter, found near the Ilissos River, Athens, Greece, ca. 340–330 BCE. Marble, 5' 6" high. National Archaeological Museum, Athens.

The emotional intensity of this stele representing an old man mourning the loss of his son and the figures' large, deeply set eyes with fleshy overhanging brows reflect the style of Skopas of Paros.

reminiscent of that of the Olympia seer (FIG. 5-31), ponders the irony of fate that has taken the life of his powerful son yet preserved him, the father, in his frail old age. Most remarkable of all, the hunter himself looks out at the viewer, inviting sympathy and creating an emotional bridge between the spectator and the artwork that was inconceivable in the art of the High Classical period.

LYSIPPOS The third great Late Classical sculptor, LYSIPPOS OF SIKYON, won such renown that Alexander the Great selected him to create his official portrait. (Alexander could afford to employ the best because the Macedonian kingdom enjoyed vast wealth. King Philip was able to hire the leading thinker of his age, Aristotle, as the young Alexander's tutor.) Lysippos introduced a new canon of proportions in which the bodies were more slender than those of Polykleitos and the heads roughly one-eighth the height of the body rather than one-seventh, as in the previous century. One of Lysippos's most famous works, a bronze statue of an *apoxyomenos* (an athlete scraping oil from his body after exercising)—known, as usual, only from Roman copies in marble (FIG. 5-65)—exhibits the new proportions. A comparison with Polykleitos's *Doryphoros* (FIG. 5-40) reveals more than a change in physique, however. A nervous energy, lacking in the bal-

5-65 LYSIPPOS, *Apoxyomenos* (*Scraper*). Roman copy of a bronze statue of ca. 330 BCE. Marble, 6' 9" high. Musei Vaticani, Rome. ◼◀

Lysippos introduced a new canon of proportions and a nervous energy to his statues. He also broke down the dominance of the frontal view and encouraged viewing his statues from multiple angles.

anced form of the *Doryphoros*, runs through Lysippos's *Apoxyomenos*. The *strigil* (scraper) is about to reach the end of the right arm, and at any moment the athlete will switch it to the other hand so that he can scrape his left arm. At the same time, he will shift his weight and reverse the positions of his legs. Lysippos also began to break down the dominance of the frontal view in statuary and encouraged the observer to view his athlete from multiple angles. Because Lysippos represented the apoxyomenos with his right arm boldly thrust forward, the figure breaks out of the shallow rectangular box that defined the boundaries of earlier statues. To comprehend the action, the observer must move to the side and view Lysippos's work at a three-quarter angle or in full profile.

Herakles holds the golden apples of the Hesperides in his right hand behind his back—unseen unless the viewer walks around the statue. Lysippos's subject is thus the same as that of the metope (FIG. 5-33) of the Early Classical Temple of Zeus at Olympia, but the fourth-century BCE Herakles is no longer serene. Instead of expressing joy, or at least satisfaction, at having completed 1 of the impossible 12 labors, he is almost dejected. Exhausted by his physical efforts, he can think only of his pain and weariness. Lysippos's portrayal of Herakles in this statue is an eloquent testimony to Late Classical sculptors' interest in humanizing the Greek gods and heroes. In this respect, despite their divergent styles, Praxiteles, Skopas, and Lysippos followed a common path.

Alexander the Great and Macedonian Court Art

Alexander the Great's favorite book was the *Iliad*, and his own life very much resembled an epic saga, full of heroic battles, exotic locales, and unceasing drama. Alexander was a man of singular character, an inspired leader with boundless energy and an almost foolhardy courage. He personally led his army into battle on the back of Bucephalus (FIG. 5-70), the wild and mighty steed only he could tame and ride.

ALEXANDER'S PORTRAITS Ancient sources reveal that Alexander believed only Lysippos had captured his essence in a portrait, and thus only he was authorized to sculpt the king's image. Lysippos's most famous portrait of the Macedonian king was a full-length, heroically nude bronze statue of Alexander holding a lance

5-66 LYSIPPOS, Weary Herakles (*Farnese Hercules*). Roman statue from the Baths of Caracalla (FIG. 7-66), Rome, Italy, signed by GLYKON OF ATHENS, based on a bronze statue of ca. 320 BCE. Marble, 10′ 5″ high. Museo Archeologico Nazionale, Naples.

Lysippos's portrayal of Herakles after the hero obtained the golden apples of the Hesperides ironically shows the muscle-bound hero as so weary that he must lean on his club for support.

To grasp the full meaning of another of Lysippos's works, a colossal statue (FIG. 5-66) depicting a weary Herakles, the viewer must walk around it. Once again, the original is lost. The most impressive of the surviving statues based on the Lysippan original is nearly twice life-size. It stood in the Baths of Caracalla in Rome, where, like the marble copy of Polykleitos's *Doryphoros* (FIG. 5-40) from the Roman palaestra at Pompeii, Lysippos's muscle-bound Greek hero provided inspiration for Romans who came to the baths to exercise. (The Roman sculptor, GLYKON OF ATHENS, signed the statue, but did not mention Lysippos. The educated Roman public needed no label to identify the famous work.) The exaggerated muscular development of Herakles is poignantly ironic, however. Lysippos depicted the hero as so weary that he must lean on his club for support. Without that prop, Herakles would topple over. Lysippos and other fourth-century BCE artists rejected stability and balance as worthy goals for statuary.

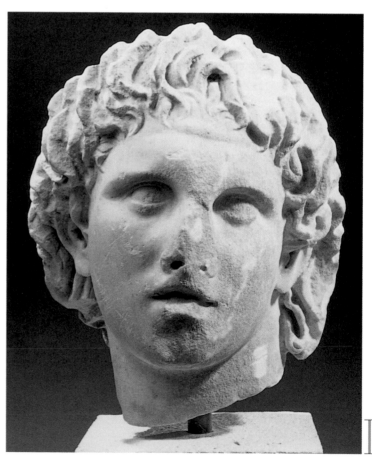

5-67 Head of Alexander the Great, from Pella, Greece, third century BCE. Marble, 1′ high. Archaeological Museum, Pella.

Lysippos was the official portrait sculptor of Alexander the Great. This third-century BCE sculpture has the sharp turn of the head and thick mane of hair of Lysippos's statue of Alexander with a lance.

and turning his head toward the sky. According to Plutarch, an epigram inscribed on the base stated the statue depicted Alexander gazing at Zeus and proclaiming, "I place the earth under my sway; you, O Zeus, keep Olympus." Plutarch also reported that Lysippos's portrait immortalized Alexander's "leonine" hair and "melting glance."[7] The Lysippan original is lost, and because Alexander was portrayed so many times, and long after his death, it is very difficult to determine which of the many surviving images is most faithful to the fourth-century BCE portrait. A leading candidate is a third-century BCE marble head (FIG. 5-67) from Pella, the capital of Macedonia and Alexander's birthplace. It has the sharp turn of the head and thick mane of hair that were key ingredients of Lysippos's portrait. The Pella sculptor's treatment of the features also is consistent with the style of the later fourth century BCE. The deep-set eyes and parted lips recall the manner of Skopas (FIG. 5-64A), and the delicate handling of the flesh brings to mind the faces of Praxitelean statues (FIG. 5-63). Although not a copy, this head very likely approximates the young king's official portrait and provides insight into Alexander's personality as well as Lysippos's art.

PELLA MOSAICS
Alexander's palace has not been excavated, but the sumptuous life of the Macedonian aristocracy is evident from the costly objects found in Macedonian graves and from the abundance of mosaics uncovered in houses at Pella. The Macedonian mosaics are *pebble mosaics* (see "Mosaics," Chapter 8, page 245). The floors consist of small stones of various colors collected from beaches and riverbanks and set into a thick coat of cement. The finest pebble mosaic yet to come to light from the Pella excavations has a stag hunt (FIG. 5-68) as its *emblema* (central framed panel), bordered in turn by an intricate floral pattern and a stylized wave motif (not shown in the illustration). The artist signed his work in the same manner as proud Greek vase painters and potters did: "GNOSIS made it." This is the earliest mosaicist's signature known,

and its prominence in the design undoubtedly attests to the artist's reputation. The home's owner wanted guests to know that Gnosis himself, not an imitator, had laid this floor.

The Pella stag hunt, with its light figures against a dark ground, has much in common with red-figure painting. In the pebble mosaic, however, thin strips of lead or terracotta define most of the contour lines and some of the interior details. Subtle gradations of yellow, brown, and red, as well as black, white, and gray pebbles, suggest the interior volumes. Gnosis used shading to model the musculature of the hunters, their billowing cloaks, and the animals' bodies. The use of light and dark to suggest volume is rare on Greek painted vases, although examples do exist. Monumental painters, however, commonly used shading, the Greek term for which was *skiagraphia* (literally, "shadow painting"). The Greeks attributed the invention of shading to an Athenian painter of the fifth century BCE named Apollodoros. Gnosis's emblema, with its sparse landscape setting, probably reflects contemporaneous panel painting.

HADES AND PERSEPHONE Excavations at Vergina have provided valuable additional information about Macedonian art and about Greek mural painting. One of the most important finds was a painted tomb with a representation of Hades, lord of the Underworld, abducting Persephone, the daughter of Demeter, the goddess of grain. The mural (FIG. 5-69) is remarkable for its intense drama and for the painter's use of foreshortening and

5-68 GNOSIS, Stag hunt, from Pella, Greece, ca. 300 BCE. Pebble mosaic, figural panel 10′ 2″ high. Archaeological Museum, Pella.

The floor mosaics at the Macedonian capital of Pella are of the early type made with pebbles of various natural colors. This stag hunt by Gnosis bears the earliest known signature of a mosaicist.

5-69 Hades abducting Persephone, detail of a wall painting in tomb 1, Vergina, Greece, mid-fourth century BCE. Fresco, detail 3′ 3½″ high.

The intense drama, three-quarter views, and shading in this representation of the lord of the Underworld kidnapping Demeter's daughter are characteristics of mural painting at the time of Alexander.

1 ft.

5-70 PHILOXENOS OF ERETRIA, *Battle of Issus,* ca. 310 BCE. Roman copy (*Alexander Mosaic*) from the House of the Faun, Pompeii, Italy, late second or early first century BCE. Tessera mosaic, 8′ 10″ × 16′ 9″. Museo Archeologico Nazionale, Naples. ◼◀

Battle of Issus reveals Philoxenos's mastery of foreshortening, of modeling figures in color, and of depicting reflections and shadows, as well as his ability to capture the psychological intensity of warfare.

shading. Hades holds the terrified seminude Persephone in his left arm and steers his racing chariot with his right as Persephone's garments and hair blow in the wind. The artist depicted the heads of both figures and even the chariot's wheels in three-quarter views. The chariot, in fact, seems to be bursting into the viewer's space. Especially noteworthy is the way the painter used short, dark brushstrokes to suggest shading on the underside of Hades' right arm, on Persephone's torso, and elsewhere. Although fragmentary, the Vergina mural is a precious document of the almost totally lost art of monumental painting in ancient Greece.

BATTLE OF ISSUS Further insight into developments in painting at the time of Alexander comes from a large mosaic (FIG. **5-70**) that decorated the floor of a room in a lavishly appointed Roman house at Pompeii. The mosaicist employed *tesserae* (cubical pieces of glass or tiny stones cut to the desired size and shape) instead of pebbles (see "Mosaics," Chapter 8, page 245). The subject is a great battle between the armies of Alexander the Great and the Achaemenid Persian king Darius III (r. 336–330 BCE), probably the battle of Issus in southeastern Turkey, when Darius fled in his chariot in humiliating defeat. The mosaic dates to the late second or early first century BCE. Most art historians believe it is a reasonably faithful copy of *Battle of Issus,* a famous panel painting of about 310 BCE made by PHILOXENOS OF ERETRIA for King Cassander, one of Alexander's successors. Some scholars have proposed, however, that the *Alexander Mosaic,* as it is commonly called, is a copy of a painting by one of the few Greek woman artists whose name is known, Helen of Egypt.

Battle of Issus is notable for the artist's technical mastery of problems that had long fascinated Greek painters. Even Euthymides would have marveled at the fourth-century BCE painter's depiction of the rearing horse seen in a three-quarter rear view below Darius. The subtle modulation of the horse's rump through shading in browns and yellows is much more accomplished than the comparable attempts at shading in the Pella mosaic (FIG. 5-68) or the Vergina mural (FIG. 5-69). Other details are even more impressive. The Persian to the right of the rearing horse has fallen to the ground and raises, backward, a dropped Macedonian shield to protect himself from being trampled. Philoxenos recorded the reflection of the man's terrified face on the polished surface of the shield. Everywhere in the scene, men, animals, and weapons cast shadows on the ground. This interest in the reflection of insubstantial light on a shiny surface, and in the absence of light (shadows), stands in sharp contrast to earlier painters' preoccupation with the clear presentation of weighty figures seen against a blank background. Philoxenos here truly opened a window into a world filled not only with figures, trees, and sky but also with light. This new, distinctly Greek notion of what a painting should be characterizes most of the history of art in the Western world from the Renaissance on.

Most impressive about *Battle of Issus,* however, is the psychological intensity of the drama unfolding before the viewer's eyes. Alexander, riding Bucephalus, leads his army into battle, recklessly one might say, without even a helmet to protect him. He drives his spear through one of Darius's trusted "Immortals," who swore to guard the king's life, while the Persian's horse collapses beneath him. The Macedonian king is only a few yards away from Darius,

5-71 POLYKLEITOS THE YOUNGER, aerial view of the theater (looking northeast), Epidauros, Greece, ca. 350 BCE.

The Greeks always situated theaters on hillsides to support the cavea of stone seats overlooking the circular orchestra. The Epidauros theater is the finest in Greece. It accommodated 12,000 spectators.

and Alexander directs his gaze at the Persian king, not at the man impaled on his now-useless spear. Darius has called for retreat. In fact, his charioteer is already whipping the horses and speeding the king to safety. Before he escapes, Darius looks back at Alexander and in a pathetic gesture reaches out toward his brash foe. But the victory has slipped from his hands. In Pliny's opinion, Philoxenos's painting of the battle between Alexander and Darius was "inferior to none."[8] It is easy to see why he reached that conclusion.

Architecture

In architecture, as in sculpture and painting, the Late Classical period was a time of innovation and experimentation.

THEATER OF EPIDAUROS In ancient Greece, actors did not perform plays repeatedly over months or years as they do today, but only during sacred festivals. Greek drama was closely associated with religious rites and was not pure entertainment. In the fifth century BCE, for example, the Athenians staged performances of the tragedies of Aeschylus, Sophocles, and Euripides during the Dionysos festival in the theater dedicated to the god on the southern slope of the Acropolis. Yet it is Epidauros, in the Peloponnesos, that boasts the finest theater (FIG. 5-71) in Greece. Constructed shortly after the birth of Alexander, the theater is still the setting for performances of ancient Greek dramas. The architect was POLYKLEITOS THE YOUNGER, possibly a nephew of the famous fifth-century BCE sculptor.

The precursor of the formal Greek theater was a circular patch of earth where actors performed sacred rites, songs, and dances. This circular hard and level surface later became the orchestra of the theater. *Orchestra* literally means "dancing place." The actors and the chorus performed there, and at Epidauros an altar to Dionysos stood at the center of the circle. The spectators sat on a slope overlooking the orchestra—the *theatron,* or "place for seeing." When the Greek theater took architectural shape, the builders always situated the auditorium (*cavea,* Latin for "hollow place, cavity") on a hillside. The cavea at Epidauros, composed of wedge-shaped sections (*cunei,* singular *cuneus*) of stone benches separated by stairs, is somewhat greater than a semicircle in plan. The auditorium is 387 feet in diameter, and its 55 rows of seats accommodated about 12,000 spectators. They entered the theater via a passageway between the seating area and the scene building (*skene*), which housed dressing rooms for the actors and also formed a backdrop for the plays. The design is simple but perfectly suited to its function. Even in antiquity, the Epidauros theater was famous for the harmony of its proportions. Although spectators sitting in some of the seats would have had a poor view of the skene, all had unobstructed views of the orchestra. Because of the open-air cavea's excellent acoustics, everyone could hear the actors and chorus.

CORINTHIAN CAPITALS The theater at Epidauros is about 500 yards southeast of the sanctuary of Asklepios, and Polykleitos the Younger worked there as well. He was the architect of the *tholos,* the circular shrine that probably housed the sacred snakes of the healing god. That building lies in ruins today, its architectural fragments removed to the local museum, but one can get an approximate idea of its original appearance from the somewhat earlier and partially reconstructed tholos (FIG. 5-72) at Delphi that THEODOROS OF PHOKAIA designed. Both tholoi had an exterior colonnade of Doric columns, but the interior columns had bases and *Corinthian capitals*

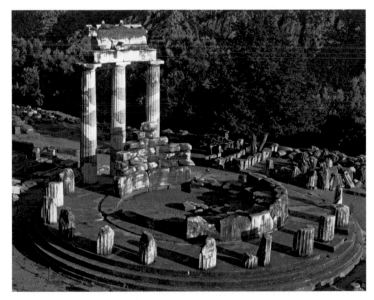

5-72 THEODOROS OF PHOKAIA, Tholos, Delphi, Greece, ca. 375 BCE.

The tholos at Delphi, although in ruins, is the best-preserved example of a round temple of the Classical period. It had Doric columns on the exterior and Corinthian columns inside.

The Corinthian Capital

The Corinthian capital (FIG. 5-73) is more ornate than either the Doric or Ionic (FIG. 5-13). It consists of a double row of acanthus leaves, from which tendrils and flowers emerge, wrapped around a bell-shaped echinus. Although architectural historians often cite this capital as the distinguishing feature of the Corinthian order, strictly speaking no Corinthian order exists. The new capital type was simply a substitute for the Ionic order's volute capital.

The sculptor Kallimachos invented the Corinthian capital during the second half of the fifth century BCE. Vitruvius recorded the circumstances that supposedly led to its creation:

> A maiden who was a citizen of Corinth . . . died. After her funeral, her nurse collected the goblets in which the maiden had taken delight while she was alive, and after putting them together in a basket, she took them to the grave monument and put them on top of it. In order that they should remain in place for a long time, she covered them with a tile. Now it happened that this basket was placed over the root of an acanthus. As time went on the acanthus root, pressed down in the middle by the weight, sent forth, when it was about springtime, leaves and stalks; its stalks growing up along the sides of the basket and being pressed out from the angles because of the weight of the tile, were forced to form volute-like curves at their extremities. At this point, Kallimachos happened to be going by and noticed the basket with this gentle growth of leaves around it. Delighted with the order and the novelty of the form, he made columns using it as his model and established a canon of proportions for it.*

Kallimachos worked on the Acropolis in Pericles' great building program. Many scholars believe a Corinthian column supported the outstretched right hand of Phidias's *Athena Parthenos* (FIG. 5-46) because one appears in some of the Roman copies of the lost statue. In any case, the earliest preserved Corinthian capital dates to the time of Kallimachos. The new type was rarely used before the mid-fourth century BCE, however, and did not become popular until Hellenistic and especially Roman times. Later architects favored the Corinthian capital because of its ornate character and because it eliminated certain problems of both the Doric and Ionic orders (see "Doric and Ionic Orders," page 116, and FIG. 5-13).

The Ionic capital, unlike the Doric, has two distinct profiles—the front and back (with the volutes) and the sides. The volutes always faced outward on a Greek temple, but architects met with a vexing problem at the corners of their buildings, which had two adjacent "fronts." They solved the problem by placing volutes on both outer faces of the corner capitals (as on the Erechtheion, FIG. 5-52, and the Temple of Athena Nike, FIG. 5-55), but that was an awkward solution.

5-73 POLYKLEITOS THE YOUNGER, Corinthian capital, from the tholos, Epidauros, Greece, ca. 350 BCE. Archaeological Museum, Epidauros.

Corinthian capitals, invented by the fifth-century BCE sculptor Kallimachos, are more ornate than Doric and Ionic capitals. They feature a double row of acanthus leaves with tendrils and flowers.

Doric design rules also presented problems for Greek architects at the corners of buildings. Doric friezes had to satisfy three supposedly inflexible rules:

❙ A triglyph must be exactly over the center of each column

❙ A triglyph must be over the center of each *intercolumniation* (the space between two columns)

❙ Triglyphs at the corners of the frieze must meet so that no space is left over

These rules are contradictory, however. If the corner triglyphs must meet, then they cannot be placed over the center of the corner column (FIGS. 5-1, 5-25, 5-30, and 5-44).

The Corinthian capital eliminated both problems. Because the capital's four sides have a similar appearance, corner Corinthian capitals do not have to be modified, as do corner Ionic capitals. And because the Corinthian "order" incorporates an Ionic frieze, architects do not have to contend with corner triglyphs.

*Vitruvius, *De architectura*, 4.1.8–10. Translated by J. J. Pollitt, *The Art of Ancient Greece: Sources and Documents* (New York: Cambridge University Press, 1990), 193–194.

(FIG. **5-73**; see "The Corinthian Capital," above), an invention of the second half of the fifth century BCE.

Consistent with the extremely conservative nature of Greek temple design, architects did not readily embrace the Corinthian capital. Until the second century BCE, Greek architects used Corin-

thian capitals only for the interiors of sacred buildings, as at Delphi and Epidauros. The earliest instance of a Corinthian capital on the exterior of a Greek building is the Choragic Monument of Lysikrates (FIG. **5-74**), which is not really a building at all. Lysikrates had sponsored a chorus in a theatrical contest in 334 BCE, and

5-74 Choragic Monument of Lysikrates, Athens, Greece, 334 BCE.

The first known use of Corinthian capitals on the exterior of a building is on the monument Lysikrates erected in Athens to commemorate the victory his chorus won in a theatrical contest.

after he won, he erected a monument to commemorate his victory. The monument consists of a cylindrical drum resembling a tholos on a square base. Engaged Corinthian columns adorn the drum of Lysikrates' monument, and a huge Corinthian capital sits atop the roof. The freestanding capital once supported the victor's trophy, a bronze tripod.

HELLENISTIC PERIOD

Alexander the Great's conquest of the Near East and Egypt ushered in a new cultural age that historians and art historians alike call *Hellenistic*. The Hellenistic period opened with the death of Alexander in 323 BCE and lasted nearly three centuries, until the double suicide of Queen Cleopatra of Egypt and her Roman consort Mark Antony in 30 BCE after their decisive defeat at the battle of Actium by Antony's rival Augustus (see page 197). That year, Augustus made Egypt a province of the Roman Empire.

The cultural centers of the Hellenistic period were the court cities of the Greek kings who succeeded Alexander and divided his far-flung empire among themselves. Chief among them were Antioch in Syria, Alexandria in Egypt (named after Alexander and the site of his tomb), and Pergamon in Asia Minor (MAP 5-1). An international culture united the Hellenistic world, and its language was Greek. Hellenistic kings became enormously rich on the spoils of the East, priding themselves on their libraries, art collections, scientific enterprises, and skills as critics and connoisseurs, as well as on the learned men they could assemble at their courts. The world of the small, austere, and heroic city-state passed away, as did the power and prestige of its center, Athens. A cosmopolitan ("citizen of the world," in Greek) civilization, much like today's, replaced it.

Architecture

The greater variety, complexity, and sophistication of Hellenistic culture called for an architecture on an imperial scale and of wide diversity, something far beyond the requirements of the Classical polis, even beyond that of Athens at the height of its power. Building activity shifted from the old centers on the Greek mainland to the opulent cities of the Hellenistic monarchs in the East.

TEMPLE OF APOLLO, DIDYMA Great scale, a theatrical element of surprise, and a willingness to break the traditional rules of Greek temple design characterize one of the most ambitious projects of the Hellenistic period, the Temple of Apollo (FIG. 5-75) at Didyma. The Hellenistic temple replaced the Archaic temple at the site the Persians burned in 494 BCE when they sacked nearby Miletos. Construction began in 313 BCE under the direction of two architects native to the area, PAIONIOS OF EPHESOS and DAPHNIS OF MILETOS. So vast was

0 25 50 75 100 feet
0 5 10   20   30 meters

Dipteral colonnade   Inner shrine   Courtyard   Oracular room

5-75 PAIONIOS OF EPHESOS and DAPHNIS OF MILETOS, aerial view (*left,* looking east) and plan (*right*) of the Temple of Apollo, Didyma, Turkey, begun 313 BCE.

This unusual Hellenistic temple was hypaethral (open to the sky) and featured a dipteral (double peripteral) colonnade framing an interior courtyard with a smaller shrine to Apollo.

the undertaking, however, that work on the temple continued off and on for more than 500 years—and still the project was never completed.

The temple was dipteral in plan and had an unusually broad facade of 10 Ionic columns almost 65 feet tall. The sides had 21 columns, consistent with the Classical formula for perfect proportions used for the Parthenon (21 = [2 × 10] + 1), but nothing else about the design is Classical. One anomaly immediately apparent to anyone who approached the building was that it had no pediment and no roof—it was *hypaethral,* or open to the sky. Also, the grand doorway to what should have been the temple's cella was nearly 5 feet off the ground and could not be entered. The explanation for the peculiar elevated doorway is that it served as a kind of stage where the oracle of Apollo could be announced to those assembled in front of the temple. Further, the unroofed dipteral colonnade did not surround a traditional cella. The columns were instead an elaborate frame for a central courtyard in which was a small prostyle shrine that housed a statue of Apollo. Entrance to the interior court was through two smaller doorways to the left and right of the great portal and down two narrow vaulted tunnels that could accommodate only a single file of people. From these dark and mysterious lateral passageways, worshipers emerged into the clear light of the courtyard, which also had a sacred spring and laurel trees in honor of Apollo. Opposite Apollo's inner temple, a stairway some 50 feet wide rose majestically toward three portals leading into the oracular room that also opened onto the front of the temple. This complex spatial planning marked a sharp departure from Classical Greek architecture, which stressed a building's exterior almost as a work of sculpture and left its interior relatively undeveloped.

HIPPODAMOS OF MILETOS When the Greeks finally expelled the Persians from Asia Minor in 479 BCE, they returned to cities in near ruin. Reconstruction of Miletos began after 466 BCE, according to a plan laid out by Hippodamos of Miletos, whom Aristotle singled out as the father of rational city planning. Hippodamos imposed a strict grid plan on the site, regardless of the terrain, so that all streets met at right angles. In fact, such *orthogonal plans* predate Hippodamos, not only in Archaic Greece and Etruscan Italy but also in the ancient Near East and Egypt. Still, Hippodamos was

so famous that his name has ever since been synonymous with this kind of urban plan. The so-called *Hippodamian plan* also designated separate quarters for public, private, and religious functions. A "Hippodamian city" was logically as well as regularly planned. This desire to impose order on nature and to assign a proper place in the whole to each of the city's constituent parts was very much in keeping with the philosophical tenets of the fifth century BCE. Hippodamos's formula for the ideal city was another manifestation of the same outlook that produced Polykleitos's *Canon* and the Parthenon.

PRIENE Hippodamian planning was still the norm in Late Classical and Hellenistic Greece. The city of Priene (FIG. **5-76**), also in Asia Minor, was laid out during the fourth century BCE. It had fewer than 5,000 inhabitants (Hippodamos thought 10,000 was the ideal number). Situated on sloping ground, many of its narrow north-south streets were little more than long stairways. Uniformly sized city blocks, the standard planning unit, were nonetheless imposed on the irregular terrain. More than one unit was reserved for major structures such as the Temple of Athena and the theater. The central agora occupied six blocks.

STOA OF ATTALOS, ATHENS Framing each side of Priene's agora was a *stoa.* These covered colonnades, or *porticos,* which often housed shops and civic offices, were ideal vehicles for shaping urban spaces, and they were staples of Hellenistic cities. Even the agora of Athens, an ancient city notable for its haphazard, unplanned development, was eventually framed to the east and south by stoas placed at right angles to one another. These new porticos joined the famous Painted Stoa (see page 143), where the Hellenistic philosopher Zeno and his successors taught. The *Stoic* school of Greek philosophy took its name from that building.

The finest of the new Athenian stoas was the Stoa of Attalos II (FIG. **5-77**), a gift to the city by a grateful alumnus, the king of Pergamon (r. 159–138 BCE), who had studied at Athens in his youth. The stoa was meticulously reconstructed under the direction of the American School of Classical Studies at Athens and today has a second life as a museum housing more than seven decades of finds from the Athenian agora, as well as the offices of the American excavation

5-76 Restored view of Priene, Turkey, fourth century BCE and later (John Burge).

Despite its irregular terrain, Priene had a strict grid plan conforming to the principles of Hippodamos of Miletos, whom Aristotle singled out as the father of rational city planning.

5-77 Stoa of Attalos II (looking southeast with the Acropolis in the background), Agora, Athens, Greece, ca. 150 BCE.

The Stoa of Attalos II in the Athenian agora has been meticulously restored. Greek stoas were covered colonnades that housed shops and civic offices. They were also ideal vehicles for shaping urban spaces.

team. The stoa has two stories, each with 21 shops opening onto the colonnade. The facade columns are Doric on the ground level and Ionic on the second story. The mixing of the two orders on a single facade had occurred even in the Late Classical period. But it became increasingly common in the Hellenistic period, when respect for the old rules of Greek architecture was greatly diminished and a desire for variety and decorative effects often prevailed. Practical considerations also governed the form of the Stoa of Attalos. The columns are far more widely spaced than in Greek temple architecture, to allow for easy access. Also, the builders left the lower third of every Doric column shaft unfluted to guard against damage from constant traffic.

Pergamon

Pergamon, the kingdom of Attalos II, was born in the early third century BCE after the breakup of Alexander's empire. Founded by Philetairos (r. 282–263 BCE), the Pergamene kingdom embraced almost all of western and southern Asia Minor. Upon the death in 133 BCE of its last king, Attalos III (r. 138–133 BCE), Pergamon was bequeathed to Rome, which by then was the greatest power in the Mediterranean world. The Attalids enjoyed immense wealth and expended much of it on the embellishment of their capital city, especially its acropolis. Located there were the royal palace, an arsenal and barracks, a great library and theater, an agora, and the sacred precincts of Athena and Zeus.

ALTAR OF ZEUS, PERGAMON The Altar of Zeus at Pergamon, erected about 175 BCE, is the most famous Hellenistic sculptural ensemble. The monument's west front (FIG. 5-78) has been reconstructed in Berlin. The altar proper was on an elevated platform, framed by an Ionic stoalike colonnade with projecting

5-78 Reconstructed west front of the Altar of Zeus, Pergamon, Turkey, ca. 175 BCE. Staatliche Museen zu Berlin, Berlin.

The gigantomachy frieze of Pergamon's monumental Altar of Zeus is almost 400 feet long. The battle of gods and giants alluded to the victory of King Attalos I over the Gauls of Asia Minor.

5-79 Athena battling Alkyoneos, detail of the gigantomachy frieze, Altar of Zeus, Pergamon, Turkey, ca. 175 BCE. Marble, 7′ 6″ high. Staatliche Museen zu Berlin, Berlin.

The tumultuous battle scenes of the Pergamon altar have an emotional power unparalleled in earlier Greek art. Violent movement, swirling draperies, and vivid depictions of suffering fill the frieze.

wings on either side of a broad central staircase. All around the altar platform was a sculpted frieze almost 400 feet long, populated by about a hundred larger-than-life-size figures. The subject is the battle of Zeus and the gods against the giants. It is the most extensive representation Greek artists ever attempted of that epic conflict for control of the world. The gigantomachy also appeared on the shield of Phidias's *Athena Parthenos* and on some of the Parthenon metopes, because the Athenians wished to draw a parallel between the defeat of the giants and the defeat of the Persians. In the third century BCE, King Attalos I (r. 241–197 BCE) had successfully turned back an invasion of the Gauls in Asia Minor. The gigantomachy of the Altar of Zeus alluded to that Attalid victory over those barbarians. The Pergamene designers also used the gigantomachy frieze to establish a connection with Athens, whose earlier defeat of the Persians was by then legendary, and with the Parthenon, which the Hellenistic Greeks already recognized as a Classical monument—in both senses of the word. The figure of Athena (FIG. 5-79), for example, closely resembles the Athena from the Parthenon's east pediment. While Gaia, the earth goddess and mother of all the giants, emerges from the ground and looks on with horror, Athena grabs the hair of the giant Alkyoneos as Nike flies in to crown her. Zeus himself (not illustrated) was based on the Poseidon of the west pediment.

The Pergamene frieze, however, is not a dry series of borrowed motifs. On the contrary, its tumultuous narrative has an emotional intensity without parallel in earlier sculpture. The battle rages everywhere, even up and down the steps used to reach Zeus's altar (FIG. 5-78). Violent movement, swirling draperies, and vivid depictions of death and suffering fill the frieze. Wounded figures writhe in pain, and their faces reveal their anguish. Deep carving creates dark shadows. The figures project from the background like bursts of light. Art historians have justly described these features as "baroque," borrowing the term from 17th-century European sculpture (see Chapter 24). Indeed, there perhaps can be no greater contrast than between the Pergamene gigantomachy frieze and the comparable frieze (FIG. 5-18) of the Archaic Siphnian Treasury at Delphi.

DYING GAULS On the Altar of Zeus, Pergamene sculptors presented the victory of Attalos I over the Gauls in mythological disguise. An earlier Pergamene statuary group explicitly depicted the defeat of the barbarians. Roman copies of some of these figures reveal that the Hellenistic sculptors carefully studied and reproduced the distinctive features of the foreign Gauls, most notably their long, bushy hair and mustaches and the *torques* (neck bands) they frequently wore. The Pergamene victors were apparently not

5-80 Epigonos(?), Gallic chieftain killing himself and his wife. Roman copy of a bronze statue from Pergamon, Turkey, of ca. 230–220 BCE. Marble, 6′ 11″ high. Museo Nazionale Romano—Palazzo Altemps, Rome.

The defeat of the Gauls was also the subject of Pergamene statuary groups. The centerpiece of one group was a Gallic chieftain committing suicide after taking his wife's life. He preferred death to surrender.

part of this group. The viewer saw only their Gallic foes and their noble and moving response to defeat.

In what was probably the centerpiece of the group, a heroic Gallic chieftain (FIG. 5-80) defiantly drives a sword into his own chest just below the collarbone, preferring suicide to surrender. He already has taken the life of his wife, who, if captured, would have been sold as a slave. In the best Lysippan tradition, the group can be fully appreciated only by walking around it. From one side, the observer sees the Gaul's intensely expressive face, from another his powerful torso, and from a third the woman's limp, lifeless body. The man's twisting posture, the almost theatrical gestures, and the emotional intensity of the suicidal act are hallmarks of the Pergamene baroque style and have close parallels in the later frieze of Zeus's altar.

The third Gaul from this group is a trumpeter (FIG. 5-81) who collapses upon his large oval shield as blood pours from the gash in his chest. He stares at the ground with a pained expression. The Hellenistic figure recalls the dying warrior (FIG. 5-28) from the east pediment of the Temple of Aphaia at Aegina, but the pathos and drama of the suffering Gaul are far more pronounced. As in the suicide group and the gigantomachy frieze, the sculptor rendered the male musculature in an exaggerated manner. Note the tautness of the chest and the bulging veins of the left leg—implying that the unseen Pergamene warrior who has struck down this noble and savage foe must have been an extraordinarily powerful man. If this figure is the *tubicen* (trumpeter) Pliny mentioned as the work of the Pergamene master EPIGONOS, then Epigonos may be the sculptor of the entire group and the creator of the dynamic Hellenistic baroque style.[9]

5-81 Epigonos(?), Dying Gaul. Roman copy of a bronze statue from Pergamon, Turkey, ca. 230–220 BCE. Marble, 3′ $\frac{1}{2}$″ high. Musei Capitolini, Rome.

A Pergamene sculptor depicted this defeated Gallic trumpeter and the other Gauls as barbarians with bushy hair, mustaches, and neck bands, but also as noble foes who fought to the death.

Sculpture

In different ways, Praxiteles, Skopas, and Lysippos had already taken bold steps in redefining the nature of Greek statuary. Still, Hellenistic sculptors went further, both in terms of style and in expanding the range of subjects considered suitable for monumental sculpture.

NIKE OF SAMOTHRACE One of the masterpieces of Hellenistic baroque sculpture is the statue of winged Victory set up in the Sanctuary of the Great Gods on the island of Samothrace. The *Nike of Samothrace* (FIG. 5-82) has just alighted on the prow of a Greek warship. She raises her (missing) right arm to crown the naval victor, just as Nike places a wreath on Athena's head on the Altar of Zeus (FIG. 5-79). But the Pergamene relief figure seems calm by comparison. The Samothracian Nike's wings still beat, and the wind sweeps her drapery. Her himation bunches in thick folds around her right leg, and her chiton is pulled tightly across her abdomen and left leg.

5-83 ALEXANDROS OF ANTIOCH-ON-THE-MEANDER, *Aphrodite* (*Venus de Milo*), from Melos, Greece, ca. 150–125 BCE. Marble, 6′ 7″ high. Musée du Louvre, Paris.

Displaying the eroticism of many Hellenistic statues, this Aphrodite is more overtly sexual than the Knidian Aphrodite (FIG. 5-62). The goddess's slipping garment teases the spectator.

1 ft.

5-82 Nike alighting on a warship (*Nike of Samothrace*), from Samothrace, Greece, ca. 190 BCE. Marble, Nike 8′ 1″ high. Musée du Louvre, Paris. ◼◀

Victory lands on a ship's prow to crown a naval victor. Her wings still beat, and the wind sweeps her drapery. The statue's placement in a fountain of splashing water heightened the dramatic visual effect.

1 ft.

5-83A Aphrodite, Eros, and Pan, Delos, ca. 100 BCE.

The statue's setting amplified this theatrical effect. The sculptor set the war galley in the upper basin of a two-tiered fountain. In the lower basin were large boulders. The fountain's flowing water created the illusion of rushing waves hitting the prow of the ship. The statue's reflection in the shimmering water below accentuated the sense of lightness and movement. The sound of splashing water added an aural dimension to the visual drama. Art and nature combined here to create one of the most successful sculptures ever fashioned. In the *Nike of Samothrace* and other works in the Hellenistic baroque manner, sculptors resoundingly rejected the Polykleitan conception of a statue as an ideally proportioned, self-contained entity on a bare pedestal. The Hellenistic statues interact with their environment and appear as living, breathing, and intensely emotive human (or divine) presences.

VENUS DE MILO In the Hellenistic period, sculptors regularly followed Praxiteles' lead in undressing Aphrodite, but they also openly explored the eroticism of the nude female form. The famous *Venus de Milo* (FIG. 5-83) is a larger-than-life-size marble

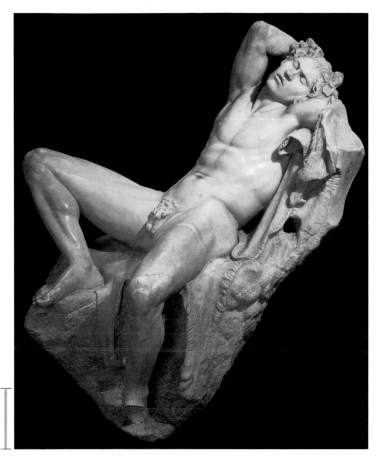

5-84 Sleeping satyr (*Barberini Faun*), from Rome, Italy, ca. 230–200 BCE. Marble, 7′ 1″ high. Glyptothek, Munich.

Here, a Hellenistic sculptor represented a restlessly sleeping, drunken satyr, a semihuman in a suspended state of consciousness—the antithesis of the Classical ideals of rationality and discipline.

statue of Aphrodite found on Melos together with its inscribed base (now lost) signed by the sculptor ALEXANDROS OF ANTIOCH-ON-THE-MEANDER. In this statue, the goddess of love is more modestly draped than the *Aphrodite of Knidos* (FIG. 5-62) but is more overtly sexual. Her left hand (separately preserved) holds the apple Paris awarded her when he judged her the most beautiful goddess. Her right hand may have lightly grasped the edge of her drapery near the left hip in a halfhearted attempt to keep it from slipping farther down her body. The sculptor intentionally designed the work to tease the spectator, instilling this partially draped Aphrodite with a sexuality absent from Praxiteles' entirely nude image of the goddess. Other Hellenistic sculptors (FIG. 5-83A), especially when creating works for private patrons, went even further in depicting the goddess of love as an object of sexual desire.

BARBERINI FAUN Archaic statues smile at the viewer, and even when Classical statues look away, they are always awake and alert. Hellenistic sculptors often portrayed sleep. The suspension of consciousness and the entrance into the fantasy world of dreams—the antithesis of the Classical ideals of rationality and discipline—had great appeal for them. This newfound interest is evident in a marble statue (FIG. 5-84) of a drunken, restlessly sleeping *satyr* (a semihuman follower of Dionysos) known as the *Barberini Faun*, after Cardinal Barberini, who acquired the statue when it was unearthed in Rome in the 17th century. Barberini hired Gianlorenzo Bernini, the great Italian Baroque sculptor (FIGS. 24-6 to 24-8), to

restore the statue. Bernini no doubt felt that this dynamic statue in the Pergamene manner was the work of a kindred spirit. The satyr has consumed too much wine and has thrown down his panther skin on a convenient rock, then fallen into a disturbed, intoxicated sleep. His brows are furrowed, and one can almost hear him snore.

Eroticism also comes to the fore in this statue. Although men had been represented naked in Greek art for hundreds of years, Archaic kouroi and Classical athletes and gods do not exude sexuality. Sensuality surfaced in the works of Praxiteles and his followers in the fourth century BCE. But the dreamy and supremely beautiful Hermes playfully dangling grapes before the infant Dionysos (FIG. 5-63) has nothing of the blatant sexuality of the *Barberini Faun*, whose wantonly spread legs focus attention on his genitals. Homosexuality was common in the male world of ancient Greece. It is not surprising that when Hellenistic sculptors began to explore the sexuality of the human body, they turned their attention to both men and women.

SLEEPING EROS Another Hellenistic depiction of sleep, but one radically different in character, is the bronze statue (FIG. 5-85) from Rhodes portraying Eros sleeping on a rock. Before the Hellenistic age, artists usually represented the winged child-god of love as an adolescent (FIG. 5-50, *center*). Here, as in the group of *Aphrodite, Eros, and Pan* (FIG. 5-83A), he is the pudgy winged infant Cupid, the form he takes in art from this point up to the present. The Hellenistic representations of Eros are noteworthy because throughout history, artists frequently painted and sculpted babies as miniature adults—often with adult personalities to match their mature bodies. Hellenistic sculptors were masters at reproducing the soft flesh and muscles of infants and portraying the spirit of young children in memorable statues. This representation of Eros differs from the contemporaneous group from Delos in one important respect. The winged child does not participate in any action. Rather, like the *Barberini Faun* (FIG. 5-84), he is asleep, one wing folded beneath him, one foot barely touching the ground, his right arm hanging limply, and his mouth open as he breathes. Eros enjoys the peaceful sleep of an infant free of the worries of the world.

5-85 Sleeping Eros, from Rhodes, ca. 150–100 BCE. Bronze, 2′ 9½″ long. Metropolitan Museum of Art, New York (Rogers Fund, 1943).

Eros, an adolescent in earlier Greek art, appears here as a pudgy winged infant sleeping on a rock. The Hellenistic sculptor skillfully represented the anatomy and personality of infants.

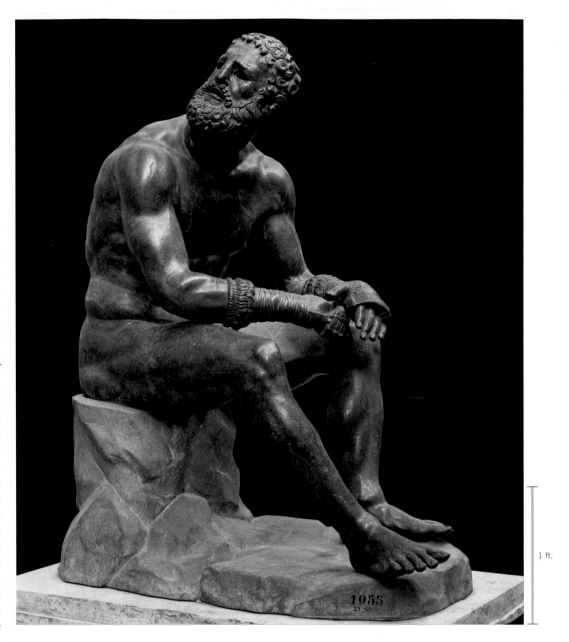

5-86 Seated boxer, from Rome, Italy, ca. 100–50 BCE. Bronze, 4′ 2″ high. Museo Nazionale Romano—Palazzo Massimo alle Terme, Rome.

Even when Hellenistic artists treated traditional themes, they approached them in novel ways. This bronze statue depicts an older, defeated boxer with a broken nose and battered ears.

1 ft.

DEFEATED BOXER Although Hellenistic sculptors tackled an expanded range of subjects, they did not abandon such traditional themes as the Greek athlete. Nevertheless, they often treated the old subjects in novel ways. This is certainly true of the magnificent bronze statue (FIG. **5-86**) of a seated boxer, a Hellenistic original found in Rome and perhaps at one time part of a group. The boxer is not a victorious young athlete with a perfect face and body but a heavily battered, defeated veteran whose upward gaze may have been directed at the man who had just beaten him. Too many punches from powerful hands wrapped in leather thongs—Greek boxers did not use the modern sport's cushioned gloves—have distorted the boxer's face. His nose is broken, as are his teeth. He has smashed "cauliflower" ears. Inlaid copper blood drips from the cuts on his forehead, nose, and cheeks. How different is this rendition of a powerful bearded man from that of the noble Riace warrior (FIGS. 5-35 and I-17) of the Early Classical period. The Hellenistic sculptor appealed not to the intellect but to the emotions when striving to evoke compassion for the pounded hulk of a once-mighty fighter.

OLD MARKET WOMAN The realistic bent of much Hellenistic sculpture—the very opposite of the Classical period's idealism—is evident above all in a series of statues of old men and women from the lowest rungs of the social order. Shepherds, fishermen, and drunken beggars are common—the kinds of people pictured earlier on red-figure vases but never before thought worthy of monumental statuary. One of the finest preserved statues of this type depicts a haggard old woman (FIG. **5-87**) bringing chickens and a basket of fruits and vegetables to sell in the market. Her face is wrinkled, her body bent with age, and her spirit broken by a lifetime of poverty. She carries on because she must, not because she derives any pleasure from life. No one knows the purpose of these statues, but they attest to an interest in social realism absent in earlier Greek statuary.

Statues of the aged and the ugly are, of course, the polar opposites of the images of the young and the beautiful that dominated Greek art until the Hellenistic age, but they are consistent with the period's changed character. The Hellenistic world was a cosmopolitan place, and the highborn could not help but encounter the poor and a growing number of foreigners (non-Greek "barbarians") on a daily basis. Hellenistic art reflects this different social climate in the depiction of a much wider variety of physical types, including different ethnicities. The sensitive portrayal of Gallic warriors with their shaggy hair, strange mustaches, and golden torques (FIGS. 5-80 and 5-81) has already been noted. Africans, Scythians, and others, formerly only the occasional subject of vase painters, also entered the realm of monumental sculpture in Hellenistic art.

DEMOSTHENES These sculptures of foreigners and the urban poor, however realistic, are not portraits. Rather, they are sensitive studies of physical types. But the growing interest in the individual beginning in the Late Classical period did lead in the Hellenistic era to the production of true likenesses of specific persons. In fact, one of the great achievements of Hellenistic artists was the redefinition of portraiture. In the Classical period, Kresilas won fame for having made the noble Pericles appear even nobler in his portrait (FIG. 5-41). In contrast, in Hellenistic times, sculptors sought not only to record the true appearance of their subjects in bronze and stone but also to capture the essence of their personalities in likenesses both accurate and moving.

1 ft.

5-87 Old market woman. Roman copy(?) of a marble statue of ca. 150–100 BCE. Marble, 4′ 1⅞″ high. Metropolitan Museum of Art, New York.

Consistent with the realism of much Hellenistic art, many statues portray the elderly of the lowest rungs of society. Earlier Greek artists did not consider them suitable subjects for statuary.

5-88 POLYEUKTOS, Demosthenes. Roman copy of a bronze original of ca. 280 BCE. Marble, 6′ 7½″ high. Ny Carlsberg Glyptotek, Copenhagen.

One of the earliest Hellenistic portraits, frequently copied, was Polyeuktos's representation of the great orator Demosthenes as a frail man who possessed great courage and moral conviction.

1 ft.

One of the earliest of these, perhaps the finest of the Hellenistic age and frequently copied in Roman times, was a bronze portrait statue of Demosthenes (FIG. 5-88) by POLYEUKTOS. The original, commissioned in 280 BCE, 42 years after the great orator's death, stood in the Athenian agora. Demosthenes was a frail man and in his youth even suffered from a speech impediment, but he had enormous courage and great moral conviction. A veteran of the disastrous battle against Philip II at Chaeronea, he repeatedly tried to rally opposition to Macedonian imperialism, both before and after Alexander's death. In the end, when it was clear the Macedonians would capture him, he took his own life by drinking poison.

Polyeuktos rejected Kresilas's and Lysippos's notions of the purpose of portraiture and did not attempt to portray a supremely confident leader with a magnificent physique. His Demosthenes has an aged and slightly stooped body. The orator clasps his hands nervously in front of him as he looks downward, deep in thought. His face is lined, his hair is receding, and his expression is one of great sadness. Whatever physical discomfort Demosthenes felt is here joined by an inner pain, his deep sorrow over the tragic demise of democracy at the hands of the Macedonian conquerors.

Hellenistic Art under Roman Patronage

In the opening years of the second century BCE, the Roman general Flamininus defeated the Macedonian army and declared the old poleis of Classical Greece free once again. The city-states never regained their former glory, however. Greece became a Roman province in 146 BCE. When Athens 60 years later sided with King Mithridates VI of Pontus (r. 120–63 BCE) in his war against Rome, the general Sulla crushed the Athenians. Thereafter, although Athens retained some of its earlier prestige as a center of culture and learning, politically it was merely another city in the ever-expanding Roman Empire. Nonetheless, Greek artists continued to be in great demand, both to furnish the Romans with an endless stream of copies of Classical and Hellenistic masterpieces and to create new statues in Greek style for Roman patrons.

5-89 Athanadoros, Hagesandros, and Polydoros of Rhodes, Laocoön and his sons, from Rome, Italy, early first century CE. Marble, 7′ 10½″ high. Musei Vaticani, Rome.

Hellenistic style lived on in Rome. Although stylistically akin to Pergamene sculpture, this statue of sea serpents attacking Laocoön and his two sons matches the account given only in the *Aeneid*.

5-90 Athanadoros, Hagesandros, and Polydoros of Rhodes, head of Odysseus, from the villa of Tiberius, Sperlonga, Italy, early first century CE. Marble, 2′ 1¼″ high. Museo Archeologico, Sperlonga.

This emotionally charged depiction of Odysseus was part of a mythological statuary group the three Laocoön sculptors made for a grotto at the emperor Tiberius's seaside villa at Sperlonga.

LAOCOÖN One work of this type is the famous group (FIG. 5-89) of the Trojan priest Laocoön and his sons, unearthed in Rome in 1506 in the presence of the great Italian Renaissance artist Michelangelo (see Chapter 22). The marble group, long believed an original of the second century BCE, was found in the remains of the palace of the emperor Titus (r. 79–81 CE), exactly where Pliny had seen it more than 14 centuries before. Pliny attributed the statue to three sculptors—ATHANADOROS, HAGESANDROS, and POLYDOROS OF RHODES—who art historians now generally think worked in the early first century CE. These artists probably based their group on a Hellenistic masterpiece depicting Laocoön and only one son. Their variation on the original added the son at Laocoön's left (note the greater compositional integration of the other two figures) to conform with the Roman poet Vergil's account in the *Aeneid*. Vergil vividly described the strangling of Laocoön and his *two* sons by sea serpents while sacrificing at an altar. The gods who favored the Greeks in the war against Troy had sent the serpents to punish Laocoön, who had tried to warn his compatriots about the danger of bringing the Greeks' wooden horse within the walls of their city.

In Vergil's graphic account, Laocoön suffered in terrible agony. Athanadoros and his colleagues communicated the torment of the priest and his sons in spectacular fashion in the marble group. The three Trojans writhe in pain as they struggle to free themselves from the death grip of the serpents. One bites into Laocoön's left hip as the priest lets out a ferocious cry. The serpent-entwined figures recall the suffering giants of the great frieze of the Altar of Zeus at Pergamon, and Laocoön himself is strikingly similar to Alkyoneos (FIG. 5-79), Athena's opponent. In fact, many scholars

believe that a Pergamene statuary group of the second century BCE was the inspiration for the three Rhodian sculptors.

SPERLONGA That the work seen by Pliny was made for Romans rather than Greeks was confirmed in 1957 by the discovery of fragments of several Hellenistic-style groups illustrating scenes from Homer's *Odyssey*. Archaeologists found the sculptures in a grotto that served as the summer banquet hall of the seaside villa of the Roman emperor Tiberius (r. 14–37 CE) at Sperlonga. One of these groups—depicting the monster Scylla attacking Odysseus's ship—bears the signatures of the same three sculptors Pliny cited as the creators of the Laocoön group. Another group, installed around a central pool in the grotto, depicted the blinding of the Cyclops Polyphemos by Odysseus and his comrades, an incident also set in a cave in the Homeric epic. The figure of Odysseus (FIG. 5-90) from this theatrical group is one of the finest sculptures of antiquity. The hero's cap can barely contain his swirling locks of hair. Even Odysseus's beard seems to be swept up in the emotional intensity of the moment. The parted lips and the deep shadows produced by sharp undercutting add drama to the head, which complemented Odysseus's agitated body.

The baroque school of Hellenistic sculpture thus lived on long after Greece ceased to be a political force. When Rome inherited the Pergamene kingdom from the last of the Attalids in 133 BCE, it also became heir to the Greek artistic legacy. What Rome adopted from Greece it passed on to the medieval and modern worlds. If Greece was peculiarly the inventor of the European spirit, Rome (see Chapter 7) was its propagator and amplifier.

ANCIENT GREECE

GEOMETRIC AND ORIENTALIZING ART ca. 900–600 BCE

▌ Homer lived during the eighth century BCE, the era when the city-states of Classical Greece took shape, the Olympic Games were founded (776 BCE), and the Greeks began to trade with their neighbors to both east and west. At the same time, the human figure returned to Greek art in the form of bronze statuettes and simple silhouettes amid other abstract motifs on Geometric vases.

▌ Increasing contact with the civilizations of Egypt and Mesopotamia precipitated the so-called Orientalizing phase (ca. 700–600 BCE) of Greek art, when Eastern monsters began to appear on black-figure vases.

Hero and centaur,
ca. 750–730 BCE

ARCHAIC ART ca. 600–480 BCE

▌ Around 600 BCE, the first life-size stone statues appeared in Greece. The earliest kouroi emulated the frontal poses of Egyptian statues, but artists depicted the young men nude, the way Greek athletes competed at Olympia. During the course of the sixth century BCE, Greek sculptors refined the proportions and added "Archaic smiles" to the faces of their statues to make them seem more lifelike.

▌ The Archaic age also brought the construction of the first stone temples with peripteral colonnades and the codification of the Doric and Ionic orders.

▌ The Andokides Painter invented red-figure vase painting around 530 BCE. Euphronios and Euthymides rejected the age-old composite view for the human figure and experimented with foreshortening.

Euphronios, Herakles and Antaios,
ca. 510 BCE

EARLY AND HIGH CLASSICAL ART ca. 480–400 BCE

▌ The Classical period opened with the Persian sack of the Athenian Acropolis in 480 BCE and the Greek victory a year later. During the Early Classical period (480–450 BCE), sculptors revolutionized statuary by introducing contrapposto (weight shift) to their figures.

▌ In the High Classical period (450–400 BCE), Polykleitos developed a canon of proportions for the perfect statue. Iktinos similarly applied mathematical formulas to temple design in the belief that beauty resulted from the use of harmonic numbers. Under the patronage of Perikles and the artistic directorship of Phidias, the Athenians rebuilt the Acropolis after 447 BCE. The Parthenon, Phidias's statue of Athena Parthenos, and the works of Polykleitos have defined what it means to be "Classical" ever since.

Parthenon, Acropolis, Athens,
447–438 BCE

LATE CLASSICAL ART ca. 400–323 BCE

▌ In the aftermath of the Peloponnesian War, which ended in 404 BCE, Greek artists, though still adhering to the philosophy that humanity was the "measure of all things," began to focus more on the real world of appearances than on the ideal world of perfect beings. Late Classical sculptors humanized the remote deities, athletes, and heroes of the fifth century BCE. Praxiteles, for example, caused a sensation when he portrayed Aphrodite undressed. Lysippos depicted Herakles as muscle-bound but so weary that he needed to lean on his club for support.

▌ In architecture, the ornate Corinthian capital became increasingly popular, breaking the monopoly of the Doric and Ionic orders.

▌ The period closed with Alexander the Great, who transformed the Mediterranean world politically and ushered in a new artistic age as well.

Praxiteles, *Aphrodite of Knidos*,
ca. 350–340 BCE

HELLENISTIC ART ca. 323–30 BCE

▌ The Hellenistic age extends from the death of Alexander until the death of Cleopatra, when Egypt became a province of the Roman Empire.

▌ In art, both architects and sculptors broke most of the rules of Classical design. At Didyma, for example, the Temple of Apollo had no roof and contained a smaller temple within it. Hellenistic sculptors explored new subjects—Gauls with strange mustaches and necklaces, impoverished old women—and treated traditional subjects in new ways—athletes with battered bodies and faces, openly erotic goddesses. Artists delighted in depicting violent movement and unbridled emotion.

Altar of Zeus, Pergamon,
ca. 175 BCE

The Tomb of the Augurs is one of the oldest tombs at Tarquinia to have frescoes on all four walls. Dominating the rear wall is a large door, probably the symbolic entrance to the Underworld.

Two men extend one arm toward the door and place one hand against the forehead in a double gesture signifying salute and mourning. The deceased may be the purple-robed official to the right.

On the right wall, the Etruscan painter depicted the funerary games in honor of the deceased. The man with a curved staff is not a Roman augur with a lituus but is the umpire at a wrestling match.

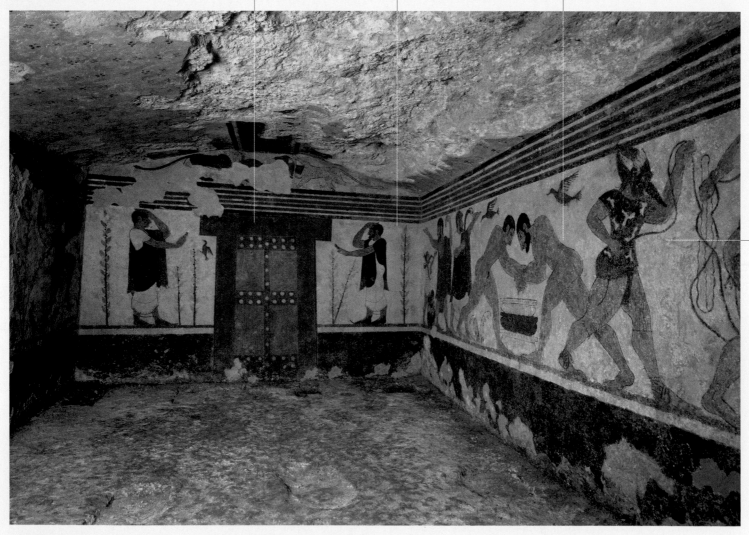

6-1 Interior of the Tomb of the Augurs, Monterozzi necropolis, Tarquinia, ca. 520 BCE.

6

THE ETRUSCANS

A masked phersu, unique to Etruria, oversees a gruesome contest between a club-wielding man whose head is covered by a sack and a fearsome dog—perhaps a precursor of Roman gladiatorial games.

THE REDISCOVERY OF ETRUSCAN ART

"The Etruscans, as everyone knows, were the people who occupied the middle of Italy in early Roman days, and whom the Romans, in their usual neighborly fashion, wiped out entirely." So opens D. H. Lawrence's witty and sensitive *Etruscan Places* (1929), one of the earliest modern essays to place a high value on Etruscan art and treat it as much more than a debased form of Greek art. ("Most people despise everything B.C. that isn't Greek, for the good reason that it ought to be Greek if it isn't," Lawrence quipped.) Fortunately, scholars and the public at large soon also came to admire the Etruscans, and it has been a long time since anyone had to argue for the importance and originality of Etruscan art. Indeed, although influenced by Greek art, Etruscan art differs in many fundamental ways.

The Tomb of the Augurs (FIG. 6-1), datable around 520 BCE, makes that point forcefully. It is one of thousands of underground tombs, laboriously carved out of the bedrock at the important Etruscan city of Tarquinia, at a time when the Greeks still buried their dead in simple earth graves. The tomb also has fresco paintings—an art form virtually unknown in sixth-century BCE Greece—on all four walls, and although the artists adhered to many Greek conventions, the subjects they depicted are distinctly Etruscan.

At the center of the rear wall is a large door, probably the symbolic portal to the Underworld. To either side of it, two men extend one arm toward the door and place one hand against the forehead in a double gesture signifying salute and mourning. At the far end of the right wall is a man in a purple robe, a mark of his elevated stature, and two attendants. One carries a chair, the official seat of the man's high office. The other sleeps, or more likely weeps, crouched on the ground. The official is likely the one who has died. The rest of the right wall as well as the left and front walls depict the funerary games in honor of the dead man. To the right of the official and his attendants is a man with a curved staff similar to the *lituus* of the Roman priests called *augurs,* hence the modern name of the tomb. But the Etruscan "augur" is really an umpire at a wrestling match. To the right, a masked man labeled *phersu* (another phersu is at the far end of the left wall) controls a fearsome dog on a leash. The phersu's leash also entangles and restrains the legs of a club-wielding man. A sack covers his head, rendering him an almost helpless victim of the dog, which has already drawn blood. Some historians regard this gruesome contest as a direct precursor of Roman gladiatorial shows. In any case, Etruscan art and architecture unquestionably provided the models for the earliest Roman painters, sculptors, and architects.

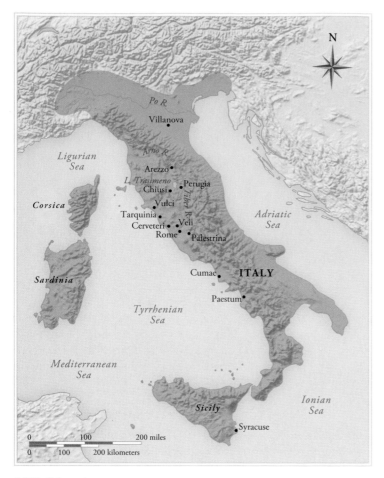

MAP 6-1 Italy in Etruscan times.

6-2 Fibula with Orientalizing lions, from the Regolini-Galassi Tomb, Sorbo necropolis, Cerveteri, Italy, ca. 650–640 BCE. Gold, 1' $\frac{1}{2}$" high. Musei Vaticani, Rome.

This huge gold pin found with other Orientalizing jewelry in a Cerveteri tomb combines repoussé and granulation and is the work of an Etruscan artist, but the lions are Egyptian and Mesopotamian motifs.

ETRURIA AND THE ETRUSCANS

The heartland of the Etruscans (who called themselves Rasenna) was the territory between the Arno and Tiber rivers of central Italy (MAP 6-1). The lush green hills still bear their name—Tuscany, the land of the people the Romans called Etrusci or Tusci, the region centered on Florence. So, too, do the blue waters that splash against the western coastline of the Italian peninsula, for the Greeks referred to the Etruscans as Tyrsenoi or Tyrrhenoi and gave their name to the Tyrrhenian Sea. Both ancient and modern commentators have debated whether the Etruscans were an indigenous people or immigrants. Their language, although written in a Greek-derived script, is unrelated to the Indo-European linguistic family and remains largely undeciphered. The fifth-century BCE Greek historian Herodotus claimed the Etruscans came from Lydia in Asia Minor

and that Tyrsenos was their king—hence their Greek name. But Dionysius of Halicarnassus, a first-century BCE Greek historian, maintained the Etrusci were native Italians. Some modern researchers have theorized the Etruscans descended from the north into Italy. No doubt some truth exists in each theory. The Etruscan people of historical times—the Rasenna—were very likely the result of a gradual fusion of native and immigrant populations. This mixing of peoples occurred in the early first millennium BCE during the so-called Villanovan period, named for an archaeological site near present-day Bologna. At that time—contemporaneous with the Geometric period in Greece—the Etruscans emerged as a people with an art-producing culture related to but distinct from those of other Italic peoples and from the civilizations of Greece and the Orient.

THE ETRUSCANS

700	Orientalizing	600	Archaic	480	Classical and Hellenistic	BCE 89
	▌ The Etruscans emerge as a distinct artistic culture during the Villanovan period (ca. 900–700 BCE) ▌ During the seventh century BCE, trade with Mesopotamia inspires the incorporation of monsters and other Orientalizing motifs in Etruscan funerary goods		▌ The Etruscans construct temples of mud brick and wood with columns and stairs only on the front and terracotta statuary on the roof ▌ At Cerveteri, the Etruscans bury their dead beneath huge earthen tumuli in multichambered tombs resembling houses ▌ Tarquinian tombs feature fresco paintings depicting funerary games and banquets		▌ Etruscan sculptors excel in bronze casting, engraving mirrors and cistae, and carving stone sarcophagi ▌ Etruscan architects construct arcuated gateways, often with columns framing the arched passageway	

During the eighth and seventh centuries BCE, the Etruscans, as highly skilled seafarers, enriched themselves through trade abroad. By the sixth century BCE, they controlled most of northern and central Italy. Their most powerful cities included Tarquinia, Cerveteri, Vulci, and Veii. These and the other Etruscan cities never united to form a state, however, so it is inaccurate to speak of an Etruscan "nation" or "kingdom," but only of Etruria, the territory the Etruscans occupied. Any semblance of unity among the independent Etruscan cities was based primarily on common linguistic ties and religious beliefs and practices.

EARLY ETRUSCAN ART

Although art historians now universally acknowledge the distinctive character of Etruscan painting, sculpture, and architecture, they still usually divide the history of Etruscan art into periods mirroring those of Greek art. The seventh century BCE is the Orientalizing period of Etruscan art (followed by the Archaic, Classical, and Hellenistic periods).

Orientalizing Art

During the Orientalizing period, the Etruscans successfully mined iron, tin, copper, and silver, creating great wealth and, in the process, transforming Etruscan society. Villages with agriculturally based economies gave way in the seventh century BCE to prosperous cities engaged in international commerce. Wealthy families could afford to acquire foreign goods, and the Etruscan elite quickly developed a taste for luxury objects incorporating Eastern motifs. To satisfy the demand, local artisans, inspired by imported goods, produced magnificent objects for both homes and tombs. As in Greece at the same time, the locally manufactured Orientalizing artifacts cannot be mistaken for their foreign models.

REGOLINI-GALASSI TOMB About 650–640 BCE, a wealthy Etruscan family in Cerveteri stocked the Regolini-Galassi Tomb (named for its excavators) with bronze cauldrons and gold jewelry produced in Etruria but of Orientalizing style. The most spectacular of the many luxurious objects in the tomb is a gold *fibula* (clasp or safety pin; FIG. **6-2**) of unique shape used to fasten a woman's gown at the shoulder. The gigantic disk-shaped fibula is in the Italic tradition, but the five lions striding across its surface are motifs originating in the Orient. The technique, also emulating Eastern imports, is masterful, combining repoussé and *granulation* (the fusing of tiny metal balls, or granules, to a metal surface). The Regolini-Galassi fibula equals or exceeds in quality anything that might have served as a model.

Etruscan Counterparts of Greco-Roman Gods and Heroes

Etruscan	*Greek*	*Roman*
Tinia	Zeus	Jupiter
Uni	Hera	Juno
Menrva	Athena	Minerva
Apulu	Apollo	Apollo
Artumes	Artemis	Diana
Hercle	Herakles	Hercules

The jewelry from the Regolini-Galassi Tomb also includes a gold *pectoral* that covered a deceased woman's chest, and two gold circlets that may be earrings, although they are large enough to be bracelets. A taste for this kind of ostentatious display is frequently the hallmark of newly acquired wealth, and this was certainly the case in seventh-century BCE Etruria.

Archaic Art and Architecture

The art and architecture of Greece also impressed Etruscan artists looking eastward for inspiration. Still, however eager those artists may have been to emulate Greek works, their distinctive Etruscan temperament always manifested itself.

ETRUSCAN TEMPLES In religious architecture, for example, the differences between temples honoring the Etruscan gods (see "Etruscan Counterparts of Greco-Roman Gods and Heroes," above) and their Greek prototypes far outweigh the similarities. Because of the materials Etruscan architects employed, usually only the foundations of their temples have survived. These are nonetheless sufficient to reveal the plans of the edifices. Supplementing the archaeological record is the Roman architect Vitruvius's treatise on architecture written near the end of the first century BCE. In it, Vitruvius provided an invaluable chapter on Etruscan temple design.

Archaeologists have constructed a model (FIG. **6-3**) of a typical Archaic Etruscan temple based on Vitruvius's account. The sixth-century BCE Etruscan temple resembled contemporaneous Greek stone gable-roofed temples, but it had wood columns, a tile-covered wood roof, and walls of sun-dried mud brick. Entrance was possible only via a narrow staircase at the center of the front of the temple, which sat on a high podium, the only part of the building made of stone. The proportions also differed markedly. Greek temples were about twice as long as wide. Vitruvius reported the typical ratio for Etruscan temples was 6:5. Greek and Etruscan architects

6-3 Model of a typical Etruscan temple of the sixth century BCE, as described by Vitruvius. Istituto di Etruscologia e di Antichità Italiche, Università di Roma, Rome. ◼◀

Etruscan temples resembled Greek temples but had widely spaced, unfluted wood columns only at the front, walls of sun-dried mud brick, and a narrow staircase at the center of the facade.

Etruscan Artists in Rome

In 616 BCE, according to the traditional chronology, Tarquinius Priscus of Tarquinia became Rome's first Etruscan king. He ruled for almost 40 years. His grandson, Tarquinius Superbus ("the Arrogant"), was Rome's last king. Outraged by his tyrannical behavior, the Romans drove him from power in 509 BCE. Before his expulsion, however, Tarquinius Superbus embarked on a grand program to embellish the city he ruled.

The king's most ambitious undertaking was the construction of a magnificent temple on the Capitoline Hill for the joint worship of Jupiter, Juno, and Minerva. For this great commission, he summoned architects, sculptors, and workers from all over Etruria. Rome's first great religious shrine was therefore Etruscan in patronage, manufacture, and form. The architect's name is unknown, but several sources preserve the identity of the Etruscan sculptor brought in to adorn the temple—Vulca of Veii, who may also have made a statue of the god Apulu (FIG. 6-4) for his native city. Pliny the Elder described Vulca's works as "the finest images of deities of that era . . . more admired than gold."* The Romans entrusted Vulca with creating the statue of Jupiter that stood in the central cella (one for each of the three deities) in the Capitoline temple. He also fashioned the enormous terracotta statuary group of Jupiter in a four-horse chariot, which he mounted on the roof at the highest point directly over the center of the temple facade. The fame of Vulca's red-faced (painted terracotta) portrayal of Jupiter was so great Roman generals would paint their faces red in emulation of the ancient statue when they paraded in triumph through Rome after a battlefield victory. (The model of a typical three-cella Etruscan temple in FIG. 6-3 also serves to give an approximate idea of the appearance of the Capitoline Jupiter temple and of Vulca's roof statue.)

Vulca is the only Etruscan artist any ancient writer named, but the signatures of other Etruscan artists appear on extant artworks. One of these is Novios Plautios (FIG. 6-13), who also worked in Rome, although a few centuries later. By then the Etruscan kings of Rome were a distant memory, and the Romans had captured Veii and annexed its territory.

*Pliny, *Natural History*, 35.157.

1 ft.

6-4 Apulu (*Apollo of Veii*), from the roof of the Portonaccio temple, Veii, Italy, ca. 510–500 BCE. Painted terracotta, 5′ 11″ high. Museo Nazionale di Villa Giulia, Rome.

The statue of Apulu was part of a group depicting a Greek myth. Distinctly Etruscan, however, are the god's vigorous motion and gesticulating arms and the placement of the statue on a temple roof.

---

also arranged the columns in distinct ways. The columns in Etruscan temples were usually all at the front of the building, creating a deep porch occupying roughly half the podium and setting off one side of the structure as the main side. In contrast, the front and rear of Greek temples were indistinguishable, and builders placed steps and columns on all sides (FIG. 5-12). The Etruscan temple was not meant to be seen as a sculptural mass from all directions, as Greek temples were.

Furthermore, although the columns of Etruscan temples resembled Greek Doric columns (FIG. 5-13, *left*), *Tuscan columns* were made of wood, were unfluted, and had bases. Also, because of the lightness of the superstructure, fewer, more widely spaced columns were the rule in Etruscan temples. Unlike their Greek counterparts, Etruscan temples also frequently had three cellas—one for each of their chief

gods, Tinia, Uni, and Menrva. Pedimental statuary was also rare in Etruria. The Etruscans normally placed life-size narrative statuary—in terracotta instead of stone—on the roofs of their temples.

APOLLO OF VEII The finest surviving Etruscan temple statue is the life-size image of Apulu (FIG. **6-4**), which displays the energy and excitement that characterize Archaic Etruscan art in general. The statue comes from the rooftop of a temple in the Portonaccio sanctuary at Veii. Popularly known as the *Apollo of Veii*, it is but one of a group of at least four painted terracotta figures that adorned the temple's ridgepole. The statues depicted one of the 12 labors of Herakles (see "Herakles," Chapter 5, page 128). Apulu confronted Hercle for possession of the hind of Ceryneia, a wondrous gold-horned beast sacred to the god's sister Artumes. The

The "Audacity" of Etruscan Women

At the instigation of the emperor Augustus at the end of the first century BCE, Titus Livy wrote a history of Rome from its legendary founding in 753 BCE to his own day. In the first book of his great work, Livy recounted the tale of Tullia, daughter of Servius Tullius, an Etruscan king of Rome in the sixth century BCE. The princess had married the less ambitious of two brothers of the royal Tarquinius family, while her sister had married the bolder of the two princes. Together, Tullia and her brother-in-law, Tarquinius Superbus (see "Etruscan Artists in Rome," page 168), arranged for the murder of their spouses. They then married each other and plotted the overthrow and death of Tullia's father. After the king's murder, Tullia ostentatiously drove her carriage over her father's corpse, spraying herself with his blood. (The Romans still call the road where the evil deed occurred the Street of Infamy.) Livy, though condemning Tullia's actions, placed them in the context of the famous "audacity" of Etruscan women.

The independent spirit and relative freedom women enjoyed in Etruscan society similarly horrified (and threatened) other Greco-Roman male authors. The stories the fourth-century BCE Greek historian Theopompus heard about the debauchery of Etruscan women appalled him. Etruscan women epitomized immorality for Theopompus, but much of what he reported is untrue. Etruscan women did not, for example, exercise naked alongside Etruscan men. But archaeological evidence confirms the accuracy of at least one of his "slurs": Etruscan women did attend banquets and recline with their husbands on a common couch (FIGS. 6-5 and 6-9). Aristotle also remarked on this custom. It was so foreign to the Greeks it both shocked and frightened them. Only men, boys, slave girls, and prostitutes attended Greek symposiums. The wives remained at home, excluded from most aspects of public life. In Etruscan Italy, in striking contrast to Greece, women also regularly attended sporting events with men. Etruscan paintings and reliefs document this as well.

1 ft.

6-5 Sarcophagus with reclining couple, from the Banditaccia necropolis, Cerveteri, Italy, ca. 520 BCE. Painted terracotta, 3′ 9½″ × 6′ 7″. Museo Nazionale di Villa Giulia, Rome. ▣◀

Sarcophagi in the form of a husband and wife on a dining couch have no parallels in Greece. The artist's focus on the upper half of the figures and the emphatic gestures are Etruscan hallmarks.

Etruscan inscriptions also reflect the higher status of women in Etruria as compared with Greece. They often give the names of both the father and mother of the person commemorated (for example, the inscribed portrait of Aule Metele, FIG. 6-16), a practice unheard of in Greece (witness the grave stele of "Hegeso, daughter of Proxenos," FIG. 5-57). Etruscan women, moreover, retained their own names (Ramtha Visnai, FIG. 6-15A) and could legally own property independently of their husbands. The frequent use of inscriptions on Etruscan mirrors and other toiletry items (FIG. 6-13) buried with women seems to attest to a high degree of female literacy as well.

bright paint and the rippling folds of Apulu's garment call to mind Archaic Greek korai in Ionian garb (FIG. 5-11). But Apulu's vigorous striding motion, gesticulating arms, fanlike calf muscles, rippling drapery, and animated face are distinctly Etruscan. Some scholars have attributed the Apulu statue to VULCA OF VEII, the most famous Etruscan sculptor of the time (see "Etruscan Artists in Rome," page 168). The statue's discovery in 1916 was instrumental in prompting a reevaluation of the originality of Etruscan art.

CERVETERI SARCOPHAGUS Although the Greeks produced statues in terracotta, Etruscan sculptors especially favored that medium. Another Archaic Etruscan terracotta masterwork is the sarcophagus (FIG. 6-5) from a Cerveteri tomb in the form of a husband and wife reclining on a banqueting couch. The sarcopha-

gus, which was once brightly painted, consists of four separately cast and fired sections. Although the man and woman on the couch are life-size, the sarcophagus contained only the ashes of the husband or wife, or perhaps both. Cremation was the most common means of disposing of the dead in Archaic Italy. This kind of funerary monument had no parallel at this date in Greece, where there were no monumental tombs that could house large sarcophagi. The Greeks buried their dead in simple graves marked by a stele or a statue. Moreover, although banquets were common subjects on Greek vases (which, by the late sixth century BCE, the Etruscans imported in great quantities and regularly deposited in their tombs), only men dined at Greek symposiums. The image of a husband and wife sharing the same banqueting couch is uniquely Etruscan (see "The 'Audacity' of Etruscan Women," above).

In the Banditaccia necropolis at Cerveteri, the Etruscans buried several generations of families in multichambered rock-cut underground tombs covered by great earthen mounds (tumuli).

The man and woman on the Cerveteri sarcophagus are as animated as the *Apollo of Veii* (FIG. 6-4), even though they are at rest. The woman may have held a perfume flask and a pomegranate in her hands, the man an egg (compare FIG. 6-9). They are the antithesis of the stiff and formal figures encountered in Egyptian funerary sculpture (compare FIG. 3-12). Also typically Etruscan, and in sharp contrast to contemporaneous Greek statues with their emphasis on proportion and balance, is the manner in which the Cerveteri sculptor rendered the upper and lower parts of each body. The artist shaped the legs only summarily, and the transition to the torso at the waist is unnatural. The sculptor's interest focused on the upper half of the figures, especially on the vibrant faces and gesticulating arms. The Cerveteri banqueters and the Veii Apulu

speak to the viewer in a way Greek statues of similar date, with their closed contours and calm demeanor, never do.

BANDITACCIA NECROPOLIS The exact findspot of the Cerveteri sarcophagus is unrecorded, but it came from the Banditaccia necropolis, where, beginning in the seventh century BCE, wealthy Etruscan families constructed enormous tombs (FIG. 6-6) in the form of a mound, or *tumulus*, not unlike the Mycenaean Treasury of Atreus (FIG. 4-20). But whereas the Mycenaeans built their tholos tombs with masonry blocks and then covered the burial chambers with an earthen mound, each Etruscan tumulus stood over one or more subterranean multichambered tombs cut out of the dark local limestone called tufa. The largest burial

6-7 Interior of the Tomb of the Shields and Chairs, Banditaccia necropolis, Cerveteri, Italy, ca. 550–500 BCE.

Terracotta statues of the deceased probably "sat" in the chairs cut out of the bedrock of this subterranean tomb chamber. The tomb's plan (FIG. 6-7A) follows that of a typical Etruscan house.

mounds at Cerveteri are truly of colossal size, exceeding 130 feet in diameter and reaching nearly 50 feet in height. Arranged in an orderly manner along a network of streets spread over 200 acres, the Banditaccia tombs constitute a veritable city of the dead—the literal meaning of the Greek word *necropolis*.

6-7A Tomb of the Shields and Chairs, Cerveteri, ca. 550–500 BCE.

TOMB OF THE SHIELDS AND CHAIRS

The aptly named Tomb of the Shields and Chairs (FIGS. **6-7** and **6-7A**) is one of the most elaborate in the Banditaccia necropolis. Sculptors carved out of the tufa bedrock six beds and two high-backed chairs with footstools, as well as door frames and ceiling beams, in imitation of the wooden furniture and timber architecture of Archaic Etruscan homes. Based on evidence from other tombs, the Etruscans probably placed terracotta figures of the deceased on the chairs. Reliefs of 14 shields adorn the walls. The technique recalls that of rock-cut Egyptian tombs such as Amenemhet's (FIG. 3-18) at Beni Hasan and highlights the very different values of the Etruscans and the Greeks. The Etruscans' temples no longer stand because they constructed them of wood and mud brick, but their grand subterranean tombs are as permanent as the bedrock itself. The Greeks employed stone for the shrines of their gods but only rarely built monumental tombs for their dead.

TOMB OF THE RELIEFS

The most elaborate Cerveteri tomb, in decoration if not in plan, is the Tomb of the Reliefs (FIG. **6-8**). Like the much earlier Tomb of the Shields and Chairs, it accommodated several generations of a single family. The Etruscans, as usual, gouged the burial chamber out of the tufa bedrock, but in this instance they covered the sculpted walls and piers with painted stucco reliefs, hence the tomb's modern name. The stools, mirrors, drinking cups, pitchers, and knives effectively suggest a domestic context, underscoring the connection between Etruscan houses of the dead and those of the living. Other reliefs—for example, the helmet and shields over the main funerary couch (the pillows are also shallow reliefs)—are signs of the elite status of this Cerveteri family. The three-headed dog beneath the same couch is Cerberus, guardian of the gate to the Underworld, a reference to the passage from this life to the next.

TARQUINIA

Large underground burial chambers hewn out of the natural rock were also the norm in the Monterozzi necropolis at Tarquinia. Earthen mounds may once have covered the Tarquinia tombs too, but the tumuli no longer exist. In contrast to Cerveteri, the subterranean rooms at Tarquinia lack carvings imitating the appearance of Etruscan houses. In around 200 tombs, however, paintings decorate the walls, as in the Tomb of the Augurs (FIG. 6-1). Painted tombs are nonetheless statistically rare, the privilege of only the wealthiest Tarquinian families. Archaeologists have succeeded in locating so many of them by using periscopes to explore tomb interiors from the surface before considering time-consuming and costly excavation. Consequently, art historians have an almost unbroken record of monumental painting in Etruria from Archaic to Hellenistic times.

6-8 Interior of the Tomb of the Reliefs, Banditaccia necropolis, Cerveteri, Italy, late fourth or early third century BCE. ◼◀

The Tomb of the Reliefs takes its name from the painted stucco reliefs covering its walls and piers. The stools, mirrors, drinking cups, and other items are reminders of the houses of the living.

The paintings in the Tomb of the Leopards, named after the guardian beasts in the rear pediment, depict banqueting couples, servants, and musicians. The men have dark skin, the women fair skin.

6-9A Tomb of the Triclinium, Tarquinia, ca. 480–470 BCE.

TOMB OF THE LEOPARDS

Two important tombs—the Tomb of the Leopards (FIG. 6-9) and the Tomb of the Triclinium (FIG. 6-9A) are about 40 years later than the Tomb of the Augurs. The Leopards tomb takes its name from the beasts that guard the burial chamber from their perch within the pediment of the rear wall. The leopards are reminiscent of the panthers on each side of Medusa in the pediment (FIG. 5-16) of the temple of Artemis at Corfu. But mythological figures, whether Greek or Etruscan, are uncommon in Tarquinian murals, and neither the Augurs nor the Leopards tomb includes any. In the later tomb, banqueting couples (the men with dark skin, the women with light skin, in conformity with the age-old convention; compare FIGS. 3-11A and 5-20A) adorn the walls—painted versions of the terracotta sarcophagus (FIG. 6-5) from Cerveteri. Pitcher- and cup-bearers serve the guests, and musicians entertain them. The banquet takes place in the open air or perhaps in a tent set up for the occasion. In characteristic Etruscan fashion, the banqueters, servants, and entertainers all make exaggerated gestures with unnaturally enlarged hands. The man on the couch at the far right on the rear wall holds up an egg, the symbol of regeneration. The tone is joyful, rather than a somber contemplation of death—a celebration of the good life of the privileged Etruscan elite.

In stylistic terms, the Etruscan figures are comparable to those on sixth-century BCE Greek vases before Late Archaic painters became preoccupied with the problem of foreshortening. Etruscan painters were somewhat backward in this respect, but in other ways they outpaced their counterparts in Greece, especially in their interest in rendering nature. In the Tomb of the Leopards, the "landscape" is but a few trees and shrubs placed between the entertainers (and leopards) and behind the banqueting couches. But in at least one Tarquinian tomb, the natural environment was the painters' chief interest.

TOMB OF HUNTING AND FISHING In the Tomb of Hunting and Fishing, scenes of Etruscans enjoying the pleasures of nature decorate all the walls of the main chamber. In the detail reproduced here (FIG. 6-10), a youth dives off a rocky promontory, while others fish from a boat and birds fill the sky all around. On another wall, youthful hunters aim their slingshots at the brightly painted birds. The scenes of hunting and fishing recall the paintings in Egyptian tombs (FIGS. 3-15 and 3-28) and may indicate knowledge of that Eastern funerary tradition. The multicolored rocks evoke those of the Theran Spring Fresco (FIG. 4-9), but art historians know of nothing similar in contemporaneous Greek art save the Tomb of the Diver (FIG. 5-61) at Paestum. That exceptional Greek work, however, is from a Greek tomb in Italy about a half century later than the Tarquinian tomb. In fact, the Paestum painter probably emulated older Etruscan designs, undermining the outdated art historical judgment that Etruscan art was merely derivative and that Etruscan artists never set the standard for Greek artists.

LATER ETRUSCAN ART

The fifth century BCE was a golden age in Greece but not in Etruria. In 509 BCE the Romans expelled the last of their Etruscan kings, Tarquinius Superbus (see "Etruscan Artists in Rome," page 168), and replaced the monarchy with a republican form of government. In 474 BCE the allied Greek forces of Cumae and Syracuse won a victory over the Etruscan fleet off Cumae, effectively ending Etruscan dominance of the seas—and with it Etruscan prosperity.

6-10 Diving and fishing, detail of the left wall of the Tomb of Hunting and Fishing, Monterozzi necropolis, Tarquinia, Italy, ca. 530–520 BCE. Fresco, detail 5′ 6½″ high. ◼◄

Scenes of young men enjoying the pleasures of nature cover the walls of this Tarquinian tomb. The Etruscan diving scene predates a similar landscape painting (FIG. 5-61) in a Greek tomb at Paestum.

1 ft.

Classical Art

These events had important consequences in the world of art and architecture. The number of grandiose Etruscan tombs, for example, decreased sharply, and the quality of the furnishings declined markedly. No longer did the Etruscan elite fill their tombs with gold jewelry and imported Greek vases or decorate the walls with paintings of the first rank. But art did not cease in Etruria. Indeed, in the areas in which Etruscan artists excelled, especially the casting of statues in bronze and terracotta, they continued to produce impressive works, even though fewer in number.

CAPITOLINE WOLF The best-known Etruscan statue of the Classical period is the *Capitoline Wolf* (FIG. **6-11**), one of the most memorable portrayals of an animal in the history of world art. The statue is a somewhat larger than life-size hollow-cast bronze image of the she-wolf that, according to legend, nursed Romulus and Remus after they were abandoned as infants. When the twins grew to adulthood, they quarreled, and Romulus killed his brother. On April 21, 753 BCE, Romulus founded Rome and became the city's king. The statue of the she-wolf seems to have been made for the new Roman Republic after the expulsion of

6-11 *Capitoline Wolf,* from Rome, Italy, ca. 500–480 BCE. Bronze, 2′ 7½″ high. Musei Capitolini, Rome.

An Etruscan sculptor cast this bronze statue of the she-wolf that nursed the infants Romulus and Remus, founders of Rome. The animal has a tense, gaunt body and an unforgettable psychic intensity.

1 ft.

6-12 *Chimera of Arezzo,* from Arezzo, Italy, first half of fourth century BCE. Bronze, 2′ 7½″ high. Museo Archeologico Nazionale, Florence.

The chimera was a composite monster, which the Greek hero Bellerophon slew. In this Etruscan statue, the artist depicted the wounded beast poised to attack and growling ferociously.

1 ft.

Tarquinius Superbus. It became the new government's totem. The appropriately defiant image has remained the emblem of Rome to this day.

The *Capitoline Wolf* is not, however, a work of Roman art, which had not yet developed a distinct identity, nor is it a medieval sculpture, as one scholar has argued. It is the product of an Etruscan workshop. (The suckling infants are Renaissance additions.) The sculptor brilliantly characterized the she-wolf physically and psychologically. The body is tense, with spare flanks, gaunt ribs, and taut, powerful legs. The lowered neck and head, alert ears, glaring eyes, and ferocious muzzle capture the psychic intensity of the fierce and protective beast as danger approaches. Not even the great animal reliefs of Assyria (FIG. 2-23) match this profound characterization of animal temperament.

CHIMERA OF AREZZO Another masterpiece of Etruscan bronze-casting is the Late Classical *Chimera of Arezzo* (FIG. **6-12**), found at Arezzo in 1553 and inscribed *tinscvil* (Etruscan, "gift"), indicating the chimera was a votive offering in a sanctuary. The *chimera* is a monster of Greek invention with a lion's head and body and a serpent's tail (restored in this case). A second head, that of a goat, grows out of the lion's left side. The goat's neck bears the wound the Greek hero Bellerophon inflicted when he hunted and slew the composite beast. As rendered by the Etruscan sculptor, the chimera, although injured and bleeding, refuses to surrender. Like the earlier *Capitoline Wolf,* the bronze chimera has muscles stretched tightly over its rib cage. The monster prepares to attack, and a ferocious cry emanates from its open jaws. Some scholars have postulated the statue was part of a group originally including Bellerophon, but the chimera could have just as well stood alone. The menacing gaze upward toward an unseen adversary need not have been answered. In this respect, too, the chimera is in the tradition of the *Capitoline Wolf.*

Etruscan Art and the Rise of Rome

At about the time an Etruscan sculptor cast the *Chimera of Arezzo,* Rome began to appropriate Etruscan territory. Veii fell to the Romans in 396 BCE after a terrible 10-year siege. The Tarquinians

6-13 NOVIOS PLAUTIOS, *Ficoroni Cista,* from Palestrina, Italy, late fourth century BCE. Bronze, 2′ 6″ high. Museo Nazionale di Villa Giulia, Rome.

Novios Plautios made this container for a woman's toiletry articles in Rome and engraved it with the Greek myth of the Argonauts. The composition is probably an adaptation of a Greek painting.

1 ft.

forged a peace treaty with the Romans in 351, but by the beginning of the next century, Rome had annexed Tarquinia too, and in 273 BCE the Romans conquered Cerveteri.

6-13A Chalchas examining a liver, ca. 400–375 BCE.

FICORONI CISTA An inscription on the *Ficoroni Cista* (FIG. **6-13**) reflects Rome's growing power in central Italy. In the fourth century BCE, Etruscan artists began to produce large numbers of *cistae* (cylindrical containers for a woman's toiletry articles) made of sheet bronze with cast handles and feet and elaborately engraved bodies. Along with engraved bronze mirrors (FIG. **6-13A**), they were popular gifts for both the living and the dead. The center of the Etruscan bronze cista industry was Palestrina, where Francesco de' Ficoroni acquired the cista that still bears his name. The inscription on the cista's handle states that Dindia Macolnia, a local noblewoman, gave the cista (the largest found to date) to her daughter and that the artist was NOVIOS PLAUTIOS. According to the inscription, his workshop was not in Palestrina but in Rome, which by this date was becoming an important Italian cultural, as well as political, center.

The engraved frieze of the *Ficoroni Cista* depicts an episode from the Greek story of the expedition of the Argonauts (the crew of the ship *Argo*) in search of the Golden Fleece. Art historians generally agree the composition is an adaptation of a lost Greek panel painting, perhaps one on display in Rome—another testimony to the burgeoning wealth and prestige of the city Etruscan kings once ruled. The Greek source for Novios Plautios's engraving is evident in the figures seen entirely from behind or in three-quarter view

and in the placement of the protagonists on several levels in the Polygnotan manner (FIG. 5-59).

PORTA MARZIA In the third century BCE, the Etruscans of Perugia formed an alliance with Rome and were spared the destruction Veii, Cerveteri, and other Etruscan cities suffered. Portions of Perugia's ancient walls still stand, as do some of its gates. One of these, the so-called Porta Marzia (Gate of Mars), was dismantled during the Renaissance, but the upper part of the gate (FIG. **6-14**) is preserved, embedded in a later wall. A series of trapezoidal stone *voussoirs* held in place by being pressed against each other (FIG. 4-17c) form the archway. Arches of similar construction have been documented earlier in Greece as well as in Mesopotamia (FIG. 2-24), but Italy, first under the Etruscans and later under the Romans, is where *arcuated* (arch-shaped) gateways and freestanding ("triumphal") arches became a major architectural type.

The use of Hellenic-inspired *pilasters* (flat columns) to frame the rounded opening of the Porta Marzia typifies the Etruscan adaptation of Greek motifs. Arches bracketed by engaged columns or pilasters have a long and distinguished history in Roman and later times. In the Porta Marzia, sculpted half-figures of Jupiter and his sons Castor and Pollux and their steeds look out from between the fluted pilasters. The divine twins had appeared miraculously on a battlefield in 484 BCE to turn the tide in favor of the Romans. The presence of these three deities at the apex of the Porta Marzia may reflect the new Roman practice of erecting triumphal arches with gilded bronze statues on top.

SARCOPHAGUS OF LARS PULENA In Hellenistic Etruria, the descendants of the magnificent Archaic terracotta sarcophagus (FIG. 6-5) from Cerveteri were coffins of local stone. The leading production center was Tarquinia, and that is where,

6-14 Porta Marzia, Perugia, Italy, second century BCE. ◼◀

The Porta Marzia was one of the gates in Perugia's walls. The use of fluted pilasters or engaged columns to frame arches typifies Etruscan builders' adaptation of Greek architectural motifs.

6-15 Sarcophagus of Lars Pulena, from Tarquinia, Italy, late third or early second century BCE. Tufa, 6′ 6″ long. Museo Archeologico Nazionale, Tarquinia.

Images of the deceased on late Etruscan sarcophagi are more somber than those on Archaic examples (FIG. 6-5), but Lars Pulena proudly displays a list of his life's achievements on an open scroll.

during the late third or early second century BCE, an Etruscan sculptor carved the sarcophagus (FIG. **6-15**) containing the remains of Lars Pulena. The scene sculpted on the front of the coffin shows the deceased in the Underworld between two *charuns* (Etruscan death demons) swinging hammers. Two *vanths* (winged female demons) stand to the left and right. The representation signifies that Lars Pulena has successfully made the journey to the afterlife. Above, the deceased reclines on a couch, as do the couple on the Cerveteri sarcophagus, but he is not

6-15A Sarcophagus of Ramtha Visnai and Arnth Tetnies, ca. 350–300 BCE.

at a festive banquet, and his wife is not present. The somber expression on his middle-aged face contrasts sharply with the smiling, confident faces of the Archaic era when Etruria enjoyed its greatest prosperity. Similar heads—realistic but generic types, not true portraits—can be found on most later Etruscan sarcophagi (FIG. **6-15A**) and in tomb paintings. They are symptomatic of the economic and political decline of the once-mighty Etruscan city-states. Nonetheless, Lars Pulena was a proud man. He wears a fillet on his head and a wreath around his neck, and he displays a partially unfurled scroll inscribed with his name and those of his ancestors as well as a record of his life's accomplishments.

AULE METELE An even later Etruscan portrait is the bronze statue (FIG. **6-16**) representing the magistrate Aule Metele raising his arm to address an assembly—hence his modern nickname *Arringatore* (*Orator*). This life-size statue, which dates to the early first century BCE, proves that Etruscan artists continued to be experts at bronze-casting long after the heyday of Etruscan prosperity. The time coincides with the Roman achievement of total hegemony over the Etruscans. The so-called Social War ended in 89 BCE with the conferring of Roman citizenship on all of Italy's inhabitants. In fact, Aule Metele—identifiable because the sculptor inscribed the magistrate's Etruscan name and those of his father and mother on the hem of his garment—wears the short *toga* and high laced boots of a Roman magistrate. His head, with its close-cropped hair and signs of age in the face, resembles portraits produced in Rome at the same time. This orator is Etruscan in name only. If the origin of the Etruscans remains the subject of debate, the question of their demise has a ready answer. Aule Metele and his compatriots became Roman citizens, and Etruscan art became Roman art.

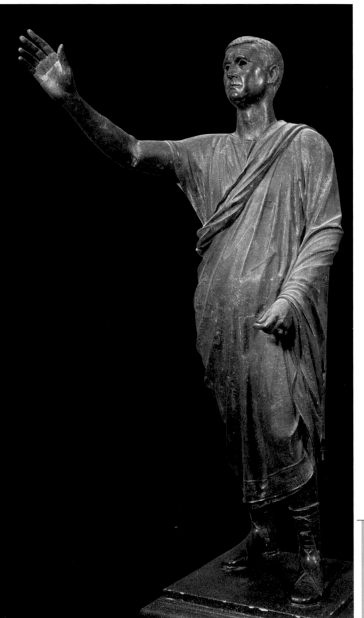

6-16 Aule Metele (*Arringatore*), from Cortona, Italy, early first century BCE. Bronze, 5′ 7″ high. Museo Archeologico Nazionale, Florence.

The life-size bronze statue portraying Aule Metele is Etruscan in name only. The orator wears the short toga and high boots of a Roman magistrate, and the portrait style is Roman as well.

THE ETRUSCANS

ORIENTALIZING ART ca. 700–600 BCE

▌ During the Villanovan period of the early first millennium BCE, the Etruscans emerged as a people with a culture distinct from those of other Italic peoples and the Greeks. Their language, although written in a Greek-derived script, is unrelated to the Indo-European linguistic family.

▌ In the seventh century BCE, the Etruscans traded metals from their mines for foreign goods and began to produce jewelry and other luxury objects decorated with motifs modeled on those found on imports from Mesopotamia. The Regolini-Galassi Tomb at Cerveteri contained a treasure trove of Orientalizing Etruscan jewelry.

Regolini-Galassi fibula, Cerveteri, ca. 650–640 BCE

ARCHAIC ART ca. 600–480 BCE

▌ The sixth century BCE was the apex of Etruscan power in Italy. Etruscan kings even ruled Rome until 509 BCE.

▌ The Etruscans admired Greek art and architecture but did not copy Greek works. They constructed their temples of wood and mud brick instead of stone and placed the columns and stairs only at the front. Terracotta statuary decorated the roof.

Model of a typical Etruscan temple, sixth century BCE

▌ Most surviving Etruscan artworks come from underground tomb chambers. At Cerveteri, great earthen mounds (tumuli) covered tombs with interiors sculptured to imitate the houses of the living.

▌ At Tarquinia, painters covered the tomb walls with monumental frescoes, often depicting funerary games, as in the Tomb of the Augurs, or banquets attended by both men and women.

Tomb of the Augurs, Tarquinia, ca. 520 BCE

CLASSICAL AND HELLENISTIC ART ca. 480–89 BCE

▌ The Greek victory over the Etruscan fleet off Cumae in 474 BCE ended Etruscan domination of the sea and marked the beginning of the decline of Etruria. Rome destroyed Veii in 396 BCE and conquered Cerveteri in 273 BCE. All of Italy became Romanized by 89 BCE.

Sarcophagus of Lars Pulena, ca. 200 BCE

▌ A very different, more somber mood pervades Etruscan art during the fifth through first centuries BCE, as seen, for example, in the sarcophagus of Lars Pulena.

▌ Later Etruscan architecture is noteworthy for the widespread use of the stone arch, often framed with Greek pilasters or engaged columns, as on the Porta Marzia at Perugia.

Porta Marzia, Perugia, second century BCE

The spiral frieze of the Column of Trajan recounts the emperor's two military campaigns in Dacia (present-day Romania). Here, Roman soldiers present severed Dacian heads to Trajan.

The campaign against the Dacians had few interludes. As soon as one skirmish ended, the Romans moved on and launched another attack. On Trajan's Column, each scene merges with the next.

The sculptors of the frieze of Trajan's Column depicted not only combat but all aspects of warfare. Here, Roman soldiers pile up logs to be transported for use at the next battle site.

7-1 Detail of three bands of the spiral frieze of the Column of Trajan (FIG. 7-45), Forum of Trajan, Rome, Italy, dedicated 112 CE. ◼◀

7

After losing a battle, a Dacian chieftain kneels before Trajan and seeks mercy. The war does not end, however, until, at the end of the frieze, the Dacian king Decebalus commits suicide.

THE ROMAN EMPIRE

FRAMING THE ERA

THE ANCIENT WORLD'S GREATEST EMPIRE

At the death of the emperor Trajan in 117 CE, for the first time in history a single government ruled an empire that extended from the Nile to the Strait of Gibraltar, from the Tigris and Euphrates to the Rhone, Danube, Thames, and beyond (MAP 7-1). No government, before or after, used art more effectively as a political tool. Trajan, perhaps Rome's greatest general, had led the imperial army to victory in both the East and West, bringing vast new territories under Roman dominion. To celebrate his successes in Dacia (roughly equivalent to present day Romania), Trajan erected a 128-foot-tall column (FIG. 7-45) in Rome. Although frequently imitated, the Column of Trajan was the first of its kind. Its distinguishing new feature was the 625-foot frieze winding around the shaft 23 times from bottom to top. It recounts the emperor's two campaigns against the Dacians.

Illustrated here (FIG. 7-1) are three of the bands midway up the column. Carving the frieze was a complex process. First, the stonemasons had to fashion enormous marble column drums, hollowed out to accommodate the internal spiral staircase running the entire length of the column shaft. The sculptors carved the figures and buildings after the drums were in place to ensure they lined up perfectly. (Note the horizontal line through the lowest frieze in the photograph corresponding to the junction between two column drums.) The sculptors carved the last scenes in the narrative first, working from the top to the bottom of the shaft so that falling marble chips or a dropped chisel would not damage the reliefs below.

At the top left of the section shown, a group of Roman soldiers storms a Dacian fortress with their shields raised and joined to form a protective turtle-shell. To the right, the battle won, Trajan, flanked by two lieutenants, views the severed Dacian heads his soldiers have brought to him as evidence of the successful completion of their mission. Further to the right, another battle begins. In the middle band, Trajan, again with an officer at each side, accepts the surrender of two Dacians. But, as before, there are still more enemies to pursue and conquer, so the Roman army cuts down more trees and piles up the logs to be transported for use at the next battle site. Another scene of surrender, this time with a Dacian kneeling before the emperor, is the subject of the lowest band, coupled with the loading of carts as the army moves on.

The repetition of standard motifs such as these characterizes the frieze as a whole. From every vantage point, Trajan could be seen directing the military operation. His personal involvement in all aspects of the Dacian campaigns—and in expanding Rome's empire on all fronts—was one of the central messages of the Column of Trajan.

MAP 7-1 The Roman Empire at the death of Trajan in 117 CE.

ROME, *CAPUT MUNDI*

The Roman Empire spanned three continents. Within its borders (MAP 7-1) lived millions of people of numerous races, religions, languages, and cultures: Britons and Gauls, Greeks and Egyptians, Africans and Syrians, Jews and Christians, to name but a few. Of all the ancient civilizations, the Roman most closely approximated today's world in its multicultural character.

Roman monuments of art and architecture are the most conspicuous and numerous remains of any ancient civilization. In Europe, the Middle East, and Africa today, Roman temples and basilicas have an afterlife as churches. The powerful concrete vaults of ancient Roman buildings form the cores of modern houses, stores, restaurants, factories, and museums. Bullfights, sports events, operas, and rock concerts are staged in Roman amphitheaters. Ships dock in what were once Roman ports, and Western Europe's highway system still closely follows the routes of Roman roads.

Ancient Rome also lives on in the Western world in concepts of law and government, in languages, in the calendar—even in the coins used daily. Roman art speaks in a language almost every Western viewer can readily understand. Its diversity and eclecticism foreshadowed the modern world. The Roman use of art, especially portraits and narrative reliefs (FIG. 7-1), to manipulate public opinion is similar to the carefully crafted imagery of contemporary political campaigns. And the Roman mastery of concrete construction began an architectural revolution still felt today.

The center of the far-flung Roman Empire was the city on the Tiber River that, according to legend, Romulus and his twin brother Remus founded on April 21, 753 BCE. Hundreds of years later, it would become the *caput mundi*, the "head (capital) of the world," but in the eighth century BCE, Rome consisted only of small huts clustered together on the Palatine Hill (FIG. 7-2, no. 3) overlooking what was then uninhabited marshland. In the Archaic period,

THE ROMAN EMPIRE

	Monarchy and Republic		Early Empire		High Empire		Late Empire	
753		27		96		192		337
	BCE		**CE**					

- Hellenization of Etruscan architecture
- Republican veristic (superrealistic) portraiture
- First and Second Styles of Pompeian painting

- Augustan revival of Classical style in art and architecture
- Third Style of Pompeian painting

- Architects realize the full potential of concrete construction
- Fourth Style of Pompeian painting

- Trajan extends the Empire and builds a new forum in Rome
- Hadrian makes beards fashionable and builds the Pantheon
- Domination of Classical style erodes under the Antonines

- Late Antique style takes root under the Severans
- Portraits of soldier emperors reveal insecurity of the age
- Constantine founds a New Rome at Constantinople

7-2 Model of the city of Rome during the early fourth century CE. Museo della Civiltà Romana, Rome. (1) Temple of Portunus, (2) Circus Maximus, (3) Palatine Hill, (4) Temple of Jupiter Capitolinus, (5) Pantheon, (6) Column of Trajan, (7) Forum of Trajan, (8) Markets of Trajan, (9) Forum of Julius Caesar, (10) Forum of Augustus, (11) Forum Romanum, (12) Basilica Nova, (13) Arch of Titus, (14) Temple of Venus and Roma, (15) Arch of Constantine, (16) Colossus of Nero, (17) Colosseum.

By the time of Constantine, the city of Rome was densely packed with temples, forums, triumphal arches, theaters, baths, racetracks, aqueducts, markets, private homes, and apartment houses.

Rome was essentially an Etruscan city, both politically and culturally. Its greatest shrine, the Temple of Jupiter Optimus Maximus (Best and Greatest) on the Capitoline Hill, was built by an Etruscan king, designed by an Etruscan architect, made of wood and mud brick in the Etruscan manner, and decorated with terracotta statuary fashioned by an Etruscan sculptor (see "Etruscan Artists in Rome," Chapter 6, page 168).

REPUBLIC

In 509 BCE, the Romans overthrew Tarquinius Superbus, the last of Rome's Etruscan kings, and established a constitutional government (see "An Outline of Roman History," page 182). The new Roman Republic vested power mainly in a *senate* (literally, "a council of elders," *senior* citizens) and in two elected *consuls*. Under extraordinary circumstances, a *dictator* could be appointed for a limited time and specific purpose, such as commanding the army during a crisis. All leaders came originally from among the wealthy landowners, or *patricians,* but later also from the *plebeian* class of small farmers, merchants, and freed slaves.

Before long, the descendants of Romulus conquered Rome's neighbors one by one: the Etruscans and the Gauls to the north, the Samnites and the Greek colonists to the south. Even the Carthaginians of North Africa, who under Hannibal's dynamic leadership had annihilated some of Rome's legions and almost brought down the Republic, fell before the mighty Roman armies.

Architecture

The year 211 BCE was a turning point both for Rome and for Roman art. Breaking with precedent, Marcellus, conqueror of the fabulously wealthy Sicilian Greek city of Syracuse, brought back to Rome not only the usual spoils of war—captured arms and armor, gold and silver coins, and the like—but also the city's artistic patrimony. Thus began, in the words of the historian Livy, "the craze for works of Greek art."[1] Exposure to Greek sculpture and painting and to the splendid marble temples of the Greek gods increased as the Romans expanded their conquests beyond Italy. Greece became a Roman province in 146 BCE, and in 133 BCE the last king of Pergamon willed his kingdom to Rome (see page 162). Nevertheless, although the Romans developed a virtually insatiable taste for Greek "antiques," the influence of Etruscan art and architecture persisted. The artists and architects of the Roman Republic drew on both Greek and Etruscan traditions.

An Outline of Roman History

MONARCHY (753–509 BCE)

Latin and Etruscan kings ruled Rome from the city's founding by Romulus and Remus until the revolt against Tarquinius Superbus (exact dates of rule unreliable).

REPUBLIC (509–27 BCE)

The Republic lasted from the expulsion of Tarquinius Superbus until the bestowing of the title of Augustus on Octavian, the grand-nephew of Julius Caesar and victor over Mark Antony in the civil war that ended the Republic. Some major figures were

- Marcellus, b. 268(?), d. 208 BCE; consul
- Marius, b. 157, d. 86 BCE; consul
- Sulla, b. 138, d. 79 BCE; consul and dictator
- Pompey, b. 106, d. 48 BCE; consul
- Julius Caesar, b. 100, d. 44 BCE; consul and dictator
- Mark Antony, b. 83, d. 30 BCE; consul

EARLY EMPIRE (27 BCE–96 CE)

The Early Empire began with the rule of Augustus and his Julio-Claudian successors and continued until the end of the Flavian dynasty. Selected emperors and their dates of rule (with names of the most influential empresses in parentheses) were

- Augustus (Livia), r. 27 BCE–14 CE
- Tiberius, r. 14–37
- Caligula, r. 37–41
- Claudius (Agrippina the Younger), r. 41–54
- Nero, r. 54–68
- Vespasian, r. 69–79

- Titus, r. 79–81
- Domitian, r. 81–96

HIGH EMPIRE (96–192 CE)

The High Empire began with the rule of Nerva and the Spanish emperors, Trajan and Hadrian, and ended with the last emperor of the Antonine dynasty. The emperors (and empresses) of this period were

- Nerva, r. 96–98
- Trajan (Plotina), r. 98–117
- Hadrian (Sabina), r. 117–138
- Antoninus Pius (Faustina the Elder), r. 138–161
- Marcus Aurelius (Faustina the Younger), r. 161–180
- Lucius Verus, coemperor with Marcus Aurelius, r. 161–169
- Commodus, r. 180–192

LATE EMPIRE (193–337 CE)

The Late Empire began with the Severan dynasty and included the so-called soldier emperors of the third century, the tetrarchs, and Constantine, the first Christian emperor. Selected emperors (and empresses) were

- Septimius Severus (Julia Domna), r. 193–211
- Caracalla (Plautilla), r. 211–217
- Severus Alexander, r. 222–235
- Philip the Arabian, r. 244–249
- Trajan Decius, r. 249–251
- Trebonianus Gallus, r. 251–253
- Diocletian, r. 284–305
- Constantine I, r. 306–337

TEMPLE OF PORTUNUS The mixing of Greek and Etruscan forms is the primary characteristic of the Republican-era Temple of Portunus (FIGS. 7-2, no. 1, and **7-3**), the Roman god of harbors. Popularly known as the Temple of Fortuna Virilis, its plan follows the Etruscan pattern with a high podium and a flight of steps only at the front (FIG. 6-3). The six freestanding columns are all in the deep porch. The structure is stone (local tufa and travertine), overlaid originally with *stucco* in imitation of Greek marble. The columns are not Tuscan but Ionic, complete with flutes and bases, and there is a matching Ionic frieze. Moreover, in an effort to approximate a peripteral Greek temple yet maintain the basic Etruscan plan, the architect added a series of engaged Ionic half columns to the sides and back of the cella. The result was a *pseudoperipteral* temple. Although the design combines Etruscan and Greek elements, the resultant mix is uniquely Roman.

7-3 Temple of Portunus (Temple of Fortuna Virilis), Rome, Italy, ca. 75 BCE. ◼◀

Republican temples combined Etruscan plans and Greek elevations. This pseudoperipteral stone temple employs the Ionic order, but it has a staircase and freestanding columns only at the front.

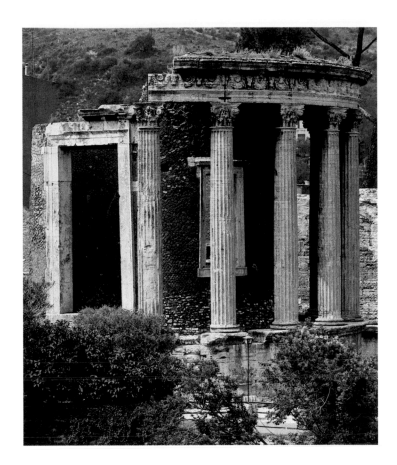

TEMPLE OF VESTA The Romans' admiration for the Greek temples they encountered in their conquests also led to the importation into Republican Italy of a temple type unknown in Etruscan architecture—the round, or tholos, temple. At Tivoli, on a dramatic site overlooking a deep gorge, a Republican architect built a Greek-inspired round temple (FIG. **7-4**) early in the first century BCE. The circular plan is standard for shrines of Vesta, and she is probably the deity honored here. The temple has travertine Corinthian columns and a frieze carved with garlands held up by ox heads, also in emulation of Greek models. But the high podium can be reached only via a narrow stairway leading to the cella door. This arrangement introduced an axial alignment not found in Greek tholoi (FIG. 5-72), where, as in Greek rectangular temples, steps continue all around the structure. Also in contrast with the Greeks, the Roman builders did not construct the cella wall using masonry blocks but a new material of recent invention: concrete.

SANCTUARY OF FORTUNA The most impressive and innovative use of concrete during the Republic was in the Sanctuary of Fortuna Primigenia (FIG. **7-5**), the goddess of good fortune, at Palestrina. Spread out over several terraces leading up the hillside to a tholos at the peak of an ascending triangle, the layout reflects

7-5 Restored view of the Sanctuary of Fortuna Primigenia, Palestrina, Italy, late second century BCE (John Burge). ◼◀

Concrete construction made possible Fortuna's hillside sanctuary at Palestrina with its terraces, ramps, shops, and porticos spread out over several levels. A tholos temple crowned the complex.

Roman Concrete Construction

The history of Roman architecture would be very different had the Romans been content to use the same building materials the Greeks, Etruscans, and other ancient peoples did. Instead, the Romans developed concrete construction, which revolutionized architectural design. Roman builders mixed *concrete* according to a changing recipe of lime mortar, volcanic sand, water, and small stones (*caementa*, from which the English word *cement* derives). After mixing the concrete, the builders poured it into wooden frames and left it to dry. When the concrete hardened completely, they removed the wooden molds, revealing a solid mass of great strength, though rough in appearance. The Romans often covered the rough concrete with stucco or with marble *revetment* (facing). Despite this lengthy procedure, concrete walls were much less costly to construct than walls of imported Greek marble or even local tufa and travertine.

The advantages of concrete went well beyond cost, however. It was possible to fashion concrete shapes unachievable in masonry construction, especially huge vaulted and domed rooms without internal supports. The new medium became a vehicle for shaping architectural space and enabled Roman architects to design buildings in revolutionary ways.

The most common types of Roman concrete vaults and domes are

▌ *Barrel Vaults* Also called the *tunnel vault*, the *barrel vault* (FIG. 7-6a) is an extension of a simple arch, creating a semi-cylindrical ceiling over parallel walls. Pre-Roman builders constructed barrel vaults using traditional ashlar masonry (FIG. 2-24), but those earlier vaults were less stable than concrete barrel vaults. If even a single block of a cut-stone vault comes loose, the whole vault may collapse. Also, masonry barrel vaults can be illuminated only by light entering at either end of the tunnel. Using concrete, Roman builders could place windows at any point in a barrel vault, because once the concrete hardened, it formed a seamless sheet of "artificial stone" in which the openings did not lessen the vault's structural integrity. Whether made of stone or concrete, barrel vaults require *buttressing* (lateral

support) of the walls below the vaults to counteract their downward and outward *thrust*.

▌ *Groin Vaults* A *groin* (or *cross*) *vault* (FIG. 7-6b) is formed by the intersection at right angles of two barrel vaults of equal size. Besides appearing lighter than the barrel vault, the groin vault needs less buttressing. Whereas the barrel vault's thrust is continuous along the entire length of the supporting wall, the groin vault's thrust is concentrated along the groins, the lines at the juncture of the two barrel vaults. Buttressing is needed only at the points where the groins meet the vault's vertical supports, usually *piers*. The system leaves the area between the piers open, permitting light to enter. Builders can construct groin vaults as well as barrel vaults, using stone blocks, but stone groin vaults have the same structural limitations when compared with concrete vaults.

When a series of groin vaults covers an interior hall (FIG. 7-6c; compare FIG. 7-47), the open lateral arches of the vaults form the equivalent of a *clerestory* of a traditional timber-roofed structure (for example, FIG. 8-10). A *fenestrated* (with openings or windows) sequence of groin vaults has a major advantage over a wooden clerestory. Concrete vaults are relatively fireproof, always an important consideration because fires were common occurrences (see "Timber Roofs and Stone Vaults," Chapter 12, page 339).

▌ *Hemispherical Domes* The largest domed space in the ancient world for more than a millennium was the corbeled, beehive-shaped tholos (FIG. 4-21) of the Treasury of Atreus at Mycenae. The Romans were able to surpass the Mycenaeans by using concrete to construct hemispherical *domes* (FIG. 7-6d), which usually rested on concrete cylindrical *drums*. If a barrel vault is a round arch extended in a line, then a hemispherical dome is a round arch rotated around the full circumference of a circle. Masonry domes, like masonry vaults, cannot accommodate windows without threat to their stability. Concrete domes can be opened up even at their apex with a circular *oculus* ("eye"), allowing light to reach the vast spaces beneath (FIGS. 7-35 and 7-51).

7-6 Roman concrete construction. (a) barrel vault, (b) groin vault, (c) fenestrated sequence of groin vaults, (d) hemispherical dome with oculus (John Burge).

Concrete domes and vaults of varying designs enabled Roman builders to revolutionize the history of architecture by shaping spaces in novel ways.

Roman Ancestor Portraits

In Republican Rome, ancestor portraits separated the old patrician families not only from the plebeian middle and lower classes of working citizens and former slaves but also from the newly wealthy and powerful of more modest origins. The case of Marius, a renowned Republican general who lacked a long and distinguished genealogy, is instructive. When his patrician colleagues in the Senate ridiculed him as a man who had no *imagines* (portrait masks) in his home, he defended himself by saying that his battle scars were his masks, the proof of his nobility.

Patrician pride in genealogy was unquestionably the motivation for a unique portrait statue (FIG. 7-7), datable to the late first century BCE, in which a man wearing a toga, the badge of Roman citizenship, holds in each hand a bust of one of his male forebears. The head of the man is ancient but unfortunately does not belong to this statue. The two heads he holds, which are probably likenesses of his father and grandfather, are characteristic examples of Republican portraiture of the first century BCE. The heads may be reproductions of wax or terracotta portraits. Marble or bronze heads would have been too heavy to carry. They are not, however, wax *imagines,* because they are sculptures in the round, not masks. The statue nonetheless would have had the same effect on the observer as the spectacle of parading ancestral portraits at a patrician funeral.

Polybius, a Greek author who wrote a history of Rome in the middle of the second century BCE, described these patrician funerals in detail:

> For whenever one of the leading men amongst [the Romans] dies . . . they place a likeness of the dead man in the most public part of the house, keeping it in a small wooden shrine. The likeness is a mask especially made for a close resemblance . . . And whenever a leading member of the family dies, they introduce [the wax masks] into the funeral procession, putting them on men who seem most like them in height and as regards the rest of their general appearance. . . . It is not easy for an ambitious and high-minded young man to see a finer spectacle than this. For who would not be won over at the sight of all the masks together of those men who had been extolled for virtue as if they were alive and breathing?*

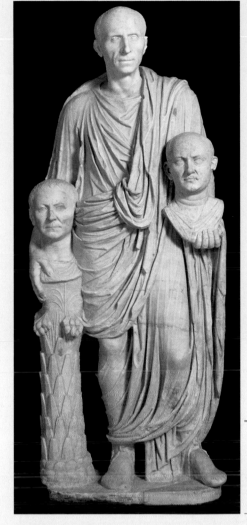

7-7 Man with portrait busts of his ancestors, from Rome, late first century BCE. Marble, 5′ 5″ high. Musei Capitolini–Centro Montemartini, Rome.

Reflecting the importance patricians placed on genealogy, this toga-clad man proudly displays the portrait busts of his father and grandfather. Both are characteristically realistic likenesses.

1 ft.

*Polybius, *History of Rome,* 6.5. Translated by Harriet I. Fowler, *Ancestor Masks and Aristocratic Power in Roman Culture* (Oxford: Clarendon Press, 1996), 309.

the new Republican familiarity with the terraced sanctuaries of the Hellenistic East. The construction method, however, was distinctly Roman. The builders used concrete barrel vaults (see "Roman Concrete Construction," page 184, and FIG. 7-6a) of enormous strength to support the imposing terraces and to cover the great ramps leading to the grand central staircase, as well as to give shape to the shops selling food, souvenirs, and the like, aligned on two levels. In this way, Roman engineers transformed the entire hillside, subjecting nature itself to human will and rational order.

Sculpture

The patrons of Republican temples and sanctuaries were in almost all cases men from old and distinguished families. Often they were victorious generals who used the spoils of war to finance public works. These aristocratic patrians were fiercely proud of their lineage. They kept likenesses of their ancestors in wooden cupboards in their homes and paraded them at the funerals of prominent relatives (see "Roman Ancestor Portraits," above, and FIG. 7-7). Portraiture was one way the patrician class celebrated its elevated position in society.

VERISM The subjects of these portraits were almost exclusively men (and to a lesser extent women) of advanced age, for generally only elders held power in the Republic. These patricians did not ask sculptors to make them appear nobler than they were, as Kresilas portrayed Pericles (FIG. 5-41). Instead, they requested brutally realistic images with their distinctive features, in the tradition of the treasured household *imagines.* One of the most striking of these

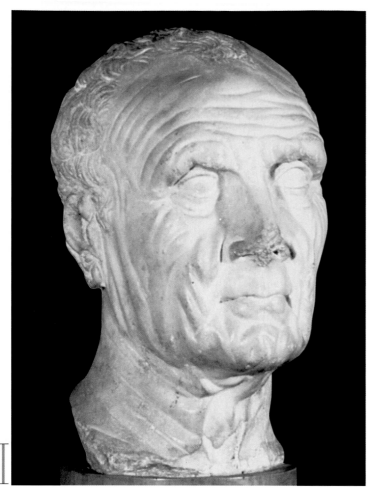

7-8 Head of an old man, from Osimo, mid-first century BCE. Marble, life-size. Palazzo del Municipio, Osimo.

Veristic (superrealistic) portraits of old men from distinguished families were the norm during the Republic. The sculptor of this head painstakingly recorded every detail of the elderly man's face.

1 in.

7-9 Portrait of a Roman general, from the Sanctuary of Hercules, Tivoli, Italy, ca. 75–50 BCE. Marble, 6' 2" high. Museo Nazionale Romano—Palazzo Massimo alle Terme, Rome.

The sculptor based this life-size portrait of a general on idealized Greek statues of heroes and athletes, but the man's head is a veristic likeness. The combination is typical of Republican portraiture.

1 ft.

so-called *veristic* (superrealistic) portraits is the head (FIG. **7-8**) of an unidentified patrician from Osimo. The sculptor painstakingly recorded each rise and fall, each bulge and fold, of the facial surface, like a mapmaker who did not want to miss the slightest detail of surface change. Scholars debate whether Republican veristic portraits were truly blunt records of individual features or exaggerated types designed to make a statement about personality: serious, experienced, determined, loyal to family and state—the most admired virtues during the Republic.

TIVOLI GENERAL The Osimo head illustrates that the Romans believed the head or bust alone (FIGS. 7-7 and 7-11) was enough to constitute a portrait. The Greeks, in contrast, believed head and body were inseparable parts of an integral whole, so their portraits were always full length (FIG. 5-87), although Roman copies often reproduced only the head (FIG. 5-41). In fact, Republican sculptors often, if incongruously, placed veristic heads on bodies to which they could not possibly belong, as in the curious and discordant seminude portrait statue (FIG. **7-9**) from Tivoli representing a Republican general. The *cuirass* (leather breastplate) at his side, which acts as a prop for the heavy marble statue, is the emblem of his rank. But the general does not appear as he would in life. Although he has a typically Republican stern and lined face, the head sits atop a powerful youthful body. The sculptor modeled the portrait on the

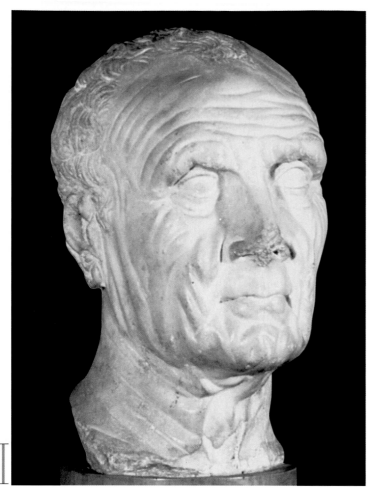

½ in.

7-10 Denarius with portrait of Julius Caesar, 44 BCE. Silver, diameter ¾″. American Numismatic Society, New York.

Julius Caesar was the first to place his own portrait on Roman coinage during his lifetime. This denarius, issued just before his assassination, shows the dictator with a deeply lined face and neck.

Art for Former Slaves

Historians and art historians alike tend to focus on the lives and monuments of famous individuals, but some of the most interesting remains of ancient Roman civilization are the artworks ordinary people commissioned, especially former slaves—*freedmen* and *freedwomen*. Slavery was common in the Roman world. Indeed, at the end of the Republic, there were approximately two million slaves in Italy—roughly one slave for every three citizens. The very rich might own hundreds of slaves, but slaves could be found in all but the poorest households. The practice was so much a part of Roman society that even slaves often became slave owners when their former masters freed them. Some gained freedom in return for meritorious service, others as bequests in their masters' wills. Most slaves died as slaves in service to their original or new owners.

The most noteworthy artworks Roman freedmen and freedwomen commissioned are the stone reliefs that regularly adorned their tomb facades. One of these reliefs (FIG. 7-11) depicts two men and a woman, all named Gessius. At the left is Gessia Fausta and at the right Gessius Primus. Both are the freed slaves of Publius Gessius, the freeborn citizen in the center, shown wearing a general's cuirass and portrayed in the standard Republican superrealistic fashion (FIGS. 7-7 and 7-8). As slaves this couple had no legal standing. They were the property of Publius Gessius. According to Roman law, however, after gaining freedom the ex-slaves became people. These stern frontal portraits proclaim their new status as members of Roman society—and their gratitude to Publius Gessius for granting them that status.

As was the custom, the ex-slaves bear their patron's name, but whether they are sister and brother, wife and husband, or unrelated is unclear. The inscriptions on the relief explicitly state Gessius Primus provided the funds for the monument in his will and Gessia Fausta, the only survivor of the three, directed the work. The relief thus depicts the living and the dead side by side, indistinguishable without the accompanying inscriptions. This theme is common in Roman art and proclaims that death does not break the bonds formed in life.

1 ft.

7-11 Funerary relief with portraits of the Gessii, from Rome(?), Italy, ca. 30 BCE. Marble, 2′ 1½″ high. Museum of Fine Arts, Boston.

Roman freedmen often placed reliefs depicting themselves and their former owners on the facades of their tombs. The portraits and inscriptions celebrated their freedom and new status as citizens.

statues of Greek athletes and heroes the Romans admired so much and often copied. The incorporation of references to Greek art in these portrait statues evoked the notion of patrician cultural superiority. To be portrayed nude also suggested the person possessed a heroic character.

7-10A Pompey the Great, ca. 55–50 BCE.

JULIUS CAESAR Beginning early in the first century BCE, the Roman desire to advertise distinguished ancestry led to the placement of portraits of illustrious forebears on Republican coins. These ancestral portraits supplanted the earlier Roman tradition (based on Greek convention) of using images of divinities on coins. No Roman, however, not even Pompey "the Great" (FIG. **7-10A**), who likened himself to Alexander, dared to place his own likeness on a coin until 44 BCE, when Julius Caesar, shortly before his assassination on the Ides of March, issued coins featuring his portrait and his newly acquired title, *dictator perpetuo* (dictator for life). The *denarius* (the standard Roman silver

coin, from which the word *penny* ultimately derives) illustrated here (FIG. **7-10**) records Caesar's aging face and receding hairline in conformity with the Republican veristic tradition. But placing the likeness of a living person on a coin violated all the norms of Republican propriety. Henceforth, Roman coins, which circulated throughout the vast territories under Roman control, would be used to mold public opinion in favor of the ruler by announcing his achievements—both real and fictional.

NONELITE PORTRAITURE
In stark contrast to the patrician tradition of displaying portraits in homes and public places, slaves and former slaves could not possess any family portraits, because, under Roman law, their parents and grandparents were not people but property. Freed slaves, however, often ordered portrait (FIG. **7-11**) and narrative (FIG. **7-11A**) reliefs for their tombs to commemorate their new status as Roman citizens (see "Art for Former Slaves," above).

7-11A Funerary procession, Amiternum, ca. 50–1 BCE.

An Eyewitness Account of the Eruption of Mount Vesuvius

7-12 Aerial view of the forum (looking northeast), Pompeii, Italy, second century BCE and later. (1) forum, (2) Temple of Jupiter (Capitolium), (3) basilica.

Before the eruption of Mount Vesuvius, the forum was the center of civic life at Pompeii. At the north end was the city's main temple, the Capitolium, and at the southwest corner, the basilica (law court).

Pliny the Elder, whose *Natural History* is one of the most important sources for the history of Greek art, was among those who tried to rescue others from danger when Mount Vesuvius erupted. Overcome by the volcano's fumes, he died. His nephew, Pliny the Younger (ca. 61–ca. 112 CE), a government official under the emperor Trajan, left an account of the eruption and his uncle's demise:

> [The volcanic cloud's] general appearance can best be expressed as being like a pine . . . for it rose to a great height on a sort of trunk and then split off into branches. . . . Sometimes it looked white, sometimes blotched and dirty, according to the amount of soil and ashes it carried with it. . . . The buildings were now shaking with violent shocks, and seemed to be swaying to and fro as if they were torn from their foundations. Outside, on the other hand, there was the danger of falling pumice-stones, even though these were light and porous. . . . Elsewhere there was daylight, [but around Vesuvius, people] were still in darkness, blacker and denser than any night that ever was. . . . When daylight returned on the 26th—two days after the last day [my uncle] had been seen—his body was found intact and uninjured, still fully clothed and looking more like sleep than death.*

*Betty Radice, trans., *Pliny the Younger: Letters and Panegyricus*, vol. 1 (Cambridge, Mass.: Harvard University Press, 1969), 427–433.

POMPEII AND THE CITIES OF VESUVIUS

On August 24, 79 CE, Mount Vesuvius, a long-dormant volcano, suddenly erupted (see "An Eyewitness Account of the Eruption of Mount Vesuvius," above). Many prosperous towns around the Bay of Naples (the ancient Greek city of Neapolis), among them Pompeii, were buried in a single day. The eruption was a catastrophe for the inhabitants of the Vesuvian cities but a boon for archaeologists and art historians. When researchers first explored the buried cities in the 18th century, the ruins had lain undisturbed for nearly 1,700 years, permitting a reconstruction of the art and life of Roman towns of the Late Republic and Early Empire to a degree impossible anywhere else.

The Oscans, one of the many early Italic population groups, were the first to settle at Pompeii, but toward the end of the fifth century BCE, the Samnites took over the town. Under the influence of their Greek neighbors, the Samnites greatly expanded the original settlement and gave monumental shape to the city center (FIG. 7-12). Pompeii fought with other Italian cities on the losing side against Rome in the so-called Social War that ended in 89 BCE, and in 80 BCE Sulla founded a new Roman colony on the site, with Latin as its official language. The colony's population had grown to between 10,000 and 20,000 when, in February 62 CE, an earthquake shook the city, causing extensive damage. When Mount Vesuvius erupted 17 years later, repairs were still in progress.

Architecture

Walking through Pompeii today is an unforgettable experience. The streets, with their heavy flagstone pavements and sidewalks, are still there, as are the stepping stones pedestrians used to cross the streets without having to step in puddles. Ingeniously, the city planners placed these stones in such a way that vehicle wheels could straddle them, enabling supplies to be brought directly to the shops, taverns, and bakeries. Tourists still can visit the impressive concrete-vaulted rooms of Pompeii's public baths, sit in the seats of its theater and amphitheater, enter the painted bedrooms and statue-filled gardens of private homes, even walk among the tombs outside the city's walls. Pompeii has been called the living city of the dead for good reason.

FORUM The center of civic life in any Roman town was its *forum,* or public square. Usually located at the city's geographic center at the intersection of the main north-south street, the *cardo,* and the main east-west avenue, the *decumanus* (FIG. 7-43), the forum was nevertheless generally closed to all but pedestrian traffic. Pompeii's forum (FIG. 7-12) lies in the southwest corner of the expanded Roman city but at the heart of the original town. The forum probably took on monumental form in the second century BCE when the Samnites, inspired by Hellenistic architecture, constructed two-story colonnades on three sides of the long and narrow plaza. At the north end they built a temple of Jupiter (FIG. 7-12, no. 2). When Pompeii became a Roman colony in 80 BCE, the Romans converted the temple into a *Capitolium*—a triple shrine of Jupiter, Juno, and Minerva, the chief Roman gods. The temple is of standard Republican type, constructed of tufa covered with fine white stucco and combining an Etruscan plan with Corinthian columns. It faces into the civic square, dominating the area. This contrasts with the siting of Greek temples (FIGS. 5-42 and 5-43), which stood in isolation and could be approached and viewed from all sides, like colossal statues on giant stepped pedestals. The Roman forum, like the Etrusco-Roman temple, had a chief side, a focus of attention.

The area within the porticos of the forum at Pompeii was empty, except for statues portraying local dignitaries and, later, Roman emperors. This is where the citizens conducted daily commerce and held festivities. All around the square, behind the colonnades, were secular and religious structures, including the town's administrative offices. Most important was the *basilica* (FIG. 7-12, no. 3) at the southwest corner. It is the earliest well-preserved building of its kind. Constructed during the late second century BCE, the basilica was Pompeii's law court and chief administrative building. In plan it resembled the forum itself: long and narrow, with two stories of internal columns dividing the space into a central *nave* and flanking *aisles.* This scheme had a long afterlife in architectural history and will be familiar to anyone who has ever entered a church.

AMPHITHEATER Shortly after the Romans took control of Pompeii, two of the town's wealthiest officials, Quinctius Valgus and Marcus Porcius, used their own funds to build a large amphitheater (FIG. 7-13) at the southeastern end of town. The earliest amphitheater known, it could seat some 20,000 spectators—more than the entire population of the town even a century and a half after its construction. The donors would have had choice reserved seats in the new entertainment center. In fact, seating was by civic and military rank. The Roman social hierarchy was therefore on display at every event.

The word *amphitheater* means "double theater," and Roman amphitheaters resemble two Greek theaters put together. Greek theaters were always on natural hillsides (FIG. 5-71), but supporting an amphitheater's continuous elliptical *cavea* (seating area) required building an artificial mountain. Only concrete, unknown to the Greeks, could easily meet that challenge. In the Pompeii amphitheater, shallow concrete barrel vaults form a giant retaining wall holding up the earthen mound and stone seats. Barrel vaults running all the way through the elliptical mountain of earth form the tunnels leading to the *arena,* the central area where the Pompeians staged bloody gladiatorial combats and wild animal hunts (see "Spectacles in the Colosseum," page 203). (*Arena* is Latin for "sand," which soaked up the blood of the wounded and killed.) Roman amphitheaters stand in sharp contrast, both architecturally and functionally, to Greco-Roman theaters, where actors performed comedies and tragedies.

A painting (FIG. 7-14) found in one of Pompeii's houses records a brawl in the amphitheater between the Pompeians and their neighbors, the Nucerians, during a gladiatorial contest in 59 CE. The fighting left many seriously wounded and led to the closing of

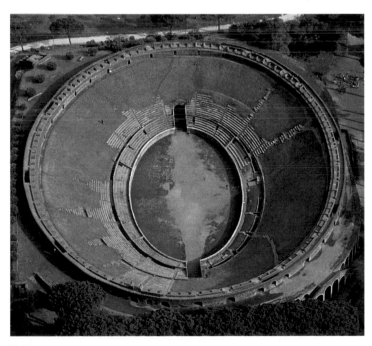

7-13 Aerial view of the amphitheater (looking southeast), Pompeii, Italy, ca. 70 BCE.

Pompeii's amphitheater is the oldest known and an early example of Roman concrete technology. In the arena, bloody gladiatorial combats and wild animal hunts took place before 20,000 spectators.

1 ft.

7-14 Brawl in the Pompeii amphitheater, wall painting from House I,3,23, Pompeii, Italy, ca. 60–79 CE. Fresco, 5' 7" × 6' 1". Museo Archeologico Nazionale, Naples.

This wall painting records a brawl that broke out in the Pompeii amphitheater in 59 CE. The painter included the awning (velarium) that could be rolled down to shield the audience from sun and rain.

The Roman House

The Roman house (FIG. 7-15) was not only a place to live. It played an important role in societal rituals. In the Roman world, individuals were frequently bound to others in a patron-client relationship whereby a wealthier, better-educated, and more powerful *patronus* would protect the interests of a *cliens,* sometimes large numbers of them. The size of a patron's clientele was one measure of his standing in society. Being seen in public accompanied by a crowd of clients was a badge of honor. In this system, a plebeian might be bound to a patrician, a freed slave to a former owner, or even one patrician to another. Regardless of rank, all clients were obligated to support their patron in political campaigns and to perform specific services on request, as well as to call on and salute the patron at the patron's home.

A client calling on a patron would enter the typical Roman *domus* (private house) through a narrow foyer (*fauces,* the "jaws" of the house), which led to a large central reception area, the *atrium.* The rooms flanking the fauces could open onto the atrium, as in FIG. 7-15, or onto the street, in which case the owner could use or rent them as shops. The roof over the atrium was partially open to the sky, not only to admit light but also to channel rainwater into a basin (*impluvium*) below to be stored in cisterns for household use. Opening onto the atrium were small bedrooms called *cubicula* (cubicles). At the back were two recessed areas (*alae,* wings) and the patron's *tablinum* or "home office," a dining room (*triclinium*), a kitchen, and sometimes a small garden.

Extant houses display endless variations of the same basic plan, dictated by the owners' personal tastes and means, the size and shape of the lot, and so forth, but all Roman houses of this type were inward-looking in nature. The design shut off the street's noise and dust, and all internal activity focused on the brightly illuminated atrium at the center of the residence. This basic module (only the front half of the typical house in FIG. 7-15) resembles the plan of the typical Etruscan house as reflected in the tombs of Cerveteri (FIGS. 6-7 and 6-7A). The early Roman house, like the early Roman temple, grew out of the Etruscan tradition.

During the second century BCE, when Roman architects were beginning to construct stone temples with Greek columns, the Roman house also took on Greek airs. Builders added a *peristyle* garden (FIG. 7-16A) behind the Etruscan-style house, providing a second internal source of illumination as well as a pleasant setting for meals served in a summer triclinium. The axial symmetry of the plan meant that on entering the fauces of the house, a visitor had a view through the atrium directly into the peristyle garden (as in FIG. 7-16), which often boasted a fountain or pool, marble statuary, mural paintings, and mosaic floors (FIG. 5-70).

Private houses of this type were typical of Pompeii and other Italian towns, but they were very rare in cities such as Rome, where the masses lived instead in multistory apartment houses (FIG. 7-54).

7-15 Restored view and plan of a typical Roman house of the Late Republic and Early Empire (John Burge). (1) fauces, (2) atrium, (3) impluvium, (4) cubiculum, (5) ala, (6) tablinum, (7) triclinium, (8) peristyle.

Older Roman houses closely followed Etruscan models and had atriums and small gardens, but during the Late Republic and Early Empire, peristyles with Greek columns became common.

the amphitheater for a decade. The painting shows the cloth awning (*velarium*) that could be rolled down from the top of the cavea to shield spectators from sun and rain as well as the distinctive external double staircases (FIG. 7-13, *lower right*) that enabled large numbers of people to enter and exit the cavea in an orderly fashion.

HOUSE OF THE VETTII The evidence from Pompeii regarding Roman domestic architecture (see "The Roman House," above, and FIG. 7-15) is unparalleled anywhere else and is the most precious by-product of the volcanic eruption of 79 CE. One of the best-preserved houses at Pompeii, partially rebuilt by Italian excavators, is the House of the Vettii, an old second-century BCE house remodeled and repainted after the earthquake of 62 CE. A photograph

(FIG. 7-16) taken in the *fauces* shows the *impluvium* in the center of the *atrium,* the opening in the roof above, and, in the background, the *peristyle* garden (FIG. 7-16A) with its marble tables and splendid mural paintings dating to the last years of the Vesuvian city. At that time, two brothers, Aulus Vettius Restitutus and Aulus Vettius Conviva, owned

7-16A Peristyle, House of the Vettii, second century BCE.

the house. They were freedmen who probably made their fortune as merchants. Their wealth enabled them to purchase and furnish the kind of fashionable townhouse that in an earlier era only patricians could have acquired.

7-16 Atrium of the House of the Vettii, Pompeii, Italy, second century BCE, rebuilt 62–79 CE.

The house of the Vettius brothers was of the later Hellenized type with a peristyle garden (FIG. 7-16A) behind the atrium. The impluvium below the open roof collected rainwater for domestic use.

Painting

The houses of Pompeii and neighboring cities and the villas in the countryside around Mount Vesuvius have yielded a treasure trove of mural paintings—the most complete record of the changing fashions in interior decoration found anywhere in the ancient world. The sheer quantity of these paintings tells a great deal about both the prosperity and the tastes of the times. How many homes today, even of the very wealthy, have custom-painted murals in nearly every room? Roman wall paintings were true frescoes (see "Fresco Painting," Chapter 14, page 408), with the colors applied while the plaster was still damp. The process was painstaking. First, the painter prepared the wall by using a trowel to apply several layers of plaster (mixed with marble dust if the patron could afford it). Only then could painting begin. Finally, when the painter completed work and the surface dried, an assistant polished the wall to achieve a marblelike finish.

In the early years of exploration at Pompeii and nearby Herculaneum, excavators focused almost exclusively on the figural panels that formed part of the overall mural designs, especially those depicting Greek myths. Workers cut the panels out of the walls and transferred them to the Naples Archaeological Museum. In time, more enlightened archaeologists put an end to the practice of cutting pieces out of the walls, and began to give serious attention to the mural designs as a whole. Toward the end of the 19th century, August Mau (1840–1909), a German art historian, divided the various mural painting schemes into four "Pompeian Styles." Mau's classification system, although later refined and modified in detail, still serves as the basis for the study of Roman painting.

7-17 First Style wall painting in the fauces of the Samnite House, Herculaneum, Italy, late second century BCE.

In First Style murals, the aim was to imitate costly marble panels using painted stucco relief. The style is Greek in origin and another example of the Hellenization of Republican architecture.

FIRST STYLE In the *First Style,* or Masonry Style, the decorator's aim was to imitate costly marble panels using painted stucco relief. The fauces (FIG. **7-17**) of an old mansion at Herculaneum, the so-called Samnite House, greets visitors with a stunning illusion of walls faced with marbles imported from quarries throughout the Mediterranean. This approach to wall decoration is comparable to the modern practice, employed in private libraries and corporate meeting rooms alike, of using cheaper manufactured materials to approximate the look and shape of genuine wood paneling. The practice is not, however, uniquely Roman. First Style walls are well documented in Greece from the late fourth century BCE on. The use of the First Style in Italian houses is yet another example of the Hellenization of Republican architecture.

7-18 Dionysiac mystery frieze, Second Style wall paintings in room 5 of the Villa of the Mysteries, Pompeii, Italy, ca. 60–50 BCE. Fresco, frieze 5′ 4″ high.

Second Style painters created the illusion of an imaginary three-dimensional world on the walls of Roman houses. The figures in this room are acting out the initiation rites of the Dionysiac mysteries.

SECOND STYLE The First Style never went completely out of fashion, but after 80 BCE a new approach to mural design became more popular. The *Second Style* is in most respects the antithesis of the First Style. Some scholars have argued that the Second Style also has precedents in Greece, but most believe it is a Roman invention. Certainly, the Second Style evolved in Italy, where it was the preferred manner until around 15 BCE, when Roman painters introduced the Third Style. Second Style painters did not aim to create the illusion of an elegant marble wall, as First Style painters sought to do. Rather, they wanted to dissolve a room's confining walls and replace them with the illusion of an imaginary three-dimensional world.

VILLA OF THE MYSTERIES An early example of the new style is the room (FIG. **7-18**) that gives its name to the Villa of the Mysteries at Pompeii. Many archaeologists believe this chamber was used to celebrate, in private, the rites of the Greek god Dionysos (Roman Bacchus). Dionysos was the focus of an unofficial mystery religion popular among women in Italy at this time. The precise nature of the Dionysiac rites is unknown, but the figural cycle in the Villa of the Mysteries, illustrating mortals (all female save for one boy) interacting with mythological figures, probably provides some evidence for the cult's initiation rites. In these rites young women, emulating Ariadne, daughter of King Minos (see page 89), united in marriage with Dionysos.

The backdrop for the nearly life-size figures is a series of painted panels imitating marble revetment, just as in the First Style but without the modeling in relief. In front of this painted marble wall, the artist created the illusion of a shallow ledge on which the human and divine actors move around the room. Especially striking is the way some of the figures interact across the corners of the room. For example, a seminude winged woman at the far right of the rear wall lashes out with her whip across the space of the room at a kneeling woman with a bare back (the initiate and bride-to-be of Dionysos) on the left end of the right wall. Nothing comparable to this room existed in Hellenistic Greece. Despite the presence of Dionysos, satyrs, and other Greek mythological figures, this is a Roman design.

BOSCOREALE In the early Second Style Dionysiac mystery frieze, the spatial illusionism is confined to the painted platform that projects into the room. But in mature Second Style designs, Roman painters created a three-dimensional setting that also extends beyond the wall, as in a cubiculum (FIG. **7-19**) from the Villa of Publius Fannius Synistor at Boscoreale, near Pompeii. The excavators removed the frescoes soon after their discovery, and today they are on display in a replica of the Roman room in New York's Metropolitan Museum of Art. All around the cubiculum the Second Style painter opened up the walls with vistas of Italian towns, marble temples, and colonnaded courtyards. Painted doors (FIG. 7-19, *left*, near the far right corner of the room; compare FIG. 6-1) and gates (FIG. 7-19, *right*) invite the viewer to walk through the wall into the magnificent world the painter created.

Although the Boscoreale painter was inconsistent in applying it, this Roman artist, like many others around the Bay of Naples, demonstrated familiarity with *linear perspective,* often incorrectly said to be an innovation of Italian Renaissance artists (see "Linear and Atmospheric Perspective," Chapter 21, page 567). In this kind of perspective, all the receding lines in a composition converge on

1 ft.

7-19 Second Style wall paintings (general view, *left,* and detail of tholos, *right*), from cubiculum M of the Villa of Publius Fannius Synistor, Boscoreale, Italy, ca. 50–40 BCE. Fresco, 8′ 9″ high. Metropolitan Museum of Art, New York.

In this Second Style bedroom, the painter opened up the walls with vistas of towns, temples, and colonnaded courtyards. The convincing illusionism is due in part to the use of linear perspective.

a single point along the painting's central axis to show depth and distance. Ancient writers state that Greek painters of the fifth century BCE first used linear perspective for the design of Athenian stage sets (hence its Greek name, *skenographia,* "scene painting"). In the Boscoreale cubiculum, the painter most successfully employed skenographia in the far corners, where a low gate leads to a peristyle framing a tholos temple (FIG. 7-19, *right*). Linear perspective was a favored tool of Second Style painters seeking to transform the usually windowless walls of Roman houses into "picture window" vistas that expanded the apparent space of the rooms.

PRIMAPORTA The ultimate example of a Second Style picture-window mural (FIG. 7-20) comes from the villa of the emperor Augustus's wife Livia (FIG. 7-28) at Primaporta, just north of Rome.

1 ft.

7-20 Gardenscape, Second Style wall paintings, from the Villa of Livia, Primaporta, Italy, ca. 30–20 BCE. Fresco, 6′ 7″ high. Museo Nazionale Romano—Palazzo Massimo alle Terme, Rome.

The ultimate example of a Second Style "picture window" wall is Livia's gardenscape. To suggest recession, the painter used atmospheric perspective, intentionally blurring the most distant forms.

There, imperial painters decorated all the walls of a vaulted room with lush gardenscapes. The only architectural element is the flimsy fence of the garden itself. To suggest recession, the painter mastered another kind of perspective, *atmospheric perspective,* indicating depth by the increasingly blurred appearance of objects in the distance (see "Linear and Atmospheric Perspective," Chapter 21, page 567). At Primaporta, the artist precisely painted the fence, trees, and birds in the foreground, whereas the details of the dense foliage in the background are indistinct. Among the wall paintings examined so far, only the landscape fresco (FIG. 4-9) from Thera offers a similar wraparound view of nature. But the Aegean fresco's white sky and red, yellow, and blue rock formations do not create a successful illusion of a world filled with air and light just a few steps away.

THIRD STYLE The Primaporta gardenscape is the polar opposite of First Style designs, which reinforce, rather than deny, the heavy presence of confining walls. But tastes changed rapidly in the Roman world, as in society today. Not long after Livia decorated her villa, Roman patrons began to favor mural designs that reasserted the primacy of the wall surface. In the *Third Style* of Pompeian painting, artists no longer attempted to replace the walls with three-dimensional worlds of their own creation. Nor did they seek to imitate the appearance of the marble walls of Hellenistic kings. Instead they adorned walls with delicate linear fantasies sketched on predominantly *monochromatic* (one-color) backgrounds.

BOSCOTRECASE One of the earliest examples of the Third Style—dating around 10 BCE—is a cubiculum (FIG. **7-21**) in the Villa of Agrippa Postumus at Boscotrecase. Nowhere did the artist use illusionistic painting to penetrate the wall. In place of the stately columns of the Second Style are insubstantial and impossibly thin *colonnettes* supporting featherweight canopies barely reminiscent of pediments. In the center of this delicate and elegant architectural frame is a tiny floating landscape painted directly on the jet black ground. It is hard to imagine a sharper contrast with the panoramic gardenscape at Livia's villa. On other Third Style walls, landscapes and mythological scenes appear in frames, like modern easel paintings hung on walls. Never could these framed panels be mistaken for windows opening onto a world beyond the room.

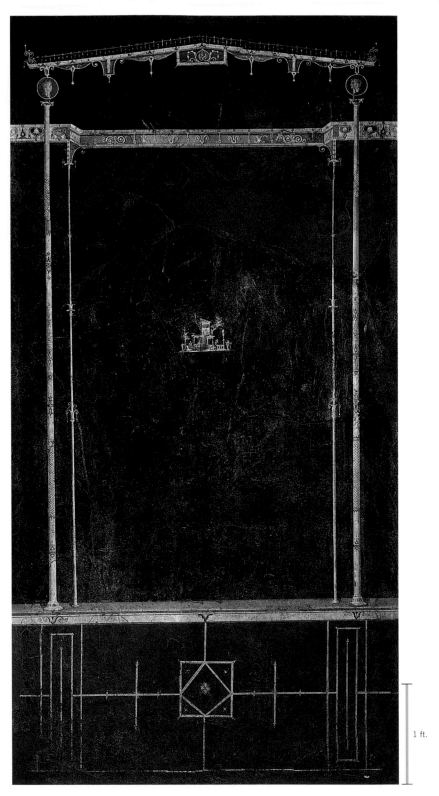

7-21 Detail of a Third Style wall painting, from cubiculum 15 of the Villa of Agrippa Postumus, Boscotrecase, Italy, ca. 10 BCE. Fresco, 7′ 8″ high. Metropolitan Museum of Art, New York.

In the Third Style, Roman painters decorated walls with delicate linear fantasies sketched on monochromatic backgrounds. Here, a tiny floating landscape on a black ground is the central motif.

1 ft.

FOURTH STYLE In the *Fourth Style,* however, a taste for illusionism returned once again. This style became popular in the 50s CE, and it was the preferred manner of mural decoration at Pompeii when the eruption of Vesuvius buried the town in volcanic ash in 79. Some examples of the new style, such as room 78 (FIG. **7-22**) in the emperor Nero's Golden House (see page 202), display a kinship with the Third Style. All the walls are an austere creamy white. In some areas the artist painted sea creatures, birds, and other motifs directly on the monochromatic background, much like the Boscotrecase landscape (FIG. 7-21). Landscapes appear in Nero's palace too—as framed paintings in the center of each large white subdivision of the wall. Views through the wall are also part of the design, but the Fourth Style architectural vistas are irrational

fantasies. The viewer looks out not on cityscapes or round temples set in peristyles but at fragments of buildings—columns supporting half-pediments, double stories of columns supporting nothing at all—painted on the same white ground as the rest of the wall. In the Fourth Style, architecture became just another motif in the Roman painter's ornamental repertoire.

IXION ROOM In the latest Fourth Style designs, painters rejected the quiet elegance of the Third Style and early Fourth Style in favor of crowded and confused compositions and sometimes garish color combinations. The Vettius brothers hired painters to decorate the Ixion Room (FIG. **7-23**)—a triclinium opening onto

7-22 Fourth Style wall paintings in room 78 of the Domus Aurea (Golden House, FIG. 7-35) of Nero, Rome, Italy, 64–68 CE.

The creamy white walls of this Neronian room display a kinship with the Third Style, but views through the wall reveal the irrational architectural vistas that characterize the new Fourth Style.

the peristyle (FIG. 7-16A) of their Pompeian house—in this manner just before the eruption of Mount Vesuvius. The decor of the dining room is a kind of summation of all the previous mural schemes, another instance of the mixing of styles noted earlier as characteristic of Roman art in general. The lowest zone, for example, is one of the most successful imitations anywhere of costly multicolored imported marbles, despite the fact the painter created the illusion without recourse to relief, as in the First Style. The large white panels in the corners of the room, with their delicate floral frames and floating central motifs, would fit naturally into the most elegant Third Style design. Unmistakably Fourth Style, however, are the fragmentary architectural vistas of the central and upper zones of the walls. They are unrelated to one another, do not constitute a unified cityscape beyond the wall, and the figures depicted would tumble into the room if they took a single step forward.

The Ixion Room takes its name from the mythological panel painting at the center of the rear wall. Ixion had attempted to seduce Hera, and Zeus punished him by binding him to a perpetually spinning wheel. The panels on the two side walls also have Greek myths as subjects. The Ixion Room is a kind of private art gallery. Many art historians believe lost Greek panel paintings were the models for the many mythological paintings on Third and Fourth Style walls. The mythological paintings on Pompeian walls attest to the Romans' continuing admiration for Greek artworks three centuries after Marcellus brought the treasures of Syracuse to Rome. Still, few, if any, of these mythological paintings can be described as true copies of famous Greek works. Unlike the replicas of Greek statues that have been found throughout the Roman world, including Pompeii (FIG. 5-40), these panels seem to be merely variations on standard compositions.

7-23 Fourth Style wall paintings in the Ixion Room (triclinium P) of the House of the Vettii (FIG. 7-16), Pompeii, Italy, ca. 70–79 CE.

Late Fourth Style murals are often garishly colored, crowded, and confused compositions with a mixture of architectural views, framed mythological panels, and First and Third Style motifs.

7-24 Neptune and Amphitrite, wall mosaic in the summer triclinium of the House of Neptune and Amphitrite, Herculaneum, Italy, ca. 62–79 CE.

In the ancient world, mosaics usually decorated floors, but this example adorns a wall. The sea deities Neptune and Amphitrite fittingly overlook an elaborate fountain in a private home.

WALL MOSAICS Mythological themes were on occasion also the subject of Roman mosaics. In the ancient world, mosaics usually covered floors. For example, the *Alexander Mosaic* (FIG. 5-70) was the floor of an *exedra* (recessed area) opening onto a peristyle in the largest house at Pompeii. But occasionally Roman mosaics decorated walls and even ceilings, foreshadowing the extensive use of wall and vault mosaics in the Middle Ages (see "Mosaics," Chapter 8, page 245). An early example of a wall mosaic (FIG. **7-24**) is in the House of Neptune and Amphitrite at Herculaneum. The statuesque figures of the sea god and his wife appropriately presided over the flowing water of the fountain in the courtyard in front of them, where the house's owners and guests enjoyed outdoor dining in warm weather.

PRIVATE PORTRAITS The themes chosen for Roman wall paintings and mosaics were diverse. Although mythological compositions were immensely popular, Roman patrons commissioned a vast range of other subjects for the walls of their homes. As noted, landscape paintings frequently appear on Second, Third, and Fourth Style walls. Paintings and mosaics depicting scenes from history include the *Alexander Mosaic* (FIG. 5-70) and the brawl in the Pompeii amphitheater (FIG. 7-14). Given the Roman custom of keeping *imagines* of illustrious ancestors in atriums, it is not surprising painted portraits also appear in Pompeian houses. The double portrait of a husband and wife illustrated here (FIG. **7-25**) originally formed part of a Fourth Style wall of an exedra opening onto the atrium of a Pompeian house. The man, who may be the lawyer Terentius Neo, holds a scroll and the woman holds a *stylus* (writing instrument) and wax writing tablet, standard attributes in Roman marriage portraits (FIG. **7-25A**). The scroll and stylus suggest the fine

education of those depicted—even if, as was sometimes true, the individuals were uneducated or even illiterate. These portraits were the Roman equivalent of modern wedding photographs of a bride and groom posing in rented formal garments never worn by them before or afterward. In contrast, the heads are not standard types but sensitive studies of the couple's individual faces. This is another instance of a realistic portrait placed on a conventional figure type (compare FIG. 7-9), a recurring phenomenon in Roman portraiture (see "Role Playing in Roman Portraiture," page 198).

7-25A Woman with stylus, Pompeii, ca. 55–70 CE.

Rarer on Pompeian walls are portraits of famous men and women of earlier eras, but several examples survive, including a full-length seated portrait of the Greek poet Menander (FIG. **7-25B**).

7-25B Menander, Pompeii, ca. 62–79 CE.

STILL-LIFE PAINTING Another genre Roman mural painters explored was *still-life* paintings (the representation of inanimate objects, artfully arranged). A still life with peaches and a carafe (FIG. **7-26**), a detail of a Fourth Style wall from a house in Herculaneum, is one of the finest extant examples. The painter was a master of illusionism and devoted as much attention to the shadows and highlights on the fruit, the stem and leaves, and the glass jar as to the objects themselves. Roman still lifes of this type are without precedent and have few successors until the 17th-century Dutch studies of food and other inanimate objects (FIGS. 25-1, 25-22, and 25-23).

7-25 Portrait of a husband and wife, wall painting from House VII,2,6, Pompeii, Italy, ca. 70–79 CE. Fresco, 1' 11" × 1' 8½".
Museo Archeologico Nazionale, Naples.

This husband and wife wished to present themselves to their guests as thoughtful and well-read. The portraits are individualized likenesses, but the poses and attributes are conventional.

7-26 Still life with peaches, detail of a Fourth Style wall painting, from Herculaneum, Italy, ca. 62–79 CE. Fresco, 1' 2" × 1' 1½".
Museo Archeologico Nazionale, Naples.

The Roman interest in illusionism explains the popularity of still-life paintings. This painter paid scrupulous attention to the play of light and shadow on different shapes and textures.

EARLY EMPIRE

The murder of Julius Caesar on the Ides of March, 44 BCE, plunged the Roman world into a bloody civil war. The fighting lasted until 31 BCE when Octavian, Caesar's grandnephew and adopted son, crushed the naval forces of Mark Antony and Queen Cleopatra of Egypt at Actium in northwestern Greece. Antony and Cleopatra committed suicide, and in 30 BCE, Egypt, once the wealthiest and most powerful kingdom of the ancient world, became another province in the ever-expanding Roman Empire.

Historians mark the passage from the Roman Republic to the Roman Empire from the day in 27 BCE when the Senate conferred the title of Augustus (the Majestic, or Exalted, One; r. 27 BCE–14 CE) on Octavian. The Empire was ostensibly a continuation of the Republic, with the same constitutional offices, but in fact Augustus, whom the Senate recognized as *princeps* (first citizen), occupied all the key positions. He was consul and *imperator* (commander in chief; root of the word *emperor*) and even, after 12 BCE, *pontifex maximus* (chief priest of the state religion). These offices gave Augustus control of all aspects of Roman public life.

PAX ROMANA With powerful armies keeping order on the Empire's frontiers and no opposition at home, Augustus brought peace and prosperity to a war-weary Mediterranean world. Known in his day as the *Pax Augusta* (Augustan Peace), the peace Augustus established prevailed for two centuries. It came to be called simply the *Pax Romana*. During this time the emperors commissioned a huge number of public works throughout the Empire: roads and bridges, theaters, amphitheaters, and bathing complexes, all on an unprecedented scale. The erection of imperial portrait statues and monuments covered with inscriptions and reliefs recounting the rulers' great deeds reminded people everywhere that the emperors were the source of peace and prosperity. These portraits and reliefs, however, often presented a picture of the emperors and their achievements bearing little resemblance to historical fact. Their purpose was not to provide an objective record but to mold public opinion. The Roman emperors and the artists they employed have had few equals in the effective use of art and architecture for propagandistic ends.

Augustus and the Julio-Claudians

When Augustus vanquished Antony and Cleopatra at Actium and became undisputed master of the Mediterranean world, he was not yet 32 years old. The rule by elders that had characterized the Roman Republic for nearly 500 years came to an abrupt end. Suddenly, Roman portraitists had to produce images of a youthful head of state. But Augustus was not merely young. The Senate had declared Caesar a god after his death, and Augustus, though never claiming to be a god himself, widely advertised himself as the son of a god. His portraits were designed to present the image of a godlike leader who miraculously never aged. Although Augustus lived until 14 CE, even official portraits made near the end of his life show him as a handsome youth (FIG. I-10). Such fictional likenesses might seem ridiculous today, when everyone can easily view photographs of world leaders as they truly appear, but in antiquity few people ever saw the emperor. His official image was all most knew. It therefore could be manipulated at will.

AUGUSTUS AS GENERAL The portraits of Augustus depict him in his many different roles in the Roman state (see "Role Playing in Roman Portraiture," page 198), but the models for many

Role Playing in Roman Portraiture

In every town throughout the vast Roman Empire, portraits of the emperors and empresses and their families were on display—in forums, basilicas, baths, and markets; in front of temples; atop triumphal arches—anywhere a statue could be placed. The rulers' heads varied little from Britain to Syria. All were replicas of official images, either imported or scrupulously copied by local artists. But the imperial sculptors combined portrait heads with many different statuary types. The type chosen depended on the position the person held in Roman society or the various fictitious guises members of the imperial family assumed. Portraits of Augustus, for example, show him not only as armed general (FIG. 7-27) but also as recipient of the civic crown for saving the lives of fellow citizens (FIG. I-10), hooded priest, toga-clad magistrate, traveling commander on horseback, heroically nude warrior, and various Roman gods, including Jupiter, Apollo, and Mercury.

Role playing was not the exclusive prerogative of emperors and princes but extended to their wives, daughters, sisters, and mothers. Portraits of Livia (FIG. 7-28) depict her as many goddesses, including Ceres, Juno, Venus, and Vesta. She also appears as the personification of Health, Justice, and Piety. In fact, it was common for imperial women to appear on Roman coins as goddesses or as embodiments of feminine virtue. Faustina the Younger, for example, the wife of Marcus Aurelius and mother of 13 children, appears as Venus and Fecundity, among many other roles. Julia Domna (FIG. 7-63), Septimius Severus's wife, is Juno, Venus, Peace, or Victory in some portraits.

Ordinary citizens also engaged in role playing. Many assumed literary pretensions in the painted portraits (FIGS. 7-25 and 7-25A) they commissioned for the walls of their homes. Others equated themselves with Greek heroes (FIG. 7-60) or Roman deities (FIG. 7-61) on their coffins. The common people followed the lead of the emperors and empresses.

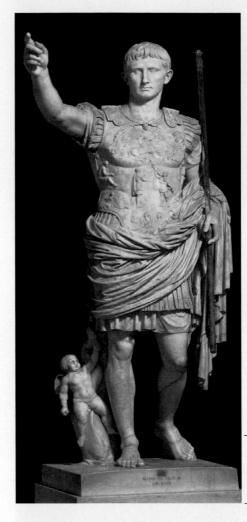

7-27 Portrait of Augustus as general, from Primaporta, Italy, early-first-century CE copy of a bronze original of ca. 20 BCE. Marble, 6′ 8″ high. Musei Vaticani, Rome. ◼◀

The models for Augustus's idealized portraits, which depict him as a never-aging god, were Classical Greek statues (FIG. 5-40). This portrait presents the emperor in armor in his role as general.

1 ft.

of them were Classical Greek statues. The portrait (FIG. **7-27**) of the emperor found at his wife Livia's villa at Primaporta (FIG. 7-20) portrays Augustus as general, standing like Polykleitos's *Doryphoros* (FIG. 5-40) but with his right arm raised to address his troops in the manner of the orator Aule Metele (FIG. 6-16). Augustus's head, although depicting a recognizable individual, also emulates the idealized Polykleitan youth's head in its overall shape, the sharp ridges of the brows, and the tight cap of layered hair. Augustus is not nude, however, and the details of the statue carry political messages. The reliefs on his cuirass advertise an important diplomatic victory—the return of the Roman military standards the Parthians had captured from a Republican general—and the Cupid at Augustus's feet proclaims his divine descent. Caesar's family, the Julians, traced their ancestry back to Venus. Cupid was the goddess's son.

LIVIA A marble portrait (FIG. **7-28**) of Livia shows the imperial women of the Augustan age shared the emperor's eternal youthfulness. Although the empress sports the latest Roman coiffure, with the hair rolled over the forehead and knotted at the nape of the neck, her blemish-free skin and sharply defined features derive from images of Classical Greek goddesses. Livia outlived Augustus by 15 years, dying at age 87. In her portraits, the coiffure changed

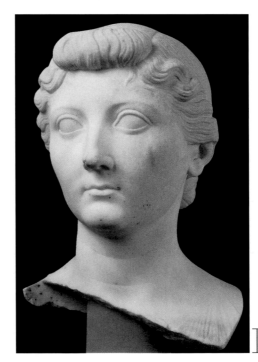

7-28 Portrait bust of Livia, from Arsinoe, Egypt, early first century CE. Marble, 1′ 1½″ high. Ny Carlsberg Glyptotek, Copenhagen.

Although Livia sports the latest Roman coiffure, her youthful appearance and sharply defined features derive from images of Greek goddesses. She died at 87, but never aged in her portraits.

1 in.

1 ft.

with the introduction of each new fashion, but her face remained ever young, befitting her exalted position in the Roman state.

ARA PACIS AUGUSTAE On Livia's birthday in 9 BCE, Augustus dedicated the Ara Pacis Augustae (Altar of the Pax Augusta, the Augustan Peace; FIG. **7-29**), the monument celebrating his most significant achievement, the establishment of peace. Figural reliefs and acanthus tendrils adorn the altar's marble precinct walls. Four panels on the east and west ends depict carefully selected mythological subjects, including a relief of Aeneas making a sacrifice (FIG. 7-29, *right*). Aeneas was the son of Venus and one of Augustus's forefathers. The connection between the emperor and Aeneas was a key element of Augustus's political ideology for his new Golden Age. It is no coincidence Vergil wrote the *Aeneid* during the rule of Augustus. Vergil's epic poem glorified the young emperor by celebrating the founder of the Julian line.

A second panel (FIG. **7-30**), on the other end of the altar enclosure, depicts a seated matron with two lively babies on her lap. Her identity is uncertain. Art historians usually call her Tellus (Mother Earth), although some scholars have identified her as Pax (Peace), Ceres (goddess of grain), or even Venus. Whoever she is, she embodies the fruits of the Pax Augusta. All around her the bountiful earth is in bloom, and animals of different species live peacefully side by side. Personifications of refreshing breezes (note their windblown drapery) flank her. One rides a bird, the other a sea creature. Earth, sky, and water are all elements of this picture of peace and fertility in the Augustan cosmos.

7-31 Procession of the imperial family, detail of the south frieze of the Ara Pacis Augustae, Rome, Italy, 13–9 BCE. Marble, 5′ 3″ high. ◼◀

Although inspired by the frieze (FIG. 5-50) of the Parthenon, the Ara Pacis processions depict recognizable individuals, including children. Augustus promoted marriage and childbearing.

1 ft.

Processions of the imperial family (FIG. **7-31**) and other important dignitaries appear on the long north and south sides of the Ara Pacis. The inspiration for these parallel friezes was very likely the Panathenaic procession frieze (FIG. 5-50, *bottom*) of the Parthenon. Augustus sought to present his new order as a Golden Age equaling that of Athens under Pericles. The emulation of Classical models thus made a political as well as an artistic statement.

Even so, the Roman procession is very different in character from its presumed Greek model. On the Parthenon, anonymous figures act out an event that recurred every four years. The frieze stands for all Panathenaic Festival processions. The Ara Pacis depicts a specific event—probably the inaugural ceremony of 13 BCE when work on the altar began—and recognizable historical figures. Among those portrayed are children, who restlessly tug on their elders' garments and talk to one another when they should be quiet on a solemn occasion—in short, children who act like children and not like miniature adults, as they frequently do in the history of art. Their presence lends a great deal of charm to the procession, but that is not why the imperial sculptors included children on the Ara Pacis when they had never before appeared on any Greek or Roman state monument. Augustus was concerned about a decline in the birthrate among the Roman nobility, and he enacted a series of laws designed to promote marriage, marital fidelity, and raising children. The portrayal of men with their families on the Altar of Peace served as a moral exemplar. The emperor used relief sculpture as well as portraiture to further his political and social agendas.

FORUM OF AUGUSTUS Augustus's most ambitious project in the capital was the construction of a new forum (FIG. 7-2, no. 10) next to Julius Caesar's forum (FIG. 7-2, no. 9), which Augustus completed. The temples and porticos in both forums were white marble from Carrara. Prior to the opening of those quarries in the second half of the first century BCE, marble had to be imported at great cost from abroad, and the Romans used it sparingly. The ready availability of Italian marble under Augustus made possible the emperor's famous boast that he found Rome a city of brick and transformed it into a city of marble.

The extensive use of Carrara marble for public monuments (including the Ara Pacis) must be seen as part of Augustus's larger program to make his city the equal of Periclean Athens. In fact, the Forum of Augustus incorporated several explicit references to Classical Athens and to the Acropolis in particular, most notably copies of the caryatids (FIG. 5-54) of the Erechtheion in the upper story of the porticos. The forum also evoked Roman history. The porticos contained dozens of portrait statues, including images of all the major figures of the Julian family going back to Aeneas. Augustus's forum became a kind of public atrium filled with *imagines*. His family history thus became part of the Roman state's official history.

NÎMES The Forum of Augustus is in ruins today, but many scholars believe some of the stonemasons from that project also constructed the so-called Maison Carrée (Square House; FIG. **7-32**)

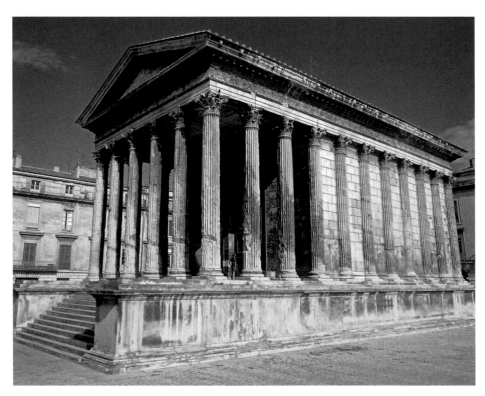

7-32 Maison Carrée, Nîmes, France, ca. 1–10 CE. ◼◀

This well-preserved Corinthian pseudoperipteral temple in France, modeled on the temple in the Forum of Augustus in Rome, exemplifies the conservative Neo-Classical Augustan architectural style.

7-33 Pont-du-Gard, Nîmes, France, ca. 16 BCE. ◼◀

Roman engineers constructed roads and bridges throughout the Empire. This aqueduct bridge brought water from a distant mountain spring to Nîmes—about 100 gallons a day for each inhabitant.

at Nîmes in southern France (Roman Gaul). This exceptionally well-preserved Corinthian pseudoperipteral temple, which dates to the opening years of the first century CE, is the best surviving example of the Augustan Neo-Classical architectural style.

An earlier Augustan project at Nîmes was the construction of the great aqueduct-bridge known today as the Pont-du-Gard (FIG. **7-33**). In the fourth century BCE, the Romans began to build aqueducts to carry water from mountain sources to their city on the Tiber River. As Rome's power spread through the Mediterranean world, its engineers constructed aqueducts, roads, and bridges to serve colonies throughout the far-flung empire. The Nîmes aqueduct provided about 100 gallons of water a day for each inhabitant from a source some 30 miles away. The water flowed over the considerable distance by gravity alone, which required channels built with a continuous gradual decline over the entire route from source to city. The three-story Pont-du-Gard maintained the height of the water channel where the water crossed

the Gard River. Each large arch spans some 82 feet and consists of blocks weighing up to two tons each. The bridge's uppermost level is a row of smaller arches, three above each of the large openings below. They carry the water channel itself. The harmonious proportional relationship between the larger and smaller arches reveals the Roman hydraulic engineer who designed the aqueduct bridge also had a keen aesthetic sense.

PORTA MAGGIORE The demand for water in the capital required the construction of many aqueducts. The emperor Claudius (r. 41–54 CE) erected a grandiose gate, the Porta Maggiore (FIG. **7-34**), at the point where two of Rome's water lines (and two major intercity roads) converged. Its huge *attic* (uppermost story) bears a lengthy dedicatory inscription concealing the stacked conduits of both aqueducts. The gate is the outstanding example of the Roman *rusticated* (rough) masonry style. Instead of using the precisely shaped blocks Greek and Augustan architects preferred, the designer of the Porta Maggiore combined smooth and rusticated surfaces. These created an exciting, if eccentric, facade with crisply carved pediments resting on engaged columns composed of rusticated drums.

NERO'S GOLDEN HOUSE In 64 CE, when Nero (r. 54–68 CE), stepson and successor of Claudius, was emperor, a great fire destroyed large sections of Rome. Afterward, Nero enacted a new building code requiring greater fireproofing, resulting in the widespread use of concrete and more opportunities for Roman architects to explore the possibilities opened up by the still relatively new material. The fire also enabled the emperor

7-34 Porta Maggiore, Rome, Italy, ca. 50 CE.

This double gateway, which supports the water channels of two important aqueducts, is the outstanding example of Roman rusticated (rough) masonry, which was especially popular under Claudius.

The Golden House of Nero

Nero's *Domus Aurea*, or Golden House, was a vast and notoriously extravagant country villa in the heart of Rome. The second-century CE Roman biographer Suetonius described it vividly:

> The entrance-hall was large enough to contain a huge statue [of Nero in the guise of Sol, the sun god; FIG. 7-2, no. 16], 120 feet high; and the pillared arcade ran for a whole mile. An enormous pool, like a sea, was surrounded by buildings made to resemble cities, and by a landscape garden consisting of ploughed fields, vineyards, pastures, and woodlands—where every variety of domestic and wild animal roamed about. Parts of the house were overlaid with gold and studded with precious stones and mother-of-pearl. All the dining-rooms had ceilings of fretted ivory, the panels of which could slide back and let a rain of flowers, or of perfume from hidden sprinklers, shower upon [Nero's] guests. The main dining-room was circular, and its roof revolved, day and night, in time with the sky. Sea water, or sulphur water, was always on tap in the baths. When the palace had been decorated throughout in this lavish style, Nero dedicated it, and condescended to remark: "Good, now I can at last begin to live like a human being!"*

Suetonius's description is a welcome reminder that the Roman ruins tourists flock to see are but a dim reflection of the magnificence of the original structures. Only in rare instances, such as the Pantheon, with its marble-faced walls and floors (FIG. 7-51), can visitors experience anything approaching the architects' intended effects. Even there, much of the marble paneling is of later date, and the gilding is missing from the dome.

*Suetonius, *Nero*, 31. Translated by Robert Graves, *Suetonius: The Twelve Caesars* (New York: Penguin, 1957; illustrated edition, 1980), 197–198.

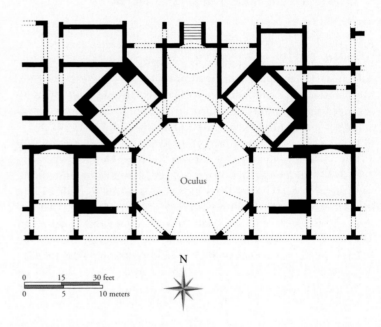

7-35 SEVERUS and CELER, section *(left)* and plan *(right)* of the octagonal hall of the Domus Aurea of Nero, Rome, Italy, 64–68 CE.

Nero's architects illuminated this octagonal room by placing an oculus in its concrete dome, and ingeniously lit the rooms around it by leaving spaces between their vaults and the dome's exterior.

to build a luxurious new palace on a huge confiscated plot of fire-ravaged land near the Forum Romanum. Nero chose two brilliant architect-engineers, SEVERUS and CELER, to design and construct his new home (see "The Golden House of Nero," above). The palace they built for the emperor had scores of rooms, many adorned with frescoes (FIG. 7-22) in the Fourth Style, others with marble paneling or painted and gilded stucco reliefs. Structurally, most of these rooms, although built of concrete, are unremarkable. One octagonal hall (FIG. **7-35**), however, stands apart from the rest and testifies to Severus and Celer's bold new approach to architectural design.

The ceiling of the octagonal room is a dome that modulates from an eight-sided to a hemispherical form as it rises toward the *oculus*—the circular opening that admitted light to the room. Radiating outward from the five inner sides (the other three, directly or indirectly, face the outside) are smaller, rectangular rooms, three covered by barrel vaults, two others (marked by a broken-line X on the plan; FIG. 7-35, *right*) by the earliest known concrete groin

vaults. Severus and Celer ingeniously lit these satellite rooms by leaving spaces between their vaulted ceilings and the central dome's exterior. But the most significant aspect of the design is that here, for the first time, the architects appear to have thought of the walls and vaults not as limiting space but as shaping it.

Today, the octagonal hall is deprived of its stucco decoration and marble *incrustation* (veneer). The concrete shell stands bare, but this serves to focus the visitor's attention on the design's spatial complexity. Anyone walking into the domed hall perceives that the space is defined not by walls but by eight angled piers. The wide square openings between the piers are so large the rooms beyond look like extensions of the central hall. The grouping of spatial units of different sizes and proportions under a variety of vaults creates a dynamic three-dimensional composition that is both complex and unified. Nero's architects were not only inventive but also progressive in their recognition of the malleable nature of concrete, a material not limited to the rectilinear forms of traditional architecture.

Spectacles in the Colosseum

A favorite pastime throughout the Roman Empire was going to the amphitheater to see two immensely popular kinds of spectacles: gladiatorial combats and animal hunts.

Gladiators were professional fighters, usually slaves who had been purchased to train in gladiatorial schools as hand-to-hand combatants. Their owners, seeking to turn a profit, rented them out for performances. Beginning with Domitian, however, all gladiators who competed in Rome were state-owned to ensure they could not be used as a private army to overthrow the government. Although every gladiator faced death each time he entered the arena, some had long careers and achieved considerable fame. Others, for example, criminals or captured enemies, entered the amphitheater without any training and without any defensive weapons. Those "gladiatorial games" were a form of capital punishment coupled with entertainment for the masses.

The participants in wild animal hunts (*venationes*) were also professionals, but often the hunts, like the gladiatorial games, were executions in thin disguise involving helpless prisoners who were easy prey for the animals. Sometimes no one entered the arena with the animals. Instead, skilled archers in the stands shot the beasts with arrows. Other times animals would be pitted against other animals—bears versus bulls, lions versus elephants, and the like—to the delight of the crowds.

The Colosseum (FIGS. 7-36 and 7-37) was the largest and most important amphitheater in the world, and the kinds of spectacles staged there were costlier and more impressive than those held anywhere else. Some ancient accounts even mention the flooding of the Colosseum so naval battles could be staged in the arena. Many scholars, however, doubt that the arena could be made watertight or that ships could maneuver in the space available. The games celebrating Titus's inauguration of the Colosseum in 80 were especially lavish. In the early third century, the historian Dio Cassius described them:

> There was a battle between cranes and also between four elephants; animals both tame and wild were slain to the number of nine thousand; and women . . . took part in despatching them. As for the men, several fought in single combat and several groups contended together both in infantry and naval battles. For Titus suddenly filled [the arena] with water and brought in horses and bulls and some other domesticated animals that had been taught to behave in the liquid element just as on land. He also brought in people on ships, who engaged in a sea-fight there. . . . On the first

7-36 Aerial view of the Colosseum (Flavian Amphitheater, looking east), Rome, Italy, ca. 70–80 CE. ◼◀

A complex system of concrete barrel vaults once held up the seats in the world's largest amphitheater, where 50,000 spectators could watch gladiatorial combats and wild animal hunts.

> day there was a gladiatorial exhibition and wild-beast hunt. . . . On the second day there was a horse-race, and on the third day a naval battle between three thousand men, followed by an infantry battle. . . . These were the spectacles that were offered, and they continued for a hundred days.*

*Dio Cassius, *Roman History*, 66.25. Translated by Earnest Cary, *Dio's Roman History*, vol. 8 (Cambridge, Mass.: Harvard University Press, 1925), 311, 313.

The Flavians

Because of his outrageous behavior, Nero faced certain assassination in 68 CE and committed suicide, bringing the Julio-Claudian dynasty to an end. A year of renewed civil strife followed. The man who emerged triumphant in this brief but bloody conflict was Vespasian (r. 69–79 CE), a general who had served under Claudius and Nero. Vespasian, whose family name was Flavius, had two sons, Titus (r. 79–81 CE) and Domitian (r. 81–96 CE). Both became emperor in turn after their father's death. The Flavian dynasty ruled Rome for more than a quarter century.

COLOSSEUM The Flavians left their mark on the capital in many ways, not the least being the construction of the Colosseum (FIGS. 7-2, no. 17, and **7-36**), the monument that, for most people, still represents Rome more than any other building. The Flavian Amphitheater, as it was then known, was one of Vespasian's first undertakings after becoming emperor. The decision to build the Colosseum was politically shrewd. The site chosen was the artificial lake on the grounds of Nero's Domus Aurea, which engineers drained for the purpose. By building the new amphitheater there, Vespasian reclaimed for the public the land Nero had confiscated for

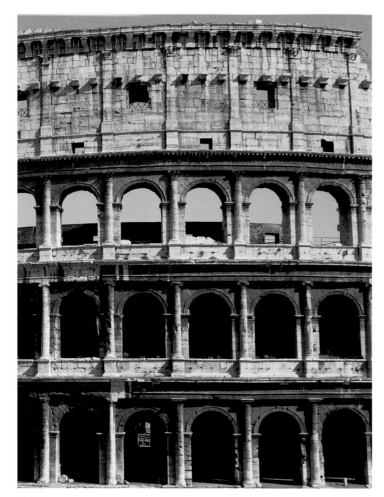

7-37 Detail of the facade of the Colosseum (Flavian Amphitheater), Rome, Italy, ca. 70–80 CE. ◼◀

For the facade of the Colosseum, an unknown architect mixed Roman arches and Greek columns—Tuscan on the lowest story, then Ionic and Corinthian. Wooden poles held up an awning over the cavea.

7-38 Portrait of Vespasian, ca. 75–79 CE. Marble, 1′ 4″ high. Ny Carlsberg Glyptotek, Copenhagen.

Vespasian's sculptors revived the veristic tradition of the Republic to underscore the elderly new emperor's Republican values in contrast to Nero's self-indulgence and extravagance.

1 in.

his private pleasure and provided Romans with the largest arena for gladiatorial combats and other lavish spectacles ever constructed. The Colosseum takes its name, however, not from its size—it could hold more than 50,000 spectators—but from its location beside the Colossus of Nero (FIG. 7-2, no. 16), the 120-foot-tall statue at the entrance to his urban villa. Vespasian did not live to see the Colosseum in use. Titus completed and formally dedicated the amphitheater in the year 80 with great fanfare (see "Spectacles in the Colosseum," page 203).

The Colosseum, like the much earlier Pompeian amphitheater (FIG. 7-13), could not have been built without concrete. A complex system of barrel-vaulted corridors held up the enormous oval seating area. This concrete "skeleton" is exposed today because in the centuries following the fall of Rome, the Colosseum served as a convenient quarry for ready-made building materials. Almost all its marble seats were hauled away, revealing the network of vaults below (FIG. 7-36). Also visible today but hidden in antiquity are the arena substructures, which in their present form date to the third century CE. They housed waiting rooms for the gladiators, animal cages, and machinery for raising and lowering stage sets as well as animals and humans. Cleverly designed lifting devices brought beasts from their dark dens into the arena's bright light. Above the seats a great velarium, as at Pompeii (FIG. 7-14), once shielded the spectators.

The exterior travertine shell (FIG. 7-37) is approximately 160 feet high, the height of a modern 16-story building. In antiquity, 76 numbered gateways provided efficient entrance and exit paths leading to and from the cavea, where the spectators sat according to their place in the social hierarchy. The decor of the exterior, however, had nothing to do with function. The architect divided the facade into four bands, with large arched openings piercing the lower three. Ornamental Greek orders frame the arches in the standard Roman sequence for multistoried buildings: from the ground up, Tuscan, Ionic, and then Corinthian. The diverse proportions of the orders formed the basis for this progression, with the Tuscan viewed as capable of supporting the heaviest load. Corinthian pilasters (and between them the brackets for the wooden poles that held up the velarium) circle the uppermost story.

The use of engaged columns and a lintel to frame the openings in the Colosseum's facade is a variation of the scheme used

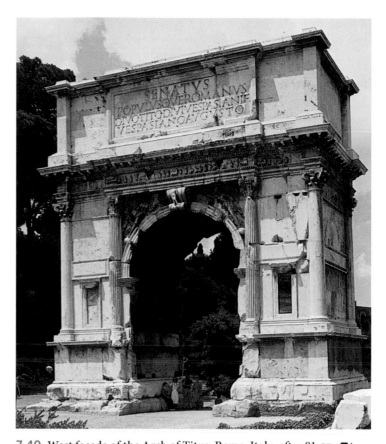

Domitian built this arch on the road leading into the Roman Forum to honor his brother, the emperor Titus, who became a god after his death. Victories fill the spandrels of the arcuated passageway.

1 in.

7-39 Portrait bust of a Flavian woman, from Rome, Italy, ca. 90 CE. Marble, 2′ 1″ high. Musco Capitolino, Rome.

The Flavian sculptor reproduced the elaborate coiffure of this elegant woman by drilling deep holes for the corkscrew curls, and carved the rest of the hair and the face with hammer and chisel.

on the Etruscan Porta Marzia (FIG. 6-14) at Perugia. The Romans commonly used this scheme from Late Republican times on, for example, at Palestrina (FIG. 7-5). Like the pseudoperipteral temple, which combines Greek orders with an Etruscan plan, this manner of decorating a building's facade mixed Greek orders with an architectural form foreign to Greek post-and-lintel architecture, namely the arch. The Roman practice of framing an arch with an applied Greek order had no structural purpose, but it added variety to the surface. In the Colosseum, it also unified a multistoried facade by casting a net of verticals and horizontals over it.

FLAVIAN PORTRAITURE Vespasian was an unpretentious career army officer who desired to distance himself from Nero's extravagant misrule. His portraits (FIG. 7-38) reflect his much simpler tastes. They also made an important political statement. Breaking with the tradition Augustus established of depicting the

Roman emperor as an eternally youthful god on earth, Vespasian's sculptors resuscitated the veristic tradition of the Republic, possibly at his specific direction. Although not as brutally descriptive as many Republican likenesses (FIG. 7-8), Vespasian's portraits frankly recorded his receding hairline and aging, leathery skin—proclaiming his traditional Republican values in contrast to Nero's.

Portraits of people of all ages survive from the Flavian period, in contrast to the Republic, when only elders were deemed worthy of depiction. A portrait bust (FIG. **7-39**) of a young woman is a case in point. Its purpose was not to project Republican virtues but rather idealized beauty—through current fashion rather than by reference to images of Greek goddesses. The portrait is notable for its elegance and delicacy and for the virtuoso way the sculptor rendered the differing textures of hair and flesh. The elaborate Flavian coiffure, with its corkscrew curls punched out using a drill instead of a chisel, is a dense mass of light and shadow set off boldly from the softly modeled and highly polished skin of the face and swanlike neck. The drill played an increasing role in Roman sculpture in succeeding periods, and when much longer hair and full beards became fashionable for men, sculptors used drills for their portraits as well (for example, FIG. 7-59A).

ARCH OF TITUS When Titus died in 81 CE, only two years after becoming emperor, his younger brother, Domitian, succeeded him. Domitian erected an arch (FIGS. 7-2, no. 13, and **7-40**) in Titus's honor on the Sacred Way leading into the Republican Forum Romanum (FIG. 7-2, no. 11). This type of freestanding arch, the so-called *triumphal arch,* has a long history in Roman art and architecture, beginning in the second century BCE. The term is something of a misnomer, however, because Roman arches celebrated more than merely military victories. Usually crowned by gilded bronze statues, they commemorated a wide variety of events, ranging from victories abroad to the building of roads and bridges at home.

The Arch of Titus is a typical early triumphal arch in having only one passageway. As on the Colosseum, engaged columns frame the *arcuated* (curved or arched) opening. The capitals are not Greek, however, but Roman *Composite capitals,* an ornate combination of Ionic volutes and Corinthian acanthus leaves. The new type became popular at about the same time as the Fourth Style in Roman painting. Reliefs depicting personified Victories (winged women, as in Greek art) fill the *spandrels* (the area between the arch's curve and the framing columns and entablature). A dedica-

tory inscription stating the Senate erected the arch to honor the god Titus, son of the god Vespasian, dominates the attic. In the vault of the passageway is a relief (FIG. **7-40A**) showing Titus's ascent to Heaven (*apotheosis*). The Senate normally proclaimed Roman emperors gods after they died, unless they ran afoul of the senators and were damned. The statues of those who suffered *damnatio memoriae* were

7-40A Apotheosis of Titus, after 81 CE.

torn down, and their names erased from public inscriptions. This was Nero's fate.

Inside the passageway of the Arch of Titus are two great relief panels. They represent the triumphal parade of Titus down the

7-41 Spoils of Jerusalem, relief panel in the passageway of the Arch of Titus, Rome, Italy, after 81 CE. Marble, 7′ 10″ high.

The reliefs inside the bay of the Arch of Titus commemorate the emperor's conquest of Judaea. Here, Roman soldiers carry in triumph the spoils taken from the Jewish temple in Jerusalem.

1 ft.

7-42 Triumph of Titus, relief panel in the passageway of the Arch of Titus, Rome, Italy, after 81 CE. Marble, 7′ 10″ high.

Victory crowns Titus in his triumphal chariot. Also present are personifications of Honor and Valor in this first known instance of the intermingling of human and divine figures in a Roman historical relief.

1 ft.

Sacred Way after his return from the conquest of Judaea at the end of the Jewish wars in 70 CE. One of the reliefs (FIG. **7-41**) depicts Roman soldiers carrying the spoils—including the sacred seven-branched candelabrum, the *menorah*—from the Jewish temple in Jerusalem. Despite considerable damage to the relief, the illusion of movement is convincing. The parade emerges from the left background into the center foreground and disappears through the obliquely placed arch in the right background. The energy and swing of the column of soldiers suggest a rapid march. The sculptor rejected the Classical low-relief style of the Ara Pacis (FIG. 7-31) in favor of extremely deep carving, which produces strong shadows. The heads of the forward figures have broken off because they stood free from the block. Their high relief emphasized their different placement in space compared with the heads in low relief, which are intact. The play of light and shadow across the protruding foreground and receding background figures enhances the sense of movement.

On the other side of the passageway, the panel (FIG. **7-42**) shows Titus in his triumphal chariot. The seeming historical accuracy of the spoils panel—it closely corresponds to the Jewish historian Josephus's contemporaneous description of Titus's triumph—gave way in this panel to allegory. Victory rides with Titus in the four-horse chariot and places a wreath on his head. Below her is a bare-chested youth who is probably a personification of Honor (*Honos*). A female personification of Valor (*Virtus*) leads the horses. These allegorical figures transform the relief from a record of Titus's battlefield success into a celebration of imperial virtues. A comparable intermingling of divine and human figures characterized the Dionysiac frieze (FIG. 7-18) of the Villa of the Mysteries at Pompeii, but the Arch of Titus panel is the first known instance of divine beings interacting with humans on an official Roman historical relief. (On the Ara Pacis, FIG. 7-29, Aeneas and "Tellus" appear in separate framed panels, carefully segregated from the procession of living Romans.) The Arch of Titus, however, honors the god Titus, not the living emperor. Soon afterward, however, this kind of interaction between mortals and immortals became a staple of Roman narrative relief sculpture, even on monuments set up while the emperor was alive.

HIGH EMPIRE

In the second century CE, under Trajan, Hadrian, and the Antonines, the Roman Empire reached its greatest geographic extent (MAP 7-1) and the height of its power. Rome's might was unchallenged in the Mediterranean world, although the Germanic peoples in Europe, the Berbers in Africa, and the Parthians and Persians in the East constantly applied pressure. Within the Empire's secure boundaries, the Pax Romana meant unprecedented prosperity for all who came under Roman rule.

Trajan

Domitian's extravagant lifestyle and ego resembled Nero's. He demanded to be addressed as *dominus et deus* (lord and god), and so angered the senators that he was assassinated in 96 CE. The Senate chose the elderly Nerva (r. 96–98 CE), one of its own, as emperor. Nerva ruled for only 16 months, but before he died he established a pattern of succession by adoption that lasted for almost a century. Nerva picked Trajan, a capable and popular general born in Italica, Spain, as the next emperor—the first non-Italian to rule Rome. Under Trajan, imperial armies brought Roman rule to ever more distant areas (MAP 7-1), and the imperial government took on ever greater responsibility for its people's welfare by instituting a number of farsighted social programs. Trajan was so popular the Senate granted him the title *Optimus* (the Best), an epithet he shared with Jupiter (who was said to have instructed Nerva to choose Trajan as his successor). In time, Trajan, along with Augustus, became the yardsticks for measuring the success of later emperors, who strove to be *felicior Augusto, melior Traiano* (luckier than Augustus, better than Trajan).

TIMGAD In 100 CE, as part of his program to extend and strengthen Roman rule on three continents, Trajan founded a new colony for army veterans at Timgad (FIG. **7-43**) in what is today Algeria. Like other colonies, Timgad became the physical embodiment of Roman authority and civilization for the local population. Roman engineers laid out the town with great precision, on the pattern of a Roman military encampment, or *castrum,* although some scholars think the castrum plan followed the scheme of Roman colonies, not vice versa. Unlike the sprawling unplanned cities of Rome and Pompeii, Timgad is a square divided into equal quarters by its two colonnaded main streets, the cardo and the decumanus, which cross at right angles. The forum is at the point where the two avenues intersect, and monumental gates marked the ends of both streets. The quarters are subdivided into square blocks, and the forum and public buildings, such as the theater and baths, occupy areas sized as multiples of these blocks. The Roman plan is a modification of the Hippodamian plan of Greek cities (FIG. 5-76), though more rigidly ordered. The Romans laid out most of their new settlements in the same manner, regardless of whether they were in North Africa, Mesopotamia, or England. This uniformity expresses concretely the centralized power of the Roman Empire at its height. But even the Romans could not regulate human behavior completely. As the satellite view reveals, when the population of Timgad grew sevenfold and burst through the Trajanic colony's walls, the colonists abandoned rational planning, and the city and its streets branched out haphazardly.

7-43 Satellite view of Timgad, Algeria, founded 100 CE.

The plan of Trajan's new colony of Timgad in North Africa features a strict grid scheme with the forum at the intersection of the two main thoroughfares, the cardo and the decumanus.

7-44 APOLLODORUS
OF DAMASCUS, Forum
of Trajan (restored view),
Rome, Italy, dedicated
112 CE (James E. Packer and
John Burge). (1) Temple of
Trajan, (2) Column of Trajan,
(3) libraries, (4) Basilica Ulpia,
(5) forum, (6) equestrian statue
of Trajan.

Funded by the spoils from two Dacian
wars, Rome's largest forum featured
a basilica with clerestory lighting, two
libraries, a commemorative column
(FIG. 7-45), and a temple of the deified
Trajan.

7-44A Funerary relief of a circus
official, ca. 110–130 CE.

FORUM OF TRAJAN Trajan completed several major building projects in Rome, including the remodeling of the Circus Maximus (FIGS. 7-2, no. 2, and **7-44A**), Rome's giant chariot-racing stadium, and the construction of a vast new bathing complex near the Colosseum constructed on top of Nero's Golden House. His most important undertaking, however, was a huge new forum (FIGS. 7-2, no. 7, and **7-44**), roughly twice the size of the century-old Forum of Augustus (FIG. 7-2, no. 10)—even excluding the enormous adjoining market complex. The new forum glorified Trajan's victories in his two wars against the Dacians (FIG. 7-1), the spoils of which paid for Trajan's building program in the capital. The architect was APOLLODORUS OF DAMASCUS, Trajan's chief military engineer during the Dacian wars. Apollodorus's plan incorporated the main features of most early forums (FIG. 7-12), except a huge basilica, not a temple, dominated the colonnaded open square. The temple (completed after the emperor's death and dedicated to the newest god in the Roman pantheon, Trajan himself) stood instead behind the basilica facing two libraries and a giant commemorative column. Entry to Trajan's forum was through an impressive gateway

7-44B Arch of Trajan,
Benevento, ca. 114–118 CE.

resembling a triumphal arch. (Trajan also erected freestanding triumphal arches in Rome and elsewhere in Italy, for example, at Benevento [FIG. **7-44B**], northeast of Naples.) Inside the forum were other reminders of Trajan's military prowess. A larger-than-life-size gilded bronze equestrian statue of the emperor stood at the center of the great court in front of the basilica. Statues of captive Dacians stood above the columns of the forum porticos.

The Basilica Ulpia (Trajan's family name was Ulpius) was a much larger and far more ornate version of the basilica in the forum of Pompeii (FIG. 7-12, no. 3). As shown in FIG. 7-44, no. 4, it had *apses,* or semicircular recesses, on each short end. Two aisles flanked the nave on each side. In contrast to the Pompeian basilica, the entrances were on the long side facing the forum. The building was

vast: about 400 feet long (without the apses) and 200 feet wide. Light entered through clerestory windows, made possible by elevating the timber-roofed nave above the colonnaded aisles. In the Republican basilica at Pompeii, light reached the nave only indirectly through aisle windows. The clerestory (used more than a thousand years before at Karnak in Egypt; FIG. 3-26) was a much better solution.

COLUMN OF TRAJAN The Column of Trajan (FIG. **7-45**) was probably also the brainchild of Apollodorus of Damascus. The idea of covering the shaft of a colossal freestanding column with a continuous spiral narrative frieze (FIG. 7-1) seems to have been invented here, but it was often copied in antiquity, during the Middle Ages (FIG. 11-24A), the Enlightenment (FIG. 26-3A), and the 19th century. The 128-foot-tall column once had a heroically nude statue of the emperor at the top. (The present statue of Saint Peter dates to the 16th century.) The tall pedestal, decorated with captured Dacian arms and armor, served as Trajan's tomb.

Art historians have likened the 625-foot band winding around the column to an illustrated scroll (FIG. 3-37) of the type housed in the neighboring libraries. The reliefs recount Trajan's two successful campaigns against the Dacians in more than 150 episodes in which some 2,500 figures appear. The band increases in width as it winds to the top of the column, in order to make the upper portions easier to see. Throughout, the relief is very low so as not to distort the contours of the shaft. Paint enhanced the legibility of the figures, but it still would have been very difficult for anyone to follow the narrative from beginning to end.

Easily recognizable compositions like those found on coin reverses and on historical relief panels—Trajan addressing his troops, sacrificing to the gods, and so on—fill most of the frieze. The narrative is not a reliable chronological account of the Dacian wars, as once thought. The sculptors nonetheless accurately recorded the general character of the campaigns. Notably, battle scenes take up only about a quarter of the frieze (FIG. 7-1). As is true of modern military operations, the Romans spent more time constructing forts, transporting men and equipment, and preparing for battle than fighting. The focus is always on the emperor, who appears repeatedly in the frieze, but the enemy is not belittled. The Romans won because of their superior organization and more powerful army, not because they were inherently superior beings.

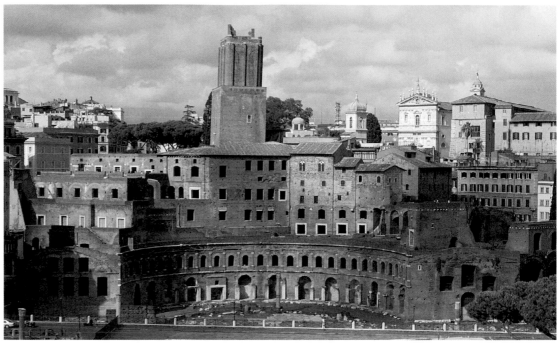

7-45 Column of Trajan, Forum of Trajan, Rome, Italy, dedicated 112 CE. ■◀

The spiral frieze of Trajan's Column tells the story of the Dacian wars in 150 episodes. The reliefs depicted all aspects of the campaigns, from battles to sacrifices to road and fort construction.

7-46 Apollodorus of Damascus, Markets of Trajan (looking northeast), Rome, Italy, ca. 100–112 CE.

Apollodorus of Damascus used brick-faced concrete to transform the Quirinal Hill overlooking Trajan's Forum into a vast multilevel complex of barrel-vaulted shops and administrative offices.

7-47 Apollodorus of Damascus, interior of the great hall, Markets of Trajan, Rome, Italy, ca. 100–112 CE.

The great hall of Trajan's Markets resembles a modern shopping mall. It housed two floors of shops, with the upper ones set back and lit by skylights. Concrete groin vaults cover the central space.

MARKETS OF TRAJAN On the Quirinal Hill overlooking the forum, Apollodorus built the Markets of Trajan (FIGS. 7-2, no. 8, 7-46, and 7-47) to house both shops and administrative offices. As earlier at Palestrina (FIG. 7-5), concrete made possible the transformation of a natural slope into a multilevel complex. Trajan's architect was a master of this modern medium as well as of the traditional stone-and-timber post-and lintel architecture of the forum below. The basic unit was the *taberna,* a single-room shop covered by a barrel vault. Each taberna had a wide doorway, usually with a

window above it through which light entered a wooden inner attic used for storage. The shops were on several levels. They opened either onto a hemicyclical facade winding around one of the great exedras of Trajan's forum, onto a paved street farther up the hill, or onto a great indoor market hall (FIG. 7-47) resembling a modern shopping mall. The hall housed two floors of shops, with the upper shops set back on each side and lit by skylights. Light from the same sources reached the ground-floor shops through arches beneath the great umbrella-like groin vaults (FIG. 7-6c) covering the hall.

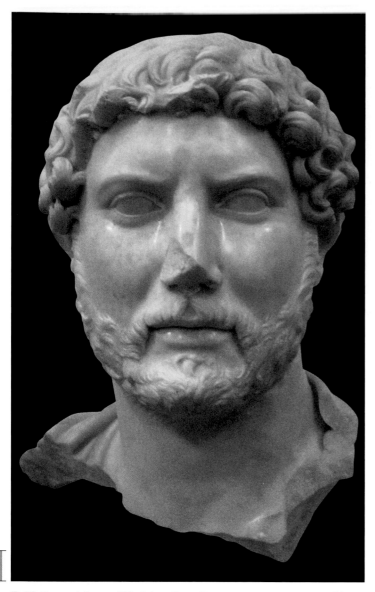

1 in.

7-48 Portrait bust of Hadrian, from Rome, ca. 117–120 CE. Marble, 1′ 4¾″ high. Museo Nazionale Romano—Palazzo Massimo alle Terme, Rome.

Hadrian, a lover of all things Greek, was the first Roman emperor to wear a beard. His artists modeled his idealized official portraits on Classical Greek statues such as Kresilas's Pericles (FIG. 5-41).

Hadrian

Hadrian (FIG. 7-48), Trajan's chosen successor and fellow Spaniard, was a connoisseur and lover of all the arts, as well as an author, architect, and hunter (FIG. 7-48A). He greatly admired Greek culture and traveled widely as emperor, often in the Greek East. Everywhere he went, local officials set up statues and arches in his honor. That is why more portraits of Hadrian exist today than of any other emperor except Augustus. Hadrian, who was 41 years old at the time of Trajan's death and who ruled for more than two decades, always appears as a mature man, but one who never ages. His likenesses more closely resemble Kresilas's portrait of Pericles (FIG. 5-41) than those of any Roman emperor before him. Fifth-century BCE statues also provided the prototypes for the idealizing official portraits of Augustus, but the Augus-

7-48A Hadrianic hunting tondi, ca. 130–138 CE.

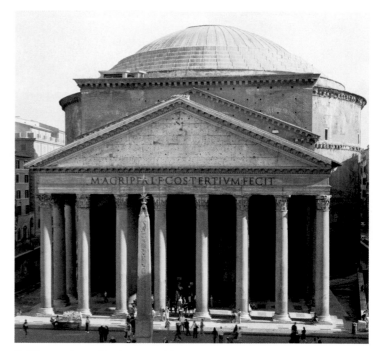

7-49 Pantheon (looking south), Rome, Italy, 118–125 CE. ◼◀

The Pantheon's traditional facade masked its revolutionary cylindrical drum and its huge hemispherical dome. The interior symbolized both the orb of the earth and the vault of the heavens.

tan models were Greek images of young athletes. The models for Hadrian's artists were Classical statues of bearded men. Hadrian's beard was a Greek affectation at the time, but thereafter beards became the norm for all Roman emperors for more than a century and a half.

PANTHEON Soon after Hadrian became emperor, work began on the Pantheon (FIGS. 7-2, no. 5, and 7-49), the temple of all the gods, one of the best-preserved buildings of antiquity. It also has been one of the most influential designs in architectural history. In the Pantheon, an unknown architect revealed the full potential of concrete, both as a building material and as a means for shaping architectural space. The original approach to the temple was from a columnar courtyard, and, like temples in Roman forums, the Pantheon stood at one narrow end of the enclosure (FIG. 7-50, *left*). Its facade of eight Corinthian columns—almost all that could be seen from ground level in antiquity—was a bow to tradition. Everything else about the Pantheon was revolutionary. Behind the columnar porch is an immense concrete cylinder covered by a huge hemispherical dome 142 feet in diameter. The dome's top is also 142 feet from the floor (FIG. 7-50, *right*). The design is thus based on the intersection of two circles (one horizontal, the other vertical). The interior space can be imagined as the orb of the earth and the dome as the vault of the heavens.

If the Pantheon's design is simplicity itself, executing that design took all the ingenuity of Hadrian's engineers. The builders constructed the cylindrical drum level by level using concrete of varied composition. Extremely hard and durable basalt went into the mix for the foundations, and the recipe gradually changed until, at the top of the dome, featherweight pumice replaced stones to lighten the load. The dome's thickness also decreases as it nears the oculus, the circular opening 30 feet in diameter that is the only light source for the interior (FIG. 7-51). The use of *coffers* (sunken

7-50 Restored cutaway view (*left*) and lateral section (*right*) of the Pantheon, Rome, Italy, 118–125 CE (John Burge).

Originally, the approach to Hadrian's "temple of all gods" was from a columnar courtyard. Like a temple in a Roman forum (FIG. 7-12), the Pantheon stood at one narrow end of the enclosure.

decorative panels) lessened the dome's weight without weakening its structure, further reduced its mass, and even provided a handsome pattern of squares within the vast circle. Renaissance drawings suggest each coffer once had a glistening gilded-bronze rosette at its center, enhancing the symbolism of the dome as the starry heavens.

Below the dome, much of the original marble veneer of the walls, niches, and floor has survived. In the Pantheon, visitors can appreciate, as almost nowhere else (compare FIG. 7-67), how magnificent the interiors of Roman concrete buildings could be. But despite the luxurious skin of the Pantheon's interior, on first entering the structure, visitors do not sense the weight of the enclosing walls but the vastness of the space they enclose. In pre-Roman architecture, the form of the enclosed space was determined by the placement of the solids, which did not so much shape space as interrupt it. Roman architects were the first to conceive of architecture in terms of units of space that could be shaped by the enclosures. The Pantheon's interior is a single unified, self-sufficient whole, uninterrupted by supporting solids. It encloses people without imprisoning them, opening through the oculus to the drifting clouds, the blue sky, the sun, and the gods. In this space, the architect used light not merely to illuminate the darkness but to create drama and underscore the symbolism of the building's shape. On a sunny day, the light passing through the oculus forms a circular beam, a disk of light that moves across the coffered dome in the course of the day as the sun moves across the sky itself. Escaping from the noise and heat of a Roman summer day into the Pantheon's cool, calm, and mystical immensity is an experience not to be missed.

7-51 Interior of the Pantheon, Rome, Italy, 118–125 CE.

The coffered dome of the Pantheon is 142 feet in diameter and 142 feet high. Light entering through its oculus forms a circular beam that moves across the dome as the sun moves across the sky.

Hadrian and Apollodorus of Damascus

Dio Cassius, a third-century CE senator who wrote a history of Rome from its founding to his day, recounted a revealing anecdote about Hadrian and Apollodorus of Damascus, architect of the Forum of Trajan (FIG. 7-44):

Hadrian first drove into exile and then put to death the architect Apollodorus who had carried out several of Trajan's building projects.... When Trajan was at one time consulting with Apollodorus about a certain problem connected with his buildings, the architect said to Hadrian, who had interrupted them with some advice, "Go away and draw your pumpkins. You know nothing about these problems." For it so happened that Hadrian was at that time priding himself on some sort of drawing. When he became emperor he remembered this insult and refused to put up with Apollodorus's outspokenness. He sent him [his own] plan for the temple of Venus and Roma [FIG. 7-2, no. 14], in order to demonstrate that it was possible for a great work to be conceived without his [Apollodorus's] help, and asked him if he thought the building was well designed. Apollodorus sent a [very critical] reply.... [The emperor did not] attempt to restrain his anger or hide his pain; on the contrary, he had the man slain.*

The story says a great deal both about the absolute power Roman emperors wielded and about how seriously Hadrian took his architectural designs. But perhaps the most interesting detail is the description of Hadrian's drawings of "pumpkins." These must have been drawings of concrete domes similar to the one in the Serapeum (FIG. 7-52) at Hadrian's Tivoli villa. Such vaults were too adventurous for Apollodorus, or at least for a public building in Trajanic Rome, and Hadrian had to try them out later at home at his own expense.

*Dio Cassius, *Roman History*, 69.4.1–5. Translated by J. J. Pollitt, *The Art of Rome, c. 753 B.C.–A.D. 337: Sources and Documents* (New York: Cambridge University Press, 1983), 175–176.

7-52 Canopus and Serapeum, Hadrian's Villa, Tivoli, Italy, ca. 125–128 CE.

Hadrian was an architect and may have personally designed some buildings at his private villa at Tivoli. The Serapeum features the kind of pumpkin-shaped concrete dome the emperor favored.

HADRIAN'S VILLA Hadrian, the amateur architect, was not the designer of the Pantheon, but the emperor became deeply involved with the development of the country villa he owned at Tivoli. One of his projects there was the construction of a pool and an artificial grotto, called the Canopus and Serapeum (FIG. **7-52**), respectively. Canopus was an Egyptian city connected to Alexandria by a canal. Its most famous temple was dedicated to the god Serapis. Nothing about the Tivoli design, however, derives from Egyptian architecture. The grotto at the end of the pool is made of concrete and has an unusual pumpkin-shaped dome Hadrian probably designed himself (see "Hadrian and Apollodorus of Damascus," above). Yet, in keeping with the persistent mixing of styles in Roman art and architecture as well as Hadrian's love of Greek art, traditional Greek columns and marble copies of famous Greek statues, including the Erechtheion caryatids (FIG. 5-54), lined the pool. The Corinthian colonnade at the curved end of the pool is, however, of a type unknown in Classical Greek architecture. The colonnade not only lacks a superstructure but has arcuated lintels, as second-century CE tomb nicknamed Al-Khazneh, the "Treasury" (FIG. **7-53**), at Petra, Jordan. It is one of the most elaborate of many tomb facades cut into the sheer rock faces of the local rose-colored mountains. As at Hadrian's villa, the architect used Greek architectural elements in a purely ornamental fashion and with a studied disregard for Classical rules.

The Treasury's facade is more than 130 feet high and consists of two stories. The lower story resembles a temple facade with six columns, but the columns are unevenly spaced and the pediment is only wide enough to cover the four central columns. On the upper level, a temple-within-a-temple sits atop the lower temple. Here the facade and roof split in half to make room for a central tholoslike cylinder, which contrasts sharply with the rectangles and triangles of the rest of the design. On both levels, the rhythmic alternation of deep projection and indentation creates dynamic patterns of light and shadow. At Petra, as at Tivoli, the architect used the vocabulary of Greek architecture, but the syntax is new and distinctively Roman. In fact, the design recalls some of the architectural fantasies painted on the walls of Roman houses—for example, the tholos seen through columns surmounted by a broken pediment (FIG. 7-19, *right*) in the Second Style cubiculum from Boscoreale.

Ostia

The average Roman, of course, did not own a luxurious country villa and was not buried in a grand tomb. About 90 percent of Rome's population of close to one million lived in multistory apartment blocks (*insulae*). After the great fire of 64 CE, these were brick-faced concrete buildings. The rents were not inexpensive, as the law of supply and demand in real estate was just as valid in antiquity as it is today. Juvenal, a Roman satirist of the early second century CE, commented that people willing to give up chariot races and the other diversions Rome had to offer could purchase a fine home in the countryside "for a year's rent in a dark hovel" in a city so noisy "the sick die mostly from lack of sleep."[2] Conditions were much the same for the inhabitants of Ostia, Rome's harbor city. After its new port opened under Trajan, Ostia's prosperity increased dramatically and so did its population. A burst of building activity began under Trajan and continued under Hadrian and throughout the second century CE.

APARTMENT HOUSES Ostia had many multistory insulae (FIG. **7-54**). Shops occupied the ground floors. Above were up to four floors of apartments. Although many of the apartments were large and had frescoed walls and ceilings, as in the aptly named

7-53 Al-Khazneh (Treasury), Petra, Jordan, second century CE.

This rock-cut tomb facade is a prime example of Roman "baroque" architecture. The designer used Greek architectural elements in a purely ornamental fashion and with a studied disregard for Classical rules.

opposed to traditional Greek horizontal lintels, between alternating pairs of columns. This simultaneous respect for Greek architecture and willingness to break the rules of Greek design typifies much Roman architecture of the High and Late Empire.

AL-KHAZNEH An even more extreme example of what many have called Roman "baroque" architecture (because of the striking parallels with 17th-century Italian buildings; see Chapter 24) is the

7-54 Model of an insula, Ostia, Italy, second century CE. Museo della Civiltà Romana, Rome.

Rome and Ostia were densely populated cities, and most Romans lived in multistory brick-faced concrete insulae (apartment houses) with shops on the ground floor. Private toilet facilities were rare.

Neptune and creatures of the sea, detail of a floor mosaic in the Baths of Neptune, Ostia, Italy, ca. 140 CE.

Black-and-white floor mosaics were popular during the second and third centuries CE. The artists conceived them as surface decorations, not as illusionistic compositions meant to rival paintings.

Insula of the Painted Vaults (FIG. 7-54A), they had neither the space nor the light of the typical Pompeian private domus (see "The Roman House," page 190). In place of peristyles, insulae had only narrow light wells or small courtyards. Consequently, instead of looking inward, large numbers of windows faced the city's noisy streets. The

7-54A Insula of the Painted Vaults, Ostia, ca. 200–220 CE.

residents cooked their food in the hallways. Only deluxe apartments had private toilets. Others shared latrines, often on a different floor from their apartments. Still, these insulae were quite similar to modern apartment houses, which also sometimes have shops on the ground floor.

Another strikingly modern feature of these multifamily residences is their brick facades, which were not concealed by stucco or marble veneers. When builders desired to incorporate a Classical motif, they added brick pilasters or engaged columns but always left the brick exposed. Ostia and Rome have many examples of apartment houses, warehouses, and tombs with intricate moldings and contrasting colors of brick. In the second century CE, brick came to be appreciated as attractive in its own right.

BATHS OF NEPTUNE Although the decoration of Ostian insulae tended to be more modest than that of the private houses of Pompeii, the finer apartments had mosaic floors as well as painted walls and ceilings (FIG. 7-54A). The most popular choice for elegant pavements at Ostia in both private and public edifices was the black-and-white mosaic. One of the largest and best-preserved examples is in the Baths of Neptune, named for the grand mosaic floor (FIG. 7-55) showing four seahorses pulling the Roman god of the sea across the waves. Neptune needs no chariot to support him as he speeds along, his mantle blowing in the strong wind. All about the god are other sea denizens, positioned so that wherever a visitor enters the room, some figures appear right side up. The second-century artist rejected the complex polychrome modeling of figures seen in Pompeian mosaics such as the *Battle of Issus* (FIG. 5-70) and used simple black silhouettes enlivened by white interior lines—an approach to pictorial representation akin in many respects to Greek black-figure vase painting (FIG. 5-19, *bottom*). Like the Archaic Greek decorators of pots, the Roman mosaicists conceived their black-and-white designs as surface decorations, not as illusionistic windows onto a three-dimensional world, and thus they were especially appropriate for floors.

ISOLA SACRA The tombs in Ostia's Isola Sacra cemetery were not the final resting places of the very wealthy but communal houses

of the dead. Constructed of brick-faced concrete, these middle-class tombs resembled the multifamily insulae of the living. Small painted terracotta plaques immortalizing the activities of merchants and professional people frequently adorned the facades. A characteristic example (FIG. 7-56) depicts a vegetable seller behind a counter. The

1 in.

7-56 **Funerary relief of a vegetable vendor, from Ostia, Italy, second half of second century CE. Painted terracotta, 1′ 5″ high. Museo Ostiense, Ostia.**

Terracotta plaques illustrating the activities of middle-class merchants frequently adorned Ostian tomb facades. In this relief of a vegetable seller, the artist tilted the counter to display the produce clearly.

artist had little interest in the Classical-revival style the emperors favored and tilted the counter forward so the observer could see the produce clearly. Comparable scenes of daily life appear on Roman funerary reliefs throughout Europe. They were as much a part of the Roman artistic legacy to the later history of Western art as the emperors' monuments, which until recently were the almost exclusive interest of art historians.

The Antonines

Early in 138 CE, Hadrian adopted the 51-year-old Antoninus Pius (r. 138–161 CE). At the same time, he required Antoninus to adopt Marcus Aurelius (r. 161–180 CE) and Lucius Verus (r. 161–169 CE),

thereby assuring a peaceful succession for at least another generation. When Hadrian died later in the year, the Senate proclaimed him a god, and Antoninus Pius became emperor. Antoninus ruled the Roman world with distinction for 23 years. After his death and deification, Marcus Aurelius and Lucius Verus became the Roman Empire's first coemperors.

COLUMN OF ANTONINUS PIUS Shortly after Antoninus Pius's death, Marcus and Lucius set up a memorial column in his honor. Its pedestal has a relief on one side illustrating the apotheosis of Antoninus and his wife, Faustina the Elder (FIG. **7-57**). On the adjacent sides are two identical representations of the *decursio* (FIG. **7-58**), or ritual circling of the imperial funerary pyre.

7-57 Apotheosis of Antoninus Pius and Faustina, pedestal of the Column of Antoninus Pius, Rome, Italy, ca. 161 CE. Marble, 8′ 1½″ high. Musei Vaticani, Rome.

This representation of the joint apotheosis of Antoninus Pius and Faustina is firmly in the Classical tradition with its elegant, well-proportioned figures, personifications, and single ground line.

7-58 Decursio, pedestal of the Column of Antoninus Pius, Rome, Italy, ca. 161 CE. Marble, 8′ 1½″ high. Musei Vaticani, Rome.

In contrast to FIG. 7-57, the Antonine decursio reliefs break sharply with Classical art conventions. The ground is the whole surface of the relief, and the figures stand on floating patches of earth.

The two figural compositions are very different. The apotheosis relief remains firmly in the Classical tradition with its elegant, well-proportioned figures, personifications, and single ground line corresponding to the panel's lower edge. The Campus Martius (Field of Mars), personified as a youth holding the Egyptian obelisk that stood in that area of Rome, reclines at the lower left corner. Roma (Rome personified) leans on a shield decorated with the she-wolf suckling Romulus and Remus (compare FIG. 6-11). Roma bids farewell to the couple being lifted into the realm of the gods on the wings of a personification of uncertain identity. Scenes of apotheosis (FIG. 7-40A) had been standard in imperial art since Augustus. New to the pictorial repertoire, however, was the fusion of time the joint apotheosis represents. Faustina had died 20 years before Antoninus Pius. By depicting the two as ascending together, the artist wished to suggest Antoninus had been faithful to his wife for two decades and now they would be reunited in the afterlife—a common conceit in Roman middle-class funerary art (FIG. 7-44A).

The decursio reliefs (FIG. 7-58) break even more strongly with Classical convention. The figures are much stockier than those in the apotheosis relief, and the sculptor did not conceive the panel as a window onto the world. The ground is the whole surface of the relief, and marching soldiers and galloping horses alike stand on floating patches of earth. This, too, had not occurred before in imperial art, only in the art of freedmen (FIG. 7-11A). After centuries of following the rules of Classical design, elite Roman artists and patrons finally became dissatisfied with them. When seeking a new direction, they adopted some of the non-Classical conventions of the art of freedmen.

MARCUS AURELIUS Another break with the past occurred in the official portraits of Marcus Aurelius, although his images retain the pompous trappings of imperial iconography. In a larger-than-life-size gilded-bronze equestrian statue (FIG. **7-59**), the emperor possesses a superhuman grandeur and is much larger than any normal human would be in relation to his horse. Marcus stretches out his right arm in a gesture that is both a greeting and an offer of clemency. Beneath the horse's raised right foreleg, an enemy once cowered, begging the emperor for mercy. The statue is a rare example of an imperial equestrian portrait, but the type was common in antiquity. For example, an equestrian statue of Trajan stood in the middle of his forum (FIG. 7-44, no. 6). Marcus's portrait survived the wholesale melting down of ancient bronze statues during the Middle Ages because it was mistakenly thought to portray Constantine, the first Christian emperor of Rome. Perhaps more than any other statuary type, the equestrian portrait expresses the Roman emperor's majesty and authority.

This message of supreme confidence is not, however, conveyed by the portrait head of Marcus's equestrian statue or any of the other portraits of the emperor in the years just before his death. Portraits of aged emperors were not new (FIG. 7-38), but Marcus's were the first ones in which a Roman emperor appeared weary, saddened, and even worried. For the first time, the strain of constant warfare on the frontiers and the burden of ruling a worldwide empire show in the emperor's face. The Antonine sculptor ventured beyond Republican verism, exposing the ruler's character, his thoughts, and his soul for all to see, as Marcus revealed them himself in his *Meditations,* a deeply moving philosophical treatise setting forth the emperor's personal worldview. This was a major turning point in the history of ancient art, and, coming as it did when relief sculptors were also challenging the Classical style (FIG. 7-58), it marked the beginning of the end of Classical art's domination in the Greco-Roman world.

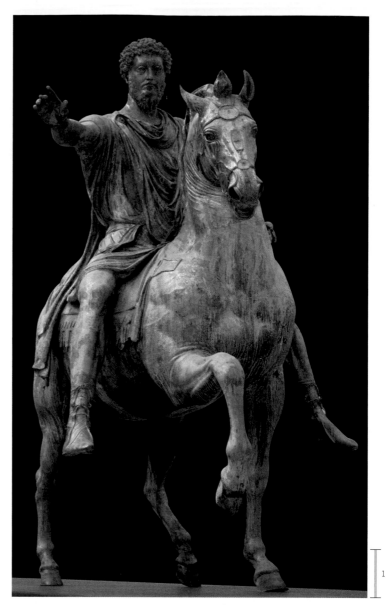

7-59 Equestrian statue of Marcus Aurelius, from Rome, Italy, ca. 175 CE. Bronze, 11′ 6″ high. Musei Capitolini–Palazzo dei Conservatori, Rome. ◼◀

In this equestrian portrait of Marcus Aurelius as omnipotent conqueror, the emperor stretches out his arm in a gesture of clemency. An enemy once cowered beneath the horse's raised foreleg.

FROM CREMATION TO BURIAL Other profound changes were taking place in Roman art and society at this time. Under Trajan and Hadrian and especially during the rule of the Antonines, Romans began to favor burial over cremation. This reversal of funerary practices may reflect the influence of Christianity and other Eastern religions, whose adherents believed in an afterlife for the human body. Although the emperors themselves continued to be cremated in the traditional Roman manner, many private citizens opted for burial. Thus they required larger containers for their remains than the ash urns that were the norm until the second century CE. This in turn led to a sudden demand for sarcophagi, which are more similar to modern coffins than any other ancient type of burial container.

ORESTES SARCOPHAGUS Greek mythology was one of the most popular subjects for the decoration of these sarcophagi. In many cases, especially in the late second and third centuries CE, Roman men and women identified themselves on their coffins with

Greek heroes and heroines, whose heads often were portraits of the deceased. These private patrons were following the model of imperial portraiture, in which emperors and empresses frequently masqueraded as gods and goddesses and heroes and heroines (see "Role Playing in Roman Portraiture," page 198, and FIG. 7-59A, a portrait of Commodus, son and successor of Marcus Aurelius, in the guise of Hercules). An early example of the type (although it lacks any portraits) is a sarcophagus (FIG. 7-60) now in Cleveland, one of many decorated with the story of the tragic Greek hero Orestes. All the examples of this type use the same basic composition. Orestes appears more than once in every case. At the center of the Cleveland sarcophagus, Orestes slays his mother, Clytaemnestra, and her lover, Aegisthus, to avenge their murder of his father, Agamemnon, and then, at the right, takes refuge at Apollo's sanctuary at Delphi (symbolized by the god's tripod).

The repetition of sarcophagus compositions indicates Roman sculptors had access to pattern books. In fact, sarcophagus production was a major industry during the High and Late Empire. Several important regional manufacturing centers existed. The sarcophagi produced in the Latin West, such as the Cleveland Orestes sarcophagus, differ in format from those made in the Greek-speaking East. Western sarcophagi have reliefs only on the front and sides, because they were placed in floor-level niches inside Roman tombs. Eastern sarcophagi have reliefs on all four sides and stood in the center of the burial chamber. This contrast parallels the essential difference between the Etrusco-Roman and the Greek temple. The former was set against the wall of a forum or sanctuary and approached from the front, whereas the latter could be reached (and viewed) from every side.

MELFI SARCOPHAGUS An elaborate sarcophagus (FIG. 7-61) of the Eastern type found at Rapolla, near Melfi in southern Italy, but manufactured in Asia Minor, attests to the vibrant export market for these luxury items in Antonine times. The distinctively Asiatic decoration of all four sides of the marble box consists of statuesque images of Greek gods and heroes in architectural frames. The figures portrayed include Venus and the legendary beauty, Helen of Troy. The lid portrait, which carries on the tradition of Etruscan sarcophagi (FIGS. 6-5, 6-15, and 6-15A), is also a feature of the most expensive Western Roman coffins. Here, the deceased woman reclines on a *kline* (bed). With her are her faithful little dog (only its forepaws remain at the left end of the lid) and

1 ft.

7-60 Sarcophagus with the myth of Orestes, ca. 140–150 CE. Marble, 2′ 7½″ high. Cleveland Museum of Art, Cleveland.

Under the Antonines, Romans began to favor burial over cremation, and sarcophagi became very popular. Themes from Greek mythology, like the tragic saga of Orestes, were common subjects.

1 ft.

7-61 Asiatic sarcophagus with kline portrait of a woman, from Rapolla, near Melfi, Italy, ca. 165–170 CE. Marble, 5′ 7″ high. Museo Nazionale Archeologico del Melfese, Melfi.

The Romans produced sarcophagi in several regions. Western sarcophagi have carvings only on the front. Eastern sarcophagi, such as this one with a woman's portrait on the lid, feature reliefs on all four sides.

Iaia of Cyzicus and the Art of Encaustic Painting

The names of very few Roman artists survive. Those that do tend to be names of artists and architects who directed major imperial building projects (Severus and Celer, Domus Aurea; Apollodorus of Damascus, Forum of Trajan), worked on a gigantic scale (Zenodorus, Colossus of Nero), or made precious objects for famous patrons (Dioscurides, gem cutter for Augustus).

An interesting exception to this rule is IAIA OF CYZICUS. Pliny the Elder reported the following about this renowned painter from Asia Minor who worked in Italy during the Republic:

> Iaia of Cyzicus, who remained a virgin all her life, painted at Rome during the time when M. Varro [116–27 BCE; a renowned Republican scholar and author] was a youth, both with a brush and with a cestrum on ivory, specializing mainly in portraits of women; she also painted a large panel in Naples representing an old woman and a portrait of herself done with a mirror. Her hand was quicker than that of any other painter, and her artistry was of such high quality that she commanded much higher prices than the most celebrated painters of the same period.*

7-62A Mummy of Artemidorus, ca. 100–120 CE.

The *cestrum* Pliny mentioned is a small spatula used in *encaustic* painting, a technique of mixing colors with hot wax and then applying them to the surface. Pliny knew of encaustic paintings of considerable antiquity, including those of Polygnotos of Thasos (see page 143). The best evidence for the technique comes, however, from Roman Egypt, where mummy cases (FIG. 7-62A) routinely incorporated encaustic portraits on wood panels (FIGS. 7-62 and 7-62B).

Artists applied encaustic to marble (FIG. 5-63A) as well as to wood. According to Pliny, when Praxiteles was asked which of his statues he preferred, the fourth-century BCE Greek artist, perhaps the ancient world's greatest marble sculptor, replied: "Those that Nikias painted."† This anecdote underscores the importance of coloration in ancient statuary.

*Pliny the Elder, *Natural History*, 35.147–148. Translated by J. J. Pollitt, *The Art of Rome, c. 753 B.C.–A.D. 337: Sources and Documents* (New York: Cambridge University Press, 1983), 87.
†Pliny the Elder, *Natural History*, 35.133.

1 in.

7-62 Mummy portrait of a priest of Serapis, from Hawara (Faiyum), Egypt, ca. 140–160 CE. Encaustic on wood, 1′ 4¾″ × 8¾″. British Museum, London.

In Roman times, the Egyptians continued to bury their dead in mummy cases, but painted portraits replaced the traditional masks. The painting medium is encaustic—colors mixed with hot wax.

Cupid (at the right). The winged infant god mournfully holds a downturned torch, a reference to the death of a woman whose beauty rivaled that of his mother, Venus, and of Homer's Helen.

MUMMY PORTRAITS In Egypt, burial had been practiced for millennia. Even after Augustus reduced the Kingdom of the Nile to a Roman province in 30 BCE, Egyptians continued to bury their dead in mummy cases (see "Mummification," Chapter 3, page 61). In Roman times, however, painted portraits on wood often replaced the traditional stylized portrait masks (see "Iaia of Cyzicus and the Art of Encaustic Painting," above). Hundreds of Roman mummy portraits (FIGS. 7-62, 7-62A, and 7-62B) have been unearthed in the cemeteries of the Faiyum district. One example

(FIG. 7-62) depicts a priest of the Egyptian god Serapis. His curly hair and beard closely emulate the Antonine fashion in Rome, but the corkscrew curls of hair on the forehead are distinctive to images of Serapis and his followers. The priest's portrait exhibits the painter's refined use of the brush and spatula, mastery of the depiction of varied textures and of the play of light over the soft and delicately modeled face, and sensitive portrayal of the deceased's calm demeanor. The Faiyum mummies enable art historians to trace the evolution of portrait painting (FIGS. 7-25 and 7-25A) after Mount Vesuvius erupted in 79 CE.

7-62B Young woman, Hawara, ca. 110–120 CE.

LATE EMPIRE

By the time of Marcus Aurelius, two centuries after Augustus established the Pax Romana, Roman power was beginning to erode. It was increasingly difficult to keep order on the frontiers, and even within the Empire many challenged the authority of Rome. The assassination of Marcus's son Commodus (FIG. 7-59A) in 192 CE brought the Antonine dynasty to an end. The economy was in decline, and the efficient imperial bureaucracy was disintegrating. Even the official state religion was losing ground to Eastern cults, Christianity among them. The Late Empire was a pivotal era in world history during which the pagan ancient world gradually gave way to the Christian Middle Ages.

The Severans

Civil conflict followed Commodus's death. When it ended, an African-born general named Septimius Severus (r. 193–211 CE) was master of the Roman world. He succeeded in establishing a new dynasty that ruled the Empire for nearly a half century.

SEVERAN PORTRAITURE Anxious to establish his legitimacy after the civil war, Septimius Severus adopted himself into the Antonine dynasty, declaring he was Marcus Aurelius's son. It is not surprising, then, that official portraits of the emperor in bronze and marble depict him with the long hair and beard of his Antonine "father"—whatever Severus's actual appearance may have been. That is also how he appears in the only preserved painted portrait (FIG. 7-63) of an emperor. Discovered in Egypt and painted in *tempera* (pigments in egg yolk) on wood (as were many of the mummy portraits from Faiyum), the portrait is of *tondo* (circular) format. It shows Severus with his wife, Julia Domna, the daughter of a Syrian priest, and their two sons, Caracalla and Geta. Painted likenesses of

7-64 Bust of Caracalla, ca. 211–217. Marble, 1' 10¾" high. Staatliche Museen, Antikensammlung, Berlin.

Caracalla's portraits introduced a new fashion in male coiffure but are more remarkable for the dramatic turn of the emperor's head and the moving characterization of his personality.

the imperial family must have been quite common in Italy and the provinces, but their perishable nature explains their almost total loss.

The Severan family portrait is of special interest for two reasons beyond its survival. Severus's hair is tinged with gray, suggesting his marble portraits—which, like all marble sculptures in antiquity, were painted—also may have revealed his advancing age in this way. (The same was very likely true of the marble likenesses of the elderly Marcus Aurelius.) The group portrait is also notable because of the erasure of Geta's face. When Caracalla (r. 211–217 CE) succeeded his father as emperor, he had his younger brother murdered and ordered the Senate to damn Geta's memory. (Caracalla also ordered the death of his wife, Plautilla.) The Severan family portrait is an eloquent testimony to that *damnatio memoriae* and to the long arm of Roman authority, which reached all the way to Egypt in this case. This kind of defacement of a rival's image is not unique to ancient Rome, but the Roman government employed damnatio memoriae as a political tool more often and more systematically than any other civilization.

CARACALLA In the Severan painted tondo, the artist portrayed Caracalla as a boy with long, curly Antonine hair. The portraits of Caracalla as emperor are very different. In a bust (FIG. 7-64) in Berlin, Caracalla appears in heroic nudity save for a mantle over one shoulder and a sword sheath across his chest. His hair and beard, although still curly, are much shorter (compare FIG. 7-64A)—initiating a new fashion in male coiffure during the third century CE. More remarkable, however, is the moving characterization of Caracalla's personality, a further development from the groundbreaking introspection of the portraits of Marcus Aurelius. Caracalla's brow is knotted, and he abruptly turns his head over his

7-64A Caracalla, ca. 211–217 CE.

7-63 Painted portrait of Septimius Severus and his family, from Egypt, ca. 200 CE. Tempera on wood, 1' 2" diameter. Staatliche Museen, Berlin.

The only known painted portrait of an emperor shows Septimius Severus with gray hair. With him are his wife, Julia Domna, and their two sons, but Geta's head was removed after his damnatio memoriae.

7-65 Chariot procession of Septimius Severus, relief from the attic of the Arch of Septimius Severus, Lepcis Magna, Libya, 203 CE. Marble, 5′ 6″ high. Castle Museum, Tripoli.

A new non-naturalistic aesthetic emerged in later Roman art. In this relief from a triumphal arch, Septimius Severus and his two sons face the viewer even though their chariot is moving to the right.

left shoulder. The sculptor probably intended the facial expression and the dramatic movement to suggest energy and strength, but it appears to the viewer as if Caracalla suspects danger from behind. The emperor had reason to be fearful. An assassin's dagger felled him in the sixth year of his rule. Assassination would be the fate of many Roman emperors during the turbulent third century CE.

LEPCIS MAGNA The hometown of the Severans was Lepcis Magna, on the coast of what is now Libya. In the late second and early third centuries CE, the Severans constructed a modern harbor there, as well as a new forum, basilica, arch, and other monuments. The rebuilt Arch of Septimius Severus has friezes on the attic on all four sides. One (FIG. **7-65**) depicts the chariot procession of the emperor and his two sons on the occasion of their homecoming in 203. Unlike the triumph panel (FIG. 7-42) on the Arch of Titus in Rome, this relief gives no sense of rushing motion. Rather, it has a stately stillness. The chariot and the horsemen behind it move forward, but the emperor and his sons are frozen in place and face the viewer. Also different is the way the figures in the second row, whether on horseback or on foot, have no connection with the ground. The sculptor elevated them above the heads of those in the first row so they could be seen more clearly.

Both the frontality and the floating figures were new to official Roman art in Antonine and Severan times, but both appeared long before in the private art of freed slaves (FIGS. 7-11 and 7-11A). Once sculptors in the emperor's employ embraced these non-Classical elements, they had a long afterlife, largely (although never totally) displacing the Classical style the Romans adopted from Greece. As is often true in the history of art, the emergence of a new aesthetic was a by-product of a period of social, political, and economic upheaval. Art historians call this new non-naturalistic, more abstract style the Late Antique style.

BATHS OF CARACALLA The Severans were also active builders in the capital. The Baths of Caracalla (FIG. **7-66**) in Rome were the greatest in a long line of bathing and recreational complexes constructed with imperial funds to win the public's favor. Caracalla's baths dwarfed the typical baths of cities and towns such as Ostia and Pompeii. All the rooms had thick brick-faced concrete walls up to 140 feet high covered by enormous concrete vaults. The design was symmetrical along a central axis, facilitating the Roman custom of taking sequential plunges in warm-, hot-, and cold-water

baths in, respectively, the *tepidarium, caldarium,* and *frigidarium.* The caldarium (FIG. 7-66, no. 4) was a huge circular chamber with a concrete drum even taller than the Pantheon's (FIGS. 7-49 to 7-51) and a dome almost as large. Caracalla's Baths also had landscaped gardens, lecture halls, libraries, colonnaded exercise courts (*palaestras*), and a giant swimming pool (*natatio*). The entire complex covered an area of almost 50 acres. Archaeologists estimate that up to 1,600 bathers at a time could enjoy this Roman equivalent of a modern health spa. A branch of one of the city's major aqueducts supplied water, and furnaces circulated hot air through hollow floors and walls throughout the bathing rooms.

7-66 Plan of the Baths of Caracalla, Rome, Italy, 212–216 CE. (1) natatio, (2) frigidarium, (3) tepidarium, (4) caldarium, (5) palaestra.

Caracalla's baths could accommodate 1,600 bathers. They resembled a modern health spa and included libraries, lecture halls, and exercise courts in addition to bathing rooms and a swimming pool.

7-67 Frigidarium, Baths of Diocletian, Rome, ca. 298–306 (remodeled by MICHELANGELO BUONARROTI as the nave of Santa Maria degli Angeli, 1563).

The groin-vaulted nave of the church of Santa Maria degli Angeli in Rome was once the frigidarium of the Baths of Diocletian. It gives an idea of the lavish adornment of imperial Roman baths.

The Baths of Caracalla also featured stuccoed vaults, mosaic floors (both black-and-white and polychrome), marble-faced walls, and marble statuary. One of the statues on display was the 10-foot-tall marble version of Lysippos's Herakles (FIG. 5-66), whose muscular body must have inspired Romans to exercise vigorously. The concrete vaults of the Baths of Caracalla collapsed long ago, but visitors can approximate the original appearance of the central bathing hall, the frigidarium, by entering the nave (FIG. 7-67) of the church of Santa Maria degli Angeli in Rome, which was once the frigidarium of the later Baths of Diocletian. The Renaissance interior (remodeled in the 18th century) of that church has, of course, many features foreign to a Roman bath, including a painted altarpiece. The ancient mosaics and marble revetment are long gone, but the present-day interior with its rich wall treatment, colossal columns with Composite capitals, immense groin vaults, and clerestory lighting provides a better sense of what it was like to be in a Roman imperial bathing complex than does any other building in the world. It takes a powerful imagination to visualize the original appearance of Roman concrete buildings from the pathetic ruins of brick-faced walls and fallen vaults at ancient sites today, but Santa Maria degli Angeli makes the task much easier.

The Soldier Emperors

The Severan dynasty ended with the murder of Severus Alexander (r. 222–235 CE). The next half century was one of almost continuous civil war. The Roman legions declared one general after another emperor, only to have each murdered in turn by another general a few years or even a few months later. (In the year 238, two coemperors selected by the Senate were dragged from the imperial palace and murdered in public after only three months in office.) In such unstable times, no emperor could begin ambitious architectural projects. The only significant building activity in Rome during the era of the "soldier emperors" occurred under Aurelian (r. 270–275 CE). He constructed a new defensive circuit wall for the capital—a military necessity and a poignant commentary on the decay of Roman power.

TRAJAN DECIUS If architects went hungry in third-century Rome, engravers and sculptors had much to do. The mint produced great quantities of coins (in debased metal) so that the troops could be paid with money stamped with the current emperor's portrait and not with the likeness of his predecessor or rival. Each new ruler set up portrait statues and busts everywhere to assert his authority. The sculpted portraits of the third century CE are among the most moving ever made, as notable for their emotional content as they are for their technical virtuosity. Portraits of Trajan Decius (r. 249–251 CE), such as the marble bust illustrated here (FIG. 7-68), show

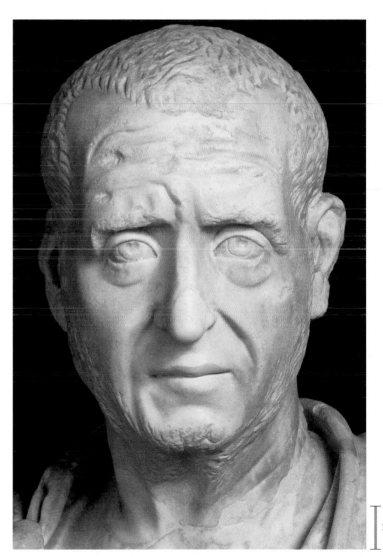

1 in.

7-68 Portrait bust of Trajan Decius, 249–251 CE. Marble, full bust 2′ 7″ high. Museo Capitolino, Rome.

This portrait of a short-lived soldier emperor depicts an older man with bags under his eyes and a sad expression. The eyes glance away nervously, reflecting the anxiety of an insecure ruler.

the emperor—best known for persecuting Christians—as an old man with bags under his eyes and a sad expression. The eyes glance away nervously rather than engage the viewer directly, revealing the anxiety of a man who knows he can do little to restore order to an out-of-control world. The sculptor modeled the marble as if it were pliant clay, compressing the sides of the head at the level of the eyes, etching the hair and beard into the stone, and chiseling deep lines in the forehead and around the mouth. The portrait reveals the anguished soul of the man—and of the times.

TREBONIANUS GALLUS Portraits of Decius's short-lived predecessor, Philip the Arabian (r. 244–249 CE), and

7-68A Philip the Arabian, 244–249 CE.

successor, Trebonianus Gallus (r. 251–253 CE), also have survived. Philip's busts (FIG. 7-68A) are marble and typical of the era, but the portrait of Trebonianus illustrated here (FIG. 7-69) is a larger-than-life-size bronze statue. Trebonianus appears in heroic nudity, as had so many emperors and generals before him. His physique, however, is not that of the strong but graceful Greek athletes Augustus and his successors admired so much. Instead, his is a wrestler's body with massive legs and a swollen trunk. The heavyset body dwarfs the head, with its nervous expression. In this portrait, the Greek ideal of the keen mind in the harmoniously proportioned body gave way to an image of brute force—an image well suited to the age of the soldier emperors.

LUDOVISI BATTLE SARCOPHAGUS By the third century, burial of the dead had become so widespread that even the imperial family practiced it in place of cremation. Sarcophagi were more popular than ever. An unusually large sarcophagus (FIG. 7-70), discovered in Rome in 1621 and purchased by Cardinal Ludovisi, is decorated on the front with a chaotic scene of battle between Romans and one of their northern foes, probably the Goths. The sculptor spread the writhing and highly emotive figures evenly across the entire relief, with no illusion of space behind them. This piling of figures is an even more extreme rejection of Classical perspective than was the use of floating ground lines in the decursio panel (FIG. 7-58) of the Column of Antoninus Pius. It underscores the increasing dissatisfaction of Late Antique artists with the Classical style.

Within this dense mass of intertwined bodies, the central horseman stands out vividly. He wears no helmet and thrusts out his open right hand to demonstrate he holds no weapon. Several scholars have identified him as one of the sons of Trajan Decius. In an age when the Roman army was far from invincible and Roman emperors were constantly felled by other Romans, the young general on the *Ludovisi Battle Sarcophagus* boasts that he is a fearless commander assured of victory. His self-assurance may stem from his having embraced one of the increasingly popular Oriental mystery religions. On the youth's forehead, the sculptor carved the emblem of Mithras, the Persian god of light, truth, and victory over death.

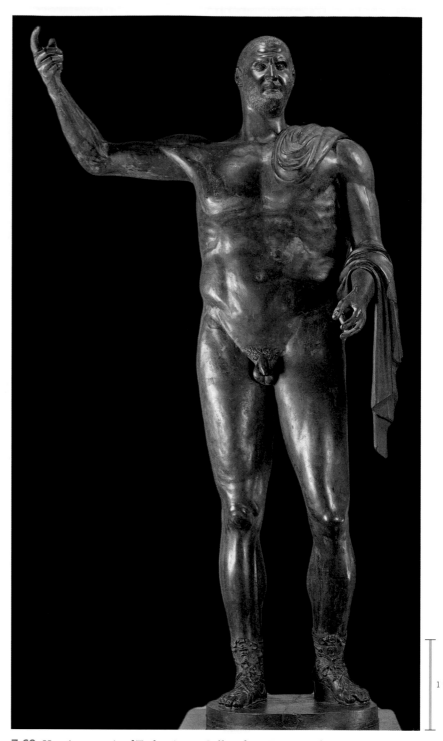

1 ft.

7-69 Heroic portrait of Trebonianus Gallus, from Rome, Italy, 251–253 CE. Bronze, 7′ 11″ high. Metropolitan Museum of Art, New York.

In this over-life-size heroically nude statue, Trebonianus Gallus projects an image of brute force. He has the massive physique of a powerful wrestler, but his face expresses nervousness.

PHILOSOPHER SARCOPHAGUS The insecurity of the times led some Romans to seek solace in philosophy. On many third-century sarcophagi, the deceased assumed the role of the learned intellectual. One especially large example depicts a seated Roman philosopher holding a scroll (FIG. 7-71). Two standing women (also with portrait features) gaze at him from left and right, confirming his importance. In the background are other philosophers, students or colleagues of the central deceased teacher. The two women may be the deceased's wife and daughter, two sisters,

7-70 Battle of Romans and barbarians (*Ludovisi Battle Sarcophagus*), from Rome, Italy, ca. 250–260 CE. Marble, 5′ high. Museo Nazionale Romano—Palazzo Altemps, Rome.

A chaotic scene of battle between Romans and barbarians decorates the front of this sarcophagus. The sculptor piled up the writhing, emotive figures in an emphatic rejection of Classical perspective.

7-71 Sarcophagus of a philosopher, ca. 270–280 CE. Marble, 4′ 11″ high. Musei Vaticani, Rome.

On many third-century CE sarcophagi, the deceased appears as a learned intellectual. Here, the seated philosopher is the central frontal figure. His two female muses also have portrait features.

every rule of Classical design. Although made of stone, the building, with its circular domed cella set behind a gabled columnar facade, is in many ways a critique of the concrete Pantheon (FIG. 7-49), which by then had achieved the status of a "classic." Many features of the Baalbek temple intentionally depart from the norm. The platform, for example, is scalloped all around the cella. The columns—the only known instance of five-sided Corinthian capitals with corresponding pentagonal bases—support a matching scalloped entablature (which serves to buttress the shallow stone dome). These concave forms and those of the niches in the cella walls play off against the cella's convex shape. Even the "traditional" facade of the Baalbek temple is eccentric. The unknown architect inserted an arch within the triangular pediment.

Diocletian and the Tetrarchy

In an attempt to restore order to the Roman Empire, Diocletian (r. 284–305 CE), whose troops proclaimed him emperor, decided to share power with his potential rivals. In 293, he established the *tetrarchy* (rule by four) and adopted the title of Augustus of the East. The other three *tetrarchs* were a corresponding Augustus of the West, and Eastern and Western Caesars (whose allegiance to the two Augusti was cemented by marriage to their daughters). Together, the four emperors ruled without strife until Diocletian retired in 305. Without his leadership, the tetrarchic form of government collapsed, and renewed civil war followed. The division of the Roman Empire into eastern and western spheres persisted throughout the Middle Ages, however, setting the Byzantine East apart from the Latin West.

GROUP PORTRAITS In art, if not in life, the four tetrarchs often appeared together, both on coins and in statues. Artists did not try to capture their individual appearances and personalities but sought instead to represent the nature of the tetrarchy itself—that is, to portray four equal partners in power. In the two pairs of porphyry (purple marble) tetrarchic portraits (FIG. **7-73**) in Venice, it is impossible to name the rulers. Each of the four emperors has lost his identity as an individual and been subsumed into the larger entity of the tetrarchy. All the tetrarchs are identically clad in cuirass and cloak. Each grasps a sheathed sword in his left hand. With their right arms they embrace one another in an overt display of concord. The figures, like those on the decursio relief (FIG. 7-58) of the Column of Antoninus Pius, have large cubical heads and squat bodies. The drapery is schematic, the bodies are shapeless, and the faces are emotionless masks, distinguished only by the beards of two of the tetrarchs (probably the older Augusti, differentiating them from the younger Caesars). Nonetheless, each pair is as alike as freehand carving can achieve. In this group portrait, carved eight centuries after Greek sculptors first freed the human form from the formal rigidity of the Egyptian-inspired kouros stance, an artist once again conceived the human figure in iconic terms. Idealism, naturalism, individuality, and personality have disappeared.

PALACE OF DIOCLETIAN When Diocletian abdicated in 305, he returned to his birthplace, Dalmatia (roughly the former Yugoslavia), where he built a palace (FIG. **7-74**) at Split on the Adriatic coast. Just as Aurelian had felt it necessary to girdle Rome with fortress walls, Diocletian instructed his architects to provide him with a walled suburban palace. The fortified complex, which covers about 10 acres, has the layout of a Roman castrum, complete with watchtowers flanking the gates. It gave the emperor a sense of security in the most insecure of times.

7-72 Restored view (*top*) and plan (*bottom*) of the Temple of Venus, Baalbek, Lebanon, third century CE.

This "baroque" temple violates almost every rule of Classical design. It has a scalloped platform and entablature, five-sided Corinthian capitals, and a facade with an arch inside the pediment.

or some other combination of family members. The composition, with a frontal central figure and two subordinate flanking figures, is typical of the Late Antique style. This type of sarcophagus became popular for Christian burials. Sculptors used the wise-man motif to portray not only the deceased (FIG. 8-7) but also Christ flanked by saints (FIG. 8-1).

BAALBEK The decline in respect for Classical art also is evident in third-century architecture. At Baalbek in present-day Lebanon, the architect of the Temple of Venus (FIG. **7-72**), following in the "baroque" tradition of the Petra Treasury (FIG. 7-53), ignored almost

7-73 Portraits of the four tetrarchs, from Constantinople, ca. 305 CE. Porphyry, 4′ 3″ high. Saint Mark's, Venice.

Diocletian established the tetrarchy to bring order to the Roman world. In group portraits, artists always depicted the four corulers as nearly identical partners in power, not as distinct individuals.

1 ft.

Within the high walls, two avenues (comparable to the cardo and decumanus of a Roman city; FIG. 7-43) intersected at the palace's center. Where a city's forum would have been situated, Diocletian's palace had a colonnaded court leading to the entrance to the imperial residence, which had a templelike facade with an arch within its pediment, as in Baalbek's Temple of Venus (FIG. 7-72). Diocletian presented himself as if he were a god in his temple when he appeared before those who gathered in the court to pay homage to him. On one side of the court was a Temple of Jupiter. On the other side was Diocletian's domed octagonal *mausoleum* (FIG. 7-74, *center right*), which towered above all the other structures in the complex. Domed tombs of this type became very popular in Late Antiquity not only for mausoleums but eventually also for churches, especially in the Byzantine East (see Chapters 8 and 9). In fact, Diocletian's mausoleum is a church today.

Constantine

An all-too-familiar period of conflict followed the short-lived concord among the tetrarchs that ended with Diocletian's abdication. This latest war among rival Roman armies lasted two decades. The eventual victor was Constantine I, son of Constantius Chlorus, Diocletian's Caesar of the West. After the death of his father, Constantine (r. 306–337 CE), called the Great, invaded Italy. In 312 CE, in a decisive battle at Rome's Milvian Bridge, he defeated and killed Maxentius and took control of the capital. Constantine attributed his victory to the aid of the Christian god. The next year, he and

7-74 Restored view of the palace of Diocletian, Split, Croatia, ca. 298–306.

Diocletian's palace resembled a fortified Roman city (compare FIG. 7-43). Within its high walls, two avenues intersected at the forumlike colonnaded courtyard leading to the emperor's residential quarters.

Licinius, Constantine's coemperor in the East, issued the Edict of Milan, ending the persecution of Christians.

In time, Constantine and Licinius became foes, and in 324 Constantine defeated and executed Licinius near Byzantium (modern Istanbul, Turkey). Constantine, now unchallenged ruler of the whole Roman Empire, founded a "New Rome" at Byzantium and named it Constantinople (City of Constantine). In 325, at the Council of Nicaea, Christianity became the de facto official religion of the Roman Empire. From this point on, the ancient cults declined rapidly. Constantine dedicated Constantinople on May 11, 330, "by the commandment of God," and in 337 the emperor was baptized on his deathbed. For many scholars, the transfer of the seat of power from Rome to Constantinople and the recognition of Christianity mark the end of antiquity and the beginning of the Middle Ages.

Constantinian art is a mirror of this transition from the ancient to the medieval world. In Rome, for example, Constantine was a builder in the grand tradition of the emperors of the first, second, and early third centuries, erecting public baths, a basilica on the road leading into the Roman Forum, and a triumphal arch. But he was also the patron of the city's first churches (see Chapter 8).

ARCH OF CONSTANTINE Between 312 and 315, Constantine erected a great triple-passageway arch (FIGS. 7-2, no. 15, and **7-75**) next to the Colosseum to commemorate his defeat of Maxentius. The arch was the largest set up in Rome since the end of the Severan dynasty. The builders, however, took much of the sculptural decoration from earlier monuments of Trajan, Hadrian (FIG. 7-48A), and Marcus Aurelius, and all of the columns and other architectural elements date to an earlier era. Constantine's sculptors refashioned the second-century reliefs to honor him by recutting the heads of the earlier emperors with his features. They also added labels to the old reliefs, such as *Liberator Urbis* (Liberator of the City) and *Fundator Quietus* (Bringer of Peace), references to the downfall of Maxentius and the end of civil war. Art historians have often cited this reuse of statues and reliefs as evidence of a decline in creativity and technical skill in the Late Roman Empire. Although such a judgment is in part deserved, it ignores the fact that the reused sculptures were carefully selected to associate Constantine with the "good emperors" of the second century. One of the arch's few Constantinian reliefs underscores that message. It shows Constantine on the speaker's platform in the Roman Forum between statues of Hadrian and Marcus Aurelius.

7-75 South facade of the Arch of Constantine, Rome, Italy, 312–315 CE. ◼◀

Much of the sculptural decoration of Constantine's arch came from monuments of Trajan, Hadrian, and Marcus Aurelius. Sculptors recut the heads of the earlier emperors to substitute Constantine's features.

7-76 Distribution of largesse, detail of the north frieze of the Arch of Constantine, Rome, Italy, 312–315 CE. Marble, 3′ 4″ high.

This Constantinian frieze is less a narrative of action than a picture of actors frozen in time. The composition's rigid formality reflects the new values that would come to dominate medieval art.

1 ft.

In another Constantinian relief (FIG. 7-76), the emperor distributes largesse to grateful citizens who approach him from right and left. Constantine is a frontal and majestic presence, elevated on a throne above the recipients of his munificence. The figures are squat in proportion, like the tetrarchs (FIG. 7-73). They do not move according to any Classical principle of naturalistic movement but, rather, with the mechanical and repeated stances and gestures of puppets. The relief is very shallow, the forms are not fully modeled, and the details are incised. The frieze is less a narrative of action than a picture of actors frozen in time so that the viewer can distinguish instantly the all-important imperial donor (at the center on a throne) from his attendants (to the left and right above) and the recipients of the largesse (below and of smaller stature).

An eminent art historian once characterized this approach to pictorial narrative as a "decline of form," and when judged by the standards of Classical art, it was. But the composition's rigid formality, determined by the rank of those portrayed, was consistent with a new set of values. It soon became the preferred mode, supplanting the Classical notion that a picture is a window onto a world of anecdotal action. Comparing this Constantinian relief with a Byzantine icon (FIG. 9-18) reveals that the compositional principles of the Late Antique style became those of medieval art. They were very different from, but not "better" or "worse" than, those of Greco-Roman art. The Arch of Constantine is the quintessential monument of its era, exhibiting a respect for the past in its reuse of second-century sculptures while rejecting the norms of Classical design in its frieze and thereby paving the way for the iconic art of the Middle Ages.

COLOSSUS OF CONSTANTINE After Constantine's victory over Maxentius, his official portraits broke with tetrarchic tradition as well as with the style of the soldier emperors, and resuscitated the Augustan image of an eternally youthful head of state. The most impressive of Constantine's preserved portraits is an eight and-one-half-foot-tall head (FIG. 7-77), one of several fragments of a colossal enthroned statue of the emperor composed of a brick core, a wooden torso covered with bronze, and a head and limbs of

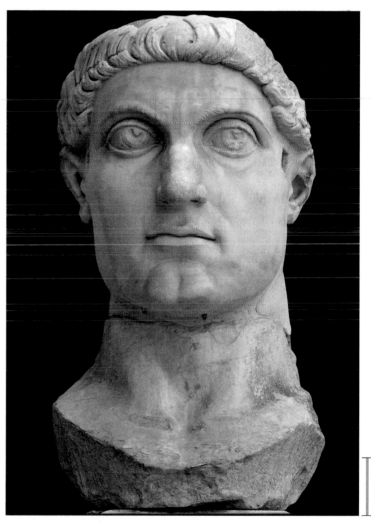

1 ft.

7-77 Colossal head of Constantine, from the Basilica Nova, Rome, Italy, ca. 315–330 CE. Marble, 8′ 6″ high. Musei Capitolini–Palazzo dei Conservatori, Rome. ◼◀

Constantine's portraits revive the Augustan image of an eternally youthful ruler. This colossal head is one fragment of an enthroned Jupiter-like statue of the emperor holding the orb of world power.

marble. Constantine's artist modeled the seminude seated portrait on Roman images of Jupiter. The emperor held an orb (possibly surmounted by the cross of Christ), the symbol of global power, in his extended left hand. The nervous glance of third-century portraits is absent, replaced by a frontal mask with enormous eyes set into the broad and simple planes of the head. The emperor's personality is lost in this immense image of eternal authority. The colossal size, the likening of the emperor to Jupiter, the eyes directed at no person or thing of this world—all combine to produce a formula of overwhelming power appropriate to Constantine's exalted position as absolute ruler.

BASILICA NOVA Constantine's gigantic portrait sat in the western apse of the Basilica Nova (New Basilica) in Rome (FIGS. 7-2, no. 12, and **7-78**), a project Maxentius had begun and Constantine completed. From its position in the apse, the emperor's image dominated the interior of the basilica in much the same way enthroned statues of Greco-Roman divinities loomed over awestruck mortals in temple cellas (compare FIG. 5-46).

The Basilica Nova ruins never fail to impress tourists with their size and mass. The original structure was 300 feet long and 215 feet wide. Brick-faced concrete walls 20 feet thick supported coffered barrel vaults in the aisles. These vaults also buttressed the groin vaults of the nave, which was 115 feet high. Marble slabs and stuccoes covered the walls and floors. The reconstruction in FIG. 7-78 effectively suggests the immensity of the interior, where the great vaults dwarf even the emperor's colossal portrait. The drawing also clearly reveals the fenestration of the groin vaults (FIG. 7-6c), a lighting system akin to the clerestory of a traditional stone-and-timber basilica. The architect here applied to basilica design the lessons learned in the design and construction of buildings such as Trajan's great market hall (FIG. 7-46) and the Baths of Caracalla and Diocletian (FIG. 7-67).

AULA PALATINA Few architects, however, followed suit. At Trier on the Moselle River in Germany, the imperial seat of Constantius Chlorus as Caesar of the West, Constantine built a traditional basilica-like audience hall, the Aula Palatina (FIG. **7-79**), as part of his new palace complex. The Trier basilica measures about 190 feet long and 95 feet wide and has an austere brick exterior, enlivened somewhat by highlighting in grayish-white stucco. The use of lead-framed panes of glass for the windows enabled the builders to give life and movement to the blank exterior surfaces.

Inside (FIG. **7-80**), the audience hall was also very simple. Its flat, coffered wood ceiling is some 95 feet above the floor. The interior has no aisles, only a wide space with two stories of large windows that provide ample light. At the narrow north end, a *chancel arch* divides the main hall from the semicircular apse (which also has a flat ceiling). The Aula Palatina's interior is quite severe, although mosaics and marble plaques originally covered the arch and apse to provide a magnificent frame for the enthroned emperor. The design of both the interior and exterior has close parallels in many Early Christian churches (see Chapter 8).

7-78 Restored cutaway view of the Basilica Nova, Rome, Italy, ca. 306–312 CE (John Burge).

Roman builders applied the lessons learned constructing baths and market halls to the Basilica Nova, where fenestrated concrete groin vaults replaced the clerestory of a stone-and-timber basilica.

7-79 Exterior of the Aula Palatina (looking southeast), Trier, Germany, early fourth century CE. ◼◀

The austere brick exterior of Constantine's Aula Palatina at Trier is typical of later Roman architecture. Two stories of windows with lead-framed panes of glass take up most of the surface area.

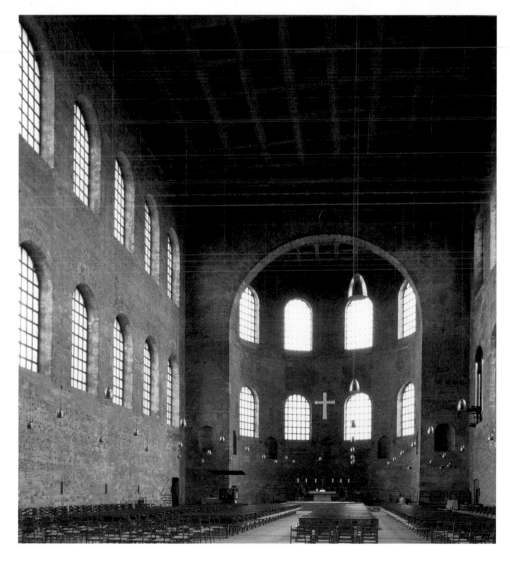

7-80 Interior of the Aula Palatina (looking north), Trier, Germany, early fourth century CE. ◼◀

The interior of the audience hall of Constantine's palace in Germany resembles a timber-roofed basilica with an apse at one end, but it has no aisles. The large windows provided ample illumination.

CONSTANTINIAN COINS The two portraits of Constantine on the coins in FIG. **7-81** reveal both the essential character of Roman imperial portraiture and the special nature of Constantinian art.

The first (FIG. 7-81, *left*) dates shortly after the death of Constantine's father, when Constantine was in his early 20s and his position was still insecure. Here, in his official portrait, he appears considerably older, because he adopted the imagery of the tetrarchs. Indeed, were it not for the accompanying label identifying this Caesar as Constantine, it would be impossible to know whom the coin engraver portrayed.

Eight years later (FIG. 7-81, *right*)—after the defeat of Maxentius and the Edict of Milan—Constantine, now the unchallenged Augustus of the West, is clean-shaven and looks his real age, having rejected the mature tetrarchic look in favor of youth. These two coins should dispel any uncertainty about the often fictive nature of imperial portraiture and the ability of Roman emperors to choose any official image that suited their needs. In Roman art, "portrait" is often not synonymous with "likeness."

The later coin is also an eloquent testimony to the dual nature of Constantinian rule. The emperor appears in his important role as imperator, dressed in armor, wearing an ornate helmet, and carrying a shield bearing the enduring emblem of the Roman state—the she-wolf nursing Romulus and Remus (compare FIG. 6-11 and Roma's shield in FIG. 7-57). Yet he does not carry the traditional eagle-topped scepter of the Roman emperor. Rather, he holds a cross crowned by an orb. At the crest of his helmet, at the front, just below the grand plume, is a disk containing the *Christogram,* the monogram ☧ made up of *chi* (X), *rho* (P), and *iota* (I), the initial letters of Christ's name in Greek (compare the shield a soldier holds in FIG. 9-13). The artist portrayed Constantine as both Roman emperor and soldier in the army of the Lord. The coin, like Constantinian art in general, belongs both to the ancient and to the medieval worlds.

½ in.   ½ in.

7-81 Two coins with portraits of Constantine. *Left:* nummus, 307 CE. Billon, diameter 1″. American Numismatic Society, New York. *Right:* medallion, ca. 315 CE. Silver, diameter 1″. Staatliche Münzsammlung, Munich.

These two coins underscore that portraits of Roman emperors were rarely true likenesses. On the earlier coin, Constantine appears as a bearded tetrarch. On the later coin, he appears eternally youthful.

THE ROMAN EMPIRE

MONARCHY AND REPUBLIC 753–27 BCE

I According to legend, Romulus and Remus founded Rome in 753 BCE. In the sixth century BCE, Etruscan kings ruled the city, and Roman art was Etruscan in character.

I In the centuries following the establishment of the Republic in 509 BCE, Rome conquered its neighbors in Italy and then moved into Greece, bringing exposure to Greek art and architecture.

I Republican temples combined Etruscan plans with the Greek orders, and houses had peristyles with Greek columns. The Romans, however, pioneered the use of concrete as a building material.

I The First Style of mural painting derived from Greece, but the illusionism of the Second Style is distinctly Roman.

I Republican portraits were usually superrealistic likenesses of elderly patricians and celebrated traditional Roman values.

Man with ancestor busts,
late first century BCE

EARLY EMPIRE 27 BCE–96 CE

I Augustus (r. 27 BCE–14 CE) defeated Mark Antony and Cleopatra at Actium in 31 BCE and became the first Roman emperor.

I Augustan art revived the Classical style with frequent references to Periclean Athens. Augustus's ambitious building program made lavish use of marble, and his portraits always depicted him as an idealized youth.

I Under the Julio-Claudians (r. 14–68 CE), builders began to realize the full potential of concrete in buildings such as the Golden House of Nero.

I The Flavian emperors (r. 68-96 CE) built the Colosseum, the largest Roman amphitheater, and arches and other monuments celebrating their victory in Judaea.

I The eruption of Mount Vesuvius in 79 CE buried Pompeii and Herculaneum. During the quarter century before the disaster, painters decorated the walls of houses in the Third and Fourth Styles.

Ara Pacis Augustae, Rome, 13–9 BCE

Colosseum, Rome,
ca. 70–80 CE

HIGH EMPIRE 96–192 CE

I The Roman Empire reached its greatest extent under Trajan (r. 98–117 CE). The emperor's new forum and markets transformed the civic center of Rome. Trajan's Column commemorated his two campaigns in Dacia in a spiral frieze with thousands of figures.

I Hadrian (r. 117–138 CE), emulating Greek statesmen and philosophers, was the first emperor to wear a beard. He built the Pantheon, a triumph of concrete technology.

I Under the Antonines (r. 138–192 CE), the dominance of Classical art began to erode, and imperial artists introduced new compositional schemes in relief sculpture and a psychological element in portraiture.

Marcus Aurelius,
ca. 175 CE

LATE EMPIRE 192–337 CE

I In the art of the Severans (r. 193–235 CE), the non-Classical Late Antique style took root. Artists represented the emperor as a central frontal figure disengaged from the action around him.

I During the chaotic era of the soldier emperors (r. 235–284 CE), artists revealed the anxiety and insecurity of the emperors in moving portraits.

I Diocletian (r. 284–305 CE) reestablished order by sharing power. Statues of the tetrarchs portray the four emperors as identical and equal rulers, not as individuals.

Arch of Constantine, Rome,
312–315 CE

I Constantine (r. 306–336 CE) restored one-man rule, ended persecution of Christians, and transferred the capital of the Empire from Rome to Constantinople in 330. The abstract formality of Constantinian art paved the way for the iconic art of the Middle Ages.

Episodes from the
Hebrew scriptures,
including Abraham's
sacrifice of Isaac, appear
side by side with scenes
from the life of Jesus
on this sarcophagus
of a recent convert to
Christianity.

Christ, long-haired and
youthful in the Early
Christian tradition, sits
above a personification of
the Roman sky god. Flanking
the new ruler of the universe
are Saints Peter and Paul.

The Jewish scenes
on Junius Bassus's
sarcophagus had
special significance
for Christians. Adam
and Eve's original sin
of eating the apple in
the Garden of Eden
necessitated Christ's
sacrifice.

1 ft.

8-1 Sarcophagus of Junius Bassus, from Rome, Italy, ca. 359. Marble, 3′ 10½″ × 8′. Museo Storico del Tesoro della Basilica di San Pietro, Rome.

8

LATE ANTIQUITY

The compositions of many Early Christian reliefs derive from Greco-Roman art. The scene of Jesus entering Jerusalem on a donkey recalls portrayals of Roman emperors entering conquered cities.

ROMANS, JEWS, AND CHRISTIANS

During the third and fourth centuries, a rapidly growing number of Romans rejected polytheism (belief in multiple gods) in favor of monotheism (the worship of a single all-powerful god)—but they did not stop commissioning works of art. A prominent example is Junius Bassus, the mid-fourth-century city prefect of Rome who converted to Christianity and, according to the inscription on his sarcophagus (FIG. 8-1), was baptized just before his death in 359. He grew up immersed in traditional Roman culture and initially paid homage to the old Roman gods, but when he died, he chose to be buried in a sarcophagus decorated with episodes from the Hebrew scriptures and the life of Jesus.

The sculptor of Junius Bassus's sarcophagus decorated it with reliefs only on the front and two short sides in the western Roman manner (see Chapter 7). The front has 10 figural scenes in two registers of five compartments, each framed by columns in the tradition of Asiatic sarcophagi (FIG. 7-61). The deceased does not appear in any of those compartments. Instead, Jewish and Christian biblical stories fill the niches. Jesus has pride of place and appears in the central compartment of each register: as a teacher enthroned between Saints Peter and Paul (top niche), and entering Jerusalem on a donkey (bottom niche). Both compositions owe a great deal to official Roman art. In the upper zone, Christ, like an enthroned Roman emperor, sits above a personification of the sky god holding a billowing mantle over his head, indicating Christ is ruler of the universe. The scene below derives in part from portrayals of Roman emperors entering conquered cities on horseback, but Jesus' steed and the absence of imperial attributes contrast sharply with the imperial models the sculptor used as compositional sources.

The Jewish scenes on the Junius Bassus sarcophagus include the stories of Adam and Eve and Abraham and Isaac, which took on added significance for Christians as foretelling events in the life of their Savior. Christians believe Adam and Eve's original sin of eating the apple in the Garden of Eden ultimately necessitated Christ's sacrifice for the salvation of humankind. At the upper left, Abraham is about to sacrifice Isaac. Christians view this Genesis story as a prefiguration of God's sacrifice of his son, Jesus.

The crucifixion, however, does not appear on the sarcophagus and was rare in Early Christian art. Artists emphasized Christ's divinity and exemplary life as teacher and miracle worker, not his suffering and death at the hands of the Romans. This sculptor, however, alluded to the crucifixion in the scenes at the upper right showing Jesus led before Pontius Pilate for judgment. The Romans condemned Jesus to death, but he triumphantly overcame it. Junius Bassus hoped for a similar salvation.

THE LATE ANTIQUE WORLD

The Roman Empire was home to an extraordinarily diverse population. In Rome alone on any given day, someone walking through the city's various quarters would have encountered people of an astonishing range of social, ethnic, racial, linguistic, and religious backgrounds. This multicultural character of Roman society became only more pronounced as the Romans expanded their territories throughout Europe, Africa, and Mesopotamia (MAP 7-1). Chapter 7 focused on the public and private art and architecture of Romans through the time of Constantine, who worshiped the traditional gods and embraced the values of the classical world.* This chapter treats primarily Late Antique Jewish and Christian artworks, created both before and after Constantine. These sculptures, paintings, mosaics, and other art forms are no less Roman than imperial

*Note: In *Art through the Ages*, the adjective "Classical," with uppercase *C*, refers specifically to the Classical period of ancient Greece, 480–323 BCE. Lowercase "classical" refers to Greco-Roman antiquity in general, that is, the period treated in Chapters 5, 6, and 7.

portraits, statues of gods and heroes, or sarcophagi with mythological scenes. Indeed, the artists may in some cases have been the same. But although they are Roman in style and technique, the Jewish and Christian sculptures, paintings, and buildings of Late Antiquity differ significantly in subject and often in function from contemporaneous Roman secular and religious art and architecture. For that reason, and because these Late Antique artworks and sacred buildings formed the foundation of the art and architecture of the Middle Ages, they are the subject of a separate chapter.

DURA-EUROPOS AND JEWISH ART

The powerful religious crosscurrents of Late Antiquity may be seen in microcosm in a distant outpost of the Roman Empire on a promontory overlooking the Euphrates River in Syria (MAP 8-1). Called Europos by the Greeks and Dura by the Romans, the town probably was founded shortly after the death of Alexander the Great by one of his successors. By the end of the second century BCE, Dura-Europos was in the hands of the Parthians. Trajan captured the city

MAP 8-1 The Mediterranean world in late antiquity.

LATE ANTIQUITY

	192	Pre-Constantinian	306	Constantine	337	Sons of Constantine to Justinian	526
		▌ Biblical murals in the Dura-Europos synagogue ▌ Earliest Christian sarcophagi and catacomb paintings		▌ Construction of the first churches in Rome, including Old Saint Peter's ▌ Dedication of Constantinople as the New Rome		▌ Capital of Western Roman Empire moved to Ravenna ▌ Mosaics become the primary medium for church decoration ▌ Earliest preserved illustrated manuscripts with biblical themes	

8-2 Interior of the synagogue, Dura-Europos, Syria, with wall paintings of biblical themes, ca. 245–256. Tempera on plaster. Reconstruction in National Museum of Damascus, Damascus.

The Dura-Europos synagogue was a converted private house. The niche housing the sacred Torah is at the center of one long wall with paintings depicting episodes from the Hebrew scriptures.

stylized gestures, and the figures, which have expressionless features and, in most of the panels, lack both volume and shadow, tend to stand in frontal rows. The painting from the book of Samuel in which *Samuel Anoints David* (FIG. **8-3**) exemplifies this Late Antique style, also seen in the friezes of the Arch of Septimius Severus (FIG. 7-65) at Lepcis Magna and the Arch of Constantine (FIG. 7-76) in Rome. The episode is on the main wall just to the right of the Torah niche. The prophet anoints the future king of Israel, as David's six older brothers look on. The painter drew attention to Samuel by depicting him larger than all the rest, a familiar convention of Late Antique art. David and his brothers are frontal figures looking out at the viewer. They seem almost weightless, and their bodies do not even have enough feet. The painter distinguished David from his brothers by the purple toga he wears. Purple was the color associated with the Roman emperor, and the Dura artist borrowed the imperial toga to signify David's royalty.

in 115,[†] but Dura reverted to Parthian control shortly thereafter. In 165, under Marcus Aurelius, the Romans retook the city and placed a permanent garrison there. Dura-Europos fell in 256 to Rome's new enemy in the East, the Sasanians, heirs to the Parthian Empire (see Chapter 2). The Sasanian siege of Dura is an important fixed point in the chronology of Late Antiquity because the inhabitants evacuated the town, leaving its buildings largely intact. This "Pompeii of the desert" has revealed the remains of more than a dozen different cult buildings, including many shrines of the polytheistic religions of the Mediterranean and Mesopotamia. But the excavators also discovered places of worship for the monotheistic creeds of Judaism and Christianity.

SYNAGOGUE PAINTINGS Dura-Europos's synagogue is remarkable not only for its very existence in a Roman garrison town but also for its extensive cycle of mural paintings depicting episodes from the sacred Jewish *Torah* (the scroll containing the *Pentateuch,* the first five books of the Hebrew scriptures). The Jews of Dura-Europos converted a private house with a central courtyard into a synagogue during the latter part of the second century. The main room (FIG. **8-2**) has a niche for the Torah at the center of one long wall. The paintings cover all the remaining wall surfaces. The discovery of an elaborate mural cycle in a Jewish temple initially surprised scholars because they had assumed the Second Commandment (Exodus 20:4–6) prohibiting Jews from worshiping images precluded the decoration of synagogues with figural scenes. Narrative scenes like those at Dura must have appeared in many Late Antique synagogues as well as in Jewish manuscripts, although no illustrated Bible of this period survives (see "Medieval Manuscript Illumination," page 249). God (YHWH, or Yahweh in the Torah), however, never appears in the Dura paintings, except as a hand emerging from the top of the framed panels.

The Dura murals are mostly devoid of action, even when the subject is a narrative theme. The artists told the stories through

8-3 *Samuel Anoints David,* detail of main interior wall of the synagogue, Dura-Europos, Syria, ca. 245–256. Tempera on plaster, 4′ 7″ high.

The figures in this scene from the book of Samuel lack volume, stand in frontal rows, and exhibit stylized gestures, features characteristic of Late Antique art, regardless of subject matter.

1 ft.

[†]In this chapter, all dates are CE unless otherwise indicated.

8-4 Ark of the Covenant and two menorahs, painted wall in a Jewish catacomb, Villa Torlonia, Rome, Italy, third century. Fresco, 3′ 11″ high.

Some of the oldest catacombs in Rome were Jewish burial places. This example features mural paintings that include depictions of the sacred Ark of the Covenant and two menorahs.

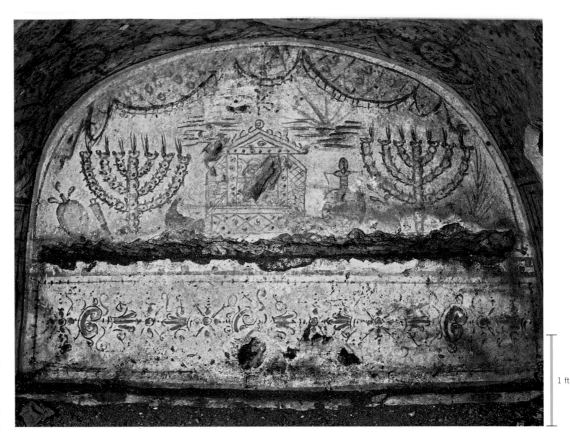

VILLA TORLONIA Mural paintings of similar date depicting Jewish themes have also been found in Rome, most notably in underground chambers on the grounds of the present Villa Torlonia, where Jewish families buried their dead beginning in the second century. Perhaps the finest of the Torlonia paintings (FIG. 8-4) depicts two seven-branched menorahs, modest versions of the sumptuous menorah (FIG. 7-41) Roman soldiers brought back from Jerusalem after Titus sacked the great Hebrew temple there. At the center is the Ark of the Covenant of the Jerusalem temple, which contained the sacred stone tablets of Moses with the Ten Commandments. These important emblems of their faith appropriately decorated one wall of the tomb in which these Roman Jews were laid to rest.

CHRISTIAN COMMUNITY HOUSE The Christian community at Dura-Europos also had a place to gather for worship and to conduct important ceremonies. As was the synagogue, the Christian meeting house (FIG. 8-5) was a remodeled private residence with a central courtyard (FIG. 8-5, no. 1). Its meeting hall (no. 2)—created by breaking down the partition between two rooms on the court's south side—could accommodate no more than about 70 people at a time. It had a raised platform at one end where the leader of the congregation sat or stood. Another room (no. 3), on the opposite side of the courtyard, had a font for *baptismal* rites, the all-important ceremony initiating a new convert into the Christian community.

Although the *baptistery* had mural paintings (poorly preserved), the place where Christians gathered to worship at Dura, as elsewhere in the Roman Empire, was a modest secondhand house, in striking contrast to the grand temples of the Roman gods. Without the approval of the state, Christian as well as Jewish communities remained small in number. Nonetheless, the emperor Diocletian (FIG. 7-73) was so concerned by the growing popularity of Christianity in the Roman army ranks that he ordered a fresh round of persecutions in 303 to 305, a half century after the last great persecutions under Trajan Decius (FIG. 7-68). As Christianity's appeal grew, so too did the Roman state's fear of weakening imperial authority, because the Christians refused to pay even token homage to the Roman state's official gods (which included deified emperors as well as the traditional pantheon of gods and goddesses). Persecution ended only in 311, when Galerius issued an edict of toleration,

and especially in 313, when Constantine (FIG. 7-77), who believed the Christian God was the source of his power rather than a threat to it (see pages 225–226), issued the Edict of Milan, which established Christianity as a legal religion with equal or superior standing to the traditional Roman cults.

8-5 Restored cutaway view of the Christian community house, Dura-Europos, Syria, ca. 240–256 (John Burge). (1) former courtyard of private house, (2) meeting hall, (3) baptistery.

The Christian community at Dura-Europos met in a remodeled private home that could accommodate only about 70 people. The house had a central courtyard, a meeting hall, and a baptistery.

THE CATACOMBS AND FUNERARY ART

Very little is known about the art of the first Christians. When art historians speak about "Early Christian art," they are referring to the earliest preserved artworks with Christian subjects, not the art of Christians at the time of Jesus. Most Early Christian art in Rome dates to the third and fourth centuries and is found in the *catacombs*—vast subterranean networks of galleries (passageways) and chambers designed as cemeteries for burying Christians and, to a lesser extent, Jews (FIG. 8-4) and others. The name derives from the Latin *ad catacumbas,* which means "in the hollows." The Christian and Jewish communities tunneled the catacombs out of the tufa bedrock, much as the Etruscans created the underground tomb chambers (FIGS. 6-7 and 6-8) in the Cerveteri necropolis. The catacombs are less elaborate than the Etruscan tombs but much more extensive. The known catacombs in Rome (others exist elsewhere), which ring the outskirts of the city, comprise galleries estimated to run for 60 to 90 miles. From the second through the fourth centuries, these burial complexes were in constant use, accommodating as many as four million bodies.

In accordance with Roman custom, the dead had to be buried outside a city's walls on private property. Christian families often pooled funds in a burial association, or *confraternity*. Each of the now-labyrinthine catacombs was initially of modest extent. First, the workers dug a gallery three to four feet wide around the perimeter of the burial ground at a convenient level below the surface. In the walls of these galleries, they cut *loculi* (openings to receive the bodies of the dead, one above another, like shelves). Often, small rooms carved out of the rock, called *cubicula* (as in Roman houses of the living), served as mortuary chapels. Once the original perimeter galleries were full of loculi and cubicula, the excavators cut other galleries at right angles to them. This process continued as long as lateral space permitted, at which point the confraternities opened lower levels connected by staircases to those above. Some Roman catacomb systems extend as deep as five levels. When adjacent burial areas belonged to members of the same confraternity, or by gift or purchase fell into the same hands, the owners opened passageways between the respective cemeteries. The galleries thus spread laterally and gradually acquired a vast extent.

After Christianity received official approval under Constantine, churches rose on the land above the catacombs so the pious could worship openly at the burial sites of some of the earliest Christian *martyrs* (men and women who chose to die rather than deny their religious beliefs), whom the Church had declared *saints*.

Painting

As already noted, Late Antique Jewish and Christian works of art do not differ from contemporaneous secular Roman artworks in style or technique, only in content. Some catacomb paintings, including many of those in the fourth-century Via Dino Compagni Catacomb (FIG. 8-5A) on the Via Latina in Rome, even depict traditional Greco-Roman myths. It is not surprising, therefore, that the painted ceiling

8-5A Via Dino Compagni Catacomb, Rome, ca. 320–360.

(FIG. 8-6) of a cubiculum in the Catacomb of Saints Peter and Marcellinus in Rome, for example, is similar in format to the painted vaults (FIG. 7-54A) of some third-century apartment houses at Ostia that have a circular frame with a central medallion and *lunettes* (semicircular frames) around the circumference. The lunettes in the Early Christian cubiculum illustrated here (FIG. 8-6) contain the key episodes from the biblical story of Jonah. Sailors throw him from his ship on the left. He emerges on the right from the "whale." (The Greek word is *ketos,* or sea dragon, and that is how the artist represented the monstrous marine creature that swallowed Jonah; compare the sea dragon, FIG. 7-30, *right*.) At the bottom, safe on land,

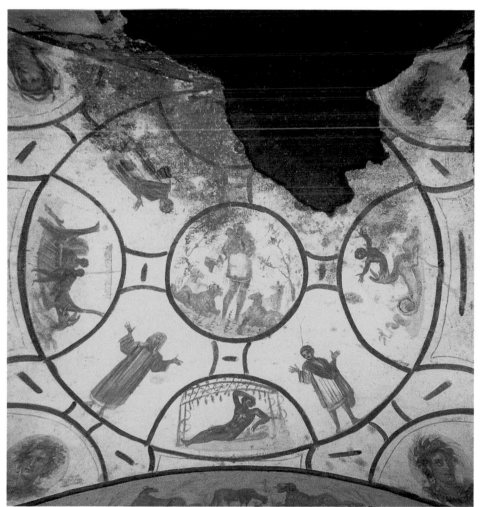

8-6 The Good Shepherd, the story of Jonah, and orants, frescoed ceiling of a cubiculum in the Catacomb of Saints Peter and Marcellinus, Rome, Italy, early fourth century.

This ceiling in a Roman catacomb is similar in format to the painted vaults of some Ostian apartment houses, but the subjects come from the Hebrew scriptures and the New Testament.

Jewish Subjects in Christian Art

When the Christians codified the Bible in its familiar form, they incorporated the Hebrew Torah and other writings, and designated the Jewish books as the "Old Testament" in contrast to the Christian books of the "New Testament." From the beginning, the Hebrew scriptures played an important role in Christian life and Christian art, in part because Jesus was a Jew and so many of the first Christians were converted Jews, but also because Christians came to view many of the persons and events of the Old Testament as prefigurations of New Testament persons and events. Christ himself established the pattern for this kind of biblical interpretation, called *typology*, when he compared Jonah's spending three days in the belly of the sea dragon (usually translated as "whale" in English) to the comparable time he would be entombed in the earth before his resurrection (Matt. 12:40). In the fourth century, Saint Augustine (354–430) confirmed the validity of this typological approach to the Old Testament when he stated that "the New Testament is hidden in the Old; the Old is clarified by the New."* Thus the Hebrew scriptures figured prominently in Early Christian art in all media. Biblical tales of Jewish faith and salvation were especially common in funerary contexts but appeared also in churches and on household objects.

*Augustine, *City of God,* 16.26.

The following are three of the most popular Jewish biblical stories depicted in Early Christian art:

- *Adam and Eve.* Eve, the first woman, tempted by a serpent, ate the forbidden fruit of the tree of knowledge, and fed some to Adam, the first man. As punishment, God expelled Adam and Eve from Paradise. This "original sin" ultimately led to Christ's sacrifice on the cross so that all humankind could be saved. Christian theologians often consider Christ the new Adam and his mother, Mary, the new Eve.

- *Sacrifice of Isaac.* God instructed Abraham, the father of the Hebrew nation, to sacrifice Isaac, his only son with his wife Sarah, as proof of his faith. (The mother of Abraham's first son, Ishmael, was Sarah's handmaiden.) When it became clear that Abraham would obey, the Lord sent an angel to restrain him and provided a ram for sacrifice in Isaac's place. Christians view this episode as a prefiguration of the sacrifice of God's only son, Jesus.

- *Jonah.* The Old Testament prophet Jonah had disobeyed God's command. In his wrath, the Lord caused a storm while Jonah was at sea. Jonah asked the sailors to throw him overboard, and the storm subsided. A sea dragon then swallowed Jonah, but God answered his prayers, and the monster spat out Jonah after three days, foretelling Christ's resurrection.

8-7 Sarcophagus with philosopher, orant, and Old and New Testament scenes, ca. 270. Marble, 1′ 11¼″ × 7′ 2″. Santa Maria Antiqua, Rome.

Early Christian sarcophagi often mixed Old and New Testament themes. Jonah was a popular subject because he emerged safely from a sea monster after three days, prefiguring Christ's resurrection.

Jonah contemplates the miracle of his salvation and the mercy of God. Jonah was a popular figure in Early Christian painting and sculpture, especially in funerary contexts. The Christians honored him as a *prefiguration* (prophetic forerunner) of Christ, who rose from death as Jonah had been delivered from the belly of the ketos, also after three days. Hebrew miracles prefiguring Christ's resurrection abound in the catacombs and in Early Christian art in general (see "Jewish Subjects in Christian Art," above).

A man, a woman, and at least one child occupy the compartments between the Jonah lunettes. They are *orants* (praying figures), raising their arms in the ancient attitude of prayer. Together they make

up a cross-section of the Christian family seeking a heavenly afterlife, although they may be generic portraits of the owners of the cubiculum. The central medallion shows Christ as the Good Shepherd, whose powers of salvation the painter underscored by placing the four episodes of the Jonah story around him. The motif of the Good Shepherd can be traced back to Archaic Greek art, but there the calf bearer (FIG. 5-8) was a bearded man offering his animal in sacrifice to Athena. In Early Christian art, Christ is the youthful and loyal protector of the Christian flock, who said to his disciples, "I am the good shepherd; the good shepherd gives his life for the sheep" (John 10:11). In the Christian motif, the sheep on Christ's shoulders is not a sacrificial offering.

It is one of the lost sheep Christ has retrieved, symbolizing a sinner who has strayed and been rescued. Early Christian artists almost invariably represented Christ either as the Good Shepherd or as a teacher. Only after Christianity became the Roman Empire's official religion in 380 did Christ take on in art such imperial attributes as the halo, the purple robe, and the throne, which denoted rulership. Eventually, artists depicted Christ with the beard of a mature adult—as in the late-fourth-century Catacomb of Commodilla in Rome (FIG. 8-6A)—which has been the standard form for centuries, supplanting the youthful imagery of most Early Christian portrayals of the Savior.

8-6A Catacomb of Commodilla, Rome, ca. 370–385.

Sculpture

Most Christians rejected cremation because they believed in the resurrection of the body, and the wealthiest Christian faithful, as other well-to-do Romans, favored impressive marble sarcophagi. Many of these coffins have survived in the catacombs and elsewhere. As expected, the most common themes painted on the walls and vaults of the Roman subterranean cemeteries were also the subjects that appeared on Early Christian sarcophagi. Often, the decoration of the marble coffins was a collection of significant Jewish and Christian themes, just as on the painted ceiling (FIG. 8-6) in the Catacomb of Saints Peter and Marcellinus.

SANTA MARIA ANTIQUA SARCOPHAGUS On the front of a sarcophagus (FIG. 8-7) in Santa Maria Antiqua in Rome, the story of Jonah occupies the left third. At the center are an orant and a seated philosopher, the latter a motif borrowed directly from Roman sarcophagi (FIG. 7-71) and popular also in Roman painting (FIG. 7-25B) and statuary. The heads of both the praying woman and the seated man reading from a scroll are unfinished. Roman workshops often produced sarcophagi before knowing who would purchase them. The sculptors added the portraits at the time of burial, if they added them at all. This practice underscores the universal appeal of the themes chosen.

At the right arc two different, yet linked, representations of Jesus—as the Good Shepherd and as a child receiving baptism in the Jordan River, though he really was baptized at age 30 (see "The Life of Jesus in Art," pages 240–241). In the early centuries of Christianity, baptism was usually delayed almost to the moment of death because it cleansed the Christian of all sin. One of those who was baptized on his deathbed was the emperor Constantine. On this sarcophagus, the newly baptized child Jesus turns his head toward the Good Shepherd and places his right hand on one of the sheep—perhaps the sculptor's way of suggesting Jesus' future ministry.

GOOD SHEPHERD STATUETTE Apart from the reliefs on privately commissioned sarcophagi such as the Santa Maria Antiqua sarcophagus and that of the city prefect Junius Bassus (FIG. 8-1), monumental sculpture became increasingly uncommon in the fourth century. Roman emperors and other officials continued to set up portraits, and sculptors still carved and cast statues of Greco-Roman gods and mythological figures, but the number of freestanding sculptures decreased sharply. In his *Apologia*, Justin Martyr, a second-century philosopher who converted to Christianity, condemned the traditional Greco-Roman practice of worshiping statues as gods, which the Second Commandment prohibited. Christians tended to suspect the freestanding statue, linking it with the false gods of the Romans, so Early Christian houses of worship, like Late

8-8 Christ as the Good Shepherd, ca. 300–350. Marble, 3' ¼" high. Musei Vaticani, Rome.

Although freestanding images of Christ were uncommon in Late Antiquity, several statuettes exist representing the Good Shepherd. The patrons were probably recent converts to Christianity.

1 ft.

Antique synagogues (FIG. 8-2), had no cult statues. Nor did churches or synagogues have any equivalent of the pedimental statues and relief friezes of Greco-Roman temples.

The Greco-Roman experience, however, was still a living part of the Mediterranean mentality, and many recently converted Christians retained some of the traditional values of the Greco-Roman world. This may account for those rare instances of freestanding Early Christian sculptures, such as the fourth-century statuettes representing Christ as the Good Shepherd (FIG. 8-8) or as a seated philosopher (FIG. 8-8A). As in Early

8-8A Christ seated, ca. 350–375.

Christian catacomb paintings (FIG. 8-6) and sarcophagi (FIG. 8-7), Christ is a long-haired young man dressed in a simple tunic. In the Good Shepherd statuette, he stands in a classical contrapposto stance with his right hip outthrust and his left leg bent. Several other marble statuettes of Christ bearing a sheep on his shoulders have been found, including one now in the Cleveland Museum of Art. It was part of a cache of sculptures from Turkey that included portraits and four marble statuettes illustrating episodes of the story of Jonah. Like the Good Shepherd statues, the Jonah figures are freestanding versions of the narrative scenes popular on Early Christian sarcophagi.

The Life of Jesus in Art

Christians believe Jesus of Nazareth is the son of God, the *Messiah* (Savior, *Christ*) of the Jews prophesied in the Hebrew scriptures. His life—his miraculous birth from the womb of a virgin mother, his preaching and miracle working, his execution by the Romans and subsequent ascent to Heaven—has been the subject of countless artworks from Roman times through the present day. The primary literary sources for these representations are the Gospels of the New Testament attributed to the four evangelists, Saints Matthew, Mark, Luke, and John (see "The Four Evangelists," Chapter 11, page 314); later apocryphal works; and medieval theologians' commentaries on these texts.

The life of Jesus dominated the subject matter of Christian art to a far greater extent than Greco-Roman religion and mythology ever did classical art. Whereas images of athletes, portraits of statesmen and philosophers, narratives of war and peace, genre scenes, and other secular subjects were staples of the classical tradition, Christian iconography held a near monopoly in the art of the Western world in the Middle Ages.

Although during certain periods artists rarely, if ever, depicted many of the events of Jesus' life, the cycle as a whole has been one of the most frequent subjects of Western art, even after the widespread revival of classical and secular themes during the Renaissance. Thus it is useful to summarize at the outset the entire cycle of events as they usually appear in artworks.

INCARNATION AND CHILDHOOD

The first "cycle" of the life of Jesus consists of the events of his conception (incarnation), birth, infancy, and childhood.

▌ *Annunciation to Mary.* The archangel Gabriel announces to the Virgin Mary that she will miraculously conceive and give birth to God's son Jesus. Artists sometimes indicated God's presence at the incarnation by a dove, the symbol of the Holy Spirit, the third "person" of the *Trinity* with God the Father and Jesus.

▌ *Visitation.* The pregnant Mary visits Elizabeth, her older cousin, who is pregnant with the future Saint John the Baptist. Elizabeth is the first to recognize that the baby Mary is bearing is the son of God, and they rejoice.

▌ *Nativity, Annunciation to the Shepherds, and Adoration of the Shepherds.* Jesus is born at night in Bethlehem and placed in a basket. Mary and her husband, Joseph, marvel at the newborn in a stable or, in Byzantine art, in a cave. An angel announces the birth of the Savior to shepherds in the field, who rush to adore the infant Jesus.

▌ *Adoration of the Magi.* A bright star alerts three wise men (*magi*) in the East that the king of the Jews has been born. They travel 12 days to find the holy family and present precious gifts to the infant Jesus.

▌ *Presentation in the Temple.* In accordance with Jewish tradition, Mary and Joseph bring their firstborn son to the temple in Jerusalem, where the aged Simeon, who God said would not die until he had seen the Messiah, recognizes Jesus as the prophesied savior of humankind.

▌ *Massacre of the Innocents and Flight into Egypt.* King Herod, fearful a rival king has been born, orders the massacre of all infants in Bethlehem, but an angel warns the holy family and they escape to Egypt.

▌ *Dispute in the Temple.* Joseph and Mary travel to Jerusalem for the feast of *Passover* (the celebration of the release of the Jews from bondage to the pharaohs of Egypt). Jesus, only 12 years old at the time, engages in learned debate with astonished Jewish scholars in the temple, foretelling his ministry.

PUBLIC MINISTRY

The public-ministry cycle comprises the teachings of Jesus and the miracles he performed.

▌ *Baptism.* Jesus' public ministry begins with his baptism at age 30 by John the Baptist in the Jordan River, where the dove of the Holy Spirit appears and God's voice is heard proclaiming Jesus as his son.

▌ *Calling of Matthew.* Jesus summons Matthew, a tax collector, to follow him, and Matthew becomes one of his 12 disciples, or *apostles* (from the Greek for "messenger"), and later the author of one of the four Gospels of the New Testament.

▌ *Miracles.* In the course of his teaching and travels, Jesus performs many miracles, revealing his divine nature. These include acts of healing and raising the dead, turning water into wine, walking on water and calming storms, and creating wondrous quantities of food. In the miracle of loaves and fishes, for example, Jesus transforms a few loaves of bread and a handful of fishes into enough food to feed several thousand people.

▌ *Delivery of the Keys to Peter.* The fisherman Peter was one of the first men Jesus summoned as a disciple. Jesus chooses Peter (whose name means "rock") as his successor. He declares Peter is the rock on which his church will be built, and symbolically delivers to Peter the keys to the kingdom of Heaven.

▌ *Transfiguration.* Jesus scales a high mountain and, in the presence of Peter and two other disciples, James and John the Evangelist, transforms into radiant light. God, speaking from a cloud, discloses Jesus is his son.

▌ *Cleansing of the Temple.* Jesus returns to Jerusalem, where he finds money changers and merchants conducting business in the temple. He rebukes them and drives them out of the sacred precinct.

PASSION

The passion (from Latin *passio,* "suffering") cycle includes the episodes leading to Jesus' trial, execution, resurrection, and ascent to Heaven.

▎*Entry into Jerusalem.* On the Sunday before his crucifixion (Palm Sunday), Jesus rides into Jerusalem on a donkey, accompanied by disciples. Crowds of people enthusiastically greet Jesus and place palm fronds in his path.

▎*Last Supper and Washing of the Disciples' Feet.* In Jerusalem, Jesus celebrates Passover with his disciples. During this last supper, Jesus foretells his imminent betrayal, arrest, and death and invites the disciples to remember him when they eat unleavened bread (symbol of his body) and drink wine (his blood). This ritual became the celebration of *Mass* (*Eucharist*) in Christian liturgy. At the same meal, Jesus sets an example of humility for his apostles by washing their feet.

▎*Agony in the Garden.* Jesus goes to the Mount of Olives in the Garden of Gethsemane, where he struggles to overcome his human fear of death by praying for divine strength. The apostles who accompanied him there fall asleep despite his request they stay awake with him while he prays.

▎*Betrayal and Arrest.* One of the disciples, Judas Iscariot, agrees to betray Jesus to the Jewish authorities in return for 30 pieces of silver. Judas leads the soldiers to Jesus and identifies the "king of the Jews" by kissing him, whereupon the soldiers arrest Jesus. Later, a remorseful Judas hangs himself from a tree.

▎*Trials of Jesus and Denial of Peter.* The soldiers bring Jesus before Caiaphas, the Jewish high priest, who interrogates Jesus about his claim to be the Messiah. Meanwhile, the disciple Peter thrice denies knowing Jesus, as Jesus predicted he would. Jesus is then brought before the Roman governor of Judaea, Pontius Pilate, on the charge of treason because he had proclaimed himself as the Jews' king. Pilate asks the crowd to choose between freeing Jesus or Barabbas, a murderer. The people choose Barabbas, and the judge condemns Jesus to death. Pilate then washes his hands, symbolically relieving himself of responsibility for the mob's decision.

▎*Flagellation and Mocking.* The Roman soldiers who hold Jesus captive tie him up, whip (flagellate) him, and mock him by dressing him as king of the Jews and placing a crown of thorns on his head.

▎*Carrying of the Cross, Raising of the Cross, and Crucifixion.* The Romans force Jesus to carry the cross on which he will be crucified from Jerusalem to Mount Calvary (Golgotha, the "place of the skull," Adam's burial place). Jesus falls three times, and his robe is stripped along the way. Soldiers erect the cross—often labeled in art *INRI* (the initial letters of "Jesus of Nazareth, King of the Jews" in Latin)—and nail his hands and feet to it. Jesus' mother, John the Evangelist, and Mary Magdalene mourn at the foot of the cross, while the Roman soldiers torment Jesus. One of them (the centurion Longinus) stabs Jesus in the side with a spear. After suffering great pain, Jesus dies. The crucifixion occurred on a Friday, and Christians celebrate the day each year as Good Friday.

▎*Deposition, Lamentation, and Entombment.* Two disciples, Joseph of Arimathea and Nicodemus, remove Jesus' body from the cross (the deposition). Sometimes those present at the crucifixion look on. His mother and his followers take Jesus to the tomb Joseph had purchased for himself, and Joseph, Nicodemus, the Virgin Mary, Saint John the Evangelist, and Mary Magdalene mourn over the dead Jesus (the lamentation). (When in art the isolated figure of the Virgin Mary cradles her dead son in her lap, it is called a *Pietà*—Italian for "pity.") In portrayals of the entombment, his followers lower Jesus into a sarcophagus in the tomb.

▎*Descent into Limbo.* During the three days he spends in the tomb, Jesus (after death, Christ) descends into Hell, or Limbo, and triumphantly frees the souls of the righteous, including Adam, Eve, Moses, David, Solomon, and John the Baptist. In Byzantine art, the label *Anastasis* (Greek, "resurrection") often identifies this episode, although the event precedes Christ's emergence from the tomb and reappearance on earth.

▎*Resurrection and Three Marys at the Tomb.* On the third day after his burial (Easter Sunday), Christ rises from the dead and leaves the tomb while the Roman guards sleep. The Virgin Mary, Mary Magdalene, and Mary, the mother of James, visit the tomb but find it empty. An angel informs them Christ has been resurrected.

▎*Noli Me Tangere, Supper at Emmaus, and Doubting of Thomas.* During the 40 days between Christ's resurrection and his ascent to Heaven, he appears on several occasions to his followers. When he encounters Mary Magdalene weeping at his tomb, Christ warns her with the words "Don't touch me" (*Noli me tangere* in Latin), but he tells her to inform the apostles of his return. At Emmaus he eats supper with two of his astonished disciples. Later, Christ invites Thomas, who cannot believe Jesus has risen, to touch the wound in his side that he received at his crucifixion.

▎*Ascension.* On the 40th day, on the Mount of Olives, with his mother and apostles as witnesses, Christ gloriously ascends to Heaven in a cloud.

ARCHITECTURE AND MOSAICS

Although the Christians conducted some ceremonies in the catacombs, regular services took place in private community houses of the type found at Dura-Europos (FIG. 8-5). Once Christianity achieved imperial sponsorship under Constantine, an urgent need suddenly arose to construct churches. The new buildings had to meet the requirements of Christian *liturgy* (the official ritual of public worship), provide a suitably monumental setting for the celebration of the Christian faith, and accommodate the rapidly growing numbers of worshipers.

Constantine believed the Christian god had guided him to victory over Maxentius, and in lifelong gratitude he protected and advanced Christianity throughout the Empire. As emperor, he was, of course, obliged to safeguard the ancient Roman religion, traditions, and monuments, and he was (for his time) a builder on a grand scale in the heart of the city (FIGS. 7-75 and 7-78). But Constantine, eager to provide buildings to house the Christian rituals and venerated burial places, especially the memorials of founding saints, also was the first major patron of Christian architecture. He constructed elaborate basilicas, memorials, and mausoleums not only in Rome but also in Constantinople, his "New Rome" in the East, and at sites sacred to Christianity, most notably Bethlehem, the birthplace of Jesus, and Jerusalem, the site of the crucifixion.

Rome

The major Constantinian churches in Rome stood on sites associated with the graves of Christian martyrs, which, in keeping with Roman burial practice, were all on the city's outskirts. The decision to erect churches at those sites also enabled Constantine to keep the new Christian shrines out of the city center and avoid any confrontation between Rome's Christians and those who continued to worship the old gods.

OLD SAINT PETER'S The greatest of Constantine's churches in Rome was Old Saint Peter's (FIG. 8-9), probably begun as early as 319. The present-day church (FIGS. 24-3 and 24-4), one of the master-

8-9 Restored cutaway view (*top*) and plan (*bottom*) of Old Saint Peter's, Rome, Italy, begun ca. 319 (John Burge).

Built by Constantine, the first imperial patron of Christianity, this huge church stood over Saint Peter's grave. The building's plan and elevation resemble those of Roman basilicas, not temples.

pieces of Italian Renaissance and Baroque architecture, is a replacement for the Constantinian structure. Old Saint Peter's stood on the western side of the Tiber River on a terrace on the irregular slope of the Vatican Hill over the ancient cemetery in which Constantine and Pope Sylvester (r. 314–335) believed Peter, the founder of the Christian community in Rome, had been buried. Excavations in the Roman cemetery beneath the church have in fact revealed a second-century memorial erected in honor of the Christian martyr at his reputed grave. Capable of housing 3,000 to 4,000 worshipers at one time, the immense church enshrined Peter's tomb, one of the most hallowed sites in Christendom, second only to the Holy Sepulcher in Jerusalem, the site of Christ's resurrection. The project also fulfilled the figurative words of Christ himself, when he said, "Thou art Peter, and upon this rock I will build my church" (Matt. 16:18). Peter was Rome's first bishop and the head of the long line of popes extending to the present.

The plan and elevation (FIG. 8-9) of Old Saint Peter's resemble those of Roman basilicas and audience halls, such as the Basilica Ulpia (FIG. 7-44, no. 4) in the Forum of Trajan and Constantine's own Aula Palatina (FIGS. 7-79 and 7-80) at Trier, rather than the design of any Greco-Roman temple. The Christians, understandably, did not want their houses of worship to mimic the form of polytheistic shrines, but practical considerations also contributed to their shunning the classical temple type. Greco-Roman temples housed only the cult statue of the deity. All rituals took place outside at open-air altars. Therefore, architects would have found it difficult to adapt the classical temple as a building accommodating large numbers of people within it. The Roman basilica, in contrast, was ideally suited as a place for congregation.

Like most Roman basilicas, Old Saint Peter's had a wide central *nave* (FIG. 8-9, *bottom*) with flanking *aisles* and an *apse* at the end. But unlike Roman basilicas, which sometimes had doorways on one long side opening onto an aisle (FIG. 7-44, no. 4), Early Christian basilicas all had a pronounced *longitudinal* axis. Worshipers entered the basilica through a *narthex*, or vestibule. When they emerged in Saint Peter's 300-foot-long nave, they had an unobstructed view of the altar in the apse, framed by the *chancel arch* dividing the nave from the transept. The *transept*, or transverse

aisle, an area perpendicular to the nave between the nave and apse, was a special feature of this Constantinian church. It housed Saint Peter's *relics,* which attracted hordes of pilgrims. (Relics are body parts, clothing, or objects associated with a saint or Christ himself; see "The Veneration of Relics," Chapter 12, page 336.) The transept became a standard element of church design in the West only much later, when it also took on, with the nave and apse, the symbolism of the Christian cross. Saint Peter's basilica also had a colonnaded courtyard in front of the narthex, very much like the forum proper in the Forum of Trajan (FIG. 7-44, no. 5) but called an *atrium,* like the central room in a Roman private house (FIG. 7-15).

Compared with Roman temples, which usually displayed statuary in pediments on their facades, most Early Christian basilicas were quite austere on the exterior. Inside, however, were frescoes and mosaics, marble columns (taken from older Roman buildings, as was customary at the time), and costly ornaments. The *Liber pontificalis,* or *Book of the Pontiffs (Popes),* compiled by an anonymous sixth-century author, lists Constantine's gifts to Old Saint Peter's. They included altars, chandeliers, candlesticks, pitchers, goblets, and plates fashioned of gold and silver and sometimes embellished with jewels and pearls, as well as jeweled altar cloths for use in the Mass and gold foil to sheathe the vault of the apse.[1] A huge marble *baldacchino* (domical canopy over an altar), supported by four spiral porphyry columns, marked the spot of Saint Peter's tomb.

SANTA SABINA Some idea of the character of the timber-roofed interior of Old Saint Peter's can be gleaned from the interior (FIG. **8-10**) of Santa Sabina in Rome. Santa Sabina, built a century later, is a basilican church of much more modest proportions than Constantine's immense Vatican basilica, but it still retains its Early Christian character, as well as its original carved wooden doors (FIG. **8-10A**). The Corinthian columns of its nave *arcade* produce a steady rhythm that focuses all attention on the chancel arch and the apse, which frame the altar. In Santa Sabina, as in Old Saint Peter's, light drenched the nave from the *clerestory*

8-10A West doors, Santa Sabina, Rome, ca. 432.

windows piercing the thin upper wall beneath the timber roof. The same light would have illuminated the frescoes and mosaics that commonly adorned the nave and apse of Early Christian churches. Outside, Santa Sabina has plain brick walls. They closely resemble the exterior of Trier's Aula Palatina (FIG. 7-79).

8-10 Interior of Santa Sabina (looking northeast), Rome, Italy, 422–432. ◼◀

Santa Sabina and other Early Christian basilican churches were timber-roofed and illuminated by clerestory windows. The nave arcade focused attention on the apse, which framed the altar.

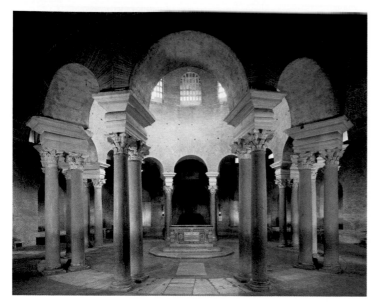

8-11 Interior of Santa Costanza (looking southwest), Rome, Italy, ca. 337–351. ◼◀

Possibly built as the mausoleum of Constantine's daughter, Santa Costanza later became a church. Its central plan, featuring a domed interior, would become the preferred form for Byzantine churches.

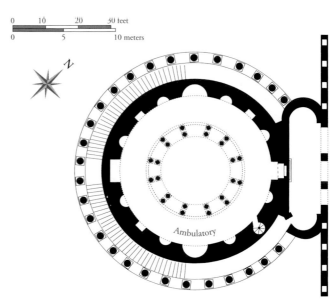

8-12 Plan of Santa Costanza, Rome, Italy, ca. 337–351.

Santa Costanza has antecedents in the domed temples (FIG. 7-51) and mausoleums (FIG. 7-74) of the Romans, but its plan, with 12 pairs of columns and a vaulted ambulatory, is unique.

SANTA COSTANZA The rectangular basilican church design was long the favorite of the Western Christian world. But Early Christian architects also adopted another classical architectural type: the *central-plan* building, in which the parts are of equal or almost equal dimensions around the center. Roman central-plan buildings were usually round or polygonal domed structures. Byzantine architects developed this form to monumental proportions and amplified its theme in numerous ingenious variations (see Chapter 9). In the West, builders generally used the central plan for structures adjacent to the main basilicas, such as mausoleums, baptisteries, and private chapels, rather than for churches, as in the East.

A highly refined example of the central-plan design is Santa Costanza (FIGS. 8-11 and 8-12), built on the northern outskirts of Rome in the mid-fourth century, possibly as the mausoleum for Constantina, the emperor Constantine's daughter. Recent excavations have called the traditional identification into question, but the building housed Constantina's monumental porphyry sarcophagus, even if the structure was not originally her tomb. The mausoleum, later converted into a church, stood next to the basilican church of Saint Agnes, who was buried in a nearby catacomb. Santa Costanza's antecedents are traceable to the tholos tombs (FIGS. 4-20 and 4-21) of the Mycenaeans, but its immediate predecessors were the domed structures of the Romans, such as the Pantheon (FIGS. 7-49 to 7-51) and especially imperial mausoleums such as Diocletian's (FIG. 7-74, *right*) at Split. At Santa Costanza, the architect modified the interior design of those Roman buildings to accommodate an *ambulatory,* a ringlike barrel-vaulted corridor separated from the central domed cylinder by a dozen pairs of columns.

Like most Early Christian basilicas, Santa Costanza has a severe brick exterior. Its interior was once richly adorned with mosaics, although most are lost. Old and New Testament themes appeared side by side, as in the catacombs and on Early Christian sarcophagi. The Santa Costanza mosaic program, however, also included subjects

8-13 Detail of the mosaic in the ambulatory vault of Santa Costanza, Rome, Italy, ca. 337–351. ◼◀

The ambulatory mosaics of Santa Costanza depict putti harvesting grapes and making wine, motifs associated with Bacchus, but for a Christian, the scenes evoked the Eucharist and Christ's blood.

Mosaics

As an art form, *mosaic* had a rather simple and utilitarian beginning, seemingly invented primarily to provide an inexpensive and durable flooring. Originally, mosaicists set small beach pebbles, unaltered from their natural form and color, into a thick coat of cement. Artisans soon discovered, however, that the stones could be arranged in decorative patterns. At first, these *pebble mosaics* were uncomplicated and confined to geometric shapes. Generally, the artists used only black and white stones. Examples of this type, dating to the eighth century BCE, have been found at Gordion in Asia Minor. Eventually, artists arranged the stones to form more complex pictorial designs, and by the fourth century BCE the technique had developed to a high level of sophistication. Mosaicists depicted elaborate figural scenes using a broad range of colors— red, yellow, and brown in addition to black, white, and gray—and shaded the figures, clothing, and setting to suggest volume. Thin strips of lead provided linear definition (FIG. 5-68).

By the middle of the third century BCE, artists had invented a new kind of mosaic that enabled the best mosaicists to create designs more closely approximating true paintings. The new technique employed *tesserae* (Latin for "cubes" or "dice"). These tiny cut stones gave artists much greater flexibility because they could adjust the size and shape of the tesserae, eliminating the need for lead strips to indicate contours and interior details. More gradual gradations of color also became possible (FIG. 5-70), and mosaicists finally could aspire to rival the achievements of painters.

In Early Christian mosaics (FIGS. 8-13, 8-13A, 8-14, and 8-16 to 8-19A), the tesserae are usually made of glass, which reflects light and makes the surfaces sparkle. Ancient mosaicists occasionally used glass tesserae, but the Romans preferred opaque marble pieces. Mosaics quickly became the standard means of decorating walls and vaults in Early Christian buildings, although mural paintings were also popular. The mosaics caught the light flooding through the windows in vibrant reflection, producing sharp contrasts and concentrations of color that could focus attention on a composition's central, most relevant features. Early Christian mosaics were not meant to incorporate the subtle tonal changes a naturalistic painter's approach would require. Artists "placed," rather than blended, colors. Bright, hard, glittering texture, set within a rigorously simplified pattern, became the rule. For mosaics situated high in an apse or ambulatory vault or over the nave colonnade, far above the observer's head, the painstaking use of tiny tesserae seen in Roman floor and wall mosaics (FIGS. 5-70 and 7-24) would be meaningless. Early Christian mosaics, designed to be seen from a distance, employed larger tesserae. The mosaicists also set the tesserae unevenly so that their surfaces could catch and reflect the light. Artists favored simple designs for optimal legibility. For several centuries, mosaic, in the service of Christian theology, was the medium of some of the supreme masterpieces of medieval art.

8-14 *The Parting of Abraham and Lot,* mosaic in the nave of Santa Maria Maggiore, Rome, Italy, 432–440.

In this Early Christian glass-tessera mosaic depicting *The Parting of Abraham and Lot,* the artist included the yet-unborn Isaac because of his importance as a prefiguration of Christ.

8-13A Christ as Sol Invictus, late third century.

common in Roman funerary art, although they were susceptible to a Christian interpretation. In one section (FIG. 8-13) of the mosaic in the ambulatory vault, for example, are scenes of putti harvesting grapes and making wine. (Similar scenes decorate Constantina's sarcophagus.) A portrait bust is at the center of a rich vine scroll. A second bust appears in another section of the mosaic vault, but both are heavily restored, and the identification of the pair as Constantina and her husband is uncertain. In the Roman world, wine was primarily associated with Bacchus, but for a Christian, the vineyards brought to mind the wine of the Eucharist and the blood of Christ. Already in the third century, however, mosaics of explicitly Christian content had been used in tombs, for example, in the Mausoleum of the Julii (FIG. 8-13A) in the ancient cemetery beneath Saint Peter's in Rome.

SANTA MARIA MAGGIORE Mosaic decoration (see "Mosaics," above) played an important role in the interiors of Early Christian buildings of all types. In churches, mosaics not only provided a beautiful setting for the Christian liturgy, but also were vehicles for instructing the congregation about biblical stories and Christian dogma. Old Testament themes are the focus of the extensive fifth-century mosaic cycle in the nave of the basilican church of Santa Maria Maggiore in Rome, the first major church in the West dedicated to the Virgin Mary. Construction of the church began in 432, the year after the Council of Ephesus officially designated Mary as the Mother of God (*Theotokos,* "bearer of god" in Greek). The council, convened to debate whether Mary had given birth to the man Jesus or to God as man, ruled that the divine and human coexisted in Christ and that Mary was indeed the Mother of God.

One mosaic panel (FIG. 8-14) dramatically represents *The Parting of Abraham and Lot,* as set forth in Genesis, the Bible's opening book. Agreeing to disagree, Abraham's nephew Lot leads his family and followers to the right, toward the city of Sodom, while Abraham heads for Canaan, moving toward a basilica-like building (perhaps symbolizing the Church) on the left. Lot's is the evil choice, and the instruments of the evil (his two daughters) stand in front of him. The figure of the yet-unborn Isaac, the instrument of good (and, as noted earlier, a prefiguration of Christ), stands before his father, Abraham.

The cleavage of the two groups is emphatic, and the mosaicist represented each group using a shorthand device called a *head cluster,* which had precedents in antiquity and a long history in Christian art. The figures engage in a sharp dialogue of glance and gesture. The wide eyes turn in their sockets, and the enlarged hands make broad gestures. This kind of simplified motion, which is characteristic of Late Antique narrative art of Roman, Jewish, and Christian subject matter alike, has great power to communicate without ambiguity. But the Abraham and Lot mosaic also reveals the heritage of classical art. The town in the background of the Abraham and Lot mosaic would not be out of place in a Roman mural (FIG. 7-19, *left*) or on the Column of Trajan (FIG. 7-1), and the figures themselves are modeled in light and dark, cast shadows, and still loom with massive solidity. Another century had to pass before Western Christian mosaicists portrayed figures as flat images, rather than as three-dimensional bodies, finally rejecting the norms of classical art in favor of a style better suited for a focus on the spiritual instead of the natural world. Early Christian art, like Late Antique Roman art in general, vacillates between these two stylistic poles.

Ravenna

In the decades after the 324 founding of Constantinople, the New Rome in the East, and the death of Constantine in 337, the pace of Christianization of the Roman Empire quickened. In 380 the emperor Theodosius I (r. 379–395) issued an edict finally establishing Christianity as the state religion. In 391 he enacted a ban against worship of the old Roman gods, and in 394 he abolished the Olympic Games, the enduring symbol of the classical world and its values.

Theodosius died in 395, and imperial power passed to his two sons, Arcadius (r. 395–408), who became Emperor of the East, and Honorius (r. 395–423), Emperor of the West. In 404, when the Visigoths, under their king, Alaric (r. 395–410), threatened to overrun Italy from the northwest, Honorius moved his capital from Milan to Ravenna, an ancient Roman city (perhaps founded by the Etruscans) near Italy's Adriatic coast, some 80 miles south of Venice. In 410, Alaric captured Rome, and in 476, Ravenna fell to Odoacer (r. 476–493), the first Germanic king of Italy. Odoacer was overthrown in turn by Theodoric (r. 471–526), king of the Ostrogoths, who established his capital at Ravenna in 493. Ravenna fell to the Byzantine emperor Justinian in 539, and the subsequent history of the city belongs with that of Byzantium (see Chapter 9).

MAUSOLEUM OF GALLA PLACIDIA The so-called Mausoleum of Galla Placidia, Honorius's half-sister, is a rather small *cruciform* (cross-shaped) structure (FIG. 8-15) with barrel-vaulted arms and a tower at the *crossing.* Built shortly after 425, almost a quarter century before Galla Placidia's death in 450, it was probably originally a chapel to the martyred Saint Lawrence. The building was once thought to be Galla Placidia's tomb, however, hence its name today. The chapel adjoined the narthex of the now greatly altered palace-church of Santa Croce (Holy Cross), which was also cruciform in plan. The chapel's cross arms are of unequal length, so that the building has a longitudinal orientation, unlike the centrally planned Santa Costanza (FIGS. 8-11 and 8-12), but because all four arms are very short, the emphasis is on the tall *crossing tower* with

8-16 Interior of the Mausoleum of Galla Placidia, Ravenna, Italy, ca. 425.

Before Late Antiquity, mosaics were usually confined to floors. Inside the so-called Mausoleum of Galla Placidia, mosaics cover every square inch of the interior above the marble-faced walls.

8-15 Mausoleum of Galla Placidia, Ravenna, Italy, ca. 425. ◼◀

This cruciform chapel with a domed crossing is an early example of the combination of central and longitudinal plans. The unadorned brick shell encloses a rich ensemble of mosaics.

Jesus sits among his flock, haloed and robed in gold and purple. The landscape and the figures, with their cast shadows, are the work of a mosaicist still rooted in the naturalistic classical tradition.

Christ as Good Shepherd is the subject of the lunette (FIG. 8-17) above the entrance. No earlier version of the Good Shepherd is as regal as this one. Instead of carrying a lamb on his shoulders (FIGS. 8-6 to 8-8), Jesus sits among his flock, haloed and robed in gold and purple. To his left and right, the sheep are distributed evenly in groups of three. But their arrangement is rather loose and informal, and they occupy a carefully described landscape extending from foreground to background beneath a blue sky. As at Santa Maria Maggiore (FIG. 8-14), all the forms have three-dimensional bulk and are still deeply rooted in the classical tradition.

its vault resembling a dome. This small, unassuming building thus represents one of the earliest successful fusions of the two basic Late Antique plans—the longitudinal, used for basilican churches, and the central, used primarily for baptisteries and mausoleums. It introduced, on a small scale, a building type that was to have a long history in church architecture: the longitudinally planned building with a vaulted or domed crossing.

The chapel's unadorned brick shell encloses one of the richest mosaic ensembles (FIG. 8-16) in Early Christian art. Mosaics cover every square inch of the interior surfaces above the marble-faced walls. Garlands and decorative medallions resembling snowflakes on a dark blue ground adorn the barrel vaults of the nave and cross arms. The tower has a large golden cross set against a star-studded sky. Representations of saints and apostles cover the other surfaces. At the end of the nave is a mosaic representing Saint Lawrence next to the gridiron on which he was tortured. The martyred saint carries a cross, suggesting faith in Christ led to his salvation.

SANT'APOLLINARE NUOVO Ravenna is famous for its treasure trove of Early Christian and Byzantine mosaics. About 30 years later than the Galla Placidia mosaics are those of Ravenna's Orthodox Baptistery (FIG. 8-17A). An especially large cycle of mosaics adorns the palace-church Theodoric built in 504, soon after he settled in Ravenna. A three-aisled basilica originally dedicated to "Our Lord Jesus Christ," the church was rededicated in the ninth century as Sant'Apollinare Nuovo, when it acquired the relics of Saint Apollinaris. The rich mosaic decoration of the nave walls (FIG. 8-18) fills three zones. Only the upper two date from Theodoric's time. Hebrew patriarchs

8-17A Orthodox Baptistery, Ravenna, ca. 458.

8-18 Interior of Sant'Apollinare Nuovo (looking east), Ravenna, Italy, dedicated 504. ◼◀

Theodoric, king of the Ostrogoths, established his capital at Ravenna in 493. His palace-church features an extensive series of mosaics depicting Hebrew prophets and scenes from the life of Christ.

8-19 *Miracle of the Loaves and Fishes,* mosaic from the top register of the nave wall (above the clerestory windows in FIG. 8-18) of Sant'Apollinare Nuovo, Ravenna, Italy, ca. 504.

In contrast to FIG. 8-17, Jesus here faces directly toward the viewer. Blue sky has given way to the otherworldly splendor of heavenly gold, the standard background color for medieval mosaics.

and prophets stand between the clerestory windows. Above them, scenes from Christ's life alternate with decorative panels.

The *Miracle of the Loaves and Fishes* mosaic (FIG. **8-19**) stands in sharp contrast to the 80-year-earlier mosaics of the Mausoleum of Galla Placidia. Jesus, beardless, in the imperial dress of gold and purple, and now distinguished by the cross-inscribed *nimbus* (halo) that signifies his divinity, faces directly toward the viewer. With extended arms he directs his disciples to distribute to the great crowd the miraculously increased supply of bread and fish he has produced. The mosaicist told the story with the least number of figures necessary to make its meaning explicit, aligning the figures laterally, moving them close to the foreground, and placing them in a shallow picture box. The composition, so different from those in the lunettes of the Mausoleum of Galla Placidia, is similar to that of the Samuel and David mural (FIG. 8-3) in the Dura-Europos synagogue two and a half centuries earlier as well as

8-19A Hagios Georgios, Thessaloniki, ca. 390–450.

the late-fourth-century mosaics (FIG. **8-19A**) in Hagios Georgios in Thessaloniki, Greece, illustrating once again that Early Christian artists inherited both classical naturalism and Late Antique abstraction from Roman art. But the Sant'Apollinare Nuovo mosaic, like those in Hagios Georgios, differs from the Dura murals as well as the Galla Placidia mosaics in having a golden background, which lifts the mosaic out of time and space and emphasizes the spiritual over the physical. The landscape setting, which the artist who decorated the Mausoleum of Galla Placidia so explicitly described (FIG. 8-17), is here merely a few rocks and bushes enclosing the figure group like parentheses. The blue sky of the physical world has given way to the otherworldly splendor of heavenly gold. The ethereal golden background as well as the weightless figures with their flat, curtainlike garments would soon become the norm in Byzantine art, although even in Byzantium echoes of classical naturalism persisted (see Chapter 9).

LUXURY ARTS

Throughout history, artists have produced so-called "minor arts"—jewelry, metalwork, cameos, ivories, among other crafts—alongside the "major arts" of sculpture and painting. Although the terminology seems to suggest a difference in importance or quality, "minor" refers only to size. Indeed, the artists who fashioned jewelry, carved ivories and cameos, and produced gold and silver vessels by casting or hammering (*repoussé*) employed the costliest materials known. Some of them, for example, Dioscurides, official gem cutter of the emperor Augustus, are among the few Roman artists whose names survive. In Late Antiquity and the Middle Ages, the minor arts—

more appropriately called "luxury arts"—enjoyed high status, and they figure prominently in the history of art through the ages.

Illuminated Manuscripts

Although few examples survive, illustrated books were common in public and private libraries in the ancient world. The long tradition of placing pictures in manuscripts began in pharaonic Egypt (FIG. 3-37) and continued in Greek and Roman times.

VATICAN VERGIL The oldest preserved painted Greek or Latin manuscript is the *Vatican Vergil,* which dates from the early fifth century and is among the earliest preserved illustrated medieval books (see "Medieval Manuscript Illumination," page 249). It originally contained more than 200 pictures illustrating all of Vergil's works. Today, only 50 painted *folios* (leaves or pages) of the *Aeneid* and *Georgics* survive. The manuscript is important not only because of its age. The *Vatican Vergil* is a prime example of traditional Roman iconography and of the classical style long after Theodosius banned worship of the old gods.

The page illustrated here (FIG. **8-20**) includes a section of text from the *Georgics* at the top and a framed illustration below. Vergil recounts his visit to a modest farm near Taranto in southern Italy belonging to an old man from Corycus in Asia Minor. In the illustration, the old farmer sits at the left. His rustic farmhouse is in the background, rendered in three-quarter view. The farmer speaks about the pleasures of the simple life in the country—a recurrent theme in Latin poetry—and on his methods of gardening. His audience is two laborers and, at the far right, Vergil himself in the guise of a farmhand. The style is reminiscent of Pompeian landscapes, with quick touches that suggest space and atmosphere. In fact, the heavy, dark frame has close parallels in the late Pompeian styles of mural painting (FIG. 7-22).

VIENNA GENESIS The oldest well-preserved painted manuscript containing biblical scenes is the early-sixth-century *Vienna Genesis,* so called because of its present location. The book is sumptuous. The pages are fine calfskin dyed with rich purple, the same dye used to give imperial cloth its distinctive color. The Greek text is in silver ink.

Medieval Manuscript Illumination

Rare as medieval books are, they are far more numerous than their ancient predecessors. An important invention during the Early Roman Empire was the *codex,* which greatly aided the dissemination of manuscripts as well as their preservation. A codex is much like a modern book, composed of separate leaves (*folios*) enclosed within a cover and bound together at one side. The new format superseded the long manuscript scroll (*rotulus*) of the Egyptians, Greeks, Etruscans, and Romans. (The Etruscan magistrate Lars Pulena, FIG. 6-15; the philosophers on Roman and Early Christian sarcophagi, FIGS. 7-71 and 8-7; and Christ himself in his role as teacher, FIGS. 8-1 and 8-8A, all hold rotuli in their hands.) Much more durable *vellum* (calfskin) and *parchment* (lambskin), which provided better surfaces for painting, also replaced the comparatively brittle *papyrus* used for ancient scrolls. As a result, luxuriousness of ornamentation became increasingly typical of sacred books in the Middle Ages, and at times the material beauty of the pages

and their illustrations overwhelm or usurp the spiritual beauty of the text. Art historians refer to the luxurious painted books produced before the invention of the printing press as *illuminated manuscripts,* from the Latin *illuminare,* meaning "to adorn, ornament, or brighten." The oldest preserved examples (FIGS. 8-20 to 8-22) date to the fifth and sixth centuries.

Illuminated books were costly to produce and involved many steps. Numerous artisans performed very specialized tasks, beginning with the curing and cutting (and sometimes the dyeing; FIGS. 8-21, 8-21A, and 8-22) of the animal skin, followed by the sketching of lines to guide the scribe and to set aside spaces for illumination, the lettering of the text, the addition of paintings, and finally the binding of the pages and attachment of covers, buckles, and clasps. The covers could be even more sumptuous than the book itself. Many preserved covers are fashioned of gold and decorated with jewels, ivory carvings, and repoussé reliefs (FIG. 11-16).

1 in.

8-20 *Old Farmer of Corycus,* **folio 7 verso of the** *Vatican Vergil,* **ca. 400–420. Tempera on parchment, 1' $\frac{1}{2}$" × 1'. Biblioteca Apostolica Vaticana, Rome.**

The earliest surviving painted Latin manuscript is a collection of the poet Vergil's works. This page includes part of the text of the *Georgics* and a pastoral scene reminiscent of Roman landscape murals.

1 in.

8-21 *Rebecca and Eliezer at the Well,* **folio 7 recto of the** *Vienna Genesis,* **early sixth century. Tempera, gold, and silver on purple vellum, 1' $\frac{1}{4}$" × 9$\frac{1}{4}$". Österreichische Nationalbibliothek, Vienna.**

This sumptuously painted book of Genesis is the oldest well-preserved manuscript containing biblical scenes. Two episodes of the Rebecca story appear in a single setting filled with classical motifs.

Folio 7 (FIG. **8-21**) of the *Vienna Genesis* illustrates *Rebecca and Eliezer at the Well* (Gen. 24:15–61). When Isaac, Abraham's son, was 40 years old, his parents sent their servant Eliezer to find a wife for him. Eliezer chose Rebecca, because when he stopped at a well, she was the first woman to draw water for him and his camels. As elsewhere in the manuscript (FIG. **8-21A**), the painter presented

more than one episode of the story within a single frame, employing an ancient manner of pictorial storytelling called *continuous narration* (compare FIG. 7-44A). In the first episode, at the left, Rebecca leaves the city of Nahor to fetch water from the well.

8-21A Story of Jacob, *Vienna Genesis,* early sixth century.

8-22 *Christ before Pilate*, folio 8 verso of the *Rossano Gospels*, early sixth century. Tempera on purple vellum, 11″ × 10¼″. Museo Diocesano d'Arte Sacra, Rossano.

The sources for medieval manuscript illustrations were diverse. The way the people form an arch around Pilate on this page suggests the composition derives from a painting in an apse.

In the second episode, she offers water to Eliezer and his camels, while one of them already laps water from the well. The artist painted Nahor as a walled city seen from above, like the cityscapes in the Santa Maria Maggiore mosaics (FIG. 8-14), the Column of Trajan (FIG. 7-1), and innumerable earlier Roman representations of cities in painting and relief sculpture. Rebecca walks to the well along the colonnaded avenue of a Roman city. A seminude female personification of a spring is the source of the well water. These are further reminders of the persistence of classical motifs and stylistic modes in Early Christian art.

Contemporaneous with, but radically different from, the mosaic panels (FIG. 8-19) of Sant'Apollinare Nuovo, the *Vienna Genesis* incorporates many anecdotal details, such as the drinking camel and Rebecca bracing herself with her raised left foot on the rim of the well as she tips up her jug for Eliezer. Nonetheless, the illuminator placed the figures in a blank landscape except for the miniature city and the road to the well. As at Ravenna, only those elements necessary to tell the story and set the scene are present, nothing else.

ROSSANO GOSPELS Closely related to the *Vienna Genesis* is another early-sixth-century Greek manuscript, the *Rossano Gospels,* the earliest preserved illuminated book containing illustrations of the New Testament. By this time a canon of New Testament iconography had been fairly well established. As in the *Vienna Genesis,* the text of the *Rossano Gospels* is in silver ink on purple-dyed vellum. The Rossano artist, however, attempted with considerable success to harmonize the colors with the purple

background. The subject of folio 8 (FIG. **8-22**) is the appearance of Jesus before Pilate, who asks the Jews to choose between Jesus and Barabbas (Matt. 27:2–26). The vividly gesturing figures are on two levels separated by a simple ground line, which not only separates the figures spatially but also temporally. In the upper level, Pilate presides over the tribunal. He sits indoors on an elevated dais, following a long-established pattern in Roman art (FIG. 7-76). The people form an arch around Pilate. (The artist may have based the composition on a painting in an apse—an appropriate setting for a seated magistrate.) They demand the death of Jesus, while a court scribe records the proceedings. Below, and outdoors, are Jesus (here a bearded adult, as soon became the norm for medieval and later depictions of Christ; compare FIG. 8-6A) and the bound Barabbas. The painter explicitly labeled Barabbas to avoid any possible confusion and make the picture as readable as the text. Neither the haloed Christ nor Pilate on his magistrate's dais, flanked by painted imperial portraits, needed any further identification.

Metalwork

Especially prized in antiquity and throughout the Middle Ages were items of tableware fashioned out of precious metals, for example, the gold Achaemenid rhyton (FIG. 2-26A) from Hamadan and the Mycenaean drinking cups (FIG. 4-23A) from Vapheio, discussed earlier.

MILDENHALL TREASURE In 1942, a farmer plowing his fields near Mildenhall, England, discovered a hoard of silver tableware dating to the mid-fourth century CE. The "Mildenhall Treasure" must have been the proud possession of a wealthy local family. The hoard consists of 34 silver pieces, including bowls, platters, ladles, and spoons. The most spectacular item is a large platter known as the "Great Dish" (FIG. **8-23**). At the center is the bearded head of the god Oceanus, framed by a ring of Nereids (sea nymphs).

8-23 Oceanus and Nereids, and drinking contest between Bacchus and Hercules, "Great Dish," from Mildenhall, England, mid-fourth century CE. Silver, 1′ 11¾″ diameter. British Museum, London.

Part of a hoard of silver tableware owned by a Christian family, this large platter nonetheless features sea deities and a drinking contest between Bacchus, the Roman god of wine, and Hercules.

Ivory Carving

Ivory has been prized since the earliest times, when sculptors fashioned the tusks of Ice Age European mammoths into pendants, beads, and other items for body adornment, and, occasionally, statuettes (FIGS. 1-4 and 1-5A). The primary ivory sources in the historical period have been the elephants of India and especially Africa, where the species is larger than the Asian counterpart and the tusks longer, heavier, and of finer grain. African elephant tusks 5 to 6 feet in length and weighing 10 pounds are common, but tusks of male elephants can be 10 feet long or more and weigh well over 100 pounds. Carved ivories are familiar, if precious, finds at Mesopotamian and Egyptian sites, and ivory objects were also coveted in the prehistoric Aegean (FIG. 4-24) and throughout the classical world. Most frequently employed then for household objects, small votive offerings, and gifts to the deceased, ivory also could be used for grandiose statues such as Phidias's *Athena Parthenos* (FIG. 5-46).

In the Greco-Roman world, people admired ivory both for its beauty and because of its exotic origin. Elephant tusks were costly imports, and Roman generals proudly displayed them in triumphal processions when they paraded the spoils of war before the people. (In FIG. 9-4, a barbarian brings tribute to a Byzantine emperor in the form of an ivory tusk.) Adding to the expense of the material itself was that only highly skilled artisans were capable of working in ivory. The tusks were very hard and of irregular shape, and the ivory workers needed a full toolbox of saws, chisels, knives, files, and gravers close at hand to cut the tusks into blocks for statuettes or thin plaques decorated with relief figures and ornamentation.

In Late Antiquity and the early medieval period, artists chose ivory most frequently for book covers, chests and boxes (FIG. 8-24),

1 in.

8-24 *Suicide of Judas* and *Crucifixion*, plaque from a box, ca. 420. Ivory, $3'' \times 3\frac{7}{8}''$. British Museum, London. ◼◀

This plaque from a luxurious ivory box is the first known representation of the *Crucifixion of Christ*, shown here as a beardless youth who experiences no pain. At the left, Judas, his betrayer, hangs himself.

and diptychs (FIGS. 8-25 and 9-2). A *diptych* is a pair of hinged tablets, usually of wood, with a wax layer on the inner sides for writing letters and other documents. (The court scribe recording Jesus' trial in the *Rossano Gospels*, FIG. 8-22, and the women in two painted portraits from Pompeii, FIGS. 7-25 and 7-25A, both hold wooden diptychs.) Diptychs fashioned from ivory generally were reserved for ceremonial and official purposes—for example, to announce the election of a consul or a marriage between two wealthy families or to commemorate the death of an elevated member of society.

A larger outer band celebrates the consumption of wine and features a drinking contest between Bacchus (with his left foot resting on a panther) and Hercules, who is so drunk two satyrs struggle to support him. Three of the spoons bear the Greek letters *chi, rho, alpha,* and *omega*—explicit references to Christ (FIG. 8-6A)—but the figural decoration of all the items in the treasure illustrates classical mythology. The hoard attests to the survival of the Roman gods and of classical iconography during the Late Antique period even in Christian contexts.

Ivory Carving

Among the other important luxury arts of Late Antiquity was ivory carving, which has an even longer history in the ancient world than does metalwork (see "Ivory Carving," above).

SUICIDE OF JUDAS **AND** *CRUCIFIXION* A century before a manuscript painter illuminated the pages of the *Rossano Gospels* (FIG. 8-22) with scenes from the passion cycle, a Roman or northern Italian sculptor produced a series of ivory plaques for a small box that dramatically recount the suffering and triumph of Christ. The narrative on the box begins with Pilate washing his hands, Jesus carrying the cross on the road to Calvary, and the denial of Peter, all compressed into a single panel. The plaque illustrated here, *Suicide of Judas* (FIG. **8-24**), is the next in the sequence and shows, at the left, Judas hanging from a tree with his open bag of silver dumped on the ground beneath his feet. The *Crucifixion* is at the right. The Virgin Mary and Joseph of Arimathea are to the left of the cross. On the other side, Longinus thrusts his spear into the side of the "king of the Jews" (the inscribed letters *REX IVD* appear above Jesus' head).

8-25 Woman sacrificing at an altar, right leaf of the diptych of the Nicomachi and the Symmachi, ca. 400. Ivory, 11¾″ × 5½″. Victoria & Albert Museum, London.

Even after Theodosius banned all pagan cults in 391, some Roman families still practiced the ancient rites. The sculptor who carved this ivory plaque also carried on the classical artistic style.

SYMMACHORVM

1 in.

The two remaining panels show two Marys and two soldiers at the open doors of a tomb with an empty coffin within and the doubting Thomas touching the wound of the risen Christ.

The series is one of the oldest cycles of passion scenes preserved today. It dates to the period when artists were beginning to establish the standard iconographical types for medieval narratives of Christ's life. On these plaques, Jesus always appears as a beardless youth. In the *Crucifixion* scene (FIG. 8-24, *right*), the earliest known rendition of the subject in the history of art, Jesus exhibits a superhuman imperviousness to pain. He is a muscular, nearly nude, heroic figure who appears virtually weightless. Jesus does not *hang* from the cross. He is *displayed* on it—a divine being with open eyes who has conquered death. The striking contrast between the powerful frontal unsuffering Jesus on the cross and the limp hanging body of his betrayer with his snapped neck is highly effective, both visually and symbolically.

DIPTYCH OF THE SYMMACHI Although Constantine endorsed Christianity and dedicated his New Rome in the East to the Christian God, not everyone converted to the new religion, even after Theodosius banned all ancient cults and closed all temples in 391. An ivory plaque (FIG. **8-25**), probably produced in Rome around 400, strikingly exhibits the endurance of the traditional Roman gods and of the classical style on the eve of Alaric's sack of the "eternal city." The ivory, one of a pair of leaves of a diptych, may commemorate either the marriage of members of two powerful Roman families of the senatorial class, the Nicomachi and the Symmachi, or the passing within a decade of two prominent male members of the two families. Whether or not the diptych refers to any specific event(s), the Nicomachi and the Symmachi here ostentatiously reaffirmed their faith in the old gods. Certainly, they favored the aesthetic ideals of the classical past, as exemplified by the stately processional friezes of the Greek Parthenon (FIG. 5-50, *bottom*) and the Roman Ara Pacis (FIG. 7-31).

The leaf inscribed "of the Symmachi" (FIG. 8-25) represents a woman sacrificing at an altar in front of a tree. She wears ivy in her hair and seems to be celebrating the rites of Bacchus—the same wine god featured on the Mildenhall silver platter (FIG. 8-23). Some scholars dispute the identity of the divinity honored, but no one questions that the deity is one of the Roman gods whose worship had been banned. The other diptych panel, inscribed "of the Nicomachi," also shows a woman at an open-air altar. On both panels, the precise yet fluent and graceful line, the relaxed poses, and the mood of spiritual serenity reveal an artist who practiced within a still-vital classical tradition that idealized human beauty as its central focus. The great senatorial magnates of Rome, who resisted the Empire-wide imposition of the Christian faith at the end of the fourth century, probably deliberately sustained the classical tradition. Despite the widespread adoption during the third and fourth centuries of the new non-naturalistic Late Antique aesthetic featuring wafer-thin frontal figures, the classical tradition in art lived on

and was never fully extinguished in the Middle Ages. Classical art survived in intermittent revivals, renovations, and restorations side by side and in contrast with the opposing nonclassical medieval styles until it rose to dominance once again in the Renaissance.

LATE ANTIQUITY

PRE-CONSTANTINIAN 192–306

▌ The Second Commandment prohibition against worshiping images once led scholars to think the Jews of the Roman Empire had no figural art, but the synagogue at Dura-Europos contains an extensive series of mural paintings illustrating episodes from the Hebrew scriptures. The Dura synagogue, like the Christian community house at the same site, was a remodeled private home.

▌ Christ was crucified ca. 33, but very little Christian art or architecture survives from the first centuries of Christianity. "Early Christian art" means the earliest art of Christian content, not the art of Christians at the time of Jesus, and comes primarily from the catacombs of Rome.

▌ During the second half of the third century, Christian sarcophagi adorned with a mixture of Old and New Testament scenes began to appear.

Synagogue, Dura-Europos, ca. 245–256

Santa Maria Antiqua sarophagus, ca. 270

CONSTANTINE 306–337

▌ Constantine's Edict of Milan of 313 granted Christianity legal status equal or superior to the cults of the traditional gods. The emperor was the first great patron of Christian art and built the first churches in Rome, including Old Saint Peter's.

▌ In a Christian ceremony, Constantine dedicated Constantinople as the new capital of the Roman Empire in 330. He was baptized on his deathbed in 337.

▌ Early Christian artists profusely decorated the walls and ceilings of the catacombs with frescoes. Popular themes were Christ as Good Shepherd and the salvation of Jonah.

Old Saint Peter's, Rome, begun ca. 319

SONS OF CONSTANTINE TO JUSTINIAN 337–526

▌ The emperor Theodosius I (r. 379–395) proclaimed Christianity the official religion of the Roman Empire in 380 and banned worship of the old Roman gods in 391.

▌ Honorius (r. 395–423) moved the capital of his Western Roman Empire to Ravenna in 404. Rome fell to the Visigothic king Alaric in 410.

▌ Mosaics became a major vehicle for the depiction of Christian themes in churches. Extensive mosaic cycles are preserved in the nave of Santa Maria Maggiore in Rome and especially in Sant'Apollinare Nuovo in Ravenna.

▌ The earliest preserved manuscripts featuring illustrations of the Old and New Testaments date to the early sixth century. Illuminated manuscripts, such as the *Vienna Genesis*, would become one of the major art forms of the Middle Ages.

▌ Late Antique artists excelled in producing luxurious items for domestic use in silver and ivory, such as tableware, boxes, and diptychs, and decorated them with reliefs depicting both Christian and traditional Roman themes.

Santa Maria Maggiore,
Rome, 432–440

Vienna Genesis,
early sixth century

The Byzantine empress Theodora holds the golden cup of wine for the Eucharist as her husband carries the platter of bread. But neither she nor Justinian was ever in Ravenna.

The apse mosaics celebrate Justinian's right to rule on earth. Christ, dressed in the purple robe worn by Byzantine emperors, sits on the orb of the world at the time of his second coming.

The emperor Justinian and Maximianus, the bishop who dedicated the church, appear in the apse. The mosaic program of San Vitale underscores the Byzantine emperor's dual political and religious roles.

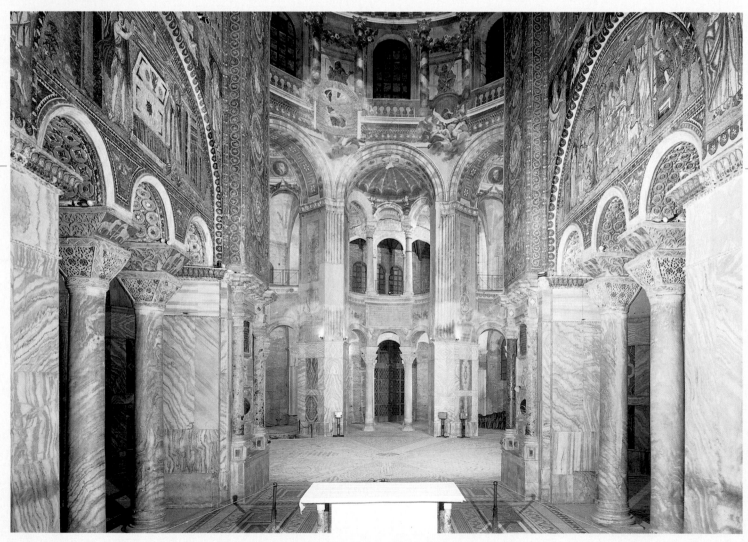

9-1 Interior of San Vitale (looking from the apse into the choir), Ravenna, Italy, 526–547. ◼◀

BYZANTIUM

San Vitale is a central-plan church with an octagonal plan modeled on churches in Constantinople. Its austere facade gives no hint of its sumptuous marble- and mosaic-covered interior.

CHURCH AND STATE UNITED

San Vitale (FIG. 9-1), dedicated by Bishop Maximianus in 547 in honor of Saint Vitalis, who died a martyr at the hands of the Romans at Ravenna in the second century, is the most spectacular building in that northern Italian outpost of the Byzantine Empire. The church is an unforgettable experience for all who have entered it and marveled at its intricate design and magnificent mosaics.

The exterior's octagonal regularity is not readily apparent inside the centrally planned church. The design features two concentric octagons. The dome-covered inner octagon rises above the surrounding octagon to provide the interior with clerestory lighting. Eight large rectilinear piers alternate with curved, columned exedrae, pushing outward into the surrounding two-story ambulatory. A rich diversity of ever-changing perspectives greets visitors walking through the building. Arches looping over arches, curving and flattened spaces, and wall and vault shapes all seem to change constantly with the viewer's position. Light filtered through alabaster-paned windows plays over the glittering mosaics and glowing marbles covering the building's complex surfaces, producing a sumptuous effect.

The mosaics in San Vitale's choir and apse, like the building itself, must be regarded as one of the greatest achievements of Byzantine art. Completed less than a decade after the Ostrogoths surrendered Ravenna (see Chapter 8), the apse and choir decorations form a unified composition, whose theme is the holy ratification of the emperor Justinian's right to rule. In the apse vault, Christ sits on the orb of the world at the time of his second coming. On the choir wall to the left of the apse mosaic appears Justinian. He stands on the Savior's right side. The two are united visually and symbolically by the imperial purple they wear and by their haloes. A dozen attendants accompany Justinian, paralleling Christ's 12 apostles. Thus, the mosaic program underscores the dual political and religious roles of the Byzantine emperor. The laws of the Church and the laws of the state, united in the laws of God, manifest themselves in the person of the emperor, whose right to rule was God-given.

Justinian's counterpart on the opposite wall of the apse is his empress, Theodora, with her corresponding retinue. Both processions move into the apse, Justinian proceeding from left to right and Theodora from right to left, in order to take part in the Eucharist. Justinian carries the paten containing the bread, and Theodora the golden cup with the wine. Neither she nor Justinian ever visited Ravenna, however. Their participation in the liturgy at San Vitale is pictorial fiction. The mosaics are proxies for the absent sovereigns. Justinian is present because he was the head of the Byzantine state, and his appearance in the mosaic underscores that his authority extends over his territories in Italy.

THE CHRISTIAN ROMAN EMPIRE

In 324, when Constantine I founded Constantinople (Greek, "Constantine's city") on the site of ancient Byzantium, he legitimately could claim to be ruler of a united Roman Empire. But when Theodosius I (r. 379–395) died, he divided the Empire between his sons. Arcadius, the elder brother, became Emperor of the East, and Honorius, Emperor of the West. Arcadius ruled from Constantinople. After the sack of Rome in 410, Honorius moved the Western capital to Milan and later to Ravenna. Though not formally codified, Theodosius's division of the Empire (which paralleled Diocletian's century-earlier division of administrative responsibility) became permanent. Centralized government soon disintegrated in the Western half and gave way to warring kingdoms (see Chapter 11).

The Eastern half of the Roman Empire, only loosely connected by religion to the West and with only minor territorial holdings there, had a long and complex history of its own. Centered at Constantinople—dubbed the New Rome—the Eastern Christian Empire remained a cultural and political entity for a millennium, until the last of a long line of Eastern Roman emperors, ironically named Constantine XI, died at Constantinople in 1453, defending the city in vain against the Ottoman Turks.

Historians refer to that Eastern Christian Roman Empire as Byzantium (MAP 9-1), employing Constantinople's original name, and use the term *Byzantine* to identify whatever pertains to Byzantium—its territory, its history, and its culture. The Byzantine emperors, however, did not use the term to define themselves. They called their empire Rome and themselves Romans. Though they spoke Greek and not Latin, the Eastern Roman emperors never

MAP 9-1 The Byzantine Empire at the death of Justinian in 565.

BYZANTIUM

324	Early Byzantine	726	843	Middle Byzantine	1204	1261	Late Byzantine	1453

- Constantine founds Constantinople, 324
- Justinian builds Hagia Sophia with a 180-foot-high dome resting on pendentives, 532–537
- Dedication of San Vitale at Ravenna with its rich mosaic program, 547
- Icon painting flourishes at Mount Sinai until Leo III bans picturing the divine in 726

- Theodora repeals iconoclasm, 843
- Churches feature exterior walls with decorative patterning, Greek-cross plans, and domes on drums resting on pendentives or squinches
- Ivory triptychs for personal prayer become popular

- Michael VIII recaptures Constantinople after the Crusader sack of 1204
- Revival of mural and icon painting
- Fall of Constantinople to the Ottoman Turks, 1453

relinquished their claim as the legitimate successors to the ancient Roman emperors (see "The Emperors of New Rome," page 259). During the long course of its history, Byzantium was the Christian buffer against the expansion of Islam into central and northern Europe, and its cultural influence was felt repeatedly in Europe throughout the Middle Ages. Byzantium Christianized the Slavic peoples of the Balkans and of Russia, giving them its Orthodox religion and alphabet, its literary culture, and its art and architecture. Byzantium's collapse in 1453 brought the Ottoman Empire into Europe as far as the Danube River, but Constantinople's fall had an impact even farther to the west. The westward flight of Byzantine scholars from the Rome of the East introduced the study of classical Greek to Italy and helped inspire there the new consciousness of antiquity historians call the Renaissance (see Chapter 14).

Art historians divide the history of Byzantine art into three periods. The first, Early Byzantine, extends from the founding of Constantinople in 324 to the onset of *iconoclasm* (the destruction of images used in religious worship) in 726 under Leo III. The Middle Byzantine period begins with the renunciation of iconoclasm in 843 and ends with the Western Crusaders' occupation of Constantinople in 1204. Late Byzantine corresponds to the two centuries after the Byzantines recaptured Constantinople in 1261 until its final loss in 1453 to the Ottoman Turks and the conversion of many churches to mosques (see Chapter 10).

EARLY BYZANTINE ART

The golden age of Early Byzantine art began with the accession of Justinian in 537, but important Byzantine artworks survive from the century before Justinian's reign, especially ivories and illuminated manuscripts—costly, treasured objects, as in the Late Antique West (see Chapter 8).

Before Justinian

ARCHANGEL MICHAEL In the early sixth century, a master carver, probably working in Constantinople, produced the largest extant Byzantine ivory panel (FIG. **9-2**). It is probably the right half of a hinged diptych and depicts Saint Michael the Archangel. The inscription opens with the words "Receive these gifts." The dedication is perhaps a reference to the cross-surmounted orb of power the archangel once offered to a Byzantine emperor depicted on the missing diptych leaf. The prototype of Michael must have been a classical winged Victory, although Victory was personified as a woman in Greco-Roman art and usually carried the palm branch of victory, as she does on a somewhat later Byzantine ivory (FIG. 9-4). The Christian artist here ingeniously adapted a classical personification and imbued it with new meaning.

The archangel's flowing drapery, which reveals the body's shape, the delicately incised wings, and the facial type and coiffure are other indications the artist who carved this ivory was still working in the classical tradition. Nonetheless, the Byzantine sculptor had little concern for the rules of naturalistic representation. The archangel dwarfs the architectural setting. Michael's feet rest on three steps at once, and his upper body, wings, and arms are in front of the column shafts, whereas his lower body is behind the column bases at the top of the receding staircase. These spatial ambiguities do not detract from the figure's striking beauty, but they do signify the emergence in Byzantium of the same aesthetic already noted in the Late Antique mosaics of Thessaloniki (FIG. 8-19A). Here, as there, the Byzantine artist rejected the goal

9-2 Saint Michael the Archangel, right leaf of a diptych, early sixth century. Ivory, 1′ 5″ × 5½″. British Museum, London.

The sculptor who carved this largest extant Byzantine ivory panel modeled Saint Michael on a classical winged Victory, but the archangel seems to float in front of the architecture rather than stand in it.

of most classical artists: to render the three-dimensional world in convincing and consistent fashion and to people that world with fully modeled figures firmly rooted on the ground. Michael seems more to float in front of the architecture than to stand in it.

9-3 **Anicia Juliana between Magnanimity and Prudence, folio 6 verso of the *Vienna Dioskorides*, from Honoratai, near Constantinople (Istanbul), Turkey, ca. 512.** Tempera on vellum, 1′ 3″ × 1′ 11″. Österreichische Nationalbibliothek, Vienna.

In gratitude for her generosity, the people of Honoratai presented Anicia Juliana, a great art patron, with a book in which she appears enthroned with personifications of Magnanimity and Prudence.

9-3A Blackberry bush, *Vienna Dioskorides*, 512.

VIENNA DIOSKORIDES The physical world was, however, the focus of one of the rare surviving early medieval secular books. In the mid-first century, a Greek physician named Dioskorides compiled an encyclopedia of medicinal herbs called *De materia medica*. An early-sixth-century copy (FIGS. **9-3** and **9-3A**) of this medical manual, nearly a thousand pages in length, is in the Austrian National Library. The so-called *Vienna Dioskorides* was a gift from the people of Honoratai, near Constantinople, to Anicia Juliana, daughter of the short-lived Emperor of the West, Anicias Olybrias (r. 472). Anicia Juliana was a leading patron of the arts and had built a church dedicated to the Virgin Mary at Honoratai in 512. She also provided the funds to construct Saint Polyeuktos in Constantinople between 524 and 527. The excavated ruins of that church indicate it was a domed basilica—an important forerunner of the pioneering design of Justinian's Hagia Sophia (FIGS. **9-5** to **9-8**).

The *Vienna Dioskorides* contains 498 illustrations, almost all images of plants (FIG. **9-3A**) rendered with a scientific fidelity to nature that stands in stark contrast to contemporaneous Byzantine paintings and mosaics of religious subjects. It is likely the *Vienna Dioskorides* painters copied the illustrations as well as the text of a classical manuscript. One page, however, cannot be a copy—the

dedication page (FIG. 9-3) featuring a portrait of Anicia Juliana in an eight-pointed star and circle frame. This earliest known illustrated dedication page shows Anicia Juliana enthroned between personifications of Magnanimity and Prudence, with a kneeling figure labeled Gratitude of the Arts at her feet. The princess holds a book in her left hand, probably this *De material medica*. The shading and modeling of the figures, the heads seen at oblique angles, the rendering of the throne's footstool in perspective, and the use of personifications establish that the painter still worked in the classical tradition most other Byzantine artists had by then rejected.

Justinianic Art and Architecture

Historians and art historians alike regard the reign of the emperor Justinian (r. 527–565) as Byzantium's first golden age, during which the Christian Roman Empire briefly rivaled the old Roman Empire in power and extent (MAP 9-1). Justinian's generals, Belisarius and Narses, drove the Ostrogoths out of Italy, expelled the Vandals from the African provinces, beat back the Bulgars on the northern frontier, and held the Sasanians at bay on the eastern borders. At home, the emperor put down a dangerous rebellion in 532 of political and religious factions in the city (the Nika revolt) and supervised the codification of Roman law in a great work known as the *Corpus juris civilis* (*Code of Civil Law*), which became the foundation of the law systems of many modern European nations. Justinian could claim, with considerable justification, to have revived the glory of Old Rome in New Rome.

At the beginning of the fourth century, Constantine recognized Christianity and became its first imperial sponsor. By the end of the century, Theodosius had established Christianity as the Roman Empire's official religion. It was Justinian, however, who proclaimed Christianity the Empire's only lawful religion, specifically the Orthodox Christian doctrine. In Orthodox Christianity, the central article of faith is the equality of the three aspects of the Trinity of Father, Son, and Holy Spirit (as stated in Roman Catholic, Protestant, and Eastern Orthodox creeds today). All other versions of Christianity were heresies, especially the Arian, which asserted that the Father and Son were distinct entities and that the Father created the Son. Therefore, Christ was not equal to God. Also classified as a heresy was the Monophysite view that Christ had only one nature, which was divine, contrary to both the Orthodox and Arian belief that Christ had a dual divine-human nature. Justinian considered it his first duty not only to stamp out the few surviving polytheistic cults but also to crush all those who professed any Christian doctrine other than the Orthodox.

BARBERINI IVORY Justinianic art, like Late Antique art, was both religious and secular. A masterwork of political art is the ivory plaque known today as the *Barberini Ivory* (FIG. **9-4**) because it was once part of the 17th-century collection of Cardinal Barberini in Rome. Carved in five parts (one is lost), the panel shows at the center an emperor, usually identified as Justinian, riding triumphantly on a rearing horse, while a startled, half-hidden barbarian recoils in fear behind him. The dynamic twisting postures of both horse and rider and the motif of the spear-thrusting equestrian emperor are familiar motifs in Roman imperial works (see "The Emperors of New Rome," page 259), as are the personifications of bountiful Earth (below the horse) and palm-bearing Victory (flying in to crown the conqueror). Also borrowed from the art of Old Rome are the barbarians at the bottom of the plaque bearing tribute and seeking clemency. Accompanying them are a lion, elephant, and tiger—exotic animals native to Africa and Asia, sites of Justinianic

The Emperors of New Rome

The emperors of Byzantium, the New Rome on the Bosporus, considered themselves the direct successors of the emperors of the Old Rome on the Tiber. Although they proclaimed Orthodox Christianity as the official state religion and suppressed all of Old Rome's polytheistic cults, the political imagery of Byzantine art displays a striking continuity between ancient Rome and medieval Byzantium. Artists continued to portray emperors sitting on thrones holding the orb of the earth in their hands, battling foes while riding on mighty horses, and receiving tribute from defeated enemies. In the Early Byzantine period, official portraits continued to be set up in great numbers throughout the territories Byzantium controlled. But, as was true of the classical world, much of imperial Byzantine statuary is forever lost. Nonetheless, some of the lost portraits of the Byzantine emperors can be visualized from miniature versions of them on ivory reliefs such as the *Barberini Ivory* (FIG. 9-4) and from descriptions in surviving texts.

One especially impressive portrait in the Roman imperial tradition, melted down long ago, depicted the emperor Justinian on horseback atop a grandiose column. Cast in glittering bronze, like the equestrian statue of Marcus Aurelius (FIG. 7-59) set up nearly 400 years earlier, it attested to the continuity between the art of Old and New Rome, where pompous imperial images were commonly displayed at the apex of freestanding columns. (Compare FIG. 7-45, where a statue of Saint Peter has replaced a lost statue of the emperor Trajan.) Procopius, the historian of Justinian's reign, described the equestrian portrait:

> Finest bronze, cast into panels and wreaths, encompasses the stones [of the column] on all sides, both binding them securely together and covering them with adornment. . . . This bronze is in color softer than pure gold, while in value it does not fall much short of an equal weight of silver. At the summit of the column stands a huge bronze horse turned towards the east, a most noteworthy sight. . . . Upon this horse is mounted a bronze image of the Emperor like a colossus. . . . He wears a cuirass in heroic fashion and his head is covered with a helmet . . . and a kind of radiance flashes forth from there. . . . He gazes towards the rising sun, steering his course, I suppose, against the Persians. In his left hand he holds a globe, by which the sculptor has signified that the whole earth and sea were subject to him, yet he carries neither sword nor spear nor any other weapon, but a cross surmounts his globe, by virtue of which alone he has won the kingship and victory in war. Stretching forth his right hand towards the regions of the East and spreading out his fingers, he commands the barbarians that dwell there to remain at home and not to advance any further.*

9-4 Justinian as world conqueror (*Barberini Ivory*), mid-sixth century. Ivory, 1′ 1½″ × 10½″. Musée du Louvre, Paris.

Classical style and motifs lived on in Byzantine art in ivories such as this one. Justinian rides a rearing horse accompanied by personifications of Victory and Earth. Above, Christ blesses the emperor.

Statues such as this one are the missing links in an imperial tradition that never really died and that lived on also in the Holy Roman Empire (FIG. 11-12) and in Renaissance Italy (FIGS. 21-16 and 21-17).

*Cyril Mango, trans., *The Art of the Byzantine Empire, 312–1453: Sources and Documents* (reprint of 1972 ed., Toronto: Toronto University Press, 1986), 110–111.

conquest. At the left, a Roman soldier carries a statuette of another Victory, reinforcing the central panel's message. The source of the emperor's strength, however, comes not from his earthly armies but from God. The uppermost panel depicts two angels holding aloft a youthful image of Christ carrying a cross in his left hand. Christ blesses Justinian with a gesture of his right hand, indicating approval of the emperor's rule.

HAGIA SOPHIA Like the emperors of Old Rome, Justinian was an ambitious builder. In Constantinople alone, he built or restored more than 30 churches of the Orthodox faith. The historian Procopius of Caesarea (ca. 500–ca. 565) declared the emperor's extravagant building program was an obsession that cost his subjects dearly in taxation. But Justinian's monuments defined the Byzantine style in architecture forever after.

9-5 ANTHEMIUS OF TRALLES and ISIDORUS OF MILETUS, aerial view of Hagia Sophia (looking north), Constantinople (Istanbul), Turkey, 532–537. ◼◀

Justinian's reign was the first golden age of Byzantine art and architecture. Hagia Sophia was the most magnificent of the more than 30 churches Justinian built or restored in Constantinople alone.

9-6 ANTHEMIUS OF TRALLES and ISIDORUS OF MILETUS, restored cutaway view of Hagia Sophia, Constantinople (Istanbul), Turkey, 532–537 (John Burge). ◼◀

Hagia Sophia is a domed basilica. Buttressing the great dome are eastern and western half-domes whose thrusts descend, in turn, into smaller half-domes surmounting columned exedrae.

The emperor's most important project was the construction of Hagia Sophia (FIGS. **9-5** and **9-6**), the church of Holy Wisdom, in Constantinople. ANTHEMIUS OF TRALLES and ISIDORUS OF MILETUS, a mathematician and a physicist (neither man an architect in the modern sense of the word), designed and built the church for Justinian between 532 and 537. They began work immediately after fire destroyed an earlier church on the site during the Nika riot in January 532. Justinian intended the new church to rival all other churches ever built and even to surpass in scale and magnificence the Temple of Solomon in Jerusalem. The result was Byzantium's grandest building and one of the supreme accomplishments of world architecture.

Hagia Sophia's dimensions are formidable for any structure not made of steel. In plan (FIG. **9-7**), it is about 270 feet long and

9-7 ANTHEMIUS OF TRALLES and ISIDORUS OF MILETUS, plan of Hagia Sophia, Constantinople (Istanbul), Turkey, 532–537 (John Burge).

In Hagia Sophia, Justinian's architects succeeded in fusing two previously independent architectural traditions: the vertically oriented central-plan building and the longitudinally oriented basilica.

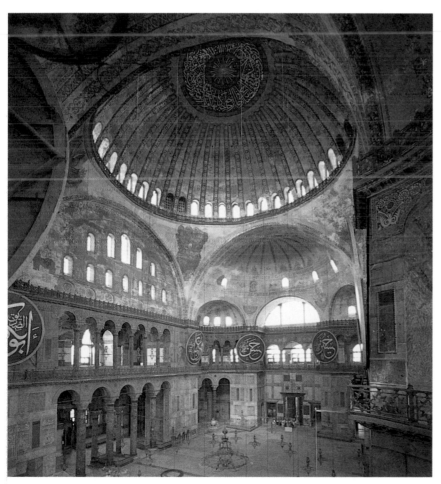

9-8 ANTHEMIUS OF TRALLES and ISIDORUS OF MILETUS, interior of Hagia Sophia (looking southwest), Constantinople (Istanbul), Turkey, 532–537. ◼◀

Pendentive construction made possible Hagia Sophia's lofty dome, which seems to ride on a halo of light. A contemporary said the dome seemed to be suspended by "a golden chain from Heaven."

240 feet wide. The dome is 108 feet in diameter, and its crown rises some 180 feet above the pavement (FIG. **9-8**). (The first dome collapsed in 558. Its replacement required repair in the 9th and 14th centuries. The present dome is steeper and more stable than the original.) In scale, Hagia Sophia rivals the architectural wonders of Rome: the Pantheon, the Baths of Caracalla, and the Basilica of Constantine (see Chapter 7). In exterior view (FIG. 9-5), the great dome dominates the structure, but the building's external aspects today are much changed from their original appearance. The huge buttresses are later additions to the Justinianic design, and after the Ottoman conquest of 1453, when Hagia Sophia became a *mosque*, the Turks constructed four towering *minarets* (see Chapter 10) at the corners of the former church. The building is now a museum.

The characteristic Byzantine plainness and unpretentiousness of the exterior scarcely prepare visitors for the building's interior (FIG. 9-8). A poet and *silentiary* (an usher responsible for maintaining silence in the palace) at Justinian's court, Paul Silentiarius, vividly described the original magnificence of Hagia Sophia's interior:

Who . . . shall sing the marble meadows gathered upon the mighty walls and spreading pavement. . . . [There is stone] from the green flanks of Carystus [and] the speckled Phrygian stone, sometimes rosy mixed with white, sometimes gleaming with purple and silver flowers. There is a wealth of porphyry stone, too, besprinkled with little bright stars. . . . You may see the bright green stone of Laconia and the glittering marble with wavy veins found in the deep gullies of the Iasian peaks, exhibiting slanting streaks of blood-red and livid white; the pale yellow with swirling red from the Lydian headland; the glittering crocus-like golden stone [of Libya]; . . . glittering [Celtic] black [with] here and there an abundance of milk; the pale onyx with glint of precious metal; and [Thessalian marble] in parts vivid green not unlike emerald. . . . It has spots resembling snow next to flashes of black so that in one stone various beauties mingle.[1]

The feature that distinguishes Hagia Sophia from equally lavishly revetted Roman buildings such as the Pantheon (FIG. 7-51) is the special mystical quality of the light flooding the interior. The soaring canopy-like dome that dominates the inside as well as the outside of the church rides on a halo of light from windows in the dome's base. Visitors to Hagia Sophia from Justinian's time to today have been struck by the light within the church and its effect on the human spirit. The 40 windows at the base of the dome create the illusion the dome rests on the light pouring through them.

Procopius observed that the dome looked as if it were suspended by "a golden chain from Heaven" and that "the space is not illuminated by the sun from the outside, but that the radiance is generated within, so great an abundance of light bathes this shrine all around."[2] Paul the Silentiary compared the dome to "the firmament which rests on air" and described the vaulting as covered with "gilded tesserae from which a glittering stream of golden rays pours abundantly and strikes men's eyes with irresistible force. It is as if one were gazing at the midday sun in spring."[3] Thus, Hagia Sophia has a vastness of space shot through with light, and a central dome that appears to be supported by the light it admits. Light is the mystic element—light that

Pendentives and Squinches

Perhaps the most characteristic feature of Byzantine architecture is the placement of a dome, which is circular at its base, over a square, as in the Justinianic church of Hagia Sophia (FIGS. 9-6 to 9-8) and countless later structures (for example, FIGS. 9-21, 9-22, and 9-26). Two structural devices that are hallmarks of Byzantine engineering made this feat possible: *pendentives* and *squinches*.

In pendentive construction (from the Latin *pendere*, "to hang"), a dome rests on what is, in effect, a second, larger dome (FIG. 9-9, *left*). The builders omit the top portion and four segments around the rim of the larger dome, producing four curved triangles, or pendentives. The pendentives join to form a ring and four arches whose planes bound a square. The pendentives and arches transfer the weight of the dome not to the walls but to the four piers from which the arches spring. The first use of pendentives on a monumental scale was in Hagia Sophia (FIGS. 9-6 and 9-8) in the mid-sixth century, although Mesopotamian architects had experimented with them earlier. In Roman and Early Christian central-plan buildings, such as the Pantheon (FIGS. 7-50 and 7-51) and Santa Costanza (FIG. 8-11), the domes spring directly from the circular top of a cylinder (FIG. 7-6d).

The pendentive system is a dynamic solution to the problem of setting a round dome over a square, making possible a union of centralized and longitudinal or basilican structures. A similar effect can be achieved using squinches (FIG. 9-9, *right*)—arches, corbels,

or lintels—that bridge the corners of the supporting walls and form an octagon inscribed within a square. To achieve even greater height, a builder can rest a dome on a cylindrical drum that in turn rests on either pendentives or squinches (FIG. 9-22), but the principle of supporting a dome over a square is the same.

Pendentives   Squinches

9-9 **Dome on pendentives (*left*) and on squinches (*right*).**

Pendentives (triangular sections of a sphere) make it possible to place a dome on a ring over a square. Squinches achieve the same goal by bridging the corners of the square to form an octagonal base.

---

glitters in the mosaics, shines forth from the marbles, and pervades and defines spaces that escape definition. Light seems to dissolve material substance and transform it into an abstract spiritual vision. Pseudo-Dionysius, perhaps the most influential mystic philosopher of the age, wrote in *The Divine Names*: "Light comes from the Good and . . . light is the visual image of God."[4]

PENDENTIVES To achieve this illusion of a floating "dome of Heaven," Anthemius and Isidorus used *pendentives* (see "Pendentives and Squinches," above) to transfer the weight from the great dome to the piers beneath rather than to the walls. With pendentives (FIG. 9-9, *left*), not only could the space beneath the dome be unobstructed but scores of windows also could puncture the walls. The pendentives created the impression of a dome suspended above, not held up by, walls. Experts today can explain the technical virtuosity of Justinian's builders, but it remained a mystery to their contemporaries. Procopius communicated the sense of wonderment experienced by those who entered Justinian's great church: "No matter how much they concentrate their attention on this and that, and examine everything with contracted eyebrows, they are unable to understand the craftsmanship and always depart from there amazed by the perplexing spectacle."[5]

By placing a hemispherical dome on a square base instead of on a circular base, as in the Pantheon (FIGS. 7-50 and 7-51), Anthemius and Isidorus succeeded in fusing two previously independent and seemingly mutually exclusive architectural traditions: the vertically oriented central-plan building and the longitudinally oriented

basilica. Hagia Sophia is, in essence, a domed basilica (FIG. 9-6)—a uniquely successful conclusion to several centuries of experimentation in Christian church architecture. However, the thrusts of the pendentive construction at Hagia Sophia made external buttresses necessary, as well as huge internal northern and southern wall piers and eastern and western half-domes (FIG. 9-5). The semidomes' thrusts descend, in turn, into still smaller half-domes surmounting columned exedrae (FIG. 9-8) that give a curving flow to the design.

The diverse vistas and screenlike ornamented surfaces mask the structural lines. The columnar arcades of the nave and second-story galleries have no real structural function. Like the walls they pierce, they are only part of a fragile "fill" between the huge piers. Structurally, although Hagia Sophia may seem Roman in its great scale and majesty, the organization of its masses is not Roman. The very fact the "walls" in Hagia Sophia are concealed (and barely adequate) piers indicates the architects sought Roman monumentality as an *effect* and did not design the building according to Roman principles. Using brick in place of concrete was a further departure from Roman practice and marks Byzantine architecture as a distinctive structural style. Hagia Sophia's eight great supporting piers are ashlar masonry, but the screen walls are brick, as are the vaults of the aisles and galleries and the dome and semicircular half-domes.

The ingenious design of Hagia Sophia provided the illumination and the setting for the solemn liturgy of the Orthodox faith. The large windows along the rim of the great dome poured light down upon the interior's jeweled splendor, where priests staged the sacred spectacle. Sung by clerical choirs, the Orthodox equivalent of the Latin Mass celebrated the sacrament of the Eucharist at the altar in the apsidal sanctuary, in spiritual reenactment of Jesus' crucifixion. Processions of chanting priests, accompanying the patriarch (archbishop) of Constantinople, moved slowly to and from the sanctuary and the vast nave. The gorgeous array of their vestments (compare FIG. 9-35A) rivaled the interior's polychrome marbles, complementing the interior's finely wrought, gleaming candlesticks and candelabra; the illuminated books bound in gold or ivory and inlaid with jewels and enamels; and the crosses, sacred vessels, and processional banners. Each, with its great richness of texture and color, glowing in shafts of light from the dome, contributed to the majestic ambience of Justinian's great church.

The nave of Hagia Sophia was reserved for the clergy, not the congregation. The laity, segregated by sex, had only partial views of the brilliant ceremony from the shadows of the aisles and galleries, restrained in most places by marble parapets. The emperor was the only layperson privileged to enter the sanctuary. When he participated with the patriarch in the liturgical drama, standing at the pulpit beneath the great dome, his rule was again sanctified and his person exalted. Church and state were symbolically made one (see "Church and State United," page 255). The church building was then the earthly image of the court of Heaven, its light the image of God and God's holy wisdom.

At Hagia Sophia, the intricate logic of Greek theology, the ambitious scale of Rome, the vaulting tradition of Mesopotamia, and the mysticism of Eastern Christianity combined to create a monument that is at once a summation of antiquity and a positive assertion of the triumph of Christian faith.

RAVENNA In 493, Theodoric, the Ostrogoths' greatest king, chose Ravenna, an Etruscan and later a Roman city near the Adriatic coast of Italy south of Venice, as the capital of his kingdom, which encompassed much of the Balkans and all of Italy (see Chapter 8). During the short history of Theodoric's unfortunate successors, Ravenna's importance declined. But in 539, Justinian's general Belisarius captured the city, initiating an important new chapter in its history. Ravenna remained the Eastern Empire's foothold in Italy for two centuries, until the Lombards and then the Franks overtook it. During Justinian's reign, Ravenna enjoyed great prosperity at a time when repeated sieges, conquests, and sackings threatened the "eternal city" of Rome with extinction. As the seat of Byzantine dominion in Italy, Ravenna and its culture became an extension of Constantinople. Its art, even more than that of the Byzantine capital (where relatively little outside of architecture has survived), clearly reveals the transition from the Early Christian to the Byzantine style.

SAN VITALE Construction of Ravenna's greatest shrine, San Vitale (FIGS. 9-1, **9-10**, and **9-11**), began under Bishop Ecclesius (r. 522–532) shortly after Theodoric's death in 526. A wealthy citizen, Julianus Argentarius (Julian the Banker), provided the enormous sum of 26,000 *solidi* (gold coins weighing in excess of 350 pounds) required to proceed with the work. San Vitale is unlike any of the Early Christian churches (FIG. 8-18) of Ravenna. It is not a basilica. Rather, it is centrally planned, like Justinian's churches in Constantinople, and it seems, in fact, to have been loosely modeled on the earlier Church of Saints Sergius and Bacchus there.

As already discussed (FIG. 9-1), San Vitale's design features a dome-covered clerestory-lit central space defined by piers alternating with curved, columned exedrae, creating an intricate eight-leafed plan (FIG. 9-11). The exedrae closely integrate the inner and

9-10 Aerial view of San Vitale (looking northwest), Ravenna, Italy, 526–547. ◼◀

Justinian's general Belisarius captured Ravenna from the Ostrogoths. The city became the seat of Byzantine dominion in Italy. San Vitale honored Saint Vitalis, a second-century Ravenna martyr.

0 10 20 30 40 50 feet
0   5   10   15   20 meters

1. Narthex
2. Domed octagon
3. Apse

9-11 Plan of San Vitale, Ravenna, Italy, 526–547.

Centrally planned like Justinian's churches in Constantinople, San Vitale has a design featuring an off-axis narthex and two concentric octagons. A dome crowns the taller, inner octagon.

youthful in the Early Christian tradition, sits atop the world and holds a scroll with seven seals (Rev. 5:1). The four rivers of Paradise flow beneath him, and rainbow-hued clouds float above. Christ extends the golden martyr's wreath to Vitalis, the patron saint of the church, whom an angel introduces. At Christ's left, another angel presents Bishop Ecclesius, who offers a model of San Vitale to Christ. The arrangement recalls Christ's prophecy of the last days of the world: "And then shall they see the Son of Man coming in the clouds with great power and glory. And then shall he send his angels, and shall gather together his elect from the four winds, from the uttermost part of Heaven" (Mark 13:26–27).

Images and symbols covering the entire sanctuary express the single idea of Christ's redemption of humanity and the reenactment of it in the Eucharist. For example, the lunette mosaic over the two columns on the northern side of the choir depicts the story of Abraham and the three angels. Sarah, Abraham's wife, was 90 years old and childless when three angels visited Abraham. They announced Sarah would bear a son, and she later miraculously gave birth to Isaac. Christians believe the Old Testament angels symbolize the Holy Trinity. Immediately to the right in the lunette is the sacrifice of Isaac, a prefiguration of Christ's crucifixion (see "Jewish Subjects in Christian Art," Chapter 8, page 238).

JUSTINIAN AND THEODORA The most distinctive elements of the mosaic program of San Vitale are the facing panels in the choir depicting Justinian (FIG. 9-13) and Theodora (FIG. 9-14). The positions of the figures are all-important. They express the formulas of precedence and rank. In the Justinian mosaic, the emperor is at the center, distinguished from the other dignitaries by his purple robe and halo, which connect him with the Savior in the vault above. At Justinian's left (at right in the mosaic)

9-14A Throne of Maximianus, ca. 546–556.

is Bishop Maximianus (r. 546–556), the man responsible for San Vitale's completion. (His magnificent ivory throne [FIG. 9-14A] is on display today in one of Ravenna's museums.) The mosaicist stressed the bishop's importance by labeling his figure with the only identifying inscription in the composition. (Some scholars think Maximianus added the inscription and the bishop represented was originally Ecclesius.)

The artist divided the figures into three groups: the emperor and his staff; the clergy; and the imperial guard, bearing a shield with the *chi-rho-iota* (☧) monogram of Christ. Each group has a leader whose feet precede (by one foot overlapping) the feet of those who follow. The positions of Justinian and Maximianus are curiously ambiguous. Although the emperor appears to be slightly behind the bishop, the golden *paten* (large shallow bowl or plate for the Eucharist bread) he carries overlaps the bishop's arm. Thus, symbolized by place and gesture, the imperial and churchly powers are in balance. The emperor's paten, the bishop's cross, and the attendant clerics' book and censer produce a slow forward movement that strikingly modifies the scene's rigid formality. The artist placed nothing in the background, wishing the observer to understand the procession as taking place in this very sanctuary. Thus, the emperor appears forever as a participant in the sacred rites and as the proprietor of this royal church and the ruler of the Western Empire.

The procession at San Vitale recalls but contrasts with that of Augustus and his entourage (FIG. 7-31) on the Ara Pacis, built more than a half millennium earlier in Rome. There, the fully modeled marble figures have their feet planted firmly on the ground. The

9-12 Choir and apse of San Vitale with mosaic of Christ between two angels, Saint Vitalis, and Bishop Ecclesius, Ravenna, Italy, 526–547. ■◀

In the apse vault, a youthful Christ, seated on the orb of the world at the time of his second coming, extends the gold martyr's wreath to Saint Vitalis. Bishop Ecclesius offers Christ a model of San Vitale.

outer spaces that otherwise would have existed simply side by side as independent units. A cross-vaulted *choir* (FIG. 9-12) preceding the apse interrupts the ambulatory and gives the plan some axial stability. Weakening this effect, however, is the off-axis placement of the narthex, whose odd angle never has been explained fully. (The atrium, which no longer exists, may have paralleled a street running in the same direction as the angle of the narthex.)

The mosaic-clad walls and vaults of San Vitale's interior are dazzling. In the apse vault is a vision of the second coming. Christ,

San Vitale's mosaics reveal the new Byzantine aesthetic. Justinian is foremost among the weightless and speechless frontal figures hovering before the viewer, their positions in space uncertain.

9-14 Theodora and attendants, mosaic on the south wall of the apse, San Vitale, Ravenna, Italy, ca. 547. ■◄

Justinian's counterpart on the opposite wall is the powerful Empress Theodora. Neither she nor Justinian ever visited Ravenna. San Vitale's mosaics are proxies for the absent sovereigns.

Romans talk among themselves, unaware of the viewer's presence. All is anecdote, all very human and of this world, even if the figures themselves conform to a classical ideal of beauty that cannot be achieved in reality. The frontal figures of the Byzantine mosaic hover before viewers, weightless and speechless, their positions in space uncertain. Tall, spare, angular, and elegant, they have lost the rather squat proportions characteristic of much Early Christian figural art. The garments fall straight, stiff, and thin from the narrow shoulders. The organic body has dematerialized, and, except for the heads, some of which seem to be true portraits, viewers see a procession of solemn spirits gliding silently in the presence of the sacrament. Indeed, the theological basis for this approach to representation was the idea that the divine was invisible and that the purpose of religious art was to stimulate spiritual seeing. Theodulf of Orleans summed up this idea around 790: "God is beheld not with the eyes of the flesh but only with the eye of the mind."[6] The mosaics of San Vitale reveal this new Byzantine aesthetic, one very different from that of the classical world but equally compelling. Byzantine art disparages matter and material values. It is an art in which blue sky has given way to heavenly gold, an art without solid bodies or cast shadows, and with the perspective of Paradise, which is nowhere and everywhere.

The figures in the Theodora mosaic (FIG. 9-14) exhibit the same stylistic traits as those in the Justinian mosaic, but the artist represented the women within a definite architecture, perhaps the atrium of San Vitale. The empress stands in state beneath an imperial canopy, waiting to follow the emperor's procession. An attendant beckons her to pass through the curtained doorway. The fact she is outside the sanctuary in a courtyard with a fountain and only about to enter attests that, in the ceremonial protocol, her rank was not quite equal to her consort's. But the very presence of Theodora at San Vitale is significant. She, like many other Byzantine empresses (see "Zoe," page 273), wielded enormous influence in the Byzantine state. Of humble origin, Theodora, who was 15 years younger than Justinian, initially attracted his attention because of her beauty, but she soon became his most trusted adviser. John the Lydian, a civil servant at Constantinople at the time, described her as "surpassing in intelligence all men who ever lived." For example, during the Nika revolt in Constantinople in 532, when all of her husband's ministers counseled flight from the city, Theodora, by the sheer force of her personality, persuaded Justinian and his generals to hold their ground—and they succeeded in suppressing the uprising. In the mosaic, the artist underscored Theodora's elevated rank by decorating the border of her garment with a representation of the three magi, suggesting the empress belongs in the company of the three monarchs bearing gifts who approached the newborn Jesus.

SANT'APOLLINARE IN CLASSE Until the ninth century, the Church of Sant'Apollinare in Classe housed the body of Saint Apollinaris, who suffered his martyrdom in Classe, Ravenna's port. The church itself is Early Christian in type, a basilica with a nave and flanking aisles, like Theodoric's palace-church (FIG. 8-18) dedicated to the same saint in Ravenna. As in the earlier church, the Justinianic building's exterior is plain and unadorned, but inside sumptuous mosaics fill the apse (FIG. 9-15). The mosaic decorating the semidome above the apse was probably in place by the time of the church's dedication in 549. The mosaics of the framing arch are of later date.

Against a gold ground, a large medallion with a jeweled cross dominates the composition. This may represent the cross Constantine erected on the hill of Calvary to commemorate the martyrdom of Jesus. Visible just above the cross is the hand of God. On either side of the medallion, in the clouds, are the Old Testament prophets Moses and Elijah, who appeared before Jesus during his Transfiguration (FIG. 9-16). Below these two figures are three sheep, symbols of the disciples John, Peter, and James, who accompanied Jesus to the foot of the mountain he ascended in order to converse with the prophets. Beneath, amid green fields with trees, flowers, and birds, stands the church's patron saint, Apollinaris. The mosaicist portrayed him in the Early Christian manner as an orant with uplifted arms. Accompanying Apollinaris are 12 sheep, perhaps representing the Christian congregation under the saint's protection, and forming, as they march in regular file across the apse, a wonderfully decorative base.

Comparison of the Early Byzantine Sant'Apollinare in Classe mosaic with the Galla Placidia mosaic (FIG. 8-17) from the Early Christian period at Ravenna shows how the style and artists' approach to the subject changed during the course of a century. Both mosaics portray a human figure and some sheep in a landscape. But in Classe, in the mid-sixth century, the artist did not try to represent voluminous figures in a naturalistic setting, but instead treated the saint, the animals, and the plants as flat symbols, lined up side by side. The mosaicist carefully avoided overlapping in what must have been an intentional effort to omit all reference to the three-

9-16 *Transfiguration of Jesus,* apse mosaic, Church of the Virgin, monastery of Saint Catherine, Mount Sinai, Egypt, ca. 548–565.

In this apse mosaic, unlike FIG. 9-15, the artist swept away all traces of landscape for a depthless field of gold. The prophets and disciples cast no shadows even though bathed in divine light.

dimensional space of the material world and physical reality. Shapes have lost the volume seen in the earlier mosaic and instead are flat silhouettes with linear details. The effect is that of an extremely rich, flat tapestry without illusionistic devices. This new Byzantine style became the ideal vehicle for conveying the extremely complex symbolism of the fully developed Christian dogma.

Indeed, the Classe apse mosaic is much richer in meaning than first meets the eye. The cross symbolizes not only Christ's own death, with its redeeming consequences, but also the death of his martyrs (in this case, Saint Apollinaris). The lamb, also a symbol of martyrdom, appropriately represents the martyred apostles. The whole scene expands above the altar, where the priests celebrated the sacrament of the Eucharist—the miraculous recurrence of the supreme redemptive act. The altars of Christian churches were, from early times, sanctified by the bones and relics of martyrs (see "The Veneration of Relics," Chapter 12, page 336). Thus, the mystery and the martyrdom joined in one concept. The death of the martyr, in imitation of Christ, is a triumph over death that leads to eternal life. The images above the altar present an inspiring vision, delivered with overwhelming force, to the eyes of believers. Looming above their eyes is the apparition of a great mystery, ordered to make perfectly simple and clear that humankind's duty is to seek salvation. Even the illiterate, who might not grasp the details of the complex theological program, could understand that the way of the martyr is open to the Christian faithful and that the reward of eternal life is within their reach.

MOUNT SINAI During Justinian's reign, almost continuous building took place, not only in Constantinople and Ravenna but throughout the Byzantine Empire. At about the time mosaicists in Ravenna were completing their work at San Vitale and Sant'Apollinare in Classe, Justinian's builders were rebuilding an important early *monastery* (an enclosed compound for monks) at Mount Sinai in Egypt where Moses received the Ten Commandments from God. Now called Saint Catherine's, the monastery marked the spot at the foot of the mountain where the Bible says God first spoke to the Hebrew prophet from a burning bush.

Monasticism began in Egypt in the third century and spread rapidly to Palestine and Syria in the East and as far as Ireland in the West (see Chapter 11). It began as a migration to the wilderness by those who sought a more spiritual way of life, far from the burdens, distractions, and temptations of town and city. In desert places, these refuge seekers lived austerely as hermits, in contemplative isolation, cultivating the soul's perfection. So many thousands fled the cities that the authorities became alarmed—noting the effect on the tax base, military recruitment, and business in general.

The origins of the monastic movement are associated with Saints Anthony and Pachomius in Egypt in the fourth century. By the fifth century, many of the formerly isolated monks had begun to live together within a common enclosure and formulate regulations governing communal life under the direction of an abbot (see "Medieval Monasteries and Benedictine Rule," Chapter 11, page 322). The monks typically lived in a walled monastery, an architectural complex that included the monks' residence (an alignment of single cells), an oratory (monastic church), a *refectory* (dining hall), a kitchen, storage and service quarters, and a guest house for pilgrims (FIG. 11-19).

Justinian rebuilt the monastery at Mount Sinai between 548 and 565 and constructed imposing walls around it. The site had been an important pilgrimage destination since the fourth century, and Justinian's fortress protected not only the monks but also the lay pilgrims during their visits. The Mount Sinai church was dedicated to the Virgin Mary, whom the Orthodox Church had officially recognized in the mid-fifth century as the Mother of God (*Theotokos,* "she who bore God" in Greek), putting to rest a controversy about the divine nature of Christ.

In the church's apse is the *Transfiguration of Jesus* mosaic (FIG. **9-16**). (Other mosaics in the church depict Moses receiving the Law and standing before the burning bush.) Jesus appears in a deep-blue almond-shaped *mandorla* (almond-shaped aureole of light). At his feet are John, Peter, and James. At the left and right are Elijah and Moses. Portrait busts of saints and prophets in medallions frame the whole scene. The artist stressed the intense

9-17 *Ascension of Christ,* folio 13 verso of the *Rabbula Gospels,* from Zagba, Syria, 586. Tempera on parchment, 1′ 1″ × 10½″. Biblioteca Medicea-Laurenziana, Florence.

The Gospels do not mention the Virgin as a witness of Christ's Ascension. Her prominent position in the *Rabbula Gospels* is an early example of the important role Mary played in medieval art.

whiteness of Jesus' transfigured, spiritualized form, from which rays stream down on the disciples. The stately figures of the prophets and the static frontality of Jesus set off the frantic terror and astonishment of the gesticulating disciples. These distinctions dramatically contrast the eternal composure of heavenly beings with the distraught responses of the earthbound. At Mount Sinai, the mosaicist swept away all traces of landscape and architectural setting for a depthless field of gold, fixing the figures and their labels in isolation from one another. A rainbow band of colors graduating from yellow to blue bounds the golden field at its base. The relationship of the figures to this multicolor ground line is ambiguous. The artist placed some figures behind it, whereas others overlap it. The bodies cast no shadows, even though supernatural light streams over them. This is not the natural world Jesus and his disciples inhabited. It is a world of mystical vision. The mosaicist subtracted all substance that might suggest the passage of time or motion through physical space, enabling the devout to contemplate the eternal and motionless world of religious truth.

Manuscript and Icon Painting

As in the Early Christian period, manuscript painting was an important art form during the Early Byzantine era. This period also marked the beginning of another Byzantine pictorial tradition with a long and distinguished history—icon painting.

RABBULA GOSPELS One of the essential Christian beliefs is that following his execution at the hands of the Romans, Christ rose from his tomb after three days and, on the 40th day, ascended from the Mount of Olives to Heaven. The *Crucifixion, Resurrection,* and *Ascension* are all subjects of full-page paintings (FIGS. **9-17** and **9-17A**) in a manuscript known as the *Rabbula Gospels.* Written in Syriac by the monk Rabbula at the monastery of Saint John the Evangelist at Zagba in

9-17A *Crucifixion* and *Resurrection, Rabbula Gospels,* 586.

Syria, it dates to 586. The page depicting the *Ascension of Christ* (FIG. 9-17) shows Christ, bearded and surrounded by a mandorla, as in the Mount Sinai *Transfiguration* (FIG. 9-16), but here angels bear the mandorla aloft. Below, Mary, other angels, and various apostles look on. The artist set the figures into a mosaic-like frame (compare FIGS. 9-13 and 9-14), and many art historians think the model for the manuscript page was a mural painting or mosaic in a Byzantine church somewhere in the Eastern Empire.

The account of Christ ascending to Heaven is not part of the accompanying text of the *Rabbula Gospels* but comes from the book of Acts. In the latter, the Virgin is not present at the miraculous event. In the *Rabbula Gospels* representation, however, the Theotokos occupies a prominent position, central and directly beneath Christ. It is an early example of the important role the Mother of God played in medieval art, both in the East and in the West. Frontal, with a nimbus, and posed as an orant, Mary stands apart from the commotion all about her and looks out at the viewer. Other details also depart from the Gospel texts. Christ, for example, does not rise in a cloud. Rather, as in the vision of Ezekiel in the book of Revelation, he ascends in a mandorla above a fiery winged chariot. The chariot carries the symbols of the four evangelists—the man, lion, ox, and eagle (see "The Four Evangelists," Chapter 11, page 314). This page therefore does not illustrate the Gospels. Rather, its purpose is to present one of the central tenets of Christian faith. Similar compositions appear on pilgrims' flasks from Palestine that were souvenir items reproducing important monuments visited. They reinforce the theory that the Byzantine painter based the *Ascension of Christ* in the *Rabbula Gospels* on a lost painting or mosaic in a major church.

ICONS Gospel books such as the *Rabbula Gospels* played an important role in monastic religious life. So, too, did *icons,* which also figured prominently in private devotion (see "Icons and Iconoclasm," page 269). Unfortunately, few early icons survive. Two of the finest examples come from Saint Catherine's monastery at Mount Sinai. One represents the enthroned Theotokos (FIG. **9-18**), and the other (FIG. **9-18A**) Christ blessing the viewer of the icon. The medium used for both icons is encaustic on wood, continuing a tradition of panel painting in Egypt that, like so much else in the Byzantine world,

9-18A Christ blessing, Mount Sinai, sixth century.

dates to the Roman Empire (FIGS. 7-62, 7-62A, 7-62B, and 7-63).

The smaller of the two illustrated icons (FIG. 9-18) is more ambitious in the number of figures depicted. In a composition reminiscent of the portrait of Anicia Juliana (FIG. 9-3) in the *Vienna Dioskorides,* the Sinai icon painter represented the enthroned Theotokos and Child with Saints Theodore and George. The two guardian saints intercede with the Virgin on the viewer's behalf. Behind

Icons and Iconoclasm

Icons ("images" in Greek) are small portable paintings depicting Christ, the Virgin, or saints (or a combination of all three, as in FIG. 9-18). Icons survive from as early as the fourth century. From the sixth century on, they became enormously popular in Byzantine worship, both public and private. Eastern Christians considered icons a personal, intimate, and indispensable medium for spiritual transaction with holy figures. Some icons (for example, FIG. 9-31) came to be regarded as wonder-working, and believers ascribed miracles and healing powers to them.

Icons, however, were by no means universally accepted. From the beginning, many Christians were deeply suspicious of the practice of imaging the divine, whether on portable panels, on the walls of churches, or especially as statues that reminded them of ancient idols. The opponents of Christian figural art had in mind the Old Testament prohibition of images the Lord dictated to Moses in the Second Commandment: "Thou shalt not make unto thee any graven image or any likeness of anything that is in heaven above, or that is in the earth beneath, or that is in the water under the earth. Thou shalt not bow down thyself to them, nor serve them" (Exod. 20:4, 5). For example, early in the fourth century, Constantia, sister of the emperor Constantine, requested an image of Christ from Eusebius of Caesarea (ca. 263–339), the first great historian of the Church. He rebuked her, referring to the Second Commandment:

> Can it be that you have forgotten that passage in which God lays down the law that no likeness should be made of what is in heaven or in the earth beneath? . . . Are not such things banished and excluded from churches all over the world, and is it not common knowledge that such practices are not permitted to us . . . lest we appear, like idol worshipers, to carry our God around in an image?*

Opposition to icons became especially strong in the eighth century, when the faithful often burned incense and knelt before the icons in prayer to seek protection or a cure for illness. Although their purpose was only to evoke the presence of the holy figures addressed in prayer, in the minds of many, icons became identified with the personages represented. Icon veneration became confused with idol worship, and this brought about an imperial ban not only on the making of icons but of all sacred images as well as edicts ordering the destruction of existing images (*iconoclasm*). The *iconoclasts* (breakers of images) and the *iconophiles* (lovers of images) became bitter and irreconcilable enemies. The anguish of the latter is evident in the following graphic description of the deeds of the iconoclasts, written in about 754:

> In every village and town one could witness the weeping and lamentation of the pious, whereas, on the part of the impious, [one saw] sacred things trodden upon, [liturgical] vessels turned to other use, churches scraped down and smeared with ashes because they contained holy images. And wherever there were venerable images of Christ or the Mother of God or the saints, these were consigned to the flames or were gouged out or smeared over.†

1 ft

9-18 Virgin (Theotokos) and Child between Saints Theodore and George, icon, sixth or early seventh century. Encaustic on wood, 2′ 3″ × 1′ 7¾″. Monastery of Saint Catherine, Mount Sinai, Egypt.

Byzantine icons are the heirs to the Roman tradition of portrait painting on small wood panels, but their Christian subjects and function as devotional objects broke sharply from classical models.

The consequences of iconoclasm for the early history of Byzantine art are difficult to overstate. For more than a century, not only did the portrayal of Christ, the Virgin, and the saints cease, but the iconoclasts also destroyed countless works from the first several centuries of Christendom. For this reason, writing a history of Early Byzantine art presents a great challenge to art historians.

*Cyril Mango, trans., *The Art of the Byzantine Empire, 312–1453: Sources and Documents* (reprint of 1972 ed., Toronto: University of Toronto Press, 1986), 17–18.
†Mango, 152.

them, two angels gaze upward to a shaft of light where the hand of God appears. The foreground figures are strictly frontal and have a solemn demeanor. Background details are few and suppressed. The shallow forward plane of the picture dominates. Traces of the Greco-Roman illusionism noted in the Anicia Juliana portrait remain in the Virgin's rather personalized features, in her sideways glance, and in the posing of the angels' heads. But the painter rendered the saints' bodies in the new Byzantine manner.

ICONOCLASM The preservation of the Early Byzantine icons at the Mount Sinai monastery is fortuitous but ironic, for opposition to icon worship was especially prominent in the Monophysite provinces of Syria and Egypt. There, in the seventh century, a series of calamities erupted, indirectly causing an imperial ban on images. The Sasanians (see Chapter 2), chronically at war with Rome, swept into the Eastern provinces, and between 611 and 617 they captured the great cities of Antioch, Jerusalem, and Alexandria. The Byzantine emperor Heraclius (r. 610–641) had hardly defeated them in 627 when a new and overwhelming power appeared unexpectedly on the stage of history. The Arabs, under the banner of the new Islamic religion, conquered not only Byzantium's Eastern provinces but also Persia itself, replacing the Sasanians in the age-old balance of power with the Christian West (see Chapter 10). In a few years the Arabs were launching attacks on Constantinople, and Byzantium was fighting for its life.

These were catastrophic years for the Eastern Roman Empire. They terminated once and for all the long story of imperial Rome, closed the Early Byzantine period, and inaugurated the medieval era of Byzantine history. The Byzantine Empire lost almost two-thirds of its territory—many cities and much of its population, wealth, and material resources. The shock of these events may have persuaded the emperor Leo III (r. 717–741) that God was punishing the Christian Roman Empire for its idolatrous worship of icons by setting upon it the merciless armies of the infidel—an enemy that, moreover, shunned the representation not only of God but of all living things in holy places (see Chapter 10). Some scholars believe another motivation for Leo's 726 ban on picturing the divine was to assert the authority of the state over the Church. In any case, for more than a century, Byzantine artists produced little new religious figurative art. In place of images of holy figures, the iconoclasts used symbolic forms already familiar in Early Christian art, for example, the cross (FIG. 9-12).

MIDDLE BYZANTINE ART

In the late eighth and ninth centuries, a powerful reaction against iconoclasm set in. The case in favor of icons had been made forcefully earlier in the eighth century by Saint John of Damascus (ca. 675–ca. 749), who argued that the invisible God the Father had made an image of himself in the son Jesus and in humankind in general and that although icons were likenesses of holy figures, they were not identical to their prototypes. To oppose making images of holy figures was contrary to the actions of God. Two female regents in particular led the movement to restore image-making in the Byzantine Empire: the empresses Irene in 780 and Theodora in 843, after the death of her husband Theophilos (r. 829–842). Unlike Irene's short-lived repeal of the prohibition against icons, Theodora's opposition proved to be definitive and permanent and led to the condemnation of iconoclasm as a heresy.

Shortly thereafter, a new line of emperors, the Macedonian dynasty, resuscitated the Early Byzantine tradition of lavish imperial patronage of religious art and architecture and the making of images of Christ, the Virgin, and saints. Basil I (r. 867–886), head of the new dynasty, regarded himself as the restorer of the Roman Empire. He denounced as usurpers the Carolingian monarchs of the West (see Chapter 11) who, since 800, had claimed the title "Roman Empire" for their realm. Basil bluntly reminded their emissary that the only true emperor of Rome reigned in Constantinople. They were not Roman emperors but merely "kings of the Germans." Iconoclasm had forced Byzantine artists westward, where doubtless they found employment at the courts of these Germanic kings (see "Theophanu, a Byzantine Princess in Ottonian Germany," Chapter 11, page 328). These Byzantine "refugees" strongly influenced the character of Western European art.

Architecture and Mosaics

The triumph of the iconophiles over the iconoclasts meant Byzantine mural painters, mosaicists, book illuminators, ivory carvers, and metalworkers once again received plentiful commissions. Basil I and his successors also undertook the laborious and costly task of refurbishing the churches the iconoclasts defaced and neglected.

THEOTOKOS, HAGIA SOPHIA In 867, the Macedonian dynasty dedicated a new mosaic (FIG. 9-19) depicting the enthroned Virgin with the Christ Child in her lap in the apse of the Justinianic church of Hagia Sophia. In the vast space beneath the dome of the great church, the figures look undersized, but the seated Theotokos is more than 16 feet tall. An accompanying inscription, now fragmentary, announced "pious emperors" (the Macedonians) had commissioned the mosaic to replace one the "impostors" (the

9-19 Virgin (Theotokos) and Child enthroned, apse mosaic, Hagia Sophia, Constantinople (Istanbul), Turkey, dedicated 867. ◼◀

After the repeal of iconoclasm, Basil I dedicated a huge new mosaic in the apse of Hagia Sophia depicting the Virgin and Child enthroned. An inscription says it replaced one the iconoclasts destroyed.

iconoclasts) had destroyed. The declaration may be purely rhetorical, however. There was probably no comparable image of the Virgin and Child in the sixth-century apse.

The ninth-century mosaic echoes the style and composition of the Early Byzantine Mount Sinai icon (FIG. 9-18) of the Theotokos, Christ, and saints. Here, however, the angular placement of the throne and footstool alleviate the strict frontality of Mother and (much older) Child. The mosaicist rendered the furnishings in a perspective that, although imperfect, recalls once more the Greco-Roman roots of Byzantine art. The treatment of the folds of Christ's robes is, by contrast, even more schematic and flatter than in earlier mosaics. These seemingly contradictory stylistic features are not uncommon in Byzantine paintings and mosaics.

Most significant about the images in the Hagia Sophia apse is their very existence, marking the end of iconoclasm in the Byzantine Empire.

HOSIOS LOUKAS Although the new emperors did not wait long to redecorate the churches of their predecessors, they undertook little new church construction in the decades after the renunciation of iconoclasm in 843. But in the 10th century and through the 12th, a number of monastic churches arose that are the flowers of Middle Byzantine architecture. They feature a brilliant series of variations on the domed central plan. From the exterior, the typical later Byzantine church building is a domed cube, with the dome rising above the square on a kind of cylinder or *drum*. The churches are small, vertical, high-shouldered, and, unlike earlier Byzantine buildings, have exterior wall surfaces decorated with vivid patterns, probably reflecting Islamic architecture.

The Katholikon (FIGS. **9-20** and **9-21**, *bottom*) at Hosios Loukas (Saint Luke) in Greece, near ancient Delphi, dates to the early 11th century. One of two churches at the site—the other is the Church of the Theotokos (FIG. 9-21, *top*) built during the second half of the 10th century—the Katholikon exemplifies church design during this second golden age of Byzantine art and architecture. Light stones framed by dark red bricks—the so-called *cloisonné* technique, a term borrowed from enamel work (FIG. 11-3)—make up the walls. The interplay of arcuated windows, projecting apses, and varying roof lines further enhances this surface dynamism. The plans of both Hosios Loukas churches show the form of a domed cross in a square with four equal-length, vaulted cross arms (the *Greek cross*). The dome of the smaller Church of the Theotokos rests on pendentives. In the larger and later Katholikon, the architect placed the dome over an octagon inscribed within a square. The octagon was formed by squinches (FIG. 9-9, *right*), which play the same role as pendentives in making the transition from a square base to a round dome but create a different visual effect on the interior. This arrangement departs from the older designs, such as Santa Costanza's circular plan (FIG. 8-12), San Vitale's octagonal plan (FIG. 9-11), and Hagia Sophia's dome on pendentives rising from a square (FIGS. 9-6 to 9-8). The Katholikon's complex core lies within two rectangles, the outermost one forming the exterior walls. Thus, in plan from the center out, a circle-octagon-square-oblong series exhibits an intricate interrelationship that is at once complex and unified.

9-20 Katholikon (looking northeast), Hosios Loukas, Greece, first quarter of 11th century.

Middle Byzantine churches typically are small and high-shouldered, with a central dome on a drum and exterior wall surfaces with decorative patterns, probably reflecting Islamic architecture.

1. Dome on pendentives
2. Dome on squinches

N

0   10   20   30 feet

0   5   10 meters

9-21 Plan of the Church of the Theotokos (*top*) and the Katholikon (*bottom*), Hosios Loukas, Greece, second half of 10th and first quarter of 11th century respectively.

The plans of the pair of monastic churches at Hosios Loukas in Greece take the form of a domed square at the center of a cross with four equal-length vaulted arms (the Greek cross).

9-22 Interior of the Church of the Dormition (looking into the dome), Daphni, Greece, ca. 1090–1100.

The Daphni dome rests on an octagon formed by squinches, which play the same role as pendentives in making the transition from a square base to a round dome but create a different visual effect.

9-23 *Christ as Pantokrator,* dome mosaic in the Church of the Dormition, Daphni, Greece, ca. 1090–1100.

The mosaic of Christ as last judge in the Daphni dome is like a gigantic icon hovering dramatically in space, connecting the awestruck worshiper below with Heaven through Christ.

9-24 *Crucifixion,* mosaic in the north arm of the east wall of the Church of the Dormition, Daphni, Greece, ca. 1090–1100.

The Daphni *Crucifixion* is a subtle blend of Hellenistic style and the more abstract Byzantine manner. The Virgin Mary and Saint John point to Christ on the cross as if to a devotional object.

DAPHNI Similar in general design to the Katholikon, but constructed at the end of the 11th century, is the monastic Church of the Dormition (from the Latin for "sleep," referring to the ascension of the Virgin Mary to Heaven at the moment of her death) at Daphni, near Athens. Like the Katholikon, the church's interior (FIG. **9-22**) creates a mystery out of space, surface, light, and dark. High and narrow, the design forces the viewer's gaze to rise and revolve. The eye is drawn upward toward the dome, but much can distract it in the interplay of flat walls and concave recesses; wide and narrow openings; groin and barrel vaults; and illuminated and dark spaces. Middle Byzantine architects aimed for the creation of complex interior spaces with dramatically shifting perspectives.

At Daphni, the main elements of the late-11th-century pictorial program are intact, although the mosaics underwent restoration in the 19th century. Gazing down from on high in the dome is the fearsome image (FIG. **9-23**) of Christ as *Pantokrator* (literally "ruler of all" in Greek but usually applied to Christ in his role as last judge of humankind). The dome mosaic is the climax of an elaborate hierarchical mosaic program including several New Testament episodes below. The Daphni Pantokrator is like a gigantic icon hovering dramatically in space. The image serves to connect the awestruck worshiper in the church below with Heaven through Christ.

Born to the Purple: Empress Zoe

Although rarely rulers in their own right, Byzantine empresses often wielded great power and influence. Theodora (ca. 500–548) was Justinian's most trusted adviser. In 780, Irene (ca. 755–802) became regent for her 10-year-old son, Constantine VI (r. 780–797), and briefly repealed the imperial ban against icons. In 843, another empress, Theodora (ca. 815–867), convened a religious council, which permanently put an end to iconoclasm. Theodora achieved sainthood as a result.

The most influential Byzantine empress of the 11th century was Zoe Porphyrogenita ("born to the purple"), the elder daughter of Constantine VIII (r. 1025–1028). Born around 978, Zoe was not permitted to marry until just before her father's death, and she remained childless throughout her life. In 1028, Zoe married Romanos III Argyros (r. 1028–1034), Constantine's chosen successor, but she soon fell in love with another member of the court, with whom she may have plotted the drowning of Romanos in his bath. In any case, Zoe married Michael IV (r. 1034–1041) the same day, even though by law widows were supposed to wait a full year before remarrying. Toward the end of Michael's reign, the couple adopted a son, Michael V (r. 1042), who succeeded his father and banished his adoptive mother to a convent. With the support of her subjects, Zoe returned to Constantinople, deposed the emperor, and ruled briefly in 1042 in her own name before marrying Constantine IX Monomachos (r. 1042–1054), who outlived her by four years. Thus, four successive emperors of Byzantium owed their coronations to Zoe.

A mosaic portrait of Zoe and her last husband flanking the enthroned Christ (FIG. 9-25) adorns the east wall of the south gallery of Hagia Sophia. The emperor holds a purse, signifying the generous donation Constantine made to the church. Zoe holds a scroll, also a reference to her gifts to the church. Inscriptions next to the portraits describe Constantine as "pious emperor and king of the Romans" and Zoe as "pious empress." Many scholars believe that the mosaic

9-25 Christ between Constantine IX Monomachus and the empress Zoe, mosaic on the east wall of the south gallery, Hagia Sophia, Constantinople (Istanbul), Turkey, ca. 1028–1035.

Zoe, who was the wife of three emperors, here appears with the enthroned Christ and her third husband. Constantine IX's portrait may have replaced successive portraits of Zoe's previous two husbands.

dates to the reign of Romanos and bore his portrait, and that Zoe twice asked the imperial artists to update the mosaic with new portraits and labels upon each of her subsequent marriages.

The Pantokrator theme was a common one in churches throughout the Byzantine Empire. A mosaic of the Pantokrator also once adorned the dome of the Hosios Loukas Katholikon.

Below the Daphni dome, on the wall beneath the barrel vault of one arm of the Greek cross, is the *Crucifixion* mosaic (FIG. 9-24) in a pictorial style characteristic of the posticonoclastic Middle Byzantine period. Like the Pantokrator mosaic in the dome, the Daphni *Crucifixion* is a subtle blend of the painterly naturalistic style of Late Antiquity and the later, more abstract and formalistic Byzantine style. The Byzantine artist fully assimilated classicism's simplicity, dignity, and grace into a perfect synthesis with Byzantine piety and pathos. The figures have regained the classical organic structure to a surprising degree, particularly compared with figures from the Justinianic period (compare FIGS. 9-13 and 9-14). The style is a masterful adaptation of classical statuesque qualities to the linear Byzantine manner.

In quiet sorrow and resignation, the Virgin and Saint John flank the crucified Christ. A skull at the foot of the cross indicates Golgotha, the "place of skulls." The artist needed nothing else to set the scene. Symmetry and closed space combine to produce an effect of the motionless and unchanging aspect of the deepest mystery of

the Christian religion, as recalled in the ceremony of the Eucharist. The picture is not a narrative of the historical event of Jesus' execution, the approach taken by the carver of the Early Christian ivory panel (FIG. 8-24) examined in the previous chapter. Nor is Christ a triumphant, beardless youth, oblivious to pain and defiant of the laws of gravity. Rather, he has a tilted head and sagging body, and although the Savior is not overtly in pain, blood and water spurt from the wound Longinus inflicted on him, as recounted in Saint John's Gospel. The Virgin and John point to the figure on the cross as if to a devotional object. They act as intercessors between the viewer below and Christ, who, in the dome, appears as the last judge of all humans. The mosaic decoration of the church is the perfect complement to Christian liturgy.

EMPRESS ZOE As in the Early Byzantine period, Middle Byzantine mosaicists also produced portraits of their imperial patrons for church interiors. Several such portraits grace the interior walls of Hagia Sophia (FIG. 9-8) in Constantinople. Perhaps the finest of these is on the east wall of the south gallery. It depicts Constantine IX and Zoe (see "Born to the Purple: Empress Zoe," above) flanking the enthroned Christ (FIG. 9-25). Like the much earlier imperial portraits (FIGS. 9-13 and 9-14) in San Vitale at Ravenna, the emperor and empress are haloed, but no longer is there a separation between the human and the divine, as in the sixth-century apse. Other Middle Byzantine mosaics depict the imperial couple flanking the Virgin.

SAINT MARK'S, VENICE The Middle Byzantine revival of church building and of figural mosaics extended beyond the Greek-speaking East in the 10th to 12th centuries. The marriage of Anna, the sister of Basil II (r. 976–1025), to the Russian prince Vladimir (r. 980–1015) in 989, marked the introduction of Orthodox Christianity to Russia. Construction of the vast five-apse, 13-dome Cathedral of Saint Sophia (FIG. **9-25A**) at Kiev followed within a half century. A resurgence of religious architecture and of the mosaicist's art also occurred in areas of the former Western Roman Empire where the ties with Constantinople were the strongest. In the Early Byzantine period, Venice, about 80 miles north of Ravenna on the eastern coast of Italy, was a dependency of that Byzantine stronghold. In 751, Ravenna fell to the Lombards,

who wrested control of most of northern Italy from Constantinople. Venice, however, became an independent power. Its *doges* (dukes) enriched themselves and the city through seaborne commerce, serving as the crucial link between Byzantium and the West.

Venice had obtained the relics of Saint Mark from Alexandria in Egypt in 829, and the doges constructed the first Venetian shrine dedicated to the evangelist—a palace chapel and *martyrium* (martyr's shrine)—shortly thereafter. Fire destroyed the ninth-century chapel in 976. The Venetians then built a second shrine on the site, but a grandiose new Saint Mark's (FIG. **9-26**) begun in 1063 by Doge Domenico Contarini (r. 1043–1071) replaced it. The model for Contarini's church was the Church of the Holy Apostles at Constantinople, built in Justinian's time. That shrine no longer exists, but its key elements were a cruciform plan with a central dome over the crossing and four other domes over the four equal arms of the Greek cross, as at Saint Mark's. Because of its importance to the city, the doges furnished the church's interior with costly altarpieces, such as the *Pala d'Oro* (FIG. **9-26A**), and other liturgical objects and deposited there many of the treasures, including icons (FIG. **9-26B**), they brought back as booty from the sack of Constantinople in 1204.

The interior (FIG. 9-26) of Saint Mark's is, like its plan, Byzantine in effect. Light enters through a row of windows at the bases of all five domes, vividly illuminating a rich cycle of mosaics. Both Byzantine and local artists worked on Saint Mark's mosaics over the course of several centuries. Most of the mosaics date to the 12th and 13th centuries. Cleaning and restoration on a grand scale have returned the mosaics to their original splendor, enabling visitors to experience the full radiance of 40,000 square feet of mosaics covering all the walls, arches, vaults, and domes like a gold-brocaded figured fabric.

In the vast central dome, 80 feet above the floor and 42 feet in diameter, Christ ascends to Heaven in the presence of the Virgin Mary and the 12 apostles. In the great arch framing the church crossing are mosaics of the *Crucifixion* and *Resurrection* and Christ's liberation from death (*Anastasis*) of Adam and Eve, Saint John the Baptist, and other biblical figures. The mosaics have explanatory labels in both Latin and Greek, reflecting Venice's position as the key link between Eastern and Western Christendom in the later Middle Ages. The insubstantial figures on the walls, vaults, and domes appear weightless, and they project no farther from their flat field than do the elegant Latin and Greek letters above them. Nothing here reflects on the world of matter, of solids, of light and shade, of perspective space. Rather, the mosaics reveal the mysteries of the Christian faith.

9-26 Interior of Saint Mark's (looking east), Venice, Italy, begin 1063.

Modeled on a church in Constantinople, Saint Mark's has a central dome over the crossing, four other domes over the arms of the Greek cross, and 40,000 square feet of Byzantine-style mosaics.

NORMAN SICILY Matching Venetian success in the western Mediterranean were the Normans, the northern French descendants of the Vikings who, having driven the Arabs from Sicily, set up a powerful kingdom there. Though they were the enemies of Byzantium, the Normans, like the Venetians, assimilated Byzantine culture and even employed Byzantine artisans. They also incorporated in their monuments elements of the Islamic art of the Arabs they had defeated. The Normans' Palatine (palace) Chapel (FIG. **9-27A**) at Palermo with its prismatic (*muqarnas*) ceiling, a characteristic Muslim form (see

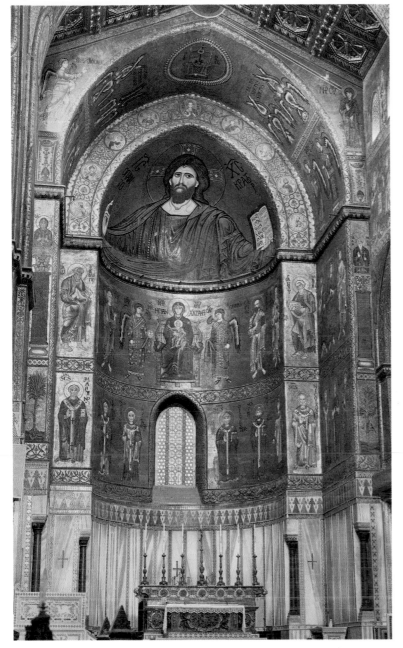

In centrally planned Byzantine churches, the image of the Pantokrator usually appears in the main dome, but Monreale's cathedral is a longitudinal basilica. The semidome of the apse is its only vault.

Chapter 10), is one example of the rich interplay of Western Christian, Byzantine, and Islamic cultures in Norman Sicily.

9-27A Cappella Palatina, Palermo, begun 1142.

The mosaics of the great basilican church of Monreale (FIG. 9-27), not far from Palermo, are striking evidence of Byzantine influence. They rival those of Saint Mark's in both quality and extent. One scholar has estimated the Monreale mosaics required more than 100 million glass and stone tesserae. The Norman king William II (r. 1087–1100) paid for the mosaics, and the artists portrayed him twice in the church, continuing the theme of royal presence and patronage of the much earlier Ravenna portraits of Justinian and Theodora (FIGS. 9-13 and 9-14) at San Vitale and the Middle Byzantine portraits of Constantine IX and Zoe (FIG. 9-25) in Hagia Sophia in Constantinople. In one panel, William stands next to the enthroned Christ, who places his hand on William's crown. In the second, the king kneels before the Virgin and presents her with a model of the Monreale church.

The apse mosaics (FIG. 9-27) are especially impressive. The image of Christ as Pantokrator is in the vault. In Byzantium, the Pantokrator's image usually appears in the main dome (FIGS. 9-22 and 9-23). But the Monreale church is a basilica, longitudinally planned in the Western tradition. The semidome of the apse, the only vault in the building and its architectural focus, was the logical choice for the most important element of the pictorial program. Below the Pantokrator in rank and dignity is the enthroned Theotokos, flanked by archangels and the 12 apostles, symmetrically arranged in balanced groups. Lower on the wall (and less elevated in the church hierarchy) are popes, bishops, and other saints. The artists observed the stern formalities of Byzantine style here, far from Constantinople. The Monreale mosaics, like those at Saint Mark's (FIG. 9-26) in Venice and in the Palatine Chapel (FIG. 9-27A) in Palermo, testify to the stature of Byzantium and of Byzantine art in medieval Italy.

Ivory Carving and Painting

Middle Byzantine artists also produced costly carved ivories in large numbers. The three-part *triptych* replaced the earlier diptych as the standard format for ivory panels.

HARBAVILLE TRIPTYCH One example of this type is the *Harbaville Triptych* (FIG. 9-28), a portable shrine with hinged wings used for private devotion. Ivory triptychs were very popular—among those who could afford such luxurious items—and they often replaced icons for use in personal prayer. Carved on

1 in.

9-28 Christ enthroned with saints (*Harbaville Triptych*), ca. 950. Ivory, central panel 9½″ × 5½″. Musée du Louvre, Paris.

In this small three-part shrine with hinged wings used for private devotion, the ivory carver depicted the figures with looser classical stances, in contrast to the frontal poses of most Byzantine figures.

9-29 *Lamentation,* **wall painting, Saint Pantaleimon, Nerezi, Macedonia, 1164.**

Working in the Balkans in an alternate Byzantine mode, this painter staged the emotional scene of the *Lamentation* in a hilly landscape below a blue sky and peopled it with fully modeled figures.

the wings of the *Harbaville Triptych,* both inside and out, are four pairs of full-length figures and two pairs of medallions depicting saints. A cross dominates the central panel on the back of the triptych (not illustrated). On the inside is a scene of *Deësis* (supplication). Saint John the Baptist and the Theotokos appear as intercessors, praying on behalf of the viewer to the enthroned Savior. Below them are five apostles.

The formality and solemnity usually associated with Byzantine art, visible in the mosaics of Ravenna and Monreale, yielded here to a softer, more fluid technique. The figures may lack true classical contrapposto, but the looser stances (most stand on bases, like freestanding statues) and three-quarter views of many of the heads relieve the hard austerity of the customary frontal pose. This more natural, classical spirit was a second, equally important stylistic current of the Middle Byzantine period. It also surfaced in mural painting and book illumination.

NEREZI When the emperors lifted the ban against religious images and again encouraged religious painting at Constantinople, the impact was felt far and wide. The style varied from region to region, but a renewed enthusiasm for picturing the key New Testament figures and events was universal. In 1164, at Nerezi in Macedonia, Byzantine painters embellished the church of Saint Pantaleimon with murals of great emotional power. One of these, *Lamentation* (FIG. **9-29**), is an image of passionate grief over the dead Christ. The artist captured Christ's followers in attitudes, expressions, and gestures of quite human bereavement. Joseph of Arimathea and the disciple Nicodemus kneel at his feet. Mary presses her cheek against her dead son's face. Saint John clings to Christ's left hand. In the Gospels, neither Mary nor John was present at the entombment of Christ. Their inclusion here, as elsewhere in Middle Byzantine art, intensified for the viewer the emotional impact of Christ's death. These

representations parallel the development of liturgical hymns recounting the Virgin lamenting her son's death on the cross.

At Nerezi, the painter set the scene in a hilly landscape below a blue sky—a striking contrast to the abstract golden world of the mosaics favored for church walls elsewhere in the Byzantine Empire. This Balkan artist strove to make utterly convincing an emotionally charged realization of the theme by staging the *Lamentation* in a more natural setting and peopling it with fully modeled actors. This alternate representational mode is no less Byzantine than the frontal, flatter figures at Constantinople and Ravenna. In time, this more naturalistic style would also be emulated in Italy (FIG. 14-8).

PARIS PSALTER Another example of this classical-revival style is a page from a book of the Psalms of David. The so-called *Paris Psalter* (FIG. **9-30**) reasserts the artistic values of the Greco-Roman past with astonishing authority. Art historians believe the manuscript dates from the mid-10th century—the so-called Macedonian Renaissance, a time of enthusiastic and careful study of the language and literature of ancient Greece, and of humanistic reverence for the classical past. It is not surprising that artists would once again draw inspiration from the Hellenistic naturalism of the pre-Christian Mediterranean world.

David, the psalmist, surrounded by sheep, goats, and his faithful dog, plays his harp in a rocky landscape with a town in the background. Similar settings appeared frequently in Pompeian murals. Befitting an ancient depiction of Orpheus, the Greek hero who could charm even inanimate objects with his music, allegorical figures accompany the Old Testament harpist. Melody looks over his shoulder, and Echo peers from behind a column. A reclining male figure points to a Greek inscription identifying him as representing the mountain of Bethlehem. These allegorical figures do not appear in the Bible. They are the stock population of Greco-Roman painting.

9-30 *David Composing the Psalms,* folio 1 verso of the *Paris Psalter,* ca. 950–970. Tempera on vellum, 1′ 2⅛″ × 10¼″. Bibliothèque Nationale, Paris.

During the Macedonian Renaissance, Byzantine artists revived the classical style. This painter portrayed David as if a Greek hero, accompanied by personifications of Melody, Echo, and Bethlehem.

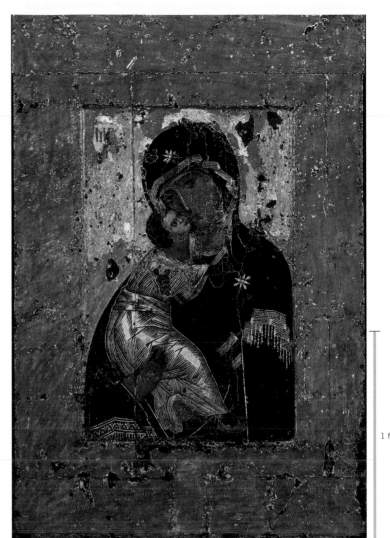

9-31 Virgin of Compassion icon (*Vladimir Virgin*), late 11th or early 12th century, with later repainting. Tempera on wood, 2′ 6½″ × 1′ 9″. Tretyakov Gallery, Moscow.

In this icon, the artist depicted Mary as the Virgin of Compassion, who presses her cheek against her son's as she contemplates his future. The reverse side shows the instruments of Christ's passion.

Apparently, the artist had seen a work from Late Antiquity or perhaps earlier and partly translated it into a Byzantine pictorial idiom. In works such as this, Byzantine artists kept the classical style alive in the Middle Ages.

VLADIMIR VIRGIN Nothing in Middle Byzantine art better demonstrates the rejection of the iconoclastic viewpoint than the painted icon's return to prominence. After the restoration of images, such icons multiplied by the thousands to meet public and private demand. In the 11th century, the clergy began to display icons in hierarchical order (Christ, the Theotokos, John the Baptist, and then other saints, as on the *Harbaville Triptych*) in tiers on the *templon,* the low columnar screen separating the sanctuary from the main body of a Byzantine church.

The *Vladimir Virgin* (FIG. **9-31**) is the most renowned Middle Byzantine icon produced in Russia. Unfortunately, the revered image has been repainted many times, and only traces of the original surface remain. Descended from works such as the Mount Sinai icon (FIG. 9-18), the *Vladimir Virgin* clearly reveals the stylized abstraction resulting from centuries of working and reworking the conventional image. Probably the work of a painter from Constantinople, the *Vladimir Virgin* displays all the characteristic traits of the Byzantine icon of the Virgin and Child: the Virgin's long,

straight nose and small mouth; the golden rays in the infant's drapery; the decorative sweep of the unbroken contour that encloses the two figures; and the flat silhouette against the golden ground. But this is a much more tender and personalized image of the Virgin than that in the Mount Sinai icon. Here Mary is the Virgin of Compassion, who presses her cheek against her son's in an intimate portrayal of Mother and Child. A deep pathos infuses the image as Mary contemplates the future sacrifice of her son. (The back of the icon bears images of the instruments of Christ's Passion.)

The icon of Vladimir, like most icons, has seen hard service. Placed before or above altars in churches or private chapels, the icon became blackened by the incense and smoke from candles that burned before or below it. It was taken to Kiev (Ukraine) in 1131, then to Vladimir (Russia) in 1155 (hence its name), and in 1395, as a wonder-working image, to Moscow to protect that city from Timur (Tamerlane) and his Mongol armies (see Chapter 10). The Russians believed the sacred picture saved the city of Kazan from later Tartar invasions and all of Russia from the Poles in the 17th century. The *Vladimir Virgin* is a historical symbol of Byzantium's religious and cultural mission to the Slavic world.

LATE BYZANTINE ART

When rule passed from the Macedonian to the Comnenian dynasty in the later 11th and 12th centuries, three events of fateful significance changed Byzantium's fortunes for the worse. The Seljuk Turks conquered most of Anatolia. The Byzantine Orthodox Church broke finally with the Church of Rome. And the Crusades brought the Latins (a generic term for the peoples of the West) into Byzantine lands on their way to fight for the Christian cross against the Saracens (Muslims) in the Holy Land (see "The Crusades," Chapter 12, page 346).

Crusaders had passed through Constantinople many times en route to "smite the infidel" and had marveled at its wealth and magnificence. Envy, greed, religious fanaticism (the Latins called the Greeks "heretics"), and even ethnic enmity motivated the Crusaders when, during the Fourth Crusade in 1203 and 1204, the Venetians persuaded them to divert their expedition against the Muslims in Palestine and to attack Constantinople instead. They took the city and sacked it. Nicetas Choniates, a contemporaneous historian, expressed the feelings of the Byzantines toward the Crusaders: "The accursed Latins would plunder our wealth and wipe out our race. . . . Between us there can be only an unbridgeable gulf

of hatred. . . . They bear the Cross of Christ on their shoulders, but even the Saracens are kinder."[7]

The Latins set up kingdoms within Byzantium, notably in Constantinople itself. What remained of Byzantium split into three small states. The Palaeologans ruled one of these, the kingdom of Nicaea. In 1261, Michael VIII Palaeologus (r. 1259–1282) succeeded in recapturing Constantinople. One of the gems of Late Byzantine architecture— the church dedicated to Saint Catherine (FIG. 9-32A) in Constantinople—dates to his reign. But Michael's empire was no more than a fragment, and even that disintegrated during the next two centuries. Isolated from the Christian West by Muslim conquests in the Balkans and

9-32A Saint Catherine, Thessaloniki, ca. 1280.

besieged by Muslim Turks to the East, Byzantium sought help from the West. It was not forthcoming. In 1453, the Ottoman Turks, then a formidable power, took Constantinople and brought to an end the long history of Byzantium (see Chapter 10). But despite the state's grim political condition under the Palaeologan dynasty, the arts flourished well into the 14th century.

9-32 *Anastasis,* fresco in the apse of the parekklesion of the Church of Christ in Chora (now the Kariye Museum), Constantinople (Istanbul), Turkey, ca. 1310–1320. ◼◀

In this Late Byzantine funerary chapel, Christ, a white apparition surrounded by a luminous mandorla, raises Adam and Eve from their tombs as John the Baptist and Kings David and Solomon look on.

Painting

During the 14th and 15th centuries, artists throughout the Byzantine world produced masterpieces of mural and icon painting rivaling those of the earlier periods. Four characteristic examples from the old capital of Constantinople and as far away as Russia illustrate the range and quality of painting during the Late Byzantine period.

CHRIST IN CHORA A fresco of the *Anastasis* (FIG. **9-32**) is in the apse of the *parekklesion* (side chapel, in this instance a funerary chapel) of the Church of Christ in Chora in Constantinople. One of many subsidiary subjects that made up the complex mosaic program of Saint Mark's (FIG. 9-26) in Venice, the *Anastasis* is here central to a cycle of pictures portraying the themes of human mortality and redemption by Christ and of the intercession of the Virgin, both appropriate for a funerary chapel. Christ, trampling Satan and all the locks and keys of his prison house of Hell, raises Adam and Eve from their tombs. Looking on are John the Baptist, King David, and King Solomon on the left, and various martyr saints on the right. Christ, central and in a luminous mandorla, reaches out equally to Adam and Eve. The action is swift and smooth, the

supple motions executed with the grace of a ballet. The figures float in a spiritual atmosphere, spaceless and without material mass or shadow-casting volume. This same smoothness and lightness also characterize the modeling of the figures and the subtly nuanced coloration. The jagged abstractions of drapery found in many earlier Byzantine frescoes and mosaics are gone in a return to the fluid delineation of drapery characteristic of the long tradition of classical illusionism.

Throughout the centuries, Byzantine artists looked back to Greco-Roman illusionism. But unlike classical artists, Byzantine painters and mosaicists did not believe the systematic observation of material nature should be the source of their representations of the eternal. They drew their images from a persistent and conventionalized vision of a spiritual world unsusceptible to change. That consistent vision is what unites works as distant in time as the sixth-century apse mosaic (FIG. 9-16) at Mount Sinai and the 14th-century fresco in the Church of Christ in Chora.

OHRID ICONS Icon painting may most intensely reveal Byzantine spirituality. In the Late Byzantine period, the Early Byzantine templon developed into an *iconostasis* (icon stand), a high screen with doors. As its name implies, the iconostasis supported tiers of painted devotional images, which began to be produced again in large numbers, both in Constantinople and throughout the diminished Byzantine Empire.

One example (FIG. **9-33**), notable for the lavish use of finely etched silver foil to frame the painted figure of Christ as Savior of Souls, dates to the beginning of the 14th century. It comes from the church of Saint Clement at Ohrid in Macedonia, where many Late Byzantine icons imported from the capital have been preserved. The painter of the Ohrid Christ, in a manner consistent with Byzantine art's conservative nature, adhered to an iconographical and stylistic tradition dating to the earliest icons from the monastery at Mount Sinai. As elsewhere (FIGS. 9-18A, 9-23, and 9-25), the Savior holds a bejeweled Bible in his left hand while he blesses the faithful with his right hand. The mixture of styles is typical of Byzantine painting. Note especially the juxtaposition of Christ's fully modeled head and neck, which reveal the Byzantine artist's Greco-Roman heritage, with the schematic linear folds of Christ's garment, which do not envelop the figure but rather seem to be placed in front of it.

Late Byzantine icons often have paintings on two sides because they were carried in processions. When the clergy brought the icons into the church, they did not mount them on the iconostasis but exhibited them on stands so they could be viewed from both sides. The Ohrid icon of Christ has a painting of the *Crucifixion* on its reverse. Another double icon

1 ft.

9-33 Christ as Savior of Souls, icon from Saint Clement, Ohrid, Macedonia, early 14th century. Tempera, linen, and silver on wood, 3′ ¼″ × 2′ 2½″. Icon Gallery of Saint Clement, Ohrid. ◼◢

Notable for the lavish use of finely etched silver foil, this icon typifies Byzantine stylistic complexity. Christ's fully modeled head and neck contrast with the schematic linear folds of his garment.

9-34 *Annunciation,* reverse of two-sided icon from the Church of the Virgin Peribleptos, Ohrid, Macedonia, early 14th century. Tempera and linen on wood, 3′ ⅝″ × 2′ 2¾″. Icon Gallery of Saint Clement, Ohrid.

Late Byzantine icons often have two painted sides because they were carried in processions. On this icon the Virgin Mary appears on the front and this *Annunciation* scene on the back.

9-35 ANDREI RUBLYEV, *Three Angels* (Old Testament Trinity), ca. 1410. Tempera on wood, 4′ 8″ × 3′ 9″. Tretyakov Gallery, Moscow. ◼◄

This exceptionally large icon featuring subtle line and vivid colors is one of the masterworks of Russian painting. It depicts the three angels who appeared to Abraham, prefiguring the Trinity.

from Ohrid, also imported from Constantinople, represents the Virgin on the front as Christ's counterpart as Savior of Souls. The *Annunciation* (FIG. **9-34**) is the subject of the reverse. With a commanding gesture of heavenly authority, the angel Gabriel announces to Mary that she is to be the Mother of God. She responds with a simple gesture conveying both astonishment and acceptance. The gestures and attitudes of the figures are again conventional, as are the highly simplified architectural props. The painter rendered the latter in inconsistent perspective derived from classical prototypes, but set the sturdy three-dimensional forms against an otherworldly golden sky, suggesting the sacred space in which the narrative unfolds. This icon therefore also exemplifies the diversity of stylistic sources that characterizes Byzantine art throughout its long history.

ANDREI RUBLYEV Icon painting flourished also in Russia. Russian icons usually have strong patterns, firm lines, and intense contrasting colors, which serve to heighten the legibility of the icons in the wavering candlelight and clouds of incense worshipers encountered in church interiors. For many art historians, Russian painting reached a climax in the work of ANDREI RUBLYEV (ca. 1370–1430). His nearly five-foot-tall panel (FIG. **9-35**) depicting the three Old Testament angels who appeared to Abraham is a work of great spiritual power. Painted during the tenure of Photius as Metropolitan (Orthodox archbishop) of Russia (FIG. **9-35A**), it is

an unsurpassed example of subtle line in union with what once were intensely vivid colors, now faded. The angels sit about a table, each framed with a halo and sweeping wings, three nearly identical figures distinguished primarily by their garment colors. The light linear play of the draperies sets off the tranquil demeanor of the figures. Juxtapositions of complementary hues add intensity to the coloration. The blue and green folds of the central figure's

9-35A Large sakkos of Photius, ca. 1417.

cloak, for example, stand out starkly against the deep-red robe and the gilded orange of the wings. In the figure on the left, the highlights of the orange cloak are an opalescent blue-green. The unmodulated saturation, brilliance, and purity of the color harmonies are the hallmark of Rublyev's style.

THE THIRD ROME With the fall of Constantinople in 1453, Russia became Byzantium's self-appointed heir, defending Christendom against the infidel. The court of the tsar (derived from Caesar) declared: "Because the Old Rome has fallen, and because the Second Rome, which is Constantinople, is now in the hands of the godless Turks, thy kingdom, O pious Tsar, is the Third Rome. . . . Two Romes have fallen, but the Third stands, and there shall be no more."[8] Rome, Byzantium, Russia—Old Rome, New Rome, and Third Rome—were a continuum, spanning two and a half millennia during which artists and architects produced many of the most significant paintings, sculptures, and buildings in the long history of art through the ages.

BYZANTIUM

EARLY BYZANTINE ART 324–726

▌ Constantine founded Constantinople on the site of the ancient Greek city of Byzantium in 324 and dedicated this "New Rome" to the Christian God in 330.

▌ The first golden age of Byzantine art was the result of the lavish patronage of Justinian (r. 527–565). In Constantinople alone, Justinian built or restored more than 30 churches. The greatest was Hagia Sophia, which rivaled the architectural wonders of Old Rome. A brilliant fusion of central and longitudinal plans, its 180-foot-high dome rests on pendentives but seemed to contemporaries to be suspended "by a golden chain from Heaven."

▌ The seat of Byzantine power in Italy was Ravenna, which also prospered under Justinian. San Vitale is Ravenna's greatest church. Its mosaics, with their weightless, hovering, frontal figures against a gold background, reveal the new Byzantine aesthetic.

▌ Justinian also rebuilt the monastery at Mount Sinai in Egypt. The preserved Sinai icons—portable devotional paintings depicting Christ, the Virgin, and saints—are the finest of the Early Byzantine period.

▌ In 726, Leo III (r. 717–741) enacted a ban against picturing the divine, initiating the era of iconoclasm (726–843) and the destruction of countless Early Byzantine artworks.

Hagia Sophia, Constantinople, 532–537

San Vitale, Ravenna, 526–547

MIDDLE BYZANTINE ART 843–1204

▌ Empress Theodora repealed iconoclasm in 843, and in 867, Basil I (r. 867–886) dedicated a new mosaic depicting the Theotokos (Mother of God) in Hagia Sophia. It marked the triumph of the iconophiles over the iconoclasts.

▌ Ivory carving and manuscript painting flourished during the Middle Byzantine period, as during the preceding era. Hinged ivory shrines, such as the *Harbaville Triptych*, were popular for use in private prayer. The *Paris Psalter* is noteworthy for the conscious revival of classical naturalism.

▌ Middle Byzantine churches, such as those at Hosios Loukas and Daphni, have highly decorative exterior walls and feature domes that rest on drums above the center of a Greek cross. The climax of the interior mosaic programs was often an image of Christ as Pantokrator in the dome.

Paris Psalter, ca. 950–970

Church of the Dormition, Daphni, ca. 1090–1100

LATE BYZANTINE ART 1261–1453

▌ In 1204, Latin Crusaders sacked Constantinople, bringing to an end the Middle Byzantine era. In 1261, Michael VIII Palaeologus (r. 1259–1282) succeeded in recapturing the city. Constantinople remained in Byzantine hands until its capture by the Ottoman Turks in 1453.

▌ Important mural paintings of the Late Byzantine period are in the Church of Christ in Chora. An extensive picture cycle portrays Christ as redeemer. In the apse, he raises Adam and Eve from their tombs.

▌ Late Byzantine icons were displayed in tiers on an iconostasis or on individual stands so that the paintings on both sides could be seen. Christ or the Virgin usually appeared on the front. The reverse depicted a narrative scene from the life of Christ.

Annunciation, Ohrid, early 14th century

The horseshoe and multilobed arches of the gates to the Mezquita at Córdoba were part of the expansion and remodeling of the mosque carried out by the Umayyad caliph al-Hakam II.

Islamic architecture draws on diverse sources. The horseshoe arches of the Córdoba mosque's prayer hall may derive from Visigothic architecture. The Arabs overthrew that Christian kingdom in 711.

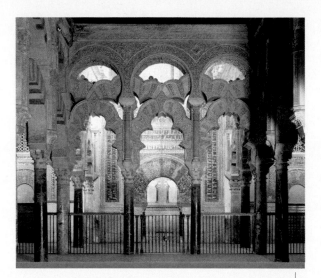

In the 10th century, al-Hakam II also added a maqsura to the Córdoba Mezquita. The hall highlights Muslim architects' bold experimentation with curvilinear shapes and different kinds of arches.

10-1 Aerial view of the Mezquita (Great Mosque), Córdoba, Spain, 8th to 10th centuries; rededicated as the Cathedral of Saint Mary, 1236.

10

THE ISLAMIC WORLD

Byzantine artists installed the mosaics in the mihrab dome in the Córdoba mosque, but the decorative patterns formed by the crisscrossing ribs and the multilobed arches are distinctly Islamic.

THE RISE AND SPREAD OF ISLAM

At the time of Muhammad's birth around 570, the Arabian peninsula was peripheral to the Byzantine and Sasanian empires. The Arabs, nomadic herders and caravan merchants who worshiped many gods, resisted the Prophet's teachings of Islam, an Arabic word meaning "submission to the one God (Allah in Arabic)." Within a decade of Muhammad's death in 632, however, Muslims ("those who submit") ruled Arabia, Palestine, Syria, Iraq, and northern Egypt. From there, the new religion spread rapidly both eastward and westward.

With the rise of Islam also came the birth of a compelling new worldwide tradition of art and architecture. In the Middle East and North Africa, Islamic art largely replaced Late Antique art. In India, the establishment of Muslim rule at Delhi in the early 13th century brought Islamic art and architecture to South Asia (see Chapter 32). In fact, perhaps the most famous building in Asia, the Taj Mahal (FIG. 32-6) at Agra, is an Islamic mausoleum. At the opposite end of the then-known world, Abd al-Rahman I (r. 756–788) founded a Spanish Muslim dynasty at Córdoba, which became the center of a brilliant court culture that profoundly influenced medieval Europe.

The jewel of the capital at Córdoba was its Great Mosque (FIG. **10-1**), begun in 784 and enlarged several times during the 9th and 10th centuries until it eventually became one of the largest mosques in the Islamic West. In 1236, the Christians rededicated and remodeled the shrine as a church (the tallest part of the complex, at the center of the aerial view, is Córdoba's cathedral) after they recaptured the city from the Muslims.

A visual feast greets all visitors to the mosque. Its Muslim designers used overlapping horseshoe-shaped arches (which became synonymous with Islamic architecture in Europe) in the uppermost zone of the eastern and western gates to the complex. Double rows of arches surmount the more than 500 columns in the mosque's huge prayer hall. Even more elaborate multilobed arches on slender columns form dazzling frames for other areas of the mosque, especially in the *maqsura,* the hall reserved for the ruler, which at Córdoba connects the mosque to the palace. Crisscrossing ribs form intricate decorative patterns in the complex's largest dome.

The Córdoba Mezquita (Spanish, "mosque") typifies Islamic architecture both in its conformity to the basic principles of mosque design and in its incorporation of distinctive regional forms.

EARLY ISLAMIC ART

The religion of Islam arose in Arabia early in the seventh century, after the Prophet Muhammad began to receive God's revelations (see "Muhammad and Islam," page 285). At that time, the Arabs were not major players on the world stage. Yet within little more than a century, the eastern Mediterranean, which Byzantium once ringed and ruled, had become an Islamic lake, and the armies of Muhammad's successors had subdued the Middle East, long the seat of Persian dominance and influence. The swiftness of the Islamic advance is among the wonders of history. By 640, Muslims ruled Syria, Palestine, and Iraq. In 642, the Byzantine army abandoned Alexandria, marking the Muslim conquest of Lower (northern) Egypt. In 651, Islamic forces ended more than 400 years of Sasanian rule in Iran (see Chapter 2). All of North Africa was under Muslim control by 710. A victory at Jerez de la Frontera in southern Spain in 711 seemed to open all of western Europe to the Muslims. By 732, they had advanced north to Poitiers in France. There, however, an army of Franks under Charles Martel (r. 714–741), the grandfather of Charlemagne, opposed them successfully (see Chapter 11), halting Islamic expansion at the Pyrenees. In Spain, in contrast, the Muslim rulers of Córdoba (FIG. 10-1) flourished until 1031, and not until 1492 did

Islamic influence and power end in Iberia. That year the army of King Ferdinand II of Aragon (r. 1479–1516) and Queen Isabella, the sponsors of Columbus's voyage to the New World, overthrew the caliphs of Granada. In the East, the Muslims reached the Indus River by 751 (see Chapter 32). Only in Anatolia did stubborn Byzantine resistance slow their advance. Relentless Muslim pressure against the shrinking Byzantine Empire eventually brought about its collapse in 1453, when the Ottoman Turks entered Constantinople (see Chapter 9).

Military might alone cannot, however, account for the irresistible and far-ranging sweep of Islam from Arabia to India to North Africa and Spain (MAP 10-1). That Islam endured in the lands Muhammad's successors conquered can be explained only by the nature of the Islamic faith and its appeal to millions of converts. Islam remains today one of the world's great religions, with adherents on all continents. Its sophisticated culture has had a major influence around the globe. Arab scholars laid the foundations of arithmetic and algebra and made significant contributions to astronomy, medicine, and the natural sciences. During the 12th and 13th centuries, Christian scholars in the West eagerly studied Arabic translations of Aristotle and other ancient Greek writers. Arabic love lyrics and poetic descriptions of nature inspired the early French troubadours.

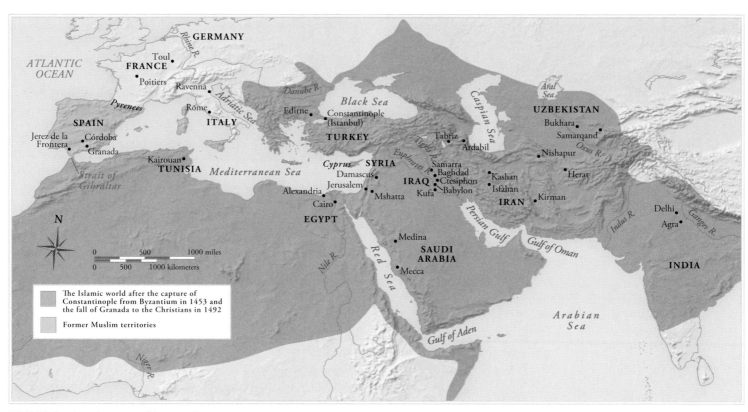

MAP 10-1 The Islamic world around 1500.

THE ISLAMIC WORLD

622	756	1453	1924
▮ Muhammad abandons Mecca for Medina, 622 ▮ Umayyads (r. 661–750), the first Islamic dynasty, build Dome of the Rock in Jerusalem and Great Mosque in Damascus	▮ Abbasids produce earliest Korans with Kufic calligraphy ▮ Spanish Umayyad dynasty builds Great Mosque in capital of Córdoba ▮ Nasrids embellish Alhambra with magnificent palaces ▮ Fatimid, Ayyubid, and Mamluk dynasties in Egypt are lavish art patrons	▮ Ottomans capture Byzantine Constantinople in 1453 and develop the domed central-plan mosque ▮ Flowering of Timurid book illumination under Shah Tahmasp ▮ Safavid artisans perfect the manufacture of cuerda seca and mosaic tiles	

Muhammad and Islam

Muhammad, revered by Muslims as the Final Prophet in the line including Abraham, Moses, and Jesus, was a native of Mecca on the west coast of Arabia. Born around 570 into a family of merchants in the great Arabian caravan trade, Muhammad was critical of the polytheistic religion of his fellow Arabs. In 610, he began to receive the revelations of God through the archangel Gabriel. Opposition to Muhammad's message among the Arabs was strong and led to persecution. In 622, the Prophet and his followers abandoned Mecca for a desert oasis eventually called Medina ("City of the Prophet"). Islam dates its beginnings from this flight, known as the *Hijra* (emigration).* Barely eight years later, in 630, Muhammad returned to Mecca with 10,000 soldiers. He took control of the city, converted the population to Islam, and destroyed all the idols. But he preserved as the Islamic world's symbolic center the small cubical building that had housed the idols, the *Kaaba* (from the Arabic for "cube"). The Arabs associated the Kaaba with the era of Abraham and Ishmael, the common ancestors of Jews and Arabs. Muhammad died in Medina in 632.

The essential tenet of Islam is acceptance of and submission to God's will. Muslims must live according to the rules laid down in the collected revelations communicated through Muhammad during his lifetime. The *Koran,* Islam's sacred book, codified by the Muslim ruler Uthman (r. 644–656), records Mohammad's revelations. The word "Koran" means "recitations"—a reference to Gabriel's instructions to Muhammad in 610 to "recite in the name of God." The Koran is composed of 114 *surahs* (chapters) divided into verses.

The profession of faith in the one God is the first of five obligations binding all Muslims. In addition, the faithful must worship five times daily facing Mecca, give alms to the poor, fast during the month of Ramadan, and once in a lifetime—if possible—make a pilgrimage to Mecca. The revelations in the Koran are not the only guide for Muslims. Muhammad's words and exemplary ways and customs, the *Hadith,* recorded in the *Sunnah,* offer models to all Muslims on ethical problems of everyday life. The reward for the faithful is Paradise.

Islam has much in common with Judaism and Christianity. Muslims think of their religion as a continuation, a completion, and in some sense a reformation of those other great monotheisms. Islam, for example, incorporates many Old Testament teachings, with their sober ethical standards and rejection of idol worship. But, unlike Jesus in the New Testament Gospels, Muhammad did not claim to be divine. Rather, he was God's messenger, the Final Prophet, who purified and perfected the common faith of Jews, Christians, and Muslims in one God. Islam also differs from Judaism and Christianity in its simpler organization. Muslims worship God directly, without a hierarchy of rabbis, priests, or saints acting as intermediaries.

In Islam, as Muhammad defined it, the union of religious and secular authority was even more complete than in Byzantium. Muhammad established a new social order, replacing the Arabs' old decentralized tribal one, and took complete charge of his community's temporal as well as spiritual affairs. After Muhammad's death, the *caliphs* (from the Arabic for "successor") continued this practice of uniting religious and political leadership in one ruler.

*Muslims date events beginning with the Hijra in the same way Christians reckon events from Christ's birth and the Romans before them began their calendar with Rome's founding by Romulus and Remus in 753 BCE. The Muslim year is, however, a 354-day year of 12 lunar months, and thus dates cannot be converted by simply adding 622 to Christian-era dates.

Architecture

During the early centuries of Islamic history, the Muslim world's political and cultural center was the Fertile Crescent of ancient Mesopotamia. The caliphs of Damascus (capital of modern Syria) and Baghdad (capital of Iraq) appointed provincial governors to rule the vast territories they controlled. These governors eventually gained relative independence by setting up dynasties in various territories and provinces, including the Umayyads in Syria (661–750) and in Spain (756–1031), the Abbasids in Iraq (750–1258, largely nominal after 945), the Samanids in Uzbekistan (819–1005), the Fatimids in Egypt (909–1171), and others.

Like other potentates before and after, the Muslim caliphs were builders on a grand scale. The first Islamic buildings, both religious and secular, are in the Middle East, but important early examples of Islamic architecture still stand also in North Africa, Spain, and Central Asia.

DOME OF THE ROCK The first great Islamic building was the Dome of the Rock (FIG. 10-2) in Jerusalem. The Muslims had taken the city from the Byzantines in 638, and the Umayyad caliph Abd al-Malik (r. 685–705) erected the monumental shrine between 687 and 692 as an architectural tribute to the triumph of Islam. The Dome of the Rock marked the coming of the new religion to the city that had been, and still is, sacred to both Jews and

10-2 Aerial view (looking southwest) of the Dome of the Rock, Jerusalem, 687–692.

Abd al-Malik built the Dome of the Rock to mark the triumph of Islam in Jerusalem on a site sacred to Muslims, Christians, and Jews. The shrine takes the form of an octagon with a towering dome.

Early Islamic Art   **285**

10-3 Interior of the Dome of the Rock, Jerusalem, 687–692.

On the interior of the Dome of the Rock, the original mosaics are largely intact. At the center of the rotunda is the rocky outcropping later associated with Adam, Abraham, and Muhammad.

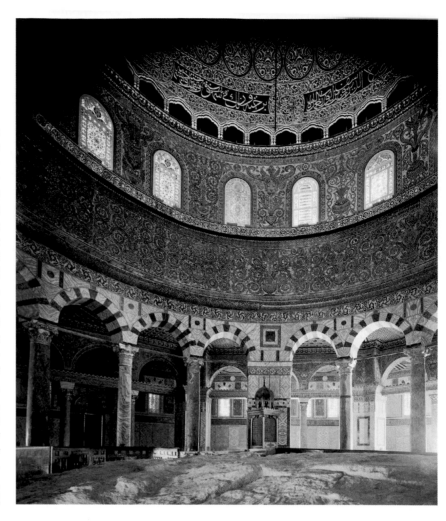

Christians. The structure rises from a huge platform known as the Noble Enclosure, where in ancient times the Hebrews built the Temple of Solomon that the Roman emperor Titus destroyed in the year 70 (see Chapter 7). In time, the site acquired additional significance as the reputed location of Adam's grave and the spot where Abraham prepared to sacrifice Isaac. The rock (FIG. 10-3) that gives the building its name also later came to be identified with the place where Muhammad began his miraculous journey to Heaven (the *Miraj*) and then, in the same night, returned to his home in Mecca.

In its form, construction, and decoration, the Dome of the Rock is firmly in the Late Antique tradition of the Mediterranean world. It is a domed central-plan structure descended from the Pantheon (FIG. 7-49) in Rome and Hagia Sophia (FIG. 9-5) in Constantinople, but it more closely resembles the octagonal San Vitale (FIG. 9-10) in Ravenna. In all likelihood, a neighboring Christian monument, Constantine's Church of the Holy Sepulcher, inspired the Dome of the Rock's designers. That fourth-century domed rotunda bore a family resemblance to the roughly contemporaneous Constantinian mausoleum later rededicated as Santa Costanza (FIGS. 8-11 and 8-12) in Rome. Crowning the Islamic shrine is a 75-foot-tall double-shelled

10-4 Aerial view (looking southeast) of the Great Mosque, Damascus, Syria, 706–715. ◼◂

The Umayyads constructed Damascus's Great Mosque after they transferred their capital from Mecca in 661. The mosque owes a debt to Late Antique architecture in its plan and decoration.

wooden dome, which so dominates the elevation as to reduce the octagon to function merely as its base. This soaring, majestic unit creates a decidedly more commanding effect than that of similar Late Antique and Byzantine domical structures (FIGS. 9-5 and 9-10). The silhouettes of those domes are comparatively insignificant when seen from the outside.

The building's exterior has been much restored. Tiling from the 16th century and later has replaced the original mosaic. Yet the vivid, colorful patterning wrapping the walls like a textile is typical of Islamic ornamentation. It contrasts markedly with Byzantine brickwork and Greco-Roman sculptured decoration. The interior's rich mosaic ornamentation (FIG. 10-3) is largely intact and suggests the original appearance of the exterior walls. Against a lush vegetal background, Abd al-Malik's mosaicists depicted crowns, jewels, chalices, and other royal motifs—probably a reference to the triumph of Islam over the Byzantine and Persian empires. Inscriptions, mostly from the Koran, underscore Islam as the superior new monotheism, superseding both Judaism and Christianity in Jerusalem. (Curiously, no inscription refers to the rock within the shrine.)

GREAT MOSQUE, DAMASCUS The Umayyads transferred their capital from Mecca to Damascus in 661. There, Abd al-Malik's son, the caliph al-Walid (r. 705–715), purchased a Byzantine church dedicated to John the Baptist (formerly a Roman temple of Jupiter) and built an imposing new mosque for the expanding Muslim population (see "The Mosque," page 288). The Umayyads demolished the church, but they used the Roman precinct walls as a foundation for their construction. Like the Dome of the Rock, Damascus's Great Mosque (FIG. 10-4) owes much to Roman and Early Christian architecture. The Islamic builders incorporated stone blocks, columns, and capitals salvaged from the earlier structures on the land acquired by al-Walid. Pier *arcades* reminiscent of Roman aqueducts (FIG. 7-33) frame the courtyard. The *minarets*, two at the southern corners and one at the northern side of the enclosure—the earliest in the Islamic world—are modifications of the preexisting Roman square towers. The grand prayer hall, taller than the rest of the complex, is on the south side of the courtyard (facing Mecca). The hall's facade, with its pediment and arches, recalls Roman and Byzantine models and faces into the courtyard, like a temple in a Roman forum (FIG. 7-12), a plan maintained throughout the long history of mosque architecture. The Damascus mosque synthesizes elements received from other cultures into a novel architectural unity, which includes the distinctive Islamic elements of *mihrab,* mihrab dome, *minbar,* and minaret.

An extensive cycle of glass mosaics once covered the walls of the Great Mosque. In one of the surviving sections (FIG. 10-5), a conch-shell niche "supports" an arcaded pavilion with a flowering rooftop flanked by structures shown in perspective. Like the architectural design, the mosaics owe much to Roman, Early Christian, and Byzantine art. Indeed, some evidence indicates they were the work of Byzantine mosaicists. Characteristically, temples, clusters of houses, trees, and rivers compose the pictorial fields, bounded by stylized vegetal designs also found in Roman, Early Christian, and Byzantine ornamentation. No zoomorphic forms, human or animal, appear either in the pictorial or ornamental spaces. This is true of all the mosaics in the Great Mosque as well as the mosaics in the earlier Dome of the Rock (FIG. 10-3). Although there is no prohibition against figural art in the Koran, Islamic tradition, based on the Hadith, shuns the representation of fauna of any kind in sacred places. Accompanying (but now lost) inscriptions explained the world shown in the Damascus mosaics, suspended miragelike in a featureless field of gold, as an image of Paradise. The imagery is consistent with many passages from the Koran describing the gorgeous places of Paradise awaiting the faithful—gardens, groves of trees, flowing streams, and "lofty chambers."

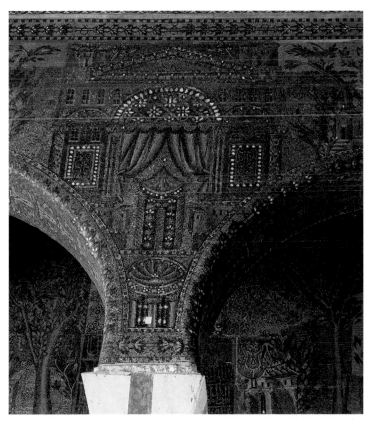

10-5 Detail of a mosaic in the courtyard arcade of the Great Mosque, Damascus, Syria, 706–715.

The mosaics of the Great Mosque at Damascus are probably the work of Byzantine artists and include buildings and landscapes, though not zoomorphic forms, common in Late Antique art.

BAGHDAD The Umayyad caliphs maintained power for nearly a century, during which they constructed numerous palatial residences throughout their domains. Perhaps the most impressive was the palace (FIGS. 10-5A and 10-5B) at Mshatta in Jordan datable just before 750 when, after years of civil war, the Abbasids, who claimed descent from Abbas, an uncle of Muhammad, overthrew the Umayyad caliphs. The new rulers moved the capital from Damascus to a site in Iraq near the old Sasanian capital of Ctesiphon (FIG. 2-28). There the caliph al-Mansur (r. 754–775) established a new capital, Baghdad, which he called Madina al-Salam, the City of Peace. Laid out in 762 at a time astrologers determined was favorable, Baghdad had a circular plan, about a mile and a half in diameter. The shape, which had precedents in ancient Assyria, Parthia, and Persia, signified the new capital was the center of the universe. The city had a moat and four gates oriented to the four compass points. At the center was the caliph's palace. No traces of al-Mansur's Round City remain today, but for almost 300 years, Baghdad was the hub of Arab power and of a brilliant Islamic culture. The Abbasid caliphs amassed great wealth and established diplomatic relations

10-5A Plan, Umayyad palace, Mshatta, 740–750.

10-5B Frieze, Umayyad palace, Mshatta, 740–750.

The Mosque

Islamic religious architecture is closely related to Muslim prayer, an obligation laid down in the Koran for all Muslims. In Islam, worshiping can be a private act and requires neither prescribed ceremony nor a special locale. Only the *qibla*—the direction (toward Mecca) Muslims face while praying—is important. But worship also became a communal act when the first Muslim community established a simple ritual for it. To celebrate the Muslim sabbath, which occurs on Friday, the community convened each Friday at noon, probably in the Prophet's house in Medina. The main feature of Muhammad's house was a large square court with rows of palm trunks supporting thatched roofs along the north and south sides. The southern side, which faced Mecca, was wider and had a double row of trunks. After the prayer, the *imam,* or leader of collective worship, stood on a stepped pulpit, or *minbar,* set up in front of the southern (qibla) wall, and preached the sermon.

These features became standard in the Islamic house of worship, the *mosque* (from Arabic "masjid," a place of prostration), where the faithful gather for the five daily prayers. The *congregational mosque* (also called the *Friday mosque* or *great mosque*) was ideally large enough to accommodate a community's entire population for the Friday noon prayer. An important feature both of ordinary mosques and of congregational mosques is the *mihrab* (FIG. 10-6, no. 2), a semicircular niche usually set into the qibla wall. Often a dome over the bay in front of the mihrab marked its position (FIGS. 10-4 and 10-6, no. 3). The niche was a familiar Greco-Roman architectural feature, generally enclosing a statue. Scholars still debate its origin, purpose, and meaning in Islamic architecture. The mihrab originally may have honored the place where the Prophet stood in his house at Medina when he led communal worship.

In some mosques, a *maqsura* precedes the mihrab. The maqsura, the area generally reserved for the ruler or his representative, can be quite elaborate in form (FIG. 10-11). Many mosques also have one or more *minarets* (FIGS. 10-4, 10-7, and 10-23), towers used to call the faithful to worship. When the Muslims converted buildings of other faiths into mosques, they clearly signaled the change on the exterior by the construction of minarets (FIG. 9-5). *Hypostyle halls,* communal worship halls with roofs held up by a multitude of columns (FIGS. 10-6, no. 4, and 10-10), are characteristic features of early mosques. Later variations include mosques with four *iwans* (vaulted rectangular recesses), one on each side of the courtyard (FIGS. 10-13 and 10-14), and *central-plan* mosques with a single large dome-covered interior space (FIGS. 10-23 and 10-24), as in Byzantine churches, some of which later became mosques (FIG. 9-8).

Today, despite many variations in design and detail (see, for example, the adobe-and-wood mosque in Mali, FIG. 19-9) and the employment of building techniques and materials unknown in Muhammad's day, the mosque's essential features remain unchanged. The orientation of all mosques everywhere, whatever their plan, is Mecca, and the faithful worship facing the qibla wall.

10-6 Aerial view (looking south; *left*) and plan (*right*) of the Great Mosque, Kairouan, Tunisia, ca. 836–875. ◼◀

Kairouan's Great Mosque is a hypostyle mosque with forecourt and columnar prayer hall. The plan most closely resembles the layout of Muhammad's house in Medina.

1. Qibla wall 5. Nave
2. Mihrab 6. Entrance dome
3. Mihrab dome 7. Forecourt
4. Hypostyle prayer hall 8. Minaret

0 25 50 75 100 feet
0 10 20 30 meters

throughout the world, even with Charlemagne in Germany. They spent lavishly on art, literature, and science and were responsible for the translation of numerous Greek texts that otherwise would have been lost. In fact, many of these ancient works first became known in medieval Europe through their Arabic versions.

GREAT MOSQUE, KAIROUAN Several decades after the founding of Baghdad, the Abbasids constructed at Kairouan in Tunisia one of the best preserved early mosques (FIG. **10-6**). Of *hypostyle* design, it most closely reflects the mosque's supposed precursor, Muhammad's house in Medina (see "The Mosque," page 288). Still in use today, the Kairouan mosque retains its carved wooden minbar of 862, the oldest known. The precinct takes the form of a slightly askew parallelogram of huge scale, some 450 by 260 feet. Built of stone, its walls have sturdy buttresses, square in profile. Lateral entrances on the east and west lead to an arcaded forecourt (FIG. 10-6, no. 7) resembling a Roman forum (FIG. 7-44), oriented north-south on axis with the mosque's impressive minaret (no. 8) and the two domes of the hypostyle prayer hall (no. 4). The first dome (no. 6) is over the entrance bay, the second (no. 3) over the bay that fronts the mihrab (no. 2) set into the *qibla* wall (no. 1). A raised nave (no. 5) connects the domed spaces and prolongs the north-south axis of the minaret and courtyard. Eight columned aisles flank the nave on either side, providing space for a large congregation.

MALWIYA MINARET, SAMARRA The three-story minaret of the Kairouan mosque is square in plan and believed to be a near-copy of a Roman lighthouse, but minarets take a variety of forms. Perhaps the most striking and novel is the minaret of the immense (more than 45,000 square yards) Great Mosque at Samarra, Iraq, on the east bank of the Tigris River north of Baghdad. Samarra was the capital of the Abbasid caliph al-Mutawakkil (r. 847–861), who built the mosque between 848 and 852. At the time of its construction the Samarra mosque was the largest in the world. Known as the Malwiya ("snail shell" in Arabic) Minaret (FIG. **10-7**), it is more than 165 feet tall. Although it now stands alone, originally a bridge linked the minaret to the mosque. The distinguishing feature of the brick tower is its stepped spiral ramp, which increases in slope from bottom to top. Once thought to be an ancient Mesopotamian *ziggurat,* the Samarra minaret inspired some European depictions of the biblical Tower of Babel (Babylon's ziggurat; see "Babylon, City of Wonders," Chapter 2, page 49). Because it is too tall to have been used to call Muslims to prayer, the Abbasids probably intended the Malwiya Minaret, visible from a considerable distance in the flat plain around Samarra, to announce the presence of Islam in the Tigris Valley. Unfortunately, since 2005 the minaret has suffered damage at the hands of various parties during the continuing unrest in Iraq.

SAMANID MAUSOLEUM, BUKHARA Dynasties of governors who exercised considerable independence while recognizing the ultimate authority of the Baghdad caliphs oversaw the eastern realms of the Abbasid Empire. One of these dynasties, the Samanids (r. 819–1005), presided over the eastern frontier beyond the Oxus River (Transoxiana) on the border with India. In the early 10th century, the Samanids erected an impressive domed brick mausoleum (FIG. **10-8**) at Bukhara in modern Uzbekistan. Monumental tombs were virtually unknown in the early Islamic period. Muhammad had been opposed to elaborate burials and instructed his followers to bury him in a simple unmarked grave. In time, however, the

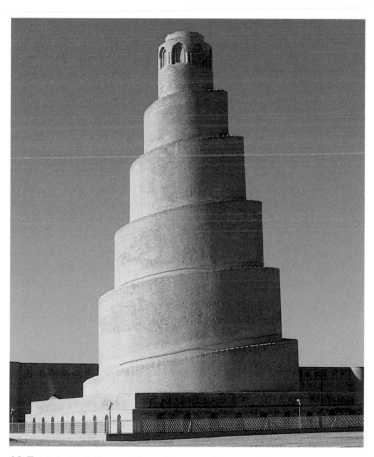

10-7 Malwiya Minaret, Great Mosque, Samarra, Iraq, 848–852.

The unique spiral Malwiya (snail shell) Minaret of Samarra's Great Mosque is more than 165 feet tall and can be seen from afar. It served to announce the presence of Islam in the Tigris Valley.

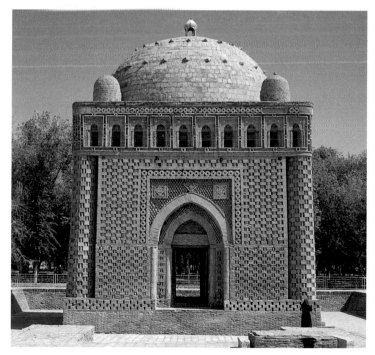

10-8 Mausoleum of the Samanids, Bukhara, Uzbekistan, early 10th century.

Monumental tombs were almost unknown in the early Islamic period. The Samanid mausoleum at Bukhara is one of the oldest. Its dome-on-cube form had a long afterlife in Islamic funerary architecture.

10-9 Prayer hall of the Mezquita (Great Mosque), Córdoba, Spain, 8th to 10th centuries.

Córdoba was the capital of the Spanish Umayyad dynasty. In the Great Mosque's hypostyle prayer hall, 36 piers and 514 columns support a unique series of double-tiered horseshoe-shaped arches.

Prophet's resting place in Medina acquired a wooden screen and a dome. By the ninth century, Abbasid caliphs were laid to rest in dynastic mausoleums.

The Samanid mausoleum at Bukhara is one of the earliest preserved tombs in the Islamic world. Constructed of baked bricks, it takes the form of a dome-capped cube with slightly sloping sides. With exceptional skill, the builders painstakingly shaped the bricks to create a vivid and varied surface pattern. Some of the bricks form *engaged columns* (half-round, attached columns) at the corners. A brick *blind arcade* (a series of arches in relief, with blocked openings) runs around all four sides. Inside, the walls are as elaborate as the exterior. The brick dome rests on arcuated brick squinches (see "Pendentives and Squinches," Chapter 9, page 262) framed by engaged *colonnettes* (thin columns). The dome-on-cube form had a long and distinguished future in Islamic funerary architecture (FIGS. 10-22 and 32-6).

GREAT MOSQUE, CÓRDOBA At the opposite end of the Muslim world, Abd al-Rahman I (r. 756–788), the only Umayyad notable to escape the Abbasid massacre of his clan in Syria, fled to Spain in 750. There, the Arabs had overthrown the Christian kingdom of the Visigoths in 711 (see Chapter 11). The Arab military governors accepted the fugitive as their overlord, and he founded the Spanish Umayyad dynasty, which lasted nearly three centuries. The capital of the Spanish Umayyads was Córdoba, which became the center of a brilliant culture rivaling that of the Abbasids at Baghdad and exerting major influence on the civilization of the Christian West.

The jewel of the capital at Córdoba was its Great Mosque (FIG. 10-1), begun in 784 by Abd al-Rahman I and enlarged

several times during the 9th and 10th centuries. Córdoba's Mezquita eventually became one of the largest mosques in the Islamic West. The hypostyle prayer hall (FIG. 10-9) has 36 piers and 514 columns topped by a unique system of double-tiered arches that carried a wooden roof (later replaced by vaults). The two-story system was the builders' response to the need to raise the roof to an acceptable height using short columns that had been employed earlier in other structures. The lower arches are horseshoe-shaped, a form perhaps adapted from earlier Mesopotamian architecture or

10-10 Detail of the upper zones of the east gate of the Mezquita (Great Mosque), Córdoba, Spain, 961–965.

The caliph al-Hakam II expanded and renovated Córdoba's Mezquita. The new gates to the complex feature intricate surface patterns of overlapping horseshoe-shaped and multilobed arches.

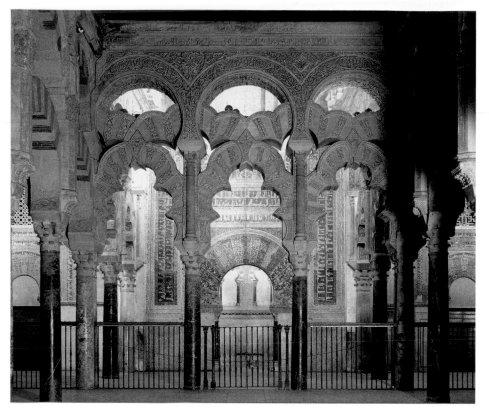

10-11 Maqsura of the Mezquita (Great Mosque), Córdoba, Spain, 961–965.

Reserved for the caliph, the maqsura of the Córdoba mosque connected the mosque to his palace. It is a prime example of Islamic experimentation with highly decorative multilobed arches.

of Visigothic origin (FIG. 11-10). In the West, the horseshoe arch quickly became closely associated with Muslim architecture. Visually, these arches seem to billow out like windblown sails, and they contribute greatly to the light and airy effect of the Córdoba mosque's interior.

In 961, al-Hakam II (r. 961–976) became caliph. A learned man who amassed a library of 400,000 volumes, he immediately undertook major renovations to the mosque. His builders expanded the prayer hall, added a series of domes, and constructed monumental gates on the complex's eastern (FIG. 10-10) and western facades. The gates are noteworthy for their colorful masonry and intricate surface patterns, especially in the uppermost zone, with its series of overlapping horseshoe-shaped arches springing from delicate colonnettes.

Also dating to the caliphate of al-Hakam II is the mosque's extraordinary maqsura (FIG. 10-11), the area reserved for the caliph and connected to his palace by a corridor in the qibla wall. The Córdoba maqsura is a prime example of Islamic experimentation with highly decorative multilobed arches (which are subsidiary motifs in the contemporaneous gate, FIG. 10-10). The Muslim builders created rich and varied abstract patterns and further enhanced the magnificent effect of the complex arches by sheathing the walls with marbles and mosaics. Al-Hakam II wished to emulate the great mosaic-clad monuments his Umayyad predecessors had erected in Jerusalem (FIG. 10-3) and Damascus (FIG. 10-5), and he brought the mosaicists and even the *tesserae* (cubical pieces) to Córdoba from Constantinople.

The same desire for decorative effect also inspired the design of the dome (FIG. 10-12) covering the area in front of the mihrab, one of the four domes built during the 10th century to emphasize the axis leading to the mihrab. The dome rests on an octagonal base of arcuated squinches. Crisscrossing ribs form an intricate pattern centered on two squares set at 45-degree angles to each other. The mosaics are the work of the same Byzantine artists responsible for the maqsura's decoration.

FRIDAY MOSQUE, ISFAHAN Muslim rulers built mosques of the hypostyle type throughout their realms during the early centuries of the new religion, but other mosque plans gradually gained favor in certain regions (see "The Mosque," page 288). At Isfahan, the third-largest city in Iran today, the Abbasids constructed the first mosque

10-12 Dome in front of the mihrab of the Mezquita (Great Mosque), Córdoba, Spain, 961–965.

The dome in front of the Córdoba mihrab rests on an octagonal base of arcuated squinches. Crisscrossing ribs form an intricate decorative pattern. Byzantine artists fashioned the mosaic ornamentation.

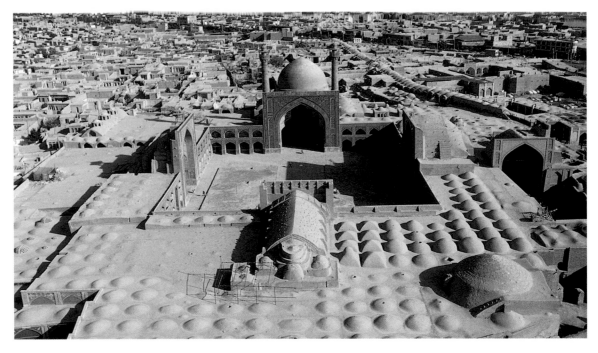

10-13 Aerial view (looking southwest) of the Friday Mosque, Isfahan, Iran, 11th to 17th centuries. ◼◀

The typical Iranian mosque plan with four vaulted iwans and a courtyard was perhaps first used in the mosque Sultan Malik Shah I built in the late 11th century at his capital of Isfahan.

1. Iwan
2. Courtyard
3. Qibla iwan
4. Domed maqsura

10-14 Plan of the Friday Mosque, Isfahan, Iran, 11th to 17th centuries.

In Isfahan's Friday Mosque, as in other four-iwan mosques, the qibla iwan is the largest. Its size and the dome-covered maqsura in front of it indicated the proper direction to face for Muslim prayer.

of hypostyle design in that formerly Sasanian city during the eighth century. In the 11th century, the Seljuks, a Turkic people who had converted to Islam, built an extensive, although short-lived empire that stretched eastward from Anatolia and included Iran. At that time, the Seljuk *sultan* (ruler) Malik Shah I (r. 1072–1092) made Isfahan his capital and transformed the Abbasid mosque in stages.

The Seljuk Friday Mosque (FIGS. **10-13** and **10-14**) underwent further modification over subsequent centuries, but still retains its basic 11th-century plan, consisting of a large courtyard bordered by a two-story arcade on each side. Four vaulted iwans open onto the courtyard, one at the center of each side. The southwestern iwan (FIG. 10-14, no. 3) leads into a dome-covered room (no. 4) in front of the mihrab that functioned as a maqsura reserved for the sultan and his attendants. It is uncertain whether Isfahan's Friday Mosque is the earliest example of a four-iwan mosque, but that plan became standard in Iranian religious architecture. In this type of mosque, the qibla iwan is always the largest. Its size (and the dome that often accompanied it) immediately indicated to worshipers the proper direction for prayer.

Luxury Arts

The furnishings of Islamic mosques and palaces reflect a love of sumptuous materials and rich decorative patterns. Muslim artisans artfully worked ivory (FIG. 10-15), metal, wood, and glass into a great variety of objects for sacred spaces or the home. They used colored glass with striking effect in mosque lamps (FIG. 10-28) and produced ceramics (FIG. 10-18) of high quality in large numbers. Muslim metalwork-

10-14A Silk textile, from Zandana, eighth century.

ers created elaborate ewers (FIG. 10-16), basins (FIG. 10-31), jewel cases, writing boxes, and other portable items (FIG. 10-32) made of bronze or brass, engraved, and inlaid with silver. Weavers employed silk (FIGS. **10-14A** and 10-26A) and wool (FIG. 10-27) to fashion textiles featuring both abstract and pictorial motifs. Because wood is scarce in most of the Islamic world, the kinds of furniture used in the West—beds, tables, and chairs—are rare in Muslim buildings. Movable furnishings, therefore, do not define Islamic architectural spaces. A room's function (eating or sleeping, for example) can change simply by rearranging the carpets and cushions.

IVORY The centers of production for these luxurious art forms were usually the courts of the Muslim caliphs and sultans. One

10-15 Pyxis of al Mughira, from Medina al-Zahra, near Córdoba, Spain, 968. Ivory, $5\frac{7}{8}''$ high. Musée du Louvre, Paris.

The royal workshops of Abd al-Rahman III produced luxurious objects such as this ivory pyxis decorated with hunting motifs and vine scrolls. It belonged to al-Mughira, the caliph's younger son.

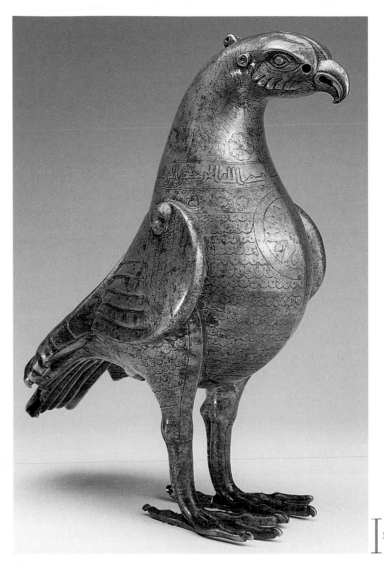

10-16 SULAYMAN, Ewer in the form of a bird, 796. Brass with silver and copper inlay, 1' 3" high. Hermitage, Saint Petersburg.

Signed and dated by its maker, this bird ewer resembles a freestanding statuette. The engraved decoration of the body combines natural feathers with abstract motifs and Arabic calligraphy.

was Córdoba (FIGS. 10-1 and 10-9 to 10-12). Abd al-Rahman III (r. 912–961), a descendant of the founder of the Umayyad dynasty in Spain, became *emir* (ruler) when he was 22. In 929, he declared himself caliph, a title previously restricted to the Muslim rulers who controlled the holy cities of Mecca and Medina. During his nearly 50-year reign, he constructed a lavish new palace for himself and his successors at Medina al-Zahra, about five miles from Córdoba. The palace complex housed royal workshops for the production of luxury items for the caliph's family and for use as diplomatic gifts, including richly carved ivory boxes (FIG. **10-15**). Befitting their prospective owners, Spanish Umayyad ivory *pyxides* (singular, *pyxis;* a cylindrical box with a hemispherical lid) usually featured motifs symbolic of royal power and privilege, including hunting scenes and musical entertainments.

The pyxis shown here (FIG. 10-15) belonged to al-Mughira, the younger son of Abd al-Rahman III. The inscription carved at the base of the lid is a prayer for the 18-year-old prince's well-being: "God's blessing, favors, and happiness to al-Mughira, son of the commander of the faithful, may God have mercy upon him,

in the year 357 [968 CE]." The anonymous ivory carver decorated the pyxis with a rich array of animals and hunters amid lush vine scrolls surrounding four eight-lobed figural medallions. In one medallion, lions attack bulls. In another (not visible in FIG. 10-15), the prince himself appears, serenaded by a lutenist.

METALWORK One striking example of early Islamic metalwork is the cast brass ewer (FIG. 10-16) in the form of a bird signed by SULAYMAN and dated 796. Some 15 inches tall, the ewer is nothing less than a freestanding statuette, although the holes between the eyes and beak function as a spout and betray its utilitarian purpose. The decoration on the body, which bears traces of silver and copper inlay, takes a variety of forms. In places, the incised lines seem to suggest natural feathers, but the rosettes on the neck, the large medallions on the breast, and the inscribed collar have no basis in anatomy. Similar motifs appear in Islamic textiles, pottery, and architectural tiles. The ready adaptability of motifs to various scales and to various techniques illustrates both the flexibility of Islamic design and its relative independence from its carrier.

Early Islamic Art   **293**

10-17 Koran page with beginning of surah 18, 9th or early 10th century. Ink and gold on vellum, $7\frac{1}{4}'' \times 10\frac{1}{4}''$. Chester Beatty Library and Oriental Art Gallery, Dublin. ◼◀

The script used in the oldest-known Korans is the stately rectilinear Kufic. This page has five text lines and a palm-tree finial but characteristically does not include depictions of animals or humans.

1 in.

KORANS In the Islamic world, the art of *calligraphy*, ornamental writing, held a place of honor. The faithful wanted to reproduce the Koran's sacred words in a script as beautiful as human hands could contrive. Passages from the Koran adorned not only the fragile pages of books but also the walls of buildings—for example, in the mosaic band above the outer ring of columns inside the Dome of the Rock (FIG. 10-3). The practice of calligraphy was itself a holy task and required long, arduous training. The scribe had to possess exceptional spiritual refinement. An ancient Arabic proverb proclaims, "Purity of writing is purity of soul." Only in China does calligraphy hold as elevated a position among the arts (see "Calligraphy and Inscriptions on Chinese Paintings," Chapter 33, page 997).

Arabic script predates Islam. It is written from right to left with certain characters connected by a baseline. Although the codification of the chief Islamic book, the sacred Koran, occurred in the mid-seventh century, the earliest preserved Korans date to the ninth century. Koran pages were either bound into books or stored as loose sheets in boxes. Most of the early examples feature texts written in the script form called *Kufic,* after the city of Kufa, one of the renowned centers of Arabic calligraphy. Kufic script—used also for the inscription on al-Mughira's 10th-century pyxis (FIG. 10-15)—is quite angular, with the uprights forming almost right angles with the baseline. As with Hebrew and other Semitic languages, the usual practice was to write in consonants only. But to facilitate recitation of the Koran, scribes often indicated vowels by red or yellow symbols above or below the line.

10-17A *Blue Koran,* from Kairouan, 9th to mid-10th century.

All of these features are present in a 9th- or early-10th-century Koran page (FIG. **10-17**) now in Dublin and in the blue-dyed page (FIG. **10-17A**) of a contemporaneous Koran at Harvard University. The Dublin page carries the heading and opening lines of surah 18 of the Koran. The five text lines are in black ink with red vowels below a decorative

band incorporating the chapter title in gold and ending in a palm-tree *finial* (a crowning ornament). This approach to page design has parallels at the extreme northwestern corner of the then-known world—in the early medieval manuscripts of Britain and Ireland, where text and ornamentation are similarly united (FIG. 11-1). But the stylized human and animal forms that populate those Christian books never appear in Korans.

CERAMICS Around the same time, potters in Nishapur in Iran and in Samarqand in Uzbekistan developed a simple but elegant type of glazed dish with calligraphic decoration. One of the best-preserved examples of *Samarqand ware* is a large dish (FIG. **10-18**) from the Nishapur region in Khurasan province of northeastern Iran. To produce dishes such as this, the ceramists formed the shape from the local dark pink clay and then immersed the dish in a tub of white slip. When the slip dried, a painter-calligrapher wrote a Kufic text in black or brown paint around the flat rim of the dish, usually, as here, extending the angular letters both horizontally and vertically to create a circular border and to fill the full width of the rim. A transparent glaze, applied last, sealed the decoration and, after firing, gave the dish an attractive sheen.

The text on this dish is an Arabic proverb, which reads: "Knowledge is bitter-tasting at first, but in the end it is sweeter than honey. Good health [to the owner of this dish]." Because the Arabic words are so similar, recently some scholars have translated "knowledge" as "magnanimity." In either case, this and similar proverbs with practical advice for secular life would have appealed to cultured individuals such as successful merchants. The proverb's reference to food is, of course, highly appropriate for the decoration of tableware.

LATER ISLAMIC ART

In 1192, a Muslim army under the command of Muhammad of Ghor won a decisive battle at Tarain, which led to the formation in 1206 of an Islamic sultanate at Delhi and eventually to the greatest Muslim

1 in.

10-18 Dish with Arabic proverb, from Nishapur, Iran, 10th century. Painted and glazed earthenware, 1′ 2½″ diameter. Musée du Louvre, Paris.

An Arabic proverb in Kufic calligraphy is the sole decoration of this dish made for a cultured owner. It states that knowledge, although bitter at first taste, is ultimately sweeter than honey.

empire in Asia, the Mughal Empire. But no sooner did the Muslims establish a permanent presence in South Asia than the Mongols, who had invaded northern China in 1210 (see Chapter 33), overthrew the Abbasid caliphs in Central Asia and Persia. Isfahan fell to the Mongols in 1236, Baghdad in 1258, and Damascus in 1260. Islamic art continued to flourish, however, and important new regional artistic centers emerged. The rest of this chapter treats the art and architec-

ture of the Nasrids (1232–1492) in Spain, the Ayyubids (1171–1250) and Mamluks (1250–1517) in Egypt, the Timurids (1370–1501) and Safavids (1501–1732) in Iran, and the Ottomans (1281–1924) in Turkey. For Islamic art in South Asia, see Chapter 32.

Architecture

In the early years of the 11th century, the Umayyad caliphs' power in Spain unraveled, and their palaces fell prey to Berber soldiers from North Africa. The Berbers ruled southern Spain for several generations but could not resist the pressure of Christian forces from the north. Córdoba fell to the Christians in 1236, the same year the Mongols captured Isfahan. From then until the final Christian triumph in 1492, the Nasrids, an Arab dynasty that had established its capital at Granada in 1232, ruled the remaining Muslim territories in Spain.

ALHAMBRA On a rocky spur at Granada, the Nasrids constructed a huge palace-fortress called the Alhambra ("the Red" in Arabic), named for the rose color of the stone used for its walls and 23 towers. By the end of the 14th century, the complex had a population of 40,000 and included at least a half dozen royal residences. Only two of these fared well over the centuries. Paradoxically, they owe their preservation to the Christian victors, who maintained a few of the buildings as trophies commemorating the expulsion of the Nasrids. The two palaces present a vivid picture of court life in Islamic Spain before the Christian reconquest.

The Palace of the Lions takes its name from its courtyard (FIG. 10-19), which contains a fountain with 12 marble lions carrying a water basin on their backs. Colonnaded courtyards with fountains and statues have a long history in the Mediterranean world, especially in the houses and villas of the Roman Empire (FIG. 7-16A). The Alhambra's lion fountain is an unusual instance of freestanding stone sculpture in the Islamic world, unthinkable in a sacred setting. But the design of the courtyard is distinctly Islamic and features many multilobed pointed arches and lavish stuccoed walls with interwoven abstract motifs and Arabic calligraphy. The palace was the residence of Muhammad V (r. 1354–1391), and its courtyards, lush gardens, and luxurious carpets and other furnishings served to conjure the image of Paradise.

10-19 Court of the Lions (looking east), Palace of the Lions, Alhambra, Granada, Spain, 1354–1391.

The Nasrid Palace of the Lions takes its name from the fountain in this courtyard, a rare Islamic example of stone sculpture. Interwoven abstract ornamentation and Arabic calligraphy cover the stucco walls.

10-20 Muqarnas dome, Hall of the Abencerrajes, Palace of the Lions, Alhambra, Granada, Spain, 1354–1391.

The structure of this dome on an octagonal drum is difficult to discern because of the intricately carved stucco muqarnas. The prismatic forms reflect sunlight, creating the effect of a starry sky.

The Palace of the Lions is noteworthy also for its elaborate stucco ceilings. A spectacular example is the dome (FIG. **10-20**) of the Hall of the Abencerrajes (a leading Spanish family). The dome rests on an octagonal drum supported by squinches and pierced by eight pairs of windows, but its structure is difficult to discern because of the intricate carved stucco decoration. Some 5,000 *muqarnas*—tier after tier of stalactite-like prismatic forms that seem aimed at denying the structure's solidity—cover the ceiling. The muqarnas catch and reflect sunlight as well as form beautiful abstract patterns. The lofty vault in this hall and others in the palace symbolize the dome of Heaven. The flickering light and shadows create the effect of a starry sky as the sun's rays glide from window to window during the day. To underscore the symbolism, the palace walls bear inscriptions with verses by the court poet Ibn Zamrak (1333–1393), who compared the Alhambra's lacelike muqarnas ceilings to "the heavenly spheres whose orbits revolve."

MAUSOLEUM OF SULTAN HASAN After the Mongol conquests, the center of Islamic power moved from Baghdad to Egypt. The lords of Egypt at the time were former Turkish slaves ("mamluks" in Arabic) who converted to Islam. The capital of the Mamluk sultans was Cairo, which became the largest Muslim city of the late Middle Ages. The Mamluks were prolific builders, and Sultan Hasan, although not an important figure in Islamic history, was the most ambitious of all. He ruled briefly as a child and was deposed but regained the sultanate from 1354 until his assassination in 1361.

Hasan's major building project in Cairo was a huge madrasa complex (FIGS. **10-21** and **10-22**) on a plot of land about 8,000 square yards in area. A *madrasa* ("place of study" in Arabic) is a theological college devoted to the teaching of Islamic law. Hasan's complex was so large it housed not only four madrasas for the study of the four major schools of Islamic law but also a mosque, mausoleum, orphanage, and hospital, as well as shops and baths. Like all Islamic building complexes incorporating religious, educational, and charitable functions, this one depended on an endowment funded by rental properties. The income from these paid the salaries of attendants and faculty, provided furnishings and supplies such as oil for the lamps or free food for the poor, and supported scholarships for needy students.

The grandiose structure has a large central courtyard (FIG. 10-21, no. 5) with a monumental fountain in the center and four vaulted iwans opening onto it, as in Iranian mosques (FIG. 10-14). In each corner of the main courtyard, between the iwans (FIG. 10-21, no. 3), is a madrasa (no. 4) with its own courtyard and four or five stories of rooms for the students. The largest iwan (no. 2) in the complex, on the southern side, served as a mosque. Contemporaries believed the soaring vault that covered this iwan was taller than the arch of the Sasanian palace (FIG. 2-28) at Ctesiphon, which was then one of the most admired engineering feats in the world. Behind the qibla wall stands the sultan's mausoleum (FIGS. 10-21, no. 1, and 10-22), a gigantic version of the Samanid tomb (FIG. 10-8) at Bukhara but with two flanking minarets. The builders intentionally placed the dome-covered cube south of the mosque so that the prayers of the faithful facing Mecca would be directed toward Hasan's tomb. (The tomb houses only the bodies of the sultan's two sons, however. They could not recover their father's remains after his assassination.)

1. Mausoleum
2. Mosque (southern iwan)
3. Iwans
4. Madrasas
5. Courtyard with fountain

N

0 25 50 75 100 feet

0   10   20   30 meters

10-21 Plan of the madrasa-mosque-mausoleum complex of Sultan Hasan, Cairo, Egypt, begun 1356.

Sultan Hasan's complex included his tomb, four madrasas, and a mosque. The plan with four iwans opening onto a central courtyard derives from Iranian mosques (FIG. 10-14).

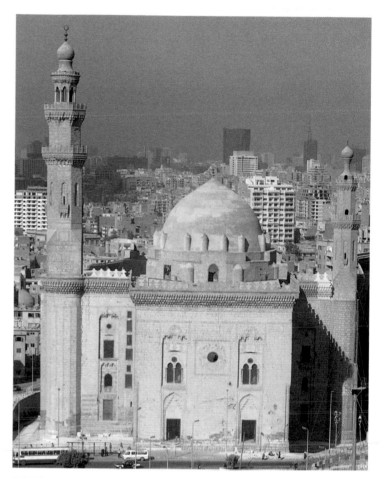

10-22 Madrasa-mosque-mausoleum complex of Sultan Hasan (looking northwest with the mausoleum in the foreground), Cairo, Egypt, begun 1356.

Hasan's mausoleum is a gigantic version of the earlier Samanid mausoleum (FIG. 10-8). Because of its location south of the complex's mosque, praying Muslims faced the Mamluk sultan's tomb.

A muqarnas cornice crowns the exterior walls of Hasan's complex, and marble plaques of several colors cover the mihrab in the mosque and the walls of the mausoleum. The complex as a whole is relatively austere, however. Its massiveness and geometric clarity present a striking contrast to the filigreed elegance of the contemporaneous Alhambra (FIGS. 10-19 and 10-20) and testify to the diversity of regional styles within the Islamic world, especially after the end of the Umayyad and Abbasid dynasties.

OTTOMAN EMPIRE After the downfall of the Seljuks (FIGS. 10-13 and 10-14), several local dynasties established themselves in Anatolia, among them the Ottomans, founded by Osman I (r. 1281–1326). Under Osman's successors, the Ottoman state expanded throughout vast areas of Asia, Europe, and North Africa. By the middle of the 15th century, the Ottoman Empire had become one of the great world powers.

The Ottoman emperors were lavish patrons of architecture, and the builders in their employ developed a new type of mosque, the core of which was a dome-covered square prayer hall. The combination of dome and square had an appealing geometric clarity and became the nucleus of all Ottoman architecture. At first used singly, the domed units came to be used in multiples, the distinctive feature of later Ottoman architecture.

After the Ottoman Turks conquered Constantinople (Istanbul) in 1453, they firmly established their architectural code. Hagia Sophia (FIGS. 9-5 to 9-8) especially impressed the new lords of Constantinople. In some respects, Justinian's great church conformed to their own ideals, and they converted the Byzantine church into a mosque with minarets. But the longitudinal orientation of Hagia Sophia's interior never satisfied Ottoman builders, and Anatolian development moved instead toward the central-plan mosque.

SINAN THE GREAT The first Ottoman central-plan mosques date to the 1520s, but the finest examples are the designs of the most famous Ottoman architect, SINAN (ca. 1491–1588), who worked for one of the greatest Ottoman sultans, Suleyman the Magnificent (r. 1520–1566; FIG. 10-22A). Sinan perfected the Ottoman architectural style. By his time, Ottoman

10-22A Tughra of Suleyman the Magnificent, ca. 1555–1560.

builders almost universally employed the basic domed unit, which could be multiplied, enlarged, or contracted as needed, and almost any number of units could be combined. Thus, the typical 16th-century Ottoman mosque was a creative assemblage of domical units and artfully juxtaposed geometric spaces. Architects usually designed domes with an extravagant margin of structural safety that has since served them well in earthquake-prone Istanbul and other Turkish cities. (Vivid demonstration of the sound construction of the Ottoman mosques came in August 1999 when a powerful earthquake centered 65 miles east of Istanbul toppled hundreds of modern buildings and killed thousands of people but caused no damage to the centuries-old mosques.) Working within this architectural tradition, Sinan searched for solutions to the problems of unifying the additive elements and of creating a monumental centralized space with harmonious proportions.

Sinan the Great and the Mosque of Selim II

Sinan, called "the Great," was truly the greatest Ottoman architect. Born a Christian around 1491, he converted to Islam, served in the Ottoman government, and trained in engineering and the art of building while in the Ottoman army. Officials quickly recognized Sinan's talent and entrusted him with increasing responsibility until, in 1538, he became chief court architect for Suleyman the Magnificent, a generous patron of art and architecture. He retained that position for a half century. Tradition associates Sinan with hundreds of building projects, both sacred and secular, although he could not have been involved with all of them.

The capstone of Sinan's distinguished career was the Edirne mosque (FIGS. 10-23 and 10-24) of Suleyman's son, Selim II, which Sinan designed when he was almost 80 years old. In it, he sought to surpass the greatest achievements of Byzantine architects, just as Sultan Hasan's builders in Cairo (FIG. 10-22) attempted to rival and exceed the Sasanian architects of antiquity. Sa'i Mustafa Çelebi, Sinan's biographer, recorded the architect's accomplishment in his own words:

> Sultan Selim Khan ordered the erection of a mosque in Edirne. . . .
> His humble servant [I, Sinan] prepared for him a drawing depicting, on a dominating site in the city, four minarets on the four

corners of a dome. . . . Those who consider themselves architects among Christians say that in the realm of Islam no dome can equal that of the Hagia Sophia; they claim that no Muslim architect would be able to build such a large dome. In this mosque, with the help of God and the support of Sultan Selim Khan, I erected a dome six cubits higher and four cubits wider than the dome of the Hagia Sophia.*

The Edirne dome is, in fact, higher than Hagia Sophia's (FIG. 9-8) when measured from its base, but its crown is not as far above the pavement as that of the dome of Justinian's church. Nonetheless, Sinan's feat won universal acclaim as a triumph. The Ottomans considered the Mosque of Selim II proof they finally had outshone the Christian emperors of Byzantium in the realm of architecture.

*Aptullah Kuran, *Sinan: The Grand Old Master of Ottoman Architecture* (Washington, D.C.: Institute of Turkish Studies, 1987), 168–169.

10-24 SINAN, interior of the Mosque of Selim II, Edirne, Turkey, 1568–1575. ◼◀

The interior of Sinan's Edirne mosque is a fusion of an octagon and a dome-covered square with four half-domes at the corners. The plan features geometric clarity and precise numerical ratios.

10-23 SINAN, Mosque of Selim II, Edirne, Turkey, 1568–1575. ◼◀

The Ottomans developed a new type of mosque with a dome-covered square prayer hall. The dome of Sinan's Mosque of Selim II is taller than Hagia Sophia's (FIG. 9-8) and is an engineering triumph.

Islamic Tilework

From the Dome of the Rock (FIGS. 10-2 and 10-3), the earliest major Islamic building, to the present day, Muslim builders have used mosaics or ceramic tiles to decorate the walls and vaults of mosques, madrasas, palaces, and tombs. The golden age of Islamic tilework was the 16th and 17th centuries. At that time, artists used two basic techniques to enliven building interiors with brightly colored tiled walls and to sheathe their exteriors with gleaming tiles that reflected the sun's rays.

In *mosaic tilework* (for example, FIG. 10-26), potters fire large ceramic panels of single colors in the kiln and then cut them into smaller pieces and set the pieces in plaster in a manner similar to the laying of mosaic *tesserae* of stone or glass (see "Mosaics," Chapter 8, page 245).

Cuerda seca (dry cord) tilework was introduced in Umayyad Spain during the 10th century—hence its Spanish name even in Middle Eastern and Central Asian contexts. Cuerda seca tiles (for example, FIG. 10-25) are polychrome and can more easily bear complex geometric and vegetal patterns as well as Arabic script than can mosaic tiles. They are also more economical to use because vast surfaces can be covered with large tiles much more quickly than they can with thousands of smaller mosaic tiles. But when builders use cuerda seca tiles to sheathe curved surfaces (vaults, domes, minarets), the ceramists must fire the tiles in the exact shape required—a daunting challenge. Polychrome tiles have other drawbacks. Because the ceramists fire all the glazes at the same temperature, cuerda seca tiles are not as brilliant in color as mosaic tiles and do not reflect light the way the more irregular surfaces of tile

10-25 Muqarnas tilework of the entrance portal of the Imam (Shah) Mosque, Isfahan, Iran, 1611–1638. ◼◀

The ceramists who produced the cuerda seca tiles of the muqarnas-filled portal to the Imam mosque had to manufacture a wide variety of shapes with curved surfaces to cover the prismatic, pointed half dome.

mosaics do. The preparation of the multicolored tiles also requires greater care. To prevent the colors from running together during firing, the potters outline the motifs on cuerda seca tiles with cords containing manganese, which leaves a matte black line between the colors after firing.

Sinan's vision found ultimate expression in the Mosque of Selim II (FIGS. **10-23** and **10-24**) at Edirne, which had been the capital of the Ottoman Empire from 1367 to 1472 and where Selim II (r. 1566–1574) maintained a palace. There, Sinan designed a mosque with a massive dome set off by four slender pencil-shaped minarets (each more than 200 feet high, among the tallest ever constructed). The dome's height surpasses that of Hagia Sophia's dome (see "Sinan the Great and the Mosque of Selim II," page 298). But it is the organization of the Edirne mosque's interior space that reveals Sinan's genius. The mihrab is recessed into an apselike alcove deep enough to permit window illumination from three sides, making the brilliantly colored tile panels of its lower walls sparkle as if with their own glowing light. The plan of the main hall is an ingenious fusion of an octagon with the dome-covered square. The octagon, formed by the eight massive dome supports, is pierced by the four half-dome-covered corners of the square. The result is a fluid interpenetration of several geometric volumes that represents the culminating solution to Sinan's lifelong search for a monumental, unified interior space. Sinan's forms are clear and legible, like mathematical equations. Height, width, and masses relate to one another in a simple but effective ratio of 1:2, and precise numerical ratios similarly characterize the complex as a whole. The forecourt

of the building, for example, covers an area equal to that of the mosque proper. Most architectural historians regard the Mosque of Selim II as the climax of Ottoman architecture. Sinan proudly proclaimed it his masterpiece.

IMAM MOSQUE, ISFAHAN While the Ottomans held sway in Turkey, the Safavids (r. 1501–1732) ruled the ancient Persian domains formerly under the control of the Abbasids, Seljuks, and Timurids (FIG. 10-29). The Safavids installed the ceramic-tile revetment on the walls and vaults of the Seljuks' Friday Mosque (FIG. 10-13) at Isfahan and built the Imam Mosque (formerly the Shah, or Royal, Mosque) in the early 17th century, which boasts some of the finest examples of Iranian tilework (FIG. **10-25**). The use of glazed tiles has a long history in the Middle East. Even in ancient Mesopotamia, builders sometimes covered walls and gates with colorful baked bricks (FIG. 2-24).

In the Islamic world, the art of ceramic tilework reached its peak in the 16th and 17th centuries in Iran and Turkey (see "Islamic Tilework," above), when, for example, the Ottomans replaced the exterior mosaics of the Dome of the Rock (FIG. 10-2) in Jerusalem with glazed tiles. In the Imam Mosque in Isfahan, Safavid tiles cover almost every surface. For the entrance portal (FIG. 10-25), the cera-

10-26 Mihrab, from the Madrasa Imami, Isfahan, Iran, ca. 1354. Glazed mosaic tilework, 11′ 3″ × 7′ 6″. Metropolitan Museum of Art, New York. ◼◄

This Iranian mihrab is a masterpiece of mosaic tilework. Every piece had to be cut to fit its specific place in the design. It exemplifies the perfect aesthetic union of Islamic calligraphy and ornamentation.

1 ft.

from the Koran in Kufic, the stately rectilinear script employed for the earliest Korans (FIGS. 10-17 and 10-17A). Many supple cursive styles also make up the repertoire of Islamic calligraphy. One of these styles, known as *Muhaqqaq,* fills the mihrab's outer rectangular frame. The mosaic tile decoration on the curving surface of the niche and the area above the pointed arch consists of tighter and looser networks of geometric and abstract floral motifs. The mosaic technique is masterful. Every piece had to be cut to fit its specific place in the mihrab—even the tile inscriptions. The ceramist smoothly integrated the subtly varied decorative patterns with the framed inscription in the center of the niche—proclaiming that the mosque is the domicile of the pious believer. The mihrab's outermost inscription—detailing the five pillars of Islamic faith (see "Muhammad and Islam," page 285)—serves as a fringelike extension, as well as a boundary, for the entire design. The unification of calligraphic and geometric elements is so complete that only the practiced eye can distinguish them. The artist transformed the architectural surface into a textile surface—the three-dimensional wall into a two-dimensional hanging—weaving the calligraphy into it as another cluster of motifs within the total pattern.

Luxury Arts

The tile-covered mosques of Isfahan, Sultan Hasan's madrasa complex in Cairo, and the architecture of Sinan the Great in Edirne are enduring testaments to the brilliant artistic culture of the Safavid, Mamluk, and Ottoman rulers of the Muslim world. Still, these are but some of the most conspicuous public manifestations of the greatness of later Islamic art and architecture (see Chapter 32 for the achievements of the Muslim rulers of India). In the smaller-scale, and often private, realm of the luxury arts, Muslim artists also excelled. From the vast array of manuscript paintings, ceramics, and metalwork, the six masterpieces illustrated here (FIGS. 10-27 to 10-32) suggest both the range and the quality of the inappropriately dubbed Islamic "minor arts" of the 13th to 16th centuries.

ARDABIL CARPETS The first of these artworks (FIG. 10-27) is by far the largest, one of a pair of carpets from Ardabil in Iran. The carpets come from the funerary mosque of Shaykh Safi al-Din (1252–1334), the founder of the Safavid line, but they date to 1540, two centuries after the construction of the mosque, during the reign of Shah Tahmasp (r. 1524–1576). Tahmasp elevated carpet weaving to a national industry and set up royal factories at Isfahan, Kashan, Kirman, and Tabriz. The name MAQSUD OF KASHAN appears as part of the design of the carpet illustrated here. Maqsud must have been the artist who supplied the master pattern to two teams of royal weavers (one for each of the two carpets). The carpet, almost 35 by 18 feet, consists of roughly 25 million knots, some 340 to the square inch. (Its twin has even more knots.)

The design consists of a central sunburst medallion, representing the inside of a dome, surrounded by 16 pendants. Mosque lamps (appropriate motifs for the Ardabil funerary mosque) hang from two pendants on the long axis of the carpet. The lamps are

mists had to manufacture a wide variety of shapes with curved surfaces to sheathe the complex forms of the muqarnas-filled, pointed half dome. The result was a technological triumph as well as a dazzling display of abstract decoration.

MADRASA IMAMI, ISFAHAN As already noted, verses from the Koran appeared in the mosaics of the Dome of the Rock (FIG. 10-3) in Jerusalem and in mosaics and other media on the walls of countless later Islamic structures. Indeed, some of the masterworks of Arabic calligraphy are not in manuscripts but on walls. A 14th-century mihrab (FIG. **10-26**) from the Madrasa Imami in Isfahan exemplifies the perfect aesthetic union between the Islamic calligrapher's art and abstract ornamentation. The pointed arch framing the mihrab niche bears an inscription

10 ft.

10-27 MAQSUD OF KASHAN, carpet from the funerary mosque of Shaykh Safi al-Din, Ardabil, Iran, 1540. Wool and silk, 34′ 6″ × 17′ 7″. Victoria & Albert Museum, London.

Maqsud of Kashan's enormous Ardabil carpet required roughly 25 million knots. It presents the illusion of a heavenly dome with mosque lamps reflected in a pool of water filled with floating lotus blossoms.

of different sizes. This may be an optical device to make the two appear equal in size when viewed from the end of the carpet at the room's threshold (the bottom end in FIG. 10-27). Covering the rich, dark blue background are leaves and flowers attached to delicate stems that spread over the whole field. The entire composition presents the illusion of a heavenly dome with lamps reflected in a pool of water full of floating lotus blossoms. No human or animal figures appear, as befits a carpet intended for a mosque, although they can be found on other Islamic textiles used in secular contexts, both earlier (FIG. 10-15A) and later.

1 in.

10-28 Mosque lamp of Sayf al-Din Tuquztimur, from Egypt, 1340. Glass with enamel decoration, 1′ 1″ high. British Museum, London.

The enamel decoration of this glass mosque lamp includes a quotation from the Koran comparing God's light with the light in a lamp. The burning wick dramatically illuminated the sacred verse.

MOSQUE LAMPS The kind of mosque lamps depicted on the Ardabil carpets were usually made of glass and lavishly decorated. Islamic artists perfected this art form, and fortunately, despite their exceptionally fragile nature, many examples survive, in large part because those who handled them did so with reverence and care. One of the finest is the mosque lamp (FIG. **10-28**) made for Sayf al-Din Tuquztimur (d. 1345), an official in the court of the Mamluk sultan al-Nasir Muhammad (r. 1309–1341). The glass lamps hung on chains from mosque ceilings. The shape of Tuquztimur's lamp is typical of the period, consisting of a conical neck, a wide body with six vertical handles, and a tall foot. Inside, a small glass container held the oil and wick. The *enamel* (colors fused to the surfaces) decoration includes Tuquztimur's emblem—an eagle over a cup (Tuquztimur served as the sultan's cup-bearer)—and cursive Arabic calligraphy giving the official's name and titles as well as a quotation of the Koranic verse (24:35) that compares God's light with the light in a lamp. The lamplight dramatically illuminated that verse (and Tuquztimur's name).

10-29 BIHZAD, *Seduction of Yusuf,* folio 52 verso of the *Bustan* of Sultan Husayn Mayqara, from Herat, Afghanistan, 1488. Ink and color on paper, $11\frac{7}{8}'' \times 8\frac{5}{8}''$. National Library, Cairo.

The most famous Timurid manuscript painter was Bihzad. This page displays vivid color, intricate decorative detailing, and a brilliant balance between two-dimensional patterning and perspective.

1 in.

TIMURID *BUSTAN* In the late 14th century, a new Islamic empire arose in Central Asia under the leadership of Timur (r. 1370–1405), known in the Western world as Tamerlane. Timur, a successor of the Mongol conqueror Genghis Khan, quickly extended his dominions to include Iran and parts of Anatolia. The Timurids, who ruled until 1501, were great patrons of art and architecture in Herat, Bukhara, Samarqand, and other cities. Herat in particular became a leading center for the production of luxurious books under the patronage of the Timurid sultan Husayn Mayqara (r. 1470–1506).

The most famous Persian painter of his age was BIHZAD, who worked at the Herat court before migrating to Tabriz. At Herat, he illustrated the sultan's copy of *Bustan* (*The Orchard*) by the Persian poet Sadi (ca. 1209–1292). One page (FIG. **10-29**) represents a story in both the Bible and the Koran—the seduction of Yusuf (Joseph) by Potiphar's wife, Zulayhka. Bihzad dispersed Sadi's text throughout the page in elegant Arabic script in a series of beige panels. According to the tale as told by Jami (1414–1492), an influential mystic theologian and poet whose Persian text appears in blue in the white pointed arch of the composition's lower center, Zulaykha lured Yusuf into her palace and led him through seven rooms, locking each door behind him. In the last room she threw herself at Yusuf, but he resisted and was able to flee when the seven doors opened miraculously. Bihzad's painting of the story highlights all the stylistic elements that brought him great renown: vivid color, intricate decorative detailing suggesting luxurious textiles and tiled walls, and a brilliant balance between two-dimensional patterning and perspective depictions of balconies and staircases. Bizhad's apprentices later worked for the Mughal court in India and introduced his distinctive style to South Asia (see Chapter 32).

SAFAVID *SHAHNAMA* The successors of the Timurids in Iran were the Safavids. Shah Tahmasp (FIG. 32-5), the Safavid ruler who commissioned the Ardabil carpets (FIG. 10-27), was also a great patron of books. Around 1525, he commissioned an ambitious decade-long project to produce an illustrated 742-page copy of the *Shahnama* (*Book of Kings*). The *Shahnama*, the Persian national epic poem by Firdawsi (940–1025), recounts the history of Iran from creation until the Muslim conquest. Tahmasp's *Shahnama* contains 258 illustrations by many artists, including some of the most admired painters of the day. It was eventually presented as a gift to Selim II, the Ottoman sultan who was the patron of Sinan's mosque (FIGS. 10-23 and 10-24) at Edirne. The manuscript later entered a private collection in the West and ultimately was auctioned as a series of individual pages, destroying its integrity but underscoring that Western collectors viewed each page as an independent masterpiece.

The page reproduced here (FIG. **10-30**) is the work of SULTAN-MUHAMMAD and depicts Gayumars, the legendary first king of Iran, and his court. According to tradition, Gayumars ruled from a mountaintop when humans first learned to cook food and clothe themselves in leopard skins. In Sultan-Muhammad's representation of the story, Gayumars presides over his court (all the figures wear leopard skins) from his mountain throne. The king is surrounded by light amid a golden sky. His son and grandson perch on multicolored rocky outcroppings to the viewer's left and right, respectively.

1 in.

The court encircles the ruler and his heirs. Dozens of human faces appear within the rocks, and many species of animals populate the lush landscape. According to the *Shahnama,* wild beasts became instantly tame in the presence of Gayumars. Sultan-Muhammad rendered the figures, animals, trees, rocks, and sky with an extraordinarily delicate touch. The sense of lightness and airiness that permeates the painting is enhanced by its placement on the page—floating, off center, on a speckled background of gold leaf. The painter gave his royal patron a singular vision of Iran's fabled past.

BAPTISTÈRE DE SAINT LOUIS Metalwork was another early Islamic art form (FIG. 10-16) that continued to play an important role in the later period. An example of the highest quality is a brass basin (FIG. 10-31) from Egypt inlaid with gold and silver and signed—six times—by the Mamluk artist MUHAMMAD IBN AL-ZAYN. The basin, used for washing hands at official ceremonies, must have been fashioned for a specific Mamluk patron. Some scholars think a court official named Salar ordered the piece as a gift for his sultan, but no inscription identifies him. The central band depicts Mamluk hunters and Mongol enemies. Running animals fill the friezes above and below. Stylized vegetal forms of inlaid silver fill the background of all the bands and roundels.

1 in.

Christian Patronage of Islamic Art

During the 11th through 13th centuries, large numbers of Christians traveled to Islamic lands, especially to the Christian holy sites in Jerusalem and Bethlehem, either as pilgrims or as Crusaders (see "Pilgrimages" and "The Crusades," Chapter 12, pages 335 and 346). Many returned with mementos of their journey, usually in the form of inexpensive mass-produced souvenirs. But some wealthy individuals commissioned local Muslim artists to produce custommade pieces using costly materials.

A unique brass canteen (FIG. 10-32) inlaid with silver and decorated with scenes of the life of Jesus appears to be the work of a 13th-century Ayyubid metalsmith in the employ of a Christian patron. The canteen is a luxurious version of the "pilgrim flasks" Christian visitors to the Holy Land often carried back to Europe. Four inscriptions in Arabic promise eternal glory, secure life, perfect prosperity, and increasing good luck to the canteen's unnamed owner, who must have been a Christian, not only because of the type of object but especially the choice of scenes engraved into the canteen. The Madonna and Christ Child appear enthroned in the central medallion, and three panels depicting New Testament events (see "The Life of Jesus in Art," Chapter 8, pages 240–241) fill most of the band around the medallion. The narrative unfolds in a counterclockwise sequence (Arabic is read from right to left), beginning with the *Nativity* (at 2 o'clock) and continuing with the *Presentation in the Temple* (10 o'clock) and Jesus' *Entry into Jerusalem* (6 o'clock). The scenes may have been chosen because the patron had visited their locales (Bethlehem and Jerusalem). Most scholars believe the artist used Syrian Christian manuscripts as the source for the canteen's Christian iconography. Many of the decorative details, however, are common in contemporaneous Islamic metalwork inscribed with the names of Muslim patrons. Whoever the owner was, the canteen testifies to the fruitful artistic interaction between Christians and Muslims in 13th-century Syria.

10-32 Canteen with episodes from the life of Jesus, from Syria, ca. 1240–1250. Brass, inlaid with silver, 1' 2½" high. Freer Gallery of Art, Washington, D.C.

This unique canteen is the work of an Ayyubid metalsmith in the employ of a Christian pilgrim to the Holy Land. The three scenes from the life of Jesus appear in counterclockwise sequence.

1 in.

Figures and animals also decorate the inside and underside of the basin, which has long been known as the *Baptistère de Saint Louis*. The association with the famous French king (see "Louis IX, the Saintly King," Chapter 13, page 385) is a myth, however. Louis died before Muhammad ibn al-Zayn made the piece. Nonetheless, the *Baptistère*, taken to France long ago, was used in the baptismal rites of newborns of the French royal family as early as the 17th century. Like the Zandana silk (FIG. 10-14A) in Toul Cathedral and a canteen (FIG. **10-32**) featuring scenes of the life of Christ (see "Christian Patronage of Islamic Art," above), the *Baptistère de Saint Louis* testifies to the prestige of Islamic art well beyond the boundaries of the Islamic world.

THE ISLAMIC WORLD

UMAYYAD SYRIA AND ABBASID IRAQ 661–1258

▌ The Umayyads (r. 661–750) were the first Islamic dynasty. They ruled from their capital at Damascus (Syria) until the Abbasids (r. 750–1258) overthrew them and established a new capital at Baghdad (Iraq).

▌ The first great Islamic building was the Dome of the Rock, a domed octagon commemorating the triumph of Islam in Jerusalem, which the Muslims captured from the Byzantines in 638.

▌ Umayyad and Abbasid mosques, for example those in Damascus and Kairouan (Tunisia), are of the hypostyle-hall type and incorporate arcaded courtyards and minarets. The mosaic decoration of early mosques was often the work of Byzantine artists but excluded zoomorphic forms.

▌ The earliest preserved Korans date to the ninth century and feature Kufic calligraphy and decorative motifs but no figural illustrations.

Dome of the Rock, Jerusalem, 687–692

ISLAMIC SPAIN 756–1492

▌ Abd-al-Rahman I established the Umayyad dynasty (r. 756–1031) in Spain when he escaped the Abbasid massacre of his clan in 750.

▌ The Umayyad capital was at Córdoba, where the caliphs constructed and expanded the Great Mosque between the 8th and 10th centuries. The mosque features horseshoe and multilobed arches and mosaic-clad domes resting on arcuated squinches.

▌ The last Spanish Muslim dynasty was the Nasrid (r. 1232–1492), whose capital was at Granada. The Alhambra is the best surviving example of Islamic palace architecture. It is famous for its stuccoed walls and arches and its muqarnas decoration on vaults and domes.

Great Mosque, Córdoba, 8th to 10th centuries

ISLAMIC EGYPT 909–1517

▌ The Fatimids (r. 909–1171) established their caliphate at Cairo (Egypt) in 909. Their successors were the Ayyubids (r. 1171–1250) and the Mamluks (r. 1250–1517).

▌ The most ambitious Mamluk builder was Sultan Hasan, whose madrasa mosque-mausoleum complex in Cairo derives from Iranian four-iwan mosque designs.

▌ Egyptian artists excelled in glassmaking, metalwork, and other luxury arts and produced magnificent mosque lamps and engraved basins.

Mosque lamp of Sayf al-Din Tuquztimur, 1340

TIMURID AND SAFAVID IRAN AND CENTRAL ASIA 1370–1732

▌ The Timurid (r. 1370–1501) and Safavid (r. 1501–1732) dynasties, which ruled Iran and Central Asia for almost four centuries, were great patrons of art and architecture.

▌ The Timurid court at Herat (Afghanistan) employed the most skilled painters of the day, who specialized in illustrating books. The most famous was Bihzad.

▌ Persian painting also flourished in Safavid Iran under Shah Tahmasp (r. 1524–1576), who in addition set up royal carpet factories in several cities.

▌ The art of tilework reached its peak under the patronage of the Safavid dynasty. Builders of the time frequently used cuerda seca and mosaic tiles to cover the walls, vaults, and domes of mosques, madrasas, palaces, and tombs.

Bihzad, *Seduction of Yusuf*, 1488

OTTOMAN TURKEY 1281–1924

▌ Osman I (r. 1281–1326) founded the Ottoman dynasty in Turkey. By the middle of the 15th century, the Ottomans had become a fearsome power and captured Byzantine Constantinople in 1453.

▌ The greatest Ottoman architect was Sinan (ca. 1491–1588), who perfected the design of the domed central-plan mosque. His Mosque of Selim II at Edirne is also an engineering triumph. Its dome is taller than Hagia Sophia's.

Sinan, Mosque of Selim II, Edirne, 1568–1575

In this opening page to the Gospel of Saint Matthew, the painter transformed the biblical text into abstract pattern, literally making God's words beautiful. The intricate design recalls early medieval metalwork.

The *chi-rho-iota* (XPI) page is not purely embellished script and abstract pattern. Half-figures of winged angels appear to the left of *chi,* accompanying the monogram as if accompanying Christ himself.

1 in.

11-1 Chi-rho-iota (**XPI**) page, folio 34 recto of the *Book of Kells,* probably from Iona, Scotland, late eighth or early ninth century. Tempera on vellum, 1′ 1″ × 9½″. Trinity College Library, Dublin.

The only unadorned letters in the opening of the passage read on Christmas Eve are the two words *autem* (abbreviated simply as *h*) and *generatio:* "Now this is how the birth of Christ came about."

EARLY MEDIEVAL EUROPE

The other figural elements on this page of the *Book of Kells* include a male head growing out of the end of the curve in the letter *rho*. Animals are at the base of *rho* to the left of *h generatio*.

MISSIONARIES SPREAD CHRISTIAN ART

The half millennium between 500 and 1000 was the great formative period of western medieval art, a time of great innovation. The patrons of many of these works were Christian missionaries, who brought to the non-Christian peoples of the former northwestern provinces of the Roman Empire not only the Gospel but the culture of the Late Antique Mediterranean world as well.

In Ireland, the most distant European outpost, the Christianization of the Celts began in the fifth century. By the end of the seventh century, monks at several Irish monasteries were producing magnificent illuminated books for use by the clergy and for impressing the illiterate with the beauty of God's words. The greatest early medieval Irish book is the *Book of Kells*, which one commentator described in the *Annals of Ulster* for 1003 as "the chief relic of the western world." The manuscript was probably the work of scribes and illuminators at the monastery at Iona. The monks kept the book in an elaborate metalwork box, as befitted a greatly revered "relic," and likely displayed it on the church altar.

The page reproduced here (FIG. 11-1) opens the account of the nativity of Jesus in the Gospel of Saint Matthew. The initial letters of Christ in Greek (XPI, *chi-rho-iota*) occupy nearly the entire page, although two words—*autem* (abbreviated simply as *h*) and *generatio*—appear at the lower right. Together they read: "Now this is how the birth of Christ came about." The page corresponds to the opening of Matthew's Gospel, the passage read in church on Christmas Eve. The illuminator transformed the holy words into extraordinarily intricate, abstract designs recalling metalwork (FIG. 11-3), but the page is not purely embellished script and abstract pattern. The letter *rho*, for example, ends in a male head, and animals are at the base of *rho* to the left of *h generatio*. Half-figures of winged angels appear to the left of *chi*. Close observation reveals many other figures, human and animal. When the priest Giraldus Cambrensis visited Ireland in 1185, he described a manuscript he saw that, if not the *Book of Kells* itself, must have been very much like it:

> Fine craftsmanship is all about you, but you might not notice it. Look more keenly at it and you . . . will make out intricacies, so delicate and subtle, so exact and compact, so full of knots and links, with colors so fresh and vivid, that you might say that all this was the work of an angel, and not of a man. For my part, the oftener I see the book, the more carefully I study it, the more I am lost in ever fresh amazement, and I see more and more wonders in the book.[1]

In the early Middle Ages, the monasteries of northern Europe were both the repositories of knowledge in the midst of an almost wholly illiterate population and the greatest centers of art production.

ART OF THE WARRIOR LORDS

Early medieval art* in western Europe (MAP **11-1**) was the result of a unique tripartite fusion of the classical heritage of Rome's northwestern provinces, the cultures of the non-Roman peoples north of the Alps, and Christianity. Although the Romans called everyone who lived beyond their empire's frontiers "barbarians," many northerners had risen to prominent positions within the Roman army and government during Late Antiquity. Others established their own areas of rule, sometimes with Rome's approval, sometimes in opposition to imperial authority. Over the centuries the various population groups merged, and a new order gradually replaced what had been the Roman Empire, resulting eventually in today's European nations.

As Rome's power waned, armed conflicts and competition for political authority became commonplace among the Huns, Vandals, Merovingians, Franks, Goths, and other non-Roman peoples of Europe. Once one group established itself in Italy or in one of Rome's European provinces, another often pressed in behind and compelled the first one to move on. The Visigoths, for example, who at one time controlled part of Italy and formed a kingdom in what is today southern France, were forced southward into Spain under pressure from the Franks, who had crossed the lower Rhine River and established themselves firmly in France, Switzerland, the Netherlands, and parts of Germany. The Ostrogoths moved from Pannonia (at the junction of modern Hungary, Austria, and the former Yugoslavia) to Italy. Under Theodoric (see page 246), they established their kingdom there, only to have it fall less than a century later to the Lombards, the last of the early Germanic powers to occupy land within the limits of the old Roman Empire. Anglo-Saxons controlled what had been Roman Britain. Celts inhabited France and parts of the British Isles, including Ireland. In Scandinavia, the seafaring Vikings held sway.

Art historians do not know the full range of art and architecture these non-Roman cultures produced. What has survived is

MAP 11-1 The Carolingian Empire at the death of Charlemagne in 814.

probably not fully representative and consists almost exclusively of small portable "status symbols"—weapons and items of personal adornment such as bracelets, pendants, and belt buckles that archaeologists have discovered in lavish burials. Earlier scholars, who viewed medieval art through a Renaissance lens, ignored these "minor arts" because of their small scale, seemingly utilitarian nature, and abstract ornamentation, and because their makers rejected the classical idea that naturalistic representation should be the focus of artistic endeavor. In the early Middle Ages, people regarded these objects, which often display a high degree of technical and stylistic

---

*The adjective *medieval* and the noun *Middle Ages* are very old terms stemming from an outmoded view of the roughly 1,000 years between the adoption of Christianity as the Roman Empire's official religion and the rebirth (Renaissance) of interest in classical antiquity. Earlier historians, following the lead of the humanist scholars of Renaissance

Italy, viewed this period as a long and artistically crude interval between—in the middle of—two great civilizations. The force of tradition dictates the retention of both terms to describe this period and its art, although scholars long ago ceased judging medieval art as unsophisticated or inferior.

EARLY MEDIEVAL EUROPE

410	Warrior Lords	768	Hiberno-Saxon and Carolingian	919	Ottonian	1024
	▌ After the fall of Rome, artists produce portable items of personal adornment featuring cloisonné ornamentation and intertwined animal and interlace patterns		▌ Christian missionaries commission sumptuous illuminated manuscripts featuring full pages devoted to embellishing the Word of God ▌ Charlemagne and his Carolingian successors (768–877) initiate a conscious revival of the art and culture of Early Christian Rome ▌ Carolingian architects introduce the twin-tower westwork and modular plans for basilican churches		▌ Ottonian painters and sculptors produce illuminated manuscripts and ivory reliefs inspired by Late Antique and Byzantine sources ▌ Ottonian architects introduce the alternate-support system and galleries into the naves of churches	

11-2 Pair of Merovingian looped fibulae, from Jouy-le-Comte, France, mid-sixth century. Silver gilt worked in filigree, with inlays of garnets and other stones, 4″ high. Musée d'Archéologie Nationale, Saint-Germain-en-Laye.

Jeweled fibulae were status symbols among early medieval warlords. This pair, probably owned by a Merovingian woman, features eagle heads and fish integrated into a highly decorative design.

MEROVINGIAN FIBULAE Most characteristic, perhaps, of the prestige adornments of the early medieval period was the *fibula*, a decorative pin the Romans wore (and the Etruscans before them; FIG. 6-2). Men and women alike used fibulae to fasten their garments. Made of bronze, silver, or gold, these pins often featured profuse decoration, sometimes incorporating inlaid precious or semi-precious stones. The pair of fibulae illustrated here (FIG. 11-2) formed part of a find of jewelry of the mid-sixth century, when Merovingian kings (r. 482–751) ruled large parts of what is now France. The pins, probably once the proud possession of a wealthy Merovingian woman, accompanied their owner into the afterlife. They resemble, in general form, the roughly contemporaneous but plain fibulae used to fasten the outer garments of some of the attendants flanking the Byzantine emperor Justinian in the apse mosaic (FIG. 9-13) of San Vitale in Ravenna. (Note how much more elaborate is the emperor's clasp. In Rome, Byzantium, and early medieval Europe alike, these fibulae were emblems of office and of prestige.)

Covering almost the entire surface of each of the Merovingian fibulae are decorative patterns adjusted carefully to the basic shape of the object. They thus describe and amplify the fibula's form and structure, becoming an organic part of the pin itself. Often the early medieval metalworkers so successfully integrated zoomorphic elements into this type of highly disciplined, abstract decorative design that the animal forms became almost unrecognizable. For example, the fibulae in FIG. 11-2 incorporate a fish just below the center of each pin. The looped forms around the edges are stylized eagles' heads with red garnets forming the eyes.

SUTTON HOO SHIP BURIAL The *Beowulf* saga also recounts the funeral of the warrior lord Scyld, whom his comrades laid to rest in a ship overflowing with arms and armor and costly adornments set adrift in the North Sea.

sophistication, as treasures. The objects enhanced their owners' prestige and testified to the stature of those buried with them. In the great early (possibly seventh-century) Anglo-Saxon epic *Beowulf*, after Beowulf dies, his comrades cremate the hero and place his ashes in a huge *tumulus* (burial mound) overlooking the sea. As an everlasting tribute to Beowulf's greatness, they "buried rings and brooches in the barrow, all those adornments that brave men had brought out from the hoard after Beowulf died. They bequeathed the gleaming gold, treasure of men, to the earth."[2]

> They laid their dear lord, the giver of rings, deep within the ship by the mast in majesty; many treasures and adornments from far and wide were gathered there. I have never heard of a ship equipped more handsomely with weapons and war-gear, swords and corselets; on his breast lay countless treasures that were to travel far with him into the waves' domain.[3]

In 1939, archaeologists uncovered a treasure-laden ship in a burial mound at Sutton Hoo, near the sea, in Suffolk, England. Although the Sutton Hoo ship never set out to sea, it epitomizes the early medieval tradition of burying great lords in ships with rich furnishings, as recorded in *Beowulf*. Among the many precious finds were a purse cover (FIG. 11-3) with gold, glass, and garnet ornamentation, a gold belt

11-3 Purse cover, from the Sutton Hoo ship burial in Suffolk, England, ca. 625. Gold, glass, and cloisonné garnets, $7\frac{1}{2}$″ long. British Museum, London (gift of Mrs. E. M. Pretty). ◼

This purse cover comes from a treasure-laden royal burial ship. The combination of abstract interlace ornamentation with animal figures is the hallmark of the art of the early Middle Ages in western Europe.

11-3A Belt buckle, Sutton Hoo, ca. 625. ◼◀

buckle (FIG. 11-3A), 10 silver bowls, a silver plate with the imperial stamp of the Byzantine emperor Anastasius I (r. 491–518), and 40 gold coins (perhaps to pay the 40 oarsmen who would row the deceased across the sea on his final voyage). Also placed in the ship were two silver spoons inscribed "Saulos" and "Paulos," Saint Paul's names in Greek before and after his baptism. They may allude to a conversion to Christianity. Some historians have associated the ship with the East Anglian king Raedwald (r. 599?–625), who was baptized a Christian before his death in 625, but the identity of the king buried at Sutton Hoo is uncertain.

The most extraordinary item found in the Sutton Hoo ship is the purse cover (FIG. 11-3). The decoration consists of seven *cloisonné* plaques within a cloisonné border. The cloisonné technique, a favorite of the early medieval "treasure givers," dates at least as early as the New Kingdom in Egypt. Metalworkers produced cloisonné jewelry by soldering small metal strips, or *cloisons* (French for "partitions"), edge up, to a metal background, and then filling the compartments with semiprecious stones, pieces of colored glass, or glass paste fired to resemble sparkling jewels. The edges of the cloisons are an important part of the design. Cloisonné is a cross between mosaic and stained glass (see "Mosaics," Chapter 8, page 245, and "Stained-Glass Windows," Chapter 13, page 375), but medieval artists used it only on a miniature scale.

On the Sutton Hoo purse cover, four symmetrically arranged groups of figures make up the lower row. The end groups consist of a man standing between two beasts. He faces front, and they appear in profile. This heraldic type of grouping has a venerable heritage in the ancient world (FIG. 2-10) but must have delivered a powerful contemporary message. It is a pictorial parallel to the epic sagas of the era in which heroes such as Beowulf battle and conquer horrific monsters. The two center groups represent eagles attacking ducks. The metalworker ingeniously composed the animal figures. For example, the convex beaks of the eagles (compare the Merovingian fibulae, FIG. 11-2) fit against the concave beaks of the ducks. The two figures fit together so snugly they seem at first to be a single dense abstract design. This is true also of the man-animals motif.

Above these figures are three geometric designs. The outer ones are purely linear, although they also rely on color contrasts for their effect. The central design is an interlace pattern in which the interlacements evolve into writhing animal figures. Elaborate intertwining linear patterns are characteristic of many times and places, notably in the art of the Islamic world (see Chapter 10). But the combination of interlace with animal figures was uncommon outside the realm of the early medieval warlords. In fact, metalcraft with interlace patterns and other motifs beautifully integrated with the animal form was, without doubt, the premier art of the early Middle Ages in northwestern Europe. Interest in it was so great that artists imitated the colorful effects of jewelry designs in the painted decorations of manuscripts (FIG. 11-1), in the masonry of churches, and in sculpture in stone and wood, the last an especially important medium of Viking art.

VIKINGS In 793, the pre-Christian traders and pirates of Scandinavia known as Vikings (named after the *viks*—coves or "trading places"—of the Norwegian shoreline) landed in the British Isles. They destroyed the Christian monastic community on Lindisfarne Island off the Northumbrian (northeastern) coast of England. Shortly after, these Norsemen (North men) attacked the monastery

at Jarrow in England as well as that on Iona Island, off the west coast of Scotland. From then until the mid-11th century, the Vikings were the terror of western Europe. From their great ships they seasonally harried and plundered harbors and river settlements. Their fast, seaworthy longboats took them on wide-ranging voyages, from Ireland eastward to Russia and westward to Iceland and Greenland and even, briefly, to Newfoundland in North America, long before Columbus arrived in the New World.

The Vikings were intent not merely on a hit-and-run strategy of destruction but also on colonizing the lands they occupied by conquest. Their exceptional talent for organization and administration, as well as for war, enabled them to conquer and govern large territories in Ireland, England, and France, as well as in the Baltic regions and Russia. For a while, in the early 11th century, the whole of England was part of a Danish empire. When Vikings settled in northern France in the early 10th century, their territory came to be called Normandy—home of the Norsemen who became Normans. (Later, a Norman duke, William the Conqueror, sailed across the English Channel and invaded and became the master of Anglo-Saxon England; FIG. 12-38.)

OSEBERG SHIP BURIAL Much of the preserved art of the Viking sea-rovers consists of decoration of their great wooden ships (FIGS. 11-4 and 11-4A). Striking examples of Viking woodcarving come from a ship burial near the sea at Oseberg, Norway. The ship, discovered beneath an

11-4A Viking ship burial, Oseberg, ca. 815–820.

earthen mound as was the earlier Sutton Hoo burial, is more than 70 feet long. The vessel contained the remains of two women. The size of the burial alone and the lavishly carved wooden ornamentation of the sleek ship attest to the importance of those laid to rest

1 in.

11-4 Animal-head post, from the Viking ship burial, Oseberg, Norway, ca. 825. Wood, head 5″ high. Viking Ship Museum, University of Oslo, Bygdoy.

The Vikings were master wood-carvers. This Viking ship post combines in one composition the head of a roaring beast with surface ornamentation in the form of tightly interwoven writhing animals.

there. The vessel also once must have carried many precious objects robbers stole long before its modern discovery.

An animal-head post (FIG. 11-4) is characteristic of the masterfully carved decoration of the Oseberg ship. It combines in one composition the image of a roaring beast with protruding eyes and flaring nostrils and the complex, controlled pattern of tightly interwoven animals that writhe, gripping and snapping, in serpentine fashion. The Oseberg animal head is a powerfully expressive example of the union of two fundamental motifs of the warrior lords' art—the animal form and the interlace pattern.

STAVE CHURCH, URNES By the 11th century, much of Scandinavia had become Christian, but Viking artistic traditions persisted. Nowhere is this more evident than in the decoration of the portal (FIG. 11-5) of the stave church (*staves* are wedge-shaped timbers placed vertically) at Urnes, Norway. The portal and a few staves are almost all that remain from the mid-11th century church. Builders later incorporated these fragments into the walls of the 12th-century church. Gracefully elongated animal forms intertwine with flexible plant stalks and tendrils in spiraling rhythm. The effect of natural growth is astonishing, yet the designer subjected

11-5 Wooden portal of the stave church at Urnes, Norway, ca. 1050–1070.

By the 11th century, Scandinavia had become mostly Christian, but Viking artistic traditions persisted, as in the intertwining animal-and-plant decoration of this Norwegian church portal.

the organic forms to a highly refined abstract sensibility. This intricate Urnes style was the culmination of three centuries of Viking inventiveness.

HIBERNO-SAXON ART

At the same time that powerful Merovingian, Anglo-Saxon, and Scandinavian warlords were amassing artworks dominated by abstract and animal motifs, Christian missionaries were establishing monasteries in northern Europe and sponsoring artworks of Christian content. The early medieval art of these monasteries, however, differs dramatically from contemporaneous works produced in Italy and the Byzantine Empire. These Christian artworks are among the most distinctive ever created and testify to the fruitful fusion of native and imported artistic traditions.

In Ireland, in part because of their isolation, the Celts who converted to Christianity, although nominally subject to the Roman popes, quickly developed a form of monastic organization that differed from the Church of Rome's. The monks often selected inaccessible and inhospitable places where they could carry on their duties far from worldly temptations and distractions. Before long, Irish monks, filled with missionary zeal, set up monastic establishments in Britain and Scotland. In 563, Saint Columba founded an important monastery on the Scottish island of Iona, where he successfully converted the native Picts to Christianity. Iona monks established the monastery at Lindisfarne off the northern coast of Britain in 635 and around 800 produced the extraordinary *Book of Kells* (FIG. 11-1).

The *Book of Kells* (named after the abbey in central Ireland that once owned it) is the outstanding example of the style art historians have named *Hiberno-Saxon* (Hibernia was the Roman name of Ireland) or *Insular* to denote the monastic art of the Irish-English islands. The most distinctive products of the Hiberno-Saxon monasteries were illuminated Christian books (see "Medieval Books," page 312). Books were the primary vehicles in the effort to Christianize Britain, Scotland, and Ireland. Indeed, they brought the word of God to a predominantly illiterate population who regarded the monks' sumptuous volumes with awe. Books were scarce and jealously guarded treasures of the libraries and *scriptoria* (writing studios) of monasteries and major churches. Illuminated books are the most important extant monuments of the brilliant artistic culture that flourished in Ireland and Northumbria during the seventh and eighth centuries.

BOOK OF DURROW Among the earliest Hiberno-Saxon illuminated manuscripts is the *Book of Durrow*, a Gospel book that may have been written and decorated in the monastic scriptorium at Iona, although it has no documented provenance. In the late Middle Ages, it was in the monastery in Durrow, Ireland—hence its modern name. The Durrow Gospels already display one of the most characteristic features of Insular book illumination—full pages devoted neither to text nor to illustration but to pure embellishment. The Hiberno-Saxon painters must have felt beautiful decoration lent prestige to books just as ornamental jewelry lent status to those who wore it. Interspersed between the Durrow text pages are so-called *carpet pages*, resembling textiles, made up of decorative panels of abstract and zoomorphic forms (compare FIG. 11-7). The *Book of Durrow* also contains pages where the illuminator enormously enlarged the initial letters of an important passage of sacred text and transformed those letters into elaborate decorative patterns (compare FIG. 11-1). Such manuscript pages have no precedents in Greco-Roman books. They reveal the striking independence of Insular artists from the classical tradition.

Medieval Books

The central role books played in the medieval Church led to the development of a large number of specialized types for priests, monks and nuns, and laypersons.

The primary sacred text came to be called the Bible ("the Book"), consisting of the Hebrew scriptures (the "Old Testament") and the Christian "New Testament," written in Greek. In the late fourth century, Saint Jerome produced the canonical Latin, or *Vulgate* (vulgar, or common tongue), version of the Bible, which incorporates 46 Old and 27 New Testament books. Before the invention of the printing press in the 15th century, all books were handwritten ("manuscripts," from the Latin *manu scriptus*). Bibles were major undertakings, and few early medieval monasteries possessed a complete Bible. Instead, scribes usually produced separate volumes containing several biblical books.

The *Pentateuch* contains the five books of the Jewish Torah, beginning with the story of Adam and Eve (Genesis). The *Gospels* ("good news") are the New Testament works of Saints Matthew, Mark, Luke, and John (see "The Four Evangelists," page 314) and tell the story of the life of Christ (see "The Life of Jesus in Art," Chapter 8, pages 240–241). Medieval Gospel books often contained *canon tables*—a concordance, or matching, of the corresponding passages of the four Gospels, which Eusebius of Caesarea compiled in the fourth century. *Psalters* collected the 150 psalms of King David, written in Hebrew and translated into both Greek and Latin.

The Church also frequently employed other types of books. The *lectionary* contains passages from the Gospels reordered to appear in the sequence that priests read them during the celebration of Mass throughout the year. *Breviaries* include the texts required for monks' daily recitations. *Sacramentaries* incorporate the prayers priests recite during Mass. *Benedictionals* contain bishops' blessings. In the later Middle Ages, scribes developed books for the private devotions of the laity, patterned after monks' readers. The

11-6 Man (symbol of Saint Matthew), folio 21 verso of the *Book of Durrow,* possibly from Iona, Scotland, ca. 660–680. Ink and tempera on parchment, $9\frac{5}{8}'' \times 6\frac{1}{8}''$. Trinity College Library, Dublin.

This early Hiberno-Saxon Gospel book has four pages devoted to the symbols of the four evangelists. The cloak of Saint Matthew's man resembles a cloisonné brooch filled with abstract ornamentation.

most popular was the *Book of Hours,* so called because it contains the prayers to be read at specified times of the day.

Medieval scribes produced many other types of books—compilations of saints' lives (*passionals*), theological treatises, secular texts on history and science, and even some classics of Greco-Roman literature—but these contained illustrations less frequently than did the various sacred texts.

In the *Book of Durrow,* each of the four Gospel books has a carpet page facing a page dedicated to the symbol of the evangelist who wrote that Gospel. An elaborate interlace design similar to those found on contemporaneous belt buckles and brooches frames each symbol. These pages served to highlight the major divisions of the text. The symbol of Saint Matthew (FIG. **11-6**) is a man (more commonly represented later as winged; see "The Four Evangelists," page 314), but the only human parts the artist—a seventh-century monk—chose to render are a schematic frontal head and two profile feet. A cloak of yellow, red, and green squares—resembling cloisons filled with intricate abstract designs and outlined in dark brown or black—envelops the rest of the "body." The *Book of Durrow* weds the abstraction of northern European early medieval personal

adornment with the Christian pictorial imagery of Italy and Byzantium. The vehicle for the transmission of those Mediterranean forms was the illustrated book itself, which Christian missionaries brought to Ireland.

LINDISFARNE GOSPELS The marriage between Christian imagery and the animal-interlace style of the northern warlords is evident in the cross-inscribed carpet page (FIG. **11-7**) of the *Lindisfarne Gospels.* Produced in the Northumbrian monastery on Lindisfarne Island, the book contains several ornamental pages and exemplifies Hiberno-Saxon art at its best. According to a later *colophon* (an inscription, usually on the last page, providing information regarding a book's manufacture), Eadfrith, bishop of Lindisfarne

11-7 Cross-inscribed carpet page, folio 26 verso of the *Lindisfarne Gospels,* from Northumbria, England, ca. 698–721. Tempera on vellum, 1′ 1½″ × 9¼″. British Library, London.

The cross-inscribed carpet page of the *Lindisfarne Gospels* exemplifies the way Hiberno-Saxon illuminators married Christian imagery and the animal-interlace style of the early medieval warlords.

1 in.

between 698 and his death in 721, wrote the *Lindisfarne Gospels* "for God and Saint Cuthbert." Cuthbert's relics recently had been deposited in the Lindisfarne church (see "The Veneration of Relics," Chapter 12, page 336).

The patterning and detail of this Lindisfarne ornamental page are much more intricate than the *Book of Durrow* pages. Serpentine interlacements of fantastic animals devour each other, curling over and returning on their writhing, elastic shapes. The rhythm of expanding and contracting forms produces a vivid effect of motion and change, but the painter held it in check by the regularity of the design and by the dominating motif of the inscribed cross. The cross—the all-important symbol of the imported religion—stabilizes the rhythms of the serpentines and, perhaps by contrast with

its heavy immobility, seems to heighten the effect of motion. The illuminator placed the motifs in detailed symmetries, with inversions, reversals, and repetitions the viewer must study closely to appreciate not only their variety but also their mazelike complexity. The zoomorphic forms intermingle with clusters and knots of line, and the whole design vibrates with energy. The color is rich yet cool. The painter adroitly adjusted shape and color to achieve a smooth and perfectly even surface.

Like most Hiberno-Saxon artworks, the Lindisfarne cross page displays the artist's preference for small, infinitely complex, and painstaking designs. Even the Matthew symbol (FIG. 11-6) in the *Book of Durrow* reveals the illuminator's concern was abstract design, not the depiction of the natural world. But exceptions exist. In some

The Four Evangelists

Evangelist derives from the Greek word for "one who announces good news," namely the Gospel of Christ. The authors of the Gospels, the first four books of the New Testament, are Saints Matthew, Mark, Luke, and John, collectively known as the four evangelists. The Gospel books provide the authoritative account of the life of Jesus, differing in some details but together constituting the literary basis for the iconography of Christian art (see "The Life of Jesus in Art," Chapter 8, pages 240–241). Each evangelist has a unique symbol derived from passages in Ezekiel (1:5–14) and the Apocalypse (4:6–8).

11-8 Saint Matthew, folio 25 verso of the *Lindisfarne Gospels,* from Northumbria, England, ca. 698–721. Tempera on vellum, $1' \frac{1}{2}'' \times 9\frac{1}{4}''$. British Library, London. ◼️

Portraits of the four evangelists frequently appeared in Gospel books. A Mediterranean book probably inspired this Hiberno-Saxon depiction of Saint Matthew with his symbol, a winged man.

- **Matthew** was a tax collector in Capernaum before Jesus called him to become an apostle. Little else is known about him, and accounts differ as to how he became a martyr. Matthew's symbol is the winged man or angel, because his Gospel opens with a description of the human ancestry of Christ.

- **Mark** was the first bishop of Alexandria in Egypt, where he suffered martyrdom. He was a companion of both Saint Peter and Saint Paul. One tradition says Peter dictated the Gospel to Mark, or at least inspired him to write it. Because Mark's Gospel begins with a voice crying in the wilderness, his symbol is the lion, the king of the desert.

- **Luke** was a disciple of Saint Paul, who refers to Luke as a physician. A later tradition says Luke painted a portrait of the Virgin Mary and the Christ Child. Consequently, late medieval painters' guilds often chose Luke as their patron saint. Luke's symbol is the ox, because his Gospel opens with a description of the priest Zacharias sacrificing an ox.

- **John** was one of the most important apostles. He sat next to Jesus at the last supper and was present at the crucifixion, lamentation, and transfiguration. John was also the author of the Apocalypse, the last book of the New Testament, which he wrote in exile on the Greek island of Patmos. The Apocalypse records John's visions of the end of the world, the last judgment, and the second coming. John's symbol is the eagle, the soaring bird connected with his apocalyptic visions.

The four evangelists appear frequently in medieval art, especially in illuminated Gospel books where they regularly serve as frontispieces to their respective Gospels. Often, artists represented them as seated authors, with or without their symbols (FIGS. I-8, 11-8, 11-13, and 11-14). In some instances, all four evangelists appear together (FIG. I-8). Frequently, both in painting and in sculpture, artists represented only the symbols (FIGS. 9-14A, 11-6, 12-1, 12-8, 12-18, and 13-6).

Insular manuscripts, the artists based their compositions on classical pictures in imported Mediterranean books. This is the case with the author portrait of Saint Matthew (FIG. **11-8**) in the *Lindisfarne Gospels.* The Hiberno-Saxon illuminator's model probably was an illustrated Gospel book a Christian missionary brought from Italy to England. Author portraits were familiar features of Greek and Latin books, and similar representations of seated philosophers or poets

writing or reading (FIGS. 7-25B, 7-71, and 8-7) abound in ancient art. The Lindisfarne Matthew sits in his study composing his account of the life of Christ. A curtain sets the scene indoors, as in classical art (FIG. 5-58), and Matthew's seat is at an angle, which also suggests a Mediterranean model employing classical perspective. The painter (or the scribe) labeled Matthew in a curious combination of Greek (*O Agios,* "saint"—written, however, using Latin rather than Greek

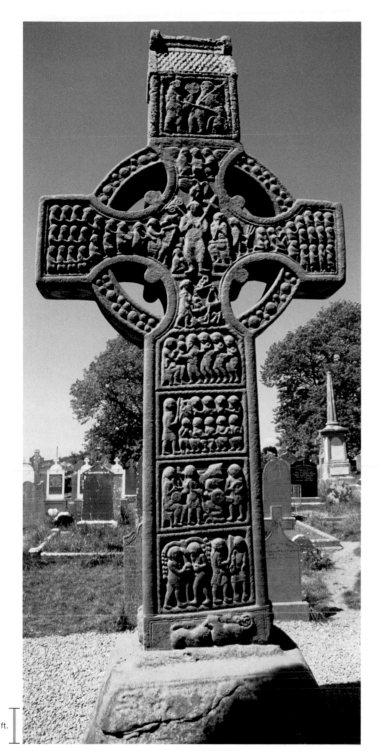

11-9 *High Cross of Muiredach* (east face), Monasterboice, Ireland, 923. Sandstone, 18′ high.

Early medieval Irish high crosses are exceptional in size. The cross marking Muiredach's grave bears reliefs depicting the *Crucifixion* and *Last Judgment*, themes suited to a Christian burial.

in contrast with the open book of Matthew's New Testament, a common juxtaposition in medieval Christian art and thought.

Although a Mediterranean manuscript inspired the Lindisfarne composition, the Northumbrian painter's goal was not to copy the model faithfully. Instead, uninterested in the emphasis on volume, shading, and perspective that are the hallmarks of the pictorial illusionism of Greco-Roman painting, the Lindisfarne illuminator conceived the subject exclusively in terms of line and color. In the Hiberno-Saxon manuscript, the drapery folds are a series of sharp, regularly spaced, curving lines filled in with flat colors. The painter converted fully modeled forms bathed in light into the linear idiom of Insular art. The result is a vivid new vision of Saint Matthew.

HIGH CROSSES Surpassing the *Lindisfarne Gospels* in richness is the *Book of Kells,* which boasts an unprecedented number of full-page illuminations, including carpet pages, evangelist symbols, portrayals of the Virgin Mary and of Christ, New Testament narrative scenes, canon tables, and several instances (for example, FIG. 11-1, already discussed) of monumentalized and embellished words from the Bible. The *Book of Kells* is a relatively small object, however, designed for display on an altar. In the Hiberno-Saxon world, the high crosses of Ireland and northern England, set up between the 8th and 10th centuries, are exceptional in their mass and scale. These majestic monuments, some more than 20 feet in height, preside over burial grounds adjoining monasteries. Freestanding and unattached to any architectural fabric, the high crosses have the imposing unity, weight, and presence of both building and statue— architecture and sculpture combined.

The *High Cross of Muiredach* (FIG. **11-9**) at Monasterboice and the *South Cross* (FIG. **11-9A**) at Ahenny are two of the largest and finest early medieval high crosses. The Monasterboice cross is larger and more unusual because of its extensive narrative relief decoration. An inscription on the bottom of the west face of the shaft asks a prayer for a man named Muiredach. Most scholars identify him as the influential Irish cleric of the same name who was abbot of Monasterboice and died in 923. The monastery he headed was one of Ireland's oldest, founded in the late fifth century. The cross probably marked the abbot's grave. Four

11-9A *South Cross,* Ahenny, late eighth century.

arcs forming a circle loop the concave arms, which expand into squared terminals (compare FIG. 11-7). The circle intersecting the cross identifies the type as Celtic. At the center of the west side of Muiredach's cross is a depiction of the crucified Christ. On the east side (FIG. 11-9), the risen Christ stands as judge of the world, the hope of the dead. Below him is a depiction of the weighing of souls on scales—a theme that two centuries later sculptors of church portals (FIG. 12-1) pursued with extraordinary force.

VISIGOTHIC AND MOZARABIC ART

The Romans never ruled Ireland, but Spain was a province of the Roman Empire for hundreds of years. The Roman conquest brought new roads to the Iberian peninsula and new cities with Roman temples, forums, theaters, and aqueducts. But in the early fifth century, the Roman cities fell to Germanic invaders, most notably the Visigoths, who had converted to Christianity. Many of the stone churches the Visigoths built in the sixth and seventh centuries still stand.

letters) and Latin (*Mattheus*), perhaps to lend the page the prestige of two classical languages. The former was the language of the New Testament, the latter that of the Church of Rome. Accompanying Matthew is his symbol, the winged man, labeled *imago hominis,* "image of the man" (see "The Four Evangelists," page 314). The identity of the figure—represented as a disembodied head and shoulders—behind the curtain is uncertain. Among the possibilities are Christ, Saint Cuthbert, and Moses holding the closed book of the Old Testament

11-10 San Juan Bautista (looking northeast), Baños de Cerrato, Spain, 661.

This three-aisled basilican church dedicated to Saint John the Baptist is typical of Visigothic architecture in Spain. It features three square apses and an entrance portal crowned by a horseshoe arch.

BAÑOS DE CERRATO An outstanding example is the church of San Juan Bautista (Saint John the Baptist, FIG. **11-10**) at Baños de Cerrato, which the Visigothic king Recceswinth (r. 649–672) constructed in 661 in thanksgiving for a cure after bathing in the waters there. The Visigothic churches are basilican in form but often have multiple square apses. (The Baños de Cerrato church has three.) They also regularly incorporate horseshoe arches, a form usually associated with Islamic architecture (FIGS. 10-9 and 10-10) but that in Spain predates the Muslim conquest of 711.

TÁBARA Although the Islamic caliphs of Córdoba swept the Visigoths away (see Chapter 10), they never succeeded in gaining control of the northernmost parts of the peninsula. There, the Christian culture called *Mozarabic* (referring to Christians living in Arab territories) continued to flourish, as did some Jewish communities. One northern Spanish monk, Beatus (ca. 730–798), abbot of San Martín at Liébana, wrote *Commentary on the Apocalypse* around 776. This influential work was widely copied and illustrated in the monastic scriptoria of medieval Europe. One copy was produced at the monastery of San Salvador at Tábara in the kingdom of Léon in 970. The colophon (FIG. **11-11**) to the illustrated *Commentary* presents the earliest known depiction of a medieval scriptorium. Because the artist provided a composite of exterior and interior views of the building, it is especially informative.

At the left is a great bell tower with a monk on the ground floor ringing the bells. The painter carefully recorded the Islamic-style glazed-tile walls of the tower, its interior ladders, and its elegant windows with their horseshoe arches, the legacy of the Visigoths. To the right, in the scriptorium proper, three monks perform their respective specialized duties. The colophon identifies the two monks in the main room as the scribe Senior and the painter EMETERIUS. To the right, a third monk uses shears to cut sheets of parchment. The colophon also pays tribute to Magius, "the worthy master painter. . . . May he deserve to be crowned with Christ,"[4] who died before he could complete his work on the book. His pupil Emeterius took his place and brought the project to fruition. He probably was the painter of the colophon.

The colophon of another Beatus manuscript, dated 975 and today in Girona Cathedral, also names Emeterius as coilluminator with the nun Ende, a "painter and servant of God." Ende's is one of the few recorded names of a woman artist in the Middle Ages, a rarity also in the ancient world (see "Iaia of Cyzicus," Chapter 7, page 218).

1 in.

11-11 EMETERIUS, the tower and scriptorium of San Salvador de Tábara, colophon (folio 168) of the *Commentary on the Apocalypse* by Beatus, from Tábara, Spain, 970. Tempera on parchment, 1′ 2⅛″ × 10″. Archivo Histórico Nacional, Madrid.

In this earliest known depiction of a medieval scriptorium, the painter carefully recorded the tower's Islamic-style glazed-tile walls and elegant windows with horseshoe arches, a Visigothic legacy.

Charlemagne's *Renovatio Imperii Romani*

Charlemagne's official seal bore the phrase *renovatio imperii Romani* (renewal of the Roman Empire). As the pope's designated Roman emperor, Charlemagne sought to revive the glory of Early Christian Rome. He accomplished this in part through artistic patronage, commissioning imperial portrait statues (FIG. 11-12) and large numbers of illustrated manuscripts (FIGS. 11-12A and 11-13), and by fostering a general revival of learning.

To make his empire as splendid as Rome's, Charlemagne invited to his court at Aachen the best minds and the finest artisans of western Europe and the Byzantine East. Among them were Theodulf of Orléans (d. 821), Paulinus of Aquileia (d. 802), and Alcuin (d. 804), master of the cathedral school at York, the center of Northumbrian learning. Alcuin brought Anglo-Saxon scholarship to the Carolingian court.

Charlemagne himself, according to Einhard (d. 840), his biographer, could read and speak Latin fluently, in addition to Frankish, his native tongue. He also could understand Greek, and he studied rhetoric and mathematics with the learned men he gathered around him. But he never learned to write properly. That was a task best left to professional scribes. In fact, one of Charlemagne's dearest projects was the recovery of the true text of the Bible, which, through centuries of errors in copying, had become quite corrupted. Various scholars undertook the great project, but Alcuin of York's revision of the Bible, prepared at the new monastery at Tours, became the most widely used.

Charlemagne's scribes also were responsible for the development of a new, more compact, and more easily written and legible version of Latin script called *Caroline minuscule*. The letters on this page are descendants of the alphabet Carolingian scribes perfected. Later generations also owe to Charlemagne's patronage the restoration and copying of important classical texts. The earliest known manuscripts of many Greek and Roman authors are Carolingian in date.

11-12 Equestrian portrait of Charlemagne or Charles the Bald, from Metz, France, ninth century. Bronze, originally gilt, $9\frac{1}{2}$″ high. Musée du Louvre, Paris.

The Carolingian emperors sought to revive the glory and imagery of the Roman Empire. This equestrian portrait depicts a crowned emperor holding a globe, the symbol of world dominion.

CAROLINGIAN ART

On Christmas Day of the year 800, Pope Leo III (r. 795–816) crowned Charles the Great (Charlemagne), king of the Franks since 768, as emperor of Rome (r. 800–814). In time, Charlemagne came to be seen as the first Holy (that is, Christian) Roman Emperor, a title his successors did not formally adopt until the 12th century. The setting for Charlemagne's coronation, fittingly, was Saint Peter's basilica (FIG. 8-9) in Rome, built by Constantine, the first Roman emperor to embrace Christianity. Born in 742, when northern Europe was still in chaos, Charlemagne consolidated the Frankish kingdom his father and grandfather bequeathed him, defeated the Lombards in Italy (MAP 11-1), and laid claim to reviving the glory of the Roman Empire. He gave his name (Carolus Magnus in Latin) to an entire era, the *Carolingian* period.

The "Carolingian Renaissance" was a remarkable historical phenomenon, an energetic, brilliant emulation of the art, culture, and political ideals of Early Christian Rome (see "Charlemagne's *Renovatio Imperii Romani*," above). Charlemagne's (Holy) Roman Empire, waxing and waning for a thousand years and with many hiatuses, existed in central Europe until Napoleon destroyed it in 1806.

Sculpture and Painting

When Charlemagne returned home from his coronation in Rome, he ordered the transfer of an equestrian statue of the Ostrogothic king Theodoric from Ravenna to the Carolingian palace complex at Aachen. That portrait is lost, as is the grand gilded-bronze statue of the Byzantine emperor Justinian that once crowned a column in Constantinople (see "The Emperors of New Rome," Chapter 9, page 259). But in the early Middle Ages, both statues stood as reminders of ancient Rome's glory and of the pretensions and aspirations of the medieval successors of Rome's Christian emperors.

EQUESTRIAN STATUETTE The portrait of Theodoric may have been the inspiration for a ninth-century bronze statuette (FIG. 11-12) of a Carolingian emperor on horseback. Charlemagne greatly admired Theodoric, the first Germanic ruler of Rome. Many scholars have identified the small bronze figure as Charlemagne himself, although others think it portrays his grandson, Charles the Bald (r. 840–877). The ultimate model for the statuette was the equestrian portrait (FIG. 7-59) of Marcus Aurelius in Rome. In the Middle Ages, people mistakenly thought the bronze statue represented Constantine, another revered predecessor of Charlemagne and his Carolingian successors. Both the Roman and the medieval sculptors portrayed their emperor as overly large so that the ruler, not the horse, is the center of attention. But unlike Marcus Aurelius, who extends his right arm in a gesture of clemency to a foe who once cowered beneath the raised foreleg of his horse, Charlemagne (or Charles the Bald) is on parade. He wears imperial robes rather than a general's cloak, although his sheathed sword is visible. On his head is a crown, and in his outstretched left hand he holds a globe, symbol of world dominion. The portrait proclaimed the *renovatio* of the Roman Empire's power and trappings.

11-12A Christ enthroned, *Godesalc Lectionary*, 781–783.

CORONATION GOSPELS Charlemagne was a sincere admirer of learning, the arts, and classical culture, even before his coronation as emperor of Rome. He placed high value on books, both sacred and secular, importing many and producing far more. One of the earliest is the *Godesalc Lectionary* (FIG. 11-12A), securely dated to 781 to 783, but the most famous is the early-ninth-century purple vellum *Coronation Gospels* (also known as the *Gospel Book of Charlemagne*), which has a text written in handsome gold letters. The major full-page illuminations, which show the four Gospel authors at work, reveal that Carolingian manuscript painters

brought a radically different stylistic sensibility to their work compared with their Hiberno-Saxon counterparts. For example, for the page depicting Saint Matthew (FIG. 11-13), the *Coronation Gospels* painter, in contrast to the Northumbrian illuminator who painted the portrait of the same evangelist in the *Lindisfarne Gospels* (FIG. 11-8), used color and modulation of light and shade, not line, to create shapes, and deft, illusionistic brushwork to define the massive drapery folds wrapped around Matthew's body. The cross-legged chair, the lectern, and the saint's toga are familiar Roman accessories. In fact, this Carolingian evangelist portrait closely follows the format and style of Greco-Roman author portraits, as exemplified by the seated Menander (FIG. 7-25B) at Pompeii. The *Coronation Gospels* landscape background also has many parallels in Roman painting, and the frame consists of the kind of acanthus leaves found in Roman temple capitals and friezes (FIG. 7-32). Almost nothing is known in the Hiberno-Saxon or Frankish world that could have prepared the way for this portrayal of Saint Matthew. If a Frankish, rather than an Italian or a Byzantine, artist painted the evangelist portraits of the *Coronation Gospels,* the Carolingian artist had fully absorbed the classical manner. Classical painting style was one of the many components of Charlemagne's program to establish Aachen as the capital of a renewed Christian Roman Empire.

11-13 Saint Matthew, folio 15 recto of the *Coronation Gospels* (*Gospel Book of Charlemagne*), from Aachen, Germany, ca. 800–810. Ink and tempera on vellum, 1′ ¾″ × 10″. Schatzkammer, Kunsthistorisches Museum, Vienna. ◼◀

The books produced for Charlemagne's court reveal the legacy of classical art (FIG. 7-25B). The Carolingian painter used light, shade, and perspective to create the illusion of three-dimensional form.

11-14 Saint Matthew, folio 18 verso of the *Ebbo Gospels* (*Gospel Book of Archbishop Ebbo of Reims*), from Hautvillers, France, ca. 816–835. Ink and tempera on vellum, 10¼″ × 8¾″. Bibliothèque Municipale, Épernay. ◼◀

Saint Matthew writes frantically, and the folds of his drapery writhe and vibrate. Even the landscape rears up alive. The painter merged classical illusionism with the northern European linear tradition.

MEA·QUAREMEREPPULIS   ADDMQUILAETIFICAT   CONFITEBORILLI·SALU
TIFTQUARETRISTISINCEDO·   IUUENTUTEMMEAM·   TAREUULTUSMEIETDSMS·
DUMADFLICITMEINIMICUS

1 in.

11-15 Psalm 44, detail of folio 25 recto of the *Utrecht Psalter,* from Hautvillers, France, ca. 820–835. Ink on vellum, full page, 1' 1" × 9⁷⁄₈"; detail, 4½" high. University Library, Utrecht.

The drawings in the *Utrecht Psalter* are rich in anecdotal detail and show figures acting out—literally—King David's psalms. The vivid animation resembles that of the *Ebbo Gospels* Matthew (FIG. 11-14).

EBBO GOSPELS The classical-revival style evident in the *Coronation Gospels* was by no means the only one that appeared suddenly in the Carolingian world. Court school and monastic scriptoria employed a wide variety of styles derived from Late Antique prototypes. Another Saint Matthew (FIG. **11-14**), in a Gospel book made for Archbishop Ebbo of Reims, France, may be an interpretation of an author portrait very similar to the one the *Coronation Gospels* master used as a model. The *Ebbo Gospels* illuminator, however, replaced the classical calm and solidity of the *Coronation Gospels* evangelist with an energy approaching frenzy. Matthew (the winged man in the upper right corner identifies him) writes in frantic haste. His hair stands on end, his eyes open wide, the folds of his drapery writhe and vibrate, the landscape behind him rears up alive. The painter even set the page's leaf border in motion. Matthew's face, hands, inkhorn, pen, and book are the focus of the composition. This presentation contrasts strongly with the settled pose of the Saint Matthew of the *Coronation Gospels* with its even stress so that no part of the composition jumps out at viewers to seize their attention. Just as the painter of the *Lindisfarne Gospels* Matthew (FIG. 11-8) transformed an imported model into an original Hiberno-Saxon idiom, so the *Ebbo Gospels* artist translated a classical prototype into a new Carolingian vernacular. This master painter brilliantly merged classical illusionism and the northern linear tradition.

UTRECHT PSALTER One of the most extraordinary medieval manuscripts is the *Utrecht Psalter* (FIG. **11-15**). The text reproduces the psalms of David in three columns of Latin capital letters (FIG. **11-15A**) in emulation of the script and page organization of ancient books. The artist illustrated each psalm with a pen-and-ink drawing stretching across the entire width of the page. Some scholars have argued that the costumes and other details indicate the artist followed one or more manuscripts created 400 years before. Even if

the *Utrecht Psalter* is not a copy, the artist's intention was to evoke earlier artworks and to make the book appear ancient.

The painter of the *Utrecht Psalter* displayed a genius for anecdotal detail throughout the manuscript. On one page (FIG. 11-15), the figures act out—literally—Psalm 44 (Psalm 43 of the Vulgate text of the Carolingian era), in which the psalmist laments the plight of the oppressed Israelites. For example, the artist drew some slain sheep fallen to the ground ("We are counted as sheep for slaughter") in front of a walled city reminiscent of cities on the Column of Trajan (FIG. 7-1) in Rome and in Early Christian mosaics (FIG. 8-14) and manuscripts (FIG. 8-21). At the left, the faithful grovel on the ground before a temple ("Our soul is bowed down to the dust; our belly cleaveth unto the earth"). In response to the six pleading angels ("Awake, why sleepest thou, O Lord?"), the artist depicted the Lord reclining in a canopied bed overlooking the slaughter below. But "the Lord" is Jesus, complete with cruciform halo, instead of David's Hebrew God. The drawing shows a vivid animation of much the same kind as the *Ebbo Gospels* Saint Matthew (FIG. 11-14). The bodies of the *Utrecht Psalter* figures are tense, with shoulders hunched and heads thrust forward. As in the *Ebbo Gospels,* even the earth heaves up around the figures. The rapid, sketchy techniques used to render the figures convey the same nervous vitality as found in the *Ebbo* evangelists.

11-15A Psalm 23, *Utrecht Psalter,* ca. 820–835.

LINDAU GOSPELS The taste for sumptuously wrought and portable objects, the hallmark of the art of the early medieval warlords, persisted under Charlemagne and his successors. The Carolingians commissioned numerous works employing costly materials, including book covers made of gold and jewels and sometimes

11-16 *Crucifixion,* front cover of the *Lindau Gospels,* from Saint Gall, Switzerland, ca. 870. Gold, precious stones, and pearls, $1' 1\frac{3}{8}'' \times 10\frac{3}{8}''$. Pierpont Morgan Library, New York. ◼◀

This sumptuous Carolingian book cover revives the Early Christian imagery of the youthful Christ (FIG. 8-24). The statuesque, crucified Christ, heedless of pain, is classical in conception and execution.

1 in.

also ivory or pearls. Gold and gems not only glorified the word of God but also evoked the heavenly Jerusalem. One of the most luxurious Carolingian book covers (FIG. **11-16**) is the one later added to the *Lindau Gospels.* The gold cover, fashioned in one of the workshops of Charles the Bald's court, is monumental in conception. A youthful Christ in the Early Christian tradition, nailed to the cross, is the central motif. Surrounding Christ are pearls and jewels (raised on golden claw feet so they can catch and reflect the light even more brilliantly and protect the delicate metal relief from denting). The statuesque open-eyed figure, rendered in *repoussé* (hammered or pressed relief), recalls the beardless, unsuffering Christ of a fifth-century ivory plaque (FIG. 8-24) from Italy. In contrast, the four angels and the personifications of the Moon and the Sun above and the crouching figures of the Virgin Mary and Saint John (and two other figures of uncertain identity) in the quadrants below display the vivacity and nervous energy of the *Utrecht Psalter* figures (FIGS. 11-15 and 11-15A). The *Lindau Gospels* cover highlights the stylistic diversity of early medieval art in Europe. Here, however, the trans-

lated figural style of the Mediterranean prevailed, in keeping with the classical tastes and imperial aspirations of the Frankish emperors of Rome.

Architecture

In his eagerness to reestablish the imperial past, Charlemagne also encouraged the use of Roman building techniques. In architecture, as in sculpture and painting, innovations made in the reinterpretation of earlier Roman Christian sources became fundamental to the subsequent development of northern European architecture. For his models, Charlemagne looked to Rome and Ravenna. One was the former heart of the Roman Empire, which he wanted to renew. The other was the long-term western outpost of Byzantine might and splendor, which he wanted to emulate in his own capital at Aachen, a site chosen because of its renowned hot springs.

AACHEN Charlemagne often visited Ravenna, and the equestrian statue of Theodoric he brought from there to display in his

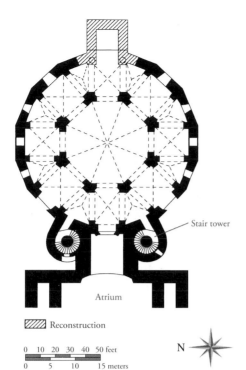

11-17 Restored plan (*left*) and west facade (*right*) of the Palatine Chapel of Charlemagne, Aachen, Germany, 792–805.

Charlemagne sought to emulate Byzantine splendor in Germany. The plan of his Aachen palace chapel is based on that of San Vitale (FIG. 9-11) at Ravenna, but the west facade is distinctly Carolingian.

Stair tower

Atrium

Reconstruction

0 10 20 30 40 50 feet
0   5   10   15 meters

N

palace complex at Aachen served as a model for Carolingian equestrian portraits (FIG. 11-12). Charlemagne also imported porphyry (purple marble) columns from Ravenna to adorn his Palatine Chapel, and historians long have thought he chose one of Ravenna's churches as the model for the new structure. The plan (FIG. **11-17**, *left*) of the Aachen chapel resembles that of San Vitale (FIG. 9-11), and a direct relationship very likely exists between the two.

A comparison between the Carolingian chapel, the first vaulted structure of the Middle Ages north of the Alps, and its southern counterpart is instructive. The Aachen plan is simpler. The architect omitted San Vitale's apselike extensions reaching from the central octagon into the ambulatory. At Aachen, the two main units stand in greater independence of each other. This solution may lack the subtle sophistication of the Byzantine building, but the Palatine Chapel gains geometric clarity. A view of its interior (FIG. **11-18**) shows that Charlemagne's builders converted the "floating" quality of San Vitale (FIG. 9-1) into massive geometric form.

The Carolingian conversion of a complex and subtle Byzantine prototype into a building that expresses robust strength and clear structural articulation foreshadows the architecture of the 11th and 12th centuries and the style called Romanesque (see Chapter 12). So, too, does the treatment of the Palatine Chapel's exterior, where two cylindrical towers with spiral staircases flank the entrance portal (FIG. 11-17, *right*). This was a first step toward the great dual-tower facades of western European churches from the 10th century to the present. Above the portal, Charlemagne could appear in a large framing arch and be seen by those gathered in the atrium in front of the chapel. (The plan includes only part of the atrium.) Directly behind that second-story arch was Charlemagne's marble throne. From there he could peer down at the altar in the apse. Charlemagne's imperial gallery followed the model of the imperial gallery at Hagia Sophia (FIGS. 9-6 to 9-8) in Constantinople. The Palatine Chapel was in every sense a royal chapel. The coronation of Charlemagne's son, Louis the Pious (r. 814–840), took place there when he succeeded his father as emperor.

11-18 Interior of the Palatine Chapel of Charlemagne (looking east), Aachen, Germany, 792–805.

Charlemagne's chapel is the first vaulted medieval structure north of the Alps. The architect transformed the complex, glittering interior of San Vitale (FIG. 9-1) into simple, massive geometric form.

Medieval Monasteries and Benedictine Rule

Since Early Christian times, monks who established monasteries also made the rules that governed communal life. The most significant of these monks was Benedict of Nursia (Saint Benedict, ca. 480–547), who founded the Benedictine Order in 529. By the ninth century, the "Rule" Benedict wrote (*Regula Sancti Benedicti*) had become standard for all western European monastic communities, in part because Charlemagne had encouraged its adoption throughout the Frankish territories.

Saint Benedict believed the corruption of the clergy that accompanied the increasing worldliness of the Church had its roots in the lack of firm organization and regulation. As he saw it, idleness and selfishness had led to neglect of the commandments of God and of the Church. The cure for this was communal association in an *abbey* under the absolute rule of an *abbot* the monks elected (or an *abbess* the nuns chose), who would ensure the clergy spent each hour of the day in useful work and in sacred reading. The emphasis on work and study and not on meditation and austerity is of great historical significance. Since antiquity, manual labor had been considered unseemly, the business of the lowborn or of slaves. Benedict raised it to the dignity of religion. The core idea of what many people today call the "work ethic" found early expression in Benedictine monasteries as an essential feature of spiritual life. By thus exalting the virtue of manual labor, Benedict not only rescued it from its age-old association with slavery but also recognized it as the way to self-sufficiency for the entire religious community.

Whereas some of Saint Benedict's followers emphasized spiritual "work" over manual labor, others, most notably the Cistercians (see "Bernard of Clairvaux," Chapter 12, page 342), put Benedictine teachings about the value of physical work into practice. These monks reached into their surroundings and helped reduce the vast areas of daunting wilderness of early medieval Europe. They cleared dense forest teeming with wolves, bear, and wild boar, drained swamps, cultivated wastelands, and built roads, bridges, and dams, as well as monastic churches and their associated living and service quarters.

The ideal monastery (FIG. 11-19) provided all the facilities necessary for the conduct of daily life—a mill, bakery, infirmary, vegetable garden, and even a brewery—so the monks would feel no need to wander outside its protective walls. These religious communities were centrally important to the revival of learning. The clergy, who were also often scribes and scholars, had a monopoly on the skills of reading and writing in an age of almost universal illiteracy. The monastic libraries and scriptoria (FIG. 11-11), where the monks and nuns read, copied, illuminated, and bound books with ornamented covers, became centers of study. Monasteries were almost the sole

1 in.

11-19 Schematic plan for a monastery, from Saint Gall, Switzerland, ca. 819. Red ink on parchment, 2′ 4″ × 3′ 8⅛″. Stiftsbibliothek, Saint Gall.

The purpose of this plan for an ideal, self-sufficient Benedictine monastery was to separate the monks from the laity. Near the center is the church with its cloister, the monks' earthly paradise.

repositories of what remained of the literary culture of the Greco-Roman world and early Christianity. Saint Benedict's requirements of manual labor and sacred reading came to include writing and copying books, studying music for chanting daily prayers, and—of great significance—teaching. The monasteries were the schools of the early Middle Ages as well as self-sufficient communities and production centers.

SAINT GALL The emperor was not the only important builder of the Carolingian age. With prosperity also came the construction and expansion of many monasteries. A unique document, the ideal plan (FIG. **11-19**) for a Benedictine monastery (see "Medieval Monasteries and Benedictine Rule," above) at Saint Gall in Switzerland, provides precious information about the design of Carolingian monastic communities. Haito, the abbot of Reichenau and bishop of Basel, ordered the preparation of the plan and sent it to the abbot of Saint Gall around 819 as a guide for the rebuilding of the Saint Gall

monastery. The design's fundamental purpose was to separate the monks from the laity (nonclergy) who also inhabited the community. Variations of the scheme may be seen in later monasteries all across western Europe. Near the center, dominating everything, was the church (*oratory*) with its *cloister*, a colonnaded courtyard not unlike the Early Christian atrium (FIG. 8-9) but situated to the side of the church instead of in front of its main portal. Reserved for the monks alone, the cloister was a kind of earthly paradise removed from the world at large. The Saint Gall cloister is an early example. Clustered around the cloister were the most essential buildings: dormitory, refectory, kitchen, and storage rooms. Other structures, including an infirmary, school, guest house, bakery, brewery, and workshops, filled the areas around this central core of church and cloister. In at least one Carolingian monastery, at Lorsch in Germany, a monumental freestanding gateway (FIG. 11-19A) stood in front of the church.

Haito invited the abbot of Saint Gall to adapt the plan as he saw fit, and indeed, the Saint Gall builders did not follow the Reichenau model precisely. Nonetheless, had the abbot wished, Haito's plan could have served as a practical guide for the Saint Gall masons because it was laid out using a *module* (standard unit) of 2.5 feet. The designer consistently employed that module, or multiples or fractions of it, for all elements of the plan. For example, the nave's width, indicated on the plan as 40 feet, is equal to 16 modules. Each monk's bed is 2.5 modules long, and the paths in the vegetable garden are 1.25 modules wide.

The prototypes carrying the greatest authority for Charlemagne and his builders were those from the Christian phase of the Late Roman Empire. The widespread adoption of the Early Christian basilica, at Saint Gall and elsewhere, rather than the domed central plan of Byzantine churches, was crucial to the subsequent development of western European church architecture. Unfortunately, no Carolingian basilica has survived in its original form. Nevertheless, it is possible to reconstruct the appearance of some of them with fair accuracy, for example, the abbey of Saint-Riquier (FIG. 11-19B) at Centula, France, which an 11th-century illuminator reproduced in a now-lost manuscript. Some Carolingian structures followed their Early Christian models quite closely. But in other instances, the ninth-century builders significantly modified the basilica plan, converting it into a much more complex form. The monastery church at Saint Gall, for example, was essentially a traditional basilica, but it had features not found in any Early Christian church. Most obvious is the addition of a second apse on the west end of the building, perhaps to accommodate additional altars and to display relics (see "The Veneration of Relics," Chapter 12, page 336). Whatever its purpose, this feature remained a characteristic regional element of German churches until the 11th century.

Not quite as evident but much more important to the subsequent development of church architecture in northern Europe was the presence of a transept at Saint Gall, a very rare feature but one that characterized the two greatest Early Christian basilicas in Rome, Saint Peter's (FIG. 8-9) and Saint Paul's, as well as the main church at the Centula abbey (FIG. 11-19B). The Saint Gall transept is as wide as the nave on the plan and was probably the same height. Early Christian builders had not been concerned with proportional relationships. On the Saint Gall plan, however, the various parts of the building relate to one another by a geometric scheme that ties them together into a tight and cohesive unit. Equalizing the widths of nave and transept automatically makes the area where they cross (the *crossing*) a square. Most Carolingian churches shared this feature. But Haito's planner also used the *crossing square* as the unit of measurement for the remainder of the church plan. The transept arms are equal to one crossing square, the distance between transept and apse is one crossing square, and the nave is 4.5 crossing squares long. In addition, the two aisles are half as wide as the nave, integrating all parts of the church in a rational and orderly plan.

The Saint Gall plan also reveals another important feature of many Carolingian basilicas, including Saint-Riquier (FIG. 11-19B) at Centula: towers framing the end(s) of the church. Haito's plan shows only two towers, both cylindrical and on the west side of the church, as at Charlemagne's Palatine Chapel (FIG. 11-17), but they stand apart from the church facade. If a tower existed above the crossing, the silhouette of Saint Gall would have shown three towers, altering the horizontal profile of the traditional basilica and identifying the church even from afar. Saint-Riquier had six towers.

CORVEY Other Carolingian basilicas had towers incorporated in the fabric of the west end of the building, thereby creating a unified monumental facade greeting all those who entered the church. Architectural historians call this feature of Carolingian and some later churches the *westwork* (from the German *Westwerk*, "western entrance structure"). Early medieval writers referred to it as a *castellum* (Latin, "castle" or "fortress") or *turris* ("tower"). The sole surviving example is the abbey church (FIG. 11-20) at Corvey. The uppermost parts are 12th-century additions (easily distinguishable from

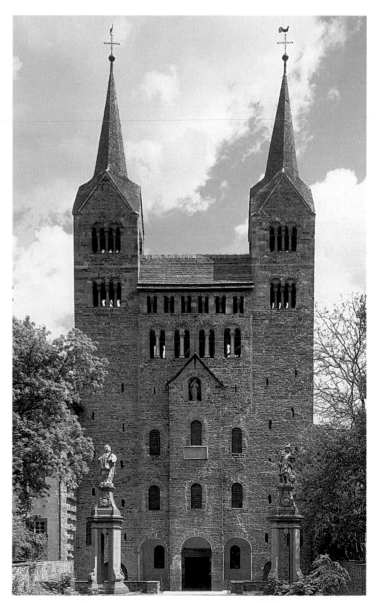

11-20 Westwork of the abbey church, Corvey, Germany, 873–885.

An important new feature of Carolingian church architecture was the westwork, a monumental western facade incorporating two towers. The sole surviving example is the abbey church at Corvey.

the original westwork by the differing masonry technique). Stairs in each tower provided access to the upper stories of the westwork. On the second floor was a two-story chapel with an aisle and a gallery on three sides. As at Aachen, the chapel opened onto the nave, and from it the visiting emperor and his entourage could watch and participate in the service below. Not all Carolingian westworks, however, served as seats reserved for the emperor. They also functioned as churches within churches, housing a second altar for special celebrations on major feast days. Boys' choirs stationed in the westwork chapel participated from above in the services conducted in the church's nave.

OTTONIAN ART

Louis the Pious laid Charlemagne to rest in the Palatine Chapel at Aachen in 814. Charlemagne had ruled for 46 years, but his empire survived him by fewer than 30. When Louis died in 840, his three sons—Charles the Bald, Lothair, and Louis the German—divided the Carolingian Empire among themselves. After bloody conflicts, the brothers signed a treaty at Verdun in 843 partitioning the Frankish lands into western, central, and eastern areas, very roughly foreshadowing the later nations of France and Germany and a third realm corresponding to a long strip of land stretching from the Netherlands and Belgium to Rome. Intensified Viking incursions in the west helped bring about the collapse of the Carolingians. The empire's breakup into weak kingdoms, ineffectual against the invasions, brought a time of confusion to Europe. Complementing the Viking scourge in the west were the invasions of the Magyars in the east and the plundering and piracy of the Saracens (Muslims) in the Mediterranean.

Only in the mid-10th century did the eastern part of the former empire consolidate under the rule of a new Saxon line of German emperors called, after the names of the three most illustrious family members, the *Ottonians*. The pope crowned the first Otto (r. 936–973) in Rome in 962, and Otto assumed the title "Emperor of Rome" that Charlemagne's weak successors held during most of the previous century. The Ottonian emperors made headway against the eastern invaders, remained free from Viking attacks, and not only preserved but also enriched the culture and tradition of the Carolingian period. The Church, which had become corrupt and disorganized, recovered in the 10th century under the influence of a great monastic reform the Ottonians encouraged and sanctioned. The new German emperors also cemented ties with Italy and the papacy as well as with Byzantium (see "Theophanu," page 328). The Ottonian line ended in the early 11th century with the death of Henry II (r. 1002–1024).

Architecture

Ottonian architects followed the course of their Carolingian predecessors, building basilican churches with towering spires and imposing westworks, but they also introduced new features that would have a long future in Western church architecture.

GERNRODE The best-preserved 10th-century Ottonian basilica is Saint Cyriakus at Gernrode, begun in 961 and completed in 973. In the 12th century, a large apse replaced the western entrance, but the upper parts of the westwork, including the two cylindrical towers, are intact. The interior (FIG. **11-21**), although heavily restored in the 19th century, retains its 10th-century character. Saint Cyriakus reveals how Ottonian architects enriched the Early Christian and Carolingian basilica. The church has a transept at the east with a square choir in front of the apse. The nave is one of the first in western Europe to incorporate a gallery between the

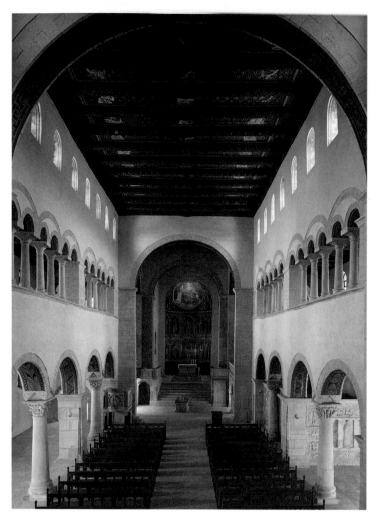

11-21 Nave of the church of Saint Cyriakus (looking east), Gernrode, Germany, 961–973.

Ottonian builders modified the interior elevation of Early Christian basilicas. The Gernrode designer added a gallery above the nave arcade and adopted an alternate-support system of piers and columns.

ground-floor arcade and the clerestory, a design that became very popular in the succeeding Romanesque era (see Chapter 12). Scholars have reached no consensus on the function of these galleries in Ottonian churches. They cannot have been reserved for women, as some think they were in Byzantium, because Saint Cyriakus is the centerpiece of a convent exclusively for nuns, founded the same year construction of the church began. The galleries may have housed additional altars, as in the westwork at Corvey, or the singers in the church's choir. The Gernrode builders also transformed the nave arcade itself by adopting the *alternate-support system,* in which heavy square piers alternate with columns, dividing the nave into vertical units. The division continues into the gallery level, breaking the smooth rhythm of the all-column arcades of Early Christian and Carolingian basilicas and leading the eye upward. Later architects would carry this verticalization of the basilican nave much further (FIG. 13-19).

HILDESHEIM A great patron of Ottonian art and architecture was Bishop Bernward (r. 993–1022) of Hildesheim, Germany. He was the tutor of Otto III (r. 983–1002) and builder of the abbey church of Saint Michael (FIGS. **11-22** and **11-23**) at Hildesheim. Bernward, who made Hildesheim a center of learning, was an eager scholar, a lover of the arts, and, according to Thangmar of

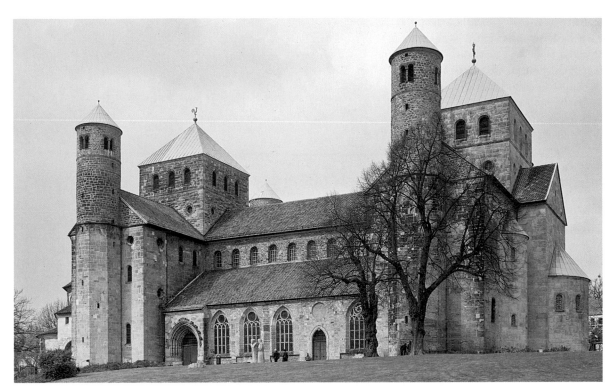

11-22 Saint Michael's (looking northwest), Hildesheim, Germany, 1001–1031. ■◀

Built by Bishop Bernward, a great art patron, Saint Michael's is a masterpiece of Ottonian basilica design. The church's two apses, two transepts, and multiple towers give it a distinctive profile.

11-23 Longitudinal section (*top*) and plan (*bottom*) of the abbey church of Saint Michael's, Hildesheim, Germany, 1001–1031.

Saint Michael's entrances are on the side. Alternating piers and columns divide the space in the nave into vertical units. These features transformed the tunnel-like horizontality of Early Christian basilicas.

Heidelberg, his biographer, an expert craftsman and bronze-caster. In 1001, Bernward traveled to Rome as the guest of Otto III. During this stay, he studied at first hand the monuments of the ancient empire the Carolingian and Ottonian emperors revered.

Constructed between 1001 and 1031 (and rebuilt after a bombing raid during World War II), Saint Michael's has a double-transept plan (FIG. 11-23, *bottom*), six towers, and a westwork. The two transepts create eastern and western centers of gravity. The nave

11-23A Nave, Saint Michael's, Hildesheim, 1001–1031.

(FIG. 11-23A) merely seems to be a hall connecting them. Lateral entrances leading into the aisles from the north and south additionally make for an almost complete loss of the traditional basilican orientation toward the east. Some ancient Roman basilicas, such as the Basilica Ulpia (FIG. 7-44, no. 4) in Trajan's Forum, also had two apses and entrances on the side, and Bernward probably was familiar with this variant basilican plan.

At Hildesheim, as in the plan of the monastery at Saint Gall (FIG. 11-19), the builders adopted a modular approach. The crossing squares, for example, are the basis for the nave's dimensions—three crossing squares long and one square wide. The placement of heavy piers at the corners of each square gives visual emphasis to the three units. These piers alternate with pairs of columns (FIG. 11-23A) as wall supports in a design similar to that of Saint Cyriakus (FIG. 11-21) at Gernrode.

Sculpture and Painting

In 1001, when Bishop Bernward was in Rome visiting the young Otto III, he resided in Otto's palace on the Aventine Hill in the neighborhood of Santa Sabina, an Early Christian church renowned for its carved wooden doors (FIG. 8-10A). Those doors, decorated with episodes from both the Old and New Testaments, may have inspired the remarkable bronze doors the bishop had cast for his new church in Germany.

HILDESHEIM DOORS The doors (FIG. 11-24) to Saint Michael's, dated by inscription to 1015, are more than 15 feet tall. They are technological marvels, because the Ottonian metalworkers cast each giant door in a single piece with the figural sculpture. Carolingian sculpture, like most sculpture since Late Antiquity, consisted primarily of small-scale art executed in ivory and precious metals, often for book covers (FIG. 11-16). The Hildesheim doors are huge in comparison, but the 16 individual panels stem from this tradition.

11-24A Column, Saint Michael's, Hildesheim, ca. 1015–1022. ◼◀

Bernward placed the bronze doors in the portal to Saint Michael's from the cloister, where the monks would see them each time they entered the church. The panels of the left door illustrate highlights from Genesis, beginning with the *Creation of Eve* (at the top) and ending with the murder of Adam and Eve's son Abel by his brother, Cain (at the bottom). The right door recounts the life of Jesus (reading from the bottom up), starting with the *Annunciation* and terminating with the appearance to Mary Magdalene of Christ after his resurrection (see "The Life of Jesus in Art," Chapter 8, pages 240–241). Together, the doors tell the story of original sin and ultimate redemption, showing the expulsion from the Garden of Eden and the path back to Paradise through the Church. (Reliefs depicting additional episodes from Jesus' life decorate a bronze column [FIG. 11-24A] that Bernward also commissioned for Saint Michael's.) As in Early Christian times, the Ottonian clergy interpreted the Hebrew scriptures as prefiguring the New Testament (see "Jewish Subjects in Christian Art," Chapter 8, page 238). For example, the Hildesheim designer juxtaposed the panel depicting the *Fall of Adam and Eve* on the left door with the *Crucifixion* on the right door. Eve nursing the infant Cain is opposite Mary with the Christ Child in her lap.

11-24 Doors with relief panels (Genesis, left door; life of Christ, right door), commissioned by Bishop Bernward for Saint Michael's, Hildesheim, Germany, 1015. Bronze, 15′ 5¾″ high. Dom-Museum, Hildesheim. ◼◀

Bernward's doors tell the story of original sin and redemption, and draw parallels between the Old and New Testaments, as in the expulsion from Paradise and the infancy and suffering of Christ.

The composition of many of the scenes on the doors derives from Carolingian manuscript illumination, and the style of the figures has an expressive strength that brings to mind the illustrations in the *Utrecht Psalter* (FIGS. 11-15 and 11-15A). For example, in the fourth panel (FIG. 11-25) from the top on the left door, God, portrayed as a man, accuses Adam and Eve after their fall from grace. He jabs his finger at them with the force of his whole body. The force is concentrated in the gesture, which becomes the psychic focus of the entire composition. The frightened pair crouch, not only to hide their shame but also to escape the lightning bolt of divine wrath. Each passes the blame—Adam pointing backward to Eve and Eve pointing downward to the deceitful serpent. The starkly flat setting throws into relief the gestures and attitudes of rage, accusation, guilt, and fear. The sculptor presented the story with simplicity, although with great emotional impact, as well as a flair for anecdotal detail. Adam and Eve both struggle to point with one arm while attempting to shield their bodies from view with the other. With an instinct for expressive pose and gesture, the artist brilliantly communicated their newfound embarrassment at their nakedness and their unconvincing denials of wrongdoing.

MAGDEBURG IVORIES The figural panels of the bronze doors of Saint Michael's at Hildesheim constitute a unique ensemble, but they are not the only series of small-scale narrative relief panels made for display in an Ottonian church. Sixteen ivory plaques remain from a set of perhaps as many as 50 that once decorated the altar, pulpit, or another important item of church furniture in Magdeburg Cathedral. The cathedral housed the relics of Saint Mauritius (Maurice), a Christian army commander from Africa whom the Romans executed in Gaul during the third century when he refused to sacrifice to the old gods. Otto transferred the saint's relics from France to Magdeburg in 960. A former monastic community on the eastern frontier of the Ottonian Empire, Magdeburg became an archbishopric in 968, the year Otto I dedicated the city's new cathedral. The 10th-century church burned down in 1207. The present cathedral is a Gothic replacement.

Most of the plaques depict scenes from the life of Jesus. The one illustrated here (FIG. **11-26**), however, features Otto I presenting Magdeburg Cathedral to Christ, who sits on a large wreath and extends his right hand to the emperor to indicate he welcomes the gift. Ottonian representations of the emperor usually depict him as the central figure and of large stature (FIG. 11-29), but the artist here represented the bearded and crowned Otto to one side and as the size of a child. The age-old principle of hierarchy of scale dictated that the artist depict the only mortal as the smallest figure.

Christ is largest, and the saints are intermediate in size. The two most prominent are Saint Peter, at the right holding the key to the kingdom of Heaven, and Saint Mauritius, who introduces the emperor to Christ. Art historians believe the plaques are the work of Milanese ivory carvers. Lombardy was part of Otto I's empire.

Theophanu, a Byzantine Princess in Ottonian Germany

The bishop of Mainz crowned Otto I king of the Saxons at Aachen in 936, but it was not until 962 that Pope John XII (r. 955–964) conferred the title of Emperor of Rome upon him in Saint Peter's basilica. Otto, known as the Great, had ambitions to restore the glory of Charlemagne's Christian Roman Empire and to enlarge the territory under his rule. In 951, he defeated a Roman noble who had taken prisoner Adelaide, the widow of the Lombard king Lothar. Otto then married Adelaide, assumed the title of King of the Lombards, and extended his power south of the Alps. Looking eastward, in 972 he arranged the marriage of his son (and co-emperor since 967), Otto II, to Theophanu (ca. 955–991), probably the niece of Emperor Nikephoros II Phokas (r. 963–969). Otto was 17 years old, his bride 16. They wed in Saint Peter's in Rome, with Pope John XIII (r. 965–972) presiding. When Otto the Great died the next year, Otto II became sole emperor (r. 973–983). The second Otto died in Italy a decade later and was buried in the atrium of Saint Peter's. His son, Otto III, only three years old at the time, nominally became king, but it was his mother, Theophanu, coregent with Adelaide until 985 and sole regent thereafter, who wielded power in the Ottonian Empire until her death in 991. Adelaide then served as regent until Otto III was old enough to rule on his own. He became Roman emperor in 996 and died six years later.

Theophanu brought the prestige of Byzantium to Germany. Artistic ties between the Ottonian court and Constantinople became even stronger, and the Ottonians imported Byzantine luxury goods, including ivory plaques, in great quantities. One surviving ivory panel (FIG. 11-27) commemorates the marriage between Otto II and Theophanu. It shows Christ, central and the largest figure, extending both arms to bless the crowned emperor and his empress. (Otto appears much older than 17, consistent with his imperial stature.) The artist depicted all three standing rigidly and looking directly at the viewer. The frontality of the figures, the tripartite composition, and the style of carving suggest the work is an import from Constantinople, as does the lengthy Greek dedicatory inscription. A few words are in Latin, however, and the inscription also identifies the donor—the tiny bowing figure clinging to Christ's stool—as an Italian bishop. Some art historians therefore think the artist may have been an Ottonian ivory carver in Lombardy. Nonetheless, the iconography is distinctively Byzantine because the imagery declares that Otto's authority to rule comes directly

11-27 Christ blessing Otto II and Theophanu, 972–973. Ivory, $7\frac{1}{8}'' \times 4''$. Musée National du Moyen Age, Paris.

Commemorating the marriage of Otto II and Theophanu, this ivory plaque is Byzantine in style and iconography. The princess promoted Byzantine art and culture at the Ottonian court.

from Christ, not from the pope. Whether of Byzantine or Ottonian manufacture, the ivory is an Ottonian commission in Byzantine style. The influence of Byzantine art is also evident in Ottonian manuscript painting (FIGS. 11-29A and 11-30).

OTTO II AND THEOPHANU On April 14, 972, Otto I arranged the marriage of his son Otto II to the Byzantine princess Theophanu (see "Theophanu, a Byzantine Princess in Ottonian Germany," above). The wedding secured the important political alliance between the Ottonian and Byzantine empires. Because the couple married in Rome with the pope administering the vows, the wedding simultaneously reaffirmed the close relationship between the Ottonians and the papacy. The marriage, commemorated on a unique ivory plaque (FIG. **11-27**), also enhanced the already strong artistic and cultural ties between Germany and Constantinople.

GERO CRUCIFIX During the Ottonian period, interest in freestanding statuary, which had been exceedingly rare for the pre-

ceding half millennium, also revived. The outstanding example of Ottonian monumental sculpture is the crucifix (FIG. **11-28**) Archbishop Gero (r. 969–976) commissioned and presented to Cologne Cathedral in 970. Carved in oak, then painted and gilded, the 6-foot-tall image of Christ nailed to the cross is both statue and *reliquary* (a shrine for sacred relics; see "The Veneration of Relics," Chapter 12, page 336). A compartment in the back of the head held bread for the Eucharist. According to one story, a crack developed in the wood of Gero's crucifix but miraculously healed. Similar tales of miracles surround many sacred Christian objects, for example, some Byzantine icons (see "Icons," Chapter 9, page 269).

The Gero crucifix presents a dramatically different conception of Christ from that seen on the *Lindau Gospels* cover (FIG. 11-16),

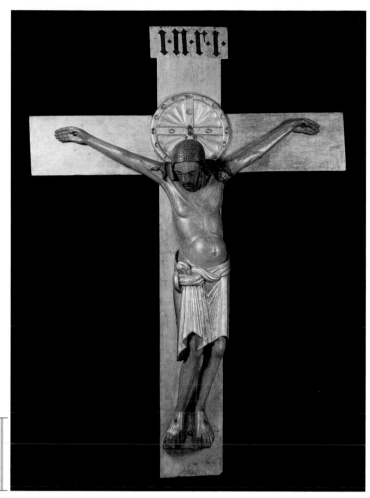

11-28 Crucifix commissioned by Archbishop Gero for Cologne Cathedral, Cologne, Germany, ca. 970. Painted wood, height of figure 6′ 2″. Cathedral, Cologne. ◼◀

In this early example of the revival of monumental sculpture in the Middle Ages, an Ottonian sculptor depicted with unprecedented emotional power the intense agony of Christ's ordeal on the cross.

1 ft.

1 in.

11-29 Otto III enthroned, folio 24 recto of the *Gospel Book of Otto III*, from Reichenau, Germany, 997–1000. Tempera on vellum, 1′ 1″ × 9⅜″. Bayerische Staatsbibliothek, Munich.

Emperor Otto III, descended from both German and Byzantine imperial lines, appears in this Gospel book enthroned and holding the scepter and cross-inscribed orb signifying his universal authority.

with its Early Christian imagery of the youthful Christ triumphant over death. Consistent with the strong Byzantine element in Ottonian art, the bearded Christ of the Cologne crucifix is more akin to Byzantine representations (FIG. 9-24) of the suffering Jesus, but the emotional power of the Ottonian work is greater still. The sculptor depicted Christ as an all-too-human martyr. Blood streaks down his forehead from the (missing) crown of thorns. His eyelids are closed, his face is contorted in pain, and his body sags under its weight. The muscles stretch to their limit—those of the right shoulder and chest seem almost to rip apart. The halo behind Christ's head may foretell his subsequent resurrection, but the worshiper can sense only his pain. Gero's crucifix is the most powerful characterization of intense agony of the early Middle Ages.

11-29A Jesus and Peter, *Gospel Book of Otto III*, 997–1000.

GOSPEL BOOK OF OTTO III In a Gospel book containing some of the finest early medieval paintings of the life of Jesus (for example, FIG. **11-29A**), one full-page representation (FIG. **11-29**) stands apart from the rest. The page shows Otto III, son of Otto II and Theophanu, enthroned and holding the scepter and cross-inscribed orb that signify his universal authority, conforming to a Christian impe-

rial iconographic tradition that began with Constantine (FIG. 7-81, *right*). At the emperor's sides are the clergy and the barons (the Church and the state), both aligned in his support. On the facing page (not illustrated), also derived from ancient Roman sources, female personifications of Slavinia, Germany, Gaul, and Rome—the provinces of the Ottonian Empire—bring tribute to the young emperor.

Of the three Ottos, the last most fervently dreamed of a revived Christian Roman Empire. Indeed, it was his life's obsession. The boy-emperor was keenly aware of his descent from both German and Byzantine imperial lines, but he apparently was prouder of his Constantinopolitan than his German roots. He moved his court, with its Byzantine rituals, to Rome and there set up theatrically the symbols and trappings of Roman imperialism. Otto's romantic dream of imperial unity for Europe, the conceit behind his self-aggrandizing portrayal in the *Gospel Book of Otto III*, never materialized, however. He died prematurely, at age 21, and, at his request, was buried beside Charlemagne at Aachen.

LECTIONARY OF HENRY II Otto III's successor, Henry II, was the last Ottonian emperor. Of the artworks produced during his reign, the *Lectionary of Henry II* is the most noteworthy. A product of the leading Ottonian scriptorium at Reichenau, as was Otto III's Gospel book, Henry's lectionary (a book of Gospel readings for the Mass; see "Medieval Books," page 312) was a gift to Bamberg Cathedral. In the full-page illumination of the announcement of Christ's

11-30 *Annunciation to the Shepherds,* folio in the *Lectionary of Henry II,* from Reichenau, Germany, 1002–1014. Tempera on vellum, 1′ 5″ × 1′ 1″. Bayerische Staatsbibliothek, Munich.

The full-page illuminations in the *Lectionary of Henry II* fuse elements of Late Antique landscapes, the Carolingian-Ottonian anecdotal narrative tradition, and the golden background of Byzantine art.

11-31 **Abbess Uta dedicating her codex to the Virgin,** folio 2 recto of the *Uta Codex,* from Regensburg, Germany, ca. 1025. Tempera on parchment, $9\frac{5}{8}$″ × $5\frac{1}{8}$″. Bayerische Staatsbibliothek, Munich.

The *Uta Codex* illustrates the important role women played both in religious life and as patrons of the arts. The dedicatory page shows Abbess Uta presenting her codex to the Virgin Mary.

birth to the shepherds (FIG. **11-30**), the angel has just alighted on a hill, his still-beating wings agitating his draperies. The angel looms immense above the startled and terrified shepherds, filling the golden sky. He extends his hand in a gesture of authority and instruction. Emphasized more than the message itself are the power and majesty of God's authority. The painting is a summation of the stylistic complexity of Ottonian art. It is a highly successful fusion of the Carolingian-Ottonian anecdotal narrative tradition, elements derived from Late Antique painting—for example, the rocky landscape setting with grazing animals (FIG. 8-17)—and the golden background of Byzantine book illumination and mosaic decoration.

UTA CODEX Another lectionary (FIG. **11-31**), one of the finest Ottonian books produced for the clergy, as opposed to the imperial court, was the work of scribes and illuminators at Regensburg. Their patron was Uta, abbess of Niedermünster from 1003 to 1025, a leading nun well known in royal circles. Uta was instrumental in bringing Benedictine reforms to the Niedermünster convent, whose nuns were usually the daughters of the local nobility. Near the end of her life, she presented the nunnery with a sumptuous manuscript containing many full-page illuminations interspersed with Gospel readings, the so-called *Uta Codex*. The lectionary's gold-jewel-and-enamel case also survives, underscoring the nature

of medieval books as sacred objects to be venerated in their own right as well as embodiments of the eternal word of God.

The dedicatory page (FIG. 11-31) at the front of the *Uta Codex* depicts the Virgin Mary with the Christ Child in her lap in the central medallion. Labeled *Virgo Virginum,* Virgin of Virgins, Mary is the model for Uta and the Niedermünster nuns. Uta is the full-length figure presenting a new book—this book—to the Virgin. An inscription accompanies the dedicatory image: "Virgin Mother of God, happy because of the divine Child, receive the votive offerings of your Uta of ready service."[5] The artist painted Uta last, superimposing her figure upon the design and carefully placing it so that Uta's head touches the Virgin's medallion but does not penetrate it, suggesting the interplay between, but also the separation of, the divine and human realms.

In many respects, the *Uta Codex* is more typical of the Middle Ages than are the artworks and buildings commissioned by the Carolingian and Ottonian emperors. The Roman Empire, in revived form, may have lived on to 1002 at Otto III's court in Rome, but after Henry II's death in 1024, a new age began, and Rome's influence waned. Romanesque Europe instead found unity in a common religious fervor (see Chapter 12).

EARLY MEDIEVAL EUROPE

ART OF THE WARRIOR LORDS 5th to 10th Centuries

▌ After the fall of Rome in 410, the Huns, Vandals, Merovingians, Franks, Goths, Vikings, and other non-Roman peoples competed for power and territory in the former northwestern provinces of the Roman Empire.

▌ Other than the ornamentation of ships used for burials, the surviving artworks of this period are almost exclusively small-scale status symbols, especially items of personal adornment such as bracelets, pins, purses, and belt buckles, often featuring cloisonné decoration. A mixture of abstract and zoomorphic motifs appears on these portable treasures. Especially characteristic are intertwined animal and interlace patterns.

Sutton Hoo purse cover, ca. 625

HIBERNO-SAXON ART 6th to 10th Centuries

▌ Art historians call the Christian art of the early medieval Britain and Ireland Hiberno-Saxon or Insular. The most important extant artworks are the illuminated manuscripts produced in the monastic scriptoria of Ireland and Northumbria.

▌ These Insular books feature folios devoted neither to text nor to illustration but to pure embellishment. "Carpet pages" consist of decorative panels of abstract and zoomorphic motifs. Some books also have full pages depicting the four evangelists or their symbols. Text pages often present the initial letters of important passages enlarged and transformed into elaborate decorative patterns.

Book of Kells, late eighth or early ninth century

CAROLINGIAN ART 768–877

▌ Charlemagne, king of the Franks since 768, expanded the territories he inherited from his father, and in 800, Pope Leo III crowned him emperor of Rome (r. 800–814). Charlemagne and his successors initiated a conscious revival of the art and culture of Early Christian Rome.

▌ Carolingian sculptors revived the imperial Roman tradition of portraying rulers on horseback and the Early Christian tradition of depicting Christ as a statuesque youth. Artists merged the illusionism of classical painting with the northern European linear tradition, replacing the calm and solid figures of those models with figures that leap from the page with frenzied energy.

▌ Carolingian architects looked to Ravenna and Early Christian Rome for models but transformed their sources, introducing, for example, the twin-tower western facade for basilicas and employing strict modular plans for entire monasteries as well as individual churches.

Charlemagne or Charles the Bald, ninth century

Utrecht Psalter, ca. 820–835

OTTONIAN ART 919–1024

▌ In the mid-10th century, a new line of emperors, the Ottonians, consolidated the eastern part of Charlemagne's former empire and sought to preserve the culture and tradition of the Carolingian period.

▌ Ottonian artists, like other early medieval artists, excelled in producing sumptuous small-scale artworks, especially ivory plaques with narrative reliefs, often influenced by Byzantine art. But Ottonian sculptors also revived the art of monumental sculpture in works such as the *Gero Crucifix* and the colossal bronze doors of Saint Michael's at Hildesheim. Ottonian painting combines motifs and landscape elements from Late Antique art with the golden backgrounds of Byzantine art.

▌ Ottonian architects built basilican churches incorporating the towers and westworks of their Carolingian models but introduced the alternate-support system and galleries into the interior nave elevation.

Saint Michael's, Hildesheim, 1001–1031

Christ presides over
the separation of
the blessed from the
damned in Gislebertus's
dramatic vision of
the *Last Judgment,*
designed to terrify those
guilty of sin and beckon
them into the church.

Above Autun Cathedral's portal, at the far left,
a trumpet-blowing angel announces the second
coming. Another obliging angel boosts one of
the blessed over the fortified walls of Heaven.

Below, the souls of the dead line up to await their fate. Two
men whose travel bags identify them as pilgrims to Jerusalem
and Santiago de Compostela can expect to be judged favorably.

1 ft.

12-1 Gislebertus, *Last Judgment,* west tympanum of Saint-Lazare, Autun, France, ca. 1120–1135. Marble, 21′ wide at base. ◼◀

ROMANESQUE EUROPE

In Gislebertus's unforgettable rendition of the weighing of souls on judgment day, angels and the Devil's agents contest at the scales, each trying to tip the balance for or against a soul.

THE REBIRTH OF MONUMENTAL SCULPTURE

As worshipers entered the western portal of Saint-Lazare (Saint Lazarus) at Autun, they passed under a dramatic representation of the *Last Judgment* (FIG. **12-1**) by the sculptor GISLEBERTUS. A renowned artist, he inscribed his name in the stone relief and added this admonition: "May this terror terrify those whom earthly error binds, for the horror of these images here in this manner truly depicts what will be."[1] The warning echoes the sentiment expressed in a mid-10th-century copy of Beatus of Liébana's *Commentary on the Apocalypse*. There, the painter Magius (teacher of Emeterius; see FIG. 11-11) explained the purpose of his work: "I have painted a series of pictures for the wonderful words of [the Apocalypse's] stories, so that the wise may fear the coming of the future judgment of the world's end."[2]

Few people in 12th-century France other than the clergy could read Gislebertus's message, but even the illiterate could, in the words of Saint Bernard of Clairvaux, "read in the marble" (see "Bernard of Clairvaux on Cloister Sculpture," page 342). Indeed, in the entire history of art, there is probably no more terrifying visualization of what awaits sinners than the *Last Judgment* at Autun. Four trumpet-blowing angels announce the second coming of Christ, enthroned at the center, far larger than any other figure. He dispassionately presides over the separation of the blessed from the damned. At the left, an obliging angel boosts one of the saved into the heavenly city. Below, the souls of the dead line up to await their fate. Two of the men near the center of the lintel carry bags emblazoned with a cross and a shell. These are the symbols of pilgrims to Jerusalem and Santiago de Compostela, respectively (see "Pilgrimage Roads in France and Spain," page 335, and MAP **12-1**). Those who had made the difficult journey would be judged favorably. To their right, three small figures beg an angel to intercede on their behalf. The angel responds by pointing to the judge above. On the right side are those who will be condemned to Hell. Giant hands pluck one poor soul from the earth. Directly above is Gislebertus's unforgettable rendition of the weighing of souls (compare FIG. 11-9). Angels and the Devil's agents try to manipulate the balance for or against a soul. Hideous demons guffaw and roar. Their gaunt, lined bodies, with legs ending in sharp claws, writhe and bend like long, loathsome insects. A devilish creature, leaning from the dragon mouth of Hell, drags souls in, while above him, a howling demon crams the damned headfirst into a furnace.

The Autun *Last Judgment* is one of the earliest examples of the rebirth of the art of monumental sculpture in the Middle Ages, one hallmark of the age art historians have dubbed *Romanesque* because of the extensive use of stone sculpture and stone vaulting in ecclesiastical architecture.

EUROPEAN CULTURE IN THE NEW MILLENNIUM

The Romanesque era is the first since Archaic and Classical Greece to take its name from an artistic style rather than from politics or geography. Unlike Carolingian and Ottonian art, named for emperors, or Hiberno-Saxon art, a regional term, *Romanesque* is a title art historians invented to describe medieval art that appeared "Roman-like." Architectural historians first employed the adjective in the early 19th century to describe European architecture of the 11th and 12th centuries. They noted that certain architectural elements of this period, principally barrel and groin vaults based on the round arch, resembled those of ancient Roman architecture. Thus, the word distinguished most Romanesque buildings from earlier medieval timber-roofed structures, as well as from later Gothic churches with vaults resting on pointed arches (see Chapter 13). Scholars in other fields quickly borrowed the term. Today "Romanesque" broadly designates the history and culture of western Europe between about 1050 and 1200.

TOWNS AND CHURCHES In the early Middle Ages, the focus of life was the *manor,* or estate, of a landholding *liege lord,* who might grant rights to a portion of his land to *vassals.* The vassals swore allegiance to their liege and rendered him military service in return for use of the land and the promise of protection. But in the Romanesque period, a sharp increase in trade encouraged the growth of towns and cities, gradually displacing *feudalism* as the governing political, social, and economic system of late medieval Europe. Feudal lords granted independence to the new towns in the form of charters, which enumerated the communities' rights, privileges, immunities, and exemptions beyond the feudal obligations the vassals owed the lords. Often located on navigable rivers, the new urban centers naturally became the nuclei of networks of maritime and overland commerce.

Separated by design from the busy secular life of Romanesque towns were the monasteries (see "Medieval Monasteries," Chapter 11, page 322) and their churches. During the 11th and 12th centuries, thousands of ecclesiastical buildings were remodeled or newly constructed. This immense building enterprise was in part a natural by-product of the rise of independent cities and the prosperity they enjoyed. But it also was an expression of the widely felt relief and thanksgiving that the conclusion of the first Christian millennium in the year 1000 had not brought an end to the world, as many had feared. In the Romanesque age, the construction of churches became almost an obsession. Raoul Glaber (ca. 985–ca. 1046), a monk who witnessed the coming of the new millennium, noted the beginning of it:

> [After the] year of the millennium, which is now about three years past, there occurred, throughout the world, especially in Italy and Gaul, a rebuilding of church basilicas. Notwithstanding, the greater number were already well established and not in the least in need, nevertheless each Christian people strove against the others to erect nobler ones. It was as if the whole earth, having cast off the old by shaking itself, were clothing itself everywhere in the white robe of the church.[3]

PILGRIMS AND RELICS The enormous investment in ecclesiastical buildings and furnishings also reflected a significant increase in pilgrimage traffic in Romanesque Europe (see "Pilgrimage Roads in France and Spain," page 335, and MAP 12-1). Pilgrims, along with wealthy landowners, were important sources of funding for those monasteries that possessed the *relics* of venerated saints (see "The Veneration of Relics," page 336). The monks of Sainte-Foy (FIG. 12-7A) at Conques, for example, used pilgrims' donations to pay for a magnificent cameo-and-jewel-encrusted gold-and-silver *reliquary* (FIG. **12-2**) to house the skull of Saint Faith. In fact, the clergy of the various monasteries vied with one another to provide the most magnificent settings for the display of their unique relics. They found justification for their lavish expenditures on buildings and furnishings in the Bible itself, for example, in Psalm 26:8, "Lord, I have loved the beauty of your house, and the place where your glory dwells." Traveling pilgrims fostered the growth of towns as well as monasteries. Pilgrimages were a major economic as well as conceptual catalyst for the art and architecture of the Romanesque period.

FRANCE AND NORTHERN SPAIN

Although art historians use the adjective "Romanesque" to describe 11th- and 12th-century art and architecture throughout Europe, pronounced regional differences exist. This chapter examines in turn Romanesque France and Spain; the Holy Roman Empire; Italy; and Normandy and England. To a certain extent, Romanesque art and architecture can be compared with the European Romance languages, which vary regionally but have a common core in Latin, the language of the Romans.

ROMANESQUE EUROPE

1000	1100	1200
▌ Romanesque architects replace the timber roofs of churches with barrel vaults in the nave and groin vaults in the aisles	▌ Architects introduce groin vaulting in church naves in conjunction with a three-story elevation (arcade-tribune-clerestory)	
▌ Builders also add radiating chapels to ambulatories for the display of relics	▌ Relief sculpture becomes commonplace on church facades, usually greeting worshipers with a vision of Christ as last judge	
▌ Sculptors revive the art of monumental stone relief carving	▌ Manuscript illumination flourishes in the scriptoria of Cluniac monasteries	

Pilgrimage Roads in France and Spain

In the Romanesque era, pilgrimage was the most conspicuous feature of public religious devotion, proclaiming pilgrims' faith in the power of saints and hope for their special favor. The major shrines—Saint Peter's and Saint Paul's in Rome and the Church of the Holy Sepulcher in Jerusalem—drew pilgrims from all over Europe, just as Muslims journeyed from afar to Mecca (see "Muhammad and Islam," Chapter 10, page 285). The pilgrims braved bad roads and hostile wildernesses infested with robbers who preyed on innocent travelers—all for the sake of salvation. The journeys could take more than a year to complete—when they were successful. People often undertook pilgrimage as an act of repentance or as a last resort in their search for a cure for some physical disability. Hardship and austerity were means of increasing pilgrims' chances for the remission of sin or of disease. The distance and peril of the pilgrimage were measures of pilgrims' sincerity of repentance or of the reward they sought.

For those with insufficient time or money to make a pilgrimage to Rome or Jerusalem (in short, most people in Europe), holy destinations could be found closer to home. In France, for example, the church at Vézelay (FIG. 12-14) housed the bones of Mary Magdalene. Pilgrims could also view Saint Lazarus's remains at Autun (FIG. 12-1), Saint Saturninus's at Toulouse (FIG. 12-5), Saint Faith's at Conques (FIGS. 12-2 and 12-7A), and Saint Martin's at Tours (see "The Veneration of Relics," page 336). Each of these great shrines was also an important way station en route to the most venerated shrine in western Europe, the tomb of Saint James at Santiago de Compostela (FIG. 12-7B) in northwestern Spain.

Large crowds of pilgrims paying homage to saints placed a great burden on the churches possessing their relics and led to changes in church design, principally longer and wider naves and aisles, transepts and ambulatories with additional chapels (FIG. 12-6), and second-story galleries (FIGS. 12-7 and 12-7B). Pilgrim traffic also established the routes that later became the major avenues of commerce and communication in western Europe. The popularity of pilgrimages gave rise to travel guides that, like modern guidebooks, provided pilgrims with information not only about saints and shrines but also about roads, accommodations, food, and drink. How widely circulated these handwritten books were remains a matter of scholarly debate, but the information they provide is invaluable.

The most famous Romanesque guidebook described the four roads leading to Santiago de Compostela through Arles and Toulouse, Conques and Moissac, Vézelay and Périgueux, and Tours and Bordeaux in France (MAP 12-1). Saint James was the symbol of Christian resistance to Muslim expansion in western Europe, and his relics, discovered in the ninth century, drew pilgrims to Santiago de Compostela from far and wide. The guidebook's anonymous 12th-century author, possibly Aimery Picaud, a Cluniac monk, was himself a well-traveled pilgrim. The text states the author wrote the guide "in Rome, in the lands of Jerusalem, in France, in Italy, in Germany, in Frisia and mainly in Cluny."* Pilgrims reading the guidebook learned about the saints and their shrines at each stop along the way to Spain. Saint Saturninus of Toulouse, for example, endured a martyr's death at the hands of the Romans when he

> was tied to some furious and wild bulls and then precipitated from the height of the citadel. . . . His head crushed, his brains knocked out, his whole body torn to pieces, he rendered his worthy soul to Christ. He is buried in an excellent location close to the city of Toulouse where a large basilica [FIGS. 12-5 to 12-7] was erected by the faithful in his honor.†

MAP 12-1 Western Europe around 1100.

*William Melczer, *The Pilgrim's Guide to Santiago de Compostela* (New York: Italica Press, 1993), 133.
† Ibid., 103.

The Veneration of Relics

The cult of *relics* was not new in the Romanesque era. For centuries, Christians had traveled to sacred shrines housing the body parts of, or objects associated with, the holy family or the saints. The faithful had long believed bones, clothing, instruments of martyrdom, and the like had the power to heal body and soul. The veneration of relics, however, reached a high point in the 11th and 12th centuries, prompting the devout to undertake often dangerous pilgrimages to hallowed shrines in Jerusalem, Rome, and throughout western Europe (see "Pilgrimage Roads in France and Spain," page 335). Churches vied with one another not only for the possession of relics but also in the magnificence of the containers (*reliquaries*) that preserved and protected them.

The case of the relics of Saint Faith (Sainte-Foy, in French), an early-fourth-century child martyr who refused to pay homage to the Roman gods, is a telling example. A monk from the abbey church at Conques (FIG. 12-7A) stole the saint's skull from the nearby abbey of Agen around 880. The monks justified the act as *furta sacra* (holy theft), claiming Saint Faith herself wished to move. The reliquary (FIG. 12-2) they provided to house the saint's remains is one of the most sumptuous ever produced. It takes the form of an enthroned statuette of the martyr. Fashioned of gold leaf and silver gilt over a wooden core, the reliquary prominently features inset jewels and cameos of various dates—the accumulated donations of pilgrims and church patrons over many years. The saint's oversize head is a reworked ancient Roman *parade helmet*—a masklike helmet worn by soldiers on special ceremonial occasions and not part of standard battle dress. The monks added a martyr's crown to the ancient helmet. The rear of the throne bears a *Crucifixion* image engraved in rock crystal, establishing a parallel between Christ's martyrdom and Saint Faith's.

Reflecting the Romanesque passion for relics, *The Song of Roland,* an 11th-century epic poem recounting a historical battle of 778 between Charlemagne's rear-guard and the Saracens, describes Durendal, the extraordinary sword the hero Roland wielded, as follows:

> Ah, Durendal, fair, hallowed, and devote,
> What store of relics lie in thy hilt of gold!
> St Peter's tooth, St Basil's blood, it holds,
> Hair of my lord St Denis, there enclosed,
> Likewise a piece of Blessed Mary's robe.*

Given the competition among Romanesque monasteries and cities for the possession of saints' relics, the 11th-century *Pilgrim's Guide to Santiago de Compostela* included comments on authenticity. For example, about Saint James's tomb, the anonymous author stated:

> May therefore the imitators from beyond the mountains blush
> who claim to possess some portion of him or even his entire relic.
> In fact, the body of the Apostle is here in its entirety, divinely lit
> by paradisiacal carbuncles, incessantly honored with immaculate
> and soft perfumes, decorated with dazzling celestial candles, and
> diligently worshipped by attentive angels.†

1 ft.

12-2 Reliquary statue of Sainte-Foy (Saint Faith), late 10th to early 11th century with later additions. Gold, silver gilt, jewels, and cameos over a wooden core, 2′ 9½″ high. Treasury, Sainte-Foy, Conques.

This enthroned image containing the skull of Saint Faith is one of the most lavish Romanesque reliquaries. The head is an ancient Roman parade helmet, and the cameos are donations from pilgrims.

*173.2344–2348. Translated by Dorothy L. Sayers, *The Song of Roland* (New York: Penguin, 1957), 141.
†William Melczer, *The Pilgrim's Guide to Santiago de Compostela* (New York: Italica Press, 1993), 127.

Architecture and Architectural Sculpture

The regional diversity of the Romanesque period is particularly evident in architecture. For example, some Romanesque churches, especially in Italy, retained the wooden roofs of their Early Christian predecessors long after stone vaulting had become commonplace elsewhere. Even in France and northern Spain, home of many of the most innovative instances of stone vaulting, some Romanesque architects continued to build timber-roofed churches.

VIGNORY The mid-11th-century church of Saint-Étienne (Saint Stephen) at Vignory in the Champagne region of central France has strong ties to Carolingian-Ottonian architecture but already incorporates features that became common only in later Romanesque buildings. The interior (FIG. **12-3**) reveals a kinship with the three-story wooden-roofed churches of the Ottonian era, for example, Saint Cyriakus (FIG. 11-21) at Gernrode. At Vignory, however, the second story is not a true *tribune* (gallery over the aisle opening onto the nave) but rather a screen with alternating piers and columns opening onto very tall flanking aisles. The east end of the church, in contrast, has an innovative plan (FIG. 12-4) with an ambulatory around the choir and three semicircular chapels opening onto it. These *radiating chapels* probably housed the church's relics, which the faithful could view without having to enter the choir where the main altar stood.

Although other 11th-century churches, for example, Sant Vicenç (FIG. **12-4A**) at Cardona, Spain, and Saint-Philibert (FIG. **12-4B**) at Tournus, France, are noteworthy as early Romanesque examples of stone vaulting, Saint-Étienne at Vignory is one of the first examples of the introduction of stone sculpture into Romanesque ecclesiastical architecture, one of the period's defining features. At Vignory, however, the only sculpture is the relief decoration of the capitals of the ambulatory and false tribunes where abstract and vegetal ornamentation, lions, and other quadrupeds are the exclusive motifs.

12-4A Sant Vicenç, Cardona, ca. 1029–1040.

12-4B Saint-Philibert, Tournus, ca. 1060. ◼◀

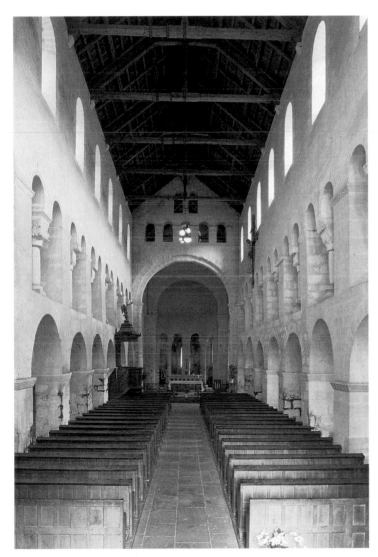

12-3 Interior of Saint-Étienne (looking east), Vignory, France, 1050–1057. ◼◀

The timber-roofed abbey church at Vignory reveals a kinship with the three-story naves of Ottonian churches (FIG. 11-21), which also feature an alternate-support system of piers and columns.

12-4 Plan of Saint-Étienne, Vignory, France, 1050–1057. (1) nave, (2) aisles, (3) choir, (4) ambulatory, (5) radiating chapels.

The innovative plan of the east end of the abbey church of Saint Stephen features an ambulatory around the choir and three semicircular radiating chapels opening onto it for the display of relics.

12-5 Aerial view of Saint-Sernin (looking northwest), Toulouse, France, ca. 1070–1120. ■◀

Pilgrimages were a major economic catalyst for the art and architecture of the Romanesque period. The clergy vied with one another to provide magnificent settings for the display of holy relics.

TOULOUSE Dwarfing the Vignory, Cardona, and Tournus churches is the immense stone-vaulted basilica of Saint-Sernin (Saint Saturninus; FIGS. **12-5** to **12-7**) at Toulouse. Construction began around 1070 to honor the city's first bishop, a martyr saint of the middle of the third century. Toulouse was an important stop on the pilgrimage road through southwestern France to Santiago de Compostela (see "Pilgrimage Roads," page 335). Large congregations gathered at the shrines along the major pilgrimage routes, and the unknown architect designed Saint-Sernin to accommo-

12-7A Sainte-Foy, Conques, mid-11th to early 12th century. ■◀

12-7B Saint James, Santiago de Compostela, ca. 1075–1120.

date them. The grand scale of the building is apparent in the aerial view (FIG. 12-5), which includes automobiles, trucks, and nearly invisible pedestrians. The church's 12th-century exterior is still largely intact, although the two towers of the western facade (at the left in FIG. 12-5) were never completed, and the prominent crossing tower dates to the Gothic and later periods. Saint-Sernin's plan (FIG. 12-6) closely resembles those of the churches of Saint Faith (FIG. **12-7A**) at Conques, Saint James (FIG. **12-7B**) at Santiago de Compostela, and Saint Martin at Tours, and exemplifies what has come to be called the "pilgrimage church" type. At Toulouse, the builders increased the length of the nave, doubled the side aisles, and added a transept, ambulatory, and radiating chapels to provide additional space for pilgrims and the clergy. Radiating chapels opening onto an ambulatory already were a feature of Vignory's abbey church (FIG. 12-4), but at Toulouse the chapels are greater in number and open onto the transept as well as the ambulatory.

The Saint-Sernin plan is extremely regular and geometrically precise. The crossing square, flanked by massive piers and marked off by heavy arches, served as the module for the entire church. Each nave bay, for example, measures exactly one-half of the crossing square, and each aisle bay measures exactly one-quarter. The builders employed similar simple ratios throughout the church. The first suggestion of this kind of planning scheme in medieval Europe was the Saint Gall monastery plan (FIG. 11-19), almost three

12-6 Plan of Saint-Sernin, Toulouse, France, ca. 1070–1120 (after Kenneth John Conant).

Increased traffic led to changes in church design. "Pilgrimage churches" have longer and wider naves and aisles, as well as transepts and ambulatories with radiating chapels for viewing relics.

centuries earlier. The Toulouse solution was a crisply rational and highly refined realization of an idea first seen in Carolingian architecture. This approach to design became increasingly common in the Romanesque period.

Another telling feature of Saint-Sernin's design is the insertion of tribunes opening onto the nave over the inner aisles (FIG. 12-7), a feature also of the nave (FIG. 12-7B) of the church of Saint James at Santiago de Compostela. These galleries housed overflow crowds on special occasions and also played an important role in buttressing the nave's continuous semicircular cut-stone *barrel vault*, in contrast to the timber roof over the nave (FIG. 12-3) of the smaller abbey church at Vignory (see "Timber Roofs and Stone Vaults," page 339).

Timber Roofs and Stone Vaults

The perils of wooden construction were the subject of frequent commentary among chroniclers of medieval ecclesiastical history. In some cases, churches burned over and over again in the course of a single century and repeatedly had to be extensively repaired or completely rebuilt. In September 1174, for example, Canterbury Cathedral, which had been dedicated only 44 years earlier, was accidentally set ablaze and destroyed. Gervase of Canterbury (1141–1210), who entered the monastery there in 1163 and wrote a history of the archbishopric from 1100 to 1199, provided a vivid eyewitness account of the disastrous fire in his *Chronica:*

> [D]uring an extraordinarily violent south wind, a fire broke out before the gate of the church, and outside the walls of the monastery, by which three cottages were half destroyed. From thence, while the citizens were assembling and subduing the fire, cinders and sparks carried aloft by the high wind were deposited upon the church, and being driven by the fury of the wind between the joints of the lead, remained there amongst the half-rotten planks, and shortly glowing with increased heat, set fire to the rotten rafters; from these the fire was communicated to the larger beams and their braces, no one yet perceiving or helping. For the well-painted ceiling below, and the sheet-lead covering above, concealed between them the fire that had arisen within. . . . But beams and braces burning, the flames arose to the slopes of the roof; and the sheets of lead yielded to the increasing heat and began to melt. Thus the raging wind, finding a freer entrance, increased the fury of the fire. . . . And now that the fire had loosened the beams from the pegs that bound them together, the half-burnt timbers fell into the choir below upon the seats of the monks; the seats, consisting of a great mass of woodwork, caught fire, and thus the mischief grew worse and worse. And it was marvellous, though sad, to behold how that glorious choir itself fed and assisted the fire that was destroying it. For the flames multiplied by this mass of timber, and extending upwards full fifteen cubits [about twenty-five feet], scorched and burnt the walls, and more especially injured the columns of the church. . . . In this manner the house of God, hitherto delightful as a paradise of pleasures, was now made a despicable heap of ashes, reduced to a dreary wilderness.*

After the fire, the Canterbury monks summoned a master builder from Sens, a French city 75 miles southeast of Paris, to supervise the construction of their new church. Gervase reported that the first task William of Sens tackled was "the procuring of stone from beyond the sea."

A quest for fireproof structures, however, apparently was not the primary rationale for stone vaulting. Although protec-

12-7 Interior of Saint-Sernin (looking east), Toulouse, France, ca. 1070–1120. ◼◀

Saint-Sernin's stone vaults helped retard fire. The groin-vaulted tribune galleries also buttressed the nave's barrel vault whose transverse arches continue the lines of the compound piers.

tion from devastating conflagrations was no doubt one of the attractions of constructing masonry vaults in an age when candles and lamps provided interior illumination, other factors probably played a greater role in the decision to make the enormous investment of time and funds required. The rapid spread of stone vaulting throughout Romanesque Europe—beginning in the 11th century at Cardona (FIG. 12-4A), Tournus (FIG. 12-4B), Toulouse (FIG. 12-7), Santiago de Compostela (FIG. 12-7B), Speyer (FIG. 12-20), and Milan (FIG. 12-22)—was most likely the result of a desire to provide a suitably majestic setting for the display of relics as well as enhanced acoustics for the Christian liturgy and the music accompanying it. Some contemporaneous texts, in fact, comment on the visual impact of costly stone vaults. For example, in 1150 at Angers in northwestern France, a church chronicler explained what the bishop sought to achieve by replacing the timber roof of his cathedral with stone vaults: "[He] took down the timber beams of the nave of the church, threatening to fall from sheer old age, and began to build stone vaults of wondrous effect."†

---

*Translated by Robert Willis. Quoted in Elizabeth Gilmore Holt, *A Documentary History of Art,* 2d ed. (Princeton, N.J.: Princeton University Press, 1981), 1:52–54.
†Translated by John Hooper Harvey, *The Medieval Architect* (London: Waylan, 1972), 39.

1 ft.

12-8 BERNARDUS GELDUINUS, *Christ in Majesty,* relief in the ambulatory of Saint-Sernin, Toulouse, France, ca. 1096. Marble, 4′ 2″ high.

One of the earliest series of large Romanesque figural reliefs decorated the pilgrimage church of Saint-Sernin. The models were probably metal or ivory Carolingian and Ottonian book covers.

Groin vaults (indicated by Xs on the plan, FIG. 12-6; compare FIG. 7-6*b*) in the tribunes as well as in the ground-floor aisles absorbed the pressure exerted by the barrel vault along the entire length of the nave and transferred the main thrust to the thick outer walls.

The builders of Saint-Sernin were not content merely to buttress the massive nave vault. They also carefully coordinated the design of the vault with that of the nave arcade below and with the modular plan of the building as a whole. The nave elevation (FIG. 12-7), which features *engaged columns* (attached half-columns) embellishing the

piers marking the corners of the bays, fully reflects the church's geometric floor plan (FIG. 12-6). Architectural historians refer to piers with columns or pilasters attached to their rectangular cores as *compound piers.* At Saint-Sernin, the engaged columns rise from the bottom of the compound piers to the vault's *springing* (the lowest stone of an arch) and continue across the nave as *transverse arches.* As a result, the Saint-Sernin nave gives the impression of being numerous identical vertical volumes of space placed one behind the other, marching down the building's length in orderly procession. Saint-Sernin's spatial organization corresponds to and renders visually the plan's geometric organization. The articulation of the building's exterior walls (FIG. 12-5), where buttresses frame each bay, also reflects the segmentation of the nave. This rationally integrated scheme, with repeated units decorated and separated by moldings, would have a long future in later European church architecture.

Saint-Sernin also boasts one of the earliest precisely dated series of large Romanesque figural reliefs—a group of seven marble slabs representing Christ, angels, and apostles. An inscription on the altar states the reliefs date to the year 1096 and identifies the artist as BERNARDUS GELDUINUS. Today, the plaques adorn the church's ambulatory wall, but their original location is uncertain. In the view of some scholars, the reliefs once formed part of a shrine dedicated to Saint Saturninus that stood in the *crypt* (a vaulted underground chamber) of the grand pilgrimage church. Others believe the plaques once decorated a choir screen or an exterior portal. The relief illustrated here (FIG. **12-8**), *Christ in Majesty,* is the centerpiece of the group. Christ sits in a mandorla, his right hand raised in blessing, his left hand resting on an open book inscribed *Pax vobis* ("Peace unto you"). The signs of the four evangelists (see "The Four Evangelists," Chapter 11, page 314) occupy the corners of the slab. Art historians debate the sources of Bernardus's style, but the composition could have been used earlier for a Carolingian or Ottonian work in metal or ivory, perhaps a book cover. The polished marble has the gloss of both materials, and the sharply incised lines and ornamentation of Christ's aureole are characteristic of pre-Romanesque metalwork.

Stone sculpture, with some notable exceptions, such as the Irish high crosses (FIGS. 11-9 and 11-9A), had almost disappeared from the art of western Europe during the early Middle Ages. The revival of stonecarving in the 11th century at Toulouse and Saint-Genis-des-Fontaines (FIG. **12-8A**) in southern France and Silos (FIG. **12-8B**) in northern Spain is a hallmark of the Romanesque age—and one reason the period is aptly named. The inspiration for stone sculpture no doubt came, at least in part, from the abundant remains of ancient statues and reliefs throughout Rome's northwestern provinces. Yet these models had been available for centuries, and they cannot explain the sudden proliferation of stone sculpture in Romanesque churches. Many art historians have noted that the reemergence of monumental stone sculpture coincided with the introduction of stone vaulting. But medieval builders had erected stone-walled churches and monumental westworks for centuries, even if the structures bore timber ceilings and roofs. The earliest Romanesque sculptures, in fact, appear in timber-roofed churches, such as Saint-Étienne (FIG. 12-3) at Vignory. Therefore, the addition of stone vaults to basilican churches cannot

12-8A Saint-Genis-des-Fontaines, 1019–1020.

12-8B Santo Domingo, Silos, ca. 1090–1100.

Restored view of the third abbey church (Cluny III), Cluny, France, 1088–1130 (John Burge).

Cluny III was the largest church in Europe for 500 years. It had a 500-foot-long, three-story (arcade-tribune-clerestory) nave, four aisles, radiating chapels, and slightly pointed stone barrel vaults.

account for the resurgence of stonecarving in the Romanesque period. But just as stone vaulting reflects the greater prosperity of the age, so too does the decoration of churches with large-scale sculptures. Both are consistent with the widespread desire in the Romanesque period to beautify the house of God and make it, in the words of Gervase of Canterbury, "a paradise of pleasures."

The popularity of stone sculpture in the 12th century also reflects the changing role of many churches in western Europe. In the early Middle Ages, most churches served small monastic communities, and the worshipers were primarily or exclusively clergy. With the rise of towns in the Romanesque period, churches, especially those on the major pilgrimage routes, increasingly served the lay public. The display of sculpture both inside and outside Romanesque churches was a means of impressing—and educating—a new and largely illiterate audience.

CLUNY The primary patrons of Romanesque sculpture were the monks of the Cluniac order. In 909, William the Pious, duke of Aquitaine (r. 893–918), donated land near Cluny in Burgundy to a community of reform-minded Benedictine monks under the leadership of Berno of Baume (d. 927). Because William waived his feudal rights to the land, the abbot of Cluny was obligated only to the pope in Rome, a unique privilege. Berno founded a new order at Cluny according to the rules of Saint Benedict (see "Medieval Monasteries and Benedictine Rule," Chapter 11, page 322). Under Berno's successors, the Cluniac monks became famous for their scholarship, music, and art. Their influence and wealth grew

rapidly, and they built a series of ever more elaborate monastic churches at Cluny.

Abbot Hugh of Semur (1024–1109) began construction of the third church at Cluny in 1088. Called Cluny III by architectural historians, the building is, unfortunately, largely destroyed today but can be reconstructed in a computer drawing (FIG. **12-9**). When work concluded in 1130, Cluny III was the largest church in Europe, and it retained that distinction for almost 500 years until the completion of the new Saint Peter's (FIG. 24-4) in Rome in the early 17th century. Contemporaries considered Cluny III a place worthy for angels to dwell if they lived on earth. The church had a bold and influential design, with a barrel-vaulted nave, four aisles, and radiating chapels, as at Saint-Sernin, but with a three-story nave elevation (arcade-tribune-clerestory) and slightly pointed nave vaults. With a nave more than 500 feet long and more than 100 feet high (both dimensions are about 50 percent greater than at Saint-Sernin), it epitomized the grandiose scale of the new stone-vaulted Romanesque churches and was a symbol of the power and prestige of the Cluniac order.

MOISSAC An important stop in southwestern France along the pilgrimage route to Saint James's tomb at Santiago de Compostela was Moissac, which boasts the most extensive preserved ensemble of early Romanesque sculpture. The monks of the Moissac abbey had joined the Cluniac order in 1047. Enriched by the gifts of pilgrims and noble benefactors, they adorned their church with an elaborate series of relief sculptures. The oldest are in the *cloister* (from the Latin word *claustrum*, an enclosed place), which

Bernard of Clairvaux on Cloister Sculpture

The most influential theologian of the Romanesque era was Bernard of Clairvaux (1090–1153). A Cistercian monk and abbot of the monastery he founded at Clairvaux in northern Burgundy, he embodied not only the reforming spirit of the Cistercian order but also the new religious fervor awakening throughout Europe. Bernard's impassioned eloquence made him a celebrity and drew him into the stormy politics of the 12th century. He intervened in high ecclesiastical and secular matters, defended and sheltered embattled popes, counseled kings, denounced heretics, and preached Crusades against the Muslims (see "The Crusades," page 346)—all in defense of papal Christianity and spiritual values. The Church declared Bernard a saint in 1174, barely two decades after his death.

In a letter Bernard wrote in 1127 to William, abbot of Saint-Thierry, he complained about the rich outfitting of non-Cistercian churches in general, and in particular, the sculptural adornment of monastic cloisters, such as those at Silos (FIG. 12-8B) and Moissac (FIG. 12-10).

> I will overlook the immense heights of the places of prayer, their immoderate lengths, their superfluous widths, the costly refinements, and painstaking representations which deflect the attention . . . of those who pray and thus hinder their devotion. . . . But so be it, let these things be made for the honor of God . . . [But] in the cloisters, before the eyes of the brothers while they read—

what . . . are the filthy apes doing there? The fierce lions? The monstrous centaurs? The creatures, part man and part beast? . . . You may see many bodies under one head, and conversely many heads on one body. On one side the tail of a serpent is seen on a quadruped, on the other side the head of a quadruped is on the body of a fish. Over there an animal has a horse for the front half and a goat for the back . . . Everywhere so plentiful and astonishing a variety of contradictory forms is seen that one would rather read in the marble than in books, and spend the whole day wondering at every single one of them than in meditating on the law of God. Good God! If one is not ashamed of the absurdity, why is one not at least troubled at the expense?*

*Apologia 12.28–29. Translated by Conrad Rudolph, *The "Things of Greater Importance": Bernard of Clairvaux's* Apologia *and the Medieval Attitude toward Art* (Philadelphia: University of Pennsylvania Press, 1990), 279, 283.

1 ft.

12-10 General view of the cloister (*left*; looking southeast) and detail of the pier with the relief of Abbot Durandus (*right*), Saint-Pierre, Moissac, France, ca. 1100–1115. Relief: limestone, 6′ high. ◼◀

The revived tradition of stonecarving probably began with historiated capitals. The most extensive preserved ensemble of sculptured early Romanesque capitals is in the Moissac cloister.

connotes being shut away from the world. Architecturally, the medieval church cloister expressed the seclusion of the spiritual life, the *vita contemplativa*. At Moissac, as elsewhere, the cloister provided the monks (and nuns) with a foretaste of Paradise. In its garden or the timber-roofed columnar walkway framing the garden (FIG. 12-10, *left*), they could read their devotions, pray, meditate,

and carry on other activites in a beautiful and centrally located space. The cloisters of the 12th century are monuments to the vitality, popularity, and influence of monasticism at its peak.

Moissac's cloister sculpture program consists of large figural reliefs on the piers as well as *historiated* (ornamented with figures) capitals on the columns. The pier reliefs portray the 12 apostles and the monastery's first Cluniac abbot (FIG. 12-10, *right*), Durandus (1047–1072), whom the monks buried in the cloister. The Durandus relief is not a portrait in the modern sense of the word but a generic, bilaterally symmetrical image of the abbot holding his staff in his left hand and raising his right hand in a gesture of blessing. The carving is very shallow—an exercise in two-dimensional design rather than an attempt at representing a fully modeled figure in space. The feet, for example, which point downward, do not rest on the ground and cannot support the abbot's weight (compare FIG. 9-2).

The 76 capitals alternately crown single and paired column shafts. They are variously decorated, some with abstract patterns, many with biblical scenes or the lives of saints, others with fantastic monsters of all sorts—basilisks, griffins, lizards, gargoyles, and more. *Bestiaries*—collections of illustrations of real and imaginary animals—became very popular in the Romanesque age. The monstrous forms were reminders of the chaos and deformity of a world without God's order. Medieval artists delighted in inventing composite multiheaded beasts and other fantastic creations. Historiated capitals were also a feature of Moissac's mother church, Cluny III, and were common in Cluniac monasteries.

Not everyone shared the Cluniac monks' enthusiasm for stone sculpture. One group of Benedictine monks founded a new order at Cîteaux in eastern France in 1098. The Cistercians (from the Latin name for Cîteaux) split from the Cluniac order to return to the strict observance of the rules of Saint Benedict (see "Medieval Monasteries and Benedictine Rule," Chapter 11, page 322), changing the color of their habits from Cluniac black to unbleached white. These White Monks emphasized productive manual labor, and their systematic farming techniques stimulated the agricultural transformation of Europe. The Cistercian movement expanded with astonishing rapidity. Within a half century, the White Monks had established more than 500 monasteries. Their churches, such as Notre-Dame at Fontenay (FIG. 12-10A), are uniformly austere. The Cistercians rejected figural sculpture as a

12-10A Notre-Dame, Fontenay, 1139–1147. ◼◀

distraction from their devotions. The most outspoken Cistercian critic of church sculpture was Abbot Bernard of Clairvaux (see "Bernard of Clairvaux on Cloister Sculpture," page 342).

Bernard directed his tirade against figural sculpture primarily at monks who allowed the carvings to distract them from their meditations. But at Moissac (FIG. 12-11) and other Cluniac churches, the most extensive sculptural

12-11 South portal of Saint-Pierre, Moissac, France, ca. 1115–1135. *Top:* general view. *Bottom:* detail of tympanum with *Second Coming of Christ.* ◼◀

A vision of the second coming of Christ on judgment day greets worshipers entering Saint-Pierre at Moissac. The sculptural program reflects the belief that Christ is the door to salvation.

The Romanesque Church Portal

One of the most significant and distinctive features of Romanesque art is the revival of monumental sculpture in stone. Large-scale carved biblical figures were extremely rare in Christian art before the year 1000. But in the late 11th and early 12th centuries, rich ensembles of figural reliefs began to appear again, most often in the grand stone portals (FIGS. 12-11 and 12-14A) through which the faithful had to pass. Sculpture had been employed in church doorways before. For example, carved wooden doors (FIG. 8-10A) greeted Early Christian worshipers as they entered Santa Sabina in Rome, and Ottonian bronze doors (FIG. 11-24) decorated with Old and New Testament scenes marked the entrance from the cloister to Saint Michael's at Hildesheim. But these were exceptions, and in the Romanesque era (and during the Gothic period that followed), sculpture usually appeared in the area *around*, rather than *on*, the doors.

Shown in FIG. 12-12 are the parts of church portals Romanesque sculptors regularly decorated with figural reliefs:

▌ *Tympanum* (FIGS. 12-1, 12-11, 12-14, and 12-14A), the prominent semicircular *lunette* above the doorway proper, comparable in importance to the triangular pediment of a Greco-Roman temple.

▌ *Voussoirs* (FIG. 12-14), the wedge-shaped blocks that together form the *archivolts* of the arch framing the tympanum.

▌ *Lintel* (FIGS. 12-8A, 12-11, 12-13B, and 12-14), the horizontal beam above the doorway.

▌ *Trumeau* (FIGS. 12-11 and 12-13), the center post supporting the lintel in the middle of the doorway.

▌ *Jambs* (FIG. 12-11), the side posts of the doorway.

12-12 **The Romanesque church portal.**

The clergy considered the church doorway the beginning of the path to salvation through Christ. Many Romanesque churches feature didactic sculptural reliefs above and beside the entrance portals.

ensembles adorned those parts of the church open to the laity, especially the facade—for example, that of Notre-Dame-la-Grande (FIG. 12-11A) at Poitiers. Saint-Pierre's richly decorated south portal faces the town square, and features figural and decorative reliefs in its *tympanum, voussoirs, lintel, trumeau,* and *jambs* (see "The Romanesque Church Portal," *left*, and FIG. 12-12). The tympanum depicts the *Second Coming* of Christ as

12-11A Notre-Dame-la-Grande, Poitiers, ca. 1130–1150. ◼◀

king and judge of the world in its last days. As befits his majesty, the enthroned Christ is at the center, reflecting a compositional rule followed since Early Christian times. Flanking him are the signs of the four evangelists and attendant angels holding scrolls to record human deeds for judgment. The figures of crowned musicians, which complete the design, are the 24 elders who accompany Christ as the kings of this world and make music in his praise. Each turns to face the enthroned judge, much as would the courtiers of a Romanesque monarch in attendance on their lord. Two courses of wavy lines symbolizing the clouds of Heaven divide the elders into three tiers.

12-13 **Old Testament prophet (Jeremiah or Isaiah?), right side of the trumeau of the south portal of Saint-Pierre, Moissac, France, ca. 1115–1130.** ◼◀

This animated prophet displays the scroll recounting his vision. His position below the apparition of Christ as last judge is in keeping with the tradition of pairing Old and New Testament themes.

Most sculptured Romanesque church portals present a larger-than-life Christ as the central motif. These facades reflect the belief, dating to Early Christian times, that Christ is the door to salvation ("I am the door; who enters through me will be saved"—John 10:9). An inscription on the tympanum of the late-11th-century monastic church of Santa Cruz de la Serós in Spain made this message explicit: "I am the eternal door. Pass through me faithful. I am the source of life."[4]

Many variations exist within the general style of Romanesque sculpture, as within Romanesque architecture. The figures of the Moissac tympanum contrast sharply with those of the earlier Saint-Sernin ambulatory reliefs (FIG. 12-8) and the Silos pier reliefs (FIG. 12-8B), as well as the contemporaneous *Last Judgment* tympanum (FIG. 12-1) at Autun and even the pier reliefs (FIG. 12-10, *right*) of the Moissac cloister. The extremely elongated bodies of the angels recording each soul's fate, the cross-legged dancing pose of Saint Matthew's angel, and the jerky, hinged movement of the elders' heads are characteristic of the nameless Moissac master's style of representing the human figure. The zigzag and dovetail lines of the draperies, the bandlike folds of the torsos, the bending back of the hands against the body, and the wide cheekbones are also common features of this distinctive style. The animation of the individual figures, however, contrasts with the stately monumentality of the composition as a whole, producing a dynamic tension in the tympanum.

The jambs and trumeau (FIG. **12-13**) of the Moissac portal have scalloped contours (FIG. 12-11), a borrowing from Spanish Islamic architecture (FIGS. 10-10 and 10-11). Six roaring interlaced lions on the front of the trumeau greet worshipers as they enter the church. The animal world was never far from the medieval mind, and people often associated the fiercest beasts with kings and barons—for example, Richard the Lionhearted, Henry the Lion, and Henry the Bear. Lions were the church's ideal protectors. In the Middle Ages, people believed lions slept with their eyes open. But the notion of placing fearsome images at the gateways to important places is of very ancient origin. Ancestors of the Moissac lions include the lions and composite monsters that guarded the palaces of Hittite, Assyrian, and Mycenaean kings (FIGS. 2-18A, 2-20, and 4-19) and the panthers and leopards in Greek temple pediments (FIG. 5-16) and Etruscan tombs (FIG. 6-9).

On the trumeau's right face is a prophet—identified by some scholars as Jeremiah, as Isaiah by others—who displays a scroll bearing his prophetic vision. His position below the apparition of Christ as the apocalyptic judge is yet another instance of the pairing of Old and New Testament themes, in keeping with an iconographic tradition established in Early Christian times (see "Jewish Subjects in Christian Art," Chapter 8, page 238). The prophet's figure is very tall and thin, in the manner of the tympanum angels, and like Matthew's angel, he executes a cross-legged step. The animation of the body reveals the passionate nature of the soul within. The flowing lines of the drapery folds ultimately derive from manuscript illumination (compare FIG. 12-15A) and here play gracefully around the elegant figure. The long, serpentine locks of hair and beard frame an arresting image of the dreaming mystic. The prophet seems entranced by his vision of what is to come, the light of ordinary day unseen by his wide eyes.

VÉZELAY At the same time sculptors were adorning Saint-Pierre at Moissac, Gislebertus and his assistants were at work on Saint-Lazare at Autun, decorating not only the west tympanum (FIG. 12-1) but also the nave (FIG. **12-13A**) and the north portal (FIG. **12-13B**). A team of stonecarvers also worked nearby at the church of La Madeleine (Mary Magdalene) at Vézelay. Vézelay is more closely associated with the Crusades (see "The Crusades," page 346) than is any other church in Europe. Pope Urban II had intended to preach the launching of the First Crusade at Vézelay in 1095, although he delivered the sermon at Clermont instead. In 1147, Bernard of Clairvaux called for the

12-13A GISLEBERTUS, *Suicide of Judas*, Autun, ca. 1120–1135. ■◆

12-13B GISLEBERTUS, *Eve*, Autun, ca. 1120–1135. ■◆

Second Crusade at Vézelay, and King Louis VII of France took up the cross there. The Magdalene church at Vézelay was also where, in 1190, King Richard the Lionhearted of England and King Philip Augustus of France set out on the Third Crusade.

The major element of the sculptural program of La Madeleine at Vézelay is the tympanum (FIG. **12-14**) of the central portal of the

12-14 *Pentecost* and *Mission of the Apostles*, tympanum of the center portal of the narthex of La Madeleine, Vézelay, France, 1120–1132. ■◆

In the tympanum of the church most closely associated with the Crusades, light rays emanating from Christ's hands instill the Holy Spirit in the apostles, whose mission is to convert the world's heathens.

The Crusades

In 1095, Pope Urban II (r. 1088–1099) delivered a stirring sermon at the Council of Clermont in which he called for an assault on the Holy Land:

> [Y]our brethren who live in the East are in urgent need of your help . . . [because] the Turks and Arabs have attacked them. . . . They have killed and captured many, and have destroyed the churches . . . I, or rather the Lord, beseech you as Christ's heralds . . . to persuade all people of whatever rank, foot-soldiers and knights, poor and rich, to carry aid promptly to those Christians and to destroy that vile race from the lands of our friends. . . . All who die by the way . . . shall have immediate remission of sins. . . . Let those who go not put off the journey, but rent their lands and collect money for their expenses . . . [and] eagerly set out on the way with God as their guide.*

Between 1095 and 1190, Christians launched three great Crusades from France. The *Crusades* ("taking of the Cross") were mass armed pilgrimages whose stated purpose was to wrest the Christian shrines of the Holy Land from Muslim control. Similar vows bound Crusaders and pilgrims. They hoped not only to atone for sins and win salvation but also to glorify God and extend the power of the Church. The joint action of the papacy and the mostly French feudal lords in this type of holy war strengthened papal authority over the long run and created an image of Christian solidarity.

The symbolic embodiment of the joining of religious and secular forces in the Crusades was the Christian warrior, the fighting priest, or the priestly fighter. From the early medieval warrior evolved the Christian knight, who fought for the honor of God rather than in defense of his chieftain. The first and most typical of the crusading knights were the Knights Templar. After the Christian conquest of Jerusalem in 1099, they stationed themselves next to the Dome of the Rock (FIGS. 10-2 and 10-3), that is, on the site of Solomon's Temple, the source of their name. Their mission was to protect pilgrims visiting the recovered Christian shrines. Formally founded in 1118, the Knights Templar order received the blessing of Bernard of Clairvaux, who gave them a rule of organization based on that of his own Cistercians. Bernard justified their militancy by declaring "the knight of Christ" is "glorified in slaying the infidel . . . because thereby Christ is glorified," and the Christian knight then wins salvation. The Cistercian abbot saw the Crusades as part of the general reform of the Church and as the defense of the supremacy of Christendom. He himself called for the Second Crusade in 1147 at Vézelay (FIG. 12-14). For the Muslims, however, the Crusaders were nothing more than violent invaders who slaughtered the population of Jerusalem (Jewish as well as Muslim) when they took the city in July 1099.

In the end, the Muslims expelled the Christian armies, and the Crusaders failed miserably in their attempt to regain the Holy Land. But in western Europe, the Crusades had a much greater impact by increasing the power and prestige of the towns. Italian port cities such as Pisa (FIG. 12-26) thrived on the commercial opportunities presented by the transportation of Crusaders overseas. Many communities purchased their charters from the barons who owned their land when the latter needed to finance their campaigns in the Holy Land. This gave rise to a middle class of merchants and artisans to rival the power of the feudal lords and the great monasteries—an economic and societal change of enormous consequence for the later history of Europe.

*As recorded by Fulcher of Chartres (1059–ca. 1127). Translated by O. J. Thatcher and E. H. McNeal, quoted in Roberta Anderson and Dominic Aidan Bellenger, eds., *Medieval Worlds: A Sourcebook* (New York: Routledge, 2003), 88–90.

---

church's narthex. It depicts the *Pentecost* and the *Mission of the Apostles*. As related in Acts 1:4–9, Christ foretold the 12 apostles would receive the power of the Holy Spirit and become witnesses of the truth of the Gospels throughout the world. The light rays emanating from Christ's hands represent the instilling of the Holy Spirit in the apostles (Acts 2:1–42) at the Pentecost (the seventh Sunday after Easter). The apostles, holding the Gospel books, receive their spiritual assignment to preach the Gospel to all nations. The Christ figure is a splendid calligraphic design. The drapery lines shoot out in rays, break into quick zigzag rhythms, and spin into whorls, wonderfully conveying the spiritual light and energy flowing from Christ over and into the equally animated apostles. The overall composition, as well as the detailed treatment of the figures, contrasts with the much more sedate representation of the second coming (FIG. 12-11) at Moissac, where a grid of horizontal and vertical lines contains almost all the figures. The sharp differences between the two tympana once again highlight the regional diversity of Romanesque art.

The world's heathen, the objects of the apostles' mission, appear on the Vézelay lintel below and in eight compartments around the tympanum. The portrayals of the yet-to-be-converted constitute a medieval anthropological encyclopedia. Present are the legendary giant-eared Panotii of India, Pygmies (who require ladders to mount horses), and a host of other races, some characterized by a dog's head, others by a pig's snout, and still others by flaming hair. The assembly of agitated figures also includes hunchbacks, mutes, blind men, and lame men. Humanity, still suffering, awaits the salvation to come. As at Autun (FIG. 12-1) and Moissac (FIG. 12-11), and also at Saint-Trophîme (FIG. 12-14A) in Arles, as worshipers passed through the portal, the tympanum established God's omnipotence and presented the Church as the road to salvation.

12-14A Saint-Trophîme, Arles, mid-12th century.

Painting and Other Arts

Unlike the practices of placing vaults over naves and aisles and decorating building facades with monumental stone reliefs, the art of painting needed no "revival" in the Romanesque period. Monasteries produced illuminated manuscripts in large numbers in the early Middle Ages, and even the Roman tradition of mural painting had never died. But the quantity of preserved frescoes and illustrated books from the Romanesque era is unprecedented.

12-15 Initial *L* and Saint Matthew, folio 10 recto of the *Codex Colbertinus,* probably from Moissac, France, ca. 1100. Tempera on vellum, 7½″ × 4″. Bibliothèque Nationale, Paris.

Probably produced in the Moissac scriptorium, the *Codex Colbertinus* illuminations are stylistically similar to the contemporaneous cloister sculptures (FIG. 12-10) of that Cluniac monastery.

12-15A *Corbie Gospels,* ca. 1120.

CODEX COLBERTINUS In addition to sponsoring the costliest sculptural programs of the Romanesque age, Cluniac monasteries produced many of the finest and most ornate illuminated manuscripts, including the *Codex Colbertinus* (FIG. **12-15**) and the *Corbie Gospels* (FIG. **12-15A**), both of which are closely related stylistically to the relief sculptures of Saint-Pierre at Moissac.

The *Codex Colbertinus* is, in fact, probably the work of scribes and painters in the Moissac scriptorium, and it is contemporaneous with the column capitals and pier reliefs of Saint-Pierre's cloister (FIG. 12-10). The major illuminations in the manuscript are the full pages featuring historiated initials and evangelist portraits. The opening page (FIG. 12-15) of the Gospel according to Saint Matthew includes both the large initial letter *L* of *Liber* (book)

12-16 Initial *R* with knight fighting dragons, folio 4 verso of the *Moralia in Job,* from Cîteaux, France, ca. 1115–1125. Ink and tempera on vellum, 1′ 1¾″ × 9¼″. Bibliothèque Municipale, Dijon.

Ornamented initials date to the Hiberno-Saxon era (FIG. 11-1), but this artist translated the theme into Romanesque terms. The duel between knight and dragons symbolized a monk's spiritual struggle.

and a "portrait" of the author. Matthew holds a book in his left hand and raises his right hand in a gesture of blessing. He stands frontally between a pair of columns supporting an arch, just as does Abbot Durandus (FIG. 12-10, *right*) on one of the Moissac cloister piers. The two figures are similar in other respects as well. For example, both artists depicted the robed men with dangling feet.

The letter *L* has no equivalent in the Moissac sculptures, but the real and imaginary animals and birds with long, twisted necks that inhabit the initial have parallels in Saint-Pierre's cloister capitals (FIG. 12-10, *left*). The intertwining forms attest to the long afterlife of the animal-interlace style of the illuminated books (FIG. 11-7) of the Hiberno-Saxon period.

MORALIA IN JOB Another major Romanesque scriptorium was at the abbey of Cîteaux, mother church of the Cistercian order. Just before Bernard of Clairvaux joined the monastery in 1112, the monks completed work on an illuminated copy of Saint Gregory's *Moralia in Job.* It is an example of Cistercian illumination before Bernard's passionate opposition to monastic figural art led in 1134 to a Cistercian ban on elaborate paintings in manuscripts as well as sculptural ornamentation in monasteries. After 1134, in sharp contrast to Cluniac Moissac, the Cistercian order prohibited full-page illustrations, and even initial letters had to be nonfigurative and of a single color.

The historiated initial illustrated here (FIG. 12-16) clearly would have been in violation of Bernard's ban had it not been ing of the torso and partitioning of the folds are evident (compare FIG. 12-13), but the master painter deftly avoided stiffness and angularity. The partitioning here accentuates the knight's verticality and elegance and the thrusting action of his servant. The flowing sleeves add a spirited flourish to the swordsman's gesture. The knight, handsomely garbed, cavalierly wears no armor and calmly aims a single stroke, unmoved by the ferocious dragons lunging at him.

SAINT-SAVIN-SUR-GARTEMPE Although the art of fresco painting never died in early medieval Europe, the murals (not true frescoes, however) of the Benedictine abbey church of Saint-Savin-sur-Gartempe have no Carolingian or Ottonian parallels, because the paintings decorate the stone barrel vault of the church's nave (FIG. **12-17**). Saint-Savin is a *hall* church—a church where the aisles are approximately the same height as the nave. The tall windows in the aisles provided more illumination to the nave than in churches having low aisles and tribunes. The abundant light streaming into the church may explain why the monks chose to decorate the nave's barrel vault with paintings. (They also painted the nave piers to imitate rich veined marble.) The subjects of Saint-Savin's nave paintings all come from the Pentateuch, but New Testament themes appear in the transept, ambulatory, and chapels, where the painters also depicted the lives of Saint Savin and another local saint. The elongated, agitated, cross-legged figures have stylistic affinities both to the reliefs of southern French portals and to illuminated manuscripts such as the *Corbie Gospels* (FIG. 12-15A) and the *Moralia in Job* (FIG. 12-16).

SANTA MARÍA DE MUR In the Romanesque period, northern Spain, home to the great pilgrimage church of Saint James at Santiago de Compostela, was one of the most important regional artistic centers. In fact, Catalonia in northeastern Spain boasts more Romanesque mural paintings today than anywhere else. Especially impressive is the *Christ in Majesty* fresco (FIG. **12-18**), now in Boston, that once filled the apse of Santa María de Mur, a monastery church not far from Lérida. The formality, symmetry, and placement of the figures are Byzantine (compare FIGS. 9-16 and 9-27). But the Spanish artist rejected Byzantine mosaic in favor of direct painting on plaster-coated walls.

The iconographic scheme in the semidome of the apse echoes the themes of the sculpted tympana of contemporaneous French (FIGS. 12-11 and 12-14A) and Spanish Romanesque church portals. The signs of the four evangelists flank Christ in a star-strewn mandorla—the Apocalypse theme that so fascinated the Romanesque imagination. Seven lamps between Christ and the evangelists' signs symbolize the seven Christian communities where Saint John addressed his revelation (the Apocalypse) at the beginning of his book (Rev. 1:4, 12, 20). Below stand apostles, paired off in formal frontality, as in the Monreale Cathedral apse (FIG. 9-27). The Spanish painter rendered the principal figures with partitioning of the drapery into volumes, here and there made tubular by local shading, and stiffened the irregular shapes of pliable cloth into geometric patterns. The overall effect is one of simple, strong, and even blunt directness of statement, reinforced by harsh, bright color, appropriate for a powerful icon.

MORGAN MADONNA Despite the widespread use of stone relief sculptures to adorn church portals, resistance to the creation of statues in the round—in any material—continued in the Romanesque period. The avoidance of anything that might be construed as an idol was still the rule, in keeping with the Second Commandment. Two centuries after Archbishop Gero commissioned a monumen-

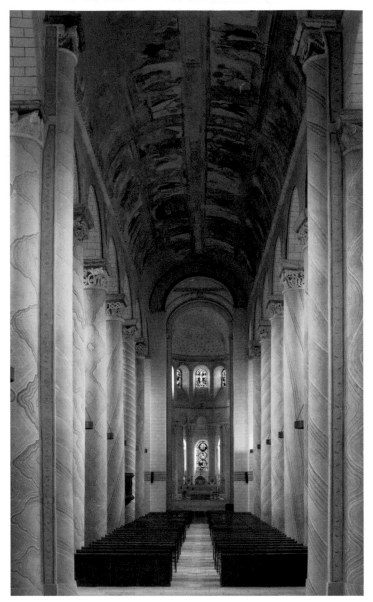

12-17 Nave of the abbey church (looking east) of Saint-Savin, Saint-Savin-sur-Gartempe, France, ca. 1100. ▮◀

Saint-Savin is a hall church with aisles approximately the same height as the nave. The tall aisle windows provide ample illumination for the biblical paintings on the nave's barrel vault.

painted before his prohibitions took effect. A knight, his squire, and two roaring dragons form an intricate letter *R,* the initial letter of the salutation *Reverentissimo.* This page is the opening of Gregory's letter to "the very reverent" Leandro, bishop of Seville, Spain. The knight is a slender, regal figure who raises his shield and sword against the dragons, while the squire, crouching beneath him, runs a lance through one of the monsters. Although the clergy viewed the duel between knight and dragons as an allegory of the spiritual struggle of monks against the Devil for the salvation of souls, Bernard opposed this kind of illumination, just as he condemned carvings of monstrous creatures and "fighting knights" on cloister capitals (see "Bernard of Clairvaux," page 342).

Ornamented initials date to the Hiberno-Saxon period (FIG. 11-1), but in the *Moralia in Job,* the artist translated the theme into Romanesque terms. The page with the initial *R* may be a reliable picture of a medieval baron's costume. The typically French Romanesque band-

12-18 *Christ in Majesty,* apse, Santa María de Mur, near Lérida, Spain, mid-12th century. Fresco, 24' high. Museum of Fine Arts, Boston.

In this fresco, formerly in the apse of Santa María de Mur, Christ appears in a mandorla between the four evangelists' signs. The fresco resembles French and Spanish Romanesque tympanum reliefs.

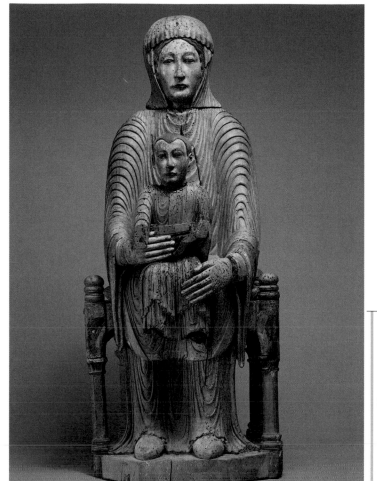

12-19 Virgin and Child (*Morgan Madonna*), from Auvergne, France, second half of 12th century. Painted wood, 2' 7" high. Metropolitan Museum of Art, New York (gift of J. Pierpont Morgan, 1916).

The veneration of relics created a demand for small-scale images of the holy family and saints to be placed on chapel altars. This wooden statuette depicts the Virgin as the "throne of wisdom."

tal wooden image of the crucified Christ (FIG. 11-28) for Cologne Cathedral, freestanding statues of Christ, the Virgin Mary, and the saints were still quite rare. The veneration of relics, however, brought with it a demand for small-scale images of the holy family and saints to be placed on the chapel altars of the churches along the pilgrimage roads. Reliquaries in the form of saints (FIG. 12-2) or parts of saints (FIG. 12-25), tabletop crucifixes, and small wooden devotional images began to be produced in great numbers.

One popular type, a specialty of the workshops of Auvergne, France, was a wooden statuette depicting the Virgin Mary with the Christ Child in her lap. The *Morgan Madonna* (FIG. **12-19**), so named because it once belonged to the American financier and collector J. Pierpont Morgan, is one example. The type, known as the "throne of wisdom" (*sedes sapientiae* in Latin), is a western European freestanding version of the Byzantine Theotokos theme popular in icons and mosaics (FIGS. 9-18 and 9-19). Christ holds a Bible in his left hand and raises his right arm in blessing (both hands are broken off). He is the embodiment of the divine wisdom contained in the holy scriptures. His mother, seated on a wooden chair, is in turn the throne of wisdom because her lap is the Christ Child's throne. As in Byzantine art, both Mother and Child sit

rigidly upright and are strictly frontal, emotionless figures. But the intimate scale, the gesture of benediction, the once-bright coloring of the garments, and the soft modeling of the Virgin's face make the group seem much less remote than its Byzantine counterparts.

HOLY ROMAN EMPIRE

The Romanesque successors of the Ottonians were the Salians (r. 1027–1125), a dynasty of Franks. They ruled an empire corresponding roughly to present-day Germany and the Lombard region of northern Italy (MAP 12-1). Like their predecessors, the Salian emperors were important patrons of art and architecture, although, as elsewhere in Romanesque Europe, the monasteries remained great centers of artistic production.

Architecture

The barrel-vaulted naves of Saint-Sernin (FIG. 12-7) at Toulouse, Saint James at Santiago de Compostela (FIG. 12-7B), Cluny III (FIG. 12-9), and Notre-Dame (FIG. 12-10A) at Fontenay admirably met French and Spanish Romanesque architects' goals of making the house of the Lord beautiful and providing excellent acoustics for church services. In addition, they were relatively fireproof compared with timber-roofed structures such as Saint-Étienne (FIG. 12-3) at Vignory. But the barrel vaults often failed in one critical requirement—lighting. Due to the great outward thrust barrel vaults exert along their full length, even when pointed (FIGS. 12-9 and 12-10A) instead of semicircular, a clerestory is difficult to construct. (The Toulouse, Santiago de Compostela, and Fontenay designers did not even attempt to introduce a clerestory, although their counterparts at Cluny III succeeded.) Structurally, the central aim of Romanesque architects in the Holy Roman Empire (and in Normandy and England; see page 357) was to develop a masonry vault system that admitted light and was aesthetically pleasing.

Covering the nave with groin vaults instead of barrel vaults became the solution. Ancient Roman builders had used the groin vault widely, because they realized its concentration of thrusts at four supporting points enabled them to introduce clerestory windows (FIGS. 7-6c, 7-67, and 7-78). Concrete, which could be poured into forms, where it solidified into a homogeneous mass (see "Roman Concrete Construction," Chapter 7, page 184), made the gigantic Roman groin vaults possible. But the technique of mixing concrete had not survived into the Middle Ages. The technical problems of building groin vaults of cut stone and heavy rubble, which had very little cohesive quality, at first limited their use to the covering of small areas, such as the individual bays of the aisles of the pilgrimage churches at Toulouse and Santiago de Compostela (FIGS. 12-7 and 12-7B). During the 11th century, however, masons in the Holy Roman Empire, using cut-stone blocks held together with mortar, developed a groin vault of monumental dimensions.

SPEYER Construction of Speyer Cathedral (FIG. **12-20**) in the German Rhineland, far from the pilgrimage routes of southern France and northern Spain, began in 1030. The church was the burial place of the Holy Roman emperors until the beginning of the 12th century, and funding for the building campaign came from imperial patrons, not traveling pilgrims and local landowners. Like all *cathedrals,* Speyer was also the seat (*cathedra* in Latin) of the powerful local bishop. In its earliest form, the church was a timber-roofed structure. When Henry IV (r. 1056–1105) rebuilt the cathedral between 1082 and 1105, his masons covered the nave with stone groin vaults. The large clerestory windows above the nave arcade provided ample light to the interior. Architectural historians disagree about where the first comprehensive use of groin vaulting occurred in Romanesque times, and nationalistic concerns sometimes color the debate. But no one doubts that the large groin vaults covering the nave of Speyer Cathedral represent one of the most daring and successful engineering experiments of the time. The nave is 45 feet wide, and the crowns of the vaults are 107 feet above the floor.

Speyer Cathedral employs an alternate-support system in the nave, as in the Ottonian churches of Saint Cyriakus (FIG. 11-21) at Gernrode and Saint Michael's (FIGS. 11-23 and 11-23A) at Hildesheim. At Speyer, however, the alternation continues all the way up into the vaults, with the nave's more richly molded compound piers marking the corners of the groin vaults. Speyer's interior shows the same striving for height and the same compartmentalized effect seen at Toulouse and Santiago de Compostela (FIGS. 12-7 and 12-7B), but by virtue of the alternate-support system, the rhythm of the Speyer nave is a little more complex. Because each compartment has its own vault, the impression of a sequence of vertical spatial blocks is even more convincing.

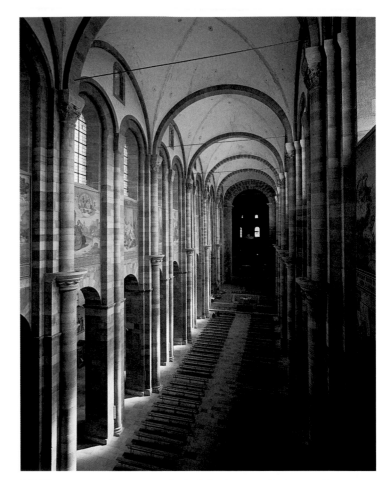

12-20 Interior of Speyer Cathedral (looking east), Speyer, Germany, begun 1030; nave vaults, ca. 1082–1105.

The imperial cathedral at Speyer is one of the earliest examples of the use of groin vaulting in a nave. Groin vaults made possible the insertion of large clerestory windows above the nave arcade.

MILAN After Charlemagne crushed the Lombards in 773, German kings held sway over Lombardy, and the Rhineland and northern Italy cross-fertilized each other artistically. No scholarly agreement exists as to which source of artistic influence was dominant in the Romanesque age, the German or the Lombard. The question, no doubt, will remain the subject of controversy until the construction date of Sant'Ambrogio (FIG. **12-21**) in Milan can be established unequivocally. The church, erected in honor of Saint Ambrose (d. 397), Milan's first bishop, is the central monument of Lombard Romanesque architecture. Some scholars think the church was a prototype for Speyer Cathedral, but Sant'Ambrogio is a remarkable building even if it was not a model for Speyer's builders. The Milanese church has an atrium in the Early Christian tradition (FIG. 8-9)—one of the last to be built—and a two-story narthex pierced by arches on both levels. Two *campaniles* (Italian, "bell towers") join the building on the west. The shorter one dates to the 10th century, and the taller north campanile is a 12th-century addition. Over the nave's east end is an octagonal tower that recalls the crossing towers of Ottonian churches (FIG. 11-22).

Sant'Ambrogio has a nave (FIG. **12-22**) and two aisles but no transept. Each bay consists of a full square in the nave flanked by two small squares in each aisle, all covered with groin vaults. The main vaults are slightly domical, rising higher than the transverse arches. The

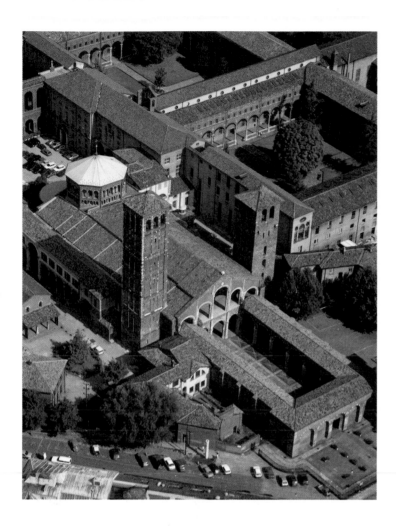

12-21 Aerial view of Sant'Ambrogio (looking southeast), Milan, Italy, late 11th to early 12th century.

With its atrium and low, broad proportions, Sant'Ambrogio recalls Early Christian basilicas. Over the nave's east end, however, is an octagonal tower resembling Ottonian crossing towers.

windows in the octagonal dome over the last bay—probably here, as elsewhere, a reference to the dome of Heaven—provide the major light source for the otherwise rather dark interior. (The building lacks a clerestory.) The emphatic alternate-support system perfectly reflects the geometric regularity of the plan. The lightest pier moldings stop at the gallery level, and the heavier ones rise to support the main vaults. At Sant'Ambrogio, the compound piers even continue into the ponderous vaults, which have supporting arches, or *ribs*, along their groins. Sant'Ambrogio is one of the first instances of *rib vaulting*, a salient characteristic of mature Romanesque and of later Gothic architecture (see "The Gothic Rib Vault," Chapter 13, page 368).

The regional diversity of Romanesque architecture quickly becomes evident by comparing the proportions of Sant'Ambrogio with those of Speyer Cathedral (FIG. 12-20) and of Saint-Sernin (FIGS. 12-5 to 12-7) at Toulouse and Saint James (FIG. 12-7B) at Santiago de Compostela. The Milanese building does not aspire to the soaring height of the French, Spanish, and German churches. Save for the later of the two towers, Sant'Ambrogio's proportions are low and broad and remain close to those of Early Christian basilicas. Italian architects, even those working within the orbit of the Holy Roman Empire, had firm roots in the venerable Early Christian style and never sought the verticality found in northern European architecture, not even during the Gothic period.

12-22 Interior of Sant'Ambrogio (looking east), Milan, Italy, late 11th to early 12th century.

Sant'Ambrogio reveals the transalpine ties of Lombard architecture. Each groin-vaulted nave bay corresponds to two aisle bays. The alternate-support system complements this modular plan.

Romanesque Countesses, Queens, and Nuns

Romanesque Europe was still a man's world, but women could and did have power and influence. Countess Matilda of Canossa (1046–1115), who ruled Tuscany after 1069, was sole heiress of vast holdings in northern Italy. She was a key figure in the political struggle between the popes and the German emperors who controlled Lombardy. With unflagging resolution, she defended the reforms of Pope Gregory VII (r. 1073–1085) and at her death willed most of her lands to the papacy.

More famous and more powerful was Eleanor of Aquitaine (1122–1204), wife of Henry II of England. She married Henry after the annulment of her marriage to Louis VII, king of France. She was queen of France for 15 years and queen of England for 35 years. During that time she bore three daughters and five sons. Two became kings—Richard I (the Lionhearted) and John. She prompted her sons to rebel against their father, for which Henry imprisoned her. Released at Henry's death, she lived on as dowager queen, managing England's government and King John's holdings in France.

Of quite different stamp was Hildegard of Bingen (1098–1179), the most prominent nun of the 12th century and one of the greatest religious figures of the Middle Ages. Hildegard was born into an aristocratic family that owned large estates in the German Rhineland. At a very early age she began to have visions. When she was eight, her parents placed her in the Benedictine *double monastery* (for monks and nuns) at Disibodenberg. She became a nun at 15. In 1141, God instructed Hildegard to disclose her visions to the world. Before then she had revealed them only to close confidants at the monastery. One of them was the monk Volmar, and Hildegard chose to dictate her visions to him for posterity (FIG. 12-23). No less a figure than Bernard of Clairvaux certified in 1147 that her visions were authentic, and Archbishop Heinrich of Mainz joined in the endorsement. In 1148, the Cistercian pope Eugenius III (r. 1145–1153) formally authorized Hildegard "in the name of Christ and Saint Peter to publish all that she had learned from the Holy Spirit." At this time Hildegard became the abbess of a new convent built for her near Bingen. As reports of Hildegard's visions spread, kings, popes, barons, and prelates sought her counsel. All of them were attracted by her spiritual insight into the Christian faith. In addition to her visionary works—the most important is the *Scivias* (FIG. 12-23)—Hildegard wrote two scientific

12-23 Hildegard reveals her visions, detail of a facsimile of a lost folio in the Rupertsberger *Scivias* by Hildegard of Bingen, from Trier or Bingen, Germany, ca. 1050–1079. Abbey of St. Hildegard, Rüdesheim/Eibingen.

Hildegard of Bingen, the most prominent nun of her time, experienced divine visions, shown here as five tongues of fire entering her brain. She also composed music and wrote scientific treatises.

treatises. *Physica* is a study of the natural world, and *Causae et curae* (*Causes and Cures*) is a medical encyclopedia. Hildegard also composed the music and wrote the lyrics of 77 songs, which appeared under the title *Symphonia*.

Hildegard was the most famous Romanesque nun, but she was by no means the only learned woman of her age. A younger contemporary, Herrad (d. 1195), abbess of Hohenberg, Austria, was also the author of an important medieval encyclopedia. Herrad's *Hortus deliciarum* (*Garden of Delights*) is a history of the world intended for instructing the nuns under her supervision, but it reached a much wider audience.

Painting and Other Arts

The number and variety of illuminated manuscripts dating to the Romanesque era attest to the great demand for illustrated religious tomes in the abbeys of western Europe. The extraordinarily productive scribes and painters who created these books were almost exclusively monks and nuns working in the scriptoria of those same isolated religious communities.

HILDEGARD OF BINGEN Among the most interesting German religious manuscripts is the *Scivias* (*Know the Ways [Scite vias] of God*) of Hildegard of Bingen. Hildegard was a nun who eventually became the abbess of the convent at Disibodenberg in the Rhineland (see "Romanesque Countesses, Queens, and Nuns," above). The manuscript, lost in 1945, exists today only in a facsimile. The original probably was written and illuminated at the monastery of Saint Matthias at Trier between 1150 and Hildegard's death in 1179, but it is possible Hildegard supervised production of the book at Bingen. The *Scivias* contains a record of Hildegard's vision of the divine order of the cosmos and of humankind's place in it. The vision came to her as a fiery light pouring into her brain from the open vault of Heaven.

On the opening page (FIG. 12-23) of the Trier manuscript, Hildegard sits within the monastery walls, her feet resting on a footstool, in much the same way the painters of the *Coronation* and *Ebbo Gospels* (FIGS. 11-13 and 11-14) represented the evangelists. The *Scivias* page is a link in a chain of author portraits with roots in classical antiquity (FIG. 7-25B). The artist showed Hildegard experiencing her divine vision by depicting five long tongues of fire emanating from above and entering her brain, just as she describes the experience in the accompanying text. Hildegard immediately sets down what has been revealed to her on a wax tablet resting on her left knee. Nearby, the monk Volmar, Hildegard's confessor, copies into a book all she has written. Here, in a singularly dramatic context, is a picture of the essential nature of ancient and medieval book manufacture—individual scribes copying and recopying texts by hand (compare FIG. 11-11). The most labor-intensive and costliest texts, such as Hildegard's *Scivias,* also were illuminated (see "Medieval Manuscript Illumination," Chapter 8, page 249). They required the collaboration of skilled painters, for example, the Weissenau monk RUFILLUS, who placed a portrait of himself at work (FIG. 12-23A) in a *passional* (book of saints' lives).

12-23A RUFILLUS, Initial *R,* ca. 1170–1200.

RAINER OF HUY The names of some Romanesque sculptors in the Holy Roman Empire are also known. One of them is RAINER OF HUY, a bronzeworker from the Meuse River valley in Belgium, an area renowned for its metalwork. Art historians have attributed an 1118 bronze baptismal font (FIG. 12-24) to him. Made for Notre-Dame-des-Fonts in Liège, the bronze basin rests on the foreparts of a dozen oxen. The oxen refer to the "molten sea . . . on twelve oxen" cast in bronze for King Solomon's temple (1 Kings 7:23–25). The Old Testament story prefigured Christ's baptism (medieval scholars equated the oxen with the 12 apostles), which is the central scene on the Romanesque font. Rainer's work, as that of so many earlier artists in the Holy Roman Empire beginning in Carolingian times, revived the classical style and the classical spirit. The figures are softly rounded, with idealized bodies and faces and heavy clinging drapery. Rainer even represented one figure (at the left in FIG. 12-24) in a three-quarter view from the rear, a popular motif in classical art, and some of the figures, including Christ himself, are naked. Nudity is very rare in the art of the Middle Ages. Adam and Eve (FIGS. 8-1, 11-24A, 12-13B, and 12-28) are exceptions, but medieval artists usually depicted the first man and woman as embarrassed by their nudity, the opposite of the high value the classical world placed on the beauty of the human body.

SAINT ALEXANDER The reliquaries of Saint Faith (FIG. 12-2) and of Saint Alexander (FIG. 12-25), a hallowed pope (Alexander II, r. 1061–1073), are among the most sumptuous of the Romanesque

12-24 RAINER OF HUY, *Baptism of Christ,* baptismal font from Notre-Dame-des-Fonts, Liège, Belgium, 1118. Bronze, 2′ 1″ high. Saint-Barthélémy, Liège.

In the work of Rainer of Huy, the classical style and the classical spirit lived on in the Holy Roman Empire. His Liège baptismal font features idealized figures and even a nude representation of Christ.

12-25 Head reliquary of Saint Alexander, from the abbey church, Stavelot, Belgium, 1145. Silver repoussé (partly gilt), gilt bronze, gems, pearls, and enamel, 1′ $5\frac{1}{2}$″ high. Musées Royaux d'Art et d'Histoire, Brussels.

The Stavelot reliquary is typical in the use of costly materials. The combination of an idealized classical head with Byzantine-style enamels underscores the stylistic diversity of Romanesque art.

age, a time when churches vied to possess the most important relics and often expended large sums on their containers (see "Relics," page 336). Made in 1145 for Abbot Wibald of Stavelot in Belgium, Saint Alexander's reliquary takes the form of an almost life-size head, fashioned in beaten (*repoussé*) silver with bronze gilding for the hair. The idealized head resembles portraits of youthful Roman emperors such as Augustus (FIG. I-10) and Constantine (FIG. 7-77), and the Romanesque metalworker may have used an ancient sculpture as a model. The saint wears a collar of jewels and enamel plaques around his neck. Enamels and gems also adorn the box on which the head is mounted. The reliquary rests on four bronze dragons—mythical animals of the kind populating Romanesque cloister capitals. Not surprisingly, Bernard of Clairvaux was as critical of lavish church furnishings like the reliquaries of Saints Faith and Alexander as he was of Romanesque cloister sculpture:

> [Men's] eyes are fixed on relics covered with gold and purses are opened. The thoroughly beautiful image of some male or female saint is exhibited and that saint is believed to be the more holy the more highly colored the image is. People rush to kiss it, they are

invited to donate, and they admire the beautiful more than they venerate the sacred. . . . O vanity of vanities, but no more vain than insane! The Church . . . dresses its stones in gold and it abandons its children naked. It serves the eyes of the rich at the expense of the poor.[5]

The central plaque on the front of the Stavelot reliquary depicts the *canonized* (declared a saint) pope. Saints Eventius and Theodolus flank him. The nine plaques on the other three sides represent female allegorical figures—Wisdom, Piety, and Humility among them. Although a local artist produced these enamels in the Meuse River region, the models were surely Byzantine. Saint Alexander's reliquary underscores the multiple sources of Romanesque art, as well as its stylistic diversity. Not since antiquity had people journeyed as extensively as they did in the Romanesque period, and artists regularly saw works of wide geographic origin. Abbot Wibald himself epitomizes the well-traveled 12th-century clergyman. He was abbot of Montecassino in southern Italy and took part in the Second Crusade. Frederick Barbarossa (Holy Roman emperor, r. 1152–1190) sent him to Constantinople to arrange Frederick's

12-26 Cathedral complex (looking northeast), Pisa, Italy; cathedral begun 1063; baptistery begun 1153; campanile begun 1174. ◼◀

Pisa's cathedral more closely resembles Early Christian basilicas than structurally more experimental French and German Romanesque churches. Separate bell towers and baptisteries are Italian features.

wedding to the niece of the Byzantine emperor Manuel Comnenus. (Two centuries before, another German emperor, Otto II, married the Byzantine princess Theophanu, which also served to promote Byzantine style in the Holy Roman Empire; see "Theophanu," Chapter 11, page 328.)

ITALY

Nowhere is the regional diversity of Romanesque art and architecture more readily apparent than in Italy, where the ancient Roman and Early Christian heritage was strongest. Although Tuscany, the ancient Etruscan heartland (see Chapter 6), and other regions south of Lombardy were part of the territory of the Salian emperors, Italy south of Milan represented a distinct artistic zone during the Romanesque period.

Architecture and Architectural Sculpture

Italian Romanesque architects designed buildings that were for the most part structurally less experimental than those erected in Germany and Lombardy. Italian builders adhered closely to the Early Christian basilican type of church.

12-27 Baptistery of San Giovanni (looking northwest), Florence, Italy, begun 1059. ◼◀

The Florentine baptistery is a domed octagon descended from Roman and Early Christian central-plan buildings. The distinctive Tuscan Romanesque marble paneling stems from Roman wall designs.

PISA The cathedral complex (FIG. **12-26**) at Pisa dramatically testifies to the prosperity that busy maritime city enjoyed. The spoils of a naval victory over the Muslims off Palermo in Sicily in 1062 provided the funds for the Pisan building program. The cathedral, its freestanding bell tower, and the baptistery, where infants and converts were initiated into the Christian community, present a rare opportunity to study a coherent group of three Romanesque buildings. Save for the upper portion of the baptistery, with its remodeled Gothic exterior, the three structures are stylistically homogeneous.

Construction of Pisa Cathedral began first—in 1063, the same year work began on Saint Mark's (FIG. 9-26) in Venice, another powerful maritime city. The cathedral is large, with a nave and four aisles, and is one of the most impressive and majestic Romanesque churches. The Pisans, according to a document of the time, wanted their bishop's church not only to be a monument to the glory of God but also to bring credit to the city. At first glance, Pisa Cathedral resembles an Early Christian basilica with a timber roof, columnar arcade, and clerestory. But the broadly projecting transept with apses, the crossing dome, and the facade's multiple arcaded galleries distinguish it as Romanesque. So too does the rich marble *incrustation* (wall decoration consisting of bright panels of different colors, as in the Pantheon's interior, FIG. 7-51). The cathedral's campanile, detached in the standard Italian fashion, is Pisa's famous Leaning Tower (FIG. 12-26, *right*). Graceful arcaded galleries mark the tower's stages and repeat the cathedral facade's motif, effectively relating the round campanile to its mother building. The tilted vertical axis of the tower is the result of a settling foundation. The tower began to "lean" even while under construction, and by the late 20th century had inclined some 5.5 degrees (about 15 feet) out of plumb at the top. In 1999, an international team of scientists began a daring project to remove soil from beneath the north side of the tower. The soil extraction has already moved the tower more than an inch closer to vertical and ensured the stability of the structure for at least 300 years. (Because of the touristic appeal of the Leaning Tower, there are no plans to restore the campanile to its original upright position.)

FLORENCE The public understandably thinks of Florence as a Renaissance city (MAP 21-1), but it was already an important independent city-state in the Romanesque period. The gem of Florentine Romanesque architecture is the baptistery (FIG. **12-27**) of San Giovanni (Saint John), the city's patron saint. Pope Nicholas II (r. 1059–1061) dedicated the building in 1059. It thus predates Pisa's baptistery (FIG. 12-26, *left*), but construction of the Florentine baptistery continued into the next century. Both baptisteries face their city's cathedral. Freestanding baptisteries are unusual, and these Tuscan examples reflect the great significance the Florentines and Pisans attached to baptismal rites. On the day of a newborn child's anointment, the citizenry gathered in the baptistery to welcome a new member into their community. Baptisteries therefore were important civic, as well as religious, structures. Some of the most renowned artists of the late Middle Ages and the Renaissance provided the Florentine and Pisan baptisteries with pulpits (FIG. 14-2), bronze doors (FIGS. 14-19, 21-2, 21-3, 21-9, and 21-10), and mosaics.

The simple and serene classicism of San Giovanni's design recalls ancient Roman architecture. The baptistery stands in a direct line of descent from the Pantheon (FIG. 7-49), imperial mausoleums (such as Diocletian's; FIG. 7-74), the Early Christian Santa Costanza (FIG. 8-11), the Byzantine San Vitale (FIG. 9-10),

12-27A San Miniato al Monte, Florence, ca. 1062–1090. ◼◀

12-27B Sant'Angelo in Formis, near Capua, ca. 1085.

and other Roman and Christian central-plan structures, including Charlemagne's Palatine Chapel (FIGS. 11-17 and 11-18) at Aachen. The distinctive Tuscan Romanesque marble incrustation patterning the walls of Florence's baptistery and the slightly later church of San Miniato al Monte (FIG. **12-27A**) stems ultimately from Roman wall designs (FIGS. 7-17 and 7-51). (The ancient tradition of decorating walls with frescoes also survived in Romanesque Italy, for example, at Sant'Angelo in Formis, FIG. **12-27B**.) The simple oblong and arcuated panels of the baptistery assert the building's structural lines and its elevation levels. In plan, San Giovanni is a domed octagon, wrapped on the exterior by an elegant arcade, three arches to a bay. It has three entrances, one each on the north, south, and east sides. On the west side an oblong sanctuary replaces the original semicircular apse. The domical vault is some 90 feet in diameter, its construction a feat remarkable for its time.

MODENA Despite the pronounced structural differences between Italian Romanesque churches and those of France, Spain, and the Holy Roman Empire, Italian church officials also frequently employed sculptors to adorn the facades of their buildings. In fact, one of the first examples of fully developed narrative relief sculpture in Romanesque art is the marble frieze (FIG. **12-28**) on the facade of Modena Cathedral in northern Italy. Carved around 1110, it represents scenes from Genesis set against an architectural backdrop of a type common on Roman and Early Christian sarcophagi, which were plentiful in the region. The segment in FIG. 12-28, *Creation and Temptation of Adam and Eve* (Gen. 2, 3:1–8), repeats the theme employed almost exactly a century earlier on Bishop Bernward's bronze doors (FIGS. 11-24 and 11-25) at Hildesheim. At Modena, as at Saint Michael's, the faithful entered the Lord's house with a reminder of original sin and the suggestion that the only path to salvation is through Christ.

On the Modena frieze, Christ is at the far left, framed by a mandorla held up by angels—a variation on the motif of the Saint-Sernin ambulatory relief (FIG. 12-8). The creation of Adam, then Eve, and the serpent's temptation of Eve are to the right. The relief carving is high, and some parts are almost entirely in the round. The frieze is the work of a master craftsman whose name, WILIGELMO, appears in an inscription on another relief on the facade. There he boasts, "Among sculptors, your work shines forth, Wiligelmo." The inscription is also an indication of how proud Wiligelmo's patrons were to obtain the services of such an accomplished sculptor for their city's cathedral.

FIDENZA The reawakening of interest in stone sculpture in the round also is evident in northern Italy, where the sculptor

12-28 WILIGELMO, *Creation and Temptation of Adam and Eve*, detail of the frieze on the west facade, Modena Cathedral, Modena, Italy, ca. 1110. Marble, 3′ high.

For Modena's cathedral, Wiligelmo represented scenes from Genesis against an architectural backdrop of a type common on Roman and Early Christian sarcophagi, which were plentiful in the area.

MECA AH 101
Romanesque and Gothic Art

[handwritten: ✻ look at plan of Gothic church]

[handwritten: Romanesque = barrel vault — stone]

Terms:
Pilgrimage
Reliquary
Ambulatory— *[handwritten: around the apse]* *[handwritten: ‑ no atrium or narthex.]*
Barrel vaults
Radiating chapels *[handwritten: ‑ directly from outside into main church]*
✻Tympanum — *[handwritten: Autun Cathedral]*
Flying buttresses *[handwritten: gothic = windows, light, flying buttresses]*
Ribbed groin vaults *[handwritten: ‑ Durham Cath.]* *[handwritten: rom. = walls]*
Pointed arches *[handwritten: focal pt. of church. Heaven vs. Hell]*

Romanesque art:
Santiago de Compostela *[handwritten: ‑ 1078‑1122 ‑ pilgrimage ‑ France ‑ Gothic tower + barrel vaults]*
Head reliquary of St. Alexander, 1145 *[handwritten: ‑ head reliquary ‑ churches vied for the best relics. Reliquary of Sainte Foy Conques 9th cent.]*
Saint-Sernin, Toulouse, France, 1070-1120 *[handwritten: ‑ tower is gothic ‑ barrel vaults]*
Abbey church of Cluny III, Cluny, France, 1088-1130 *[handwritten: ‑ one of the largest churches in Europe ‑ determined the struct. evol. of Ely Cathedral ‑ wooden ceiling]*
Durham Cathedral, England, 1093-1130 *[handwritten: ‑ 1st ex. of rib groin vault ‑ (The Gothic Rib Vault) of Gothic archi.]*
Saint-Étienne, Caen, France, 1068-1115 *[handwritten: ‑ Gothic Spires ‑ abbey church ‑ a lot of light]*
✻Last Judgment tympanum by Gislebertus, Saint-Lazare, Autun, France, 1120-1135 *[handwritten: ‑ Tympanum]*
Virgin and Child, from Auvergne, France, 12th century *[handwritten: ‑ simple, pure, austere ‑ relic for chapel altar ‑ rigid]*

Gothic art:
Saint-Denis, Paris, France, 1140-1144 —
Chartres Cathedral, France, 1145-1220 —
  Royal portal, 1145-1155
  St. Theodore, south transept, 1230
Amiens Cathedral, France, 1220-1236
Notre Dame, Paris, 1180-1250
Reims Cathedral, France, 1225-1290
  Reims, Annunciation and Visitation, 1220-55
Sainte-Chapelle, Paris, 1243-48 *[handwritten: ‑ all windows]*
[handwritten: Wells Cathedral ‑ England ‑ 1330s]

[handwritten: Abbot Suger ‑ wants to show how important the church is. lighter + relevant to by means of town ‑ light = Christ]
[handwritten: Gislebertus, Eve. 3 Wise Men. Autum Cathedral]
[handwritten: ✻ anagogical = uplifting; light]
[handwritten: ✻ Artes ‑ Monestaries ‑ Monks]

Questions for sections:

1. Compare and contrast the architectural styles of a specific Romanesque church and a specific Gothic church. Consider the plans, exterior, and interiors. What are the new architectural features of the Gothic church? What theological ideas influenced the differences between these styles?

2. Why were stained glass windows and light so important in the Gothic cathedral?

3. Discuss the importance of pilgrimage and relics for the development of the Romanesque architectural style. What role did monasticism play in the development of this style?

to life in a monastery

4. Compare the jamb statues of the Old Testament Kings and Queens on the central doorway at Chartres Cathedral (Fig. 18-7) with the *Annunciation* and *Visitation* on Reims Cathedral. How do you account for the stylistic differences? What role does classicism play?

Architecture:

Romanesque –
   ○ regional diversity
   ○ esp. Italy – wooden roofs – Early Christian
   ○ despite the innovation of stone vaulting, some preferred timber

ambulatory
choir — radiating chapels
nave → aisles
} Saint Étienne 1050-1057

12-29 BENEDETTO ANTELAMI, King David, statue in a niche on the west facade of Fidenza Cathedral, Fidenza, Italy, ca. 1180–1190.

Benedetto Antelami's King David on the facade of Fidenza Cathedral is a rare example of life-size freestanding statuary in the Romanesque period. The style is unmistakably rooted in Greco-Roman art.

BENEDETTO ANTELAMI was active in the last quarter of the 12th century. Several reliefs by his hand exist, including Parma Cathedral's pulpit and the portals of that city's baptistery. But his most unusual works are the two monumental marble statues of biblical figures he carved for the west facade of Fidenza Cathedral. Benedetto's King David (FIG. 12-29) seems confined within his niche. His elbows are kept close to his body. Absent is the weight shift that is the hallmark of classical statuary. Yet the sculptor's conception of this prophet is unmistakably rooted in Greco-Roman art. Comparison of the Fidenza David with the prophet on the Moissac trumeau (FIG. 12-13), who also displays an unfurled scroll, reveals how much the Italian sculptor freed his figure from its architectural setting. Other sculptors did not immediately emulate Antelami's classical approach to portraying figures in stone. But the idea of placing freestanding statues in niches would be taken up again in Italy by Early Renaissance sculptors (FIGS. 21-4 to 21-6).

NORMANDY AND ENGLAND

After their conversion to Christianity in the early 10th century, the Vikings (see Chapter 11) settled on the northern coast of France in present-day Normandy. Almost at once, they proved themselves not only aggressive warriors but also skilled administrators and builders, active in Sicily (FIG. 9-27) as well as in northern Europe.

Architecture

The Normans quickly developed a distinctive Romanesque architectural style that became the major source of French Gothic architecture.

CAEN Most critics consider the abbey church of Saint-Étienne at Caen the masterpiece of Norman Romanesque architecture. Begun by William of Normandy (William the Conqueror; see page 361) in 1067, work must have advanced rapidly, because the Normans buried the duke in the church in 1087. Saint-Étienne's west facade (FIG. 12-30) is a striking design rooted in the tradition of

12-30 West facade of Saint-Étienne, Caen, France, begun 1067. ◼◀

The division of Saint-Étienne's facade into three parts corresponding to the nave and aisles reflects the methodical planning of the entire structure. The towers also have a tripartite design.

12-31 Interior of Saint-Étienne (looking east), Caen, France, vaulted ca. 1115–1120. ◼◄

The groin vaults of Saint-Étienne made clerestory windows possible. The three-story elevation with its large arched openings provides ample light and makes the nave appear taller than it is.

Carolingian and Ottonian westworks, but it reveals a new unified organizational scheme. Four large buttresses divide the facade into three bays corresponding to the nave and aisles. Above the buttresses, the towers also display a triple division and a progressively greater piercing of their walls from lower to upper stages. (The culminating spires are a Gothic addition.) The tripartite division extends throughout the facade, both vertically and horizontally, organizing it into a close-knit, well-integrated composition consistent with the careful and methodical planning of the entire structure.

The original design of Saint-Étienne called for a wooden roof, as originally at Speyer Cathedral. But the Caen nave (FIG. **12-31**) had compound piers with simple engaged half-columns alternating with piers with half-columns attached to pilasters. When the Normans decided to install groin vaults around 1115, the existing alternating compound piers in the nave proved a good match. Those piers soar all the way to the vaults' springing. Their branching ribs divide the large square-vault compartments into six sections—a *sexpartite vault* (FIG. **12-32**). The vaults rise high enough to provide room for clerestory windows. The resulting three-story elevation,

12-32 Plan of Saint-Étienne, Caen, France.

The early-12th-century nave vaults of Saint-Étienne spring from compound piers with alternating half-columns and pilasters. The diagonal and transverse ribs divide the vaults into six compartments.

with its large arched openings, allows ample light to reach the interior. It also makes the nave appear taller than it is. As in the Milanese church of Sant'Ambrogio (FIG. 12-22), the Norman building has rib vaults. The diagonal and transverse ribs form a structural skeleton that partially supports the still fairly massive paneling between them. But despite the heavy masonry, the large windows and reduced interior wall surface give Saint-Étienne's nave a light and airy quality unusual in the Romanesque period.

DURHAM William of Normandy's conquest of Anglo-Saxon England in 1066 began a new epoch in English history. In architecture, it signaled the importation of Norman Romanesque building and design methods. Durham Cathedral (FIGS. **12-33** and **12-34**) sits majestically on a cliff overlooking the Wear River in northern England, the centerpiece of a monastery, church, and fortified-castle complex on the Scottish frontier. Unlike Speyer Cathedral and Saint-Étienne, Durham Cathedral, begun around 1093—before the remodeling of the Caen church—was a vaulted structure from the beginning. Consequently, the pattern of the ribs of the nave's groin vaults corresponds perfectly to the design of the arcade below. Each seven-part nave vault covers two bays. Large, simple pillars ornamented with abstract designs (diamond, chevron, and cable patterns, all originally painted) alternate with compound piers that carry the transverse arches of the vaults. The pier-vault relationship scarcely could be more visible or the building's structural rationale better expressed.

The bold surface patterning of the pillars in the Durham nave is a reminder that the raising of imposing stone edifices such as the Romanesque churches of England and Normandy required more than just the talents of master designers. A corps of expert masons had to transform rough stone blocks into the precise shapes necessary for their specific place in the church's fabric. Although thousands of simple quadrangular blocks make up the great walls of these buildings, the stonecutters also had to produce large numbers of blocks of far more complex shapes. To cover the nave and aisles, the masons had to carve blocks with concave faces to conform to the curve of the vault. Also required were blocks with projecting moldings for the ribs, blocks with convex surfaces for the pillars or with multiple profiles for the compound piers, and so forth. It was an immense undertaking, and it is no wonder medieval building campaigns often lasted for decades.

12-33 Interior (*left*; looking east) and lateral section (*right*) of Durham Cathedral, Durham, England, begun ca. 1093.

Durham Cathedral is the first example of a rib groin vault placed over a three-story nave. Quadrant arches replaced groin vaults in the tribune as buttresses of the nave vaults.

12-34 Plan of Durham Cathedral, Durham, England (after Kenneth John Conant).

Durham Cathedral is typically English in its long, slender proportions. In the nave, simple pillars alternate with compound piers that support the transverse arches of the seven-part groin vaults.

Durham Cathedral's plan (FIG. 12-34) is typically English with its long, slender proportions. It does not employ the modular scheme with the same care and logic seen at Caen. But in other ways, this English church is even more innovative than the French church. It is the earliest example known of a rib groin vault placed over a three-story nave. In the nave's western parts, completed before 1130, the rib vaults have slightly pointed arches, bringing together for the first time two key elements that determined the structural evolu-

tion of Gothic architecture (see "The Gothic Rib Vault," Chapter 13, page 368). Also of great significance is the way the English builders buttressed the nave vaults. The lateral section (FIG. 12-33, *right*) exposes the simple *quadrant arches* (arches whose curve extends for one-quarter of a circle's circumference) that take the place of groin vaults in the Durham tribune. The structural descendants of these quadrant arches are the flying buttresses that epitomize the mature Gothic solution to church construction (see "The Gothic Cathedral," Chapter 13, page 373, and FIG. 13-12).

Painting and Other Arts

Many of the finest illustrated manuscripts of the Romanesque age were the work of monks in English scriptoria, following in the tradition of Hiberno-Saxon book production (see Chapter 11).

BURY BIBLE The *Bury Bible* (FIG. **12-35**), produced at the Bury Saint Edmunds abbey in England around 1135, exemplifies the sumptuous illumination common to the large Bibles produced in wealthy Romanesque abbeys not subject to the Cistercian restrictions on painted manuscripts. These costly books lent prestige to monasteries that could afford them (see "Medieval Books," Chapter 11, page 312). The artist responsible for the *Bury Bible* is known: MASTER HUGO, who was also a sculptor and metalworker. With Gislebertus (FIGS. 12-1, 12-13A, and 12-13B), Bernardus Gelduinus (FIG. 12-8), Rufillus (FIG. 12-23A), Rainer of Huy (FIG. 12-24), Wiligelmo (FIG. 12-28), and Benedetto Antelami (FIG. 12-29), Hugo was one of the small but growing number of Romanesque

12-35 MASTER HUGO, *Moses Expounding the Law,* folio 94 recto of the *Bury Bible,* from Bury Saint Edmunds, England, ca. 1135. Ink and tempera on vellum, 1′ 8″ × 1′ 2″. Corpus Christi College, Cambridge.

Master Hugo was a rare Romanesque lay artist, one of the emerging class of professional artists and artisans who depended for their livelihood on commissions from wealthy monasteries.

artists who signed their works or whose names were recorded. In the 12th century, artists, illuminators as well as sculptors, increasingly began to identify themselves. Although most medieval artists remained anonymous, the contrast of the Romanesque period with the early Middle Ages is striking. Hugo apparently was a secular artist, one of the emerging class of professional artists and artisans who depended for their livelihood on commissions from well-endowed monasteries. These artists resided in towns rather than within secluded abbey walls, and they traveled frequently to find work. They were the exception, however, and most Romanesque scribes and illuminators continued to be monks and nuns working anonymously in the service of God. The Benedictine rule, for example, specified that "artisans in the

12-35A Winchester Psalter, ca. 1145–1155.

12-36 EADWINE THE SCRIBE(?), Eadwine the Scribe at work, folio 283 verso of the *Eadwine Psalter,* ca. 1160–1170. Ink and tempera on vellum, 1′ 3½″ × 11⅝″. Trinity College, Cambridge. ◼◀

Although he humbly offered his book as a gift to God, the English monk Eadwine added an inscription to his portrait declaring himself a "prince among scribes" whose fame would endure forever.

monastery . . . are to practice their craft with all humility, but only with the abbot's permission."[6] Some monks, however, produced illuminated volumes not for use in the abbey but on royal commission, for example, the *Winchester Psalter* (FIG. 12-35A).

One page (FIG. 12-35) of the *Bury Bible* shows two scenes from Deuteronomy framed by symmetrical leaf motifs in softly glowing harmonized colors. In the upper register, Master Hugo painted *Moses Expounding the Law,* in which he represented the prophet with horns, consistent with Saint Jerome's translation of the Hebrew word that also means "rays" (compare Michelangelo's similar conception of the Hebrew prophet, FIG. 22-14). The lower panel portrays Moses pointing out the clean and unclean beasts. The gestures are slow and gentle and have quiet dignity. The figures of Moses and Aaron seem to glide. This presentation is quite different from the abrupt emphasis and spastic movement seen in earlier Romanesque paintings. The movements of the figures appear more integrated and smooth. Yet patterning remains in the multiple divisions of the draped limbs, the lightly shaded volumes connected with sinuous lines and ladderlike folds. Hugo still thought of the drapery and body as somehow the same. The frame has a quite definite limiting function, and the painter carefully fit the figures within it.

12-37 Funeral procession to Westminster Abbey, detail of the *Bayeux Tapestry,* from Bayeux Cathedral, Bayeux, France, ca. 1070–1080. Embroidered wool on linen, 1′ 8″ high (entire length of fabric 229′ 8″). Centre Guillaume le Conquérant, Bayeux. ◼◀

The *Bayeux Tapestry* is unique in medieval art. Like historical narratives in Roman art, it depicts contemporaneous events in full detail, as in the scroll-like frieze of Trajan's Column (FIG. 7-1).

EADWINE PSALTER The *Eadwine Psalter* is the masterpiece of an English monk known as EADWINE THE SCRIBE. It contains 166 illustrations, many of them variations of those in the Carolingian *Utrecht Psalter* (FIGS. 11-15 and 11-15A). The last page (FIG. 12-36), however, presents a rare picture of a Romanesque artist at work (compare FIG. 12-23A). The style of the Eadwine portrait resembles that of the *Bury Bible,* but although the patterning is still firm (notably in the cowl and the thigh), the drapery falls more softly and follows the movements of the body beneath it. Here, the abstract patterning of many Romanesque painted and sculpted garments yielded slightly, but clearly, to the requirements of more naturalistic representation. The Romanesque artist's instinct for decorating the surface remained, as is apparent in the gown's whorls and spirals. Significantly, however, the artist painted those interior lines very lightly so that they would not conflict with the functional lines containing them.

The "portrait" of Eadwine—it is probably a generic type and not a specific likeness—is in the long tradition of author portraits in ancient and medieval manuscripts (FIGS. 11-8, 11-13, 11-14, and 12-23; compare FIG. 7-25B), although the true author of the *Eadwine Psalter* is King David. Eadwine exaggerated his importance by likening himself to an evangelist writing his Gospel and by including an inscription within the inner frame identifying himself and proclaiming that he is a "prince among scribes." He declares the excellence of his work will cause his fame to endure forever, and consequently he can offer his book as an acceptable gift to God. Eadwine, like other Romanesque sculptors and painters who signed their works, may have been concerned for his fame, but these artists, whether clergy or laity, were as yet unaware of the concepts of fine art and fine artist. To them, their work existed not for its own sake but for God's. Nonetheless, works such as this one are an early sign of a new attitude toward the role of the artist in society that presages the reemergence in the Renaissance of the classical notion of individual artistic genius.

BAYEUX TAPESTRY The most famous work of English Romanesque art is neither a book nor Christian in subject. The so-called *Bayeux Tapestry* (FIGS. 12-37 and 12-38) is unique in medieval art. It is an embroidered fabric—not, in fact, a woven tapestry—made of wool sewn on linen (see "Embroidery and Tapestry," page 362). Closely related to Romanesque manuscript illumination, its borders contain the kinds of real and imaginary animals found in contemporaneous books, and an explanatory Latin text sewn in thread accompanies many of the pictures. Some 20 inches high and about 230 feet long, the *Bayeux Tapestry* is a continuous, friezelike, pictorial narrative of a crucial moment in England's history and of the events leading up to it. The Norman defeat of the Anglo-Saxons at Hastings in 1066 brought England under the control of the Normans, uniting all of England and much of France under one rule. The dukes of Normandy became the kings of England. Commissioned by Bishop Odo, the half brother of the conquering Duke William, the embroidery may have been sewn by women at the Norman court. Many art historians, however, believe it was the work of English stitchers in Kent, where Odo was earl after the Norman conquest. Odo donated the work to Bayeux Cathedral (hence its nickname), but it is uncertain whether it was originally intended for display in the church's nave, where the theme would have been a curious choice.

The events that precipitated the Norman invasion of England are well documented. In 1066, Edward the Confessor (r. 1042–1066), the Anglo-Saxon king of England, died. The Normans believed Edward had recognized William of Normandy as his rightful heir. But the crown went to Harold, earl of Wessex, the king's Anglo-Saxon brother-in-law, who had sworn an oath of allegiance to William. The betrayed Normans, descendants of the seafaring Vikings, boarded their ships, crossed the English Channel, and crushed Harold's forces.

Embroidery and Tapestry

The most famous embroidery of the Middle Ages is, ironically, known as the *Bayeux Tapestry* (FIGS. 12-37 and 12-38). Embroidery and tapestry are related—but different—means of decorating textiles. *Tapestry* designs are woven on a loom as part of the fabric. *Embroidery* patterns are sewn onto fabrics with threads.

The needleworkers who fashioned the *Bayeux Tapestry* were either Norman or English women. They employed eight colors of dyed wool yarn—two varieties of blue, three shades of green, yellow, buff, and terracotta red—and two kinds of stitches. In *stem stitching*, short overlapping strands of thread form jagged lines. *Laid-and-couched work* creates solid blocks of color. In the latter technique, the needleworker first lays down a series of parallel and then a series of cross stitches. Finally, the stitcher tacks down the cross-hatched threads using couching (knotting).

On the *Bayeux Tapestry,* the embroiderers left the natural linen color exposed for the background, human flesh, building walls, and other "colorless" design elements. Stem stitches define the contours of figures and buildings and delineate interior details, such as facial features, body armor, and roof tiles. The clothing, animal bodies, and other solid areas are laid-and-couched work.

12-38 Battle of Hastings, detail of the *Bayeux Tapestry,* from Bayeux Cathedral, Bayeux, France, ca. 1070–1080. Embroidered wool on linen, 1′ 8″ high (entire length of fabric 229′ 8″). Centre Guillaume le Conquérant, Bayeux. ◼◀

The *Bayeux Tapestry* is really an embroidery. The needleworkers employed eight colors of dyed wool yarn and sewed the threads onto linen using both stem stitching and laid-and-couched work.

Illustrated here are two episodes of the epic tale as represented in the *Bayeux Tapestry.* The first detail (FIG. 12-37) depicts King Edward's funeral procession. The hand of God points the way to the church in London where he was buried—Westminster Abbey, consecrated on December 28, 1065, just a few days before Edward's death. The church was one of the first Romanesque buildings erected in England, and the embroiderers took pains to record its main features, including the imposing crossing tower and the long nave with tribunes. Here William was crowned king of England on Christmas Day, 1066. (The coronation of every English monarch since then also has occurred in Westminster Abbey.) The second detail (FIG. 12-38) shows the Battle of Hastings in progress. The Norman cavalry cuts down the English defenders. Filling the lower border are the dead and wounded, although the upper register continues the animal motifs of the rest of the embroidery. The Romanesque artists co-opted some of the characteristic motifs of Greco-Roman battle scenes, for example, the horses with twisted necks and contorted bodies (compare FIG. 5-70), but rendered the figures in the Romanesque manner. Linear patterning and flat color replaced classical three-dimensional volume and modeling in light and dark hues.

The *Bayeux Tapestry* stands apart from all other Romanesque artworks in depicting in full detail an event at a time shortly after it occurred, recalling the historical narratives of ancient Roman art. Art historians have often likened the Norman embroidery to the scroll-like frieze of the Column of Trajan (FIGS. 7-1 and 7-45). Like the Roman account, the story told on the textile is the conqueror's version of history, a proclamation of national pride. As in the ancient frieze, the narrative is not confined to battlefield successes. It is a complete chronicle of events. Included are the preparations for war, with scenes depicting the felling and splitting of trees for ship construction, the loading of equipment onto the vessels, the cooking and serving of meals, and so forth. In this respect, the *Bayeux Tapestry* is the most *Roman*-esque work of Romanesque art.

ROMANESQUE EUROPE

FRANCE AND NORTHERN SPAIN

▌ *Romanesque* takes its name from the Roman-like barrel and groin vaults based on round arches employed in many European churches built between 1050 and 1200. Romanesque vaults, however, are made of stone, not concrete.

▌ Numerous churches sprang up along the pilgrimage roads leading to the shrine of Saint James at Santiago de Compostela. These churches were large enough to accommodate crowds of pilgrims who came to view the relics displayed in radiating chapels off the ambulatory and transept.

▌ The Romanesque period also brought the revival of monumental stone relief sculpture in cloisters and especially in church portals, where scenes of Christ as last judge often greeted the faithful as they entered the doorway to the road to salvation.

▌ The leading patrons of Romanesque sculpture and painting were the monks of the Cluniac order. In contrast, the Cistercians, under the leadership of Bernard of Clairvaux, condemned figural art in churches and religious books.

Saint-Sernin, Toulouse, ca. 1070–1120

Saint-Lazare, Autun,
ca. 1120–1135

HOLY ROMAN EMPIRE

▌ In the Romanesque period, the Salian dynasty (r. 1027–1125) ruled an empire corresponding roughly to present-day Germany and northern Italy.

▌ Architects in the Holy Roman Empire built structurally innovative churches. Speyer Cathedral and Sant'Ambrogio in Milan are two of the earliest examples of the use of groin vaults in naves.

▌ In Belgium, sculptors excelled in metalwork, producing costly reliquaries of silver, jewels, and enamel, such as that containing the remains of Pope Alexander II. Rainer of Huy, one of several Romanesque artists whose name is known, cast a bronze baptismal font in a single piece.

Reliquary of
Saint Alexander, 1145

ITALY

▌ The regional diversity of Romanesque art and architecture is especially evident in Italy, where the heritage of ancient Rome and Early Christianity was strongest.

▌ Romanesque churches in Pisa and Florence have timber roofs in contrast to the vaulted interiors of northern European buildings. The exteriors often feature marble paneling of different colors. Church campaniles were usually freestanding, as were baptisteries, which took the form of independent central-plan buildings facing the cathedral.

Baptistery of San Giovanni,
Florence, begun 1059

NORMANDY AND ENGLAND

▌ After their conversion to Christianity in the early 10th century, the Vikings settled on the northern coast of France. From there, Duke William of Normandy crossed the channel and conquered England in 1066. The *Bayeux Tapestry* chronicles that war—a unique example of contemporaneous historical narrative art in the Middle Ages.

▌ Norman and English Romanesque architects introduced new features to church design that later greatly influenced French Gothic architecture. Saint-Étienne at Caen and Durham Cathedral are the earliest examples of the use of rib groin vaults over a three-story (arcade-tribune-clerestory) nave. The Durham builders also experimented with quadrant arches in the tribune to buttress the nave vaults.

Durham Cathedral,
begun ca. 1093

Chartres Cathedral is the key monument of both Early and High Gothic architecture. The west facade still has much in common with Romanesque designs but features statues on the door jambs.

Architectural historians consider the rebuilt Chartres Cathedral the first great monument of High Gothic architecture. It is the first church planned from the beginning to have flying buttresses.

Chartres set the pattern for High Gothic cathedrals in the use of four-part rib vaults springing from pointed arches and in the introduction of a three-story nave elevation (arcade, triforium, clerestory).

13-1 Aerial view of Chartres Cathedral (looking north), Chartres, France, as rebuilt after 1194. ◼◀

GOTHIC EUROPE

Flying buttresses made possible the replacement of heavy masonry walls with immense stained-glass windows, which transformed natural sunlight into divine light of various hues.

THE AGE OF THE GREAT CATHEDRALS

In 1550, Giorgio Vasari (1511–1574) first used *Gothic* as a term of ridicule to describe late medieval art and architecture, which he attributed to the Goths and regarded as "monstrous and barbarous."[1] With the publication that year of his influential *Introduction to the Three Arts of Design,* Vasari codified for all time the notion the early Renaissance artist Lorenzo Ghiberti (1378–1455) had already advanced in his *Commentarii,* namely that the Middle Ages was a period of decline. The Italian humanists, who regarded Greco-Roman art as the standard of excellence, believed the uncouth Goths were responsible both for the downfall of Rome and for the decline of the classical style in art and architecture. They regarded "Gothic" art with contempt and considered it ugly and crude.

In the 13th and 14th centuries, however, Chartres Cathedral (FIG. **13-1**) and similar French buildings set the standard throughout most of Europe. For the clergy and the lay public alike, the great cathedrals towering over their towns were not distortions of the classical style but *opus modernum* ("modern work"), glorious images of the City of God, the Heavenly Jerusalem, which they were privileged to build on earth.

The Gothic cathedral was the unique product of an era of peace and widespread economic prosperity, deep spirituality, and extraordinary technological innovation. The essential ingredients of these towering holy structures were lofty masonry rib vaults on pointed arches invisibly held in place by external ("flying") buttresses, and interiors illuminated with mystical light streaming through huge colored-glass windows (see "The Gothic Cathedral," page 373).

The key monument of this exciting new style is Chartres Cathedral, discussed in detail later. Begun around 1145, the church dedicated to Our Lady (Notre Dame), the Virgin Mary, housed her mantle, a precious relic. The lower parts of the massive west towers and the portals between them are all that remain of that Early Gothic cathedral destroyed by fire in 1194 before it had been completed. Reconstruction of the church began immediately but in the High Gothic style with flying buttresses, rib vaults on pointed arches, and immense stained-glass windows. Chartres Cathedral is therefore a singularly instructive composite of a 12th-century facade and a 13th-century nave and transept, and documents the early and mature stages of the development of Gothic architecture in the place of its birth, the region around Paris called the Île-de-France.

FRANCE

As in the Romanesque period, the great artistic innovations of the Gothic age were in large part the outgrowth of widespread prosperity. This was a time of profound change in European society. The focus of both intellectual and religious life shifted definitively from monasteries in the countryside to rapidly expanding secular cities. In these new urban centers, prosperous merchants made their homes and formed *guilds* (professional associations), scholars founded the first modern universities, and vernacular literature, especially courtly romances, exploded in popularity. Although the papacy was at the height of its power, and Christian knights still waged Crusades against the Muslims, the independent secular nations of modern Europe were beginning to take shape. Foremost among them was France, and that is where, around 1140, the Gothic style first appeared.

By the 13th century, the opus modernum of the region around Paris had spread throughout western Europe (MAP 13-1), and in the next century reached farther still. Saint Vitus Cathedral in Prague (Czech Republic), for example, begun in 1344, closely emulates French Gothic architecture. In fact, some late medieval writers referred to Gothic buildings anywhere in Europe as *opus francigenum* ("French work"). Nevertheless, many regional variants existed within European Gothic, just as distinct regional styles characterized the Romanesque period (see Chapter 12). Therefore, this chapter deals with contemporaneous developments in the major regions—France, England, and the Holy Roman Empire—in separate sections. The art and architecture of 13th- and 14th-century Italy are the subject of Chapter 14.

Architecture, Sculpture, and Stained Glass

Art historians generally agree Saint-Denis, a few miles north of Paris, was the birthplace of Gothic architecture. Dionysius (Denis in French) was the legendary saint who brought Christianity to Gaul and who died a martyr's death there in the third century. The Benedictine order founded the abbey at Saint-Denis in the seventh century on the site of the saint's burial. (According to legend, after

MAP 13-1 Europe around 1200.

his execution, Dionysius miraculously stood up and marched to his grave carrying his severed head in his hands.) In the ninth century, the monks constructed a basilica at Saint-Denis, which housed the saint's tomb and those of nearly all the French kings dating back to the sixth century, as well as the crimson military banner that reputedly belonged to Charlemagne. The Carolingian basilica became France's royal church, the very symbol of the monarchy—just as Speyer Cathedral (FIG. 12-20) was the burial place of the German rulers of the Holy Roman Empire.

SUGER AND SAINT-DENIS   By 1122, when a monk named Suger (ca. 1081–1151) became abbot of Saint-Denis, the old church was in disrepair and had become too small to accommodate the growing number of pilgrims. Suger also believed the basilica was of insufficient grandeur to serve as the official church of the French kings (see "Abbot Suger and the Rebuilding of Saint-Denis," page 367). In 1135, Suger began to rebuild the church (FIGS. 13-2 and 13-3) by

GOTHIC EUROPE

1140	Early Gothic	1194	High Gothic	1300	Late Gothic	1500

- Abbot Suger begins rebuilding the French royal abbey church at Saint-Denis with rib vaults on pointed arches and stained-glass windows
- As at Saint-Denis, sculpted jamb figures adorn all three portals of the west facade of Chartres Cathedral
- The builders of Laon Cathedral insert a triforium as the fourth story in the nave elevation

- The rebuilt Chartres Cathedral sets the pattern for High Gothic churches: four-part nave vaults braced by external flying buttresses, three-story elevation (arcade, triforium, clerestory), and stained-glass windows in place of heavy masonry
- At Chartres and Reims in France, at Naumburg in Germany, and elsewhere, statues become more independent of their architectural setting
- Manuscript illumination moves from monastic scriptoria to urban lay workshops, especially in Paris

- The Flamboyant style in France and the Perpendicular style in England emphasize surface embellishment over structural clarity. Characteristic features are delicate webs of flamelike tracery and fan vaults with pendants resembling stalactites
- The humanization of holy figures in statuary continues, especially in Germany, where sculptors dramatically record the suffering of Jesus

Abbot Suger and the Rebuilding of Saint-Denis

Abbot Suger of Saint-Denis (1081–1151) rose from humble parentage to become the right-hand man of both Louis VI (r. 1108–1137) and Louis VII (r. 1137–1180). When the latter, accompanied by his queen, Eleanor of Aquitaine, left to join the Second Crusade (1147–1149), Suger served as regent of France. From his youth, Suger wrote, he had dreamed of the possibility of embellishing the church in which most French monarchs since Merovingian times had been buried. Within 15 years of becoming abbot of Saint-Denis, Suger began rebuilding its Carolingian basilica. In his time, the French monarchy's power, except for scattered holdings, extended over an area not much larger than the Île-de-France, the region centered on Paris. But the kings had pretensions to rule all of France. Suger aimed to increase the prestige both of his abbey and of the monarchy by rebuilding France's royal church in grand fashion.

Suger wrote three detailed treatises about his activities as abbot, recording how he summoned masons and artists from many regions to help design and construct his new church. In one important passage, he described the special qualities of the new east end (FIGS. 13-2 and 13-3) dedicated in 1144:

> [I]t was cunningly provided that—through the upper columns and central arches which were to be placed upon the lower ones built in the crypt—the central nave of the old [Carolingian church] should be equalized, by means of geometrical and arithmetical instruments, with the central nave of the new addition; and, likewise, that the dimensions of the old side-aisles should be equalized with the dimensions of the new side-aisles, except for that elegant and praiseworthy extension in [the form of] a circular string of chapels, by virtue of which the whole [church] would shine with the wonderful and uninterrupted light of most sacred windows, pervading the interior beauty.*

The abbot's brief discussion of Sain-Denis's new ambulatory and chapels is key to understanding Early Gothic architecture. Suger wrote at much greater length, however, about his church's glorious golden and gem-studded furnishings. Here, for example, is his description of the *altar frontal* (the decorated panel on the front of the altar) in the choir:

> Into this panel, which stands in front of [Saint-Denis's] most sacred body, we have put . . . about forty-two marks of gold [and] a multifarious wealth of precious gems, hyacinths, rubies, sapphires, emeralds and topazes, and also an array of different large pearls.†

The costly furnishings and the light-filled space caused Suger to "delight in the beauty of the house of God" and "called [him] away from external cares." The new church made him feel as if he were "dwelling . . . in some strange region of the universe which neither exists entirely in the slime of the earth nor entirely in the purity of Heaven." In Suger's eyes, his splendid new church, permeated with light and outfitted with gold and precious gems, was a way station on the road to Paradise, which "transported [him] from this inferior to that higher world."‡ He regarded a lavish investment in art as a spiritual aid, not as an undesirable distraction for the pious monk, as did Bernard of Clairvaux (see "Bernard of Clairvaux," Chapter 12, page 342). Suger's forceful justification of art in the church set the stage for the proliferation of costly stained-glass windows and sculptures in the cathedrals of the Gothic age.

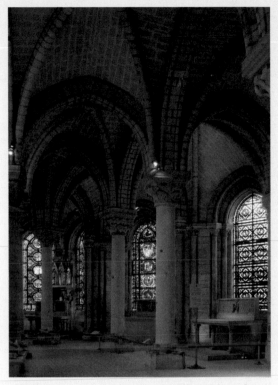

13-2 Ambulatory and radiating chapels (looking northeast), abbey church, Saint-Denis, France, 1140–1144. ◼◀

Abbot Suger's remodeling of Saint-Denis marked the beginning of Gothic architecture. Rib vaults with pointed arches spring from slender columns. Stained-glass windows admit lux nova.

13-3 Plan of the east end, abbey church, Saint-Denis, France, 1140–1144 (after Sumner Crosby).

The innovative plan of the east end of Saint-Denis dates to Abbot Suger's lifetime. By using very light rib vaults, the builders were able to eliminate the walls between the radiating chapels.

---

*Translated by Erwin Panofsky, *Abbot Suger on the Abbey Church of Saint-Denis and Its Art Treasures*, 2d ed. (Princeton: Princeton University Press, 1979), 101.
†Ibid., 55.
‡Ibid., 65.

The Gothic Rib Vault

The ancestors of the Gothic *rib vault* are the Romanesque vaults found at Caen (FIG. 12-31), Durham (FIG. 12-33), and elsewhere. The rib vault's distinguishing feature is the crossed, or diagonal, arches under its groins, as seen in the Saint-Denis ambulatory and chapels (FIG. 13-2; compare FIG. 13-21). These arches form the *armature*, or skeletal framework, for constructing the vault. Gothic vaults generally have more thinly vaulted *webs* (the masonry between the ribs) than found in Romanesque vaults. But the chief difference between the two types of vaults is the *pointed arch,* an integral part of the Gothic skeletal armature. The first wide use of pointed (or *ogival*) arches was in Sasanian architecture (FIG. 2-28), and Islamic builders later adopted them. French Romanesque architects (FIGS. 12-10A and 12-11) borrowed the form from Muslim Spain and passed it to their Gothic successors. Pointed arches enabled Gothic builders to make the crowns of all the vault's arches approximately the same level, regardless of the space to be vaulted. Romanesque architects could not achieve this with their semicircular arches.

The drawings in FIG. 13-4 illustrate this key difference. In FIG. 13-4*a,* the rectangle *ABCD* is an oblong nave bay to be vaulted. *AC* and *DB* are the diagonal ribs; *AB* and *DC,* the transverse arches; and *AD* and *BC,* the nave arcade's arches. If the architect uses semi-circular arches (*AFB, BJC,* and *DHC*), their radii and, therefore, their heights (*EF, IJ,* and *GH*), will be different, because the width of a semicircular arch determines its height. The result will be a vault (FIG. 13-4*b*) with higher transverse arches (*DHC*) than the arcade's arches (*CJB*). The vault's crown (*F*) will be still higher. If the builder uses pointed arches (FIG. 13-4*c*), the transverse (*DLC*) and arcade (*BKC*) arches can have the same heights (*GL* and *IK* in FIG. 13-4*a*). The result will be a Gothic rib vault where the points of the arches (*L* and *K*) are at the same level as the vault's crown (*F*).

A major advantage of the Gothic vault is its flexibility, which permits the vaulting of compartments of varying shapes, as at Saint-Denis (FIG. 13-3). Pointed arches also channel the weight of the vaults more directly downward than do semicircular arches. The vaults therefore require less buttressing to hold them in place, in turn permitting the stonemasons to open up the walls and place large windows beneath the arches. Because pointed arches also lead the eye upward, they make the vaults appear taller than they are. In FIG. 13-4, the crown (*F*) of both the Romanesque (*b*) and Gothic (*c*) vaults is the same height from the pavement, but the Gothic vault seems taller. Both the physical and visual properties of rib vaults with pointed arches aided Gothic builders in their quest for soaring height in church interiors (FIG. 13-10).

13-4 Diagram (a) and drawings of rib vaults with semicircular (b) and pointed (c) arches.

Pointed arches channel the weight of the rib vaults more directly downward than do semicircular arches, requiring less buttressing. Pointed arches also make the vaults appear taller than they are.

13-3A West facade, Saint-Denis, 1135–1140. ◼◀

erecting a new west facade (FIG. **13-3A**) with sculptured portals. Work began on the east end (FIGS. 13-2 and 13-3) in 1140. Suger died before he could remodel the nave, but he attended the dedication of the new choir, ambulatory, and radiating chapels on June 11, 1144. Also in attendance were King Louis VII of France, Queen Eleanor of Aquitaine (see "Romanesque Countesses, Queens, and Nuns," Chapter 12, page 352), and five archbishops.

Because the French considered the old church a relic in its own right, the new east end had to conform to the dimensions of the crypt below it. Nevertheless, the remodeled portion of Saint-Denis represented a sharp break from past practice. Innovative rib vaults resting on pointed arches (see "The Gothic Rib Vault," above, and FIG. **13-4***c*) cover the ambulatory and chapels (FIGS. 13-2 and 13-3). These pioneering, exceptionally lightweight vaults spring from slender columns in the ambulatory and from the thin masonry walls framing the chapels. The lightness of the vaults enabled the builders to eliminate the walls between the chapels and open up the outer walls and fill them with stained-glass windows (see "Stained-Glass Windows," page 375). Suger and his contemporaries marveled at the "wonderful and uninterrupted light" pouring in through the

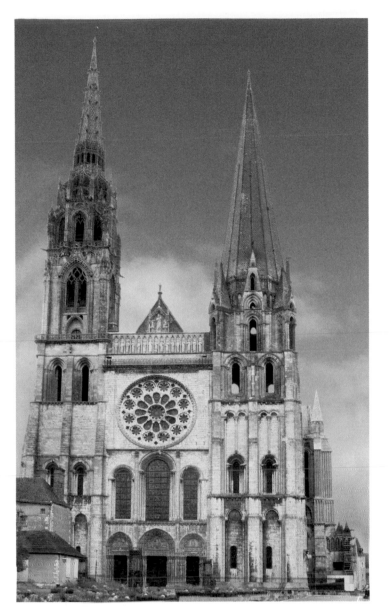

The Early Gothic west facade was all that remained of Chartres Cathedral after the 1194 fire. The design still has much in common with Romanesque facades. The rose window is an example of plate tracery.

"most sacred windows." The abbot called the colored light *lux nova* ("new light"). Both the new type of vaulting and the use of stained glass became hallmarks of French Gothic architecture.

Saint-Denis is also the key monument of Early Gothic sculpture. Little of the sculpture Suger commissioned for the west facade (FIG. 13-3A) of the abbey church survived the French Revolution of the late 18th century (see Chapter 26). Old engravings reveal Suger carried on the artistic heritage of Romanesque Burgundy (see Chapter 12) by filling all three portals with sculpture, but Suger's sculptors also introduced figures of Old Testament kings, queens, and prophets attached to columns on the jambs of all three doorways.

ROYAL PORTAL, CHARTRES This innovative treatment of the Saint-Denis portals appeared immediately afterward at the Cathedral of Notre Dame (FIG. 13-1) at Chartres, also in the Île-de-France. Work on the west facade (FIG. **13-5**) began around 1145. The west entrance, the Royal Portal (FIG. **13-6**)—so named because of the figures of kings and queens flanking its three doorways, as at Saint-Denis—constitutes the most complete surviving ensemble of Early Gothic sculpture. Thierry of Chartres, chancellor of the Cathedral School of Chartres from 1141 until his death 10 years later, may have conceived the complex iconographical program. The archivolts of the right portal, for example, depict the seven female personifications of the liberal arts with the learned men of antiquity at their feet. The figures celebrate the revival of classical scholarship in the 12th century and symbolize human knowledge, which Thierry and other leading intellectuals of the era believed led to true faith (see "Paris, Schoolmen, and Scholasticism" page 372).

The sculptures of the Royal Portal (FIG. 13-6) proclaim the majesty and power of Christ. To unite the three doorways iconographically and visually, the sculptors carved episodes from the lives of the Virgin (Notre Dame) and Christ on the capitals, which form a kind of frieze linking one entrance to the next. Christ's *Ascension* into Heaven appears in the tympanum of the left portal. All around, in the archivolts, are the signs of the zodiac and scenes representing the various labors of the months of the year. They are symbols of the cosmic and earthly worlds. The *Second Coming* is the subject of the central tympanum, as at Moissac

13-6 Royal Portal, west facade, Chartres Cathedral, Chartres, France, ca. 1145–1155. ◼◀

The sculptures of the Royal Portal proclaim the majesty and power of Christ. The tympana depict, from left to right, Christ's *Ascension*, the *Second Coming*, and Jesus in the lap of the Virgin Mary.

13-7 Old Testament kings and queen, jamb statues, right side of the central doorway of the Royal Portal, Chartres Cathedral, Chartres, France, ca. 1145–1155. ◼◀

The biblical kings and queens of the Royal Portal are the royal ancestors of Christ. These Early Gothic jamb figures display the first signs of a new naturalism in European sculpture.

(FIG. 12-11). The signs of the four evangelists, the 24 elders of the Apocalypse, and the 12 apostles appear around Christ or on the lintel. In the tympanum of the right portal, Christ appears in the lap of the Virgin Mary. Scenes of the Savior's childhood fill the lintel below, where Jesus appears on an altar, connecting the sculptures at the entrance to the church with the symbolic sacrifice of the Eucharist within.

The depiction of Mary in the right tympanum recalls Byzantine representations of the Theotokos (FIGS. 9-18 and 9-19), as well as the Romanesque "throne of wisdom" (FIG. 12-19). But the Virgin's prominence on the Chartres facade has no parallel in the sculptural programs of Romanesque church portals. At Chartres, Mary assumes a central role, a position she maintained throughout the Gothic period, during which time her cult reached a high point. As the Mother of Christ, she stood compassionately between the last judge and the horrors of Hell, interceding for all her faithful (compare FIG. 13-38B). Worshipers in the later 12th and 13th centuries sang hymns to the Virgin and dedicated great cathedrals to her. Soldiers carried her image into battle on banners, and Mary's name joined Saint Denis's as part of the French king's battle cry. The Virgin ("Our Lady") became the spiritual lady of chivalry, and the Christian knight dedicated his life to her. The severity of Romanesque themes stressing the last judgment yielded to the gentleness of Gothic art, in which Mary is the kindly queen of Heaven.

JAMB STATUES Statues of Old Testament kings and queens occupy the jambs flanking each doorway of the Royal Portal (FIGS. 13-6 and **13-7**). They are the royal ancestors of Christ and, both figuratively and literally, support the New Testament figures above the doorways. They wear 12th-century clothes, and medieval observers may have regarded them as images of the kings and queens of France. (This was the motivation for vandalizing the comparable figures at Saint-Denis during the French Revolution.) The figures stand rigidly upright with their elbows held close against their hips. The linear folds of their garments—inherited from the Romanesque style, along with the elongated proportions—generally echo the vertical lines of the columns behind them. (In this respect, Gothic jamb statues differ significantly from classical caryatids; FIG. 5-54. The Gothic figures are *attached* to columns. The classical statues *replaced* the columns.) Yet, within and despite this architectural straitjacket, the statues display the first signs of a new naturalism. Although technically high reliefs, the kings and queens stand out from the plane of the wall, and, consistent with medieval (and ancient) practice, artists originally painted the statues in vivid colors, enhancing their lifelike appearance. The new naturalism is noticeable particularly in the statues' heads, where kindly human faces replace the masklike features of most Romanesque figures. At Chartres, a personalization of appearance began that led first to idealized portraits of the perfect Christian and finally, by 1400, to the portraiture of specific individuals. The sculptors of the Royal Portal figures initiated an era of artistic concern with personality and individuality.

LAON CATHEDRAL Both Chartres Cathedral and the abbey church of Saint-Denis had lengthy construction histories, and only small portions of the structures date to the Early Gothic period. Laon Cathedral (FIGS. **13-8** and **13-9**), however, begun about 1160 and finished shortly after 1200, provides a comprehensive picture of French church architecture of the second half of the 12th century. Although the Laon builders retained many Romanesque features in their design, they combined them with the rib vault resting on pointed arches, the essential element of Early Gothic architecture.

Among the Laon plan's Romanesque features are the nave bays with their large sexpartite rib vaults, flanked by two small groin-vaulted squares in each aisle. The vaulting system (except for the pointed arches), as well as the vaulted gallery above the aisles, derived from Norman Romanesque churches such as Saint-Étienne (FIG. 12-31) at Caen. The Laon architect also employed the Romanesque alternate-support system in the nave arcade. Above the piers, alternating bundles of three and five shafts frame the aisle bays. A new feature found in the Laon interior, however, is the *triforium*, the band of arcades below the clerestory (FIGS. 13-9 and **13-10a**). The triforium occupies the space corresponding to the exterior strip of wall covered by the sloping timber roof above the galleries. The insertion of the triforium into the Romanesque three-story nave elevation reflected a growing desire to break up all continuous wall surfaces. The new horizontal zone produced the characteristic four-story Early Gothic interior elevation: nave arcade, vaulted gallery, triforium, and clerestory with single *lancets* (tall, narrow windows ending in pointed arches).

Laon Cathedral's west facade (FIG. 13-8) signals an even more pronounced departure from the Romanesque style still lingering at Saint-Denis (FIG. 13-3A) and Chartres (FIG. 13-5). Typically Gothic are the huge central rose window, the deep porches in front of the doorways, and the open structure of the towers. A comparison of the facades of Laon Cathedral and Saint-Étienne (FIG. 12-30) at Caen reveals a much deeper penetration of the wall mass in the later building. At Laon, as in Gothic architecture generally, the

13-8 West facade of Laon Cathedral, Laon, France, begun ca. 1190. ◼◀

The huge central rose window, the deep porches in front of the doorways, and the open structure of the towers distinguish Laon's Early Gothic facade from Romanesque church facades.

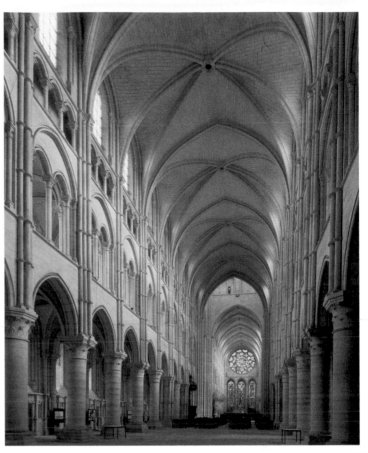

13-9 Interior of Laon Cathedral (looking northeast), Laon, France, begun ca. 1190. ◼◀

The insertion of a triforium at Laon broke up the nave wall and produced the characteristic four-story Early Gothic interior elevation: nave arcade, vaulted gallery, triforium, and clerestory.

a Laon
height of nave, 80'
width of nave, 37'6"
ratio, 2.13:1

b Paris
height of nave, 115'
width of nave, 40'
ratio, 2.88:1

c Chartres
height of nave, 120'
width of nave, 45'6"
ratio, 2.64:1

d Amiens
height of nave, 144'
width of nave, 48'
ratio, 3.00:1

13-10 Nave elevations of four French Gothic cathedrals at the same scale (after Louis Grodecki).

Gothic naves evolved from a four-story elevation (arcade, tribune gallery, triforium, clerestory) to a three-story elevation (without tribune). The height of the vaults also increased dramatically.

Paris, Schoolmen, and Scholasticism

A few years before the formal consecration of the altar of the Cathedral of Notre-Dame (FIG. 13-11) in Paris, Philip II Augustus (r. 1180–1223) succeeded to the throne. Philip brought the feudal barons under his control and expanded the royal domains to include Normandy in the north and most of Languedoc in the south, laying the foundations for the modern nation of France. Renowned as "the maker of Paris," he gave the city its walls, paved its streets, and built the palace of the Louvre (now one of the world's great museums) to house the royal family. Although Rome remained the religious center of Western Christendom, the Île-de-France and Paris in particular became its intellectual capital as well as the leading artistic center of the Gothic world. The University of Paris attracted the best minds from all over Europe. Virtually every thinker of note in the Gothic age at some point studied or taught at Paris.

Even in the Romanesque period, Paris was a center of learning. Its Cathedral School professors, known as Schoolmen, developed the philosophy called *Scholasticism*. The greatest of the early Schoolmen was Peter Abelard (1079–1142), a champion of logical reasoning. Abelard and his contemporaries had been introduced to the writings of the Greek philosopher Aristotle through the Arabic scholars of Islamic Spain. Abelard applied Aristotle's system of rational inquiry to the interpretation of religious belief. Until the 12th century, both clergy and laymen considered truth the exclusive property of divine revelation as given in the holy scriptures. But the Schoolmen, using Aristotle's method, sought to demonstrate reason alone could lead to certain truths. Their goal was to prove the central articles of Christian faith by argument (*disputatio*). In Scholastic argument, Schoolmen state a possibility, then cite an authoritative view in objection, next reconcile the positions, and, finally, offer a reply to each of the rejected original arguments.

One of Abelard's greatest critics was Bernard of Clairvaux (see "Bernard of Clairvaux," Chapter 12, page 342), who believed Scholasticism

was equivalent to questioning Christian dogma. Although Bernard succeeded in 1140 in having the Church officially condemn Abelard's doctrines, the Schoolmen's philosophy developed systematically until it became the dominant Western philosophy of the late Middle Ages. By the 13th century, the Schoolmen of Paris already had organized as a professional guild of master scholars, separate from the numerous Church schools the bishop of Paris oversaw. The structure of the Parisian guild served as the model for many other European universities.

The greatest advocate of Abelard's Scholasticism was Thomas Aquinas (1225–1274), an Italian monk who became a saint in 1323. Aquinas settled in Paris in 1244. There, the German theologian Albertus Magnus (d. 1280) instructed him in Aristotelian philosophy. Aquinas went on to become an influential teacher at the University of Paris. His most famous work, *Summa Theologica* (left unfinished at his death), is a model of the Scholastic approach to knowledge. Aquinas divided his treatise into books, the books into questions, the questions into articles, each article into objections with contradictions and responses, and, finally, answers to the objections. He set forth five ways to prove the existence of God by rational argument. Aquinas's work remains the foundation of contemporary Catholic teaching.

13-11 Notre-Dame (looking north), Paris, France, begun 1163; nave and flying buttresses, ca. 1180–1200; remodeled after 1225. ◼◀

King Philip II initiated a building boom in Paris, which quickly became the intellectual capital of Europe. Notre-Dame in Paris was the first great cathedral built using flying buttresses.

operating principle was to reduce sheer mass and replace it with intricately framed voids.

NOTRE-DAME, PARIS About 1130, Louis VI moved his official residence to Paris, spurring much commercial activity and a great building boom. Paris soon became the leading city and intellectual capital of France, indeed of all northern Europe (see "Paris, Schoolmen, and Scholasticism," above). A new cathedral became a necessity. Notre-Dame (FIG. 13-11) occupies a picturesque site on an island in the Seine River called the Île-de-la-Cité. The Gothic church (see "The Gothic Cathedral," page 373), which replaced a large Merovingian basilica, has a complicated building

history. The choir and transept were completed by 1182, the nave by about 1225, and the facade not until 1250 to 1260. Sexpartite vaults cover the nave, as at Laon. The original elevation (the builders modified the design as work progressed) had four stories, but the scheme (FIG. 13-10b) differed from Laon's (FIG. 13-10a). In each bay, in place of the triforium over the gallery, was a stained-glass *oculus* (small round window), opening up the wall below the clerestory lancet. As a result, windows filled two of the four stories, further reducing the masonry area.

To hold the much thinner—and taller (compare FIGS. 13-10a and 13-10b)—walls of Notre-Dame in place, the unknown architect introduced *flying buttresses* that spring from the lower roofs over the

The Gothic Cathedral

The great cathedrals erected throughout Europe in the later 12th and 13th centuries are the enduring symbols of the Gothic age. They are eloquent testimonies to the extraordinary skill of the architects, engineers, carpenters, masons, sculptors, glassworkers, and metalsmiths who constructed and embellished them. Most of the architectural components of Gothic cathedrals had appeared in earlier structures, but Gothic architects combined the elements in new ways. The essential ingredients of their formula for constructing churches in the *opus modernum* style were rib vaults with pointed arches (see "The Gothic Rib Vault," page 368), flying buttresses, and huge colored-glass windows (see "Stained-Glass Windows," page 375). These three features and other important terms used in describing Gothic buildings are listed and defined here and illustrated in FIG. 13-12.

▌ *Pinnacle* (FIG. 13-12, no. 1) A sharply pointed ornament capping the piers or flying buttresses; also used on cathedral facades.

▌ *Flying buttresses* (2) Masonry struts that transfer the thrust of the nave vaults across the roofs of the side aisles and ambulatory to a tall pier rising above the church's exterior wall.

▌ *Vaulting web* (3) The masonry blocks filling the area between the ribs of a groin vault.

▌ *Diagonal rib* (4) In plan, one of the ribs forming the X of a groin vault. In FIG. 13-4, the diagonal ribs are the lines AC and DB.

▌ *Transverse rib* (5) A rib crossing the nave or aisle at a 90-degree angle (lines *AB* and *DC* in FIG. 13-4).

▌ *Springing* (6) The lowest stone of an arch; in Gothic vaulting, the lowest stone of a diagonal or transverse rib.

▌ *Clerestory* (7) The windows below the vaults in the nave elevation's uppermost level. By using flying buttresses and rib vaults on pointed arches, Gothic architects could build huge clerestory windows and fill them with *stained glass* held in place by ornamental stonework called *tracery*.

▌ *Oculus* (8) A small, round window.

▌ *Lancet* (9) A tall, narrow window crowned by a pointed arch.

▌ *Triforium* (10) The story in the nave elevation consisting of arcades, usually blind arcades but occasionally filled with stained glass.

▌ *Nave arcade* (11) The series of arches supported by piers separating the nave from the side aisles.

▌ *Compound pier (cluster pier) with shafts (responds)* (12) A pier with a group, or cluster, of attached shafts, or responds, extending to the springing of the vaults.

13-12 Cutaway view of a typical French Gothic cathedral (John Burge). ▪◀

The major elements of the Gothic formula for constructing a church in the *opus modernum* style were rib vaults with pointed arches, flying buttresses, and stained-glass windows.

aisles and ambulatory (FIG. 13-11; compare FIG. **13-12**) and counter the outward thrust of the nave vaults. Gothic builders introduced flying buttresses as early as 1150 in a few smaller churches, but at Notre-Dame in Paris they circle a great urban cathedral. The internal quadrant arches (FIG. 12-33, *right*) beneath the aisle roofs at Durham, also employed at Laon, perform a similar function and may be regarded as precedents for exposed Gothic flying buttresses. The combination of precisely positioned flying buttresses and rib vaults with pointed arches was the ideal solution to the problem of constructing lofty naves with huge windows. The flying buttresses, which function as extended fingers holding up the walls, are key components of the distinctive "look" of Gothic cathedrals (FIG. 13-12).

CHARTRES AFTER 1194 Churches burned frequently in the Middle Ages (see "Timber Roofs," Chapter 12, page 339), and church officials often had to raise money unexpectedly for new building campaigns. In contrast to monastic churches, which usually were small and often could be completed quickly, the construction histories of urban cathedrals frequently extended over decades and sometimes over centuries. Their financing depended largely on collections and public contributions (not always voluntary), and a lack of funds often interrupted building programs. Unforeseen events, such as wars, famines, or plagues, or friction between the town and cathedral authorities would also often halt construction, which then might not resume for years. At Reims (FIG. 13-23), the clergy offered *indulgences* (pardons for sins committed) to those who helped underwrite the enormous cost of erecting the cathedral. The rebuilding of Chartres Cathedral (FIG. 13-1) after the devastating fire of 1194 took a relatively short 27 years, but at one point the townspeople revolted against the prospect of a heavier tax burden. They stormed the bishop's residence and drove him into exile for four years.

Chartres Cathedral's mid-12th-century west facade (FIG. 13-5) and the masonry of the crypt to the east were the only sections left standing after the 1194 conflagration. The crypt housed the most precious relic of Chartres—the mantle of the Virgin, which miraculously survived the fire. For reasons of piety and economy, the builders used the crypt for the foundation of the new structure. The retention of the crypt and west facade determined the new church's dimensions but not its plan or elevation. Architectural historians usually consider the post-1194 Chartres Cathedral the first High Gothic building.

The Chartres plan (FIG. **13-13**) reveals a new kind of organization. Rectangular nave bays replaced the square bays with sexpartite

vaults and the alternate-support system, still present in Early Gothic churches such as Laon Cathedral (FIG. 13-9). The new system, in which a single square in each aisle (rather than two, as before) flanks a single rectangular unit in the nave, became the High Gothic norm. A change in vault design and the abandonment of the alternate-support system usually accompanied this new bay arrangement. The High Gothic nave vault, which covered only one bay and therefore could be braced more easily than its Early Gothic predecessor, had only four parts. The visual effect of these changes was to unify the interior (FIG. **13-14**), because the nave now consisted of a sequence of identical units. The level crowns of the successive nave vaults, which pointed arches made possible, enhanced this effect.

The 1194 Chartres Cathedral was also the first church planned from its inception to have flying buttresses, another key High Gothic feature. The flying buttresses enabled the builders to eliminate the tribune above the aisle, which had partially braced Romanesque and Early Gothic naves (compare FIG. 13-10c with FIGS. 13-10a and 13-10b). The new High Gothic tripartite nave elevation consisted of arcade, triforium, and clerestory with greatly enlarged windows. The Chartres windows are almost as tall as the main arcade and consist of double lancets with a single crowning oculus. The strategic placement of flying buttresses made possible the construction of nave walls with so many voids that heavy masonry played merely a minor role.

CHARTRES STAINED GLASS Despite the vastly increased size of its clerestory windows, the Chartres nave (FIG. 13-14) is relatively dark. This seeming contradiction is the result of using light-muffling colored glass for the windows instead of clear glass. The purpose of the Chartres windows was not to illuminate the interior with bright sunlight but to transform natural light into Suger's mystical lux nova (see "Stained-Glass Windows," page 375, and FIG. **13-15**).

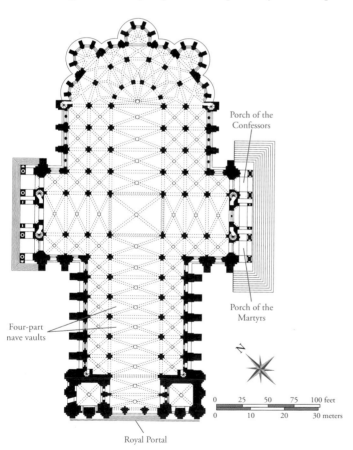

Porch of the Confessors

Porch of the Martyrs

Four-part nave vaults

Royal Portal

0 25 50 75 100 feet
0 10 20 30 meters

13-13 Plan of Chartres Cathedral, Chartres, France, as rebuilt after the 1194 fire (after Paul Frankl).

The Chartres plan, in which one square (instead of two) in each aisle flanks a single rectangular unit in the nave with a four-part vault, became the norm for High Gothic church architecture.

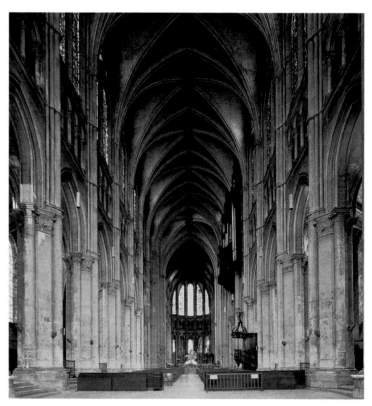

13-14 Interior of Chartres Cathedral (looking east), Chartres, France, begun 1194. ◼◂

Chartres Cathedral established the High Gothic model also in its tripartite elevation consisting of nave arcade, triforium, and clerestory with stained-glass windows almost as tall as the main arcade.

Stained-Glass Windows

Stained-glass windows, although not a Gothic invention, are almost synonymous with Gothic architecture. No other age produced windows of such rich color and beauty. The technology of manufacturing colored glass is very old, however. Egyptian artists excelled at fashioning colorful glass objects for both home and tomb, and archaeologists have uncovered thousands of colored-glass artifacts at classical sites. But Gothic artists used stained glass in new ways. In earlier eras, the clergy introduced color and religious iconography into church interiors mainly with mural paintings and mosaics, often with magnificent effect. Stained-glass windows differ from those techniques in one all-important respect. They do not conceal walls. They replace them. Moreover, they transmit rather than reflect light, filtering and transforming the natural sunlight.

Abbot Suger called this colored light *lux nova* (see "Abbot Suger," page 367). Suger's contemporary, Hugh of Saint-Victor (1096–1142), a prominent Parisian theologian, also commented on the special mystical quality of stained-glass windows: "Stained-glass windows are the Holy Scriptures . . . and since their brilliance lets the splendor of the True Light pass into the church, they enlighten those inside."* William Durandus (ca. 1237–1296), bishop of Mende (southern France), expressed a similar sentiment at the end of the 13th century: "The glass windows in a church are Holy Scriptures, which expel the wind and the rain, that is, all things hurtful, but transmit the light of the True Sun, that is, God, into the hearts of the faithful."†

According to Suger, the 12th-century stained-glass windows of Saint-Denis (FIG. 13-2) were "painted by the exquisite hands of many masters from different regions," proving the art was well established at that time.‡ In fact, colored windows appeared in some churches as early as the fourth century, and several sophisticated Romanesque examples of figural stained-glass windows survive. The manufacture of these windows was costly and labor-intensive. A German Benedictine monk named Theophilus recorded the full process around 1100. First, the master designer drew the exact composition of the planned window on a wooden panel, indicating all the linear details and noting the colors for each section. Glassblowers provided flat sheets of glass of different colors to *glaziers* (glassworkers), who cut the window-panes to the required size and shape with special iron shears. Glaziers produced an even greater range of colors by *flashing* (fusing one layer of colored glass to another). Next, painters added details such as faces, hands, hair, and clothing in enamel by tracing the master design on the wood panel through the colored glass. Then they heated the painted glass to fuse the enamel to the surface. Next the glaziers "leaded" the various fragments of glass—that is, they joined them by strips of lead called *cames*. The *leading* not only held the pieces together but also separated the colors to heighten the effect of the design as a whole. The distinctive character of Gothic stained-glass windows is largely the result of this combination of fine linear details with broad flat expanses of color framed by black lead. Finally, the glassworkers strengthened the completed window with an armature of iron bands, which in the 12th century formed a grid over the entire design (FIG. 13-16). In the 13th century, the bands followed the outlines of the medallions and of the surrounding areas (FIGS. 13-15, 13-17, and 13-25).

The form of the stone frames for the stained-glass windows also evolved. At Saint-Denis (FIG. 13-3A), Laon (FIG. 13-8), and on Chartres Cathedral's 12th-century west facade (FIG. 13-5), *plate tracery* holds the rose window in place. The glass fills only the "punched holes" in the heavy ornamental stonework. *Bar tracery*, a later development, is much more slender. The stained-glass windows of the Chartres transepts (FIG. 13-17) and on the facades of Amiens (FIG. 13-21) and Reims (FIG. 13-23) cathedrals fill almost the entire opening, and the stonework is unobtrusive, resembling delicate leading more than masonry wall.

*Hugh of Saint-Victor, *Speculum de mysteriis ecclesiae*, sermon 2.
†William Durandus, *Rationale divinorum officiorum*, 1.1.24. Translated by John Mason Neale and Benjamin Webb, *The Symbolism of Churches and Church Ornaments* (Leeds: T. W. Green, 1843), 28.
‡Translated by Erwin Panofsky, *Abbot Suger*, 73.

13-15 Stonemasons and sculptors, detail of a stained-glass window in the northernmost radiating chapel in the ambulatory, Chartres Cathedral, Chartres, France, ca. 1200–1220. ◼◀

Glaziers made stained-glass windows by fusing layers of colored glass, joining the pieces with lead strips, and painting the details in enamel. The windows transformed natural light into divine light.

13-16 Virgin and Child and angels (*Notre Dame de la Belle Verrière*), detail of a window in the choir of Chartres Cathedral, Chartres, France, ca. 1170, with 13th-century side panels. Stained glass, 12′ 9″ high. ◼◢

This stained-glass window miraculously survived the devastating Chartres fire of 1194. It has an armature of iron bands forming a grid over the entire design, an Early Gothic characteristic.

Chartres Cathedral retains almost the full complement of its original stained glass, paid for by workers' guilds (FIG. 13-15) and royalty (FIG. 13-17) alike. Although the tinted windows have a dimming effect, they transform the character of the church's interior in dramatic fashion. Gothic buildings that no longer have their original stained-glass windows give a false impression of what their designers intended.

One Chartres window that survived the fire of 1194 is the tall single lancet called *Notre Dame de la Belle Verrière* (Our Lady of the Beautiful Window, FIG. **13-16**). The central section with a red background, which depicts the Virgin Mary enthroned with the Christ Child in her lap, dates to about 1170. High Gothic glaziers added framing angels seen against a blue ground when they reinstalled the window in the south aisle of the 13th-century choir. Mary is here the beautiful young queen of Heaven, haloed, crowned, and accompanied by the dove of the Holy Spirit. Comparing this Virgin and Child with the enthroned Theotokos and Child (FIG. 9-19) of Hagia Sophia highlights not only the greater severity and aloofness of the Byzantine image but also the sharp difference between the light-reflecting mosaic medium and Gothic light-filtering stained glass. Gothic and Byzantine builders used light to transform the material world into the spiritual, but in opposite ways. In Gothic architecture, light entered from outside the building through a screen of stone-set colored glass. In Byzantine architecture, light reflected off myriad glass tesserae set into the thick masonry wall.

Chartres's 13th-century Gothic windows are even more spectacular than the *Belle Verrière* because the introduction of flying buttresses made it possible for builders to plan from the outset on filling entire walls with stained glass. The immense rose window (approx-

13-17 Rose window and lancets, north transept, Chartres Cathedral, Chartres, France, ca. 1220. Stained glass, rose window 43′ in diameter. ◼◢

Immense stained-glass rose and lancet windows, held in place by an intricate armature of bar tracery, fill almost the entire facade wall of the High Gothic north transept of Chartres Cathedral.

imately 43 feet in diameter) and tall lancets of the north transept (FIG. **13-17**) were the gift of Queen Blanche of Castile, around 1220. The royal motifs of yellow castles on a red ground and yellow *fleurs-de-lis*—three-petaled iris flowers (compare FIG. 25-24), France's royal floral emblem—on a blue ground fill the eight narrow windows in the rose's lower spandrels. The iconography is also fitting for a queen. The enthroned Virgin and Child appear in the roundel at the center of the rose, which resembles a gem-studded book cover or cloisonné brooch. Around her are four doves of the Holy Spirit and eight angels. Twelve square panels contain images of Old Testament kings, including David and Solomon (at the 12 and 1 o'clock positions respectively). These are the royal ancestors of Christ. Isaiah (11:1–3) had prophesied the Messiah would come from the family of the patriarch Jesse, father of David. The genealogical "tree of Jesse" is a familiar motif in medieval art. Below, in the lancets, are Saint Anne and the baby Virgin. Flanking them are four of Christ's Old Testament ancestors, Melchizedek, David, Solomon, and Aaron, echoing the royal genealogy of the rose

13-18 Saint Theodore, jamb statue, left portal, Porch of the Martyrs, south transept, Chartres Cathedral, Chartres, France, ca. 1230.

Although the statue of Theodore is still attached to a column, the setting no longer determines its pose. The High Gothic sculptor portrayed the saint in a contrapposto stance, as in classical statuary.

but at a larger scale. Many Gothic stained-glass windows also present narrative scenes, and their iconographical programs are often more complex than those of the sculptured church portals. (The representation of masons and sculptors at work in FIG. 13-15, for example, is the lowest section of a lancet dedicated to the life of Caraunus—Chéron in French—a legendary local sixth-century martyr who was probably the patron saint of the Chartres stonemasons' guild.)

The rose and lancets change in hue and intensity with the hours, turning solid architecture into a floating vision of the celestial heavens. Almost the entire mass of wall opens up into stained glass, held in place by an intricate stone armature of bar tracery. Here, the Gothic passion for luminous colored light led to a most daring and successful attempt to subtract all superfluous material bulk just short of destabilizing the structure. That this vast, complex fabric of stone-set glass has maintained its structural integrity for almost 800 years attests to the Gothic builders' engineering genius.

13-18A Porch of the Confessors, Chartres, ca. 1220–1230. ■◄

CHARTRES SOUTH TRANSEPT

The sculptures adorning the portals of the two Chartres transepts erected after the 1194 fire are also prime examples of the new High Gothic spirit. As at Laon (FIG. 13-8) and Paris (FIG. 13-11) cathedrals, the Chartres transept portals project more forcefully from the church than do the Early Gothic portals of its west facade (compare FIGS. 13-1 and 13-5). Similarly, the statues of saints (FIGS. **13-18** and **13-18A**) on the portal jambs, which date from 1220 to 1230, are more independent from the architectural framework. Although the figures

are still attached to columns, the architectural setting does not determine their poses as much as it did on the west portals (FIG. 13-7).

The masterpiece of the south transept is the figure of Saint Theodore (FIG. 13-18), the martyred warrior on the left jamb of the left portal (the Porch of the Martyrs). It reveals the great changes Gothic sculpture had undergone since the Royal Portal statues of the mid-12th century. The High Gothic sculptor portrayed Theodore as the ideal Christian knight, clothing him in the cloak and chain-mail armor of 13th-century Crusaders. The handsome, long-haired youth holds his spear firmly in his right hand and rests his left hand on his shield. He turns his head to the left and swings out his hip to the right. The body's resulting torsion and pronounced sway recall ancient Greek statuary, especially the contrapposto stance of Polykleitos's *Spear Bearer* (FIG. 5-40). The changes that occurred in 13th-century Gothic sculpture echo the revolutionary developments in ancient Greek sculpture during the transition from the Archaic to the Classical style (see Chapter 5) and could appropriately be described as a second "Classical revolution."

AMIENS CATHEDRAL Chartres Cathedral was one of the most influential buildings in the history of architecture. Its builders set a pattern many other Gothic architects followed, even if they refined the details. Construction of Amiens Cathedral (FIG. **13-19**) began in 1220 while work was still in progress at Chartres. The architects were ROBERT DE LUZARCHES, THOMAS DE CORMONT, and RENAUD

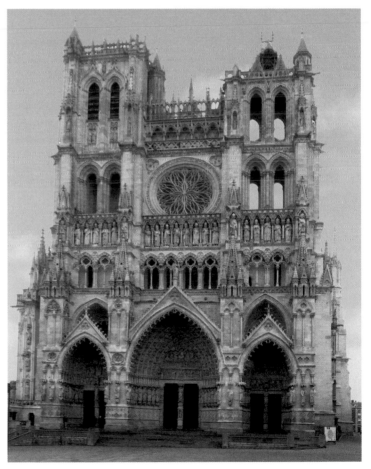

13-19 ROBERT DE LUZARCHES, THOMAS DE CORMONT, and RENAUD DE CORMONT, west facade of Amiens Cathedral, Amiens, France, begun 1220. ■◄

The deep piercing of the Amiens facade left few surfaces for decoration, but sculptors covered the remaining ones with colonnettes, pinnacles, and rosettes that nearly dissolve the structure's masonry.

France **377**

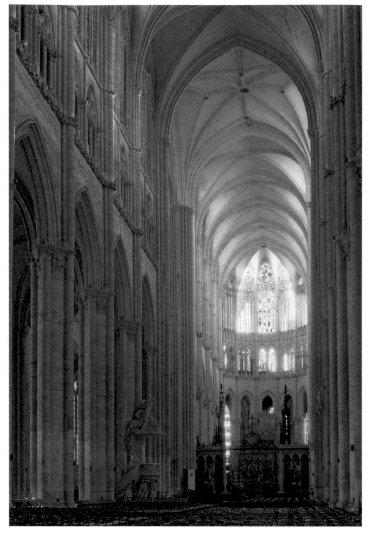

13-20 ROBERT DE LUZARCHES, THOMAS DE CORMONT, and RENAUD DE CORMONT, interior of Amiens Cathedral (looking east), Amiens, France, begun 1220. ◼◀

The concept of a self-sustaining skeletal architecture reached full maturity at Amiens Cathedral. The four-part vaults on pointed arches rise an astounding 144 feet above the nave floor.

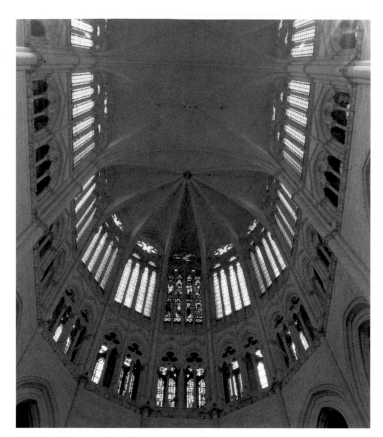

13-21 ROBERT DE LUZARCHES, THOMAS DE CORMONT, and RENAUD DE CORMONT, vaults, clerestory, and triforium of the choir of Amiens Cathedral, Amiens, France, begun 1220. ◼◀

The Amiens choir vaults resemble a canopy on bundled masts. The light entering from the clerestory and triforium creates a buoyant lightness not normally associated with stone architecture.

DE CORMONT. The builders finished the nave (FIG. 13-20) by 1236 and the radiating chapels by 1247, but work on the choir (FIG. 13-21) continued until almost 1270. The Amiens elevation (FIG. 13-10d) derived from the High Gothic formula of Chartres (FIG. 13-10c). But Amiens Cathedral's proportions are more slender, and the number and complexity of the lancet windows in both its clerestory and triforium are greater. The whole design reflects the builders' confident use of the complete High Gothic structural vocabulary: the rectangular-bay system, the four-part rib vault, and a buttressing system that made possible the almost complete elimination of heavy masses and thick weight-bearing walls. At Amiens, the concept of a self-sustaining skeletal architecture reached full maturity. The remaining stretches of wall seem to serve no purpose other than to provide a weather screen for the interior.

Amiens Cathedral is one of the most impressive examples of the French Gothic obsession with constructing ever-taller cathedrals. Using their new skeletal frames of stone, French builders attempted goals almost beyond limit, pushing to new heights with increasingly slender supports. The nave vaults at Laon rise to a

height of about 80 feet, at Paris 115 feet, and at Chartres 120 feet. Those at Amiens are 144 feet above the floor (FIG. 13-10). The most daring quest for exceptional height occurred at Beauvais (FIG. I-2), where the choir vaults are 157 feet high—but the builders never completed the cathedral. The Beauvais vaults are unstable and require additional buttressing today.

At Amiens, the lines of the vault ribs converge to the colonnettes and speed down the shell-like walls to the compound piers (FIG. 13-20). Almost every part of the superstructure has its corresponding element below. The overall effect is of effortless strength, of a buoyant lightness not normally associated with stone architecture. Viewed directly from below, the choir vaults (FIG. 13-21) resemble a canopy, tentlike and suspended from bundled masts. The light flooding in from the clerestory makes the vaults seem even more insubstantial. The effect recalls another great building, one utterly different from Amiens but where light also plays a defining role: Hagia Sophia (FIG. 9-8) in Constantinople. At Amiens, the designers also reduced the building's physical mass by structural ingenuity and daring, and light further dematerializes what remains. If Hagia Sophia is the perfect expression of Byzantine spirituality in architecture, Amiens, with its soaring vaults and giant windows admitting divine colored light, is its Gothic counterpart.

Work began on the Amiens west facade (FIG. 13-19) at the same time as the nave (1220). Its lower parts reflect the influence of Laon Cathedral (FIG. 13-8) in the spacing of the funnel-like and gable-covered portals. But the Amiens builders punctured the upper parts

13-22 Christ (*Beau Dieu*), trumeau statue of the central doorway of the west facade, Amiens Cathedral, Amiens, France, ca. 1220–1235. ■◀

The *Beau Dieu* blesses all who enter Amiens Cathedral. He tramples a lion and dragon symbolizing the evil forces in the world. This benevolent Gothic Christ gives humankind hope in salvation.

13-23 GAUCHER DE REIMS and BERNARD DE SOISSONS, west facade of Reims Cathedral, Reims, France, ca. 1225–1290.

Reims Cathedral's facade reveals the High Gothic architect's desire to replace heavy masonry with intricately framed voids. Stained-glass windows, not stone reliefs, fill the three tympana.

of the facade to an even greater degree than did the Laon designer. The deep piercing of walls and towers at Amiens left few areas for decoration, but sculptors covered the remaining surfaces with a network of colonnettes, arches, pinnacles, rosettes, and other decorative stonework that visually screens and nearly dissolves the structure's solid core. Sculpture also extends to the areas above the portals, especially the band of statues (the so-called kings' gallery) running the full width of the facade directly below the rose window (with 15th-century tracery). The uneven towers were later additions. The shorter one dates from the 14th century, the taller one from the 15th century.

BEAU DIEU Greeting worshipers as they enter the cathedral is the statue the French call *Beau Dieu* (Beautiful God; FIG. **13-22**) on the central doorway's trumeau. The High Gothic sculptor fully modeled Christ's figure, enveloping his body with massive drapery folds cascading from his waist. Compared with the kings and queens (FIG. 13-7) of the Royal Portal, the *Beau Dieu* is almost independent of its architectural setting. Nonetheless, the statue is still attached to the trumeau, and the sculptor placed an architectural canopy over Christ's head. The canopy mimics the east end of a 13th-century cathedral with a series of radiating chapels boasting elegant lancet windows in the latest Gothic style. Above the *Beau Dieu* is the great central tympanum with the representation of Christ as last judge. The trumeau Christ does not strike terror into sinners, however. Instead he blesses those who enter the church and tramples a lion and a dragon symbolizing the evil forces in the world. This image of Christ gives humankind hope in salvation. The *Beau*

Dieu epitomizes the bearded, benevolent Gothic image of Christ that replaced the youthful Early Christian Christ (FIG. 8-8) and the stern Byzantine Pantocrator (FIG. 9-23) as the preferred representation of the Savior in later European art. The handsome figure's quiet grace and grandeur also contrast sharply with the emotional intensity of the twisting Romanesque prophet (FIG. 12-13) carved in relief on the Moissac trumeau.

REIMS CATHEDRAL Construction of Reims Cathedral, for centuries the site of all French kings' coronations, began only a few years after work commenced at Amiens. GAUCHER DE REIMS and BERNARD DE SOISSONS, who were primarily responsible for the west facade (FIG. **13-23**), carried the High Gothic style of Amiens still further, both architecturally and sculpturally. The Amiens and Reims facades, although similar, display some significant differences. The *kings' gallery* of statues at Reims is *above* the great rose window, and the figures stand in taller and more ornate frames. In fact, the builders "stretched" every detail of the facade. The openings in the towers and those to the left and right of the rose window are taller, narrower, and more intricately decorated, and they more closely

13-23A Interior of Reims Cathedral, begun 1211. ◼◀

resemble the elegant lancets of the clerestory within (FIG. **13-23A**). A pointed arch also frames the rose window itself, and the pinnacles over the portals are taller and more elaborate than those at Amiens. Most striking, however, is the treatment of the tympana over the doorways, where stained-glass windows replaced the stone relief sculpture of earlier facades. The contrast with Romanesque heavy masonry construction (FIG. 12-30) is extreme. No less noteworthy, however, is the rapid transformation of the Gothic facade since the 12th-century designs of Saint-Denis (FIG. 13-3A) and Chartres (FIG. 13-5) and even Laon (FIG. 13-8).

Reims Cathedral is also a prime example of the High Gothic style in sculpture. The statues and reliefs of the west facade celebrate the Virgin Mary. Above the central gable, Mary is crowned as queen of Heaven. On the trumeau, she is the youthful Mother of God above reliefs depicting original sin. (Many medieval theologians considered Mary the new Eve.) The jamb statues to her left and right relate episodes from the infancy cycle (see "The Life of Jesus in Art," Chapter 8, pages 240–241), including *Annunciation* and *Visitation* (FIG. **13-24**). The statues appear completely detached from their architectural background because the sculptors shrank the supporting columns into insignificance. The columns in no way restrict the free and easy movements of the full-bodied figures. These 13th-century jamb statues contrast strikingly with those of the Early Gothic Royal Portal (FIG. 13-7), where the background columns occupy a volume equal to that of the figures.

The Reims statues also vividly illustrate how long it frequently took to complete the sculptural ornamentation of a large Gothic cathedral. Sculptural projects of this magnitude normally required decades to complete and entailed hiring many sculptors often working in diverse styles. Art historians believe three different sculptors carved the four statues in FIG. 13-24 at different times during the quarter century from 1230 to 1255. The *Visitation* group (FIG. 13-24, *right*) is the work of one of the many artists of the era—in Germany and Italy as well as France—who must

have studied classical statuary. Reims was an ancient Roman city. The heads of both Mary and Saint Elizabeth resemble Roman portraits, and the rich folds of the garments they wear also recall Roman statuary (FIG. 7-61). The Gothic statues closely approximate the classical naturalistic style and feature contrapposto postures in which the swaying of the hips is much more pronounced than in the Chartres's Saint Theodore (FIG. 13-18). The right legs of the Reims figures bend, and the knees press through the rippling folds of the garments. The sculptor also set the holy figures' arms in motion. Mary and Elizabeth turn their faces toward each other, and they converse through gestures. In the Reims *Visitation* group, the formerly isolated Gothic jamb statues became actors in a biblical narrative.

The statues in the *Annunciation* group (FIG. 13-24, *left*) also stand free from their architectural setting, but they are products of different workshops. Mary is a slender figure with severe drapery. This artist preferred broad expanses of fabric to the multiplicity of folds of the *Visitation* Mary. The angel Gabriel, the latest of the four statues, exhibits the elegant style of the Parisian court at the middle of the 13th century. Gabriel has a much more elongated body and is far more animated than his neighbors. He pivots gracefully, almost as if dancing, and smiles broadly. Like a courtier, Gabriel exudes charm. Mary, in contrast, is serious and introspective and does not respond overtly to the news the angel has brought.

SAINTE-CHAPELLE, PARIS The stained-glass windows inserted into the portal tympana of Reims Cathedral exemplify the wall-dissolving High Gothic architectural style. The architect of Sainte-Chapelle (FIG. 13-25) in Paris extended this style to an entire building. Louis IX built Sainte-Chapelle, joined to the royal palace, as a repository for the crown of thorns and other relics of Christ's

13-24 *Annunciation* and *Visitation*, jamb statues on the right side of the central doorway of the west facade, Reims Cathedral, Reims, France, ca. 1230–1255. ◼◀

Several sculptors working in diverse styles carved the Reims jamb statues, but all the figures resemble freestanding statues with bodies and arms in motion. The biblical figures converse through gestures.

passion he had purchased in 1239 from his cousin Baldwin II (r. 1228–1261), the Latin emperor of Constantinople. The chapel is a masterpiece of the so-called *Rayonnant* (radiant) style of the High Gothic age, which dominated the second half of the 13th century. It was the preferred style of the Parisian court of Saint Louis (see "Louis IX," page 385). Sainte-Chapelle's architect carried the dissolution of walls and the reduction of the bulk of the supports to the point that some 6,450 square feet of stained glass make up more than three-quarters of the structure. The supporting elements are hardly more than large *mullions,* or vertical stone bars. The emphasis is on the extreme slenderness of the architectural forms and on linearity in general. Although the chapel required restoration in the 19th century (after suffering damage during the French Revolution), it retains most of its original 13th-century stained glass. Sainte-Chapelle's enormous windows filter the light and fill the interior with an unearthly rose-violet atmosphere. Approximately 49 feet high and 15 feet wide, they were the largest stained-glass windows designed up to their time.

VIRGIN OF PARIS The "court style" of Sainte-Chapelle has its pictorial parallel in the mannered elegance of the roughly contemporaneous Gabriel of the Reims *Annunciation* group (FIG. 13-24,

left), but the style long outlived Saint Louis and his royal artists and architects. An example of the court style in Late Gothic sculpture is the early-14th-century statue nicknamed the *Virgin of Paris* (FIG. 13-26) because of its location in the Parisian Cathedral of Notre-Dame. The sculptor portrayed Mary in an exaggerated S-curve posture typical of Late Gothic sculpture. She is a worldly queen and wears a heavy gem-encrusted crown. The princely Christ Child reaches toward his young mother. The tender, anecdotal characterization of mother and son seen here is a later manifestation of the humanization of the portrayal of religious figures in Gothic sculpture that began at Chartres and developed especially in Germany (FIGS. 13-48 to 13-50). Late Gothic statuary is very different in tone from the solemnity of most High Gothic figures, just as Late Classical Greek statues of the Olympian gods differ from High Classical depictions (compare FIG. 13-26 with FIG. 5-63).

SAINT-MACLOU, ROUEN Late French Gothic architecture also represents a departure from the norms of High Gothic. The change from Rayonnant architecture to the *Flamboyant* style (named for the flamelike appearance of its pointed bar tracery) occurred in the 14th century. The new manner reached its florid maturity nearly a century later in Rouen, the capital of Normandy,

13-25 Interior of the upper chapel (looking northeast), Sainte-Chapelle, Paris, France, 1243–1248. ◼◀

At Louis IX's Sainte-Chapelle, the architect succeeded in dissolving the walls to such an extent that 6,450 square feet of stained glass account for more than three-quarters of the Rayonnant Gothic structure.

13-26 Virgin and Child (*Virgin of Paris*), Notre-Dame, Paris, France, early 14th century. ◼◀

Late Gothic sculpture is elegant and mannered. Here, the solemnity of Early and High Gothic religious figures gave way to a tender, anecdotal portrayal of Mary and Jesus as royal mother and son.

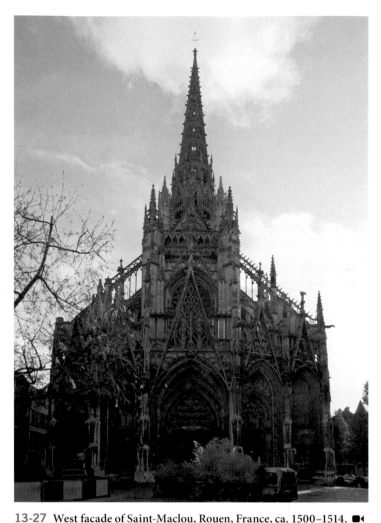

13-27 West facade of Saint-Maclou, Rouen, France, ca. 1500–1514. ◼◀

Saint-Maclou is the masterpiece of Late Gothic Flamboyant architecture. Its ornate tracery of curves and countercurves forms brittle decorative webs masking the building's structure.

in the church of Saint-Maclou (FIG. **13-27**). The shrine is tiny (only about 75 feet high and 180 feet long) compared with 13th-century cathedrals, and its facade breaks sharply from the High Gothic style (FIGS. 13-21 and 13-23). The five portals (two of them false doors) bend outward in an arc. Ornate gables crown the doorways, pierced through and filled with wiry, "flickering" Flamboyant tracery. Made up of curves and countercurves forming brittle decorative webs, the ornate Late Gothic tracery masks the building's structure. The transparency of the pinnacles over the doorways enables visitors to see the central rose window and the flying buttresses, even though they are set well back from the facade. The overlapping of all features, pierced as they are, confuses the structural lines and produces a bewildering complexity of views that is the hallmark of the Flamboyant style.

CARCASSONNE The Gothic period may have been the age of the great cathedrals, but widespread prosperity also stimulated the construction of major secular buildings such as town halls, palaces, and private residences. In a time of frequent warfare, the feudal barons often had constructed fortified castles in places enemies could not easily reach. Sometimes thick defensive wall circuits or *ramparts* enclosed entire towns. In time, however, purely defensive wars became obsolete due to the invention of artillery and improvements in siege craft. The fortress era gradually passed, and throughout Europe once-mighty ramparts fell into ruin.

Carcassonne (FIG. **13-28**) in Languedoc in southern France, once the regional center of resistance to the northern forces of royal France, is the best-preserved example of a Gothic fortified town. Restored in the 19th century by EUGÈNE VIOLLET-LE-DUC (1814–1879), Carcassonne occupies a site on a hill bounded by the Aude River. Fortified since Roman times, it has Visigothic walls dating from the 6th century, reinforced in the 12th century. *Battlements* (low parapets) with *crenellations* (composed of alternating solid *merlons* and open *crenels*) protected guards patrolling the stone ring surrounding the town. Carcassonne might be forced to surrender but could not easily be taken by storm. Within the town's double

13-28 Aerial view of the fortified town of Carcassonne (looking west), France. Bastions and towers, 12th–13th centuries, restored by EUGÈNE VIOLLET-LE-DUC in the 19th century.

Carcassonne provides a rare glimpse of what was once a familiar sight in Gothic France: a tight complex of castle, cathedral, and town with a crenellated and towered wall circuit for defense.

13-29 Hall of the cloth guild, Bruges, Belgium, begun 1230.

The Bruges cloth guild's meeting hall is an early example of a new type of secular architecture in the late Middle Ages. Its lofty tower competed for attention with the towers of the cathedral.

13-30 Inner facade and courtyard of the house of Jacques Coeur, Bourges, France, 1443–1451. ◀

The townhouse of the wealthy Bourges financier Jacques Coeur is both a splendid example of Late Gothic architecture with elaborate tracery and a symbol of the period's new secular spirit.

walls was a fortified castle (FIG. 13-28, *right*) with a massive attached *keep*, a secure tower that could serve as a place of last refuge. Balancing that center of secular power was the bishop's seat, the cathedral of Saint-Nazaire (FIG. 13-28, *left*). The small church, built between 1269 and 1329, may have been the work of an architect brought in from northern France. In any case, Saint-Nazaire's builders were certainly familiar with the latest developments in architecture in the Île-de-France. Today, Carcassonne provides a rare glimpse of what was once a familiar sight in Gothic France: a tightly contained complex of castle, cathedral, and town within towered walls.

GUILD HALL, BRUGES One of the many signs of the growing secularization of urban life in the late Middle Ages was the erection of monumental meeting halls and warehouses for the increasing number of craft guilds being formed throughout Europe. An early example is the imposing market and guild hall (FIG. **13-29**) of the clothmakers of Bruges, begun in 1230. Situated in the city's major square, it testifies to the important role of artisans and merchants in Gothic Europe. The design combines features of military construction (the corner watchtowers with their crenellations) and ecclesiastical architecture (lancet windows with crowning oculi). The uppermost, octagonal portion of the tower with its flying buttresses and pinnacles dates to the 15th century, but even the original two-story

tower is taller than the rest of the hall. Lofty towers, a common feature of late medieval guild and town halls (compare FIGS. 14-15 and 14-18B), were designed to compete for attention and prestige with the towers of city cathedrals.

HOUSE OF JACQUES COEUR The new class of wealthy merchants who rose to prominence throughout Europe in the late Middle Ages may not have accumulated fortunes equaling those of the hereditary royalty, but they still wielded enormous power and influence. The career of the French financier Jacques Coeur (1395–1456) illustrates how enterprising private citizens could win and quickly lose—wealth and power. Coeur had banking houses in every major city of France and many cities abroad. He employed more than 300 agents and competed with the great trading republics of Italy. His merchant ships filled the Mediterranean, and with the papacy's permission, he imported spices and textiles from Muslim lands to the east. He was the treasurer of King Charles VII (r. 1422–1461) of France and a friend of Pope Nicholas V (r. 1447–1455). In 1451, however, his enemies framed him on an absurd charge of having poisoned Agnes Sorel (1421–1450), the king's mistress. The judges who sentenced Coeur to prison and confiscated his vast wealth and property were among those who owed him money. Coeur escaped in 1454 and made his way to Rome, where the pope warmly received him. He died of fever while leading a fleet of papal war galleys in the eastern Mediterranean.

Jacques Coeur's great townhouse still stands in his native city of Bourges. Built between 1443 and 1451 (with special permission to encroach upon the town ramparts), it is the best-preserved example of Late Gothic domestic architecture. The house's plan is irregular, with the units arranged around an open courtyard (FIG. **13-30**). The service areas (maintenance shops, storage rooms, servants' quarters, and baths—a rare luxury anywhere until the 20th century) occupy the ground level. The upper stories house the great hall and auxiliary rooms used for offices and family living rooms. Over the main entrance is a private chapel. One of the towers served as a treasury. The exterior and interior facades have steep pyramidal roofs of different heights. Decorative details include Flamboyant tracery and large pointed-arch stained-glass windows. An elegant canopied niche facing the street once housed a royal equestrian statue. A comparable statue of Coeur on horseback dominated the facade opening onto the interior courtyard. Jacques Coeur's house is both a splendid example of Late Gothic architecture and a monumental symbol of the period's new secular spirit.

Book Illumination and Luxury Arts

Paris's claim as the intellectual center of Gothic Europe (see "Paris," page 372) did not rest solely on the stature of its university faculty and the reputation of its architects, masons, sculptors, and stained-glass makers. The city was also a renowned center for the production of fine books. Dante Alighieri (1265–1321), the famous Florentine poet, in fact, referred to Paris in his *Divine Comedy* (ca. 1310–1320) as the city famed for the art of illumination.[2] During the Gothic period, bookmaking shifted from monastic scriptoria shut off from the world to urban workshops of professional artists—and Paris boasted the most and best workshops. The owners of these new for-profit secular businesses sold their products to the royal family, scholars, and prosperous merchants. The Parisian shops were the forerunners of modern publishing houses.

VILLARD DE HONNECOURT One of the most intriguing Parisian manuscripts preserved today was not, however, a book for sale but a personal sketchbook. Compiled by VILLARD DE HONNECOURT, an early-13th-century master mason, its pages contain plans of choirs with radiating chapels and drawings of church towers, lifting devices, a sawmill, stained-glass windows, and other subjects of obvious interest to architects and masons. But also sprinkled liberally throughout the pages are pictures of religious and worldly figures as well as animals, some realistic and others purely fantastic. On the page reproduced here (FIG. 13-31), Villard demonstrated the value of the *ars de geometria* (art of geometry) to artists, showing how both natural forms and buildings are based on simple geometric shapes such as the square, circle, and triangle. Even when he claimed he drew his animals from nature, he composed his figures around a skeleton not of bones but of abstract geometric forms. Geometry was, in Villard's words, "strong help in drawing figures."

GOD AS CREATOR Geometry also played a symbolic role in Gothic art and architecture. Gothic artists, architects, and theolo-

1 in.

13-31 VILLARD DE HONNECOURT, figures based on geometric shapes, folio 18 verso of a sketchbook, from Paris, France, ca. 1220–1235. Ink on vellum, $9\frac{1}{4}'' \times 6''$. Bibliothèque Nationale, Paris.

On this page from his private sketchbook, the master mason Villard de Honnecourt sought to demonstrate how simple geometric shapes are the basis of both natural forms and buildings.

1 in.

13-32 *God as Creator of the World,* folio 1 verso of a moralized Bible, from Paris, France, ca. 1220–1230. Ink, tempera, and gold leaf on vellum, $1' 1\frac{1}{2}'' \times 8\frac{1}{4}''$. Österreichische Nationalbibliothek, Vienna.

Paris boasted renowned workshops for the production of illuminated manuscripts. In this book, the artist portrayed God in the process of creating the universe using a Gothic builder's compass.

Louis IX, the Saintly King

The royal patron behind the Parisian Rayonnant court style of Gothic art and architecture was King Louis IX (1215–1270; r. 1226–1270), grandson of Philip Augustus. Louis inherited the throne when he was only 12 years old, so until he reached adulthood 6 years later, his mother, Blanche of Castile (FIG. 13-33), granddaughter of Eleanor of Aquitaine (see "Romanesque Countesses, Queens, and Nuns," Chapter 12, page 352), served as France's regent.

The French regarded Louis as the ideal king. In 1297, only 27 years after Louis's death, Pope Boniface VIII (r. 1294–1303) declared the king a saint. In his own time, Louis was revered for his piety, justice, truthfulness, and charity. His almsgiving and his donations to religious foundations were extravagant. He especially favored the *mendicant* (begging) orders, the Dominicans and Franciscans (see "Mendicant Orders," Chapter 14, page 404), as he admired their poverty, piety, and self-sacrificing disregard of material things.

Louis launched two unsuccessful Crusades (see "Crusades," Chapter 12, page 346), the Seventh (1248–1254, when, in her son's absence, Blanche was again French regent) and the Eighth (1270). He died in Tunisia during the latter. As a crusading knight who lost his life in the service of the Church, Louis personified the chivalric virtues of courage, loyalty, and self-sacrifice. Saint Louis united in his person the best qualities of the Christian knight, the benevolent monarch, and the holy man. He became the model of medieval Christian kingship.

Louis's political accomplishments were also noteworthy. He subdued the unruly French barons, and between 1243 and 1314 no one seriously challenged the crown. He negotiated a treaty with Henry III (r. 1216–1272), king of France's traditional enemy, Eng-

13-33 Blanche of Castile, Louis IX, and two monks, dedication page (folio 8 recto) of a moralized Bible, from Paris, France, 1226–1234. Ink, tempera, and gold leaf on vellum, $1' 3'' \times 10\frac{1}{2}''$. Pierpont Morgan Library, New York.

The dedication page of this royal book depicts Saint Louis, his mother and French regent Blanche of Castile, a monk, and a lay scribe at work on the paired illustrations of a moralized Bible.

1 in.

land. Such was his reputation for integrity and just dealing that he served as arbiter in at least a dozen international disputes. So successful was he as peacekeeper that despite civil wars through most of the 13th century, international peace prevailed. Under Saint Louis, medieval France was at its most prosperous, and its art and architecture were admired and imitated throughout Europe.

gians alike thought the triangle, for example, embodied the Trinity of God the Father, Christ, and the Holy Spirit. The circle, which has neither a beginning nor an end, symbolized the eternity of the one God. The book of Revelation (21.12–21) describes the Heavenly Jerusalem as a walled city in the form of a perfect square with 12 gates. When Gothic architects based their designs on the art of geometry, building their forms out of abstract shapes laden with symbolic meaning, they believed they were working according to the divinely established laws of nature.

A vivid illustration of this concept appears as the frontispiece (FIG. **13-32**) of a moralized Bible produced in Paris during the 1220s. *Moralized Bibles* are heavily illustrated, each page pairing paintings of Old and New Testament episodes with explanations of their moral significance. The page reproduced here does not conform to this formula because it is the introduction to all that follows. Above the illustration, the scribe wrote (in French rather than Latin): "Here God creates heaven and earth, the sun and moon, and all the elements." The painter depicted God in the process of creating the world, shaping the universe with the aid of a compass. Within the perfect circle already created are the spherical sun and

moon and the unformed matter that will become the earth once God applies the same geometric principles to it. In contrast to the biblical account of creation, in which God created the sun, moon, and stars after the earth had been formed, and made the world by sheer force of will and a simple "Let there be" command, the Gothic artist portrayed God as systematically creating the universe with what Villard would describe as "the strong help of geometry."

BLANCHE OF CASTILE Not surprisingly, some of the finest Gothic books known today belonged to the French monarchy. Saint Louis in particular was an avid collector of both secular and religious books (see "Louis IX, the Saintly King," above). He and his royal predecessors and successors formed a vast library that eventually became the core of France's national library, the Bibliothèque Nationale.

One book the royal family commissioned is a moralized Bible now in the collection of New York's Pierpont Morgan Library. Louis's mother, Blanche of Castile, ordered the Bible during her regency (1226–1234) for her teenage son. The dedication page (FIG. **13-33**) has a costly gold background and depicts Blanche and Louis enthroned beneath triple-lobed arches and miniature cityscapes. The latter are comparable to the architectural canopies above the heads of contemporaneous French portal statues (FIGS. 13-18 and 13-22). With vivid gestures, Blanche instructs the young Louis, underscoring her superior position. (The prominence of Mary as queen of Heaven in Gothic art parallels the rising influence of secular queens in Gothic Europe.) Below Blanche and Louis, in similar architectural frames, are a monk and a professional lay scribe. The older clergyman instructs the scribe, who already has divided his page into two columns of four roundels each, a format often used for the paired illustrations of moralized Bibles. The inspirations for such pages filled with circular frames were probably the roundels of Gothic stained-glass windows (compare the windows of Louis's own later Sainte-Chapelle, FIG. 13-25, in Paris).

The picture of Gothic book production on the dedication page of Blanche of Castile's moralized Bible is a very abbreviated one, as was the view of a monastic scriptorium discussed earlier (FIG. 11-11). Indeed, the manufacturing processes used in the workshops of 13th-century Paris and 10th-century Tábara did not differ significantly. Bookmaking involved many steps and numerous specialized artists, scribes, and assistants of varying skill levels. The Benedictine abbot Johannes Trithemius (1462–1516) described the way books were still made in his day in his treatise *In Praise of Scribes*:

> If you do not know how to write, you still can assist the scribes
> in various ways. One of you can correct what another has writ-
> ten. Another can add the rubrics [headings] to the corrected text.
> A third can add initials and signs of division. Still another can
> arrange the leaves and attach the binding. Another of you can
> prepare the covers, the leather, the buckles and clasps. All sorts
> of assistance can be offered the scribe to help him pursue his
> work without interruption. He needs many things which can be
> prepared by others: parchment cut, flattened and ruled for script,
> ready ink and pens. You will always find something with which to
> help the scribe.[3]

Preparation of the illuminated pages also involved several hands. Some artists, for example, specialized in painting borders or initials. Only the workshop head or one of the most advanced assistants would paint the main figural scenes. Given this division of labor and the assembly-line nature of Gothic book production, it is astonishing how uniform the style is on a single page, as well as from page to page, in most illuminated manuscripts.

PSALTER OF SAINT LOUIS The golden background of Blanche's Bible is unusual and has no parallel in Gothic windows. But the radiance of stained glass probably inspired the glowing color of other 13th-century Parisian illuminated manuscripts. In some cases, masters in the same urban workshop produced both glass and books. Many art historians believe the *Psalter of Saint Louis* (FIG. **13-34**) is one of several books produced in Paris for Louis IX by artists associated with those who made the stained glass for his Sainte-Chapelle. Certainly, the painted architectural setting in Louis's book of Psalms reflects the pierced screenlike lightness and transparency of royal Rayonnant buildings such as Sainte-Chapelle. The intense colors, especially the blues, emulate stained glass, and the lines in the borders resemble leading. The gables, pierced by rose windows with bar tracery, are standard Rayonnant architectural features.

On the page from the *Psalter of Saint Louis* shown here (FIG. 13-34), the illuminator represented *Abraham and the Three*

13-34 *Abraham and the Three Angels,* folio 7 verso of the *Psalter of Saint Louis,* from Paris, France, 1253–1270. Ink, tempera, and gold leaf on vellum, 5″ × 3½″. Bibliothèque Nationale, Paris.

The architectural settings in the *Psalter of Saint Louis* reflect the lightness and transparency of Parisian royal buildings, such as Sainte-Chapelle (FIG. 13-25). The colors emulate stained glass.

1 in.

Angels, the Old Testament story Christians believed prefigured the Trinity (see "Jewish Subjects in Christian Art," Chapter 8, page 238). Two episodes appear on the same page, separated by the tree of Mamre mentioned in the Bible. At the left, Abraham greets the three angels. In the other scene, he entertains them while his wife, Sarah, peers at them from a tent. The figures' delicate features and the linear wavy strands of their hair have parallels in Blanche of Castile's moralized Bible, as well as in Parisian stained glass. The elegant proportions, facial expressions, theatrical gestures, and swaying poses are characteristic of the Parisian court style admired throughout Europe. Compare, for example, the angel in the left foreground with the Gabriel statue (FIG. 13-24, *left*) of the Reims *Annunciation* group.

BREVIARY OF PHILIPPE LE BEL As in the Romanesque period, some Gothic manuscript illuminators signed their work. The names of others appear in royal accounts of payments made and similar official documents. One of the artists who produced books for the French court was MASTER HONORÉ, whose Parisian workshop was on the street known today as rue Boutebrie. Honoré illuminated a *breviary* (see "Medieval Books," Chapter 11, page 312) for Philippe le Bel (Philip the Fair, r. 1285–1314) in 1296. On the page illustrated here (FIG. **13-35**), Honoré painted two Old Testament scenes involving David. In the upper panel, Samuel

13-35 MASTER HONORÉ, *Samuel Anointing David* and *Battle of David and Goliath*, folio 7 verso of the *Breviary of Philippe le Bel*, from Paris, France, 1296. Ink and tempera on vellum, $7\frac{7}{8}'' \times 4\frac{7}{8}''$. Bibliothèque Nationale, Paris.

Master Honoré was one of the Parisian lay artists who produced books for the French monarchy. His figures are noteworthy for their sculptural volume and the play of light and shade on their bodies.

13-36 JEAN PUCELLE, *David before Saul*, folio 24 verso of the *Belleville Breviary*, from Paris, France, ca. 1325. Ink and tempera on vellum, $9\frac{1}{2}'' \times 6\frac{3}{4}''$. Bibliothèque Nationale, Paris.

Pucelle's fully modeled figures in architectural settings rendered in convincing perspective reveal his study of contemporaneous painting in Italy. He was also a close observer of plants and fauna.

anoints the youthful David. Below, while King Saul looks on, David prepares to aim his slingshot at his most famous opponent, the giant Goliath (who already touches the wound on his forehead). Immediately to the right, David slays Goliath with his sword.

Master Honoré's linear treatment of hair, his figures' delicate hands and gestures, and their elegant swaying postures are typical of Parisian painting of the time. But this painter was much more interested than most of his colleagues in giving his figures sculptural volume and showing the play of light on their bodies. Honoré showed little concern for locating his figures in space, however. The Goliath panel in Philippe's breviary has a textilelike decorative background, and the feet of the artist's figures frequently overlap the border. Compared with his contemporaries, Master Honoré pioneered naturalism in figure painting. Still, he approached the art of book illumination as a decorator of two-dimensional pages.

He did not embrace the classical notion that a painting should be an illusionistic window into a three-dimensional world.

BELLEVILLE BREVIARY David and Saul also are the subjects of a miniature painting at the top left of an elaborately decorated text page (FIG. **13-36**) in the *Belleville Breviary*, which JEAN PUCELLE of Paris painted around 1325. In this manuscript and the Book of Hours (FIG. **13-36A**) which he illuminated for Queen Jeanne d'Evreux, wife of Charles IV (r. 1322–1328), Pucelle outdid Honoré and other French artists by placing his fully modeled figures in three-dimensional architectural settings rendered in convincing perspective.

13-36A PUCELLE, *Hours of Jeanne d'Evreux*, ca. 1325–1328.

For example, he painted Saul as a weighty figure seated on a throne seen in three-quarter view, and he meticulously depicted the receding coffers of the barrel vault over the young David's head. Similar "stage sets" already had become commonplace in Italian painting, and art historians believe Pucelle visited Italy and studied Duccio di Buoninsegna's work (FIGS. 14-9 to 14-11) in Siena. Pucelle's (or an assistant's) renditions of plants, a bird, butterflies, a dragonfly, a fish, a snail, and a monkey also reveal a keen interest in and close observation of the natural world. Nonetheless, in the *Belleville Breviary,* the text still dominates the page, and the artist (and his patron) delighted in ornamental flourishes, fancy initial letters, and abstract patterns. In that respect, comparisons with panel paintings such as Duccio's are inappropriate. Pucelle's breviary remains firmly in the tradition of book illumination.

The *Belleville Breviary* is of special interest because Pucelle's name and those of some of his assistants appear at the end of the book, in a memorandum recording the payment they received for their work. Inscriptions in other Gothic illuminated books regularly state the production costs—the prices paid for materials, especially gold, and for the execution of initials, figures, flowery script, and other embellishments. By this time, illuminators were professional guild members, and their personal reputation guaranteed the quality of their work. Although the cost of materials was still the major factor determining a book's price, individual skill and "brand name" increasingly decided the value of the illuminator's services. The centuries-old monopoly of the Church in book production had ended.

VIRGIN OF JEANNE D'EVREUX The royal family also patronized goldsmiths, silversmiths, and other artists specializing in the production of luxury works in metal and enamel for churches, palaces, and private homes. Especially popular were statuettes of sacred figures, which the wealthy purchased either for private devotion or as gifts to churches. The Virgin Mary was a favored subject, reflecting her new prominence in the iconography of Gothic portal sculpture.

Perhaps the finest of these costly statuettes is the large silver-gilt figurine known as the *Virgin of Jeanne d'Evreux* (FIG. **13-37**). The French queen donated the image of the Virgin and Child to the royal abbey church of Saint-Denis in 1339. Mary stands on a rectangular base decorated with enamel scenes of Christ's passion. (Some art historians think the enamels are Jean Pucelle's work.) But no hint of grief appears in the beautiful young Mary's face. The Christ Child, also without a care in the world, playfully reaches for his mother. The elegant proportions of the two figures, Mary's emphatic swaying posture, the heavy drapery folds, and the intimate human characterization of mother and son are also features of the roughly contemporaneous *Virgin of Paris* (FIG. 13-26). The sculptor of large stone statues and the royal silversmith working at small scale approached the representation of the Virgin and Child in a similar fashion. In both instances, Mary appears not only as the Mother of Christ but also as the queen of Heaven. The Saint-Denis Mary originally had a crown on her head, and the scepter she holds is in the form of the *fleur-de-lis* (compare FIG. 13-17). The statuette also served as a reliquary. The Virgin's scepter contained hairs believed to come from Mary's head.

THE CASTLE OF LOVE Gothic artists produced luxurious objects for secular as well as religious contexts. Sometimes they decorated these costly pieces with stories of courtly love inspired by the romantic literature of the day, such as the account of Lancelot and Queen Guinevere, wife of King Arthur of Camelot. The French poet Chrétien de Troyes recorded their love affair in the late 12th century.

An interesting object of this type is a woman's jewelry box adorned with ivory relief panels. The theme of the panel illustrated here (FIG. **13-38**) is related to the allegorical poem *Romance of the*

1 in.

13-37 *Virgin of Jeanne d'Evreux,* **from the abbey church of Saint-Denis, France, 1339. Silver gilt and enamel, 2′ 3½″ high. Musée du Louvre, Paris.** ◼◀

Queen Jeanne d'Evreux donated this sumptuous reliquary-statuette to the royal abbey of Saint-Denis. It shares with the *Virgin of Paris* (FIG. 13-26) the intimate human characterization of the holy figures.

Rose by Guillaume de Lorris, written around 1225 to 1235 and completed by Jean de Meung between 1275 and 1280. At the left, the sculptor carved the allegory of the siege of the Castle of Love. Gothic knights attempt to capture love's fortress by shooting flowers from their bows and hurling baskets of roses over the walls from catapults. Among the castle's defenders is Cupid, who aims his arrow at one of the knights while a comrade scales the walls on a ladder. In the lid's central sections, two knights joust on horseback. Several maidens survey the contest from a balcony and cheer the knights on as trumpets blare. A youth in the crowd holds a hunting falcon. The

13-38 *Castle of Love,* lid of a jewelry box, from Paris, France, ca. 1330–1350. Ivory and iron, $4\frac{1}{2}'' \times 9\frac{3}{4}''$. Walters Art Museum, Baltimore.

French Gothic artists also created luxurious objects for homes. Adorning this jewelry casket are ivory reliefs inspired by the romantic literature of the day. Knights joust and storm the Castle of Love.

sport was a favorite pastime of the leisure class in the late Middle Ages. At the right, the victorious knight receives his prize (a bouquet of roses) from a chastely dressed maiden on horseback. The scenes on the sides of the box include the legend of the unicorn—a white horse with a single ivory horn, a medieval allegory of female virtue. Only a virgin could attract the rare animal, and any woman who could do so thereby demonstrated her moral purity. Although religious themes monopolized artistic production for churches in the Gothic age, secular themes figured prominently in private contexts. Unfortunately, very few examples of the latter survive.

ENGLAND

13-38A Santa María, Léon, begun 1254.

In 1269, the prior (deputy abbot) of the church of Saint Peter at Wimpfen-im-Tal in the German Rhineland hired "a very experienced architect who had recently come from the city of Paris" to rebuild his monastery church.[4] The architect reconstructed the church *opere francigeno* (in the French manner)—that is, in the Gothic style, the *opus modernum* of the Île-de-France. A French architect may also have designed the Cathedral of Santa María (FIG. 13-38A) at Léon in northern Spain, begun in 1254. The spread of the Parisian Gothic style had begun even earlier, but in the second half of the 13th century, the new style became dominant throughout the Continent. European architecture did not, however, turn Gothic all at once or even uniformly. Almost everywhere, patrons and builders modified the court style of the Île-de-France according to local preferences. Because the old Romanesque traditions lingered on in many places, each area,

marrying its local Romanesque design to the new style, developed its own brand of Gothic architecture.

Beginning with the Norman conquest in 1066 (see Chapter 12), French artistic and architectural styles quickly had an influence in England, but in the Gothic period, as in the Romanesque, English artworks (for example, RICHARD DE BELLO'S *mappamundi* in Hereford Cathedral, FIG. 13-38B) have a distinctive character.

13-38B *Mappamundi* of Henry III, ca. 1277–1289.

SALISBURY CATHEDRAL English Gothic churches cannot be mistaken for French ones. The English Gothic style reflects an aesthetic sensibility quite different from French Gothic in emphasizing linear pattern and horizontality instead of structural logic and verticality. Salisbury Cathedral (FIGS. **13-39** to **13-41**), begun in 1220—the same year work started on Amiens Cathedral (FIGS. 13-19 to 13-21)—embodies these essential characteristics. The building campaign lasted about 40 years. The two cathedrals thus are almost exactly contemporaneous, and the differences between them are instructive. Although Salisbury's facade incorporates some of the superficial motifs of French Gothic architecture—for example, lancet windows and blind arcades with pointed arches as well as statuary—it presents a striking contrast to French High Gothic designs (FIGS. 13-21 and 13-23). The English facade is a squat screen in front of the nave, wider than the building behind it. The architect did not seek to match the soaring height of French facades or try to make the facade correspond to the three-part division of the interior (nave and two aisles). Different, too, is the emphasis on the great crossing tower (added around 1320–1330), which

13-41 Interior of Salisbury Cathedral (looking east), Salisbury, England, 1220–1258.

Salisbury Cathedral's interior differs from contemporaneous French Gothic designs in the strong horizontal emphasis of its three-story elevation and the use of dark Purbeck marble for moldings.

13-39 Aerial view of Salisbury Cathedral (looking northeast), Salisbury, England, 1220–1258; west facade completed 1265; spire ca. 1320–1330. ◼◀

Exhibiting the distinctive regional features of English Gothic architecture, Salisbury Cathedral has a squat facade that is wider than the building behind it. The architects used flying buttresses sparingly.

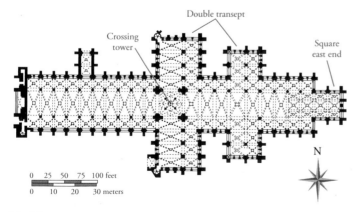

13-40 Plan of Salisbury Cathedral, Salisbury, England, 1220–1258.

The long rectilinear plan of Salisbury Cathedral, with its double transept and flat eastern end, is typically English. The four-part rib vaults of the nave follow the Chartres model (FIG. 13-13).

dominates the silhouette. Salisbury's height is modest compared with that of Amiens and Reims. Because height is not a decisive factor in the English building, the architect used the flying buttress sparingly.

Equally distinctive is Salisbury Cathedral's long rectilinear plan (FIG. 13-40), with its double transept and flat eastern end. The latter feature was characteristic of Cistercian (FIG. 12-10A) and English churches since Romanesque times. The interior (FIG. 13-41), although Gothic in its three-story elevation, pointed arches, four-part rib vaults, compound piers, and the tracery of the triforium, conspicuously departs from the French Gothic style. The pier colonnettes stop at the springing of the nave arches and do not connect with the vault ribs (compare FIGS. 13-19, 13-20, and 13-23A). Instead, the vault ribs rise from corbels in the triforium, producing a strong horizontal emphasis. Underscoring this horizontality is the rich color contrast between the light stone of the walls and vaults and the dark marble (from the Isle of Purbeck in southeastern England) used for the triforium moldings and corbels, compound pier responds, and other details. In short, French Gothic architecture may have inspired the design of Salisbury Cathedral, but its builders transformed the French style in accordance with English taste.

GLOUCESTER CATHEDRAL The elaboration of architectural pattern for its own sake had long been a distinguishing feature of English architecture. The decorative motifs on the Romanesque piers

13-42 Choir of Gloucester Cathedral (looking east), Gloucester, England, 1332–1357.

The Perpendicular style of Late English Gothic architecture takes its name from the pronounced verticality of its linear details. The multiplication of ribs in the vaults is also a characteristic feature.

13-43 ROBERT and WILLIAM VERTUE, fan vaults of the chapel of Henry VII, Westminster Abbey, London, England, 1503–1519. ◼◀

The chapel of Henry VII epitomizes the decorative and structure-disguising qualities of the Perpendicular style in the use of fan vaults with lacelike tracery and pendants resembling stalactites.

13-42A Tomb of Edward II, Gloucester, ca. 1330–1335.

of Durham Cathedral (FIG. 12-33, *left*) are an early example. The pier, wall, and vault elements, still relatively simple at Salisbury, became increasingly complex and decorative in the 14th century, culminating in what architectural historians call the *Perpendicular* style. This Late English Gothic style is on display in the choir (FIG. **13-42**) of Gloucester Cathedral, remodeled about a century after Salisbury under Edward III (r. 1327–1357), who also installed a Perpendicular style tomb (FIG. **13-42A**) in the church in honor of his father, Edward II (r. 1307–1327). The Perpendicular style takes its name from the pronounced verticality of its decorative details, in contrast to the horizontal emphasis of Salisbury and Early English Gothic.

A single enormous window divided into tiers of small windows of similar shape and proportion fills the characteristically flat east end of Gloucester Cathedral. At the top, two slender lancets flank a wider central section that also ends in a pointed arch. The design has much in common with the screen facade of Salisbury, but the proportions are different. Vertical, as opposed to horizontal, lines dominate. In the choir wall, the architect also erased Salisbury's strong horizontal accents, as the vertical wall elements lift directly from the floor to the vaulting, unifying the walls with the vaults in the French manner. The vault ribs, which designers had begun to multiply soon after Salisbury, are at Gloucester a dense thicket of entirely ornamental strands serving no structural purpose. The choir, in fact, does not have any rib vaults at all but a continuous Romanesque barrel vault with applied Gothic ornamentation. In the Gloucester choir, the taste for decorative surfaces triumphed over structural clarity.

CHAPEL OF HENRY VII The decorative, structure-disguising qualities of the Perpendicular style became even more pronounced in its late phases. A primary example is the early-16th-century ceiling (FIG. **13-43**) of the chapel of Henry VII adjoining Westminster Abbey in London. Here, ROBERT and WILLIAM VERTUE turned the earlier English linear play of ribs into a kind of architectural embroidery. The architects pulled the ribs into uniquely English *fan vaults* (vaults with radiating ribs forming a fanlike pattern) with large hanging *pendants* resembling stalactites. The vault looks as if it had been some organic mass hardened in the process of melting. Intricate tracery resembling lace overwhelms the cones hanging from the ceiling. The chapel represents the dissolution of structural Gothic into decorative fancy. The architects released the Gothic style's original lines from their function and multiplied them into the uninhibited architectural virtuosity and theatrics of the Perpendicular style. A parallel phenomenon in France is the Flamboyant style of Saint-Maclou (FIG. 13-27) at Rouen.

13-44 NICHOLAS OF VERDUN, *Sacrifice of Isaac,* detail of the *Klosterneuburg Altar,* from the abbey church at Klosterneuburg, Austria, 1181. Gilded copper and enamel, $5\frac{1}{2}''$ high. Stiftsmuseum, Klosterneuburg.

Nicholas of Verdun was the leading artist of the Meuse valley region, renowned for its enamel- and metalwork. His gold figures twist and turn and stand out vividly from the blue enamel background.

HOLY ROMAN EMPIRE

As part of his plan to make his new church at Saint-Denis an earthly introduction to the splendors of Paradise (see "Abbot Suger," page 367), Suger selected artists from the Meuse River valley in present-day Belgium to fashion for the choir a magnificent crucifix on a sumptuous base decorated with 68 enamel scenes pairing Old and New Testament episodes. The Mosan region long had been famous for the quality of its metalworkers and enamelers (FIGS. 12-24 and 12-25). Indeed, as Suger's treatises demonstrate, in the Middle Ages the artists who worked at small scale with precious metals, ivory, and jewels produced the most admired objects in a church, far more important in the eyes of contemporaries than the jamb figures and tympanum reliefs that form the core of modern histories of medieval art.

NICHOLAS OF VERDUN The leading Mosan artist of the late 12th and early 13th centuries was NICHOLAS OF VERDUN. In 1181, Nicholas completed work on a gilded-copper and enamel *ambo* (a pulpit for biblical readings) for the Benedictine abbey church at Klosterneuburg, near Vienna in Austria. After a fire damaged the pulpit in 1330, the church hired artists to convert the pulpit into an *altarpiece.* The pulpit's sides became the wings of a *triptych* (three-part altarpiece). The 14th-century artists also

added six scenes to Nicholas's original 45. The *Klosterneuburg Altar* in its final form (FIG. **13-44A**) has a central row of enamels depicting New Testament episodes, beginning with the *Annunciation,* and bearing the label *sub gracia,* or the world "under grace," that is, after the coming of Christ. The upper and lower registers contain Old Testament scenes labeled, respectively, *ante legem,* "before the law" Moses received on Mount Sinai, and *sub lege,* "under the law" of the Ten Commandments. In this scheme, prophetic Old Testament events appear above and below the New Testament episodes they prefigure. For example, framing the *Annunciation* to Mary of the coming birth of Jesus are enamels of angels announcing the births of Isaac and Samson. In the central section of the triptych, the Old Testament counterpart of Christ's *Crucifixion* is Abraham's *Sacrifice of Isaac* (FIG. **13-44**), a parallel already established in Early Christian times (see "Jewish Subjects in Christian Art," Chapter 8, page 238, and FIG. 8-1). Here, the angel flies in at the last moment to grab the blade of Abraham's sword before he can slay the bound Isaac on the altar.

Nicholas of Verdun's Klosterneuburg enamels may give an idea of the appearance of the Old and New Testament enamels on the lost Saint-Denis crucifix. Universally admired, Mosan enamels and metalwork were instrumental in the development of the French Gothic figural style. The gold figures stand out vividly from the blue enamel background. The biblical actors twist and turn, make emphatic gestures, and wear garments almost overwhelmed by the intricate linear patterns of their folds.

Sculpted versions of the Klosterneuburg figures appear on the *Shrine of the Three Kings* (FIG. **13-45**) in Cologne Cathedral. Nicholas of Verdun probably began work on the huge reliquary (six feet long and almost as tall) in 1190. Philip von Heinsberg, archbishop of Cologne from 1167 to 1191, commissioned the shrine to contain relics of the three magi. Holy Roman Emperor Frederick Barbarossa (r. 1155–1190) acquired them in the conquest of Milan in 1164 and donated them to the German cathedral. Possession of the magi's relics gave the Cologne archbishops the right to crown German kings. Nicholas's reliquary, made of silver and bronze with ornamentation in enamel and gemstones, is one of the most luxurious ever fashioned, especially considering its size. The shape resembles that of a basilican church. Repoussé figures of the Virgin Mary, the three magi, Old Testament prophets, and New Testament apostles in arcuated frames are variations of those on the Klosterneuburg pulpit. The deep channels and tight bunches of drapery folds are hallmarks of Nicholas's style.

The *Klosterneuburg Altar* and *Shrine of the Three Kings,* together with Suger's treatises on the furnishings of Saint-Denis, are welcome reminders of how magnificently outfitted medieval church interiors were. The sumptuous small-scale objects exhibited in the choir and chapels, which also housed the church's most precious relics, played a defining role in creating a special otherworldly atmosphere for Christian ritual. These Gothic examples continued a tradition dating to the Roman emperor Constantine and the first imperial patronage of Christianity (see Chapter 8).

STRASBOURG CATHEDRAL About the time Nicholas of Verdun was at work on the *Klosterneuburg Altar,* construction began on a new cathedral for Strasbourg in present-day France, then an important city in the German Rhineland ruled by the successors of the Ottonian dynasty. The apse, choir, and transepts, begun in

Cologne's archbishop commissioned this huge reliquary in the shape of a church to house relics of the three magi. The deep channels of drapery folds are hallmarks of Nicholas's influential style.

1 ft.

1176, were in place by around 1230. Stylistically, these sections of Strasbourg Cathedral are Romanesque. But the reliefs of the two south-transept portals are fully Gothic and reveal the same interest in the antique style as in contemporaneous French sculpture, especially that of Reims, as well as in the earlier work of Nicholas of Verdun. By the mid 13th century, artists throughout Europe were producing antique-looking statuary and relief sculpture.

The left tympanum (FIG. **13-46**) presents *Death of the Virgin.* A comparison of the Strasbourg Mary on her deathbed with the Mary of the Reims *Visitation* group (FIG. 13-24, *right*) shows the stylistic kinship of the Strasbourg and Reims masters. The 12 apostles gather around the Virgin, forming an arc of mourners well suited to the semicircular frame. The sculptor adjusted the heights of the figures to fit the available space (the apostles at the right are the shortest)

13-46 *Death of the Virgin,* tympanum of the left doorway of the south transept, Strasbourg Cathedral, Strasbourg, France, ca. 1230.

Stylistically akin to the *Visitation* group (FIG. 13-24, *right*) of Reims Cathedral, the figures in Strasbourg's south-transept tympanum express profound sorrow through dramatic poses and gestures.

13-47 NAUMBURG MASTER, *Crucifixion*, west choir screen of Naumburg Cathedral, Naumburg, Germany, ca. 1249–1255. Painted limestone statues, life size.

The emotional pathos of the crucified Christ and the mourning Virgin and Saint John are characteristic of German medieval sculpture. The choir screen is also notable for its preserved coloration.

and, as in many depictions of crowds in the history of art, some of the figures have no legs or feet. At the center, Christ receives his mother's soul (the doll-like figure he holds in his left hand). Mary Magdalene, wringing her hands in grief, crouches beside the deathbed. The sorrowing figures express emotion in varying degrees of intensity, from serene resignation to gesturing agitation. The sculptor organized the group both by dramatic pose and gesture and by the rippling flow of deeply incised drapery passing among them like a rhythmic electric pulse. The sculptor's objective was to imbue the sacred figures with human emotions and to stir emotional responses in observers. In Gothic France, as already noted, art became increasingly humanized and natural. In the Holy Roman Empire, artists carried this humanizing trend even further by emphasizing passionate drama.

NAUMBURG CATHEDRAL During his tenure as bishop (1244–1272), Dietrich II of Wettin completed the rebuilding of the Romanesque cathedral at Naumburg in northern Germany. The church had two choirs, and the western choir, which Dietrich commissioned, was the most distinctive aspect of the project. The bishop built the choir as a memorial to 12 donors of the original 11th-century church. The artist who oversaw this project, known as the NAUMBURG MASTER, directed the team of sculptors responsible for the monumental screen (FIG. **13-47**) that functioned as a portal to the western choir. Based loosely on contemporaneous church portals having statues on the trumeau and jambs, the Naumburg screen includes life-size figures of Christ on the cross and of the distraught Virgin Mary and John the Evangelist. John, openly crying, turns his head away, unable to look at the suffering Christ. Mary also does not look at her son, but she faces and gestures toward the approaching worshipers, suggesting she can intercede on their behalf at the last judgment (compare FIG. 13-38B).

The heightened emotionalism of the Naumburg statues had been a persistent characteristic of German medieval art since the Ottonian era. Indeed, the crucified Christ in the Naumburg choir is the direct descendant of the Christ of the *Gero Crucifix* (FIG. 11-28). Like that earlier statue, these indoor sculptures have retained their color, whereas almost all the statues on church exteriors, exposed to sun and rain for centuries, have lost their original paint. The

Naumburg choir screen gives modern viewers an excellent idea of the original appearance of portal sculptures of Romanesque and Gothic churches.

EKKEHARD AND UTA Within the choir, the same workshop carved the statues of the 12 original donors, some of whom were the bishop's ancestors. Two of the figures (FIG. **13-48**) stand out from the group of solemn men and women because of their exceptional quality. They represent the margrave (military governor) Ekkehard II of Meissen and his wife, Uta. The statues are attached to columns and stand beneath architectural canopies, following the pattern of French Gothic portal statuary, but they project from the architecture more forcefully and move more freely than contemporaneous French jamb figures. The period costumes and the individualized features and personalities of the margrave and his wife give the impression they posed for their own portraits, although

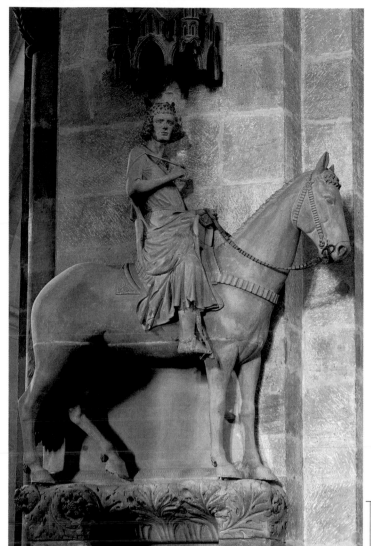

13-49 Equestrian portrait (*Bamberg Rider*), statue in the east choir, Bamberg Cathedral, Germany, ca. 1235–1240. Sandstone, 7′ 9″ high.

Probably a portrait of a German emperor, perhaps Frederick II, the *Bamberg Rider* revives the imagery of the Carolingian Empire. The French-style architectural canopy cannot contain the statue.

1 ft.

13-48 NAUMBURG MASTER, Ekkehard and Uta, statues in the west choir, Naumburg Cathedral, Naumburg, Germany, ca. 1249–1255. Painted limestone, Ekkehard 6′ 2″ high.

The period costumes and individualized features of these donor portraits give the impression Ekkehard and Uta posed for their statues, but they lived long before the Naumburg Master's time.

the subjects lived well before the Naumburg Master's time. Ekkehard, the intense knight, contrasts with the beautiful and aloof Uta. With a wonderfully graceful gesture, she draws the collar of her cloak partly across her face while she gathers up a soft fold of drapery with a jeweled, delicate hand. The sculptor subtly revealed the

shape of Uta's right arm beneath her cloak and rendered the fall of drapery folds with an accuracy suggesting the sculptor used a living model. The two statues are arresting images of real people, even if they bear the names of aristocrats the artist never met. By the mid-13th century, in the Holy Roman Empire as well as in England (FIG. 13-42A) and elsewhere, life-size images of secular personages had found their way into churches.

BAMBERG RIDER Somewhat earlier in date than the Naumburg donor figures is the *Bamberg Rider* (FIG. 13-49), the earliest preserved large-scale equestrian statue of the Middle Ages. For centuries, this statue has been mounted against a pier in Bamberg Cathedral beneath an architectural canopy that frames the rider's body but not his horse. Scholars debate whether the statue was made for this location or moved there, perhaps from the church's exterior. Whatever the statue's original location, it revives the imperial imagery of Byzantium (see "The Emperors of New Rome," Chapter 9, page 259) and the Carolingian Empire (FIG. 11-12), derived in turn from ancient Roman statuary (FIG. 7-59).

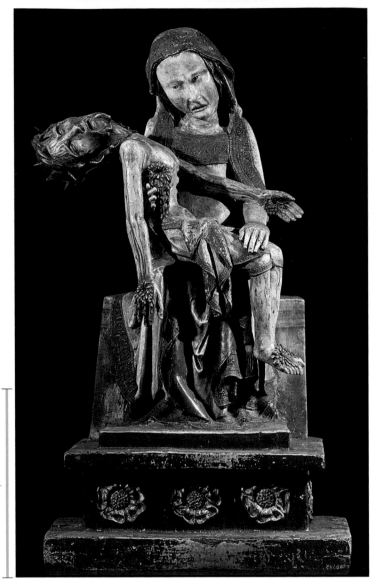

13-50 *Röttgen Pietà*, from the Rhineland, Germany, ca. 1300–1325. Painted wood, 2′ 10½″ high. Rheinisches Landemuseum, Bonn. ◼◀

This statuette of the Virgin grieving over the distorted dead body of Christ in her lap reflects the increased interest in the 13th and 14th centuries in Jesus' suffering and the Virgin's grief.

1 ft.

Unlike Ekkehard and Uta, the *Bamberg Rider* seems to be a true portrait of a living person. Some art historians believe it represents a Holy Roman emperor, perhaps Frederick II (r. 1220– 1250), who was a benefactor of Bamberg Cathedral. The many other identifications include Saint George and one of the three magi, but a historical personality is most likely the subject. The placement of a portrait of a Holy Roman emperor in the cathedral would have underscored the unity of church and state in 13th-century Germany. The artist carefully represented the rider's costume, the high saddle, and the horse's trappings. The *Bamberg Rider* turns toward the observer, as if presiding at a review of troops. The torsion of this figure reflects the same impatience with subordination to architecture found in the sculptures of Naumburg Cathedral (FIGS. 13-47 and 13-48).

RÖTTGEN PIETÀ The confident 13th-century portraits at Naumburg and Bamberg stand in marked contrast to a haunting 14th-century German painted wooden statuette (FIG. **13-50**) of the Virgin Mary holding the dead Christ in her lap. Like the *Crucifixion* (FIG. 13-47) of Naumburg's west choir, this *Pietà* (Italian, "pity" or "compassion") reflects the increased interest during the 13th and 14th centuries in humanizing biblical figures and in the suffering of Jesus and grief of his mother and followers. This expressed emotionalism accompanied the shift toward representation of the human body in motion. As the figures of the church portals began to twist on their columns, then move within their niches, and then stand independently, their details became more outwardly related to the human audience as indicators of recognizable human emotions.

The sculptor of the *Röttgen Pietà* (named after a collector) portrayed Christ as a stunted, distorted human wreck, stiffened in death and covered with streams of blood gushing from a huge wound. The Virgin, who cradles him as if he were a child in her lap, is the very image of maternal anguish, her oversized face twisted in an expression of unbearable grief. This statue expresses nothing of the serenity of Romanesque and earlier Gothic depictions of Mary (FIGS. 12-19 and 13-16). Nor does it have anything in common with the aloof, iconic images of the Theotokos with the infant Jesus in her lap common in Byzantine art (FIGS. 9-18 and 9-19). Here the artist forcibly confronts the devout with an appalling icon of agony, death, and sorrow. The work calls out to the horrified believer, "What is your suffering compared to this?"

COLOGNE CATHEDRAL The architecture of the Holy Roman Empire remained conservatively Romanesque well into the 13th century. In many German churches, the only Gothic feature was the rib vault, buttressed solely by the heavy masonry of the walls. By mid-century, though, the French Gothic style began to have a profound influence.

Cologne Cathedral (FIG. **13-51**), begun in 1248 under the direction of GERHARD OF COLOGNE, was not completed until more than 600 years later, making it one of the longest construction projects on record. Work halted entirely from the mid-16th to the mid-19th century, when church officials unexpectedly discovered the 14th-century design for the facade. *Gothic Revival* architects then completed the building according to the original plans, adding the nave, towers, and facade to the east end, which had stood alone for several centuries. The Gothic/Gothic Revival structure is the largest cathedral in northern Europe and boasts a giant (422-foot-long) nave (FIG. **13-52**) with two aisles on each side.

The 150-foot-high 14th-century choir is a skillful variation of the Amiens Cathedral choir (FIGS. 13-20 and 13-21) design, with double lancets in the triforium and tall, slender single windows in the clerestory above and choir arcade below. Completed four decades after Gerhard's death but according to his plans, the choir expresses the Gothic quest for height even more emphatically than do many French Gothic buildings. Despite the cathedral's seeming lack of substance, proof of its stability came during World War II, when the city of Cologne suffered extremely heavy aerial bombardments. The church survived the war by virtue of its Gothic skeletal design. Once the first few bomb blasts blew out all of its windows, subsequent explosions had no adverse effects, and the skeleton remained intact and structurally sound.

SAINT ELIZABETH, MARBURG A different type of design, also probably of French origin (FIG. 12-17) but developed especially in Germany, is the *Hallenkirche* (hall church), in which the height of the aisles is the same as the height of the nave. Hall

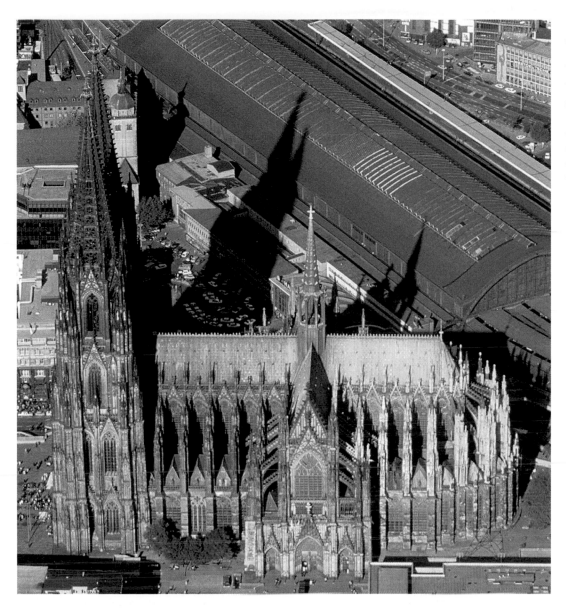

13-51 GERHARD OF COLOGNE, aerial view of Cologne Cathedral (looking north), Cologne, Germany, begun 1248; nave, facade, and towers completed 1880.

Cologne Cathedral, the largest church in northern Europe, took more than 600 years to build. Only the east end dates to the 13th century. The 19th-century portions follow the original Gothic plans.

13-52 GERHARD OF COLOGNE, interior of Cologne Cathedral (looking east), Cologne, Germany. Choir completed 1322.

Cologne Cathedral's nave is 422 feet long. The 150-foot-high choir, a taller variation on the Amiens Cathedral choir (FIGS. 13-20 and 13-21), is a prime example of Gothic architects' quest for height.

13-53 Interior of Saint Elizabeth (looking west), Marburg, Germany, 1235–1283.

This German church is an early example of a Hallenkirche, in which the aisles are the same height as the nave. Because of the tall windows in the aisle walls, sunlight brightly illuminates the interior.

13-54 PETER PARLER, interior (looking east) of Heiligkreuzkirche (Church of the Holy Cross), Schwäbisch Gmünd, Germany, begun 1351.

As in the Gloucester choir (FIG. 13-42), the vaults of this German church are structurally simple but visually complex. The multiplication of ribs characterizes Late Gothic architecture throughout Europe.

churches, consequently, have no tribune, triforium, or clerestory. An early German example of this type is the church of Saint Elizabeth (FIG. **13-53**) at Marburg, built between 1235 and 1283. It incorporates French-inspired rib vaults with pointed arches and tall lancet windows. The facade has two spire-capped towers in the French manner but no tracery arcades or portal sculpture. Because the aisles provide much of the bracing for the nave vaults, the exterior of Saint Elizabeth is without the dramatic parade of flying buttresses typically circling French Gothic churches. But the Marburg interior, lighted by double rows of tall windows in the aisle walls, is more unified and free flowing, less narrow and divided, and more brightly illuminated than the interiors of most French and English Gothic churches.

HEINRICH AND PETER PARLER A later German hall church is the Heiligkreuzkirche (Church of the Holy Cross) at Schwäbisch Gmünd, begun in 1317 by HEINRICH PARLER (ca. 1290–ca. 1360). Heinrich was the founder of a family of architects who worked in Germany and later in northern Italy. His name first surfaces in the early 14th century, when he played a role in supervising the construction of Cologne Cathedral (FIGS. 13-51 and 13-52). Work continued on the Schwäbisch Gmünd church into the 16th century, but the nave was substantially complete when one of his sons, PETER PARLER (1330–1399), began work on the choir (FIG. **13-54**) in 1351.

As in the nave of the church, the choir aisles are as tall as the central space. The light entering the choir through the large win-

dows in the aisle walls and in the chapels ringing the choir provides ample illumination for the clergy conducting services. It also enables worshipers to admire the elaborate patterns of the vault ribs. The multiplication of ribs in this German church is consistent with 14th-century taste throughout Europe and has parallels in the Flamboyant style of France and especially the Perpendicular style of England. As in the choir (FIG. 13-42) of Gloucester Cathedral, begun two decades before, the choir vaults at Schwäbisch Gmünd are structurally simple but visually complex. Parler's vaults form an elegant canopy for the severe columnar piers from which they spring, creating a very effective contrast.

One of Peter Parler's brothers, named Heinrich after their father, was also an architect. He was among those who formed a committee in 1386 to advise the Milanese on the design and construction of their new cathedral. The case of the Parler family is symptomatic both of the dramatic increase in the number of recorded names of artists and architects during the Gothic period, and of the international character of Gothic art and architecture, despite sometimes pronounced regional variations.

GOTHIC EUROPE

FRANCE

▌ The birthplace of Gothic art and architecture was Saint-Denis, where Abbot Suger used rib vaults with pointed arches to rebuild the Carolingian royal church and filled the windows of the ambulatory with stained glass. On the west facade, Suger introduced sculpted figures on the portal jambs, a feature that appeared shortly later on the Royal Portal of Chartres Cathedral. Saint-Denis, the west facade of Chartres, and Laon Cathedral are the key monuments of Early Gothic (1140–1194) architecture.

▌ After a fire in 1194, Chartres Cathedral was rebuilt with flying buttresses, four-part nave vaults, and a three-story elevation of nave arcade, triforium, and clerestory. These features set the pattern for High Gothic (1194–1300) cathedrals. French architects sought to construct naves of soaring height. The vaults of Amiens Cathedral are 144 feet high.

▌ Flying buttresses made possible huge stained-glass windows. High Gothic windows employed delicate lead cames and bar tracery. The colored glass converted natural sunlight into divine light (*lux nova*), dramatically transforming the character of church interiors.

▌ High Gothic jamb statues broke out of the architectural straitjacket of their Early Gothic predecessors. At Chartres, Reims, and elsewhere, the sculpted figures move freely and sometimes converse with their neighbors.

▌ The High Gothic Rayonnant court style of Louis IX gave way in the Late Gothic (1300–1500) period to the Flamboyant style, in which flamelike tracery formed brittle decorative webs, as at Saint-Maclou in Rouen.

▌ The prosperity of the era also led to a boom in secular architecture. Important examples are the fortified circuit wall of Carcassonne, the hall of the cloth guild in Bruges, and the house of the financier Jacques Coeur in Bourges.

▌ In the 13th century, Paris was the intellectual capital of Europe and home to numerous workshops of professional lay artists specializing in the production of luxurious illuminated manuscripts. These urban for-profit ancestors of modern publishing houses usurped the role of monastic scriptoria.

Royal Portal, Chartres Cathedral, ca. 1145–1155

Amiens Cathedral, begun 1220

Psalter of Saint Louis, 1253–1270

ENGLAND

▌ The Parisian Gothic style spread rapidly throughout Europe during the 13th century, but many regional styles developed, as in the Romanesque period. English Gothic churches, such as Salisbury Cathedral, differ from their French counterparts in their wider and shorter facades, flat east ends, double transepts, and sparing use of flying buttresses.

▌ Especially characteristic of English Gothic architecture is the elaboration of architectural patterns, which often disguise the underlying structure of the buildings. For example, the fan vaults of the chapel of Henry VII at Westminster Abbey in London transform the logical rib vaults of French buildings into decorative fancy in the Late Gothic Perpendicular style.

Salisbury Cathedral, Salisbury, 1220–1258

HOLY ROMAN EMPIRE

▌ Nicholas of Verdun was the leading artist of the Meuse River valley, an area renowned for enamel- and metalwork. Nicholas's altars and shrines provide an idea of the sumptuous nature of the furnishings of Gothic churches. His innovative figural style influenced the development of Gothic sculpture.

▌ German architects eagerly embraced the French Gothic architectural style at Cologne Cathedral and elsewhere. German originality manifested itself most clearly in the Gothic period in sculpture, which often featured emotionally charged figures in dramatic poses and also revived the art of portraiture. Statues of secular historical figures are key elements of the sculptural programs of Naumburg and Bamberg cathedrals.

Nicholas of Verdun, *Shrine of the Three Kings,* ca. 1190

Giotto's cycle of biblical frescoes in the Arena Chapel includes 38 framed panels depicting the lives of the Virgin, her parents, and Jesus. The passion cycle opens with *Entry into Jerusalem.*

Giotto's vision of the *Last Judgment* fills the west wall above the entrance to the Arena Chapel. The Paduan banker Enrico Scrovegni built the chapel to expiate the moneylender's sin of usury.

Giotto was a pioneer in pursuing a naturalistic approach to representation based on observation. In *Betrayal of Jesus,* he revived the classical tradition of depicting some figures from the rear.

14-1 GIOTTO DI BONDONE, interior of the Arena Chapel (Cappella Scrovegni; looking west), Padua, Italy, 1305–1306.

Giotto was also a master of composition. In *Lamentation*, the rocky slope behind the figures leads the viewer's eye toward the heads of Mary and the dead Jesus at the lower left.

LATE MEDIEVAL ITALY

LATE MEDIEVAL OR PROTO-RENAISSANCE?

Art historians debate whether the art of Italy between 1200 and 1400 is the last phase of medieval art or the beginning of the rebirth, or *Renaissance*, of Greco-Roman *naturalism*. All agree, however, the pivotal figure of this age was the Florentine painter GIOTTO DI BONDONE (ca. 1266–1337), whose masterwork was the fresco cycle of the Arena Chapel (FIG. **14-1**) in Padua. A banker, Enrico Scrovegni, built the chapel on a site adjacent to his palace in the hope it would expiate the moneylender's sin of usury. Consecrated in 1305, the chapel takes its name from an ancient Roman arena (*amphitheater*) nearby.

Some scholars have suggested Giotto himself may have been the chapel's architect, because its design so perfectly suits its interior decoration. The rectangular hall has only six windows, all in the south wall, leaving the other walls as almost unbroken and well-illuminated surfaces for painting. In 38 framed panels, Giotto presented the most poignant incidents from the lives of the Virgin and her parents, Joachim and Anna, in the top level, and, in the middle and lower levels, the life and mission (middle), and the passion and resurrection (bottom) of Jesus. The climactic event of the cycle of human salvation, *Last Judgment*, covers most of the west wall above the chapel's entrance.

The *Entry into Jerusalem, Betrayal of Jesus,* and *Lamentation* panels reveal the essentials of Giotto's style. In contrast to the common practice of his day, Giotto based his method of pictorial expression on observation of the natural world—the approach championed by the ancient Greeks and Romans but largely abandoned in the Middle Ages. Subtly scaled to the chapel's space, Giotto's stately and slow-moving half-life-size figures act out the religious dramas convincingly and with great restraint. The biblical actors are sculpturesque, simple, and weighty, often *foreshortened* (seen from an angle) and modeled with light and shading in the classical manner. They convey individual emotions through their postures and gestures. Giotto's naturalism displaced the Byzantine style in Italy (see Chapter 9), inaugurating an age some scholars call "early scientific." By stressing the preeminence of sight for gaining knowledge of the world, Giotto and his successors contributed to the foundation of empirical science. They recognized that the visual world must be observed before it can be analyzed and understood. Praised in his own and later times for his fidelity to nature, Giotto was more than a mere imitator of it. He showed his generation a new way of seeing. With Giotto, Western painters turned away from the spiritual world—the focus of medieval European artists—and once again moved resolutely toward the visible world as the inspiration for their art.

13TH CENTURY

When the Italian humanists of the 16th century condemned the art of the late Middle Ages in northern Europe as *"Gothic"* (see Chapter 13), they did so by comparing it with the contemporaneous art of Italy, which consciously revived *classical** art. Italian artists and scholars regarded medieval artworks as distortions of the noble art of the Greeks and Romans. Interest in the art of classical antiquity was not entirely absent during the medieval period, however, even in France, the center of the Gothic style. For example, on the west front of Reims Cathedral, the 13th-century statues of Christian *saints* and angels (FIG. 13-24) reveal the unmistakable influence of ancient Roman art on French sculptors. However, the classical revival that took root in Italy during the 13th and 14th centuries was much more pervasive and longer-lasting.

Sculpture

Italian admiration for classical art surfaced early on at the court of Frederick II, king of Sicily (r. 1197–1250) and Holy Roman emperor (r. 1220–1250). Frederick's nostalgia for Rome's past grandeur fostered a revival of classical sculpture in Sicily and southern Italy not unlike the classical *renovatio* (renewal) Charlemagne encouraged in Germany and France four centuries earlier (see Chapter 11).

NICOLA PISANO The sculptor Nicola d'Apulia (Nicholas of Apulia), better known as NICOLA PISANO (active ca. 1258–1278) after his adopted city (see "Italian Artists' Names," page 405, and MAP 14-1), received his early training in southern Italy under Frederick's rule. In 1250, Nicola traveled northward and eventually settled in Pisa. Then at the height of its political and economic power, the maritime city was a magnet for artists seeking lucrative commissions. Nicola specialized in carving marble reliefs and ornamentation for large *pulpits* (raised platforms from which priests led church services), completing the first (FIG. **14-2**) in 1260 for Pisa's century-old baptistery (FIG. 12-26, *left*). Some elements of the pulpit's design carried on medieval traditions—for example, the *trefoil* (triple-curved) *arches* and the lions supporting some of the *columns*—but Nicola also incorporated classical elements. The large *capitals* with two rows of thick overlapping leaves crowning the columns are a Gothic variation of the *Corinthian capital* (see page 151 and FIG. 5-73, or page xxii–xxiii in Volume II and Book D). The arches are round, as in Roman architecture, rather than pointed (*ogival*), as in Gothic buildings. Also, each of the large rectangular relief panels resembles the sculptured front of a Roman *sarcophagus* (coffin; for example, FIG. 7-70).

1 ft.

14-2 NICOLA PISANO, **pulpit of the baptistery, Pisa, Italy, 1259–1260. Marble, 15′ high.** ◼◀

Nicola Pisano's Pisa baptistery pulpit retains many medieval features, for example, the trefoil arches and the lions supporting columns, but the figures derive from ancient Roman sarcophagus reliefs.

*In *Art through the Ages* the adjective "Classical," with uppercase C, refers specifically to the Classical period of ancient Greece, 480–323 BCE. Lowercase "classical" refers to Greco-Roman antiquity in general, that is, the period treated in Chapters 5, 6, and 7.

LATE MEDIEVAL ITALY

13th Century	14th Century
▮ Bonaventura Berlinghieri and Cimabue are the leading painters working in the Italo-Byzantine style, or *maniera greca*	▮ In Florence, Giotto, considered the first Renaissance artist, pioneers a naturalistic approach to painting based on observation
▮ Nicola and Giovanni Pisano, father and son, represent two contrasting sculptural styles, the classical and the Gothic respectively	▮ In Siena, Duccio softens the maniera greca and humanizes religious subject matter
▮ Fresco cycles in Rome and Assisi foreshadow the revolutionary art of Giotto	▮ Secular themes emerge as important subjects in civic commissions, as in the frescoes of Siena's Palazzo Pubblico
	▮ Florence, Siena, and Orvieto build new cathedrals that are stylistically closer to Early Christian basilicas than to French Gothic cathedrals

14-3 NICOLA PISANO, *Annunciation, Nativity,* and *Adoration of the Shepherds,* relief panel on the baptistery pulpit, Pisa, Italy, 1259–1260. Marble, 2′ 10″ × 3′ 9″. ◼◂

Classical sculpture inspired the faces, beards, coiffures, and draperies, as well as the bulk and weight of Nicola's figures. The *Nativity* Madonna resembles lid figures on Roman sarcophagi.

1 ft.

14-4 GIOVANNI PISANO, *Annunciation, Nativity,* and *Adoration of the Shepherds,* relief panel on the pulpit of Sant'Andrea, Pistoia, Italy, 1297–1301. Marble, 2′ 10″ × 3′ 4″.

The French Gothic style had a greater influence on Giovanni Pisano, Nicola's son. Giovanni arranged his figures loosely and dynamically. They display a nervous agitation, as if moved by spiritual passion.

1 ft.

The densely packed large-scale figures of the individual panels also seem to derive from the compositions found on Roman sarcophagi. One of these panels (FIG. 14-3) depicts scenes from the infancy cycle of Christ (see "The Life of Jesus in Art," Chapter 8, pages 240–241, or pages xxx–xxxi, in Volume II and Book D), including *Annunciation* (*top left*), *Nativity* (*center* and *lower half*), and *Adoration of the Shepherds* (*top right*). Mary appears twice, and her size varies. The focus of the composition is the reclining Virgin of *Nativity,* whose posture and drapery are reminiscent of those of the lid figures on Etruscan (FIGS. 6-5 and 6-15) and Roman (FIG. 7-61) sarcophagi. The face types, beards, and coiffures, as well as the bulk and weight of Nicola's figures, also reveal the influence of classical relief sculpture. Art historians have even been able to pinpoint the models of some of the pulpit figures on Roman sarcophagi in Pisa.

GIOVANNI PISANO Nicola's son, GIOVANNI PISANO (ca. 1250–1320), likewise became a sought-after sculptor of church pulpits. Giovanni's pulpit in Sant'Andrea at Pistoia also has a panel (FIG. 14-4) featuring *Nativity* and related scenes. The son's version of the subject offers a striking contrast to his father's thick carving and placid, almost stolid presentation of the religious narrative. Giovanni arranged the figures loosely and dynamically. They twist and bend in excited animation, and the deep spaces between them suggest their motion. In *Annunciation* (*top left*), the Virgin shrinks from the angel's sudden appearance in a posture of alarm touched with humility. The same spasm of apprehension contracts her supple body as she reclines in *Nativity* (*center*). The drama's principals share in a peculiar nervous agitation, as if spiritual passion suddenly moves all of them. Only the shepherds and the sheep (*right*)

The Great Schism, Mendicant Orders, and Confraternities

In 1305, the College of Cardinals (the collective body of all cardinals) elected a French pope, Clement V (r. 1305–1314), who settled in Avignon. Subsequent French popes remained in Avignon, despite their announced intentions to return to Rome. Understandably, the Italians, who saw Rome as the rightful capital of the universal Church, resented the Avignon papacy. The conflict between the French and Italians resulted in the election in 1378 of two popes—Clement VII, who resided in Avignon (and who does not appear in the Catholic Church's official list of popes), and Urban VI (r. 1378–1389), who remained in Rome. Thus began what became known as the Great Schism. After 40 years, Holy Roman Emperor Sigismund (r. 1410–1437) convened a council that resolved this crisis by electing a new Roman pope, Martin V (r. 1417–1431), who was acceptable to all.

The pope's absence from Italy during much of the 14th century contributed to an increase in prominence of *monastic orders*. The Augustinians, Carmelites, and Servites became very active, ensuring a constant religious presence in the daily life of Italians, but the largest and most influential monastic orders were the *mendicants* (begging friars)—the Franciscans, founded by Francis of Assisi (FIG. 14-5), and the Dominicans, founded by the Spaniard Dominic de Guzman (ca. 1170–1221). These mendicants renounced all worldly goods and committed themselves to spreading God's word, performing good deeds, and ministering to the sick and dying. The Dominicans, in particular, contributed significantly to establishing urban educational institutions. The Franciscans and Dominicans became very popular in Italy because of their devotion to their faith and the more personal relationship with God they encouraged. Although both mendicant orders worked for the glory of God, a degree of rivalry nevertheless existed between the two. For example, in Florence they established their churches on opposite sides of the city—Santa Croce (FIG. I-4), the Franciscan church, on the eastern side, and the Dominicans' Santa Maria Novella (FIG. 14-6A) on the western (MAP 21-1).

14-5 BONAVENTURA BERLINGHIERI, *Saint Francis Altarpiece,* San Francesco, Pescia, Italy, 1235. Tempera on wood, 5′ × 3′ × 6′. 📹

Berlinghieri painted this altarpiece in the Italo-Byzantine style, or maniera greca, for the mendicant (begging) order of Franciscans. It is the earliest known representation of Saint Francis of Assisi.

1 ft.

Confraternities, organizations consisting of laypersons who dedicated themselves to strict religious observance, also grew in popularity during the 14th and 15th centuries. The mission of confraternities included tending the sick, burying the dead, singing hymns, and performing other good works. The confraternities as well as the mendicant orders continued to play an important role in Italian religious life through the 16th century. The numerous artworks and monastic churches they commissioned have ensured their enduring legacy.

do not yet share in the miraculous event. The swiftly turning, sinuous draperies, the slender figures they enfold, and the general emotionalism of the scene are features not found in Nicola Pisano's interpretation. The father worked in the classical tradition, the son in a style derived from French Gothic. These styles were two of the three most important ingredients in the formation of the distinctive and original art of 14th-century Italy.

Painting and Architecture

The third major stylistic element in late medieval Italian art was the Byzantine tradition (see Chapter 9). Throughout the Middle Ages, the Byzantine style dominated Italian painting, but its influence

was especially strong after the fall of Constantinople in 1204, which precipitated a migration of Byzantine artists to Italy.

BONAVENTURA BERLINGHIERI One of the leading painters working in the Italo-Byzantine style, or *maniera greca* (Greek style), was BONAVENTURA BERLINGHIERI (active ca. 1235–1244) of Lucca. His most famous work is the *Saint Francis Altarpiece* (FIG. 14-5) in the church of San Francesco (Saint Francis) in Pescia. Painted in 1235 using *tempera* on wood panel (see "Tempera and Oil Painting," Chapter 20, page 539), the *altarpiece* honors Saint Francis of Assisi (ca. 1181–1226), whose most important shrine (FIG. 14-5A), at Assisi itself, boasts the most extensive cycle of

Italian Artists' Names

In contemporary societies, people have become accustomed to a standardized method of identifying individuals, in part because of the proliferation of official documents such as driver's licenses, passports, and student identification cards. Modern names consist of given names (names selected by the parents) and family names, although the order of the two (or more) names varies from country to country. In China, for example, the family name precedes the given name (see Chapters 16 and 33).

This kind of regularity in names was not, however, the norm in premodern Italy. Many individuals were known by their place of birth or adopted hometown. Nicola Pisano (FIGS. 14-2 and 14-3) was "Nicholas the Pisan," Giulio Romano was "Julius the Roman," and Domenico Veneziano was "the Venetian." Leonardo da Vinci ("Leonard from Vinci") hailed from the small town of Vinci, near Florence (MAP 14-1). Art historians therefore refer to these artists by their given names, not the names of their towns. (The title of Dan Brown's best-selling novel should have been *The Leonardo Code,* not *The Da Vinci Code.*)

Nicknames were also common. Giorgione was "Big George." People usually referred to Tommaso di Cristoforo Fini as Masolino ("Little Thomas") to distinguish him from his more famous pupil, Masaccio ("Brutish Thomas"). Guido di Pietro was called Fra Angelico (the Angelic Friar). Cenni di Pepo is remembered as Cimabue (FIG. 14-6), which means "bull's head."

Names were also impermanent and could be changed at will. This flexibility has resulted in significant challenges for historians, who often must deal with archival documents and records referring to the same artist by different names.

MAP 14-1 Italy around 1400.

14-5A San Francesco, Assisi, 1228–1253.

14-5B ST. FRANCIS MASTER, *Preaching to the Birds,* ca. 1290–1300.

frescoes from 13th-century Italy. Berlinghieri depicted Francis wearing the costume later adopted by all Franciscan monks: a coarse clerical robe tied at the waist with a rope. The saint displays the *stigmata*—marks resembling Christ's wounds—that miraculously appeared on his hands and feet. Flanking Francis are two angels, whose frontal poses, prominent halos, and lack of modeling reveal the Byzantine roots of Berlinghieri's style. So, too, does the use of *gold leaf* (gold beaten into tissue-paper-thin sheets, then applied to surfaces), which emphasizes the image's flatness and spiritual nature. The narrative scenes along the sides of the panel provide an active contrast to the stiff formality of the large central image of Francis. At the upper left, taking pride of place at the saint's right, Francis receives the stigmata. Directly below, the saint preaches to the birds, a subject that also figures prominently in the fresco program (FIG. 14-5B) of San Francesco at Assisi, the work of a painter art historians call the SAINT FRANCIS MASTER. These and the scenes depicting Francis's

miracle cures strongly suggest Berlinghieri's source was one or more Byzantine *illuminated manuscripts* (compare FIG. 9-17) with biblical narrative scenes.

Berlinghieri's *Saint Francis Altarpiece* also highlights the increasingly prominent role of religious orders in late medieval Italy (see "The Great Schism, Mendicant Orders, and Confraternities," page 404). Saint Francis's Franciscan order worked diligently to impress on the public the saint's valuable example and to demonstrate the order's commitment to teaching and to alleviating suffering. Berlinghieri's Pescia altarpiece, painted only nine years after Francis's death, is the earliest known signed and dated representation of the saint. Appropriately, Berlinghieri's panel focuses on the aspects of the saint's life the Franciscans wanted to promote, thereby making visible (and thus more credible) the legendary life of this holy man. Saint Francis believed he could get closer to God by rejecting worldly goods, and to achieve this he stripped himself bare in a public square and committed himself to a strict life of fasting, prayer, and meditation. His followers considered the appearance of stigmata on Francis's hands and feet (clearly visible in the saint's frontal image, which resembles a Byzantine *icon*) as God's blessing, and viewed Francis as a second Christ. Fittingly, four of the six narrative scenes on the altarpiece depict miraculous healings, connecting Saint Francis even more emphatically to Christ.

13th Century   **405**

14-6 CIMABUE, *Madonna Enthroned with Angels and Prophets,* from Santa Trinità, Florence, ca. 1280–1290. Tempera and gold leaf on wood, 12′ 7″ × 7′ 4″. Galleria degli Uffizi, Florence. ◼◢

Cimabue was one of the first artists to break away from the *maniera greca.* Although he relied on Byzantine models, Cimabue depicted the Madonna's massive throne as receding into space.

14-6A Santa Maria Novella, Florence, begun ca. 1246. ◼◢

CIMABUE One of the first artists to break from the Italo-Byzantine style that dominated 13th-century Italian painting was Cenni di Pepo, better known as CIMABUE (ca. 1240–1302). Cimabue challenged some of the major conventions of late medieval art in pursuit of a new naturalism, the close observation of the natural world—the core of the classical tradition. He painted *Madonna Enthroned with Angels and Prophets* (FIG. 14-6) for Santa Trinità (Holy Trinity) in Florence, the Benedictine church near the Arno River built between 1258 and 1280, roughly contemporaneous with the Dominican church of Santa Maria Novella (FIG. 14-6A). The composition and the gold background reveal the painter's reliance on Byzantine models (compare FIG. 9-18).

Cimabue also used the gold embellishments common to Byzantine art for the folds of the Madonna's robe, but they are no longer merely decorative patterns. In his panel they enhance the three-dimensionality of the drapery. Furthermore, Cimabue constructed a deeper space for the Madonna and the surrounding figures to inhabit than was common in Byzantine art. The Virgin's throne, for example, is a massive structure and Cimabue convincingly depicted it as receding into space. The overlapping bodies of the angels on each side of the throne and the half-length prophets who look outward or upward from beneath it reinforce the sense of depth.

14TH CENTURY

In the 14th century, Italy consisted of numerous independent *city-states,* each corresponding to a geographic region centered on a major city (MAP 14-1). Most of the city-states, such as Venice, Florence, Lucca, and Siena, were republics—constitutional oligarchies governed by executive bodies, advisory councils, and special commissions. Other powerful 14th-century states included the Papal States, the Kingdom of Naples, and the Duchies of Milan, Modena, Ferrara, and Savoy. As their names indicate, these states were politically distinct from the republics, but all the states shared in the prosperity of the period. The sources of wealth varied from state to state. Italy's port cities expanded maritime trade, whereas the economies of other cities depended on banking or the manufacture of arms or textiles.

The outbreak of the Black Death (bubonic plague) in the late 1340s threatened this prosperity, however. Originating in China, the Black Death swept across Europe. The most devastating natural disaster in European history, the plague eliminated between 25 and 50 percent of the Continent's population in about five years. The Black Death devastated Italy's inhabitants. In large Italian cities, where people lived in relatively close proximity, the death tolls climbed as high as 50 to 60 percent of the population. The bubonic plague had a significant effect on art. It stimulated religious bequests and encouraged the commissioning of devotional images. The focus on sickness and death also led to a burgeoning in hospital construction.

Another significant development in 14th-century Italy was the blossoming of a vernacular (commonly spoken) literature, which dramatically affected Italy's intellectual and cultural life. Latin remained the official language of Church liturgy and state documents. However, the creation of an Italian vernacular literature (based on the Tuscan dialect common in Florence) expanded the audience for philosophical and intellectual concepts because of its greater accessibility. Dante Alighieri (1265–1321, author of *The Divine Comedy*), the poet and scholar Francesco Petrarch (1304–1374), and Giovanni Boccaccio (1313–1375, author of *Decameron*) were most responsible for establishing this vernacular literature.

RENAISSANCE HUMANISM The development of a vernacular literature was one important sign that the essentially religious view of the world dominating medieval Europe was about to change dramatically in what historians call the *Renaissance.* Although religion continued to occupy a primary position in the lives of Europeans, a growing concern with the natural world, the individual, and humanity's worldly existence characterized the Renaissance period—the 14th through the 16th centuries. The word *renaissance* in French and English (*rinascità* in Italian) refers to a "rebirth" of art and culture. A revived interest in classical cultures—indeed, the veneration of classical antiquity as a model—was central to this rebirth. The notion of the Renaissance representing the restoration of the glorious past of Greece and Rome gave rise to the concept of the "Middle Ages" as the era falling between antiquity and the Renaissance. The transition from the medieval to the Renaissance, though dramatic, did not come about abruptly, however. In fact, much that is medieval persisted in the Renaissance and in later periods.

Fundamental to the development of the Italian Renaissance was *humanism,* which emerged during the 14th century and became a central component of Italian art and culture in the 15th and 16th centuries. Humanism was more a code of civil conduct, a theory of education, and a scholarly discipline than a philosophical system. As their name suggests, Italian humanists were concerned chiefly with human values and interests as distinct from—but not opposed to—religion's otherworldly values. Humanists pointed to classical cultures as particularly praiseworthy. This enthusiasm for antiquity, represented by the elegant Latin of Cicero (106–43 BCE) and the Augustan age, involved study of Latin literature and a conscious emulation of what proponents believed were the Roman civic virtues. These included self-sacrificing service to the state, participation in government, defense of state institutions (especially the administration of justice), and stoic indifference to personal misfortune in the performance of duty. With the help of a new interest in and knowledge of Greek, the humanists of the late 14th and 15th centuries recovered a large part of Greek as well as Roman literature and philosophy that had been lost, left unnoticed, or cast aside in the Middle Ages. Indeed, classical cultures provided humanists with a model for living in this world, a model primarily of human focus derived not from an authoritative and traditional religious dogma but from reason.

Ideally, humanists sought no material reward for services rendered. The sole reward for heroes of civic virtue was fame, just as the reward for leaders of the holy life was sainthood. For the educated, the lives of heroes and heroines of the past became as edifying as the lives of the saints. Petrarch wrote a book on illustrious men, and his colleague Boccaccio complemented it with 106 biographies of famous women—from Eve to Joanna, queen of Naples (r. 1343–1382). Both Petrarch and Boccaccio were famous in their own day as poets, scholars, and men of letters—their achievements equivalent in honor to those of the heroes of civic virtue. In 1341 in Rome, Petrarch received the laurel wreath crown, the ancient symbol of victory and merit. The humanist cult of fame emphasized the importance of creative individuals and their role in contributing to the renown of the city-state and of all Italy.

Giotto

14-6B CAVALLINI, *Last Judgment,* ca. 1290–1295.

Critics from Giorgio Vasari[†] to the present day have regarded Giotto di Bondone (FIG. 14-1) as the first Renaissance painter. A pioneer in pursuing a naturalistic approach to representation based on observation, he made a much more radical break with the past than did Cimabue, whom Vasari identified as Giotto's teacher. Scholars still debate the sources of Giotto's style, however. One formative influence must have been Cimabue's work,

[†]Giorgio Vasari (1511–1574) was both a painter and an architect. Today, however, people associate him primarily with his landmark book, *Lives of the Most Eminent Painters, Sculptors, and Architects,* first published in 1550. Despite inaccuracies, Vasari's *Lives* is an invaluable research tool. It is the major contemporaneous source of information about Italian Renaissance art and artists.

although Vasari lauded Giotto as having eclipsed his master by abandoning the "crude maniera greca." The 13th-century *murals* of San Francesco at Assisi (FIGS. 14-5A and 14-5B) and those of PIETRO CAVALLINI (ca. 1240–ca. 1340) in Rome (FIG. 14-6B) may also have influenced the young Giotto. French Gothic sculpture (which Giotto may have seen but which was certainly familiar to him from the work of Giovanni Pisano, who had spent time in Paris) and ancient Roman art probably also contributed to Giotto's artistic education. Yet no mere synthesis of these varied influences could have produced the significant shift in artistic approach that has led some scholars to describe Giotto as the father of Western pictorial art. Renowned in his own day, his reputation has never faltered. Regardless of the other influences on his artistic style, his true teacher was nature—the world of visible things.

MADONNA ENTHRONED On nearly the same great scale as Cimabue's enthroned Madonna (FIG. 14-6) is Giotto's panel (FIG. 14-7) depicting the same subject, painted for the high altar

1 ft.

14-7 GIOTTO DI BONDONE, *Madonna Enthroned,* from the Church of Ognissanti, Florence, ca. 1310. Tempera and gold leaf on wood, 10′ 8″ × 6′ 8″. Galleria degli Uffizi, Florence.

Giotto displaced the Byzantine style in Italian painting and revived classical naturalism. His figures have substance, dimensionality, and bulk, and give the illusion they could throw shadows.

Fresco Painting

Fresco painting has a long history, particularly in the Mediterranean region, where the Minoans (FIGS. 4-7 to 4-9B) used it as early as the 17th century BCE. *Fresco* (Italian for "fresh") is a mural-painting technique involving the application of permanent limeproof pigments, diluted in water, on freshly laid lime plaster. Because the surface of the wall absorbs the pigments as the plaster dries, fresco is one of the most durable painting techniques. The stable condition of the ancient Minoan frescoes, as well as those found at Pompeii and other Roman sites (FIGS. 7-17 to 7-26), in San Francesco (FIGS. 14-5A and 14-5B) at Assisi, and in the Arena Chapel (FIGS. 14-1 and 14-8 to 14-8B) at Padua, testify to the longevity of this painting method. The colors have remained vivid (although dirt and soot have necessitated cleaning—most famously in the Vatican's Sistine Chapel; FIG. 22-18B) because of the chemically inert pigments the artists used. In addition to this *buon fresco* (good, that is, true fresco) technique, artists used *fresco secco* (dry fresco). Fresco secco involves painting on dried lime plaster, the method the ancient Egyptians favored (FIGS. 3-28 and 3-29). Although the finished product visually approximates buon fresco, the plaster wall does not absorb the pigments, which simply adhere to the surface, so fresco secco is not as permanent as buon fresco.

The buon fresco process is time-consuming and demanding and requires several layers of plaster. Although buon fresco methods vary, generally the artist prepares the wall with a rough layer of lime plaster called the *arriccio* (brown coat). The artist then transfers the composition to the wall, usually by drawing directly on the arriccio with a burnt-orange pigment called *sinopia* (most popular during the 14th century), or by transferring a *cartoon* (a full-size preparatory drawing). Cartoons increased in usage in the 15th and 16th centuries, largely replacing sinopia underdrawings. Finally, the painter lays the *intonaco* (painting coat) smoothly over the drawing in sections (called *giornate*—Italian for "days") only as large as the artist expects to complete in that session. (In Giotto's *Lamentation*

1 ft.

14-8 GIOTTO DI BONDONE, *Lamentation,* Arena Chapel (Cappella Scrovegni), Padua, Italy, ca. 1305. Fresco, 6' 6¾" × 6' ¾". ◼◀

Giotto painted *Lamentation* in several sections, each corresponding to one painting session. Artists employing the buon fresco technique must complete each section before the plaster dries.

[FIG. 14-8], the giornate are easy to distinguish.) The buon fresco painter must apply the colors quickly, because once the plaster is dry, it will no longer absorb the pigment. Any unpainted areas of the intonaco after a session must be cut away so that fresh plaster can be applied for the next giornata.

In areas of high humidity, such as Venice, fresco was less appropriate because moisture is an obstacle to the drying process. Over the centuries, fresco became less popular, although it did experience a revival in the 1930s with the Mexican muralists (FIGS. 29-73 and 29-74).

of Florence's Church of the Ognissanti (All Saints). Although still portrayed against the traditional gold background, Giotto's Madonna rests within her Gothic throne with the unshakable stability of an ancient marble goddess (compare FIG. 7-30). Giotto replaced Cimabue's slender Virgin, fragile beneath the thin ripplings of her drapery, with a weighty, queenly mother. In Giotto's painting, the Madonna's body is not lost—indeed, it is asserted. Giotto even showed Mary's breasts pressing through the thin fabric of her white undergarment. Gold highlights have disappeared from her heavy robe. Giotto aimed instead to construct a figure with substance, dimensionality, and bulk—qualities suppressed in favor of a spiritual immateriality in Byzantine and Italo-Byzantine art. Works painted in the new style portray statuesque figures projecting into the light and giving the illusion they could throw shadows. Giotto's *Madonna Enthroned* marks the end of medieval painting in Italy and the beginning of a new naturalistic approach to art.

14-8A GIOTTO, *Entry into Jerusalem*, ca. 1305.

14-8B GIOTTO, *Betrayal of Jesus*, ca. 1305.

ARENA CHAPEL Projecting on a flat surface the illusion of solid bodies moving through space presents a double challenge. Constructing the illusion of a weighty, three-dimensional body also requires constructing the illusion of a space sufficiently ample to contain that body. In his *fresco* cycles (see "Fresco Painting," page 408), Giotto constantly strove to reconcile these two aspects of illusionistic painting. His murals in Enrico Scrovegni's Arena Chapel (FIG. 14-1) at Padua show his art at its finest. In 38 framed scenes (FIGS. **14-8, 14-8A,** and **14-8B**), Giotto presented one of the most impressive and complete Christian pictorial cycles ever rendered. The narrative unfolds on the north and south walls in three zones, reading from top to bottom. Below, imitation marble veneer—reminiscent of ancient Roman decoration (FIG. 7-51), which Giotto may have seen—alternates with personified Virtues and Vices painted in *grisaille* (monochrome grays, often used for modeling in paintings) to resemble sculpture. On the west wall above the chapel's entrance is Giotto's dramatic *Last Judgment,* the culminating scene also of Pietro Cavallini's late-13th-century fresco cycle (FIG. 14-6B) in Santa Cecilia in Trastevere in Rome. The chapel's vaulted ceiling is blue, an azure sky dotted with golden stars symbolic of Heaven. Medallions bearing images of Christ, Mary, and various prophets also appear on the vault. Giotto painted the same blue in the backgrounds of the narrative panels on the walls below. The color thereby functions as a unifying agent for the entire decorative scheme.

The panel in the lowest zone of the north wall, *Lamentation* (FIG. 14-8), illustrates particularly well the revolutionary nature of Giotto's style. In the presence of boldly foreshortened angels, seen head-on with their bodies receding into the background and darting about in hysterical grief, a congregation mourns over the dead Savior just before his entombment. Mary cradles her son's body, while Mary Magdalene looks solemnly at the wounds in Christ's feet and Saint John the Evangelist throws his arms back dramatically. Giotto arranged a shallow stage for the figures, bounded by a thick diagonal rock incline defining a horizontal ledge in the foreground. Though narrow, the ledge provides firm visual support for the figures. The rocky setting recalls the landscape of a 12th-century Byzantine mural (FIG. 9-29) at Nerezi in Macedonia. Here, the steep slope leads the viewer's eye toward the picture's dramatic focal point at the lower left. The postures and gestures of Giotto's figures convey a broad spectrum of grief. They range from Mary's almost fierce despair to the passionate outbursts of Mary Magdalene and John to the philosophical resignation of the two disciples at the right and the mute sorrow of the two hooded mourners in the foreground. In *Lamentation,* a single event provokes a host of individual responses in figures that are convincing presences both physically and psychologically. Painters before Giotto rarely attempted, let alone achieved, this combination of naturalistic representation, compositional complexity, and emotional resonance.

The formal design of the *Lamentation* fresco—the way Giotto grouped the figures within the constructed space—is worth close study. Each group has its own definition, and each contributes to the rhythmic order of the composition. The strong diagonal of the rocky ledge, with its single dead tree (the tree of knowledge of good and evil, which withered after Adam and Eve's original sin), concentrates the viewer's attention on the heads of Christ and his mother, which Giotto positioned dynamically off center. The massive bulk of the seated mourner in the painting's left corner arrests and contains all movement beyond Mary and her dead son. The seated mourner to the right establishes a relation with the center figures, who, by gazes and gestures, draw the viewer's attention back to Christ's head. Figures seen from the back, which are frequent in Giotto's compositions (compare FIG. 14-8B), represent an innovation in the development away from the formal Italo-Byzantine style. These figures emphasize the foreground, aiding the visual placement of the intermediate figures farther back in space. This device, the very contradiction of Byzantine frontality, in effect puts viewers behind the "observer figures," who, facing the action as spectators, reinforce the sense of stagecraft as a model for painting.

Giotto's new devices for depicting spatial depth and body mass could not, of course, have been possible without his management of light and shade. He shaded his figures to indicate both the direction of the light illuminating their bodies and the shadows (the diminished light), thereby giving the figures volume. In *Lamentation,* light falls upon the upper surfaces of the figures (especially the two central bending figures) and passes down to dark in their garments, separating the volumes one from the other and pushing one to the fore, the other to the rear. The graded continuum of light and shade, directed by an even, neutral light from a single steady source—not shown in the picture—was the first step toward the development of *chiaroscuro* (the use of contrasts of dark and light to produce modeling) in later Renaissance painting (see Chapter 21).

The stagelike settings made possible by Giotto's innovations in *perspective* (the depiction of three-dimensional objects in space on a two-dimensional surface) and lighting suited perfectly the dramatic narrative the Franciscans emphasized then as a principal method for educating the faithful in their religion. In this new age of humanism, the old stylized presentations of the holy mysteries had evolved into *mystery plays.* Actors extended the drama of the Mass into one- and two-act tableaus and scenes and then into simple narratives offered at church portals and in city squares. (Eventually, confraternities also presented more elaborate religious dramas called *sacre rappresentazioni*—holy representations.) The great increase in popular sermons to huge city audiences prompted a public taste for narrative, recited as dramatically as possible. The arts of illusionistic painting, of drama, and of sermon rhetoric with all their theatrical flourishes developed simultaneously and were mutually influential. Giotto's art masterfully synthesized dramatic narrative, holy lesson, and truth to human experience in a visual idiom of his own invention, accessible to all. Not surprisingly, Giotto's frescoes served as textbooks for generations of Renaissance painters.

Siena

Among 14th-century Italian city-states, the Republics of Siena and Florence were the most powerful. Both were urban centers of bankers and merchants with widespread international contacts and large sums available for the commissioning of artworks (see "Artists' Guilds, Artistic Commissions, and Artists' Contracts," page 410).

Artists' Guilds, Artistic Commissions, and Artists' Contracts

The structured organization of economic activity during the 14th century, when Italy had established a thriving international trade and held a commanding position in the Mediterranean world, extended to many trades and professions. *Guilds* (associations of master craftspeople, apprentices, and tradespeople), which had emerged during the 12th century, became prominent. These associations not only protected members' common economic interests against external pressures, such as taxation, but also provided them with the means to regulate their internal operations (for example, work quality and membership training).

Because of today's international open art market, the notion of an "artists' union" may seem strange. The general public tends to think of art as the creative expression of an individual artist. However, artists did not always enjoy this degree of freedom. Historically, they rarely undertook major artworks without receiving a specific commission. The patron contracting for the artist's services could be a civic group, religious entity, private individual, or even the artists' guild itself. Guilds, although primarily business organizations, contributed to their city's religious and artistic life by subsidizing the building and decoration of numerous churches and hospitals. For example, the wool manufacturers' guild oversaw the start of Florence Cathedral (FIGS. 14-18 and 14-18A) in 1296, and the wool merchants' guild supervised the completion of its dome (FIG. 21-30A). The guild of silk manufacturers and goldsmiths provided the funds to build Florence's foundling hospital, the Ospedale degli Innocenti (FIG. 21-31).

Monastic orders, confraternities, and the popes were also major art patrons. In addition, wealthy families and individuals—for example, the Paduan banker Enrico Scrovegni (FIG. 14-1)—commissioned artworks for a wide variety of reasons. Besides the aesthetic pleasure these patrons derived from art, the images often also served as testaments to the patron's piety, wealth, and stature. Because artworks during this period were the product of service contracts, a patron's needs or wishes played a crucial role in the final form of any painting, sculpture, or building. Some early contracts between patrons and artists still exist. Patrons normally asked artists to submit drawings or models for approval, and they expected the artists they hired to adhere closely to the approved designs. The contracts usually stipulated certain conditions, such as the insistence on the artist's own hand in the production of the work, the quality of pigment and amount of gold or other precious items to be used, completion date, payment terms, and penalties for failure to meet the contract's terms.

A few extant 13th- and 14th-century painting contracts are especially illuminating. Although they may specify the subject to be represented, these binding legal documents always focus on the financial aspects of the commission and the responsibilities of the painter to the patron (and vice versa). In a contract dated November 1, 1301, between Cimabue (FIG. 14-6) and another artist and the Hospital of Santa Chiara in Pisa, the artists agree to supply an altarpiece

> with colonnettes, tabernacles, and predella, painted with histories of the divine majesty of the Blessed Virgin Mary, of the apostles,

of the angels, and with other figures and pictures, as shall be seen fit and shall please the said master of or other legitimate persons for the hospital.*

Other terms of the Santa Chiara contract specify the size of the panel and require the artists to use gold and silver gilding for parts of the altarpiece.

The contract for the construction of an altarpiece was usually a separate document, because it necessitated employing the services of a master carpenter. For example, on April 15, 1285, the leading painter of Siena, Duccio di Buoninsegna (FIGS. 14-9 to 14-11), signed a contract with the rectors of the Confraternity of the Laudesi, the lay group associated with the Dominican church of Santa Maria Novella (FIG. 14-6A) in Florence. The contract specified only that Duccio was to provide the painting, not its frame—and it imposed conditions the painter had to meet if he was to be paid.

> [The rectors] promise . . . to pay the same Duccio . . . as the payment and price of the painting of the said panel that is to be painted and done by him in the way described below . . . 150 lire of the small florins. . . . [Duccio, in turn, promises] to paint and embellish the panel with the image of the blessed Virgin Mary and of her omnipotent Son and other figures, according to the wishes and pleasure of the lessors, and to gild [the panel] and do everything that will enhance the beauty of the panel, his being all the expenses and the costs. . . . If the said panel is not beautifully painted and it is not embellished according to the wishes and desires of the same lessors, they are in no way bound to pay him the price or any part of it.†

Sometimes patrons furnished the materials and paid artists by the day instead of a fixed amount. That was the arrangement Duccio made on October 9, 1308, when he agreed to paint the *Maestà* (FIG. 14-9) for the high altar of Siena Cathedral.

> Duccio has promised to paint and make the said panel as well as he can and knows how, and he further agreed not to accept or receive any other work until the said panel is done and completed. . . . [The church officials promise] to pay the said Duccio sixteen solidi of the Sienese denari as his salary for the said work and labor for each day that the said Duccio works with his own hands on the said panel . . . [and] to provide and give everything that will be necessary for working on the said panel so that the said Duccio need contribute nothing to the work save his person and his effort.‡

In all cases, the artists worked for their patrons and could count on being compensated for their talents and efforts only if the work they delivered met the standards of those who ordered it.

*Translated by John White, *Duccio: Tuscan Art and the Medieval Workshop* (London: Thames & Hudson, 1979), 34.
†Translated by James H. Stubblebine, *Duccio di Buoninsegna and His School* (Princeton, N.J.: Princeton University Press, 1979), 1: 192.
‡Stubblebine, *Duccio*, 1: 201.

14-9 DUCCIO DI BUONINSEGNA, *Virgin and Child Enthroned with Saints,* principal panel of the *Maestà* altarpiece, from Siena Cathedral, Siena, Italy, 1308–1311. Tempera and gold leaf on wood, 7′ × 13′. Museo dell'Opera del Duomo, Siena. ◼◀

Duccio derived the formality and symmetry of his composition from Byzantine painting, but relaxed the rigidity and frontality of the figures, softened the drapery, and individualized the faces.

14-10 DUCCIO DI BUONINSEGNA, *Life of Jesus,* 14 panels from the back of the *Maestà* altarpiece, from Siena Cathedral, Siena, Italy, 1308–1311. Tempera and gold leaf on wood, 7′ × 13′. Museo dell'Opera del Duomo, Siena.

On the back of the *Maestà* altarpiece, Duccio painted Jesus' passion in 24 scenes on 14 panels, beginning with *Entry into Jerusalem* (FIG. 14-10A), at the lower left, through *Noli me tangere,* at top right.

DUCCIO The works of DUCCIO DI BUONINSEGNA (active ca. 1278–1318) represent Sienese art at its most supreme. His most famous painting, the immense altarpiece called *Maestà* (*Virgin Enthroned in Majesty;* FIG. 14-9), replaced a much smaller painting of the Virgin Mary on the high altar of Siena Cathedral (FIG. 14-12A). The Sienese believed the Virgin had brought them victory over the Florentines at the battle of Monteperti in 1260, and she was the focus of the religious life of the republic. Duccio and his assistants began work on the prestigious commission in 1308 and completed *Maestà* in 1311, causing the entire city to celebrate. Shops closed and the bishop led a great procession of priests, civic officials, and the populace at large in carrying the altarpiece from Duccio's studio outside the city gate through the Campo (FIG. 14-15) up to its home on Siena's highest hill. So great was Duccio's stature that church officials permitted him to include his name in the dedicatory inscription on the front of the altarpiece on the Virgin's footstool: "Holy Mother of God, be the cause of peace for Siena and of life for Duccio, because he painted you thus."

As originally executed, Duccio's *Maestà* consisted of the seven-foot-high central panel (FIG. 14-9) with the dedicatory inscription, surmounted by seven *pinnacles* above, and a *predella,* or raised shelf, of panels at the base, altogether some 13 feet high. Painted in tempera front and back (FIG. 14-10), the work unfortunately can no longer be seen in its entirety, because of its dismantling in subsequent centuries. Many of Duccio's panels are on display today as single masterpieces, scattered among the world's museums.

The main panel on the front of the altarpiece represents the Virgin enthroned as queen of Heaven amid choruses of angels and saints. Duccio derived the composition's formality and symmetry, along with the figures and facial types of the principal angels and saints, from Byzantine tradition. But the artist relaxed the strict frontality and rigidity of the figures. They turn to each other in quiet conversation. Further, Duccio individualized the faces of the four saints kneeling in the foreground, who perform their ceremonial gestures without stiffness. Similarly, he softened the usual Byzantine hard body outlines and drapery patterning. The folds of the garments, particularly those of the female saints at both ends of the panel, fall and curve loosely. This is a feature familiar in French Gothic works (FIG. 13-37) and is a mark of the artistic dialogue between Italy and northern Europe in the 14th century.

Despite these changes revealing Duccio's interest in the new naturalism, he respected the age-old requirement that as an altarpiece, *Maestà* would be the focus of worship in Siena's largest and most important church, its *cathedral*, the seat of the bishop of Siena. As such, Duccio knew *Maestà* should be an object holy in itself—a work of splendor to the eyes, precious in its message and its materials. Duccio thus recognized how the function of the altarpiece naturally limited experimentation in depicting narrative action and producing illusionistic effects (such as Giotto's) by modeling forms and adjusting their placement in pictorial space.

Instead, the queen of Heaven panel is a miracle of color composition and texture manipulation, unfortunately not fully revealed in photographs. Close inspection of the original reveals what the Sienese artist learned from other sources. In the 13th and 14th centuries, Italy was the distribution center for the great silk trade from China and the Middle East (see "The Silk Road," Chapter 16, page 458). After processing the silk in city-states such as Lucca and Florence, the Italians exported the precious fabric throughout Europe to satisfy an immense market for sumptuous dress. (Dante, Petrarch, and many other humanists decried the appetite for luxury in costume, which to them represented a decline in civic and moral virtue.) People throughout Europe (Duccio and other artists among them) prized fabrics from China, Persia, Byzantium, and the Islamic world. In *Maestà*, Duccio created the glistening and shimmering effects of textiles, adapting the motifs and design patterns of exotic materials. Complementing the luxurious fabrics and the (lost) gilded wood frame are the halos of the holy figures, which feature tooled decorative designs in gold leaf (*punchwork*). But Duccio, like Giotto (FIG. 14-7), eliminated almost all the gold patterning of the figures' garments in favor of creating three-dimensional volume. Traces remain only in the Virgin's red dress.

In contrast to the main panel, the predella and the back (FIG. 14-10) of *Maestà* present an extensive series of narrative panels of different sizes and shapes, beginning with *Annunciation* and culminating with Christ's *Resurrection* and other episodes following his *Crucifixion* (see "The Life of Jesus in Art," Chapter 11, pages 240–241, or pages xxx–xxxi in Volume II and Book D). The section reproduced here, consisting of 24 scenes in 14 panels, relates Christ's passion. Duccio drew the details of his scenes from the accounts in all four Gospels. The viewer reads the pictorial story in zig-zag fashion, beginning with *Entry into Jerusalem* (FIG. 14-10A) at the lower left. *Crucifixion* is at the top cen-

14-10A Duccio, *Entry into Jerusalem*, 1308–1311.

14-11 Duccio di Buoninsegna, *Betrayal of Jesus*, panel on the back of the *Maestà* altarpiece, from Siena Cathedral, Siena, Italy, 1309–1311. Tempera and gold leaf on wood, 1' 10½" × 3' 4". Museo dell'Opera del Duomo, Siena.

In this dramatic depiction of Judas's betrayal of Jesus, the actors display a variety of individual emotions. Duccio here took a decisive step toward the humanization of religious subject matter.

ter. The narrative ends with Christ's appearance to Mary Magdalene (*Noli me tangere*) at the top right. Duccio consistently dressed Jesus in blue robes in most of the panels, but beginning with *Transfiguration*, he gilded the Savior's garment.

On the front panel, Duccio showed himself as the great master of the formal altarpiece. However, he allowed himself greater latitude for experimentation in the small accompanying panels, front and back. (Worshipers could always view both sides of the altarpiece because the high altar stood at the center of the sanctuary.) *Maestà*'s biblical scenes reveal Duccio's powers as a narrative painter. In *Betrayal of Jesus* (FIG. 14-11; compare FIG. 14-8B), for example, the artist represented several episodes of the event—the betrayal of Jesus by Judas's false kiss, the disciples fleeing in terror, and Peter cutting off the ear of the high priest's servant. Although the background, with its golden sky and rock formations, remains traditional, the style of the figures before it has changed radically. The bodies are not the flat frontal shapes of Italo-Byzantine art. Duccio imbued them with mass, modeled them with a range of tonalities from light to dark, and arranged their draperies around them convincingly. Even more novel and striking is the way the figures seem to react to the central event. Through posture, gesture, and even facial expression, they display a variety of emotions. Duccio carefully differentiated among the anger of Peter, the malice of Judas (echoed in the faces of the throng about Jesus), and the apprehension and timidity of the fleeing disciples. These figures are actors in a religious drama the artist interpreted in terms of thoroughly human actions and reactions. In this and the other narrative panels, for example, Jesus' *Entry into Jerusalem* (FIG. 14-10A), a theme treated also by Giotto in the Arena Chapel (FIG. 14-8A), Duccio took a decisive step toward the humanization of religious subject matter.

ORVIETO CATHEDRAL While Duccio was working on *Maestà* for Siena's most important church, a Sienese architect, Lorenzo Maitani, received the commission to design Orvieto's Cathedral (FIG. 14-12). The Orvieto *facade*, like the earlier facade of Siena Cathedral (FIG. 14-12A), begun by Giovanni Pisano (FIG. 14-4), demonstrates the appeal of the decorative vocabulary of French Gothic architecture in Italy at the end of the 13th and beginning of the 14th century. Characteristically French are the pointed gables over Orvieto Cathedral's three doorways, the *rose window* and

14-12 LORENZO MAITANI, Orvieto Cathedral (looking northeast), Orvieto, Italy, begun 1310. ◼️◀

The pointed gables over the doorways, the rose window, and the large pinnacles derive from French Gothic architecture, but the facade of Orvieto Cathedral masks a traditional timber-roofed basilica.

statues in niches in the upper zone, and the four large *pinnacles* dividing the facade into three *bays* (see "The Gothic Cathedral," Chapter 13, page 373, or page xxvi in Volume II and Book D). The outer pinnacles serve as miniature substitutes for the tall northern European west-front towers. Maitani's facade, however, is a Gothic overlay masking a marble-revetted *basilican* structure in the Tuscan *Romanesque* tradition, as the three-quarter view of the cathedral in FIG. 14-12 reveals. Few Italian architects fully embraced the Gothic style. The Orvieto facade resembles a great altar screen, its single plane covered with carefully placed carved and painted decoration. In principle, Orvieto belongs with Pisa Cathedral (FIG. 12-26) and other earlier Italian buildings, rather than with the French cathedrals at Amiens (FIG. 13-19) and Reims (FIG. 13-23). Inside, Orvieto Cathedral has a timber-roofed *nave* with a two-story *elevation* (columnar *arcade* and *clerestory*) in the Early Christian manner. Both the *chancel arch* framing the *apse* and the nave arcade's arches are round as opposed to pointed.

14-12A Siena Cathedral, begun ca. 1226. ◼️◀

SIMONE MARTINI Duccio's successors in the Sienese school also produced innovative works. SIMONE MARTINI (ca. 1285–1344) was a pupil of Duccio's and may have assisted him in painting *Maestà*. Martini was a close friend of Petrarch's, and the poet praised him highly for his portrait of "Laura" (the woman to whom Petrarch dedicated his sonnets). Martini worked for the French kings in Naples and Sicily and, in his last years, produced paintings for the papal court at Avignon, where he came in contact with French painters. By adapting the insubstantial but luxuriant patterns of the Gothic style to Sienese art and, in turn, by acquainting painters north of the Alps with the Sienese style, Martini was instrumental in creating the so-called *International style*. This new style swept Europe during the late 14th and early 15th centuries because it appealed to the aristocratic taste for brilliant colors, lavish costumes, intricate ornamentation, and themes involving splendid processions.

The *Annunciation* altarpiece (FIG. 14-13) Martini created for Siena Cathedral features elegant shapes and radiant color, fluttering line, and weightless figures in a spaceless setting—all hallmarks of the artist's style.

1 ft.

14-13 SIMONE MARTINI and LIPPO MEMMI, *Annunciation* altarpiece, from Siena Cathedral, 1333 (frame reconstructed in the 19th century). Tempera and gold leaf on wood, center panel 10′ 1″ × 8′ 8¾″. Galleria degli Uffizi, Florence.

A pupil of Duccio's, Martini was instrumental in the creation of the International style. Its hallmarks are elegant shapes, radiant color, flowing line, and weightless figures in golden, spaceless settings.

Artistic Training in Renaissance Italy

In Italy during the 14th through 16th centuries, training to become a professional artist capable of earning membership in the appropriate guild (see "Artists' Guilds," page 410) was a laborious and lengthy process. Aspiring artists started their training at an early age, anywhere from age 7 to 15. Their fathers would negotiate an arrangement with a master artist whereby each youth lived with that master for a specified number of years, usually five or six. During that time, the boys served as apprentices to the master of the workshop, learning the trade. (This living arrangement served as a major obstacle for female artists, because it was inappropriate for young girls to live in a male master's household.) The guilds supervised this rigorous training. They wanted not only to ensure their professional reputations by admitting only the most talented members but also to control the number of artists (and thereby limit competition). Toward this end, they frequently tried to regulate the number of apprentices working under a single master.

The skills apprentices learned varied with the type of studio they joined. Those apprenticed to painters learned to grind pigments, draw, prepare wood panels for painting, gild, and lay plaster for fresco. Sculptors in training learned to manipulate different materials—wood, stone, *terracotta* (baked clay), wax, bronze, or stucco—although many sculpture workshops specialized in only one or two of these materials. For stone carving, apprentices learned their craft by blocking out the master's designs for statues. As their skills developed, apprentices took on increasingly difficult tasks.

Cennino Cennini (ca. 1370–1440) explained the value of this apprenticeship system, and in particular, the advantages for young artists in studying and copying the works of older masters, in an influential book he published in 1400, *Il Libro dell'Arte* (*The Handbook of Art*):

> Having first practiced drawing for a while, . . . take pains and pleasure in constantly copying the best things which you can find done by the hand of great masters. And if you are in a place where many good masters have been, so much the better for you. But I give you this advice: take care to select the best one every time, and the one who has the greatest reputation. And, as you go on from day to day, it will be against nature if you do not get some grasp of his style and of his spirit. For if you undertake to copy after one master today and after another one tomorrow, you will not acquire the style of either one or the other, and you will inevitably, through

enthusiasm, become capricious, because each style will be distracting your mind. You will try to work in this man's way today, and in the other's tomorrow, and so you will not get either of them right. If you follow the course of one man through constant practice, your intelligence would have to be crude indeed for you not to get some nourishment from it. Then you will find, if nature has granted you any imagination at all, that you will eventually acquire a style individual to yourself, and it cannot help being good; because your hand and your mind, being always accustomed to gather flowers, would ill know how to pluck thorns.*

After completing their apprenticeships, artists entered the appropriate guilds. For example, painters, who ground pigments, joined the guild of apothecaries. Sculptors were members of the guild of stoneworkers, and goldsmiths entered the silk guild, because metalworkers often stretched gold into threads wound around silk for weaving. Guild membership served as certification of the artists' competence, but did not mean they were ready to open their own studios. New guild-certified artists usually served as assistants to master artists, because until they established their reputations, they could not expect to receive many commissions, and the cost of establishing their own workshops was high. In any case, this arrangement was not permanent, and workshops were not necessarily static enterprises. Although well-established and respected studios existed, workshops could be organized around individual masters (with no set studio locations) or organized for a specific project, especially an extensive decoration program.

Generally, assistants to painters were responsible for gilding frames and backgrounds, completing decorative work, and, occasionally, rendering architectural settings. Artists regarded figures, especially those central to the represented subject, as the most important and difficult parts of a painting, and the master reserved these for himself. Sometimes assistants painted secondary or marginal figures but only under the master's close supervision. That was probably the case with Simone Martini's *Annunciation* altarpiece (FIG. 14-13), in which the master painted the Virgin and angel, and the flanking saints are probably the work of his assistant, Lippo Memmi.

*Translated by Daniel V. Thompson Jr., *Cennino Cennini, The Craftsman's Handbook* (*Il Libro dell'Arte*) (New York: Dover Publications, 1960; reprint of 1933 ed.), 14–15.

The complex etiquette of the European chivalric courts probably dictated the presentation. The angel Gabriel has just alighted, the breeze of his passage lifting his mantle, his iridescent wings still beating. The gold of his sumptuous gown signals he has descended from Heaven to deliver his message. The Virgin, putting down her book of devotions, shrinks demurely from Gabriel's reverent genuflection—an appropriate act in the presence of royalty. Mary draws about her the deep blue, golden-hemmed mantle, colors befitting the queen of Heaven. Between the two figures is a vase of white lilies, symbolic of the Virgin's purity. Despite Mary's modesty and diffidence and the tremendous import of the angel's message, the scene subordinates drama to court ritual, and structural experimentation to surface splendor. The intricate *tracery* of the richly

tooled (reconstructed) French Gothic–inspired frame and the elaborate punchwork halos (by then a characteristic feature of Sienese panel painting) enhance the tactile magnificence of *Annunciation*.

Simone Martini and his student and assistant, LIPPO MEMMI (active ca. 1317–1350), signed the altarpiece and dated it (1333). The latter's contribution to *Annunciation* is still a matter of debate, but most art historians believe he painted the two lateral saints. These figures, which are reminiscent of the jamb statues of Gothic church portals, have greater solidity and lack the linear elegance of Martini's central pair. Given the nature of medieval and Renaissance workshop practices, it is often difficult to distinguish the master's hand from those of assistants, especially if the master corrected or redid part of the pupil's work (see "Artistic Training in Renaissance Italy," page 414).

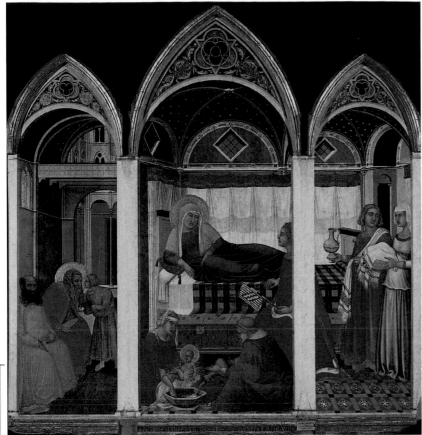

14-14 PIETRO LORENZETTI, *Birth of the Virgin*, from the altar of Saint Savinus, Siena Cathedral, Siena, Italy, 1342. Tempera on wood, 6' 1" × 5' 11". Museo dell'Opera del Duomo, Siena.

In this triptych, Pietro Lorenzetti revived the pictorial illusionism of ancient Roman murals and painted the architectural members dividing the panel as if they extended back into the painted space.

PIETRO LORENZETTI Another of Duccio's students, PIETRO LORENZETTI (active 1320–1348), contributed significantly to the general experiments in pictorial realism taking place in 14th-century Italy. Surpassing even his renowned master, Lorenzetti achieved a remarkable degree of spatial illusionism in his *Birth of the Virgin* (FIG. 14-14), a large *triptych* (three-part panel painting) created for the altar of Saint Savinus in Siena Cathedral. Lorenzetti painted the wooden architectural members dividing the altarpiece into three sections as though they extended back into the painted space. Viewers seem to look through the wooden frame (added later) into a boxlike stage, where the event takes place. That one of the vertical members cuts across a figure, blocking part of it from view, strengthens the illusion. In subsequent centuries, artists exploited this use of architectural elements to enhance the illusion of painted figures acting out a drama a mere few feet away. This kind of pictorial illusionism characterized ancient Roman mural painting (FIGS. 7-18 and 7-19, *right*) but had not been practiced in Italy for a thousand years.

Lorenzetti's setting for his holy subject also represented a marked step in the advance of worldly realism. Saint Anne—who, like Nicola Pisano's Virgin in *Nativity* (FIG. 14-3), resembles a reclining figure on the lid of a Roman sarcophagus (FIG. 7-61)—props herself up wearily as the midwives wash the child and the women bring gifts. She is the center of an episode occurring in an upper-class Italian house of the period. A number of carefully observed domestic details and the scene at the left, where Joachim eagerly awaits news of the delivery, create the illusion that the viewer has opened the walls of Saint Anne's house and peered inside. Lorenzetti's altarpiece is noteworthy both for the painter's innovations in spatial illusionism and for his careful inspection and recording of details of the everyday world.

PALAZZO PUBBLICO Not all Sienese painting of the early 14th century was religious in character. One of the most important fresco cycles of the period (FIGS. 14-16 and 14-17) was a civic commission for Siena's Palazzo Pubblico ("public palace" or city hall). Siena was a proud commercial and political rival of Florence. The secular center of the community, the civic meeting hall in the main square (the Campo, or Field), was almost as great an object of civic pride as the city's cathedral (FIG. 14-12A). The Palazzo Pubblico (FIG. 14-15) has a slightly concave

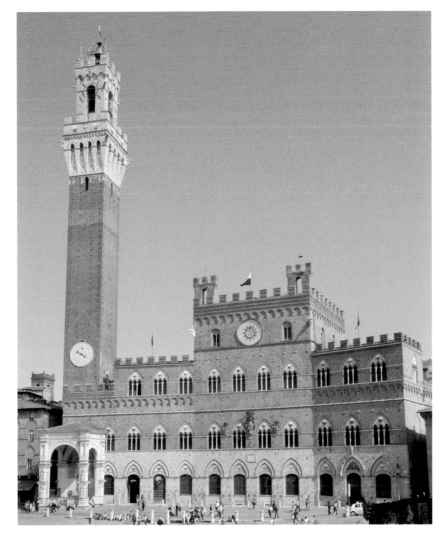

14-15 Palazzo Pubblico (looking east), Siena, Italy, 1288–1309. ◼◀

Siena's Palazzo Pubblico has a concave facade and a gigantic tower visible for miles around. The tower served as both a defensive lookout over the countryside and a symbol of the city-state's power.

14th Century **415**

14-16 AMBROGIO LORENZETTI, *Peaceful City,* detail from *Effects of Good Government in the City and in the Country,* east wall, Sala della Pace, Palazzo Pubblico, Siena, Italy, 1338–1339. Fresco. ◼◀

In the Hall of Peace (FIG. 14-16A) of Siena's city hall (FIG. 14-15), Ambrogio Lorenzetti painted an illusionistic panorama of the bustling city. The fresco served as an allegory of good government in the Sienese republic.

facade (to conform to the irregular shape of the Campo) and a gigantic tower visible from miles around (compare FIGS. 13-29 and 14-18B). The imposing building and tower must have earned the admiration of Siena's citizens as well as of visitors to the city, inspiring in them respect for the republic's power and success. The tower served as a lookout over the city and the countryside around it and as a bell tower (*campanile*) for ringing signals of all kinds to the populace. Siena, as other Italian city-states, had to defend itself against neighboring cities and often against kings and emperors. In addition, it had to secure itself against internal upheavals common in the history of the Italian city-republics. Class struggle, feuds among rich and powerful families, and even uprisings of the whole populace against the city governors were constant threats in medieval Italy. The heavy walls and *battlements* (fortified *parapets*) of the Sienese town hall eloquently express how frequently the city governors needed to defend themselves against their own citizens. The Palazzo Pubblico tower, out of reach of most missiles, incorporates *machicolated galleries* (galleries with holes in their floors to enable defenders to dump stones or hot liquids on attackers below) built out on *corbels* (projecting supporting architectural members) for defense of the tower's base.

AMBROGIO LORENZETTI

The painter entrusted with the major fresco program in the Palazzo Pubblico was Pietro Loren-

14-16A Sala della Pace, Siena, 1338–1339.

zetti's brother AMBROGIO LORENZETTI (active 1319–1348). In the frescoes Ambrogio produced for the Sala della Pace (Hall of Peace; FIG. 14-16A), he elaborated his brother's advances in illusionistic representation in spectacular fashion while giving visual form to Sienese civic concerns. The subjects of Ambrogio's murals are *Allegory of Good Government, Bad Government and the Effects of Bad Government in the City,* and *Effects of Good Government in the City and in the Country.* The turbulent politics of the

Italian cities—the violent party struggles, the overthrow and reinstatement of governments—called for solemn reminders of fair and just administration, and the city hall was just the place to display these allegorical paintings. Indeed, the leaders of the Sienese government who commissioned this fresco series had undertaken the "ordering and reformation of the whole city and countryside of Siena."

In *Effects of Good Government in the City and in the Country,* Ambrogio depicted the urban and rural effects of good government. *Peaceful City* (FIG. 14-16) is a panoramic view of Siena, with its clustering palaces, markets, towers, churches, streets, and walls, reminiscent of the townscapes of ancient Roman murals (FIG. 7-19, *left*). The city's traffic moves peacefully, guild members ply their trades and crafts, and radiant maidens, clustered hand in hand, perform a graceful circling dance. Dancers were regular features of festive springtime rituals. Here, their presence also serves as a metaphor for a peaceful commonwealth. The artist fondly observed the life of his city, and its architecture gave him an opportunity to apply Sienese artists' rapidly growing knowledge of perspective.

As the viewer's eye passes through the city gate to the countryside beyond its walls, Ambrogio's *Peaceful Country* (FIG. 14-17) presents a bird's-eye view of the undulating Tuscan terrain with its villas, castles, plowed farmlands, and peasants going about their occupations at different seasons of the year. Although it is an allegory, not a mimetic picture of the Sienese countryside on a specific day, Lorenzetti particularized the view of Tuscany—as well as the city view—by careful observation and endowed the painting with the character of a portrait of a specific place and environment. *Peaceful Country* represents one of the first appearances of *landscape* in Western art since antiquity (FIG. 7-20).

An allegorical figure of Security hovers above the hills and fields, unfurling a scroll promising safety to all who live under the rule of law. But Siena could not protect its citizens from the plague sweeping through Europe in the mid-14th century. The Black Death (see page 406) killed thousands of Sienese and may have ended the careers of both Lorenzettis. They disappear from historical records in 1348.

14-17 AMBROGIO LORENZETTI, *Peaceful Country*, detail from *Effects of Good Government in the City and in the Country*, east wall, Sala della Pace (FIG. 14-16A), Palazzo Pubblico (FIG. 14-15), Siena, Italy, 1338–1339. Fresco. ◼◀

This sweeping view of the countryside is one of the first instances of landscape painting in Western art since antiquity. The winged figure of Security promises safety to all who live under Sienese law.

Florence

Like Siena, the Republic of Florence was a dominant city-state during the 14th century. The historian Giovanni Villani (ca. 1270–1348), for example, described Florence as "the daughter and the creature of Rome," suggesting a preeminence inherited from the Roman Empire. Florentines were fiercely proud of what they perceived as their economic and cultural superiority. Florence controlled the textile industry in Italy, and the republic's gold *florin* was the standard coin of exchange everywhere in Europe.

FLORENCE CATHEDRAL Florentines translated their pride in their predominance into such landmark buildings as Santa Maria del Fiore (FIGS. **14-18** and **14-18A**), Florence's cathedral, the center for the most important religious observances in the city. ARNOLFO DI CAMBIO (ca. 1245–1302) began work on the cathedral (*Duomo* in Italian) in 1296, three years before he received the commission to build the city's town hall, the Palazzo della Signoria (FIG. **14-18B**). Intended as the "most beautiful and honorable church in Tuscany," the cathedral reveals the competitiveness Florentines felt with cities such as Siena (FIG. 14-12A) and Pisa (FIG. 12-26). Church authorities planned for the

14-18A Nave, Florence Cathedral, begun 1296.

14-18B Palazzo della Signoria, Florence, 1299–1310.

14-18 ARNOLFO DI CAMBIO and others, aerial view of Santa Maria del Fiore (and the Baptistery of San Giovanni; looking northeast), Florence, Italy, begun 1296. Campanile designed by GIOTTO DI BONDONE, 1334. ◼◀

The Florentine Duomo's marble revetment carries on the Tuscan Romanesque architectural tradition, linking this basilican church more closely to Early Christian Italy than to Gothic France.

Duomo to hold the city's entire population, and although its capacity is only about 30,000 (Florence's population at the time was slightly less than 100,000), the building seemed so large even the noted architect Leon Battista Alberti (see Chapter 21) commented it seemed to cover "all of Tuscany with its shade." The builders ornamented the cathedral's surfaces, in the old Tuscan fashion, with marble-encrusted geometric designs, matching the *revetment* (decorative wall paneling) to that of the facing 11th-century Romanesque baptistery of San Giovanni (FIGS. 12-27 and 14-18, *left*).

The vast gulf separating Santa Maria del Fiore from its northern European counterparts becomes evident in a comparison between the Florentine church and the High Gothic cathedrals of Amiens (FIG. 13-19), Reims (FIG. 13-23), and Cologne (FIG. 13-52). Gothic architects' emphatic stress on the vertical produced an awe-inspiring upward rush of unmatched vigor and intensity. The French and German buildings express organic growth shooting heavenward, as the pierced, translucent stone tracery of the spires merges with the atmosphere. Florence Cathedral, in contrast, clings to the ground and has no aspirations to flight. All emphasis is on the horizontal elements of the design, and the building rests firmly and massively on the ground. The clearly defined simple geometric volumes of the cathedral show no tendency to merge either into each other or into the sky.

Giotto di Bondone designed the Duomo's campanile in 1334. In keeping with Italian tradition (FIGS. 12-21 and 12-26), it stands apart from the church. In fact, it is essentially self-sufficient and could stand anywhere else in the city without looking out of place. The same cannot be said of the towers of Amiens, Reims, and Cologne cathedrals. They are essential elements of the structures behind them, and it would be unthinkable to detach one of them and place it somewhere else. No individual element of Gothic churches seems capable of an independent existence. One form merges into the next in a series of rising movements pulling the eye upward and never permitting it to rest until it reaches the sky. The Florentine campanile is entirely different. Neatly subdivided into cubic sections, Giotto's tower is the sum of its component parts. Not only could this tower be removed from the building without adverse effects, but also each of the parts—cleanly separated from each other by continuous moldings—seems capable of existing independently as an object of considerable aesthetic appeal. This compartmentalization is reminiscent of the Romanesque style, but it also forecasts the ideals of Renaissance architecture. Artists hoped to express structure in the clear, logical relationships of the component parts and to produce self-sufficient works that could exist in complete independence. Compared with northern European towers, Giotto's campanile has a cool and rational quality more appealing to the intellect than to the emotions.

14-19 ANDREA PISANO, south doors of the Baptistery of San Giovanni (FIG. 12-27), Florence, Italy, 1330–1336. Gilded bronze, doors 16′ × 9′ 2″; individual panels 1′ 7$\frac{1}{4}$″ × 1′ 5″. (The door frames date to the mid-15th century.)

Andrea Pisano's bronze doors have 28 panels with figural reliefs in French Gothic quatrefoil frames. The lower eight depict Christian virtues. The rest represent the life of Saint John the Baptist.

The facade of Florence Cathedral was not completed until the 19th century, and then in a form much altered from its original design. In fact, until the 17th century, Italian builders exhibited little concern for the facades of their churches, and dozens remain unfinished to this day. One reason for this may be that Italian architects did not conceive the facades as integral parts of the structures but rather, as in the case of Orvieto Cathedral (FIG. 14-12), as screens that could be added to the church exterior at any time.

A generation after work began on Florence's church, the citizens decided also to beautify their 11th-century baptistery (FIGS. 12-27 and 14-18, *left*) with a set of bronze doors (FIG. **14-19**) for the south entrance to the building. The sponsors were the members of

Florence's guild of wool importers, who competed for business and prestige with the wool manufacturers' association, an important sponsor of the cathedral building campaign. The wool-importers' guild hired ANDREA PISANO (ca. 1290–1348), a native of Pontedera in the territory of Pisa—unrelated to Nicola and Giovanni Pisano (see "Italian Artists' Names," page 405)—to create the doors. Andrea designed 28 bronze panels for the doors, each cast separately, of which 20 depict episodes from the life of Saint John the Baptist, to whom the Florentines dedicated their baptistery. Eight panels (at the bottom) represent personified Christian virtues. The *quatrefoil* (four-lobed, cloverlike) frames are of the type used earlier for reliefs flanking the doorways of Amiens Cathedral (FIG. 13-19), suggesting French Gothic sculpture was one source of Andrea's style. The gilded figures stand on projecting ledges in each quatrefoil. Their proportions and flowing robes also reveal a debt to French sculpture, but the compositions, both in general conception (small groups of figures in stagelike settings) and in some details, owe a great deal to Giotto, for whom Andrea had earlier executed reliefs for the cathedral's campanile, perhaps according to Giotto's designs.

The wool importers' patronage of the baptistery did not end with this project. In the following century, the guild paid for the even more prestigious east doors (FIGS. 21-9 and 21-10), directly across from the cathedral's west facade, and also for a statue of Saint John the Baptist on the facade of Or San Michele, a multipurpose building housing a 14th-century tabernacle (FIG. 14-19A) by ANDREA ORCAGNA (active ca. 1343–1368) featuring the painting *Madonna and Child Enthroned with Saints* by BERNARDO DADDI (active ca. 1312–1348).

14-19A ORCAGNA, Or San Michele tabernacle, 1355–1359.

Pisa

Siena and Florence were inland centers of commerce. Pisa was one of Italy's port cities, which, with Genoa and Venice (MAP 14-1), controlled the rapidly growing maritime avenues connecting western Europe with the lands of Islam, with Byzantium and Russia, and with China. As prosperous as Pisa was as a major shipping power, however, it was not immune from the disruption the Black Death wreaked across all of Italy and Europe in the late 1340s. Concern with death, a significant theme in art even before the onset of the plague, became more prominent in the years after midcentury.

CAMPOSANTO *Triumph of Death* is a tour de force of death imagery (FIG. 14-20). The creator of this large-scale (over 18 by 49 feet) fresco remains disputed. Some art historians attribute the work to FRANCESCO TRAINI (active ca. 1321–1363), while others argue for BUONAMICO BUFFALMACCO (active 1320–1336). Painted on the wall of the Camposanto (Holy Field), the enclosed burial ground adjacent to Pisa's cathedral (FIG. 12-26), the fresco captures the horrors of death and forces viewers to confront their mortality. The painter rendered each scene with naturalism and emotive power. In the left foreground (FIG. 14-20, *top*), young aristocrats, mounted in a stylish cavalcade, encounter three coffin-encased corpses in differing stages of decomposition. As the horror of the confrontation with death strikes them, the ladies turn away with delicate disgust, while a gentleman holds his nose. (The animals, horses and dogs, sniff excitedly.) At the far left, the hermit Saint Macarius unrolls a scroll bearing an inscription commenting on the folly of pleasure and

1 ft.

1 ft.

14-20 FRANCESCO TRAINI or BUONAMICO BUFFALMACCO, two details of *Triumph of Death*, 1330s. Full fresco, 18′ 6″ × 49′ 2″. Camposanto, Pisa. ◼◄

Befitting its location on a wall in Pisa's Camposanto, the enclosed burial ground adjacent to the cathedral, this fresco captures the horrors of death and forces viewers to confront their mortality.

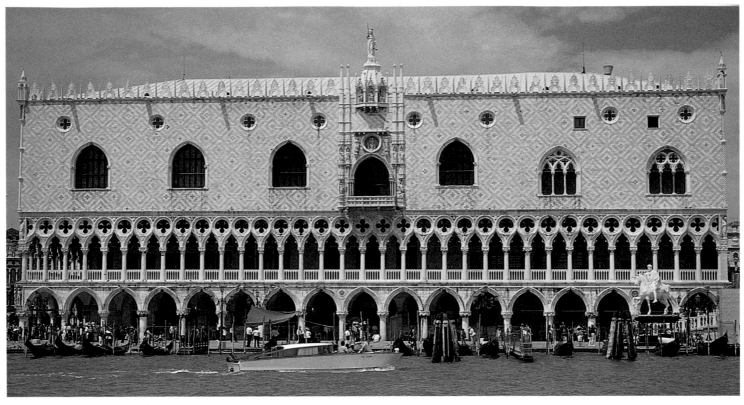

14-21 Doge's Palace, Venice, Italy, begun ca. 1340–1345; expanded and remodeled, 1424–1438.

The delicate patterning in cream- and rose-colored marbles, the pointed and ogee arches, and the quatrefoil medallions of the Doge's Palace constitute a Venetian variation of northern Gothic architecture.

the inevitability of death. On the far right, ladies and gentlemen ignore dreadful realities, occupying themselves in an orange grove with music and amusements while above them (FIG. 14-20, *bottom*) angels and demons struggle for the souls of the corpses heaped in the foreground.

In addition to these direct and straightforward scenes, the mural contains details conveying more subtle messages. For example, the painter depicted those who appear unprepared for death— and thus unlikely to achieve salvation—as wealthy and reveling in luxury. Given that the Dominicans—an order committed to a life of poverty (see "Mendicant Orders," page 404)—participated in the design for this fresco program, this imagery surely was a warning against greed and lust.

Venice

One of the wealthiest cities of late medieval Italy—and of Europe— was Venice, renowned for its streets of water. Situated on a lagoon on the northeastern coast of Italy, Venice was secure from land attack and could rely on a powerful navy for protection against invasion from the sea. Internally, Venice was a tight corporation of ruling families that, for centuries, provided stable rule and fostered economic growth.

DOGE'S PALACE The Venetian republic's seat of government was the Doge's (Duke's) Palace (FIG. **14-21**). Begun around 1340 to 1345 and significantly remodeled after 1424, it was the most ornate public building in medieval Italy. In a stately march, the first level's short and heavy columns support rather severe *pointed arches* that look strong enough to carry the weight of the upper structure. Their rhythm doubles in the upper arcades, where more slender columns carry *ogee arches* (made up of double-curving lines), which terminate in flamelike tips between medallions pierced with quatrefoils. Each story is taller than the one beneath it, the topmost as high as the two lower arcades combined. Yet the building does not look top-heavy. This is due in part to the complete absence of articulation in the top story and in part to the walls' delicate patterning, in cream- and rose-colored marbles, which makes them appear paper-thin. The Doge's Palace represents a delightful and charming variant of Late Gothic architecture. Colorful, decorative, light and airy in appearance, the Venetian palace is ideally suited to this unique Italian city that floats between water and sky.

LATE MEDIEVAL ITALY

13TH CENTURY

▌ Diversity of style characterizes the art of 13th-century Italy, with some artists working in the *maniera greca*, or Italo-Byzantine style, some in the mode of Gothic France, and others in the newly revived classical tradition.

▌ The leading painters working in the Italo-Byzantine style were Bonaventura Berlinghieri and Cimabue. Both drew inspiration from Byzantine icons and illuminated manuscripts. Berlinghieri's *Saint Francis Altarpiece* is the earliest dated portrayal of Saint Francis of Assisi, who died in 1226.

▌ Trained in southern Italy in the court style of Frederick II (r. 1197–1250), Nicola Pisano was a master sculptor who settled in Pisa and carved pulpits incorporating marble panels that, both stylistically and in individual motifs, derive from ancient Roman sarcophagi. Nicola's son, Giovanni Pisano, also was a sculptor of church pulpits, but his work more closely reflects the Gothic sculpture of France.

▌ At the end of the century, in Rome and Assisi, Pietro Cavallini and other fresco painters created mural programs foreshadowing the revolutionary art of Giotto.

Bonaventura Berlinghieri, *Saint Francis Altarpiece*, 1235

Nicola Pisano, Pisa Baptistery pulpit, 1259–1260

14TH CENTURY

▌ During the 14th century, Italy suffered the most devastating natural disaster in European history—the Black Death—but it was also the time when Renaissance humanism took root. Although religion continued to occupy a primary position in Italian life, scholars and artists became increasingly concerned with the natural world.

▌ Art historians regard Giotto di Bondone of Florence as the first Renaissance painter. An architect as well, Giotto designed the bell tower of Florence's Cathedral. His masterpiece is the fresco program of the Arena Chapel in Padua, where he established himself as a pioneer in pursuing a naturalistic approach to representation based on observation, which was at the core of the classical tradition in art. The Renaissance marked the rebirth of classical values in art and society.

▌ The greatest master of the Sienese school of painting was Duccio di Buoninsegna, whose *Maestà* still incorporates many elements of the *maniera greca*. He relaxed the frontality and rigidity of his figures, however, and in the narrative scenes on the back of the gigantic altarpiece in Siena Cathedral took a decisive step toward humanizing religious subject matter by depicting actors displaying individual emotions.

▌ Secular themes also came to the fore in 14th-century Italy, most notably in Ambrogio Lorenzetti's frescoes for Siena's Palazzo Pubblico. His depictions of the city and its surrounding countryside are among the first landscapes in Western art since antiquity.

▌ The prosperity of the 14th century led to many major building campaigns, including new cathedrals in Florence, Siena, and Orvieto, and new administrative palaces in Florence, Siena, and Venice. Florence's 11th-century baptistery also received new bronze doors by Andrea Pisano.

▌ The 14th-century architecture of Italy underscores the regional character of late medieval art. Orvieto Cathedral's facade, for example, incorporates some elements of the French Gothic vocabulary, but it is a screen masking a timber-roofed structure with round arches in the nave arcade in the Early Christian tradition.

Giotto, Arena Chapel, Padua, ca. 1305

Duccio, *Maestà*, Siena Cathedral, 1308–1311

Orvieto Cathedral, begun 1310

This frieze is one of the earliest pictorial narratives of the Buddha's life. At the left, Queen Maya gives birth to Prince Siddhartha, the future Buddha, who emerges from her right hip.

Here, the Buddha, seated in the Deer Park at Sarnath with his right hand raised in a gesture of blessing, preaches his first sermon in which he reveals the Eightfold Path to nirvana.

In the next scene, the Buddha sits beneath the Bodhi tree while the soldiers and demons of the evil Mara attempt to distract him from his quest for knowledge, but they are not successful.

15-1 The life and death of the Buddha, frieze from Gandhara, Pakistan, second century CE. Schist, 2′ 2⅜″ × 9′ 6⅛″. Freer Gallery of Art, Washington, D.C.

In the final scene, the Buddha lies dying among his devotees, who wail in grief, save for one meditating monk who realizes the Buddha has achieved nirvana and release from suffering.

SOUTH AND SOUTHEAST ASIA BEFORE 1200

THE LIFE OF THE BUDDHA

The Buddha (Enlightened One) was born around 563 BCE as Prince Siddhartha Gautama, the eldest son of the king of the Shakya clan. A prophecy foretold he would grow up to be either a world conqueror or a great religious leader. His father preferred the secular role for young Siddhartha and groomed him for kingship by shielding the boy from the hardships of the world. When he was 29, however, the prince rode out of the palace, abandoned his wife and family, and encountered for himself the pain of old age, sickness, and death. Siddhartha responded to the suffering he witnessed by renouncing his opulent life and becoming a wandering ascetic searching for knowledge through meditation. Six years later, he achieved complete enlightenment, or buddhahood, while meditating beneath a pipal tree (the Bodhi tree) at Bodh Gaya ("place of enlightenment") in eastern India. Known from that day on as Shakyamuni ("wise man of the Shakya clan"), the Buddha preached his first sermon in the Deer Park at Sarnath. There he set in motion the Wheel (*chakra*) of the Law (*dharma*) and expounded the Four Noble Truths, the core insights of Buddhism: (1) life is suffering; (2) the cause of suffering is desire; (3) one can overcome and extinguish desire; (4) the way to conquer desire and end suffering is to follow the Buddha's Eightfold Path of right understanding, right thought, right speech, right action, right livelihood, right effort, right mindfulness, and right concentration. The Buddha's path leads to *nirvana,* the cessation of the endless cycle of painful life, death, and rebirth. The Buddha continued to preach until his death at age 80.

One of the earliest pictorial narrative cycles of the Buddha's life is a stone frieze (FIG. **15-1**) from Gandhara, a region largely in Pakistan today, close to the Afghanistan border. Depicted, in chronological order from left to right, are the Buddha's birth at Lumbini, the enlightenment at Bodh Gaya, the first sermon at Sarnath, and the Buddha's death at Kushinagara. At the left, Queen Maya gives birth to Prince Siddhartha, who emerges from her right hip. Receiving him is the god Indra. Elegantly dressed ladies, one with a fan of peacock feathers, suggest the opulent court life the Buddha left behind. In the next scene, the Buddha sits beneath the Bodhi tree while the soldiers and demons of the evil Mara attempt to distract him from his quest for knowledge. They are unsuccessful, and the Buddha then preaches the Eightfold Path to nirvana in the Deer Park at Sarnath. The sculptor set the scene by placing two deer and the Wheel of the Law beneath the figure of the Buddha. In the final section of the frieze, the parinirvana, the Buddha lies dying among his devotees, some of whom wail in grief, while one monk, who realizes the Buddha has been permanently released from suffering, remains tranquil in meditation.

SOUTH ASIA

In the third millennium BCE, a great civilization arose over a wide geographic area along the Indus River in Pakistan and extended into India as far south as Gujarat and east beyond Delhi (MAP **15-1**). Thus, when Alexander the Great and his army reached India in 326 BCE, they encountered a civilization already more than 2,000 years old. In fact, the remains of the first cities in the Indus Valley predate the palaces of Homer's Trojan War heroes (FIGS. 4-15 and 4-19) by a millennium. Archaeologists have dubbed this early South Asian culture the Indus Civilization.

Indus Civilization

The Indus Civilization flourished from about 2600 to 1500 BCE. The most important excavated Indus sites are Mohenjo-daro and Harappa in present-day Pakistan. Both were fully developed cities featuring streets oriented to compass points and multistoried houses built of carefully formed and precisely laid kiln-baked bricks. Their inhabitants engaged in trade with cities as far away as modern Iraq, but in sharp contrast to the contemporaneous civilizations of Mesopotamia and Egypt (see Chapters 2 and 3), no surviving Indus building has yet been identified as a temple or a palace.

MAP 15-1 South and Southeast Asian sites before 1200.

SOUTH AND SOUTHEAST ASIA BEFORE 1200

2600	Indus	1500	323	Maurya	185	Shunga, Andhra, Kushan	320	Gupta and Post-Gupta	647	Medieval	1200

BCE   CE

- First South Asian cities in the Indus Valley have rational plans and sophisticated water-supply and sewage systems
- Indus art is small-scale and has stylistic parallels in the art of Mesopotamia

- Ashoka (r. 272–231 BCE) converts to Buddhism and builds the original Great Stupa at Sanchi. He also sets up pillars with animal capitals throughout his kingdom—the oldest preserved monumental stone artworks in India

- Construction of stupas and rock-cut chaitya halls in Buddhist monasteries
- First representations of the Buddha in human form based on prototypes in Greco-Roman art

- Gupta sculptors establish the canonical image of the Buddha
- Earliest mural paintings in the Buddhist caves of Ajanta
- Oldest preserved Hindu monumental stone temples and sculptures

- Emergence of distinct regional styles in South Asian Hindu temple architecture
- Regional variations on Indian architectural and sculptural prototypes appear throughout Southeast Asia

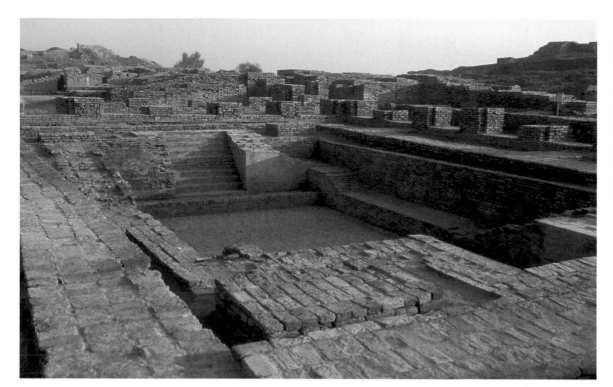

The Indus cities of the third millennium BCE had sophisticated water-supply and sewage systems, which made possible this brick complex used for ritual bathing of a kind still practiced in South Asia today.

MOHENJO-DARO The Indus cities also boasted one of the world's first sophisticated systems of water supply and sewage. Throughout Mohenjo-daro, hundreds of wells provided fresh water to homes incorporating some of the oldest recorded private bathing areas and toilet facilities, with drainage into public sewers. In the heart of the city stood the so-called Great Bath, a complex of rooms centered on a sunken brick pool (FIG. 15-2) 39 feet long, 23 feet wide, and 8 feet deep. The Indus builders made the pool watertight by sealing the joints between the bricks with bitumen, an asphaltlike material also used in Mesopotamia. The bath was probably not a purely recreational facility but rather a place for ritual bathing of the kind still practiced in South Asia today.

Surprisingly, excavators have discovered little art from the long-lived Indus Civilization, and all of the objects found are small. Perhaps the most impressive preserved sculpture represents a robed male figure (FIG. 15-3) with half-closed eyes, a low forehead, and a closely trimmed beard with shaved upper lip. He wears a headband with a central circular emblem, matched by a similar armband. Holes on each side of his neck suggest he also wore a necklace of precious metal. *Trefoils* (cloverlike designs with three stylized leaves) decorate his elegant robe. They, as well as the circles of the head- and armbands, originally held red paste and shell inlays, as did the eyes. Scholars often compare the Mohenjo-daro statuette with Sumerian sculptures, where the trefoil motif appears in sacred contexts, and refer to the person portrayed as a "priest-king," the ambiguous term used for some Sumerian leaders. The identity and rank of the Mohenjo-daro figure are uncertain, however. Nonetheless, the elaborate costume and precious materials make clear he was an elite individual.

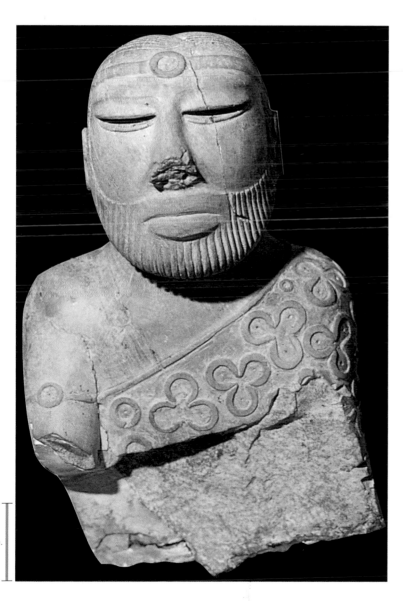

1 in.

15-3 Robed male figure, from Mohenjo-daro, Pakistan, ca. 2000–1900 BCE. Steatite, $6\frac{7}{8}$″ high. National Museum of Pakistan, Karachi.

Little art survives from the Indus Civilization, and all of it is of small scale. This bearded figure, which scholars think represents a priest-king, has iconographic similarities to some Sumerian sculptures.

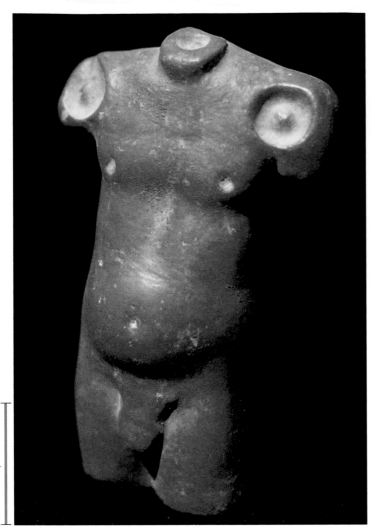

15-4 Nude male torso, from Harappa, Pakistan, ca. 2000–1900 BCE. Red sandstone, $3\frac{3}{4}''$ high. National Museum, New Delhi.

This miniature figure, with its emphasis on sensuous polished surfaces and swelling curves, already displays many of the stylistic traits common to South Asian sculpture for thousands of years.

HARAPPA Quite different in style is the fragmentary miniature red sandstone male figure (FIG. **15-4**) found at Harappa. Scholars usually compare this nude figure, which is less than 4 inches in height, with Greek statues of much later date, but the treatment of anatomy separates it sharply from the classical tradition. The highly polished surface of the stone and the swelling curves of the abdomen reveal the Indus artist's interest in the fluid movement of a living body, not in the logical anatomical structure of Greek sculpture. This sense of pulsating vigor and the emphasis on sensuous surfaces would continue to be chief characteristics of South Asian sculpture for thousands of years.

INDUS SEALS The most common Indus art objects are steatite seals with incised designs. They are similar in many ways to the stamp seals found at contemporaneous sites in Mesopotamia (see "Mesopotamian Seals," Chapter 2, page 39). Most of the Indus examples have an animal or tiny narrative carved on the face, along with an as-yet-untranslated script. On the back, a *boss* (circular knob) with a hole permitted insertion of a string so that the owner could wear the seal or hang it on a wall. As in the ancient Near East, the Indus peoples sometimes used the seals to make impressions on clay, apparently for securing trade goods wrapped in textiles. The animals most frequently represented include the humped bull,

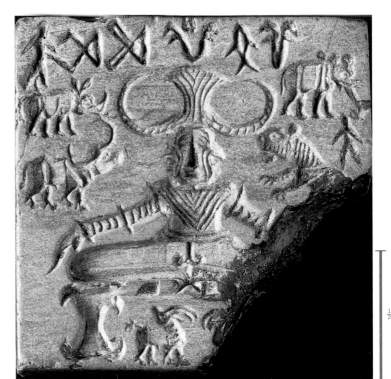

15-5 Seal with seated figure in yogic posture, from Mohenjo-daro, Pakistan, ca. 2300–1750 BCE. Steatite coated with alkali and baked, $1\frac{3}{8}'' \times 1\frac{3}{8}''$. National Museum, New Delhi.

This seal depicting a (three-faced?) figure wearing a horned headdress and seated in a yogic posture indicates this important Indian meditative practice began as early as the Indus Civilization.

elephant, rhinoceros, and tiger. The seal carvers portrayed all the animals in strict profile, as did the painters and relief sculptors of all other early cultures. Some of the narrative seals indicate the Indus peoples considered trees sacred, as both Buddhists and Hindus did later. Many scholars have suggested religious and ritual continuities between the Indus Civilization and later Indian culture.

One of the most elaborate seals (FIG. **15-5**) depicts a male figure with a horned headdress and, perhaps, three faces, seated (with erect penis) among the profile animals that regularly appear alone on other seals. The figure's position—folded legs with heels pressed together and arms resting on the knees—suggests a yogic posture (compare FIG. 15-12). *Yoga* is a method for controlling the body and relaxing the mind used in later Indian religions to yoke, or unite, the practitioner to the divine. Although most scholars reject the identification of this figure as a prototype of the multiheaded Hindu god Shiva (FIG. 15-18) as Lord of Beasts, the yogic posture proves this important Indian meditative practice began as early as the Indus Civilization.

Vedic and Upanishadic Period

By 1700 BCE, the urban phase of the Indus Civilization had ended in most areas. The production of sculptures, seals, and script gradually ceased, and village life replaced urban culture. Very little art survives from the next thousand years, but the religious foundations laid during this period helped define most later South and Southeast Asian art.

VEDAS The basis for the new religious ideas were the oral hymns of the Aryans, a mobile herding people from Central Asia who occupied the Punjab, an area of northwestern India, in the second

Buddhism and Buddhist Iconography

The earliest form of Buddhism is Theravada (Path of the Elders) Buddhism. Practiced by the historical Buddha's disciples at the monasteries they founded after his death, Theravada Buddhism seeks to aid individuals wishing to follow Shakyamuni Buddha's path to enlightenment and nirvana. The new religion developed and changed over time, however, as the Buddha's teachings spread from India throughout Asia. The second major school of Buddhist thought, Mahayana (Great Path) Buddhism, emerged around the beginning of the Common Era (CE). Mahayana Buddhists refer to Theravada Buddhism as Hinayana (Lesser Path) Buddhism and believe in a larger goal than nirvana for an individual—namely, buddhahood for all. Mahayana Buddhists also revere *bodhisattvas* (Buddhas-to-be), exemplars of compassion who restrain themselves at the threshold of nirvana to aid others in earning merit and achieving buddhahood. Theravada Buddhism became the dominant sect in southern India, Sri Lanka, and mainland Southeast Asia, whereas Mahayana Buddhism took root in northern India and spread to China, Korea, Japan, and Nepal.

A third important Buddhist sect, especially popular in East Asia, venerates the Amitabha Buddha (Amida in Japanese), the Buddha of Infinite Light and Life. The devotees of this Buddha hope to be reborn in the Pure Land Paradise of the West, where the Amitabha resides and can grant them salvation. In Pure Land teachings, people have no possibility of attaining enlightenment on their own but can achieve paradise by faith alone.

The earliest (first century CE) depictions of the Buddha in human form show him as a robed monk. Artists distinguished the Enlightened One from monks and bodhisattvas by *lakshanas*, body attributes indicating the Buddha's suprahuman nature. These distinguishing marks include an *urna*, or curl of hair between the eyebrows, shown as a dot; an *ushnisha*, a cranial bump shown as hair on the earliest images (FIGS. 15-1, 15-11, 15-11A, and 15-12) but later as part of the head (FIG. 15-13); and, less frequently, palms and soles imprinted with a wheel (FIG. 15-12). Artists also often depicted the Buddha with elongated ears, the result of wearing heavy royal jewelry in his youth, but the enlightened Shakyamuni is rarely bejeweled, though many bodhisattvas are (FIG. 15-14). Sometimes the Buddha appears with a halo, or sun disk, behind his head (FIGS. 15-11, 15-11A, 15-12, and 15-13).

Representations of the Buddha also feature a repertory of *mudras*, or hand gestures, conveying fixed meanings. These include the *dhyana* (meditation) mudra, with the right hand over the left, palms upward (FIG. 15-11); the *bhumisparsha* (earth-touching) mudra, right hand down reaching to the ground, calling the earth to witness the Buddha's enlightenment (FIG. 15-1); the *dharmachakra* (Wheel of the Law, or teaching) mudra, a two-handed gesture with right thumb and index finger forming a circle (FIG. 15-13); and the *abhaya* (do not fear) mudra, right hand up, palm outward, a gesture of protection or blessing (FIGS. 15-1, 15-11A, and 15-12).

Episodes from the Buddha's life are among the most popular subjects in all Buddhist artistic traditions. No single text provides the complete or authoritative narrative of the Buddha's life and death. Thus, numerous versions and variations exist, allowing for a rich artistic repertory. Four of the most important events (see "The Life of the Buddha," page 423) are his birth at Lumbini from the side of his mother, Queen Maya (FIG. 15-1); the achievement of buddhahood while meditating beneath the Bodhi tree at Bodh Gaya (FIG. 15-1); the Buddha's first sermon at Sarnath (FIGS. 15-1 and 15-13); and his attainment of nirvana (*parinirvana*) when he died at Kushinagara (FIGS. 15-1 and 15-28). Buddhists established monasteries and monuments at the four sites where these key events occurred, although the Buddha himself disapproved of all luxury, including lavish religious shrines featuring costly figural art.

millennium BCE. The Aryans ("Noble Ones") spoke Sanskrit, the earliest language yet identified in South Asia. Around 1500 BCE, they composed the first of four *Vedas*. These Sanskrit compilations of religious learning (*Veda* means "knowledge") included hymns intended for priests (called Brahmins) to chant or sing. The Brahmins headed a social hierarchy, or caste system, perhaps of pre-Aryan origin, that still forms the basis of Indian society today. Below the priests were the warriors, traders, and manual laborers (including artists and architects), respectively. The Aryan religion centered on sacrifice, the ritual enactment of often highly intricate and lengthy ceremonies in which the priests placed materials, such as milk and soma (an intoxicating drink), into a fire that carried the sacrifices to the gods in the heavens. If the Brahmins performed these rituals accurately, the gods would fulfill the prayers of those who sponsored the sacrifices. These gods, primarily male, included Indra, Varuna, Surya, and Agni, gods associated, respectively, with rain, the ocean, the sun, and fire. The Aryans apparently did not create images of these deities.

UPANISHADS The next phase of South Asian urban civilization developed east of the Indus heartland, in the Ganges River valley. Here, from 800 to 500 BCE, religious thinkers composed a variety of texts called the *Upanishads*. Among the innovative ideas in the Upanishads were *samsara, karma,* and *moksha* (or *nirvana*). *Samsara* is the belief that individuals are born again after death in an almost endless round of rebirths. The type of rebirth can vary. One can be reborn as a human being, an animal, or even a god. An individual's past actions (*karma*), either good or bad, determine the nature of future rebirths. The ultimate goal of a person's religious life is to escape—*moksha* (liberation) or *nirvana* (cessation)—from the cycle of birth and death by merging the individual self into the vital force of the universe.

HINDUISM AND BUDDHISM Hinduism and Buddhism, the two major modern religions originating in Asia, developed in the late centuries BCE and the early centuries CE. Hinduism, the dominant religion in India today, discussed in more detail later, has its origins in Aryan religion. The founder of Buddhism was the Buddha (see "The Life of the Buddha," page 423), who advocated the path of *asceticism,* or self-discipline and self-denial, as the means to free oneself from attachments to people and possessions, thus ending rebirth (see "Buddhism and Buddhist Iconography," above). Buddhists call the escape from the cycle of birth, death, and rebirth "nirvana" (cessation). Hindus call it "moksha" (liberation). Unlike

Ashoka's Conversion to Buddhism

The reign of the Maurya king Ashoka marks both the beginning of monumental stone art and architecture (FIGS. 15-6, 15-6A, and 15-6B) in India and the first official sponsorship of Buddhism. The effect of Ashoka's conversion to Buddhism on the later history of art and religion in Asia cannot be overstated. An edict carved into a rock at Dhauli in the ancient region of Kalinga (roughly equivalent to the modern state of Orissa on the Bay of Bengal) records Ashoka's embrace of nonviolence and of the Buddha's teachings after an especially bloody conquest that claimed more than 100,000 lives. The inscription also captures Ashoka's missionary zeal, which spread Buddhism far beyond the boundaries of his kingdom.

> The Beloved of the Gods [Ashoka], conqueror of the Kalingas, is moved to remorse now. For he has felt profound sorrow and regret because the conquest of a people previously unconquered involves slaughter, death, and deportation.... [King Ashoka] now thinks that even a person who wrongs him must be forgiven ... [and he] considers moral conquest [conquest by dharma] the most important conquest. He has achieved this moral conquest repeatedly both here and among the peoples living beyond the borders of his kingdom.... Even in countries which [King Ashoka's] envoys have not reached, people have heard about dharma and about [the king's] ordinances and instructions in dharma.... This edict on dharma has been inscribed so that my sons and great-grandsons who may come after me should not think new conquests worth achieving.... Let them consider moral conquest the only true conquest.*

The story of Ashoka's renunciation of violent aggression at Kalinga still resonates today. It inspired one of the most important 20th-century Indian sculptors to take up the theme and imbue it with contemporary meaning (FIG. 32-11).

*Rock Edict XIII. Translated by N. A. Nikam and Richard McKeon, *The Edicts of Asoka* (Chicago: University of Chicago Press, 1959), 27–30.

15-6 Lion capital of the column set up by Ashoka at Sarnath, India, ca. 250 BCE. Polished sandstone, 7′ high. Archaeological Museum, Sarnath.

Ashoka formulated a legal code based on the Buddha's teachings and inscribed those laws on columns he set up throughout his kingdom. The lions on this capital supported the Wheel of the Law.

1 ft.

---

their predecessors in South Asia, both Hindus and Buddhists use images of gods and holy persons in religious rituals. To judge from surviving works, Buddhism has the older artistic tradition. The earliest Buddhist monuments date to the Maurya period.

Maurya Dynasty

In 326 BCE, after conquering the Persian Empire (see Chapter 5), Alexander the Great reached the Indus River, but his troops refused to go forward. Reluctantly, Alexander abandoned his dream of conquering India and headed home. After Alexander's death three years later, his generals divided his empire among themselves. One of them, Seleucus Nicator, reinvaded India, but Chandragupta Maurya (r. 323–298 BCE), founder of the Maurya dynasty, defeated

him in 305 BCE and eventually consolidated almost all of present-day India under his domain. Chandragupta's capital was Pataliputra (modern Patna) in northeastern India, far from the center of the Indus Civilization (MAP 15-1). Megasthenes, Seleucus's ambassador to the Maurya court, described Pataliputra in his book on India as a large and wealthy city enclosed within mighty wooden walls so extensive the circuit had 64 gates and 570 towers.

ASHOKA The greatest Maurya ruler was Ashoka (r. 272–231 BCE), who left his imprint on history by converting to Buddhism and spreading the Buddha's teaching throughout and beyond India (see "Ashoka's Conversion to Buddhism," above). Ashoka formulated a legal code based on the Buddha's dharma and inscribed his laws on enormous *monolithic* (one-piece stone) columns set up throughout his kingdom. Ashoka's pillars, one of which (FIG. 15-6A) still stands at Lauriya Nandangarh, reached 30 to 40 feet high and were the first monumental stone artworks in India. The pillars penetrated deep into the ground, connecting earth and sky, forming an "axis of the universe," a pre-Buddhist concept that became an important motif in Buddhist architecture. The columns stood along pilgrimage routes to sites associated with the Buddha and on the roads leading to Pataliputra.

15-6A Lion pillar, Lauriya Nandangarh, ca. 245 BCE.

Capping Ashoka's pillars were elaborate *capitals,* also carved from a single block of stone. The finest (FIG. 15-6) comes from Sarnath, where the Buddha gave his first sermon and set the Wheel of the Law into motion. At 7 feet high, it and a contemporaneous statue representing a fertility goddess (FIG. 15-6B) found near the Mauryan capital are among the earliest works of monumental sculpture in South Asia. Stylistically, the Sarnath lion capital owes much to ancient Mesopotamia and Persia, especially the Achaemenid art of Persepolis (FIG. 2-26), but its iconography is Buddhist. Two pairs of back-to-back lions (texts often refer to the Buddha as "the lion") stand on a round *abacus* decorated with four wheels and four animals symbolizing the four quarters of the world. The lions once carried a large stone wheel on their backs. The wheel (*chakra*) is a reference to the Wheel of the Law but also indicated Ashoka's stature as a *chakravartin* ("holder of the wheel"), a universal king imbued with divine authority. The open mouths of the four lions facing the four quarters of the world may signify the worldwide announcement of the Buddha's message.

15-6B Yakshi with fly whisk, Didarganj, mid-third century BCE.

Shunga, Andhra, and Kushan Dynasties

The Maurya dynasty came to an abrupt end when its last ruler was assassinated by one of his generals, who founded a new dynasty in his own name. The Shungas, however, never ruled an empire as extensive as the Maurya kingdom. The Shunga realm comprised only central India, and the Andhras, who controlled the Deccan plateau to the south, usurped their power in the early first century BCE. By the middle of that century, an even greater empire, the Kushan, rose in northern India. Its most celebrated king was Kanishka, who came to power during the late first or early second century CE and who set up capitals at Peshawar and other sites in Gandhara. The Kushans grew rich on trade between China and the west along one of the main caravan routes bringing the luxuries of the Orient to the Roman Empire (see "The Silk Road," Chapter 16, page 458). Kanishka even struck coins modeled on the imperial coinage of Rome, some featuring Greco-Roman deities, but Kanishka's coins also carried portraits of himself and images of the Buddha and various Hindu deities.

SANCHI The unifying characteristic of this age of regional dynasties in South Asia was the patronage of Buddhism. One important Buddhist monastery, founded during Ashoka's reign and in use for more than a thousand years, is at Sanchi in central India. It consists of many buildings constructed over the centuries, including *viharas* (celled structures where monks live), large *stupas* (see "The Stupa," page 430), *chaitya halls* (halls with rounded, or *apsidal*, ends for housing smaller stupas), and temples for sheltering images.

The Great Stupa at Sanchi dates originally to Ashoka's reign, but its present form (FIG. 15-7), with its tall stone fence and four gates, dates from about 50 BCE to 50 CE. The solid earth-and-rubble dome stands 50 feet high. Worshipers enter through one of

1 ft.

15-7 *Top:* Great Stupa (looking north), Sanchi, India, third century BCE to first century CE. *Bottom:* Elephants and yakshi, detail of the east torana, mid-first century BCE to early first century CE. Sandstone, 5′ high.

The Sanchi stupa is an earthen mound containing relics of the Buddha. Buddhists walk around stupas in a clockwise direction. They believe the circular movement brings devotees into harmony with the cosmos.

The Stupa

An essential element of Buddhist sanctuaries is the *stupa*, a large circular mound modeled on earlier South Asian burial mounds of a type familiar in many other ancient cultures (FIGS. 4-20 and 6-6). The stupa was not a tomb, however, but a monument housing relics of the Buddha. When the Buddha died, his followers placed his cremated remains in eight *reliquaries*, or containers, similar in function to the later reliquaries housed in medieval churches at pilgrimage sites throughout the Christian world (see "The Veneration of Relics," Chapter 12, page 336). But unlike their Western equivalents, which were put on display, the Buddha's relics were buried in solid earthen mounds (stupas) that could not be entered. In the mid-third century BCE, Ashoka opened the original eight stupas and spread the Buddha's relics among thousands of stupas in all corners of his realm. Buddhists venerated the Buddha's remains by *circumambulation*, walking around the stupa in a clockwise direction. The circular movement, echoing the movement of the earth and the sun, brought the devotee into harmony with the cosmos. Stupas come in many sizes, from tiny handheld objects to huge structures, such as the Great Stupa at Sanchi (FIG. 15-7), constructed originally by Ashoka and later enlarged.

The monumental stupas are three-dimensional *mandalas*, or sacred diagrams of the universe. The domed stupa itself represents the world mountain, with the cardinal points marked by *toranas*, or gateways (FIGS. 15-8 and 15-8A). The *harmika*, positioned atop the stupa dome, is a stone fence or railing that encloses a square

15-8 Diagram of the Great Stupa, Sanchi, India, third century BCE to first century CE.

Stupas are three-dimensional mandalas (sacred diagrams of the universe). The domed stupa represents the world mountain with a yasti at the top corresponding to the axis of the universe. Toranas mark the cardinal points.

area symbolizing the sacred domain of the gods. At the harmika's center, a *yasti*, or pole, corresponds to the axis of the universe, a motif already present in Ashoka's pillars (FIG. 15-6A). Three *chatras*, or stone disks, assigned various meanings, crown the yasti. The yasti rises from the mountain-dome and passes through the harmika, thus uniting this world with the heavenly paradise. A stone fence often encloses the entire structure, clearly separating the sacred space containing the Buddha's relics from the profane world outside.

the gateways, walk on the lower circumambulation path, then climb the stairs on the south side to circumambulate at the second level (FIG. 15-8). Carved onto different parts of the Great Stupa are more than 600 brief inscriptions of donors to the project. Hundreds of individuals (more than a third of them women) made the monument's construction possible. Veneration of the Buddha was open to all, not just the monks, and common laypeople, who hoped to accrue merit for future rebirths with their gifts, made most of the dedications.

15-8A East torana, Great Stupa, Sanchi, ca. 50 BCE–50 CE.

The reliefs on the four toranas (FIG. 15-8A) at Sanchi depict the story of the Buddha's life and those of his past lives (*jatakas*). In Buddhist belief, everyone has had innumerable past lives, including Siddhartha. During Siddhartha's former lives, as recorded in the jatakas, he accumulated sufficient merit to achieve enlightenment and become the Buddha. In the life stories recounted in the Sanchi torana reliefs, however, the Buddha never appears in human form. Instead, the artists used symbols, for example, footprints, a parasol, or an empty seat, to indicate the Buddha's presence. Some scholars regard these symbols as markers of where the Buddha once was so that others can follow in his footsteps.

Also carved on the east torana is a scantily clad, sensuous woman called a *yakshi* (FIG. 15-7, *bottom*). These goddesses, worshiped throughout India, personify fertility and vegetation and were long-established statuary types (FIG. 15-6B) in the repertoire of South Asian sculptors. The Sanchi yakshi reaches up to hold a mango tree branch while pressing her left foot against the trunk, which causes the tree to flower. Buddhist artists later adopted this pose, with its rich associations of procreation and abundance, for representing the Buddha's mother, Maya, giving birth (FIG. 15-1). Thus, South Asian artists adopted pan-Indian symbolism, such as the woman under the tree, when formulating Buddhist iconography.

KARLE The chaitya hall (FIGS. 15-9 and 15-10) carved out of the living rock at Karle in imitation of earlier wooden structures is the best early example of a Buddhist stupa hall. Datable around 50 to 100 CE, the Karle hall has a pillared *ambulatory* (walking path), enabling worshipers to circumambulate the stupa placed at the back of the sacred cave. The hall also has excellent acoustics for devotional chanting. At nearly 45 feet high and 125 feet long, it surpasses in size even the rock-cut chamber (FIG. 3-23) of the temple of the Egyptian pharaoh Ramses II. Elaborate capitals atop the rock-cut pillars depict men and women riding on elephants (compare FIG. 15-8). Outside,

15-9 Interior of the chaitya hall, Karle, India, ca. 50–100 CE.

Chaitya halls in Buddhist monasteries house stupas. The rock-cut cave at Karle imitates earlier wooden halls. The massive interior (45 feet tall, 125 feet long) has excellent acoustics for devotional chanting.

15-10 Plan (*top*) and section (*bottom*) of the chaitya hall, Karle, India, ca. 50–100 CE.

An early example of Buddhist architecture, the chaitya hall at Karle is carved out of the rock. It has a pillared ambulatory enabling worshipers to circumambulate the stupa in the apse of the cave.

amorous couples (*mithunas*) flank the entrance. As do the yakshis at Sanchi, these auspicious figures symbolize the creative life force.

GANDHARA The first anthropomorphic representations of the Buddha probably appeared in the first century CE. Scholars still debate what brought about this momentous shift in Buddhist iconography, but one factor may have been the changing perception of the Buddha himself. Originally revered as an enlightened mortal, the Buddha increasingly became regarded as a divinity. Consequently, the Buddha's followers desired images of him to worship.

Many early portrayals of the Buddha in human form come from the Gandhara region. A second-century CE statue (FIG. **15-11**) carved in gray schist, the local stone, shows the Buddha, with halo, ushnisha, and urna, dressed in a monk's robe, seated in a cross-legged yogic posture similar to that of the male figure with horned headdress on the Indus seal (FIG. 15-5). The Buddha's hands overlap, palms upward, in the dhyana mudra, the gesture of meditation see "Buddhism," page 427). This statue and similar

15-11 Meditating Buddha, from Gandhara, Pakistan, second century CE. Gray schist, 3′ 7½″ high. National Museums of Scotland, Edinburgh. ◼◀

Many early portrayals of the Buddha in human form come from Gandhara and depict the Enlightened One as a robed monk. The style of this Gandharan Buddha owes much to Greco-Roman art.

15-11A Standing Buddha, Gandhara, second to third century CE.

Gandharan representations of the Buddha, standing (FIG. **15-11A**) as well as seated, owe a great deal to Greco-Roman art, both in the treatment of body forms, such as the sharp, arching brows and continuous profile of forehead and nose (FIG. 5-41), and in the draping of the togalike garment (FIG. 7-71).

One of the earliest pictorial narratives in which the Buddha appears in human form also comes from Gandhara: the frieze (FIG. 15-1) in the Freer Gallery depicting the Buddha's birth at Lumbini, the enlightenment at Bodh Gaya, the first sermon at Sarnath, and the Buddha's death at Kushinagara. Although the iconography of the frieze is Buddhist with roots in earlier South Asian art—the representation of Queen Maya giving birth to Prince Siddhartha derives from depictions of yakshis (FIG. 15-7, *bottom*)—Roman reliefs must have served as stylistic models for the sculptors. For example, the distribution of standing and equestrian figures over the relief ground, with those behind the first row seemingly suspended in the air, is familiar in Roman art of the second and third centuries CE (FIGS. 7-65 and 7-70). The figure of the Buddha on his deathbed has parallels in the reclining figures on the lids of Roman sarcophagi (FIG. 7-61). The type of hierarchical composition in which a large central figure sits between balanced tiers of smaller onlookers is also common in Roman imperial art (FIG. 7-76).

MATHURA Contemporaneous with but stylistically distinct from the Gandharan sculptures are the Buddha images from Mathura, a city about 90 miles south of Delhi that was also part of the Kushan Empire. The Mathura statues (for example, FIG. **15-12**) have closer links to the Indian portrayals of *yakshas*, the male equivalents of the yakshis. Indian artists represented yakshas as robust, powerful males with broad shoulders and open, staring eyes. Mathura Buddhas, carved from red sandstone, as was the Harappa nude man (FIG. 15-4), retain these characteristics but wear a monk's robe (with right shoulder bare) and lack the yakshas' jewelry and other signs of wealth. The robe appears almost transparent, revealing the full, fleshy body beneath. In FIG. 15-12, the Buddha sits in a yogic posture on a lion throne under the Bodhi tree, attended by fly-whisk bearers. He raises his right hand palm-out in the abhaya

15-12 Buddha seated on lion throne, from Mathura, India, second century CE. Red sandstone, 2′ 3½″ high. Archaeological Museum, Muttra.

Stylistically distinct from the Gandharan Buddhas are those of Mathura. In this statue depicting the Buddha under the Bodhi tree, the Buddha has the body type of a yaksha but wears a monk's robe.

15-13 Seated Buddha preaching first sermon, from Sarnath, India, second half of fifth century. Tan sandstone, 5′ 3″ high. Archaeological Museum, Sarnath.

Gupta artists formulated the canonical sculpted image of the Buddha, combining the Gandharan monastic-robe type with the Mathuran soft, full-bodied figure attired in clinging garments.

The Painted Caves of Ajanta

Art historians assume India had a rich painting tradition in ancient times, but because early Indian artists often used perishable materials, such as palm leaf and wood, and because of the tropical climate in much of India, nearly all early Indian painting has disappeared. At Ajanta in the Deccan region, however, paintings cover the walls, pillars, and ceilings of several caves datable to the second half of the fifth century.

The detail reproduced here (FIG. 15-14) comes from one of the restored murals in cave 1 at Ajanta. The bodhisattva Padmapani sits among a crowd of devotees, both princes and commoners. With long, dark hair hanging down below a jeweled crown, he stands holding his attribute, a blue lotus flower, in his right hand. The painter rendered with finesse the sensuous form of the richly attired bodhisattva, gently modeling the figure with gradations of color and delicate highlights and shading, especially evident in the face and neck. The artist also carefully considered the placement of the painting in the cave, putting it on the left wall of the entrance to the antechamber of the main shrine. From that location the bodhisattva gazes downward at worshipers entering the antechamber on their way to the rock-cut Buddha image in a cell at the back of the cave.

To create the Ajanta murals, the painters—professional lay artists rather than monks—first applied two layers of clay mixed with straw and other materials to the walls. They then added a third layer of fine white lime plaster. Unlike true fresco painting (see "Fresco Painting," Chapter 14, page 408), in which painters apply colors to wet plaster, the Indian painters waited for the lime to dry. This method produces less durable results, and the Ajanta murals have suffered water damage over the centuries. The artists next outlined the figures in dark red and painted in the details of faces,

15-14 Bodhisattva Padmapani, detail of a wall painting in the antechamber of cave 1, Ajanta, India, second half of fifth century.

In this early example of Indian painting in an Ajanta cave, the artist rendered the sensuous form of the richly attired bodhisattva with gentle gradations of color and delicate highlights and shadows.

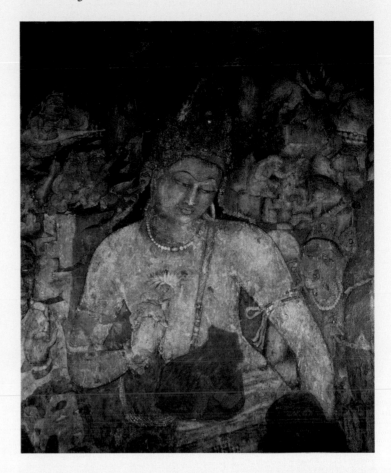

costumes, and jewelry. The Ajanta palette consisted of six basic water-soluble colors, produced mostly from local minerals: white, from lime; black, from soot; red and yellow, from ocher; and green, from glauconite. Blue, used sparingly, came from costly lapis lazuli imported from Afghanistan. The last step was to polish the painted surface with a smooth stone.

gesture, indicating to worshipers they need have no fear. His hands and feet bear the mark of the Wheel of the Law. The inscription reveals a Buddhist nun named Amoha-asi dedicated the sculpture "to the welfare and happiness of all sentient beings."

The Gupta and Post-Gupta Periods

Around 320* a new empire arose in north-central India. The Gupta emperors chose Pataliputra as their capital, deliberately associating themselves with the prestige of the former Maurya Empire. The heyday of this dynasty was under Chandragupta II (r. 375–415), whose very name recalled the first Maurya emperor. The Guptas were great patrons of art and literature.

SARNATH Under the Guptas, artists formulated what became the canonical image of the Buddha, combining the Gandharan monastic robe covering both shoulders (FIGS. 15-1, 15-11, and 15-11A)

_____
* From this point on, all dates in this chapter are CE unless otherwise stated.

with the soft, full-bodied Buddha figures with clinging garments of Mathuran sculpture (FIG. 15-12). These disparate styles beautifully merge in a fifth-century statue (FIG. **15-13**) of the Buddha from Sarnath. The statue's smooth, unadorned surfaces conform to the Indian notion of perfect body form and emphasize the figure's spirituality. The Buddha's eyes are downcast in meditation, and he holds his hands in front of his body in the Wheel-turning gesture, preaching his first sermon. Below the Buddha is a scene with the Wheel of the Law at the center between two (now partially broken) deer symbolizing the Deer Park at Sarnath. Buddha images such as this one became so popular that temples housing Buddha statues seem largely to have superseded the stupa as the norm in Buddhist sacred architecture.

BUDDHIST AJANTA The new popularity of Buddha imagery is evident in the mural and ceiling paintings of cave 1 (FIG. **15-14**) and the many other caves carved into the mountainside at Ajanta, northeast of Bombay (see "The Painted Caves of Ajanta," above). Ajanta owes its fame today to those paintings, but the site had been added more than 20 new caves to the site. Another Ajanta Buddhist monument is cave 19, which boasts a chaitya hall (FIG. 15-15) contemporaneous with the murals in cave 1. The typological similarity of the fifth-century Ajanta chaitya hall to the earlier example at Karle (FIG. 15-9) is immediately clear and is consistent with the conservative nature of religious architecture in all cultures. At Ajanta, however, sculptors carved on the front of the stupa an image of the Buddha standing between columns.

HINDU AJANTA At Ajanta, as at many other sites in India, Buddhists and Hindus (and adherents of other faiths) practiced their religions side by side. For example, at the same time painters were at work on the Buddhist murals in cave 1, the Hindu Vakataka king Harishena (r. 462–481) and members of his court were the sponsors of new Hindu caves at the monastery. Buddhism and Hinduism are not monotheistic religions, such as Judaism, Christianity, and Islam. Instead, Buddhists and Hindus approach the spiritual through many gods and varying paths, which permits mutually tolerated differences. In fact, in Hinduism, the Buddha was one of the 10 incarnations of Vishnu, one of the three principal Hindu deities (see "Hinduism and Hindu Iconography," page 435).

UDAYAGIRI More early Buddhist than Hindu art has survived in India because the Buddhists constructed their monasteries with durable materials such as stone and brick. But in the Gupta period, Hindu stone sculpture and architecture began to rival the great Buddhist monuments of South Asia. The oldest Hindu cave temples are at Udayagiri, near Sanchi. They date to the early fifth century, some 600 years after the first Buddhist examples. Although the Udayagiri temples are architecturally simple and small, the site boasts monumental relief sculptures showing an already fully developed religious iconography. One of these reliefs (FIG. 15-16), carved in a shallow niche of rock, shows a 13-foot-tall Vishnu in his incarnation as the boar Varaha. The avatar has a human body and a boar's head. Vishnu assumed this form when he rescued the earth—personified as the goddess Bhudevi clinging to the boar's tusk—from being carried off to the bottom of the ocean. Vishnu stands with one foot resting on the coils of a snake king (note the

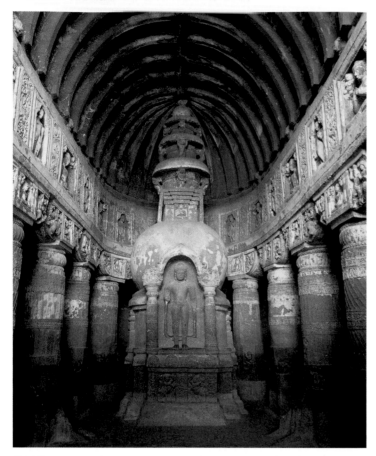

15-15 Interior of cave 19, Ajanta, India, second half of fifth century.

The popularity of Gupta Buddha statues led to a transformation in Indian religious architecture. Cave 19 at Ajanta is a chaitya hall with an image of the Buddha carved on the front of its stupa.

home to a small Buddhist monastery for centuries. During the second half of the fifth century, that is, about the same time a Gupta sculptor created the classic seated Buddha of Sarnath, royal patrons of the local Vakataka dynasty, allied to the Guptas by marriage,

15-16 *Boar Avatar of Vishnu Rescues the Earth,* cave 5, Udayagiri, India, early fifth century. Relief 22′ × 13′; Vishnu 12′ 8″ high.

The oldest Hindu cave temples are at Udayagiri, a site that also boasts some of the earliest Hindu stone sculptures, such as this huge relief of Vishnu as the boar Varaha rescuing the earth.

1 ft.

Hinduism and Hindu Iconography

Unlike Buddhism (and Christianity, Islam, and other religions), Hinduism recognizes no founder or great prophet. Hinduism also has no descriptive definition but means "the religion of the Indians." Both "India" and "Hindu" have a common root in the name of the Indus River. The practices and beliefs of Hindus vary tremendously, but the literary origins of Hinduism date to the Vedic period, and some aspects of Hindu practice apparently were already present in the Indus Civilization of the third millennium BCE. Ritual sacrifice by Brahmin priests is central to Hinduism, as it was to the Aryans. The goal of sacrifice is to please a deity in order to achieve release (*moksha*, liberation) from the endless cycle of birth, death, and rebirth (*samsara*) and become one with the universal spirit.

Not only is Hinduism a religion of many gods, but the Hindu deities have various natures and take many forms. This multiplicity suggests the all-pervasive nature of the Hindu gods. The three most important deities are the gods Shiva and Vishnu and the goddess Devi. Each of the three major sects of Hinduism today considers one of these three to be supreme—Shiva in Shaivism, Vishnu in Vaishnavism, and Devi in Shaktism. (*Shakti* is the female creative force.)

Shiva is the Destroyer, but, consistent with the multiplicity of Hindu belief, he is also a regenerative force. In the latter role, Shiva can be represented in the form of a *linga* (a phallus or cosmic pillar). When Shiva appears in human form in Hindu art, he frequently has multiple limbs and heads (FIGS. 15-17, 15-18, and 15-27), signs of his suprahuman nature, and matted locks piled atop his head, crowned by a crescent moon. Sometimes he wears a serpent scarf and has a third eye on his forehead (the emblem of his all-seeing nature). Shiva rides the bull **Nandi** (FIG. 15-17) and often carries a *trident*, a three-pronged pitchfork.

Vishnu is the Preserver of the Universe. Artists frequently portray him with four arms (FIGS. 15-20 and 15-31) holding various attributes, including a conch-shell trumpet and discus. He sometimes reclines on a serpent floating on the waters of the cosmic sea (FIGS. 15-20 and 15-31). When the evil forces of the universe become too strong, he descends to earth to restore balance and assumes different forms (*avatars*, or incarnations), including a boar (FIG. 15-16), fish, and tortoise, as well as **Krishna**, the divine lover (FIG. 32-7), and even the Buddha himself.

Devi is the Great Goddess who takes many forms and has many names. Hindus worship her alone or as a consort of male gods (**Parvati** or **Uma**, wife of Shiva; **Lakshmi**, wife of Vishnu), as

15-17 Dancing Shiva, rock-cut relief, cave 1, Badami, India, late sixth century.

Shiva here dances the cosmic dance and has 18 arms, some holding objects, others forming mudras. Hindu gods often have multiple limbs to indicate their suprahuman nature and divine powers.

well as **Radha**, lover of Krishna (FIG. 32-7). She has both benign and horrific forms; she both creates and destroys. In one manifestation, she is **Durga**, a multiarmed goddess who often rides a lion (FIG. 15-22). Her son is the elephant-headed **Ganesha** (FIG. 15-17).

The stationary images of deities in Hindu temples are often made of stone. Hindus periodically remove portable images of their gods, often of bronze (FIG. 15-27), from the temple, particularly during festivals to enable many worshipers to take *darshan* (seeing the deity and being seen by the deity) at one time. In temples dedicated to Shiva, the stationary form is the linga.

multiple hoods behind his human head), who represents the conquered demon that attempted to abduct the earth. Rows of gods and sages form lines to witness the event.

The relief served a political as well as a religious purpose. The patron of the relief was a local king who honored the great Gupta king Chandragupta II in a nearby inscription dated to the year 401. Many scholars believe the local king wanted viewers to see Chandragupta (who had visited the site) as saving his kingdom by ridding it of its enemies in much the same way Varaha saved the earth.

BADAMI During the sixth century, the Huns brought down the Gupta Empire, and various regional dynasties rose to power. In the Deccan plateau of central India, the Chalukya kings ruled from their capital at Badami. There, Chalukya sculptors carved a series of reliefs in the walls of halls cut into the cliff above the city. One relief (FIG. **15-17**), datable to the late sixth century, shows Shiva dancing the cosmic dance, his 18 arms swinging rhythmically in an arc. Some of the hands hold objects, and others form prescribed mudras. At the lower right, the elephant-headed Ganesha tentatively

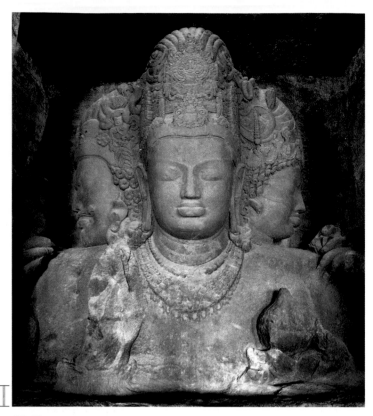

15-18 Shiva as Mahadeva, cave 1, Elephanta, India, ca. 550–575. Basalt, Shiva 17′ 10″ high.

This immense rock-cut image of Shiva as Mahadeva ("Great God") emerges out of the depths of the Elephanta cave as worshipers' eyes adjust to the darkness. Shiva has both male and female faces.

1 ft.

sents Shiva's destructive side. Shiva holds these two opposing forces in check, and the central face expresses their balance. The cyclic destruction and creation of the universe, which the side faces also symbolize, are part of Indian notions of time, matched by the cyclic pattern of death and rebirth (samsara).

DEOGARH The excavated cave shrines just considered are characteristic of early Hindu religious architecture, but temples constructed using quarried stone became more important as Hinduism evolved over the centuries. As they did with the cave temples, the Hindus initially built rather small and simple temples but decorated them with narrative reliefs displaying a fully developed iconography. The Vishnu Temple (FIG. **15-19**) at Deogarh in north-central India, datable to the early sixth century, is among the first Hindu temples constructed with stone blocks. A simple square structure, it has an elaborately decorated doorway at the front and a relief in a niche on each of the other three sides. Sculpted guardians and mithunas protect the doorway at Deogarh, because it is the transition point between the dangerous outside and the sacred. The temple culminates in a tall tower, originally at least 40 feet high.

The reliefs in the three niches of the Deogarh temple depict important episodes in the saga of Vishnu. On the south (FIG. **15-20**), Vishnu sleeps on the coils of the giant serpent Ananta, whose multiple heads form a kind of umbrella around the god's face. While Lakshmi massages her husband's legs (he has cramps as he gives birth), the four-armed Vishnu dreams the universe into reality. A lotus plant (said to have grown out of Vishnu's navel) supports the four-headed Hindu god of creation, Brahma. Flanking him are other important Hindu divinities, including Shiva on his bull. Below are six figures. The four at the right are personifications of Vishnu's various powers. They will defeat the two armed demons at the left. The

mimics Shiva. Nandi, Shiva's bull mount, stands at the left. Artists often represented Hindu deities as part human and part animal (FIG. 15-16) or, as in the Badami relief, as figures with multiple body parts. Such composite and multilimbed forms indicate the subjects are not human but suprahuman gods with supernatural powers.

ELEPHANTA Another portrayal of Shiva as a suprahuman being is in a third Hindu cave site, on Elephanta, an island in Bombay's harbor that early Portuguese colonizers named after a life-size stone elephant sculpture there. A king of the Kalachuri dynasty took control of Elephanta in the sixth century, and he may have commissioned the largest of the island's cave temples. Just inside the west entrance to the cave is a shrine housing Shiva's linga, the god's emblem. Deep within the temple, in a niche once closed off with wooden doors, is a nearly 18-foot-high rock-cut image (FIG. **15-18**) of Shiva as Mahadeva, the "Great God" or Lord of Lords. Mahadeva appears to emerge out of the depths of the cave as worshipers' eyes become accustomed to the darkness. This image of Shiva has three faces, each showing a different aspect of the deity. (A fourth, unseen at the back, is implied—the god has not emerged fully from the rock.) The central face expresses Shiva's quiet, balanced demeanor. The clean planes of the face contrast with the richness of the piled hair encrusted with jewels. The two side faces differ significantly. The one on the right is female, with framing hair curls. The left face is a grimacing male with a curling mustache who wears a cobra as an earring. The female (Uma) indicates the creative aspect of Shiva. The fierce male (Bhairava) repre-

15-19 Vishnu Temple (looking north), Deogarh, India, early sixth century.

One of the first masonry Hindu temples, the Vishnu Temple at Deogarh is a simple square building with a tower. Sculpted guardians protect its entrance. Narrative reliefs adorn the three other sides.

15-20 *Vishnu Asleep on the Serpent Ananta,* relief panel on the south facade of the Vishnu Temple, Deogarh, India, early sixth century.

Sculptors carved the reliefs of the Vishnu Temple at Deogarh in classic Gupta style. In the south panel, the four-armed Vishnu sleeps on the serpent Ananta as he dreams the universe into reality.

sculptor carved all the figures in the classic Gupta style, with smooth bodies and clinging garments (compare FIG. 15-13).

Early Medieval Period

During the several centuries corresponding to the early medieval period in Europe (see Chapter 11), the early Islamic period in Mesopotamia and Persia (see Chapter 10), the Tang and Song dynasties in China (see Chapter 16), and the Hakuho, Nara, and Heian periods in Japan (see Chapter 17), regional dynasties ruled parts of India. Among the most important of these kingdoms were the Palas and Chandellas in northern India and the Pallavas and Cholas in the south. Whereas Buddhism spread rapidly throughout eastern Asia, in medieval India it gradually declined, and the various local kings vied with one another to build glorious shrines to the Hindu gods.

MAMALLAPURAM In addition to cave temples and masonry temples, Indian architects created a third type of monument: freestanding temples carved out of rocky outcroppings. Sculpted monolithic temples are rare. Some of the earliest and most impressive are at Mamallapuram, south of Madras on the Bay of Bengal, where they are called *rathas,* or "chariots" (that is, vehicles of the gods). In the late seventh century, the Pallava dynasty ordered five rathas (FIG. **15-21**) carved out of a

15-21 Rock-cut rathas (looking southwest), Mamallapuram, India, second half of seventh century. From *left* to *right:* Dharmaraja, Bhima, and Arjuna rathas.

Indian architects also created temples by sculpting them from the living rock. The seventh-century rathas ("chariots" of the gods) at Mamallapuram were all carved from a single huge granite outcropping.

15-22 *Durga Slaying the Buffalo Demon Manisha,* rock-cut relief in the Mahishasuramardini cave temple, Mamallapuram, India, seventh century CE. Granite, 9' high.

The supreme Hindu goddess Devi here takes the form of Durga riding a lion. Wielding weapons in her eight hands, Durga defeats the demon Manisha, symbolizing the triumph of good over evil.

1 ft.

single huge granite boulder jutting out from the sand. The group is of special interest because it illustrates the variety of temple forms at this period, based on earlier wooden structures, before a standard masonry type of temple became the norm in southern India.

The largest Mamallapuram ratha, the Dharmaraja (FIG. 15-21, *left*), dedicated to Shiva, is an early example of the typical southern-style temple with stepped-pyramid *vimana* (see "Hindu Temples," page 439). The tower ascends in pronounced tiers of cornices decorated with miniature shrines. The lower walls include carved columns and figures of deities inside niches. The Bhima ratha to the right, dedicated to Vishnu, has a rectangular plan and a rounded roof. The next ratha, the Arjuna, is a smaller example of the southern Indian type. At the end of the row (not visible in FIG. 15-21) sits the very small Draupadi ratha, modeled on a thatched hut and dedicated to Durga, a form of the supreme Hindu goddess Devi. The two largest temples were never finished.

DURGA AND MANISHA The Hindu warrior goddess who defends civilization against the evil forces at work in the world is Durga ("She who is difficult to oppose"). On one wall of the Mahishasuramardini cave temple at Mamallapuram, Durga rides into battle on the back of a lion, leading an army of chubby dwarfs against the buffalo-headed, human-bodied demon Manisha (FIG. **15-22**), as recounted in one of the most important early works of Hindu literature, the *Devi Mahatmya*. The combat symbolizes for Hindus the struggle between good and evil, order and disorder.

In the Mamallapuram cave relief, the buffalo demon is a giant, far larger than the slender and elegantly dressed eight-armed goddess who stretches her bow to launch an arrow against her foe. Her other arms wield additional weapons given to her by the male Hindu deities when they beseeched her to do battle on their behalf against the terrible Manisha. Durga is therefore a fearsome force despite her delicate appearance. The club-bearing demon recoils from her onslaught. He and his allies have begun their retreat, although he turns his head to look back at Durga. The victory of the goddess over the physically more powerful demon eloquently conveys the message that for the Hindu faithful, good will triumph over evil.

The horizontal format of the relief, the piling up of figures over the surface, and the dramatic and effective way the sculptor has communicated the chaos of hand-to-hand combat all recall Late Antique Roman sarcophagi, such as the *Ludovisi Battle Sarcophagus* (FIG. 7-70). The relief is one of several major works of narrative relief sculpture at Mamallapuram. By far the largest—featuring life-size figures—probably represents the *Descent of the Ganges River* (FIG. **15-22A**).

15-22A *Descent of the Ganges,* Mamallapuram, ca. 600–650.

15-22B Kailasanatha Temple, Ellora, second half of eighth century.

THANJAVUR More ambitious than the rathas of Mamallapuram is the eighth-century rock-cut Kailasanatha Temple (FIG. **15-22B**) at Ellora, a forerunner of the largest known freestanding Hindu temples in the southern Indian tradition (see "Hindu Temples," page 439). Under the Cholas, whose territories extended into part of Sri Lanka and even Java, architects constructed southern-type temples of unprecedented size. The Rajarajeshvara Temple (FIG. 15-23) at Thanjavur, dedicated in 1010 to Shiva as the Lord of Rajaraja, was the largest and tallest temple (210 feet high) in India at the time. The temple stands inside a walled precinct. It consists of a stairway leading to two flat-roofed mandapas, the larger one having 36 pillars, and to the garbha griha in the base of the enormous pyramidal vimana, which is as much an emblem of the Cholas' secular power as of their devotion to Shiva. On the exterior walls of the lower stories are numerous reliefs in niches depicting the god in his various forms.

KHAJURAHO At the same time the Cholas were building the Rajarajeshvara Temple at Thanjavur in the south, the Chandella dynasty was constructing northern-style temples at Khajuraho. The Vishvanatha Temple (FIG. 15-24) is one of more than 20 large, elaborate temples at that site. Vishvanatha ("Lord of the World") is

Hindu Temples

The Hindu temple is the home of the gods on earth and the place where they make themselves visible to humans. At the core of all Hindu temples is the *garbha griha* ("womb chamber"), which houses images or symbols of the deity—for example, Shiva's linga (see "Hinduism," page 435). Only Brahmin priests may enter this inner sanctuary and make offerings to the gods. Worshipers, however, may stand at the threshold and behold the deity as manifest by its image. In the elaborate multiroomed temples of later Hindu architecture, the worshipers and priests progress through a series of ever more sacred spaces, usually on an east-west axis. Hindu priests and architects attached great importance to each temple's plan and sought to make it conform to the sacred geometric diagram (*mandala*) of the universe.

Architectural historians, following ancient Indian texts, divide Hindu temples into two major typological groups tied to geography. The most important distinguishing feature of the **northern** style of temple (FIG. 15-24) is its beehivelike tower or *shikhara* ("mountain peak"), capped by an *amalaka,* a ribbed cushionlike form, derived from the shape of the amala fruit (believed to have medicinal powers). Amalakas appear on the corners of the lower levels of the shikhara too. Northern temples also have smaller towerlike roofs over the halls (*mandapas*) leading to the garbha griha.

Southern temples (FIG. 15-23) can easily be recognized by the flat roofs of their pillared mandapas and by their shorter towered shrines, called *vimanas,* which lack the curved profile of their northern counterparts and resemble multilevel pyramids.

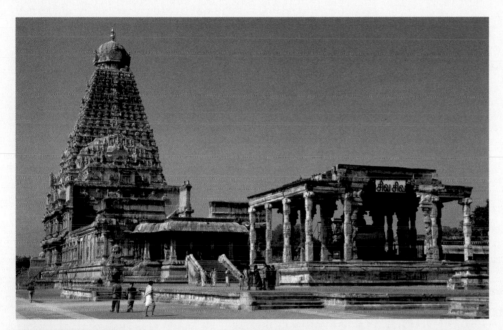

15-23 Rajarajeshvara Temple (looking southeast), Thanjavur, India, ca. 1010.

The Rajarajeshvara Temple at Thanjavur is an example of the southern type of Hindu temple. Two flat-roofed mandapas lead to the garbha griha in the base of its 210-foot-tall pyramidal vimana.

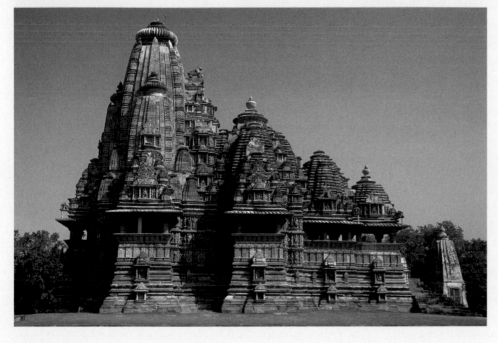

15-24 Vishvanatha Temple (looking north), Khajuraho, India, ca. 1000.

The Vishvanatha Temple is a northern Hindu temple type. It has four towers, each taller than the preceding one, symbolizing Shiva's mountain home. The largest tower is the beehive-shaped shikhara.

another of the many names for Shiva. Dedicated in 1002, the structure has three towers over the mandapas, each rising higher than the preceding one, leading to the tallest tower at the rear, in much the same way the foothills of the Himalayas, Shiva's home, rise to meet their highest peak. The mountain symbolism applies to the interior plan (FIG. 15-25) of the Vishvanatha Temple as well. Under

the tallest tower, the shikhara, is the garbha griha, the small and dark inner sanctuary chamber, like a cave, which houses the image of the deity. Thus, temples such as the Vishvanatha symbolize constructed mountains with caves, comparable to the cave temples at Elephanta and other Indian sites. In all cases, the deity manifests himself or herself within the cave and takes various forms in sculptures. The temple-mountains, however, are not intended to appear natural but rather are perfect mountains designed using ideal mathematical proportions.

The reliefs of Thanjavur's Rajarajeshvara Temple are typical of southern temple decoration, which is generally limited to images of deities. The exterior walls of Khajuraho's Vishvanatha Temple are equally typical of northern temples in the profusion of sculptures (FIG. 15-26) depicting mortals as well as gods, especially pairs of men and women (mithunas) embracing or engaged in sexual intercourse in an extraordinary range of positions. The use of seminude yakshis and amorous couples as motifs on religious buildings in India has a very long history, going back to the earliest architectural traditions, both Hindu and Buddhist (Sanchi, FIG. 15-8, and Karle). As in the earlier examples, the erotic sculptures of Khajuraho suggest fertility and the propagation of life and serve as auspicious protectors of the sacred precinct.

SHIVA AS NATARAJA Portable objects also play an important role in Hinduism. The statuette (FIG. 15-27) of Shiva from Tamil Nadu, cast in solid bronze around 1000, recalls the sixth-century

15-25 Plan of the Vishvanatha Temple, Khajuraho, India, ca. 1000.

Under the shikhara of the Vishvanatha Temple is the garbha griha, the dark inner sanctuary chamber resembling a cave, which houses the image of the deity. Only priests can enter the garbha griha.

15-26 Mithuna reliefs, detail of the north side of the Vishvanatha Temple, Khajuraho, India, ca. 1000.

Northern Hindu temples usually feature reliefs depicting deities and amorous couples (mithunas). The erotic sculptures suggest the propagation of life and serve as protectors of the sacred precinct.

One of many portable images of the gods used in Hindu worship, this solid-bronze statuette of Shiva as Lord of the Dance depicts the god balancing on one leg atop a dwarf representing ignorance.

of the god but the god itself. All must treat the image as a living being. Worship of the deity involves caring for him as if he were an honored person. Bathed, clothed, given foods to eat, and taken for outings, the image also receives gifts—songs, lights (lit oil lamps), good smells (incense), and flowers, things the god can enjoy through the senses. The food given to the god is particularly important, as he eats the "essence," leaving the remainder for the worshiper. The food is then *prasada* ("grace"), sacred because it came in contact with the divine. In an especially religious household, the deity resides as an image and receives the food for each meal before the family eats. When the god resides in a temple, it is the duty of the priests to feed, clothe, and take care of him.

The Chola dynasty ended in the 13th century, a time of political, religious, and cultural change in South Asia. At this point, Buddhism survived in only some areas of India. It soon died out completely there, although the late form of northern Indian Buddhism continued in Tibet and Nepal. At the same time, Islam, which had arrived in India as early as the eighth century, became a potent political force with the establishment of the Delhi sultanate in 1206. Hindu and Islamic art assumed preeminent roles in India in the 13th century (see Chapter 32).

SOUTHEAST ASIA

Art historians once considered the art of Southeast Asia an extension of Indian civilization. Because of the Indian character of many Southeast Asian monuments, scholars hypothesized that Indian artists had constructed and decorated them and that Indians had colonized Southeast Asia. Today, researchers have concluded no Indian colonization occurred. The expansion of Indian culture to Southeast Asia during the first millennium CE was peaceful and nonimperialistic, a by-product of trade. In the early centuries CE, ships bringing trade goods from India and China to Rome passed through Southeast Asia on the monsoon winds. The local tribal chieftains quickly saw an opportunity to participate, mainly with their own forest products, such as aromatic woods, bird feathers, and spices. Accompanying the trade goods from India were Sanskrit, Buddhism, and Hinduism—and Buddhist and Hindu art. But the Southeast Asian peoples soon modified Indian art to make it their own. Art historians now recognize Southeast Asian art and architecture as a distinctive and multifaceted tradition.

relief (FIG. 15-17) in the Badami cave, but it is one of many examples of moveable images of deities created under the Chola kings and still used in Hindu rituals today. Here, Shiva dances as Nataraja ("Lord of the Dance") by balancing on one leg atop Apasmara, the dwarf of ignorance, which the god stamps out as he dances. Shiva extends all four arms, two of them touching the flaming *nimbus* ("light of glory") encircling him. These two upper hands also hold a small drum (right hand) and a flame (left hand). Shiva creates the universe to the drumbeat's rhythm. The small fire represents destruction. Shiva's lower left hand points to his upraised foot, indicating the foot as the place where devotees can find refuge and enlightenment. The god's lower right hand, raised in the abhaya mudra, tells worshipers to come forward without fear. As Shiva spins, his matted hair comes loose and spreads like a fan on both sides of his head.

At times, worshipers insert poles into the holes on the base of the Tamil Nadu Shiva to carry it, but even when stationary, the statuette would not appear as it does in FIG. 15-27. Rather, when Hindus worship the Shiva Nataraja, they dress the image, cover it with jewels, and garland it with flowers. The only bronze part visible is the face, marked with colored powders and scented pastes. Considered the embodiment of the deity, the image is not a symbol

15-28 *Death of the Buddha* (*Parinirvana*), Gal Vihara, near Polonnaruwa, Sri Lanka, 11th to 12th century. Granulite, Buddha 10′ × 46′.

The sculptor of this colossal recumbent Sri Lankan Buddha emulated the classic Gupta style of a half millennium earlier in the figure's clinging robe, rounded face, and coiffure.

10 ft.

15-29 Aerial view of Borobudur, Java, Indonesia, ca. 800.

Borobudur is a gigantic, unique Buddhist monument. Built on nine terraces with more than 1,500 stupas and 1,500 statues and reliefs, it takes the form of a cosmic mountain, which worshipers circumambulate.

Sri Lanka

Sri Lanka (formerly Ceylon) is an island located at the very tip of the Indian subcontinent. Theravada Buddhism, the oldest form of Buddhism, stressing worship of the historical Buddha (Shakyamuni Buddha), arrived in Sri Lanka as early as the third century BCE. From there it spread to other parts of Southeast Asia. With the demise of Buddhism in India in about the 13th century, Sri Lanka now has the longest-lived Buddhist tradition in the world.

15-28A Ananda Temple, Bagan, begun 1091.

GAL VIHARA One of the largest sculptures in Southeast Asia is the 46-foot-long recumbent Buddha (FIG. **15-28**) carved out of a rocky outcropping at Gal Vihara in the 11th or 12th century. To the left of the Buddha, much smaller in scale, stands his cousin and chief disciple, Ananda, arms crossed, mourning Shakyamuni's death. (At about the same time, the Burmese built a temple [FIG. **15-28A**] in honor of Ananda at Bagan.) Although more than a half millennium later in date, the Sri Lankan representation of the Buddha's parinirvana reveals its sculptor's debt to the classic Gupta sculptures of India, with their clinging garments, rounded faces, and distinctive renditions of hair (compare FIG. 15-13). Other Southeast Asian monuments, in contrast, exhibit a marked independence from Indian models.

Java

On the island of Java, part of the modern nation of Indonesia, the period from the 8th to the 10th centuries brought construction of both Hindu and Buddhist monuments.

BOROBUDUR Unique in both form and meaning, Borobudur (FIG. **15-29**) is a Buddhist monument of colossal size, measuring about 400 feet per side at the base and about 98 feet tall. Built over a small hill on nine terraces accessed by four stairways aligned with the cardinal points, the structure contains literally millions of blocks of volcanic stone. Visitors ascending the massive monument on their way to the summit encounter more than 500 life-size Buddha images, at least 1,000 relief panels, and some 1,500 stupas of various sizes.

Scholars debate the intended meaning of Borobudur. Most think it is a constructed cosmic mountain, a three-dimensional mandala where worshipers pass through various realms on their way to ultimate enlightenment. As they circumambulate the structure, pilgrims first see reliefs illustrating the karmic effects of different kinds of human behavior, then reliefs depicting jatakas of the Buddha's earlier lives, and, farther up, events from the life of Shakyamuni. On the circular terraces near the summit, each stupa is hollow and houses

15-29A Bodhisattva Maitreya, Prakhon Chai, eighth to ninth century.

a statue of the seated Buddha, who has achieved spiritual enlightenment and preaches using the Wheel-turning mudra. At the very top is the largest, sealed stupa. It may once have contained another Buddha image, but it may also have been left empty to symbolize the formlessness of true enlightenment. Although scholars have interpreted the iconographic program in different ways, all agree on two essential points: that Borobudur is dependent on Indian art, literature, and religion, and that nothing comparable exists in India itself. Borobudur's sophistication, complexity, and originality underline how completely the Javanese, and Southeast Asians in general, had absorbed, rethought, and reformulated Indian religion and art by 800. (In Thailand, for example, sculptors created a unique iconography for bodhisattvas [FIG. 15-29A] combining Buddhist and Hindu elements.)

Cambodia

In 802, at about the same time the Javanese built Borobudur, the Khmer king Jayavarman II (r. 802–850) founded the Angkor dynasty, which ruled Cambodia for the next 400 years and sponsored the construction of hundreds of monuments, including gigantic Buddhist monasteries (*wats*). For at least two centuries before the founding of Angkor, the Khmer (the predominant ethnic group in Cambodia) produced Indian-related sculpture of exceptional quality. Images of Vishnu were particularly important during the pre-Angkorian period.

HARIHARA A statue of Vishnu (FIG. **15-30**) from Prasat Andet shows the Hindu god in his manifestation as Harihara (Shiva-Vishnu). To represent Harihara, the sculptor divided the statue

15-30 Harihara, from Prasat Andet, Cambodia, early seventh century. Stone, 6′ 3″ high. National Museum, Phnom Penh.

Harihara is a composite of Shiva (the god's right side) and Vishnu (on the left). Stylistically indebted to Gupta sculpture, the Khmer statue is freestanding so that it could be viewed from all sides.

1 ft.

15-31 *Vishnu Lying on the Cosmic Ocean,* from the Mebon Temple on an island in the western baray, Angkor, Cambodia, 11th century. Bronze, fragment 8′ long.

This fragmentary hollow-cast bronze statue was originally more than 20 feet long and inlaid with gold, silver, and jewels. It portrays Vishnu asleep on the cosmic ocean at the moment of the universe's creation.

1 ft.

vertically, with Shiva on the god's right side, Vishnu on his left. The tall headgear reflects the division most clearly. The Shiva half, embellished with the winding locks of an ascetic, contrasts with the kingly Vishnu's plain miter. Attributes (now lost) held in the four hands also helped differentiate the two sides. Stylistically, the Cambodian statue, like the Sri Lankan parinirvana group (FIG. 15-28), derives from Indian sculptures (FIG. 15-13) of Gupta style. But unlike almost all stone sculpture in India, carved in relief on slabs or stelae, this Khmer image is in the round. The Harihara's broken arms and ankles vividly attest to the vulnerability of this format. The Khmer sculptors, however, wanted their statues to be seen from all sides in the center of the garbha grihas of brick temples.

VISHNU ON THE COSMIC OCEAN The Khmer kings were exceedingly powerful and possessed enormous wealth. A now-fragmentary statue (FIG. **15-31**) portraying Vishnu lying on the cosmic ocean testifies to both the luxurious nature of much Khmer art and to the mastery of Khmer bronze-casters. The surviving portion is about 8 feet long. In complete form, at well over 20 feet long, the Vishnu statue was among the largest bronzes of the ancient and medieval worlds, surpassed only by such lost wonders as the statue of Athena (FIG. 5-46) in the Parthenon and the 120-foot-tall colossus of the Roman emperor Nero (see "The Golden House of Nero," Chapter 7, page 202). Originally, gold and silver inlays and jewels embellished the Vishnu image, and the god wore a separate miter on his head. The subject of the gigantic statue is the same as that carved in relief (FIG. 15-20) on the Deogarh Vishnu Temple. Vishnu lies asleep on the cosmic ocean at the moment of the creation of the universe. In the myth, a lotus stem grows from Vishnu's navel, its flower supporting Brahma, the creator god. In this statue, Vishnu probably had a waterspout emerging from his navel, indicating his ability to create the waters as well as to create Brahma and protect the earth. The statue occupied an island temple in the western *baray* (reservoir) of Angkor.

ANGKOR WAT For more than four centuries, successive kings worked on construction of the Angkor site. Founded by Indravarman (r. 877–889), Angkor is an engineering marvel, a vast complex of temples and palaces within a rectangular grid of canals and reservoirs fed by local rivers. Each of the Khmer kings built a temple mountain at Angkor and installed his personal god—Shiva, Vishnu, or the Buddha—on top and gave the god part of his own royal name, implying the king was a manifestation of the deity. When the king died, the Khmer believed the god reabsorbed him, because he had been the earthly portion of the deity during his lifetime, so they worshiped the king's image as the god. This concept of kingship approaches deification of the ruler, familiar in many other societies, such as pharaonic Egypt (see Chapter 3).

Of all the Khmer kings' monuments, Angkor Wat (FIG. **15-32**) is the most spectacular. Built by Suryavarman II (r. 1113–1150), it is the largest of the many Khmer temple complexes. Angkor Wat rises from a huge rectangle of land delineated by a moat measuring about 5,000 by 4,000 feet. Like the other Khmer temples, its purpose was to associate the king with his personal god, in this case Vishnu. The centerpiece of the complex is a tall stepped tower surrounded by four smaller towers connected by covered galleries. The five towers symbolize the five peaks of Mount Meru, the sacred mountain at the center of the universe. Two more circuit walls with galleries, towers, and gates enclose the central block. Thus, as one progresses inward through the complex, the towers rise ever higher, paralleling the towers of Khajuraho's Vishvanatha Temple (FIG. 15-24) but in a more complex sequence and on a much grander scale.

Throughout Angkor Wat, stone reliefs glorify both Vishnu in his various avatars and Suryavarman II. A relief (FIG. **15-33**) on the inner wall of the lowest gallery shows the king holding court. Suryavarman II sits on an elaborate wooden throne, its bronze legs rising as cobra heads. Kneeling retainers, smaller than the king because they are lesser figures in the Khmer hierarchy, hold a forest of umbrellas and fans, emblems of Suryavarman's exalted rank. In the reliefs of Angkor Wat, religion and politics are united.

15-32 Aerial view of Angkor Wat (looking northeast), Angkor, Cambodia, first half of 12th century.

Angkor Wat, built by Suryavarman II to associate the Khmer king with the god Vishnu, has five towers symbolizing the five peaks of Mount Meru, the sacred mountain at the center of the universe.

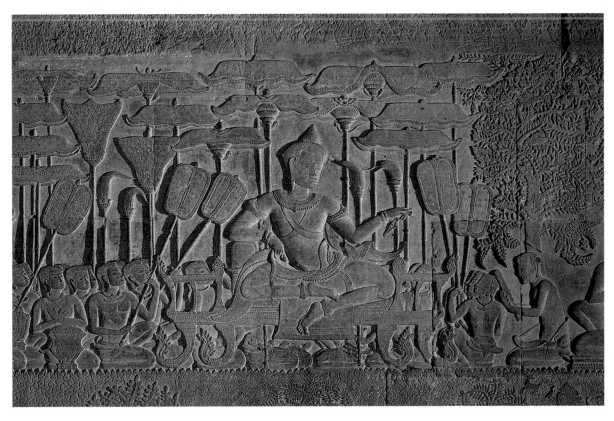

15-33 King Suryavarman II holding court, detail of a stone relief, lowest gallery, south side, Angkor Wat, Angkor, Cambodia, first half of 12th century.

The reliefs of Angkor Wat glorify Vishnu in his various incarnations and Suryavarman II, whom the sculptor depicted holding court and surrounded by his attendants, all of smaller scale than the king.

Jayavarman VII embraced Buddhism
instead of Hinduism. His most important
temple, the Bayon, has towers carved with
giant faces probably depicting either the
bodhisattva Lokeshvara or the king himself.

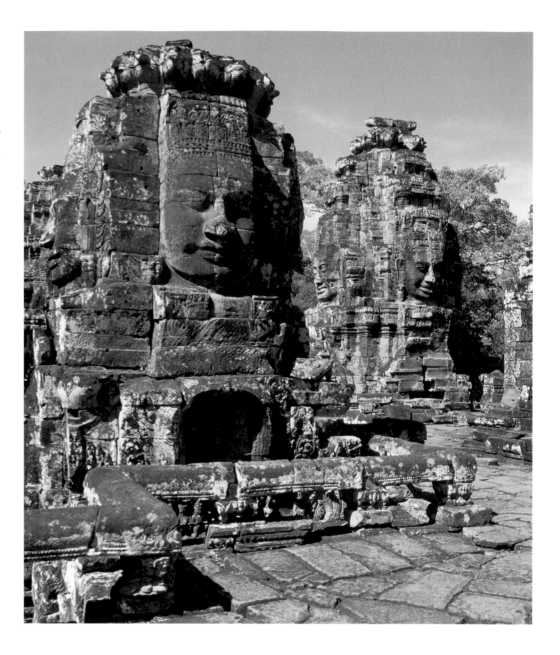

BAYON Jayavarman VII (r. 1181–1219), Suryavarman II's son, ruled over much of mainland Southeast Asia and built more during his reign than all the Khmer kings preceding him combined. His most important temple, the Bayon (FIG. 15-34), is a complicated monument constructed with unique circular terraces surmounted by towers carved with giant faces. Jayavarman turned to Buddhism from the Hinduism the earlier Khmer rulers embraced, but he adapted his new creed to make the Buddha and the bodhisattva Lokeshvara ("Lord of the World") into divine prototypes of the king, in the Khmer tradition. The faces on the Bayon towers perhaps portray Lokeshvara, intended to indicate the watchful compassion emanating in all directions from the capital. Other

researchers have proposed that the faces depict Jayavarman himself. The king's great experiment in religion and art was short-lived, but it also marked the point of change in Southeast Asia when Theravada Buddhism began to dominate most of the mainland. Chapter 32 chronicles this important development.

During the first to fourth centuries, Buddhism also spread to other parts of Asia—to China, Korea, and Japan. Although the artistic traditions in these countries differ greatly from one another, they share, along with Southeast Asia, a tradition of Buddhist art and an ultimate tie with India. Chapters 16 and 17 trace the changes Buddhist art underwent in East Asia, along with the region's other rich artistic traditions.

SOUTH AND SOUTHEAST ASIA BEFORE 1200

INDUS CIVILIZATION ca. 2600–1500 BCE

- One of the world's earliest civilizations arose in the Indus Valley in the third millennium BCE. Indus cities, such as Mohenjo-daro and Harappa, had streets oriented to the compass points and sophisticated water-supply and sewage systems.
- Little Indus art survives, mainly seals with incised designs and small-scale sculptures such as the statue of a priest-king from Mohenjo-daro. Indus sculptures have stylistic parallels with the art of Mesopotamia, with which the South Asian cities engaged in trade.

Robed male figure, Mohenjo-daro, ca. 2600–1900 BCE

MAURYA DYNASTY 323–185 BCE

- Chandragupta Maurya (r. 323–298 BCE), founder of the dynasty bearing his name, established his capital at Pataliputra in northeastern India and repelled the Greeks from South Asia in 305 BCE.
- The greatest Maurya ruler was Ashoka (r. 272–231 BCE), who converted to Buddhism and spread the Buddha's teaching throughout South Asia. Ashoka was the builder of the original Great Stupa at Sanchi and set up 30- to 40-foot-tall pillars with animal capitals throughout his kingdom. These columns, the first monumental stone artworks in India, owe a stylistic debt to Achaemenid Persian sculpture, but the iconography is Buddhist.

Lion capital of Ashoka, Sarnath, ca. 250 BCE

SHUNGA, ANDHRA, AND KUSHAN DYNASTIES ca. 185 BCE–320 CE

- The unifying characteristic of this age of regional dynasties in South Asia was the patronage of Buddhism. In addition to the stupa, the chief early type of Buddhist sacred architecture was the pillared rock-cut chaitya hall.
- The first representations of the Buddha in human form probably date to the first century CE. Gandharan Buddha statues owe a strong stylistic debt to Greco Roman art.
- By the second century CE, the iconography of the life of the Buddha from his birth at Lumbini to his death at Kushinagara was well established.

Chaitya hall, Karle, ca. 50 CE

GUPTA AND POST-GUPTA PERIODS ca. 320–647

- Gupta sculptors formulated the canonical Buddha image in the fifth century, combining Gandharan iconography with a soft, full-bodied figure in clinging garments.
- The Gupta-period Buddhist caves of Ajanta are the best surviving examples of early mural painting in India.
- The oldest Hindu monumental stone temples and sculptures date to the fifth and sixth centuries, including the rock-cut reliefs of Udayagiri, Badami, and Elephanta, and the Vishnu Temple at Deogarh.

Dancing Shiva, Badami, late sixth century

MEDIEVAL PERIOD 7th to 12th Centuries

- Several distinctive South Asian regional styles emerged in Hindu religious architecture during the medieval period. Northern temples, such as the Vishvanatha Temple at Khajuraho, feature a series of small towers leading to a tall beehive-shaped tower, or shikhara, over the garbha griha. Southern temples, such as the Rajarajeshvara Temple at Thanjavur, have flat-roofed pillared halls (mandapas) leading to a pyramidal tower (vimana).
- In Southeast Asia, medieval art and architecture reflect Indian prototypes, but many local styles developed. The most distinctive monuments of the period are Borobudur on Java and the temples of the Khmer kings at Angkor in Cambodia.

Borobudur, Java, ca. 800

The tomb of the marquise of Dai contained many treasures, most notably a T-shaped painted silk banner draped over her coffin. The upper part represents Heaven, with the silvery moon and red sun.

In the celestial realm at the top of the T, between and below the two heavenly orbs—the moon and its symbol, the toad, and the sun and its symbol, the raven—are dragons and immortal beings.

At the center of the vertical section of the banner, the standing figure on the first white platform is probably the marquise of Dai, awaiting her ascent to Heaven, where she can gain immortality.

1 ft.

16-1 Funeral banner, from tomb 1 (tomb of the marquise of Dai), Mawangdui, China, Han dynasty, ca. 168 BCE. Painted silk, 6′ 8¾″ × 3′ ¼″. Hunan Provincial Museum, Changsha.

CHINA AND KOREA TO 1279

The lowest portion of the banner found in the marquise's tomb depicts the noblewoman's funeral. The two representations of her are among the earliest portraits in Chinese art.

CHINESE SILK FOR THE AFTERLIFE

In 1972, archaeologists excavated the tomb of the marquise of Dai at Mawangdui. The tomb contained a rich array of goods for use during burial ceremonies and to accompany the noblewoman into the afterlife. Among the finds were decorated lacquer utensils, rich textiles, and an astonishingly well-preserved corpse in the innermost of four nested *sarcophagi*. Most remarkable, however, was the discovery of a painted T-shaped silk banner (FIG. 16-1) draped over the marquise's coffin.

Silk is the finest natural fabric ever produced. It comes from the cocoons of caterpillars called silkworms. The manufacture of silk was a well-established industry in China by the second millennium BCE. Silk farmers raise silkworms from eggs, which they place in trays. The farmers also must grow mulberry trees or purchase mulberry leaves, the silkworms' only food source. The silkworms form cocoons out of very fine filaments they extrude as liquid from their bodies. The filaments soon solidify with exposure to air. Before the transformed caterpillars emerge as moths and badly damage the silk, the farmers kill them with steam or high heat. They soften the cocoons in hot water and unwind the filaments onto a reel. The filaments are so fine that workers generally unwind the threads from five to ten cocoons together to bond into a single strand while the filaments are still soft and sticky. Later, the silk workers twist several strands together to form a thicker yarn and then weave the yarn on a loom to produce silk cloth. Both the yarn and the cloth can be dyed, and the silk fabric can be decorated by weaving threads of different colors together in special patterns (*brocades*) or by stitching in threads of different colors (*embroidery*). Greatly admired, Chinese silk and the secrets of its production gradually spread across the ancient world along what came to be called the Silk Road (see "The Silk Road," page 458).

The marquise's funerary banner is an early masterpiece of painting on silk. Scholars generally agree the area within the cross at the top of the T represents Heaven. Most of the vertical section below is the human realm. At the very bottom is the Underworld. In the heavenly realm, dragons and immortal beings appear between and below two orbs—the red sun and its symbol, the raven, on the right, and the silvery moon and its symbol, the toad, on the left. Below, the standing figure on the first white platform near the center of the vertical section is probably the marquise of Dai herself—one of the first portraits in Chinese art. The woman awaits her ascent to Heaven, where she can attain immortality. Nearer the bottom, the artist depicted her funeral. Between these two sections are two intertwining dragons. Their tails reach down to the Underworld and their heads point to Heaven, unifying the entire composition.

CHINA

East Asia is a vast area, varied both topographically and climatically. Dominated by the huge land mass of China, the region also encompasses the peninsula of Korea and the islands of Japan (MAP 16-1). China's landscape includes sandy plains, mighty rivers, towering mountains, and fertile farmlands. Its political and cultural boundaries have varied over the millennia, and at times it has grown geographically to about twice the area of the United States, encompassing Tibet, Chinese Turkestan (Xinjiang), Mongolia, Manchuria, and parts of Korea. China boasts the world's largest population and is ethnically diverse. The spoken language varies so much that speakers of different dialects do not understand one another. The written language, however, which employs *characters* (signs recording spoken words, even if those words are spoken differently in the various dialects), has made possible a shared Chinese literary, philosophic, and religious tradition.

Neolithic Age

Discoveries in recent decades have expanded the already rich Chinese archaeological record enormously and have provided evidence of settled village life as far back as the seventh or early sixth millennium BCE. Excavators have uncovered Neolithic sites with large multifamily houses constructed of wood, bamboo, wattle, daub, and mud plaster and equipped with hearths. These early villages

MAP 16-1 China during the Tang dynasty.

CHINA AND KOREA TO 1279

	Neolithic to Shang		Zhou and Qin		Han and Period of Disunity			Tang		Song and Liao	
7000		1500	1050		206	581	618		907		1279

Neolithic to Shang	Zhou and Qin	Han and Period of Disunity	Tang	Song and Liao
I Chinese ceramists produce sophisticated pottery before the invention of the potter's wheel I Shang artists perfect the piece-mold technique of bronze-casting	I Zhou artists excel in fashioning luxurious objects in bronze, lacquer, and jade I The First Emperor of Qin builds an immense burial mound guarded by 6,000 terracotta soldiers	I Han buildings feature interlocking clusters of wooden brackets I Earliest Chinese image of the Buddha, 338 CE I Xie He formulates "Six Canons" of Chinese painting, early sixth century	I Chang'an, the Tang capital, is the most magnificent city in the world I Golden age of Chinese painting on silk scrolls I Major sculpted and painted Buddhist temples	I China becomes the world's most technologically advanced society I Apogee of landscape painting under the Song emperors I Liao dynasty builds the world's tallest wooden building

Chinese Earthenwares and Stonewares

China has no rival in the combined length and richness of its ceramic history. Beginning with the makers of the earliest pots in prehistoric villages (FIG. 16-2), ancient Chinese potters showed a flair for shaping carefully prepared and kneaded clay into diverse, often dramatic and elegant vessel forms. Until Chinese potters developed true *porcelains* (extremely fine, hard white ceramics; see "Chinese Porcelain," Chapter 33, page 997) around 1300, they produced only two types of clay vessels or objects—earthenwares and stonewares. For both types, potters used clays colored by mineral impurities, especially iron compounds ranging from yellow to brownish-black.

The clay bodies of *earthenwares* (FIG. 16-2), fired at low temperatures in open pits or simple kilns, remain soft and porous, thus allowing liquids to seep through. Chinese artists also used the low-fire technique to produce terracotta sculptures, even life-size figures of humans and animals (FIG. 16-6). Over time, Chinese potters developed kilns enabling them to fire their clay vessels at much higher temperatures—more than 2,000 degrees Fahrenheit. These elevated temperatures produce *stonewares,* named for their stone-like hardness and density.

Potters in China excelled at the various techniques commonly used to decorate earthenwares and stonewares. Most of these decorative methods depend on changes occurring in the kiln to chemical compounds found in clay as natural impurities. When fired, many compounds change color dramatically, depending on the conditions in the kiln. For example, if little oxygen remains in a hot kiln, iron oxide (rust) turns either gray or brownish-black, whereas an abundance of oxygen produces a reddish hue (see "Greek Vase Painting," Chapter 5, page 110).

Chinese potters also decorated vessels simply by painting their surfaces. In one of the oldest decorative techniques, the potters applied *slip* (a mixture of clay and water like a fine, thin mud)—by painting, pouring, or dipping—to a clay body not yet fully dry. The natural varieties of clay produced a broad, if not bright, range of colors, as seen in Neolithic vessels (FIG. 16-2). But Chinese potters often added compounds such as iron oxide to the slip to change or intensify the colors. After the vessels had partially dried, the potters could incise lines through the slip down to the clay body to produce designs such as those seen in later Chinese stonewares (FIG. 16-21). Chinese artists also inlaid designs, carving them into plain vessel surfaces and then filling them with slip or soft clay of a contrasting color. These techniques spread throughout East Asia (FIG. 16-29).

16-2 Yangshao Culture vases, from Gansu Province, China, mid-third millennium BCE.

Chinese artists produced vessels of many different shapes even before the invention of the potter's wheel and decorated them with abstract motifs in red and brownish-black on a cream-colored ground.

To produce a hard, glassy surface after firing, potters coated plain or decorated vessels with a *glaze,* a finely ground mixture of minerals. They often used clear or highly translucent glazes, but opaque, richly colored glazes also became common. Sometimes painters allowed the thick glazes to run down the side of a vase or a figurine (FIG. 16-18) to produce dramatic effects.

---

also had pens for domesticated animals, kilns for pottery production, pits for storage and refuse, and cemeteries for the dead. Chinese Neolithic artisans produced impressive artworks, especially from jade and clay.

YANGSHAO POTTERY Mastery of the art of pottery occurred at a very early date in China. The potters of the Yangshao Culture, which arose along the Yellow River in northeastern China, produced fine decorated *earthenware* bowls (see "Chinese Earthenwares and Stonewares," above) even before the invention of the potter's wheel in the fourth millennium BCE. In the third millennium, the Yangshao potters of Gansu Province formed by hand and then painted vessels (FIG. **16-2**) of astonishing sophistication. The multiplicity of shapes suggests the vessels served a wide variety of functions in daily life, but most of the finds come from graves. Decoration is in red and brownish-black on a cream-colored ground. Some pots and bowls include stylized animal motifs, but most feature abstract designs. The painters reveal a highly refined aesthetic sensibility, effectively integrating a variety of angular and curvilinear geometric motifs, including stripes, zigzags, lozenges, circles, spirals, and waves.

Shang Bronze-Casting

Among the finest bronzes of the second millennium BCE are those that Shang artists created using piece molds. The Shang bronze-workers began the process by producing a solid clay model of the desired object. When the model dried to durable hardness, they pressed damp clay around it to form a mold that hardened but remained somewhat flexible. At that point, they carefully cut the mold in pieces, removed the pieces from the model, and baked the pieces in a kiln to form hard earthenware sections. Sculptors then carved the intricate details of the relief decoration into the inner surfaces of the piece molds. Next, the artists shaved the model to reduce its size to form a core for the piece mold. They next reassembled the mold around the model using bronze spacers to preserve a void between the model and the mold—a space equivalent to the layer of wax used in the lost-wax method (see "Hollow-Casting Life-Size Bronze Statues," Chapter 5, page 130). The Shang bronze-casters then added a final clay layer on the outside to hold everything together, leaving open ducts for pouring molten bronze into the space between the model and the mold and for venting gases. Once the mold cooled, they broke it apart, removed the new bronze vessel, and cleaned and polished it.

Shang bronzes show mastery in casting rivaling that of any other ancient civilization. The great numbers of cast-bronze vessels strongly suggest well-organized workshops. Shang bronzes held wine, water, grain, or meat for sacrificial rites. Each vessel's shape matched its intended purpose. All feature surfaces densely covered with abstract and animal motifs. On the guang illustrated here (FIG. 16-3), the multiple designs and their fields of background spirals integrate so closely with the form of the libation-pouring vessel that they are not merely an external embellishment but an

16-3 Guang, probably from Anyang, China, Shang dynasty, 12th or 11th century BCE. Bronze, 6½" high. Asian Art Museum of San Francisco (Avery Brundage Collection).

Shang artists perfected casting elaborate bronze vessels covered with animal motifs. The animal forms, real and imaginary, on this libation guang are probably connected with the world of spirits.

1 in.

integral part of the sculptural whole. Some motifs on the guang's side may represent the eyes of a tiger and the horns of a ram. A horned animal forms the front of the lid, and at the rear is a horned head with a bird's beak. Another horned head appears on the handle. Fish, birds, elephants, rabbits, and more abstract composite creatures swarm over the surface against a background of spirals. The fabulous animal forms, real and imaginary, on Shang bronzes are unlikely to have been purely decorative. They probably inhabit the world of spirits addressed in the rituals.

Shang Dynasty and Sanxingdui

During the past century, archaeologists have begun to confirm the existence of China's earliest royal dynasties, long thought to have been mythical. In 1959, for example, at Yanshi in Henan Province, excavators found what they believe to be traces of the Xia (ca. 2000–1600 BCE), China's oldest dynasty. Much better documented, however, is the Shang dynasty (ca. 1600–1050 BCE), the first great Chinese dynasty of the Bronze Age. The Shang kings ruled from a series of royal capitals in the Yellow River valley and vied for power and territory with the rulers of neighboring states. In 1928, excavations at Anyang (ancient Yin) brought to light the last Shang capital. There, archaeologists found a large number of objects—turtle shells, animal bones, and bronze containers—inscribed in the earliest form of the Chinese language. These fragmentary records and the other finds at Anyang provide important information about the

Shang kings and their affairs. They reveal a warlike, highly stratified society. Walls of pounded earth protected Shang cities. Servants, captives, and even teams of charioteers with chariots and horses accompanied Shang kings to their tombs, a practice also documented in Mesopotamia at the Royal Cemetery at Ur (see Chapter 2).

The excavated tomb furnishings include weapons and a great wealth of objects in jade, ivory, lacquer, and bronze. Not only the kings received lavish burials. The tomb of Fu Hao, the wife of Wu Ding (r. ca. 1215–1190 BCE), contained an ivory beaker inlaid with turquoise and more than a thousand jade and bronze objects. The Chinese used many of the vessels found in Shang tombs, for example, the guang (FIG. 16-3), shaped like a covered gravy boat, in sacrifices to ancestors and in funerary ceremonies. In some cases families set up shrines for ancestor worship above the burial sites. Shang artists cast their elaborate bronze vessels in piece molds (see "Shang Bronze-Casting," above).

ters with distinct aesthetic traditions. In 1986, pits at Sanxingdui, near Chengdu in southwestern China, yielded a treasure of elephant tusks and objects in gold, bronze, jade, and clay of types never before discovered. They attest to an independent kingdom of enormous wealth contemporaneous with the better-known Shang dynasty.

The most dramatic find at Sanxingdui was a bronze statue (FIG. 16-4) more than 8 feet tall. Chinese representations of the human figure on this scale are otherwise unknown at this early date. The Sanxingdui statue matches anything from Anyang in masterful casting technique. Very different in subject and style from the Shang bronzes, the over-life-size bronze figure initially shocked art historians who had formed their ideas about Bronze Age Chinese aesthetics based solely on Shang material. The figure—of unknown identity—is highly stylized, with elongated proportions and large, staring eyes. It stands on a base composed of four legs formed of fantastic animal heads with horns and trunklike snouts. The statue tapers gently as it rises, and the figure gradually becomes rounder. Just below the neck, great arms branch dramatically outward, ending in oversized hands that once held an object, most likely one of the many elephant tusks buried in pit 2 with the bronze statue. Surface decorations of squared spirals and hook-pointed curves are all that link this monumental statue with the small-scale and intricate Shang piece-mold bronze vessels (FIG. 16-3). Systematic excavations and chance finds will probably produce more surprises in the future and cause art historians to revise once again their picture of Chinese art in the second half of the second millennium BCE.

Zhou Dynasty

Around 1050 BCE, the Zhou, former vassals of the Shang, captured Anyang and overthrew their Shang overlords. The Zhou dynasty proved to be the longest lasting in China's history—so long historians divide the Zhou era into two periods: Western Zhou (ca. 1050–771 BCE) and Eastern Zhou (770–256 BCE). The dividing event is the transfer of the Zhou capital from Chang'an (modern Xi'an) in the west to Luoyang in the east. The closing centuries of Zhou rule include a long period of warfare among competing states (Warring States Period, ca. 475–221 BCE). The Zhou fell to one of these states, the Qin, in 256 BCE.

ZHOU JADE Under the Zhou, the development of markets and the introduction of bronze coinage brought heightened prosperity and a taste for lavish products, such as bronzes inlaid with gold and silver. Late Zhou bronzes feature scenes of hunting, religious rites, and magic practices. These may relate to the subjects and compositions of lost paintings mentioned in Zhou literature. Other materials favored in the late Zhou period were *lacquer*, a varnishlike substance made from the sap of the Asiatic sumac, used to decorate wood furniture and other objects (see "Lacquered Wood," Chapter 33, page 995, and FIG. 33-8), and jade (see "Chinese Jade," page 454).

The manufacture of jade objects for burial with the dead, beginning in Neolithic times, reached a peak of technical perfection during the Zhou dynasty. Among the most common finds in tombs of the period are *bi* disks (FIG. 16-5)—thin, flat circular pieces of jade with a hole in the center, which may have symbolized the circle of Heaven. Bi disks were status symbols in life as well as treasured items the dead took with them to the afterlife. After a battle, for example, the victors forced their defeated foes to relinquish their bi disks as symbols of their submission. The disks also had high monetary value.

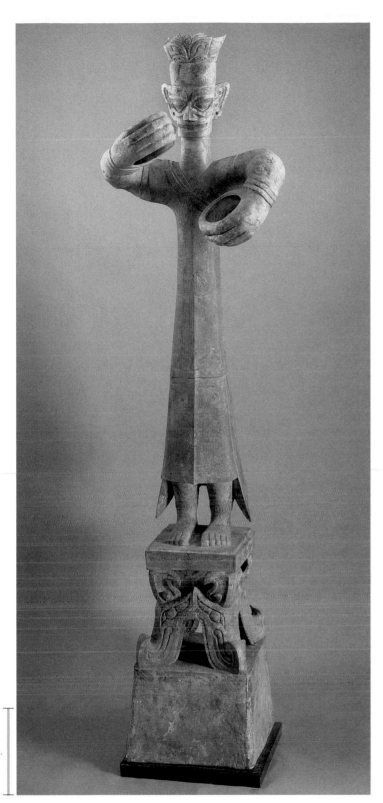

1 ft.

16-4 Standing male figure, from pit 2, Sanxingdui, China, ca. 1200–1050 BCE. Bronze, 8′ 5″ high, including base. Museum, Sanxingdui.

Excavations at Sanxingdui have revealed a civilization contemporaneous with the Shang but with a different artistic aesthetic. This over-life-size statue has elongated proportions and large, staring eyes.

SANXINGDUI Recent excavations in other regions of China have greatly augmented historical understanding of the Bronze Age. They suggest that at the same time Anyang flourished under its Shang rulers in northern China, so did other major cen-

Chinese Jade

The Chinese first used jade—or more precisely, nephrite—for artworks and ritual objects in the Neolithic period. Nephrite polishes to a more lustrous, slightly buttery finish than jadeite (the stone Chinese sculptors preferred from the 18th century on), which is quite glassy. Both stones are beautiful, come in colors other than the well-known green, and are tough, hard, and heavy. In China, those qualities became metaphors for the fortitude and moral perfection of superior persons. The Chinese also believed jade possessed magical qualities that could protect the dead. In one Han dynasty tomb, for example, archaeologists discovered the bodies of a prince and princess dressed in suits composed of more than 2,000 jade pieces sewn together with gold wire.

Because of its extreme hardness, jade could not be carved with the Neolithic sculptor's stone tools. Researchers have speculated on how these early artists were able to cut, shape, and incise the nephrite objects found at many Neolithic Chinese sites. The sculptors probably used cords embedded with sand to incise lines into the surfaces. Sand placed in a bamboo tube drill could perforate the hard stone, but the process would have been long and arduous, requiring great patience as well as superior skill.

Even after the invention of bronze tools, Chinese sculptors still had to rely on grinding and abrasion rather than simple drilling and chiseling to produce their intricately shaped, pierced, and engraved works. An example is the *bi* (FIG. 16-5) shown here, said to have come from a royal Eastern Zhou tomb at Jincun. Rows of raised spirals, created by laborious grinding and polishing, decorate the disk itself. Within the inner circle and around the outer edge of the bi are elegant dragons. The Chinese thought dragons inhabited the water and flew between Heaven and Earth, bringing rain, so these animals long have been symbols of good fortune in East Asia. They also symbolized the rulers' power to mediate between Heaven and Earth. To sculpt the dragons on the bi from Jincun required long hours of work to pierce through the hard jade. The bi testifies to the Zhou sculptor's mastery of this difficult material.

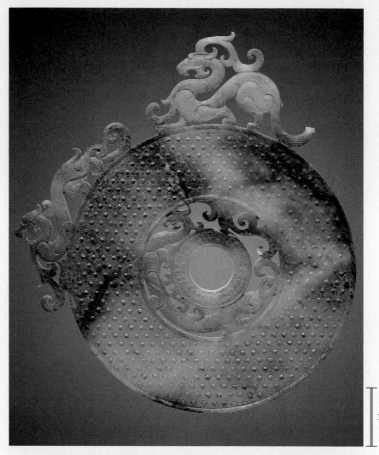

1 in.

16-5 Bi disk with dragons, from Jincun(?), near Luoyang, China, Eastern Zhou dynasty, fourth to third century BCE. Nephrite, $6\frac{1}{2}''$ in diameter. Nelson-Atkins Museum of Art, Kansas City.

This intricately shaped jade bi required hours of grinding, piercing, engraving, and polishing to produce. Dragons were Chinese symbols of good fortune and flew between Heaven and Earth.

Qin Dynasty

During the Warring States Period, China endured more than two centuries of political and social turmoil. This was also a time of intellectual and artistic upheaval, when conflicting schools of philosophy, including Legalism, Daoism, and Confucianism, emerged. Order was finally restored when the powerful armies of the ruler of the state of Qin (from which the modern name "China" derives) conquered all rival states. Known to history by his title, Qin Shi Huangdi (First Emperor of Qin), between 221 and 210 BCE he controlled an area equal to about half of modern China, much larger than the territories of any of the earlier Chinese dynasties. During his reign, Shi Huangdi ordered the linkage of active fortifications along the northern border of his realm to form the famous Great Wall. The wall defended China against the fierce nomadic peoples of the north, especially the Huns, who eventually made their way to eastern Europe. By sometimes brutal methods, the First Emperor

consolidated rule through a centralized bureaucracy and adopted standardized written language, weights and measures, and coinage. He also repressed all schools of thought other than Legalism, which espoused absolute obedience to the state's authority and advocated strict laws and punishments. Chinese historians have harshly condemned the First Emperor, but the bureaucratic system he put in place long outlasted his reign. Its success was due in large part to Shi Huangdi's decision to replace the feudal lords with talented salaried administrators and to reward merit rather than to favor high birth.

TERRACOTTA ARMY, LINTONG In 1974, excavations started at the site of the immense burial mound of the First Emperor of Qin at Lintong. For its construction, the ruler conscripted more than 700,000 laborers, and the project continued after his death. The mound itself remains unexcavated, but archae-

16-6 Army of the First Emperor of Qin in pits next to his burial mound, Lintong, China, Qin dynasty, ca. 210 BCE. Painted terracotta, average figure 5′ 10$\frac{7}{8}$″ high. ◼◀

The First Emperor was buried beneath an immense mound guarded by more than 6,000 life-size terracotta soldiers. Although produced from common molds, every figure has an individualized appearance.

ologists believe it contains a vast treasure-filled underground funerary palace designed to match the fabulous palace the emperor occupied in life. The historian Sima Qian (136–85 BCE) described both palaces, but scholars did not take his account seriously until the discovery of pits around the tomb containing more than 6,000 life-size painted terracotta figures (FIG. **16-6**) of soldiers and horses, as well as bronze horses and chariots. The terracotta army served as the First Emperor's bodyguard deployed in perpetuity outside his tomb.

The Lintong army, consisting of statues of cavalry, chariots, archers, lancers, and hand-to-hand fighters, was one of the 20th century's greatest archaeological discoveries. Lesser versions of Shi Huangdi's army have since been uncovered at other Chinese sites, suggesting the First Emperor's tomb became the model for many others. The huge assemblage at Lintong testifies to a high degree of organization in the Qin imperial workshop. Manufacturing this army of statues required a veritable army of sculptors and painters as well as a large number of huge kilns. The First Emperor's artisans could have opted to use the same molds over and over again to produce thousands of identical soldiers standing in strict formation. In fact, they did employ the same molds repeatedly for different parts of the statues but assembled the parts in many different combinations. Consequently, the stances, arm positions, garment folds, equipment, coiffures, and facial features vary, sometimes slightly, sometimes markedly, from statue to statue. Additional hand modeling of the cast body parts before firing enabled the sculptors to differentiate the figures even more. The Qin painters undoubtedly added further variations to the appearance of the terracotta army. The result of these efforts was a brilliant balance of uniformity and individuality.

Han Dynasty

Soon after the First Emperor's death, the people who had suffered under his reign revolted, assassinated his corrupt and incompetent son, and founded the Han dynasty in 206 BCE. The Han ruled China for four centuries, integrating many of the Qin reforms in a more liberal governing policy. They also extended China's southern and western boundaries, penetrating far into Central Asia (present-day Xinjiang). Han merchants even traded indirectly with distant Rome via the so-called Silk Road (see "The Silk Road," page 458).

WU FAMILY SHRINES Excavations of Han dynasty tombs have uncovered some of the finest examples of Chinese painting, such as the silk funerary banner of the marquise of Dai (FIG. 16-1), and of bronze-casting, for example, the *boshan* (incense burner) of Prince Liu Sheng (FIG. **16-6A**). The most important stone sculptures of this period are the pictorial narratives on the walls of the Wu family shrines in a cemetery at Jiaxiang in Shandong Province. The shrines, which date between 147 and 168 CE, document the emergence under the Han dynasty of private, nonaristocratic families as patrons of religious and mythological art having political overtones. Dedicated to deceased male family members, the Wu shrines are simple in form, consisting of three low walls and a pitched roof. On the interior surfaces, sculptors carved flat polished images that stand out against an equally flat, though roughly textured, ground. The historical scenes include a representation of the third-century BCE hero Jing Ke's attempt to assassinate the tyrannical First Emperor of Qin.

16-6A Incense burner of Prince Liu Sheng, ca. 113 BCE.

16-7 The archer Yi(?) and a reception in a mansion, Wu family shrine, Jiaxiang, China, Han dynasty, 147–168 CE. Rubbing of a stone relief, 3′ × 5′.

The Wu family shrines depict legendary, historical, and contemporaneous subjects. Here, the hero Yi shoots down suns to save Earth from scorching. To the right is a ceremonial scene in a Han mansion.

1 ft.

On the slab shown in FIG. **16-7**, a *rubbing* (an impression made by placing dampened paper over the surface and rubbing ink onto the portions adhering to the relief carving) taken from the shrine wall depicts an archer at the upper left who is probably the hero Yi. He saves Earth from scorching by shooting down the nine extra suns, represented as crows in the Fusang tree. (The small orbs below the sun on the marquise of Dai's banner [FIG. 16-1] probably allude to the same story.) The lowest zone shows a procession of umbrella-carriages moving to the left. Above, underneath the overhanging eaves of a two-story mansion, robed men bearing gifts pay homage to a central figure of uncertain identity, represented as larger and therefore more important. Two men kneel before the larger figure. Women occupy the upper story. Again, one figure, at the center and

facing forward, is singled out as the most important. The identities of the individual figures are unknown. Interpretations vary widely, and in the past decade, scholars have discovered some of the Wu reliefs have recarved inscriptions, leading them to question even the traditional date of the slab. Nonetheless, these scenes of homage and loyalty are consistent with the Confucian ideals of Han society (see "Daoism and Confucianism," page 463).

WUWEI FLYING HORSE Han sculptors also excelled in bronze-casting. Of the many surviving bronze figurines of this period, those discovered in 1969 at Wuwei in Gansu Province in the brick tomb of Governor-General Zhang are of special interest. The tomb contained almost 100 cast-bronze sculptures of horses, chariots, and soldiers—a miniature version of the life-size army (FIG. 16-6) guarding the tomb of the First Emperor of Qin. The figurine illustrated here (FIG. 16-8) represents a distinctive breed of horse from Turkestan. It differs from all the others in Zheng's tomb because it is not prancing or standing still but galloping, or, more accurately, flying, because one hoof rests on a swallow with spread wings. The sculptor posed the horse with its head tilted to one side but presented the animal's body in a pure profile. (Compare the horses pulling carts in the reliefs [FIG. 16-7] of the Wu family shrine.) The Wuwei horse has an even more elegant silhouette, with its legs spread widely and its tail lifted behind it like a fifth leg, balancing the curved neck and the rear left leg. Zhang's airborne horse suggests the journey from his tomb will take him heavenward to an immortal afterlife.

HAN HOUSES AND PALACES No remains of Han domestic buildings survive, but ceramic models of houses deposited in Han tombs, together with representations such as those in the Wu family shrines, provide information about Chinese residential architecture and construction techniques during the early centuries CE. An unusually large painted earthenware model (FIG. **16-9**) reproduces a Han house with sharply projecting tiled roofs resting on a framework of timber posts, lintels, and brackets. This construction method (FIG. **16-10**) typifies much Chinese architecture even today (see "Chinese Wooden Construction," page 457). Descriptions of Han palaces suggest they were grandiose versions of the type of house reproduced in this model but with more luxurious decoration, including mural paintings and walls of lacquered wood.

1 in.

16-8 Flying horse, from the tomb of Governor-General Zhang, Wuwei, China, Han dynasty, late second century CE. Bronze, 1′ 1½″ high. Gansu Provincial Museum, Lanzhou.

Found in a late Han dynasty tomb, this cast-bronze galloping, flying horse has one hoof on a swallow with spread wings, suggesting the deceased's heavenward journey to the afterlife.

Chinese Wooden Construction

Although the basic unit of Chinese architecture, the rectangular hall with columns supporting a roof, was common in many ancient civilizations, Chinese buildings have two major distinguishing features: the curving silhouettes of their roofs and their method of construction. The Chinese, like other ancient peoples, used wood to construct their earliest buildings. Although those structures do not survive, scholars believe many of the features giving East Asian architecture its distinctive character may date to the Zhou dynasty. Even the simple buildings reproduced on Han stone carvings (FIG. 16-7) and in clay models (FIG. 16-9) reveal a style and a method of construction long basic to China.

The typical Chinese hall has a pitched roof with projecting eaves. Wooden columns, lintels, and brackets provide the support. The walls have no weight-bearing function but serve only as screens separating inside from outside and room from room. The colors of Chinese buildings, predominantly red, black, yellow, and white, are also distinctive. Chinese timber architecture is customarily multicolored throughout, save for certain parts left in natural color, such as railings made of white marble. The builders usually painted the screen walls and the columns red. Chinese designers often chose dazzling combinations of colors and elaborate patterns for the beams, brackets, eaves, rafters, and ceilings. Artists painted or lacquered the surfaces to protect the timber from rot and wood parasites, as well as to produce an arresting aesthetic effect.

The drawing reproduced here (FIG. 16-10) shows the basic construction method of Chinese architecture, with the major components of a Chinese building labeled. The builders laid *beams* between columns, decreasing the length of the beams as the structure rose. The beams supported vertical *struts*, which in turn supported higher beams and eventually the *purlins* running the length of the building and carrying the roof's sloping *rafters*. Unlike the rigid elements of the triangular trussed timber roof common in the West, which produce flat sloping rooflines, the varying lengths of the Chinese cross beams and the variously placed purlins can create curved profiles. Early Chinese roofs have flat profiles (FIGS. 16-7 and 16-9), but curving rafters (FIGS. 16-10 and 16-22) later became the norm, not only in China but throughout East Asia. The interlocking clusters of brackets were capable of supporting roofs with broad overhanging *eaves*, another typical feature of Chinese architecture. Multiplication of the *bays* (spaces between the columns) could extend the building's length to any dimension desired, although each bay could be no wider or longer than the length of a single tree trunk. The proportions of the structural elements could be fixed into *modules* (basic units), allowing for standardization of parts and thus rapid construction. The Chinese wooden construction system was so sophisticated that highly skilled workers could fit the parts together without using any adhesive substance, such as mortar or glue, and still build very large, stable structures capable of standing for centuries.

16-9 Model of a house, Han dynasty, first century CE. Painted earthenware, 4′ 4″ high. Nelson-Atkins Museum of Art, Kansas City.

This Han house model provides invaluable information about the form, coloration, and construction methods of Chinese architecture. The flat profile of the rooflines is typical of earlier Chinese buildings.

16-10 Chinese raised beam construction (after L. Liu).

Chinese walls have no weight-bearing function. They serve only as screens separating inside from outside and room from room. Tang dynasty and later buildings usually have curved rafters and eaves.

Rafters
Purlin
Strut
Beam
Eaves

1 ft.

The Silk Road

The Chinese began to produce silk (see "Chinese Silk for the Afterlife," page 449) as early as the second millennium BCE, and people soon coveted the luxury fabric throughout Asia and beyond. Romans knew of silk as early as the second century BCE and treasured it for garments and hangings. Silk came to Rome along the ancient fabled Silk Road—a network of caravan routes across Central Asia linking China and the Mediterranean world (MAP 16-1). The western part, between the Mediterranean region and India, developed first, due largely to the difficult geographic conditions in northeastern India. In Central Asia, the caravans had to skirt the Taklimakan Desert, one of the most inhospitable environments on earth, as well as climb high, dangerous mountain passes. Very few traders traveled the entire distance. Along the way, goods usually passed through the hands of people from many lands, who often only dimly understood the ultimate origins and destinations of what they traded. The Roman passion for silk ultimately led to the modern name for these caravan routes, but silk was far from the only product traded along the way. Gold, ivory, gems, glass, lacquer, incense, furs, spices, cotton, linens, exotic animals, and other merchandise precious enough to warrant the risks passed along the Silk Road.

Ideas moved along the Silk Road as well. Most important perhaps, the caravans brought Buddhism to China from India in the first century CE, opening a significant new chapter in both the history of religion and the history of art in China.

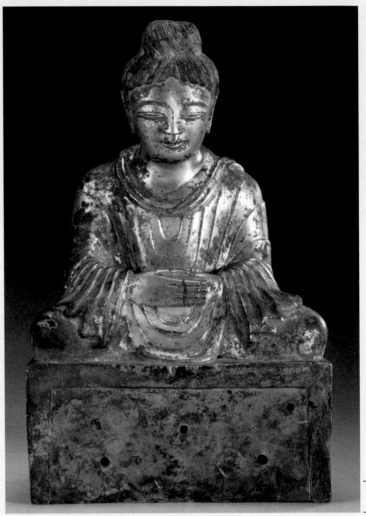

16-11 Shakyamuni Buddha, from Hebei Province, Later Zhao dynasty, Period of Disunity, 338. Gilded bronze, 1′ 3½″ high. Asian Art Museum of San Francisco, San Francisco (Avery Brundage Collection).

The Silk Road brought not only trade goods to China but also Buddhism. This earliest datable Chinese Buddha image is stylistically indebted to Gandharan prototypes (FIG. 15-11).

1 in.

Period of Disunity

For three and a half centuries, from 220 to 581,* civil strife divided China into competing states. Scholars variously refer to this era as the Period of Disunity or the period of the Six Dynasties or of the Northern and Southern Dynasties. In the history of this extremely complex era, one development deserves special mention—the occupation of northern China by peoples who were not ethnically Han Chinese and who spoke non-Chinese languages. It was in the northern states, connected to India by the desert caravan routes of the Silk Road (see "The Silk Road," above), that Buddhism first took root in China during the Han dynasty. Certain practices shared with Daoism (see "Daoism and Confucianism," page 463), such as withdrawal from ordinary society, helped Buddhism gain an initial foothold in the north. But Buddhism's promise of hope beyond the troubles of this world earned it an ever broader audience during the upheavals of the Period of Disunity. In addition, the fully developed Buddhist system of thought attracted intellectuals. Buddhism never fully

displaced Confucianism and Daoism, but it did prosper throughout China for centuries and had a profound influence on the further development of the religious forms of those two native traditions.

ZHAO BUDDHA A gilded bronze statuette (FIG. 16-11) in San Francisco representing Shakyamuni, the historical Buddha, bears an inscription giving its date as 338. Although some scholars have argued that the inscription is a later addition, many art historians accept the statuette as the earliest precisely datable Chinese image of the Buddha, created during the Later Zhao dynasty (319–351). The oldest Chinese Buddhist texts describe the Buddha as golden and radiating light. This no doubt accounts for the choice of gilded bronze as the sculptor's medium. In both style and iconography, this early Buddha resembles the prototype conceived and developed at Gandhara (FIGS. 15-1, 15-11, and 15-11A). The Chinese figure recalls its presumed South Asian models in the flat, relieflike handling of the robe's heavy concentric folds, the ushnisha (cranial bump) on the head, and the cross-legged position. So new were the icon and its meaning, however, that the Chinese sculptor misrepresented the canonical dhyana mudra, or meditation gesture (see "Buddhism and Buddhist Iconography," Chapter 15, page 427).

*From this point on, all dates in this chapter are CE unless otherwise stated.

Chinese Painting Materials and Formats

Mural paintings in caves (FIG. 16-15) were popular in China, as they were in South Asia (FIG. 15-14), but Chinese artists also employed several other materials and formats for their works. The basic requirements for paintings not on walls were the same as for writing—a round tapered brush, soot-based ink, and either silk or paper. The Chinese were masters of the brush. Sometimes they used modulated lines for contours and interior details that elastically thicken and thin to convey depth and mass. In other works, they used *iron-wire lines* (thin, unmodulated lines with a suggestion of tensile strength) to define each figure in their paintings. Chinese painters also used richly colored minerals as pigments, finely ground and suspended in a gluey medium, and watery washes of mineral and vegetable dyes. The formats of Chinese paintings on silk or paper tend to be personal and intimate, and they are usually best viewed by only one or two people at a time. The most common types are listed here.

Hanging scrolls (FIGS. 16-14A, 16-19, 16-24, and 16-25). Chinese painters often mounted pictures on, or painted directly on, unrolled vertical scrolls for display on walls.

Handscrolls (FIGS. 16-12, 16-16, 16-20, and 16-23A). Artists also frequently attached paintings to, or painted directly on, long, narrow scrolls the viewer unrolled horizontally, section by section from right to left.

Album leaves (FIGS. 16-23 and 33-15). Many Chinese artists painted small panels on paper leaves, which collectors placed in albums.

Fans (FIG. 33-14). Stiff round or arched folding fans were also popular painting formats.

16-12 Attributed to GU KAIZHI, *Lady Feng and the Bear*, detail of *Admonitions of the Instructress to the Court Ladies*, Period of Disunity, late fourth century. Handscroll, ink and colors on silk, $9\frac{3}{4}$″ × 11′ $4\frac{1}{2}$″. British Museum, London.

Chinese handscrolls are unrolled and read from right to left. This section of an early scroll depicts Lady Feng's act of heroism to save the life of her emperor, a perfect model of Confucian behavior.

1 in.

Here, the Buddha clasps his hands across his stomach. In South Asian art, the Buddha turns his palms upward, with thumbs barely touching in front of his torso.

LADY FENG'S HEROISM Secular arts also flourished in the Period of Disunity, as rulers sought calligraphers and painters to lend prestige to their courts. The most famous early Chinese painter with whom extant works can be associated was GU KAIZHI (ca. 344–406). Gu was a friend of important members of the Eastern Jin dynasty (317–420) and won renown as a calligrapher, a painter of court portraits, and a pioneer of landscape painting. A *handscroll* (see "Chinese Painting Materials and Formats," above) attributed to Gu Kaizhi in the 11th century is not by his hand, but it exemplifies the key elements of his art. Called *Admonitions of the Instructress to the Court Ladies,* the horizontal scroll contains

painted scenes and accompanying explanatory text. Like all Chinese handscrolls, this one was unrolled and read from right to left, with only a small section exposed for viewing at one time.

The section illustrated here (FIG. **16-12**) records a well-known act of heroism—Lady Feng saving her emperor's life by placing herself between him and an attacking bear, a perfect model of Confucian behavior. As in many early Chinese paintings, the artist set the figures against a blank background with only a minimal setting for the scene, although in other works Gu provided landscape settings for his narratives. The figures' poses and fluttering drapery ribbons, in concert with individualized facial expressions, convey a clear quality of animation. This style accords well with painting ideals expressed in texts of the time, when representing inner vitality and spirit took precedence over reproducing surface appearances (see "Xie He's Six Canons," page 460).

Xie He's Six Canons

China has a long and rich history of scholarship on painting, preserved today in copies of texts from as far back as the fourth century and in citations to even earlier sources. Few of the first texts on painting survive, but later authors often quoted them, preserving parts of some important works for posterity. Thus, educated Chinese painters and their clients could steep themselves in a rich art historical tradition. Perhaps the most famous subject of later commentary is a set of six "canons" (laws) of painting Xie He formulated in the early sixth century. The canons, as translated by James Cahill, are as follows:

1. Engender a sense of movement through spirit consonance.

2. Use the brush with the bone method.

3. Responding to things, depict their forms.

4. According to kind, describe appearances [with color].

5. Dividing and planning, positioning and arranging.

6. Transmitting and conveying earlier models through copying and transcribing.*

Xie employed only four characters for each of these succinct and cryptic laws. Several variant translations have been proposed, and scholars actively debate the precise meaning of each canon. Interpreting the canons in connection with extant paintings is often difficult but nonetheless offers valuable insights into what the Chinese of Xie's day and later valued in painting.

The simplest canons to understand are the third, fourth, and fifth, because they show Chinese painters' concern for accuracy in rendering forms and colors and for care in composition, artistic concerns common in many cultures. However, separating form and color into different laws gives written expression to a distinctive feature of early Chinese painting. Painters such as Gu Kaizhi (FIG. 16-12) and Yan Liben (FIG. 16-16) used an outline-and-color technique. Their brushed-ink outline drawings employ flat applications of color. To suggest volume, they used ink shading along edges, such as drapery folds.

Also noteworthy is the order of the laws, suggesting Chinese painters' primary concern: to convey the vital spirit of their subjects and their own sensitivity to that spirit. Next in importance was the handling of the brush and the careful placement of strokes, especially of ink. The sixth canon also speaks to a standard Chinese painting practice: copying. Chinese painters, like painters in other cultures throughout history, trained by copying the works of their teachers and other artists (see "Artistic Training in Renaissance Italy," Chapter 14, page 414). In addition, Chinese artists often copied famous paintings as sources of forms and ideas for their own works and to preserve great works created using fragile materials. In China, as elsewhere, change and individual development occurred in constant reference to the past, the artists always preserving some elements of it.

*James Cahill, "The Six Laws and How to Read Them," *Ars Orientalis* 4 (1961), 372–381.

MEETING OF TWO BUDDHAS A gilded bronze statuette (FIG. **16-13**) shows how the sculptors of the Northern Wei dynasty (386–534) transformed the Gandhara-derived style of earlier Buddhist art in China (FIG. 16-11). Dated 518, the piece was probably a private devotional object in a domestic setting or a votive offering in a temple. It represents the meeting of Shakyamuni Buddha (at the viewer's right) and Prabhutaratna, the Buddha who had achieved nirvana in the remote past, as recounted in the *Lotus Sutra*, an encyclopedic collection of Buddhist thought and poetry. When Shakyamuni was preaching on Vulture Peak, Prabhutaratna's stupa miraculously appeared in the sky. Shakyamuni opened it and revealed Prabhutaratna himself, who had promised to be present whenever the Lotus Sutra was preached. Shakyamuni sat beside him and continued to expound the Lotus Sutra's teachings. The meeting of the two Buddhas symbolized the continuity of Buddhist thought across the ages.

Behind each Buddha is a *mandorla* (flamelike almond-shaped nimbus). Both figures sit in the *lalitasana* pose—one leg folded and the other hanging down. This standard pose, which indicates

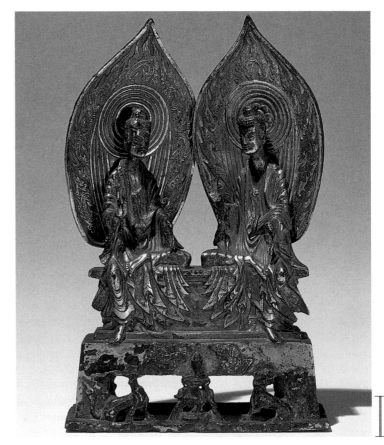

16-13 Shakyamuni and Prabhutaratna, from Hebei Province, Northern Wei dynasty, 518. Gilded bronze, 10¼″ high. Musée Guimet, Paris.

The sculptor of this statuette transformed the Gandhara-derived style of earlier Chinese Buddhist art (FIG. 16-11). The bodies have elongated proportions, and the garment folds form sharp ridges.

1 in.

relaxation, underscores the ease of communication between the two Buddhas. Their bodies have elongated proportions, and their smiling faces have sharp noses and almond eyes. The folds of the garments drop like a waterfall from their shoulders to their knees and spill over onto the pedestal, where they form sharp ridges resembling the teeth of a saw. The rhythmic sweep and linear elegance of the folds recall the brushwork of contemporaneous Chinese painting.

BUDDHIST CAVES The Northern Wei dynasty was also responsible for beginning work at the great Longmen Cave complex near Luoyang, further developed under the Tang dynasty (FIG. 16-14). Modeled on the cave temples of India (see Chapter 15), the Longmen and other Chinese complexes feature rock-cut shrines decorated with sculptures and paintings. The Longmen site alone eventually grew to encompass 2,345 shrines and more than 100,000 statues and 2,800 inscriptions, attesting to the importance of Buddhism in China at this time. The Northern Wei emperors also sponsored Buddhist caves at the Yungang Grottoes near Datong, notably cave 20 with its colossal rock-cut image of the seated Buddha (FIG. **16-13A**).

16-13A Seated Buddha, cave 20, Yungang, ca. 460–470.

Sui and Tang Dynasties

16-13B Sui altarpiece with Amitabha and attendants, 593.

The emperors of the short-lived Sui dynasty (r. 581–618) succeeded in reuniting China and prepared the way for the brilliant Tang dynasty, but few high quality works survive from the 37-year Sui reign. One Sui masterpiece is a small altarpiece (FIG. **16-13B**) now in Boston, dated by inscription to 593.

Under the Tang emperors (r. 618–907), China entered a period of unequaled magnificence (MAP 16-1). Chinese armies marched across Central Asia, prompting an influx of foreign peoples, wealth, and ideas into China. Traders, missionaries, and other travelers journeyed to the cosmopolitan Tang capital at Chang'an, and the Chinese, in turn, ventured westward. Chang'an, laid out on a grid scheme, occupied more than 30 square miles. It was the greatest city in the world during the seventh and eighth centuries.

VAIROCANA BUDDHA In its first century, the new dynasty continued to support Buddhism and to sponsor great monuments for Buddhist worshipers. One of the most spectacular Tang Buddhist sculptures is carved into the face of a cliff in the Longmen Cave complex. The colossal relief (FIG. **16-14**), which dominates the entire site, features a central figure of the Buddha 44 feet tall—seated. An inscription records that the project was completed in 676 when Gaozong (r. 649–683) was the Tang emperor and that in 672 the empress Wu Zetian underwrote a substantial portion of the considerable cost with her private funds. Wu Zetian was an exceptional woman by any standard, and when Gaozong died in 683, she declared herself emperor and ruled until 705, when she was forced to abdicate at age 82.

Wu Zetian's Buddha is the Vairocana Buddha, not the historical Buddha of FIGS. 16-11, 16-13, and 16-13A, but the Mahayana Cosmic Buddha, the Buddha of Boundless Space and Time (see "Buddhism," Chapter 15, page 427). Flanking him are two of his monks, attendant bodhisattvas, and guardian figures—all smaller than the Buddha but still of colossal size. The sculptors represented the Buddha in serene majesty. An almost geometric regularity of contour and smoothness of planes emphasize the volume of the massive figure. The folds of his robes fall in a few concentric arcs. The artists suppressed surface detail in the interest of monumental simplicity and dignity.

DUNHUANG GROTTOES The westward expansion of the Tang Empire increased the importance of Dunhuang, the westernmost gateway to China on the Silk Road. Dunhuang long had been a wealthy, cosmopolitan trade center, a Buddhist pilgrimage destination, and home to thriving communities of Buddhist monks and nuns of varied ethnicity, as well as to adherents of other religions. In the course of several centuries beginning in the Period of Disunity, the Chinese cut hundreds of sanctuaries with painted murals into the soft rock of the cliffs near Dunhuang. Known today as the Mogao Grottoes and in antiquity as the Caves of a Thousand

16-14 Vairocana Buddha, disciples, and bodhisattvas, Fengxian Temple, Longmen Caves, Luoyang, China, Tang dynasty, completed 676. Limestone, Buddha, 44' high. ◼◀

Empress Wu Zetian sponsored these colossal rock-cut sculptures. The Tang artists represented the Mahayana Cosmic Buddha in serene majesty, suppressing surface detail in favor of monumental simplicity.

16-14A *Bodhisattva Guanyin*, Dunhuang, late 9th or early 10th century.

Buddhas, the Dunhuang cave temples also contain sculptured images of painted unfired clay and stucco and painted silk scrolls (FIG. 16-14A). The earliest recorded dedication of a cave at Dunhuang was in 366, but the oldest extant caves date to the early fifth century. The Dunhuang Grottoes are especially important because in 845 the emperor Wuzong instituted a major persecution, destroying 4,600 Buddhist temples and 40,000 shrines and forcing the return of 260,500 monks and nuns to lay life. Wuzong's policies did not affect Dunhuang, then under Tibetan rule, so the site preserves much of the type of art lost elsewhere.

Paradise of Amitabha (FIG. 16-15) in Dunhuang cave 172 shows how the splendor of the Tang era and religious teachings could come together in a powerful image. Buddhist Pure Land sects, especially those centered on Amitabha, Buddha of the West, had captured the popular imagination in the Period of Disunity under the Six Dynasties and continued to flourish during the Tang dynasty. Pure Land teachings asserted that individuals had no hope of attaining enlightenment through their own power because of the waning of the Buddha's law. Instead, they could obtain rebirth in a realm free from spiritual corruption simply through faith in Amitabha's promise of salvation. Richly detailed, brilliantly colored pictures steeped in the opulence of the Tang dynasty, such as this one, greatly aided worshipers in gaining faith by visualizing the wonders of the Pure Land Paradise. Amitabha sits in the center of a raised platform against a backdrop of ornate buildings characteristic of the Tang era (compare the Foguang Si [Buddha Radiance Temple] at Mount Wutai [FIG. 16-15A]).

16-15A Foguang Si, Mount Wutai, ca. 857.

The Buddha's principal bodhisattvas and lesser divine attendants surround him. Before them a celestial dance takes place. Bodhisattvas had strong appeal in East Asia as compassionate beings ready to achieve buddhahood but dedicated to humanity's salvation. Some received direct worship and became the main subjects of sculpture and painting.

YAN LIBEN Although few examples of Tang painting exist today, many art historians regard the early Tang dynasty as the golden age of Chinese figure painting. In perfect accord with contemporaneous and later Chinese poets' and critics' glowing descriptions of Tang painting style are the unrestored portions of *The Thirteen Emperors* (FIG. 16-16), a masterpiece of line drawing and colored washes long attributed to YAN LIBEN (d. 673). Born into an aristocratic family and the son of a famous artist, Yan was prime minister under the emperor Gaozong as well as a celebrated painter. This handscroll depicts 13 Chinese rulers from the Han to the Sui dynasties. Its purpose was to portray these historical figures as exemplars of moral and political virtue, in keeping with the Confucian ideal of learning from the past (see "Daoism and Confucianism," page 463). Each emperor stands or sits in an undefined space. The emperor's greater size relative to his attendants immediately establishes his superior stature. Simple shading in the faces and the robes gives the figures an added semblance of volume and presence.

The detail in FIG. 16-16 represents Emperor Xuan of the Chen dynasty (557–589) seated among his attendants, two of whom carry the ceremonial fans that signify his rank and focus the viewer's attention on him. Xuan stands out from the others also because of his dark robes. His majestic serenity contrasts with his attendants' animated poses, which vary sharply from figure to figure, lending vitality to the composition.

TOMB OF YONGTAI Wall paintings in the tomb of the Tang princess Yongtai (684–701) at Qianxian, near Chang'an, permit an analysis of court painting styles unobscured by problems of

16-15 *Paradise of Amitabha,* cave 172, Dunhuang, China, Tang dynasty, mid-eighth century. Wall painting, 10′ high.

This richly detailed, brilliantly colored mural aided worshipers at Dunhuang to visualize the wonders of the Pure Land Paradise promised to those who had faith in Amitabha, the Buddha of the West.

1 ft.

Daoism and Confucianism

Daoism and Confucianism are both philosophies and religions native to China. Both schools of thought attracted wide followings during the Warring States Period (ca. 475–221 BCE) when political turbulence led to social unrest.

Daoism emerged out of the metaphysical teachings attributed to Laozi (604?–531? BCE) and Zhuangzi (370?–301? BCE). It takes its name from Laozi's treatise *Daodejing* (*The Way and Its Power*). Daoist philosophy stresses an intuitive awareness, nurtured by harmonious contact with nature, and shuns everything artificial. Daoists seek to follow the universal path, or principle, called the Dao, whose features cannot be described but only suggested through analogies. For example, the Dao is said to be like water, always yielding but eventually wearing away the hard stone that does not yield. For Daoists, strength comes from flexibility and inaction. Historically, Daoist principles encouraged retreat from society in favor of personal cultivation in nature and the achievement of a perfect balance between *yang,* active masculine energy, and *yin,* passive feminine energy.

Confucius (Kong Fuzi, or Master Kong, 551–479 BCE) was born in the state of Lu (roughly modern Shandong Province) to an aristocratic family that had fallen on hard times. From an early age, he showed a strong interest in the rites and ceremonies that helped unite people into an orderly society. As he grew older, he developed a deep concern for the suffering the civil conflict of his day caused. Thus, he adopted a philosophy he hoped would lead to order and stability. The *junzi* ("superior person" or "gentleman") who possesses *ren* ("human-heartedness") personified the ideal social order Confucius sought. Although the term *junzi* originally assumed noble birth, in Confucian thought anyone can become a junzi by cultivating the virtues Confucius espoused, especially empathy for suffering, pursuit of morality and justice, respect for ancient ceremonies, and adherence to traditional social relationships, such as those between parent and child, elder and younger sibling, husband and wife, and ruler and subject.

Confucius's disciple Mencius (or Mengzi, 371?–289? BCE) developed his master's ideas further, stressing that the deference to age and rank at the heart of the Confucian social order brings a reciprocal responsibility. For example, a king's legitimacy depends on the goodwill of his people. A ruler should share his joys with his subjects and will know his laws are unjust if they bring suffering to the people.

Confucius spent much of his adult life trying to find rulers willing to apply his teachings, but he died in disappointment. However, he and Mencius profoundly influenced Chinese thought and social practice. Chinese traditions of venerating deceased ancestors and outstanding leaders encouraged the development of Confucianism as a religion as well as a philosophic tradition. Eventually, Emperor Wu (r. 140–87 BCE) of the Han dynasty established Confucianism as the state's official doctrine. Thereafter, it became the primary subject of the civil service exams required for admission into and advancement within government service.

Confucian and *Daoist* are broad, imprecise terms scholars often use to distinguish aspects of Chinese culture stressing social responsibility and order (Confucian, for example, FIGS. 16-12 and 16-16) from those emphasizing cultivation of individuals, often in reclusion (Daoist, for example, FIGS. 16-19 and 16-23). But both philosophies share the idea that anyone can cultivate wisdom or ability, regardless of birth.

16-16 Attributed to YAN LIBEN, *Emperor Xuan and Attendants,* detail of *The Thirteen Emperors,* Tang dynasty, ca. 650. Handscroll, ink and colors on silk, detail 1' 8¼" × 1' 5½"; full scroll 17' 5" long. Museum of Fine Arts, Boston.

This handscroll portrays 13 Chinese rulers as Confucian exemplars of moral and political virtue. Yan Liben, a celebrated Tang painter, was a master of line drawing and colored washes.

1 in.

16-17 Palace ladies, detail of a wall painting, tomb of Princess Yongtai, Qianxian, China, Tang dynasty, 706. Detail, 5′ 10″ high.

The paintings in this Tang princess's tomb depict scenes of pleasant court life. The muralist used thick, even contour lines and did not provide any setting, but the composition effectively conveys depth.

1 ft.

authenticity and reconstruction. When she was 17 years old, Yongtai was either murdered or forced to commit suicide by Wu Zetian, sponsor of the colossal rock-cut image of the Vairocana Buddha (FIG. 16-14) at Luoyang. Yongtai's underground tomb dates to 706, however, because her formal burial had to await Wu Zetian's death. The murals illustrated here (FIG. **16-17**) depict palace ladies and their attendants, images of pleasant court life to accompany the princess into her afterlife. The figures appear as if on a shallow stage, but the artist did not provide any indications of background or setting. The women, arranged in two rows, assume a variety of poses, some seen full-face, others in three-quarter views, both from the front and the back. The device of paired figures facing into and out of the picture space appears often in paintings of this period and effectively conveys depth. Thick, even contour lines describe full-volumed faces and suggest solid forms beneath the drapery, all with the utmost economy. This simplicity of form and line, along with the measured cadence of the poses, results in an air of monumental dignity.

TANG CERAMIC SCULPTURE Tang ceramists also achieved renown and produced thousands of earthenware figures of people, domesticated animals, and fantastic creatures for burial in tombs. These statuettes attest to a demand for ceramic sculpture by a much wider group of patrons than ever before, but terracotta funerary sculpture has a long history in China. The most spectacular example is the ceramic army (FIG. 16-6) of the First Emperor of Qin. The subjects of the Tang figurines are also much more diverse than in earlier periods. The depiction of a broad range of foreigners, including Semitic traders and Central Asian musicians on camels, accurately reflects the cosmopolitanism of Tang China.

The artists painted some figurines with colored slips and decorated others, such as the spirited, handsomely adorned neighing horse in FIG. **16-18**, with colorful lead glazes that ran in dramatic streams down the objects' sides when fired (see "Chinese Earthenwares and Stonewares," page 451). The popularity of the horse as a

subject of Chinese art (compare FIG. 16-8) reflects the importance the emperors placed on the quality of their stables. The breed represented here is powerful in build. Its beautifully arched neck terminates in a small, elegant head. Richly harnessed and saddled, the horse testifies to its rider's nobility.

1 in.

16-18 Neighing horse, Tang dynasty, eighth to ninth century. Glazed earthenware, 1′ 8″ high. Victoria & Albert Museum, London.

Tang ceramists achieved renown for their earthenware figurines decorated with colorful lead glazes that ran in dramatic streams down the sides when a piece was fired, as in this statuette.

Song and Liao Dynasties

The last century of Tang rule brought many popular uprisings and the empire's gradual disintegration. After an interim of internal strife known as the Five Dynasties period (907–960), General Zhao Kuangyin succeeded in consolidating the country once again. He established himself as the first emperor (r. 960–976) of the Song dynasty (960–1279), which ruled China from a capital in the north at Bianliang (modern Kaifeng) during the Northern Song period (960–1127). The Song emperors curtailed many of the hereditary privileges of the elite class. They also made political appointments on the basis of scores on civil service examinations, and education became a more important prerequisite for Song officials than high birth.

The three centuries of Song rule, including the Southern Song period (1127–1279) when the capital was at Lin'an (modern Hangzhou) in southern China, were also a time of extraordinary technological innovation. Under the Song dynasty, the Chinese invented the magnetic compass for sea navigation, printing with moveable clay type, paper money, and gunpowder. Song China was the most technologically advanced society in the world in the early second millennium.

FAN KUAN For many art historians, the Song dynasty also marks the apogee of Chinese landscape painting, which first emerged as a major subject during the Period of Disunity. Although many of the great Northern Song masters worked for the imperial court, FAN KUAN (ca. 960–1030) was a Daoist recluse (see "Daoism and Confucianism," page 463) who shunned the cosmopolitan life of Bianliang. He believed nature was a better teacher than were other artists, and he spent long days in the mountains studying configurations of rocks and trees and the effect of sunlight and moonlight on natural forms. Just as centuries later, Giorgio Vasari (1511–1574) would credit Italian Renaissance artists with the exploration and perfection of naturalistic painting (see Chapter 21), so did Song critics laud Fan and other leading Chinese painters of the day as the first masters of the recording of light, shade, distance, and texture—several centuries earlier than in Europe. Yet, the comparison with 15th- and 16th-century Italy is misleading. Chinese landscape painters did not aim to produce portraits of specific places seen from a fixed viewpoint. They did not seek to imitate or to reproduce nature. Rather, they sought to capture the essence of nature and of its individual elements using brush and ink on silk. Their paintings are tributes to nature, not representations of unique rock or tree formations.

In *Travelers among Mountains and Streams* (FIG. **16-19**), Fan painted a vertical landscape of massive mountains rising from the distance. The overwhelming natural forms dwarf the few human and animal figures (for example, the mule train in the lower right corner), which the artist reduced to minute proportions. The nearly seven-foot-long silk hanging scroll cannot contain nature's grandeur, and the landscape continues in all directions beyond its borders. Fan showed some elements from level ground (for example, the great boulder in the foreground), and others obliquely from the top (the shrubbery on the highest cliff). The shifting perspectives lead the viewer's eye on a journey through the mountains. To appreciate the painted landscape fully, an observer must focus not only on the larger composition but also on intricate details and on the character of each brushstroke. Numerous "texture strokes" help model massive forms and convey a sense of tactile surfaces. For the face of the mountain, for example, Fan employed small, pale brush marks, the kind of texture stroke the Chinese call "raindrop strokes."

16-19 FAN KUAN, *Travelers among Mountains and Streams,* Northern Song period, early 11th century. Hanging scroll, ink and colors on silk, 6′ 7¼″ × 3′ 4¼″. National Palace Museum, Taibei.

Fan Kuan, a Daoist recluse, spent long days in the mountains studying the effects of light on rock formations and trees. He was one of the first masters at recording light, shade, distance, and texture.

HUIZONG A century after Fan Kuan painted in the mountains of Shanxi, HUIZONG (1082–1135; r. 1101–1126) assumed the Song throne at Bianliang. Less interested in governing than in the arts, the new emperor brought the country to near bankruptcy and lost much of China's territory to the armies of the Tartar Jin dynasty (1115–1234), who captured the Song capital in 1126 and took Huizong as a prisoner. He died in their hands nine years later. An

清曉飄逸棣彩霄仙禽告瑞忽來儀飄

祥瑞故作詩以紀其實

經時不散迤邐歸飛västの北陽散感兹

往來都民無不稽首瞻望歎異久之

之端頗甚閒道餘皆如應奏師

飛鳴太空十餘首有二鶴對止於鴟尾

低映端門眾皆仰而視之條有群鶴

政如宣和壬辰上元之次夕忽有祥雲拂鬱

16-20 Attributed to HUIZONG, *Auspicious Cranes*, Northern Song period, 1112. Section of a handscroll, ink and colors on silk, 1′ 8⅛″ × 4′ 6⅜″. Liaoning Provincial Museum, Shenyang.

The Chinese regarded the white cranes that appeared at Huizong's palace as an auspicious sign. This painting of the event is a masterful combination of elegant composition and realistic observation.

accomplished poet, calligrapher, and painter, Huizong reorganized the imperial painting academy and required the study of poetry and calligraphy as part of the official training of court painters. *Calligraphy,* or the art of writing, was highly esteemed in China throughout its history, and prominent inscriptions are frequent elements of Chinese paintings (see "Calligraphy and Inscriptions on Chinese Paintings," Chapter 33, page 997). Huizong also promoted the careful study both of nature and of the classical art of earlier periods, and was an avid art collector as well as the sponsor of a comprehensive catalogue of the vast imperial art holdings.

A short handscroll (FIG. 16-20) usually attributed to Huizong is more likely the work of court painters under his direction, but it displays the emperor's style as both calligrapher and painter. Huizong's characters represent one of many styles of Chinese calligraphy. They consist of thin strokes, and each character is meticulously aligned with its neighbors to form neat vertical rows. The painting depicts cranes flying over the roofs of Bianliang. It is a masterful combination of elegant composition and realistic observation. The painter carefully recorded the black and red feathers of the white cranes and depicted the birds from a variety of viewpoints to suggest they were circling around the roof. Huizong did not, however, choose this subject because of his interest in the anatomy and flight patterns of birds. The painting was a propaganda piece commemorating the appearance of 20 white cranes at the palace gates during a festival in 1112. The Chinese interpreted the

16-21 Meiping vase, from Xiuwi, China, Northern Song period, 12th century. Stoneware, Cizhou type, with sgraffito decoration, 1′ 7½″ high. Asian Art Museum of San Francisco, San Francisco (Avery Brundage Collection).

Chinese potters developed the sgraffito technique (incising through a colored slip) during the Northern Song period. This vase features vines and flowers created by cutting through a black slip.

appearance of the cranes as an auspicious sign, proof Heaven had blessed Huizong's rule. Although few would ever have viewed the handscroll, painted banners featuring the cranes were displayed on special occasions, where they could be seen by a larger public.

CIZHOU POTTERY Song artists also produced superb ceramics. Some reflect their patrons' interests in antiquities and imitate the powerful forms of the Shang and Zhou bronzes. However, Song ceramics more commonly had elegant shapes with fluid silhouettes. Many featured monochrome glazes, such as the famous celadon wares, also produced in Korea (FIG. 16-29), but a quite different kind of pottery emerged in northern China, loosely classed as Cizhou (after the city in Hebei Province that was the center of production). The example shown here (FIG. 16-21) is a vase of the high-shouldered shape known as *meiping*. Chinese potters developed the subtle techniques of *sgraffito* (incising the design through a colored slip) during the Northern Song period. They achieved the intricate black-and-white design on this meiping by cutting through a black slip (see "Chinese Earthenwares and Stonewares," page 451). The vase's tightly twining vine and flower-petal motifs closely embrace the vessel in a perfect accommodation of surface design to vase shape.

FOGUANG SI PAGODA For two centuries during the Northern Song period, the Liao dynasty (907–1125) ruled part of northern China. The Liao emperors were important patrons of architecture, painting, and sculpture (for example, the statue of Bodhi-

sattva Guanyin, FIG. 16-21A). In 1056, the Liao dynasty built the Foguang Si Pagoda (FIG. 16-22), the tallest wooden building ever constructed, at Yingxian in Shanxi Province. The *pagoda,* or tower—the building type most often associated with Buddhism in China and other parts of East Asia—is the most eye-catching feature of a Buddhist temple complex. It somewhat resembles the tall towers of Indian temples (see "Hindu Temples," Chapter 15, page 439) and their distant ancestor, the Bud-

16-21A Bodhisattva Guanyin seated on Potalaka, 11th or early 12th century.

dhist stupa (see "The Stupa," Chapter 15, page 430). As did stupas, many early pagodas housed relics and provided a focus for devotion to the Buddha. Later pagodas served other functions, such as housing sacred images and texts. The Chinese and Koreans built both stone and brick pagodas, but wooden pagodas were also common and became the standard in Japan (FIG. 17-9).

The nine-story octagonal pagoda at Yingxian is 216 feet tall and made entirely of wood (see "Chinese Wooden Construction," page 457). Sixty giant, four-tiered bracket clusters carry the floor beams and projecting eaves of the five main stories. They rest on two concentric rings of columns at each level. Alternating main stories and windowless mezzanines with cantilevered balconies, set back farther on each story as the tower rises, form a combined elevation of nine stories. Along with the open veranda on the ground level and the soaring pinnacle, the balconies visually lighten the building's mass.

16-22 View (*left*) and cross-section (*right;* after L. Liu) of Foguang Si Pagoda, Yingxian, China, Liao dynasty, 1056.

The tallest wooden building in the world is this Buddhist pagoda at Yingxian. The nine-story tower shows the Chinese wooden beam-and-bracket construction system at its most ingenious.

16-23 MA YUAN, *On a Mountain Path in Spring*, Southern Song period, early 13th century. Album leaf, ink and colors on silk, 10¾″ × 17″. National Palace Museum, Taibei.

In contrast to Fan (FIG. 16-19), Ma reduced the landscape on this album leaf to a few elements and confined them to one part of the page. A large, solitary figure gazes into the infinite distance.

1 in.

The cross-section (FIG. 16-22, *right*) shows the symmetrical placement of statues of the Buddha inside, the colossal scale of the ground-floor statue, and the intricacy of the beam-and-bracket system at its most ingenious.

SOUTHERN SONG PERIOD When the Jin captured Bianliang and the emperor Huizong in 1126 and took control of northern China, Gaozong (r. 1127–1162), Huizong's sixth son, escaped and eventually established a new Song capital in the south at Lin'an (present-day Hangzhou). From there, he and his successors during the Southern Song period ruled their reduced empire until 1279.

Court sponsorship of painting continued in the new capital, and, as in the Northern Song period, some emperors took a direct interest in the painters of the imperial painting academy. During the reign of Ningzong (r. 1194–1224), members of the court, including Ningzong himself and Empress Yang, frequently added brief poems to the paintings created under their direction. Some painters belonged to families that had worked for the Song emperors for several generations.

MA YUAN The most famous Song painters came from the Ma family, which began working for the Song dynasty during the Northern Song period. MA YUAN (ca. 1160–1225) painted *On a Mountain Path in Spring* (FIG. **16-23**), a silk album leaf, for Ningzong in the early 13th century. In his composition, as in those of his contemporary,

16-23A XIA GUI, *Twelve Views from a Thatched Hut*, ca. 1200–1225.

XIA GUI (active ca. 1195–1230; FIG. **16-23A**), in striking contrast to Fan Kuan's much larger *Travelers among Mountains and Streams* (FIG. 16-19), Ma reduced the landscape to a few elements and confined the natural setting to the foreground and left side of the page. A large, solitary figure gazes out into the infinite distance. Framing him are the carefully placed diagonals of willow branches. Near the upper right corner, a bird flies toward the couplet Ningzong added in ink, demonstrating his mastery of both poetry and calligraphy:

Brushed by his sleeves, wild flowers dance in the wind;
Fleeing from him, hidden birds cut short their songs.

Some scholars have suggested the author of the two-line poem was Empress Yang, but the inscription is in Ningzong's hand. In any case, landscape paintings such as this one are perfect embodiments of the Chinese ideals of peace and unity with nature.

ZHOU JICHANG Other Southern Song painters focused on religious themes. Although Neo-Confucianism, a blend of traditional Chinese thought and selected Buddhist concepts, became the leading philosophy, traditional Buddhist themes remained popular subjects for paintings. ZHOU JICHANG (ca. 1130–1190) painted *Lohans Giving Alms to Beggars* (FIG. **16-24**) around 1178 as part of a series of 100 scrolls produced at the southern coastal city of Ningbo for an abbot who invited individual donors to pay for the paintings as offerings in the nearby Buddhist temple. *Lohans* are enlightened disciples of the Buddha who have achieved freedom from rebirth (nirvana) by suppression of all desire for earthly things. Their charge was to protect Buddhist law until the arrival of the Buddha of the Future. In his Ningbo scroll, Zhou arranged the foreground, middle ground, and background vertically to clarify the lohans' positions relative to one another and to the beggars. The lohans move with slow dignity in a plane above the ragged wretches who scramble miserably for the alms their serene benefactors throw down. The extreme difference in deportment between the two groups distinguishes their status, as do their contrasting features. The lohans' vividly colored attire, flowing draperies, and quiet gestures set them off from the dirt-colored and jagged shapes of the people physically and spiritually beneath them. In this painting, consistent with Xie's principles (see "Xie He's Six Canons," page 460), Zhou used color for symbolic and decorative purposes, not to imitate nature or depict the appearance of individual forms. The composition of the landscape—the cloudy platform and lofty peaks of the lohans and the desertlike setting of the beggars—also distinguishes the two spheres of being.

LIANG KAI A new school of Buddhist thought, Chan Buddhism (see "Chan Buddhism," page 470), which stressed the quest for personal enlightenment through meditation, also flourished under the Song dynasty. LIANG KAI (active early 13th century) was a master of an abbreviated, expressive style of ink painting that found great favor among Chan monks in China, Korea, and Japan. He served in the painting academy of the imperial court in Hangzhou, and his early works include poetic landscapes typical of the Southern Song. Later in life, he left the court and concentrated on figure painting, including Chan subjects.

1 in.

16-24 Zhou Jichang, *Lohans Giving Alms to Beggars,* Southern Song period, ca. 1178. Hanging scroll, ink and colors on silk, 3′ 7$\frac{7}{8}$″ × 1′ 8$\frac{7}{8}$″. Museum of Fine Arts, Boston.

Zhou chose a vertical arrangement of the figures in the fore-, middle-, and background in order to elevate the enlightened lohans in their bright attire above the ragged, dirt-colored beggars.

Surviving works attributed to Liang include an ink painting (FIG. **16-25**) of the Sixth Chan Patriarch, Huineng, crouching as he chops bamboo. In Chan thought, the performance of even mundane tasks such as chopping bamboo had the potential to become a spiritual exercise. In fact, this scene specifically depicts the patriarch's "Chan moment," when the sound of the blade striking the bamboo resonated within his spiritually attuned mind to propel him through the final doorway to enlightenment. The scruffy,

1 in.

16-25 Liang Kai, *Sixth Chan Patriarch Chopping Bamboo,* Southern Song period, early 13th century. Hanging scroll, ink on paper, 2′ 5$\frac{1}{4}$″ high. Tokyo National Museum, Tokyo.

On this hanging scroll, Liang, a renowned master of ink painting, depicted the Sixth Chan Patriarch's "Chan moment," when the chopping sound of his blade propelled the patriarch to enlightenment.

caricature-like representation of the revered figure suggests that worldly matters, such as physical appearance or signs of social status, do not burden Huineng's mind.

Chan Buddhism

Under the Song emperors (960–1279), the new school of *Chan* Buddhism gradually gained importance, until it was second only to Neo-Confucianism. The Chan school traced its origins through a series of patriarchs (the founder and early leaders, joined in a master–pupil lineage). The First Chan Patriarch was Bodhidharma, a semilegendary sixth-century Indian missionary. By the time of the Sixth Chan Patriarch, Huineng (638–713; FIG. 16-25), in the early Tang period, the religious forms and practices of the school were already well established.

Although Chan monks adapted many of the rituals and ceremonies of other schools over the course of time, they focused on the cultivation of the mind or spirit of the individual in order to break through the illusions of ordinary reality, especially by means of meditation. In Chan thought, the means of enlightenment lie within the individual, and direct personal experience with some ultimate reality is the necessary step to its achievement. Meditation

is a critical practice. In fact, the word *Chan* is a translation of the Sanskrit word for "meditation." Bodhidharma is said to have meditated so long in a cave his arms and legs withered away.

Chan Buddhism has two major schools of thought. The Northern school holds that enlightenment comes only gradually after long meditation, but the Southern school believes the breakthrough to enlightenment can be sudden and spontaneous. Huineng, for example, achieved his "Chan moment" when he heard the sharp sound of a cutting blade strike a bamboo stick—the subject of an early-13th-century hanging scroll (FIG. 16-25) by the Southern Song painter Liang Kai.

Chan Buddhist beliefs influenced art and aesthetics as they developed in China and spread to Korea and Japan. In Japan, Chan (Japanese *Zen*) had an especially extensive, long-term influence on the arts and remains an important school of Buddhism there today (see "Zen Buddhism," Chapter 34, page 1007).

Liang used a variety of brushstrokes in the execution of this deceptively simple picture. Most are pale and wet, ranging from the fine lines of Huineng's beard to the broad texture strokes of the tree. A few darker strokes, which define the vine growing around the tree and the patriarch's clothing, offer visual accents in the painting. This kind of quick and seemingly casual execution of paintings has traditionally been interpreted as a sign of a painter's ability to produce compelling pictures spontaneously as a result of superior training and character, or, in the Chan setting, progress toward enlightenment.

KOREA

Korea is a northeast Asian peninsula that shares borders with China and Russia and faces the islands of Japan (MAPS 16-1 and 17-1). Korea's pivotal location is a key factor in understanding the relationship of its art to that of China and the influence of Korea's art on that of Japan. Ethnically, the Koreans are related to the peoples of eastern Siberia and Mongolia as well as to the Japanese. At first, the Koreans used Chinese characters to write Korean words, but later they invented their own phonetic alphabet. Korean art, although frequently based on Chinese models, is not merely derivative but has, like Korean civilization, a distinct identity.

Three Kingdoms Period

Pottery-producing cultures appeared on the Korean peninsula in the Neolithic period no later than 6000 BCE, and the Korean Bronze Age dates from about 1000 BCE. Bronze technology came to Korea from the area that is today northeastern China (formerly known as Manchuria). About 100 BCE, during the Han dynasty, the Chinese established outposts in Korea. The most important was Lolang, which became a prosperous commercial center. By the middle of the century, however, three native kingdoms—Goguryeo, Baekje, and Silla—controlled most of the Korean peninsula and reigned for more than seven centuries until Silla completed its conquest of its neighbors in 668. During this era, known as the Three Kingdoms period (ca. 57 BCE–688 CE), Korea remained in continuous contact with both China and Japan. Buddhism came to Korea from China

in the fourth century CE, first in Goguryeo and Baekje and then in the Silla kingdom. The Koreans in turn transmitted it from the peninsula to Japan in the sixth century.

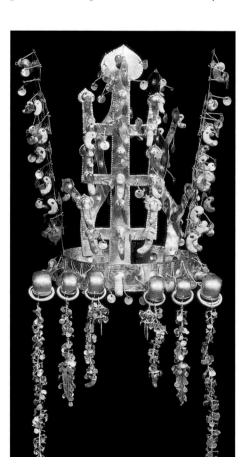

16-26 Crown, from the north mound of the Cheonmachong tomb (tomb 98), Hwangnam-dong, near Gyeongju, Korea, Three Kingdoms Period, fifth to sixth century. Gold and jade, $10\frac{3}{4}''$ high. Gyeongju National Museum, Gyeongju.

This gold-and-jade crown from a Silla tomb attests to the wealth of that kingdom and the skill of its artists. The uprights may be stylized tree and antler forms symbolizing life and supernatural power.

1 in.

SILLA CROWN Tombs of the Silla kingdom have yielded spectacular artifacts representative of the wealth and power of its rulers. Finds in the region of Gyeongju, the Silla capital, justify the city's ancient name—Kumsong (City of Gold). The gold-and-jade crown (FIG. 16-26) from the Cheonmachong (Heavenly Horse) tomb at Hwangnam-dong, near Gyeongju, dated to the fifth or sixth century, also attests to the high quality of artisanship among Silla artists. The crown's major elements, the band and the uprights, as well as the myriad spangles adorning them, were cut from sheet gold and embossed along the edges. Gold rivets and wires secure the whole, as do the comma-shaped pieces of jade further embellishing the crown. Archaeologists interpret the uprights as stylized tree and antler forms believed to symbolize life and supernatural power. The Cheonmachong crown has no Chinese counterpart, although the technique of working sheet gold may have come to Korea from northeast China.

BODHISATTVA MAITREYA The introduction of Buddhism to Korea in the fourth century created a demand for images of the Buddha and of bodhisattvas. The style and iconography of early Korean Buddhist art usually depended on Chinese models, but later examples depart from Chinese prototypes and mark the maturation of a distinct regional artistic tradition. A three-foot-tall gilt cast-bronze statue (FIG. 16-27), made either in the Baekje or Silla kingdom in the early seventh century CE, represents Bodhisattva Maitreya seated in meditation. Maitreya, the future Buddha who will succeed Shakyamuni, the historical Buddha, wears only a simple necklace, in contrast to the rich jewelry of most Chinese bodhisattvas, and his trilobed crown is also a characteristic Korean feature. The bodhisattva's chest is bare, but he wears a long skirt over his lower body, the folds of which cascade over his seat and onto the ground. Maitreya has crossed his right leg and placed his right foot on his left thigh. He leans his chin on his right hand, a posture connoting contemplation. His right elbow in turn rests on his right thigh. The slender proportions of the figure have parallels in Chinese bronzes of the Northern Wei dynasty, for example, the group of Shakyamuni and Prabhutaratna (FIG. 16-13) from Hebei Province, but the treatment of the drapery folds differs sharply.

Unified Silla Kingdom

Aided by China's emperor, the Silla kingdom conquered the Goguryeo and Baekje kingdoms and unified Korea in 668. The era of the Unified Silla Kingdom (688–935) is roughly contemporaneous with the Tang dynasty's brilliant culture in China, and many consider the era Korea's golden age.

SEOKGURAM The Silla rulers embraced Buddhism both as a source of religious enlightenment and as a protective force. They considered the magnificent Buddhist temples they constructed in and around their capital of Gyeongju to be supernatural defenses against external threats as well as places of worship. Unfortunately, none of these temples survived Korea's turbulent history. However, there remains at Seokguram, near the summit of Mount Toham, northeast of the city, a splendid granite Buddhist monument (FIG. 16-28). Scant surviving records suggest it was built under the supervision of Kim Tae-song, a member of the royal family who

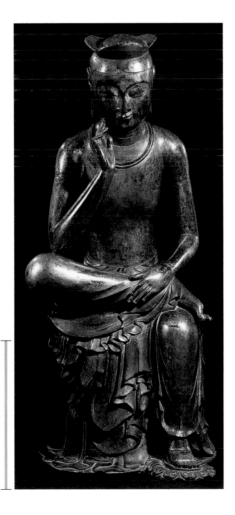

16-27 Meditating Bodhisattva Maitreya, Three Kingdoms period, early seventh century CE. Gilt bronze, 2′ 11⅞″ high. National Museum of Korea, Seoul.

The introduction of Buddhism to Korea created a demand for Buddhist images. An early masterpiece of Korean Buddhist sculpture is this gilt-bronze statue of Maitreya, the Buddha of the Future.

1 ft.

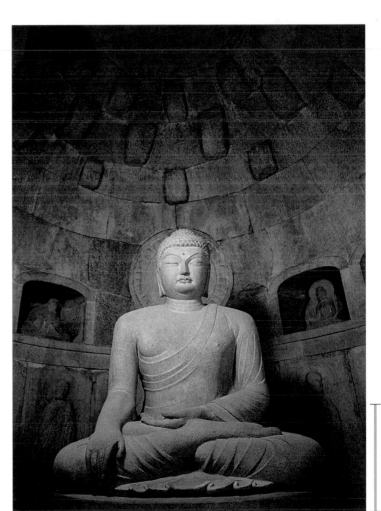

1 ft.

16-28 Shakyamuni Buddha, in the rotunda of the cave temple, Seokguram, Korea, Unified Silla Kingdom, 751–774. Granite, 11′ high.

Unlike rock-cut Chinese Buddhist shrines, this Korean cave temple was constructed of granite blocks. Dominating the rotunda is a huge statue depicting the Buddha at the moment of enlightenment.

1 in.

16-29 Maebyeong vase, Goryeo dynasty, 12th century. Porcellaneous stoneware with incised decoration under celadon glaze, 1′ 4″ tall. Philadelphia Museum of Art, Philadelphia (purchased with the Fiske Kimball Fund and the Marie Kimball Fund, 1974).

Celadon wares feature highly translucent iron-pigmented glazes with incised designs. This green maebyeong vase has herons interspersed among mallow and lotus blossoms.

served as prime minister. He initiated construction in 742 to honor his parents in his previous life. Certainly, the intimate scale of Seokguram and the quality of its reliefs and freestanding figures support the idea it was a private chapel for royalty.

The main *rotunda* (circular area under a dome) measures about 21 feet in diameter. Despite its modest size, the Seokguram project required substantial resources. Unlike the Chinese Buddhist caves at Yungang (FIG. 16-13A), Longmen (FIG. 16-14), and Dunhuang (FIG. 16-15), the interior wall surfaces and sculpture were not cut from the rock in the process of excavation. Instead, workers assembled hundreds of granite pieces of various shapes and sizes, attaching them with stone rivets instead of mortar.

Sculpted images of bodhisattvas, lohans, and guardians line the lower zone of the wall. Above, 10 niches contain miniature statues of seated bodhisattvas and believers. All these figures face inward toward the 11-foot-tall statue of Shakyamuni, which dominates the chamber and faces the entrance. Carved from a single block of granite, the image represents the Buddha as he touched the earth to call it to witness the realization of his enlightenment at Bodh Gaya (FIG. 15-1). Although remote in time and place from the Sarnath Buddha in India (FIG. 15-13), this majestic image remains faithful to its iconographic prototype. More immediately, the Korean statue draws on the robust, round-faced figures of Tang China (FIG. 16-14), and its drapery is a more schematic version of the fluid type found in Tang sculpture. However, no close precedents exist for the figure's distinctly broad-shouldered dignity combined with harmonious proportions. Art historians consider this Korean statue one of the finest images of the Buddha in East Asia.

Goryeo Dynasty

Although Buddhism was the established religion of Korea, Confucianism, introduced from China during the Silla era, increasingly shaped social and political conventions. In the ninth century, the three old kingdoms began to reemerge as distinct political entities, and although the Unified Silla and Goryeo kingdoms overlapped (between about 918 and 935), by 935 the Goryeo (from Goguryeo) had taken control, and they dominated for the next three centuries. In 1231 the Mongols, who had invaded China, pushed into Korea, beginning a war lasting 30 years. In the end, the Goryeo had to submit to forming an alliance with the Mongols, who eventually conquered all of China (see Chapter 33).

CELADON WARE Goryeo potters in the 12th century produced the famous Korean *celadon* wares, admired worldwide. The finest celadon wares feature ornate engraved and inlaid designs over which the ceramists applied highly translucent iron-pigmented glazes, fired in an oxygen-deprived kiln to become gray, pale blue, pale green, or brownish-olive. A masterful example of celadon ware is the plum-shaped (*maebyeong* in Korean, *meiping* in Chinese, FIG. 16-21) vase (FIG. **16-29**) that once belonged to the American financier and art collector J. P. Morgan. Dating to the later Goryeo period, it is the largest maebyeong vase known and was decorated using the inlay technique for which Goryeo potters were famous. The artist incised delicate motifs of herons interspersed among mallow and lotus blossoms into the clay's surface and then filled the grooves with white and colored slip. Then the potter scraped the surface of the vessel and finally covered the entire maebyeong with the celadon blue-green glaze. The incised motifs are broader at the top than at the bottom, reflecting the potter's sure sense of the dynamic relationship between ornamentation and ceramic volume.

CHINA, KOREA, AND JAPAN China's achievements in virtually every field spread beyond even the boundaries of the vast empires it sometimes controlled. Although Buddhism was born in India, the Chinese adaptations and transformations of its teachings, religious practices, and artistic forms were those that spread farther east. China's neighbors owe China an immense cultural debt, but Korea was the crucial artistic, cultural, and religious link between the mainland and the islands of Japan, the subject of Chapter 17.

CHINA AND KOREA BEFORE 1280

NEOLITHIC TO SHANG DYNASTY ca. 7000–1050 BCE

▌ The history of Chinese art begins with the production of Neolithic earthenware pottery in the fourth millennium BCE.

▌ The Shang dynasty (r. ca. 1600–1050 BCE), which ruled the Yellow River valley, was the first great Chinese dynasty of the Bronze Age. Shang bronze-workers were among the best in the ancient world and created a wide variety of elaborately decorated vessels using a sophisticated piece-mold casting process.

Guang, Anyang,
12th or 11th century BCE

ZHOU AND QIN DYNASTIES 1050–206 BCE

▌ The Zhou dynasty was the longest in China's history. The Western Zhou kings (r. ca. 1050–771 BCE) ruled from Chang'an and the Eastern Zhou kings (r. 770–256 BCE) from Luoyang. During the last centuries of Zhou rule, Daoism and Confucianism gained wide followings in China. Zhou artists produced lavish works in bronze, lacquer, and especially jade.

▌ China's First Emperor founded the short-lived Qin dynasty (r. 221–206 BCE) after defeating the Zhou and all other rival states. A terracotta army of more than 6,000 soldiers guarded the First Emperor's burial mound at Lintong. The tomb itself remains unexcavated.

Army of the First Emperor of Qin,
Lintong, ca. 210 BCE

HAN DYNASTY AND PERIOD OF DISUNITY 206 BCE–581 CE

▌ The Han dynasty (r. 206 BCE–220 CE) extended China's boundaries to the south and west and even traded indirectly with Rome via the fabled Silk Road. Han tombs have yielded rich finds, including painted silks, bronze figurines, jade burial suits, and earthenware models of wooden buildings.

▌ Civil strife divided China into competing states from 220 to 581 CE. The earliest Chinese images of the Buddha date to this so-called Period of Disunity, during which Xie He (early sixth century) formulated his six canons of Chinese painting.

Shakyamuni and
Prabhutaratna, 518

TANG DYNASTY AND UNIFIED SILLA KINGDOM 618–935

▌ China enjoyed unequaled prosperity and power under the Tang emperors (r. 618–907), whose capital at Chang'an became the greatest and most cosmopolitan city in the world.

▌ The Tang dynasty was the golden age of Chinese figure painting. The few surviving works include *The Thirteen Emperors* handscroll by Yan Liben illustrating historical figures as exemplars of Confucian ideals. The Dunhuang caves provide evidence of the magnificence of Tang Buddhist art, especially mural painting.

▌ Korea also enjoyed an artistic golden age at this time under the Unified Silla Kingdom (r. 688–935).

Yan Liben,
The Thirteen Emperors, ca. 650

SONG AND LIAO DYNASTIES 960–1279

▌ Song China (Northern Song, r. 960–1127, capital at Bianliang; Southern Song, r. 1127–1279, capital at Lin'an) was the most technologically advanced society in the world in the early second millennium. The Song era also marked the apogee of Chinese landscape painting. Among the leading artists were Fan Kuan and Ma Yuan.

▌ For part of this period, the Liao dynasty (r. 907–1125) controlled northern China and erected the tallest wooden building in the world, the Foguang Si Pagoda.

Foguang Si Pagoda,
Yingxian, 1056

The pagoda of a Japanese Buddhist temple complex housed relics of the Buddha. The Horyuji pagoda is 122 feet tall. The towering height connoted the soaring spirit of Buddhist faith.

The Horyuji kondo was a replacement for an earlier hall destroyed by fire. Priests rescued its Buddha triad, carved by the master sculptor Tori Busshi, and reinstalled the group in the later structure.

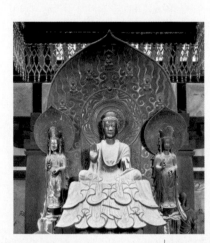

The kondo, or Golden Hall, of a Buddhist temple complex housed statues of the Buddha and bodhisattvas. The Horyuji kondo follows Chinese models in its construction method and curved roofline.

17-1 Aerial view of the Horyuji temple complex (looking northwest), Nara Prefecture, Japan, Nara period, ca. 680.

Adorning the Horyuji Golden Hall were mural paintings of the Buddhas of the Four Directions, including Amida, the Buddha of Immeasurable Light and Infinite Life, seated in his Western Pure Land.

17

JAPAN BEFORE 1333

FRAMING THE ERA

BUDDHISM SPREADS TO JAPAN

The Japanese archipelago (MAP 17-1) consists of four main islands—Hokkaido, Honshu, Shikoku, and Kyushu—and hundreds of smaller ones, a surprising number of them inhabited. Japanese culture, however, does not share the isolation of some island civilizations, but rather has long demonstrated responsiveness to imported ideas—Buddhism among them.

Buddhism arrived in Japan in 552 CE in the form of a gift of Buddhist scriptures and a Buddha statue from a Korean king to the Japanese emperor. The most important early Japanese Buddhist temple complex is at Horyuji (FIG. 17-1), seven miles south of present-day Nara. Fire destroyed the first (sixth-century) temple on the site, which housed a bronze *Buddha triad* (Buddha flanked by two bodhisattvas) dated 632. Shaka—the Japanese name for the historical Buddha (Shakyamuni in Sanskrit)—sits in front of a flaming mandorla (a lotus-petal-shaped nimbus). The sculptor was TORI BUSSHI (*busshi* means "maker of Buddhist images").

Temple officials later installed Tori's group in the rebuilt seventh-century *kondo* of the Nara complex. The kondo, or Golden Hall, was the main hall for worship and contained statues of the Buddha and the bodhisattvas the temple honored. Other key buildings in the Horyuji and similar Japanese Buddhist temple complexes include the *kodo,* or lecture hall, for both monks and laypersons to listen to the reading of sacred texts, and a pagoda, which housed relics of the Buddha. The Horyuji pagoda is five stories and 122 feet tall. The towering height—accentuated by the decreasing size of the roofs from bottom to top—connotes the soaring spirit of Buddhist faith. Both the Horyuji kondo and pagoda underscore Japan's openness to other East Asian artistic traditions. Following Chinese models, the Japanese builders used ceramic tiles as roofing material and adopted the distinctive curved roofline of Tang (FIG. 16-15A) and later Chinese architecture.

In addition to Tori's Buddha triad, the Horyuji kondo boasted some of the finest examples of Buddhist wall painting in East Asia. The pictorial program celebrated the Buddhas of the Four Directions, including Amida (Amitabha in Sanskrit), the Buddha of Immeasurable Light and Infinite Life, who was ruler of the Western Pure Land Paradise. Some scholars believe the painters who executed the Horyuji murals were not Japanese but Chinese or Korean—further evidence of the fruitful artistic and cultural exchanges between the Japanese islands and the mainland. The introduction of Buddhism to Japan in 552 CE so profoundly changed the character of Japanese art and architecture that scholars traditionally divide the early history of art in Japan into pre-Buddhist and Buddhist eras.

JAPAN BEFORE BUDDHISM

Japan's earliest distinct culture antedated the birth of the Buddha (see "The Life of the Buddha," Chapter 15, page 423) by roughly 10,000 years and lasted for several millennia, far longer than the entire later history of art in Japan.

Jomon

Art historians call the earliest art-producing culture of Japan the Jomon (ca. 10,500–300 BCE). The term *jomon* ("cord markings") refers to the technique Japanese potters of this era used to decorate earthenware vessels. The Jomon people were hunter-gatherers, but unlike most such societies, which were nomadic, the Jomon enjoyed surprisingly settled lives. Their villages consisted of pit dwellings—shallow round excavations with raised earthen rims and thatched roofs. Their settled existence permitted the Jomon people to develop distinctive ceramic technology, even before their development of agriculture. In fact, archaeologists have dated some ceramic *sherds* (pottery fragments) found in Japan to before 10,000 BCE—older than sherds from any other area of the world.

MAP 17-1 Japan before 1333.

JAPAN BEFORE 1333

BCE	CE					
Jomon and Yayoi	Kofun	Asuka and Nara		Heian	Kamakura	
10,500 — 300	300 — 552	552 — 784	794	794 — 1185	1185 — 1332	

- Neolithic Jomon ceramists produce distinctive pottery having cordlike decoration
- Yayoi metalworkers cast bronze bells modeled on Han Chinese prototypes

- Japanese elite patrons construct monumental keyhole-shaped burial mounds and place cylindrical clay figures (haniwa) around and on top of them

- Buddhism arrives in Japan from Korea in 552, initiating the Asuka period
- The imperial government establishes its capital at Nara in 710 and builds Buddhist temple complexes following Chinese models

- The imperial capital moves to Heiankyo (Kyoto) in 794, and Esoteric Buddhism takes hold in Japan
- Narrative scroll painting becomes a major art form

- Power shifts from the Japanese emperor to the shoguns of Kamakura
- Sculptors create realistic portraits in wood with rock-crystal eyes

MIDDLE JOMON POTTERY In addition to rope markings, incised lines and applied coils of clay adorned Jomon pottery surfaces. The most impressive examples come from the Middle Jomon period (2500–1500 BCE). Much of the population then lived in the mountainous inland region, where local variations in ceramic form and surface treatment abounded. However, all Jomon potters shared a highly developed feeling for modeled, rather than painted, ceramic ornamentation. Jomon pottery displays such a wealth of applied clay coils, striped incisions, and sometimes quasi-figural motifs that the sculptural treatment in certain instances even jeopardizes the basic functionality of the vessel. Jomon vessels served a wide variety of purposes, from storage to cooking to bone burial. Some of the most elaborate pots may have been used in communal rituals. A dramatic example (FIG. **17-2**) from Miyanomae characteristically shows an intricately modeled surface and a partially sculpted rim. Jomon pottery contrasts strikingly with China's most celebrated Neolithic earthenwares (FIG. 16-2), which emphasize basic ceramic form and painted decoration.

Yayoi

Jomon culture gradually gave way to Yayoi (ca. 300 BCE–300 CE). The period takes its name from the Yayoi district of Tokyo, where archaeologists initially discovered evidence of this first post-Jomon civilization, but the culture emerged in Kyushu, the southernmost of the main Japanese islands, and spread northward. Increased interaction with both China and Korea and immigration from Korea brought dramatic social and technological transformations during the Yayoi period. The Japanese continued to live in pit dwellings, but their villages grew in size, and they developed fortifications, indicating a perceived need for defense. In the third century CE, Chinese visitors noted Japan had walled towns, many small kingdoms, and a highly stratified social structure. Wet-rice agriculture provided the social and economic foundations for this development. The Yayoi period was a time of tremendous change in Japanese material culture as well. Yayoi ceramists produced vessels that were less sculptural than Jomon pottery and sometimes polychrome, and they developed bronze-casting and loom weaving.

DOTAKU Among the most intriguing objects Yayoi artisans fashioned were *dotaku,* or bells. They resemble Han Chinese bell forms, but the Yayoi did not use dotaku as musical instruments. The bronze bells, which are oval in section and range in height from 5 inches to more than 4 feet, were treasured ceremonial objects, and the Japanese often deposited them in graves. Cast in clay molds, these bronzes generally featured raised geometric decoration presented in bands or blocks. On some of the hundreds of surviving dotaku, including the medium-size example illustrated here (FIG. **17-3**), the ornamentation consists of simple line drawings of people, animals, and boats, often in scenes of hunting and fishing or agricultural activities. The dotaku engravings are the earliest extant examples of pictorial art in Japan.

1 in.

17-2 Vessel, from Miyanomae, Nagano Prefecture, Japan, Middle Jomon period, ca. 2500–1500 BCE. Earthenware, 1′ 11⅔″ high. **Tokyo National Museum, Tokyo.**

Jomon pottery is the earliest art form of Japan. Characteristic features are the applied clay coils, striped incisions, and quasi-figural motifs that sometimes jeopardize the functionality of the vessel.

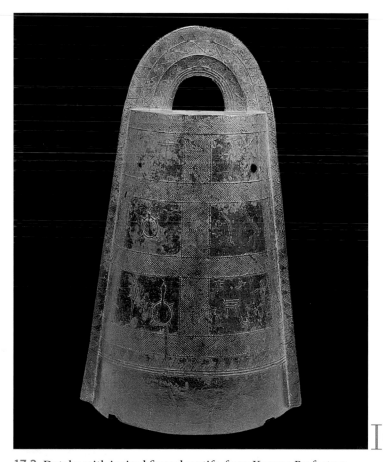

1 in.

17-3 Dotaku with incised figural motifs, from Kagawa Prefecture, Japan, late Yayoi period, ca. 100–300 CE. Bronze, 1′ 4⅞″ high. **Tokyo National Museum, Tokyo.**

Yayoi dotaku were based on Han Chinese bells, but they were not musical instruments. Dotaku feature geometric decoration and the earliest Japanese images of humans and animals.

Kofun

Historians named the succeeding Kofun period (ca. 300–552)* after the enormous earthen burial mounds, or *tumuli*, that had begun to appear in the third century. (*Ko* means "old"; *fun* means "tomb.") The tumuli grew dramatically in number and scale in the fourth century and, as in Greece (FIG. 4-20) and Italy (FIG. 6-6) many centuries earlier, served to proclaim the power and wealth of those buried in them.

TOMB OF NINTOKU The largest tumulus (FIG. 17-4) in Japan is at Sakai. Most scholars identify it as the tomb of Emperor Nintoku, although others think the tumulus postdates his death in 399. The central mound, which takes the "keyhole" form that was standard for tumuli during the Kofun period, is 1,574 feet long and rises to a height of 114 feet. Surrounded by three moats, the entire site covers 458 acres. The best-preserved Kofun tumuli have a stone-walled burial chamber near the summit of the mound. Inside were the deceased's coffin and numerous objects to take into the afterlife. The objects buried with exalted individuals such as Emperor Nintoku included imperial regalia, swords, comma-shaped jewels, and bronze mirrors. The mirrors, which the Japanese believed offered magical protection, came from China, but the form of the Kofun keyhole tombs and many of the other burial goods suggest even closer connections with Korea. For example, the comma-shaped jewels closely resemble those found on Korean Silla crowns (FIG. 16-26), but the Japanese counterparts are simpler and fashioned of gilt bronze.

HANIWA The Japanese also placed unglazed ceramic sculptures called *haniwa* on and around Kofun tumuli. These sculptures, usually several feet in height, as is the warrior shown here (FIG. 17-5), are distinctly Japanese. Compared with the Chinese terracotta soldiers and horses (FIG. 16-6) buried with the First Emperor of Qin, these statues appear deceptively whimsical as variations on a cylindrical theme (*hani* means "clay," *wa* means "circle"). Yet haniwa sculptors skillfully adapted the basic clay cylinder into a host of forms, from abstract shapes to objects, animals (for example, deer, bears, horses, and monkeys), and human figures, such as warriors and female shamans. These artists altered the shapes of the cylinders, emblazoned them with applied ornaments, excised or built up forms, and then painted the haniwa. The variety of figure types suggests the haniwa did not function as military guards but perhaps rather represented the realm the deceased ruled during his life. The Japanese set the statues both in curving rows around the tumulus and in groups around a haniwa house placed directly over the deceased's

*From this point on, all dates in this chapter are CE unless otherwise stated.

17-4 Tomb of Emperor Nintoku (looking northeast), Sakai, Osaka Prefecture, Japan, Kofun period, late fourth to early fifth century.

The largest Kofun tumulus, attributed to Emperor Nintoku, has a keyhole shape and three surrounding moats. About 20,000 clay haniwa originally stood on the gigantic earthen mound.

17-5 Haniwa warrior, from Gunma Prefecture, Japan, Kofun period, fifth to mid-sixth century. Low-fired clay, 4′ 3¼″ high. Tokyo National Museum, Tokyo. ■◀

During the Kofun period, the Japanese set up cylindrical clay statues (haniwa) of humans, animals, and objects on burial tumuli. They may represent the realm the deceased ruled during his life.

burial chamber. Presumably, the number of sculptures reflected the stature of the dead person. The arrangement may mimic a funeral procession in honor of the dead. Emperor Nintoku's tumulus had about 20,000 haniwa statues placed around the mound.

SHINTO The religious system the Japanese embraced during the Yayoi and Kofun eras is Shinto (see "Shinto," page 479). The Japanese imperial clan traces its origins to the Shinto sun goddess Amaterasu. Her shrine (FIG. 17-6) at Ise in a forest near the Isuzu River is the most important Shinto religious center. The location, use, and ritual reconstruction of the Ise Jingu (Ise Shrine) every 20 years reflect the primary characteristics of Shinto—sacred space, ritual renewal, and purification.

Shinto

The early beliefs and practices of pre-Buddhist Japan, which form a part of the belief system later called Shinto ("Way of the Gods"), did not derive from the teachings of any individual founding figure or distinct leader. Nor do formal scriptures, in the strict sense, exist for these beliefs and practices. Shinto developed in Japan in conjunction with the advent of agriculture during the Yayoi period. Japanese religious practices thus originally focused on the needs of this agrarian society and included agricultural rites surrounding planting and harvesting. Villagers venerated and prayed to a multitude of local deities or spirits called *kami*. The early Japanese believed kami existed in mountains, waterfalls, trees, and other features of nature, as well as in charismatic people, and they venerated not only the kami themselves but also the places the kami occupied, which the ancient Japanese considered sacred.

Each clan (a local group claiming a common ancestor, and the basic societal unit during the Kofun period) had its own protector kami, to whom members offered prayers in the spring for successful planting and in the fall for good harvests. Clan members built shrines consisting of several buildings for the veneration of kami. Priests made offerings of grains and fruits at these shrines and prayed on behalf of the clans. Rituals of divination, water purifica-

tion, and ceremonial cleansing at the shrines proliferated. Visitors to the shrine area had to wash before entering in a ritual of spiritual and physical purification.

Purity was such a critical aspect of Japanese religious beliefs that people would abandon buildings and even settlements if negative events, such as poor harvests, suggested spiritual defilement. Even the early imperial court moved several times to newly built towns to escape impurity and its consequences. Such purification concepts are also the basis for the cyclical rebuilding of the sanctuaries at grand shrines. The buildings of the inner shrine (FIG. 17-6) at Ise, for example, have been rebuilt every 20 years for more than a millennium with few interruptions. Rebuilding rids the sacred site of physical and spiritual impurities that otherwise might accumulate. During reconstruction, the old shrine remains standing until carpenters build an exact duplicate next to it. In this way, the Japanese have preserved ancient forms with great precision.

When Buddhism arrived in Japan from the mainland in the sixth century, Shinto practices changed. For example, until the introduction of Buddhism, painted or carved images of Shinto deities did not exist. Yet despite the eventual predominance of Buddhism in Japan, Shinto remains a vital religion for many Japanese.

17-6 **Main hall (looking northwest) of the Ise Jingu, Ise, Mie Prefecture, Japan, Kofun period or later; rebuilt in 1993.**

The most important Shinto shrine in Japan honors the sun goddess Amaterasu. Constructed of wood with a thatch roof and rebuilt every 20 years, the shrine reflects the form of early Japanese granaries.

Traditionally attributed to the Kofun period, the shrine is probably of later date, but it still serves as a representative example of sacred architecture in ancient Japan. Although Japanese shrine architecture varies tremendously, scholars believe the Ise Shrine preserves some of the earliest design elements. Yet the shrine is unique because of its connection to the Japanese imperial family. No other shrines may

be constructed with the identical design. The original source for the form of the Ise complex's main hall appears to be Japanese granaries, which were among the most important buildings in Japan's early agrarian society. Not every aspect of the Ise Shrine is equally ancient. The three main structures of the inner shrine nonetheless convey some sense of Japanese architecture before the introduction of

Buddhism and before the development of more elaborately constructed and adorned buildings.

Aside from the thatched roofs and some metallic decorations, the sole construction material at Ise is wood, fitted together in a *mortise-and-tenon* system, in which the builders slip the wallboards into slots in the pillars. Two massive freestanding posts (once great cypress trunks), one at the center of each end of the main sanctuary, support most of the weight of the *ridgepole,* the beam at the crest of the roof. The golden-hued cypress columns and planks contrast in color and texture with the white gravel covering the sacred grounds. The roof was thatch, which the Japanese smoked, sewed into bundles, and then laid in layers. The smooth shearing of the entire surface produced a gently changing contour. Today, cypress bark covers the roof. Decorative elements (originally having a structural function) enhance the roofline, and include *chigi,* extensions of the rafters at each end of the roof, and *katsuogi,* wooden logs placed at right angles across the ridgepole to hold the thatch of the roof in place. The Ise Shrine highlights the connection, central to Shinto, between nature and spirit. Not only are the construction materials derived from the natural world, but the shrine also stands at a specific location where the builders believed a kami had taken up residence.

BUDDHIST JAPAN

In 552, according to traditional interpretation, King Syong Myong, ruler of Baekje, one of Korea's Three Kingdoms (see Chapter 16), sent Emperor Kimmei (r. 539–571) of Japan a gilded-bronze statue of the Buddha along with *sutras* (Buddhist scriptures) translated into Chinese, at the time the written language of East Asia. The Korean king urged the Japanese emperor to convert to Buddhism. Resistance to the new religion was initially fierce and led to civil strife and armed conflict between opposing Japanese factions. Syong Myong's gift nonetheless marked the beginning of the Asuka period (552–645), during which the ruling elite embraced major elements of continental culture that had been gradually filtering into Japan. These cultural components, which ultimately became firmly established in Japan, included Chinese writing, Confucianism (see "Daoism and Confucianism," Chapter 16, page 463), and Buddhism (see "Buddhism and Buddhist Iconography," Chapter 15, page 427). Older beliefs and practices (those that came to be known as Shinto) continued to have significance (and do to the present day), especially as agricultural rituals and imperial court rites. As time passed, Shinto deities even gained new identities as local manifestations of Buddhist deities.

In 645, a series of reforms led to the establishment of a centralized government in place of the individual clans that controlled Japan's different regions. This shift marked the beginning of the Nara period (645–784), when the Japanese court, ruling from a series of capitals south of modern Kyoto, increasingly adopted the forms and rites of the Chinese court. In 710, the Japanese finally established what they intended as a permanent capital at Heijo (present-day Nara). City planners laid out the new capital on a symmetrical grid closely modeled on the plan of the Chinese capital of Chang'an.

Asuka and Nara

In the arts associated with Buddhist practices, Japan followed Korean and Chinese prototypes very closely, especially during the Asuka and Nara periods. In fact, early Buddhist architecture in Japan adhered so closely to mainland standards (although generally with a considerable time lag) that surviving Japanese temples have helped greatly in the reconstruction of what has been almost completely lost on the Asian continent.

TORI BUSSHI Among the earliest extant examples of Japanese Buddhist sculpture is the bronze Buddha triad (FIG. **17-7**) by Tori Busshi at Horyuji (FIG. 17-1), dated 632. According to the inscription on the Buddha's halo, Empress Suiko (r. 593–628) commissioned the work as a votive offering when her nephew, Prince Shotuku Taishi, the leading champion of Buddhism and Confucian principles of governance in Asuka Japan, fell ill in 621. When Shotuku died, the empress dedicated the triad to the prince's well-being in his next life and to his hoped-for rebirth in Paradise. The central figure in the triad is Shaka, seated with his right hand raised in the abhaya mudra ("fear-not gesture"; see "Buddhism and Buddhist Iconography," Chapter 15, page 427). The flaming mandorla that forms a backdrop to the historical Buddha incorporates small figures of other Buddhas. The sculptor was a descendant of a Chinese immigrant, and the Horyuji Buddha triad reflects the style of the early to mid-sixth century in China and Korea, a style that featured elongated heads and elegant drapery folds forming gravity-defying swirls. The vibrant patterns of the Buddha's garment contrast with the serenity of his pose and expression.

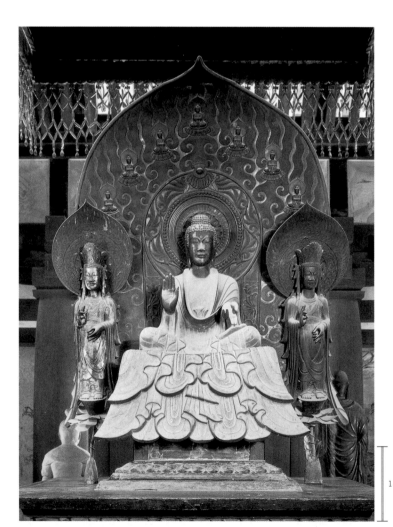

17-7 TORI BUSSHI, Shaka triad, kondo, Horyuji, Nara Prefecture, Japan, Asuka period, 623. Bronze, central figure 2′ 10″ high. ▪◀

Tori's Shaka triad (the historical Buddha and two bodhisattvas) is among the earliest Japanese Buddhist sculptures. The elongated heads and elegant swirling drapery reflect Chinese models.

17-8 Yakushi triad, kondo, Yakushiji, Nara Prefecture, Japan, Nara period, late seventh or early eighth century. Bronze, central figure 8′ 4″ high, including base and mandorla. ◼◀

The sculptor of this Buddha triad favored greater anatomical definition and shape-revealing drapery than did Asuka artist Tori Busshi. The Nara statues display the sensuality of Indian sculpture.

1 ft.

YAKUSHI TRIAD In the early Nara period, Japanese sculptors began to move beyond the Asuka style in favor of new ideas and forms coming out of Tang China and Korea. More direct relations with China also narrowed the time lag between developments there and their transfer to Japan. In the bronze (originally gilded) triad of Yakushi (the Indian Bhaisajyaguru, the Buddha of Healing who presides over the Eastern Pure Land; FIG. **17-8**) in the kondo of the late-seventh-century Yakushiji temple complex in Nara, the sculptor favored greater anatomical definition and shape-revealing drapery over the dramatic stylizations of Tori's triad. The statues of

the attendant Bodhisattvas Nikko and Gakko, especially, reveal the long stylistic trail back through China (FIG. 16-14) to the sensuous fleshiness and outthrust-hip poses of Indian sculpture (FIGS. 15-7, *bottom,* and 15-13).

HORYUJI KONDO Tori Busshi created his Shaka triad for an Asuka Buddhist temple complex at Horyuji (FIG. 17-1), founded by Prince Shotuku near his own estate outside Nara. Fire destroyed the Asuka temple, but the priests rescued Tori's statue and reinstalled it around 680 in the kondo (FIG. **17-9**) of the successor Nara-era

17-9 Kondo (looking southeast), Horyuji, Nara Prefecture, Japan, Nara period, ca. 680.

The kondo, or Golden Hall, of a Buddhist temple complex housed statues of the Buddha and bodhisattvas. The Horyuji kondo follows Chinese models in its construction method and curved roofline.

1 ft.

17-10 Amida triad, photograph before fire damage of the mural formerly in the kondo, Horyuji, Nara Prefecture, Japan, Nara period, ca. 710. Ink and colors, 10′ 3″ × 8′ 6″. Original mural now in the Horyuji Treasure House, Nara.

The murals of the Horyuji kondo represented the Buddhas of the Four Directions. Amida, the Buddha of the Western Pure Land, has red iron-wire lines and reflects Chinese Tang painting style.

complex. Although periodically repaired and somewhat altered (the covered porch is an eighth-century addition; the upper railing dates to the 17th century), the structure retains its graceful but sturdy forms beneath the modifications. The main pillars (not visible in FIG. 17-9 due to the porch addition) decrease in diameter from bottom to top. The tapering provides an effective transition between the more delicate brackets above and the columns' stout forms. Also somewhat masked by the added porch is the harmonious reduction in scale from the first to the second story.

Until a disastrous fire in 1949, visitors to the Horyuji complex could view important early examples of Japanese Buddhist mural painting. Executed around 710, when Nara became the Japanese capital, these

17-11 Daibutsuden (looking north), odaiji, Nara, Japan, Nara period, 743; rebuilt ca. 1700.

The Daibutsuden of the Todaiji temple complex is the largest wooden building in the world. Commissioned by Emperor Shomu in 743, the Great Buddha Hall originally had 11 bays instead of the current 7.

paintings are poorly preserved today and best studied in old color photographs. The most important paintings depicted the Buddhas of the Four Directions. As do the other three, Amida (FIG. **17-10**), the Buddha of the Western Pure Land, sits enthroned in his fabled paradise, attended by bodhisattvas. The exclusive worship of Amida later became a major trend in Japanese Buddhism, and much grander depictions of his paradise appeared, resembling those at Dunhuang (FIG. 16-15) in China. Here, however, the representation is simple and iconic.

Although executed on a dry wall, the Japanese painting process involved techniques similar to fresco, such as transferring designs from paper to wall by piercing holes in the paper and pushing colored powder through the perforations (*pouncing*). As in the Buddha triad (FIG. 17-8) at Yakushiji, the mature Tang style, with its echoes of Indian sensuality, surfaces in this work. The smooth brush lines, thoroughly East Asian, give the figures their substance and life. These lines, often seen in Buddhist painting, are called *iron-wire lines* because they are thin and of unvarying width with a suggestion of tensile strength. As in many other Buddhist paintings, the lines are red instead of black. The identity of the painters of these pictures is unknown, but they may have been Chinese or Korean rather than Japanese.

DAIBUTSUDEN, TODAIJI At the Todaiji temple complex at Nara, the kondo is known as the Daibutsuden (FIG. **17-11**), or Great Buddha Hall. Originally constructed in the eighth century, the current Daibutsuden dates to the early 18th century. The Nara-period temple housed a 53-foot-tall bronze image of the Cosmic Buddha, Roshana (Sanskrit, Vairocana), inspired by Chinese colossal stone statues (FIG. 16-14) of this type. The commissioning of Todaiji and its Great Buddha (Daibutsu) by Emperor Shomu (r. 724–749) in 743 was historically important as part of an imperial attempt to unify and strengthen the country by enlisting religious authority to reinforce imperial power. The temple served as the administrative center of a network of branch temples built in every province. Thus, the consolidation of imperial authority and thorough penetration of Buddhism throughout the country went hand in hand. The dissemination of a common religion contributed to the eventual disruption of the clan system and the unification of disparate political groups. The building and the Daibutsu within were so important that court and government officials as well as Buddhist dignitaries from China and India attended the opening ceremonies on April 9, 752. Chinese Buddhist monks also arrived in Japan in large numbers and were instrumental in spreading Buddhist teachings throughout Japan. Sadly, the current building is significantly smaller than the original. Today, the Daibutsuden has 7 bays, the original had 11. Yet even in its diminished size, the Todaiji Great Buddha Hall is the largest wooden building in the world.

Heian

In 784, possibly to escape the power of the Buddhist priests in Nara, the imperial house moved its capital north, eventually relocating in 794 in what became its home until modern times. Originally called Heiankyo ("capital of peace and tranquility"), its name today is Kyoto. The Heian period (794–1185) of Japanese art takes its name from the new capital. Early in the period, Japan maintained fairly close ties with China, but from the middle of the ninth century on, relations between Japan and China deteriorated so rapidly that by the end of that century, court-sponsored contacts had ceased. Japanese culture became much more self-directed than it had been in the preceding few centuries.

ESOTERIC BUDDHISM Among the major developments during the early Heian period was the introduction of Esoteric Buddhism to Japan from China. The name reflects the secret transmission of its teachings. Two Esoteric sects made their appearance: Tendai in 805 and Shingon in 806. The teachings of Tendai were based on the *Lotus Sutra,* one of the Buddhist scriptural narratives, and *Shingon* (True Word) teachings on two other sutras. Both Tendai and Shingon Buddhists believe all individuals possess buddha nature and can achieve enlightenment through meditation rituals and careful living. To aid focus during meditation, Shingon disciples use special hand gestures (mudras) and recite particular words or syllables (*mantras* in Sanskrit, *shingon* in Japanese). Shingon became the primary form of Buddhism in Japan through the mid-10th century.

TAIZOKAI MANDARA Because of the emphasis on ritual and meditation in Shingon, the arts flourished during the early Heian period. Both paintings and sculptures provided followers with visualizations of specific Buddhist deities and allowed them to contemplate the transcendental concepts central to the religion. Of particular importance in Shingon meditation was the *mandara* (*mandala* in Sanskrit), a diagram of the cosmic universe. The most famous Japanese mandaras are the Womb World (Taizokai) and the Diamond World (Kongokai). Together they formed a complementary pair on the wall of a Shingon kondo. The central motif in the Womb World is the lotus of compassion. In the Diamond World it is the diamond scepter of wisdom. The Womb World is composed of 12 zones, each representing one of the various dimensions of buddha nature (for example, universal knowledge, wisdom, achievement, and purity). The Taizokai mandara illustrated here (FIG. **17-12**) is among the oldest and best preserved in Japan. It is on display today with a corresponding Kongokai mandara at Kyoogokokuji (Toji), the Shingon teaching center established at Kyoto in 823. Many of the figures hold lightning bolts, symbolizing the power of the mind to destroy human passion. Both the Toji Womb World mandara and its Diamond World counterpart reflect Chinese models.

PHOENIX HALL, UJI During the middle and later Heian period, belief in the vow of Amida, the Buddha of the Western Pure Land, to save believers through rebirth in his realm gained great prominence among the Japanese aristocracy. Eventually, the simple message of Pure Land (Jodo, in Japanese) Buddhism—universal salvation—facilitated the spread of Buddhism to all classes of Japanese society. The most important surviving monument in Japan related to Pure Land beliefs is the

1 ft.

17-12 Taizokai (Womb World) mandara, Kyoogokokuji (Toji), Kyoto, Japan, Heian period, second half of ninth century. Hanging scroll, color on silk, $6' \times 5' \frac{3}{8}''$.

The Womb World mandara is a diagram of the cosmic universe composed of 12 zones representing the dimensions of Buddha nature. Mandaras played a central role in Esoteric Buddhist meditation.

17-13 Phoenix Hall (looking west), Byodoin, Uji, Kyoto Prefecture, Japan, Heian period, 1053.

The Phoenix Hall's elaborate winged form evokes images of Amida's palace in the Western Pure Land. Situated on a pond, the temple suggests the floating weightlessness of celestial architecture.

17-13A JOCHO, Seated Amida, Phoenix Hall, Uji, 1053.

Phoenix Hall (FIG. **17-13**) of the Byodoin, a Heian Buddhist temple complex at Uji, south of Kyoto. Fujiwara Yorimichi (990–1074), the powerful regent for three emperors between 1016 and 1068, built the temple in memory of his father, Fujiwara no Michinaga (966–1027), on the grounds of Michinaga's summer villa at Uji. Dedicated in 1053, the Phoenix Hall houses a gilded and lacquered wood statue (FIG. **17-13A**) of Amida by the master sculptor JOCHO (d. 1057). The building's elaborate winged form evokes images of the Buddha's palace in his Pure Land, as depicted in East Asian paintings (FIG. 16-15) in which the architecture reflects the design of Chinese palaces. By placing only light pillars on the exterior, elevating the wings, and situating the whole on a reflective pond, the Phoenix Hall builders suggested the floating weightlessness of celestial architecture. The building's name derives from its overall birdlike shape and from two bronze phoenixes decorating the ridgepole ends. In eastern Asia, people believed these birds alighted on lands properly ruled. Here, they represent imperial might, sometimes associated especially with the empress. The authority of the Fujiwara family derived primarily from the marriage of daughters to the imperial line.

TALE OF GENJI Japan's most admired literary classic is *Tale of Genji*, written around 1000 by Murasaki Shikubu (usually referred to as Lady Murasaki; ca. 978–ca. 1025), a lady-in-waiting at the court. Recounting the lives and loves of Prince Genji and his descendants, *Tale of Genji* provides readers with a view of Heian court culture (see "Heian Court Culture," page 485). The oldest extant examples of illustrated copies are fragments from

17-13B FUJIWARA NO SADANOBU, *Ishiyama-gire*, early 12th century.

a deluxe set of early-12th-century handscrolls (see "Chinese Painting Materials and Formats," Chapter 16, page 459). From textual and physical evidence, scholars have suggested the set originally consisted of about 10 handscrolls produced by 5 teams of artisans. Each team consisted of a nobleman talented in calligraphy, a chief painter who drew the compositions in ink, and assistants who added the color. The script is primarily *hiragana*, a sound-based writing system developed in Japan from Chinese characters. Whereas Japanese scribes employed Chinese characters for Chinese poetry, hiragana became the primary script for Japanese court poetry. One Heian master of hiragana calligraphy was FUJIWARA NO SADANOBU (1088–ca. 1156; FIG. **17-13B**). In *the Genji* handscrolls, pictures alternate with text, as in Gu Kaizhi's *Admonitions* scrolls (FIG. 16-12). However, the Japanese work focuses on emotionally charged moments in personal relationships, rather than on lessons in exemplary behavior.

In the scene illustrated here (FIG. **17-14**), Genji meets with his greatest love near the time of her death. The bush-clover in the garden identifies the season as autumn, a time associated with the fading of life and love. A radically upturned ground plane and strong diagonal lines suggest three-dimensional space. The painter omitted roofs and ceilings to provide a privileged view of the interior spaces where the action takes place. The unusual angles were also metaphors for the emotions of the characters depicted. Flat fields of unshaded color emphasize the painting's two-dimensional character. Rich patterns in the textiles and architectural ornamentation produce a feeling of sumptuousness. The human figures appear constructed of stiff layers of contrasting fabrics, and the artist

Heian Court Culture

During the Nara and especially the Heian periods, the Japanese imperial court developed as the center of an elite culture. In a time of peace and prosperity, the aristocracy had the leisure to play musical instruments and write poetry. Exchanging poems became a common social practice and a frequent preoccupation of lovers. Both men and women produced poems as well as paintings and calligraphy that critics generally consider "classical" today. Heian court members, especially those from the great Fujiwara clan that dominated the court for a century and a half and built the Phoenix Hall (FIG. 17-13) at Uji, compiled the first great anthologies of Japanese poetry and wrote Japan's most influential secular prose.

A lady-in-waiting to an empress of the early 11th century wrote the best-known work of literature in Japan, *Tale of Genji*.

Known as Lady Murasaki, the author is one of many women who were important writers, especially of diaries and poems. Generally considered the world's first lengthy novel (the English translation is almost a thousand pages), *Tale of Genji* tells of the life and loves of Prince Genji and, after his death, of his heirs. The novel and much of Japanese literature consistently display sensitivity to the sadness inherent in the transience of love and life. These human sentiments are often intertwined with the seasonality of nature. For example, the full moon, flying geese, crying deer, and certain plants symbolize autumn, which in turn evokes somber emotions, fading love, and dying. These concrete but evocative images frequently appear in paintings, such as the illustrated scrolls of *Tale of Genji* (FIG. 17-14).

1 in.

17-14 *Genji Visits Murasaki,* from the Minori chapter, *Tale of Genji,* Heian period, first half of 12th century. Handscroll, ink and color on paper, $8\frac{5}{8}''$ high. Goto Art Museum, Tokyo. ◼◀

In this handscroll of Lady Murasaki's *Tale of Genji,* the upturned ground and diagonal lines suggest three-dimensional space. Flat color fields emphasize the painting's two-dimensionality.

simplified and generalized the aristocratic faces, using a horizontal line for each eye and a hook for the nose. This lack of individualization may reflect societal restrictions on looking directly at exalted persons. Later Japanese critics considered several formal features of the *Genji* illustrations—native subjects, bright mineral pigments, lack of emphasis on strong brushwork, and general flatness—typical of *yamato-e,* or "native-style painting." (*Yamato* means "Japan" and the term describes anything characteristically Japanese.)

LEGENDS OF MOUNT SHIGI Heian painting was diverse in both style and subject matter. *Legends of Mount Shigi,* painted

during the late 12th century, represents a different facet of Heian narrative handscroll painting. The stories belong to a genre of pious Buddhist tales devoted to miraculous events involving virtuous individuals. Unlike the *Genji* scrolls, short segments of text and pictures do not alternate. Instead, the painters took advantage of the scroll format to present several scenes in a long, unbroken stretch. For example, the first scroll shows the same travelers at several stages of their journey through a continuous landscape.

The *Mount Shigi* scrolls illustrate three miracles associated with a Buddhist monk named Myoren who resided in a hut close to a small temple on the slopes of Mount Shigi near Nara. The

17-15 *The Flying Storehouse*, from *Legends of Mount Shigi*, Heian period, late 12th century. Handscroll, ink and colors on paper, 1′ ½″ high. Chogosonshiji, Nara.

This Heian handscroll illustrating a Buddhist miracle differs from the *Genji* scroll (FIG. 17-14) in both subject and style. The artist exaggerated each feature of the gesticulating and scurrying figures.

first relates the story of the flying storehouse (FIG. **17-15**) and depicts Myoren's *begging bowl* (the bowl Buddhist monks use to collect alms, either money or food) lifting the rice-filled granary of a greedy farmer and, through the power of the monk's faith, carrying it off to Myoren's mountaintop hut. The painter used a multitude of rapid brushstrokes and pale colors to depict the astonished landowner, his attendants, and several onlookers in various attitudes and poses. Some grimace, others gesticulate wildly and scurry about in frantic amazement. As in the *Genji* scroll, the *Shigi* painter represented the architecture from above, but in striking contrast to the generic faces of the *Genji* illustrations, the artist exaggerated each figure's features.

Kamakura

In the late 12th century, a series of civil wars between rival warrior families led to the end of the Japanese imperial court as a major political and social force. The victors, headed by the Minamoto family, established their *shogunate* (military government) at Kamakura in eastern Japan. The imperial court remained in Kyoto as the theoretical source of political authority, but real power resided with the *shoguns*. The first shogun was Minamoto Yoritomo (1147–1199), on whom the emperor officially bestowed the title in 1185. The ensuing period of Japanese art is called the Kamakura period (1185–1332), named for the shogunate's headquarters. Under the Kamakura shoguns, more frequent and positive contact with China brought with it an appreciation for recent cultural developments there, ranging from new architectural styles to Zen Buddhism.

SHUNJOBO CHOGEN Rebuilding in Nara after the destruction the civil wars inflicted presented an early opportunity for architectural experimentation. A leading figure in planning and directing the reconstruction efforts was the priest Shunjobo Chogen (1120–1206), who sources say made three trips to China between 1166 and 1176. After learning about contemporary Chinese architecture, he oversaw the rebuilding of Todaiji (FIG. 17-11), among other projects, with generous donations from Minamoto Yoritomo. Chogen's portrait statue (FIG. **17-16**), probably carved shortly after his death at age 86, is one of the most striking examples of the high level of naturalism prevalent in the early Kamakura period. It features finely painted details and a powerful rendering of the signs of aging, including sunken cheeks and eye sockets, lined face and neck, and

slumping posture. Details such as the nervous handling of prayer beads capture the personality as well as the appearance of the priest. The statue displays fine Heian carving techniques combined with an increased concern for natural volume and detail learned from studying, among other sources, surviving Nara-period works and sculptures imported from Song China. Enhancing the natural quality of this and other Kamakura portrait statues is the use of inlaid rock crystal for the eyes, a technique unique to Japan.

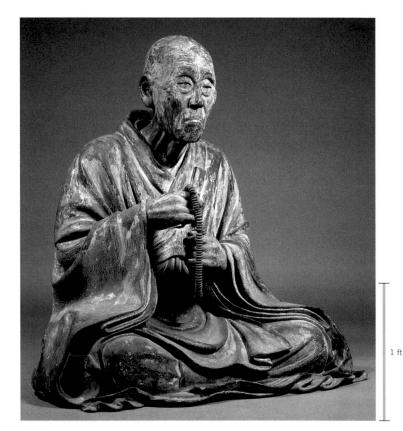

17-16 Portrait statue of the priest Shunjobo Chogen, Todaiji, Nara, Japan, Kamakura period, ca. 1206. Painted cypress wood, 2′ 8⅜″ high.

Kamakura artists' interest in naturalism is evident in this moving portrait of a seated priest. The statue is noteworthy for its finely painted details and powerful rendering of personality and old age.

Heian and Kamakura Artistic Workshops

Until the late Heian period, major artistic commissions came almost exclusively from the imperial court or the great temples. As shogun warrior families gained wealth and power, they too became great art patrons—in many cases closely following established preferences in subject and style.

Artists, for the most part, did not work independently but rather were affiliated with workshops. Indeed, until recently, hierarchically organized male workshops produced most Japanese art. Membership in these workshops was often based on familial relationships. Dominating each workshop was a master, and many of his main assistants and apprentices were relatives. Outsiders of considerable skill sometimes joined workshops, often through marriage or adoption. The eldest son usually inherited the master's position, after rigorous training in the necessary skills from a very young age. Therefore, one meaning of the term *art school* in Japan is a network of workshops tracing their origins to the same master, a kind of artistic clan. Inside the workshops, the master and senior assistants handled the most important production stages, but artists of lower rank helped with the more routine work. The Kamakura portrait statue (FIG. 17-17) of the priest Kuya preaching, for example, was the work of Kosho, whose family workshop traced its artistic roots to a sculptor who lived 150 years before Kosho learned his craft.

Artistic cooperation also surfaced in court bureaus, an alternative to family workshops. These official bureaus, housed at the imperial palace, had emerged by the Heian period. The imperial painting bureau accrued particular fame. Teams of court painters, led by the bureau director, produced pictures such as the scenes in the *Tale of Genji* handscrolls (FIG. 17-14). This system remained vital into the Kamakura period and well beyond. Under the direction of a patron or the patron's representative, the master painter laid out the composition by brushing in the initial outlines and contours. Under his supervision, junior painters applied the colors. The master then completed the work by brushing in fresh contours and details such as facial features. Very junior assistants and apprentices assisted in the process by preparing paper, ink, and pigments. Unlike mastership in hereditarily run workshops, competition among several families determined control of the court painting bureau during the Heian and Kamakura periods.

17-17 Kosho, Portrait statue of the priest Kuya preaching, Kamakura period, early 13th century. Painted wood with inlaid eyes, 3′ 10¼″ high. Rokuharamitsuji, Kyoto.

Kosho, a leading Kamakura sculptor, depicted Kuya as a frail priest roaming the countryside chanting the six syllables of the prayer to Amida, shown as six tiny Buddhas emerging from his mouth.

1 ft.

The bureaus and family workshops did not control all art production, however. Priest-artists trained in temple workshops to make Buddhist art objects for public viewing as well as images for private priestly meditation. Amateur painting was common among aristocrats of all ranks. As they did for poetry composition and calligraphy, aristocrats frequently sponsored painting competitions, in which both women and men participated. In fact, court ladies probably played a significant role in developing the painting style seen in the *Genji* scrolls, and a few participated in public projects.

KOSHO The name of the sculptor of Shunjobo Chogen's portrait is not known, but a contemporaneous portrait (FIG. **17-17**) of the highest quality survives by Kosho (d. 1237), one of the great Kamakura masters of realistic sculpture. Kosho was the fourth of six sons of the sculptor Unkei (d. 1223; FIG. **17-17A**), who was in turn the son of a sculptor of the impor-

17-17A Unkei, *Agyo*, Todaiji, 1203.

tant Kei School (see "Heian and Kamakura Artistic Workshops," above), which traced its lineage to the mid-11th-century master Jocho (FIG. 17-13A). Art historians generally regard the portrait statue of the priest Kuya (903–972) to be Kosho's best work. Kuya converted to Amidism, an early form of Pure Land Buddhism (see "Buddhism," Chapter 15, page 427), after killing a deer. Horrified at what he had done, he devoted the rest of his life to roaming the countryside preaching faith in Amida. Kuya always dressed in ragged clothes and held a walking staff topped by the antlers of the

17-18 *Night Attack on the Sanjo Palace,* from *Events of the Heiji Period,* Kamakura period, 13th century. Handscroll, ink and colors on paper, 1′ 4¼″ high; complete scroll, 22′ 10″ long. Museum of Fine Arts, Boston (Fenollosa-Weld Collection).

The *Heiji* scroll is an example of historical narrative painting. Staccato brushwork and vivid flashes of color beautifully capture the drama of the night attack and burning of Goshirakawa's palace.

1 in.

deer whose life he took. Everywhere he went he chanted the six-syllable *nembutsu* prayer professing total faith in the compassion of Amida Buddha (*Namu Amida Butsu*) while beating a gong.

Kosho's wooden statue is an imaginary portrait, but it is so convincing in its naturalistic depiction of a frail old man of faith it seems as if Kuya posed for the portrait, even though he had been dead for more than two centuries when Kosho carved this statue for the Rokuharamitsuji temple in Kyoto. Kuya walks with his left foot advanced and his antler-topped staff in his left hand. His gong

hangs from a yoke over his shoulders, and he holds his striker in his right hand. Most remarkable is the way Kosho represented Kuya chanting. He placed six miniature Buddhas on a wire emerging from Kuya's mouth, one for each syllable of his chant.

ATTACK ON SANJO PALACE All the painting types flourishing in the Heian period continued to prosper in the Kamakura period. A striking example of handscroll painting is *Events of the Heiji Period,* which dates to the 13th century and illustrates another facet of Japanese painting—historical narrative. The scroll depicts some civil-war battles at the end of the Heian period. The section reproduced here (FIG. **17-18**) represents the nighttime attack on the Sanjo palace during which the retired emperor Goshirakawa (r. 1155–1158) was taken prisoner and his palace burned. Swirling flames and billowing clouds of smoke dominate the composition. Below, soldiers on horseback and on foot do battle. As in other Heian and Kamakura scrolls, the artist represented the buildings from above at a sharp angle. Noteworthy here are the painter's staccato brushwork and the vivid flashes of color that beautifully capture the drama of the event.

AMIDA DESCENDING Buddhism and Buddhist painting also remained vital in the Kamakura period, and elite patrons continued to commission major Pure Land artworks. Pure Land Buddhism in Japan stressed the saving power of Amida, who, if called on, hastened to believers at the moment of death and conveyed them to his Pure Land. Pictures of this scene were often hung in the presence of a dying person, who recited Amida's name to ensure salvation. In *Amida Descending over the Mountains* (FIG. **17-19**), a gigantic Amida rises from behind the mountains against the backdrop of a dark sky. His two main attendant bodhisattvas, Kannon and Seishi, have already descended. The painter depicted them as if they were addressing the deceased directly. Below, two boys point to the approaching divinities. In contrast to these gesticulating figures, Amida is still and frontal, which gives his image an iconic quality. Particularly striking is the way in which Amida's halo (nimbus) resembles a rising moon, an image long admired in Japan for its spiritual beauty.

The Kamakura period ended the way it began—with civil war. After several years of conflict beginning in 1332, one shogun emerged supreme and governed Japan from his headquarters in the Muramachi district of Kyoto. The art and architecture of Japan from 1336 to 1980 are the subject of Chapter 34.

1 ft.

17-19 *Amida Descending over the Mountains,* Zenrinji, Kyoto, Japan, Kamakura period, 13th century. Hanging scroll, ink and colors on silk, 4′ 3⅛″ × 3′ 10½″.

Scrolls depicting Amida descending to convey the dead to the Pure Land Paradise were often hung in the room of a dying person. Here, the rendering of Amida has an iconic character.

JAPAN BEFORE 1333

JOMON AND YAYOI PERIODS ca. 10,500 BCE–300 CE

I The Jomon (ca. 10,500–300 BCE) is Japan's earliest distinct culture. It takes its name from the applied clay cordlike coil decoration of Jomon pottery.

I Archaeologists unearthed the first evidence for the Yayoi culture (ca. 300 BCE–300 CE) in the Yayoi district of Tokyo, but the culture emerged in Kyushu and spread northward. Increasing contact with the East Asian mainland is evident in the form of Yayoi dotaku, which were modeled on Han Chinese bells but were not musical instruments.

Middle Jomon vessel,
ca. 2,500–1,500 BCE

KOFUN PERIOD ca. 300–552

I Kofun means "old tomb," and great earthen keyhole-shaped burial mounds are the primary characteristic of the last pre-Buddhist period of Japanese art. The largest tumulus in Japan, attributed to Emperor Nintoku, who died in 399, is at Sakai.

I About 20,000 clay cylindrical figures (haniwa) stood around and atop the Sakai tumulus. Haniwa sculptures depict inanimate objects and animals as well as human figures, including warriors. The haniwa may represent the realm the deceased ruled during life.

Tomb of Emperor Nintoku, Sakai,
late 4th to early 5th century

ASUKA AND NARA PERIODS 552–784

I Buddhism came to Japan from Korea in 552, and the first Japanese Buddhist artworks, such as Tori Busshi's Shaka triad at Horyuji, date to the Asuka period (552–645).

I During the Nara period (645–784), a centralized imperial government was established, with its capital at Nara from 710 to 784. Nara architecture, for example, the Horyuji kondo, followed Tang Chinese models in the use of ceramic roof tiles and the adoption of a curved roofline. The Daibutsuden constructed at Todaiji in 743 is the largest wooden building in the world.

Tori Busshi, Shaka triad, 623

HEIAN PERIOD 794–1185

I In 794 the imperial family moved the capital to Heiankyo (Kyoto). Shortly thereafter, Esoteric Buddhism arrived in Japan and created demand for painted mandaras of the Womb World and the Diamond World in order to facilitate meditation.

I A masterpiece of Heian Buddhist architecture is the Phoenix Hall of the Byodoin at Uji, which evokes images of the celestial architecture of the Buddha's Pure Land of the West.

I Narrative scroll painting was a major Heian art form. Illustrated scrolls of Lady Murasaki's *Tale of Genji* feature the distinctive combination of elevated viewpoints that suggest three-dimensional space and flat colors that emphasize the painting's two-dimensional character.

Tale of Genji, first half
of 12th century

KAMAKURA PERIOD 1185–1332

I In 1185, power shifted from the Japanese emperor to the first shogun of Kamakura. The shoguns became great patrons of art and architecture.

I Kamakura painting is diverse in both subject and style and includes historical narratives, such as *Events of the Heiji Period,* and Buddhist hanging scrolls.

I Kamakura wood portraits—for example, the seated statue of the priest Shunjobo Chogen—are noteworthy for their realism and the use of rock crystal for the eyes.

Shunjobo Chogen, ca. 1206

One of the most unusual Maya buildings is the Caracol ("snail shell") at Chichén Itzá. It encloses a spiral staircase and was probably both a temple to Kulkulcán and an astronomical observatory.

Chichén Itzá boasts the largest ball court in Mesoamerica. The rules of the ball game remain obscure, but the games were important rituals that often ended in the death of captured enemies.

The characteristic Maya temple was a stepped pyramidal platform with a shrine on the top. Chichén Itzá's, which has 365 steps on four sides, was a temple to Kulkulcán, the feathered-serpent god.

18-1 Aerial view (looking southwest) of the Maya city of Chichén Itzá, Mexico, centered on the Castillo, ca. 800–900 CE. ◼◀

18

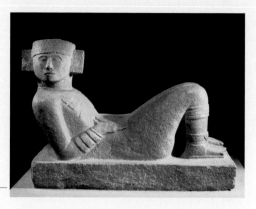

Inside the Kulkulcán temple was a *chacmool* statue similar to this one from the nearby Platform of the Eagles. Chacmools are fallen warriors with receptacles on their chests to receive sacrificial offerings.

NATIVE ARTS OF THE AMERICAS BEFORE 1300

ANCIENT CITIES IN A NEW WORLD

During the millennium and a half before Europeans discovered what for them was a "New World," the native peoples of the Western Hemisphere constructed some of the world's largest cities. Teotihuacán, for example, near present-day Mexico City, was a great metropolis covering nine square miles. The city, which had a population of nearly 200,000 at its peak in the sixth century CE, was widely influential throughout Mesoamerica.

The most famous of the many civilizations that flourished in the Americas before 1300 was the Maya. Renowned for their great urban centers and imposing temple-pyramids carved out of the dense rain and scrub forests of Mexico, Guatemala, Honduras, and Belize, the Maya were also skilled in mathematics and astronomy, developed a complex written language, and kept detailed historical records.

One of the best preserved Maya sites—and most frequently visited because of its proximity to the popular vacation destination of Cancún in the Yucatán Peninsula—is Chichén Itzá (FIG. **18-1**). The city dates to the period archaeologists have dubbed the Postclassic, that is, the late period, beginning around 900 CE. Some of its major buildings are typical, however, of earlier Classic sites, such as Copán in Honduras and Tikal in Guatemala.

Dominating Chichén Itzá's main northern plaza is a gigantic pyramidal stepped platform crowned by a temple to Kukulcán, the feathered-serpent god. Oriented to the four cardinal points, the pyramid has nine levels and 365 steps collectively on its four sides. Solar connections abound in Maya architecture, and during the winter and summer equinoxes, the sun's rays create the illusion of the serpent-god on the pyramid's steps.

Chichén Itzá also boasts the largest ball court in Mesoamerica, almost 500 feet long. There, skilled athletes competed in ball games that are poorly understood today, but that often resulted in the sacrifice of captives forced to play—and always lose. Archaeologists have found sculptures representing fallen warriors (*chacmools*) at several locations around the main plaza, including the pyramid-temple of Kukulcán. The chacmools probably figured in the sacrificial rites connected with the ritual ball games. More unusual is the round and domed temple nicknamed the Caracol ("snail-shell") by the Spanish conquerors because of its internal spiral staircase. It probably doubled as an astronomical observatory. Eventually, Chichén Itzá, as so many other abandoned Maya cities, became absorbed into the thick vegetation that still hems in the site—to be rediscovered and explored centuries later by modern archaeologists.

THE ANCIENT AMERICAS

The origins of the indigenous peoples of the Americas are still uncertain. Sometime no later than 30,000 to 10,000 BCE, these first Americans probably crossed the now-submerged land bridge called Beringia, which connected the shores of the Bering Strait between Asia and North America. Some migrants may have reached the Western Hemisphere via boats traveling along the Pacific coast of North America. These Stone Age nomads were hunter-gatherers. They made tools only of bone, pressure-flaked stone, and wood. They had no knowledge of agriculture but possibly some of basketry. They could control fire and probably built simple shelters. For many centuries, they spread out until they occupied the two American continents. But they were always few in number. When the first Europeans arrived at the end of the 15th century (see Chapter 35), the total population of the Western Hemisphere may not have exceeded 40 million.

Between 8000 and 2000 BCE, some of the migrants learned to fish, farm cotton, and domesticate plants such as squash and maize (corn). The nomads settled in villages and learned to make ceramic utensils and figurines. Metal technology developed only in the Andean region of South America (eventually spreading north into present-day Mexico) and, although extremely refined, generally met only the need for ornamentation, not for tools. With these skills as a base, many cultures rose and fell over long periods.

Several of the peoples of North, Central, and South America had already reached a high level of social complexity and technological achievement by the early centuries CE. Although most relied on stone tools, did not use the wheel (except for toys), and had no pack animals but the llama (in South America), the early Americans developed complex agricultural techniques and excelled in the engineering arts associated with the planning and construction of cities, civic and domestic buildings, roads and bridges, and irrigation and drainage systems. They carved monumental stone statues and reliefs, painted extensive murals, and mastered the arts of weaving, pottery, and metalwork. In Mesoamerica, the Maya and other cultural groups even had a highly developed writing system and knowledge of mathematical calculation that enabled them to keep precise records and create a sophisticated calendar and a highly accurate astronomy.

These advanced civilizations went into rapid decline, however, in the 16th century when the Europeans introduced new diseases to the Western Hemisphere, and Hernán Cortés (1485–1547), Francisco Pizarro (1471–1541), and their armies conquered the Aztec and Inka empires. Some native elites survived and adapted to the Spanish presence, but the conquerors destroyed most of the once-glorious American cities in their zeal to obliterate all traces of non-Christian worship. The forces of nature—erosion and the encroachment of tropical forests—caused the abandonment of other sites. But despite the ruined state of the pre-Hispanic cities of the Americas today, archaeologists and art historians have been able to reconstruct much of the art and architectural history of the Western Hemisphere before its inhabitants made contact with Europeans. This chapter examines in turn the artistic achievements of the native peoples of Mesoamerica, South America, and North America before 1300. Chapter 35 treats the art and architecture of the Americas from 1300 to the present.

MESOAMERICA

The term *Mesoamerica* describes the region comprising part of present-day Mexico, Guatemala, Belize, Honduras, and the Pacific coast of El Salvador (MAP **18-1**). Mesoamerica was the homeland of several of the great *pre-Columbian* civilizations—those that flourished before the arrival of Christopher Columbus (1451–1506) and the subsequent European invasion.

The principal regions of pre-Columbian Mesoamerica are the Gulf Coast region (Olmec and Classic Veracruz cultures); the states of Jalisco, Colima, and Nayarit (collectively known as West Mexico); Chiapas, Yucatán, Quintana Roo, and Campeche states in Mexico, the Petén area of Guatemala, Belize, and Honduras (Maya culture); southwestern Mexico and the state of Oaxaca (Zapotec and Mixtec cultures); and the central plateau surrounding modern Mexico City (Teotihuacán, Toltec, and Aztec cultures). These civilizations were often influential over extensive areas.

The Mexican highlands are a volcanic and seismic region. In highland Mexico, great reaches of arid plateau land, fertile for maize and other crops wherever water is available, lie between heavily forested mountain slopes, which at some places rise to a perpetual snow level. The moist tropical rain forests of the coastal plains yield

NATIVE ARTS OF THE AMERICAS BEFORE 1300

	BCE	CE		
1200	**400**	**300**	**900**	**1300**
▌ Colossal ruler portraits of the Olmec (ca. 900–400 BCE), the "mother culture" of Mesoamerica ▌ Temple complexes and relief stelae set up at Chavín de Huántar (ca. 800–200 BCE) in Andean South America	▌ Construction of the Avenue of the Dead and the pyramids of Teotihuacán in Preclassic (ca. 400 BCE–300 CE) Mesoamerica ▌ The Paracas (ca. 400 BCE–200 CE) culture in Peru produces extraordinary textiles ▌ Adena (ca. 500–1 BCE) build the first great mounds in North America	▌ The Maya construct vast complexes of temple-pyramids, palaces, plazas, and ball courts in Classic (ca. 300–900) Mesoamerica ▌ The Nasca (ca. 200 BCE–600 CE) create 800 miles of earth drawings around 500 CE ▌ The Tiwanaku (ca. 100–1000) and Wari (ca. 500–800) cultures flourish in northern Bolivia and southern Peru	▌ Construction of a huge pyramid-temple and the largest ball court in Mesoamerica at the Postclassic (ca. 900–1521) Maya site of Chichén Itzá ▌ Cahokia, Illinois, with 120 mounds is the largest city in North America during the Mississippian culture (ca. 800–1500) ▌ In the American Southwest, the Mimbres (ca. 1000–1250) produce black-and-white painted bowls, and the Ancestral Puebloans build a complex with 800 rooms at Chaco Canyon (ca. 850–1050)	

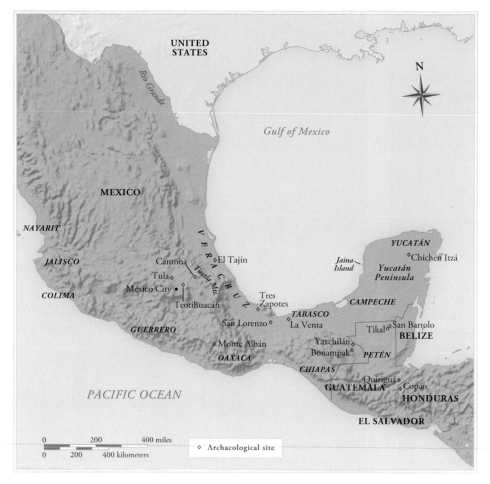

MAP 18-1 Early sites in Mesoamerica.

Scholars can now list many Maya rulers by name and fix the dates of their reigns with precision. Other writing systems, such as that of the Zapotec, who began to record dates at a very early time, are less well understood, but researchers are making rapid progress in their interpretation. Historians have now established a widely accepted Mesoamerican chronology divided into three epochs, with some overlapping of subperiods. The Preclassic (Formative), which marks the rise of elites and the first major works of art and architecture, extends from 2000 BCE to about 300 CE. The Classic period runs from about 300 to 900. The Postclassic begins about 900 and ends with the Spanish conquest in 1521.

Olmec and Preclassic West Mexico

Archaeologists often refer to the Olmec culture of the present-day states of Veracruz and Tabasco as the "mother culture" of Mesoamerica, because many distinctive Mesoamerican religious, social, and artistic traditions can be traced to it. Recent excavations, however, have revealed other important centers during the Preclassic period. The notion of a linear evolution of all Mesoamerican art and architecture from the Olmec is giving way to a more complex, multicenter picture of early Mesoamerica.

Settling in the tropical lowlands of the Gulf of Mexico, the Olmec peoples cultivated a terrain of rain forest and alluvial lowland washed by numerous rivers flowing into the gulf. Here, between approximately 1500 and 400 BCE, social organization assumed the form later Mesoamerican cultures adapted and developed. The mass of the population—food-producing farmers scattered in hinterland villages—provided the sustenance and labor that maintained a hereditary caste of rulers, hierarchies of priests, functionaries, and artisans. The nonfarming population presumably lived, arranged by rank, within precincts that served ceremonial, administrative, and residential functions and perhaps also were marketplaces. At regular intervals, the whole community convened for ritual observances at the religious-civic centers of towns such as San Lorenzo and La Venta. These centers were the formative architectural expressions of the structure and ideals of Olmec society.

OLMEC RULER PORTRAITS At La Venta, low clay-and-earthen platforms and stone fences enclosed two great courtyards. At one end of the larger area was a mound almost 100 feet high. Although now very eroded, this early pyramid, built of earth and adorned with colored clays, may have been intended to mimic a mountain, held sacred by Mesoamerican peoples as both a life-giving source of water and a feared destructive force. (Volcanic eruptions and earthquakes still wreak havoc in this region.) The La Venta layout is an early form of the temple-pyramid-plaza complex aligned on a north-south axis that characterized later Mesoamerican ceremonial center design.

rich crops, when the land can be cleared. In Yucatán, a subsoil of limestone furnishes abundant material for both building and carving. This limestone tableland merges with the vast Petén region of Guatemala, which separates Mexico from Honduras. Yucatán and the Petén, where dense rain forest alternates with broad stretches of grassland, boast some of the most spectacular Maya ruins, including the site of Chichén Itzá (FIG. 18-1). The great mountain chains of Mexico and Guatemala extend into Honduras and slope sharply down to tropical coasts. Highlands and mountain valleys, with their chill and temperate climates, alternate dramatically with the humid climate of tropical rain forest and coastlines.

The variegated landscape of Mesoamerica may have much to do with the diversity of languages its native populations speak. Researchers have documented no fewer than 14 linguistic families. Many of the languages spoken in the pre–Spanish conquest period survive to this day. Various Mayan languages linger in Guatemala and southern Mexico. The Náhuatl of the Aztecs endures in the Mexican highlands. The Zapotec and Mixtec languages persist in Oaxaca and its environs. Diverse as the languages of these peoples were, their cultures otherwise had much in common. The Mesoamerican peoples shared maize cultivation, religious beliefs and rites, myths, social structures, customs, and arts.

Archaeologists, with ever-increasing refinement of technique, have been uncovering, describing, and classifying Mesoamerican monuments for more than a century. In the 1950s, linguists made important breakthroughs in deciphering the Maya *hieroglyphic* script, and epigraphers have made further progress in recent decades.

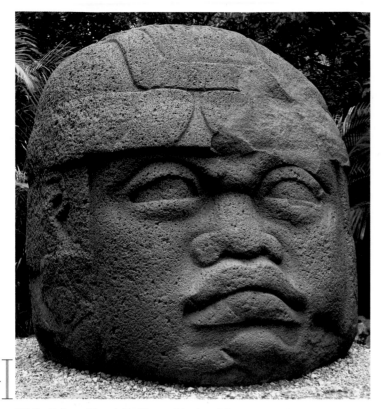

18-2 Colossal head, La Venta, Mexico, Olmec, ca. 900–400 BCE. Basalt, 9′ 4″ high. Museo-Parque La Venta, Villahermosa.

The identities of the Olmec colossi are uncertain, but their individualized features and distinctive headgear as well as later Maya practice suggest these heads portray rulers rather than deities.

Four colossal basalt heads (FIG. **18-2**), weighing about 10 tons each and standing between 6 and 10 feet high, face out from the plaza. Archaeologists have discovered more than a dozen similar heads at San Lorenzo and Tres Zapotes. Almost as much of an achievement as the carving of these huge stones with stone tools was their transportation across the 60 miles of swampland from the nearest known basalt source, the Tuxtla Mountains. Although the identities of these colossi are uncertain, their individualized features and distinctive headgear and ear ornaments, as well as the later Maya practice of carving monumental ruler portraits, suggest the Olmec heads portray rulers rather than gods. The sheer size of the heads and their intensity of expression evoke great power, whether mortal or divine.

JADE CELTS The Olmec also made paintings in caves, fashioned ceramic figurines, and carved sculptures in jade, a prized, extremely hard, dark green stone they acquired from unknown sources far from their homeland. Sometimes the Olmec carved jade into ax-shaped polished forms art historians call *celts,* which they then buried under their ceremonial courtyards or platforms, perhaps in connection with rites associated with maize agriculture. The celt shape could be modified into a figural form, combining relief carving with incising. Olmec sculptors used stone-tipped drills and abrasive materials, such as sand, to carve jade. The subjects represented include figures combining human and animal features and postures, such as the *were-jaguar* illustrated here (FIG. **18-3**), which may be a maize deity. The Olmec human-animal representations may also refer to the belief that religious practitioners underwent dangerous transformations to wrest power from supernatural forces and harness it for the good of the community.

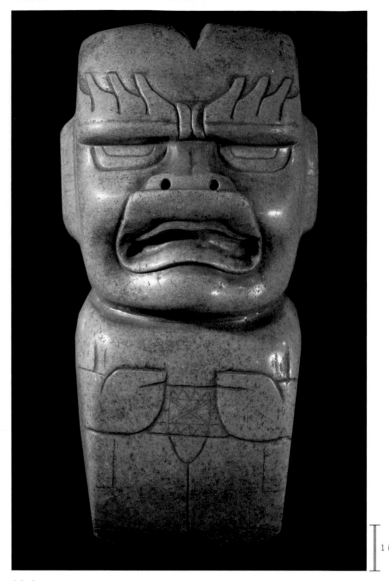

18-3 Ceremonial ax in the form of a were-jaguar, from La Venta, Mexico, Olmec, ca. 900–400 BCE. Jadeite, 11½″ high. British Museum, London.

Olmec celts often represent composite human-animal figures. They may reflect the Mesoamerican belief that religious practitioners underwent dangerous transformations on behalf of the community.

WEST MEXICO Far to the west of the tropical heartland of the Olmec are the Preclassic sites along Mexico's Pacific coast. Historians have long thought the ancient peoples of the modern West Mexican states of Nayarit, Jalisco, and Colima existed at Mesoamerica's geographic and cultural fringes. Recent archaeological discoveries, however, have revealed that although the West Mexicans did not produce large-scale stone sculpture, they did build permanent structures. These included tiered platforms and ball courts (see "The Mesoamerican Ball Game," page 501), architectural features found in nearly all Mesoamerican cultures and as far north as the North American Southwest. Yet West Mexico is best known for its rich tradition of clay sculpture. The sculptures come from tombs consisting of shafts as deep as 50 feet with chambers at their base. Because scientific excavations began only recently, much of what is known about West Mexican tomb contents derives primarily from the artifacts grave robbers found and sold. Researchers believe, however, the West Mexicans built most of these tombs and filled them with elaborate offerings during the late Preclassic period, the half millennium before 300 CE.

18-4 Seated figure with drinking cup, from Colima, Mexico, ca. 200 BCE–500 CE. Clay with orange and red slip, 1′ 1″ high. Los Angeles County Museum of Art (Proctor Stafford Collection, purchased with funds provided by Mr. and Mrs. Allan C. Balch).

Preclassic West Mexico is famous for its ceramic sculptures. This one may depict a religious practitioner with a horn on his forehead or a political leader wearing a shell ornament—or someone serving both roles.

1 in.

The large ceramic figures found in the Colima tombs are consistently a highly burnished red orange, in contrast to the distinctive polychrome surfaces of the majority of other West Mexican ceramics. The area also is noted for small-scale clay narrative scenes that include modeled houses and temples and numerous solid figurines shown in a variety of lively activities. These sculptures, which almost exclusively depict elite ritual activities, are not found in any other ancient Mesoamerican culture, and their meaning is often uncertain. For example, scholars are unsure whether the figure illustrated here (FIG. **18-4**) is a religious practitioner with a horn on his forehead (a common indigenous symbol of special powers) or a political leader wearing a shell ornament (often a Mesoamerican emblem of rulership)—or a person serving both roles.

Teotihuacán

At Olmec sites, the characteristic later Mesoamerican temple-pyramid-plaza layout appeared in embryonic form. At Teotihuacán (FIG. **18-5**), northeast of modern Mexico City, the Preclassic scheme

18-5 Aerial view of Teotihuacán (looking south), Mexico. Pyramid of the Moon (*foreground*), Pyramid of the Sun (*top left*), and the Citadel (*background*), all connected by the Avenue of the Dead; main structures ca. 50–250 CE. ◼◀

At its peak around 600 CE, Teotihuacán was the world's sixth-largest city. It featured a grid plan, a two-mile-long main avenue, and monumental pyramids echoing the shapes of nearby mountains.

underwent a massive expansion into a genuine city. Teotihuacán was a large, densely populated metropolis that fulfilled a central civic, economic, and religious role for the region and indeed for much of Mesoamerica. Built up between about 100 BCE and 600 CE, when fire ravaged the city, the site's major monuments date to the late Preclassic period between 50 and 250 CE. Teotihuacán covers nine square miles, laid out in a grid pattern with the axes oriented by sophisticated surveying. The city's orientation and the placement of some of its key monuments apparently relate to astronomical phenomena.

At its peak, around 600 CE, Teotihuacán may have had as many as 125,000 to 200,000 residents, which would have made it then the sixth-largest city in the world. Divided into numerous wardlike sectors, this metropolis must have had a uniquely cosmopolitan character, with Zapotec peoples located in the city's western wards, and merchants from Veracruz living in the eastern wards, importing their own pottery and building their houses and tombs in the style of their homelands. The city's urbanization did nothing to detract from its sacred nature. In fact, it vastly augmented Teotihuacán's importance as a religious center. The Aztecs, who visited Teotihuacán regularly and reverently long after it had been abandoned, gave it its current name, which means "the place of the gods." Because the city's inhabitants left only a handful of undeciphered hieroglyphs, linguists do not yet even know what language they spoke. The names of many major features of the site are unknown. The Avenue of the Dead and the Pyramids of the Sun and Moon are later Aztec designations that do not necessarily relate to the original names of these streets and buildings.

North-south and east-west axes, each four miles in length, divide the grid plan into quarters. The scheme recalls Hellenistic and Roman urban planning (compare FIGS. 5-76 and 7-43) and is very unusual in Mesoamerica before the Aztecs. The main north-south axis, the Avenue of the Dead (FIG. 18-5), is 130 feet wide and connects the Pyramid of the Moon complex with the Citadel and its Temple of Quetzalcoatl. This two-mile stretch is not a continuously flat street but is broken by sets of stairs, giving pedestrians a constantly changing view of the surrounding buildings and landscape.

PYRAMIDS The largest structures at Teotihuacán are the stepped temple platforms popularly called pyramids, as in Egypt (see Chapter 3), but there is no connection between these two ancient cultures. The Preclassic Pyramid of the Sun (FIG. 18-5, *top left*), facing west on the east side of the Avenue of the Dead, dates to the first century CE. The city's centerpiece, it rises to a height of more than 200 feet in its restored state, which may not accurately reflect the pyramid's original appearance. The Pyramid of the Moon (FIG. 18-5, *foreground*) is a century or more later, around 150 to 250 CE. The shapes of the monumental structures at Teotihuacán echo the surrounding mountains. Their imposing mass and scale surpass those of all other Mesoamerican sites. Rubble-filled and faced with the local volcanic stone, the pyramids consist of stacked squared platforms diminishing in perimeter from the base to the top. Unlike the Stepped Pyramid of Djoser (FIG. 3-4) in Egyptian Saqqara, the Teotihuacán pyramids have ramped stairways that once led to crowning temples constructed of perishable materials such as wood and thatch. A distinctive feature of Teotihuacán construction is the alternation of sloping (*talud*) and vertical (*tablero*) rubble layers. The employment of *talud-tablero construction* at other sites is a sure sign of Teotihuacán influence.

The Teotihuacanos built the Pyramid of the Sun over a cave, which they reshaped and filled with ceramic offerings. The pyramid

18-6 Temple of Quetzalcoatl (looking southeast), the Citadel, Teotihuacán, Mexico, third century CE. ◼◂

The stone heads of Quetzalcoatl decorating this temple are the earliest Mesoamerican representations of the feathered-serpent god. Excavators found sacrificial victims beneath and around the pyramid.

18-7 Goddess, wall painting from the Tetitla apartment complex at Teotihuacán, Mexico, 650–750 CE. Pigments over clay and plaster.

Elaborate mural paintings adorned Teotihuacán's elite residential compound. This example may depict the city's principal deity, a goddess wearing a jade mask and a large feathered headdress.

may have marked a sacred spring within the now-dry cave. Excavators found children buried at the four corners of each of the pyramid's tiers. The Aztec sacrificed children to bring rainfall, and Teotihuacán art abounds with references to water, so the Teotihuacanos may have shared the Aztec preoccupation with rain and agricultural fertility. The city's inhabitants rebuilt the Pyramid of the Moon (currently being excavated) at least five times in Teotihuacán's early history. It may have been positioned to mimic the shape of Cerro Gordo, the volcanic mountain behind it, undoubtedly an important source of life-sustaining streams.

QUETZALCOATL At the south end of the Avenue of the Dead is the great quadrangle of the Citadel (FIG. 18-5, *background*). It encloses a smaller pyramidal shrine datable to the third century CE, the Temple of Quetzalcoatl (FIG. **18-6**). Quetzalcoatl, the "feathered serpent," was a major god in the Mesoamerican pantheon at the time of the Spanish conquest, hundreds of years after the fall of Teotihuacán. The Aztecs associated him with wind, rain clouds, and life. Beneath the temple, archaeologists found a tomb looted in antiquity, perhaps belonging to a Teotihuacano ruler. The discovery has led them to speculate the Teotihuacanos buried their elite in or under pyramids, as did the Maya. Surrounding the tomb both beneath and around the pyramid were the remains of at least a hundred sacrificial victims. Some wore necklaces made of strings of human jaws, both real and sculpted from shell. As did most other Mesoamerican groups, the Teotihuacanos invoked and

appeased their gods through human sacrifice. The presence of such a large number of victims also may reflect Teotihuacán's militaristic expansion. Throughout Mesoamerica, the victors often sacrificed captured warriors.

The temple's sculptured panels, which feature projecting stone heads of Quetzalcoatl alternating with heads of a long-snouted scaly creature with rings on its forehead, decorate each of the temple's six terraces. This is the first unambiguous representation of the feathered serpent in Mesoamerica. The scaly creature's identity is unclear. Linking these alternating heads are low-relief carvings of feathered-serpent bodies and seashells. The latter both reflect Teotihuacán contact with the peoples of the Mexican coasts and symbolize water, an essential ingredient for the sustenance of an agricultural economy.

MURAL PAINTING As in most ancient Mesoamerican cities, brightly painted stucco once covered Teotihuacán's buildings and streets. Elaborate murals also decorated the walls of the rooms of its elite residential compounds. The paintings (FIGS. **18-7** and **18-7A**) chiefly depict deities, ritual

18-7A Bloodletting mural, Teotihuacán, ca. 600–700 CE.

activities, and processions of priests, warriors, and even animals. Experimenting with a variety of surfaces, materials, and techniques over the centuries, Teotihuacán muralists finally settled on applying pigments to a smooth lime-plaster surface coated with clay. They then polished the surface to a high sheen. Although some Teotihuacán paintings have a restricted palette of varying tones of red (largely derived from the mineral hematite), creating subtle contrasts between figure and ground, most employ vivid hues arranged in flat, carefully outlined patterns.

The mural illustrated here (FIG. 18-7) depicts an earth or nature goddess. Some scholars think she was the city's principal deity. Always shown frontally with her face covered by a jade mask, she is dwarfed by her large feathered headdress and reduced to a bust placed upon a stylized pyramid. She stretches her hands out to provide liquid streams filled with bounty—a motif common in many cultures, including ancient Mesopotamia (FIGS. 2-17 and 2-18A). The stylized human hearts flanking the frontal bird mask in the Teotihuacano goddess's headdress reflect the ancient Mesoamerican belief that human sacrifice is essential to agricultural renewal.

The influence of Teotihuacán was all-pervasive in Mesoamerica. The Teotihuacanos established colonies as far away as the southern borders of Maya civilization, in the highlands of Guatemala, some 800 miles from Teotihuacán.

Classic Maya

The Olmec and Teotihuacán civilizations made a strong contribution to the development of Classic Maya culture. As was true of Teotihuacán, the foundations of Maya civilization date to the Preclassic period, perhaps 600 BCE or even earlier. At that time, the Maya, who occupied the moist lowland areas of Belize, southern Mexico, Guatemala, and Honduras, seem to have abandoned their early, somewhat egalitarian pattern of village life and adopted a hierarchical autocratic society. This system evolved into the typical Maya city-state governed by hereditary rulers and ranked nobility. How and why this happened are still unknown, but the Classic Maya culture endured for 600 years.

Although the causes of the beginning and end of Classic Maya civilization are obscure, researchers are gradually revealing its history, religion, ceremonies, conventions, and patterns of daily life through scientific excavation and progress made in decoding Mayan script. Two important breakthroughs have radically altered the understanding of both Mayan writing and the Maya worldview. The first was the realization that the Maya depicted their rulers (rather than gods or anonymous priests) in their art and noted their rulers' achievements in their texts. The second was that Mayan writing is largely phonetic—that is, the hieroglyphs consist of signs representing sounds in the Mayan language. Fortunately, the Spaniards recorded the various Mayan languages in colonial texts and dictionaries. Descendants of the Maya still speak most of the ancient languages today, facilitating the translation of many ancient Mayan hieroglyphs.

The Maya possessed a highly developed knowledge of arithmetic calculation and the ability to observe and record the movements of the sun, the moon, and numerous planets. They contrived an intricate but astonishingly accurate calendar with a fixed-zero date, and although their structuring of time was radically different in form from the Western calendar used today, it was just as precise and efficient. With their calendar, the Maya established the genealogical lines of their rulers, which certified their claim to rule, and created the only true written history in ancient America. Although other ancient Mesoamerican societies, even in the Preclassic period, also possessed calendars, only the Maya calendar can be translated directly into today's system of measuring time.

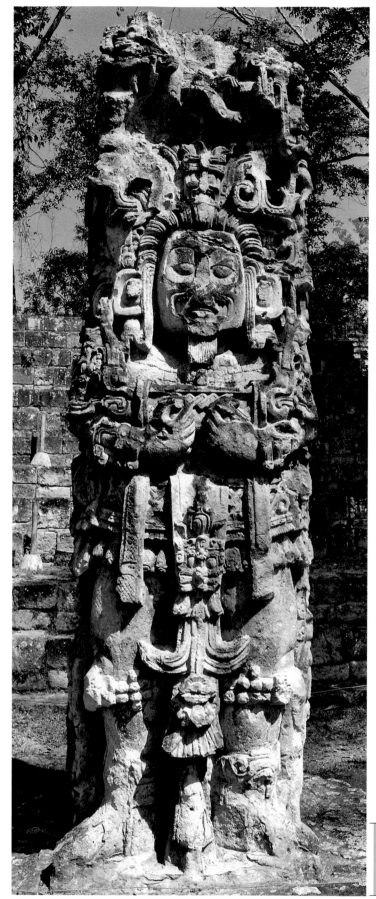

1 ft.

18-8 Stele D portraying Ruler 13 (Waxaklajuun-Ub'aah-K'awiil), Great Plaza, Copán, Honduras, Maya, 736 CE. Stone, 11′ 9″ high.

This 12-foot stele portrays one of Copán's most important rulers as an over-life-size figure wearing an elaborate headdress and holding a double-headed serpent bar, symbol of his sacred authority.

ARCHITECTURE AND RITUAL Vast complexes of terraced temple-pyramids, palaces, plazas, ball courts (see "The Mesoamerican Ball Game," page 501), and residences of the governing elite dotted the Maya area. Unlike Teotihuacán, no single Maya site ever achieved complete dominance as the center of power. The new architecture, and the art embellishing it, advertised the power of the rulers, who appropriated cosmic symbolism and stressed their descent from gods to reinforce their claims to legitimate rule.

The Maya erected their most sacred and majestic buildings in enclosed, centrally located precincts within their cities. Archaeologists call these areas the "site core"—the religious and administrative nucleus for a population of dispersed farmers settled throughout a suburban area of many square miles. There, the Maya rulers staged dramatic rituals within spacious sculpture-filled plazas. In both life and art, the ruling families and troops of priests, nobles, and retainers wore extravagant, vividly colorful cotton textiles, feathers, jaguar skins, and jade, all emblematic of rank and wealth. On the different levels of the painted and polished temple platforms, the ruling classes performed the rites in clouds of incense to the music of maracas, flutes, and drums. The Maya thus transformed the architectural complex at each city's center into a theater of religion and statecraft.

COPÁN Because Copán, on the western border of Honduras, has more hieroglyphic inscriptions and well-preserved carved monuments than any other site in the Americas, it was one of the first Maya sites excavated. It also has proved one of the richest in the trove of architecture, sculpture, and artifacts recovered. Conspicuous plazas dominated the heart of the city. In Copán's Great Plaza, the Maya set up tall, sculpted stone *stelae*. Carved with the portraits of the rulers who erected them, these stelae also recorded their names, dates of reign, and notable achievements in glyphs on the front, sides, or back.

Stele D (FIG. 18-8), set up in 736 CE, represents one of the city's foremost rulers, Waxaklajuun-Ub'aah-K'awiil (r. 695–738), whose name means "18 are the apparitions of the god K'awiil." Scholars often call him Ruler 13 in the Copán dynastic sequence of 16 rulers. During his long reign, the city may have reached its greatest physical extent and range of political influence. On Stele D, Ruler 13 wears an elaborate headdress and ornamented kilt and sandals. He holds across his chest a double-headed serpent bar, symbol of his sacred authority. His features are distinctly Maya, although highly idealized. The Maya elite usually required sculptors and painters to depict them as eternally youthful. The dense, deeply carved ornamental details framing the face and figure in florid profusion stand almost clear of the block and wrap around the sides of the stele. The high relief, originally painted, gives the impression of an over-life-size freestanding statue, although an incised hieroglyphic text is on the flat back side of the stele. A powerful ruler who erected many stelae and buildings at Copán, including one of Mesoamerica's best-preserved (and carefully restored) ball courts (FIG. 18-9; see "The Mesoamerican Ball Game," page 501), Ruler 13 eventually suffered a humiliating end. In 738, the king of neighboring Quiriguá captured and beheaded him.

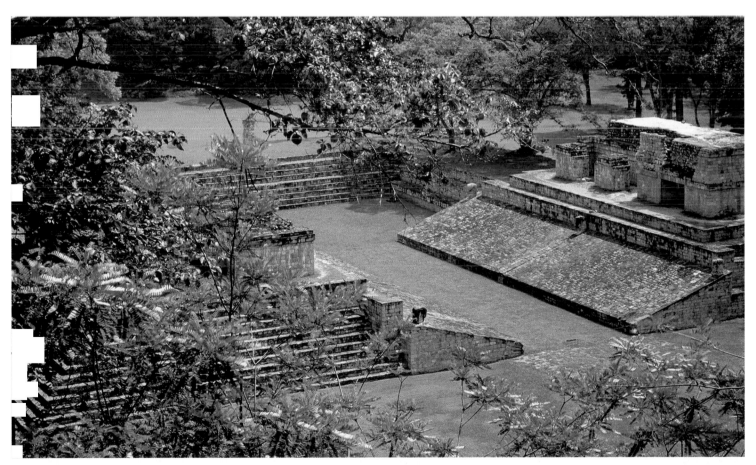

18-9 Ball court (looking northeast), Middle Plaza, Copán, Honduras, Maya, 738 CE.

Ball courts were common in Mesoamerican cities. Copán's is 93 feet long. The rules of the ball game itself are unknown, but games sometimes ended in human sacrifice of captives taken in battle.

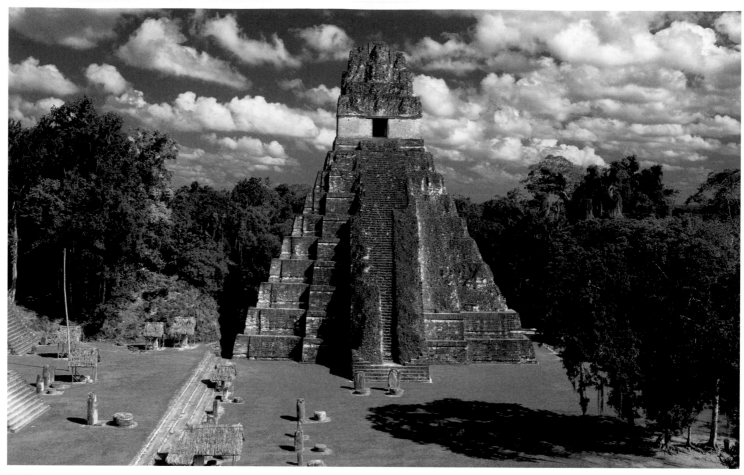

18-10 Temple I (Temple of the Giant Jaguar), Tikal, Guatemala, Maya, ca. 732 CE.

Temple I at Tikal is a 145-foot-tall pyramid that was the temple-mausoleum of Hasaw Chan K'awiil, who died in 732 CE. The nine tiers of the pyramid probably refer to the nine levels of the Underworld.

18-10A Temple of the Inscriptions, Palenque, ca. 675–690 CE.

TIKAL Another great Maya site of the Classic period is Tikal in Guatemala, some 150 miles north of Copán. Tikal is one of the oldest and largest Maya cities. Together with its suburbs, Tikal originally covered some 75 square miles and served as the ceremonial center of a population of perhaps 75,000. The Maya did not lay out central Tikal on a grid plan as did the designers of contemporaneous Teotihuacán. Instead, causeways connected irregular groupings. Modern surveys have uncovered the remains of as many as 3,000 separate structures in an area of about six square miles. The site's nucleus is the Great Plaza, an open area studded with stelae and bordered by large stone structures. The Maya engineers graded the plaza and other areas of the city to conduct rainwater into the city's reservoirs. Dominating the Great Plaza are two soaring pyramids, taller than the surrounding rain forest, which face each other across the open square. The larger pyramid (FIG. **18-10**), Temple I (also called the Temple of the Giant Jaguar after a motif on one of its carved wooden lintels), reaches a height of about 145 feet, about twice the height of the late-seventh-century Temple of the Inscriptions (FIG. **18-10A**) at Palenque in Mexico, but more than 50 feet shorter and much narrower than the Preclassic Pyramid of the Sun (FIG. 18-5, *top left*) at Teotihuacán. Considerable evidence indicates the builders of Palenque and Tikal and other Maya sites painted the exteriors of their temples red or red, white, and other bright colors.

The Temple of the Giant Jaguar at Tikal is the temple-mausoleum of one of the city's greatest rulers, Hasaw Chan K'awiil, who died in 732 CE. The Maya buried him in a vaulted chamber under the pyramid's base. The towering structure consists of nine sharply inclining platforms, probably a reference to the nine levels of the Underworld, and a three-chambered temple reached by a narrow stairway. Surmounting the temple is an elaborately sculpted *roof comb,* a vertical architectural projection that once bore the ruler's gigantic portrait modeled in stucco.

JAINA As did their West Mexican predecessors (FIG. 18-4), the Maya excelled at modeling small-scale figures in clay. The extant examples are remarkably lifelike and display an almost unlimited variety of postures and gestures, made possible by the malleable nature of the medium. The figures, often cast in molds, also represent a wider range of human types and activities than is commonly depicted on Maya stelae. Ball players (FIG. **18-11**), women weaving, older men, dwarfs, supernatural beings, and amorous couples, as well as elaborately attired rulers and warriors, are the most common subjects. Many of the hollow figurines are also whistles. All are products of ceramic workshops on the mainland, but burials on the island cemetery of Jaina, off the western coast of Yucatán, have yielded hundreds of clay statuettes, including the ball player illustrated here. Traces of blue remain on the man's belt, remnants of the vivid pigments that once covered many of these figurines. The Maya used "Maya blue," a combination of a particular kind of clay and indigo, a vegetable dye, to paint both ceramics and murals.

The Mesoamerican Ball Game

After witnessing the native ball game of Mexico soon after their arrival, the 16th-century Spanish conquerors took Aztec ball players back to Europe to demonstrate the novel sport. Their chronicles remark on the athletes' great skill, the heavy wagering that accompanied the competition, and the ball itself, made of rubber, a substance the Spaniards had never seen before.

Native Americans played the game throughout Mesoamerica and into the southwestern United States, beginning at least 3,400 years ago, the date of the earliest known ball court. The Olmec were apparently avid players. Their very name—a modern invention in Náhuatl, the Aztec language—means "rubber people," after the latex-growing region they inhabited. Not only do ball players appear in Olmec art, but archaeologists also have found remnants of sunken earthen ball courts and even rubber balls at Olmec sites.

The Olmec earthen playing field evolved in other Mesoamerican cultures into a plastered masonry surface, I- or T-shaped in plan, flanked by two parallel sloping or straight walls. Sometimes the walls were wide enough to support small structures on top, as at Copán (FIG. 18-9). At other sites, temples stood at either end of the ball court. These structures were common features of Mesoamerican cities. At Cantona in the Mexican state of Puebla, for example, archaeologists have uncovered 22 ball courts even though only a small portion of the site has been excavated. Teotihuacán (FIG. 18-5) is an exception. Excavators have not yet found a ball court there, but mural paintings at the site illustrate people playing the game with portable markers and sticks. Most ball courts were adjacent to the important civic structures of Mesoamerican cities, such as palaces and temple-pyramids, as at Copán.

Historians know surprisingly little about the rules of the ball game itself, not even how many players were on the field or how they scored goals. Unlike a modern soccer field with its standard dimensions, Mesoamerican ball courts vary widely in size. The largest known—at Chichén Itzá (FIG. 18-1)—is nearly 500 feet long. Copán's is about 93 feet long. Some have stone rings set high up on their walls at right angles to the ground, but many courts lack this feature, so it is uncertain whether the players aimed to get the ball through a ring in order to score a point. Alternatively, players may have scored goals by bouncing the ball against the walls and into the end zones. As in soccer, players could not touch the ball with their hands but used their heads, elbows, hips, and legs. They wore thick leather belts, and sometimes even helmets, and padded their knees and arms against the blows of the fast-moving, solid rubber ball. Typically, the Maya portrayed ball players wearing heavy protective clothing and kneeling, poised to deflect the ball (FIG. 18-11).

Although widely enjoyed as a competitive spectator sport, the ball game did not serve solely for entertainment. The ball, for example, may have represented a celestial body such as the sun, its move-

18-11 Ball player, from Jaina Island, Mexico, Maya, 700–900 CE. Painted clay, 6¼″ high. Museo Nacional de Antropología, Mexico City.

Maya ceramic figurines represent a wide range of human types and activities. This kneeling ball player wears a thick leather belt and arm- and kneepads to protect him from the hard rubber ball.

ments over the court imitating the sun's daily passage through the sky. Reliefs on the walls of ball courts at certain sites make clear the game sometimes culminated in human sacrifice, probably of captives taken in battle and then forced to participate in a game they were predestined to lose.

Accounts of ball games also appear in Mesoamerican mythology. In the Maya epic known as the *Popol Vuh* (*Council Book*), first written down in Spanish in the colonial period, the evil lords of the Underworld force a legendary pair of twins to play ball. The brothers lose, and the victors sacrifice them. The sons of one twin eventually travel to the Underworld and, after a series of trials including a ball game, outwit the lords and kill them. They revive their father, buried in the ball court after his earlier defeat at the hands of the Underworld gods. The younger twins rise to the heavens to become the sun and the moon, and the father becomes the god of maize, principal sustenance of all Mesoamerican peoples. The ball game and its aftermath, then, were a metaphor for the cycle of life, death, and regeneration that permeated Mesoamerican religion.

This pigment has proved virtually indestructible, unlike other colors the Maya used, which have mostly disappeared over time. Like the larger terracotta figures of West Mexico, these figurines accompanied the dead on their inevitable voyage to the Underworld.

The excavations at Jaina, however, have revealed nothing more that might clarify the meaning and function of the figures. Male figurines do not come exclusively from burials of male individuals, for example.

18-12 Presentation of captives to Lord Chan Muwan, room 2 of structure 1, Bonampak, Mexico, Maya, ca. 790 CE. Mural, 17′ × 15′; watercolor copy by Antonio Tejeda. Peabody Museum, Harvard University, Cambridge.

The figures in this mural—a cross between fresco and tempera—may be standing on a pyramid's steps. At the top, the richly attired Chan Muwan reviews naked captives, with mutilated hands, awaiting death.

1 ft.

BONAMPAK The vivacity of the Jaina figurines and their variety of pose, costume, and occupation have parallels in the mural paintings of Bonampak (Mayan for "painted walls") in southeastern Mexico. Three chambers in one Bonampak structure contain murals recording important aspects of Maya court life. The illustrated example (FIG. **18-12**) shows warriors surrounding captives on a terraced platform. The figures have naturalistic proportions and overlap, twist, turn, and gesture. The artists used fluid lines to outline the figures, working with color to indicate both texture and volume. The Bonampak painters combined their pigments—both mineral and organic—with a mixture of water, crushed limestone, and vegetable gums and applied them to their stucco walls in a technique best described as a cross between *fresco* and *tempera.*

Circumstantial details abound in the Bonampak murals. The information revealed is comprehensive, explicit, and presented with the fidelity of an eyewitness report. Royal personages are identifiable by both their physical features and their costumes, and accompanying inscriptions provide the precise day, month, and year for the events recorded. All the scenes at Bonampak relate the events and ceremonies welcoming a new royal heir (shown as a toddler in some scenes). They include presentations, preparations for a royal fete, dancing, battle, and the taking and sacrificing of prisoners. On all occasions of state, public bloodletting was an integral part of Maya ritual. The ruler, his consort, and certain members of the nobility drew blood from their bodies and sought union with the supernatural world. The slaughter of captives taken in war regularly accompanied this ceremony. Indeed, Mesoamerican cultures

undertook warfare largely to provide victims for sacrifice. The torture and eventual execution of prisoners served both to nourish the gods and to strike fear into enemies and the general populace.

The scene (FIG. 18-12) in room 2 of structure 1 depicts the presentation of prisoners to Lord Chan Muwan. The painter arranged the figures in registers that may represent a pyramid's steps. On the uppermost step, against a blue background, is a file of gorgeously appareled nobles wearing animal headgear. Conspicuous among them on the right are retainers clad in jaguar pelts and jaguar headdresses. Also present is Chan Muwan's wife (third from right). The ruler himself, in jaguar jerkin and high-backed sandals, stands at the center, facing a crouching victim who appears to beg for mercy. Naked captives, anticipating death, crowd the middle level. One of them, already dead, sprawls at the ruler's feet. Others dumbly contemplate the blood dripping from their mutilated hands. The lower zone, cut through by a doorway into the structure housing the murals, shows clusters of attendants who are doubtless of inferior rank to the lords of the upper zone. The stiff formality of the victors contrasts graphically with the supple imploring attitudes and gestures of the hapless victims. The Bonampak victory was short-lived, however. The artists never finished the murals, and soon after the dates written on the walls, the Maya apparently abandoned the site.

The Bonampak murals are the most famous Maya wall paintings, but they are not unique. In 2001 at San Bartolo in northeastern Guatemala, American archaeologists discovered the earliest examples yet found. They date to around 100 BCE, almost a millennium before the Bonampak murals.

18-13 Enthroned Maya lord and attendants, cylinder vase, probably from Altamira, Mexico, Maya, ca. 672–830 CE. Polychrome ceramic, 8″ high. Dumbarton Oaks Research Library and Collections, Washington, D.C.

Maya polychrome ceramics depict a variety of subjects ranging from mythology to daily life. This cylinder vase shows an enthroned Maya lord at a ritual involving drinking and dancing.

18-14 Shield Jaguar and Lady Xoc, lintel 24 of temple 23, Yaxchilán, Mexico, Maya, ca. 725 CE. Limestone, 3′ 7″ × 2′ 6½″. British Museum, London.

The carved lintels of this eighth-century temple document the central role elite women played in Maya society. Lady Xoc pierces her tongue in a bloodletting ritual intended to induce a visionary state.

CYLINDER VASES Frescoes such as those at Bonampak and San Bartolo once liberally adorned the walls of Maya civic and religious buildings, but surviving examples are rare. Fortunately, as in ancient Greece (see Chapter 5), painted ceramics have been found in large numbers at Maya sites. But Maya painted pottery, in contrast to most Greek vase paintings, is polychrome. Produced using colored slips fired at low temperatures in open pits to achieve a lustrous surface, Maya vases approximate the appearance of mural painting much more closely than do the black-and-red compositions on Greek vases. Hieroglyphic labels are common and identify many of the figures and events depicted and also record individual artist's names. Sometimes the texts describe the contents of the vessels. Cylinder vases often contained cacao, a much-prized chocolate drink, but others were gifts to the dead and never used in daily life.

The scene on the cylinder vase illustrated here (FIG. 18-13), like those on similar vessels, wraps around the entire exterior surface. At the center is an enthroned, bare-chested Maya lord wearing a feathered headdress. He engages in animated conversation with two seated noblemen to his right. A lidded cylinder vase is at his side. A kneeling attendant at his left offers him a bowl. The drawing style is typical of Maya ceramics. Black contour lines are prominent, and the artist filled in the outlines with flat colors—mostly red, orange, and brown—on a creamy slip background. The painted hieroglyphs describe this as a ritual scene involving drinking and dancing. The inscriptions also name the participants and the artist.

YAXCHILÁN Elite women played an important role in Maya society, and some surviving artworks document their high status. The painted reliefs on the lintels of temple 23 at Yaxchilán represent an elite woman as a central figure in Maya ritual. Lintel 24 (FIG. 18-14) depicts the ruler Itzamna B'ahlam II (r. 681–742 CE), known as Shield Jaguar, and his principal wife, Lady Xoc. She is magnificently outfitted in an elaborate woven garment, headdress, and jewels. With a barbed cord she pierces her tongue in a bloodletting ceremony (compare FIG. 18-7A) that, according to accompanying inscriptions, celebrated the birth of a son to one of the ruler's other wives as well as an alignment between the planets Saturn and Jupiter. The celebration must have taken place in a dark chamber or at night because Shield Jaguar provides illumination with a blazing torch. These ceremonies induced an altered state of consciousness in order to connect the bloodletter with the supernatural world. (Lintel 25 depicts Lady Xoc and her vision of an ancestor emerging from the mouth of a serpent.)

18-15 Pyramid of the Niches (looking northeast), El Tajín, Mexico, Classic Veracruz, sixth century CE.

The Pyramid of the Niches, although only 66 feet tall, has 365 niches, one for each day of the solar year. It is one of many Mesoamerican monuments connected with astronomy and the calendar.

Classic Veracruz

The Maya is the most famous Classic Mesoamerican culture today, and its remains are the most abundant. Still, other cultures also flourished, and some of their surviving monuments rival those of the Maya in size and sophistication. In the Veracruz plain, for example, the heir to the Olmec culture was a civilization archaeologists call Classic Veracruz. The name of the people who occupied the area at the time is unknown.

EL TAJÍN The major Classic Veracruz site is El Tajín, which explorers discovered in the dense rain forest of the Gulf of Mexico coast in 1785. At its peak, El Tajín was a thriving city of hundreds of acres and tens of thousands of inhabitants. The excavated portion of the city has already revealed 17 ball courts. The building that dominates the ceremonial center of El Tajín is the so-called Pyramid of the Niches (FIG. **18-15**), a sixth-century CE structure of unusual form. In spite of its small size (only 66 feet tall), the Pyramid of the Niches encases an earlier smaller pyramid. The later structure has a steep staircase on its east side and six stories, each one incorporating a row of niches on each of the four sides, 365 in all. The number of niches, which corresponds to the number of days in a solar year, is unlikely to be coincidental. The Pyramid of the Niches is one of many examples of the close connection between the form of Mesoamerican monuments and astronomical observations and the measurement of time.

Postclassic Mexico

Throughout Mesoamerica, the Classic period ended at different times with the disintegration of the great civilizations. Teotihuacán's political and cultural empire, for example, began to wane around 600, when fire destroyed the city center. Archaeologists have not yet determined the cause, but within a century, the Teotihuacanos had deserted the formerly great metropolis. Around 900, the Maya abandoned many of their sites to the jungle, leaving a few northern Maya cities to flourish for another century or two before they, too, became depopulated. The Classic culture of the Zapotecs, centered at Monte Albán in the state of Oaxaca, came to an end around 700, and the neighboring Mixtec peoples assumed supremacy in this area during the Postclassic period. Classic El Tajín survived the general crisis afflicting the others but burned sometime in the 12th century. War and confusion followed the collapse of the Classic civilizations and facilitated the breakup of the great states into small, local political entities isolated in fortified sites. The disintegration encouraged even more warlike regimes and chronic aggression. The militant city-state of Chichén Itzá (FIG. 18-1) dominated Yucatán, while in central Mexico the Toltec and the later Aztec peoples, both ambitious migrants from the north, forged empires by force of arms.

CHICHÉN ITZÁ Yucatán, a flat, low limestone peninsula covered with scrub vegetation, lies north of the rolling and densely forested region of the Guatemalan Petén. During the Classic period, Mayan-speaking peoples sparsely inhabited this northern region. For reasons still the subject of debate, when the southern Maya abandoned their Classic sites after 900, the northern Maya continued to build many new temples in this area. They also experimented with construction techniques and materials to a much greater extent than their counterparts farther south. Piers and columns appeared in doorways, and stone mosaics enlivened facades. The northern groups also invented a new type of construction, a solid core of coarse rubble faced on both sides with a veneer of square limestone plates.

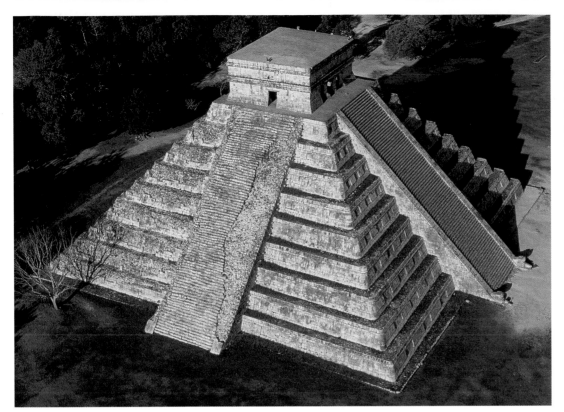

A temple to Kulkulcán sits atop this pyramid featuring a total of 365 stairs on its four sides. At the winter and summer equinoxes, the sun casts a shadow in the shape of a serpent along the northern staircase.

Dominating the main northern plaza (FIG. 18-1) of Chichén Itzá today is the 98-foot-high pyramid (FIG. 18-16) the Spaniards nicknamed the Castillo (Castle). Like Temple I at Tikal (FIG. 18-10), this pyramid has nine levels. Atop the structure is a temple dedicated to Kukulcán, the Maya equivalent of Quetzalcoatl, and, as at El Tajín (FIG. 18-15), the design of the Castillo is tied to the solar year. The north side has 92 steps and the other three sides 91 steps each for a total of 365. At the winter and summer equinoxes, the sun casts a shadow along the northern staircase of the pyramid.

Because of the pyramid's silhouette and the angle of the sun, the shadow takes the shape of a serpent that slithers along the pyramid's face as the sun moves across the sky.

Excavations inside the Castillo in 1937 revealed an earlier nine-level pyramid within the later and larger structure. Inside was a chamber with a throne in the form of a red jaguar and a stone figure of the chacmool type depicting a fallen warrior. Chacmools (for example, FIG. 18-17, found on the so-called Platform of the Eagles near the Castillo) recline on their backs and have receptacles on

1 ft.

18-17 Chacmool, from the Platform of the Eagles, Chichén Itzá, Mexico, Maya, ca. 800–900 CE. Stone, 4′ 10½″ high. Museo Nacional de Antropología, Mexico City. ◼◀

Chacmools represent fallen warriors reclining on their backs with receptacles on their chests to receive sacrificial offerings. Excavators discovered one in the throne chamber inside an earlier pyramid within the Castillo (FIG. 18-16).

Caracol means "snail shell," and this unusual round northern Maya structure encloses a circular staircase. The building may have been a temple to Kulkulcán with an astronomical observatory at its summit.

their chests to receive ritual offerings, probably of sacrificial victims. The name, coined by Augustus Le Plongeon (1826–1908), an early explorer of Maya (and Peruvian) sites, means "red jaguar paw" in Mayan. The distinctive forms of Mesoamerican chacmools made a deep impression upon some 20th-century sculptors.

The Caracol (FIG. **18-18**) at Chichén Itzá, with its snail-shaped interior stairway, establishes that the northern Maya were as inventive with architectural form as they were experimental with construction and materials. A cylindrical tower rests on a broad terrace that is in turn supported by a larger rectangular platform measuring 169 by 232 feet. The tower, composed of two concentric walls, encloses a circular staircase that leads to a small chamber near the top of the structure. In plan, the building recalls the cross-section of a conch shell (hence the building's Spanish nickname), which was an attribute of the feathered serpent, and round temples were dedicated to him in central Mexico. This building may therefore also have been a temple to Kukulcán. Windows along the Caracol's staircase and an opening at the summit probably were used for astronomical observation.

TULA The rulers of the Aztec Empire, the most powerful in Mesoamerican history (see Chapter 35), claimed descent from the Toltecs, whose name means "makers of things." Little is known about the Toltecs, and scholars are rethinking the traditional view that they were invaders from the north whose arrival in central Mexico contributed to the fall of the Classic civilizations. In any case, the Toltecs occupied Tula, north of Mexico City, from about 900 to 1200. Feared warriors as well as master artisans and farmers, they also constructed imposing temples and set up stone statues. Most impressive are the four colossal *atlantids* (male statue-columns; FIG. **18-19**) built up of four stone drums each that stand atop Pyramid B at Tula. Whether the atlan-

tids portray rulers in military dress or anonymous armed warriors is uncertain, but their function is clear. These images of brutal authority stand eternally at attention, warding off all hostile forces. They wear feathered headdresses and, as breastplates, stylized butterflies, heraldic symbols of the Toltecs. In one hand they clutch a bundle of darts and in the other an *atlatl* (spear-thrower), typical weapons of highland Mexico. The figures originally supported a temple roof, now missing. Their architectural function dictated the rigidity of pose, compactness, and strict simplicity of contour of the figures.

By 1180, the last Toltec ruler abandoned Tula, and most of his people followed. Some years later, the city was catastrophically destroyed, its ceremonial buildings burned to their foundations, its walls torn down, and the straggling remainder of its population scattered. The exact reasons for the Toltecs' departure and for their city's destruction are unknown, but they left a power vacuum in Mexico that the Aztecs eventually filled three centuries later.

18-19 Colossal atlantids, Pyramid B, Tula, Mexico, Toltec, ca. 900–1180 CE. Stone, each 16' high.

Little is known about the Toltecs, but they left behind these colossal stone statue-columns atop a pyramid-temple at Tula. The atlantids portray warriors or rulers armed with darts and spear-throwers.

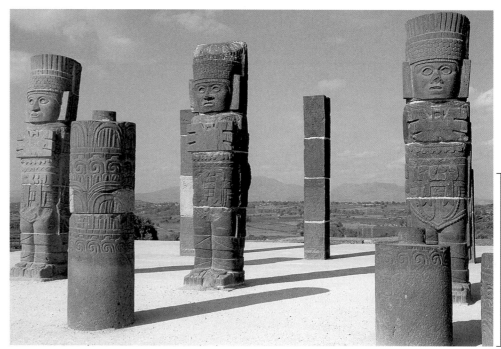

10 ft.

INTERMEDIATE AREA

Between the highly developed civilizations of Mesoamerica and the South American Andes lies a region archaeologists have dubbed the "Intermediate Area." Comprising parts of El Salvador, Honduras, Ecuador, and Venezuela, and all of Panama, Costa Rica, Nicaragua, and Colombia, at the time of the European invasion it was by no means a unified political territory but rather was divided among many small rival chiefdoms. Although the people of the Intermediate Area did not produce monumental architecture on the scale of their neighbors to the north and south and, unlike the Mesoamericans, left no written records, they too were consummate artists. Potters in the Intermediate Area made some of the earliest ceramics of the Americas, and they continued to create an astonishing variety of terracotta vessels and figures until the time of the Spanish conquest. Among the other arts practiced in the Intermediate Area were stone sculpture, jade carving, and especially the highly prized art of goldworking. The first Europeans to make contact here were astonished to see the natives appearing in public nearly naked but covered in gold jewelry. The legend of El Dorado, a Colombian chief who coated himself in gold as part of his accession rites, was largely responsible for the Spanish invaders' ruthless plunder of the region.

TAIRONA In northern Colombia (MAP 18-2), the Sierra Nevada de Santa Marta rises above the Caribbean. The topography of lofty mountains and river valleys provided considerable isolation and the independent development of various groups. The inhabitants of this region after about 1000 CE included a group known as the Tairona, whose goldsmiths were among the finest in the Western Hemisphere. They produced technologically advanced and aesthetically sophisticated work in gold mostly by cutting and hammering thin gold sheets. The Tairona smiths, however, who had to obtain gold by trade, used the *lost-wax process* in part to preserve

the scarce amount of the precious metal available to them. Tairona pendants were not simply rich accessories for costumes but amulets or talismans representing powerful beings who gave the wearer protection and status. The pendant shown here (FIG. **18-20**), cast in a gold-and-copper alloy called tumbaga, represents a bat-faced man—perhaps a masked man rather than a composite being, or a man in the process of spiritual transformation. In local mythology, the first animal created was the bat. This bat-man wears an immense headdress composed of two birds in the round, two great beaked heads, and a series of spirals crowned by two overarching stalks. The harmony of repeated curvilinear motifs, the rhythmic play of their contours, and the precise delineation of minute detail attest to the artist's technical control and aesthetic sensitivity.

SOUTH AMERICA

As in Mesoamerica, until their defeat at the hands of the Spanish conquistadors, the indigenous peoples of Andean South America (MAP **18-2**) erected towering monuments and produced sophisticated paintings, sculptures, ceramics, and textiles. Although less well studied than the ancient Mesoamerican cultures, the South American civilizations are older, and in some ways they surpassed the accomplishments of their northern counterparts. Andean peoples, for example, mastered metalworking much earlier, and their monumental architecture predates that of the earliest Mesoamerican culture, the Olmec, by more than a millennium. The peoples of northern Chile even began to mummify their dead at least 500 years before the Egyptians.

The Central Andean region of South America lies between Ecuador and northern Chile, its western border the Pacific Ocean.

MAP 18-2 Early sites in Andean South America.

18-20 Pendant in the form of a bat-faced man, from northeastern Colombia, Tairona, after 1000 CE. Tumbaga, 5¼″ high. Metropolitan Museum of Art, New York (Jan Mitchell and Sons Collection).

The peoples of the Intermediate Area between Mesoamerica and Andean South America were expert goldsmiths. This pendant depicting a bat-faced man with a large headdress served as an amulet.

It consists of three well-defined geographic zones, running north and south and roughly parallel to one another. The narrow western coastal plain is a desert crossed by rivers, creating habitable fertile valleys. Next, the high peaks of the great Cordillera of the Andes hem in plateaus of a temperate climate. The region's inland border, the eastern slopes of the Andes, is a hot and humid jungle.

Andean civilizations flourished both in the highlands and on the coast. Highland cave dwellers fashioned the first rudimentary art objects by 8800 BCE. Weavers began to fashion sophisticated textiles as early as 2500 BCE, and the firing of clay began in Peru before 1800 BCE. Beginning about 800 BCE, Andean chronology alternates between periods historians call "horizons," when a single culture appears to have dominated a broad geographic area for a relatively long period, and "intermediate periods" characterized by more independent regional development. The Chavín culture (ca. 800–200 BCE) represents the first period, Early Horizon; the Tiwanaku and Wari cultures (ca. 600–1000 CE) the Middle Horizon; and the Inka Empire (discussed in Chapter 35) the Late Horizon. Among the many regional styles that flourished between these horizons, the most important are the Early Intermediate period (ca. 200 BCE–700 CE) Paracas and Nasca cultures of the south coast of Peru, and the Moche in the north.

The discovery of complex ancient communities documented by radiocarbon dating is changing the picture of early South American cultures. Planned communities boasting organized labor systems and monumental architecture dot the narrow river valleys that drop from the Andes to the Pacific Ocean. In the Central Andes, these early sites began to develop around 3000 BCE, about a millennium before the invention of pottery there. Carved gourds and some fragmentary cotton textiles survive from this early period. They depict composite creatures, such as crabs turning into snakes, as well as doubled and then reversed images, both hallmarks of later Andean art.

The architecture of the early coastal sites typically consists of large U-shaped flat-topped platforms—some as high as a 10-story building—around sunken courtyards. Many had numerous small chambers on top. Construction materials included both uncut fieldstones and handmade *adobes* (sun-dried mud bricks) in the shape of cones, laid point to point in coarse mud plaster to form walls and platforms. These complexes almost always faced toward the Andes, source of the life-giving rivers on which these communities depended for survival. Mountain worship, which continues in the Andean region to this day, was probably the focus of early religious practices as well. In the highlands, archaeologists also have discovered large ceremonial complexes. In place of the numerous interconnecting rooms found atop many coastal mounds, the highland examples have a single small chamber at the top, often with a stone-lined firepit in the center. These pits probably played a role in ancient fire rituals. Excavators have found burnt offerings in the pits, often of exotic objects such as marine shells and tropical bird feathers.

Chavín

Named after the ceremonial center of Chavín de Huántar, located in the northern highlands of Peru, the Chavín culture of the Early Horizon period developed and spread throughout much of the coastal region and the highlands during the first millennium BCE. Once thought to be the "mother culture" of the Andean region, archaeologists now view the Chavín culture as the culmination of developments that began elsewhere some 2,000 years earlier.

The Old Temple of Chavín de Huántar was an important pilgrimage site. Dated to the first millennium BCE, it resembles some of the sacred complexes of the earliest Andean cultures but is much larger. It is a U-shaped, stone-faced structure with wings up to

83 yards long facing east between two rivers. Although at first glance its three stories appear to be a solid stepped platform, in fact narrow passageways, small chambers, and stairways penetrate the temple in a labyrinthine pattern. No windows, however, light the interior spaces. The few members of Chavín society with access to these rooms must have witnessed secret and sacred torch-lit ceremonies. Fronting the temple are sunken courts, an arrangement also adopted from earlier coastal sites.

The temple complex at Chavín de Huántar is famous for its extensive stone carvings. The most common subjects are composite creatures combining feline, avian, reptilian, and human features. Consisting largely of low relief on panels, cornices, and columns, and some rarer instances of freestanding sculpture, Chavín carving is essentially shallow, linear incision. An immense oracular cult image stood in the center of the temple's oldest part. Other examples of sculpture in the round include heads of mythological creatures pegged into the exterior walls.

RAIMONDI STELE Found in the main temple at Chavín de Huántar and named after its discoverer, the *Raimondi Stele* (FIG. **18-21**) represents a figure called the "staff god." He appears in various versions from Colombia to northern Bolivia but always holds staffs. Seldom, however, do the representations have the

18-21 *Raimondi Stele,* from the main temple, Chavín de Huántar, Peru, ca. 800–200 BCE. Green diorite, 6′ high. Instituto Nacional de Cultura, Lima.

The *Raimondi Stele* staff god wears a headdress of faces and snakes. Seen upside down, the god's face becomes two faces. The ability of gods to transform themselves is a core aspect of Andean religion.

1 ft.

degree of elaboration found at Chavín. The Chavín staff god gazes upward, frowns, and bares his teeth. His elaborate headdress dominates the upper two-thirds of the slab. Inverting the image reveals that the headdress consists of a series of fanged jawless faces, each emerging from the mouth of the one above it. Snakes abound. They extend from the deity's belt, make up part of the staffs, serve as whiskers and hair for the deity and the headdress creatures, and form a braid at the apex of the composition. The *Raimondi Stele* clearly illustrates the Andean artistic tendency toward both multiplicity and dual readings. Upside down, the god's face turns into two faces. The ability of gods to transform before viewers' eyes is a core aspect of Andean religion.

Chavín iconography spread widely throughout the Andean region via portable media such as goldwork, textiles, and ceramics. For example, more than 300 miles from Chavín on the south coast of Peru, archaeologists have discovered cotton textiles with imagery recalling Chavín sculpture. Painted staff-bearing female deities, apparently local manifestations or consorts of the highland staff god, decorate these large cloths, which may have served as wall hangings in temples. Ceramic vessels found on the north coast of Peru also carry motifs similar to those found on Chavín stone carvings.

Paracas, Nasca, and Moche

Several coastal traditions developed during the millennium from about 400 BCE to 700 CE. The most prominent were the Paracas (ca. 400 BCE–200 CE), Nasca (ca. 200 BCE–600 CE), and Moche (ca. 1–700 CE). Together they exemplify the great variations within Peruvian art styles.

PARACAS The Paracas culture occupied a desert peninsula and a nearby river valley on the south coast of Peru. Outstanding among the Paracas arts are the funerary textiles used to wrap the bodies of the dead in multiple layers. These textiles, buried in shaft tombs beneath the sands and preserved because of the dry desert climate, are among the enduring masterpieces of Andean art (see "Andean Weaving," page 510). Most are of woven cotton with designs embroidered onto the fabric in alpaca or vicuña wool imported from the highlands. The weavers, probably exclusively women, used more than 150 vivid colors, the majority derived from plants. Feline, bird, and serpent motifs appear on many of the textiles, but the human figure, real or mythological, predominates. Humans dressed up as or changing into animals are common motifs on the grave mantles—consistent with the Andean transformation theme noted on the *Raimondi Stele* (FIG. 18-21). On one well-preserved mantle (FIG. 18-22), a figure with prominent eyes appears scores of times over the surface. The flowing hair and the slow kicking motion of the legs suggest the figure is flying or floating while carrying batons and fans, or according to some scholars, knives and hallucinogenic mushrooms. On other mantles, the figures carry the skulls or severed heads of enemies. Art historians have interpreted the flying figures either as Paracas religious practitioners dancing or flying during an ecstatic trance or as images of the deceased. Despite endless repetitions of the figure, variations of detail occur throughout each textile, notably in the figures' positions and in subtle color changes.

1 ft.

18-22 Embroidered funerary mantle, from the southern coast of Peru, Paracas, first century CE. Plain-weave camelid fiber with stem-stitch embroidery of camelid wool, 4′ 7⅞″ × 7′ 10⅞″. Museum of Fine Arts, Boston (William A. Paine Fund).

Paracas weavers created elaborate mantles to wrap around the bodies of the dead. The flying or floating figure repeated endlessly on this mantle is probably the deceased or a religious practitioner.

Andean Weaving

When the Inka first encountered the Spanish conquistadors, they found the Europeans' fixation on gold and silver puzzling. The Inka valued finely woven cloth just as highly as precious metal. Textiles and clothing dominated every aspect of their existence. Storing textiles in great warehouses, their leaders demanded cloth as tribute, gave it as gifts, exchanged it during diplomatic negotiations, and even burned it as a sacrificial offering. Although both men and women participated in cloth production, the Inka rulers selected the best women weavers from around the empire and sequestered them for life to produce textiles exclusively for the elite.

Andean weavers manufactured their textiles by spinning into yarn the cotton grown in five different shades on the warm coast and the fur sheared from highland llamas, alpacas, vicuñas, or guanacos, and then weaving the yarn into cloth. Rare tropical bird feathers and small plaques of gold and silver were sometimes sewn onto cloth destined for the nobility. Andean weavers mastered nearly every textile technique known today, many executed with a simple device known as a *backstrap loom*. Similar looms are still in use in the Andes. The weavers stretch the long *warp* (vertical) threads between two wooden bars. The top bar is tied to an upright. A belt or backstrap, attached to the bottom bar, encircles the waist of the seated weaver, who maintains the tension of the warp threads by leaning back. The weaver passes the *weft* (horizontal) threads over and under the warps and pushes them tightly against each other to produce the finished cloth. In ancient textiles, the sturdy cotton often formed the warp, and the wool, which can be dyed brighter colors, served to create complex designs in the weft.

Embroidery, the sewing of threads onto a finished ground cloth to form contrasting designs, was the specialty of the Paracas culture (FIG. 18-22).

The dry deserts of coastal Peru have preserved not only numerous textiles from different periods but also hundreds of finely worked baskets containing spinning and weaving implements. These tools are invaluable sources of information about Andean textile production processes. The baskets found in documented contexts came from women's graves, attesting to the close identity between weaving and women, the reverence for the cloth-making process, and the Andean belief that textiles were necessary in the afterlife.

A special problem all weavers confront is they must visualize the entire design in advance and cannot easily change it during the weaving process. No records exist of how Andean weavers learned, retained, and passed on the elaborate patterns they wove into cloth, but some painted ceramics depict weavers at work, apparently copying designs from finished models. However, the inventiveness of individual weavers is evident in the endless variety of colors and patterns in surviving Andean textiles. This creativity often led Andean artists to design textiles that are highly abstract and geometric. Paracas embroideries (FIG. 18-22), for example, may depict humans, down to the patterns on the tunics they wear, yet the weavers reduced the figures to their essentials in order to focus on their otherworldly role. The Wari compositions (FIG. 18-28) are the culmination of this tendency toward abstraction in which figural motifs become stunning blocks of color that overwhelm the subject matter itself.

NASCA The Nasca culture takes its name from the Nasca River valley south of Paracas. The early centuries of the Nasca civilization ran concurrently with the closing centuries of the Paracas culture, and Nasca style emulated Paracas style. The Nasca won renown for their pottery, and thousands of their ceramic vessels survive. These usually have round bottoms, double spouts connected by bridges, and smoothly burnished polychrome surfaces. The subjects of their painted decoration vary greatly, but plants, animals, and composite mythological creatures, part human and part animal, are most common. Nasca painters often represented ritual impersonators, some of whom, like the Paracas flying figures (FIG. 18-22), hold trophy heads and weapons. On the vessel illustrated here (FIG. 18-23) are two costumed flying figures. The painter reduced their bodies and limbs to abstract appendages and focused on the heads. The figures wear a multicolored necklace, a whiskered gold mouthpiece, circular disks hanging from the ears, and a rayed crown on the forehead. Masks or heads with streaming hair,

18-23 Bridge-spouted vessel with flying figures, from the Nasca River valley, Peru, Nasca, ca. 50–200 CE. Painted ceramic, 5½″ high. Art Institute of Chicago, Chicago (Kate S. Buckingham Endowment).

The Nasca were masters of pottery painting. The painter of this bridge-spouted vessel depicted two crowned and bejeweled flying figures, probably ritual impersonators with trophy heads.

1 in.

the Greeks and the Maya (FIG. 18-13) surpassed the Moche in the information recorded on their ceramics. Moche pots illustrate architecture, metallurgy, weaving, the brewing of chicha (fermented maize beer), human deformities and diseases, and even sexual acts. Moche vessels are predominantly flat-bottomed stirrup-spouted jars derived from Chavín prototypes. The potters generally decorated them with a *bichrome* (two-color) slip. Although the Moche made early vessels by hand without the aid of a potter's wheel, they fashioned later ones in two-piece molds. Thus, numerous near-duplicates survive. Moche potters continued to refine the stirrup spout, making it an elegant slender tube, much narrower than the Chavín examples. The portrait vessel illustrated here (FIG. 18-25) is an elaborate example of a common Moche type. It may depict the face of a warrior, a ruler, or even a royal retainer whose image may have been buried with many other pots to accompany his dead master. The realistic rendering of the physiognomy is particularly striking.

possibly more trophy heads, flow over the impersonators' backs, increasing the sense of motion.

Nasca artists also depicted figures on a gigantic scale. Some 800 miles of lines drawn in complex networks on the dry surface of the Nasca Plain have long attracted world attention because of their colossal size, which defies human perception from the ground. Preserved today are about three dozen images of birds, fish, and plants, including a hummingbird (FIG. 18-24) several hundred feet long. The Nasca artists also drew geometric forms, such as trapezoids, spirals, and straight lines running for miles. Artists produced the Nasca Lines, as art historians have dubbed these immense earth drawings, by selectively removing the dark top layer of stones to expose the light clay and calcite below. The Nasca created the lines quite easily from available materials and using rudimentary geometry. Small groups of workers have made modern reproductions of them with relative ease. The lines seem to be paths laid out using simple stone-and-string methods. Some lead in traceable directions across the deserts of the Nasca River drainage. Others have many shrinelike nodes punctuating the lines, like the knots on a cord. Some lines converge at central places usually situated close to water sources and seem to be associated with water supply and irrigation. They may have marked pilgrimage routes for those who journeyed to local or regional shrines on foot. Altogether, the vast arrangement of the Nasca Lines is a system—not a meaningless maze but a traversable map that plotted the whole terrain of Nasca material and spiritual concerns. Remarkably, until quite recently, the peoples of highland Bolivia made and used similar ritual pathways in association with shrines, demonstrating the tenacity of the Andean indigenous belief systems.

MOCHE Among the most famous art objects the ancient Peruvians produced are the painted clay vessels of the Moche, who occupied a series of river valleys on the north coast of Peru around the same time the Nasca flourished to the south. Among ancient civilizations, only

18-25 Vessel in the shape of a portrait head, from the northern coast of Peru, Moche, fifth to sixth century CE. Painted clay, 1' $\frac{1}{2}$" high. Museo Arqueológico Rafael Larco Herrera, Lima.

1 in.

18-26 Ear ornament, from Sipán, Peru, Moche, ca. 300 CE. Gold and turquoise, 4⅘" diameter. Bruning Archaeological Museum, Lambayeque.

This ear ornament from a Sipán tomb depicts a warrior priest and two retainers. The priest carries a war club and shield and wears an owl-head-bead necklace. The costume corresponds to archaeological finds.

SIPÁN Elite men, along with retinues of sacrificial victims, appear to be the occupants of several rich Moche tombs excavated near the village of Sipán on the arid northwest coast of Peru. The Sipán burials have yielded a treasure of golden artifacts and more than a thousand ceramic vessels. The discovery of the tombs in the late 1980s created a great stir in the archaeological world, contributing significantly to the knowledge of Moche culture. Beneath a large adobe platform adjacent to two high but greatly eroded pyramids, excavators found the most impressive of several lavish graves, the tomb of a man known today as the Lord of Sipán or the Warrior Priest. The splendor of the trappings adorning his corpse, the quantity and quality of the sumptuous accessories, and the bodies of the retainers buried with him indicate he was a personage of the highest rank. Indeed, the Lord of Sipán may have been one of the warrior priests so often depicted on Moche ceramic wares and murals (and on a golden pyramid-shaped rattle in this very tomb) assaulting his enemies and participating in sacrificial ceremonies.

18-27 Gateway of the Sun, Bolivia, Tiwanaku, ca. 375–700 CE. Stone, 9′ 10″ high.

The Gateway of the Sun probably led into a sacred area. The central figure is a version of the Chavín staff god (FIG. 18-21). Originally painted, the relief was also inlaid with turquoise and covered with gold.

An ear ornament (FIG. 18-26) of turquoise and gold found in one Sipán tomb shows a warrior priest clad much like the Lord of Sipán. Two retainers appear in profile to the left and right of the central figure. Represented frontally, he carries a war club and shield and wears a necklace of owl-head beads. The figure's bladelike, crescent-shaped helmet is a replica of the large golden one buried with the Sipán lord. The war club and shield also match finds in the Warrior Priest's tomb. The figure wears an ear ornament that is a simplified version of the ornament it decorates. Other details also correspond to excavated objects—for example, the removable nose ring hanging down over the mouth. The value of the Sipán find is incalculable for what it reveals about elite Moche culture and for its confirmation of the accuracy of the iconography of Moche artworks.

Tiwanaku and Wari

The bleak highland country of southeastern Peru and southwestern Bolivia contrasts markedly with the warm valleys of the coast. In the Bolivian mountains, the Tiwanaku culture (ca. 100–1000 CE) developed beginning in the second century CE. North of the Paracas society in Peru, the Wari culture (ca. 500–800 CE) dominated parts of the dry coast.

TIWANAKU Named after its principal archaeological site on the southern shore of Lake Titicaca, the Tiwanaku culture flourished for nearly a millennium, spreading to the adjacent coastal area as well as to other highland regions, eventually extending from southern Peru to northern Chile. Tiwanaku was an important ceremonial center. Its inhabitants constructed grand buildings using the region's fine sandstone, andesite, and diorite.

Tiwanaku's imposing Gateway of the Sun (FIG. 18-27) is a huge monolithic block of andesite pierced by a single doorway. Moved in ancient times from its original location within the site, the gateway now forms part of an enormous walled platform. Relief sculpture crowns the gate. The central figure is a Tiwanaku version of the Chavín staff god (FIG. 18-21). Larger than all the other figures and presented frontally, he dominates the composition and presides over the passageway. Rays project from his head. Many terminate in puma heads, representing the power of the highlands' fiercest predator. The staff god—possibly a sky and weather deity rather than the sun deity the rayed head suggests—appears in art throughout the Tiwanaku horizon, associated with smaller attendant figures. Those of the Gateway of the Sun are winged and have human or condor heads. Like the puma, the condor is an impressive carnivore, the largest raptor in the world. Sky and earth beings thus converge on the gate, which probably served as the doorway to a sacred area, a place of transformation. The reliefs were once colorfully painted. The figures' eyes apparently also had turquoise inlays, and gold covered the surfaces. The effect undoubtedly was dazzling.

WARI The flat, abstract, and repetitive figures surrounding the central figure on the Gateway of the Sun recall woven textile designs. Indeed, the people of the Tiwanaku culture, like those of the Paracas, were consummate weavers, although many fewer textiles survive from the damp highlands. Many examples of weaving, especially tunics, survive from the contemporaneous Wari culture in Peru, however.

Although Wari weavers fashioned cloth from both wool and cotton fibers, as did their Paracas predecessors (FIG. 18-22), the resemblance between the two textile styles ends there. Whereas Paracas weavers embroidered motifs onto the plain woven surface, their Wari counterparts wove the designs directly into the fabric, the weft threads packed densely over the warp threads in a technique known as *tapestry* (see "Embroidery and Tapestry," Chapter 12, page 362). Some particularly fine pieces have more than 200 weft threads per inch. Furthermore, unlike the relatively naturalistic individual figures depicted on Paracas mantles, those appearing on Wari textiles are so closely connected and so abstract as to be nearly unrecognizable. In the tunic shown here, known as the *Lima Tapestry* (FIG. **18-28**), the Wari designer expanded or compressed each figure in a different way and placed them in vertical rows pressed between narrow red bands of plain cloth. Elegant tunics such as this one must have been prestige garments made for the elite. A close connection existed between clothing and status in many ancient American societies, especially in the Inka Empire that eventually dominated Andean South America (see Chapter 35).

18-28 *Lima Tapestry,* tunic, from Peru, Wari, ca. 500–800 CE. 3′ 3$\frac{3}{8}$″ × 2′ 11$\frac{3}{8}$″. Museo Nacional de Antropología Arqueología e Historia del Perú, Lima.

Whereas Paracas mantles (FIG. 18-22) are embroideries, Wari textiles are tapestries with the motifs woven directly into the fabric. The figures on this tunic are so abstract as to be nearly unrecognizable.

1 ft.

NORTH AMERICA

In many parts of the United States and Canada, archaeologists have identified indigenous cultures dating as far back as 12,000 years ago. Most of the surviving art objects, however, come from the last 2,000 years. Scholars divide the vast and varied territory of North America (MAP 18-3) into cultural regions based on the geography and relative homogeneity of language and social and artistic patterns. Native lifestyles varied widely over the continent, ranging from small bands of migratory hunters to settled—at times even urban—agriculturalists. Among the art-producing peoples who inhabited the continent before the arrival of Europeans are the Eskimos of Alaska and the Inuit of Canada, who hunted and fished across the Arctic from Greenland to Siberia, and the maize farmers of the American Southwest, who wrested water from their arid environment and built effective irrigation systems as well as roads and spectacular cliff dwellings. Farmers also settled in the vast, temperate Eastern Woodlands—ranging from eastern Canada to Florida and from the Atlantic to the Great Plains west of the Mississippi. Some of them left behind great earthen mounds that once functioned as their elite residences or burial places.

Eskimo

The Eskimoan peoples originally migrated to North America across the Bering Strait. During the early first millennium CE, a community of Eskimo sea-mammal hunters and tool makers occupied parts of Alaska during the Norton, or Old Bering Sea, culture that began around 500 BCE.

IPIUTAK MASK Archaeologists have uncovered major works of Eskimo art at the Ipiutak site at Point Hope. The finds include a variety of burial goods as well as tools. A burial mask (FIG. **18-29**) datable to around 100 CE is of special interest. The artist fashioned the mask out of walrus ivory, the material used for most Arctic artworks because of the scarcity of wood in the region. The mask consists of nine carefully shaped parts, interrelated to produce several faces, both human and animal, echoing the transformation theme noted in other ancient American cultures. The confident, subtle composition in shallow relief is a tribute to the artist's imaginative control over the material. The mask's abstract circles and curved lines are common motifs on the decorated tools discovered at Point Hope. For centuries, the Eskimo also carved human and animal figures, always at small scale, reflecting a nomadic lifestyle requiring the creation of portable objects.

Woodlands

Early Native American artists also excelled in working stone into a variety of utilitarian and ceremonial objects. Some early cultures, such as those of the Woodlands east of the Mississippi River, also

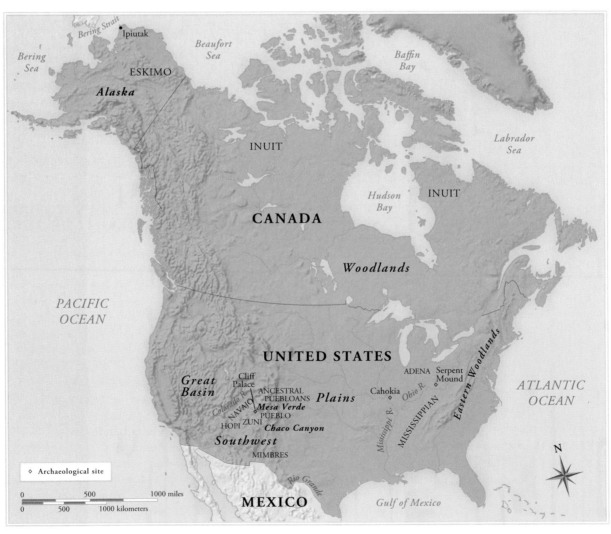

MAP 18-3 Early Native American sites in North America. ◼◀

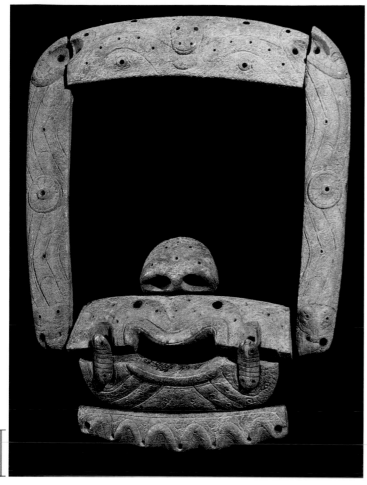

18-29 Burial mask, from Point Hope, Alaska, Ipiutak, ca. 100 CE. Ivory, greatest width 9½". American Museum of Natural History, New York.

Carved out of walrus ivory, this mask consists of nine parts that can be combined to produce several faces, both human and animal, echoing the transformation theme common in ancient American art.

established great urban centers with populations sometimes exceeding 20,000.

ADENA Archaeologists have found remains of the Adena culture of Ohio at about 500 sites in the Central Woodlands. The Adena buried their elite in great earthen mounds and often placed ceremonial pipes in the graves. Smoking was an important social and religious ritual in many Native American cultures, and pipes were treasured status symbols men wanted to take with them into the afterlife. The Adena pipe shown here (FIG. **18-30**), carved between 500 BCE and the end of the millennium, takes the shape of a standing man. The figure has naturalistic joint articulations and musculature, a lively flexed-leg pose, and an alert facial expression—all combining to suggest movement. In form and costume (note the prominent ear spools), the figure resembles some Mesoamerican sculptures.

MISSISSIPPIAN The Adena were the first great mound builders of North America, but the Mississippian culture, which emerged around 800 CE and eventually encompassed much of the eastern United States, surpassed all earlier Woodlands groups in the size and complexity of their communities. One Mississippian mound site, Cahokia in southern Illinois, was the largest city in North America in the early second millennium CE, with a population

18-30 Pipe, from a mound in Ohio, Adena, ca. 500–1 BCE. Stone, 8" high. Ohio Historical Society, Columbus.

Smoking was an important ritual in ancient North America, and the Adena often buried pipes with men for use in the afterlife. This example resembles some Mesoamerican sculptures in form and costume.

of at least 20,000 and an area of more than six square miles. There were approximately 120 mounds at Cahokia. The grandest, 100 feet tall and built in stages between about 900 and 1200 CE, was Monk's Mound

18-30A Monk's Mound, Cahokia, ca. 1050–1200 CE.

(FIG. **18-30A**). It aligns with the position of the sun at the equinoxes and may have served as an astronomical observatory as well as the site of agricultural ceremonies. Topping each stage were wooden structures the Mississippians eventually destroyed in preparation for the building of a new layer.

Serpent Mound

Serpent Mound (FIG. 18-31) is one of the largest and best known of the Woodlands effigy mounds, but it is the subject of considerable controversy. First excavated in the 1880s, Serpent Mound represents one of the first efforts at preserving a Native American site from destruction at the hands of pot hunters and farmers. For a long time after its exploration, archaeologists attributed construction of the mound to the Adena culture, which flourished in the Ohio area during the last several centuries BCE. Radiocarbon dates taken from the mound, however, indicate the people known as Mississippians built it much later. Unlike most other ancient mounds, for example, Monk's Mound (FIG. 18-30A) in Cahokia, Illinois, Serpent Mound contained no evidence of burials or temples. Serpents, however, were important in Mississippian iconography, appearing, for instance, etched on shell gorgets similar to the one reproduced in FIG. 18-32. The Mississippians strongly associated snakes with the earth and the fertility of crops. A stone figurine found at one Mississippian site depicts a woman digging her hoe into the back of a large serpentine creature whose tail turns into a vine of gourds.

Some researchers have proposed another possible meaning for the construction of Serpent Mound. The date suggested for it is 1070, not long after the brightest appearance in recorded history of Halley's Comet in 1066, an astronomical event recorded on the 11th-century *Bayeux Tapestry* (FIGS. 12-37 and 12-38) as an important omen. Could Serpent Mound have been built in response to the same comet lighting up the North American heavens? Scholars have even suggested the serpentine form of the mound replicates Halley's Comet streaking across the night sky. Whatever its meaning, an earthwork as large and elaborate as Serpent Mound could only have been built by a large labor force under the firm direction of a powerful elite eager to leave its mark on the landscape forever.

18-31 Serpent Mound, Ohio, Mississippian, ca. 1070 CE. 1200′ long, 20′ wide, 5′ high.

The Mississippians constructed effigy mounds in the form of animals and birds. This mound seems to depict a serpent. Some scholars, however, think it replicates the path of Halley's Comet in 1066.

1 in.

18-32 Incised gorget with running warrior, from Sumner County, Tennessee, Mississippian, ca. 1250–1300 CE. Shell, 4″ wide. National Museum of the American Indian, Washington, D.C.

This neck pendant was probably a gift to the dead to ensure safe passage to the afterlife. It represents a running Mississippian warrior holding a mace in one hand and a severed human head in the other.

1 in.

18-33 Bowl with two cranes and geometric forms, from New Mexico, Mimbres, ca. 1250 CE. Painted ceramic, diameter 1′ $\frac{1}{2}$″. Art Institute of Chicago, Chicago (Hugh L. and Mary T. Adams Fund).

Native Americans have been producing pottery for more than 2,000 years, long before the introduction of the potter's wheel. Mimbres bowls feature black-and-white animals and abstract patterns.

The Mississippians also constructed *effigy mounds* (mounds built in the form of animals or birds). One of the best preserved is Serpent Mound (FIG. 18-31), a twisting earthwork on a bluff overlooking a creek in Ohio. It measures nearly a quarter mile from its open jaw (FIG. 18-31, *top right*), which seems to clasp an oval-shaped mound in its mouth, to its tightly coiled tail (*far left*). Both its date and meaning are controversial (see "Serpent Mound," page 516).

The Mississippian peoples, like their predecessors in North America, also manufactured small portable art objects. The shell *gorget,* or neck pendant, was a favorite item. One example (FIG. 18-32), found at a site in Tennessee, dates from around 1250 to 1300 CE and depicts a running warrior, shown in the same kind of composite profile and frontal view with bent arms and legs used to suggest motion in other ancient cultures (compare, for instance, FIG. 5-16). The Tennessee warrior wears an elaborate headdress incorporating an arrow. He carries a mace in his left hand and a severed human head in his right. On his face is the painted forked eye of a falcon. Most Mississippian gorgets come from burial and temple mounds, and archaeologists believe they were gifts to the dead to ensure their safe arrival and prosperity in the land of the spirits. Other art objects found in similar contexts include fine mica cutouts and embossed copper cutouts of hands, bodies, snakes, birds, and other presumably symbolic forms.

Southwest

In the Southwest, Native Americans have been producing pottery since the late first millennium BCE, but the most impressive examples of decorated pottery date to after 1000 CE.

MIMBRES The Mimbres culture of southwestern New Mexico, which flourished between approximately 1000 and 1250 CE, is renowned for its black-on white painted bowls. Mimbres bowls have been found in burials under house floors, inverted over the head of the deceased and ritually "killed" by puncturing a small hole at the base, perhaps to allow the spirits of the deceased to join their ancestors in the sky (which contemporary Southwestern peoples view as a dome). The bowl illustrated here (FIG. 18-33) dates to around 1250 and features an animated graphic rendering of two black cranes on a white ground. The contrast between the bowl's abstract border designs and the birds creates a dynamic tension. Thousands of different compositions appear on Mimbres pottery. They range from lively and complex geometric patterns to abstract renditions of humans, animals, and composite mythological beings. Almost all are imaginative creations by artists who seem to have been determined not to repeat themselves. Their designs emphasize linear rhythms balanced and controlled within a clearly defined border. Because the potter's wheel was unknown in the Americas, the artists constructed their pots out of coils of clay, creating countless sophisticated shapes of varied size, always characterized by technical excellence. Although historians have no direct knowledge about the potters' identities, the fact that pottery making was usually women's work in the Southwest during the historical period (see "Gender Roles in Native American Art," Chapter 35, page 1030) suggests the Mimbres potters also may have been women.

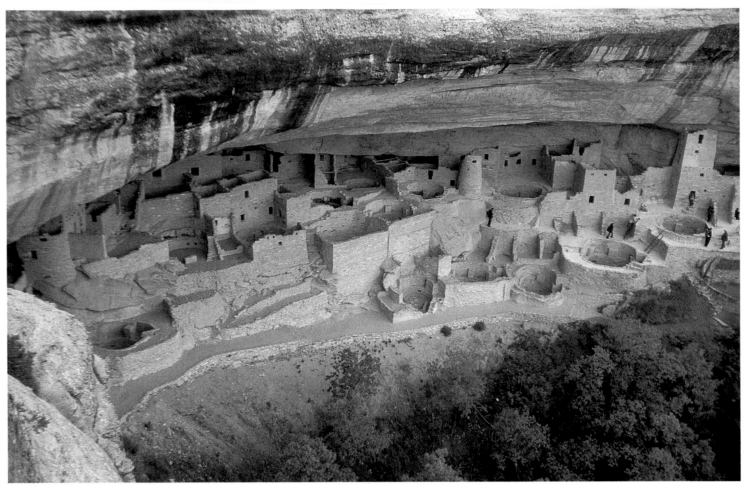

18-34 Cliff Palace (looking northeast), Mesa Verde National Park, Colorado, Ancestral Puebloan, ca. 1150–1300 CE.

Cliff Palace, wedged into a sheltered ledge to heat the pueblo in winter and shade it during the hot summer months, contains about 200 stone-and-timber rooms plastered inside and out with adobe.

ANCESTRAL PUEBLOANS

18-33A Pueblo Bonito, Chaco Canyon, ca. 850–1050 CE.

The Ancestral Puebloans, formerly known as the Anasazi, were northern neighbors of the Mimbres. (Anasazi means "enemy ancestors" in Navajo, a term the descendants of these early Native Americans have understandably rejected.) The Ancestral Puebloans emerged as an identifiable culture around 200 CE, but their art did not reach its peak until about 1000. The many ruined *pueblos* (urban settlements) scattered throughout the Southwest reveal the Ancestral Puebloans' masterful building skills. In Chaco Canyon (FIG. **18-33A**), New Mexico, for example, they built a great semicircle of 800 rooms reaching to five stepped-back stories, the largest of several similar sites in and around the canyon. Chaco Canyon was the center of a wide trade network extending as far as Mexico.

Sometime in the late 12th century, a drought occurred, and the Ancestral Puebloans largely abandoned their open canyon-floor dwelling sites to move farther north to the steep-sided canyons and lusher environment of Mesa Verde in southwestern Colorado. Cliff Palace (FIG. **18-34**) is wedged into a sheltered ledge above a valley floor. It contains about 200 rectangular rooms (mostly communal dwellings) of carefully laid stone and timber, once plastered inside and out with adobe. The location for Cliff Palace was not accidental. The Ancestral Puebloans designed it to take advantage of the sun to heat the pueblo in winter and the sheltering ledge to shade it during the hot summer months. Scattered in the foreground of FIG. 18-34 are two dozen large circular roofed semisubterranean structures called *kivas*. The Ancestral Puebloans entered the kivas using a ladder extending through a hole in the flat roof. These rooms were the spiritual centers of native Southwest life, male council houses where the elders stored ritual regalia and where private rituals and preparations for public ceremonies took place—and still do.

The Ancestral Puebloans did not disappear but gradually evolved into the various Pueblo peoples who still live in Arizona, New Mexico, Colorado, and Utah. They continue to speak their native languages, practice deeply rooted rituals, and make pottery in the traditional manner. Their art is discussed in Chapter 35.

NATIVE ARTS OF THE AMERICAS BEFORE 1300

MESOAMERICA

▌ The Olmec (ca. 1200–400 BCE) is often called the "mother culture" of Mesoamerica. At La Venta and elsewhere, the Olmec built pyramids and ball courts and carved colossal basalt portraits of their rulers during the Preclassic period.

▌ In contrast to the embryonic civic centers of the Olmec, Teotihuacán in the Valley of Mexico was a huge metropolis laid out on a strict grid plan. Its major pyramids and plazas date to the late Preclassic period (ca. 50–250 CE).

▌ The Maya occupied parts of Mexico, Belize, Guatemala, and Honduras. During the Classic period (ca. 300–900 CE), at Copán, Tikal, and other sites, they built vast complexes of temple-pyramids, palaces, plazas, and ball courts and decorated them with monumental sculptures and mural paintings glorifying their rulers and gods. The Maya also left extensive written records and possessed a sophisticated knowledge of astronomy and arithmetic calculation.

▌ The most famous Postclassic (ca. 900–1521) Maya site is Chichén Itzá in the Yucatán Peninsula, which boasts a huge pyramid-temple to Kulkulcán and the largest ball court in Mesoamerica.

Colossal head, La Venta, Olmec, ca. 900–400 BCE

Temple I, Tikal, Maya, ca. 732 CE

SOUTH AMERICA

▌ The ancient civilizations of South America are even older than those of Mesoamerica. The earliest Andean sites began to develop around 3000 BCE.

▌ At Chavín de Huántar in Peru, archaeologists have excavated U-shaped temple complexes and monumental statues and reliefs dating between about 800 and 200 BCE, during the Early Horizon period.

▌ The Paracas (ca. 400 BCE–200 CE), Nasca (ca. 200 BCE–600 CE), and Moche (ca. 1–700 CE) cultures of the Early Intermediate period in Peru produced extraordinary textiles, distinctive painted ceramics, and turquoise-inlaid goldwork. The subjects range from composite human-animals to ruler portraits. Most monumental are the Nasca Lines, which may have marked pilgrimage routes.

▌ The Tiwanaku (ca. 100–1000 CE) and Wari (ca. 500–800 CE) cultures of northern Bolivia and southern Peru flourished during the Middle Horizon period. Tiwanaku is noteworthy for its monumental stone architecture. The Wari produced magnificent tapestries.

Hummingbird, Nasca, ca. 500 CE

Lima Tapestry, Wari, ca. 500–800 CE

NORTH AMERICA

▌ The indigenous cultures of the United States and Canada date as far back as 10,000 BCE, but most of the surviving art objects date from the last 2,000 years. The Eskimo, for example, produced small-scale artworks in ivory beginning in the early first millennium CE, reflecting a nomadic lifestyle requiring portable objects.

▌ The peoples of the Mississippian culture (ca. 800–1500 CE) were great mound builders. Cahokia in Illinois encompassed about 120 mounds and was the largest city in North America during the early second millennium CE.

▌ In the Southwest, Native Americans have been producing pottery for more than 2,000 years. The black-and-white painted bowls of the Mimbres (ca. 1000–1250 CE) are among the finest. The Ancestral Puebloans were master builders of pueblos, urban settlements of stone and wood, often plastered with adobe. The pueblo at Chaco Canyon, New Mexico, had about 800 rooms. Cliff Palace, Colorado, is noteworthy for its sophisticated design, wedged into a sheltered ledge to take advantage of the winter sun and the summer shade.

Cliff Palace, Colorado, Ancestral Puebloan, ca. 1150–1300 CE

One of the Benin king's praise names is "great head," and on this cast-bronze royal altar, the artist represented him larger than all other figures and with a disproportionately large head.

The unknown artist who cast this *ikegobo* drew attention to the king by placing attendant figures to his left and right who each raise one arm to point to his head.

An *ikegobo* is an altar to the hand, the symbol of personal achievement in Benin society. The band at the bottom of this altar features hands alternating with other emblems of royal power.

1 in.

19-1 Altar to the Hand (ikegobo), from Benin, Nigeria, ca. 1735–1750. Brass, 1′ 5½″ high. British Museum, London (gift of Sir William Ingram). ◼◀

19

AFRICA BEFORE 1800

The sacred king, or *oba,* depicted twice on this portable altar is probably Eresonyen, who ruled Benin about 1735–1750. He wears a multistrand coral necklace emblematic of his high office.

SACRED KINGSHIP IN BENIN

Some of the oldest paintings yet discovered, for example those from the Apollo 11 Cave in Namibia (FIG. 1-3), come from Africa, and African art is as diverse as the continent is vast. Most African artworks created before 1800 are difficult to date and interpret. The art of the Benin kingdom, just west of the lower reaches of the Niger River in what is today Nigeria (not to be confused with the modern Republic of Benin), is exceptional. The kingdom, most likely established in the 13th century, reached the apex of its wealth and power in the 16th century. Benin kingship was hereditary and considered sacred, and the purpose of the finest preserved Benin artworks was to honor the ruling *oba,* his family, and his ancestors. The names and dates of many of the Benin kings are known, and numerous extant artworks can even be confidently attributed to specific rulers.

The 18th-century cast-brass royal shrine illustrated here (FIG. **19-1**), on which the oba appears twice, underscores the centrality of the sacred king in Benin culture. Called an *ikegobo* and about a foot and a half tall, it is a portable altar to the hand, which symbolized personal achievement in Benin society, both on the battlefield and in peacetime. The altar features symmetrical hierarchical compositions centered on the dominant king, probably Eresonyen, who ruled Benin around 1735 to 1750, and who appears on the altar wearing the multistrand coral necklace emblematic of his high office. He is the central figure on the top of the altar, flanked by smaller (and therefore lesser) members of his court, usually identified as priests. In front of the king and his attendant priests is a pair of leopards, animals the sacred king sacrificed and symbolic of his power over all creatures. Similar compositions are common in Benin arts, as exemplified by the royal plaque (FIG. I-1) discussed in the Introduction. On the ikegobo, as was the norm throughout Africa, the artist distorted the king's proportions to emphasize his head, the seat of his will and power. Benin men celebrate a festival of the head called Igue, and one of the king's praise names is "great head."

King Eresonyen appears again as the largest figure on the cylindrical body of the altar. As in the freestanding group at the top, the size of the figures in relief varies with their importance at the Benin court. The sculptor drew attention to the sacred oba by placing him at the center, where two attendant figures raise their arms to point to his head. Around the base are more leopards, ram and elephant heads, and crocodiles (not all visible in FIG. 19-1), and the all-important hands symbolizing royal power and accomplishment. The oba and other high-ranking officials offered sacrifices at the ikegobo to ensure the king's continued strength and achievement.

FRAMING THE ERA

AFRICAN PEOPLES AND ART FORMS

Africa (MAP **19-1**, page 524) is a vast continent of 52 nations comprising more than one-fifth of the world's land mass and many distinct topographical and ecological zones. Parched deserts occupy northern and southern regions, high mountains rise in the east, and three great rivers—the Niger, the Congo, and the Nile—and their lush valleys support agriculture and large settled populations. More than 2,000 distinct ethnic, cultural, and linguistic groups, often but inaccurately called "tribes," long have inhabited the African continent. These population groups historically have ranged in size from a few hundred, in hunting and gathering bands, to 20 million or more. Councils of elders often governed smaller groups, whereas larger populations sometimes formed a centralized state under a king, as in Benin (FIG. 19-1).

Despite this great variety, African peoples share many core beliefs and practices. These include honoring ancestors, worshiping nature deities, and elevating rulers to sacred status. Most Africans also consult diviners or fortune tellers. These beliefs have given rise to many richly expressive art traditions. Some have close equivalents in Western cultures, for example, figural sculpture, sacred and secular architecture, and rock engraving and painting. But other art forms, poorly documented until recent times because of their perishable nature and because they did not conform to Western notions of "artworks," also played key roles in African life. These include the art of body decoration and modification, costumes, and masks.

Given the size of the African continent and the diversity of ethnic groups, it is not surprising that African art varies enormously in subject, materials, and function. Nomadic and seminomadic peoples excel in the arts of personal adornment and also produce rock engravings and paintings depicting animals and rituals. Farmers, in contrast, often create figural sculpture in terracotta, wood, and metal for display in shrines to legendary ancestors or nature deities held responsible for the health of crops and the well-being of the people. The regalia, art, and architecture of kings and their courts, as elsewhere in the world, celebrate the wealth and power of the rulers themselves. Nearly all African peoples lavish artistic energy on the decoration of their bodies to express their identity and status, and many communities mount richly layered festivals, including masquerades, to celebrate harvests and the New Year and to commemorate the deaths of leaders.

This chapter surveys the early, and often difficult to date, art and architecture of sub-Saharan Africa from prehistoric times through the 18th century (see "Dating African Art and Identifying African Artists," page 523). The discussion includes the effects on Africans and African art of the first contacts with Europeans, which began along the seacoasts in the late 15th century, but excludes the art and architecture of Egypt and of Roman and Islamic North Africa, already treated in Chapters 3, 7, and 10 respectively. Chapter 37 treats African art of the past two centuries, from the beginning of European colonization to 1980. Contemporary African art is considered in its global context in Chapter 31.

PREHISTORY AND EARLY CULTURES

Thousands of rock engravings and paintings found at hundreds of sites across the continent constitute the earliest known African art. Some painted animals (FIG. 1-3) from the Apollo 11 Cave in southwestern Africa date to perhaps as long ago as 25,000 years, earlier than all but the oldest *Paleolithic* (Old Stone Age) art of Europe (see Chapter 1). Because humankind apparently originated in Africa, archaeologists may yet discover the world's earliest art there as well.

Rock Art

The greatest concentrations of rock art are in the Sahara to the north, the Horn of Africa in the east, and the Kalahari Desert to the south, as well as in caves and on rock outcroppings in southern Africa. Accurately naturalistic renderings as well as stylized images on rock surfaces show animals and humans in many different positions and activities, singly or in groups, stationary or in motion. Most of these works date to within the past 4,000 to 6,000 years, but some may have been created as early as 8000 BCE. They provide a rich record of the environment, human activities, and animal species in prehistoric times.

TASSILI N'AJJER A 7,000-year-old painting (FIG. **19-2**) from Tassili n'Ajjer in southeastern Algeria in the central Sahara (at that time a verdant savannah) is one of the earliest and finest surviving examples of rock art. The painter depicted a running woman with convincing animation and significant detail. The dotted marks on her shoulders, legs, and torso probably indicate she is wearing body paint applied for a ritual. Her face, however, is featureless, a common

AFRICA BEFORE 1800

	BCE	CE		
25,000	1000	0	1500	1800
	▌ Oldest paintings in Africa are among the earliest artworks known ▌ Most examples of rock art date after 6000 BCE	▌ Earliest African sculptures in the round produced by the Nok culture	▌ Bronze-casting using the lost-wax method practiced at Igbo Ukwu ▌ The markedly different style of sculptures from Ile-Ife and from Djenne underscores the regional diversity of African art ▌ Major Islamic and Christian shrines dedicated at Djenne and Lalibela ▌ Construction of the royal palace complex of the Great Zimbabwe Empire	▌ Benin sculptors produce a wide range of ivories and cast bronzes glorifying the royal family ▌ Earliest interaction between African artists and European patrons

Dating African Art and Identifying African Artists

Most African objects bear neither labels nor signatures, and consequently it is nearly impossible to date them precisely or to identify their makers definitively. As in the West, this is especially true for the oldest surviving artworks (FIGS. I-1 and 19-2), but in Africa the absence of documentary information persisted until quite recently. Early collectors did not even bother to ask the names of living artists or when they made their works. Although a firm chronology for the full range of African arts is currently beyond reach, broad historical trends are reasonably clear. Still, until archaeologists conduct more extensive fieldwork in sub-Saharan Africa, many artworks will remain difficult to date even within a century, and whole cultures will continue to be poorly documented. Some African peoples, however, have left written documents that help date their artworks, even when their methods of measuring time differ from those used today. Other cultures, such as the Benin kingdom (FIGS. I-1, 19-1, and 19-13), preserve detailed oral records of past events. Historians can check these against the accounts of European travelers and traders.

When artists are members of craft or occupational guilds—such as blacksmiths and brass-casters in Western Sudan—commissions go to the group chief, and the specific artist who worked on the commission may never be known. Nevertheless, art historians can identify individual hands if an artist's work is distinctive. Documentation now exists for several hundred artists, even if most of their names are lost. For some sculptors who worked in the late 19th or early 20th centuries, however, scholars have been able to compile fairly detailed biographies (see "African Artists," Chapter 37, page 1071).

Where documentation on authorship or dating is fragmentary or unavailable, art historians sometimes try to establish chronology from an object's style, although, as discussed in the Introduction, stylistic analysis is a subjective tool. Scientific techniques such as *radiocarbon dating* (measuring the decay rate of carbon isotopes in organic matter to provide dates for wood, fiber, and ivory) and *thermoluminescence* (dating the amounts of radiation found in fired clay objects) have also proved useful but cannot provide precise dates. Nonetheless, art historians are slowly writing the history of African art, even if large gaps remain to be filled.

One major problem impeding compilation of an accurate history of art in Africa is illegal and uncontrolled excavation. By removing artworks from the ground, treasure hunters disturb or ruin the objects' original contexts and reduce or eliminate the possibility of establishing accurate chronologies. This phenomenon is not unique to Africa, however (see "Archaeology, Art History, and the Art Market," Chapter 4, page 88). Archaeologists on all continents

19-2 Running woman, rock painting, from Tassili n'Ajjer, Algeria, ca. 6000–4000 BCE.

Prehistoric rock paintings are difficult to date and interpret. This Algerian example represents a running woman wearing body paint, raffia skirt, and horned headgear, apparently in a ritual context.

confront the problem of looting and the consequent loss of knowledge about the provenance and original function of objects collectors wish to acquire. That is the unfortunate result of the worldwide appreciation of African art that began in the early 20th century, when many European artists looked to "primitive art" for inspiration (see "Primitivism and Colonialism," Chapter 29, page 846).

trait in the earliest art of Europe as well as Africa (see Chapter 1). The white parallel patterns attached to her arms and waist probably represent flowing raffia decorations and a raffia skirt. Horns are also part of her ceremonial attire—shown, as typically in prehistoric art (see Chapter 1), in the *twisted perspective,* or *composite view,* that is, seen from the front even though on a profile head. Notably, the artist painted this detailed image over a field of much smaller painted human beings, an example of why it is often so difficult to date and interpret art on rock surfaces, as subsequent superimpositions are frequent. Nonetheless, scholars have been able to establish a rough chronology for African rock art, an art form that continues to the present day.

Although the precise meaning of most African rock art also remains uncertain, a considerable literature exists describing, analyzing, and interpreting the varied human and animal activities shown, as well as the evidently symbolic, more abstract patterns.

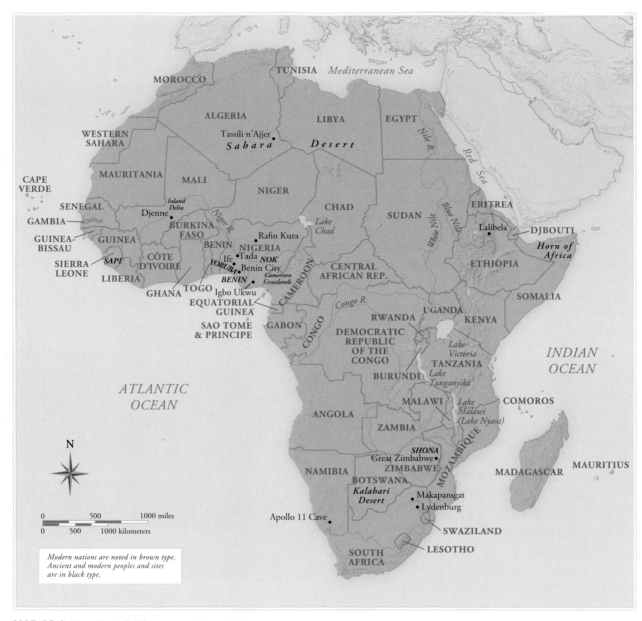

MAP 19-1 Precolonial African peoples and sites.

The human and humanlike figures may include representations of supernatural beings as well as mortals. Some scholars have, in fact, interpreted the woman from Tassili n'Ajjer as a horned deity instead of a human wearing ceremonial headgear.

Nok and Lydenburg

Outside Egypt and neighboring Nubia (see Chapter 3), the earliest African sculptures in the round have been found at several sites in central Nigeria archaeologists collectively call the Nok culture. Scholars disagree on whether the Nok sites were unified politically or socially. Named after the site where these sculptures were first discovered in 1928, Nok art dates between 500 BCE and 200 CE. Hundreds of Nok-style human and animal heads, body parts, and figures have been found accidentally during tin-mining operations, but unfortunately not in their original context.

NOK A representative Nok terracotta head (FIG. **19-3**), found at Rafin Kura, is a fragment of what was originally a full figure. Preserved

fragments of other statues indicate the Nok sculptors fashioned a variety of types, including standing, seated, and kneeling figures. The heads are disproportionately large compared with the bodies. The head shown here has an expressive face with large alert eyes, flaring nostrils, and parted lips. The pierced eyes, mouth, and ear holes are characteristic of Nok sculpture and probably helped to equalize the heating of the hollow clay head during the firing process. The coiffure with incised grooves, the raised eyebrows, the perforated triangular eyes, and the sharp jaw line suggest the sculptor carved some details of the head while modeling the rest. The function of the Nok terracottas is unclear, but the broken tube around the neck of the Rafin Kura figure may be a bead necklace, an indication the person portrayed held an elevated position in Nok society. The gender of the Nok artists is also unknown, but because the primary ceramists and clay sculptors across the continent have traditionally been women, Nok women may have sculpted these heads as well (see "Gender Roles in African Art Production," Chapter 37, page 1070).

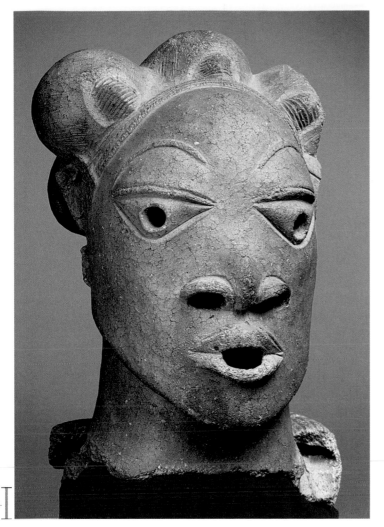

19-3 Nok head, from Rafin Kura, Nigeria, ca. 500 BCE–200 CE. Terracotta, 1′ 2 3/16″ high. National Museum, Lagos.

The earliest African sculptures in the round come from Nigeria. The Nok culture produced expressive terracotta heads with large eyes, mouths, and ears. Piercing equalized the heat during the firing process.

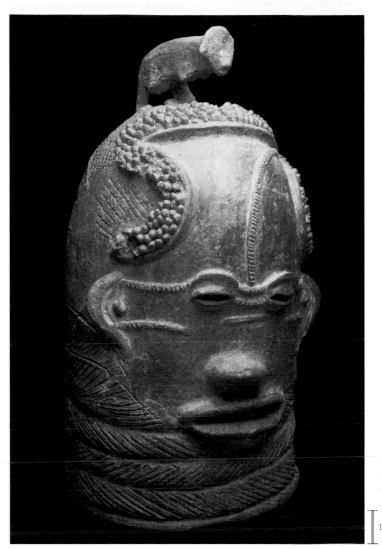

19-4 Head, from Lydenburg, South Africa, ca. 500 CE. Terracotta, 1′ 2 15/16″ high. IZIKO Museums of Cape Town, Cape Town.

This Lydenburg head resembles an inverted terracotta pot and may have been a helmet mask. The sculptor depicted the features by applying thin clay fillets. The scarification marks are signs of beauty.

LYDENBURG Later than the Nok examples are the seven life-size terracotta heads discovered carefully buried in a pit outside the town of Lydenburg in present-day South Africa. Radiocarbon evidence indicates the heads date to about 500 CE. The Lydenburg head illustrated here (FIG. **19-4**), reconstructed from fragments, has a humanlike form, although its inverted pot shape differs markedly from the more naturalistic Nok heads. The artist formed the eyes, ears, nose, and mouth, as well as the hairline, by applying thin clay fillets onto the head. The same method produced what are probably *scarification* marks (scars intentionally created to form patterns on the flesh) on the forehead, temples, and between the eyes. Incised linear patterns also adorn the back of the head. (This head is among the earliest artworks documenting the ancient African practice of beautifying the body through the creation of scars, a custom different from, but comparable to, the Polynesian tradition of tattooing bodies; see "Tattoo in Polynesia," Chapter 36, page 1055). The horizontal neck bands, with their incised surfaces, resemble the ringed or banded necks Africans still consider signs of beauty in many parts of the continent. In Africa, it is not uncommon for the human body itself to become a work of art. A small, unidentifiable animal sits atop the Lydenburg head (compare FIG. 4-12). In the absence of contemporaneous written documents, scholars can only guess at the use and meaning of a head such as this one, but it is noteworthy that animals appear only on those Lydenburg heads large enough to have served as helmet masks. The head, therefore, probably had a ceremonial function.

Igbo Ukwu

By the 9th or 10th century, a West African bronze-casting tradition of great sophistication had developed in the lower Niger area, just east of that great river. Dozens of objects in an intricate refined style have been unearthed at Igbo Ukwu. The ceramic, copper, bronze, and iron artifacts include basins (FIG. **19-4A**), bowls, altar stands, staffs, swords, scabbards, knives, and pendants. In one grave, archaeologists discovered numerous prestige objects—copper anklets, armlets, spiral ornaments, a fan handle, and more than 100,000 beads, which may have been used as a form of currency. The tomb also contained three elephant tusks, a beaded arm-

19-4A Roped water basin, Igbo Ukwu, 9th to 10th centuries CE.

Art and Leadership in Africa

The relationships between leaders and art forms are strong, complex, and universal in Africa. Political, spiritual, and social leaders—kings, chiefs, titled people, and religious specialists—have the power and wealth to obtain the services of the best artists and acquire the most sumptuous materials to adorn themselves (FIG. 37-23), furnish their homes and palaces (FIGS. 37-6, 37-16, and 37-16A), and make visible the cultural and religious organizations they lead (FIGS. 19-1 and 37-13). Leaders also possess the power to dispense art or the prerogative to use it.

A number of formal or structural principles or trends characterize leaders' arts and thus set them off from the popular arts of ordinary Africans. Leaders' arts—for example, the lavish layered regalia of chiefs and kings (FIG. 19-6)—tend to be durable and fashioned of costly materials, such as ivory (FIG. 19-13), beads, copper alloys, and other metals. Some of the objects made specifically for African leaders, such as stools or chairs (FIG. 37-6), ornate clothing (FIG. 37-23), and special weaponry, draw attention to their superior status. Handheld objects, for example, staffs (FIG. 19-1), spears, knives, scepters, pipes, and fly whisks (FIG. 19-5), extend a leader's reach and magnify his or her gestures. Other objects associated with leaders, such as fans (FIG. I-1), shields, and umbrellas, protect the leaders both physically and spiritually. Sometimes the regalia and implements of an important person are so heavy they render the leader virtually immobile (FIG. 37-23), suggesting the temporary holder of an office is less significant than the eternal office itself. In African art, leaders not only appear wearing and holding the trappings of their high offices. Artists commonly portrayed them as larger-than-life figures flanked by diminutive attendants (FIGS. I-1 and 19-1) or mounted on undersized horses (FIGS. I-1 and 19-5). Often the leaders, both male and female, have facial scars (FIGS. 19-5, 19-6A, and 19-13) denoting their elevated status in society.

Although leaders' arts are easy to recognize in centralized, hierarchical societies, such as the Benin kingdom (FIGS. I-1, 19-1, 19-13, and 37-13), leaders among less centralized peoples have been no less conversant with the power of art to move people and effect change. For example, African leaders often oversee religious rituals in which they may be less visible than the forms they commission and manipulate: shrines, altars, festivals, and rites of passage such as funerals, the last being especially elaborate and festive in many parts of Africa. The arts that leaders control thus help create pageantry, mystery, and spectacle, enriching and changing the lives of the people.

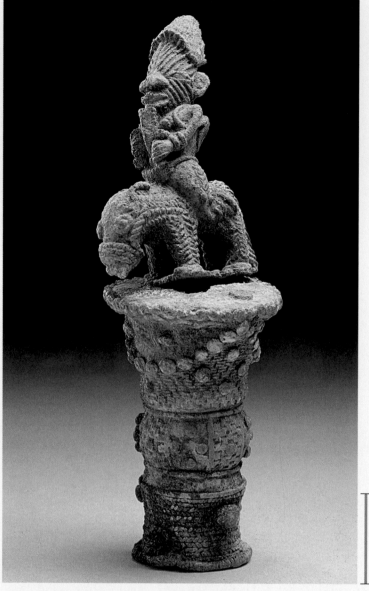

1 in.

19-5 Equestrian figure on fly-whisk hilt, from Igbo Ukwu, Nigeria, 9th to 10th centuries CE. Copper-alloy bronze, figure $6\frac{3}{16}''$ high. National Museum, Lagos. ◼◂

The oldest preserved African lost-wax cast bronze is this fly-whisk hilt, which a leader used to extend his reach and magnify his gestures. The artist exaggerated the size of the ruler compared with his steed.

let, a crown, and a bronze leopard's skull. These items, doubtless the regalia of a leader (see "Art and Leadership in Africa," above), whether secular or religious, are the earliest cast-metal objects known from regions south of the Sahara.

EQUESTRIAN FLY WHISK A lost-wax cast-bronze sculpture (FIG. 19-5), the earliest yet found in Africa, came from the same grave at Igbo Ukwu. It depicts an equestrian figure on a fly-whisk handle. The African artist made the handle using a casting method similar to that documented much earlier in Mesopotamia (FIG. 2-12)

and the Mediterranean (see "Hollow-Casting," Chapter 5, page 130). The sculpture's upper section comprises a figure seated on a horse, a symbol of power in many parts of West Africa, and the lower part is an elaborately embellished handle with beaded and threadlike patterns. As is common in African art, the sculptor intentionally represented the rider as much larger than his steed and also exaggerated the size of the man's head. The prominent facial stripes are another instance of scarification. Here the scars probably are marks of titled status. Similar examples of facial modification can still be found among Igbo-speaking peoples today.

Ruler Portraiture at Ile-Ife

Just after the turn of the 19th century, the German anthropologist Leo Frobenius (1873–1938) "discovered" the sculpture of Ile-Ife in the Lower Niger River region. Because of the refinement and naturalism of the statues and heads he saw, Frobenius, who, like most Europeans, had preconceived notions about the "primitive" nature of African art, could not believe these sculptures were the work of local artists. Rather, he ascribed authorship to ancient Greece, where he knew many instances of similarly lifelike statuary. Other scholars traced the Ile-Ife works to ancient Egypt, along with patterns of sacred kingship they also believed originated several thousand miles away in the Nile Valley. But excavations in and around Ile-Ife, especially near the king's palace, have conclusively established that ancient Nigerian sculptors were indeed the artists who made the extraordinary sculptures in stone, terracotta, and copper alloys found at Ile-Ife. Radiocarbon dating places these works as early as the 11th or 12th century. Most of the finds date to what archaeologists have dubbed the "Pavement Era" of the 12th to 14th centuries, when the Yoruba paved several rectangular areas of their capital at Ile-Ife with bricklike ceramic sherds. These paved precincts were probably ritual centers where the Yoruba displayed the images of their deceased rulers on altars. The sculptures served the kings in ceremonies of installation, in funerals, and in annual festivals reaffirming the sacred power of the ruler and the allegiance of his people.

As is the case with the full-length portrait of the king illustrated here (FIG. 19-6) and the head (FIG. 19-6A) from the royal palace complex, the Ife sculptors usually modeled both heads and bodies in a strikingly naturalistic manner, apart from blemishes or signs of age, which they intentionally omitted. Thus, Ife style is lifelike but at the same time idealized. The artists portrayed most people as young adults in the prime of life and without any disfiguring warts or wrinkles. Some life-size heads, although still idealized, take naturalism so far as to give the impression of being individual portraits. This is especially true of a group of 19 heads cast in copper alloys that scholars are quite certain record the features of specific persons, although nearly all their names are lost. Several of the Ife heads have small holes above the forehead (FIG. 19-6A) and around the lips and jaw, and were found with black beads. The perforations and beads suggest the heads once had beaded crowns with veils, such as those known among Yoruba kings today, and perhaps human hair as well. Elaborate beadwork, a Yoruba royal prerogative, is also a salient feature of the Ife king's image in FIG. 19-6.

The hundreds of terracotta and copper-alloy heads, body parts and fragments, animals, and ritual vessels from Ile-Ife attest to a

19-6 King, from Ita Yemoo (Ife), Nigeria, 11th to 12th centuries. Zinc-brass, 1' 6½" high. Museum of Ife Antiquities, Ife. ◼◀

Unlike most African sculptures, this royal figure has a naturalistically modeled torso and facial features approaching portraiture. The head, however, the locus of wisdom, is disproportionately large.

⌶ 1 in.

remarkable period of African art during which sensitive, meticulously rendered idealized naturalism prevailed. To this day, works in this style stand in vivid contrast to the vast majority of African objects, which show the human figure in many different, quite strongly conventionalized styles. Diversity of style in the art of a continent as vast and ancient as Africa should surprise no one, however.

11TH TO 18TH CENTURIES

Although kings ruled some African population groups from an early date, the best evidence for royal arts in Africa comes from the several centuries between about 1000 and the beginning of European colonization in the 19th century.* During this period, Africans also constructed major houses of worship for the religions of Christianity and Islam, both of which originated in the Middle East but quickly gained adherents south of the Sahara.

*From this point on, all dates in this chapter are CE unless otherwise stated.

Ile-Ife

Africans have long considered Ile-Ife, about 200 miles west of Igbo Ukwu in southwestern Nigeria, the cradle of Yoruba civilization, the place where the gods Oduduwa and Obatala created the earth and its peoples. Tradition also names Oduduwa the first *oni* (ruler) of Ile-Ife and the ancestor of all Yoruba kings.

ILE-IFE KING Ife artists often portrayed their sacred kings in sculpture. One of the most impressive examples is a statuette (FIG. 19-6) of an Ife *oni* (king), cast in a zinc-brass alloy, datable to the 11th or 12th century. This and many similar representations

19-6A Head of a king, Ile-Ife, 12th to 13th centuries. ■◀

of Ife rulers—for example, a 12th- or 13th-century head (FIG. 19-6A) found in the Wunmonije palace complex—are exceptional in Africa because of the artists' naturalism in recording facial features and fleshy anatomy (see "Ruler Portraiture at Ile-Ife," page 527). The naturalism does not extend to body proportions, however. The heads of the Ife rulers, for example, are disproportionately large compared with their bodies. For modern Yoruba, the head is the locus of wisdom, destiny, and the essence of being, and these ideas probably developed at least 800 years ago, accounting for the emphasis on the head in Ife statuary. In the statuette illustrated here, the artist also took great care to indicate the man's status as a sacred ruler by precisely reproducing the details of the king's heavily beaded costume, crown, and jewelry.

TADA SEATED MAN Usually thought to be the work of a sculptor from Ile-Ife but perhaps attesting to an independent artistic center is a statuette (FIG. 19-7) of a seated figure found about 120 miles from the Yoruba capital on the banks of the Niger River near the village of Tada. Although the naturalistic rendition of the head and body of the Tada figure is typical of sculptures (FIGS. 19-6 and 19-6A) found at or near Ile-Ife, the relaxed seated posture is unique. The Tada figure also wears only a simple cap and a patterned fabric wrapped around the hips, and it is unlikely the sculpture portrays a king. The seated posture, however, suggests the figure, cast in several pieces, may have been placed on a throne. It is possible the Yoruba dressed the statue in royal regalia, now lost. Also distinguishing this sculpture from those of Ile-Ife is the more naturalistic proportional relationship between the head and body. The material—almost pure copper—also separates the Tada figure from contemporaneous Ile-Ife sculptures.

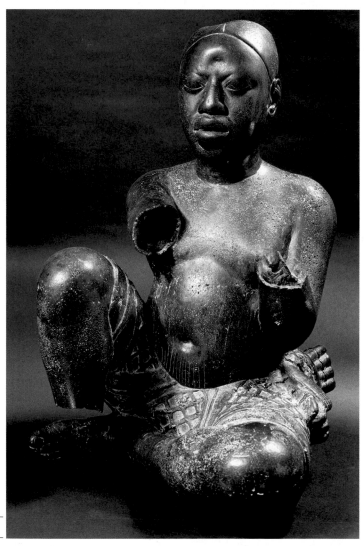

1 in.

19-7 Seated man, from Tada, Nigeria, 13th to 14th centuries. Copper, 1′ 9⅛″ high. National Museum, Lagos.

Although stylistically related to the naturalistic zinc-brass sculptures of Ile-Ife, this unique copper seated figure found 120 miles away may be the product of a distinct regional workshop.

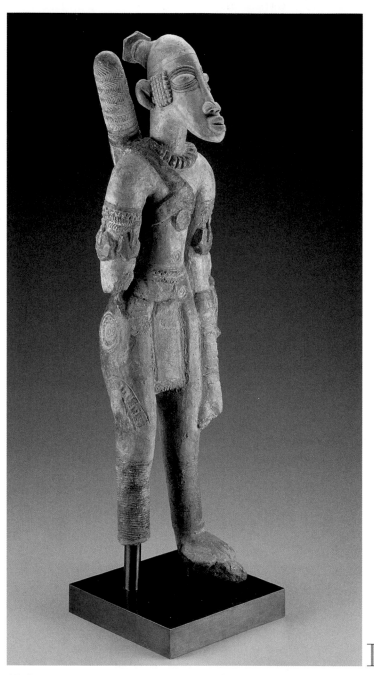

1 in.

19-8 Archer, from Djenne, Mali, 13th to 15th centuries. Terracotta, 2′ ⅜″ high. National Museum of African Art, Washington, D.C.

Djenne terracottas present a striking contrast to statues from Ile-Ife. This archer is thin with tubular limbs and an elongated head featuring a prominent chin, bulging eyes, and large nose.

Discoveries such as this one are reminders of how incomplete is the record of early African art. Additional finds may one day establish whether Ile-Ife was a unique center for the production of naturalistic statuary during the first half of the second millennium or rather one of several stylistically related regional workshops.

Djenne and Lalibela

The inland floodplain of the Niger River was for the African continent a kind of "fertile crescent" analogous to ancient Mesopotamia (see Chapter 2). By about 800, a walled town, Djenne in present-day Mali, had been built on high ground left dry during the flooding season. At this site, archaeologists have uncovered evidence of many specialist workshops of blacksmiths, sculptors, potters, and other artisans.

DJENNE TERRACOTTAS Hundreds of sensitively modeled terracotta sculptures, most dating to between 1100 and 1500, have been found at numerous sites in the Djenne region. Production tapered off sharply, however, with the arrival of Islam, whose adherents shunned figural art in religious contexts (see Chapter 10). Unfortunately, as is true of the Nok terracottas, the vast majority of the surviving Djenne sculptures came from illegal excavations, and all contextual information about them has been destroyed. The subject matter includes male and female couples, people with what some scholars interpret as lesions and swellings, and snake-entwined figures. The Djenne sculptors depicted the human figures in a variety of postures—seated, reclining, kneeling, standing, and on horseback. Some are warriors. Others wear elaborate jewelry, but many are without adornment or attributes. The range of subjects and postures is extraordinary at this date.

The terracotta figure illustrated here (FIG. 19-8) dates to the 13th to 15th centuries and represents a Djenne warrior with a quiver of arrows on his back and knives strapped to his left arm. The proportions of the figure present a striking contrast to those from Ile-Ife and Tada (FIGS. 19-6 and 19-7)—thin and tall with tubular limbs and an elongated head with a prominent chin, bulging eyes, and large nose, characteristic features of the distinctive Djenne style.

GREAT MOSQUE, DJENNE One of the most ambitious examples of *adobe* (sun-dried mud-brick) architecture in the world is at Djenne's Great Mosque (FIG. 19-9), first built in the 13th century and reconstructed in 1906–1907 after a fire destroyed the earlier building in 1830. The mosque has a large courtyard in front of a roofed prayer hall, emulating the plan of many of the oldest mosques known (see "The Mosque," Chapter 10, page 288), and the *qibla* wall faces Mecca, as in all mosques. The facade, however, is unlike any in the Middle East and features soaring adobe towers and vertical buttresses resembling engaged columns that produce a majestic rhythm. The many rows of protruding wooden beams further enliven the walls but also serve a practical function as perches for workers undertaking the essential recoating of sacred clay on the exterior that occurs during an annual festival.

BETA GIORGHIS, LALIBELA Many early African cultures maintained trade networks that sometimes extended well beyond the continent. The exchange of goods also brought an exchange of artistic ideas and forms. One striking example is Lalibela in the rugged highlands of present-day Ethiopia, where land travel is difficult. Christianity arrived in Ethiopia in the early fourth

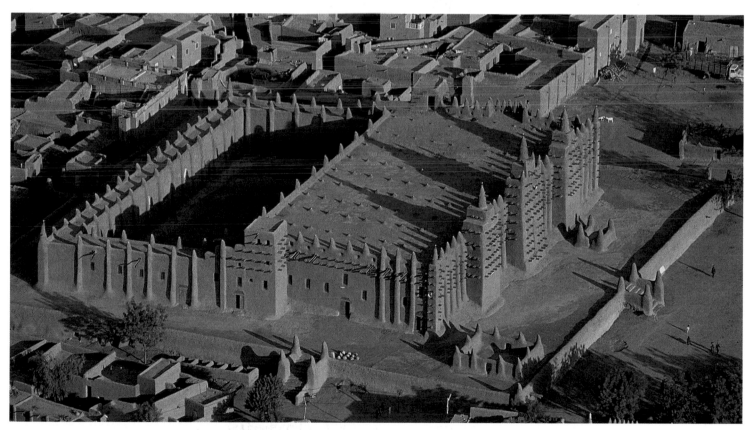

19-9 Aerial view of the Great Mosque (looking northwest), Djenne, Mali, begun 13th century, rebuilt 1906–1907.

The Great Mosque at Djenne resembles Middle Eastern mosques in plan (large courtyard in front of a roofed prayer hall), but the construction materials—adobe and wood—are distinctly African.

19-10 Beta Giorghis (Church of Saint George), Lalibela, Ethiopia, ca. 1220.

The Christian king Lalibela sought to build a New Jerusalem in Ethiopia. The rock-cut church of Saint George emulates Byzantine models and has a Greek-cross plan and internal dome.

century, when the region was part of the indigenous Aksum Empire. In the early 13th century, King Lalibela (r. 1181–1211) of the Zagwe dynasty commissioned 11 churches to be cut from the bedrock at his capital of Roha (renamed Lalibela in his honor after his death). The king wished to transform his city into a "New Jerusalem," a pilgrimage site for Ethiopian Christians, which it still is today. Pilgrims can visit all 11 churches because they are linked by tunnels and walkways below ground level.

Not the largest but probably the latest and in many ways the most interesting of these rock-cut churches is Beta Giorghis (FIG. **19-10**), the Church of Saint George, which Lalibela's stonemasons cut out of the red tufa in the form of a Greek cross, revealing a familiarity with contemporaneous Byzantine architecture (see Chapter 9). About 43 feet tall, the roof of the structure has a 40-by-40-foot Greek cross sculpted in relief, underscoring the sacred shape of the church. Inside is a hollowed-out dome beneath the cruciform roof. Rock-cut buildings are rare but well documented in Egypt, Jordan, and India (see Chapters 3, 7, and 15). Some of the most complex designs are at Lalibela. Carving from the bedrock a complex building such as Beta Giorghis, with all its details, required careful planning and highly skilled labor. The volcanic bedrock is soft and easily worked, but the designer had to visualize all aspects of the complete structure before the work began because there was no possibility of revision or correction.

Great Zimbabwe

Many of the earliest artworks found in Africa come from the southern part of the continent (for example, FIG. 1-3). The most famous southern African site is a complex of stone ruins at the large southeastern political center called Great Zimbabwe. First occupied in the 11th century, the site features walled enclosures and towers dating from about the late 13th to the middle of the 15th centuries. At that time, the Great Zimbabwe Empire had a wide trade network. Finds of beads and pottery from the Near East and China, along with copper and gold objects, underscore that Great Zimbabwe was a prosperous trade center long before Europeans began their coastal voyaging in the late 15th century.

GREAT ENCLOSURE Most scholars agree Great Zimbabwe was a royal residence with special areas for the ruler, his wives, and nobles, including an open court for ceremonial gatherings (the royal hill complex). At the zenith of the empire's power, as many as 18,000 people may have lived in the surrounding area, with most of the commoners residing outside the enclosed complex reserved for royalty. Although the habitations themselves have not survived, the enclosures remain. They are unusual for their size and the excellence of their stonework. Some perimeter walls are 30 feet tall. One of these, known as the Great Enclosure (FIG. **19-11**), houses one large and several small conical, towerlike stone structures, which archaeologists have interpreted symbolically as masculine (large) and feminine (small) forms, but their precise significance is unknown. The form of the large tower suggests a granary. Grain bins were symbols of royal power and generosity, as the ruler received tribute in grain and dispensed it to the people in times of need.

19-11 Walls and tower, Great Enclosure, Great Zimbabwe, Zimbabwe, 14th century.

The Great Zimbabwe Empire in southern Africa had a trade network that extended to Mesopotamia and China. Thirty-foot-high stone walls and conical towers surrounded the royal residence.

SOAPSTONE MONOLITHS Explorations at Great Zimbabwe have yielded eight soapstone *monoliths* (sculptures carved from a single block of stone). Seven came from the royal hill complex and probably stood in shrines to ancestors. The eighth monolith (FIG. **19-12**), found in an area now considered the ancestral shrine of the ruler's first wife, stands several feet tall. Some have interpreted the bird at the top as symbolizing the king or his ancestors. (Ancestral spirits among the present-day Shona-speaking peoples of the area take the form of birds, especially eagles, believed to communicate between the sky and the earth.) The crocodile on the front of the monolith may represent the wife's elder male ancestors. The circles beneath the bird are called "eyes of the crocodile" in Shona and may symbolically represent elder female ancestors. The double- and single-chevron motifs may stand for young male and young female ancestors, respectively. The bird seems to be a bird of prey, such as an eagle, but this and other bird sculptures from the site have feet with five humanlike toes, rather than an eagle's three-toed talons. The Great Zimbabwe birds are of no known species, and some scholars have speculated the five-toed bird and the crocodile symbolize previous rulers who would have acted as messengers between the living and the dead, as well as between the sky and the earth.

Benin

According to oral tradition, the first Benin king in the 13th century was the grandson of a Yoruba king of Ile-Ife. Benin reached its greatest power and geographical extent in the 16th century. The kingdom's vicissitudes and slow decline thereafter culminated in 1897, when the British burned and sacked the Benin palace and city. Benin City thrives today, however, and the palace, where the Benin king continues to live, has been partially rebuilt. In addition to expertly cast copper-alloy sculptures (FIGS. I-1 and 19-1), Benin artists have produced sophisticated artworks in ivory, wood, ceramic, and wrought iron. The hereditary oba and his court still use and dispense art objects as royal favors to title holders and other chiefs (see "Art and Leadership," page 526).

QUEEN MOTHER IVORY Among the masterworks of Benin art are the cast-brass altar (FIG. 19-1) honoring Oba Eresonyen, already discussed, and an extraordinary ivory head of a woman, now in the Metropolitan Museum of Art (FIG. **19-13**), which a Benin king almost certainly wore at his waist. A nearly identical pendant, fashioned from the same piece of ivory, is in the British Museum. Oba Esigie (r. ca. 1504–1550), under whom the Benin kingdom flourished and expanded with Portuguese aid, probably commissioned the pair.

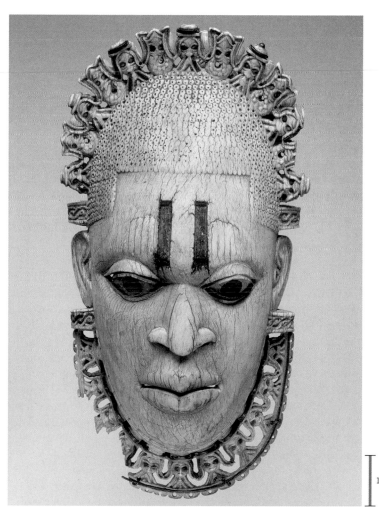

1 in.

19-12 Monolith with bird and crocodile, from Great Zimbabwe, Zimbabwe, 15th century. Soapstone, bird 1' 2½" high. Great Zimbabwe Site Museum, Great Zimbabwe.

This soapstone monolith stood in the ancestral shrine of a Great Zimbabwe ruler's wife. The bird and crocodile may symbolize previous rulers who act as messengers between the living and dead.

1 in.

19-13 Waist pendant of a queen mother, from Benin, Nigeria, ca. 1520. Ivory and iron, 9⅜" high. Metropolitan Museum of Art, New York (Michael C. Rockefeller Memorial Collection, gift of Nelson A. Rockefeller, 1972).

This head probably portrays Idia, mother of Oba Esigie, who wore it on his waist. Above Idia's head are Portuguese heads and mudfish, symbols of trade and of the sea god Olokun.

Esigie's mother, Idia, helped him in warfare, and in return he created for her the title of Queen Mother, *iy'oba*, and built her a separate palace and court. He and his successors also set up altars to their mothers on which they displayed bronze portraits (for example, FIG. **19-13A**) of them.

The ivory pendant illustrated here (FIG. 19-13) most likely represents Idia and is remarkable for its sensitive naturalism. On its crown are alternating bearded Portuguese heads and mudfish, symbolic references respectively to Benin's trade and diplomatic relationships with the Portuguese and to Olokun, god of the sea, wealth, and creativity. The mudfish, equally at home on land and in the sea, also symbolized the dual human/divine aspect of the ruler. Another series of Portuguese heads adorns the lower part of the carving. In the late 15th and 16th centuries, the Benin people probably associated the Portuguese, with their large ships from across the sea, their powerful weapons, and their wealth in metals, cloth, and other goods, with Olokun, the deity they deemed responsible for abundance and prosperity.

Sapi

Between 1490 and 1540, some peoples on the Atlantic coast of Africa in present-day Sierra Leone, whom the Portuguese collectively called the Sapi, created art not only for themselves but also for Portuguese explorers and traders, who brought the objects back to Europe.

SAPI SALTCELLARS The Portuguese commissions included delicate spoons, forks, and elaborate containers usually referred to as saltcellars, as well as boxes, hunting horns, and knife handles. Salt was a valuable commodity, used both as a flavoring and as a food preservative. Costly saltcellars were prestige items that graced the tables of the European elite (compare FIG. 22-52). Sapi sculptors meticulously carved the saltcellars from elephant tusk ivory, which was plentiful in those early days and was one of the coveted exports in early West and Central African trade with Europe. The ivories the Sapi produced for export are a fascinating hybrid art form. Characterized by refined detail and careful finish, they are the earliest examples of African tourist art.

Art historians have attributed the saltcellar shown here (FIG. **19-14**), almost 17 inches high, to the MASTER OF THE SYMBOLIC EXECUTION, one of the three major Sapi ivory carvers during the period. This saltcellar, which depicts an execution scene, is one of the artist's best pieces and the source of the assigned name. A kneeling figure with a shield in one hand holds an ax (restored) in the other hand over another seated figure about to lose his head. On the ground before the executioner, six severed heads grimly testify to the executioner's power. A double zigzag line separates the lid of the globular container from the rest of the vessel. This vessel rests in turn on a circular platform held up by slender rods adorned with crocodile images. Two male and two female figures sit between these rods, grasping them. The men wear European-style pants and have long, straight hair. The women wear skirts, and the elaborate raised patterns on their upper chests surely represent decorative scars.

The European components of this saltcellar are the overall design of a spherical container on a pedestal and some of the geometric patterning on the base and the sphere, as well as certain elements of dress, such as the shirts and hats. Distinctly African are the style of the human heads and figures and their proportions, the latter skewed here to emphasize the head, as so often seen in African art. Identical large noses with flaring nostrils, as well as the conventions for rendering eyes and lips, characterize Sapi stone figures

19-14 MASTER OF THE SYMBOLIC EXECUTION, saltcellar, Sapi-Portuguese, from Sierra Leone, ca. 1490–1540. Ivory, 1′ 4⅞″ high. Museo Nazionale Preistorico e Etnografico Luigi Pigorini, Rome.

The Sapi exported saltcellars combining African and Portuguese traits. This one represents an execution scene with an African-featured man wearing European pants seated among severed heads.

from the same region and period. Scholars do not know whether it was the African carver or the European patron who specified the subject matter and the configurations of various parts, but the Sapi works testify to a fruitful artistic interaction between Africans and Europeans during the early 16th century.

The impact of European art became much more pronounced in the late 19th and especially the 20th centuries. These developments and the continuing vitality of the native arts in Africa are examined in Chapter 37.

AFRICA BEFORE 1800

PREHISTORY, CA. 25,000–1000 BCE

▌ Humankind apparently originated in Africa, and some of the oldest known artworks come from the Apollo 11 Cave (FIG. 1-3) in southwestern Africa. Most African rock art, however, is no earlier than 6000 BCE. Some of the oldest examples are at Tassili n'Ajjer in northwestern Africa.

Running woman, Tassili n'Ajjer,
ca. 6000–4000 BCE

EARLY CULTURES, CA. 1000 BCE–1000 CE

▌ The Nok culture of central Nigeria produced the oldest African examples of sculpture in the round between 500 BCE and 200 CE. The pierced eyes, noses, and mouths helped equalize the heat during the firing process.

▌ The earliest examples of African bronze-casting using the lost-wax method are the 9th- or 10th-century CE sculptures found at Igbo Ukwu (Nigeria).

Nok terracotta head,
ca. 500 BCE–200 CE

11TH TO 15TH CENTURIES

▌ The sculptors of Ile-Ife (Nigeria) fashioned images of their kings in an unusually naturalistic style during the 11th and 12th centuries, but the heads of the figures are disproportionately large, as in most African artworks.

▌ The terracotta sculptures of Djenne (Mali), datable about 1100–1500, encompass an extraordinary variety of subjects, including warriors and equestrian figures. They display a distinctive style featuring tubular limbs and elongated heads.

Ife king, 11th to 12th centuries

▌ In northern Africa, converts to Islam and Christianity constructed major religious shrines that emulated foreign models but employed different building materials and methods, for example, the adobe Great Mosque at Djenne and the rock-cut church of Beta Giorghis (Saint George) at Lalibela (Ethiopia).

▌ In southern Africa, the Great Zimbabwe Empire conducted prosperous trade with Mesopotamia and China long before the first contact with Europeans. Impressive stone walls and towers enclosed the royal palace complex.

Great Mosque, Djenne, 13th century

16TH TO 18TH CENTURIES

▌ The Benin kingdom in the Lower Niger region, probably founded in the 13th century, reached its zenith in the 16th century. Benin sculptors excelled in ivory carving and bronze-casting, producing artworks that glorified the royal family.

▌ An early example of the interaction between African artists and European patrons is the series of Sapi ivory saltcellars from Sierra Leone datable between 1490 and 1540.

Benin altar to the hand,
ca. 1735–1750

NOTES

Introduction

1. Quoted in George Heard Hamilton, *Painting and Sculpture in Europe, 1880–1940,* 6th ed. (New Haven, Conn.: Yale University Press, 1993), 345.
2. Quoted in *Josef Albers: Homage to the Square* (New York: Museum of Modern Art, 1964), n.p.

Chapter 2

1. Translated by Françoise Tallon, in Prudence O. Harper et al., *The Royal City of Susa* (New York: Metropolitan Museum of Art, 1991), 132.

Chapter 3

1. The chronology adopted in this chapter is that of John Baines and Jaromír Malék, *Atlas of Ancient Egypt* (Oxford: Oxford University Press, 1980), 36–37. The division of kingdoms is that of, among others, Mark Lehner, *The Complete Pyramids* (New York: Thames & Hudson, 1997), 89, and David P. Silverman, ed., *Ancient Egypt* (New York: Oxford University Press, 1997), 20–39.
2. Translated by James P. Allen, *The Ancient Egyptian Pyramid Texts* (Atlanta, Ga.: Society of Biblical Literature, 2005), 31.
3. Allen, 57.
4. Allen, 56.

Chapter 4

1. Homer, *Iliad,* 2.466–649.

Chapter 5

1. Diodorus Siculus, *Library of History,* 1.91.
2. Pausanias, *Description of Greece,* 5.16.1.
3. Plutarch, *Life of Pericles,* 12.
4. Pliny, *Natural History,* 34.74.
5. Ibid., 36.20.
6. Lucian, *Amores,* 13–14; *Imagines,* 6.
7. Plutarch, *Moralia,* 335A–B. Translated by J. J. Pollitt, *The Art of Ancient Greece: Sources and Documents* (New York: Cambridge University Press, 1990), 99.
8. Pliny, *Natural History,* 35.110.
9. Ibid., 34.88.

Chapter 7

1. Livy, *History of Rome,* 25.40.1–3.
2. Juvenal, *Satires,* 3.225, 232.

Chapter 8

1. Translated by Raymond Davis, *The Book of Pontiffs* (Liverpool: Liverpool University Press, 1989), 18–19.

Chapter 9

1. Paulus Silentiarius, *Descriptio Sanctae Sophiae,* 617–646. Translated by Cyril Mango, *The Art of the Byzantine Empire, 312–1453: Sources and Documents* (reprint of 1972 ed., Toronto: University of Toronto Press, 1986), 85–86.
2. Procopius, *De aedificiis,* 1.1.23ff. Translated by Mango, 74.
3. Paulus Silentiarius, *Descriptio,* 489, 668. Translated by Mango, 83, 86.
4. Translated by Colin Luibheid, *Pseudo-Dionysius: The Complete Works* (New York: Paulist Press, 1987), 68ff.
5. Procopius, 1.1.23ff. Translated by Mango, 75.
6. *Libri Carolini,* 4.2. Translated by Herbert L. Kessler, *Spiritual Seeing: Picturing God's Invisibility in Medieval Art* (Philadelphia: University of Pennsylvania Press, 2000), 119.
7. Nina G. Garsoïan, "Later Byzantium," in John A. Garraty and Peter Gay, eds., *The Columbia History of the World* (New York: Harper & Row, 1972), 453.
8. Garsoïan, 460.

Chapter 11

1. Translated by Françoise Henry, *The Book of Kells* (New York: Alfred A. Knopf, 1974), 165.
2. *Beowulf,* 3162–3164. Translated by Kevin Crossley-Holland (New York: Farrar, Straus & Giroux, 1968), 119.
3. *Beowulf,* 33.
4. Translated by John W. Williams, in *The Art of Medieval Spain A.D. 500–1200* (New York: Metropolitan Museum of Art, 1993), 156.
5. Translated by Adam S. Cohen, *The Uta Codex* (University Park: Pennsylvania University Press, 2000), 11, 41.

Chapter 12

1. Translated by Calvin B. Kendall, *The Allegory of the Church: Romanesque Portals and Their Verse Inscriptions* (Toronto: University of Toronto Press, 1998), 207.
2. Translated by John Williams, *A Spanish Apocalypse: The Morgan Beatus Manuscript* (New York: George Braziller, 1991), 223.
3. Translated by Charles P. Parkhurst Jr., in Elizabeth G. Holt, *A Documentary History of Art* (Princeton, N.J.: Princeton University Press, 2d ed., 1981), 1: 18.
4. Translated by Giovanna De Appolonia, Boston University.
5. Bernard of Clairvaux, *Apologia* 12.28. Translated by Conrad Rudolph, *The "Things of Greater Importance": Bernard of Clairvaux's Apologia and the Medieval Attitude toward Art* (Philadelphia: University of Pennsylvania Press, 1990), 281, 283.
6. *Rule of Saint Benedict,* 57.1. Translated by Timothy Fry, *The Rule of St. Benedict* (Collegeville, Minn.: Liturgical Press, 1981), 265.

Chapter 13

1. Giorgio Vasari, "Introduzione alle tre arti del disegno" (1550), ch. 3, in Paul Frankl, *The Gothic: Literary Sources and Interpretation through Eight Centuries* (Princeton, N.J.: Princeton University Press, 1960), 290–291, 859–860.
2. Dante, *Divine Comedy,* Purgatory, 11.81.
3. Translated by Roland Behrendt, *Johannes Trithemius, In Praise of Scribes: De laude scriptorum* (Lawrence, Kansas: Coronado Press, 1974), 71.
4. Frankl, *The Gothic,* 55.

GLOSSARY

abacus—The uppermost portion of the *capital* of a *column,* usually a thin slab. (116)

abbess—See *abbey.* (322)

abbey—A religious community under the direction of an abbot (for monks) or an abbess (for nuns). (322)

abbot—See *abbey.* (322)

abhaya—See *mudra.* (427)

abrasion—The rubbing or grinding of stone or another material to produce a smooth finish (64)

abstract—Non-representational; forms and colors arranged without reference to the depiction of an object. (5)

acropolis—Greek, "high city." In ancient Greece, usually the site of the city's most important temple(s). (117)

additive light—Natural light, or sunlight, the sum of all the wavelengths of the visible *spectrum.* See also *subtractive light* (7)

additive sculpture—A kind of sculpture *technique* in which materials (for example, clay) are built up or "added" to create form. (11)

adobe—The clay used to make a kind of sundried mud brick of the same name; a building made of such brick. (508, 529)

agora—An open square or space used for public meetings or business in ancient Greek cities. (138)

aisle—The portion of a *basilica* flanking the *nave* and separated from it by a row of *columns* or *piers.* (12, 189, 243)

ala (pl. alae)—One of a pair of rectangular recesses at the back of the *atrium* of a Roman house. (190)

album leaf—A painting on a single sheet of paper for a collection stored in an album. (459)

altar frontal—A decorative panel on the front of a church altar. (367)

altarpiece—A panel, painted or sculpted, situated above and behind an altar. (392, 404)

alternate-support system—In church architecture, the use of alternating wall supports in the *nave,* usually *piers* and *columns* or *compound piers* of alternating form. (324)

amalaka—In Hindu temple design, the large flat disk with ribbed edges surmounting the beehive-shaped tower (*shikara*). (439)

Amazonomachy—In Greek mythology, the battle between the Greeks and Amazons. (136)

ambo—A church *pulpit* for biblical readings. (392)

ambulatory—A covered walkway, outdoors (as in a church *cloister*) or indoors; especially the passageway around the *apse* and the *choir* of a church. In Buddhist architecture, the passageway leading around the *stupa* in a *chaitya hall.* (244, 430)

amphiprostyle—A *classical* temple *plan* in which the *columns* are placed across both the front and back but not along the sides. (115)

amphitheater—Greek, "double theater." A Roman building type resembling two Greek theaters put together. The Roman amphitheater featured a continuous elliptical *cavea* around a central *arena.* (189, 401)

amphora—An ancient Greek two-handled jar used for general storage purposes, usually to hold wine or oil. (110)

amulet—An object worn to ward off evil or to aid the wearer. (61)

antae—The molded projecting ends of the walls forming the *pronaos* or *opisthodomos* of an ancient Greek temple. (115)

ante legem—Latin, "before the law." In Christian thought, the period before Moses received the Ten Commandments. See also *sub lege.* (392)

apadana—The great audience hall in ancient Persian palaces. (51)

apostle—Greek, "messenger." One of the 12 disciples of Jesus. (240)

apotheosis—Elevated to the rank of gods, or the ascent to heaven. (206, 18-10A)

apotropaic—Capable of warding off evil. (118)

apoxyomenos—Greek, "athlete scraping oil from his body." (147)

apse—A recess, usually semicircular, in the wall of a building, commonly found at the east end of a church. (28, 134, 208, 243, 413)

apsidal—Rounded; *apse*-shaped. (429)

arcade—A series of *arches* supported by *piers* or *columns.* (52, 243, 287, 290, 413)

arch—A curved structural member that spans an opening and is generally composed of wedge-shaped blocks (*voussoirs*) that transmit the downward pressure laterally. See also *thrust.* (48, 12-10A)

Archaic—The artistic style of 600–480 BCE in Greece, characterized in part by the use of the *composite view* for painted and *relief* figures and of Egyptian stances for statues. (111)

Archaic smile—The smile that appears on all *Archaic* Greek statues from about 570 to 480 BCE. The smile is the Archaic sculptor's way of indicating that the person portrayed is alive. (112)

architrave—The *lintel* or lowest division of the *entablature;* also called the epistyle. (116)

archivolt—The continuous molding framing an *arch.* In *Romanesque* and *Gothic* architecture, one of the series of concentric bands framing the *tympanum.* (344)

arcuated—*Arch*-shaped. (48, 175, 206)

arena—In a Roman *amphitheater,* the central area where bloody *gladiatorial* combats and other boisterous events took place. (189)

armature—The crossed, or diagonal, *arches* that form the skeletal framework of a *Gothic rib vault.* In sculpture, the framework for a clay form. (11, 368)

arriccio—In *fresco* painting, the first layer of rough lime plaster applied to the wall. (408)

asceticism—Self-discipline and self-denial. (427)

ashlar masonry—Carefully cut and regularly shaped blocks of stone used in construction, fitted together without mortar. (62)

atlantid—A male figure that functions as a supporting *column.* See also *caryatid.* (72, 506)

atlatl—Spear-thrower, the typical weapon of the Toltecs of ancient Mexico. (506)

atmospheric perspective—See *perspective.* (194)

atrium—The central reception room of a Roman house that is partly open to the sky. Also the open, *colonnaded* court in front of and attached to a Christian *basilica.* (190, 243)

attic—The uppermost story of a building, *triumphal arch,* or city gate. (201)

attribute—(n.) The distinctive identifying aspect of a person, for example, an object held, an associated animal, or a mark on the body. (v.) To make an *attribution.* (5)

attribution—Assignment of a work to a maker or makers. (6)

augur—A Roman priest who determined the will of the gods from the flight of birds and whose attribute is the *lituus.* (165)

avatar—A manifestation of a deity incarnated in some visible form in which the deity performs a sacred function on earth. In Hinduism, an incarnation of a god. (435)

axial plan—See *plan*. (72)

axis mundi—Latin, "axis of the universe." In South Asia, a tall pillar planted deep in the ground, connecting earth and sky. (15-6A)

backstrap loom—A simple Andean loom featuring a belt or backstrap encircling the waist of the seated weaver. (510)

baldacchino—A canopy on *columns*, frequently built over an altar. (243)

baptism—The Christian bathing ceremony in which an infant or a convert becomes a member of the Christian community. (236)

baptistery—In Christian architecture, the building used for *baptism*, usually situated next to a church. Also, the designated area or hall within a church for baptismal rites. (236)

bar tracery—See *tracery*. (375)

baray—One of the large reservoirs laid out around Cambodian *wats* that served as means of transportation as well as irrigation. A network of canals connected the reservoirs. (444)

barrel vault—See *vault*. (184, 338)

base—In ancient Greek architecture, the molded projecting lowest part of *Ionic* and *Corinthian* *columns*. (*Doric* columns do not have bases.) (51, 116)

basilica (adj. **basilican**)—In Roman architecture, a public building for legal and other civic proceedings, rectangular in plan with an entrance usually on a long side. In Christian architecture, a church somewhat resembling the Roman basilica, usually entered from one end and with an *apse* at the other. (189, 413)

bas-relief—See *relief*. (12)

battlement—A low parapet at the top of a circuit wall in a fortification. (382, 416)

bay—The space between two columns, or one unit in the *nave arcade* of a church; also, the passageway in an *arcuated* gate. (411, 413, 457)

beam—A horizontal structural member that carries the load of the superstructure of a building; a timber *lintel*. (457)

begging bowl—The bowl Buddhist monks use to collect alms, either money or food. (486)

ben-ben—A pyramidal stone; an emblem of the Egyptian god Re. (57, 61)

benedictional—A Christian religious book containing bishops' blessings. (312)

bent-axis plan—A *plan* that incorporates two or more angular changes of direction, characteristic of Sumerian architecture. (33)

bestiary—A collection of illustrations of real and imaginary animals. (343)

bhumisparsha—See *mudra*. (427)

bi—In ancient China, jade disks carved as ritual objects for burial with the dead. They were often decorated with piercings that extended entirely through the object, as well as with surface carvings. (453, 454)

bichrome—Two-color. (511)

bilateral symmetry—Having the same *forms* on either side of a central axis. (64)

bilingual vases—Experimental Greek vases produced for a short time in the late sixth century BCE; one side featured *black-figure* decoration, the other *red-figure*. (121)

black-figure painting—In early Greek pottery, the silhouetting of dark figures against a light background of natural, reddish clay, with linear details cut into the surface through the silhouettes. (111)

blind arcade—An *arcade* having no true openings, applied as decoration to a wall surface. (52, 290)

block statue—In ancient Egyptian sculpture, a cubic stone image with simplified body parts. (74)

bodhisattva—In Buddhist thought, a potential Buddha who chooses not to achieve enlightenment in order to help save humanity. (427)

Book of Hours—A Christian religious book for private devotion containing prayers to be read at specified times of the day. (312)

boshan—A Chinese incense burner. (455, 16-6A)

boss—A circular knob. (426)

breviary—A Christian religious book of selected daily prayers and Psalms. (312, 386, 550)

bucranium (pl. **bucrania**)—Latin, "bovine skull." A common motif in classical architectural ornament. (1-16A)

Buddha triad—A three-figure group with a central Buddha flanked on each side by a *bodhisattva*. (475)

buon fresco—See *fresco*. (408)

bust—A freestanding sculpture of the head, shoulders, and chest of a person. (12)

buttress—An exterior masonry structure that opposes the lateral *thrust* of an *arch* or a *vault*. A pier buttress is a solid mass of masonry. A flying buttress consists typically of an inclined member carried on an arch or a series of arches and a solid buttress to which it transmits lateral thrust. (184)

Byzantine—The art, territory, history, and culture of the Eastern Christian Empire and its capital of Constantinople (ancient Byzantium). (256)

caduceus—In ancient Greek mythology, a magical rod entwined with serpents, the attribute of Hermes (Roman, Mercury), the messenger of the gods. (107)

caldarium—The hot-bath section of a Roman bathing establishment. (220)

caliph(s)—Islamic rulers, regarded as successors of Muhammad. (285)

calligrapher—One who practices *calligraphy*. (294, 466)

calligraphy—Greek, "beautiful writing." Handwriting or penmanship, especially elegant writing as a decorative art. (294, 466)

came—A lead strip in a *stained-glass* window that joins separate pieces of colored glass. (375)

campanile—A bell tower of a church, usually, but not always, freestanding. (350, 416)

canon—A rule, for example, of proportion. The ancient Greeks considered beauty to be a matter of "correct" proportion and sought a canon of proportion, for the human figure and for buildings. The fifth-century BCE sculptor Polykleitos wrote the *Canon*, a treatise incorporating his formula for the perfectly proportioned statue. (10, 66)

canon table—A concordance, or matching, of the corresponding passages of the four *Gospels* as compiled by Eusebius of Caesarea in the fourth century. (312)

canonized—Declared a saint by the Catholic Church. (354, 14-5A)

canopic jar—In ancient Egypt, the container in which the organs of the deceased were placed for later burial with the mummy. (61)

capital—The uppermost member of a *column*, serving as a transition from the *shaft* to the *lintel*. In *classical* architecture, the form of the capital varies with the *order*. (51, 60, 116, 402, 429)

Capitolium—An ancient Roman temple dedicated to the gods Jupiter, Juno, and Minerva. (189)

caput mundi—Latin, "head (capital) of the world." (180)

cardo—The north-south street in a Roman town, intersecting the *decumanus* at right angles. (189)

Caroline minuscule—The alphabet that *Carolingian* scribes perfected, from which the modern English alphabet was developed. (317)

Carolingian (adj.)—Pertaining to the empire of Charlemagne (Latin, "Carolus Magnus") and his successors. (317)

carpet page—In early medieval manuscripts, a decorative page resembling a textile. (311)

cartography—The art of mapmaking. (13-38B)

cartoon—In painting, a full-size preliminary drawing from which a painting is made. (408)

carving—A *technique* of sculpture in which the artist cuts away material (for example, from a stone block) in order to create a *statue* or a *relief*. (11)

caryatid—A female figure that functions as a supporting *column*. See also *atlantid*. (72, 117)

castellum—See *westwork*. (323)

casting—A sculptural *technique* in which the artist pours liquid metal, plaster, clay, or another material into a *mold*. When the material dries, the sculptor removes the cast piece from the mold. (11)

castrum—A Roman military encampment. (207)

catacombs—Subterranean networks of rock-cut galleries and chambers designed as cemeteries for the burial of the dead. (237)

cathedra—Latin, "seat." See *cathedral*. (350)

cathedral—A bishop's church. The word derives from *cathedra*, referring to the bishop's chair. (350, 412)

cavea—Latin, "hollow place or cavity." The seating area in ancient Greek and Roman theaters and *amphitheaters*. (151, 189)

celadon—A Chinese-Korean pottery *glaze*, fired in an oxygen-deprived kiln to a characteristic gray-green or pale blue color. (472)

cella—The chamber at the center of an ancient temple; in a *classical* temple, the room (Greek, *naos*) in which the *cult statue* usually stood. (33, 115)

celt—In Olmec Mexico, an ax-shaped form made of polished jade; generally, a prehistoric metal or stone implement shaped like a chisel or ax head. (494)

centaur—In ancient Greek mythology, a creature with the front or top half of a human and the back or bottom half of a horse. (105)

centauromachy—In ancient Greek mythology, the battle between the Greeks and *centaurs*. (120)

central plan—See *plan*. (244, 288)

cestrum—A small spatula used in *encaustic* painting. (218)

chacmool—A *Mesoamerican* statuary type depicting a fallen warrior on his back with a receptacle on his chest for sacrificial offerings. (491)

chaitya hall—A South Asian rock-cut temple hall having a votive *stupa* at one end. (429)

chakra—The Buddha's wheel, set in motion at Sarnath. (423, 429)

chakravartin—In South Asia, the ideal king, the Universal Lord who ruled through goodness. (429)

Chan—See *Zen*. (470)

chancel arch—The arch separating the chancel (the *apse* or *choir*) or the *transept* from the *nave* of a basilica or church. (228, 243, 413)

chantry—An endowed chapel for the chanting of the mass for the founder of the chapel. (13-42A)

chaplet—A metal pin used in hollow-casting to connect the *investment* with the clay core. (130)

characters—In Chinese writing, signs that record spoken words. (450)

charun—An Etruscan death demon. (176)

chatra—See *yasti*. (430)

chiaroscuro—In drawing or painting, the treatment and use of light and dark, especially the gradations of light that produce the effect of *modeling*. (409)

chigi—Decorative extensions of the *rafters* at each end of the roof of a Japanese shrine. (480)

chimera—A monster of Greek invention with the head and body of a lion and the tail of a serpent. A second head, that of a goat, grows out of one side of the body. (174)

chisel—A tool with a straight blade at one end for cutting and shaping stone or wood. (18)

chiton—A Greek tunic, the essential (and often only) garment of both men and women, the other being the *himation*, or mantle. (115)

choir—The space reserved for the clergy and singers in the church, usually east of the *transept* but, in some instances, extending into the *nave*. (12, 264)

Christ—Savior. (240)

Christogram—The three initial letters (chi-rho-iota, or ☧) of Christ's name in Greek, which came to serve as a monogram for Christ. (230, 264, 307)

chronology—In art history, the dating of art objects and buildings. (2)

chryselephantine—Fashioned of gold and ivory. (94)

circumambulation—In Buddhist worship, walking around the *stupa* in a clockwise direction, a process intended to bring the worshiper into harmony with the cosmos. (430)

cire perdue—See *lost-wax process*. (130, 507)

cista (pl. **cistae**)—An Etruscan cylindrical container made of sheet bronze with cast handles and feet, often with elaborately engraved bodies, used for women's toiletry articles. (175)

city-state—An independent, self-governing city. (31, 406)

Classical—The art and culture of ancient Greece between 480 and 323 BCE. Lowercase *classical* refers more generally to Greco-Roman art and culture. (402)

clerestory—The *fenestrated* part of a building that rises above the roofs of the other parts. The oldest known clerestories are Egyptian. In Roman *basilicas* and medieval churches, clerestories are the windows that form the *nave*'s uppermost level below the timber ceiling or the *vaults*. (73, 184, 243, 373, 413)

cloison—French, "partition." A cell made of metal wire or a narrow metal strip soldered edge-up to a metal base to hold *enamel*, semi-precious stones, pieces of colored glass, or glass paste fired to resemble sparkling jewels. (310)

cloisonné—A decorative metalwork technique employing *cloisons*; also, decorative brickwork in later Byzantine architecture. (271, 310)

cloister—A *monastery* courtyard, usually with covered walks or *ambulatories* along its sides. (322, 341)

cluster pier—See *compound pier*. (340, 373, 12-4A, 14-12A)

codex (pl. **codices**)—Separate pages of *vellum* or *parchment* bound together at one side; the predecessor of the modern book. The codex superseded the *rotulus*. In *Mesoamerica*, a painted and inscribed book on long sheets of bark paper or deerskin coated with fine white plaster and folded into accordion-like pleats. (249)

coffer—A sunken panel, often ornamental, in a *vault* or a ceiling. (210)

collage—A composition made by combining on a flat surface various materials, such as newspaper, wallpaper, printed text and illustrations, photographs, and cloth. (8)

colonnade—A series or row of *columns*, usually spanned by *lintels*. (70)

colonnette—A thin *column*. (194, 290)

colophon—An inscription, usually on the last page, giving information about a book's manufacture. In Chinese painting, written texts on attached pieces of paper or silk. (312)

color—The value, or tonality, of a color is the degree of its lightness or darkness. The intensity, or saturation, of a color is its purity, its brightness or dullness. See also *primary colors, secondary colors,* and *complementary colors*. (7)

column—A vertical, weight-carrying architectural member, circular in cross-*section* and consisting of a *base* (sometimes omitted), a *shaft*, and a *capital*. (10, 51, 402)

complementary colors—Those pairs of *colors*, such as red and green, that together embrace the entire *spectrum*. The complement of one of the three *primary colors* is a mixture of the other two. (7)

compose—See *composition*. (7, 21, 38)

Composite capital—A capital combining *Ionic* volutes and *Corinthian* acanthus leaves, first used by the ancient Romans. (206)

composite view—A convention of representation in which part of a figure is shown in profile and another part of the same figure is shown frontally; also called twisted perspective. (23, 523)

composition—The way in which an artist organizes *forms* in an artwork, either by placing shapes on a flat surface or arranging forms in space. (7, 21, 38)

compound pier—A *pier* with a group, or cluster, of attached *shafts,* or *responds,* especially characteristic of *Gothic* architecture. (340, 373, 12-4A, 14-12A)

conceptual representation—The representation of the fundamental distinguishing properties of a person or object, not the way a figure or object appears in space and light at a specific moment. See *composite view*. (35)

concrete—A building material invented by the Romans and consisting of various proportions of lime mortar, volcanic sand, water, and small stones. (184)

confraternity—In Late Antiquity, an association of Christian families pooling funds to purchase property for burial. In late medieval Europe, an organization founded by laypersons who dedicated themselves to strict religious observances. (237, 404)

congregational mosque—A city's main *mosque*, designed to accommodate the entire Muslim (believers in Islam) population for the Friday noonday prayer. Also called the great mosque or Friday mosque. (288)

connoisseur—An expert in *attributing* artworks to one artist rather than another. More generally, an expert on artistic *style*. (6)

consuls—In the Roman Republic, the two chief magistrates. (181)

continuous narration—The depiction of the same figure more than once in the same space at different stages of a story. (7-44A)

contour line—In art, a continuous line defining the outer shape of an object. (7)

contrapposto—The disposition of the human figure in which one part is turned in opposition to another part (usually hips and legs one way, shoulders and chest another), creating a counterpositioning of the body about its central axis. Sometimes called "weight shift" because the weight of the body tends to be thrown to one foot, creating tension on one side and relaxation on the other. (129)

corbel—A projecting wall member used as a support for some element in the superstructure. Also, *courses* of stone or brick in which each course projects beyond the one beneath it. Two such walls, meeting at the topmost course, create a corbeled *arch* or corbeled *vault*. (416)

corbeled arch—An *arch* formed by the piling of stone blocks in horizontal *courses*, cantilevered inward until the blocks meet at a *keystone*. (99)

corbeled vault—A *vault* formed by the piling of stone blocks in horizontal *courses*, cantilevered inward until the two walls meet in an *arch*. (27, 99)

Corinthian capital—A more ornate form than *Doric* or *Ionic*; it consists of a double row of acanthus leaves from which tendrils and flowers grow, wrapped around a bell-shaped *echinus*. Although this *capital* form is often cited as the distinguishing feature of the Corinthian *order*, no such order exists, in strict terms, but only this type of capital used in the *Ionic* order. (151, 402)

cornice—The projecting, crowning member of the *entablature* framing the *pediment*; also, any crowning projection. (116)

corona civica—Latin, "civic crown." A Roman honorary wreath worn on the head. (7)

course—In masonry construction, a horizontal row of stone blocks. (28, 62)

crenel—See *crenellation*. (382)

crenellation—Alternating solid merlons and open crenels in the notched tops of walls, as in *battlements*. (382)

crossing—The space in a *cruciform* church formed by the intersection of the *nave* and the *transept*. (246, 323, 14-18A)

cross vault—See *vault*. (184)

crossing square—The area in a church formed by the intersection (*crossing*) of a *nave* and a *transept* of equal width, often used as a standard *module* of interior proportion. (323)

crossing tower—The tower over the *crossing* of a church. (246)

cruciform—Cross-shaped. (246)

Crusades—In medieval Europe, armed pilgrimages aimed at recapturing the Holy Land from the Muslims (believers in Islam). (346)

crypt—A *vaulted* space under part of a building, wholly or partly underground; in churches, normally the portion under an *apse*. (340)

cubiculum (pl. **cubicula**)—A small cubicle or bedroom that opened onto the *atrium* of a Roman house. Also, a chamber in an Early Christian *catacomb* that served as a mortuary chapel. (190, 237)

cuerda seca—A type of polychrome tilework used in decorating Islamic buildings. (299)

cuirass—A military leather breastplate. (186)

cult statue—The *statue* of the deity that stood in the *cella* of an ancient temple. (115)

cuneiform—Latin, "wedge-shaped." A system of writing used in ancient Mesopotamia, in which wedge-shaped characters were produced by pressing a *stylus* into a soft clay tablet, which was then baked or otherwise allowed to harden. (33)

cuneus (pl. **cunei**)—In ancient Greek and Roman theaters and *amphitheaters*, the wedge-shaped

section of stone benches separated by stairs. (151)

cupola—An exterior architectural feature composed of a *drum* with a shallow cap; a *dome*. (9-32A)

cutaway—An architectural drawing that combines an exterior view with an interior view of part of a building. (12)

Cycladic—The prehistoric art of the Aegean Islands around Delos, excluding Crete. (87)

Cyclopean masonry—A method of stone construction, named after the mythical *Cyclopes*, using massive, irregular blocks without mortar, characteristic of the Bronze Age fortifications of Tiryns and other *Mycenaean* sites. (97)

Cyclops (pl. **Cyclopes**)—A mythical Greek one-eyed giant. (97)

cylinder seal—A cylindrical piece of stone usually about an inch or so in height, decorated with an design cut into the surface, so that a raised pattern is left when the seal is rolled over soft clay. In the ancient Near East, documents, storage jars, and other important possessions were signed, sealed, and identified in this way. Stamp seals are an earlier, flat form of seal used for similar purposes. (39)

Daedalic—The Greek *Orientalizing* sculptural style of the seventh century BCE named after the legendary artist Daedalus. (111)

damnatio memoriae—The Roman decree condemning those who ran afoul of the Senate. Those who suffered damnatio memoriae had their memorials demolished and their names erased from public inscriptions. (206, 219)

darshan—In Hindu worship, seeing images of the divinity and being seen by the divinity. (435)

decumanus—The east-west street in a Roman town, intersecting the *cardo* at right angles. (189)

decursio—The ritual circling of a Roman funerary pyre. (215)

Deësis—Greek, "supplication." An image of Christ flanked by the figures of the Virgin Mary and John the Baptist, who intercede on behalf of humankind. (276)

demos—Greek, "the people," from which the word *democracy* is derived. (106)

demotic—Late Egyptian writing. (56)

denarius—The standard Roman silver coin from which the word *penny* ultimately derives. (187)

dharma—In Buddhism, moral law based on the Buddha's teaching. (423, 15-8A)

dharmachakra—See *mudra*. (427)

dhyana—See *mudra*. (427)

diagonal rib—See *rib*. (373)

diaphragm arch—A transverse, wall-bearing *arch* that divides a *vault* or a ceiling into compartments, providing a kind of firebreak. (12-27A)

dictator—In the Roman Republic, the supreme magistrate with extraordinary powers, appointed during a crisis for a specified period. Julius Caesar eventually became *dictator perpetuo*, dictator for life. (181, 187)

dictator perpetuo—See *dictator*. (181, 187)

dipteral—See *peristyle*. (115)

diptych—A two-paneled painting or *altarpiece*; also, an ancient Roman, Early Christian, or Byzantine hinged writing tablet, often of ivory and carved on the external sides. (251)

disputatio—Latin, "logical argument." The philosophical methodology used in *Scholasticism*. (372)

documentary evidence—In art history, the examination of written sources in order to determine the date of an artwork, the circumstances of its creation, or the identity of the artist(s) who made it. (2)

doge—Duke; a ruler of the Republic of Venice, Italy. (274)

dome—A hemispherical *vault*; theoretically, an *arch* rotated on its vertical axis. In *Mycenaean* architecture, domes are beehive-shaped. (99, 184, 14-18A)

domus—A Roman private house. (190)

Doric—One of the two systems (or *orders*) invented in ancient Greece for articulating the three units of the elevation of a *classical* building—the platform, the *colonnade*, and the superstructure (*entablature*). The Doric order is characterized by, among other features, *capitals* with funnel-shaped *echinuses*, *columns* without *bases*, and a *frieze* of *triglyphs* and *metopes*. See also *Ionic*. (116)

doryphoros—Greek, "spear bearer." (132)

dotaku—Ancient Japanese bronze ceremonial bells, usually featuring raised decoration. (477)

double monastery—A *monastery* for both monks and nuns. (352)

dressed masonry—Stone blocks shaped to the exact dimensions required, with smooth faces for a perfect fit. (62)

dromos—The passage leading to a *tholos tomb*. (99)

drum—One of the stacked cylindrical stones that form the *shaft* of a *column*. Also, the cylindrical wall that supports a *dome*. (116, 184, 271)

duomo—Italian, "cathedral." (417)

earthenware—Pottery made of clay that is fired at low temperatures and is slightly porous. Also, clay figurines and statues produced in the same manner. (451)

eaves—The lower part of a roof that overhangs the wall. (457)

echinus—The convex element of a *capital* directly below the *abacus*. (116)

effigy mounds—Ceremonial mounds built in the shape of animals or birds by native North American peoples. (517)

elevation—In architecture, a head-on view of an external or internal wall, showing its features and often other elements that would be visible beyond or before the wall. (12, 413)

emblema—The central framed figural panel of a *mosaic* floor. (149)

embroidery—The technique of sewing threads onto a finished ground to form contrasting designs. Stem stitching employs short overlapping strands of thread to form jagged lines.

Laid-and-couched work creates solid blocks of color. (362, 449, 510)

emir—A Muslim ruler. (293)

enamel—A decorative coating, usually colored, fused onto the surface of metal, glass, or ceramics. (301)

encaustic—A painting *technique* in which pigment is mixed with melted wax and applied to the surface while the mixture is hot. (111, 218)

engaged column—A half-round *column* attached to a wall. See also *pilaster*. (60, 290, 340)

ensi—A Sumerian ruler. (36)

entablature—The part of a building above the *columns* and below the roof. The entablature has three parts: *architrave, frieze,* and *pediment.* (116)

entasis—The convex profile (an apparent swelling) in the *shaft* of a *column*. (118)

Eucharist—In Christianity, the partaking of the bread and wine, which believers hold to be either Christ himself or symbolic of him. (241)

evangelist—One of the four authors (Matthew, Mark, Luke, John) of the New Testament *Gospels*. (314)

exedra—Recessed area, usually semicircular. (196)

facade—Usually, the front of a building; also, the other sides when they are emphasized architecturally. (52, 412)

faience—A low-fired opaque glasslike silicate. (94)

fan vault—See *vault*. (391)

fauces—Latin, "jaws." In a Roman house, the narrow foyer leading to the *atrium*. (190)

fenestrated—Having windows. (184)

fenestration—The arrangement of the windows of a building. (184)

feudalism—The medieval political, social, and economic system held together by the relationship between landholding *liege lords* and the *vassals* who were granted tenure of a portion of their land and in turn swore allegiance to the liege lord. (334)

fibula (pl. **fibulae**)—A decorative pin, usually used to fasten garments. (167, 309)

findspot—Place where an artifact was found; *provenance*. (18)

finial—A crowning ornament. (294)

First Style mural—The earliest style of Roman *mural* painting. Also called the Masonry style, because the aim of the artist was to imitate, using painted *stucco relief,* the appearance of costly marble panels. (191)

Flamboyant—A Late French *Gothic* style of architecture superseding the *Rayonnant* style and named for the flamelike appearance of its pointed bar *tracery*. (381)

flashing—In making *stained-glass* windows, fusing one layer of colored glass to another to produce a greater range of *colors*. (375)

fleur-de-lis—A three-petaled iris flower; the royal flower of France. (376, 388)

florin—The denomination of gold coin of *Renaissance* Florence that became an international currency for trade. (417)

flute or **fluting**—Vertical channeling, roughly semicircular in cross-*section* and used principally on *columns* and *pilasters*. (51, 68, 116, 3-5A)

flying buttress—See *buttress*. (12, 372, 373)

folio—A page of a manuscript or book. (248, 249)

foreshortening—The use of *perspective* to represent in art the apparent visual contraction of an object that extends back in space at an angle to the perpendicular plane of sight. (10, 44, 123, 401)

form—In art, an object's shape and structure, either in two dimensions (for example, a figure painted on a surface) or in three dimensions (such as a *statue*). (7)

formal analysis—The visual analysis of artistic *form*. (7)

forum—The public square of an ancient Roman city. (189)

Fourth Style mural—In Roman *mural* painting, the Fourth Style marks a return to architectural *illusionism,* but the architectural vistas of the Fourth Style are irrational fantasies. (194)

freedmen, freedwomen—In ancient and medieval society, men and women who had been freed from servitude, as opposed to having been born free. (187)

freestanding sculpture—See *sculpture in the round*. (12, 18)

fresco—Painting on lime plaster, either dry (dry fresco, or fresco secco) or wet (true, or buon, fresco). In the latter method, the pigments are mixed with water and become chemically bound to the freshly laid lime plaster. Also, a painting executed in either method. (408, 409, 502)

fresco secco—See *fresco*. (74, 408)

Friday mosque—See *congregational mosque*. (288)

frieze—The part of the *entablature* between the architrave and the cornice; also, any sculptured or painted band in a building. See *register*. (31, 116)

frigidarium—The cold-bath section of a Roman bathing establishment. (220)

furta sacra—Latin, "holy theft." (336)

garbha griha—Hindi, "womb chamber." In Hindu temples, the *cella*, the holy inner sanctum often housing the god's image or *symbol*. (439)

genre—A *style* or category of art; also, a kind of painting that realistically depicts scenes from everyday life. (5, 551)

Geometric—The *style* of Greek art during the ninth and eighth centuries BCE, characterized by *abstract* geometric ornament and schematic figures. (108)

gigantomachy—In ancient Greek mythology, the battle between gods and giants. (118)

giornata (pl. **giornate**)—Italian, "day." The section of plaster that a *fresco* painter expects to complete in one session. (408)

gladiator—An ancient Roman professional fighter, usually a slave, who competed in an *amphitheater*. (203)

glaze—A vitreous coating applied to pottery to seal and decorate the surface; it may be col-

ored, transparent, or opaque, and glossy or a dull finish called *matte*. (110, 451)

glazier—A glassworker. (375)

gold leaf—Gold beaten into tissue-paper-thin sheets that then can be applied to surfaces. (405)

gopis—South Asian herdswomen. (32-7A)

gorget—A neck pendant, usually made of shell. (517)

gorgon—In ancient Greek mythology, a hideous female demon with snake hair. Medusa, the most famous gorgon, was capable of turning anyone who gazed at her into stone. (118)

Gospels—The four New Testament books that relate the life and teachings of Jesus. (312)

Gothic—Originally a derogatory term named after the Goths, used to describe the history, culture, and art of western Europe in the 12th to 14th centuries. Typically divided into periods designated Early (1140–1194), High (1194–1300), and Late (1300–1500). (365)

granulation—A decorative technique in which tiny metal balls (granules) are fused to a metal surface. (167)

great mosque—See *congregational mosque*. (288)

Greek cross—A cross with four arms of equal length. (271)

griffin—An eagle-headed winged lion. (51, 99, 4-9B, 10-5B)

grisaille—A *monochrome* painting done mainly in neutral grays to simulate sculpture. (409, 13-36A)

groin—The edge formed by the intersection of two barrel *vaults*. (184)

groin vault—See *vault*. (184, 340, 350, 14-12A)

ground line—In paintings and *reliefs*, a painted or carved baseline on which figures appear to stand. (20, 31)

guang—An ancient Chinese covered vessel, often in animal form, holding wine, water, grain, or meat for sacrificial rites. (152)

guild—An association of merchants, craftspersons, or scholars in medieval and *Renaissance* Europe. (366, 410)

Hadith—The words and exemplary deeds of the Prophet Muhammad. (285)

hall church—See *Hallenkirche*. (348)

Hallenkirche—German, "hall church." A church design favored in Germany, but also used elsewhere, in which the *aisles* rise to the same height as the *nave*. (396)

handscroll—In Asian art, a horizontal painted scroll that is unrolled right to left, section by section, and often used to present illustrated religious texts or *landscapes*. (459)

hanging scroll—In Asian art, a vertical scroll hung on a wall with pictures mounted or painted directly on it. (459)

haniwa—Sculpted fired pottery cylinders, modeled in human, animal, or other forms and placed on Japanese *tumuli* of the Kofun period. (478)

hard-edge painting—In Buddhist architecture, a stone fence or railing that encloses an area surmounting the *dome* of a *stupa* that represents one of the Buddhist heavens; from the center arises the *yasti*. (430)

haruspex (pl. **haruspices**)—An Etruscan priest who foretells events by studying animal livers. (6-13A)

head cluster—An abbreviated way of representing a crowd by painting or carving many heads close together, usually with too few bodies for the number of heads. (246)

Helladic—The prehistoric art of the Greek mainland (*Hellas* in Greek). (87)

Hellas—The ancient name of Greece. (106)

Hellenes (adj. **Hellenic**)—The name the ancient Greeks called themselves as the people of *Hellas*. (106)

Hellenistic—The term given to the art and culture of the roughly three centuries between the death of Alexander the Great in 323 BCE and the death of Queen Cleopatra in 30 BCE, when Egypt became a Roman province. (153)

henge—An arrangement of *megalithic* stones in a circle, often surrounded by a ditch. (28)

heraldic composition—A *composition* that is symmetrical on either side of a central figure. (38)

herm—A bust on a quadrangular *pillar*. (133)

Hiberno-Saxon—An art *style* that flourished in the *monasteries* of the British Isles in the early Middle Ages. Also called Insular. (311)

hierarchy of scale—An artistic convention in which greater size indicates greater importance. (11, 31, 14-16A)

hieroglyphic—A system of writing using *symbols* or pictures. (55, 493)

high relief—See *relief*. (12, 65)

Hijra—The flight of Muhammad from Mecca to Medina in 622, the year from which Islam dates its beginnings. (285)

himation—An ancient Greek mantle worn by men and women over the *chiton* and draped in various ways. (115)

Hippodamian plan—A city *plan* devised by Hippodamos of Miletos ca. 466 BCE, in which a strict grid was imposed on a site, regardless of the terrain, so that all streets would meet at right angles. (154)

hiragana—A phonetic cursive script developed in Japan from Chinese *characters;* it came to be the primary script for Japanese court poetry. (484, 17-13B)

historiated—Ornamented with representations, such as plants, animals, or human figures, that have a narrative—as distinct from a purely decorative—function. (342)

hubris—Greek, "arrogant pride." (143)

hue—The name of a *color*. See also *primary colors, secondary colors,* and *complementary colors.* (7)

humanism—In the *Renaissance,* an emphasis on education and on expanding knowledge (especially of *classical* antiquity), the exploration of individual potential and a desire to excel, and a commitment to civic responsibility and moral duty. (407)

hydria—An ancient Greek three-handled water pitcher. (145)

hypaethral—A building having no *pediment* or roof, open to the sky. (154)

hypostyle hall—A hall with a roof supported by *columns*. (73, 288, 289)

icon—A portrait or image; especially in Byzantine churches, a panel with a painting of sacred personages that are objects of veneration. In the visual arts, a painting, a piece of sculpture, or even a building regarded as an object of veneration. (268, 269, 405)

iconoclasm—The destruction of religious or sacred images. In Byzantium, the period from 726 to 843 when there was an imperial ban on such images. The destroyers of images were known as iconoclasts. Those who opposed such a ban were known as iconophiles. (257, 269)

iconoclast—See *iconoclasm*. (257, 269)

iconography—Greek, the "writing of images." The term refers both to the content, or subject, of an artwork and to the study of content in art. It also includes the study of the symbolic, often religious, meaning of objects, persons, or events depicted in works of art. (5)

iconophile—See *iconoclasm*. (269)

iconostasis—Greek, "icon stand." In Byzantine churches, a screen or a partition, with doors and many tiers of *icons,* separating the sanctuary from the main body of the church. (279)

ikegobo—A Benin royal shrine. (520, 521)

illuminated manuscript—A luxurious handmade book with painted illustrations and decorations. (249, 405)

illusionism (adj. **illusionistic**)—The representation of the three-dimensional world on a two-dimensional surface in a manner that creates the illusion that the person, object, or place represented is three-dimensional. See also *perspective*. (8)

imagines—In ancient Rome, wax portraits of ancestors. (185, 196, 200)

imam—In Islam, the leader of collective worship. (288)

imperator—Latin, "commander in chief," from which the word *emperor* derives. (197)

impluvium—In a Roman house, the basin located in the *atrium* that collected rainwater. (190)

in antis—In ancient Greek architecture, the area between the *antae*. (115)

incrustation—Wall decoration consisting of bright panels of different *colors*. (202, 355)

indulgence—A religious pardon for a sin committed. (374)

insula (pl. **insulae**)—In Roman architecture, a multistory apartment house, usually made of brick-faced *concrete;* also refers to an entire city block. (213)

Insular—See *Hiberno-Saxon*. (311)

intensity—See *color*. (7)

interaxial or **intercolumniation**—The distance between the center of the lowest *drum* of a *column* and the center of the next. (135)

intercolumniation—See *interaxial*. (135)

internal evidence—In art history, the examination of what an artwork represents (people, clothing, hairstyles, and so on) in order to determine its date. Also, the examination of the *style* of an artwork to identify the artist who created it. (3)

International style—A *style* of 14th- and 15th-century painting begun by Simone Martini, who adapted the French *Gothic* manner to Sienese art fused with influences from northern Europe. This style appealed to the aristocracy because of its brilliant *color,* lavish costumes, intricate ornamentation, and themes involving splendid processions of knights and ladies. Also, a style of 20th-century architecture associated with Le Corbusier, whose elegance of design came to influence the look of modern office buildings and skyscrapers. (413)

intonaco—In *fresco* painting, the last layer of smooth lime plaster applied to the wall; the painting layer. (408)

investment—In hollow-casting, the final clay *mold* applied to the exterior of the wax model. (130)

Ionic—One of the two systems (or *orders*) invented in ancient Greece for articulating the three units of the elevation of a *classical* building: the platform, the *colonnade,* and the superstructure (*entablature*). The Ionic order is characterized by, among other features, *volutes, capitals, columns* with *bases,* and an uninterrupted *frieze*. (116)

iron-wire lines—In ancient Chinese painting, thin brush lines suggesting tensile strength. (459, 482)

iwan—In Islamic architecture, a *vaulted* rectangular recess opening onto a courtyard. (52, 288)

iy'oba—Benin queen mother. (532, 19-13A)

jambs—In architecture, the side posts of a doorway. (344)

jataka—Tales of the past lives of the Buddha. See also *sutra*. (430)

joined-wood technique—A Japanese sculptural *technique* in which a statue is assembled from multiple wood blocks, each hollowed out to make the pieces lighter. (17-13A)

jomon—Japanese, "cord markings." A type of Japanese ceramic technique characterized by ropelike markings. (476)

junzi—Chinese, "superior person" or "gentleman." A person who is a model of Confucian behavior. (463)

ka—In ancient Egypt, the immortal human life force. (57, 61)

Kaaba—Arabic, "cube." A small cubical building in Mecca, the Islamic world's symbolic center. (285)

kami—Shinto deities or spirits, believed in Japan to exist in nature (mountains, waterfalls) and in charismatic people. (479)

karma—In Vedic religions (see *Veda*), the ethical consequences of a person's life, which determine his or her fate. (427)

katsuogi—Wooden logs placed at right angles to the *ridgepole* of a Japanese shrine to hold the thatched roof in place. (480)

keep—A fortified tower in a castle that served as a place of last refuge. (383)

keystone—See *voussoir*. (175, 344)

khan—An Ottoman lord, or *sultan*. (10-23A)

king's gallery—The band of *statues* running the full width of the *facade* of a *Gothic cathedral* directly above the *rose window*. (379, 380)

kiva—A square or circular underground structure that is the spiritual and ceremonial center of Pueblo Indian life. (518)

kline (pl. **klinai**)—A couch or funerary bed. A type of *sarcophagus* with a reclining portrait of the deceased on its lid. (217)

kodo—The lecture hall in a Japanese Buddhist temple complex. (475)

kondo—Japanese, "golden hall." The main hall for worship in a Japanese Buddhist temple complex. The kondo contained *statues* of the Buddha and the *bodhisattvas* to whom the temple was dedicated. (475)

Koran—Islam's sacred book, composed of *surahs* (chapters) divided into verses. (285)

kore (pl. **korai**)—Greek, "young woman." An *Archaic* Greek *statue* of a young woman. (111)

kouros (pl. **kouroi**)—Greek, "young man." An *Archaic* Greek *statue* of a young man. (112)

krater—An ancient Greek wide-mouthed bowl for mixing wine and water. (102)

Kufic—An early form of Arabic script, characterized by angularity, with the uprights forming almost right angles with the baseline. (294)

kylix—An ancient Greek drinking cup with a wide bowl and two horizontal handles. (5-23A)

labrys—Minoan double ax. (90)

labyrinth—Maze. The English word derives from the mazelike plan of the *Minoan* palace at Knossos. (90)

lacquer—A varnishlike substance made from the sap of the Asiatic sumac tree, used to decorate wood and other organic materials. Often colored with mineral pigments, lacquer cures to great hardness and has a lustrous surface. (453)

laid-and-couched work—See *embroidery*. (362)

lakshana—One of the distinguishing marks of the Buddha. The lakshanas include the *urna* and *ushnisha*. (427)

lalitasana—In Buddhist iconography, the body pose with one leg folded and the other hanging down, indicating relaxation. (460)

lamassu—Assyrian guardian in the form of a man-headed winged bull. (46)

lancet—In *Gothic* architecture, a tall narrow window ending in a narrow arch of pointed profile. (370, 373, 14-5A)

landscape—A picture showing natural scenery, without narrative content. (5, 27, 416)

lateral section—See *section*. (12)

leading—In the manufacture of *stained-glass* windows, the joining of colored glass pieces using lead *cames*. (375)

lectionary—A book containing passages from the *Gospels,* arranged in the sequence that they are to be read during the celebration of religious services, including the *Mass,* throughout the year. (312)

lekythos (pl. **lekythoi**)—A flask containing perfumed oil; lekythoi were often placed in Greek graves as offerings to the deceased. (142)

libation—The pouring of liquid as part of a religious ritual. (36)

liege lord—In *feudalism*, a landowner who grants tenure of a portion of his land to a *vassal*. (334)

line—The extension of a point along a path, made concrete in art by drawing on or chiseling into a *plane*. (7)

linear perspective—See *perspective*. (192)

linga—In Hindu art, the depiction of Shiva as a phallus or cosmic *pillar*. (435)

lintel—A horizontal *beam* used to span an opening. (73, 99, 344)

liturgy (adj. **liturgical**)—The official ritual of public worship. (242)

lituus—The curved staff carried by an *augur*. (165)

loculi—Openings in the walls of *catacombs* to receive the dead. (237)

loggia—A gallery with an open *arcade* or a *colonnade* on one or both sides. (576, 14-19A)

lohan—A Buddhist holy person who has achieved enlightenment and *nirvana* by suppression of all desire for earthly things. (468)

longitudinal plan—See *plan*. (243)

longitudinal section—See *section*. (12)

lost-wax (cire perdue) process—A bronze-*casting* method in which a figure is modeled in wax and covered with clay; the whole is fired, melting away the wax (French, *cire perdue*) and hardening the clay, which then becomes a *mold* for molten metal. (130)

low relief—See *relief*. (12)

lunette—A semicircular area (with the flat side down) in a wall over a door, niche, or window; also, a painting or *relief* with a semicircular frame. (237, 344, 7-54A)

lux nova—Latin, "new light." Abbot Suger's term for the light that enters a *Gothic* church through *stained-glass* windows. (369, 375)

machicolated gallery—A gallery in a defensive tower with holes in the floor to allow stones or hot liquids to be dumped on enemies below. (416)

madrasa—An Islamic theological college adjoining and often containing a *mosque*. (296)

maebyeong—A Korean vase similar to the Chinese *meiping*. (472)

magus (pl. **magi**)—One of the three wise men from the East who presented gifts to the infant Jesus. (240)

mandala—Sanskrit term for the sacred diagram of the universe; Japanese, mandara. (430, 439, 483)

mandapa—*Pillared* hall of a Hindu temple. (439)

mandara—See *mandala*. (430, 439, 483)

mandorla—An almond-shaped *nimbus* surrounding the figure of Christ or other sacred figure. In Buddhist Japan, a lotus-petal-shaped nimbus. (267, 460)

maniera greca—Italian, "Greek manner." The Italo-*Byzantine* painting *style* of the 13th century. (404, 14-7A)

manor—In *feudalism,* the estate of a *liege lord*. (334)

mantra—Sanskrit term for the ritual words or syllables recited in *Shingon* Buddhism. (483)

maqsura—In some *mosques,* a screened area in front of the *mihrab* reserved for a ruler. (283, 288)

martyr—A person who chooses to die rather than deny his or her religious belief. See also *saint*. (237)

martyrium—A shrine to a Christian *martyr*. (274)

Masonry Style—See *First Style mural*. (191)

mass—The bulk, density, and weight of matter in *space*. (8)

Mass—The Catholic and Orthodox ritual in which believers understand that Christ's redeeming sacrifice on the cross is repeated when the priest consecrates the bread and wine in the *Eucharist*. (241)

mastaba—Arabic, "bench." An ancient Egyptian rectangular brick or stone structure with sloping sides erected over a subterranean tomb chamber connected with the outside by a shaft. (58)

matins—In Christianity, early morning prayers. (550, 13-36A)

mausoleum—A monumental tomb. The name derives from the mid-fourth-century BCE tomb of Mausolos at Halikarnassos, one of the Seven Wonders of the ancient world. (225)

meander—An ornament, usually in bands but also covering broad surfaces, consisting of interlocking geometric motifs. An ornamental pattern of contiguous straight lines joined usually at right angles. (108)

medium (pl. **media**)—The material (for example, marble, bronze, clay, *fresco*) in which an artist works; also, in painting, the vehicle (usually liquid) that carries the pigment. (7)

megalith (adj. **megalithic**)—Greek, "great stone." A large, roughly hewn stone used in the construction of monumental prehistoric structures. (27)

megaron—The large reception hall and throne room in a *Mycenaean* palace, fronted by an open, two-*columned* porch. (97)

meiping—A Chinese vase of a high-shouldered shape; the *sgrafitto technique* was used in decorating such vases. (467, 472)

mendicants—In medieval Europe, friars belonging to the Franciscan and Dominican orders, who renounced all worldly goods, lived by contributions of laypersons (the word *mendicant* means "beggar"), and devoted themselves to preaching, teaching, and doing good works. (385, 404)

menorah—In antiquity, the Jewish sacred seven-branched candelabrum. (207)

merlon—See *crenellation*. (382)

Mesoamerica—The region that comprises Mexico, Guatemala, Belize, Honduras, and the Pacific coast of El Salvador. (492)

Mesolithic—The "middle" Stone Age, between the *Paleolithic* and the *Neolithic* ages. (16)

Messiah—The savior of the Jews prophesied in Hebrew scripture. Christians believe that Jesus of Nazareth was the Messiah. (240)

metope—The square panel between the *triglyphs* in a *Doric frieze*, often sculpted in *relief*. (116)

mihrab—A semicircular niche set into the *qibla* wall of a *mosque*. (287, 288)

minaret—A distinctive feature of *mosque* architecture, a tower from which the faithful are called to worship. (134, 261, 287, 288)

minbar—In a *mosque*, the *pulpit* on which the *imam* stands. (287, 288)

Minoan—The prehistoric art of Crete, named after the legendary King Minos of Knossos. (87)

Minotaur—The mythical beast, half man and half bull, that inhabited the *labyrinth* of the *Minoan* palace at Knossos. (86)

Miraj—The ascension of the Prophet Muhammad to Heaven. (286)

mithuna—In South Asian art, a male-female couple embracing or engaged in sexual intercourse. (431)

modeling—The shaping or fashioning of three-dimensional forms in a soft material, such as clay; also, the gradations of light and shade reflected from the surfaces of matter in space, or the illusion of such gradations produced by alterations of value in a drawing, painting, or print. (113, 145, 146)

module (adj. **modular**)—A basic unit of which the dimensions of the major parts of a work are multiples. The principle is used in sculpture and other art forms, but it is most often employed in architecture, where the module may be the dimensions of an important part of a building, such as the diameter of a *column*. (10, 323, 457)

moksha—See *nirvana*. (427, 435)

mold—A hollow form for *casting*. (11)

molding—In architecture, a continuous, narrow surface (projecting or recessed, plain or ornamented) designed to break up a surface, to accent, or to decorate. (82)

monastery—A group of buildings in which monks live together, set apart from the secular community of a town. (267)

monastic—Relating to life in a *monastery*. (267, 404)

monastic order—An organization of monks living according to the same rules, for example, the Benedictine, Franciscan, and Dominican orders. (404)

monochrome (adj. **monochromatic**)—One color. (194)

monolith (adj. **monolithic**)—A stone *column shaft* that is all in one piece (not composed of *drums*); a large, single block or piece of stone used in *megalithic* structures. Also, a colossal statue carved from a single piece of stone. (116, 428)

monotheism—The worship of one all-powerful god. (233)

moralized Bible—A heavily illustrated Bible, each page pairing paintings of Old and New Testament episodes with explanations of their moral significance. (385)

mortise-and-tenon system—See *tenon*. (480)

mortuary temple—In Egyptian architecture, a temple erected for the worship of a deceased *pharaoh*. (62)

mosaic—Patterns or pictures made by embedding small pieces (*tesserae*) of stone or glass in cement on surfaces such as walls and floors; also, the *technique* of making such works. (245)

mosaic tilework—An Islamic decorative *technique* in which large ceramic panels are fired, cut into smaller pieces, and set in plaster. (299)

moschophoros—Greek, "calf bearer." (112)

mosque—The Islamic building for collective worship. From the Arabic word *masjid*, meaning a "place for bowing down." (261, 288)

Mozarabic—Referring to the Christian culture of northern Spain during the time Islamic *caliphs* ruled southern Spain. (316)

mudra—In Buddhist and Hindu iconography, a stylized and symbolic hand gesture. The dhyana (meditation) mudra consists of the right hand over the left, palms upward, in the lap. In the bhumisparsha (earth-touching) mudra, the right hand reaches down to the ground, calling the earth to witness the Buddha's enlightenment. The dharmachakra (Wheel of the Law, or teaching) mudra is a two-handed gesture with right thumb and index finger forming a circle. The abhaya (do not fear) mudra, with the right hand up, palm outward, is a gesture of protection or blessing. (427)

Muhaqqaq—A cursive style of Islamic *calligraphy*. (300)

mullion—A vertical member that divides a window or that separates one window from another. (381)

mummification—A *technique* used by ancient Egyptians to preserve human bodies so that they may serve as the eternal home of the immortal *ka*. (61)

muqarnas—Stucco decorations of Islamic buildings in which stalactite-like forms break a structure's solidity. (274, 296, 9-27A)

mural—A wall painting. (22, 407, 408, 409)

Mycenaean—The prehistoric art of the Late *Helladic* period in Greece, named after the citadel of Mycenae. (87)

mystery play—A dramatic enactment of the holy mysteries of the Christian faith performed at church portals and in city squares. (409, 12-35A)

naos—See *cella*. (33, 115)

narthex—A porch or vestibule of a church, generally *colonnaded* or *arcaded* and preceding the *nave*. (243)

natatio—The swimming pool in a Roman bathing establishment. (220)

naturalism—The style of painted or sculptured representation based on close observation of the natural world that was at the core of the *classical* tradition. (401)

nave—The central area of an ancient Roman *basilica* or of a church, demarcated from *aisles* by *piers* or *columns*. (189, 243, 413)

nave arcade—In *basilica* architecture, the series of *arches* supported by *piers* or *columns* separating the *nave* from the *aisles*. (373)

necropolis—Greek, "city of the dead." A large burial area or cemetery. (58, 171)

nembutsu—The six-syllable Japanese prayer professing faith in the compassion of Amida Buddha. (488)

nemes—In ancient Egypt, the linen headdress worn by the *pharaoh*, with the *uraeus* cobra of kingship on the front. (64)

Neolithic—The "new" Stone Age. (16)

niello—A black metallic alloy. (100)

nimbus—A halo or aureole appearing around the head of a holy figure to signify divinity. (248, 441)

nio—A Japanese guardian figure. (17-17A)

nirvana—In Buddhism and Hinduism, a blissful state brought about by absorption of the individual soul or consciousness into the supreme spirit. Also called moksha. (423, 427)

nomarch—Egyptian, "great/overlord." A regional governor during the Middle Kingdom. (3-16A)

Nun—In ancient Egypt, the primeval waters from which the creator god emerged. (57)

nymphs—In *classical* mythology, female divinities of springs, caves, and woods. (107)

oba—An African sacred king. (521, 19-13A)

oculus (pl. **oculi**)—Latin, "eye." The round central opening of a *dome*. Also, a small round window in a *Gothic cathedral*. (184, 202, 373, 14-6A)

ogee arch—An *arch* composed of two double-curving lines meeting at a point. (420, 13-42A)

ogive (adj. **ogival**)—The diagonal *rib* of a *Gothic vault*; a pointed, or Gothic, *arch*. (369, 402)

oni—An African ruler. (527)

opere francigeno—See *opus francigenum*. (366, 389)

opisthodomos—In ancient Greek architecture, a porch at the rear of a temple, set against the blank back wall of the *cella*. (115)

optical representation—The representation of people and objects seen from a fixed viewpoint. (35)

opus francigenum—Latin, "French work." Architecture in the *style* of *Gothic* France; *opere francigeno* (adj.), "in the French manner." (366, 389)

opus modernum—Latin, "modern work." The late medieval term for *Gothic* art and architecture. Also called *opus francigenum*. (365, 373, 389)

opus reticulatum—An ancient Roman method of facing *concrete* walls with lozenge-shaped bricks or stones to achieve a netlike ornamental surface pattern. (11-19A)

oracle—A prophetic message. (5-17A)

orant—In Early Christian art, a figure with both arms raised in the ancient gesture of prayer. (238)

oratory—The church of a Christian *monastery*. (267)

orchestra—Greek, "dancing place." In ancient Greek theaters, the circular piece of earth with a hard and level surface on which the performance took place. (151)

order—In *classical* architecture, a *style* represented by a characteristic design of the *columns* and *entablature*. See also *superimposed orders*. (116)

Orientalizing—The early phase of *Archaic* Greek art (seventh century BCE), so named because of the adoption of forms and motifs from the ancient Near East and Egypt. See also *Daedalic*. (109)

orthogonal plan—The imposition of a strict grid *plan* on a site, regardless of the terrain, so that all streets meet at right angles. See also *Hippodamian plan*. (154)

Ottonian (adj.)—Pertaining to the empire of Otto I and his successors. (324)

oxidizing—The first phase of the ancient Greek ceramic firing process, which turned both the pot and the clay *slip* red. During the second (reducing) phase, the oxygen supply into the kiln was shut off, and both pot and slip turned black. In the final (reoxidizing) phase, the pot's coarser material reabsorbed oxygen and became red again, whereas the smoother slip did not and remained black. (110)

pagoda—An East Asian tower, usually associated with a Buddhist temple, having a multiplicity of winged *eaves*; thought to be derived from the Indian *stupa*. (467)

pala—A panel placed behind and over the altar in a church. (9-26A)

palaestra—An ancient Greek and Roman exercise area, usually framed by a *colonnade*. In Greece, the palaestra was an independent building; in Rome, palaestras were also frequently incorporated into a bathing complex. (133, 220)

Paleolithic—The "old" Stone Age, during which humankind produced the first sculptures and paintings. (16, 522)

palette—A thin board with a thumb hole at one end on which an artist lays and mixes *colors*; any surface so used. Also, the colors or kinds of colors characteristically used by an artist. In ancient Egypt, a slate slab used for preparing makeup. (20, 55)

Pantokrator—Greek, "ruler of all." Christ as ruler and judge. (272)

papyrus—A plant native to Egypt and adjacent lands used to make paperlike writing material; also, the material or any writing on it. (56, 249)

parade helmet—A masklike helmet worn by Roman soldiers on special ceremonial occasions. (336)

parapet—A low, protective wall along the edge of a balcony, roof, or bastion. (416)

parchment—Lambskin prepared as a surface for painting or writing. (249)

parekklesion—The side chapel in a Byzantine church. (279)

parinirvana—Image of the reclining Buddha, a position often interpreted as representing his death. (427)

parthenos—Greek, "virgin." The epithet of Athena, the virgin goddess. (107)

passage grave—A prehistoric tomb with a long stone corridor leading to a burial chamber covered by a great *tumulus*. (27)

Passional—A Christian book containing the lives of *saints*. (312)

Passover—The annual feast celebrating the release of the Jews from bondage to the *pharaohs* of Egypt. (240)

paten—A large shallow bowl or plate for the bread used in the *Eucharist*. (264)

patrician—A Roman freeborn landowner. (181)

patron—The person or entity that pays an artist to produce individual artworks or employs an artist on a continuing basis. (6)

pebble mosaic—A *mosaic* made of irregularly shaped stones of various *colors*. (149, 245)

pectoral—An ornament on the chest. (167)

pediment—In *classical* architecture, the triangular space (gable) at the end of a building, formed by the ends of the sloping roof above the *colonnade*; also, an ornamental feature having this shape. (105, 116)

pendant—The large hanging terminal element of a *Gothic* fan *vault*. (391)

pendentive—A concave, triangular section of a hemisphere, four of which provide the transition from a square area to the circular base of a covering *dome*. Although pendentives appear to be hanging (pendant) from the dome, they in fact support it. (262)

Pentateuch—The first five books of the Old Testament. (235, 312)

peplos (pl. **peploi**)—A simple, long belted garment of wool worn by women in ancient Greece. (114)

period style—See *style*. (3)

peripteral—See *peristyle*. (115)

peristyle—In *classical* architecture, a *colonnade* all around the *cella* and its porch(es). A peripteral colonnade consists of a single row of *columns* on all sides; a dipteral colonnade has a double row all around. (115, 190)

Perpendicular—A Late English *Gothic style* of architecture distinguished by the pronounced verticality of its decorative details. (391)

personal style—See *style*. (4)

personification—An *abstract* idea represented in bodily form. (5)

perspective—A method of presenting an illusion of the three-dimensional world on a two-dimensional surface. In linear perspective, the most common type, all parallel lines or surface edges converge on one, two, or three vanishing points located with reference to the eye level of the viewer (the horizon line of the picture), and associated objects are rendered smaller the farther from the viewer they are intended to seem. Atmospheric, or aerial, perspective creates the illusion of distance by the greater diminution of color intensity, the shift in color toward an almost neutral blue, and the blurring of contours as the intended distance between eye and object increases. (8, 409)

pharaoh (adj. **pharaonic**)—An ancient Egyptian king. (55)

phersu—A masked man who appears in scenes of Etruscan funerary games. (165)

Phoibos—Greek, "radiant." The epithet of the Greek god Apollo. (107)

physical evidence—In art history, the examination of the materials used to produce an artwork in order to determine its date. (2)

pictograph—A picture, usually stylized, that represents an idea; also, writing using such means; also, painting on rock. See also *hieroglyphic*. (32)

pier—A vertical, freestanding masonry support. (12, 72, 184)

Pietà—A painted or sculpted representation of the Virgin Mary mourning over the body of the dead Christ. (241, 396)

pilaster—A flat, rectangular, vertical member projecting from a wall of which it forms a part. It usually has a *base* and a *capital* and is often *fluted*. (175)

pillar—Usually a weight-carrying member, such as a *pier* or a *column*; sometimes an isolated, freestanding structure used for commemorative purposes. (71, 72)

pinakotheke—Greek, "picture gallery." An ancient Greek building for the display of paintings on wood panels. (139)

pinnacle—In *Gothic* churches, a sharply pointed ornament capping the *piers* or flying *buttresses*; also used on church *facades*. (373, 411, 413)

plan—The horizontal arrangement of the parts of a building or of the buildings and streets of a city or town, or a drawing or diagram showing such an arrangement. In an axial plan, the parts of a building are organized longitudinally, or along a given axis; in a central plan, the parts of the structure are of equal or almost equal dimensions around the center. (12)

plane—A flat surface. (7)

plate tracery—See *tracery*. (375)

plebeian—The Roman social class that included small farmers, merchants, and freed slaves. (181)poesia—A term describing "poetic" art, notably Venepointed arch—A narrow *arch* of pointed profile, in contrast to a semicircular arch. (3, 368, 402, 420, 12-10A)

polis (pl. **poleis**)—An independent *city-state* in ancient Greece. (106)

polytheism—The belief in multiple gods. (233)

pontifex maximus—Latin, "chief priest." The high priest of the Roman state religion, often the emperor himself. (197)

porcelain—Extremely fine, hard, white ceramic. Unlike *stoneware*, porcelain is made from a fine white clay called kaolin mixed with ground petuntse, a type of feldspar. True porcelain is translucent and rings when struck. (451)

portico—A roofed *colonnade*; also an entrance porch. (154)

post-and-lintel system—A system of construction in which two posts support a *lintel*. (28)

pouncing—The method of transferring a sketch onto paper or a wall by tracing, using thin paper or transparent gazelle skin placed on top of the sketch, pricking the contours of the design into the skin or paper with a pin, placing the skin or paper on the surface to be painted, and forcing black pigment through the holes. (482)

prasada—In Hindu worship, food that becomes sacred by first being given to a god. (441)

pre-Columbian (adj.)—The cultures that flourished in the Western Hemisphere before the arrival of Christopher Columbus and the beginning of European contact and conquest. (492)

predella—The narrow ledge on which an *altarpiece* rests on an altar. (411)

prefiguration—In Early Christian art, the depiction of Old Testament persons and events as prophetic forerunners of Christ and New Testament events. (238)

primary colors—Red, yellow, and blue—the *colors* from which all other colors may be derived. (7)

princeps—Latin, "first citizen." The title Augustus and his successors as Roman emperor used to distinguish themselves from Hellenistic monarchs. (197)

pronaos—The space, or porch, in front of the *cella*, or naos, of an ancient Greek temple. (115)

proportion—The relationship in size of the parts of persons, buildings, or objects, often based on a *module*. (10)

prostyle—A *classical* temple *plan* in which the *columns* are only in front of the *cella* and not on the sides or back. (115)

protome—The head, forelegs, and part of the body of an animal. (51)

provenance—Origin or source; *findspot*. (3)

psalter—A book containing the Psalms. (312)

pseudoperipteral—In Roman architecture, a pseudoperipteral temple has a series of engaged *columns* all around the sides and back of the *cella* to give the appearance of a *peripteral colonnade*. (182)

pueblo—A communal multistoried dwelling made of stone or *adobe* brick by the Native Americans of the Southwest. Uppercase *Pueblo* refers to various groups that occupied such dwellings. (518)

pulpit—A raised platform in a church or *mosque* on which a priest or *imam* stands while leading the religious service. (402)

pulque—An intoxicating drink, similar to tequila, consumed during *Mesoamerican* religious rituals. (18-7A)

punchwork—Tooled decorative work in *gold leaf*. (412)

purlins—Horizontal *beams* in a roof structure, parallel to the *ridgepoles*, resting on the main *rafters* and giving support to the secondary rafters. (457)

pylon—The wide entrance gateway of an Egyptian temple, characterized by its sloping walls. (72)

pyxis (pl. **pyxides**)—A cylindrical container with a hemispherical lid. (293)

qibla—The direction (toward Mecca) Muslims face when praying. (288, 289, 529)

quadrant arch—An *arch* whose curve extends for one-quarter of a circle's circumference. (359)

quatrefoil—A shape or plan in which the parts assume the form of a cloverleaf. (419)

radiating chapels—In medieval churches, chapels for the display of *relics* that opened directly onto the *ambulatory* and the *transept*. (337)

radiocarbon dating—A method of measuring the decay rate of carbon isotopes in organic matter to determine the age of organic materials such as wood and fiber. (22, 523)

rafters—The sloping supporting timber planks that run from the *ridgepole* of a roof to its edge. (457)

raking cornice—The *cornice* on the sloping sides of a *pediment*. (116)

ramparts—Defensive wall circuits. (382)

ratha—Small, freestanding Hindu temple *carved* from a huge boulder. (437)

Rayonnant—The "radiant" style of *Gothic* architecture, dominant in the second half of the 13th century and associated with the French royal court of Louis IX at Paris. (381)

red-figure painting—In later Greek pottery, the silhouetting of red figures against a black background, with painted linear details; the reverse of *black-figure painting*. (121)

reducing—See *oxidizing*. (110)

refectory—The dining hall of a Christian *monastery*. (267)

regional style—See *style*. (3)

register—One of a series of superimposed bands or *friezes* in a pictorial narrative, or the particular levels on which motifs are placed. (31)

relics—The body parts, clothing, or objects associated with a holy figure, such as the Buddha or Christ or a Christian *saint*. (243, 336)

relief—In sculpture, figures projecting from a background of which they are part. The degree of relief is designated *high, low (bas)*, or *sunken*. In the last, the artist cuts the design into the surface so that the highest projecting parts of the image are no higher than the surface itself. See also *Archaic, carving, First Style mural, ground line, lunette, metope, relief sculpture, repoussé, rubbing, sunken, tondo*.

relief sculpture—See *relief*. (12, 18)

relieving triangle—In *Mycenaean* architecture, the triangular opening above the *lintel* that serves to lighten the weight to be carried by the lintel itself. (99)

reliquary—A container for holding *relics*. (328, 334, 336, 430)

ren—Chinese, "human-heartedness." The quality that the ideal Confucian *junzi* possesses. (463)

Renaissance—French, "rebirth." The term used to describe the history, culture, and art of 14th- through 16th-century western Europe during which artists consciously revived the *classical* style. (401, 406)

renovatio—Latin, "renewal." During the *Carolingian* period, Charlemagne sought to revive the culture of ancient Rome (renovatio imperi Romani). (317, 318, 402)

reoxidizing—See *oxidizing*. (110)

repoussé—Formed in *relief* by beating a metal plate from the back, leaving the impression on the face. The metal sheet is hammered into a hollow *mold* of wood or some other pliable material and finished with a *graver*. See also *relief*. (100, 248, 320, 354, 2-26A)

respond—An engaged *column, pilaster*, or similar element that either projects from a *compound pier* or some other supporting device or is bonded to a wall and carries one end of an *arch*. (373)

revetment—In architecture, a wall covering or facing. (184, 418)

rhyton—A pouring vessel. (51)

rib—A relatively slender, molded masonry *arch* that projects from a surface. In *Gothic* architecture, the ribs form the framework of the *vaulting*. A diagonal rib is one of the ribs that form the X of a *groin vault*. A transverse rib crosses the *nave* or aisle at a 90° angle. (12, 351)

rib vault—A *vault* in which the diagonal and transverse *ribs* compose a structural skeleton that partially supports the masonry *web* between them. (351, 368, 14-5A)

ridgepole—The *beam* running the length of a building below the peak of the gabled roof. (117, 480)

Romanesque—"Roman-like." A term used to describe the history, culture, and art of medieval western Europe from ca. 1050 to ca. 1200. (333, 413)

roof comb—The elaborately sculpted vertical projection surmounting a Maya temple-pyramid. (500)

rose window—A circular *stained-glass* window. (412, 13-3A)

rotulus—The manuscript scroll used by Egyptians, Greeks, Etruscans, and Romans; predecessor of the *codex*. (249)

rotunda—The circular area under a *dome*; also a domed round building. (472)

roundel—See *tondo*. (219, 10-15A)

rubbing—An impression of a *relief* made by placing paper over the surface and rubbing with a pencil or crayon. (456)

rusticate (n. rustication)—To give a rustic appearance by roughening the surfaces and beveling the edges of stone blocks to emphasize the joints between them. Rustication is a technique employed in ancient Roman architecture, and was also popular during the *Renaissance*, especially for stone *courses* at the ground-floor level. (201)

sacra rappresentazione (pl. **sacre rappresentazioni**)—Italian, "holy representation." A more elaborate version of a *mystery play* performed for a lay audience by a *confraternity*. (409)

sacramentary—A Christian religious book incorporating the prayers priests recite during *Mass*. (312)

saint—From the Latin word *sanctus*, meaning "made holy by God." Applied to persons who suffered and died for their Christian faith or who merited reverence for their Christian devotion while alive. In the Roman Catholic Church, a worthy deceased Catholic who is canonized by the pope. (237, 402)

sakkos—The tunic worn by a Byzantine priest. (9-35A)

Samarqand ware—A type of Islamic pottery produced in Samarqand and Nishapur in which the ceramists formed the shape of the vessel from dark pink clay and then immersed it in a tub of white slip, over which they painted ornamental or *calligraphic* decoration and which they sealed with a transparent glaze before firing. (294)

samsara—In Hindu belief, the rebirth of the soul into a succession of lives. (427, 435)

sangha—The Buddhist *monastic* order. (15-8A)

sarcophagus (pl. **sarcophagi**)—Greek, "consumer of flesh." A coffin, usually of stone. (402, 449)

saturation—See *color.* (7)

satyr—A Greek mythological follower of Dionysos having a man's upper body, a goat's hindquarters and horns, and a horse's ears and tail. (159)

saz—Ottoman design of sinuous curved leaves and complex blossoms, a Turkish term recalling an enchanted forest. (10-27A)

scarab—An Egyptian gem in the shape of a beetle. (61)

scarification—Decorative markings on the human body made by cutting or piercing the flesh to create scars. (525)

Scholasticism—The *Gothic* school of philosophy in which scholars applied Aristotle's system of rational inquiry to the interpretation of religious belief. (372)

school—A chronological and stylistic classification of works of art with a stipulation of place. (6)

screen facade—A *facade* that does not correspond to the structure of the building behind it. (12-11A)

scriptorium (pl. **scriptoria**)—The writing studio of a *monastery.* (311)

sculpture in the round—Freestanding figures, *carved* or *modeled* in three dimensions. (12, 18)

secco—Italian, "dry." See also *fresco.* (408)

Second Style mural—The style of Roman *mural* painting in which the aim was to dissolve the confining walls of a room and replace them with the illusion of a three-dimensional world constructed in the artist's imagination. (192)

secondary colors—Orange, green, and purple, obtained by mixing pairs of *primary colors* (red, yellow, blue). (7)

section—In architecture, a diagram or representation of a part of a structure or building along an imaginary *plane* that passes through it vertically. Drawings showing a theoretical slice across a structure's width are lateral sections. Those cutting through a building's length are longitudinal sections. See also *elevation* and *cutaway.* (12)

sedes sapientiae—Latin, "throne of wisdom." A Romanesque sculptural type depicting the Virgin Mary with the Christ Child in her lap. (349)

senate—Latin senatus, "council of elders." The Senate was the main legislative body in Roman constitutional government. (181)

serdab—A small concealed chamber in an Egyptian *mastaba* for the *statue* of the deceased. (58)

Severe Style—The Early *Classical* style of Greek sculpture, ca. 480–450 BCE. (128)

sexpartite vault—See *vault.* (358)

sgrafitto—A Chinese ceramic technique in which the design is cut into the surface through a colored *slip.* (467)

shaft—The tall, cylindrical part of a *column* between the *capital* and the *base.* (51, 116, 373)

shakti—In Hinduism, the female power of the deity Devi (or Goddess), which animates the matter of the cosmos. (435)

sherd—A fragmentary piece of a broken ceramic vessel. (476)

shikara—The beehive-shaped tower of a northern-style Hindu temple. (439)

Shingon—The primary form of Buddhism in Japan through the mid-10th century. Lowercase *shingon* is the Japanese term for the words or syllables recited in Buddhist rituals. (483)

shogun—In 12th- through 19th-century Japan, a military governor who managed the country on behalf of a figurehead emperor. (486)

shogunate—The Japanese military government of the 12th through 19th centuries. (486)

silentiary—An usher responsible for maintaining silence in the *Byzantine* imperial palace in Constantinople. (261)

sinopia—A burnt-orange pigment used in *fresco* painting to transfer a *cartoon* to the *arriccio* before the artist paints the plaster. (408)

siren—In ancient Greek mythology, a creature that was part bird and part woman. (110)

sistrum—An Egyptian percussion instrument or rattle. (95)

skene—Greek, "stage." The stage of a *classical* theater. (151)

skenographia—Greek, "scene painting"; the Greek term for *perspective* painting. (193)

skiagraphia—Greek, "shadow painting." The Greek term for shading, said to have been invented by Apollodoros, an Athenian painter of the fifth century BCE. (149)

slip—A mixture of fine clay and water used in ceramic decoration. (110, 451)

solidus (pl. **solidi**)—A Byzantine gold coin. (263)

space—In art history, both the actual area an object occupies or a building encloses, and the *illusionistic* representation of space in painting and sculpture. (8)

spandrel—The roughly triangular space enclosed by the curves of adjacent *arches* and a horizontal member connecting their vertexes; also, the space enclosed by the curve of an *arch* and an enclosing right angle. The area between the arch proper and the framing *columns* and *entablature.* (206)

spectrum—The range or band of visible colors in natural light. (7)

sphinx—A mythical Egyptian beast with the body of a lion and the head of a human. (63)

springing—The lowest stone of an *arch,* resting on the *impost block.* In *Gothic* vaulting, the lowest stone of a diagonal or transverse *rib.* (340, 373)

squinch—An architectural device used as a transition from a square to a polygonal or circular base for a *dome.* It may be composed of *lintels, corbels,* or *arches.* (262)

stained glass—In *Gothic* architecture, the colored glass used for windows. (12, 373, 375)

stamp seal—See *cylinder seal.* (39)

statue—A three-dimensional sculpture. (12)

stave—A wedge-shaped timber; vertically placed staves embellish the architectural features of a building. (311)

stele (pl. **stelae**)—A *carved* stone slab used to mark graves or to commemorate historical events. (36, 499)

stem stitching—See *embroidery.* (362)

stigmata—In Christian art, the wounds Christ received at his crucifixion that miraculously appear on the body of a *saint.* (405)

still life—A picture depicting an arrangement of inanimate objects. (5, 196)

stoa—In ancient Greek architecture, an open building with a roof supported by a row of *columns* parallel to the back wall. A covered *colonnade* or *portico.* (154)

Stoic—A philosophical school of ancient Greece, named after the *stoas* in which the philosophers met. (154)

stoneware—Pottery fired at high temperatures to produce a stonelike hardness and density. (451)

strategos—Greek, "general." (133)

strigil—A tool ancient Greek athletes used to scrape oil from their bodies after exercising. (147)

stringcourse—A raised horizontal *molding,* or band, in masonry. Its principal use is ornamental but it usually reflects interior structure. (11-19A)

strut—A timber plank or other structural member used as a support in a building. Also a short section of marble used to support an arm or leg in a *statue.* (457)

stucco—A type of plaster used as a coating on exterior and interior walls. Also used as a sculptural *medium.* (182)

stupa—A large, mound-shaped Buddhist shrine. (429, 430)

style—A distinctive artistic manner. Period style is the characteristic style of a specific time. Regional style is the style of a particular geographical area. Personal style is an individual artist's unique manner. (3)

stylistic evidence—In art history, the examination of the *style* of an artwork in order to determine its date or the identity of the artist. (3)

stylobate—The uppermost course of the platform of a *classical* Greek temple, which supports the *columns.* (116)

stylus—A needlelike tool used in *engraving* and *incising;* also, an ancient writing instrument used to inscribe clay or wax tablets. (33, 196)

sub gracia—Latin, "under grace." In Christian thought, the period after the coming of Christ. (392)

sub lege—Latin, "under the law." In Christian thought, the period after Moses received the

Ten Commandments and before the coming of Christ. See also *sub gracia*. (392)

subtractive light—The painter's light in art; the light reflected from pigments and objects. See also *additive light*. (7)

subtractive sculpture—A kind of sculpture technique in which materials are taken away from the original mass; *carving*. (11, 64)

sultan—A ruler of the Islamic religion; Muslim ruler. (292)

sunken relief—See *relief*. (73)

Sunnah—The collection of the Prophet Muhammad's moral sayings and descriptions of his deeds. (285)

superimposed orders—*Orders* of architecture that are placed one above another in an *arcaded* or *colonnaded* building, usually in the following sequence: *Doric* (the first story), *Ionic*, and *Corinthian*. Superimposed orders are found in later Greek architecture and were used widely by Roman and *Renaissance* builders. (204)

surah—A chapter of the *Koran*, divided into verses. (285)

sutra—In Buddhism, an account of a sermon by or a dialogue involving the Buddha. A scriptural account of the Buddha. See also *jataka*. (480)

symbol—An image that stands for another image or encapsulates an idea. (5)

symmetria—Greek, "commensurability of parts." Polykleitos's treatise on his *canon* of proportions incorporated the principle of symmetria. (135)

symposium—An ancient Greek banquet attended solely by men (and female servants and prostitutes). (108)

taberna—In Roman architecture, a single-room shop usually covered by a barrel *vault*. (209)

tablero—See *talud-tablero construction*. (496)

tablinum—The study or office in a Roman house. (190)

talud-tablero construction—The alternation of sloping (talud) and vertical (tablero) rubble layers, characteristic of Teotihuacan architecture in Mesoamerica. (496)

tapestry—A weaving *technique* in which the *weft* threads are packed densely over the *warp* threads so that the designs are woven directly into the fabric. (362, 513)

technique—The processes artists employ to create *form*, as well as the distinctive, personal ways in which they handle their materials and tools. (7)

tempera—A *technique* of painting using pigment mixed with egg yolk, glue, or casein; also, the *medium* itself. (219, 404, 502)

templon—The columnar screen separating the sanctuary from the main body of a *Byzantine* church. (277)

tenon—A projection on the end of a piece of wood that is inserted into a corresponding hole (mortise) in another piece of wood to form a joint. (480)

tephra—The volcanic ash produced by the eruption on the *Cycladic* island of Thera. (92)

tepidarium—The warm-bath section of a Roman bathing establishment. (220)

terminus ante quem—Latin, "point [date] before which." (2)

terminus post quem—Latin, "point [date] after which." (2)

terracotta—Hard-baked clay, used for sculpture and as a building material. It may be *glazed* or painted. (90, 414)

tessera (pl. tesserae)—Greek, "cube." A tiny stone or piece of glass cut to the desired shape and size for use in forming a *mosaic*. (150, 245, 291, 299)

tetrarch—One of four corulers. (224)

tetrarchy—Greek, "rule by four." A type of Roman government established in the late third century CE by Diocletian in an attempt to foster order by sharing power with potential rivals. (224)

texture—The quality of a surface (rough, smooth, hard, soft, shiny, dull) as revealed by light. In represented texture, a painter depicts an object as having a certain texture even though the pigment is the real texture. (8)

theatron—Greek, "place for seeing." In ancient Greek theaters, the slope overlooking the *orchestra* on which the spectators sat. (151)

Theotokos—Greek, "she who bore God." The Virgin Mary, the mother of Jesus. (245, 267)

thermoluminescence—A method of dating by measuring amounts of radiation found within the clay of ceramic or sculptural forms, as well as in the clay cores from metal castings. (523)

Third Style mural—In Roman *mural* painting, the style in which delicate linear fantasies were sketched on predominantly *monochromatic* backgrounds. (194)

tholos (pl. tholoi)—A temple with a circular plan. Also, the burial chamber of a *tholos tomb*. (99, 151)

tholos tomb—In *Mycenaean* architecture, a beehive-shaped tomb with a circular plan. (99)

thrust—The outward force exerted by an *arch* or a *vault* that must be counterbalanced by a *buttress*. (184)

toga—The garment worn by an ancient Roman male citizen. (176)

tonality—See *color*. (7)

tondo (pl. tondi)—A circular painting or *relief* sculpture. (219, 585, 10-15A)

Torah—The Hebrew religious scroll containing the *Pentateuch*. (235)

torana—Gateway in the stone fence around a *stupa*, located at the cardinal points of the compass. (430, 15-8A)

torque—The distinctive necklace worn by the Gauls. (156)

tracery—Ornamental stonework for holding *stained glass* in place, characteristic of *Gothic cathedrals*. In plate tracery, the glass fills only the "punched holes" in the heavy ornamental stonework. In bar tracery, the stained-glass

windows fill almost the entire opening, and the stonework is unobtrusive. (373, 414)

tramezzo—A screen placed across the *nave* of a church to separate the clergy from the lay audience. (14-6A)

transept—The part of a church with an axis that crosses the *nave* at a right angle. (243, 14-5A)

transubstantiation—The transformation of the Eucharistic bread and wine into the body and blood of Christ. (24-18A)

transverse arch—An *arch* separating one *vaulted bay* from the next. (340)

transverse barrel vault—In medieval architecture, a semicylindrical *vault* oriented at a 90° angle to the *nave* of a church. (12-10A)

transverse rib—See *rib*. (373)

treasury—In ancient Greece, a small building set up for the safe storage of *votive offerings*. (119)

trefoil—A cloverlike ornament or symbol with stylized leaves in groups of three. (425)

trefoil arch—A triple-lobed *arch*. (402)

tribune—In church architecture, a gallery over the inner *aisle* flanking the *nave*. (337)

triclinium—The dining room of a Roman house. (190, 6-9A)

trident—The three-pronged pitchfork associated with the ancient Greek sea god Poseidon (Roman, Neptune). (107, 435)

triforium—In a *Gothic cathedral*, the *blind arcaded* gallery below the *clerestory*; occasionally, the *arcades* are filled with *stained glass*. (370, 373)

triglyph—A triple projecting, grooved member of a *Doric frieze* that alternates with *metopes*. (116)

trilithon—A pair of *monoliths* topped with a *lintel*; found in *megalithic* structures. (28)

Trinity—In Christianity, God the Father, his son Jesus Christ, and the Holy Spirit. (240)

tripod—An ancient Greek deep bowl on a tall three-legged stand. (5-17A)

triptych—A three-paneled painting, ivory plaque, or *altarpiece*. Also, a small, portable shrine with hinged wings used for private devotion. (275, 392, 415)

triratna—A tripartite symbol of the three jewels of Buddhism—the Buddha himself, his *dharma*, and the *sangha*. (15-8A)

triumphal arch—In Roman architecture, a freestanding *arch* commemorating an important event, such as a military victory or the opening of a new road. (205)

true fresco—See *fresco*. (408, 409, 502)

trumeau—In church architecture, the *pillar* or center post supporting the *lintel* in the middle of the doorway. (344)

tubicen—Latin, "trumpet player." (157)

tughra—The official signature of an Ottoman emperor. (10-23A)

tumulus (pl. tumuli)—Latin, "burial mound." In Etruscan architecture, tumuli cover one or more subterranean multichambered tombs cut out of the local tufa (limestone). Also characteristic of the Japanese Kofun period of the third and fourth centuries. (27, 170, 309, 478)

tunnel vault—See *vault*. (12, 52, 184, 338)

turris—See *westwork*. (323)

Tuscan column—The standard type of Etruscan *column*. It resembles ancient Greek *Doric* columns but is made of wood, is unfluted, and has a *base*. Also a popular motif in *Renaissance* architecture. (168)

twisted perspective—See *composite view*. (23, 523)

tympanum (pl. **tympana**)—The space enclosed by a *lintel* and an *arch* over a doorway. (344, 14-12A)

typology—In Christian theology, the recognition of concordances between events, especially between episodes in the Old and New Testaments. (238)

Upanishads—South Asian religious texts of ca. 800–500 BCE that introduced the concepts of *samsara, karma,* and *moksha*. (427)

uraeus—An Egyptian cobra; one of the emblems of *pharaonic* kingship. (63)

urna—A whorl of hair, represented as a dot, between the brows; one of the *lakshanas* of the Buddha. (427)

ushabti—In ancient Egypt, a figurine placed in a tomb to act as a servant to the deceased in the afterlife. (61)

ushnisha—A knot of hair on the top of the head; one of the *lakshanas* of the Buddha. (427)

valley temple—The temple closest to the Nile River associated with each of the Great Pyramids at Gizeh in ancient Egypt. (62)

value—See *color*. (7)

vanth—An Etruscan female winged demon of death. (176)

vassal—In *feudalism,* a person who swears allegiance to a *liege lord* and renders him military service in return for tenure of a portion of the lord's land. (334)

vault (adj. **vaulted**)—A masonry roof or ceiling constructed on the *arch* principle, or a concrete roof of the same shape. A barrel (or tunnel) vault, semicylindrical in cross-*section,* is in effect a deep arch or an uninterrupted series of arches, one behind the other, over an oblong space. A quadrant vault is a half-barrel vault. A groin (or cross) vault is formed at the point at which two barrel vaults intersect at right angles. In a ribbed vault, there is a framework of *ribs* or arches under the intersections of the vaulting

sections. A sexpartite vault is one whose ribs divide the vault into six compartments. A fan vault is a vault characteristic of English *Perpendicular Gothic* architecture, in which radiating ribs form a fanlike pattern. (12, 52)

vaulting web—See *web*. (373)

Veda—Sanskrit, "knowledge." One of four second-millennium BCE South Asian compilations of religious learning. (427)

velarium—In a Roman *amphitheater,* the cloth awning that could be rolled down from the top of the *cavea* to shield spectators from sun or rain. (190)

vellum—Calfskin prepared as a surface for writing or painting. (249)

venationes—Ancient Roman wild animal hunts staged in an *amphitheater*. (203)

veristic—True to natural appearance; super-realistic. (185)

vihara—A Buddhist *monastery,* often cut into a hill. (429)

vimana—A pyramidal tower over the *garbha griha* of a Hindu temple of the southern style. (438, 439)

vita contemplativa—Latin, "contemplative life." The secluded spiritual life of monks and nuns. (342)

vizier—An Egyptian pharaoh's chief administrator. (3-11B)

volume—The *space* that *mass* organizes, divides, or encloses. (8)

volute—A spiral, scroll-like form characteristic of the ancient Greek *Ionic* and the Roman *Composite capital*. (51, 116)

votive offering—A gift of gratitude to a deity. (35)

voussoir—A wedge-shaped stone block used in the construction of a true *arch*. The central voussoir, which sets the arch, is called the keystone. (175, 344)

warp—The vertical threads of a loom or cloth. (510)

wat—A Buddhist *monastery* in Cambodia. (443)

web—The masonry blocks that fill the area between the *ribs* of a *groin vault*. Also called vaulting web. (368)

wedjat—The eye of the Egyptian falcon-god Horus, a powerful *amulet*. (57, 61)

weft—The horizontal threads of a loom or cloth. (510)

weld—To join metal parts by heating, as in assembling the separate parts of a *statue* made by *casting*. (11)

were-jaguar—A composite human-jaguar; a common motif in Olmec art. (494)

westwork—German, "western entrance structure." The *facade* and towers at the western end of a medieval church, principally in Germany. In contemporaneous documents the westwork is called a castellum (Latin, "castle" or "fortress") or turris ("tower"). (323)

white-ground painting—An ancient Greek vase-painting *technique* in which the pot was first covered with a *slip* of very fine white clay, over which black *glaze* was used to outline figures, and diluted brown, purple, red, and white were used to color them. (142)

yaksha (m.), **yakshi** (f.)—Lesser local male and female Buddhist and Hindu divinities. Yakshis are goddesses associated with fertility and vegetation. Yakshas, the male equivalent of yakshis, are often represented as fleshy but powerful males. (430, 432, 15-6B)

yamato-e—Also known as native-style painting, a purely Japanese style that often involved colorful, decorative representations of Japanese narratives or *landscapes*. (485)

yang—In Chinese cosmology, the principle of active masculine energy, which permeates the universe in varying proportions with yin, the principle of passive feminine energy. (463)

yasti—In Buddhist architecture, the mast or pole that arises from the dome of the *stupa* and its *harmika* and symbolizes the axis of the universe; it is adorned with a series of chatras (stone disks). (430)

yin—See *yang*. (463)

yoga—A method for controlling the body and relaxing the mind used in later Indian religions to yoke, or unite, the practitioner to the divine. (426)

yosegi—Japanese *joined-wood technique*. (17-13A)

Zen—A Japanese Buddhist sect and its doctrine, emphasizing enlightenment through intuition and introspection rather than the study of scripture. In Chinese, Chan. (470)

ziggurat—In ancient Mesopotamian architecture, a monumental platform for a temple. (33, 289)

BIBLIOGRAPHY

This list of books is very selective but comprehensive enough to satisfy the reading interests of the beginning art history student and general reader. Significantly expanded from the previous edition, the 14th edition bibliography can also serve as the basis for undergraduate research papers. The resources listed range from works that are valuable primarily for their reproductions to those that are scholarly surveys of schools and periods or monographs on individual artists. The emphasis is on recent in-print books and on books likely to be found in college and municipal libraries. No entries for periodical articles appear, but the bibliography begins with a list of some of the major journals that publish art historical scholarship in English.

Selected Periodicals

African Arts
American Art
American Indian Art
American Journal of Archaeology
Antiquity
Archaeology
Archives of American Art
Archives of Asian Art
Ars Orientalis
Art Bulletin
Art History
Art in America
Art Journal
Artforum International
Artnews
Burlington Magazine
Gesta
History of Photography
Journal of Egyptian Archaeology
Journal of Roman Archaeology
Journal of the Society of Architectural Historians
Journal of the Warburg and Courtauld Institutes
Latin American Antiquity
October
Oxford Art Journal
Women's Art Journal

General Studies

Baxandall, Michael. *Patterns of Intention: On the Historical Explanation of Pictures*. New Haven, Conn.: Yale University Press, 1985.

Bindman, David, ed. *The Thames & Hudson Encyclopedia of British Art*. London: Thames & Hudson, 1988.

Boström, Antonia. *The Encyclopedia of Sculpture*. 3 vols. London: Routledge, 2003.

Broude, Norma, and Mary D. Garrard, eds. *The Expanding Discourse: Feminism and Art History*. New York: Harper Collins, 1992.

Bryson, Norman. *Vision and Painting: The Logic of the Gaze*. New Haven, Conn.: Yale University Press, 1983.

Bryson, Norman, Michael Ann Holly, and Keith Moxey. *Visual Theory: Painting and Interpretation*. New York: Cambridge University Press, 1991.

Burden, Ernest. *Illustrated Dictionary of Architecture*. 2d ed. New York: McGraw-Hill, 2002.

Büttner, Nils. *Landscape Painting: A History*. New York: Abbeville, 2006.

Carrier, David. *A World Art History and Its Objects*. University Park: Pennsylvania State University Press, 2009.

Chadwick, Whitney. *Women, Art, and Society*. 4th ed. New York: Thames & Hudson, 2007.

Cheetham, Mark A., Michael Ann Holly, and Keith Moxey, eds. *The Subjects of Art History: Historical Objects in Contemporary Perspective*. New York: Cambridge University Press, 1998.

Chilvers, Ian, and Harold Osborne, eds. *The Oxford Dictionary of Art*. 3d ed. New York: Oxford University Press, 2004.

Corbin, George A. *Native Arts of North America, Africa, and the South Pacific: An Introduction*. New York: Harper Collins, 1988.

Crouch, Dora P., and June G. Johnson. *Traditions in Architecture: Africa, America, Asia, and Oceania*. New York: Oxford University Press, 2000.

Curl, James Stevens. *Oxford Dictionary of Architecture and Landscape Architecture*. 2d ed. New York: Oxford University Press, 2006.

Duby, Georges, ed. *Sculpture: From Antiquity to the Present*. 2 vols. Cologne: Taschen, 1999.

Encyclopedia of World Art. 17 vols. New York: McGraw-Hill, 1959–1987.

Fielding, Mantle. *Dictionary of American Painters, Sculptors, and Engravers*. 2d ed. Poughkeepsie, N.Y.: Apollo, 1986.

Fine, Sylvia Honig. *Women and Art: A History of Women Painters and Sculptors from the Renaissance to the 20th Century*. Rev. ed. Montclair, N.J.: Alanheld & Schram, 1978.

Fleming, John, Hugh Honour, and Nikolaus Pevsner. *The Penguin Dictionary of Architecture and Landscape Architecture*. 5th ed. New York: Penguin, 2000.

Frazier, Nancy. *The Penguin Concise Dictionary of Art History*. New York: Penguin, 2000.

Freedberg, David. *The Power of Images: Studies in the History and Theory of Response*. Chicago: University of Chicago Press, 1989.

Gaze, Delia., ed. *Dictionary of Women Artists*. 2 vols. London: Routledge, 1997.

Hall, James. *Dictionary of Subjects and Symbols in Art*. 2d ed. Boulder, Colo.: Westview, 2008.

Harris, Anne Sutherland, and Linda Nochlin. *Women Artists: 1550–1950*. Los Angeles: Los Angeles County Museum of Art; New York: Knopf, 1977.

Hauser, Arnold. *The Sociology of Art*. Chicago: University of Chicago Press, 1982.

Hults, Linda C. *The Print in the Western World: An Introductory History*. Madison: University of Wisconsin Press, 1996.

Kemp, Martin. *The Science of Art: Optical Themes in Western Art from Brunelleschi to Seurat*. New Haven, Conn.: Yale University Press, 1990.

Kostof, Spiro, and Gregory Castillo. *A History of Architecture: Settings and Rituals*. 2d ed. Oxford: Oxford University Press, 1995.

Kultermann, Udo. *The History of Art History*. New York: Abaris, 1993.

Lucie-Smith, Edward. *The Thames & Hudson Dictionary of Art Terms*. 2d ed. New York: Thames & Hudson, 2004.

Moffett, Marian, Michael Fazio, and Lawrence Wadehouse. *A World History of Architecture*. Boston: McGraw-Hill, 2004.

Morgan, Anne Lee. *Oxford Dictionary of American Art and Artists*. New York: Oxford University Press, 2008.

Murray, Peter, and Linda Murray. *A Dictionary of Art and Artists*. 7th ed. New York: Penguin, 1998.

Nelson, Robert S., and Richard Shiff, eds. *Critical Terms for Art History*. Chicago: University of Chicago Press, 1996.

Pazanelli, Roberta, ed. *The Color of Life: Polychromy in Sculpture from Antiquity to the Present*. Los Angeles: J. Paul Getty Museum, 2008.

Penny, Nicholas. *The Materials of Sculpture*. New Haven, Conn.: Yale University Press, 1993.

Pevsner, Nikolaus. *A History of Building Types*. London: Thames & Hudson, 1987. Reprint of 1979 ed.

———. *An Outline of European Architecture*. 8th ed. Baltimore: Penguin, 1974.

Pierce, James Smith. *From Abacus to Zeus: A Handbook of Art History*. 7th ed. Upper Saddle River, N.J.: Pearson Prentice Hall, 1998.

Placzek, Adolf K., ed. *Macmillan Encyclopedia of Architects*. 4 vols. New York: Macmillan, 1982.

Podro, Michael. *The Critical Historians of Art*. New Haven, Conn.: Yale University Press, 1982.

Pollock, Griselda. *Vision and Difference: Femininity, Feminism, and Histories of Art*. London: Routledge, 1988.

Pregill, Philip, and Nancy Volkman. *Landscapes in History Design and Planning in the Eastern and Western Traditions.* 2d ed. Hoboken, N.J.: Wiley, 1999.

Preziosi, Donald, ed. *The Art of Art History: A Critical Anthology.* New York: Oxford University Press, 1998.

Read, Herbert. *The Thames & Hudson Dictionary of Art and Artists.* Rev. ed. New York: Thames & Hudson, 1994.

Reid, Jane D. *The Oxford Guide to Classical Mythology in the Arts 1300–1990s.* 2 vols. New York: Oxford University Press, 1993.

Rogers, Elizabeth Barlow. *Landscape Design: A Cultural and Architectural History.* New York: Abrams, 2001.

Roth, Leland M. *Understanding Architecture: Its Elements, History, and Meaning.* 2d ed. Boulder, Colo.: Westview, 2006.

Schama, Simon. *The Power of Art.* New York: Ecco, 2006.

Slatkin, Wendy. *Women Artists in History: From Antiquity to the 20th Century.* 4th ed. Upper Saddle River, N.J.: Prentice Hall, 2000.

Steer, John, and Antony White. *Atlas of Western Art History: Artists, Sites, and Monuments from Ancient Greece to the Modern Age.* New York: Facts on File, 1994.

Stratton, Arthur. *The Orders of Architecture: Greek, Roman, and Renaissance.* London: Studio, 1986.

Summers, David. *Real Spaces: World Art History and the Rise of Western Modernism.* London: Phaidon, 2003.

Sutton, Ian. *Western Architecture: From Ancient Greece to the Present.* New York: Thames & Hudson, 1999.

Trachtenberg, Marvin, and Isabelle Hyman. *Architecture, from Prehistory to Post Modernism.* 2d ed. Upper Saddle River, N.J.: Prentice Hall, 2003.

Turner, Jane, ed. *The Dictionary of Art.* 34 vols. New ed. New York: Oxford University Press, 2003.

Watkin, David. *A History of Western Architecture.* 4th ed. London: Laurence King, 2010.

West, Shearer. *Portraiture.* New York: Oxford University Press, 2004.

Wittkower, Rudolf. *Sculpture Processes and Principles.* New York: Harper & Row, 1977.

Wren, Linnea H., and Janine M. Carter, eds. *Perspectives on Western Art: Source Documents and Readings from the Ancient Near East through the Middle Ages.* New York: Harper & Row, 1987.

Zijlmans, Kitty, and Wilfried van Damme, eds. *World Art Studies: Exploring Concepts and Approaches.* Amsterdam: Valiz, 2008.

Ancient Art, General

Aruz, Joan, and Ronald Wallenfels, eds. *Art of the First Cities: The Third Millennium BC from the Mediterranean to the Indus.* New York: Metropolitan Museum of Art, 2003.

Beard, Mary, and John Henderson. *Classical Art: From Greece to Rome.* New York: Oxford University Press, 2001.

Boardman, John. *The World of Ancient Art.* London: Thames & Hudson, 2006.

———, ed. *The Oxford History of Classical Art.* New York: Oxford University Press, 1997.

Chitham, Robert. *The Classical Orders of Architecture.* 2d ed. Boston: Architectural Press, 2005.

Clayton, Peter A., and Martin J. Price, eds. *The Seven Wonders of the Ancient World.* New York: Routledge, 1988.

Connolly, Peter, and Hazel Dodge. *The Ancient City: Life in Classical Athens and Rome.* New York: Oxford University Press, 1998.

De Grummond, Nancy Thomson, ed. *An Encyclopedia of the History of Classical Archaeology.* 2 vols. Westport, Conn.: Greenwood, 1996.

Dunbabin, Katherine. *Mosaics of the Greek and Roman World.* New York: Cambridge University Press, 1999.

Gates, Charles. *Ancient Cities: The Archaeology of Urban Life in the Ancient Near East and Egypt, Greece, and Rome.* London: Routledge, 2003.

Grossman, Janet Burnett. *Looking at Greek and Roman Sculpture in Stone: A Guide to Terms, Styles, and Techniques.* Los Angeles: J. Paul Getty Museum, 2003.

Kampen, Natalie B., ed. *Sexuality in Ancient Art.* New York: Cambridge University Press, 1996.

Lexicon Iconographicum Mythologiae Classicae. 10 vols. Zurich: Artemis, 1981–1999.

Ling, Roger. *Ancient Mosaics.* Princeton, N.J.: Princeton University Press, 1998.

Lloyd, Seton, and Hans Wolfgang Muller. *Ancient Architecture: Mesopotamia, Egypt, Crete.* New York: Electa/Rizzoli, 1980.

Oliphant, Margaret. *The Atlas of the Ancient World: Charting the Great Civilizations of the Past.* New York: Simon & Schuster, 1992.

Onians, John. *Classical Art and the Cultures of Greece and Rome.* New Haven, Conn.: Yale University Press, 1999.

Renfrew, Colin, and Paul G. Bahn. *Archaeology: Theories, Methods, and Practices.* London: Thames & Hudson, 1991.

Stillwell, Richard, William L. MacDonald, and Marian H. McAllister, eds. *The Princeton Encyclopedia of Classical Sites.* Princeton, N.J.: Princeton University Press, 1976.

Trigger, Bruce. *Understanding Early Civilizations: A Comparative Study.* New York: Cambridge University Press, 2003.

Ward-Perkins, John B. *Cities of Ancient Greece and Italy: Planning in Classical Antiquity.* Rev. ed. New York: Braziller, 1987.

Wolf, Walther. *The Origins of Western Art: Egypt, Mesopotamia, the Aegean.* New York: Universe, 1989.

Chapter 1: Art before History

Aujoulat, Norbert. *Lascaux: Movement, Space, and Time.* New York: Abrams, 2005.

Bahn, Paul G. *The Cambridge Illustrated History of Prehistoric Art.* New York: Cambridge University Press, 1998.

———. *Cave Art: A Guide to the Decorated Ice Age Caves of Europe.* London: Frances Lincoln, 2007.

Bahn, Paul G., and Jean Vertut. *Journey through the Ice Age.* Berkeley: University of California Press, 1997.

Beltrán, Antonio, ed. *The Cave of Altamira.* New York: Abrams, 1999.

Berhgaus, Guner. *New Perspectives on Prehistoric Art.* Westport, Conn.: Praeger, 2004.

Burl, Aubrey. *Great Stone Circles.* New Haven, Conn.: Yale University Press, 1999.

Chauvet, Jean-Marie, Eliette Brunel Deschamps, and Christian Hillaire. *Dawn of Art: The Chauvet Cave.* New York: Abrams, 1996.

Chippindale, Christopher. *Stonehenge Complete.* 3d ed. New York: Thames & Hudson, 2004.

Clottes, Jean. *Cave Art.* London: Phaidon, 2008.

———. *Chauvet Cave: The Art of Earliest Times.* Salt Lake City: University of Utah Press, 2003.

Cunliffe, Barry, ed. *The Oxford Illustrated Prehistory of Europe.* New York: Oxford University Press, 2001.

Guthrie, R. Dale. *The Nature of Paleolithic Art.* Chicago: University of Chicago Press, 2005.

Hodder, Ian. *The Leopard's Tale: Revealing the Mysteries of Çatalhöyük.* London: Thames & Hudson, 2006.

Kenyon, Kathleen M. *Digging up Jericho.* New York: Praeger, 1974.

Leroi-Gourhan, André. *The Dawn of European Art: An Introduction to Paleolithic Cave Painting.* Cambridge: Cambridge University Press, 1982.

Marshack, Alexander. *The Roots of Civilization: The Cognitive Beginnings of Man's First Art, Symbol and Notation.* 2d ed. Wakefield, R.I.: Moyer Bell, 1991.

Pfeiffer, John E. *The Creative Explosion: An Inquiry into the Origins of Art and Religion.* New York: Harper & Row, 1982.

Renfrew, Colin, ed. *British Prehistory: A New Outline.* London: Noyes, 1975.

Ruspoli, Mario. *The Cave of Lascaux: The Final Photographs.* New York: Abrams, 1987.

Scarre, Chris. *Exploring Prehistoric Europe.* New York: Oxford University Press, 1998.

Wainwright, Geoffrey. *The Henge Monuments: Ceremony and Society in Prehistoric Britain.* London: Thames & Hudson, 1990.

White, Randall. *Prehistoric Art: The Symbolic Journey of Humankind.* New York: Abrams, 2003.

Chapter 2: Mesopotamia and Persia

Akurgal, Ekrem. *Art of the Hittites.* New York: Abrams, 1962.

Allen, Lindsay. *The Persian Empire.* Chicago: University of Chicago Press, 2005.

Amiet, Pierre. *Art of the Ancient Near East.* New York: Abrams, 1980.

Ascalone, Enrico. *Mesopotamia: Assyrians, Sumerians, Babylonians.* Berkeley and Los Angeles: University of California Press, 2007.

Bahrani, Zainab. *The Graven Image: Representation in Babylonia and Assyria.* Philadelphia: University of Pennsylvania Press, 2003.

Bienkowski, Piotr, and Alan Millard, eds. *Dictionary of the Ancient Near East.* Philadelphia: University of Pennsylvania Press, 2000.

Collins, Paul. *Assyrian Palace Sculptures.* Austin: University of Texas Press, 2008.

Collon, Dominique. *Ancient Near Eastern Art.* Berkeley: University of California Press, 1995.

———. *First Impressions: Cylinder Seals in the Ancient Near East.* 2d ed. London: British Museum, 1993.

———. *Near Eastern Seals.* Berkeley: University of California Press, 1990.

Crawford, Harriet. *Sumer and the Sumerians.* 2d ed. New York: Cambridge University Press, 2004.

Curatola, Giovanni, ed. *The Art and Architecture of Mesopotamia.* New York: Abbeville, 2007.

Curtis, John E. *Ancient Persia.* Cambridge, Mass.: Harvard University Press, 1990.

Curtis, John E., and Julian E. Reade. *Art and Empire: Treasures from Assyria in the British Museum.* New York: Metropolitan Museum of Art, 1995.

Curtis, John E., and Nigel Tallis, eds. *Forgotten Empire: The World of Ancient Persia.* Berkeley: University of California Press, 2005.

Finkel, Irving L., and Michael J. Seymour, eds. *Babylon.* New York: Oxford University Press, 2008.

Foster, Benjamin R., and Karen Polinger Foster. *Civilizations of Ancient Iraq.* Princeton, N.J.: Princeton University Press, 2009.

Frankfort, Henri. *The Art and Architecture of the Ancient Orient.* 5th ed. New Haven, Conn.: Yale University Press, 1996.

Ghirshman, Roman. *The Arts of Ancient Iran: From Its Origins to the Time of Alexander the Great.* New York: Golden, 1964.

———. *Persian Art: The Parthian and Sassanian Dynasties, 249 BC–AD 651.* New York: Golden, 1962.

Gunter, Ann C., ed. *Investigating Artistic Environments in the Ancient Near East.* Washington, D.C.: Arthur M. Sackler Gallery, 1990.

Harper, Prudence O., Joan Aruz, and Françoise Tallon, eds. *The Royal City of Susa: Ancient Near Eastern Treasures in the Louvre*. New York: Metropolitan Museum of Art, 1992.

Leick, Gwendolyn. *Mesopotamia: The Invention of the City*. New York: Penguin, 2003.

Lloyd, Seton. *The Archaeology of Mesopotamia: From the Old Stone Age to the Persian Conquest*. London: Thames & Hudson, 1984.

Macqueen, James G. *The Hittites and Their Contemporaries in Asia Minor*. Rev. ed. New York: Thames & Hudson, 1986.

Meyers, Eric M., ed. *The Oxford Encyclopedia of Archaeology in the Near East*. 5 vols. New York: Oxford University Press, 1997.

Moortgat, Anton. *The Art of Ancient Mesopotamia*. New York: Phaidon, 1969.

Oates, Joan. *Babylon*. Rev. ed. London: Thames & Hudson, 1986.

Parrot, André. *The Arts of Assyria*. New York: Golden, 1961.

———. *Sumer: The Dawn of Art*. New York: Golden, 1961.

Porada, Edith. *Man and Images in the Ancient Near East*. Wakefield, R.I.: Moyer Bell, 1995.

Porada, Edith, and Robert H. Dyson. *The Art of Ancient Iran: Pre-Islamic Cultures*. Rev. ed. New York: Greystone, 1969.

Postgate, J. Nicholas. *Early Mesopotamia: Society and Economy at the Dawn of History*. London: Routledge, 1992.

Potts, Daniel T. *The Archaeology of Elam: Formation and Transformation of an Ancient Iranian State*. New York: Cambridge University Press, 1999.

Reade, Julian E. *Assyrian Sculpture*. Cambridge, Mass.: Harvard University Press, 1999.

———. *Mesopotamia*. Cambridge, Mass.: Harvard University Press, 1991.

Roaf, Michael. *Cultural Atlas of Mesopotamia and the Ancient Near East*. New York: Facts on File, 1990.

Russell, John M. *Sennacherib's Palace without Rival at Nineveh*. Chicago: University of Chicago Press, 1991.

Saggs, H.W.F. *Babylonians*. London: British Museum, 1995.

Sasson, Jack M., ed. *Civilizations of the Ancient Near East*. 4 vols. New York: Scribner, 1995.

Snell, Daniel C. *Life in the Ancient Near East: 3100–332 BC*. New Haven, Conn.: Yale University Press, 1997.

Strommenger, Eva, and Max Hirmer. *5,000 Years of the Art of Mesopotamia*. New York: Abrams, 1964.

Van de Mieroop, Marc. *The Ancient Mesopotamian City*. New York: Oxford University Press, 1997.

Zettler, Richard L., and Lee Horne. *Treasures from the Royal Tombs of Ur*. Philadelphia: University of Pennsylvania Museum of Archaeology and Anthropology, 1998.

Chapter 3: Egypt under the Pharaohs

Allen, James P., ed. *Egyptian Art in the Age of the Pyramids*. New York: Abrams, 1999.

Arnold, Dieter. *Building in Egypt: Pharaonic Stone Masonry*. New York: Oxford University Press, 1991.

Arnold, Dorothea. *The Royal Women of Amarna*. New York: Metropolitan Museum of Art, 1996.

———. *When the Pyramids Were Built: Egyptian Art of the Old Kingdom*. New York: Rizzoli, 1999.

Baines, John, and Jaromír Málek. *Atlas of Ancient Egypt*. New York: Facts on File, 1980.

Bard, Kathryn A. *An Introduction to the Archaeology of Ancient Egypt*. Oxford: Blackwell, 2007.

———, ed. *Encyclopedia of the Archaeology of Ancient Egypt*. London: Routledge, 1999.

Bianchi, Robert S. *Cleopatra's Egypt: Age of the Ptolemies*. Brooklyn: Brooklyn Museum, 1988.

———. *Splendors of Ancient Egypt from the Egyptian Museum, Cairo*. London: Booth-Clibborn, 1996.

Capel, Anne K., and Glenn E. Markoe, eds. *Mistress of the House, Mistress of Heaven: Women in Ancient Egypt*. New York: Hudson Hills, 1996.

D'Auria, Sue, Peter Lacovara, and Catharine H. Roehrig. *Mummies and Magic: The Funerary Arts of Ancient Egypt*. Boston: Museum of Fine Arts, 1988.

Davis, Whitney. *The Canonical Tradition in Ancient Egyptian Art*. New York: Cambridge University Press, 1989.

Dodson, Aidan, and Salima Ikram. *The Tomb in Ancient Egypt*. New York: Thames & Hudson, 2008.

Hawass, Zahi. *Valley of the Golden Mummies*. New York: Abrams, 2000.

Ikram, Salima, and Aidan Dodson. *The Mummy in Ancient Egypt: Equipping the Dead for Eternity*. New York: Thames & Hudson, 1998.

Kemp, Barry J. *Ancient Egypt: Anatomy of a Civilization*. 2d ed. New York: Routledge, 2006.

Kozloff, Arielle P., and Betsy M. Bryan. *Egypt's Dazzling Sun: Amenhotep III and His World*. Cleveland: Cleveland Museum of Art, 1992.

Lange, Kurt, and Max Hirmer. *Egypt: Architecture, Sculpture, and Painting in Three Thousand Years*. 4th ed. London: Phaidon, 1968.

Lehner, Mark. *The Complete Pyramids: Solving the Ancient Mysteries*. New York: Thames & Hudson, 1997.

Mahdy, Christine, ed. *The World of the Pharaohs: A Complete Guide to Ancient Egypt*. London: Thames & Hudson, 1990.

Málek, Jaromír. *Egypt: 4,000 Years of Art*. New York: Phaidon, 2003.

———. *Egyptian Art*. London: Phaidon, 1999.

———, ed. *Egypt: Ancient Culture, Modern Land*. Norman: University of Oklahoma Press, 1993.

Redford, Donald B. *Akhenaton, the Heretic King*. Princeton, N.J.: Princeton University Press, 1984.

———, ed. *The Oxford Encyclopedia of Ancient Egypt*. 3 vols. New York: Oxford University Press, 2001.

Reeves, C. Nicholas. *The Complete Tutankhamun: The King, the Tomb, the Royal Treasure*. London: Thames & Hudson, 1990.

Robins, Gay. *The Art of Ancient Egypt*. Rev. ed. Cambridge, Mass.: Harvard University Press, 2008.

———. *Egyptian Painting and Relief*. Aylesbury: Shire, 1986.

———. *Proportion and Style in Ancient Egyptian Art*. Austin: University of Texas Press, 1994.

———. *Women in Ancient Egypt*. London: British Museum, 1993.

Romer, John. *Valley of the Kings: Exploring the Tombs of the Pharaohs*. New York: Holt, 1994.

Russmann, Edna R. *Egyptian Sculpture: Cairo and Luxor*. Austin: University of Texas Press, 1989.

Schäfer, Heinrich. *Principles of Egyptian Art*. Rev. ed. Oxford: Clarendon, 1986.

Schulz, Regina, and Matthias Seidel, eds. *Egypt: The World of the Pharaohs*. Cologne: Könemann, 1999.

Shafer, Byron E., ed. *Temples of Ancient Egypt*. Ithaca, N.Y.: Cornell University Press, 1997.

Shaw, Ian, and Paul Nicholson. *The Dictionary of Ancient Egypt*. London: British Museum, 1995.

Silverman, David P., ed. *Ancient Egypt*. New York: Oxford University Press, 1997.

Smith, William Stevenson, and William Kelly Simpson. *The Art and Architecture of Ancient Egypt*. Rev. ed. New Haven, Conn.: Yale University Press, 1998.

Tiradritti, Francesco. *Egyptian Wall Paintings*. New York: Abbeville, 2008.

Weeks, Kent R. *The Treasures of Luxor and the Valley of the Kings*. Vercelli: White Star, 2005.

———, ed. *Valley of the Kings*. Vercelli: White Star, 2001.

Wildung, Dietrich. *Egypt: From Prehistory to the Romans*. Cologne: Taschen, 1997.

Chapter 4: The Prehistoric Aegean

Andreadaki-Vlazaki, Maria, ed. *From the Land of the Labyrinth: Minoan Crete 3000–1100 B.C.* New York: Alexander S. Onassis Public Benefit Foundation, 2008.

Barber, R.L.N. *The Cyclades in the Bronze Age*. Iowa City: University of Iowa Press, 1987.

Betancourt, Philip P. *A History of Minoan Pottery*. Princeton, N.J.: Princeton University Press, 1965.

———. *Introduction to Aegean Art*. New York: Institute for Aegean Prehistory, 2007.

Cadogan, Gerald. *Palaces of Minoan Crete*. London: Methuen, 1980.

Castleden, Rodney. *Mycenaeans*. London: Routledge, 2005.

Chadwick, John. *The Mycenaean World*. New York: Cambridge University Press, 1976.

Cullen, Tracey, ed. *Aegean Prehistory: A Review*. Boston: Archaeological Institute of America, 2001.

Demargne, Pierre. *The Birth of Greek Art*. New York: Golden, 1964.

Dickinson, Oliver P.T.K. *The Aegean Bronze Age*. New York: Cambridge University Press, 1994.

Doumas, Christos. *Thera, Pompeii of the Ancient Aegean: Excavations at Akrotiri, 1967–1979*. New York: Thames & Hudson, 1983.

———. *The Wall-Paintings of Thera*. Athens: Thera Foundation, 1992.

Fitton, J. Lesley. *Cycladic Art*. 2d ed. Cambridge, Mass.: Harvard University Press, 1999.

———. *The Discovery of the Greek Bronze Age*. London: British Museum, 1995.

Forsyth, Phyllis Young. *Thera in the Bronze Age*. New York: Peter Lang, 1997.

Getz-Preziosi, Patricia. *Sculptors of the Cyclades: Individual and Tradition in the Third Millennium BC*. Ann Arbor: University of Michigan Press, 1987.

Graham, James W. *The Palaces of Crete*. Princeton, N.J.: Princeton University Press, 1987.

Hampe, Roland, and Erika Simon. *The Birth of Greek Art: From the Mycenaean to the Archaic Period*. New York: Oxford University Press, 1981.

Higgins, Reynold. *Minoan and Mycenaean Art*. Rev. ed. New York: Thames & Hudson, 1997.

Hood, Sinclair. *The Arts in Prehistoric Greece*. New Haven, Conn.: Yale University Press, 1992.

Immerwahr, Sarah A. *Aegean Painting in the Bronze Age*. University Park: Pennsylvania State University Press, 1990.

MacGillivray, J. A. *Minotaur: Sir Arthur Evans and the Archaeology of the Minoan Myth*. New York: Hill and Wang, 2000.

Marinatos, Nanno. *Art and Religion in Thera: Reconstructing a Bronze Age Society*. Athens: Mathioulakis, 1984.

Marinatos, Spyridon, and Max Hirmer. *Crete and Mycenae*. London: Thames & Hudson, 1960.

McDonald, William A., and Carol G. Thomas. *Progress into the Past: The Rediscovery of Mycenaean Civilization*. 2d ed. Bloomington: Indiana University Press, 1990.

Preziosi, Donald, and Louise A. Hitchcock. *Aegean Art and Architecture*. New York: Oxford University Press, 1999.

Schofield, Louise. *The Mycenaeans*. London: British Museum, 2007.

Shelmerdine, Cynthia W., ed. *The Cambridge Companion to the Aegean Bronze Age*. New York: Cambridge University Press, 2008.

Taylour, Lord William. *The Mycenaeans*. London: Thames & Hudson, 1990.

Vermeule, Emily. *Greece in the Bronze Age.* Chicago: University of Chicago Press, 1972.

Warren, Peter. *The Aegean Civilisations from Ancient Crete to Mycenae.* 2d ed. Oxford: Elsevier-Phaidon, 1989.

Chapter 5: Ancient Greece

Arias, Paolo. *A History of One Thousand Years of Greek Vase Painting.* New York: Abrams, 1962.

Ashmole, Bernard. *Architect and Sculptor in Classical Greece.* New York: New York University Press, 1972.

Barletta, Barbara A. *The Origins of the Greek Architectural Orders.* New York: Cambridge University Press, 2001.

Berve, Helmut, Gottfried Gruben, and Max Hirmer. *Greek Temples, Theatres, and Shrines.* New York: Abrams, 1963.

Biers, William. *The Archaeology of Greece: An Introduction.* 2d ed. Ithaca, N.Y.: Cornell University Press, 1996.

Boardman, John. *Athenian Black Figure Vases.* Rev. ed. New York: Thames & Hudson, 1991.

——. *Athenian Red Figure Vases: The Archaic Period.* New York: Thames & Hudson, 1988.

——. *Athenian Red Figure Vases: The Classical Period.* New York: Thames & Hudson, 1989.

——. *Early Greek Vase Painting, 11th–6th Centuries BC.* New York: Thames & Hudson, 1998.

——. *Greek Sculpture: The Archaic Period.* Rev. ed. New York: Thames & Hudson, 1985.

——. *Greek Sculpture: The Classical Period.* New York: Thames & Hudson, 1987.

——. *Greek Sculpture: The Late Classical Period and Sculpture in Colonies and Overseas.* New York: Thames & Hudson, 1995.

——. *The Parthenon and Its Sculpture.* Austin: University of Texas Press, 1985.

Camp, John M. *The Archaeology of Athens.* New Haven, Conn.: Yale University Press, 2001.

Carpenter, Thomas H. *Art and Myth in Ancient Greece.* New York: Thames & Hudson, 1991.

Charbonneaux, Jean, Roland Martin, and François Villard. *Archaic Greek Art.* New York: Braziller, 1971.

——. *Classical Greek Art.* New York: Braziller, 1972.

——. *Hellenistic Art.* New York: Braziller, 1973.

Clark, Andrew J., Maya Elston, and Mary Louise Hart. *Understanding Greek Vases: A Guide to Terms, Styles, and Techniques.* Los Angeles: J. Paul Getty Museum, 2002.

Cohen, Beth, ed. *The Colors of Clay: Special Techniques in Athenian Vases.* Los Angeles: J. Paul Getty Museum, 2006.

Coldstream, J. Nicholas. *Geometric Greece.* New York: St. Martin's, 1977.

Coulton, J. J. *Ancient Greek Architects at Work.* Ithaca, N.Y.: Cornell University Press, 1982.

Donohue, A. A. *Greek Sculpture and the Problem of Description.* New York: Cambridge University Press, 2005.

Fullerton, Mark D. *Greek Art.* New York: Cambridge University Press, 2000.

Haynes, Denys E. L. *The Technique of Greek Bronze Statuary.* Mainz: von Zabern, 1992.

Houser, Caroline. *Greek Monumental Bronze Sculpture.* New York: Vendome, 1983.

Hurwit, Jeffrey M. *The Acropolis in the Age of Pericles.* New York: Cambridge University Press, 2004.

——. *The Art and Culture of Early Greece, 1100–480 BC.* Ithaca, N.Y.: Cornell University Press, 1985.

——. *The Athenian Acropolis: History, Mythology, and Archaeology from the Neolithic Era to the Present.* New York: Cambridge University Press, 1999.

Jenkins, Ian. *Greek Architecture and Its Sculpture.* Cambridge, Mass.: Harvard University Press, 2006.

——. *The Parthenon Frieze.* Austin: University of Texas Press, 1994.

Lawrence, Arnold W., and R. A. Tomlinson. *Greek Architecture.* Rev. ed. New Haven, Conn.: Yale University Press, 1996.

Martin, Roland. *Greek Architecture: Architecture of Crete, Greece, and the Greek World.* New York: Electa/Rizzoli, 1988.

Mattusch, Carol C. *Classical Bronzes: The Art and Craft of Greek and Roman Statuary.* Ithaca, N.Y.: Cornell University Press, 1996.

——. *Greek Bronze Statuary from the Beginnings through the Fifth Century BC.* Ithaca, N.Y.: Cornell University Press, 1988.

Mee, Christopher. *Greek Archaeology.* Hoboken, N.J.: Wiley-Blackwell, 2011.

Mee, Christopher, and Tony Spawforth. *Greece: An Oxford Archaeological Guide.* New York: Oxford University Press, 2001.

Morris, Sarah P. *Daidalos and the Origins of Greek Art.* Princeton, N.J.: Princeton University Press, 1992.

Neer, Richard T. *The Emergence of the Classical Style in Greek Sculpture.* Chicago: University of Chicago Press, 2010.

Osborne, Robin. *Archaic and Classical Greek Art.* New York: Oxford University Press, 1998.

Palagia, Olga. *The Pediments of the Parthenon.* Leiden: E. J. Brill, 1993.

——, ed. *Greek Sculpture: Functions, Materials, and Techniques in the Archaic and Classical Periods.* New York: Cambridge University Press, 2006.

Palagia, Olga, and Jerome J. Pollitt. *Personal Styles in Greek Sculpture.* New York: Cambridge University Press, 1996.

Pedley, John Griffiths. *Greek Art and Archaeology.* 4th ed. Upper Saddle River, N.J.: Prentice Hall, 2007.

——. *Sanctuaries and the Sacred in the Ancient Greek World.* New York: Cambridge University Press, 2005.

Petrakos, Vasileios. *Great Moments in Greek Archaeology.* Los Angeles: J. Paul Getty Museum, 2007.

Pollitt, Jerome J. *Art and Experience in Classical Greece.* New York: Cambridge University Press, 1972.

——. *Art in the Hellenistic Age.* New York: Cambridge University Press, 1986.

——. *The Art of Ancient Greece: Sources and Documents.* 2d ed. New York: Cambridge University Press, 1990.

Pugliese Carratelli, G. *The Greek World: Art and Civilization in Magna Graecia and Sicily.* New York: Rizzoli, 1996.

Reeder, Ellen D., ed. *Pandora: Women in Classical Greece.* Baltimore: Walters Art Gallery, 1995.

Rhodes, Robin F. *Architecture and Meaning on the Athenian Acropolis.* New York: Cambridge University Press, 1995.

Richter, Gisela M. *The Portraits of the Greeks.* Rev. ed. by R.R.R. Smith. Ithaca, N.Y.: Cornell University Press, 1984.

Ridgway, Brunilde S. *The Archaic Style in Greek Sculpture.* 2d ed. Chicago: Ares, 1993.

——. *Fifth-Century Styles in Greek Sculpture.* Princeton, N.J.: Princeton University Press, 1981.

——. *Fourth-Century Styles in Greek Sculpture.* Madison: University of Wisconsin Press, 1997.

——. *Hellenistic Sculpture I: The Styles of ca. 331–200 BC.* Madison: University of Wisconsin Press, 1990.

——. *Hellenistic Sculpture II: The Styles of ca. 200–100 BC.* Madison: University of Wisconsin Press, 2000.

——. *Prayers in Stone: Greek Architectural Sculpture.* Berkeley: University of California Press, 1999.

——. *Roman Copies of Greek Sculpture: The Problem of the Originals.* Ann Arbor: University of Michigan Press, 1984.

——. *The Severe Style in Greek Sculpture.* Princeton, N.J.: Princeton University Press, 1970.

Robertson, Martin. *The Art of Vase-Painting in Classical Athens.* New York: Cambridge University Press, 1992.

——. *A History of Greek Art.* Rev. ed. 2 vols. New York: Cambridge University Press, 1986.

——. *A Shorter History of Greek Art.* New York: Cambridge University Press, 1981.

Shapiro, H. Alan. *Art and Cult in Athens under the Tyrants.* Mainz: von Zabern, 1989.

——. *Myth into Art: Poet and Painter in Classical Greece.* New York: Routledge, 1994.

Smith, R.R.R. *Hellenistic Sculpture.* New York: Thames & Hudson, 1991.

Spawforth, Tony. *The Complete Greek Temples.* London, Thames & Hudson, 2006.

Spivey, Nigel. *Greek Art.* London: Phaidon, 1997.

Stansbury-O'Donnell, Mark D. *Pictorial Narrative in Ancient Greek Art.* New York: Cambridge University Press, 1999.

Stewart, Andrew. *Art, Desire, and the Body in Ancient Greece.* New York: Cambridge University Press, 1997.

——. *Classical Greece and the Birth of Western Art.* New York: Cambridge University Press, 2008.

——. *Greek Sculpture: An Exploration.* 2 vols. New Haven, Conn.: Yale University Press, 1990.

Whitley, James. *The Archaeology of Ancient Greece.* New York: Cambridge University Press, 2001.

Wycherley, Richard E. *How the Greeks Built Cities.* New York: Norton, 1976.

Chapter 6: The Etruscans

Banti, Luisa. *The Etruscan Cities and Their Culture.* Berkeley: University of California Press, 1973.

Barker, Graeme, and Tom Rasmussen. *The Etruscans.* Oxford: Blackwell, 1998.

Boethius, Axel. *Etruscan and Early Roman Architecture.* 2d ed. New Haven, Conn.: Yale University Press, 1978.

Bonfante, Larissa, ed. *Etruscan Life and Afterlife: A Handbook of Etruscan Studies.* Detroit: Wayne State University Press, 1986.

Brendel, Otto J. *Etruscan Art.* 2d ed. New Haven, Conn.: Yale University Press, 1995.

Cristofani, Mauro. *The Etruscans: A New Investigation.* London: Orbis, 1979.

De Grummond, Nancy Thomson. *Etruscan Myth, Sacred History, and Legend.* Philadelphia: University of Pennsylvania Museum, 2006.

Haynes, Sybille. *Etruscan Civilization: A Cultural History.* Los Angeles: J. Paul Getty Museum, 2000.

Heurgon, Jacques. *Daily Life of the Etruscans.* London: Weidenfeld & Nicolson, 1964.

Pallottino, Massimo. *The Etruscans.* Harmondsworth: Penguin, 1978.

Richardson, Emeline. *The Etruscans: Their Art and Civilization.* Rev. ed. Chicago: University of Chicago Press, 1976.

Ridgway, David, and Francesca Ridgway, eds. *Italy before the Romans.* New York: Academic, 1979.

Spivey, Nigel. *Etruscan Art.* New York: Thames & Hudson, 1997.

Spivey, Nigel, and Simon Stoddart. *Etruscan Italy: An Archaeological History.* London: Batsford, 1990.

Sprenger, Maja, Gilda Bartoloni, and Max Hirmer. *The Etruscans: Their History, Art, and Architecture.* New York: Abrams, 1983.

Steingräber, Stephan. *Abundance of Life: Etruscan Wall Painting.* Los Angeles: J. Paul Getty Museum, 2006.

Torelli, Mario, ed. *The Etruscans.* New York: Rizzoli, 2001.

Chapter 7: The Roman Empire

Aldrete, Gregory S. *Daily Life in the Roman City: Rome, Pompeii, and Ostia.* Westport, Conn.: Greenwood, 2004.

Anderson, James C., Jr. *Roman Architecture and Society.* Baltimore: Johns Hopkins University Press, 1997.

Andreae, Bernard. *The Art of Rome.* New York: Abrams, 1977.

Barton, Ian M., ed. *Roman Domestic Buildings.* Exeter: University of Exeter Press, 1996.

———. *Roman Public Buildings.* 2d ed. Exeter: University of Exeter Press, 1995.

Bianchi Bandinelli, Ranuccio. *Rome: The Center of Power: Roman Art to AD 200.* New York: Braziller, 1970.

———. *Rome: The Late Empire: Roman Art AD 200–400.* New York: Braziller, 1971.

Brendel, Otto J. *Prolegomena to the Study of Roman Art.* New Haven, Conn.: Yale University Press, 1979.

Claridge, Amanda. *Rome: An Oxford Archaeological Guide.* 2d ed. New York: Oxford University Press, 2010.

Clarke, John R. *The Houses of Roman Italy, 100 BC–AD 250.* Berkeley: University of California Press, 1991.

Coarelli, Filippo. *Rome and Environs: An Archaeological Guide.* Berkeley and Los Angeles: University of California Press, 2007.

Cornell, Tim, and John Matthews. *Atlas of the Roman World.* New York: Facts on File, 1982.

D'Ambra, Eve. *Roman Art.* New York: Cambridge University Press, 1998.

———, ed. *Roman Art in Context.* Upper Saddle River, N.J.: Prentice Hall, 1994.

Dobbins, John J., and Pedar W. Foss, eds. *The World of Pompeii.* London: Routledge, 2007.

Dyson, Stephen L. *Rome: A Living Portrait of an Ancient City.* Baltimore: Johns Hopkins University Press, 2010.

Gazda, Elaine K., ed. *Roman Art in the Private Sphere.* Ann Arbor: University of Michigan Press, 1991.

Grant, Michael. *Cities of Vesuvius: Pompeii and Herculaneum.* Harmondsworth: Penguin, 1976.

Hannestad, Niels. *Roman Art and Imperial Policy.* Aarhus: Aarhus University Press, 1986.

Henig, Martin, ed. *A Handbook of Roman Art.* Ithaca, N.Y.: Cornell University Press, 1983.

Kent, John P. C., and Max Hirmer. *Roman Coins.* New York: Abrams, 1978.

Kleiner, Diana E. E. *Roman Sculpture.* New Haven, Conn.: Yale University Press, 1992.

Kleiner, Diana E. E., and Susan B. Matheson, eds. *I Claudia: Women in Ancient Rome.* New Haven, Conn.: Yale University Art Gallery, 1996.

Kleiner, Fred S. *A History of Roman Art.* Enhanced ed. Belmont, Calif.: Wadsworth, 2010.

Kraus, Theodor. *Pompeii and Herculaneum: The Living Cities of the Dead.* New York: Abrams, 1975.

Lancaster, Lynne. *Concrete Vaulted Construction in Imperial Rome.* New York: Cambridge University Press, 2006.

Ling, Roger. *Roman Painting.* New York: Cambridge University Press, 1991.

L'Orange, Hans Peter. *The Roman Empire: Art Forms and Civic Life.* New York: Rizzoli, 1985.

MacCormack, Sabine G. *Art and Ceremony in Late Antiquity.* Berkeley: University of California Press, 1981.

MacDonald, William L. *The Architecture of the Roman Empire I: An Introductory Study.* Rev. ed. New Haven, Conn.: Yale University Press, 1982.

———. *The Architecture of the Roman Empire II: An Urban Appraisal.* New Haven, Conn.: Yale University Press, 1986.

———. *The Pantheon: Design, Meaning, and Progeny.* Cambridge, Mass.: Harvard University Press, 1976.

Mattusch, Carol C., ed. *Pompeii and the Roman Villa: Art and Culture around the Bay of Naples.* New York: Thames & Hudson, 2008.

Mazzoleni, Donatella. *Domus: Wall Painting in the Roman House.* Los Angeles: J. Paul Getty Museum, 2004.

McKay, Alexander G. *Houses, Villas, and Palaces in the Roman World.* Ithaca, N.Y.: Cornell University Press, 1975.

Nash, Ernest. *Pictorial Dictionary of Ancient Rome.* 2d ed. 2 vols. New York: Praeger, 1962.

Pollitt, Jerome J. *The Art of Rome, 753 BC–AD 337: Sources and Documents.* Rev. ed. New York: Cambridge University Press, 1983.

Richardson, Lawrence, Jr. *A New Topographical Dictionary of Ancient Rome.* Baltimore: Johns Hopkins University Press, 1992.

———. *Pompeii: An Architectural History.* Baltimore: Johns Hopkins University Press, 1988.

Sear, Frank. *Roman Architecture.* Rev. ed. Ithaca, N.Y.: Cornell University Press, 1989.

Stambaugh, John E. *The Ancient Roman City.* Baltimore: Johns Hopkins University Press, 1988.

Stamper, John W. *The Architecture of Roman Temples: The Republic to the Middle Empire.* New York: Cambridge University Press, 2005.

Stewart, Peter. *The Social History of Roman Art.* New York: Cambridge University Press, 2008.

Taylor, Rabun. *Roman Builders.* New York: Cambridge University Press, 2003.

Toynbee, Jocelyn M. C. *Death and Burial in the Roman World.* London: Thames & Hudson, 1971.

Wallace-Hadrill, Andrew. *Herculaneum: Past and Future.* London: Frances Lincoln, 2011.

———. *Houses and Society in Pompeii and Herculaneum.* Princeton, N.J.: Princeton University Press, 1994.

Ward-Perkins, John B. *Roman Architecture.* New York: Electa/Rizzoli, 1988.

———. *Roman Imperial Architecture.* 2d ed. New Haven, Conn.: Yale University Press, 1981.

Wilson-Jones, Mark. *Principles of Roman Architecture.* New Haven, Conn.: Yale University Press, 2000.

Wood, Susan. *Roman Portrait Sculpture AD 217–260.* Leiden: E. J. Brill, 1986.

Yegül, Fikret. *Baths and Bathing in Classical Antiquity.* Cambridge, Mass.: MIT Press, 1992.

Zanker, Paul. *Pompeii: Public and Private Life.* Cambridge, Mass.: Harvard University Press, 1998.

———. *The Power of Images in the Age of Augustus.* Ann Arbor: University of Michigan Press, 1988.

———. *Roman Art.* Los Angeles: J. Paul Getty Museum, 2010.

Chapter 8: Late Antiquity

Bowersock, G. W., Peter Brown, and Oleg Grabar, eds. *Late Antiquity: A Guide to the Postclassical World.* Cambridge, Mass.: Harvard University Press, 1998.

Brody, Lisa R., and Gail L. Hoffman, eds. *Dura Europos: Crossroads of Antiquity.* Chestnut Hill, Mass.: McMullen Museum of Art, Boston College, 2010.

Cioffarelli, Ada. *Guide to the Catacombs of Rome and Its Surroundings.* Rome: Bonsignori, 2000.

Elsner, Jas'. *Art and the Roman Viewer: The Transformation of Art from the Pagan World to Christianity.* New York: Cambridge University Press, 1995.

———. *Imperial Rome and Christian Triumph.* New York: Oxford University Press, 1998.

Fine, Steven. *Art and Judaism in the Greco-Roman World: Toward a New Jewish Archaeology.* New York: Cambridge University Press, 2005.

Finney, Paul Corby. *The Invisible God: The Earliest Christians on Art.* New York: Oxford University Press, 1994.

Grabar, André. *The Beginnings of Christian Art, 200–395.* London: Thames & Hudson, 1967.

———. *Christian Iconography.* Princeton, N.J.: Princeton University Press, 1980.

Gutmann, Joseph. *Sacred Images: Studies in Jewish Art from Antiquity to the Middle Ages.* Northampton, Mass.: Variorum, 1989.

Janes, Dominic. *God and Gold in Late Antiquity.* New York: Cambridge University Press, 1998.

Jensen, Robin Margaret. *Understanding Early Christian Art.* New York: Routledge, 2000.

Koch, Guntram. *Early Christian Art and Architecture.* London: SCM, 1996.

Krautheimer, Richard. *Rome, Profile of a City: 312–1308.* Princeton, N.J.: Princeton University Press, 1980.

Krautheimer, Richard, and Slobodan Ćurčić. *Early Christian and Byzantine Architecture.* 4th ed. New Haven, Conn.: Yale University Press, 1986.

Lowden, John. *Early Christian and Byzantine Art.* London: Phaidon, 1997.

Mathews, Thomas P. *The Clash of Gods: A Reinterpretation of Early Christian Art.* Rev. ed. Princeton, N.J.: Princeton University Press, 1999.

Milburn, Robert. *Early Christian Art and Architecture.* Berkeley: University of California Press, 1988.

Nicolai, Vincenzo Fiocchi, Fabrizio Bisconti, and Danilo Mazzoleni. *The Christian Catacombs of Rome: History, Decoration, Inscriptions.* Regensburg: Schnell & Steiner, 2006.

Perkins, Ann Louise. *The Art of Dura-Europos.* Oxford: Clarendon, 1973.

Poeschke, Joachim. *Italian Mosaics, 300–1300.* New York: Abbeville, 2010.

Rutgers, Leonard V. *Subterranean Rome: In Search of the Roots of Christianity in the Catacombs of the Eternal City.* Leuven: Peeters, 2000.

Spier, Jeffrey, ed. *Picturing the Bible: The Earliest Christian Art.* New Haven, Conn.: Yale University Press, 2007.

Volbach, Wolfgang, and Max Hirmer. *Early Christian Art.* New York: Abrams, 1962.

Webb, Matilda. *The Churches and Catacombs of Early Christian Rome: A Comprehensive Guide.* Brighton: Sussex Academic Press, 2001.

Webster, Leslie, and Michelle Brown, eds. *The Transformation of the Roman World, AD 400–900.* Berkeley: University of California Press, 1997.

Weitzmann, Kurt. *Late Antique and Early Christian Book Illumination.* New York: Braziller, 1977.

———, ed. *Age of Spirituality: Late Antique and Early Christian Art, Third to Seventh Century.* New York: Metropolitan Museum of Art, 1979.

Chapter 9: Byzantium

Barber, Charles. *Figure and Likeness: On the Limits of Representation in Byzantine Iconoclasm.* Princeton, N.J.: Princeton University Press, 2002.

Borsook, Eve. *Messages in Mosaic: The Royal Programmes of Norman Sicily.* Oxford: Clarendon, 1990.

Cormack, Robin. *Byzantine Art.* New York: Oxford University Press, 2000.

———. *Icons.* Cambridge, Mass.: Harvard University Press, 2007.

———. *Painting the Soul: Icons, Death Masks, and Shrouds.* London: Reaktion, 1997.

———. *Writing in Gold: Byzantine Society and Its Icons.* New York: Oxford University Press, 1985.

Cormack, Robin, and Maria Vassiliki. *Byzantium, 330–1453.* London: Royal Academy of Arts, 2008.

Cutler, Anthony. *The Hand of the Master: Craftsmanship, Ivory, and Society in Byzantium, 9th–11th Centuries.* Princeton, N.J.: Princeton University Press, 1994.

Deliyannis, Deborah Mauskopf. *Ravenna in Late Antiquity.* New York: Cambridge University Press, 2010.

Demus, Otto. *The Mosaic Decoration of San Marco, Venice.* Chicago: University of Chicago Press, 1990.

Evans, Helen C. *Byzantium: Faith and Power (1261–1557).* New York: Metropolitan Museum of Art, 2004.

Evans, Helen C., and William D. Wixom, eds. *The Glory of Byzantium: Art and Culture of the Middle Byzantine Era AD 843–1261.* New York: Metropolitan Museum of Art, 1997.

Freely, John. *Byzantine Monuments of Istanbul.* New York: Cambridge University Press, 2004.

Grabar, André. *The Golden Age of Justinian: From the Death of Theodosius to the Rise of Islam.* New York: Odyssey, 1967.

Grabar, André, and Manolis Chatzidakis. *Greek Mosaics of the Byzantine Period.* New York: New American Library, 1964.

Kleinbauer, W. Eugene. *Hagia Sophia.* London: Scala, 2004.

Lowden, John. *Early Christian and Byzantine Art.* London: Phaidon, 1997.

Maguire, Eunice Dauterman, and Henry Maguire. *Other Icons: Art and Power in Byzantine Secular Culture.* Princeton, N.J.: Princeton University Press, 2007.

Maguire, Henry. *Art and Eloquence in Byzantium.* Princeton, N.J.: Princeton University Press, 1981.

———. *The Icons of Their Bodies: Saints and Their Images in Byzantium.* Princeton, N.J.: Princeton University Press, 1996.

Mainstone, Rowland J. *Hagia Sophia: Architecture, Structure, and Liturgy of Justinian's Great Church.* 2d ed. New York: Thames & Hudson, 2001.

Mango, Cyril. *Art of the Byzantine Empire, 312–1453: Sources and Documents.* Toronto: University of Toronto Press, 1986. Reprint of 1972 ed.

———. *Byzantine Architecture.* New York: Electa/Rizzoli, 1985.

Mark, Robert, and Ahmet S. Cakmak, eds. *Hagia Sophia from the Age of Justinian to the Present.* New York: Cambridge University Press, 1992.

Mathews, Thomas F. *Byzantium: From Antiquity to the Renaissance.* New York: Abrams, 1998.

McClanan, Anne. *Representations of Early Byzantine Empresses: Image and Empire.* New York: Palgrave Macmillan, 2002.

Ousterhout, Robert. *Master Builders of Byzantium.* Princeton, N.J.: Princeton University Press, 2000.

Pelikan, Jaroslav. *Imago Dei: The Byzantine Apologia for Icons.* Princeton, N.J.: Princeton University Press, 1990.

Poeschke, Joachim. *Italian Mosaics, 300–1300.* New York: Abbeville, 2010.

Rodley, Lyn. *Byzantine Art and Architecture: An Introduction.* New York: Cambridge University Press, 1994.

Von Simson, Otto G. *Sacred Fortress: Byzantine Art and Statecraft in Ravenna.* Princeton, N.J.: Princeton University Press, 1986.

Weitzmann, Kurt. *The Icon.* New York: Dorset, 1987.

———. *Illustrations in Roll and Codex.* Princeton, N.J.: Princeton University Press, 1970.

Chapter 10: The Islamic World

Allan, James, and Sheila R. Canby. *Hunt for Paradise: Court Arts of Safavid Iran 1501–76.* Geneva: Skira, 2004.

Atil, Esin. *The Age of Sultan Suleyman the Magnificent.* Washington, D.C.: National Gallery of Art, 1987.

Baker, Patricia L. *Islam and the Religious Arts.* London: Continuum, 2004.

———. *Islamic Textiles.* London: British Museum, 1995.

Blair, Sheila S., and Jonathan Bloom. *The Art and Architecture of Islam 1250–1800.* New Haven, Conn.: Yale University Press, 1994.

Bloom, Jonathan M., and Sheila S. Blair. *The Grove Encyclopedia of Islamic Art and Architecture.* New York: Oxford University Press, 2009.

———. *Islamic Arts.* London: Phaidon, 1997.

Brend, Barbara. *Islamic Art.* Cambridge, Mass.: Harvard University Press, 1991.

Canby, Sheila R. *Persian Painting.* London: British Museum, 1993.

Dodds, Jerrilynn D., ed. *Al-Andalus: The Art of Islamic Spain.* New York: Metropolitan Museum of Art, 1992.

Ettinghausen, Richard, Oleg Grabar, and Marilyn Jenkins-Madina. *The Art and Architecture of Islam, 650–1250.* Rev. ed. New Haven, Conn.: Yale University Press, 2001.

Ferrier, Ronald W., ed. *The Arts of Persia.* New Haven, Conn.: Yale University Press, 1989.

Frishman, Martin, and Hasan-Uddin Khan. *The Mosque: History, Architectural Development, and Regional Diversity.* New York: Thames & Hudson, 1994.

Goodwin, Godfrey. *A History of Ottoman Architecture.* 2d ed. New York: Thames & Hudson, 1987.

Grabar, Oleg. *The Alhambra.* Cambridge, Mass.: Harvard University Press, 1978.

———. *The Formation of Islamic Art.* Rev. ed. New Haven, Conn.: Yale University Press, 1987.

———. *Islamic Visual Culture, 1100–1800.* New York: Ashgate, 2006.

Grube, Ernst J. *Architecture of the Islamic World: Its History and Social Meaning.* 2d ed. New York: Thames & Hudson, 1984.

Hattstein, Markus, and Peter Delius, eds. *Islam: Art and Architecture.* Cologne: Könemann, 2000.

Hillenbrand, Robert. *Islamic Architecture: Form, Function, Meaning.* Edinburgh: Edinburgh University Press, 1994.

———. *Islamic Art and Architecture.* New York: Thames & Hudson, 1999.

Irwin, Robert. *The Alhambra.* Cambridge, Mass.: Harvard University Press, 2004.

———. *Islamic Art in Context: Art, Architecture, and the Literary World.* New York: Abrams, 1997.

Michell, George, ed. *Architecture of the Islamic World.* New York: Thames & Hudson, 1978.

Necipoglu, Gulru. *The Age of Sinan: Architectural Culture in the Ottoman Empire.* Princeton, N.J.: Princeton University Press, 2005.

Petruccioli, Attilio, and Khalil K. Pirani, eds. *Understanding Islamic Architecture.* London: Routledge, 2002.

Porter, Venetia. *Islamic Tiles.* London: British Museum, 1995.

Robinson, Frank. *Atlas of the Islamic World.* Oxford: Equinox, 1982.

Schimmel, Annemarie. *Calligraphy and Islamic Culture.* New York: New York University Press, 1984.

Stierlin, Henri. *Islam I: Early Architecture from Baghdad to Cordoba.* Cologne: Taschen, 1996.

———. *Islamic Art and Architecture from Isfahan to the Taj Mahal.* New York: Thames & Hudson, 2002.

Tadgell, Christopher. *Four Caliphates: The Formation and Development of the Islamic Tradition.* London: Ellipsis, 1998.

Ward, Rachel M. *Islamic Metalwork.* New York: Thames & Hudson, 1993.

Welch, Anthony. *Calligraphy in the Arts of the Islamic World.* Austin: University of Texas Press, 1979.

Medieval Art, General

Alexander, Jonathan J. G. *Medieval Illuminators and Their Methods of Work.* New Haven, Conn.: Yale University Press, 1992.

The Art of Medieval Spain, AD 500–1200. New York: Metropolitan Museum of Art, 1993.

Benton, Janetta Rebold. *Art of the Middle Ages.* New York: Thames & Hudson, 2002.

Binski, Paul. *Painters (Medieval Craftsmen).* Toronto: University of Toronto Press, 1991.

Calkins, Robert G. *Illuminated Books of the Middle Ages.* Ithaca, N.Y.: Cornell University Press, 1983.

———. *Medieval Architecture in Western Europe: From AD 300 to 1500.* New York: Oxford University Press, 1998.

Coldstream, Nicola. *Masons and Sculptors (Medieval Craftsmen).* Toronto: University of Toronto Press, 1991.

———. *Medieval Architecture.* New York: Oxford University Press, 2002.

Cross, Frank L., and Livingstone, Elizabeth A., eds. *The Oxford Dictionary of the Christian Church.* 3d ed. New York: Oxford University Press, 1997.

De Hamel, Christopher. *A History of Illuminated Manuscripts.* Oxford: Phaidon, 1986.

———. *Scribes and Illuminators (Medieval Craftsmen).* Toronto: University of Toronto Press, 1992.

Doig, Allan. *Liturgy and Architecture: From the Early Church to the Middle Ages.* New York: Ashgate, 2008.

Holcomb, Melanie, ed. *Pen and Parchment: Drawing in the Middle Ages.* New York: Metropolitan Museum of Art, 2009.

Kessler, Herbert L. *Seeing Medieval Art.* Toronto: Broadview, 2004.

———. *Spiritual Seeing: Picturing God's Invisibility in Medieval Art.* Philadelphia: University of Pennsylvania Press, 2000.

Lasko, Peter. *Ars Sacra, 800–1200.* 2d ed. New Haven, Conn.: Yale University Press, 1994.

Murray, Peter, and Linda Murray. *The Oxford Companion to Christian Art and Architecture.* New York: Oxford University Press, 1996.

Pelikan, Jaroslav. *Mary through the Centuries: Her Place in the History of Culture.* New Haven, Conn.: Yale University Press, 1996.

Prache, Anne. *Cathedrals of Europe.* Ithaca, N.Y.: Cornell University Press, 1999.

Raguin, Virginia Chieffo. *Stained Glass from Its Origins to the Present.* New York: Abrams, 2003.

Ross, Leslie. *Medieval Art: A Topical Dictionary.* Westport, Conn.: Greenwood, 1996.

Schütz, Bernard. *Great Cathedrals.* New York: Abrams, 2002.

Sekules, Veronica. *Medieval Art.* New York: Oxford University Press, 2001.

Snyder, James, Henry Luttikhuizen, and Dorothy Verkerk. *Art of the Middle Ages.* 2d ed. Upper Saddle River, N.J.: Prentice Hall, 2006.

Stokstad, Marilyn. *Medieval Art.* 2d ed. Boulder, Colo.: Westview, 2004.

Tasker, Edward G. *Encyclopedia of Medieval Church Art.* London: Batsford, 1993.

Chapter 11: Early Medieval Europe

Alexander, Jonathan J. G. *Insular Manuscripts, Sixth to the Ninth Century.* London: Miller, 1978.

The Art of Medieval Spain, AD 500–1200. New York: Metropolitan Museum of Art, 1993.

Backhouse, Janet, D. H. Turner, and Leslie Webster, eds. *The Golden Age of Anglo-Saxon Art, 966–1066.* Bloomington: Indiana University Press, 1984.

Bandmann, Günter. *Early Medieval Architecture as Bearer of Meaning.* New York: Columbia University Press, 2005.

Barral i Altet, Xavier. *The Early Middle Ages: From Late Antiquity to AD 1000.* Cologne: Taschen, 1997.

Brown, Katharine Reynolds, Dafydd Kidd, and Charles T. Little, eds. *From Attila to Charlemagne.* New York: Metropolitan Museum of Art, 2000.

Brown, Michelle P. *The Lindisfarne Gospels: Society, Spirituality, and the Scribe.* Toronto: University of Toronto Press, 2003.

Carver, Martin. *Sutton Hoo: A Seventh-Century Princely Burial Ground and Its Context.* London: British Museum, 2005.

Collins, Roger. *Early Medieval Europe, 300–1000.* New York: St. Martin's, 1991.

Conant, Kenneth J. *Carolingian and Romanesque Architecture, 800–1200.* 4th ed. New Haven, Conn.: Yale University Press, 1992.

Davis-Weyer, Caecilia. *Early Medieval Art, 300–1150: Sources and Documents.* Toronto: University of Toronto Press, 1986. Reprint of 1971 ed.

Diebold, William J. *Word and Image: An Introduction to Early Medieval Art.* Boulder, Colo.: Westview Press, 2000.

Dodwell, Charles R. *Anglo-Saxon Art: A New Perspective.* Ithaca, N.Y.: Cornell University Press, 1982.

———. *The Pictorial Arts of the West, 800–1200.* New Haven, Conn.: Yale University Press, 1993.

Farr, Carol. *The Book of Kells: Its Function and Audience.* London: British Library, 1997.

Harbison, Peter. *The Golden Age of Irish Art: The Medieval Achievement 600–1200.* New York: Thames & Hudson, 1999.

Henderson, George. *From Durrow to Kells: The Insular Gospel-Books, 650–800.* London: Thames & Hudson, 1987.

Hubert, Jean, Jean Porcher, and Wolfgang Fritz Volbach. *The Carolingian Renaissance.* New York: Braziller, 1970.

———. *Europe of the Invasions.* New York: Braziller, 1969.

Mayr-Harting, Henry. *Ottonian Book Illumination: An Historical Study.* 2 vols. London: Miller, 1991–1993.

McClendon, Charles. *The Origins of Medieval Architecture: Building in Europe, AD 600–900.* New Haven, Conn.: Yale University Press, 2005.

Megaw, Ruth, and John Vincent Megaw. *Celtic Art: From Its Beginning to the Book of Kells.* New York: Thames & Hudson, 1989.

Mütherich, Florentine, and Joachim E. Gaehde. *Carolingian Painting.* New York: Braziller, 1976.

Nees, Lawrence J. *Early Medieval Art.* New York: Oxford University Press, 2002.

Nordenfalk, Carl. *Celtic and Anglo-Saxon Painting: Book Illumination in the British Isles, 600–800.* New York: Braziller, 1977.

O'Brien, Jacqueline, and Peter Harbison. *Ancient Ireland: From Prehistory to the Middle Ages.* New York: Oxford University Press, 2000.

Richardson, Hilary, and John Scarry. *An Introduction to Irish High Crosses.* Dublin: Mercier, 1990.

Stalley, Roger. *Early Medieval Architecture.* New York: Oxford University Press, 1999.

Wilson, David M. *From Viking to Crusader: Scandinavia and Europe 800–1200.* New York: Rizzoli, 1992.

Wilson, David M., and Ole Klindt-Jensen. *Viking Art.* 2d ed. Minneapolis: University of Minnesota Press, 1980.

Chapter 12: Romanesque Europe

Armi, C. Edson. *Masons and Sculptors in Romanesque Burgundy: The New Aesthetics of Cluny III.* 2 vols. University Park: Pennsylvania State University Press, 1983.

Ashley, Kathleen, and Marilyn Deegan. *Being a Pilgrim: Art and Ritual on the Medieval Routes to Santiago.* Burlington, Vt.: Lund Humphries, 2009.

Bagnoli, Martina, Holger A. Kleiner, C. Griffith Mann, and James Robinson, eds. *Treasures of Heaven: Saints, Relics, and Devotion in Medieval Europe.* New Haven, Conn.: Yale University Press: 2010.

Barral i Altet, Xavier. *The Romanesque: Towns, Cathedrals, and Monasteries.* Cologne: Taschen, 1998.

Burnett, Charles, and Peter Dronke. *Hildegard of Bingen: The Context of Her Thought and Art.* London: Warburg Institute, 1998.

Cahn, Walter. *Romanesque Bible Illumination.* Ithaca, N.Y.: Cornell University Press, 1982.

———. *Romanesque Manuscripts: The Twelfth Century.* 2 vols. London: Miller, 1998.

Conant, Kenneth J. *Carolingian and Romanesque Architecture, 800–1200.* 4th ed. New Haven, Conn.: Yale University Press, 1992.

Demus, Otto. *Romanesque Mural Painting.* New York: Thames & Hudson, 1970.

Dodwell, Charles R. *The Pictorial Arts of the West, 800–1200.* New Haven, Conn.: Yale University Press, 1993.

Fergusson, Peter. *Architecture of Solitude: Cistercian Abbeys in Twelfth-Century Europe.* Princeton, N.J.: Princeton University Press, 1984.

Grape, Wolfgang. *The Bayeux Tapestry: Monument to a Norman Triumph.* New York: Prestel, 1994.

Hearn, Millard F. *Romanesque Sculpture: The Revival of Monumental Stone Sculpture in the Eleventh and Twelfth Centuries.* Ithaca, N.Y.: Cornell University Press, 1981.

Hourihane, Colum, ed. *Romanesque Art and Thought in the Twelfth Century.* Princeton, N.J.: Index of Christian Art, 2008.

Kahn, Deborah, ed. *The Romanesque Frieze and Its Spectator.* London: Miller, 1992.

Kubach, Hans E. *Romanesque Architecture.* New York: Electa, 1988.

Male, Émile. *Religious Art in France: The Twelfth Century.* Rev. ed. Princeton, N.J.: Princeton University Press, 1978.

Minne-Sève, Viviane, and Hervé Kergall. *Romanesque and Gothic France: Architecture and Sculpture.* New York: Abrams, 2000.

Nichols, Stephen G. *Romanesque Signs: Early Medieval Narrative and Iconography.* New Haven, Conn.: Yale University Press, 1983.

Nordenfalk, Carl. *Early Medieval Book Illumination.* New York: Rizzoli, 1988.

Petzold, Andreas. *Romanesque Art.* New York: Abrams, 1995.

Schapiro, Meyer. *The Sculpture of Moissac.* New York: Thames & Hudson, 1985.

Seidel, Linda. *Legends in Limestone: Lazarus, Gislebertus, and the Cathedral of Autun.* Chicago: University of Chicago Press, 1999.

Stalley, Roger. *Early Medieval Architecture.* New York: Oxford University Press, 1999.

Tate, Robert B., and Marcus Tate. *The Pilgrim Route to Santiago.* Oxford: Phaidon, 1987.

Toman, Rolf, ed. *Romanesque: Architecture, Sculpture, Painting.* Cologne: Könemann, 1997.

Wilson, David M. *The Bayeux Tapestry: The Complete Tapestry in Color.* New York: Thames & Hudson, 2004.

Zarnecki, George, Janet Holt, and Tristram Holland, eds. *English Romanesque Art, 1066–1200.* London: Weidenfeld & Nicolson, 1984.

Chapter 13: Gothic Europe

Barnes, Carl F. *The Portfolio of Villard de Honnecourt.* New York: Ashgate, 2009.

Binski, Paul. *Becket's Crown: Art and Imagination in Gothic England, 1170–1300.* New Haven, Conn.: Yale University Press, 2004.

Bony, Jean. *The English Decorated Style: Gothic Architecture Transformed, 1250–1350.* Ithaca, N.Y.: Cornell University Press, 1979.

———. *French Gothic Architecture of the Twelfth and Thirteenth Centuries.* Berkeley: University of California Press, 1983.

Branner, Robert. *Manuscript Painting in Paris during the Reign of St. Louis.* Berkeley: University of California Press, 1977.

———. *St. Louis and the Court Style in Gothic Architecture.* London: Zwemmer, 1965.

———, ed. *Chartres Cathedral.* New York: Norton, 1969.

Brown, Sarah, and David O'Connor. *Glass-Painters (Medieval Craftsmen).* Toronto: University of Toronto Press, 1991.

Camille, Michael. *Gothic Art: Glorious Visions.* New York: Abrams, 1996.

———. *The Gothic Idol: Ideology and Image-Making in Medieval Art.* New York: Cambridge University Press, 1989.

Courtenay, Lynn T., ed. *The Engineering of Medieval Cathedrals.* Aldershot: Scolar, 1997.

Crosby, Sumner McKnight. *The Royal Abbey of Saint-Denis from Its Beginnings to the Death of Suger, 475–1151.* New Haven, Conn.: Yale University Press, 1987.

Erlande-Brandenburg, Alain. *The Cathedral: The Social and Architectural Dynamics of Construction.* New York: Cambridge University Press, 1994.

———. *Gothic Art.* New York: Abrams, 1989.

Favier, Jean. *The World of Chartres.* New York: Abrams, 1990.

Fitchen, John. *The Construction of Gothic Cathedrals: A Study of Medieval Vault Erection.* Chicago: University of Chicago Press, 1981.

Frankl, Paul. *The Gothic: Literary Sources and Interpretations through Eight Centuries.* Princeton, N.J.: Princeton University Press, 1960.

Frankl, Paul, and Paul Crossley. *Gothic Architecture.* New Haven, Conn.: Yale University Press, 2000.

Frisch, Teresa G. *Gothic Art 1140–c. 1450: Sources and Documents.* Toronto: University of Toronto Press, 1987. Reprint of 1971 ed.

Gerson, Paula, ed. *Abbot Suger and Saint-Denis.* New York: Metropolitan Museum of Art, 1986.

Givens, Jean A. *Observation and Image-Making in Gothic Art.* New York: Cambridge University Press, 2004.

Grodecki, Louis. *Gothic Architecture.* New York: Electa/Rizzoli, 1985.

Grodecki, Louis, and Catherine Brisac. *Gothic Stained Glass, 1200–1300.* Ithaca, N.Y.: Cornell University Press, 1985.

Jantzen, Hans. *High Gothic: The Classic Cathedrals of Chartres, Reims, Amiens.* Princeton, N.J.: Princeton University Press, 1984.

Male, Émile. *Religious Art in France: The Thirteenth Century.* Rev. ed. Princeton, N.J.: Princeton University Press, 1984.

Minne-Sève, Viviane, and Hervé Kergall. *Romanesque and Gothic France: Architecture and Sculpture.* New York: Abrams, 2000.

Nussbaum, Norbert. *German Gothic Church Architecture.* New Haven, Conn.: Yale University Press, 2000.

Panofsky, Erwin. *Abbot Suger on the Abbey Church of St. Denis and Its Art Treasures.* 2d ed. Princeton, N.J.: Princeton University Press, 1979.

Radding, Charles M., and William W. Clark. *Medieval Architecture, Medieval Learning.* New Haven, Conn.: Yale University Press, 1992.

Recht, Roland. *Believing and Seeing: The Art of Gothic Cathedrals.* Chicago: University of Chicago Press, 1999.

Rudolph, Conrad. *Artistic Change at St-Denis: Abbot Suger's Program and the Early Twelfth-Century Controversy over Art.* Princeton, N.J.: Princeton University Press, 1990.

Sauerländer, Willibald, and Max Hirmer. *Gothic Sculpture in France, 1140–1270.* New York: Abrams, 1973.

Scott, Robert A. *The Gothic Enterprise: A Guide to Understanding the Medieval Cathedral.* Berkeley and Los Angeles: University of California Press, 2003.

Simson, Otto G. von. *The Gothic Cathedral: Origins of Gothic Architecture and the Medieval Concept of Order.* 3d ed. Princeton, N.J.: Princeton University Press, 1988.

Toman, Rolf, ed. *The Art of Gothic: Architecture, Sculpture, Painting.* Cologne: Könemann, 1999.

Williamson, Paul. *Gothic Sculpture, 1140–1300.* New Haven, Conn.: Yale University Press, 1995.

Wilson, Christopher. *The Gothic Cathedral: The Architecture of the Great Church, 1130–1530.* London: Thames & Hudson, 1990.

Chapter 14: Late Medieval Italy

Bomford, David. *Art in the Making: Italian Painting before 1400.* London: National Gallery, 1989.

Borsook, Eve, and Fiorelli Superbi Gioffredi. *Italian Altarpieces 1250–1550: Function and Design.* Oxford: Clarendon, 1994.

Bourdua, Louise. *The Franciscans and Art Patronage in Late Medieval Italy.* New York: Cambridge University Press, 2004.

Cole, Bruce. *Sienese Painting: From Its Origins to the Fifteenth Century.* New York: Harper Collins, 1987.

Derbes, Anne. *Picturing the Passion in Late Medieval Italy: Narrative Painting, Franciscan Ideologies, and the Levant.* New York: Cambridge University Press, 1996.

Derbes, Anne, and Mark Sandona, eds. *The Cambridge Companion to Giotto.* New York: Cambridge University Press, 2004.

Hills, Paul. *The Light of Early Italian Painting.* New Haven, Conn.: Yale University Press, 1987.

Maginnis, Hayden B. J. *Painting in the Age of Giotto: A Historical Reevaluation.* University Park: Pennsylvania State University Press, 1997.

——— *The World of the Early Sienese Painter.* University Park: Pennsylvania State University Press, 2001.

Meiss, Millard. *Painting in Florence and Siena after the Black Death.* Princeton, N.J.: Princeton University Press, 1976.

Moskowitz, Anita Fiderer. *Italian Gothic Sculpture, c. 1250–c. 1400.* Cambridge: Cambridge University Press, 2001.

———. *Nicola & Giovanni Pisano: The Pulpits: Pious Devotion, Pious Diversion.* London: Harvey Miller, 3005.

Norman, Diana, ed. *Siena, Florence, and Padua: Art, Society, and Religion 1280–1400.* New Haven, Conn.: Yale University Press, 1995.

Poeschke, Joachim. *Italian Frescoes: The Age of Giotto, 1280–1400.* New York: Abbeville, 2005.

Pope-Hennessy, John. *Italian Gothic Sculpture.* 3d ed. Oxford: Phaidon, 1986.

Stubblebine, James H. *Duccio di Buoninsegna and His School.* Princeton, N.J.: Princeton University Press, 1979.

White, John. *Art and Architecture in Italy: 1250–1400.* 3d ed. New Haven, Conn.: Yale University Press, 1993.

———. *Duccio: Tuscan Art and the Medieval Workshop.* London: Thames & Hudson, 1979.

Asian Art, General

Béguin, Giles. *Buddhist Art. An Historical and Cultural Journey.* Bangkok: River Books, 2009.

Brown, Rebecca M., and Deborah S. Hutton. *Asian Art (Blackwell Anthologies in Art History).* Malden, Mass.: Blackwell, 2006.

Leidy, Denise Patry. *The Art of Buddhism: An Introduction to Its History and Meaning.* Boston: Shambhala, 2008.

McArthur, Meher. *The Arts of Asia: Materials, Techniques, Styles.* New York: Thames & Hudson, 2005.

Chapter 15: South and Southeast Asia before 1200

Asher, Frederick M. *The Art of Eastern India, 300–800.* Minneapolis: University of Minnesota Press, 1980.

Behl, Benoy K. *The Ajanta Caves: Ancient Paintings of Buddhist India.* New York: Thames & Hudson, 2005.

Blurton, T. Richard. *Hindu Art.* Cambridge, Mass.: Harvard University Press, 1993.

Chaturachinda, Gwyneth, Sunanda Krishnamurty, and Pauline W. Tabtiang. *Dictionary of South and Southeast Asian Art.* Chiang Mai, Thailand: Silkworm Books, 2000.

Chihara, Daigoro. *Hindu-Buddhist Architecture in Southeast Asia.* Leiden: E. J. Brill, 1996.

Craven, Roy C. *Indian Art: A Concise History.* Rev. ed. London: Thames & Hudson, 1997.

Dehejia, Vidya. *The Body Adorned: Dissolving Boundaries between Sacred and Profane in India's Art.* New York: Columbia University Press, 2009.

———. *Early Buddhist Rock Temples.* Ithaca, N.Y.: Cornell University Press, 1972.

———. *Indian Art.* London: Phaidon, 1997.

Desai, Vishakha N., and Darielle Mason. *Gods, Guardians, and Lovers: Temple Sculptures from North India AD 700–1200.* New York: Asia Society Galleries, 1993.

Dhavalikar, Madhukar Keshav. *Ellora.* New York: Oxford University Press, 2003.

Encyclopedia of Indian Temple Architecture. 8 vols. New Delhi: American Institute of Indian Studies; Philadelphia: University of Pennsylvania Press, 1983–1996.

Fisher, Robert E. *Buddhist Art and Architecture.* New York: Thames & Hudson, 1993.

Frederic, Louis. *Borobudur.* New York: Abbeville, 1996.

Gopinatha Rao, T. A. *Elements of Hindu Iconography.* 2d ed. 4 vols. New York: Paragon, 1968.

Hardy, Adam. *The Temple Architecture of India.* Chichester: Wiley, 2007.

Harle, James C. *The Art and Architecture of the Indian Subcontinent.* 2d ed. New Haven, Conn.: Yale University Press, 1994.

Huntington, Susan L., and John C. Huntington. *The Art of Ancient India: Buddhist, Hindu, Jain.* New York: Weatherhill, 1985.

Jacques, Claude. *The Khmer Empire: Cities and Sanctuaries from the 5th to the 13th Century.* Bangkok: River Books, 2007.

Jacques, Claude, and Michael Freeman. *Angkor: Cities and Temples.* Bangkok: River Books, 1997.

Jessup, Helen Ibbitson. *Art & Architecture of Cambodia.* New York: Thames & Hudson, 2004.

Jessup, Helen Ibbitson, and Thierry Zephir, eds. *Sculpture of Angkor and Ancient Cambodia: Millennium of Glory.* Washington, D.C.: National Gallery of Art, 1997.

Kerlogue, Fiona. *Arts of Southeast Asia.* New York: Thames & Hudson, 2004.

McIntosh, Jane R. *A Peaceful Realm: The Rise and Fall of the Indus Civilization.* Boulder, Colo.: Westview, 2002.

Michell, George. *Elephanta.* Mumbai: India Book House, 2002.

———. *Hindu Art and Architecture.* New York: Thames & Hudson, 2000.

———. *The Hindu Temple: An Introduction to Its Meaning and Forms.* Chicago: University of Chicago Press, 1988.

Mitter, Partha. *Indian Art.* New York: Oxford University Press, 2001.

Possehl, Gregory L. *The Indus Civilization: A Contemporary Perspective.* Lanham, Md.: AltaMira, 2002.

Rawson, Phillip. *The Art of Southeast Asia.* New York: Thames & Hudson, 1990.

Seth, Mira. *Indian Painting: The Great Mural Tradition.* New York: Harry N. Abrams, 2006.

Srinivasan, Doris Meth. *Many Heads, Arms, and Eyes: Origin, Meaning, and Form of Multiplicity in Indian Art.* Leiden: E. J. Brill, 1997.

Stierlin, Henri. *Hindu India from Khajuraho to the Temple City of Madurai.* Cologne: Taschen, 1998.

Williams, Joanna G. *The Art of Gupta India: Empire and Province.* Princeton, N.J.: Princeton University Press, 1982.

Chapter 16: China and Korea to 1279

Bush, Susan, and Shio-yen Shih. *Early Chinese Texts on Painting.* Cambridge, Mass.: Harvard University Press, 1985.

Cahill, James. *The Painter's Practice: How Artists Lived and Worked in Traditional China.* New York: Columbia University Press, 1994.

Clunas, Craig. *Art in China.* New York: Oxford University Press, 1997.

Fahr-Becker, Gabriele, ed. *The Art of East Asia.* Cologne: Könemann, 1999.

Fisher, Robert E. *Buddhist Art and Architecture.* New York: Thames & Hudson, 1993.

Fong, Wen C. *Beyond Representation: Chinese Painting and Calligraphy, 8th–14th Century.* New Haven, Conn.: Yale University Press, 1992.

———. *The Great Bronze Age of China: An Exhibition from the People's Republic of China.* New York: Metropolitan Museum of Art, 1980.

Fong, Wen C., and James C. Y. Watt. *Preserving the Past: Treasures from the National Palace Museum, Taipei.* New York: Metropolitan Museum of Art, 1996.

Fraser, Sarah Elizabeth. *Performing the Visual: The Practice of Buddhist Wall Painting in China and Central Asia, 618–960.* Palo Alto: Stanford University Press, 2004.

Howard, Angela Falco, Li Song, Wu Hong, and Yang Hong. *Chinese Sculpture.* New Haven, Conn.: Yale University Press, 2006.

Kim, Kumja Paik. *Goryeo Dynasty: Korea's Age of Enlightenment, 918–1392.* San Francisco: Asian Art Museum, 2003.

Kim, Lena. *Buddhist Sculpture of Korea.* Elizabeth, N.J.: Hollym, 2007.

Lee, Hui-Shu. *Empresses, Art, and Agency in Song Dynasty China.* Seattle: University of Washington Press, 2010.

Li, Chu-tsing, ed. *Artists and Patrons: Some Social and Economic Aspects of Chinese Painting.* Lawrence, Kans.: Kress Department of Art History, in cooperation with Indiana University Press, 1989.

Little, Stephen, and Shawn Eichman. *Taoism and the Arts of China.* Chicago: Art Institute of Chicago, 2000.

Murck, Alfreda. *Poetry and Painting in Song China: The Subtle Art of Dissent.* Cambridge, Mass.: Harvard University Press, 2000.

Nelson, Sarah Milledge. *The Archaeology of Korea.* New York: Cambridge University Press, 1993.

Pak, Youngsook, and Roderick Whitfield. *Earthenware and Celadon (Handbook of Korean Art).* London: Laurence King, 2003.

———. *Buddhist Sculpture (Handbook of Korean Art).* London: Laurence King, 2003.

Portal, Jane. *Korea: Art and Archaeology.* New York: Thames & Hudson, 2000.

Powers, Martin J. *Art and Political Expression in Early China.* New Haven, Conn.: Yale University Press, 1991.

Rawson, Jessica. *Ancient China: Art and Archaeology.* New York: Harper & Row, 1980.

———, ed. *The British Museum Book of Chinese Art.* New York: Thames & Hudson, 1992.

Sickman, Laurence, and Alexander C. Soper. *The Art and Architecture of China.* 3d ed. New Haven, Conn.: Yale University Press, 1992.

Silbergeld, Jerome. *Chinese Painting Style: Media, Methods, and Principles of Form.* Seattle and London: University of Washington Press, 1982.

Steinhardt, Nancy S., ed. *Chinese Architecture.* New Haven, Conn.: Yale University Press, 2002.

Sullivan, Michael. *The Arts of China.* 5th ed. Berkeley: University of California Press, 2009.

———. *The Birth of Landscape Painting.* Berkeley: University of California Press, 1962.

Thorp, Robert L., and Richard Ellis Vinograd. *Chinese Art and Culture.* New York: Abrams, 2001.

Vainker, S. J. *Chinese Pottery and Porcelain: From Prehistory to the Present.* New York: Braziller, 1991.

Watson, William. *The Arts of China to AD 900.* New Haven, Conn.: Yale University Press, 1995.

———. *The Arts of China 900–1620.* New Haven, Conn.: Yale University Press, 2000.

Weidner, Marsha, ed. *Flowering in the Shadows: Women in the History of Chinese and Japanese Painting.* Honolulu: University of Hawaii Press, 1990.

Whitfield, Roderick. *Dictionary of Korean Art and Archaeology.* Elizabeth, N.J.: Hollym, 2004.

Whitfield, Roger, and Anne Farrer. *Caves of the Thousand Buddhas: Chinese Art of the Silk Route.* New York: Braziller, 1990.

Whitfield, Roderick, Susan Whitfield, and Neville Agnew. *Cave Temples of Dunhuang: Art and History on the Silk Road.* Los Angeles: J. Paul Getty Museum, 2000.

———. *Cave Temples of Mogao: Art and History on the Silk Road.* Los Angeles: J. Paul Getty Museum, 2000.

Wu, Hung. *Monumentality in Early Chinese Art.* Palo Alto, Calif.: Stanford University Press, 1996.

———. *The Wu Liang Shrine: The Ideology of Early Chinese Pictorial Art.* Palo Alto, Calif.: Stanford University Press, 1989.

Xin, Yang, Nie Chongzheng, Lang Shaojun, Richard M. Barnhart, James Cahill, and Hung Wu. *Three Thousand Years of Chinese Painting.* New Haven, Conn.: Yale University Press, 1997.

Zhiyan, Li, Virginia L. Bower, and He Li. *Chinese Ceramics: From the Paleolithic Period through the Qing Dyansty.* New Haven, Conn.: Yale University Press, 2010.

Chapter 17: Japan before 1333

Aikens, C. Melvin, and Takayama Higuchi. *Prehistory of Japan.* New York: Academic, 1982.

Coaldrake, William H. *Architecture and Authority in Japan.* London: Routledge, 1996.

Elisseeff, Danielle, and Vadime Elisseeff. *Art of Japan.* Translated by I. Mark Paris. New York: Abrams, 1985.

Kidder, J. Edward, Jr. *The Art of Japan.* New York: Park Lane, 1985.

Kurata, Bunsaku. *Horyu-ji: Temple of the Exalted Law.* Translated by W. Chie Ishibashi. New York: Japan Society, 1981.

Mason, Penelope. *History of Japanese Art.* 2d ed. New York: Abrams, 2004.

Mizoguchi, Koji. *An Archaeological History of Japan: 30,000 B.C. to A.D. 700.* Philadelphia, University of Pennsylvania Press, 2002.

Murase, Miyeko. *The Tale of Genji: Legends and Paintings.* New York: Braziller, 2001.

Nishi, Kazuo, and Kazuo Hozumi. *What Is Japanese Architecture?* Translated by H. Mack Horton. New York: Kodansha International, 1985.

Nishikawa, Kyotaro, and Emily Sano. *The Great Age of Japanese Buddhist Sculpture AD 600–1300.* Fort Worth, Tex.: Kimbell Art Museum, 1982.

Noma, Seiroku. *The Arts of Japan: Ancient and Medieval.* New York: Kodansha, 1966.

Okudaira, Hideo. *Narrative Picture Scrolls.* Adapted by Elizabeth ten Grotenhuis. New York: Weatherhill, 1973.

Pearson, Richard J. *Ancient Japan.* New York: Braziller, 1992.

Pearson, Richard J., Gina Lee Barnes, and Karl L. Hutterer, eds. *Windows on the Japanese Past.* Ann Arbor: Center for Japanese Studies, University of Michigan, 1986.

Rosenfield, John M. *Japanese Art of the Heian Period, 794–1185.* New York: Asia Society, 1967.

Shimizu, Yoshiaki, ed. *The Shaping of Daimyo Culture 1185–1868.* Washington, D.C.: National Gallery of Art, 1988.

Stanley-Baker, Joan. *Japanese Art.* Rev. ed. New York: Thames & Hudson, 2000.

Suzuki, Kakichi. *Early Buddhist Architecture in Japan.* Translated and adapted by Mary Neighbor Parent and Nancy Shatzman Steinhardt. New York: Kodansha International, 1980.

Ten Grotenhuis, Elizabeth. *Japanese Mandalas: Representations of Sacred Geography.* Honolulu: University of Hawaii Press, 1999.

Weidner, Marsha, ed. *Flowering in the Shadows: Women in the History of Chinese and Japanese Painting.* Honolulu: University of Hawaii Press, 1990.

Chapter 18: Native Arts of the Americas before 1300

Alva, Walter, and Christopher Donnan. *Royal Tombs of Sipán.* Los Angeles: Fowler Museum of Cultural History, 1993.

Andrews, E. Wyllys, and William L. Fash, eds. *Copán: The History of an Ancient Maya Kingdom.* Santa Fe, N.M.: School of American Research, 2005.

Benson, Elizabeth P., and Beatriz de la Fuente, eds. *Olmec Art of Ancient Mexico.* Washington, D.C.: National Gallery of Art, 1996.

Berlo, Janet Catherine, ed. *Art, Ideology, and the City of Teotihuacan.* Washington, D.C.: Dumbarton Oaks, 1992.

Berlo, Janet Catherine, and Ruth B. Phillips. *Native North American Art.* New York: Oxford University Press, 1998.

Berrin, Kathleen, and Virginia M. Fields. *Olmec: Colossal Masterworks of Ancient Mexico.* New Haven, Conn.: Yale University Press, 2010.

Berrin, Kathleen, ed. *The Spirit of Ancient Peru: Treasures from the Museo Arqueologico Rafael Larco Herrera.* San Francisco: Fine Arts Museums of San Francisco, 1997.

Bourget, Steve, and Kimberly L. Jones, eds. *The Art and Archaeology of the Moche: An Ancient Andean Society of the Peruvian North Coast.* Austin: University of Texas Press, 2008.

Brody, J. J., and Rina Swentzell. *To Touch the Past: The Painted Pottery of the Mimbres People.* New York: Hudson Hills, 1996.

Brose, David. *Ancient Art of the American Woodland Indians.* New York: Abrams, 1985.

Bruhns, Karen O. *Ancient South America.* New York: Cambridge University Press, 1994.

Burger, Richard. *Chavín and the Origins of Andean Civilization.* New York: Thames & Hudson, 1992.

Carrasco, David. *The Oxford Encyclopedia of Mesoamerican Cultures: The Civilizations of Mexico and Central America.* New York: Oxford University Press, 2001.

Clark, John E., and Mary E. Pye, eds. *Olmec Art and Archaeology in Mesoamerica.* Washington, D.C.: National Gallery of Art, 2000.

Coe, Michael D. *The Maya.* 8th ed. New York: Thames & Hudson, 2011.

———. *Mexico: From the Olmecs to the Aztecs.* 6th ed. New York: Thames & Hudson, 2008.

Conklin, William J., and Jeffrey Quilter, eds. *Chavín: Art, Architecture, and Culture.* Los Angeles: Cotsen Institute of Archaeology, 2008.

Cordell, Linda S. *Ancient Pueblo Peoples.* Washington, D.C.: Smithsonian Institution, 1994.

Donnan, Christopher. *Moche Portraits from Ancient Peru.* Austin: University of Texas Press, 2003.

Fagan, Brian. *Ancient North America: The Archaeology of a Continent.* 4th ed. New York: Thames & Hudson, 2005.

———. *The First North Americans.* New York: Thames & Hudson, 2011.

Fash, William. *Scribes, Warriors, and Kings: The City of Copan and the Ancient Maya.* New York: Thames & Hudson, 1991.

Feest, Christian F. *Native Arts of North America.* 2d ed. New York: Thames & Hudson, 1992.

Foster, Michael S., and Shirley Gorenstein, eds. *Greater Mesoamerica: The Archaeology of West and Northwest Mexico.* Salt Lake City: University of Utah Press, 2000.

Grube, Nikolai, ed. *Maya: Divine Kings of the Rain Forest.* Cologne: Könemann, 2000.

Janusek, John Wayne. *Ancient Tiwanaku.* New York: Cambridge University Press, 2008.

Kolata, Alan. *The Tiwanaku: Portrait of an Andean Civilization.* Cambridge: Blackwell, 1993.

Kubler, George. *The Art and Architecture of Ancient America: The Mexican, Maya, and Andean Peoples.* 3d ed. New Haven, Conn.: Yale University Press, 1992.

Marken, Damien B., ed. *Palenque: Recent Investigations at the Classic Maya Center.* Lanham, Md.: Altamira, 2007.

Miller, Mary Ellen. *The Art of Mesoamerica, from Olmec to Aztec.* 4th ed. New York: Thames & Hudson, 2006.

———. *Maya Art and Architecture.* New York: Thames & Hudson, 1999.

Miller, Mary Ellen, and Karl Taube. *The Gods and Symbols of Ancient Mexico and the Maya: An Illustrated Dictionary of Mesoamerican Religion.* New York: Thames & Hudson, 1993.

Milner, George R. *The Moundbuilders: Ancient Peoples of Eastern North America.* New York: Thames & Hudson, 2004.

Morris, Craig, and Adriana von Hagen. *The Inka Empire and Its Andean Origins.* New York: Abbeville, 1993.

Nabokov, Peter, and Robert Easton. *Native American Architecture.* New York: Oxford University Press, 1989.

Pasztory, Esther. *Pre-Columbian Art.* New York: Cambridge University Press, 1998.

Pasztory, Esther. *Teotihuacan: An Experiment in Living*. Norman: University of Oklahoma Press, 1997.

Paul, Anne. *Paracas Ritual Attire: Symbols of Authority in Ancient Peru*. Norman: University of Oklahoma Press, 1990.

Penney, David, and George C. Longfish. *Native American Art*. Hong Kong: Hugh Lauter Levin and Associates, 1994.

Pillsbury, Joanne, ed. *Moche Art and Archaeology in Ancient Peru*. Washington, D.C.: National Gallery of Art, 2005.

Pool, Christopher A. *Olmec Archaeology and Early Mesoamerica*. New York: Cambridge University Press, 2007.

Rohm, Arthur H., and William M. Ferguson. *Puebloan Ruins of the Southwest*. Albuquerque: University of New Mexico Press, 2006.

Schele, Linda, and Peter Mathews. *The Code of Kings: The Language of Seven Sacred Maya Temples and Tombs*. New York: Scribner, 1998.

Schele, Linda, and Mary E. Miller. *The Blood of Kings: Dynasty and Ritual in Maya Art*. Fort Worth, Tex.: Kimbell Art Museum, 1986.

Schmidt, Peter, Mercedes de la Garza, and Enrique Nalda, eds. *Maya*. New York: Rizzoli, 1998.

Sharer, Robert J., and Loa P. Traxler. *The Ancient Maya*. 6th ed. Palo Alto: Stanford University Press, 2006.

Silverman, Helaine, and William H. Isbell, eds. *Handbook of South American Archaeology*. New York: Springer, 2008.

Stone-Miller, Rebecca. *Art of the Andes from Chavín to Inca*. 2d ed. New York: Thames & Hudson, 2002.

———. *To Weave for the Sun: Ancient Andean Textiles*. New York: Thames & Hudson, 1994.

Townsend, Richard F., ed. *Ancient West Mexico*. Chicago: Art Institute of Chicago, 1998.

Von Hagen, Adriana, and Craig Morris. *The Cities of the Ancient Andes*. New York: Thames & Hudson, 1998.

Wardwell, Allen. *Ancient Eskimo Ivories of the Bering Strait*. New York: Rizzoli, 1986.

Whiteford, Andrew H., Stewart Peckham, and Kate Peck Kent. *I Am Here: Two Thousand Years of Southwest Indian Arts and Crafts*. Santa Fe: Museum of New Mexico Press, 1989.

Chapter 19: Africa before 1800

Bacquart, Jean-Baptiste. *The Tribal Arts of Africa*. New York: Thames & Hudson, 2002.

Bassani, Ezio. *Arts of Africa: 7,000 Years of African Art*. Milan: Skira, 2005.

Ben-Amos, Paula. *The Art of Benin*. New York: Thames & Hudson, 1980.

Berzock, Kathleen Bickford. *Benin: Royal Arts of a West African Kingdom*. Chicago: Art Institute of Chicago, 2008.

Blier, Suzanne P. *Royal Arts of Africa: The Majesty of Form*. New York: Abrams, 1998.

Campbell, Alec, and David Coulson. *African Rock Art: Paintings and Engravings on Stone*. New York: Abrams, 2001.

Connah, Graham. *African Civilizations*. 2d ed. Cambridge: Cambridge University Press, 2001.

Coulson, David, and Alec Campbell. *African Rock Art: Painting and Engravings on Stone*. New York: Abrams, 2001.

Dewey, William J. *Legacies of Stone: Zimbabwe Past and Present*. Tervuren: Royal Museum for Central Africa, 1997.

Drewal, Henry J., John Pemberton, and Rowland Abiodun. *Yoruba: Nine Centuries of African Art and Thought*. New York: Center for African Art, in association with Abrams, 1989.

Drewal, Henry John, and Enid Schildkrout. *Dynasty and Divinity: Ife Art in Ancient Nigeria*. Seattle: University of Washington Press, 2010.

Eyo, Ekpo, and Frank Willett. *Treasures of Ancient Nigeria*. New York: Knopf, 1980.

Fagg, Bernard. *Nok Terracottas*. Lagos: Ethnographica, 1977.

Garlake, Peter. *Early Art and Architecture of Africa*. Oxford: Oxford University Press, 2002.

———. *Great Zimbabwe*. London: Thames & Hudson, 1973.

Grunne, Bernard de. *The Birth of Art in Africa: Nok Statuary in Nigeria*. Paris: Biro, 1998.

Huffman, Thomas N. *Snakes and Crocodiles: Power and Symbolism in Ancient Zimbabwe*. Johannesburg: Witwatersrand University Press, 1996.

Lajoux, Jean-Dominique. *The Rock Paintings of Tassili*. Cleveland: World Publishing, 1963.

Le Quellec, Jean-Loïc. *Rock Art in Africa: Mythology and Legend*. Paris: Flammarion, 2004.

Perani, Judith, and Fred T. Smith. *The Visual Arts of Africa: Gender, Power, and Life Cycle Rituals*. Englewood Cliffs, N.J.: Prentice Hall, 1998.

Phillips, Tom, ed. *Africa, the Art of a Continent*. New York: Prestel, 1995.

Phillipson, D. W. *African Archaeology*. 3d ed. New York: Cambridge University Press, 2005.

———. *Ancient Ethiopia: Aksum, Its Antecedents and Successors*. London: British Museum Press, 1998.

Schädler, Karl-Ferdinand. *Earth and Ore: 2,500 Years of African Art in Terra-Cotta and Metal*. Munich: Panterra Verlag, 1997.

Shaw, Thurstan. *Nigeria: Its Archaeology and Early History*. London: Thames & Hudson, 1978.

———. *Unearthing Igbo-Ukwu: Archaeological Discoveries in Eastern Nigeria*. New York: Oxford University Press, 1977.

Visonà, Monica B., ed. *A History of Art in Africa*. 2d ed. Englewood Cliffs, N.J.: Prentice Hall, 2007.

Willett, Frank. *Ife in the History of West African Sculpture*. New York: McGraw-Hill, 1967.

CREDITS

Introduction—Opener: © The Metropolitan Museum of Art/Art Resource, NY; **I-2:** © The Clyfford Still Estate. Photo: akg images; **I-3:** © Paul Maeyaert/The Bridgeman Art Library International; **I-4:** akg-images/Rabatti-Domingie; **I-5:** National Gallery of Art, Alfred Stieglitz Collection, Bequest of Georgia O'Keeffe 1987.58.3; **I-6:** Art © Estate of Ben Shahn/Licensed by VAGA, New York, NY. Photo: Whitney Museum of American Art, New York. (gift of Edith and Milton Lowenthal in memory of Juliana Force); **I-7:** © Jonathan Poore/Cengage Learning; **I-8:** akg-images; **I-9:** © The Metropolitan Museum of Art/Art Resource, NY; **I-10:** Courtesy Saskia Ltd., © Dr. Ron Wiedenhoeft; **I-11:** © 2011 The Josef and Anni Albers Foundation/Artists Rights Society (ARS), New York. Photo: © Whitney Museum of American Art; **I-12:** National Gallery, London. NG14. Bought, 1824; **I-13:** Photograph © 2011 Museum of Fine Arts, Boston; **I-14:** © bpk, Berlin/Staatsgemaeldesammlungen, Munich, Germany/Art Resource, NY; **I-15:** Jürgen Liepe, Berlin; **I-16:** © Nimatallah/Art Resource, NY; **I-17:** © Scala/Art Resource, NY; **I-18:** © Cengage Learning; **I-19a:** National Library of Australia, Canberra, Australia/The Bridgeman Art Library International; **I-19b:** Public Domain.

Chapter 1—Opener: © Jean Vertut; **1-2:** Dr. Paul G. Bahn; **1-3:** With permission: Namibia Archaeological Trust; **1-4:** © Ulmer Museum. Photo: Thomas Stephan; **Map 1-1:** © Cengage Learning; timeline © Jean Vertut; **1-5:** © Erich Lessing/Art Resource, NY; **1-5A:** © Réunion des Musées Nationaux/Art Resource, NY; **1-6A:** Louis de Seille/Courtesy Jean Clottes; **1-6:** © Giraudon/The Bridgeman Art Library International; **1-7:** © Jean Vertut; **1-8:** © Réunion des Musées Nationaux/Art Resource, NY; **1-9:** © Jean Vertut; **1-10:** © Jean Vertut; **1-11:** French Ministry of Culture and Communication, Regional Direction for Cultural Affairs-Rhone-Alpes region- Regional Department of Archaeology; **1-12:** © Jean Vertut; **01-12A:** akg-images; **1-13:** © Israel/Ancient Art and Architecture Collection Ltd./The Bridgeman Art Library; **Map 1-2:** © Cengage Learning; **1-14:** The Art Archive/Archaeological Museum Amman Jordan/Gianni Dagli Orti/Picture Desk; **1-15:** © Erich Lessing/Art Resource, NY; **1-16:** © Gianni Dagli Orti/Corbis; **1-16A:** © John Swogger/The Çatalhöyük Research Project; **1-17:** © James Mellaart/Catalhoyuk Research Project; **1-18:** The Art Archive/Gianni Dagli Orti/Picture Desk; **1-19:** Bob Krist/Corbis; **1-19A:** © Adam Woolfitt/Corbis; **1-20:** © Adam Woolfitt/Corbis; **UNF 1-1:** © Erich Lessing/Art Resource, NY; **UNF 1-2:** © Jean Vertut; **UNF 1-3:** The Art Archive/Archaeological Museum Amman Jordan/Gianni Dagli Orti/Picture Desk; **UNF 1-4:** © Adam Woolfitt/Corbis.

Chapter 2—Opener: © The Trustees of The British Museum/Art Resource, NY; **Map 2-1:** © Cengage Learning; **timeline:** © The Trustees of The British Museum/Art Resource, NY; **2-2:** © Richard Ashworth/Robert Harding; **2-3:** © Cengage Learning; **2-4:** akg-images/Bildarchiv Steffens; **2-5:** © bpk, Berlin/National Museum of Iraq, Baghdad/Art Resource, NY; **2-6:** © Erich Lessing/Art Resource, NY; **2-6A:** Hirmer Fotoarchiv, Munich; **2-7:** © Réunion des Musées Nationaux/Art Resource, NY; **2-8:** © The Trustees of the British Museum/Art Resource, NY; **2-9:** © The Trustees of the British Museum/Art Resource, NY; **2-10:** University of Pennsylvania Museum of Archaeology and Anthropology, Philadelphia; **2-11:** © The Trustees of the British Museum; **2-12:** Iraq Museum/akg-images; **2-13:** © Réunion des Musées Nationaux/Art Resource, NY; **2-14:** University of Pennsylvania Museum of Archaeology and Anthropology, Philadelphia.; **2-15:** Silvio Fiore/Superstock/Photolibrary; **2-16:** © Erich Lessing/Art Resource, NY; **2-17:** © Erich Lessing/Art Resource, NY; **2-18A:** © Erich Lessing/Art Resource, NY; **2-18:** © Réunion des Musées Nationaux/Art Resource, NY; **2-18B:** © Borromeo/Art Resource, NY; **2-19:** © Réunion des Musées Nationaux/Art Resource, NY; **2-19A:** © Lauros/Giraudon/The Bridgeman Art Library International; **2-20:** © The Bridgeman Art Library International; **2-20A:** © Cengage Learning; **2-21:** © The Trustees of The British Museum/Art Resource, NY; **2-22:** © The Trustees of The British Museum/Art Resource, NY; **2-23:** © The Trustees of the British Museum; **2-24:** © Bildarchiv Preussischer Kulturbesitz/Art Resource, NY; **2-25:** The Art Archive/Alfredo Dagli Orti/Picture Desk; **2-26:** © age fotostock/SuperStock; **2-26A:** © Scala/Art Resource, NY; **2-27:** © David Poole/Robert Harding Picture Library; **2-28:** akg-images/Gérard Degeorge; **2-28A:** Courtesy Saskia Ltd., © Dr. Ron Wiedenhoeft; **UNF 2-1:** © The Trustees of the British Museum/Art Resource, NY; **UNF 2-2:** Iraq Museum/akg-images; **UNF 2-3:** © Silvio Fiore/Superstock/Photolibrary; **UNF 2-4:** © The Trustees of the British Museum/Art Resource, NY; **UNF 2-5:** © David Poole/Robert Harding Picture Library.

Chapter 3—Opener: © Werner Forman/Art Resource, NY; **timeline:** © Werner Forman/Art Resource, NY; **3-2:** © Werner Forman/Art Resource, NY; **3-1A:** J.E. Quibell and F.W. Geen, Hierakonpolis vol.2 (London 192) p. 76/Egyptian Museum; **3-5A:** Ancient Art and Architecture Collection; **3-4:** © Werner Forman/Art Resource, NY; **3-6:** © Erich Lessing/Art Resource, NY; **3-7:** © Yann Arthus-Bertrand/Corbis; **3-9:** Courtesy of the Semitic Museum, Harvard University.; **3-10:** © Robert Harding Picture Library; **3-11:** © Araldo de Luca; **3-11A:** akg-images/Andrea Jemolo; **3-11B:** © Erich Lessing/Art Resource, NY; **3-12:** Photograph © 2011 Museum of Fine Arts, Boston; **3-13:** © Erich Lessing/Art Resource, NY; **3-13A:** Jürgen Liepe, Berlin; **3-13B:** Roemer-und Pelizaeus Museum Hildesheim; **3-14:** © Jean Vertut; **3-15:** © The Bridgeman Art Library International; **3-16:** © The Metropolitan Museum of Art/Art Resource, NY; **3-16A:** Photograph © 2011 Museum of Fine Arts, Boston; **3-17:** © Marburg/Art Resource, NY; **3-18:** akg-images/Francois Guenet; **3-19:** © De Agostini/SuperStock; **3-20:** © Scala/Art Resource, NY; **3-21:** © The Metropolitan Museum of Art/Art Resource, NY; **3-22:** akg-images/Robert O'Dea; **3-23:** © Carmen Redondo/Corbis Art/Corbis; **3-24:** © JD. Dallet/age fotostock/Photolibrary; **3-24A:** © Yann Arthus-Bertrand/Corbis; **3-25:** © Robert Harding Picture Library; **3-26:** © The Metropolitan Museum of Art/Art Resource, NY; **3-27:** © Bildarchiv Preussischer Kulturbesitz/Art Resource, NY; **3-28:** © The Trustees of the British Museum/Art Resource, NY; **3-29:** © The Trustees of the British Museum/Art Resource, NY; **3-30:** © Araldo de Luca; **3-31:** © Sean Gallup/Getty Images; **3-32:** © Bildarchiv Preussischer Kulturbesitz/Art Resource, NY; **3-33:** © Bildarchiv Preussischer Kulturbesitz/Art Resource, NY; **3-34:** © Boltin Picture Library/The Bridgeman Art Library; **3-35:** Robert Harding/Getty Images; **3-36:** The Art Archive/Egyptian Museum Cairo/Gianni Dagli Orti/Picture Desk; **3-37:** © British Museum/HIP/Art Resource, NY; **3-38:** Jürgen Liepe, Berlin; **3-39:** © The Trustees of the British Museum/Art Resource, NY; **3-40:** © Yann Arthus-Bertrand/Corbis; **UNF 3-1:** © Werner Forman/Art Resource, NY; **UNF 3-2:** © Yann Arthus-Bertrand/Corbis; **UNF 3-3:** akg-images/Francois Guenet; **UNF 3-4:** © Yann Arthus-Bertrand/Corbis.

Chapter 4—Opener: © Nimatallah/Art Resource, NY; **4-2:** © Erich Lessing/Art Resource, NY; **4-3:** The Art Archive/National Archaeological Museum Athens/Gianni Dagli Orti; **4-4:** © Yann Arthus-Bertrand/Terra/CORBIS; **4-6:** © Roger Wood/Corbis; **4-7:** Courtesy Saskia Ltd., © Dr. Ron Wiedenhoeft; **4-8:** © The Art Archive/Heraklion Museum/Gianni Dagli Orti; **4-9:** © Nimatallah/Art Resource, NY; **4-9A:** Copyright: Photo Henri Stierlin, Geneve; **4-9B:** Ch. Doumas, "The Wall Paintings of Thera," Idryma Theras-Petros M. Nomikos, Athens, 1992.; **4-10:** STUDIO KONTOS/PHOTOSTOCK; **4-11:** © Scala/Art Resource, NY; **4-12:** The Art Archive/Heraklion Museum/Gianni Dagli Orti; **4-13:** British School at Athens; **4-14:** © Erich Lessing/Art Resource, NY; **4-15:** STUDIO KONTOS/PHOTOSTOCK; **4-16:** © Erich Lessing/Art Resource, NY; **4-18A:** The Art Archive/Archaeological Museum Chora Greece/Gianni Dagli Orti/Picture Desk; **4-19:** © SIME/eStock Photo; **4-20:** © Vanni Archive/Corbis Art/Corbis; **4-21:** © Vanni Archive/Corbis Art/Corbis; **4-22A:** © George Gerster/Photo Researchers, Inc.; **4-22:** © Joe Vogan/SuperStock; **4-23:** The Art Archive/National Archaeological Museum Athens/Gianni Dagli Orti/Picture Desk; **4-23a** © Erich Lessing/Art Resource, NY; **4-24:** © Nimatallah/Art Resource, NY; **4-25:** The Art Archive/National Archaeological Museum Athens/Gianni Dagli Orti/Picture Desk; **UNF 4-01:** akg-images; **UNF 4-2:** The Art Archive/Heraklion Museum/Gianni Dagli Orti; **UNF 4-3:** The Art Archive/Heraklion Museum/Gianni Dagli Orti; **UNF 4-4:** © Joe Vogan/SuperStock; **UNF 4-5:** © Vanni Archive/Corbis Art/Corbis.

Chapter 5—Opener (bottom and detail 1): © Herbert SA House -Lank/Superstock/Photolibrary; **(detail 2):** © British Museum, London, UK/The Bridgeman Art Library; **(detail 3):** R Sheridan/Ancient Art & Architecture Collection Ltd; **(detail 4):** Royal Ontario Museum, Toronto; **timeline:** © Herbert SA House - Lank/Superstock/Photolibrary; **5-2:** Photograph © 1996 The Metropolitan Museum of Art/Art Resource, NY (14.130.14); **5-2A:** © Nimatallah/Art Resource, NY; **5-3:** © The Metropolitan Museum of Art/Art Resource, NY; **5-4:** Photograph © 2011 Museum of Fine Arts, Boston; **5-5:** © The Trustees of the British Museum; **5-6:** © Réunion des Musées Nationaux/Art Resource, NY; **5-6b:** Alison Frantz Photographic Collection, American School of Classical Studies, Athens; **5-7:** Image copyright © The Metropolitan Museum of Art/Art Resource, NY; **5-8:** © Nimatallah/Art Resource, NY; **5-9:** Gianni Dagli Orti/The Picture Desk Limited/Corbis; **5-10:** © Nimatallah/Art Resource, NY; **5-11:** © Marie Mauzy/Scala/Art Resource, NY; **5-13:** © John Burge/Cengage Learning; **5-14:** © 208 Fred S. Kleiner; **5-16:** © Vanni/Art Resource, NY; **5-17:** © Cengage Learning; **5-17A:** © De Agostini Picture Library/Learning Pictures; **5-18:** © Nimatallah/Art Resource, NY; **5-19:** Canali Photobank; **5-19b:** © Cengage Learning; **5-20A:** The Trustees of The British Museum/Art Resource, NY; **5-20:** © Scala/Art Resource, NY; **5-21a:** Photograph © 2011 Museum of Fine Arts, Boston; **5-21b:** Photograph © 2011 Museum of Fine Arts, Boston; **5-22:** © Réunion des Musées Nationaux/Art Resource, NY; **5-22A:** © Scala/Ministero per i Beni e le Attività culturali/Art Resource, NY; **5-23:** Courtesy Saskia Ltd., © Dr. Ron Wiedenhoeft; **5-23A:** Musées royaux d'Art et d'Histoire; **5-24:** Copyright: Photo Henri Stierlin, Geneve; **5-25a:** Courtesy Saskia Ltd., © Dr. Ron Wiedenhoeft; **5-26:** © Gianni Dagli Orti/The Picture Desk Limited/Corbis; **5-27:** Saskia Ltd., © Dr. Ron Wiedenhoeft; **5-28:** SASKIA Ltd. Cultural Documentation. © Dr. Ron Wiedenhoeft; **5-29:** © 208 Fred S. Kleiner; **5-30:** STUDIO KONTOS/PHOTOSTOCK; **5-31:** akg-images/John Hios; **5-32:** The Art Archive/Olympia Museum Greece/Gianni Dagli Orti/Picture Desk; **5-32A:** © Vanni/Art Resource, NY; **5-33:** The Art Archive/Olympia Museum Greece/Gianni Dagli Orti/Picture Desk; **5-34:** © Marie Mauzy/Scala/Art Resource, NY; **5-35:** © Scala/Art Resource, NY; **5-37:** © Erich Lessing/Art Resource, NY; **5-38:** © Nimatallah/Art Resource, NY; **5-39:** © Scala/Art Resource, NY; **5-40:** © Scala/Ministero per i Beni e le Attività culturali/Art Resource, NY; **5-41:** © Bildarchiv Preussischer Kulturbesitz/Art Resource, NY; **5-42:** © Yann Arthus-Bertrand/Terra/Corbis; **5-43:** © Cengage Learning; **5-44:** © Scala/Art Resource, NY; **5-46:** Royal Ontario Museum; **5-47:** © British Museum, London, UK/The Bridgeman Art Library; **5-48:** STUDIO KONTOS/PHOTOSTOCK; **5-49:** R Sheridan/Ancient Art & Architecture Collection Ltd; **5-50a:** © British Museum, London, UK/The Bridgeman Art Library, NY; **5-50b:** STUDIO KONTOS/PHOTOSTOCK; **5-50c:** Ancient Art and Architecture Collection Ltd.; **5-51:** Copyright: Photo Henri Stierlin, Geneve; **5-52:** © Scala/Art Resource, NY; **5-54:** Hervé Champollion/akg-images; **5-55:** Saskia Ltd., © Dr. Ron Wiedenhoeft; **5-56:** © Marie Mauzy/Scala, Florence/Art Resource, NY; **5-57:** © Nimatallah/Art Resource, NY; **5-58:** © Scala/Art Resource, NY; **5-58A:** © Scala/Art Resource, NY; **5-59:** © Réunion des Musées Nationaux/Art Resource, NY; **5-60:** © Scala/Art Resource, NY; **5-61:** © Mimmo Jodice/Corbis Art/Corbis; **5-62:** © Scala/Art Resource, NY;

MUSEUM INDEX

Note: *Figure numbers in blue indicate bonus images.*

SUBJECT INDEX

Notes:
- *Page numbers in italics indicate illustrations.*
- *Page numbers in italics followed by* b *indicate bonus images in the text.*
- *Page numbers in italics followed by* map *indicate maps.*
- *Figure numbers in* blue *indicate bonus images.*

begging bowls, 486
Belisarius (Byzantine general), 258, 263
Bellerophon, 128
Belleville Breviary (Pucelle), 387–388, *387*
belt buckle, Sutton Hoo ship burial, 11-3A
ben-ben, 57, 61
Benedetto Antelami, 359
    King David, Fidenza Cathedral
        (sculpture), 356–357, *357*, 12-14A
Benedict of Nursia (Saint Benedict), 322
Benedictine Rule, 322, 330, 341, 343
benedictionals, 312
Benevento (Italy): Arch of Trajan, 208, *208b*,
    7-44A, 7-44B
Beni Hasan (Egypt): rock-cut tombs, 68, *68*,
    72, 171
Benin (Nigeria)
    head of a queen mother (sculpture), *532b*,
        19-13A
    waist pendate of a queen mother,
        531–532, *531*
Benin art, 533
    sculpture, xvi, 11, 12, 520, 521, 531–532,
        19-13A
bent-axis plan, 33, 2-20A
Beowulf, 309, 11-3A
Berbers, 295
Berlinghieri, Bonaventura: *Saint Francis
    Altarpiece*, San Francesco, Pescia,
    404–405, *404*, 14-5B
Bernard de Soissons. *See* Reims Cathedral
Bernard of Clairvaux, Saint
    on church art, 333, 342, 343, 354, 367,
        12-13A
    and Crusades, 345, 346
    on Hildegard of Bingen, 352
    on illuminated manuscripts, 347–348
    on Scholasticism, 372
Bernardus Gelduinus, 359, 12-23A
    Christ in Majesty, Saint-Sernin, 340, *340*,
        356
Bernini, Gianlorenzo: *Barberini Faun*
    restoration, 159
Berno of Baume, 341
Bernward (bishop of Hildesheim), 324–325,
    326, 11-24A
bestiaries, 343
Beta Giorghis (Church of Saint George),
    Lalibela, 529–530, *530*
Bethlehem, 242
Betrayal of Christ, Hours of Jeanne d'Evreux
    (Pucelle), 13-36A
Betrayal of Jesus, 241
    in Early Christian art, 251, 12-13A
    in French/Spanish Romanesque art,
        12-13A
    in Gothic art, 13-36A
    in Italian 14th century art, 400, 401, 412,
        14-8B
Betrayal of Jesus, Arena Chapel, Padua
    (Giotto), *400*, 401, 14-8B
Betrayal of Jesus, Maestà altarpiece, Siena
    Cathedral (Duccio), 412, *412*, 14-8B
Bhagiratha, 15-22A
Bhairava (Hindu deity), 436
Bhaisajyaguru (Yakushi), 481
bhumisparsha mudra (earth-touching
    mudra), 427
bi disk with dragons, Jincun(?), 454, *454*
bi disks, 453, 454
Bible
    Alcuin's revision, 317
    Babylon ziggurat in, 34, 48, 49
    Book of Apocalypse, 314
    moralized, 384–386
    See also Christianity; Gospels; Jesus,
        life of
bichrome, 511
Bihzad: illustrator of *Bustan* (Sadi), 302, *302*
bilateral symmetry, 64
    See also symmetry
bilingual vases, 121, 121–122
Birth of the Virgin, Siena Cathedral
    (Lorenzetti), 415, *415*
Bishapur (Iran): Triumph of Shapur I over
    Valerian (relief sculpture), 52, *52b*,
    2-28A
bison: in Paleolithic art, 19, 20–21, 23, 26, 58

bison, painted cave ceiling, Altamira, 20–21,
    20, 58
bison licking its flank, fragmentary spear-
    thrower, La Madeleine, 19, *19*
bitumen, 425
Black Death, 406, 416, 419, 14-19A
black-figure painting, 110, 111, 120–121,
    5-20A
Blanche of Castile, 385–386
Blanche of Castile, Louis IX, and two monks,
    moralized Bible, *385*
blind arcades, 52, 290
block statues, 74
Blouet, Guillaume-Abel: Temple of Aphaia
    restored view, *124*
Blue Koran, 294, *294b*, 10-17A
Boar Avatar of Vishnu Rescues the Earth,
    Udayagiri (cave sculpture), 434–435,
    434
Boccaccio, Giovanni, 406, 407
Bodhidharma (Chan patriarch), 470
Bodhisattva Guanyin as the Guide of Souls,
    Dunhuang Grottoes (wall painting),
    462b, 16-14A
Bodhisattva Guanyin seated on Potalaka,
    Shanxi (sculpture), 467, *467b*, 16-21A
Bodhisattva Maitreya, Prakhon Chai
    (sculpture), *443b*, 15-29A
Bodhisattva Padmapani, cave painting,
    Ajanta, 433, *433*
bodhisattvas, 427, 433, 443, 15-29A, 16-13B
Bonampak (Mexico): presentation of
    captives to Lord Chan Muwan (mural),
    502, *502*
Bonaventura, Saint, 14-5B
Boniface VIII (Pope), 385
Book of Durrow, 311–312, *312*
Book of Kells, 306, 307, 311, 315
Book of the Dead (Egyptian), 61, 80
books
    Byzantine, 258, 268, 276–277, 405, 9-3A,
        9-17A
    Carolingian, 5, 317, 318–320, 11-13A,
        11-15A
    and Christianity, 312
    Early Islamic, 294, 10-17A
    French Gothic, 384–388, 13-36A
    French/Spanish Romanesque, 347–348,
        12-15A
    Hiberno-Saxon, 306, 307, 311–315, 318
    Holy Roman Empire Romanesque,
        352–353, 12-23A
    Japanese, 484–485
    Late Antique, 248–250
    later Islamic, 302–303
    materials and techniques, 249
    Norman Romanesque, 359–361, 12-35A
    Ottonian, 329–330, 11-29A
Books of Hours, 312, 13-36A
Borobudur, Java, *442*, 443
Boscoreale (Italy): Villa of Publius Fannius
    Synistor, 192–193, *193*, 213
Boscotrecase (Italy): Villa of Agrippa
    Postumus, 194, *194*
boshan, 455, 16-6A
bosses, 426
Bourges (France): Jacques Coeur house,
    383–384, *383*
bowl with two cranes and geometric forms,
    Mimbres, 517, *517*
Brahmins, 427, 435, 439
Brassempouy (France): head of a woman
    (ivory carving), *18b*, 1-5A
brawl in the Pompeii amphitheater, wall
    painting from House I,3,23, Pompeii,
    189–190, *189*, 196
breviaries, 312, 386–387
Breviary of Philippe le Bel (Master Honoré),
    386–387, *387*
brick, 214, 262, 290, 9-32A
bridge-spouted vessel with flying figures,
    Nasca, 510–511, *510*
brocades, 449
bronze casting
    African, 520, 521, 525–526, 19-4A, 19-13A
    Chinese, 452, 453, 456, 16-6A, 16-13B
    Early Byzantine, 259
    Elamite, 45

Etruscan, 176
    Greek Early/High Classical period, 11,
        129–131
    Korean, 471
    Neo-Sumerian, 40–41
    Southeast Asian, 444
Bruce, Thomas (Lord Elgin), 134
Bruges (Belgium): guild hall, 383, *383*
Brunelleschi, Filippo: Ospedale degli
    Innocenti (Foundling Hospital),
    Florence, 410
bubonic plague (Black Death), 406, 416, 419,
    14-19A
Bucephalus, 148, 150
bucranium/bucrania, 1-16A
Buddha seated on lion throne, Mathura,
    432–433, *432*
Buddha triad, 475
Buddha triad, Horyuji temple (Tori Busshi),
    474, 475, 480, *480*, 481
buddhas. *See* Amitabha Buddha; Shakyamuni
    Buddha; Vairocana Buddha
Buddhism, 427–428
    Ashoka's conversion to, 428, 15-6A
    Chan/Zen, 468–469, 470
    in China, 458
    Esoteric, 483
    in Japan, 475, 480
    in Korea, 470
    life of Buddha, 422, 423, 427, 432, 15-8A
    medieval Indian decline of, 437, 441
    Nara period Japanese, 481–483
    and the Silk Road, 458
    in Southeast Asia, 15-28A, 15-29A
    and stupas, 429–430
    Theravada, 427, 446, 15-28A
    See also Pure Land Buddhism
Buddhist art
    Korean, 471–472
    Southeast Asian, 442, 443, 446, 15-28A,
        15-29A
    See also Chinese Buddhist art; Japanese
        Buddhist art; South Asian Buddhist
        art
Buffalmacco, Buonamico: *Triumph of Death*,
    419–420, *419*
Bukhara (Uzbekistan): Samanid
    Mausoleum, 289–290, *289*
Bulgars, 258
bull-headed harp, tomb 789 ("King's
    Grave"), Ur, 38–39, *38*, 88
bull-headed harp with inlaid sound box,
    tomb of Pu-abi, Ur, 38, *38*, 88
bull-leaping, palace, Knossos (fresco), 91, *91*
bulls
    in Paleolithic art, 14–15, 15, 20, 22–23
    in Sumerian art, 38–39
buon fresco, 408
    See also fresco painting
Buonarroti, Michelangelo. *See* Michelangelo
    Buonarroti
Burge, John, 97, 116, 119, 134, 154, 183, 190,
    208, 211, 228, 236, 242, 260, 261, 341,
    344, 373
burial mask, Eskimo, Ipiutak, 514, *515*
burials. *See* funerary customs
Burmese art (Myanmar art), 443, 15-28A
Bury Bible (Master Hugo), 359–360, 12-23A,
    12-35A
busshi, 475
bust of Augustus wearing the corona civica
    (sculpture), 6, *7*
bust of Caracalla, 219–220, *219*
Bustan (Sadi) (ill. by Bihzad), 302, *302*
busts, 12
buttressing
    in early Byzantine architecture, 262
    in English Gothic architecture, 390
    in French Gothic architecture, 365, 378,
        13-3A
    in French/Spanish Romanesque
        architecture, 12-10A
    in Norman Romanesque architecture,
        357
    in Roman Republic architecture, 184
    See also flying buttresses
Byodoin, Uji, *484*
Byzantine, 256

Byzantine architecture
    Early, 254, 255, 259–264, 267
    early Christian architecture and, 244
    Late, 9-32A
    Middle, 271–272, 274–275, 9-25A, 9-27A
Byzantine art, 254–281, *256map*
    and African art, 530
    and Gothic art, 370
    and Holy Roman Empire Romanesque
        art, 354
    and iconoclasm, 257, 269, 270
    and Islamic art, 274–275, 287, 9-27A
    and Italian 13th century art, 404–405,
        406
    and Italian 14th century art, 409, 411
    and Italian Romanesque art, 12-27B
    Late, 278–280, 281, 9-35A
    maniera greca, 404–405, 407, 14-7A,
        14-8B
    and Ottonian art, 328
    societal contexts, 255, 256–257, 258, 263,
        270, 278
    See also Early Byzantine art; Middle
        Byzantine art
Byzantine Empire
    and Carolingian Empire, 270
    empresses, 266, 273
    and the Ottonian Empire, 256, 257, 270,
        278, 284, 324, 328, 329
    and Salian dynasty, 354–355
    timeline, 256
    See also Byzantine art

C

caduceus, 107
caementa, 184
Caen (France): Saint-Étienne, 357–358, *357*,
    358, 358, 368, 370, 13-3A
Cahill, James, 460
Cahokia, Illinois (U.S.A.): Monk's Mound,
    515, *515b*, 18-30A
Caiaphas, 241
Cairo (Egypt): madrasa-mosque-mausoleum
    complex of Sultan Hasan, 296–297, *297*
caldarium, 220
calf bearer (dedicated by Rhonbos), Athens
    (sculpture), 112, *113*, 114, 238
caliphs, 285
calligraphy
    architectural inscriptions, 287, 294, 300
    Chinese, 466, 468
    Islamic, 294, 295, 300, 301, 10-17A, 10-23A
    Japanese, 484, 17-13B
Calling of Matthew, 240
Calvert, Frank, 86
Cambodian art, 443–446
cames, 375
campaniles, 350, 355, 416, 418
Camposanto, Pisa, 419–420, *419*
Canon (Polykleitos). *See* *Doryphoros*
canon table, 312
canonization, 354, 14-5A
canons, 10
    Egyptian, 66
    of Polykleitos, 132, 135, 145, 154, 158
canopic jars, 61
Canopus and Serapeum, Hadrian's Villa,
    Tivoli, *212*
canteen with episodes from the life of Jesus,
    304, *304*
Canterbury Cathedral, 339
capitals (of columns)
    in Egyptian New Kingdom architecture,
        3-24A
    in Egyptian Predynastic architecture, 60
    in Greek architecture, 116, 123, 134–135,
        151–153
    historiated, 342–343, 12-13A
    in Italian late medieval architecture, 402
    in Minoan architecture, 90
    in Persian architecture, 51
    in Roman Early Empire architecture, 206
    in South Asian architecture, 429, 430
    See also Composite capitals; Corinthian
        capitals
Capitoline Wolf (sculpture), 173–174, *173*
Capitolium, 189
Capitolium, Pompeii, *188*, 189

florins, 417
fluted columns, 51, 68, 116, 175, 3-5A
flying buttresses, 12
  in Gothic architecture, 359, 364, 365, 372, 372–373, 373, 374, 376, 383, 390
flying horse, tomb of Governor-General Zhang, Wuwei (sculpture), 456, *456*
The Flying Storehouse, Legends of Mount Shigi (handscroll), 485–486, *486*
Foguang Si (Buddha Radiance Temple), Mount Wutai, 462, *462b*, 16-15A
Foguang Si Pagoda, Yingxian, 467–468, *467*
folios, 248, 249
Fontenay (France): Notre-Dame, 343, *343b*, 349–350, 12-10A
foreshortening, 10
  in Babylonian art, 44
  in Baroque art, 10
  in Greek art, 123, 143, 149–150, 5-22A, 5-23A, 5-58A
  in Italian 14th century art, 401, 409, 14-8B
forgeries: Cycladic art, 88
form, 7
formal analysis, 7
Fortuna Primigenia (Roman deity), 183
forum, 189, 207
forum, Pompeii, *188*, 189
Forum of Augustus, Rome, 200, 208
Forum of Trajan, Rome (Apollodorus of Damascus), 178, 208, *208*, 326
found objects, 16
Fountain (Duchamp), 16
four evangelists
  attributes of, 5, 268, 314, 12-15A
  in Carolingian art, 11-13A
  in Early Byzantine art, 268
  in French/Spanish Romanesque art, 340, 344, 348, 349, 12-11A, 12-14A, 12-15A
  in Hiberno-Saxon art, 312, 314
  on life of Jesus, 240
  in Middle Byzantine art, 9-27A
  and Pompeian/Vesuvius area author portraits, 7-25B
  See also Gospels
The Four Horsemen of the Apocalypse (Dürer), 6, *6*, 7
Four Noble Truths, 423
Fourth Style, 194–195, 7-16A
Fourth Style wall paintings, Domus Aurea (Golden House) (Severus and Celer), Rome, 194, *195*
Fourth Style wall paintings, Ixion Room, House of the Vettii, Pompeii, 195, *195*
Foy, Saint, 12-7A
Fra Angelico, 405
fragmentary head of Senusret III (sculpture), 67–68, *67*
Francis of Assisi, Saint, 404–405, 14-5A, 14-5B
Franciscan order, 385, 404, 405, 14-6A
François Vase, Chiusi (Kleitias and Ergotimos), 120, *120*
Franks, 284, 308, 317
  See also Carolingian art
Frederick II (Holy Roman Emperor), 396, 402
Frederick Barbarossa (Holy Roman Emperor), 354–355, 392
freedmen/freedwomen, 187, 190, 216, 220, 7-11A, 7-16A
freestanding sculpture. *See* sculpture in the round
French Baroque art: Claude Lorrain, 8, 9
French Gothic art, 366–389, 399
  architecture, 2–3, 12, 364, 365, 366–369, 370–374, 377–379, 380–384
  illuminated manuscripts, 384–388, 13-36A
  and Italian 14th century art, 407, 411, 419, 14-12A
  sculpture, 369–370, 377, 379, 380, 381, 388, 13-3A, 13-18A, 13-23A
  See also French Gothic stained-glass windows
French Gothic stained-glass windows, 373
  Chartres Cathedral, 365, 374, 375, 376–377, 386
  Jacques Coeur house, 384

Reims Cathedral, 380, 13-23A
Saint-Denis abbey church, 368–369, 375, 13-3A
Sainte-Chapelle, 381
French Revolution: and Gothic art, 369, 370, 13-3A
French/Spanish Romanesque art, 334–349, 363
  architecture, 335, 337–340, 341, 344–345, 348, 12-4A, 12-4B, 12-10A, 12-14A
  illuminated manuscripts, 347–348, 12-15A
  metalwork, 334, 336
  See also French/Spanish Romanesque sculpture
French/Spanish Romanesque sculpture
  Gislebertus, 5, 11, 12, 332, 333, 346, 12-13A, 12-13B
  La Madeleine, Vézelay, 345–346
  Morgan Madonna, 348–349
  Notre-Dame-la-Grande, 12-11A
  Saint-Étienne, Vignory, 337
  Saint-Genis-des-Fontaines abbey church, 12-8A
  Saint-Pierre, Moissac, 341–345
  Saint-Sernin, 340, 356
  Saint-Trophîme, 12-14A
  Santo Domingo, Silos, 12-8B
fresco painting
  Byzantine, 278, 279, 9-25A
  Etruscan, 172, 173, 6-9A
  Greek, 144, 149–150
  Italian 13th century, 14-5A, 14-5B
  Italian 14th century, 400, 401, 408, 409, 416–417, 419–420, 14-8A, 14-8B
  Italian Romanesque, 12-27B
  Late Antique Jewish, 236
  Mesoamerican, 502
  Minoan, 90–93, 194, 4-9A, 4-9B
  Mycenaean, 4-18A
  Pompeian/Vesuvius area, 189–190, 191–195, 196, 7-25A
  See also fresco secco; mural painting
fresco secco, 74, 75, 408
Friday Mosque, Isfahan, 291–292, *292*, 299
Friday mosques. *See* great mosques (congregational mosques)
frieze of the south façade, Umayyad palace, Mshatta, 10-5B
friezes
  in Akkadian art, 41
  in Greek architecture, 116, 117, 119, 136, 138
  in Roman art, 178, 179, 208–209, 362
  in Sumerian art, 31
  See also registers
frigidarium, 220, 221
Frobenius, Leo, 527
Fu Hao, 452
Fujiwara no Michinaga, 484, 17-13A
Fujiwara no Sadanobu, 484
  Ishiyama-gire, *484b*, 17-13B
Fujiwara Yorimichi, 484
funeral banner, tomb of the marquise of Dai, Mawangdui, *448*, 449, 455
funerary chapel of Rekhmire, Thebes, *64b*, 3-11B
funerary customs
  Aegean, 84, 85, 88, 99, 100, 4-22A
  Andean South America, 509
  China, 452, 454–456, 464
  Early Christian, 224, 237, 239, 8-17A
  early medieval pre-Christian, 309–311, 11-3A, 11-4A
  Egypt, 58, 59, 60, 61, 68, 74
  Etruscan, 164, 165, 169, 170–171, 6-7A, 6-13A, 6-15A
  Gothic Europe, 13-42A
  Greece, 108, 112, 113, 142, 143, 5-2A, 5-58A, 5-64B
  Islam, 289–290, 296
  Japan, 477, 478
  Mesoamerica, 497, 18-10A
  Mesopotamia, 37, 2-19A
  Native North America, 514, 515, 517
  Neolithic, 25, 27
  Preclassic period Mesoamerica, 494

Roman Empire, 187, 214, 216–217, 218, 222–224, 7-11A, 7-62A, 7-62B
  See also mortuary temples
funerary mask, Grave Circle A, Mycenae, 100, *100*
funerary relief of an official in the Circus Maximus, *208b*, 7-44A
funerary relief with portraits of the Gessii, 187, *187*
furta sacra, 336

G

Gabriel, Archangel
  in Italian 14th century art, 414
  See also Annunciation to Mary
Gaia/Ge (Greek/Roman deity), 107, 128, 156
Gakko, 481
Gal Vihara (Sri Lanka): *Death of the Buddha (Parinirvana)* (sculpture), 442, 443
Galen, 132
Galerius (Roman emperor), 236, 8-19A
galleries, 324, 416, 12-7A
  See also tribunes
Gallic chieftain killing himself and his wife (Epigonos(?)) (sculpture), 157, *157*
Gandhara (Pakistan)
  life and death of Buddha (frieze), *422*, 423, 432
  meditating Buddha (sculpture), 431–432, *431*
  standing Buddha, *432b*, 15-11A
Ganesha (Hindu deity), 435, 435–436
Gaozong (Chinese emperor), 461, 462, 468
garbha griha, 438, 439, 440
Garden of Gethsemane, 241
gardens, Babylonian, 48, 49
gardenscape, Villa of Livia, Primaporta (mural), 193–194, *193*
Gateway of the Sun, Tiwanaku, 512–513, *512*
Gaucher de Reims. *See* Reims Cathedral
Gauls, 156–157
Gautama, Siddhartha. *See* Shakyamuni Buddha
Ge. *See* Gaia
Geb (Egyptian deity), 57
Gellée, Claude. *See* Claude Lorrain
genre subjects, 5
Geometric amphora with mourning scene, Dipylon cemetery, Athens (Dipylon Painter), 108, *108b*, 5-2A
Geometric krater, Dipylon cemetery, Athens, 108–109, *108*
Geometric period Greek art, 108–109, 128, 163, 5-2A
geometry, 384–385
George, Saint, 268, 269
Georgics (Vergil), 248
Gerhard of Cologne: Cologne Cathedral, 396, *397*, *397*
Gernrode (Germany): Saint Cyriakus, 324, *324*, 326, 337, 350, 11-23A
Gero (archbishop of Cologne), 328
Gero crucifix, 328–329, *329*, 348–349, 394
Gervase of Canterbury, 339, 341
Geta, 219
Ghiberti, Lorenzo, 365
Ghurab (Egypt): Tiye (sculpture), 77, *77*
gigantomachy, 118, 119, 136, 156
gigantomachy, Siphnian Treasury, Delphi (relief sculpture), *119*, 156
Giorgione da Castelfranco, 405
giornata/giornate, 408
Giotto di Bondone, 407–409, 14-7A
  Arena Chapel, Padua, *400*, 401, *408*, 409, 412, 14-8A, 14-8B, 14-10A
  campanile, Santa Maria del Fiore (Florence Cathedral), Florence, *417*, 418
  Madonna Enthroned, Church of Ognissanti, Florence, 407–408, *407*, 14-19A
  and Andrea Pisano, 419
  and Saint Francis Master, 14-5B
Giraldus Cambrensis, 307
girl preparing to bathe (Onesimos), Chiusi (vase painting), 123, *123b*, 145, 5-23A

Girsu (Telloh) (Iraq)
  Gudea seated, holding the plan of a temple (sculpture), 42, *42*
  Gudea standing, holding an overflowing water jar (sculpture), 43, *43*
  Stele of the Vultures, 34, 36, *37*
Gislebertus, 359, 12-23A
  Eve, Saint-Lazare, 12-13B
  Last Judgment, Saint-Lazare, *5*, 11, 12, *332*, 333, 346, 12-8A, 12-13B
  Suicide of Judas, Saint-Lazare, *345b*, 12-13A
Giulio Romano, 405
Gizeh (Egypt)
  Great Pyramids, 49, 60–62, *60*, *62*, *63*, 72, 73
  Great Sphinx, 63, *63*
  Hemiunu seated statue, 66, *66b*, 3-13B
  Khafre enthroned (sculpture), 64, *64*, 3-11A, 3-11B, 3-13A
  Menkaure and Khamerernebty(?) (sculpture), 64–65, *65*, 3-11A, 3-13A
gladiators, 165, 189, 203
glazes (in ceramics), 110, 451
glaziers, 375
Gloucester Cathedral, 390–391, *391b*, *391*, 398, 13-42A
Glykon of Athens: copy of weary Herakles (Farnese Hercules) (Lysippos of Sikyon), 148, *148*
Gnosis: stag hunt, Pella (mosaic), 149, *149*, 150
goats treading seed and cattle fording a canal, mastaba of Ti, Saqqara (relief sculpture), 66, *67*
Göbekli Tepe (Turkey), 24, 26
God accusing Adam and Eve, Saint Michael's, Hildesheim (relief sculpture), 326–327, *327*
God as Creator of the World, moralized Bible, 384–385, *384*
goddess, Tetitla apartment complex, Teotihuacán (mural), *497*, 498
Godescalc Lectionary, 318, *318b*, 11-13A
gods/goddesses. *See* religion and mythology
Goguryeo kingdom (Korea), 470
gold leaf, 34, 38, 95, 405, 412
Golden House (Domus Aurea) (Severus and Celer), Rome, 194, *195*, 201–202, *202*, 203–204
Good Friday, 241
Good Shepherd, story of Jonah, and orants, Catacomb of Saints Peter and Marcellinus, Rome (fresco), 237–239, *237*
Gordian III (Roman emperor), 7-68A
Gordion (Asia Minor), 245
gorgets, 517
gorgons, 118
Goryeo dynasty (Korea), 472
Goshirakawa (Japanese emperor), 488
Gospel Book of Archbishop Ebbo of Reims. *See* Ebbo Gospels
Gospel Book of Otto III, 329, *329b*, *329*, 11-29A
Gospels, 311–312, *312*, 314, 318, 11-13A
  See also Aachen Gospels; Corbie Gospels; Coronation Gospels; Ebbo Gospels; four evangelists; Lindau Gospels; Lindisfarne Gospels; Rabbula Gospels; Rossano Gospels
Gothic architecture
  cathedrals, 359, 373
  English, 389–391, 13-42A
  French, 2–3, 12, 364, 365, 366–369, 370–374, 377–379, 380–384
  Holy Roman Empire, 392–393, 396–398
  Spanish, 13-38A
Gothic art, 363–399, 365, *366map*
  English, 389–391, 399, 13-38A, 13-38B, 13-42A
  French. *See* French Gothic art
  Holy Roman Empire, 392–398, 399, 13-44A
  societal contexts, 366, 372, 385
  timeline, 366
  See also Gothic Revival
Gothic Revival, 396

Gothic sculpture
  English, 13-42A
  French, 369–370, 377, 379, 380, 381, 388, 13-3A, 13-18A, 13-23A
  Holy Roman Empire, 393–396
Gournia (Crete), 86
Granada (Spain): Alhambra, 295–296, *295, 296*, 297
granulation, 167
Grave Circle A, Mycenae, 99–100, *99b, 100, 4-22A, 4-23A*
grave stele of a young hunter (Illisos stele), Athens, 146–147, *147, 5-64A*
grave stele of Hegeso, Dipylon cemetery, Athens, 142, *142*, 143, 146, 169
graves. *See* funerary customs
Great Bath, Mohenjo-daro, 425, *425*
"Great Dish," Mildenhall Treasure, 250–251, *250*
Great Enclosure, Great Zimbabwe, 530
Great Mosque, Córdoba, *282*, 283, 290–291, *290, 291*
Great Mosque, Damascus, *286, 287*, 287
Great Mosque, Djenne, 288, 529, *529*
Great Mosque, Kairouan, *288*, 289
Great Mosque, Samarra, 289, *289*
great mosques (congregational mosques), 288
  Friday Mosque, Isfahan, 291–292, 299
  See also Great Mosque . . . , *above*
Great Pyramids of Gizeh, 49, 60–62, *60, 62, 63, 72*, 73
Great Schism, 404
Great Sphinx, Gizeh, 63, *63*
Great Stupa, Sanchi, 429–430, *429, 429, 430, 15-8A*
Great Wall of China, 454
Great Zimbabwe (Zimbabwe), 530–531, 533
  Great Enclosure, 530
  monolith with bird and crocodile (sculpture), 531, *531*
Greco-Roman influences. *See* classical influences on later art
Greece (ancient)
  law in, 44
  Persian sack of Athens (480 BCE), 114, 124–125, 133, 136
  Roman Empire and, 161
  women, 108, 142, 169
  See also Greek art; Greek religion and mythology
Greek Archaic period art, 111–124, 163
  architecture, 115–119, *115*, 123–124, 3-5A, 5-17A
  and Early Christian art, 238
  sculpture, 111–115, 117, 118, 119, 124, 125
  vase painting, 120–123, 5-20A, 5-22A, 5-23A
Greek architecture, 189
  Archaic period, 115–119, *115*, 123–124, 3-5A, 5-17A
  Early/High Classical period, 125–126, 134–136, 138–141
  Egyptian architecture and, 68
  Hellenistic period, 153–156, 185
  Late Classical period, 49, 151–153, 5-64A, 5-64B
  Orientalizing period, 111, 5-6A, 5-6B
Greek art, 104–163, *106map*
  Archaic period. *See* Greek Archaic period art
  Daedalic style, 111, 112, 5-6B
  Early/High Classical period. *See* Greek Early/High Classical period art
  and Egyptian art, 68, 107, 109, 111, 112, 3-5A
  and Etruscan art, 110, 165, 169, 175, 6-9A
  Geometric period, 108–109, 128, 163, 5-2A
  Hellenistic period. *See* Hellenistic period Greek art
  Late Classical period. *See* Greek Late Classical period art
  and linear perspective, 193
  Orientalizing period, 109–111, 163, 169, 5-6A, 5-6B
  and Persian art, 51, 2-26A

and Roman art. *See* Greek influences on Roman art
and Seven Wonders of the ancient world, 49, 146, 5-64B
societal contexts, 106–108, 124–125, 133, 144–145, 153, 155, 161
temple plans, 115, 189
timeline, 106
See also classical influences on later art
Greek cross, 271, 530, 9-25A
Greek Early/High Classical period art, 124–144, 163
  architecture, 125–126, 134–136, 138–141
  painting, 142–144, 5-58A
  sculpture, 11, 105, 126–134, 136–138, 140, 141, 142, 5-32A
  societal contexts, 124–125
  urban planning, 154, 207
Greek influences on Roman art, 162, 190
  Early Empire, 198, 200
  High Empire, 212, 213
  Pompeii/Vesuvius area, 191, 195
  Republic, 181, 182, 183, 186–187, 7-10A
  Roman copies, 131, 132, 133, 145, 147, 148, 157, 161, 195
Greek Late Classical period art, 144–153, 163
  architecture, 49, 151–153, 5-64A, 5-64B
  mural painting, 149–150, 191
  sculpture, 145–149, 5-62A, 5-63A, 5-64A
  societal contexts, 144–145
  vase painting, 5-63A
Greek religion and mythology, 106, 107, 128
  Archaic period, 120
  and Delphi, 5-17A
  and drama, 151
  Early/High Classical period, 126, 138
  Late Classical period, 145, 146, 148, 5-62A
  and Mycenae, 101
  Roman art and, 192, 195, 216–217, 7-59A
  and ziggurats, 33
  See also classical influences on later art; Roman religion and mythology; *specific deities*
Greek sculpture
  Archaic period, 111–115, 117, 118, 119, 124, 125
  Early/High Classical period, 11, 105, 126–134, 136–138, 140, 141, 142, 5-32A
  Geometric period, 109, 128
  Hellenistic period, 156–157, 158–161, 162, 5-83A
  Late Classical period, 145–149, 5-62A, 5-63A, 5-64A
  Orientalizing period, 109–110, 111, 5-6B
Gregory I (the Great), Saint (Pope): *Moralia in Job*, 347–348, *347*
Gregory VII (Pope), 352
Gregory IX (Pope), 14-5A
Greppe Sant'Angelo (Italy): death of Sarpedon (Euphronios) (vase painting), *122b*, 5-22A
griffins, 51, 99, 4-9B, 4-18A, 10-5B
grisaille, 409, 13-36A
groin, 184
groin vaults (cross vaults), 184, *184*
  in French/Spanish Romanesque architecture, 340, 12-4A, 12-4B, 12-7A, 12-7B
  in Gothic architecture, 370
  in Holy Roman Empire Romanesque architecture, 350
  in Italian 14th century architecture, 14-12A
  in Norman Romanesque architecture, 358, 359
  in Roman architecture, 184, 202, 209, 221, 228
ground line, 20–21
  in Early Byzantine art, 268
  in Paleolithic art, 1-12A
  in Roman Republic art, 7-11A
  in Sumerian art, 30, 31, 35
  See also composition
Gu Kaizhi, 460
  Lady Feng and the Bear, Admonitions of the Instructress to the Court Ladies, 459, *459*, 484

guang, 452
guang, Anyang (bronze vessel), 452, *452*
Guanyin (Kannon), 467, 16-13B, 16-14A, 16-21A
Gudea (ensi of Lagash), 34, 42, 43
Gudea seated, holding the plan of a temple, Girsu (sculpture), 42, *42*
Gudea standing, holding an overflowing water jar, Girsu (sculpture), 43, *43*
guild hall, Bruges, 383, *383*
guilds
  Gothic era, 366, 372, 383, 388
  Italian 14th century, 410, 414
Guillaume de Lorris: *Romance of the Rose*, 388–389
Gunma Prefecture (Japan): haniwa warrior (sculpture), 478, *478*
Gupta period art (South Asia), 432, 433–435, 447

H

Hacilar (Turkey), 26
Hades (Pluto) (Greek/Roman deity), 107, 149–150
Hades abducting Persephone, Vergina (fresco), 149–150, *149, 150*
Hadith, 285
Hadrian (Roman emperor), 210–213
Hadrian's Villa, Tivoli, 212–213, *212*
Hagar Qim (Malta), 28, *28*
Hagesandros
  head of Odysseus, Sperlonga (sculpture), 162, *162*
  Laocoön and his sons (sculpture), 162, *162*
Hagia Sophia (Anthemius of Tralles and Isidorus of Miletus), Constantinople
  architecture, 259–263, *260, 261*
  and Carolingian architecture, 321
  Christ between Constantine IX Monomachus and the empress Zoe, 273–274, *273*, 275
  and Gothic architecture, 378
  and Islamic architecture, 286, 297
  and Saint Polyeuktos, Constantinople, 258
  Virgin (Theotokos) and Child enthroned (mosaic), 270–271, *270*, 376
Hagia Triada (Crete)
  archaeology, 86
  Harvesters Vase, 95, *95*, 102, 4-23A
  sarcophagus, *84*, 85, 88, 91
Hagios Georgios (Church of Saint George), Thessaloniki, 248, 257, 8-17A
Haito (bishop of Basel), 322, 323
al-Hakam II (Umayyad caliph), 282, 291
Halikarnassos (Turkey): tomb of Mausolos (Mausoleum), 49, *146b*, 5-64A, 5-64B
hall churches, 348
  See also Hallenkirche
Hall of the Bulls, Lascaux, *14*, 15, 20, 22–23
Hallenkirche, 396, 398
halos
  in Buddhist art, 427, 431, 15-11A, 16-13B
  in Byzantine art, 255, 264, 274, 280, 9-18A
  in Early Christian art, 239, 247, 248, 250, 8-6A, 8-13A
  in early medieval art, 319, 329
  in Gothic art, 376
  in Italian 13th century art, 405
  in Italian 14th century art, 412, 414
Hamadan (Iran): rhyton in the form of a winged lion, 51, *51b*, 2-26A
Hammurabi (king of Babylon), 34, 43, 44, 45, 2-18A
Han dynasty Chinese art, 448, 449, 455–456, 457, 473, 16-6A
handprints, 21–22, *21*
handscrolls, 459, 462, 463, 466, 484, 485–486, 16-23A
hanging scrolls, 459
  Heian period Japanese, 483
  Song dynasty Chinese, 465, 468–470
  Tang dynasty Chinese, 16-14A
haniwa, 478
haniwa warrior, Gunma Prefecture (sculpture), 478, *478*

Hannibal (Carthaginian leader), 181
Harappa, Pakistan, 424
  nude male torso, 426, *426*
Harbaville Triptych (Christ enthroned with saints) (ivory carving), 275–276, *275*, 277
Harihara, Prasat Andet (sculpture), 443–444, *443*
Harishena (Vakataka king), 434
harmika, 430
harmony. *See* proportion
haruspex/haruspices, 6-13A
Harvesters Vase, Hagia Triada, 95, *95*, 102, 4-23A
Hasan (Mamluk sultan of Cairo), 296
Hasaw Chan K'awiil (Maya ruler), 500
Hastings, Battle of (1066), 361–362
Hathor (Egyptian deity), 54, 55, 57, 75, 82
Hatshepsut (queen of Egypt), 41, 69–71, 72, 73, 74
Hatshepsut mortuary temple, Deir el-Bahri, 69–71, *69, 70*, 73
Hatshepsut with offering jars, Deir el-Bahri (sculpture), 70–71, *70*
Hattusa (Turkey): Lion Gate, *45b*, 2-18B
Hawes, Harriet Boyd, 86
head, Lydenburg (sculpture), 525, *525*
head clusters, 246
head of a queen mother, Benin (sculpture), *532b*, 19-13A
head of a warrior, sea off Riace (sculpture), 11, *11*
head of a woman, Brassempouy (ivory carving), *18b*, 1-5A
head of a woman, Chios (sculpture), 145, *145b*, 5-62A
head of Alexander the Great, Pella (sculpture), *148*, 149
head of an Akkadian ruler, Nineveh (sculpture), 40–41, *40*
head of an Ife king, Wunmonije compound, Ile-Ife (sculpture), 528, *528b*, 19-6A
head of an old man, Osimo (sculpture), 186, *186*
head of Caracalla (sculpture), *219b*, 7-64A
head of Herakles or Telephos (school of Skopas of Paros), Temple of Athena Alea, Tegea (sculpture), *146b*, 5-64A
head of Odysseus, Sperlonga (Athanadoros, Hagesandros, and Polydoros of Rhodes) (sculpture), 162, *162*
head of Pompey the Great (sculpture), *187b*, 7-10A
head reliquary of Saint Alexander, 353–354, *353*
Hegeso grave stele, Dipylon cemetery, Athens, 142, *142*, 143, 146, 169
Heian period Japanese art, 483–486, 487, 489, 17-13A, 17-13B
Heiligkreuzkirche, Schwäbisch Gmünd (Heinrich and Peter Parler), 398, *398*
Heinrich (bishop of Mainz), 352
Helen of Egypt, 150
Helios (Sol) (Greek/Roman deity), 107
Helios and his horses, and Dionysos (Herakles?), Parthenon east pediment, Athens (sculpture), 137, *137*
Helladic art, 87
  See also Greek art
Hellas, 106
Hellenes, 106
Hellenistic period Etruscan art, 174–176, 177, 6-13A, 6-15A
Hellenistic period Greek art, 153–162, 163, 5-64A
  architecture, 153–156, 185
  sculpture, 156–157, 158–161, 162, 5-83A
  societal contexts, 153, 161
hemispherical domes, 184
Hemiunu (Egyptian vizier), 62, 66, 3-13B
Hemiunu seated statue, Gizeh, 66, *66b*, 3-13B
henges, 28
Henry II (Holy Roman emperor), 324
Henry II (king of England), 352
Henry III (king of England), 385
Henry IV (Holy Roman emperor), 350

Henry of Blois (bishop of Winchester), 12-35A
Hepdjefai (nomarch of Asyut), 3-16A
Hephaistos (Vulcan) (Greek/Roman deity), 107
Hera (Juno) (Greek/Roman deity), 107, 117, 128, 144, 167, 189
Heraclius (Byzantine emperor), 270
Herakles (Hercules) (Greek/Roman hero), 128
    in Early Christian art, 8-5A
    in Etruscan art, 167, 168
    in Greek Archaic period art, 122, 5-17A
    in Greek Early/High Classical period art, 128, 137
    in Greek Geometric period art, 109
    in Greek Late Classical period art, 148, 5-63A, 5-64A
    in Roman art, 7-59A
Herakles wrestling Antaios (Euphronios), Cerveteri (vase painting), 122–123, 122
heraldic composition, 38, 310, 3-1A
Hercle (Etruscan deity), 167
Herculaneum (Italy)
    House of Neptune and Amphitrite, 196, 196
    Samnite House, 191, 191
    See also Pompeian/Vesuvius area art
Hercules. See Herakles
Hermes (Mercury) (Greek/Roman deity), 107, 144, 146, 5-22A
Hermes and the infant Dionysos (Praxiteles(?)) (sculpture), 145–146, 146
Hermes bringing the infant Dionysos to Papposilenos (Phiale Painter), Vulci (vase painting), 144, 144, 146
herms, 133
hero and centaur (Herakles and Nessos?), Olympia (sculpture), 109, 109
Herodotus, 49, 56, 125, 166, 2-26A
heroic portrait of Trebonianus Gallus, 222, 222
Herrad (abbess of Hohenberg): Hortus deliciarum (Garden of Delights), 352
Hesiod, 107
Hesire, relief from his tomb at Saqqara (relief sculpture), 10, 10, 12
Hestia (Vesta) (Greek/Roman deity), 107, 137, 183
Hiberno-Saxon art, 306, 307, 311–315, 318, 331
    and early Islamic art, 294
    societal contexts, 311
    and Sutton Hoo ship burial, 11-3A
Hierakonpolis (Egypt), 56–57
    palette of King Narmer, 54–55, 55, 57–58, 57, 66, 3-1A
    Tomb 100 wall paintings, 56–57, 57b, 3-1A
hierarchy of scale, 11
    in African art, xvi, 520, 521, 526, 528
    in Akkadian art, 41
    in Assyrian art, 46
    in Egyptian art, 54, 55, 66, 74, 78, 79
    in Greek art, 109, 124
    in Italian 14th century art, 14-16A
    in Late Antique Jewish art, 235
    in Ottonian art, 327
    in South Asian art, 432
    in Sumerian art, 30, 31, 36, 38, 39
hieroglyphics
    Egyptian, 54, 55, 56, 74, 3-13B
    Mesoamerican, 493
High Cross of Muiredach, Monasterboice, 315, 315
high crosses, 315
High Gothic art, 378, 379, 380–381
    See also Chartres Cathedral
high-relief sculpture, 12, 64–65
Hijra, 285
Hildegard of Bingen, 352
    Physica, 352
    Scivias (Know the Ways of God), 352–353, 352
Hildesheim (Germany): Saint Michael's, 324–327, 326b, 326, 327, 344, 350, 8-10A, 11-23A, 11-24A
himation, 115

Hindu art
    early medieval, 437–438, 440–441
    Gupta period, 434–435
    post-Gupta period, 435–437
    Southeast Asia, 443–444
    temples, 439
    and Thai Buddhist art, 15-29A
Hinduism, 427–428, 435
    See also Hindu art
Hippodamian plan, 154, 207
Hippodamos of Miletos, 154
hiragana, 484, 17-13B
historiated capitals, 342–343, 12-13A
Hittites, 45, 2-18B
Hohle Fels (Germany): ivory figurine, 18
Hohlenstein-Stadel (Germany): human with feline head, 17, 17, 18, 23, 25
hollow-casting, 41, 45, 130
Holy Roman Empire
    Carolingian dynasty, 270, 317–324
    Ottonian dynasty, 324–330
    Salian dynasty, 349–355, 363
    See also Holy Roman Empire . . . art
Holy Roman Empire Gothic art, 392–398, 399, 13-44A
Holy Roman Empire High Renaissance/ Mannerist art: Dürer, 6
Holy Roman Empire Romanesque art, 349–355, 363, 12-23A
Homage to the Square (Albers), 8, 8
Homage to the Square: "Ascending" (Albers), 8, 8
Homer
    on Achilles, 120
    Alexander the Great and, 148
    and archaeology, 85, 86
    on Greek religion and mythology, 107
    and Hellenistic period Greek art, 162
    on Kalchas, 6-13A
    on Mycenae, 95, 100cap, 4-23A
    on Pylos, 97, 4-18A
    recording of, 108
    on Tiryns, 96
homosexuality, 159
Honoré, Master: Breviary of Philippe le Bel, 386–387, 387
Honorius (Roman emperor), 246, 256
horses in Paleolithic art, 21, 22, 23, 1-12A
Horus (Egyptian deity), 55, 57, 75, 80, 82
Horus temple, Edfu, 82, 82, 3-1A
Horyuji temple, Nara Prefecture, 474, 475, 480, 480, 481–482, 481, 482
Hosios Loukas (Greece)
    Church of the Theotokos, 271, 271, 9-25A
    Katholikon, 271, 271
Hours of Jeanne d'Evreux (Pucelle), 387, 387b, 13-36A
House of Neptune and Amphitrite, Herculaneum, 196, 196
House of the Menander, Pompeii, 7-25B
House of the Vettii, Pompeii, 190, 191, 194–195, 195, 7-16A
hubris, 143
hue, 7
Hugh of Saint-Victor, 375
Hugh of Semur (abbot of Cluny), 341
Hugo, Master: Bury Bible, 359–360, 12-23A, 12-35A
Huineng (Chan patriarch), 469, 470
Huizong (Chinese emperor), 465–466, 468
    Auspicious Cranes, 466–467, 466
human face
    in Aegean art, 90, 95, 101
    in African art, 522–523, 524, 527, 532, 19-6A, 19-13A
    in Andean South American art, 511
    in Byzantine art, 270, 277, 9-18A
    in Chinese art, 459, 16-13B
    in Egyptian Amarna period art, 76–77
    in Egyptian first millenium BCE art, 80
    in Egyptian Middle Kingdom art, 67–68
    in Egyptian Old Kingdom art, 3-13A
    in Etruscan art, 169, 176, 6-9A
    in Gothic art, 370, 380, 13-18A
    in Greek Archaic period art, 112, 121, 124

in Greek Early/High Classical period art, 126, 143, 5-58A
    in Greek Geometric period art, 108
    in Greek Late Classical period art, 145, 5-62A, 5-64A
    in Italian 13th century art, 403
    in Italian 14th century art, 411, 14-8A, 14-8B
    in Japanese art, 485, 486, 17-13A
    in Late Antique Jewish art, 235
    in Mesopotamian art, 36, 46, 47, 2-6A
    in Neolithic art, 25
    in Paleolithic art, 1-5A
    in Roman Early Empire art, 198
    in Roman Late Empire art, 219–220, 222, 224, 228, 7-64A, 7-68A
    in Roman Republic art, 185–186, 187, 7-10A
    in Romanesque art, 345, 349
    in South Asian art, 432, 436, 15-11A
human figure
    in Aegean art, 85, 91, 95
    in African art, 522, 529, 532
    in Andean South American art, 509, 510–511
    in Assyrian art, 46
    in Carolingian art, 319, 320, 11-15A
    in Chinese art, 468, 469
    in Early Byzantine art, 265, 270
    in Early Christian art, 246, 8-19A, 8-21A
    in Egyptian Amarna period art, 76
    Egyptian canon, 66
    in Egyptian first millenium BCE art, 81
    in Egyptian Middle Kingdom art, 3-16A
    in Egyptian New Kingdom art, 74–75
    in Egyptian Old Kingdom art, 64, 66, 67cap, 3-11A, 3-13A, 3-13B
    in Egyptian post-Amarna period art, 80
    in Egyptian Predynastic art, 54, 55, 58
    in Elamite art, 45
    in Etruscan art, 169, 170, 172, 6-9A
    in French/Spanish Romanesque art, 11, 345, 348, 349, 12-13B, 12-14A, 12-15A
    in Gothic art, 370, 379, 380, 381, 387, 388, 395, 13-18A, 13-36A
    in Greek Archaic period art, 112–115, 120, 122, 123, 5-22A, 5-23A
    Greek canon, 132, 135, 145, 154, 158
    in Greek Early/High Classical period art, 128–131, 132, 137
    in Greek Geometric period art, 108–109, 5-2A
    in Greek Late Classical period art, 146, 147, 148
    in Greek Orientalizing period art, 109–110
    in Hellenistic period Greek art, 157
    in Italian 13th century art, 403–404
    in Italian 14th century art, 408, 412
    in Italian Romanesque art, 356–357
    in Japanese art, 484–485, 17-13A, 17-17A
    in Korean art, 471
    in Late Antique Jewish art, 235
    in Late Byzantine art, 279, 280
    in Middle Byzantine art, 273, 274, 276, 9-26A, 9-26B
    in Native North American art, 515
    in Neo-Sumerian art, 43
    in Neolithic art, 25, 26
    in Norman Romanesque art, 360, 361
    in Ottonian art, 326–327
    in Paleolithic art, 18–19, 23, 1-6A
    in Roman Early Empire art, 198
    in Roman Late Empire art, 220, 222, 224, 227
    in Roman Republic art, 186–187
    in South Asian art, 426, 15-6B, 15-11A
    in Sumerian art, 30, 35, 36, 39, 2-6A
    See also women as subjects
human sacrifice in Mesoamerica, 497, 498, 502
human skull with restored features, Jericho, 25, 25
human with feline head, Hohlenstein-Stadel (sculpture), 17, 17, 18, 23, 25
humanism
    in Greece, 107

and Italian late medieval art, 406–407, 412
    See also classical influences on later art
hummingbird, Nasca Plain, 511, 511
Hunefer, tomb of, Thebes, 80, 80
Hunefer's scroll, Thebes, 80, 80
Huns, 435
hunter capturing a bull, Vapheio (drinking cup), 100, 100b, 4-23A
hunting
    in Assyrian art, 48
    in Egyptian art, 66, 74, 75
    in Etruscan art, 172, 173
    in Greek art, 146–147, 149
    in Mycenaean art, 100, 4-23A
    in Roman art, 7-48A
Husayn Bayqara (Timurid sultan), 302
Hussein, Saddam, 40
Hwangnam-dong (Korea): Cheonmachong tomb, 470, 471
hydria, 145
Hyksos, 69
hypaethral, 154
hypostyle halls, 73, 3-24A
    in Islamic architecture, 288, 289, 290

I

Iaia of Cyzicus, 218
Ibn Zamrak, 296
iconoclasm, 257, 269, 270
iconography, 5
    Christian, 240–241, 314
    Hindu, 435
iconophiles, 269
iconostasis, 279
icons, 405
    Early Byzantine, 268–270, 269, 271, 9-18A
    Late Byzantine, 279–280
    Middle Byzantine, 274, 277, 9-26B
Ife art. See Ile-Ife
Igbo Ukwu (Nigeria)
    equestrian figure on fly-whisk hilt (sculpture), 526, 526
    roped water basin on a stand, 525b, 19-4A
Igbo Ukwu art, 525–526, 533, 19-4A
ikegobo, 520, 521
Iktinos. See Parthenon
Ile-Ife (Nigeria), 533
    head of an Ife king, Wunmonije compound (sculpture), 528, 528b, 19-6A
    king, Ita Yemoo (sculpture), 527–528, 527
Ile-Ife art, 527–529, 533, 19-6A
Iliad (Homer), 85, 86, 96cap, 107, 120, 148, 4-18A, 6-13A
    See also Homer
Illisos stele (grave stele of a young hunter), Athens, 146–147, 147, 5-64A
illuminated manuscripts, 405
    Byzantine, 258, 268, 276–277, 405, 9-3A, 9-17A
    Carolingian, 317, 318–320, 11-13A, 11-15A
    French Gothic, 384–388, 13-36A
    French/Spanish Romanesque, 347–348, 12-15A
    Hiberno-Saxon, 306, 307, 311–315
    Holy Roman Empire Romanesque, 352–353, 12-23A
    Late Antique, 248–250
    Norman Romanesque, 359–361, 12-35A
    Ottonian, 329–330, 11-29A
    See also books
illuminated tughra of Suleyman the Magnificent, 297b, 10-23A
illusionism, 8
    in Byzantine art, 270, 279
    in Carolingian art, 318, 319
    in Italian 14th century art, 408, 409, 415
    in Pompeian/Vesuvius area art, 192–193, 196
    See also perspective
illustrated books. See books; illuminated manuscripts
imagines, 185, 196, 200
imago hominis, 315
imam, 288

Imam (Shah) Mosque, Isfahan, 299–300, *299*
Imhotep
    mortuary precinct of Djoser, 58, *58b, 59, 60, 60,* 3-5A
    stepped pyramid of Djoser, 58, *59,* 496
imperator, 197
impluvium, 190, *191*
in antis (columns), 115, 117
In Praise of Scribes (Johannes Trithemius), 386
Inanna (Ishtar) (Mesopotamian deity), 34, 35
incense burner (boshan) from the tomb of Prince Liu Sheng, Mancheng, 455, *455b,* 16-6A
incised gorget with running warrior, Sumner County, Tennessee, 517, *517*
incrustation, 202, 355, 12-27A
India. *See* South Asian art
Indra (Aryan deity), 427
Indravarman (Khmer king), 444
indulgences, 374
Indus Civilization art, 424–426, 447
Inka art, 510
inlaid dagger blade with lion hunt, Grave Circle A, Mycenae, 100, *100,* 4-23A
Insula of the Painted Vaults, Ostia, 214, *214b,* 7-54A
insulae, 213–214, *213*
Insular art. *See* Hiberno-Saxon art
intensity, 7
interaxial (intercolumniation), 135, 152
intercolumniation (interaxial), 135, 152
interlace
    in Carolingian art, 11-13A
    in French/Spanish Romanesque art, 347
    in Hiberno-Saxon art, 312, 313, 315, 11-9A
    in Viking art, 311, 11-4A
Intermediate Area Native American art, 507
internal evidence, 3
International Style (medieval Europe), 413–414
intonaco, 408
Introduction to the Three Arts of Design (Vasari), 365
investiture of Zimri-Lim, palace, Mari (mural), 43, *43b,* 44, 45, 46, 2-18A
investment (in lost-wax process), 130
Ionic order, 116, *116*
    and Composite capitals, 206
    in Greek architecture, 117, 119, 136, 141, 152, 5-17A
    in Roman Republic architecture, 182
iota. *See* chi-rho-iota (Christogram)
Ipiutak, Alaska (U.S.A.): burial mask, Eskimo, 514, *515*
Irene (Byzantine empress), 270, 273, 9-26A
iron-wire lines, 459, 482
Isaac, 246
    See also Abraham and Isaac
Isabella (queen of Castile), 284
Ise (Japan): Ise Jingu, 478–480, *479*
Ise Jingu, Ise, 478–480, *479*
Isfahan (Iran)
    Friday Mosque, 291–292, *292,* 299
    Imam (Shah) Mosque, 299–300, *299*
    Madrasa Imami, 300, *300*
Ishiyama-gire (Fujiwara no Sadanobu), *484b,* 17-13B
Ishtar (Inanna) (Mesopotamia deity), 34, 35, 48, 2-18A
Ishtar Gate, Babylon, 34, 48, *49*
Ishtar temple, Mari, 36, *36b,* 2-6A
Isidorus of Miletus. *See* Hagia Sophia
Isis (Egyptian deity), 57, 80, 7-62A
Islam, 284, 285
    in Africa, 529
    in South Asia, 441
    See also Crusades; Islamic art; Ottoman Empire
Islamic art, 282–305, *284map*
    Byzantine art and, 274–275, 287, 9-27A
    Christian patronage of, 304
    and Romanesque art, 345
    societal contexts, 284, 285, 294–295
    timeline, 284
    See also early Islamic art; later Islamic art

Isola Sacra, Ostia, 214–215
Issus, battle of, 150
Istanbul. *See* Constantinople
Ita Yemoo (Nigeria): king, Ife (sculpture), 527–528, *527*
Italian 13th century art, 3–4, 402–406, 421, 14-6A
Italian 14th century art, 406–420, 421
    Cavallini, 407, 409, 14-7A
    Florence (Florentine), 417–419, 14-18A, 14-18B, 14-19A
    Giotto di Bondone, 400, 401, 407–409, 14-7A, 14-8A, 14-8B
    Pisa, 419–420
    Siena, 409, 411–416, 417, 14-10A, 14-12A, 14-16A
    societal contexts, 406–407, 409, 410, 14-16A
    Venice, 420
Italian Cinquecento Renaissance sculpture: Michelangelo Buonarroti, 11
Italian late medieval art, 400–421, *405map*
    13th century, 402–406, 421, 14-6A
    14th century. *See* Italian 14th century art
    societal contexts, 404, 406–407
    timeline, 402
    See also Renaissance
Italian Romanesque art, 354, 355–357, 363, 12-27A, 12-27B
Itzamna B'ahlam II (Maya ruler), 503
ivory carvings
    African, 531–532
    Early Byzantine, 257, 258–259, 264, 9-14A
    Early Christian, 251–252, 12-13A
    Early Islamic, 292–293
    Gothic, 388–389
    Middle Byzantine, 275–276, 277
    Minoan, 94–95
    Mycenaean, 100–101
    Ottonian, 327, 328
    Paleolithic, 17, 19, 1-5A
ivory figurine, Hohle Fels, 18
iwans, 52, *52,* 288, 292, 296
Ixion Room: House of the Vettii, Pompeii, 194–195, *195,* 7-16A
iy'oba, 532, 19-13A

J

Jack in the Pulpit No. 4 (O'Keeffe), 4, *4*
Jacob, 8-21A
Jacques Coeur house, Bourges, 383–384, *383*
jade, 453, 454, 494
Jaina Island (Mexico): ball player, Maya (sculpture), 500–501, *501*
jambs, 344, 369, 370, 380, 13-3A, 13-18A
    See also portals
James, Saint, 335, 336, 12-7B
Jami, 302
Japanese architecture
    Heian period, 483–484
    Kofun period, 478–480
    Nara period, 474, 475, 481–483
Japanese art, 474–489, *476map*
    Asuka period, 480, 489
    Edo period, 8–9
    Heian period, 483–486, 487, 489, 17-13A, 17-13B
    Jomon period, 476–477, 489
    Kamakura period, 486–488, 489, 17-17A
    Kofun period, 478–480, 489
    Nara period, 474, 475, 481–483, 489
    societal contexts. *See* societal contexts of Japanese art
    timelines, 476
    Yayoi period, 477, 489
    See also Japanese Buddhist art; Japanese painting
Japanese Buddhist art
    Asuka period, 480
    Heian period, 485–486
    Kamakura period, 486, 487–488, 17-17A
    Nara period, 474, 481–483
Japanese painting
    Edo period, 8–9
    Heian period, 483, 484–486, 487
    Kamakura period, 487, 488
    Nara period, 475, 482

Jarmo (Iraq), 24
jatakas, 430
Javan art, 442, 443
Jayavarman II (Khmer king), 443
Jayavarman VII (Khmer king), 446
Jean d'Orbais. *See* Reims Cathedral
Jean de Loup. *See* Reims Cathedral
Jean de Meung: *Romance of the Rose,* 388–389
Jeong Seon: *Geumgangsan Mountains,* 102
Jericho (Palestine), 24–25
    human skull with restored features, 25, *25*
    stone tower built into the settlement wall, *24*
Jerusalem, 242
    Church of the Holy Sepulcher, 286
    Crusader conquest of (1099), 346
    Dome of the Rock, 285–287, *285, 286,* 294, 299, 300, 346
    in Gothic cartography, 13-38B
    in Italian 14th century art, 14-10A
    Roman sack of (70), 206–207, 236, 286
Jesus, life of, 240–241, 411, 11-24A
    See also Christ; Passion of Christ; *specific events*
Jesus washing the feet of Saint Peter, *Gospel Book of Otto III,* 329b, 11-29A
jewelry. *See* luxury arts; metalwork
Jewish art in Late Antiquity, 235–236, 237
Jiaxiang (China): Wu family shrines, 455–456, *456*
Jin dynasty (China), 465, 468
Jincun (China): bi disk with dragons, 454, *454*
Jocho
    seated Amida, Phoenix Hall, Byodoin, Uji (sculpture), 484, *484b,* 17-13A
    and Unkei, 17-17A
Jodo. *See* Pure Land Buddhism: in Japan
Johannes Trithemius, 386
John (king of England), 352
John VIII Palaeologus (Byzantine emperor), 9-35A
John XII (Pope), 328
John XIII (Pope), 328
John of Damascus, Saint, 270
John the Baptist, Saint, 240
    in Byzantine art, 276, 277, 9-14A
    See also Baptism of Jesus
John the Evangelist, Saint, 241, 314
    in Byzantine art, 273, 276
    in Gothic art, 394
    in Italian 14th century art, 409
    in Italian Romanesque art, 12-27B
John the Lydian, 266
joined-wood technique (yosegi), 17-13A, 17-17A
jomon, 476
Jomon period Japanese art, 476–477, 489
Jonah, 237–238, 239, 8-13A
Joseph, Saint, 241, 9-14A
Joseph of Arimathea, 276, 12-27B
Jubilee Festival (Egypt), 60
Judaism, 33
Judas Iscariot. *See* Betrayal of Jesus
Judgment Day. *See* Last Judgment
Julia Domna (Roman empress), 198, 219
Julio-Claudians, 201–202
Julius Caesar (Roman emperor), 186, 187, 197, 7-10A, 7-40A
Junius Bassus sarcophagus, *232,* 233, 8-8A, 12-13B
Juno. *See* Hera
junzi, 463
Jupiter. *See* Zeus
Justin Martyr, 239
Justinian (Byzantine emperor)
    Barberini Ivory, 258–259
    conquest of Ravenna, 246, 263
    equestrian statue of, 259, 317
    San Vitale mosaic, 254, 255, 264–265, 275, 309
Justinian, Bishop Maximianus, and attendants, San Vitale, Ravenna (mosaic), *254,* 255, 264–265, *265,* 275, 309

Justinian and Theodora mosaics, San Vitale, Ravenna, *254,* 255, 264–266, *265,* 275, 309
Justinian as world conqueror (*Barberini Ivory*), 258–259, *259*
Juvenal, 213

K

ka (life force), 57, 61, 64, 65, 66, 74, 3-11A
Ka-Aper portrait statue, Saqqara, *66b,* 3-13A
Kaaba, 285
Kagawa Prefecture (Japan): dotaku with incised figural motifs (bell), 477, *477*
Kairouan (Tunisia): Great Mosque, *288,* 289
Kalhu (Iraq)
    Ashurnasirpal II with attendants and soldier (mural), 46, *47*
    Assyrian archers pursuing enemies (relief sculpture), 46–47, *47*
Kallikrates
    Temple of Athena Nike, Athens, 134, 141, *141,* 152
    See also Parthenon
Kallimachos, 152
Kamakura period Japanese art, 486–488, 489, 17-17A
Kamares Ware jar, Phaistos, 93, *93*
kami, 479, 480
Kanishka (Kushan king), 429
Karle (India): chaitya hall, 430–431, *431,* 434
karma, 427
Karnak (Egypt)
    Akhenaton statue, 76, *76,* 78
    Amen-Re temple, 70, 72–73, *72, 73,* 82, 115, 3-24A
    Mentuemhet portrait statue, 80–81, *81*
Katholikon, Hosios Loukas, 271, *271*
katsuogi, 480
Kawa (Sudan): Taharqo as a sphinx (sculpture), 81, *81*
keeps, 383
Kekrops (king of Athens), 140
Kerma (Sudan): Lady Sennuwy seated statue, *67b,* 3-16A
Keros (Greece): male harp player (sculpture), 88, *88*
ketos, 237
keystones. *See* voussoirs
Khafre (pharaoah of Egypt), 61, 64, *64,* 3-11A, 3-11B, 3-13A
Khafre enthroned, Gizeh (sculpture), 64, *64,* 3-11A, 3-11B, 3-13A
Khajuraho (India): Vishvanatha Temple, 438, *439,* 440, *440,* 444
Khamerernebty (queen of Egypt), 64–65, 3-11A
khan, 10-23A
Al-Khazneh (Treasury), Petra, 213, *213,* 224, 8-19A
Khmer art, 443–446
Khonsu (Egyptian deity), 57, 3-24A
Khorsabad (Iraq). *See* Dur Sharrukin
Khufu (pharaoah of Egypt), 61, 62, 3-13B
Ki no Tsurayuki, 17-13B
Kiev (Russia): Saint Sophia, 274, *274b,* 9-25A, 9-32A
Kim Tae-song, 471–472
Kimmei (Japanese emperor), 480
king, Ita Yemoo, Ile-Ife (sculpture), 527–528, *527*
king and queen of Punt and attendants, Deir el-Bahri (relief sculpture), 70, *70*
King David, Fidenza Cathedral (Benedetto Antelami) (sculpture), 356–357, *357,* 12-14A
king on horseback with attendants, Benin (bronze sculpture), *xvi,* 11, 12
King Suryavarman III holding court, Angkor Wat (relief sculpture), 444, *445*
"King's Grave" bull-headed harp, Ur, 38–39, *38, 38*
K'inich Janaab' Pakal (Maya ruler), 18-10A
kivas, 518
Kleitias: *François Vase,* Chiusi, 120, *120*
kline/klinai, 217
Klosterneuburg Altar (Nicholas of Verdun), *392b, 392,* 13-44A

Mahishasuramardini cave temple, Mamallapuram, 438, *438*
Maidum (Egypt): seated statues of Rahotep and Nofret, *64b*, 65, 3-11A, 3-13B
Maison Carrée (Square House), Nimes, 200–201, *200*
Maitani, Lorenzo: Orvieto Cathedral, 412–413, *413*, 418
Maitreya, *443b*, 471, 15-29A
Makapansgat (South Africa): waterworn pebble resembling a human face, 16, *16*
male harp player, Keros (sculpture), 88, *88*
Malik Shah I (Seljuk sultan), 292
Malta, 28
Malwiya Minaret, Samarra, 289, *289*
Mamallapuram (India)
    Descent of the Ganges River (relief sculpture), *438*, *438b*, 15-22A
    Mahishasuramardini cave temple, 438, *438*
    rock-cut rathas, 437–438, *437*
Mamluks, 296
man with ancestor busts, Rome (sculpture), 185, *185*
Mancheng (China): incense burner (boshan) from the tomb of Prince Liu Sheng, 455, *455b*, 16-6A
mandalas, 430, 439, 443, 483
mandapas, 438, 439, 15-22B
mandaras. *See* mandalas
mandorlas
    in Byzantine art, 267, 268, 279
    in Chinese art, 460
    in French/Spanish Romanesque art, 340, 348, 349, 12-8A, 12-11A
    in Japanese art, 480, 17-13A
Manetho, 56, 58
maniera greca, 404–405, 407, 14-7A, 14-8B
Manisha (Hindu deity), 438
manors, 334
al-Mansur (Abbasid caliph), 287
Mantiklos Apollo, Thebes (sculpture), 109–110, *109*, 112
mantras, 483
manuscripts, illuminated. *See* illuminated manuscripts
Maori art. *See* New Zealand art
mapmaking, 13-38B
mappamundi, 389, 13-38B
Mappamundi of Henry III (Richard de Bello), 389, *389b*, 13-38B
maps
    Aegean, *86*
    Africa, *524*
    Byzantine Empire, *256*
    China/Korea, *450*
    early medieval Europe, *308*
    Egypt, *56*
    Etruscans, *166*
    Gothic era, *366*
    Greek world, *106*
    Islamic world, *284*
    Japan, *476*
    Late Antiquity, *234*
    late medieval Italy, *405*
    Mesoamerica, *493*
    Mesopotamia, *32*
    Native North American sites, *514*
    Persia, *32*
    prehistoric sites, *17*, *24*
    Roman Empire, *180*
    South American Native sites, *507*
    South Asia, *424*
    Western Europe (1100), *335*
Maqsud of Kashan: carpet from the funerary mosque of Safi al-Din, 300–301, *301*
maqsuras, 282, 283, 288, 291
Marathon, battle of, 125, 141
Marburg (Germany): Saint Elizabeth, 398, *398*
Marcellus (Roman general), 181
Marcus Aurelius (Roman emperor), 215, 216, 235, 259, 317–318, 7-59A
Marcus Porcius, 189
Marduk (Mesopotamian deity), 34, 48
Mari (Syria)
    investiture of Zimri-Lim, palace (mural), 43, *43b*, 44, 45, 46, 2-18A

Ishtar temple, 36, *36b*, 2-6A
Marinatos, Spyridon, 92
Marine Style octopus flask, Palaikastro, 93, *93*
Marius, 185
Mark, Saint, 314, 12-15A
Mark Antony, 153, 197
Markets of Trajan, Rome (Apollodorus of Damascus), 209, *209*, 228
Mars. *See* Ares
Martin V (Pope), 404
Martini, Simone: *Annunciation* altarpiece, Siena Cathedral, 413–415, *413*
martyrium, 274
martyrs, 237, 247, 267, 8-6A
    See also specific martyrs
Mary (mother of Jesus). *See* Mother of God; Theotokos; Virgin Mary
Mary Magdalene, 241
    in Byzantine art, 9-17A
    in Gothic art, 394
    in Italian 14th century art, 409
    relics of, 335, 388
Marys at the Tomb, 241, 252
Masaccio (Tommaso di ser Giovanni di Mone Cassai): name of, 405
masks
    Egyptian, 61, 78, 79
    Mycenaean, 99, 100, 4-22A
Masolino da Panicale, 503
Masonry Style (First Style), 191
mass, 8
Mass. *See* Eucharist
Massacre of the Innocents, 240
mastabas, 58, *58*, 61, 3-13B
Master of the Symbolic Execution: saltcellar, Sapi-Portuguese, 532, *532*
Materials and Techniques boxes
    Ajanta painted caves, 433
    Andean weaving, 510
    Chinese ceramics, 451
    Chinese jade, 454
    Chinese painting, 459
    embroidery, 362
    encaustic painting, 218
    fresco painting, 408
    Greek vase painting, 110
    hollow-casting, 130
    illuminated manuscripts, 249
    Islamic tilework, 299
    ivory carving, 251
    Mesopotamian seals, 39
    mosaics, 245
    Paleolithic cave painting, 20, 22
    Shang bronze casting, 452
    stained-glass windows, 375
Mathura (India): Buddha seated on lion throne, 432–433, *432*
Matilda (countess of Canossa), 352
matins, 13-36A
Matthew, Saint, 240, 312, 314
Mau, August, 191
Mauritius (Maurice), Saint, 327
Maurya dynasty art, 428–429, 447
mausoleum, 225
Mausoleum, Halikarnassos, 49, *146b*, 5-64A, 5-64B
Mausoleum of Galla Placidia, Ravenna, 246–247, *246*, *246*, *247*, 248, 266, 8-17A
Mausoleum of the Julii, Rome, 245, *245b*, 8-13A
Mawangdui (China): tomb of the marquise of Dai, *448*, 449
Maxentius (Roman emperor), 225, 226, 228
Maximianus (bishop of Ravenna), 254, 255, 264, 9-14A
Maya art
    Classic period, 498–503, 18-10A
    Postclassic period, 490, 491, 504–506
meander, 108
Mebon Temple, Angkor, 444, *444*
medallion with portrait of Constantine, 230, *230*
Medes, 40
medieval art
    International Style, 413–414
    South Asia, 437–441

See also early Islamic art; early medieval European art; Gothic art; Heian period Japanese art; Italian late medieval art; Nara period Japanese art; Postclassic Mesoamerican art; Romanesque art; Song dynasty Chinese art; Tang dynasty Chinese art
meditating Bodhisattva Maitreya, Three Kingdoms period (sculpture), 471, *471*
meditating Buddha, Gandhara (sculpture), 431–432, *431*
meditation mudra (dhyana mudra), 427, 431, 458–459, 16-13A
Meditations (Marcus Aurelius), 216
medium/media, 7
Medusa, 118, 128, 143
megalithic architecture, 27, 27–28
megaliths, 27
megaron, 97, 115, 4-18A, 5-6A
Megasthenes, 428
meiping, 467, 472
meiping vase, Xiuwei, *466*, 467
Melfi sarcophagus, 217–218, *217*
Memmi, Lippo: *Annunciation* altarpiece, Siena Cathedral, 413–415, *413*
Menander portrait, Pompeii, *196b*, 318, 7-25B
Mencius (Mengzi), 463
mendicant orders, 385, 404, 405, 420, 14-6A
Menes (pharaoh of Egypt), 57
Mengzi (Mencius), 463
Menkaure (pharaoah of Egypt), 61, 64–65, 3-11A, 3-13A
Menkaure and Khamerernebty(?), Gizeh (sculpture), 64–65, *65*, 3-11A, 3-13A
menorahs, 207
Menrva (Etruscan deity), 167, 168
Mentuemhet (Egyptian priest), 80–81
Mentuemhet portrait statue, Karnak, 80–81, *81*
Mentuhotep II (pharoah of Egypt), 67
Mercury. *See* Hermes
merlons, 382
Merovingian art, 309
Merovingian looped fibulae, 309, *309*
Mesa Verde National Park, Colorado (U.S.A.): Cliff Palace, 518, *518*
Mesoamerican art, 492–507, *493map*, 519
    and ball games, 499, 500–501, 501
    Classic Maya, 498–503, 18-10A
    Classic Veracruz, 504
    Olmec, 493–494, 501
    Postclassic, 490, 491, 504–507
    Preclassic period West Mexican, 494–495
    societal contexts, 492–493, 497, 498, 502
    Teotihuacán, 491, 495–498, 501, 504, 18-7A
Mesolithic art/period, 16, 23
Mesopotamia
    and Greece, 107
    Neolithic art, 16, 24, 26–28, 29, 32, 1-16A, 1-19A
    religion and mythology, 32, 33–34, 35–36, 41, 43, 107, 2-18A
    timeline, 32
    See also Mesopotamian art
Mesopotamian art, 30–48, *32map*, 53
    Akkadian, 40–41, 53
    Assyrian, 32, 45–48, 53, 2-18B, 2-20A
    Babylonian, 34, 43–45, 49, 53
    and Egyptian Predynastic art, 3-1A
    Elamite, 45, 2-19A
    and Greek Geometric period art, 109
    and Greek Orientalizing period art, 109
    Hittite, 45, 2-18B
    Neo-Babylonian, 48, 49, 53
    Neo-Sumerian, 42, 43, 53, 2-18A
    and Paleolithic art, 17
    societal contexts, 32–33, 34, 40, 44, 45–46, 2-20A
    Sumerian, 30–31, 32–39, 53, 2-6A
    timeline, 32
Messiah, 240
metalwork
    Aegean, 94–95, 99, 100, 4-22A, 4-23A
    Akkadian, 40–41
    Andean South American, 512

Byzantine, 9-26A, 9-26B
Carolingian, 320
Chinese, 452, 453, 456, 16-6A, 16-13B
early medieval pre-Christian, 309–310, 11-3A
Egyptian, 77, 78, 79
Etruscan, 166, 167, 174, 175, 6-13A
Gothic, 388, 392, 393, 13-44A
Greek Early/High Classical period, 105, 136
Greek Orientalizing period, 109–110
Intermediate Area Native American, 507
Islamic, 293, 303–304
Japanese, 477
Korean, 470
Late Antique, 248, 250–251
Persian, 2-26A
Romanesque, 334, 336, 353–354
Southeast Asian, 441
    See also bronze casting
metopes, 116, 118, 128, 136–137
Mexica. *See* Aztecs
Mezquita. *See* Great Mosque, Córdoba
Michael, Archangel, 257, 9-26B
Michael IV (Byzantine emperor), 273
Michael V (Byzantine emperor), 273
Michael VIII Paleologus (Byzantine emperor), 278, 9-32A
Michelangelo Buonarroti
    and Laocoön and his sons (Athanadoros, Hagesandros, and Polydoros of Rhodes) (sculpture), 162
    Moses, tomb of Julius II, 360
    Santa Maria degli Angeli, 221, *221*
    tomb of Julius II, 360
    unfinished statue, 11, *11*
Middle Byzantine art, 270–277, 281
    architecture, 271–272, 274–275, 9-25A, 9-27A
    icons, 274, 277, 9-26B
    illuminated manuscripts, 276–277
    ivory carvings, 275–276, 277
    metalwork, 9-26A, 9-26B
    mosaics, 270–271, 272–274, 275, 9-25A, 9-27A
    painting, 276
Middle Kingdom period Egyptian art, 67–68, 83, 171, 3-16A
mihrab, 287, 288, 299, 10-5A
Milan (Italy): Sant'Ambrogio, 350–351, *351*, *351*, 358
Mildenhall Treasure, 250–251, *250*
Miletos (Turkey), 154
Mimbres art, 517
Minamoto Yoritomo (Japanese shogun), 486, 17-17A
minarets, 134, 261, 287, 288, 289, 299
minbar, 287, 288, 289
Minerva. *See* Athena
Miniature Ships Fresco, Akrotiri, *93b*, 4-9A
Minoan art, 89–95
    and archaeology, 86–87
    architecture, 89–90
    fresco painting, 90–93, 194, 4-9A, 4-9B
    ivory carvings, 94–95
    and Mycenaean art, 100, 101, 4-23A
    sarcophagi, 84, 85, 88, 91
Minoan woman or goddess (*La Parisienne*), Knossos (fresco), 90–91, *90*, *92*, 94
Minoans, 3-11B
    See also Minoan art
minor arts. *See* luxury arts
Minos (king of Crete), 85, 86, 89
Minotaur, 86, 89–90
mithuna reliefs, Vishvanatha Temple, Khajuraho, 440, *440*
Miracle of the Loaves and Fishes, Sant'Apollinare Nuovo (Orthodox Baptistery), Ravenna (mosaic), 248, *248*, 8-19A, 12-27B
Miracles of Jesus, 248
    in Early Christian art, 248, 8-10A, 8-19A
Miraj, 286
mirrors: Etruscan, 6-13A
Mission of the Apostles, 346
Mississippian culture, 515, 516, 517, 18-30A
Mithras, 222
Mithridates VI (king of Pontus), 161
mithuna reliefs, Vishvanatha Temple, Khajuraho, 440, *440*

mithunas, 431, 440
Mixtecs, 504
Miyanomae (Japan): vessel, Middle Jomon period, 477, *477*
Mnesikles: Propylaia, Athens, 134, 138–139, *139*
Moche art, 511–512
Mocking of Jesus, 241
model of a house, Han dynasty, 456, 457, *457*
modeling, 113, 146, 258, 349
   in Byzantine art, 279
   in late medieval Italian art, 409, 412
   in Romanesque art, 349
   in South Asian art, 433
   See also chiaroscuro
Modena Cathedral, 356, *356*, 12-13B
modules, 10
   in Carolingian architecture, 323
   in Chinese architecture, 457
   in Romanesque architecture, 338
Mogao Grottoes. *See* Dunhuang Grottoes
Mohenjo-daro, Pakistan, 424, 425
   Great Bath, 425, *425*
   robed male figure, 425, *425*
   seal with seated figure in yogic posture, 426, *426*
Moissac (France). *See* Saint-Pierre
moksha, 427, 435
   See also nirvana
moldings
   in Carolingian architecture, 11-19A
   in Egyptian architecture, 82
   in Gothic architecture, 390
   in Greek architecture, 117
   in Italian late medieval art, 418
   in Romanesque architecture, 340, 351, 358
molds, 11
Monasterboice (Ireland): High Cross of Muiredach, 315, *315*
monasteries
   Byzantine, 267
   early medieval European, 311, 322–323, 330
   Romanesque era, 334, 349, 352
   See also specific monasteries
monastic orders, 404
   Benedictine Rule, 322, 330, 341, 343
   Cistercian order, 322, 342, 343, 347, 12-10A
   Cluniac order, 341–342, 343, 347
   Dominican order, 385, 404, 420, 14-6A
   Franciscan order, 385, 404, 405, 14-6A
monasticism, 267, 311, 322, 341–342
   See also monastic orders
Mongols, 295, 472
Monk's Mound, Cahokia, 515, *515b*, 18-30A
monochrome
   in Pompeian/Vesuvius area art, 194
   in Roman art, 194
monolith with bird and crocodile, Great Zimbabwe (sculpture), 531, *531*
monolithic columns, 116, 428–429
monoliths, 531
   See also monolithic columns
Monophysite heresy, 258, 270
monotheism, 233, 235, 285
Monreale cathedral, 275, *275*, 348, 9-26A
Monte Albán (Mexico), 504
Monterozzi necropolis, Tarquinia, 164, *164*, 165, 171–172, *172, 173*, 6-9A
Moorish art. *See* Islamic art
Moralia in Job (Saint Gregory), 347–348, *347*
moralized Bibles, 384–386
Morgan Madonna, 349, *349*
mortise-and-tenon system, 480
mortuary precinct of Djoser, Saqqara, 58, *58b*, 59, 60, *60*, 68, 3-5A
mortuary temples, 62
   Djoser mortuary precinct, Saqqara, 58, 60, *60*, 3-5A
   Great Pyramid complex, 62
   Hatshepsut mortuary temple, Deir el-Bahri, 69–71, 73
mosaic tilework, 299–300
mosaics
   Early Byzantine, 254, 255, 264–268

Early Christian, 244–245, 245, 247–248, 8-13A, 8-17A, 8-19A
   Greek Late Classical period, 149, 150–151, 196, 214
   Islamic, 287, 291, 299–300
   Mesoamerican, 504
   Middle Byzantine, 270–271, 272–274, 275, 9-25A, 9-27A
   Roman, 196, 214
moschophoros, 112
Moses, 33, 360, 8-10A
Moses, tomb of Julius II (Michelangelo Buonarroti), 360
Moses Expounding the Law, Bury Bible (Master Hugo), 360, *360*
mosque lamp of Sayf al-Din Tuquztimur, 301, *301*
mosque lamps, 301
Mosque of Selim II, Edirne (Sinan the Great), 298, *298*, 299
mosques, 261, 287, 288, 290–292, 297, 10-5A
   See also great mosques; *specific mosques*
Mother of God, 245, 267, 280, 380
   See also Theotokos; Virgin Mary
Mount Sinai (Egypt): monastery of Saint Catherine, 267–268, *267*, 269, *269*, 270, 277, 279, 9-18A
Mount Vesuvius, eruption of, 188
   See also Pompeian/Vesuvius area art
Mount Wutai (China): Foguang Si (Buddha Radiance Temple), 462, *462b*, 16-15A
Mouth of Hell, Winchester Psalter, 12-35A
Mozarabic art, 316
Mshatta (Jordan): Umayyad palace, 287, *287b*, 10-5A, 10-5B
mudras, 427
   abhaya mudra, 427, 432–433, 480, 15-11A, 16-13B
   bhumisparsha mudra, 427
   dharmachakra mudra, 427, 443
   dhyana mudra, 427, 431, 458–459, 16-13A
   in Shingon, 483
Mughal Empire art, 294–295, 302
Muhammad, 284, 285, 289–290
Muhammad V (sultan of Granada), 295
Muhammad ibn al-Zayn: basin *(Baptistère de Saint Louis)*, 303–304, *303*
Muhammad of Ghor, 294
Muhaqqaq, 300
mullions, 381
mummification, 61, 78, 218, 7-62A
mummy portrait of a priest of Serapis, Hawara (encaustic painting), *218*
mummy portrait of a young woman, Hawara (encaustic painting), *218b*, 7-62B
mummy portrait of Artemidorus, Hawara (encaustic painting), 218, *218b, 218*, 7-62A
mummy portraits, 218, 7-62A, 7-62B
muqarnas, 274, 296, 297, 9-27A
mural painting
   Byzantine, 9-25A
   Chinese, 462, 16-14A
   Early Christian, 237–239, 8-5A, 8-6A
   Egyptian, 56–57, *57b*, 58, 74–75, 3-1A, 3-11B
   Greek, 144, 149–150, 191
   Italian 13th century, 407, 14-5A, 14-5B
   Italian 14th century, 400, 401, 408, 409, 416–417, 419–420, 14-8A, 14-8B
   Italian Romanesque, 12-27B
   Japanese, 482, 17-13A
   Late Antique Jewish, 235–236
   Mesoamerican, 497–498, 18-7A
   Mesopotamian, 46, 47, 2-18A
   Minoan, 90–93
   Ottonian, 11-23A
   Pompeian/Vesuvius area, 189–190, 191–195, 196, 197, 248, 7-25A, 7-25B
   prehistoric, 22, 26–27
   Roman High Empire, 7-54A
   Romanesque, 348
   See also cave paintings
Murasaki Shikubu: *Tale of Genji*, 484–485, *485*, 486, 487
museums: Greek forerunner of, 139
musical instruments, 38–39, 88

musicians and dancers, tomb of Nebamun, Thebes (mural), *75*
Mut (Egyptian deity), 57, 3-24A
Myanmar art (Burmese art), 443, 15-28A
Mycenae (Greece)
   female head (sculpture), 101, *101*
   funerary mask, Grave Circle A, 100, *100*
   Grave Circle A, 99–100, *99b, 100*, 4-22A, 4-23A
   inlaid dagger blade with lion hunt, 100, *100*, 4-23A
   Lion Gate, 98, 99, 101, 4-18A
   Treasury of Atreus, 98, 99, *99*, 170, 184
   two goddesses(?) and a child (sculpture), 100–101, *101*
   Warrior Vase, 102, *102*
   See also Mycenaean art
Mycenaean art, 95–102
   and archaeology, 85, 86, 87
   architecture, 96–99, 115, 170, 184, 244, 4-18A, 4-22A, 5-6A
   ivory carvings, 100–101
   metalwork, 99–100, 4-23A
   sculpture, 98, 99, 101–102
   societal contexts, 95
   vase painting, 102
Myron: *Diskobolos (Discus Thrower)*, 131–132, *131*
mystery plays, 409, 12-35A
mythology. *See* religion and mythology

N

Nabu (Mesopotamian deity), 34, 48
Nandi (bull), 435, 436, 15-22B
Nanna (Mesopotamian deity), 34, 41
naos. *See* cella
Napir-Asu (queen of Elam), 45
Napoleon Bonaparte, 56
Nara (Japan): Todaiji, 482–483, *482*, 486
Nara period Japanese art, 474, 475, 481–483, 489
Nara Prefecture (Japan)
   Horyuji temple, *474*, 475, 480, *480*, 481–482, *481, 482*
   Yakushi triad, Yakushiji, 481, *481*
Naram-Sin (king of Akkad), 40, 41
Naram-Sin victory stele, Susa, *40*, 41, 44, 47
Narmer (pharaoh of Egypt), 54, 55, 57
narrative art
   Akkadian, 40, 41
   early Christian, 249–250, 251–252, 8-21A
   early medieval, 319, 326–327, 11-15A
   Egyptian, 55, 58, 66, 78
   Gothic, 369–370, 377, 13-3A
   Greek Archaic period, 118, 119, 120, 122–123
   Greek Early/High Classical period, 104, 105, 126, 128, 143
   Greek Geometric period, 109, 128
   Greek late Classical period, 150–151
   Hellenistic period Greek, 156
   Italian 14th century, 409, 412, 14-8A
   Italian late medieval, 405
   Japanese, 488
   Late Antique Jewish, 235
   Mycenaean, 102, 4-23A
   Neolithic, 27
   Paleolithic, 22, 23
   Pompeian/Vesuvius area, 192
   Roman, 179, 187, 206–207, 208, 7-44A
   Romanesque, 356, 361–362, 12-8B, 12-11A
   South Asian, 422, 423, 426, 432, 436, 438, 15-22A
   Sumerian, 30, 31, 35, 36, 37, 38
narthex, 243, 264, 350, 8-19A
Nasca art, 510–511
Nasca Plain (Peru): hummingbird, 511, *511*
al-Nasir Muhammad, 301
Nasrid dynasty, 295
Native American art, 490–519
   Intermediate Area, 507
   Mesoamerica. *See* Mesoamerican art
   North America. *See* Native North American art
   societal contexts, 492–493

South America. *See* Andean South American art
   timelines, 492
Native North American art, *514map*, 519
   Alaska, 514, 515
   Northwest Coast, 514
   Southwest, 517–518, 18-33A
   Woodlands, 514–517, 18-30A
Nativity, 240, 403–404, 415
Natural History (Pliny), 132, 188
naturalism, 401
   See also naturalism/realism
naturalism/realism
   in African art, 527, 528, 532, 19-6A
   in Akkadian art, 40–41
   in Andean South American art, 511
   in Byzantine art, 273, 276, 9-3A, 9-18A, 9-26B
   in Chinese art, 465
   in Early Christian art, 248, 8-17A, 8-19A
   in Egyptian art, 65–66, 67–68, 3-13A
   in Gothic art, 370, 387, 388, 394, 396
   in Greek art, 126, 146
   in Italian 14th century art, 407, 408, 419, 14-7A, 14-8B, 14-10A
   in Italian late medieval art, 401, 406
   in Japanese art, 486, 488
   in Mesoamerican art, 502
   in Minoan art, 4-9A
   in Native North American art, 515
   in Roman art, 185–186, 187, 196, 205, 7-10A
Naumburg Cathedral (Naumburg Master), 394–395, *394, 395*
Naumburg Master: Naumburg Cathedral, 394–395, *394, 395*
nave arcades
   in Early Christian architecture, 243
   in early medieval architecture, 324
   in Gothic architecture, 370, 373
   in Italian late medieval architecture, 413
   in Romanesque architecture, 340, 350
naves, 373
   in Byzantine architecture, 263
   in Early Christian architecture, 243
   in early medieval architecture, 323, 324, 325–326, 11-23A
   in French Gothic architecture, 364, *371*, 374, 378, 13-23A
   in French/Spanish Romanesque architecture, 340, 341, 348, 12-4A, 12-4B, 12-7B, 12-10A
   in Holy Roman Empire Gothic architecture, 396, 398
   in Holy Roman Empire Romanesque architecture, 350
   in Islamic architecture, 289
   in Italian 13th century architecture, 14-6A
   in Italian 14th century architecture, 413, 14-18A
   in Italian Romanesque architecture, 355, 12-27A
   in Norman Romanesque architecture, 358
   in Roman architecture, 189, 208
   in Spanish Gothic architecture, 13-38A
Nebamun (Egyptian scribe), 74–75
Nebamun, tomb of, Thebes, 74–75, *75*
Nebamun hunting fowl, tomb of Nebamun, Thebes (mural), *75*
Nebuchadnezzar II (king of Babylon), 48, 49
necropolis, 58, 171
Nefertari (queen of Egypt), 72
Nefertiti (queen of Egypt), 76–77, 78
Nefertiti (Thutmose) (sculpture), 76–77, *77, 78*
Nefrura (princess of Egypt), 74
neighing horse, Tang dynasty (sculpture), 464, *464*
nembutsu, 488
nemes, 64
Neo-Babylonian art, 48, 49, 53
Neo-Confucianism, 468
Neolithic art, 23–28, *24map*, 29
   animals in, 16
   architecture, 24–25, 27, 28, 450–451, 1-16A, 1-19A

South Asian art (continued)
  Maurya dynasty, 428–429, 447, 15-6A, 15-6B
  Mughal Empire, 294–295, 302
  post-Gupta period, 435–437, 447
  Shunga/Andhra/Kushan dynasties, 422, 423, 429–433, 447, 15-8A, 15-11A
  societal contexts, 424, 427
  Sultanate of Delhi, 441
  timeline, 424
  Vedic/Upanishadic period, 426–428
  See also South Asian Buddhist art; South Asian sculpture
South Asian Buddhist art
  Gupta period, 432, 433–434
  Maurya period, 428–429, 15-6A
  Shunga/Andhra/Kushan period, 429–433, 15-8A, 15-11A
South Asian sculpture
  early medieval, 438, 440–441, 15-22A
  Gupta period, 434–435
  Maurya dynasty, 428, 429, 15-6A, 15-6B
  post-Gupta period, 436–437
  Shunga/Andhra/Kushan period, 422, 423, 430, 431–433, 15-8A, 15-11A
South Cross, Ahenny, 315, 315b, 11-9A
Southeast Asian art, 424map, 441–446
  Cambodia, 443–446
  Java, 443, 15-29A
  societal contexts, 441
  Sri Lanka, 443, 15-28A
  timelines, 424
southern Hindu temple style, 439
Southwest Native American art, 517–518, 18-33A
space, 8
spandrels, 206
Spanish art. See French/Spanish Romanesque art
spectrum, 7
Sperlonga (Italy), 162
Speyer Cathedral, 339, 350, 350, 351
sphinx, 63, 81
Split (Croatia): palace of Diocletian, 224–225, 225, 244, 356, 8-19A, 10-5A
Spoils of Jerusalem, relief panel, Arch of Titus, 206–207, 206
spotted horses and negative hand imprints, Pech-Merle (cave painting), 21
Spring Fresco (landscape with swallows), Akrotiri, 92–93, 92, 172, 194
springing, 340, 373
Square Temple, Eshnunna, 35–36, 43, 45
squinches, 262, 262, 271, 290, 296, 9-27A, 12-4A
Sri Lankan art, 442, 443
stag hunt, Pella (Gnosis) (mosaic), 149, 149, 150
stained-glass windows, 12
  in English Gothic architecture, 391, 13-38A
  French Gothic. See French Gothic stained-glass windows
  in Italian 13th century architecture, 14-5A
stamp seals, 39, 426
The Standard of Ur, 30, 31, 37–38, 37, 39, 2-6A
standing Buddha, Gandhara, 432b, 15-11A
standing male figure, Sanxingdui (sculpture), 453, 453
statue of Queen Napir-Asu, Susa, 45, 45
statues, 12
  See also sculpture
statuettes of two worshipers, Eshnunna, 35–36, 36, 43, 45
stave church, Urnes, 311, 311
staves, 311
Stele D, Waxaklajuun-Ub'aah-K'awiil, Copán, 498, 499
Stele of the Vultures (battle scenes, victory stele of Eannatum), Girsu, 34, 36, 37
stele with the laws of Hammurabi, Susa, 34, 44, 44
stele/stelae
  Akkadian, 40, 41
  Andean South American, 508–509
  Assyrian, 47

Babylonian, 41, 44
  Greek, 146–147, 5-64A
  Mesoamerican, 498, 499
  Sumerian, 34, 36
stem stitching, 362
stepped pyramid of Djoser (Imhotep), 58, 59, 496
stepped pyramids, 58, 59, 438, 490, 491, 496–497, 504, 18-10A
Stewart, Andrew, 135
stigmata, 405
Still, Clyfford: 1948-C, 1, 2
still life, 5
  in Pompeian/Vesuvius area art, 196, 197
still life with peaches, Herculaneum, 196, 197
stirrup spouts, 511
Stoa of Attalos II, Athens, 154–155, 155
Stoa Poikile (Painted Stoa) (Polygnotos of Thasos), Athens, 143, 154
stoas, 154
Stoic school of philosophy, 154
stone tower built into the settlement wall, Jericho, 24
stone vaulting
  in French/Spanish Romanesque architecture, 337, 338, 339, 340–341
  in Norman Romanesque architecturee, 358–359
Stonehenge (England), 28, 28, 1-19A
stonemasons and sculptors, Chartres Cathedral (stained-glass window), 375, 377
stoneware, 451
Story of Jacob, Vienna Genesis, 8-21A
storytelling. See narrative art
Strasbourg Cathedral, 392–394, 393
strategos, 133
strigil, 147
stringcourses, 11-19A
struts, 457
stucco, 182, 189, 7-62A
stupas, 429–430, 443
style, 3–5
stylistic evidence, 3
stylobate, 116, 135
stylus, 33, 196
sub gracia, 392
sub lege, 392
subtractive light, 7
subtractive sculpture, 11, 64
Suetonius, 202
Suger (abbot of Saint-Denis), 366, 367, 368–369, 374, 375, 392, 13-3A
Sui dynasty Chinese art, 461, 16-13B
Suicide of Judas (ivory carving), 251–252, 251, 12-13A
Suicide of Judas, Saint-Lazare (Gislebertus), 345b, 12-13A
Suiko (Japanese empress), 480
Sulayman (artist): ewer in the form of a bird, 293, 293
Suleyman the Magnificent (Ottoman sultan), 297, 10-23A
Sulla (Roman general), 161
Sultan-Muhammad: Shahnama (Book of Kings), 302–303, 303
Sultanate of Delhi, 441
sultans, 292
Sumerian art, 32–39, 53
  and archaeology, 32
  bull-headed harps, 38–39, 88
  cylinder seals, 39
  female head (Inanna?), Uruk (sculpture), 34–35
  societal contexts, 32–33, 34
  The Standard of Ur, 30, 31, 37–38, 39, 2-6A
  temple statuettes, 35–36, 2-6A
  Warka Vase, 35
Summa Theologica (Thomas Aquinas), 372
Sumner County, Tennessee (U.S.A.): incised gorget with running warrior, 517, 517
sunken relief sculpture, 73
Sunnah, 285
Supper at Emmaus, 241
surahs, 285
Surya (Aryan deity), 427

Suryavarman II (Khmer king), 444
Susa (Iran)
  beaker with animal decoration, 45b, 2-19A
  statue of Queen Napir-Asu, 45, 45
  stele with the laws of Hammurabi, 34, 44, 44
  victory stele of Naram-Sin, 40, 41, 44, 47
sutras, 480
Sutton Hoo ship burial, Suffolk, 309–310, 309, 11-3A
Swogger, John, 1-16A
Sylvester (Pope), 243
Sylvester, John Henry: Portrait of Te Pehi Kupe, 13, 13
symbols, 5
  See also attributes
symmetria, 135
symmetry, 64, 115, 146, 273, 313, 11-3A
  See also axial plans
symposium, 108
synagogue, Dura-Europa, 235, 235, 248
Syong Mong (Baekje king), 480
Syros (Greece): figurine of a woman, 87, 87

T
Tábara (Spain): monastery of San Salvador, 316
taberna, 209
tabernacle, Or San Michele, Florence (Orcagna), 419, 419b, 14-19A
tablero. See talud-tablero construction
tablinum, 190, 7-16A
Tada (Nigeria): seated man (sculpture), 528, 528
Taharqo (pharaoh of Egypt), 81
Taharqo as a sphinx, Kawa (sculpture), 81, 81
Tahmasp (Savafid shah), 300, 302
Tairona (Colombia): pendant in the form of a bat-faced man, 507, 507
Tairona art, 507
Taizokai (Womb World) mandara, Kyoogokokuji (Toji) (hanging scroll), 483, 483
Taj Mahal, Agra, 283
Tale of Genji (Murasaki Shikubu), 484–485, 485, 486, 487
talud-tablero construction, 496
Tang dynasty Chinese art, 461–462, 464, 472, 473, 16-14A, 16-15A
tapestries, 362, 513
Tarquinia (Italy)
  Monterozzi necropolis, 164, 164, 165, 171–172, 172, 173, 6-9A
  sarcophagus of Lars Pulena, 175–176, 176, 249
  Tomb of Hunting and Fishing, 172, 173
  Tomb of the Augurs, 164, 165, 171
  Tomb of the Leopards, 172, 172
  Tomb of the Triclinium, 172b, 6-9A
Tarquinius Superbus (Etruscan king of Rome), 168, 169, 172, 173–174, 181, 182
Tassili n'Ajjer (Algeria): running woman, 522–524, 523
tattoo (tatu/tatau), 13, 525
Te Pehi Kupe: Self-Portrait, 13, 13
technique, 3
Tefnut (Egyptian deity), 57
Tegea (Greece): Temple of Athena Alea (Skopas of Paros), 5-64A
tempera painting
  in Italian 13th century art, 404–405
  in Italian 14th century art, 407–408, 411–412, 413–415, 14-10A
  in Late Antique Jewish art, 235
  in Mesoamerican art, 502
  in Roman art, 219
  See also mural painting; painting
Temple A, Prinias, 111, 111b, 115, 5-6A, 5-6B
Temple of Aphaia, Aegina, 123–124, 123, 124, 125, 126
Temple of Apollo, Didyma (Paionios of Ephesos and Daphnis of Miletos), 153–154, 153
Temple of Artemis, Corfu, 118, 118, 124
Temple of Artemis, Ephesos, 49
Temple of Athena Alea (Skopas of Paros), Tegea, 5-64A

Temple of Athena Nike (Kallikrates), Athens, 134, 141, 141, 152
Temple of Fortuna Virilis (Temple of Portunus), Rome, 182, 182
Temple of Geshtinanna, Girsu, 43
Temple of Hera, Olympia, 115, 146
Temple of Hera I ("Basilica"), Paestum, 117–118, 117, 123, 135
Temple of Hera II or Apollo, Paestum, 125–126, 126
Temple of Horus, Edfu, 82, 82, 3-1A
Temple of Jupiter Optimus Maximus, Capitoline Hill, Rome (Vulca of Veii), 168, 181
Temple of Portunus (Temple of Fortuna Virilis), Rome, 182, 182
Temple of Quetzalcoatl, Teotihuacán, 496, 497
Temple of Ramses II, Abu Simbel, 71–72, 71
Temple of the Giant Jaguar, Tikal, 500, 500
Temple of the Inscriptions, Palenque, 500, 500b, 18-10A
Temple of Venus, Baalbek, 224, 224, 225
Temple of Vesta(?), Tivoli, 183, 183
Temple of Zeus, Olympia (Libon of Elis), 125–126, 126, 127, 128, 146–147, 148, 5-32A
templon, 277
Tendai Buddhism, 483
tenons. See mortise-and-tenon system
Teotihuacán (Mexico), 491
  architecture, 495–497, 495, 496
  Aztecs and, 496
  and ball games, 501
  destruction of, 504
  murals, 497–498, 18-7A
  Tetitla apartment complex, 497, 498
tephra, 92
tepidarium, 220
terminus ante quem, 2
terminus post quem, 2
terracotta
  in African art, 524, 525, 528, 529
  in Chinese art, 451, 454–455
  in Etruscan art, 168, 169, 181
  in Intermediate Area Native American art, 507
  in Italian 14th century art, 414
  in Minoan architecture, 90
  in Roman art, 214–215
tesserae, 150, 245, 291, 299
tetrarchs, 224
  See also tetrarchy
tetrarchy, 224–225
textiles
  Andean South American, 509, 510, 513
  Chinese, 448, 449, 458, 10-15A, 16-14A
  early Islamic, 10-15A
  and Italian 14th century art, 412
  Japanese, 483
  Late Byzantine, 9-35A
  later Islamic, 300–301, 10-27A
  Norman Romanesque, 361–362
texture, 8
Thai art, 443, 15-29A
Thangmar of Heidelberg, 324–325
Thanjavur (India): Rajarajeshvara Temple, 438, 439, 15-22B
theater of Epidauros (Polykleitos the Younger), 151, 151
theatron, 151
Thebes (Egypt), 69
  first millenium BCE, 80–81
  funerary chapel of Rekhmire, 64b, 3-11B
  Senmut with Princess Nefrura (sculpture), 74, 74
  tomb of Hunefer, 80, 80
  tomb of Nebamun, 74–75, 75
  tomb of Tutankhamen, 78, 78, 79, 100
  Valley of the Kings, 72
  See also Luxor
Thebes (Greece): Mantiklos Apollo (sculpture), 109–110, 109, 112
Theodora (Byzantine empress, wife of Justinian), 254, 255, 264, 265, 266, 275, 309

Theodora (Byzantine empress, wife of Theophilos), 270, 273
Theodora and attendants, San Vitale, Ravenna (mosaic), *254, 255, 264, 265, 266, 275, 309
Theodore, Saint, 268, 269, 377
Theodoric (king of the Ostrogoths), 246, 247, 263, 308, 317
Theodoros of Phokaia: tholos, Delphi, 151–152, *151*
Theodosius I (Roman emperor), 246, 256
Theodulf of Orléans, 265, 317
Theogony (Genealogy of the Gods) (Hesiod), 107
Theophanu, 328
Theopompus, 169
Theotokos
    in Early Byzantine art, 267, 268–270, *269*
    in Early Christian art, 245
    in Gothic art, 370, 396
    in Middle Byzantine art, 270–271, *271, 275, 275, 276, 277*
    western European version, 349
    See also Virgin and Child; Virgin Mary
Thera (Cyclades), 87, 91–92, 194
Theravada Buddhism, 427, 446, 15-28A
thermoluminescence, 523
Theseus (king of Athens), 89–90, 120, 137, 5-17A
Thessaloniki (Greece)
    Hagios Georgios (Church of Saint George), 248, *248b*, 257, 8-17A, 8-19A
    Saint Catherine, 278, *278b*, 9-32A
Thierry of Chartres, 369
Third Dynasty of Ur, 42, 43
Third Style, 194
Third Style wall painting, Villa of Agrippa Postumus, Boscotrecase, 194, *194*
The Thirteen Emperors (Yan Liben), 462, *463*
tholos, Delphi (Theodoros of Phokaia), 151–152, *151*
tholos tombs, 98, 99, 170, 244
tholos/tholoi, 99, 151, 183, 184
Thomas, Saint, 241, 12-8B
Thomas Aquinas, Saint, 372
Thomas de Cormont: Amiens Cathedral, *371*, 375, 377–379, *377, 377, 379*, 396, 418, 13-38A
Thoth (Egyptian deity), 57, 61
Three Angels (Rublyev), 280, *280*
Three goddesses (Hestia, Dione, and Aphrodite?), Parthenon east pediment, Athens (sculpture), 137, *137*
Three Kingdoms period (Korea), 470–471
Three Marys at the Tomb, 241
three revelers (Euthymides), Vulci (vase painting), 123, *123*
Throne of Maximianus (ivory furniture), 264, *264b*, 9-14A
thrust, 184
Thutmose (sculptor): Nefertiti, 76–77, *77*, 78
Thutmose I (pharaoh of Egypt), 70, 72
Thutmose II (pharaoh of Egypt), 69
Thutmose III (pharaoh of Egypt), 69, 70, 73, 3-11B
Ti, mastaba of, Saqqara, 66, *66*, 67, 74
Ti watching a hippopotamus hunt, mastaba of Ti, Saqqara (relief sculpture), 66, *66*
Tiberius (Roman emperor), 162
Tikal (Guatemala)
    Temple of the Giant Jaguar, 500, *500*
    urban planning, 500
tilework, 299–300
timelines
    Aegean art, 86
    African art, 522
    Byzantine Empire, 256
    Chinese/Korean art, 450
    early medieval European art, 308
    Egyptian art, 56
    Etruscan art, 166
    Gothic art, 366
    Greece, 106
    Islamic art, 284
    Italian late medieval art, 402
    Japanese art, 476
    Late Antique art, 234

Mesopotamian art, 32
    Native American art, 492
    Persian art, 32
    prehistoric art, 16
    Roman art, 180
    Romanesque art, 334
    South Asian art, 424
Timgad, Algeria, 207, *207*
Timur (Tamerlane), 302
Timurid dynasty, 302, 305
Tinia (Etruscan deity), 167, 168
Tiryns (Greece): citadel, 96–97, *96, 97*
Titans, 107
Titus (Roman emperor), 203, 204, 205, 236, 286
Tivoli (Italy)
    Hadrian's Villa, 212–213, *212*
    Temple of Vesta(?), 183, *183*
Tiwanaku (Bolivia): Gateway of the Sun, 512–513, *512*
Tiwanaku art, 512–513
Tiye (queen of Egypt), 77
Tiye, Ghurab (sculpture), 77, *77*
Todaiji, Nara, 482–483, *482*, 486, 17-17A
togas, 176
Tokugawa shogunate. *See* Edo period Japanese art
Toltecs, 506
Tomb 100 wall paintings, Hierakonpolis, 56–57, *57b*, 3-1A
Tomb of Edward II, Gloucester Cathedral, *391b*, 13-42A
tomb of Emperor Nintoku, Sakai, 478, *478*
Tomb of Hunting and Fishing, Monterozzi necropolis, Tarquinia, 172, *173*
tomb of Julius II (Michelangelo Buonarroti), 360
tomb of Mausolos (Mausoleum): Halikarnassos, 49, *146b*, 5-64A, 5-64B
tomb of Nebamun, Thebes, 74–75, *75*
Tomb of the Augurs (Tarquinia), 164, 165, 171
Tomb of the Diver, Paestum, 144, *144*, 172
Tomb of the Leopards, Monterozzi necropolis, Tarquinia, 172, *172*
tomb of the marquise of Dai, Mawangdui, *448*, 449
Tomb of the Reliefs, Banditaccia necropolis, Cerveteri, 171, *171*
Tomb of the Shields and Chairs, Banditaccia necropolis, Cerveteri, 170, 171, *171b*, 6-7A
Tomb of the Triclinium, Monterozzi necropolis, Tarquinia, *172b*, 6-9A
tomb of Ti, Saqqara, 66, *66*, 67
tomb of Tutankhamen, Thebes, 78, *78, 79*, 100
Tomb of Yongtai, Qianxian, 462, 464, *464*
tombs. *See* funerary customs
tonality, 7
tondo/tondi, 219, 7-48A, 10-15A
Torah, 235
toranas, 430, 15-8A
Torhalle, Lorsch, 232, *323b*, 11-19A
Tori Busshi: Shaka triad, Horyuji temple (sculpture), *474*, 475, 480, *480*, 481
torques, 156
Toulouse (France). *See* Saint-Sernin
Tournus (France): Saint-Philibert, 337, *337b*, 339, 12-4B
Tours (France): Saint Martin's, 335, 338
Tower of Babel (Babylon ziggurat), 34, 48, 49, 289
tracery, 373, 375, 414, 13-23A
Traini, Francesco: *Triumph of Death*, 419–420, *419*
Trajan (Roman emperor), 178, 179, 207–209, 216, 234–235, 7-44A, 7-44B
Trajan Decius (Roman emperor), 221–222, 236
Trajan's Arch, Benevento, 208, *208b*, 7-44A, 7-44B
Trajan's Column. *See* Column of Trajan
tramezzo, 14-6A
transepts
    in Early Christian architecture, 243
    in early medieval architecture, 323, 324, 325

in French/Spanish Romanesque architecture, 12-4A, 12-7B
    in Gothic architecture, 390
    in Italian 13th century architecture, 14-5A
Transfiguration of Christ, 240, 267–268, 412
Transfiguration of Jesus, Church of the Virgin, Mount Sinai, 267–268, *267*, 279
transverse arches
    in French/Spanish Romanesque architecture, 339, 340, 12-4A, 12-4B, 12-7B
    in Gothic architecture, 368
    in Holy Roman Empire Romanesque architecture, 350
    in Norman Romanesque architecture, 358, 359
transverse barrel vaults, 12-10A
transverse ribs, 373
Trastavere (Italy)
    Santa Cecilia, *407b*, 409, 14-7A
    Santa Maria, 14-7A
Travelers among Mountains and Streams (Fan Kuan), 465, *465*, 468, 16-23A
treasuries, 119
Treasury of Atreus, Mycenae, 98, 99, *99*, 170, 184
Trebonianus Gallus (Roman emperor), 222
tree of Jesse, 376
trefoil arches, 402, 14-18B
trefoils, 425
Trials of Jesus, 233, 241, 250
tribunes, 337, 338, 340, 12-7A
    See also galleries
triclinium, 190, 6-9A
trident, 107, 435
triforium, 364, 370, 373, 374, 390, 13-38A
triglyphs, 116, 152
trilithons, 28
Trinity, 240
    and Byzantine Christianity, 258, 264, 280cap
    in Gothic art, 385, 386
tripods, 5-17A
Triptolemos, 101
triptychs, 275–276, 392, 415
triratnas, 15-8A
Triumph of Death (Traini or Buffalmacco), 419–420, *419*
Triumph of Shapur I over Valerian, Bishapur (relief sculpture), 52, *52b*, 2-28A
Triumph of Titus, relief panel, Arch of Titus, 206, 207, 220
triumphal arches, 175, 205–207, 226–227
Trojan War, 86, 118, 124, 162, 5-20A
trumeaus, 344
trumeaus, 344
tubicen, 157
tughras, 10-23A
Tula (Mexico): colossal atlantids (sculpture), 506, *506*
Tullia, 169
tumulus/tumuli, 27, 170, 309, 478
tunnel vaults. *See* barrel vaults
Tuquztimur, Sayf al-Din, 301
turris. *See* westwork
Tuscan columns, 168
Tutankhamen (pharaoh of Egypt), 78, 79, 80, 100
Tutankhamen, tomb of, Thebes, 78, *78, 79*, 100
Twelve Views from a Thatched Hut (Xia Gui), *468b*, 16-23A
twisted perspective. *See* composite view
two bison cave reliefs, Le Tuc D'Audoubert, 19, *19*
two goddesses(?) and a child, Mycenae (sculpture), 100–101, *101*
two saints, Hagios Georgios (Church of Saint George), Thessaloniki (mosaic), 8-19A
tympanum/tympana, 332, 344, 345–346, 13-3A, 13-23A, 13-38A, 14-12A
typology, 238

U

Udayagiri (India): cave sculptures, 434–435
Uji (Japan): Phoenix Hall, Byodoin, 483–484, *484*, 17-13A
Uma (Parvati) (Hindu deity), 435, 436

Umayyad dynasty, 285, 287, 289, 290, 305, 10-5A, 10-5B
Umayyad palace, Mshatta, 287, *287b*, 10-5A, 10-5B
Unas (pharaoah of Egypt), 61
unfinished statue (Michelangelo), 11, *11*
Uni (Etruscan deity), 167, 168
unicorn legend, 389
Unified Silla Kingdom (Korea), 471–472, 473
Unkei, 487
    Agyo, Todaiji (sculpture), *487b*, 17-17A
Untash-Napirisha (king of Elam), 45
Upanishads, 427
Ur (Tell Muqayyar) (Iraq)
    banquet scene cylinder seal, tomb of Pu-abi, 39, *39*
    bull-headed harp, tomb 789 ("King's Grave"), 38–39, *38*, 88
    bull-headed harp with inlaid sound box, tomb of Pu-abi, 38, *38*, 88
    Royal Cemetery, 32, 58, 60
    The Standard of Ur, 30, 31, 37–38, *37*, 39, 2-6A
    votive disk of Enheduanna, 41, *41*
    ziggurat, 42, *42*
uraeus, 63, 64, 79, 81
Urban II (Pope), 346
Urban VI (Pope), 404
urban planning
    China, 461
    early Islamic, 287
    Gothic era, 382–383
    Greek Early/High Classical period, 154, 207
    Japan, 480
    Mesoamerica, 496, 500
    Roman Empire, 207, 14-18B
urna, 427, 15-11A
Urnanshe statuette, Mari, 36, *36b*, 43, 45, 2-6A
Urnes (Norway): stave church, 311, *311*
Ursus (bishop of Ravenna), 8-17A
Uruk (Iraq)
    female head (Inanna?) (sculpture), 34–35, *34*
    Warka Vase (presentation of offerings to Inanna), 35, *35*
    White Temple and ziggurat, 33, *33*, 34
ushabtis, 61
ushnisha, 427, 458, 15-11A, 16-13A
Uta (abbess of Niedermünster), 330
Uta Codex, 330, *330*
Utrecht Psalter, 319, *319*, 326, 361, 11-15A
Utu (Shamash) (Mesopotamian deity), 34, 44

V

Vairocana Buddha, 461, 482
Vairocana Buddha, disciples, and bodhisattvas, Longmen Caves, Luoyang (sculpture), 461
Valerian (Roman emperor), 52, 2-28A
Valley of the Golden Mummies, 61
Valley of the Kings, Thebes, 72
valley temples, 62, 70
    Great Pyramid complex, 62, 63, 64, 73
Vallon-Pont-d'Arc (France): Chauvet Cave, 22, *22*, 23
value, 7
Vandals, 258
vanths, 176
Vapheio (Greece): hunter capturing a bull (drinking cup), 100, *100b*, 4-23A
Varuna (Aryan deity), 427
Vasari, Giorgio
    on Giotto, 407, 14-7A
    on Gothic art, 365
    on naturalism, 465
vase painting
    Greek Archaic period, 120–123, 5-20A, 5-22A, 5-23A
    Greek Early/High Classical period, 142–144, 5-58A
    Greek Geometric period, 108–109, 5-2A
    Greek Late Classical period, 5-63A
    Greek Orientalizing period, 110–111, 169, 6-9A
    Greek techniques, 110
    Mycenaean, 102